In the last century, a new way of looking at the Bible developed. Research into the ancient Near East and its texts recreated for us the civilizations out of which the Bible emerged. In this century, there has been a revival of Jewish biblical scholarship; Israeli and American scholars, in particular, concentrating in the fields of archaeology, biblical history, Semitic languages, and the religion of Israel, have opened exciting new vistas into the world of the Scriptures. For the first time in history, we have at our disposal information and methodological tools that enable us to explore the biblical text in a way that could never have been done before. This new world of knowledge, as seen through the eyes of contemporary Jewish scholars and utilizing at the same time the insights of over twenty centuries of traditional Jewish exegesis, is now available for the first time to a general audience in *The JPS Torah Commentary*.

The Commentary is published in five volumes, each by a single author who has devoted himself to the study of the text. Given the wide range of perspectives that now exist in biblical scholarship, the JPS has recognized the individual expertise of these authors and made no attempt to impose uniformity on the methodology or content of their work.

The Hebrew text is essentially that of the Leningrad Codex B 19A, the oldest dated manuscript of the complete Hebrew Bible. Copied from a text written by the distinguished Masoretic scholar Aaron ben Moses ben Asher, who lived in the first half of the 10th century C.E., the manuscript was completed in 1009 C.E. In this edition it has been arranged according to the weekly synagogue Torah readings. The format has been adjusted to correspond to that adopted by the TANAKH, the new translation of the Hebrew Bible, published by the Jewish Publication Society and utilized in the present *Commentary*. In this text, the cantillation differs in minor details from that in the *tikkunim* used by Torah readers and should not be used to prepare Torah readings for the synagogue or to "correct" Torah readers.

The Jewish Publication Society has completed this project with a full awareness of the great tradition of Jewish Bible commentary, with a profound sense of the sanctity of the biblical text and an understanding of the awe and love that our people has accorded its Bible. The voice of our new *Commentary* resounds with the spirit and concerns of our times — just as the Jewish spirit has always found its most sincere and heartfelt expression in its appreciation of the Bible; yet it acknowledges the intrinsic value of the tools of modern scholarship in helping to establish the original sense and setting of Scripture.

With all this fixed firmly in mind, the Jewish Publication Society commits its good name and its decades of pioneering in the world of English-language Jewish publishing to this *Torah Commentary* with the hope that it will serve as the contemporary addition to the classic commentaries created by Jews during past epochs in Jewish history.

Nahum M. Sarna, GENERAL EDITOR
Chaim Potok, LITERARY EDITOR

Society Torah Commentary

וְהַמַּשְׂכִּלִים יַזְהִרוּ כְּזֹהַר הָרָקִיעַ
וּמַצְדִּיקֵי הָרַבִּים כַּכּוֹכָבִים לְעוֹלָם וָעֶד

Sander H., Alan, and David C. Mendelson

Joseph and Rebecca Meyerhoff

Warren G. and Gay H. Miller

Mr. and Mrs. Hershel Muchnick
    In memory of Max and Annie Sherman
    and Lt. Louis O. Sherman

Joseph Muchnick
    In memory of his wife, Mollie

Nancy and Morris W. Offit

Mr. and Mrs. Mitchell E. Panzer
    In memory of their parents

Edith and Charles Pascal
    In memory of their parents,
    Harry and Lena Chidakel
    Harry and Marion Pascal

Mr. and Mrs. Frank J. Pasquerilla

Leon J. Perelman

Mr. and Mrs. Ronald O. Perelman

Harry M. and Esther L. Plotkin

Anne and Henry S. Reich

Arleen and Robert S. Rifkind

Judy and Arthur Robbins
    In honor of Sheila F. Segal

Mr. and Mrs. Daniel Rose

Sam Rothberg

Rabbi Stephen A. and Nina Berman Schafer
    In memory of Joel Michael Schafer

Drs. Amiel and Chariklia-Tziraki Segal

Bernard G. Segal

Norma L. Shapiro
    In memory of her parents,
    Jane K. and Bert Levy

Lola and Gerald Sherman
    In memory of Jean and Al Sherman
    and Ada and Jack Kay

Jerome J. and Marciarose Shestack
    In memory of Olga and Isadore Shestack
    and Clara Ruth Schleifer

Jonathan and Jennifer Shestack
    In memory of their great-grandfathers,
    Rabbi Israel Shankman and
    Rabbi Judah Shestack

Dr. and Mrs. Edward B. Shils

Charles E. Smith
    In honor of Mr. and Mrs. Robert P. Kogod
    and Mr. and Mrs. Robert H. Smith

Marian Scheuer Sofaer

William and Radine Spier

The Oscar and Lillian Stempler Foundation
    In memory of Rose and Isadore Engel
    and Lillian Stempler
    In honor of Oscar Stempler

David B. Sykes
    In memory of his wife, Shirley

Mr. and Mrs. Sylvan M. Tobin

Sami and Annie Totah
    In honor of their parents

Adele and Bert M. Tracy
    In memory of their parents

Elizabeth R. and Michael A. Varet

Edna and Charles Weiner

Simon and Trudy Weker
    In honor of their children,
    Laurie, Jonathan, and Robert

Morton H. Wilner

Mr. and Mrs. Seymour D. Wolf
    In memory of their parents,
    Abraham and Dora Wolf
    Abraham and Sarah Krupsaw

Dr. Allen M. and Eleanor B. Wolpe

Ben Zevin

Benjamin Bernard Zucker
    In honor of Lotty Gutwirth Zucker

PATRONS of The Jewish Publication

And the knowledgeable will be radiant like the bright expanse of sky,
And those who lead the many to righteousness will be like the stars forever and ever.

DANIEL 12:3

Mr. and Mrs. Robert P. Abrams
In memory of Peter Abrams

D.F. Antonelli, Jr.

Mr. and Mrs. Marvin Anzel and Sons
In memory of Rose and Samuel Anzel

Stephen and Stephanie Axinn

Mr. and Mrs. Ronald S. Baron

Dr. Muriel M. Berman

Nancy Berman and Alan Bloch

Philip I. Berman

Steven M. Berman

Herbert and Nancy Bernhard

Mr. and Mrs. Arthur H. Bienenstock

Goldene and Herschel Blumberg
In memory and in honor of their parents

Irvin J. Borowsky and Laurie Wagman

Elmer Cerin
In memory of Sylvia S. Cerin

Dr. and Mrs. D. Walter Cohen
In honor of their parents,
Abram and Goldie Cohen
Joseph and Bessie Axelrod

Melvin and Ryna Cohen

Rosalie and Joseph Cohen

Elsie B. and Martin D. Cohn
In honor of their children and grandchildren

Mr. and Mrs. Charles M. Diker

Carole and Richard Eisner

Edward E. Elson

The Endowment Fund of the
Greater Hartford Jewish Federation

Edith Brenner Everett and Henry Everett
In memory of their father, Eli Brenner,
and brother, Fred Brenner

Federation of Jewish Agencies
of Greater Philadelphia

Peter I. Feinberg

Myer and Adrienne Arsht Feldman
In honor of Bella Feldman

Mr. Joseph M. and Dr. Helen G. First

Libby and Alan Fishman

Selma and William Fishman

The Foundation for Conservative Judaism
of Greater Philadelphia

Bernard and Muriel Frank

Aaron and Cecile Goldman

Evelyn and Seymour C. Graham

Dorothy Gitter Harman
In memory of her parents,
Morris and Maria Gitter

Irving B. Harris

Shirley and Stanley Hayman
In memory of their parents

Evelyn and Sol Henkind

Erica and Ludwig Jesselson

Leonard Kapiloff

Sol and Rita Kimerling

Lillian and Sid Klemow

Mr. and Mrs. Ronald A. Krancer

William B. and Elaine Kremens

Mr. and Mrs. Harvey M. Krueger

Simon and Rosa Laupheimer

Fanney N. Litvin
In memory of her husband, Philip Litvin

Ruth Meltzer
In memory of her husband, Leon

Martha H. and Joseph L. Mendelson

Martha H. and Joseph L. Mendelson
In memory of their parents,
Alexander and Celia Holstein
Abraham and Dora Mendelson

SPONSORS OF THE COMMENTARY ON DEUTERONOMY

The LORD will ordain blessings for you

וּבָאוּ עָלֶיךָ כָּל־הַבְּרָכוֹת הָאֵלֶּה

DEUTERONOMY 28:8

PATRONS

Leon J. Perelman

Dr. and Mrs. Edward B. Shils

Rabbi Benjamin Z. Kreitman

Martha H. and Joseph L. Mendelson
In memory of their parents,
Alexander and Celia Holstein
Abraham and Dora Mendelson

CONTRIBUTORS

D. F. Antonelli, Jr.

Mr. and Mrs. Marvin Anzel and Sons
In memory of Rose and Samuel Anzel

Bauman Rare Books

Herbert Berman
In memory of Leo Guzik

Irvin J. Borowsky and Laurie Wagman

Dr. D. Walter Cohen
In memory of Betty Ann Cohen and
Joseph and Bessie Axelrod

Louise and Daniel C. Cohen

Elsie B. and Martin D. Cohn
In honor of their children
and grandchildren

Mr. and Mrs. Charles M. Diker

Libby and Alan Fishman

Bernard and Muriel Frank

The Foundation for Conservative Judaism
of Greater Philadelphia

Aaron and Cecile Goldman

Joseph and Rebecca Meyerhoff

Vivien G. and Lipman Redman
In honor of our families

Arleen and Robert S. Rifkind

Norma L. Shapiro
In memory of her parents,
Jane K. and Bert Levy

Jerome J. and Marciarose Shestack
In memory of Olga and Isadore Shestack
and Clara Ruth Schleifer

Constance and Joseph Smukler

Carolyn Engel Temin
In loving memory of
David Morton Engel
and in honor of Ethel Berman Engel

Simon and Trudy Weker
In honor of their children
Laurie, Jonathan, and Robert

Mr. and Mrs. Seymour D. Wolf
In memory of their parents,
Abraham and Dora Wolf
Abraham and Sarah Krupsaw

A volume of this magnitude could not have been completed without the efforts of a very dedicated team of professionals and lay leaders who comprise the family of The Jewish Publication Society. It was my privilege to be part of this effort. I would like to pay special tribute to all of the professionals at JPS whose patience and diligence brought this project to fruition.

In addition, it has been our privilege to work in the company of devoted lay leadership who have been so consistently supportive of our work on this project and on so many others. We are indebted to the many individuals whose gifts supported this project from its inception. We are especially grateful to our benefactors, Muriel and Philip Berman, without whose generosity this and so many other outstanding publications would not have been possible.

Dr. Ellen Frankel, Editor-in-Chief

THE JPS TORAH COMMENTARY

DEUTERONOMY דברים

GENERAL EDITOR   *Nahum M. Sarna*
LITERARY EDITOR   *Chaim Potok*

GENESIS   *Nahum M. Sarna*
EXODUS   *Nahum M. Sarna*
LEVITICUS   *Baruch A. Levine*
NUMBERS   *Jacob Milgrom*
DEUTERONOMY   *Jeffrey H. Tigay*

THE JPS TORAH
COMMENTARY

DEUTERONOMY

The Traditional Hebrew Text with the New JPS Translation

Commentary by JEFFREY H. TIGAY

THE JEWISH PUBLICATION SOCIETY

PHILADELPHIA   5756 / 1996

Deuteronomy Commentary © 1996 by The Jewish Publication Society

Masoretic Hebrew text, Codex Leningrad B19ᴬ, taken from
Biblia Hebraica Stuttgartensia (BHS) © 1967/77, 1983, by the Deutsche Bibelgesellschaft, Stuttgart
Synagogue adaptation and revised format © 1996 by The Jewish Publication Society

English translation of the Torah © 1962, 1985, 1989 by The Jewish Publication Society

Composed by Varda Graphics in Galliard (English text) and Keter (Hebrew text);
lead typesetter: Betsalel Perel.

Library of Congress Cataloging-in-Publication Data

Tigay, Jeffrey H.
    Deuteronomy = [Devarim] : the traditional Hebrew text with
the new JPS translation / commentary by Jeffrey H. Tigay.
    p. cm. — (The JPS Torah commentary)
    Includes bibliographical references.
    ISBN 0–8276–0330–4
    1. Bible O.T. Deuteronomy—Commentaries. I. Bible O.T.
Deuteronomy. Hebrew. 1996. II. Bible. O.T. Deuteronomy.
English. Jewish Publication Society. 1996. III. Title.
IV. Series.
BS1275.3.T54   1996   96–3778
222'. 15077—dc20   CIP

GENESIS   ISBN 0–8276–0326–6
EXODUS   ISBN 0–8276–0327–4
LEVITICUS   ISBN 0–8276–0328–2
NUMBERS   ISBN 0–8276–0329–0
DEUTERONOMY   ISBN 0–8276–0330–4
Five-volume set   ISBN 0–8276–0331–2

THE JPS TORAH COMMENTARY PROJECT
    JEROME J. SHESTACK   *Chairman*
    JOSEPH L. MENDELSON   *Vice Chairman*

Designed by ADRIANNE ONDERDONK DUDDEN

10   9

For our sons

Eytan Amichai
Hillel Yair
Chanan Ben-Zion
and
Yisrael Shalom

ושננתם לבניך ודברת בם
(Deuteronomy 6:7)

ACKNOWLEDGMENTS

מודה אני לפניך ה׳ אלהי ששמת חלקי מיושבי בית המדרש

On the completion of this commentary I give thanks to God, who has guided me to a life of Jewish scholarship and has brought me in good health to this occasion. I do not know of an intellectual privilege greater than constant engagement with the Book of Books and its great commentators of the past and present, and the opportunity to further its understanding. For this I am grateful as well to my parents for the influences to which they exposed me, and to the teachers who instructed me.

I wish to express my deep appreciation to Nahum M. Sarna for inviting me to write this commentary, and to both him and Chaim Potok for their wise and skillful editing and for their friendship and collegiality as I wrote. I am greatly indebted to the scholarship of Moshe Greenberg for his seminal studies on biblical law and religion, for his course on Deuteronomy in 1964–65, and for his kindness in making his personal notes on the entire book available to me, and to Moshe Weinfeld and Alexander Rofé, whose extensive and penetrating studies of Deuteronomy have greatly advanced modern scholarship on the book. I have benefitted as well from the generous counsel of Judah Goldin, Barry Eichler, and the late Jonas C. Greenfield, and from all that I have learned from the earlier *JPS Torah Commentary* volumes of Nahum M. Sarna, Baruch A. Levine, and Jacob Milgrom. Several colleagues were kind enough to provide valuable references and materials, particularly Frank M. Cross, who provided me with photocopies of the Deuteronomy manuscripts from Qumran cave 4, and Eugene Ulrich, who provided me with an advance copy of DJD 14 with the official edition of those manuscripts; Edward F. Campbell, who provided me with photographs of Mounts Gerizim and Ebal; Sol Cohen, who gave freely of his erudition; and S. Dean McBride, from whose stimulating lectures and articles on Deuteronomy I have learned much. Several friends and colleagues were also kind enough to read individual chapters and offer valuable comments on them: Barry Eichler, Yisrael Eph'al, Moshe Greenberg, Alexander Rofé, Sheila Segal, Emanuel Tov, Yair Zakovitch, and the late Jacob Licht. Over the past sixteen years I have been helped by many other colleagues too numerous to name, as well as physicians, veterinarians, scientists, zoo keepers, butchers, culinary specialists, gardeners, and others who kindly offered expert advice about questions I addressed to them; I am grateful to them all. In the publication process, the professionalism of Diane Zuckerman, managing editor of the Jewish Publication Society, David Murphy, production manager, and Leslie Cohen, project editor, smoothed the complexities involved in bringing together all the elements required to produce a volume of this nature. I am grateful as well to Rabbi David Sulomm Stein, Rabbi Ivan Caine, Daniel Cohen, Esq., Shawn Zelig Aster, and Daniel Levy, for their skillful proofreading.

Much of the research for this commentary was facilitated by sabbaticals, fellowships, grants, and other assistance generously awarded to me by the University of Pennsylvania, its Israel Exchange Program, the Annenberg Institute (now the University's Center

for Judaic Studies) and its superb staff, the Muriel and Philip Berman Endowment Fund of the Jewish Publication Society, and the Memorial Foundation for Jewish Culture.

I owe the greatest debt to my dear wife, Helene, who read and critiqued early drafts of the commentary, and to our sons Eytan, Hillel, Chanan, and Yisrael, who helped me by listening, discussing, reading, and providing references, and in numerous other ways. As I looked forward to the privilege of fulfilling the commandment of Deuteronomy 6:7 and 11:19, they were never out of my thoughts when I studied and wrote, and this commentary is lovingly dedicated to them.

Jeffrey H. Tigay

CONTENTS

EXCURSUSES TO THE DEUTERONOMY COMMENTARY

WEEKLY TORAH READINGS FROM THE BOOK OF DEUTERONOMY

INTRODUCTION

The Title

Deuteronomy has two Hebrew names. The popular name, *Sefer Devarim*, is short for *(Sefer) ve-'elleh ha-devarim*, "The Book of 'These are the words,'" a name based on the ancient practice of naming books after their key opening word or phrase. A second name, *Mishneh Torah*, "the Repetition of the Torah," appears frequently in rabbinic literature. Philo and the Septuagint used its Greek translation, *Deuteronomion*, whence it came to the Latin Vulgate and then to English as "Deuteronomy." Ironically, this name stems from a misunderstanding of Deuteronomy 17:18, where the phrase first appears but actually means "a copy of the Teaching." Nevertheless, it is an apt designation for the book, which recapitulates the teachings of Genesis through Numbers.

Deuteronomy regularly refers to itself as "this Teaching" (*sefer ha-torah ha-zo't*) and "this book of Teaching" (*sefer ha-torah ha-zeh*),[1] but it seems to use these phrases as generic designations rather than formal titles. Perhaps closest to a title is "the Teaching of Moses" (*torat mosheh*, found in Josh. 8:32; 2 Kings 23:25; Mal. 3:22).

The Text

Deuteronomy, like the rest of the Torah, was copied with extreme care and its text is among the best preserved in the Bible. The received Masoretic Text is based on manuscripts of the ninth and tenth centuries C.E., themselves based on older manuscripts. Hundreds of variant readings are found in the Samaritan Pentateuch, known from medieval manuscripts; in verses cited in postbiblical, particularly rabbinic, texts;[1a] in fragments of thirty two manuscripts from the Dead Sea region (all from prior to 70 C.E.);[2] and in the Septuagint, the Greek translation made from a Hebrew original in the third century B.C.E. The vast majority are insignificant differences in spelling and grammar that do not affect the sense of the text. Some, however, are more original, while others seek to clarify or even change the meaning of the text; these are cited in the Commentary.

The Hebrew text in this volume contains paragraph breaks that parallel those in the English translation. These represent modern scholars' sense of the flow and coherence of the text. The chapter divisions, a Christian innovation adopted for Hebrew Bibles from the Vulgate, represent a medieval perception of the same. Since interpretation depends on context, and division of the text helps define context, it is important to get as close as possible to the way ancient readers divided the text.[3] In order to do so, special attention was paid in preparing this commentary to the paragraph (Heb. *parashah*) breaks in the Masoretic, Samaritan, and Dead Sea texts. These represent the perceptions of Hebrew readers who lived closer to biblical times; the Dead Sea texts show that many of the Masoretic and Samaritan breaks are ancient.

The Character and Structure of the Book

In form, Deuteronomy consists of farewell discourses and poems that Moses delivered to Israel in the last weeks of his life, and brief narratives about his final activities: commissioning Joshua as his successor, writing down the discourses, and Moses' death.

Deuteronomy may be outlined as follows (the discourses and poems are represented in italics):

I.   Heading (1:1–5)

II. *Prologue: First Discourse* (1:6–4:43)

   A. *Retrospective: The journey from Horeb to Moab* (1:6–3:29)
   B. *Exhortation to observe God's laws* (4:1–40)
   C. Appendix: Selection of asylum cities (4:41–43)

III. *Second Discourse: The covenant made in Moab* (4:44–chap. 28)

   A. Heading (4:44–49)
   B. *Prologue: The theophany and covenant at Horeb* (5)
   C. *Preamble to the laws given in Moab* (6:1–11:30)
   D. *The laws given in Moab* (11:31–26:15)
   E. Conclusion to the laws (26:16–28:68)
      1. *Mutual commitments between God and Israel* (26:16–19)
      2. Digression: Ceremonies to reaffirm the covenant upon entering the promised land (27)
      3. *Promises and warnings consequent upon fulfilling or violating the covenant* (28:1–68)
   F. Subscription (28:69)

IV. *Third Discourse: Exhortations to observe the covenant made in Moab* (29–30)

V.   Epilogue: Moses' last days (31–34)

   A. Moses' preparations of Israel for the future (31–32)
      1. Preparatory acts (31)
      2. *Moses' poem* (32:1–43)
      3. God's final instructions to Moses (32:44–52)
   B. *Moses' farewell blessings of Israel* (33)
   C. Moses' death (34)

The Main Themes of Deuteronomy

Several themes are unique to Deuteronomy, or receive greater emphasis in it than in any other book of the Torah.

Monotheism.   The fundamental principle underlying Deuteronomy is monotheism. The Lord (YHVH), God of Israel, is not only "the God of gods and the Lord of lords" (10:17), but the only true God (the "living God," 5:23). Of course, the preceding books of the Torah also recognize only Him as God, but they concentrate on prohibiting Israel from worshiping other gods, not on refuting belief in their existence (see Excursus 6). It is Deuteronomy that first states explicitly that no other god exists and demonstrates that

point, showing that the Lord alone has performed deeds that prove divinity (4:32–40; cf. 3:24). Deuteronomy also gives one of the only explanations in the Torah for the prohibition of idols (4:9–20; see Comment to 4:15–18).

An aspect of Deuteronomy's monotheism is its teaching that Israel's God guides the history of all peoples. He defeated Israel's enemies and overpowered mighty Egypt, which stood helplessly by as He removed Israel from its control. He gave Israel's neighbors their lands, too, and enabled them to defeat the earlier inhabitants (2:20–23). It was He who determined that other peoples should worship other "gods" (4:19).[4]

Loyalty to the Lord. The main theme of Deuteronomy is the ardent and exclusive loyalty that Israel owes the Lord, as expressed in 6:4–5: "Hear, O Israel! The LORD is Our God, the LORD alone. You shall love the LORD your God with all your heart and with all your soul and with all your might." Moses constantly exhorts Israel to worship the Lord alone and to shun pagan occult practices. No other book demands such a vehement campaign to prevent Israelites from worshiping other gods: it prescribes execution for Israelites who do so, or even advocate doing so; it requires the destruction of the native Canaanites to prevent them from influencing Israel to adopt their gods and abhorrent practices, such as ritual murder; and it warns that worshiping other gods will lead to Israel's destruction and exile.[5] In times of war, as a corollary of loyalty, Israel must trust God completely and face the enemy without hesitation.[6]

The concept of God. The Lord is a just and caring God, giver of just laws (4:8), who "shows no favor and takes no bribe, but upholds the cause of the fatherless and the widow, and befriends the stranger, providing him with food and clothing" (10:18). He is faithful, keeping His commitments (7:8–9; 32:4).

In striking contrast to the earlier books of the Torah, particularly those parts reflecting the priestly viewpoint,[7] Deuteronomy emphasizes God's transcendence. He is near to Israel (4:7), but only in a spiritual sense, since He is not physically present on earth. While passages in Exodus describe the sanctuary as God's dwelling,[8] Deuteronomy speaks of Him as dwelling in heaven (26:15); only His name dwells in the sanctuary (e. g., 12:5). Exodus 25 conceives of the Ark, which contains the Tablets of the Covenant, as God's footstool, and the cherubs above it as His throne where He is present when speaking with Moses; whereas Deuteronomy describes the Ark as only a chest for the Tablets (10:1–2). And in retelling episodes from Numbers that describe God as travelling with Israel above the Ark, Deuteronomy omits references to the Ark so as not to localize Him (1:33,42). Deuteronomy generally avoids reference to God's *kavod*, the term used in the earlier books to refer to His physical Presence. In describing the theophany at Horeb where, according to Exodus, God came down onto the mountain (Exod. 19:11,18,19), Deuteronomy carefully emphasizes that God spoke from heaven; only his fire, from which His voice was heard, was present on earth (Deut. 4:36).

Deuteronomy also describes God in less physical terms than do the earlier books of the Torah. In the Decalogue it eliminates the statement of Exodus 20:11 that God rested on the seventh day; it states instead that the purpose of the Sabbath is to enable servants to rest, and adds a reminder that God freed Israel from slavery in Egypt (Deut. 5:14–15). But avoidance of physical anthropomorphism does not mean that Deuteronomy conceives of the Lord as impassive. To Deuteronomy, as to the Bible as a whole, He is a feeling God. He is "drawn in love" to Israel (7:7; 10:15) and is merciful (4:31). Yet He also becomes angry at sin (7:4; 29:26; 31:17) and "jealous," like a burning fire, in defense of His claim to Israel's sole allegiance (4:24; 5:9; 6:15).

Covenant. All the books of the Torah use the metaphor of "covenant" (*berit*) to describe the relationship between God and Israel. Deuteronomy emphasizes this metaphor so frequently that it was later referred to as "the Book of the Covenant."[9] In fact, Deuteronomy refers to several covenants. The first, which established the original relationship between God and Israel, is the covenant He made on oath to Israel's ancestors to give their descendants the promised land and make them a large, prosperous, secure and victorious nation because of the ancestors' loyal obedience to Him;[10] in this sense, "covenant" means promise.[11] "Covenant" refers also to the compact between God and Israel, consisting of the stipulations required by God, Israel's promise to obey them, and God's promise to reward obedience and punish disobedience. Covenant in this sense establishes God as Israel's sovereign and serves as the basis for the relationship between them. Deuteronomy describes three such *obligatory* covenants that are essentially affirmations of the same agreement. The first consists of the stipulations God presented to Israel in the Decalogue at Horeb (Sinai) (5:6–18).[12] Because Israel was too frightened by the theophany to hear God present the remaining stipulations, God communicated them only to Moses (5:19–6:3), who transmitted them to the people forty years later in Moab, shortly before his death. Moses then reconfirmed the Horeb covenant with a second one covering these additional stipulations (these stipulations are the laws presented in chaps. 12–26, introduced by chaps. 5–11 and sanctioned by the promises and warnings in chap. 28).[13] Chapter 27 ordains that this covenant be affirmed a third time, as soon as Israel enters the promised land, in a covenant ceremony to be performed at Mounts Ebal and Gerizim.

The covenant relationship between God and Israel is summed up concisely in 26:16–19, a passage which shows that the covenant metaphor, which is rooted in the political and legal spheres, implies that the relationship between God and Israel is not a purely emotional or spiritual association, but one that also entails specific obligations that were mutually agreed upon and have consequences.[14]

The background of the covenant metaphor has been richly illuminated by modern scholarship. God's promissory covenant with the patriarchs is comparable to ancient Near Eastern promissory covenants in which a king grants land or some other gift to a servant and his descendants, unconditionally and in perpetuity, in recognition of the servant's past loyal service. The perpetual, unconditional character of such grants underlies the assurances that even if Israel betrays God and is exiled, He will restore them if they repent of their sins "because He will not forget the covenant which He made on oath with [their] fathers" (4:29–31; 30:1–10). The obligatory compact between God and Israel resembles vassal treaties in which the king of a superpower takes the king of a smaller state as his vassal and stipulates the terms of their relationship, demanding future loyalty. God, in this metaphor, becomes Israel's suzerain and Israel His vassal. The very logic of Israel's obligation to worship YHVH alone, because He alone freed Israel from Egypt, is the logic of the treaty in which the suzerain's demand for the vassal's exclusive loyalty is based on his past benefactions to the vassal, often his delivering them from enemies.[15] Deuteronomy shows numerous similarities to the form and wording of such treaties, as in the requirement that Israel love the Lord with all her heart, keep His words constantly in mind, and instruct her children about the terms of the covenant and the duty of following it.[16] Invocation of heaven and earth as witnesses (4:26; 30:19; 31:28) is common in treaties, and the blessings and curses in chapter 28 are very similar to series of blessings and curses that invoke divine rewards and punishments to sanction compliance with treaties. The provisions for depositing the Tablets of the Covenant in the Ark, and the Teaching next to the Ark, and reading the Teaching every seven years (31:10–12,25–26) are comparable to

provisions requiring the vassal to deposit the treaty in a sanctuary and read it periodically as a reminder of its terms.[17]

The suzerain-vassal treaty is not a completely adequate model for the biblical covenant metaphor since it belongs to the realm of international relations, creating a relationship between a foreign sovereign and his subjects. Such treaties are concerned only with the vassal's loyalty to the suzerain and are comparable to those provisions of God's covenant with Israel that deal with worship and loyalty to Him. They do not provide a model for God's concern for justice and human welfare as expressed in His legislation concerning Israel's internal relations, the social laws and moral regulations that make up so much of biblical law. The model for such legislation is the king giving instructions to his own people, such as we find in various ancient Near Eastern law collections and instructions to royal officials.[18] Possibly, the proximate model of the covenant in which God became Israel's king was a "royal covenant" in which a people accepted a human king who legislated for every sphere of its life.[19]

Deuteronomy does not limit itself to the covenant metaphor to describe Israel's relationship with God. It uses the metaphor of father and child to explain the nature of God's creation and guidance of Israel (8:5; 32:6,18) and Israel's obligations to Him (14:1), and to characterize Israel's rebellion as unfilial conduct (32:5–6,18–20). It also draws terms from the vocabulary of marriage and adoption because the covenant creates a familylike relationship between Israel and God (see Comments to 5:7; 26:17; 29:12; 32:6). Finally, it describes Israel as God's inheritance to express His sovereignty over them and His attachment to them (4:20; 32:9).

Love. Deuteronomy emphasizes that the bond between God and Israel is not merely legal, but spiritual and emotional as well. It reminds Israel of God's love for her[20] and calls on her to love and revere Him with all her heart, soul, and might, devoting her entire being to Him.[21] It conceives of a relationship so intense that it can be described in terms normally used of romantic love: God was "drawn in His love for Israel's ancestors" (10:15) and Israel is to "hold fast" to Him (4:4; 10:20; 11:22).

Israel. Israel owes her very existence to God, who created her, redeemed her from Egypt, guided her safely through the wilderness, fights Israel's wars, and will give Israel her land.[22] God chose Israel for a special relationship with Him. As a nation, Israel is a polity headed by God who gives it laws through His spokesman Moses and will send future instructions through other prophets (18:15–22). As God's children, all Israelites are brothers with mutual obligations to care for each other.[23] They are sacrosanct to God and must shun all conduct that is incompatible with that status.[24] They are God's "treasured people."[25] In return for their service, God promises to make them the most successful and preeminent of peoples.[26]

This relationship is not conceived in chauvinistic terms. Moses points out that Israel's election by God was no sign of merit. Indeed, Israel had been rebellious for as long as Moses knew her.[27] Rather, God chose Israel because of His love for her ancestors. Election is indeed a privilege, but one granted so that Israel would learn God's ways and follow them. Fulfilling this obligation is a precondition for Israel's well-being.[28] As God explains in Genesis 18:19, "I have singled [Abraham] out that he may instruct his children and his posterity to keep the way of the Lord by doing what is just and right, in order that the Lord may bring about for Abraham what He has promised him." The responsibility imposed by election is also expressed in Amos 3:2, where God declares to Israel: "You

alone have I singled out of all the families of the earth—That is why I will call you to account for all your iniquities."

Israel and the nations.   Deuteronomy teaches that because of Israel's election for God's service, only she worships the true God. Other nations worship His subordinates or insubstantial idols. Since God Himself assigned the other nations their objects of worship, Deuteronomy does not consider it sinful for them to worship those objects.[29] But it does consider the Canaanites' religion sinful because of the abominable rituals they perform on behalf of their deities, especially child sacrifice. For these sins, God will destroy the Canaanites and give their land to Israel.[30] As Ruler of all peoples, God also gave Israel's Transjordanian neighbors their lands and cautioned Israel that it has no right to those lands.[31] Deuteronomy envisages friendly relations with most other nations. It values their good opinion (4:6). It expects foreigners to visit and trade with Israel,[32] and permits most (including escaped slaves) to settle in Israel, marry Israelites, and eventually to join the popular Assembly (21:10–14; 23:27). Members of a few nations are denied this privilege, temporarily or permanently, because of unfriendly actions toward Israel in the past. Like the rest of the Torah, Deuteronomy grants resident aliens equal protection under civil law and extends the benefits of many religious laws to them, such as Sabbath rest.[33] But it does not require Israelites to grant them interest-free loans or remit their debts in the seventh year; financial sacrifices of that nature are obligatory only toward fellow Israelites.[34]

The Land.   All of Deuteronomy looks toward Israel's life in the promised land. The land of Israel, the focus of God's promises to the patriarchs, is His ultimate gift to their descendants. It is the place where God's laws are to be carried out and where a society pursuing justice and righteousness (4:5–8) and living in harmony with God (7:12–13) can be established. Deuteronomy's praise of the land is unstinting: it is a land oozing milk and honey, abundant in natural and man-made resources, and under God's constant supervision (6:3,10–11; 8:7–9; 11:9–12). But Deuteronomy regularly iterates that possession of the land is conditional: Israel must obey God in order to occupy it successfully (4:1), to enjoy its bounty (7:12–16), and to retain possession of it (11:21). Disobedience delayed possession (chap. 1) and may later bring expulsion (e. g., 4:25–27), and only repentance and a return to obedience can lead to restoration (30:1–10).

Law.   As noted, Israel's welfare depends on maintaining a society governed by God's social and religious laws, as presented in chapters 12–26. These laws are a divine gift to Israel, unsurpassed in their justice and their ability to secure God's closeness (4:5–8). It is the responsibility of society to enforce the laws—failing that, God will. Nevertheless, the laws are to be observed not because of a social compact among the people, or out of good citizenship, or as an authoritarian imposition from above, but because they are just and right, and because of feelings of gratitude and moral obligation toward their Author, who chose Israel and redeemed her (6:20–25), and, finally, because Israel accepted His laws and covenant freely (5:24; 26:17). To Deuteronomy, then, the laws require not only obedience, but also the proper attitude.

The laws presented in Deuteronomy—indeed, the laws of the Torah as a whole—are not a complete, systematic code that could have sufficed to govern the entire life of ancient Israel. Certain areas of life, such as commercial transactions, civil damages, and marriage, are mentioned barely or not at all. One gains the impression that only a part of the existing laws have been selected, perhaps to illustrate certain ideal principles of social justice and religious devotion.[35] Even in the topics that are covered, practical details of how the law

was to be applied are rarely spelled out. Deuteronomy in particular, perhaps keeping its general audience in mind, devotes more attention to the basic provisions of its laws than to their practical details. The latter must have been provided by custom, by an interpretive tradition developed by courts (17:8–12), as in postbiblical times, and perhaps by administrative agencies.

Centralization of Sacrificial Worship. Unique in Deuteronomy's laws is the rule that sacrificial worship may take place only in a single sanctuary. This law transfers virtually all important activities that were previously performed at sanctuaries throughout the country—sacrifice, festivals, rites of purification, and certain judicial activities—to the central sanctuary in the religious capital.[36] The reason behind it has been debated for centuries. Apparently, Deuteronomy perceived worship at multiple sites as inherently pagan.[37]

Desacralization. The limitation of sacrificial worship to a single place would inevitably remove a sacral dimension from the life of most Israelites. Most people lived far from the Temple and could not visit it often. They would have to forgo certain purificatory rites and regular sacrificing. The need to permit secular slaughter eliminated the sacral dimension of meat meals (12:15–16,20–22). These consequences of the law do not seem to have been viewed by Deuteronomy as undesirable; to the contrary, they give every indication of having been one of its aims. This is suggested by the fact that even where Deuteronomy might have shown solicitude for the sacral it does not do so. It discourages people from making vows, which usually involved sacrificing (23:23). It requires the entire people to visit the Temple for the spiritual experiences it offers (14:23), but it no longer regards the Temple as the abode of God, and it contains no laws enjoining the public to revere it or guard its purity, such as we find in the priestly literature.[38] It drastically diminishes the financial support of the Temple by taking the tithes and firstlings—the old mainstays of the Temple staff—away from the clergy and letting the laity consume them (14:22–29). Military laws are also much desacralized, with the priests' role reduced to an encouraging speech before battle (20:2).

This trend in Deuteronomy has sometimes been termed "secularization," but this term can be misleading if it is understood to mean antireligious. Deuteronomy is a profoundly religious book that seeks unceasingly to teach love and reverence for God to every Israelite and to encourage rituals which have that effect. Deuteronomy's aim is to spiritualize religion by freeing it from excessive dependence on sacrifice and priesthood.[39]

Intellectual orientation. Deuteronomy has a pronounced intellectual orientation. This is shown at the outset as Moses begins to "expound" the Teaching (1:5) and from his frequent description of himself as "teaching" the laws (4:1,5). All Israelites must learn the Teaching and teach it to their children (4:9; 6:7,20–25; 11:19). The book must be read to the entire nation publicly every seven years (31:11–13) and the king must make a personal copy to study from (17:18–19). Moses urges Israel to obey God's laws because "that will be proof of your wisdom and discernment to other peoples" (4:6). The book regularly refers to what Israel learned from personal experience. Deuteronomy regards moral and spiritual qualities, especially those required for leadership, as forms of wisdom. It often expresses this viewpoint when it paraphrases passages from the other books of the Torah: thus Moses imbues Joshua with wisdom (34:9; according to Num. 27:18–20 he imbued him with authority); the chiefs had to be "wise, discerning, and experienced" (1:13; according to Exod. 18:11 they were to be capable, Godfearing, and honest); and according to 16:19

judges must reject bribes because "bribes blind the eyes of the discerning" (lit., "wise"; according to Exod. 23:8, "bribes blind the clear-sighted").

As M. Weinfeld has shown, this intellectual orientation points unmistakably to Wisdom Literature as one of the main influences on Deuteronomy's ideas and values, and indeed, this influence is visible throughout the book.[40] The phraseology of the book has many contacts with Wisdom Literature.[41] Certain of its teachings have nearly verbatim counterparts in Wisdom Literature, such as the exhortations against partiality in judgment (1:17), moving a neighbor's landmark (19:14), having dishonest weights (25:13–16), and delaying payment of vows (23:22).[42]

Humanitarianism.   The Torah's humanitarianism is most fully developed in Deuteronomy's legislation and exhortations on behalf of the poor and disadvantaged: debtors, indentured servants, escaped slaves, resident aliens, orphans, widows and Levites, as well as animals and even convicted criminals. Humanitarian rules of this sort are found in all of the Pentateuchal laws, but they are most extensive in Deuteronomy.[43] Characteristically, 10:19 cites the duty to treat aliens lovingly among Israel's duties to God, in the same context as loving and serving God Himself. As is done elsewhere in the Torah, Deuteronomy explains that humanitarian duties toward the disadvantaged are based on Israel's similar experience in the past (10:19; 15:15; 24:18,22).

Style.   The most notable feature of Deuteronomy's style is its exhortatory, didactic, sermonic character. Whether recalling past events, presenting theological arguments, or proclaiming laws, Moses' style is not that of the historical narrative, theological treatise, or legal code. He constantly goes beyond the immediate subject to point out its religious and ethical implications and to appeal for faith and obedience. When he recalls the Exodus and the events at Horeb (Sinai), he does so in order to show that these events prove that the Lord is the only true God and that Israel should therefore obey His laws and shun false gods (4:9–20,32–40). When he recounts the journey from Horeb to the promised land, it is only to point out that Israel's faithlessness caused an entire generation to perish in the wilderness (1:1–46). When he mentions how God fed Israel with manna, it is to show that God controls nature and can make anything He chooses nourishing, for which reason Israel should always obey Him (8:1–6). It is this use of historical events that gives Moses' addresses their sermonic character: the events serve as the premises on which he bases messages. In Deuteronomy these events play the same role that biblical verses do in the midrashic sermons of talmudic times.

Underlying this style is the realization that people must be persuaded to obey the laws, especially those that require self-sacrifice, and those that are not so much laws as ethical exhortations, such as 15:7–11. Therefore, Moses regularly explains the laws and their reasons so as to secure Israel's willing and understanding compliance. At times, he devotes as much attention to explaining and justifying the laws as he does to presenting their particulars.[44] Fully fifty percent of the laws in Deuteronomy are accompanied by clauses that explain the laws or motivate people to obey them by showing their logic, justice, or consequences.[45] It is these aspects of the book that are reflected in the description of Moses as "expounding" the Teaching (1:5) and "instructing" (that is, "teaching," not merely "commanding") Israel to observe the laws (4:1,5).

As befits Moses' purpose, Deuteronomy has adopted a rhetorical style well suited to oral presentation.[46] Its sentences are long and flowing. They are marked by assonance, key words,[47] and stereotyped expressions, all valued features of oral presentation. Themes are repeated frequently, a practice that enables listeners in a large audience to catch everything

that is said. Even the laws are lucid and free of technical details, intelligible to all ranks of the people. And instead of adopting the impersonal style typical of law codes, Deuteronomy, more than any other book in the Torah, addresses the laws directly to people.

Deuteronomy's stereotyped expressions are closely tied to its main themes. Examples are "love the LORD your God with all your heart and with all your soul"; "the commandments that I enjoin upon you this day"; "the LORD freed us from Egypt by a mighty hand and an outstretched arm"; "a land flowing with milk and honey"; "the site which the LORD your God will choose to establish His name"; "do what is right (or evil) in the sight of the LORD"; "bless you in all your undertakings"; "sweep out evil from your midst"; "other gods (whom you have not experienced)"; and "abhorrent to the LORD."[48]

The Date and Background of Deuteronomy

Whereas the predominant view in Judaism is that God dictated the entire Torah to Moses, ever since talmudic times there have been sages and scholars who held that the matter was more complex than that. Deuteronomy has provided some of the most important evidence in the discussion. One talmudic sage held that Deuteronomy 34:5–12 could not have been written by Moses or in his lifetime. These verses relate Moses' ascent up Mount Nebo and tell of his death, burial, and the month of mourning that followed (34:5–12). Although some sages held that Moses had already written this down at God's dictation, Rabbi Judah b. Ilai held that it must have been written by Joshua.[49] In the Middle Ages, Rabbi Abraham ibn Ezra (1089–1164) and others noted several other verses in the Torah that could not have been written in Moses' lifetime.[50] These verses contain information not available when he was alive, or reflect conditions that did not exist then. The verses from Deuteronomy include 34:1–4 (Moses could not have written what Deuteronomy says about his ascent up Mount Nebo because he never returned from there)[51] and 31:9, which says that Moses wrote down the Teaching and gave it to the priests and elders (Moses could not have written this verse, in the past tense, in the Teaching because when he was writing the Teaching he had not yet given it to them).[52] As for any theological questions these observations might raise, Rabbi Joseph Bonfils (fourteenth century), who wrote a commentary on Ibn Ezra's commentary, held that since the additions were also made by prophets and were based on tradition and were true, it made no difference whether they were written by Moses or a later prophet because the essential thing is belief in tradition and prophecy.[53]

In 1670, Benedict (Baruch) Spinoza cited Ibn Ezra's comments and similar observations and argued that all of the Pentateuch was compiled long after Moses by Ezra the Scribe in the fifth century B.C.E. Spinoza held that Ezra used the writings of Moses, but that he modified and supplemented them considerably.

Modern study of the origin of Deuteronomy is rooted in another observation made in the Middle Ages. Some of the Church fathers and Jewish commentators had observed that "the book of Teaching" (2 Kings 22:8,11: 23:24,25) found in the Temple in 622 B.C.E., which prompted King Josiah to undertake a major religious reformation, was Deuteronomy.[54] According to 2 Kings 22–23, the book was discovered by Hilkiah the High Priest while the Temple was being renovated and was immediately brought to the king's attention.[55] When it was read to him, the king was shocked and terrified because the people had been violating its laws, for which the book threatened disaster. He convoked a public assembly

in which he read this "book of the covenant" to the people and led them in making a covenant to obey fully "the terms of this covenant as inscribed in this book" (2 Kings 23:2–3). In this covenant, the king and people canonized the book, making it the national "constitution." Then Josiah undertook an extensive reformation in which he purged the Temple and the country of paganism, including the *kadesh*-functionaries and worship of the sun, moon, and host of heaven; closed and defiled all sanctuaries except for the Jerusalem Temple; and then ordered that the *pesah* sacrifice be offered, for the first time since the days of the Chieftains (the "Judges"), as prescribed in the book, apparently meaning that the whole nation was to gather in Jerusalem for the sacrifice rather than offering it all across the country.

Josiah's actions were clearly inspired by Deuteronomy.[56] Deuteronomy is the only book of the Torah that is called a "Book of Teaching" (see p. xi), whose contents are described as "the terms of the covenant" (Deut. 28:69; 29:8), and which calls upon the people to accept its laws as the basis of their national life. It is the only book of the Torah that prohibits *kadesh*-functionaries (23:18) and that explicitly mentions the worship of the sun, moon, and the host of heaven in its laws about idolatry (4:19; 17:3). It is the only one that prohibits sacrifice outside the single chosen Temple once Israel settles in the land (chap. 12); Exodus 20:21, in contrast, envisages multiple places of sacrifice.[57] As a corollary of this prohibition, Deuteronomy is the only book that requires the entire nation to offer the *pesah* sacrifice in a single Temple (Deut. 16:2,5–7).[58] The dire warnings that so terrified Josiah point to the curses of Deuteronomy 28, which threaten the king with exile (v. 36).[59]

Building on these observations, modern scholars since W. M. L. De Wette (1805) have argued cogently that several of the Deuteronomic prescriptions that Josiah carried out were actually created for the first time shortly before he did so, in the late eighth and seventh centuries B.C.E. Before then there was no need to explicitly prohibit the worship of heavenly bodies because such rites do not seem to have been practiced—at least not widely—in Israel.[60] Nor is there any earlier indication that sacrificing at more than one sanctuary was considered wrong. The first attempt to centralize sacrifice was made about a century before Josiah by King Hezekiah (late eighth–early seventh century B.C.E.).[61] Hosea (early-mid eighth century B.C.E.) was the first prophet who criticized the proliferation of altars.[62] Earlier, no prophets or pious kings attacked or suppressed the practice, and no less a prophet than Elijah (ninth century) built an altar and offered sacrifices on Mount Carmel (1 Kings 18). As for the united national *pesah* sacrifice, Kings itself says that nothing of the sort had been done ever since the days of the Chieftains.[63] If these Deuteronomic prescriptions did not exist prior to the eighth-seventh centuries, then Deuteronomy itself could not have existed earlier. In other words, Deuteronomy was composed many centuries after Moses, closer to the time when it was discovered in the Temple in 622 B.C.E.

De Wette thought that Deuteronomy was composed during Josiah's reign to serve as the blueprint for his reforms, but this is unlikely since there are discrepancies between the book and the reforms. Deuteronomy 18:6–8 permits provincial priests who come to the Temple to serve on an equal footing with those already there, but during the reform they were not allowed to do so (2 Kings 23:9). Furthermore, some aspects of the reform are not explicitly covered by Deuteronomy. For example, whereas Josiah had to suppress idolatrous priests (2 Kings 23:5,20), Deuteronomy 13:2–6 prescribes only a procedure for dealing with apostate prophets. These differences suggest that while Josiah's reform was inspired by Deuteronomy, the book itself was not composed by those who carried it out. Finally,

key aspects of Josiah's reform and of Deuteronomy—centralizaton of sacrifice, destruction of shrines other than the Temple, and destruction of cultic pillars and sacred posts—had already been undertaken a century earlier by Hezekiah. Since Hezekiah's short-lived reformation is not said to have been based on a book, we cannot be certain that Deuteronomy existed then, but the ideas that produced the book were clearly developing. It seems likely, then, that Deuteronomy was composed in the eighth-seventh centuries.

Many features of Deuteronomy, particularly its vigorous monotheism and fervent opposition to pagan practices in Israel, are very understandable as a reaction to conditions in the eighth-seventh centuries. This was a time of intense exposure to an attractive, cosmopolitan foreign culture.[64] Between 740 and 640, the Assyrian empire dominated Syria and Palestine. It fostered international trade and diplomatic travel, it settled new foreign populations nearby, and drafted Israelite units into its army. The culture of the empire was an amalgam of Assyrian, Aramaic, and Phoenician elements. Its impact on Israel was evident in art and architecture. The leading assimilators were the royal court and the commercial elite. They adopted foreign rites, including many of those that Deuteronomy forbids. King Ahaz "passed his children through fire" like a Canaanite and replaced the Temple altar with a new one copied from an altar he saw in Damascus.[65] Although religious assimilation was temporarily curbed by Hezekiah, it was resumed with greater force by his son Manasseh, who rebuilt the shrines that Hezekiah destroyed, built altars to Baal, worshiped the host of heaven and placed altars to it and an idol of the goddess Asherah in the Temple of the Lord, passed his son through fire, and practiced divination and necromancy.[66] Other kings of Judah placed horses and chariots for the sun in the Temple.[67] In Jerusalem, courtiers and members of the royal family could be seen "donning a foreign vestment . . . and skipping over the threshold," evidently a Philistine religious custom.[68] A cult of the "Queen of Heaven," favored by women, caught on.[69] Some in Judah went so far as to dismiss Israel's God as irrelevant, "doing nothing, good or bad" (Zeph. 1:12).

Deuteronomy reflects the expanded horizons and contacts of this imperial age. It speaks of Israel lending money to foreign nations (15:6; 28:12). Some of the curses in Deuteronomy 28 may be based on Assyrian models.[70] Deuteronomy threatens attack not by neighboring states but by "a nation from afar, from the end of the earth" (28:49), and it recognizes the temptation to worship the gods of *distant* nations "anywhere from one end of the earth to another" (13:8).

In view of all this, Deuteronomy's passionate assertion of monotheism can be seen as a reaction to the rampant assimilation to paganism that was entering the land, at least among the upper classes, during the century from 740–640 B.C.E.

However, there is much in the book that seems considerably older than this. The society reflected in Deuteronomy's laws is a good deal less advanced than that of seventh century Judah.[71] It consists primarily of farmers and herders.[72] There are no laws about merchants, artisans, professional soldiers, or other professionals. There are none dealing with commerce, real estate, or written contracts, and none dealing with commercial loans. Such loans as are mentioned are those made to financially pressed individuals who must borrow to get by.[73] There is no mention of royal officials or the royal power to tax and confiscate property and draft citizens.[74] The monarchy itself is mentioned only once, as an optional figurehead institution that has no authority or role in society (17:14–20). Law enforcement is not strong enough to protect accidental manslayers from the families of their victims, and they must flee to cities of refuge for safety.[75] Nor does the book have legal remedies to offer the poor who are maltreated; it can only call for people to show them compassion and warn that if they are maltreated, they will appeal to God for help.[76]

Features like these are typical of all the biblical law collections. The society they reflect is essentially that of the period of the Chieftains ("Judges"). But they do contain some later elements. Deuteronomy in particular reflects some conditions that developed in monarchic times. It recognizes the monarchy, however grudgingly.[77] Although local judges are not appointed by the king,[78] the establishment of a central court to hear difficult cases implies a central government.[79] Subjection of defeated populations to forced labor and the use of siege warfare (20:11–12,19–20) are also phenomena of monarchic regimes.[80] The book presumes that literacy has spread to some extent among the public as well as to the king.[81] Enough of the population lives in walled cities that Deuteronomy can refer to the city gate as the place of the court,[82] and can use the metonymy "gates" as the standard term for all of the country's provincial towns and settlements.[83]

Combining all of these chronological clues, it appears that the civil laws of Deuteronomy go back to a time in the United Monarchy or the early Divided Monarchy—the tenth and ninth centuries B.C.E.—during the transition from the old tribal-agrarian society to a more urbanized, monarchic one. It is difficult to tell whether Deuteronomy selected these laws individually or in groups, or whether they were already a collection. It is also difficult to tell whether the selection was made because society was still at the social and political stage reflected in them, or the compiler considered that stage ideal and wanted to return to it. In any case, these laws were supplemented and partly revised during the Assyrian age, primarily for the purpose of centralizing sacrificial worship and countering the threat of pagan religious belief and practice to which Israel was exposed in that period. At this time too, or perhaps later, the laws were further supplemented with the Heading, Prologue, and Preamble in 4:44–11:30, as well as the concluding declaration in 26:16–19 and the sanctions and subscription in chapter 28. This is how the Second Discourse—the core of Deuteronomy—was composed.

Precisely who was responsible for these developments is difficult to determine. Deuteronomy reflects views and interests of various groups in ancient Israelite society, but it is impossible to confidently identify any single one of them as its author(s).

The Jerusalem priesthood and the royal court were involved in the discovery and promulgation of the book. Certainly, their political and economic interests would be advanced by making the capital the sole center of worship and pilgrimage (see Excursus 14), but other details of Deuteronomy prejudice their interests. The monarchy is undercut by its portrayal as an optional institution, pejoratively characterized as reflecting a desire to imitate other nations. Deuteronomy assigns the king no authority (such as appointing judges or commanding the army), it severely restricts his freedom to accumulate capital, and describes him as a figurehead whose main role is studying God's Teaching so as not to become arrogant (Deut. 17:13–20). Deuteronomy is costly to the priests because tithes and firstlings are no longer donated to them. It also requires the Jerusalem priests to share their duties and income with any provincial Levites who come to Jerusalem—a requirement they apparently resisted when Josiah's reform was carried out.[84] Theologically, too, the book seems at odds with the Jerusalem priests. The belief that God's *kavod*, or physical Presence, resides in the Temple seems to have been the belief of the Jerusalem priesthood,[85] but Deuteronomy shuns this belief and teaches that God's *name* is present. In fact, M. Weinfeld has shown that Deuteronomy presents a radically different conception of religion from that of the priestly literature.[86] Nor are the provincial Levites' interests advanced by Deuteronomy. To be sure, the book permits them to go to Jerusalem and share in the priestly office and income. But it cuts off the livelihood of those who remain in the provinces and treats them as objects of charity dependent on the good will of others.[87]

The strong intellectual orientation of the book and its affinities with Wisdom Literature have inspired the suggestion by Weinfeld that the book was authored by scribes and sages connected with the royal court.[88] The style, values, and literary affinities of the book definitely show its authors to have belonged to an educated class, and the students of Wisdom Literature included those training for royal service. But Deuteronomy never assigns any role to scribes or sages, or sets intellectual qualifications for future offices (as it did for Moses' aides in 1:13,15), and its attitude toward the king and royal officials makes it unlikely that it was authored by anybody who had their interests at heart. Prophetic authorship would be compatible with the exhortatory style of the book, with the authority Deuteronomy assigns prophets, and with its comparison of future prophets to Moses (18:15–22). We shall see, too, that Deuteronomy may have been influenced by the prophet Hosea. But it seems unlikely that the book was authored by a prophet. Not only are prophets given no extraordinary prominence in the book, but Deuteronomy subjects them to a test, on pain of death, that almost every prophet was bound to fail at some time (Deut. 18:21–22). Deuteronomy must have been created independently of all these interests.

There is a geographical aspect to the question of Deuteronomy's authorship. The law corpus of Deuteronomy 12–26 is framed by instructions telling Israel to proceed directly upon entering the land to Mounts Gerizim and Ebal, near the city of Shechem, and perform a number of ceremonies reaffirming their covenant relationship with God (11:26–32; chap. 27). Had Deuteronomy been written in Jerusalem, it would hardly have conferred on a holy site in northern Israel a prestigious role that could potentially undermine Jerusalem's claim to be God's chosen place of worship. These instructions suggest that the core of the book was actually composed in the north. This view is strengthened by Deuteronomy's affinities with the language and teachings of the northern prophet Hosea (early eighth century), who, as noted above (p. xx), criticized the proliferation of altars. He also criticized the use of cult pillars, which are forbidden in Deuteronomy 16:22.[89] Deuteronomy's command to destroy Canaanite shrines "whether on lofty mountains and on hills or under any luxuriant tree" (12:2) closely echoes Hosea's denunciation of his contemporaries who "sacrifice on the mountaintops and offer on the hills, under oaks, poplars, and terebinths whose shade is so pleasant" (Hos. 4:13). Deuteronomy's denigration of false gods as "gods whom you have not experienced" (e. g., Deut. 11:28) is explained by Hosea's declaration "Only I the LORD have been your God ever since the land of Egypt; you have never experienced a [true] God but Me" (Hos. 13:4). Deuteronomy's warning "lest . . . when you have eaten and become sated . . . your heart grow haughty and you forget the LORD your God" (Deut. 8:12–14) echoes Hosea's criticism "When they grazed, they were sated; when they were sated, their heart grew haughty; and so they forgot Me" (Hos. 13:6). And Deuteronomy's attitude toward the monarchy and its officials is reminiscent of Hosea's oracles about the political chaos in the northern kingdom, in which God declares "they have made kings, but not with My sanction; they have made officers, but not of My choice" and "Where now is your king? Let him save you! Where are the chieftains in all your towns whom you demanded [saying]: 'Give me a king and officers'? I give you kings in My ire, and take them away in My wrath" (Hos. 8:4; 13:10–11).

These connections with the northern kingdom make it seem likely that the Deuteronomic ideology crystallized there as a reform program, partly inspired by Hosea, during the final years of the kingdom as a response to the assimilatory pressures of the Assyrian age and to the excesses of the northern monarchy.[90] Its exponents must have come south to Judah as refugees after the kingdom fell, bringing their ideas either in written or oral form. The fall must have prompted serious soul-searching in the south, encouraging a

favorable hearing for their program and leading to Hezekiah's reform. At some point, before or after the reform, the program was put in writing as the book of Deuteronomy or an early version thereof. Suppressed, or at least hidden, during the reign of the paganizing king Manasseh, the book reemerged and became the program of Josiah's sweeping reform.

The Composition and History of Deuteronomy

Deuteronomy was not written in a vacuum. Written and oral sources about Israel's history, law, and religion already existed, and Deuteronomy made use of them in its own unique ways. It draws particularly on the narratives in the source that scholars call "JE"[91] and on laws from a collection that must have resembled the "Book of the Covenant" of Exodus 21–23 (though it was not identical to it).[92] For example, the recounting of the golden calf episode in chapters 9–10 often hews closely to the wording of Exodus 32–24, but it is modified in accordance with Deuteronomy's emphases. The instructions about destroying the Canaanites in Deuteronomy 7:1–6 are based partly on Exodus 23:20–33, but they omit Exodus's statement that God's angel will lead Israel, because Deuteronomy insists that God alone guides Israel. An example from the laws is the modification of Exodus 23:8 in Deuteronomy 16:19, cited above (pp. xvii–xviii). The law about releasing bondsmen in 15:12–18 is close to that of Exodus 21:2–6, but it adds the requirement to give the newly freed servant capital and supplies to live on, a typically Deuteronomic humanitarian touch. Deuteronomy does not draw on the narratives of the priestly literature (P),[93] but it draws on a number of laws from priestly sources, most notably in the dietary laws in 14:3–20 and the law about mixing species in 22:9–11.[94]

Deuteronomy not only uses these and other sources, but expects its audience to know their contents (if not necessarily the sources themselves), so that Moses can refer to things that God said in them[95] and, without explanation, allude to incidents narrated in them, such as God's anger at Aaron during the golden calf incident, the gift of manna, the Baal-peor incident, and "what happened to Miriam."[96]

Deuteronomy also draws on sources not paralleled elsewhere in the Torah. The poems in chapters 32 and 33 are old, pre-Deuteronomic texts.[97] Some of the laws seem to incorporate the text of older laws with Deuteronomic revisions appended.[98] In the homiletic sections of Moses' addresses in chapters 4–11 and 30, Deuteronomy may have incorporated brief sermons or teachings attributed to Moses (or précis of such) that were originally composed for oral delivery.[99] This impression is based on the fact that these sections of the book sometimes consist of short units that have no inherent connection to each other. Frequently, after a few verses, the text changes topics, sometimes without any transition.[100] In Deuteronomy these short units have been brought together into larger groups because of shared themes or extrinsic similarities between them (such as key words), and given literary coherence by being arranged in esthetic patterns (such as chiasmus) and framed by similar opening and closing verses. This kind of editing is similar to that of the rabbinic homiletic midrashim which literarily group together précis of sermons that were originally given in synagogues in talmudic times.[101] Since the sermons in Deuteronomy are all Deuteronomic in style, vocabulary and content, if they were originally presented as oral sermons this would imply that Deuteronomy is the product of a movement that campaigned for its views publicly.

It is unlikely that the book discovered in 622 included all of the present Deuteronomy.

Some verses are not Deuteronomic in style, vocabulary, or content, but come directly from the other Pentateuchal sources, P and JE, namely 1:3; 32:48–52, and parts of chapters 31 and 34.[102] Even those parts of the book that are clearly Deuteronomic seem to contain material from various hands, which implies that there was more than one Deuteronomic writer. First, verses 1:1–4:40 do not seem like original parts of the book. As an introduction, 1:1–5 is redundant with 4:44–49, and there are several inconsistencies between these chapters and the rest of the book. Verses 5:24–6:3 imply that it was during his farewell speech, in the land of Moab, that Moses gave the people the laws he received from God on Horeb, but in 1:18 he says that he gave them laws earlier, when they left Horeb. Verse 23:5 states that the Moabites and Ammonites did not give the Israelites food and water, but 2:28–29 states that the Moabites did do so, and 2:37 implies that Israel could not have asked the Ammonites for supplies.

Verses 1:1–4:40 seem to stem from two different authors. The point of chapters 1–3 is the importance of obeying God, but only with reference to His orders about conquering the promised land. These chapters do not appear to have been written with 4:1–40 in mind. The emphasis of the latter—and the rest of Deuteronomy—is obedience to God's laws as a way of life in the land; *ad hoc* orders are not a central theme of the book. Hence, the transitional "And now" in 4:1 looks like an editorial link, and despite many similarities and connections between these two divisions of Moses' first discourse, they may have had separate authors.[103]

Furthermore, there seem to be two groups of later interpolations within 1:1–4:40. The parenthetic notes in 2:10–12,20–23 and 3:9,11,13 are not part of Moses' address to Israel but later interpolations, addressed to the book's readers; this is shown by 2:10–12, which interrupts Moses' address to the Israelites and refers to them in the third person, and speaks of Israel's conquest of the promised land as a past event. And the promise in 4:29–31 that God will accept Israel's repentance in exile, like a similar promise in 30:1–10, is probably an interpolation from the exilic period.[104]

These considerations have led scholars to conclude that the original book—"core-Deuteronomy"—probably consisted of something like 4:44 through chapter 28 or 30, the main sections of the book. Even within this core, there are later interpolations, such 10:6–7 and chapter 27. The latter interrupts chapters 26 and 28, which clearly belong together. Many scholars take the numerous repetitions in chapter 12, and the change from plural to singular addresses there, to indicate that it combines different strata, though others question the significance of these criteria.[105] Certain laws are inconsistent with basic principles of Deuteronomy, such as 22:20–21, which allows for an execution without requiring the testimony of two witnesses, contrary to 17:6 and 19:15; this raises the possibility, noted by A. Rofé, that this law was not part of the original book.[106]

These examples illustrate one of the main foci of recent research on Deuteronomy, the attempt to distinguish between the original book and subsequent revisions, so as to appreciate the contribution of each to the final work and to identify the stage of religious thought and legal development that each reflects. The main stimulus to this research has been Martin Noth's theory that Deuteronomy 1–4:40 and chaps. 31–34 were added to the book by an exilic writer, or writers, who composed the books of Joshua through Kings. These books are suffused with the language, style, and ideas of Deuteronomy, particularly the book of Kings, which judges every king by Deuteronomic standards. Scholars call the work of this writer(s) "Deuteronomistic," and its author(s) the "Deuteronomist(s)," to distinguish them from Deuteronomy itself, which is termed "Deuteronomic." According to Noth, this writer(s) wanted to show that all of Israel's history depended on her

adherence to Deuteronomic teachings. He therefore placed Deuteronomy 4:44–30:20—the original book, in Noth's view—at the beginning of his book, and wrote the historical-biographical chapters 1–4:40 and parts of 31 and 34 to provide it with a chronological framework.[107] A corrective to Noth's view has been F. M. Cross's argument that the original Deuteronomistic edition of Kings was preexilic, composed prior to Josiah's death; accordingly, those parts of Deuteronomy attributable to the same writer are also preexilic. According to Cross, Kings was revised by a second Deuteronomist during the exile, and only a small part of Kings and such verses as Deuteronomy 4:29–31 and 30:1–10 are attributable to him.[108]

Based on these studies, a good deal of research in recent years has been devoted to identifying other passages in Deuteronomy that might be attributable to one or another of the Deuteronomists. In principle this is a plausible approach, but in practice it has proven problematic since there are few objective criteria on which to base the investigation, and the individual analyses of scholars have not commanded a consensus. In this commentary, we have not suggested analyses of this sort, partly because of their subjective nature, but especially out of a conviction that our task here is primarily to explain the text "holistically," as it has come down to us.[109] Literary-historical analyses are more suited to special monographs. Nevertheless, the implications of this approach are cautionary: because context is so important in determining the meaning of a passage, it is important to know what was the original context for which a verse was written. Undoubtedly, in the commentary that follows, we have explained some passages according to meanings that they were given only when the text reached its present form.

If the literary history of Deuteronomy traced above is anywhere near correct, it implies that Deuteronomy, or most of it, was not composed by Moses. Yet, there is a sense in which the book is Mosaic. According to a talmudic tale, when Moses was on Sinai receiving the Torah he was shown the classroom of Rabbi Akiba, the great legal scholar of many centuries later. Moses grieved when he could not understand the discussion, until he heard a student ask Akiba for the source of what he was saying, and Akiba answered, "This is a law given to Moses at Sinai."[110] The great structure of Jewish law that eventuated from Moses' original teachings is ultimately his, even if he would not recognize the forms it would eventually take. In that sense the writers of Deuteronomy, too, have given us the teaching of Moses, that is, a statement of his fundamental monotheistic teaching, designed to resist the assimilatory temptations of the writers' age and to preserve monotheism for the future.

Deuteronomy in the Ongoing Jewish Tradition

Deuteronomy had a powerful impact on later Jewish tradition. This began in the biblical period itself. The book of the prophet Jeremiah, who lived in the time of King Josiah, is suffused with Deuteronomistic language and allusions. So, too, are the historical books of Joshua, Judges, Samuel, and Kings, which all underwent Deuteronomistic editing, and may even have been compiled by Deuteronomists, as noted above (p. xxv). Echoes of Deuteronomy also appear in the prophetic books of Ezekiel and the "Second Isaiah," who lived in Babylonia during the exile; of the postexilic prophets Haggaai, Zechariah, and Malachi; and of Daniel.

Part of Deuteronomy's impact on Judaism lies in the fact that it was made the last

book of the Torah. Since God's promises to the patriarchs would be completely fulfilled only with Israel's settlement in the promised land, and many of the Torah's laws could only be put into effect there, why did the Torah not continue on through the book of Joshua, which tells how Israel took possession of the land? Why did the Torah end with Moses' death?

According to M. Greenberg, this is because the covenant between God and Israel was predicated on the Exodus, not the gift of the land.[111] The covenant was concluded in the wilderness and its fundamental obligations, such as monotheism, Sabbath, and Pesaḥ, took effect then. Once Moses finished teaching the covenant obligations and passed from the scene, Israel knew all that it needed to know in order to live in accordance with God's will. As important as the land is to the life prescribed by the covenant, the validity of the covenant is independent of the land; on the contrary, Israel's future possession of the land was dependent on her fidelity to the covenant. The separation between the Torah and the story of the conquest of the land expresses the absoluteness of the covenant and its independence of the land.

Recognizing this, the Jews in the Babylonian exile were convinced that the covenant was still binding on them outside the land; just as keeping the covenant had been a precondition for Israel's initial possession of the land, so it was for their return to it. This recognition enabled the covenant to survive the Babylonian exile, and subsequent exiles as well. It may not be too much to say that the survival of Judaism owes much to the perception that the promised land is ahead of us, but our duties to God are now.

By the time of Ezra and Nehemiah (fifth century B.C.E.), Deuteronomy and the other Pentateuchal sources were combined into the Torah essentially as we now know it, and the Jewish community that returned from exile pledged to live its life by it, ratifying and canonizing the entire Torah, as Deuteronomy had been in the days of Josiah. One of the first tasks of Ezra and his colleagues was to enforce the laws of the Torah. This included enforcing the remission of debts (Deut. 15:1–3)[112] and dissolving intermarriages, on the basis of Deuteronomy 23:4–9 and 7:1–4, so as to protect the identity and cohesiveness of the renascent Jewish community.[113] Ezra's successors set about interpreting inconsistencies between the laws of Deuteronomy and other books of the Torah in order to establish consistent laws by which to live.[114] This activity marked the first flowering of Jewish legal exegesis.

In rabbinic times, Deuteronomy helped shape many of the fundamental aspects of Jewish belief and practice that are still followed today. Fully two hundred of the traditional 613 commandments are based on Deuteronomy. One of the most far-reaching influences of the book was achieved through the interpretation of 17:11 by means of which the rabbis found the warrant to create new laws when necessary, and not only to interpret the Torah. This extraordinary understanding of the verse played a major role in allowing Judaism to develop and meet the needs of new historic situations, and not become fundamentalistic and stagnant.

Deuteronomy's contribution to Jewish worship has been extensive and profound. Parts of the book are recited in the daily liturgy and on special occasions. Deuteronomy 6:4–9 and 11:13–21 are recited twice daily as part of *Keriʾat Shema*, and its first verse is also recited on numerous other occasions.[115] Phrases from Deuteronomy (like other books of the Bible) are woven into the wording of numerous important prayers: the attributes of God in the first paragraph of the *ʿAmidah* begin with a citation from 10:17; the declaration of monotheism in *ʿAleinu* is drawn from 4:39; the life-giving power of God's laws in the second paragraph of the evening service is expressed in the words of 30:20; and the

modern prayer for the welfare of the State of Israel quotes the promise of 30:4. Today, 4:4 is recited in many communities before every Torah reading, and 4:44 at the conclusion.

Three passages from Deuteronomy figure prominently in the Haggadah of Pesaḥ. The child's question in 6:20 is one of the passages on which the parable about four types of children is based.[116] Deuteronomy 6:21, "You shall say to your children, 'We were slaves to Pharaoh in Egypt and the Lord freed us from Egypt with a mighty hand,'" introduces the first answer to the children's Four Questions about the unique procedures at the seder banquet. The epitome of Israel's history in 26:5–8, and a midrashic interpretation of it, are considered the core of the Haggadah, according to the Mishnah.[117]

But Deuteronomy's impact on worship goes beyond the recitation of its verses. Notwithstanding the fact that Psalms is the Bible's book of prayer, it was Deuteronomy that shaped the very form of Jewish worship. As noted above (p. xvii), Deuteronomy sought to free religion from excessive attachment to sacrifice and priesthood, and to encourage rituals that teach love and reverence for God to every Israelite. These attempts prepared Judaism to develop new forms of worship that enabled it to survive and flourish after the loss of the Second Temple. In the true spirit of Deuteronomy, the rabbis interpreted its exhortation to "serve Him with all your heart" as proving that prayer is a religious obligation no less than sacrifice, since service "with the heart" must mean prayer.[118] The core of Jewish worship is the recitation of the Shema, as noted, and the public reading of the Torah, which is rooted in 31:11.[119] The duty of blessing God after every meal (*Birkat Ha-Mazon*) is based on 8:10, "when you have eaten your fill, give thanks [lit., "bless"] to the Lord," and the recitation of *Kiddush* on the Sabbath is based on the rabbinic interpretation of *le-kaddesho*, "to sanctify it," in the fifth commandment (5:12).

Apart from the liturgy, Deuteronomy is the source of the idea that religious life should be based on a sacred book, and hence of the obligation of all Jews, not only an elite class, to learn the Torah and teach it to their children (5:1; 6:7). Deut. 6:4 and 33:4 are the first verses to be taught to a child as soon as the child is able to speak. The dietary laws are based in part on Deuteronomy 14:3–21. The Sabbath and pilgrimage festivals (5:12–15; 16:1–17) lie at the heart of the Jewish calendar. Other fundamental practices rooted in Deuteronomy are affixing *mezuzot* to doorposts and the wearing of *tefillin* (6:8–9; 11:18,20)[120] and fringes (*tsitsit*) (22:12). One of the sources of the obligation to give charity is 15:8. Among the laws of mourning, the thirty-day mourning period is based on 21:13 and 34:8 as well as Numbers 20:29.

Deuteronomy plays a major role in Jewish theology, since it is the book of the Bible that deals most explicitly with matters of belief and attitude. This is shown in *Sefer ha-Maddaꜥ* ("The Book of Knowledge"), the theological-ethical introduction of Maimonides' classic digest of Jewish law and theology, the *Mishneh Torah*, itself named after Deuteronomy. There, Maimonides cites Deuteronomy far more often than any other book of the Bible.[121] At the very outset, he cites Deuteronomy as the source of some of the most fundamental commandments, including the commands to believe in God, and Him alone, and to love, revere, and worship Him.

It would be difficult to overstate the extent of Deuteronomy's impact on Jewish life. No idea has done more to shape Jewish history than monotheism, which Deuteronomy asserts so passionately. And no verse has done more to shape Jewish consciousness and identity than the one that Judaism chose as the classic expression of the monotheistic idea, the Shema.

Notes to the Introduction

1. E.g., Deut. 1:5; 4:8,44; 29:20; 30:10.

1a. See E. Tov, *Textual Criticism of the Hebrew Bible* (Minneapolis: Fortress, 1992), 34 n. 10.

2. F. G. Martinez et al., eds., *Studies in Deuteronomy* (Leiden: Brill, 1994), 64–66.

3. For the difference between ancient and modern perceptions of where to start a paragraph, see Excursus 13 n. 12.

4. See Excursus 7.

5. Deut. 4:25–28; 7:1–4; 11:16–17; 13; 17:2–5; 20:16–18; 28:15–68.

6. Deut. 1:29ff.; 7:17ff.; 20:1ff.

7. These parts are found primarily in the Tabernacle and sacrificial laws of Exodus 25–40, Leviticus, and Numbers, as well as parts of the narratives in Genesis through Numbers.

8. Exod. 25:8,22; 29:45–46; 40:34–35.

9. 2 Kings 23:2; cf. v. 3 (this is not the "Book of the Covenant" of Exod. 24:7).

10. Gen. 17:7–8; 22:16–18; 26:2–5; Exod. 6:4–5.

11. Deut. 4:31; 7:9,12; 8:18.

12. See Deut. 4:13,23; 5:2–3; 17:2; 28:69.

13. See 4:44–49 and 28:69; 29:8,11,13,20,24.

14. This passage does not use the term "covenant," but it is implied by the mutual affirmations between God and Israel and its allusions to Exod. 19:5–6.

15. See Comment to 5:6–7.

16. See Comments to 5:10; 6:5–7.

17. See Comments to 10:1–2; 31:26; and Excursus 28.

18. See ANET, 159–198, 207–211, 353–354; M. Weinfeld, "The Origin of the Apodictic Law," VT 23 (1973): 63–75.

19. M. Greenberg, "Three Conceptions of the Torah in Hebrew Scriptures," in E. Blum et al., eds., *Die Hebräische Bibel und ihre zweifache Nachgeschichte* (Neukirchen-Vluyn: Neukirchener Verlag, 1990), 370; idem, "On the Refinement of the Conception of Prayer in Hebrew Scriptures," AJSR 1 (1976): 66 n. 11; cf. Weinfeld, DDS, 81–91; A. Malamat, "Organs of Statecraft in the Israelite Monarchy," in E. F. Campbell and D. N. Freedman, eds., *Biblical Archaeologist Reader* (Garden City, N.Y.: Doubleday, 1970), 163–171. Cf. 2 Sam. 5:2–3, which relates how David became king of the northern tribes by means of a covenant made in the presence of God.

20. Deut. 4:37; 7:7–8; 10:15; 23:6.

21. E.g., Deut. 4:10; 5:26; 6:2,5,13,24.

22. See, e.g., Deut. 1:8,10,30–33; 3:22; 4:20; 7:8; 32:6,18.

23. See Comment to Deut. 1:16.

24. Deut. 7:6; 14:2,21; 26:19; 28:9.

25. Deut. 7:6; 26:19.

26. Deut. 7:14; 15:6; 26:19; 28:1,12–13.

27. Deut. 9:4–24; cf. 31:16–29.

28. See, e.g., Deut. 4:37; 7:7–8; 9:4–5; 10:15.

29. Deut. 4:19–20; 32:8–9; see Excursus 7.

30. Deut. 7:4; 12:30–31; 18:9–12; 20:17–18.

31. See Comment to 2:5.

32. See Comments to 14:21; 23:21.

33. Deut. 7:6; 14:2; 26:18.

34. See Comment to 23:21.

35. Weinfeld, DDS, 282–293; idem, Commentary, 20–24. For the social ideals of biblical law, see M. Greenberg, "Biblical Attitudes Toward Power," in E. B. Firmage et al., eds., *Religion and Law* (Winona Lake, Ind.: Eisenbrauns, 1990), 111–112.

36. See Deut. 12 passim; 14:23–25; 15:20; 16:2–15; 17:8,10; 18:6; 26:2.

37. See Excursus 14.

38. Lev. 12:3–4; 15:31; 19:30; 26:2.

39. Weinfeld, DDS, 190–243.

40. See ibid., 244–319. Note the reservations of Rofé, *Mavo'*, 315–323 (translated in *Christian News from Israel*, New Series 24/4 [Spring 1974]: 204–209); C. Brekelmans, "Wisdom Influence on Deuteronomy," in D. L. Christiansen, ed., *A Song of Power and the Power of Song* (Winona Lake, Ind.: Eisenbrauns, 1993), 123–134.

41. See Weinfeld, DDS, 362–363.

42. See Prov. 24:23; 22:28; 20:10; Eccl. 5:3.

43. Deut. 12:12,18–19; 14:28–29; 15:1–18; 16:11,14; 22:6–7,10,22–23; 23:16–17,20,25–26; 24:6,10–15,17–22; 25:1–4; cf. 14:21.

44. See introductory Comments to chaps. 12 and 15.

45. See R. Sonsino, *Motive Clauses in Hebrew Law* (Chico, Calif.: Scholars Press, 1980), 197.

46. See Driver, lxxxvii–lxxxviii, and cf. W. Ong, *Orality and Literacy* (London and New York: Methuen, 1982), 38–45 (ref. courtesy of Rachel Anisfeld).

47. See introductory Comments to chaps. 1; 4; 7–8 (regarding *r-b-h*); endnote to 1:35; Comments to 2:14–16; 3:23–26a.

48. See Driver, lxxviii–lxxxiv; Weinfeld, DDS, 320–359.

49. BB 15a; Men. 30a; Sifrei 357 and parallels.

50. See the sources collected by A. J. Heschel, *The Theology of Ancient Judaism* (Hebrew) (London: Soncino,

by Joseph Bonfils in his commentary on Ibn Ezra. See D. Herzog, *Joseph Bonfils (Ṭobh 'Elem) und seine Werk Sophnath Pane'ah* (Heidelberg: Carl Winters Universitätsbuchhandlung, 1911).

51. Ibn Ezra at Deut. 1:2 (see Bonfils ad loc.) and 34:1.

52. Bonfils at Deut. 1:2. Other verses cited are Deut. 1:1–5 and 3:11; see Ibn Ezra and Bonfils at Deut. 1:2.

53. Bonfils at Gen. 12:6.

54. See H. H. Rowley, *Studies in Old Testament Prophecy* (Edinburgh: T. and T. Clark, 1957), 163 n. 28 (Ginzberg, *Legends* 6:377 n. 116, thinks that Jerome heard this from his Jewish teachers); Pseudo-Rashi at 2 Chron. 34:14.

55. For reported discoveries (some spurious) of old documents in ancient temples, see M. Cogan and H. Tadmor, *II Kings* (New York: Doubleday, 1988), 294; Weinfeld, Commentary, 18–19.

56. 2 Chron. 34–35 implies that parts of Josiah's reform began before the book was discovered, but Chronicles' chronology is not original. See M. Cogan, "The Chronicler's Use of Chronology," in J. Tigay, ed., *Empirical Models for Biblical Criticism* (Philadelphia: University of Pennsylvania, 1985), 197–209. The historicity of the account in 2 Kings, and hence its implication that Deuteronomy inspired Josiah's reform, is challenged by scholars who believe that the Deuteronomistic language of the account implies that it was composed long after the events and without the benefit of authentic sources. However, F. M. Cross has shown that Kings' story belongs to the Deuteronomistic edition written in Josiah's lifetime; see his *Canaanite Myth and Hebrew Epic* (Cambridge: Harvard University Press, 1973), 274–289. See discussion and bibliography by N. Lohfink, "Recent Discussion on 2 Kings 22–23," in Christiansen, *A Song of Power*, 36–61; idem, "The Cult Reform of Josiah," in P. D. Miller et al., eds., *Ancient Israelite Religion* (Philadelphia: Fortress Press, 1987), 459–475. For a balanced treatment of the account in 2 Kings, see Cogan and Tadmor, *II Kings*, 277–300.

57. It is debated whether the restriction in Lev. 17:1–9 means that, once settled in the land, there would be only a single legitimate sanctuary, or whether the Tent of Meeting stands for any legitimate sanctuary that would be established in the land. See Y. Kaufmann, *The Religion of Israel*, trans. M. Greenberg (Chicago: University of Chicago Press, 1960), 180–184; contrast M. Haran, "The Idea of Centralization of the Cult in the Priestly Apprehension," *Beer Sheva* 1 (1973): 114–121; Levine, *Leviticus*, xxviii and at 17:6.

58. Lev. 23:4–8 is silent on the location. Exod. 23:14–19 and 34:18–25 describe the Feast of Unleavened Bread as a pilgrimage festival, but do not say that everybody must go to the same sanctuary; not even the requirement to bring first fruits to "the house of the LORD" (23:26; 34:19) necessarily implies that. When that is the point, it is made explicit as in Deut. 16.

59. Lev. 26 contains equally terrifying threats (though not to the king), but none of the other features of Josiah's reform points uniquely to Leviticus. 2 Kings 23:8, which reflects a partly incomplete application of Deut. 18:6–8, also points to Deuteronomy.

60. The practice is first mentioned before 720 B.C.E. (2 Kings 17:16). Passing children through fire (Deut. 18:10) is first mentioned in connection with Ahaz (second half of eighth century; 2 Kings 16:3).

61. 2 Kings 18:4,22.

61. Hosea 8:11; 10:1–2,8; 12:12.

63. Perhaps alluding to the united Passover celebration that was held as soon as Israel arrived in the land (Josh. 5:10–11).

64. For the following see M. Cogan, *Imperialism and Religion* (Missoula, Mont.: Scholars Press, 1974), 65–96, esp. 88–96; M. Greenberg, "Religion: Stability and Ferment," in WHJP 4/2, 116–118.

65. 2 Kings 16:3,10–16.

66. 2 Kings 21:2–7. For celestial worship see also 23:4–5,12; Jer. 7:18; 8:2; 19:13; Ezek. 8:16; Zeph. 1:5; cf. chap. 4, n. 62.

67. 2 Kings 23:11.

68. Zeph. 1:9; cf. 1 Sam. 5:5.

69. Jer. 7:18ff.; 44:15–25.

70. See Excursus 27.

71. See S. E. Loewenstamm, "Law," in WHJP 3, 238–240; M. Noth, *The Laws in the Pentateuch* (Philadelphia: Fortress Press, 1967), 1–107.

72. See, e.g., 14:22–29; 15:18–23; 26:2,10.

73. Deut. 15:1–11; 23:20–21; see Comment there.

74. See 1 Sam. 8:11–17.

75. Deut. 19:1–13. The cities of refuge are no later than the United Monarchy. See Loewenstamm, "Law," 259–260; Greenberg, s.v. *'arei miklat*, EM 6:387; Milgrom, *Numbers*, Excursus 75.

76. Deut. 15:9; 24:15.

77. Deut. 17:14–20.

78. See Comment to 16:18. The chiefs of thousands, etc., in 1:15 do imply a monarchic background; see Excursus 2.

79. Deut. 17:8–13. According to 2 Chron. 19:5–11, King Jehoshaphat appointed judges throughout the country and a central court in Jerusalem.

80. On siege warfare see I. Eph'al, "*Darkhei leḥimah u-mishtar ḥevrati bi-tekufat ha-mikra*'," in *Hagut ba-Mikra' le-zekher Yishai Ron* (Israel: 'Am 'Oved and Israel Society for Biblical Research, 1974). So far as is known, forced labor was first used in Israel by David and Solomon.

81. Deut. 6:8; 11:20; 17:18–19; 24:1.

82. Deut. 17:5; 21:19; 22:15,24; 25:7.

83. E.g., Deut. 5:14; 12:12.

84. 2 Kings 23:9.

85. E.g., 1 Kings 8:11; cf. Isa. 6; Ezek. 1:28.

86. Weinfeld, DDS, 191–243; idem, Commentary, 25–37.

87. Deut. 12:12,18,19; 14:27,29; 16:11,14; 26:11–13.

88. Weinfeld, DDS, 158–178, 244–319; idem, Commentary, 62–65; cf. the critiques of Rofé, *Mavo*', and Brekelmans, "Wisdom Influence."

89. Hos. 10:1–2.

90. See A. Alt, *Kleine Schriften* (Munich: Beck, 1959) 2:250–275; Wright, 323–326; Weinfeld, DDS, 366–370; idem, Commentary, 44–56; H. L. Ginsberg, *The Israelian Heritage of Judaism* (New York: Jewish Theological Seminary, 1982), 19–24 (see B. A. Levine's review in *AJSR* 12 [1987]: 143–157).

91. JE itself combines two earlier sources, "J" and "E," standing for the "Yahwistic" source and the "Elohistic" one; these designations are based on the name of God that each prefers. Scholars believe that Deuteronomy has a particularly strong, some would say exclusive, affinity to E.

92. See Weinfeld, Commentary, 19–23; Kaufmann, *Religion*, 167–168.

93. In chap. 1, the scouts follow the itinerary of JE, not of P (see Excursus 2); 11:6 omits P's Korah. Exceptions, cited below, are from a different layer of Deuteronomy.

94. See Weinfeld, Commentary, 30ff.

95. Deut. 1:11; 6:3; 11:25; 13:18; 18:2; 19:8; 26:18. See J. Milgrom, "Profane Slaughter and a Formulaic Key to the Composition of Deuteronomy," HUCA 47 (1976): 1–17.

96. Deut. 4:3; 8:3; 9:20,22; 24:9.

97. See Excursuses 30 and 33.

98. Cf. Excursus 19; chap. 23, n. 47; Rofé, *Mavo*'.

99. Cf. Brekelmans, "Wisdom Influence," 125–127.

100. See, e.g., 4:1–40; 6:4–25; 11:1–25.

101. See J. Heinemann, "Profile of a Midrash," *Journal of the American Academy of Religion* 39 (1971): 141–150; R. Hammer, "Section 38 of Sifre Deuteronomy," HUCA 50 (1979): 165–178.

102. See endnote to 1:3 and Excursuses 29 and 32. On the sources of chap. 34 see Driver; Smith; L. Perlitt, "Priesterschrift im Deuteronomium?" ZAW 100 Supplement (1988): 65–87; Ph. Stoellger, "Deuteronomium 34 ohne Priesterschrift," ZAW 105 (1993): 26–51; Weinfeld, DDS, 7n., 181; Mayes.

103. See M. Noth, *The Deuteronomistic History* (Sheffield: University of Sheffield, 1981), 13–14, 33–34.

104. See Excursus 5.

105. See chap. 12, n. 3.

106. See Excursus 20, citing Rofé, *Mavo*', 147–150. Rofé's book is a systematic study, based on keen textual analyses, of the evolution of Deuteronomic law from pre-Deuteronomic sources in northern Israel, through successive Deuteronomic editions and later interpolations. See particularly his summary (66–71) and the review, with chart, by M. Anbar, *Beth Mikra* 33 (1989): 255–260.

107. See Noth, *Deuteronomistic History*, 13–17, 26–35.

108. Cross, *Canaanite Myth and Hebrew Epic*, 274–289; Richard E. Friedman, *Who Wrote the Bible* (New York: Summit, 1987), 107–116.

109. See M. Greenberg, *Ezekiel 1–20* (Garden City, N.Y.: Doubleday, 1983), 18–27.

110. Men. 29b.

111. M. Greenberg, *Understanding Exodus* (New York: Behrman House, 1969), 13–16.

112. Neh. 10:32; cf. 5:1–13.

113. See Excursus 21.

114. E.g., 2 Chron. 35:7–13 harmonizes Exod. 12:8–9 with Deut. 16:7 and Exod. 12:3–5,21 with Deut. 16:2. See Comments to Deut. 16:2,7 and Excursus 2.

115. See Excursus 10.

116. MdRY Pisḥa 18 (Lauterbach 1:166–167). In its original form, as found in manuscripts and TJ Pes. 10:4, 37d, this parable was based on the reading "upon *us*," found in the LXX of Deut. 6:20. See N. Glatzer, *The Passover Haggadah* (New York: Schocken, 1969), 24–29.

117. Mish. Pes. 10:4; Pes. 116a.

118. Sifrei 41; Maimonides, Hilkhot Tefillah 1:1; idem, Sefer Ha-Mitsvot, positive no. 5; Sefer Ha-Ḥinnukh, no. 431.

119. See Excursus 28.

120. See Excursus 11.

121. M. Greenberg, "Bible Interpretation as Exhibited in the First Book of Maimonides' Code," in *The Judeo-Christian Tradition and the U.S. Constitution* (Philadelphia: Annenberg Research Institute, 1989), 31–32.

GLOSSARY

Abravanel, Isaac ben Judah (1437–1508). Statesman, Bible commentator, religious philosopher. Portugal and Spain. His commentary is cited from the Benei Arbel edition (Jerusalem, 1979).

Aggadah   The nonhalakhic (nonlegal) homiletic side of rabbinic teaching, mostly anchored to the biblical text.

Akkadian   An ancient Semitic language spoken in Mesopotamia and widely diffused in the ancient Near East from before 3000 B.C.E. through the biblical period. Its chief dialects were Babylonian and Assyrian.

Aleppo Codex   The most famous Masoretic manuscript of the entire Hebrew Bible, in codex (book) rather than scroll form. Produced in the tenth century, it was the model followed by Maimonides in making his own copy of the Torah and in formulating his rules for writing Torah scrolls.

Amarna letters   An archive of more than three hundred official letters to and from Canaan and elsewhere in western Asia from the fourteenth century B.C.E., found at El-Amarna, Egypt, the site of the Egyptian capital under Amenophis IV (also known as Akhenaton, 1369-1353).

Aquila   A convert to Judaism from Pontus, Anatolia, and a disciple of Rabbi Akiba. He translated the standardized biblical Hebrew text into Greek in the second century C.E.

Aramaic   A Semitic language closely related to biblical Hebrew and known in many dialects and phases, including Syriac. Aramaic flourished throughout the biblical period and thereafter, and is the language of the Targums, the Gemaras, and large sections of Midrash.

Avot de-Rabbi Nathan   An exposition of an early form of Mishnah Avot (Ethics of the Fathers), transmitted in two versions.

Baal ha-Turim   Commentary on the Torah by Jacob ben Asher (?1270-1340). Germany and Spain.

Baḥya ben Asher (thirteenth century).   Bible commentator and kabbalist. Saragossa, Spain.

Bekhor Shor, Joseph ben Isaac (twelfth century).   Bible commentator. Northern France.

Chiasm(us), chiastic   A symmetrical arrangement of words or larger units of a text, in which the second group of words or units inverts the order of the first, producing patterns such as ABBA, ABCB'A'; see, for example, Comments to Deuteronomy 1:1–5; 2:15; and chapters 29–30.

Da'at Zekenim   Anthology of comments on the Torah by the authors of the Tosafot (northern France, thirteenth century).

Deuteronomy Rabba   Aggadic midrash on Deuteronomy. There are two main editions, one printed in traditional editions of Midrash Rabba, the other published from manuscript by Saul Liebermann (third ed., 1974).

Dittography   A scribal error in which the same letter or letters are accidentally written twice.

Elephantine papyri   Collection of Aramaic papyri from the Jewish and Aramean garrison of the Persian Empire based on the island of Elephantine, Egypt, in the fifth century B.C.E.

Exodus Rabba   Aggadic midrash on the book of Exodus, originally two separate compositions, combined ca. eleventh or twelfth centuries.

Fragment Targum   A series of targums to the Torah that are preserved only in fragmentary form. Also known as Jerusalem Targum (Targum Yerushalmi).

Gemara   An exposition of the Mishnah in Aramaic and Hebrew.

Genesis Apocryphon   An Aramaic elaboration of the Genesis narratives, from first century B.C.E. or C.E., found in cave 1 at Qumran.

Genesis Rabba   Palestinian aggadic midrash on the book of Genesis, edited ca. 425 C.E.

Gersonides   See Ralbag.

Halakhah   The individual and collective rabbinic legal rulings that regulate all aspects of Jewish life, both individual and corporate.

Hapax legomenon (plural: *legomena*).   A word or phrase that occurs only once in a body of literature, such as the Bible.

Haplography   A scribal error in which two successive, identical letters or groups of letters are accidentally written only once.

Ḥazzekuni   Commentary on the Torah by Hezekiah ben Rabbi Manoah, mid-thirteenth century. France.

Hendiadys   Two nouns expressing a single notion, such as "covenant and sanctions" meaning "a covenant guarded by imprecations" (Deuteronomy 29:11,13).

Ibn Ezra, Abraham (1089–1164).   Poet, grammarian, Bible commentator. Spain.

Ibn Janaḥ, Jonah (first half eleventh century).   Grammarian, lexicographer. Spain. He wrote a dictionary, *Sefer Ha-Shorashim*, and a grammar, *Sefer Ha-Rikmah*, of biblical Hebrew.

Judah Halevi (before 1075–1141).   Poet, philosopher, and author of *The Kuzari*. Spain.

Kara, Joseph (born ca. 1060).   Bible commentator. Northern France.

Kaspi, Joseph ibn (1279–1340).   Philosopher, grammarian, and commentator. Spain.

Keli Yakar   Homiletic commentary by R. Ephraim Shelomo ben Aaron of Luntschitz, Poland (1550–1619).

Kere   The way the Masorah requires a word to be read, especially when it diverges from the *ketiv*.

Keter Torah   A Karaite Torah commentary written by Aaron ben Elijah of Nicomedia, Turkey (1328?–1369).

Ketiv   The way a word, usually unvocalized, is written in the Bible; cf. *Kere*.

Kimḥi   See Radak.

Lekaḥ Tov   A midrashic compilation on the Torah and the Five Megillot by Tobias ben Eliezer, eleventh century. Balkans.

Leviticus Rabba   Palestinian aggadic midrash on the book of Leviticus, edited in the fifth century C.E.

Maimonides, Moses ben Maimon, known as the Rambam (1135–1204).   Halakhic codifier (*Ha-Yad Ha-Ḥazakah=Mishneh Torah*), philosopher (*Moreh Nevukhim=Guide of the Perplexed*), and commentator on the Mishnah. Spain and Egypt.

Malbim (1809–1879).   Acronym for Meir Loeb ben Yehiel Michael. Rabbi, preacher, and Bible commentator. Eastern Europe.

Mari   A city on the Middle Euphrates in Syria where over 20,000 cuneiform texts, mostly from the eighteenth century B.C.E., exhibiting many similarities to the Bible, have been found.

Masorah   The traditional, authoritative Hebrew text of the Bible with its consonants, vowels, and cantillation signs, as well as marginal notes that relate to orthographic, grammatical, and lexicographic oddities; developed by the school of Masoretes in Tiberias between the sixth and ninth centuries.

Mekhilta   Tannaitic Halakhic midrash on the book of Exodus in two forms, the Mekhilta de-R. Ishmael and the Mekhilta de-R. Simeon ben Yohai, first and second centuries C.E.

Meklenburg, J. Z. (1785–1865).   Author of *Ha-Ketav ve-ha-Kabbalah*. Poland.

Merism   A "polar expression," a phrase that refers to the totality of a phenomenon by naming the items at its two extremities; two examples are "when you stay at home and when you are away,

when you lie down and when you get up," meaning wherever you are and at all times (Deuteronomy 6:7).

Metonymy   A figure of speech in which a term is used in place of another that is associated with it.

Meyuḥas ben Elijah   Bible commentator and Talmudist. Greece. Probably fifteenth century.

Midrash   Legal and homiletical expositions of the biblical text, and anthologies and compilations of such.

Mishnah   The written compilation of orally transmitted legal teachings covering all aspects of Jewish law, arranged in six orders that, in turn, are divided into tractates; edited by Rabbi Judah Ha-Nasi, ca. 200 C.E. Palestine.

Motive clause   A clause in a law seeking to explain the law or motivate the listener to observe it.

Nahmanides   See Ramban.

Neveh Shalom   Commentary to Saadia's translation of the Torah, by Rabbi Amram Koraḥ (Yemen and Israel, 1871–1953). Published in *Sefer Keter Torah. Ha-"Taj" Ha-Gadol* (Jerusalem: Yosef Ḥasid, 1970).

Numbers Rabba   Aggadic midrash on the book of Numbers, originally two separate compositions, combined ca. thirteenth century.

Onomatopoeia   A word formed by imitating the sound of the object or action that it represents.

Peshitta   A translation of the Bible into Syriac, parts of which are said to have been made in the first century C.E.

Pesikta de-Rav Kahana   Homilies on the synagogue lectionaries. Fifth (?) century C.E. Palestine.

Pesikta Rabbati   Medieval midrash on the festival lectionaries.

Pirkei de-Rabbi Eliezer   Aggadic work on scriptural narratives. Eighth century. Palestine.

Punic   The phase of the Phoenician language used primarily in the western Phoenician colonies, such as Carthage, in North Africa, from around the beginning of the fifth century B.C.E.

Qumran   Site overlooking the Dead Sea where a Jewish sect lived ca. 135 B.C.E.–70 C.E. Numerous documents, including the oldest known Bible manuscripts, were found in caves nearby.

Radak   Acronym for Rabbi David ben Joseph Kimḥi (1160?–1235?). Grammarian, lexicographer, and Bible commentator. Narbonne, Provence.

Ralbag   Acronym for Rabbi Levi ben Gershom, known as Gersonides (1248–1344). Mathematician, astronomer, philosopher, Bible commentator. Southeastern France.

Ramban   Acronym for Rabbi Moses ben Naḥman, known as Nahmanides (1194–1270). Philosopher, halakhist, Bible commentator. Spain.

Rashbam   Acronym for Rabbi Samuel ben Meir (ca. 1080–1174). Commentator on Bible and Talmud, grandson of Rashi. Northern France.

Rashi   Acronym for Rabbi Solomon ben Isaac (1040–1105). Commentator on Bible and Talmud. Troyes, France.

Saadia ben Joseph (882–942).   Philosopher, halakhist, liturgical poet, grammarian, and Bible commentator and translator. Gaon (head of academy) of Pumbedita, Babylonia.

Samaritan Pentateuch   The Torah text of the Samaritans, a non-Jewish sect centered around a sanctuary on Mount Gerizim, claiming descent from the tribes of the northern kingdom of Israel. Apart from a few sectarian elements, the text is based on a type of manuscript found among Jews in Second Temple times. The text is cited here from A. and R. Sadaqa, *Jewish and Samaritan Version of the Pentateuch* (Tel Aviv and Holon, 1961–65), in which Deuteronomy is based on a manuscript said to be from the eleventh century.

Seder Olam (Rabba)   Midrashic chronological work ascribed to Yose ben Ḥalafta, second century C.E. Palestine.

Sefer Ha-Ḥinnukh   "The Book of [Mitsvah] Education." A thirteenth or fourteenth century compilation of the 613 traditional commandments of the Torah in the order of their appearance, with philosophical explanations and references to their talmudic amplification. Attributed to one Aaron ha-Levi of Barcelona, its authorship is uncertain.

Sforno, Obadiah ben Jacob (ca. 1470–ca. 1550).   Bible commentator. Italy.

Septuagint   The Greek translation of the Torah made for the Jewish community of Alexandria, Egypt, third century B.C.E.

Shadal   Samuel David Luzzatto (1800–1865). Italian philosopher, Bible translator, and commentator.

Shalag   Samuel Leib Gordon (1865–1933). Author of a Bible commentary for students and teachers. Palestine.

Shulḥan 'Arukh   The classic codification of Jewish law by Joseph Karo (1488–1575) of Safed, traditionally published with glosses by Moses Isserles (1525–1572) of Poland.

Sifra or **Torat Kohanim**   Tannaitic midrashic commentary to the book of Leviticus, probably compiled about the end of the fourth century C.E. Palestine.

Sifrei   Tannaitic midrashic commentary to the books of Numbers and Deuteronomy, probably compiled at the end of the fourth century C.E. Palestine.

Sumerian   A non-Semitic language, written in cuneiform, spoken in the southern part of ancient Babylonia in the late third millennium B.C.E.

Syriac   The Aramaic dialect of the ancient and medieval Syrian Churches.

Talmud   The body of rabbinic law, dialectic, and lore comprising the Mishnah and Gemara, the latter being an exposition and elaboration of the former in Hebrew and Aramaic. Two separate talmudic compilations exist: the Babylonian Talmud (redacted ca. 500 C.E.) and the Palestinian Talmud (also known as the Jerusalem Talmud; redacted ca. 400 C.E.).

Tanḥuma (Yelammedenu)   Collection of homiletical midrashim on the Torah, arranged according to the triennial lectionary cycle. Attributed to Tanḥum bar Abba, Palestinian preacher, fourth century C.E.

Tanna(im)   The Palestinian sages of the first and second centuries C.E., whose rulings are cited in the Mishnah.

Targum   Literally, "translation," specifically of the Bible into Aramaic.

Targum Jonathan   An unofficial free Aramaic translation of the Torah, erroneously ascribed to Jonathan ben Uzziel through misinterpretation of the initials "T.J." (= Jerusalem Targum). That scholar is the reputed author of the Targum to the Prophets.

Targum Neofiti   A targum of the Torah preserved in Vatican Manuscript "Neofiti 1," discovered in 1956.

Targum Onkelos   The standard, official Aramaic translation of the Torah. Attributed to Onkelos, reputed nephew of the Roman emperor Hadrian and convert to Judaism; second century C.E. The name is probably a corruption of Aquila.

Theodotion   Reviser of the Septuagint (second century C.E.).

Torah Temimah   Anthology of talmudic interpretations of the Torah, and penetrating analyses of them, arranged in order of the biblical verses, by Baruch ha-Levi Epstein of Pinsk (1860–1942).

Tosafot   Supplementary comments to the Talmud and to Rashi's commentary on it by his disciples (France and Germany, twelfth and thirteenth centuries).

Tosefet Berakhah   Supplementary comments by the author of Torah Temimah.

Tosefta   A compilation of tannaitic rulings either omitted from the Mishnah or containing material parallel or supplementary to it. It is arranged according to the six orders of the Mishnah.

Ugaritic   A Semitic language, closely related to Hebrew, used in the ancient city-state of Ugarit (Ras Shamra), on the Syrian coast, in the second millennium B.C.E.

Vulgate   The Latin translation of the Bible made by the Church father Jerome about 400 C.E. It became the official Bible of the Roman Catholic Church.

Wisdom Literature   Books exhorting to moral behavior and discussing theological problems on the basis of experience, such as Proverbs, Job, Ecclesiastes and similar extrabiblical works.

Yalkut Shimoni   Midrashic anthology on the Bible attributed to a certain Simeon, thirteenth century.

ABBREVIATIONS

AB	Anchor Bible
ABD	Anchor Bible Dictionary
Abr.	Philo, De Abrahamo
ADAJ	*Annual of the Department of Antiquities of Jordan*
AfO	*Archiv für Orientforschung*
AHw	W. von Soden, *Akkadisches Handwörterbuch*
AJBI	*Annual of the Japanese Biblical Institute*
AJSL	*American Journal of Semitic Languages and Literatures*
AJSR	*Association for Jewish Studies Review*
Akk.	Akkadian
Albeck	C. Albeck, ed., *Shishah Sidrei Mishnah*
ANEP	J. B. Pritchard, ed., *The Ancient Near East in Pictures Relating to the Old Testament*, 2nd ed.
ANET	J. B. Pritchard, ed., *Ancient Near Eastern Texts Relating to the Old Testament*, 3rd ed. (Pages are cited by quarters as a, b, c, or d.)
Ant.	Josephus, *Antiquities*
AOAT	*Alter Orient und Altes Testament*
AP	A. E. Cowley, *Aramaic Papyri of the Fifth Century B.C.*
Aq.	Aquila
Arab.	Arabic
Arakh.	Arakhin
Aram.	Aramaic
ARM	*Archives royales de Mari*
ARN[1,2]	Avot de-Rabbi Nathan, versions 1 and 2, ed. S. Schechter
AT	*The Bible: An American Translation*
Av.Zar.	Avodah Zarah
BA	*Biblical Archaeologist*
BAR	*Biblical Archaeology Review*
BASOR	*Bulletin of the American Schools of Oriental Research*
BB	Bava Batra
BDB	F. Brown, S. R. Driver, and C. A. Briggs, *Hebrew and English Lexicon of the Old Testament*
Bek.	. Bekhorot
Ben Yehudah	Eliezer Ben Yehudah, *Thesaurus Totius Hebraitatis*
Ber.	Berakhot
Beyerlin	W. Beyerlin, *Near Eastern Religious Texts Relating to the Old Testament*
BHK	*Biblia Hebraica*, ed. R. Kittel et al., 7th ed. (1951)
BHS	*Biblia Hebraica Stuttgartensia*
Bik.	Bikkurim
BK	Bava Kamma
BL	G. R. Driver and J. C. Miles, *The Babylonian Laws*
BM	Bava Metsia
BMAP	E. G. Kraeling, ed., *The Brooklyn Museum Aramaic Papyri*
BRL	K. Galling, ed., *Biblisches Reallexikon*, 2nd ed.
Buhl	F. Buhl, ed., *Wilhelm Gesenius' Handwörterbuch über das Alte Testament*, 16th ed.
BWL	W. G. Lambert, *Babylonian Wisdom Literature*
BZ	*Biblische Zeitschrift*
CAD	*The Assyrian Dictionary of the Oriental Institute of the University of Chicago*
CBQ	*Catholic Biblical Quarterly*
CD	Damascus Document from the Cairo Genizah
Charles	R. H. Charles, ed., *The Apocrypha and Pseudepigrapha of the Old Testament*
Craigie	P. C. Craigie, *The Book of Deuteronomy* (1976)
Da'at Soferim	C. D. Rabinowitz, *Da'at Soferim, Devarim* (Jerusalem: C. Rabinowitz, 1957)

Dalman	G. Dalman, *Arbeit und Sitte in Palästina*
Decal.	Philo, De Decalogo
Deut. R.	Deuteronomy Rabba
Dillmann	A. Dillmann, *Die Bücher Numeri, Deuteronomium, und Josua*, 2nd ed. (1886)
DISO	C.-F. Jean and J. Hoftijzer, *Dictionnaire des inscriptions sémitiques de l'ouest*
DJD	Discoveries in the Judaean Desert
DOTT	D. Winton Thomas, ed., *Documents from Old Testament Times*
Driver	S. R. Driver, *A Critical and Exegetical Commentary on Deuteronomy*, 3rd ed. (1902)
EA	Amarna letters
EAEHL	*Encyclopaedia of Archaeological Excavations in the Holy Land*
EB	*Encyclopaedia Britannica*
Ehrlich, *Mikra*	A. B. Ehrlich, *Mikrâ Ki-Pheshutô* (1899–1901)
Ehrlich, *Randglossen*	
	A. B. Ehrlich, *Randglossen zur Hebräischen Bibel* (1908–14)
EI	Eretz Israel
EM	*'Entsiklopediah Mikra'it* (Jerusalem: Mosad Bialik, 1950–88)
EncJud	*Encyclopaedia Judaica* (1971)
Eruv.	Eruvin
Exod. R.	Exodus Rabba
Finkelstein	L. Finkelstein, ed., *Sifrei on Deuteronomy*
Gen. R.	Genesis Rabba
Ginzberg, *Legends*	
	L. Ginzberg, *Legends of the Jews*
Git.	Gittin
Gk.	Greek
GKC	*Gesenius' Hebrew Grammar*, ed. E. Kautzsch, trans. A. E. Cowley
Gordon	S. L. Gordon, *Ḥamishah Ḥumshe Torah 'im Be'ur Ḥadash* (1938)
Guide	Maimonides, *Guide for the Perplexed*
Ḥag.	Ḥagigah
HALAT	W. Baumgartner et al., *Hebräisches und aramäisches Lexicon zum Alten Testament*
HAR	*Hebrew Annual Review*
HDB	*Hastings' Dictionary of the Bible*
Heb.	Hebrew
Hertz	J. H. Hertz, ed., *The Pentateuch and Haftorahs* (1937)
HJP	S. Lieberman, *Hellenism in Jewish Palestine*
HL	*The Hittite Laws* (ANET, 188–197)
Hoffmann	D. Z. Hoffmann, *Sefer Devarim* (1913–22; Hebrew trans. 1959–61)
Hor.	Horayot
HTR	*Harvard Theological Review*
HUCA	*Hebrew Union College Annual*
Ḥul.	Ḥullin
ICC	International Critical Commentary
IDB	*Interpreter's Dictionary of the Bible*
IDBS	*Interpreter's Dictionary of the Bible,* Supplementary Volume (1976)
IEJ	*Israel Exploration Journal*
IOS	*Israel Oriental Studies*
IR	*Inscriptions Reveal (Ketovot Mesapperot)*
JANES	*Journal of the Ancient Near Eastern Society of Columbia University*
JAOS	*Journal of the American Oriental Society*
Jastrow	M. Jastrow, *A Dictionary of the Targumim, the Talmud Babli and Yerushalmi, and the Midrashic Literature* (1903)
JBL	*Journal of Biblical Literature*
JCS	*Journal of Cuneiform Studies*
JE	*Jewish Encyclopedia*
JESHO	*Journal of the Economic and Social History of the Orient*
JJS	*Journal of Jewish Studies*

JLA	*Jewish Law Annual*
JNES	*Journal of Near Eastern Studies*
Joüon	P. Joüon, *Grammaire de l'Hébreu Biblique*
JPOS	*Journal of the Palestine Oriental Society*
JQR	*Jewish Quarterly Review*
JSJ	*Journal for the Study of Judaism in the Persian, Hellenistic, and Roman Period*
JSOT	*Journal for the Study of the Old Testament*
JSOTSup	*Journal for the Study of the Old Testament, Supplement Series*
JSS	*Journal of Semitic Studies*
JTS	*Journal of Theological Studies*
KAI	H. Donner and W. Röllig, eds., *Kanaanäische und Aramäische Inschriften*
Keil-Delitzsch	C. F. Keil and F. Delitzsch, *Commentary on the Old Testament* (1876; reprint, 1985)
Kel.	Kelim
Ket.	Ketubbot
Kid.	Kiddushin
Kil.	Kilayim
KJV	King James Version
Lauterbach	J. Z. Lauterbach, *Mekilta de-Rabbi Ishmael*
LCL	Loeb Classical Library edition
LE	*The Laws of Eshnunna* (ANET, 161–163)
Lev. R.	Leviticus Rabba
Levine, *Leviticus*	
	B. A. Levine, *The JPS Torah Commentary: Leviticus*
LFM	A. L. Oppenheim, *Letters from Mesopotamia*
LH	*The Laws of Hammurabi* (ANET, 163–180)
LLI	*Lipit-Ishtar Lawcode* (ANET, 159–161)
LOB	Y. Aharoni, *The Land of the Bible: A Historical Geography*, 2nd ed., trans. and ed. by A. F. Rainey
LU(N)	*The Laws of Ur-Nammu* (ANET, 523–525)
LXX	Septuagint
M	Parashah breaks in the Masoretic text as prescribed by Maimonides
Maʿas.	Maʿaserot
Maʿas. Sh.	Maʿaser Sheni
Mak.	Makkot
MAL	*The Middle Assyrian Laws* (ANET, 180–188)
Mayes	A.D.H. Mayes, *Deuteronomy* (1981)
MdRY	Mekhilta de-R. Ishmael
MdRSbY	Mekhilta de-R. Simeon ben Yoḥai
Meg.	Megilla
Mekh.	Mekhilta
Men.	Menaḥot
MG	Mikraʾot Gedolot
Mid.	Midrash
Mid. Hag.	Midrash Ha-Gadol
Mik.	Mikvaʾot
Milgrom, *Numbers*	
	J. Milgrom, *The JPS Torah Commentary: Numbers*
Mish.	Mishnah
MK	Moʿed Katan
Moffatt	James Moffatt, *The Bible: A New Translation*
Moran	W. L. Moran, "Deuteronomy," in *A New Catholic Commentary on Holy Scripture* (1969)
MT	Masoretic Text
MTvar.	Variant parashah breaks in Masoretic texts that differ from those prescribed by Maimonides
NAB	*New American Bible*
NEB	*New English Bible*
Ned.	Nedarim
NJPS	New Jewish Publication Society translation (1985)

OCD	*Oxford Classical Dictionary*, 2nd ed.
OJPS	Old Jewish Publication Society translation (1917)
Op.	Philo, De Opificio Mundi
OTS	*Oudtestamentische Studiën*
PAAJR	*Proceedings, American Academy of Jewish Research*
PEQ	*Palestine Exploration (Fund) Quarterly*
Pes.	Pesaḥim
Pesh.	Peshitta
Phillips	A. Phillips, *Deuteronomy* (1973)
Plaut	W. Gunther Plaut, ed., *The Torah: A Modern Commentary* (1981)
PRU	*Le Palais royale d'Ugarit*
PTU	F. Gröndahl, *Die Personennamen der Texte aus Ugarit*
1Q, etc.	Sigla for Qumran texts: the number preceding Q refers to the cave in which the text was found; the word or number following it refers to the composition; raised letters identify different manuscripts of the same work. Thus 1Q5 = text 5 from Qumran cave 1; 4QDeut^c = third manuscript of Deuteronomy from Qumran cave 4.
1QM	War between the Children of Light and the Children of Darkness from Qumran cave 1
1QS	Rule of the Congregation from Qumran cave 1
1QSa	Appendix to 1QS
11QTemple	Temple Scroll from Qumran cave 11
RA	*Revue d'assyriologie et d'archéologie orientale*
von Rad	G. von Rad, *Deuteronomy: A Commentary* (1966)
RB	*Revue biblique*
RH	Rosh Hashanah
RLA	E. Ebeling et al., eds., *Reallexikon der Assyriologie*
Rofé, *Mavo'*	A. Rofé, *Mavo' le-sefer Devarim* (Jerusalem: Akademon, 1988)
RQ	*Revue de Qumran*
RSP	L. Fisher, ed., *Ras Shamra Parallels*
Sam.	Samuel
Sanh.	Sanhedrin
Sarna, *Exodus*	N. M. Sarna, *The JPS Torah Commentary: Exodus*
Sarna, *Genesis*	N. M. Sarna, *The JPS Torah Commentary: Genesis*
Shab.	Shabbat
Shek.	Shekalim
Shev.	Shevi'it
Sif. Zut.	Sifrei Zuta
Smith	G. A. Smith, *The Book of Deuteronomy* (1918)
SOR	Seder Olam Rabba
Sot.	Sotah
SP	Samaritan Pentateuch
Spec.	Philo, De Specialibus Legibus
Suk.	Sukkah
SVT	*Supplements to Vetus Testamentum*
Syr.	Syriac
TA	*Tel Aviv*
Ta'an.	Ta'anit
Tanḥ.	Tanḥuma
Targ.	Targum
Targ. Jon.	Targum Jonathan
Targ. Neof.	Targum Neofiti
Targ. Onk.	Targum Onkelos
Targ. Yer.	Targum Yerushalmi
TDOT	G. J. Botterweck and H. Ringgren, eds., *Theological Dictionary of the Old Testament*
Ter.	Terumot
Thompson	J. A. Thompson, *Deuteronomy* (1974)
TJ	Jerusalem Talmud

TK	*Tosefta Ki-fshuṭah*
Toh.	Tohorot
Tosef.	Tosefta
Tur Sinai	Tur Sinai, *Peshuto shel Mikra'*
TWAT	G. J. Botterweck and H. Ringgren, eds., *Theologisches Wörterbuch zum alten Testament*
2 Mos.	Philo, De Vita Mosis, part 2
UF	*Ugarit-Forschungen*
Uffenheimer	*Ḥamishah Ḥumshe Torah 'im Peirush Ḥadash . . . me-'et S. L. Gordon*, Vol. 5, *Sefer Devarim*, newly revised by B. Uffenheimer (1972)
Ugar.	Ugaritic
UT	C. H. Gordon, *Ugaritic Textbook* (1965)
VBW	*Views of the Biblical World*
Virt.	Philo, De Virtutibus
VT	*Vetus Testamentum*
VTE	*Vassal Treaties of Esarhaddon* (ANET, 534–541)
Vulg.	Vulgate
WCJS	World Congress of Jewish Studies, Papers
Weinfeld, Commentary	
	M. Weinfeld, *Deuteronomy 1–11* (1991)
Weinfeld, DDS	M. Weinfeld, *Deuteronomy and the Deuteronomic School*
Weiss	I. H. Weiss, *Sifra Devei Rav* (Vienna, 1862; reprint, New York: Om, 1946)
WHJP	*World History of the Jewish People*, First Series: Ancient Times
WHJP 1	E. A. Speiser, ed., *At the Dawn of Civilization: A Background of Biblical History*
WHJP 2	B. Mazar, ed., *Patriarchs*
WHJP 3	B. Mazar, ed., *Judges*
WHJP 4	A. Malamat and I. Eph'al, eds., *The Age of the Monarchies*. 2 vols. Vol. 1, *Political History*; Vol. 2, *Culture and Society*
WO	*Die Welt des Orients*
Wright	G. E. Wright, "The Book of Deuteronomy," in *The Interpreter's Bible*, vol. 2 (1953)
Yad.	Yadayim
Yal.	Yalkut Shimoni
Yev.	Yevamot
ZA	*Zeitschrift für Assyriologie*
ZAW	*Zeitschrift für die alttestamentliche Wissenschaft*
Zev.	Zevaḥim

The editors have adopted a popular system for transliteration of Hebrew, except for the following letters, which have no English equivalent:

> ' = alef
> ' = ayin
> ḥ = ḥet (pronounced as the guttural "ch" in German)
> kh = khaf (pronounced as the guttural "ch" in German)

With reference to other Semitic languages, the following letters and diacritics are sometimes used: ḫ for velar ḥet, ṭ for tet, ṯ for th (as in thin), š for shin, ś for sin, and ṣ for tsadi.

Where verses are subdivided into parts, *a* and *b* following the verse number signify the part of the verse before and after the 'etnaḥta, respectively, and numerals following *a* and *b* stand for the parts of each subdivision; hence, for example, 1b2 stands for the second part of the second half of verse 1.

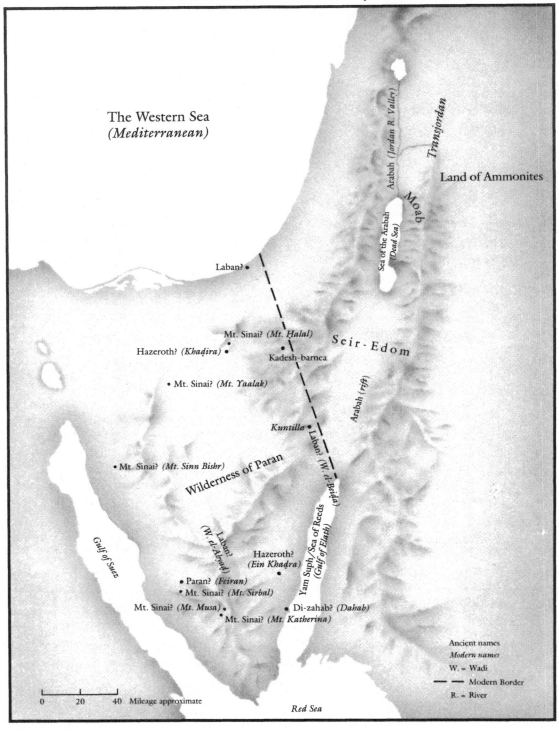

The Western Sea
(Mediterranean)

Land of Ammonites

Arabah (Jordan R. Valley)

Transjordan

Moab

Sea of the Arabah
(Dead Sea)

Laban? •

Seir-Edom

Mt. Sinai? *(Mt. Halal)*

Hazeroth? *(Khadira)* •

Kadesh-barnea

Arabah (rift)

• Mt. Sinai? *(Mt. Yaalak)*

Kuntilla •

Laban? *(W. el-Beida)*

• Mt. Sinai? *(Mt. Sinn Bishr)*

Wilderness of Paran

Yam Suph/Sea of Reeds
(Gulf of Elath)

Gulf of Suez

Laban?
(W. el-Abyad)

Hazeroth?
(Ein Khadra) •

• Paran? *(Feiran)*
• Mt. Sinai? *(Mt. Sirbal)*

Mt. Sinai? *(Mt. Musa)* •

• Di-zahab? *(Dahab)*

• Mt. Sinai? *(Mt. Katherina)*

Ancient names
Modern names
W. = Wadi
— — Modern Border
R. = River

0   20   40   Mileage approximate

Red Sea

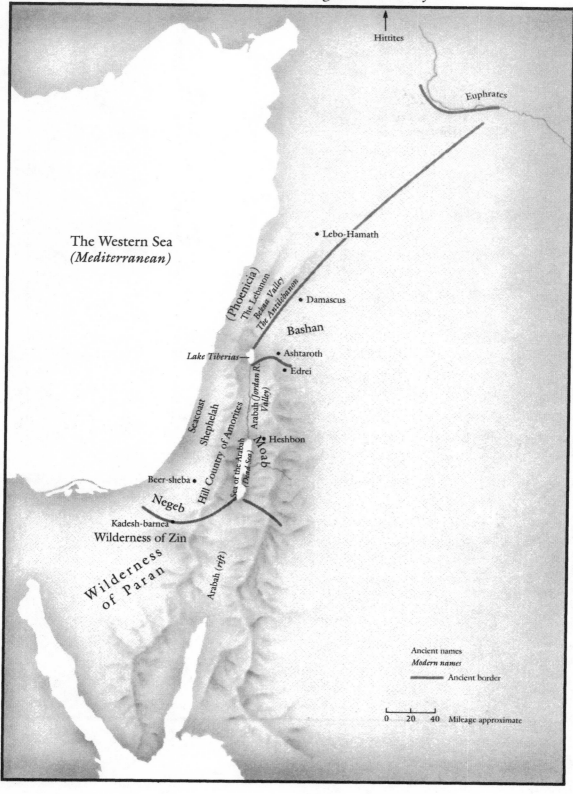

Hittites

Euphrates

The Western Sea
(Mediterranean)

• Lebo-Hamath

(Phoenicia)
The Lebanon
Beqaa Valley
The Antilebanon

• Damascus

Bashan

Lake Tiberias —

• Ashtaroth

• Edrei

Seacoast
Shephelah
Hill Country of Amorites
Arabah (Jordan R. Valley)
Sea of the Arabah (Dead Sea)
Moab

Heshbon

Beer-sheba •

Negeb

Kadesh-barnea •

Wilderness of Zin

Wilderness
of Paran

Arabah (rift)

Ancient names
Modern names
———— Ancient border

0   20   40   Mileage approximate

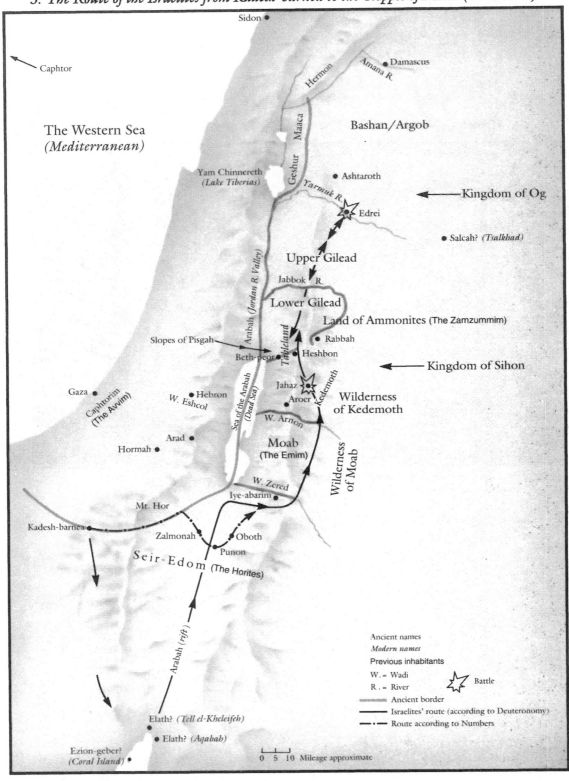

4. *Mounts Gerizim and Ebal (Deutronomy 11 and 27)*

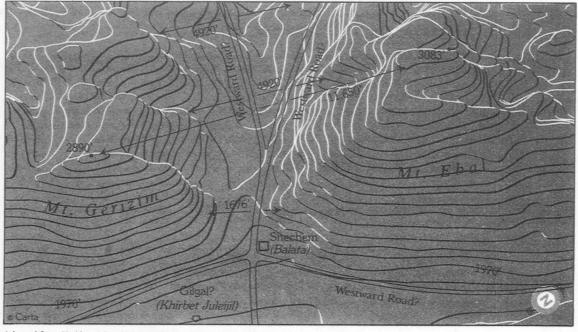

Adapted from Y. Aharoni and M. Avi-Yonah. *The Macmillan Bible Atlas*,
Revised edition (New York: Macmillan, 1977; © Carta, 1968, 1977).

5. The Scene of Deuteronomy

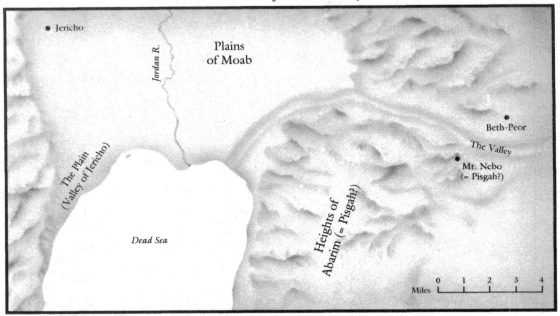

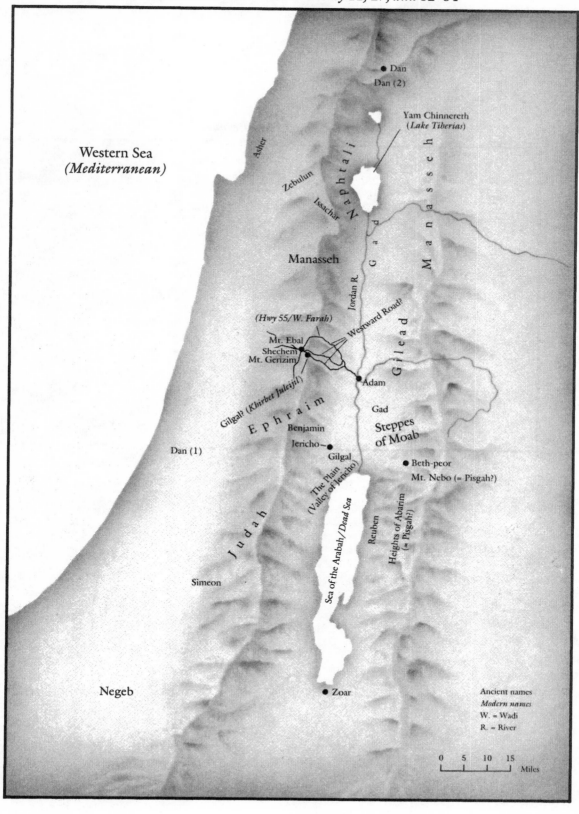

THE COMMENTARY TO DEUTERONOMY

DEVARIM

1 These are the words that Moses addressed to all Israel on the other side of the Jordan.—Through the wilderness,

דברים

א אֵ֣לֶּה הַדְּבָרִ֗ים אֲשֶׁ֨ר דִּבֶּ֤ר מֹשֶׁה֙ אֶל־כָּל־יִשְׂרָאֵ֔ל בְּעֵ֖בֶר הַיַּרְדֵּ֑ן בַּמִּדְבָּ֨ר בָּעֲרָבָה֙ מ֣וֹל ס֔וּף

CHAPTER 1

HEADING (vv. 1–5)

Devarim

The first five verses are the heading to Deuteronomy, giving the time and place of the addresses that make up the book. Verses 3–5 indicate that what follows consists of the laws and teachings that Moses addressed to the people in the land of Moab, at the end of their wanderings, shortly before they would enter the promised land. Verse 1 indicates that he had previously spoken these words at various places during the wanderings.

These verses are arranged chiastically as follows:

> A. The site of Moses' addresses—"on the other side of the Jordan," and so forth (1)
> B. The foreshadowing of the first message of the first address (2)
> C. The date when Moses began these addresses (3)
> B'. The foreshadowing of the second message of the first address (4)
> A'. The site where he delivered his addresses—"on the other side of the Jordan" (5)

It is not clear how much of Deuteronomy these verses introduce. Verses 1, 3, and 5 seem partly redundant and contradictory, and the relationship of verse 2 to its context is obscure. Critical theory holds that these verses do not all originate from the same author. But even if this is the case, the chiastic design indicates that they were brought together quite deliberately, and traditional commentators, as we shall see, have made perceptive suggestions about their coherence.

1. ***These are the words that Moses addressed to all Israel*** Apart from a few connecting passages and the narratives about Moses' last days,[1] the speaker in Deuteronomy is Moses himself, not an unnamed narrator as in the previous books of the Torah. Even the narratives and laws appear as parts of addresses in which Moses reviews the past forty years and prepares Israel for the future. Deuteronomy is thus Moses' valedictory: he sums up the laws that he gave the people and the lessons of the period in which he led them, and urges them to observe those laws and keep those lessons in mind always.[2]

on the other side of the Jordan.—Through the wilderness . . . Rather, "on the other side of the Jordan, in the wilderness. . . ."[3] This part of the verse indicates where the addresses were delivered. The most natural way to understand it is as the continuation of verse 1a. It implies that the teachings that follow were delivered at various places where the Israelites stayed during the past forty years.

Since most of the places named are in the Sinai Peninsula and the Aravah south of the Dead Sea, this verse seems inconsistent with verse 3 and most of Deuteronomy, which date the addresses of Deuteronomy to late in the fortieth year after the Exodus, *after* the Israelites had left the Sinai, passed the Aravah, and encamped in Moab.[4] To resolve the inconsistency, some medieval commentators assumed that verse 1 refers to where the addresses were *originally* delivered, while verse 3 and other passages indicate when and where they were recapitulated and explained.[5] Thus understood, the verse makes Deuteronomy consistent with the rest of the Torah by indicating that although much of its content was not reported earlier in the Torah, it is not essentially new, but is a recapitulation and exposition of what Moses had said earlier (see v. 5).[6]

The verse refers to three areas: (1) the other side of the Jordan; (2) the wilderness, in a place further defined as being "in the Arabah, near Suph"; and (3) another place, or places, somewhere between Paran and Tophel, Laban, Hazeroth, and Di-zahab. This list moves from north to south, from Transjordan to the Aravah south of the Dead Sea and then to places in the Sinai. In other words, it lists the areas where Moses addressed the people in reverse chronological order, starting where they are encamped and moving back in time.[7]

in the Arabah near Suph, between Paran and Tophel, Laban, Hazeroth, and Di-zahab, ²it is eleven days from Horeb to Kadesh-barnea by the Mount Seir route.—³It

בֵּין־פָּארָן וּבֵין־תֹּפֶל וְלָבָן וַחֲצֵרֹת וְדִי זָהָב: ² אַחַד עָשָׂר יוֹם מֵחֹרֵב דֶּרֶךְ הַר־שֵׂעִיר עַד קָדֵשׁ בַּרְנֵעַ: 3 וַיְהִי בְּאַרְבָּעִים שָׁנָה בְּעַשְׁתֵּי־

on the other side of the Jordan   In Transjordan, east of the River Jordan (4:47). Moses never crossed over to the western side of the Jordan (1:37; 3:27).

the wilderness   The text goes on to identify this wilderness as being in the Aravah, or Arabah, the rift that continues the Jordan Valley south of the Dead Sea down to the Gulf of Elath, as in 2:8. The rift is known as the Aravah to this day. For another meaning of Aravah, see verse 7.

near Suph   The ancient translations take this to be Yam Suph, "the Sea of Reeds," the biblical name for the Gulf of Elath. (The sea the Israelites crossed when leaving Egypt had the same name, but that cannot be the meaning here since Moses had no time to preach when the Israelites crossed the sea.) Suph could also be a name for some site on the shore of Yam Suph. If "in the Arabah" and "near Suph" go together, the phrase refers to the southern Aravah, where the Israelites began their march through Seir-Edom toward Moab (2:1–8).[8]

The remaining five sites, except for the unknown Tophel, can be identified with places in the Sinai Peninsula (see Map 1 and Excursus 1). They are probably mentioned to indicate that Moses delivered addresses at one or more places (perhaps including Horeb) within a region encompassed by them. It is less likely that he spoke at each site, since the five do not appear to be listed in geographical order.

2.   It was an eleven-day journey[9] from Horeb (Mount Sinai) to Kadesh-barnea, the gateway to the promised land (see vv. 19–20). Since the journey from Horeb to Kadesh is mentioned again in verse 19, this verse is probably preparatory to verse 19. Its point is that the journey took only eleven days and, had Israel trusted in God, it could have entered the land immediately and not wandered in the wilderness for thirty-eight years.[10] Although one might have expected the distance to be given in verse 19 rather than here, biblical narrative often gives information in advance, parenthetically, to prepare the reader for a subsequent narrative.[11] The events at Kadesh are the first of the two pivotal themes in Moses' first address and serve as the basis of its first message, the consequences of not trusting in God (1:20–46). Had verse 2 appeared within verse 19, it might have attracted little attention except as a chronological note. By placing the verse before the narrative with which it belongs, the text highlights and underscores the message that, had Israel trusted God, its long years of wandering would never have occurred.

Horeb   Deuteronomy's name for Mount Sinai. It is located in the Sinai peninsula, but precisely where is not known; see Excursus 1.

Kadesh-barnea   Kadesh-barnea (sometimes called simply Kadesh), near the western border of Seir-Edom, was on the southern boundary of the promised land—in essence the gateway to it (see vv. 19 and 20 and Excursus 1). The fateful events that took place at Kadesh were related in Numbers 13–14 and are recapitulated below in verses 19–46.

by the Mount Seir route   Or "by the Seir Highlands route"; Hebrew *har* can refer to a single mountain or a mountainous region. Seir is practically synonymous with Edom, which is best known as the southernmost of the Transjordanian kingdoms (see Comment to 2:2–8). Its territory also extended west of the Aravah into the highlands of the eastern Negev. Seir usually refers to this part of Edom, west of the Aravah and south of the promised land. See Excursus 1.

The "Mount Seir, or Seir Highlands, route" is probably one that terminated at Mount Seir, or the Seir highlands, since "routes which are given names in the Bible are usually designated by their terminal point."[12] A road leading to Seir could well pass through Kadesh-barnea, which was near the western border of Seir-Edom (Num. 20:16). The text does not indicate whether this road led to Seir directly from Mount Sinai or by a connecting route. In either case, since we do not know the location of Mount Sinai, it is impossible to identify the road.

3.   This verse integrates Deuteronomy into the chronological framework of the previous books of the Torah (Deuteronomy does not otherwise give precise dates).[13] It also indicates, as

was in the fortieth year, on the first day of the eleventh month, that Moses addressed the Israelites in accordance with the instructions that the LORD had given him for them, ⁴after he had defeated Sihon king of the Amorites, who dwelt in Heshbon, and King Og of Bashan, who dwelt at Ashtaroth [and] Edrei. ⁵On the other side of the Jordan, in the land of Moab, Moses undertook to expound this Teaching. He said:

עֲשָׂר חֹדֶשׁ בְּאֶחָד לַחֹדֶשׁ דִּבֶּר מֹשֶׁה אֶל־בְּנֵי יִשְׂרָאֵל כְּכֹל אֲשֶׁר צִוָּה יְהֹוָה אֹתוֹ אֲלֵהֶם: 4 אַחֲרֵי הַכֹּתוֹ אֵת סִיחֹן מֶלֶךְ הָאֱמֹרִי אֲשֶׁר יוֹשֵׁב בְּחֶשְׁבּוֹן וְאֵת עוֹג מֶלֶךְ הַבָּשָׁן אֲשֶׁר־יוֹשֵׁב בְּעַשְׁתָּרֹת בְּאֶדְרֶעִי: 5 בְּעֵבֶר הַיַּרְדֵּן בְּאֶרֶץ מוֹאָב הוֹאִיל מֹשֶׁה בֵּאֵר אֶת־הַתּוֹרָה הַזֹּאת לֵאמֹר:

verse 1 does not, that although Moses speaks here in his own name, he does so at God's command, not on his own initiative. In the context of verses 1–5 the verse means that all the words that Moses had spoken to Israel earlier, in the places mentioned in verse 1, he now repeated in the fortieth year.

the eleventh month The month known later as Shevat, which falls in January-February. According to *Seder Olam Rabba*, Moses' exposition took thirty-six days, ending (in 31:1) on the sixth of Adar.[14] This would imply that the following discourses were delivered piecemeal, not all at once.

4. In place of verse 3's calendrical date, verse 4 dates Moses' address in terms of significant events: it was after the victories over the Amorite kings Sihon and Og (Num. 21:21–22:1, recapitulated below in 2:24–3:17). According to Numbers 22:1, it was after these victories that the Israelites reached the steppes of Moab where, as verse 5 notes, Moses delivered the coming addresses. The victories are mentioned not merely as a chronological marker but because they constitute the second pivotal theme in the coming address. They are the mirror image of the events at Kadesh: they begin to reverse the disastrous effects of those events and serve as the evidence for the address's second message, that Israel should put its trust in God. Verse 4 thus foreshadows the second message of the coming address just as verse 2 foreshadows its first one. Prepared by verse 4, the attentive reader who reads of the events at Kadesh is aware of how foolishly the Israelites acted there.

Ashtaroth [and] Edrei[15] Og's two capital cities. See Excursus 1.

5. This verse serves as a more immediate introduction to what follows.

in the Land of Moab In the steppes of Moab, so-called because the area had belonged to Moab before its conquest by Sihon, from whom Israel wrested it. See introductory Comment to 2:9–16. For the precise location where Moses delivered his addresses, see 3:29; 4:46, and Map 5.

undertook Rather, "began," as understood by the ancient translations.[16]

expound This translation preserves the ambiguity of the Hebrew *be'er*. "Expound" means both "set forth or state in detail" and "explain," just as *be'er* may mean either "state clearly" or "clarify."[17] The meaning "set forth" agrees with the fact that this verse introduces the addresses of Deuteronomy, which were not previously delivered. On the other hand, "clarify" agrees with verses 1–2, which imply that these addresses recapitulate and clarify earlier teachings (see Comment to 1:18). The ancient translations understood the verse in the latter sense.[18]

this Teaching "Instruction" would better convey the wide range of meanings expressed by *Torah*, since it expresses both the intellectual and legal connotations of the term. Derived from *horah*, "teach, instruct," *Torah* refers to rules of civil and ritual procedure,[19] prophetic teaching and reproof,[20] moral exhortation,[21] and didactic narrative.[22] Moses frequently refers to Deuteronomy as "this *Torah*."[23] Here the term refers to the exhortations of chapters 5–11 and the laws of chapters 12–28 (see 4:8,44; 17:18–19; 31:12), and perhaps also to the didactic narrative and exhortations of 1:6–4:40. Of all the terms for God's instructions, none better characterizes Deuteronomy, since it connotes both law and an instruction that must be taught, studied, and pondered,[24] and it is expected to shape the character, attitudes, and conduct of those who do so (see, e.g., 6:1–2,6–9; 17:18–19; 31:10–13). This characterization of Deuteronomy reflects its strong interest in wisdom and learning, as in verses 1:13; 4:1,6; 5:1; 16:19.[25] In later times the term Torah was applied to the entire Pentateuch as "the Teaching" or "Instruction" *par excellence*.

MOSES' FIRST DISCOURSE (1:6–4:40)

Moses' first discourse serves as a prologue to the book, describing the historical events leading up to the laws he proclaims in 4:44 through chapter 28. The prologue consists of two divisions, a retrospective (1:6–3:29) and an exhortation, based on historical experience, to obey God's laws (4:1–40). Both divisions emphasize the importance of obedience to God. In the retrospective the theme is obedience to God's orders about conquering the promised land, and in the exhortation it is obedience to His laws as a way of life in the land. The latter theme leads naturally to the exposition of the laws in the second, and main, address of the book (4:44–28:69).

RETROSPECTIVE ON THE FORTY-YEAR SOJOURN IN THE WILDERNESS AND THE LESSONS OF THAT PERIOD (1:6–3:29)

Themes

In the first division of the prologue, Moses reviews the major events following Israel's departure from Horeb. These events are related more fully in Exodus and Numbers. The details recalled here emphasize important themes that the events demonstrated, of which the people need to be reminded as they prepare to enter the promised land. The most important of these themes constitute two messages: that mistrusting and disobeying God lead to disaster, and that trusting and obeying Him lead to success. These themes are expressed in the account of how God brought the Israelites to the border of the land and placed it at their disposal, how their fear and refusal to march on the land despite the assurance of God's help led to defeat by the Amorites and condemnation to death in the wilderness, and how the next generation's trust in God and obedience to His commands led to victories over powerful kings. This lengthy demonstration of the importance of trust and obedience prepares the way for Moses' subsequent exhortations to obey God's laws (as in 4:1–40) and to approach the coming battles with the Amorites with full trust and confidence in God (as in 9:1–3 and 20:1–4).

The theme of trusting God in battle reflects a concept of war according to which God is the warrior who does the actual fighting for Israel. This theme is discussed in Excursus 3.

Structure and Formulation

The themes of obedience and disobedience are underscored by the structure and formulation of the narrative. Pre-modern Hebrew texts of the Torah highlight these themes by the way they divide the narrative into units.[26] Unlike the paragraphs in the English translation, which divide the text into a large number of units that begin where there are shifts in time, place, action, speaker, and other narrative details, these Hebrew texts divide the narrative into fewer units and frequently consider speeches, especially statements by God, as the turning points in the events.[27] This makes it clear that the drama in the events, as it is throughout the Bible, is in the relationship between God's commands and promises and the people's responses to them.

The divisions in the pre-modern Hebrew texts suggest that the narrative consists of two major parts, each composed of several sections. The major parts are (1) 1:1–2:1 and (2) 2:2–3:29. Part 1, following the heading (1:1–5), covers events that occurred in the year following the Exodus, starting

with God's declaration to Israel, "You have stayed long enough at this mountain" (Horeb, i.e., Sinai) and His command that they head for the promised land (1:6–8). Part 2, covering events at the end of the forty-year sojourn in the wilderness, opens with God's declaration to Israel, "You have been skirting this hill country long enough" and His renewed command to head for the promised land (2:3). The similarity between God's two declarations is even more pronounced in the Hebrew, since the words rendered "mountain" and "hill country" are the same word (*har*) and the verbs, though different, have similar sounds (*shevet* and *sov 'et*). That these two parts of the narrative open with practically the same command underscores the fact that the events occuring between them aborted the fulfillment of the first command and that the parts are mirror images of each other. The first part ends in disaster brought on by the people's faithless disobedience; the second ends in victory resulting from their trust in God and compliance with His commands.

The way in which the people's fate depends on their response to God's commands and promises is constantly emphasized by the phraseology of the narrative. Key phrases first appear in God's commands and promises, phrases such as "you have done such-and-such long enough," "turn about and make your way," "go up," and God "swearing." These phrases are later echoed when the people obey or disobey the commands, when they trust or refuse to trust in the promises, when God reverses or renews the commands, and when He suspends or renews the promises. As a result, these phrases reverberate throughout the narrative in contrasting senses; sometimes they express God's intention to bring the people into the land and at other times they express His decision to keep them out. As we shall see in the Comments, the division of these parts into smaller sections and units highlights these themes by calling attention to the key phrases that express them.

History and Belief

The historical content of Moses' address reflects the importance of history as the basis of biblical religion. Religious belief in the Bible is based mostly on Israel's experience of God rather than on theological speculation. This experience is an important component of the covenantal relationship between God and Israel, since covenant relations between political entities were likewise based on their past experiences with each other. Moses' review of the relations between God and Israel in the recent past parallels similar historical surveys at the beginning of treaties between suzerains and vassal states in the ancient Near East. These surveys include such details as descriptions of the land granted to the vassal and reminders of the vassal's past rebellion (cf. 1:7, 26ff.).[28] Several such details will be cited in the course of the commentary.

Previous Accounts of the Events

Moses' review of the events sometimes adheres closely to the earlier narratives about them in Exodus and Numbers. There are even places where the text presupposes the audience's ability to fill in details known to us from those earlier narratives, as in the reference to Caleb's exemption from God's condemnation of his contemporaries (1:36; for other examples, see the Introduction). In other passages, however, the text deviates from the earlier accounts. Some of the differences may be simply differences in emphasis for the sake of the message that Moses seeks to convey. Others are difficult to reconcile with the earlier accounts. These differences are discussed in Excursus 2.

The First Command to Proceed to the Promised Land and Israel's Disobedience (1:6–2:1)

Themes and Structure

If we divide the text at the beginning of statements by God, we find three sections in this part of Moses' address: (A) verses 6–33, (B) 34–41, and (C) 42–2:1 (some of these are composed of several smaller units). Section A begins with God's command that Israel proceed to the promised land and take possession of it. When the people reach the border of the land, Moses exhorts them: "Go up,

6The Lord our God spoke to us at Horeb, saying: You have stayed long enough at this mountain. 7Start out and make your way to the hill country of the Amorites and to all their neighbors in the Arabah, the hill country, the Shephelah, the Negeb, the seacoast, the land of the

ו יְהוָה אֱלֹהֵינוּ דִּבֶּר אֵלֵינוּ בְּחֹרֵב לֵאמֹר רַב־לָכֶם שֶׁבֶת בָּהָר הַזֶּה: 7 פְּנוּ | וּסְעוּ לָכֶם וּבֹאוּ הַר הָאֱמֹרִי וְאֶל־כָּל־שְׁכֵנָיו בָּעֲרָבָה בָהָר וּבַשְּׁפֵלָה וּבַנֶּגֶב וּבְחוֹף הַיָּם אֶרֶץ הַכְּנַעֲנִי וְהַלְּבָנוֹן עַד־הַנָּהָר

take possession. . . . Fear not and be not dismayed." By the end of this section the people have disregarded both exhortations: they panic at the scouts' report and they refuse to go up. Sections B and C describe the consequences of their response. In Section B, verses 34–41, God reverses His promise to give this generation the land He swore to give their ancestors; He now swears that none of this generation (save Caleb and Joshua) will see the land, and He commands the people to march away from it into the wilderness. The people, shaken, reverse their own declaration and proclaim that they *will* go up to the promised land and fight for it, as the Lord had commanded.

In Section C, 1:42–2:1, the reversal of intentions becomes complete. God orders the people not to go up and fight because He will no longer accompany them, while the people flout this new command by attempting to attack the land on their own. The attack, which was once God's will, is now a violation of it and leads to a rout. After this, the people finally obey God's new command and march into the wilderness, where they remain for a long time. The people's disobedience and refusal to place their faith in God have brought about a reversal of all that was promised them.

FROM HOREB TO REBELLION   (vv. 6–33)

THE COMMAND TO PROCEED TO THE PROMISED LAND (vv. 6–8)

Moses opens his address by reminding his audience—the generation that is about to enter the promised land—that Israel had been directed to do so a generation earlier, when God commanded Israel to proceed from Horeb to the promised land and formally tendered the land to them. The command was first mentioned in Exodus 32:34–33:3, after the golden calf incident. The departure was recounted in Numbers 10:11–34. The entire retrospective that follows, through the end of chapter 3, deals with Israel's response to God's command and the consequences of that response. Moses begins by quoting the command, showing the gravity of the Israelites' refusal to proceed: having received an explicit command to proceed and assurance of success, their refusal was an act of insubordination and faithlessness.

6. you have stayed long enough God's first words in Deuteronomy express impatience, indicating that He was eager for Israel to enter the land immediately. The nearly forty-year delay was not God's intention but the result of Israel's failure to trust and obey Him.

7. The promised land is described here in terms of its main regions. See Map 2.

the hill country of the Amorites This refers to the central highlands running south to north, which would become the heartland of Israelite settlement. The Amorites were the inhabitants of these mountains, especially the southern ones, which, entering from the Sinai, the Israelites would reach first (see also vv. 19–20 and 44).[29] In verse 20, "the hill country of the Amorites" seems to refer to the promised land as a whole.

all their neighbors That is, neighboring regions.[30]

the Arabah Here the Aravah has its more common meaning, the Jordan Valley from Lake Tiberias to the Dead Sea, as in 3:17 and 4:49. The Aravah rift south of the Dead Sea (1:1) was in Edomite territory (see Comment to v. 2) and was not part of the promised land.

the hill country The neighboring regions of the Amorites in the central highlands included the territories of the Hittites, Jebusites, Amalekites, Canaanites, and Perizzites.[31]

the Shephelah The "lowland," the low hills between the Judahite part of the central highlands and the coastal plain.[32]

Canaanites, and the Lebanon, as far as the Great River, the river Euphrates. ⁸See, I place the land at your disposal. Go, take possession of the land that the LORD swore to your fathers, Abraham, Isaac, and Jacob, to assign to them and to their heirs after them.

הַגָּדֹ֖ל נְהַר־פְּרָֽת: ⁸ רְאֵ֛ה נָתַ֥תִּי לִפְנֵיכֶ֖ם אֶת־
הָאָ֑רֶץ בֹּ֚אוּ וּרְשׁ֣וּ אֶת־הָאָ֔רֶץ אֲשֶׁ֣ר נִשְׁבַּ֣ע יְהוָ֗ה
לַאֲבֹֽתֵיכֶ֛ם לְאַבְרָהָ֛ם לְיִצְחָ֥ק וּֽלְיַעֲקֹב֙ לָתֵ֣ת לָהֶ֔ם
וּלְזַרְעָ֖ם אַחֲרֵיהֶֽם:

the Negeb In the Bible this is but the northern section of what is called the Negeb, or Negev, today. It begins ten to fifteen miles north of Beer-sheba and extends about thirty miles southward to the wilderness of Zin, the southern boundary of the promised land.[33] Here the western part of the Negev is meant; the eastern part, like the Aravah, was part of Seir-Edom.[34] The name Negev, from n-g-b, "dry," reflects the relative aridity of the region: the average annual rainfall is three hundred millimeters at its northern end and one hundred millimeters at the southern end.

the seacoast Of the Mediterranean.[35]

the land of the Canaanites The translation construes this phrase as one part of the promised land, in which case it refers to parts of the seacoast, especially the area later called Phoenicia, and part of the Jordan valley, as in Genesis 10:15 and 19 and Numbers 13:29. Some later Phoenician sources likewise term Phoenicia "Canaan." The Masoretic punctuation, on the other hand, implies that the phrase is in apposition to all the regions named in the first part of the verse, and takes the phrase in its common biblical meaning of the entire promised land, as, for example, in 11:30 and Genesis 12:5. This meaning corresponds to the use of "Canaan" in Egyptian sources in which it refers to the region of the land under Egyptian control.[36]

the Lebanon This refers to the inland mountain range of that name, not to the entire territory of modern Lebanon. Here it probably refers to both the Lebanon and the Antilebanon ranges, including the Bekaa Valley between them.

as far as the Great River, the river Euphrates The phrase "the Lebanon . . . as far as the Euphrates" implies that the text is referring to that part of the Euphrates which is on a direct line with the Lebanon range, in other words, the northwestern sector of the river in northern Syria. The Euphrates, therefore, represents the northern extremity of the promised land, as in 11:24 and elsewhere.[37] For another conception of the northern boundary, see Excursus 2.

8. See, I place the land at your disposal Literally, "See, I have given the land before you." Whereas "give *to* you" means "give you title," the expression "give *before* you" means "place at your disposal," "deliver into your control."[38] This expression has both military and legal connotations that are important for the dynamic of Moses' narrative. God's assurance that "I have placed X at your disposal" or "into your hand" is a common element in divine commands to attack an enemy.[39] The past tense of the verb implies that the giving is already complete, thus expressing certainty. This connotation befits the fact that verses 6–8 initiate the military campaign to take possession of the land. The same terms are used again in verse 21, where the military theme is developed further.

The legal connotations of "I have given" are indicated by its use in contracts and in narratives describing the transfer of property. In such contexts the past tense means "I *hereby* give," indicating that the action is already completed, since uttering the phrase constitutes the act of giving.[40] The present verse therefore means that legally the land was already given to Israel; they had only to go and take it, as the next clause states.

Both connotations highlight the fact that Israel was responsible for the long delay in entering the promised land: God had already given Israel title to it and assured them of victory the moment He commanded them to depart from Horeb.[41]

take possession God's gift of the land to the Israelite people was viewed as analogous to the way a sovereign would grant land to a loyal servant. It is noteworthy that a Hittite king made a similar declaration to his vassal: "See, I gave you the Zippashla mountain land; occupy it." Documents recording such grants also specify the boundaries of the territory given the servant, much as verse 7 does here.[42]

the LORD swore Here God refers to Himself in the third person, after using the first person

9Thereupon I said to you, "I cannot bear the burden of you by myself. 10The LORD your God has multiplied you until you are today as numerous as the stars in the

ט וָאֹמַר אֲלֵכֶם בָּעֵת הַהִוא לֵאמֹר לֹא־אוּכַל לְבַדִּי שְׂאֵת אֶתְכֶם: 10 יְהוָה אֱלֹהֵיכֶם הִרְבָּה אֶתְכֶם וְהִנְּכֶם הַיּוֹם כְּכוֹכְבֵי הַשָּׁמַיִם לָרֹב:

in verses 6–8a. Such grammatical variation is common in the Bible and other ancient Near Eastern literature.[43]

God's reference to His oath to the patriarchs shows the people that He fulfills His promises. As Moses explains later, this oath is the basis of the relationship between God and the present generation (see 4:37; 7:8; 9:5). Because of the patriarchs' devotion to Him, God promised them that He would give the land to their descendants (see, for example, Gen. 12:7; 26:3–4; 28:13). Genesis 15:13–21 makes clear that the promise was to be fulfilled following the Exodus from Egypt.

THE APPOINTMENT OF CHIEFS FOR THE JOURNEY (vv. 9–18)

Moses now recalls how, after receiving God's command to set out from Horeb to the promised land, he appointed chiefs to assist him in leading the people. That he took this action at that time is suggested elsewhere in the Torah. It is not clear why he did so then, and why he recalls that action here in a speech focusing on the people's refusal to enter the land. The administrative structure Moses created was essentially a military one (see v. 15). He expected that Israel would shortly enter the land and battle its inhabitants. By mentioning these appointments here, Moses perhaps intends to underscore that all was ready and that Israel would have conquered the land immediately had it obeyed God.[44] Another reason for recalling the appointments may be the fact that when he made them Moses explained that they were necessitated by the people's extraordinary growth, in accordance with God's promise. This should have assured them that God would fulfill the remainder of His promise to give them possession of the land.

9. *Thereupon* Literally, "at that time." Although the appointment of the chiefs is recounted in Exodus 18:13–27, before the account of Israel's arrival at Mount Sinai-Horeb (19:1), commentators have long recognized that that action must have taken place later, shortly before the departure from Horeb.[45] Jethro, who first proposed the system of chiefs while visiting the Israelites, did not arrive until some time after the Israelites reached Horeb (Exod. 18:5), and he left them right after Moses appointed the chiefs (Exod. 18:27). We know from Numbers 10:29–32 that Jethro left as the Israelites were preparing to leave Horeb almost a year after they arrived there. The appointment therefore took place at that later date, as indicated here. (According to Exodus 19:1 and Numbers 10:11, they arrived at Sinai-Horeb on the first day of the third month [later called Sivan, which falls in May-June] after leaving Egypt and left the following year on the twentieth of the second month [later called Iyyar, which falls in April-May].) For the relationship of this account to that in Exodus 18:13–26 and to the similar incident in Numbers 11, see Excursus 2.

I cannot bear the burden of you by myself The translation "bear the burden" reflects Moses' feeling that the burden of leadership is wearing him out (see v. 12). Literally, however, the text means "I cannot carry you by myself," as in Numbers 11:14 where Moses speaks not only of carrying a burden but of leading the people to their destination (cf. Num. 11:12 and v. 31 here). Abravanel argues for the latter meaning in our verse as well, since the appointment of military officers (v. 15) indicates that here, too, Moses is concerned about his ability to bring the Israelites to their destination. The same verb is used in Isaiah 40:11, which describes God as a shepherd leading Israel back to its land after the exile.

10. It is the great size of the people that makes Moses' task too much for one man. With the simile "as numerous as the stars in the sky," Moses alludes to God's promises in Genesis where the same simile is used to describe Israel's future size (see Gen. 15:5; 22:17; 26:4). In so doing, Moses reminds his audience that God has already fulfilled part of the ancient promises and implies that He will fulfill the rest as well. According to biblical tradition, the Israelites numbered over 600,000 males of military age at the time of the Exodus. Assuming that each of these men had a wife and at least two children and one living parent or parent-in-law, this implies a population of at least three million people. This number raises several difficult questions and it is not certain what historical reality it corresponds to.[46]

sky.—11May the LORD, the God of your fathers, increase your numbers a thousandfold, and bless you as He promised you.—12How can I bear unaided the trouble of you, and the burden, and the bickering! 13Pick from each of your tribes men who are wise, discerning, and experienced, and I will appoint them as your heads." 14You answered me and said, "What you propose to do is good." 15So I took your tribal leaders, wise and experienced men, and appointed them heads over you: chiefs of thousands, chiefs

11 יְהֹוָה אֱלֹהֵי אֲבוֹתֵכֶם יֹסֵף עֲלֵיכֶם כָּכֶם
אֶלֶף פְּעָמִים וִיבָרֵךְ אֶתְכֶם כַּאֲשֶׁר דִּבֶּר
לָכֶם: 12 אֵיכָה אֶשָּׂא לְבַדִּי טָרְחֲכֶם
וּמַשַּׂאֲכֶם וְרִיבְכֶם: 13 הָבוּ לָכֶם אֲנָשִׁים חֲכָמִים
וּנְבֹנִים וִידֻעִים לְשִׁבְטֵיכֶם וַאֲשִׂימֵם בְּרָאשֵׁיכֶם:
14 וַתַּעֲנוּ אֹתִי וַתֹּאמְרוּ טוֹב־הַדָּבָר אֲשֶׁר־דִּבַּרְתָּ
לַעֲשׂוֹת: 15 וָאֶקַּח אֶת־רָאשֵׁי שִׁבְטֵיכֶם אֲנָשִׁים
חֲכָמִים וִידֻעִים וָאֶתֵּן אֹתָם רָאשִׁים עֲלֵיכֶם שָׂרֵי

11. Lest his audience think that he is complaining about their growth, Moses adds that he hopes that God will continue to increase their numbers.[47]

the LORD, the God of your fathers Deuteronomy normally refers to God as "the LORD your God" and uses "God of your fathers" only when referring to the covenant or the promises God made to the patriarchs.[48]

12. Here Moses does refer to the burdensome nature of his responsibilities. The burden that originally prompted the appointment of the officers was, according to Exodus 18:13–18, Moses' need to adjudicate legal disputes all day long. The term "burden" (*massa'*) recalls Jethro's comment that the officers would share this burden with Moses (Exod. 18:22). That Moses has his judicial role in mind is indicated by the term *riv*, "bickering," which also means "legal dispute." But the terms "burden" and "bickering" also call to mind Moses' need to worry about food and water for the people and to bear their quarrels (another meaning of *riv*) with him about shortages.[49]

13. Pick Exodus 18:21,24 mention that Moses selected the appointees, but he could not have acted without recommendations by the people. Chiefs of tens, fifties, hundreds, and thousands would number in the thousands (according to the Talmud, there were 78,600).[50] Moses could not possibly have known that many qualified people, especially since he had never lived among the Israelites before the Exodus.

wise, discerning, and experienced Exodus says that the appointees must be "capable men who fear God, trustworthy men who spurn ill-gotten gain" (Exod. 18:21). Rabbinic exegesis held that Jethro recommended seven qualities in all, those in our verse and those in Exodus 18:21.[51] It seems, however, that the present list is simply a paraphrase of that in Exodus, restating the qualifications in the light of Deuteronomy's emphasis on the intellectual aspect of morality. Deuteronomy regards justice and piety as expressions of wisdom (see 4:6,8, and contrast 16:19; 32:6), and wisdom literature regards the very qualities named in Exodus as expressions of wisdom.[52]

experienced Literally, "knowing."[53] It is evident from Ecclesiastes 9:11 that "wise, discerning, and knowing," like the equivalent nouns "wisdom, discernment, and knowledge" (*hokhmah, tevunah, da'at*), form a standard triad.[54]

15. The people recommended their tribal leaders and Moses appointed them "heads," a term that refers to tribal leaders whose responsibilities include both military and judicial matters. The titles such as "chief of thousands" and "chief of hundreds" usually refer to military officers.[55] That Moses appointed military officers to provide for the people and to adjudicate civil disputes is consistent with the integration of leadership roles in ancient societies. The commander of the Hittite border guards held judicial responsibilities as well as the duty of providing for various people and religious institutions. At Elephantine, Egypt, the commander of the Persian garrison was a member of the judiciary.[56] Such integration of roles was especially common in tribal societies. Later, ultimate military and judicial authority were combined in the king.[57]

    Since the problems that prompted Moses to appoint the chiefs did not involve military affairs, it seems that his solution was not shaped solely by immediate needs but by the long-range mission of the Israelites to conquer the promised land. In preparation for this mission the Israelites were organized as an army. From the moment of the Exodus they were called "the ranks of the LORD"

of hundreds, chiefs of fifties, and chiefs of tens, and officials for your tribes. [16]I charged your magistrates at that time as follows, "Hear out your fellow men, and decide justly between any man and a fellow Israelite or a stranger. [17]You shall not be partial in judgment: hear out low and

אֲלָפִים וְשָׂרֵי מֵאוֹת וְשָׂרֵי חֲמִשִּׁים וְשָׂרֵי עֲשָׂרֹת וְשֹׁטְרִים לְשִׁבְטֵיכֶם: 16 וָאֲצַוֶּה אֶת־שֹׁפְטֵיכֶם בָּעֵת הַהִוא לֵאמֹר שָׁמֹעַ בֵּין־אֲחֵיכֶם וּשְׁפַטְתֶּם צֶדֶק בֵּין־אִישׁ וּבֵין־אָחִיו וּבֵין גֵּרוֹ: 17 לֹא־תַכִּירוּ פָנִים בַּמִּשְׁפָּט כַּקָּטֹן כַּגָּדֹל תִּשְׁמָעוּן לֹא תָגוּרוּ

(Exod. 6:26; 12:17,41,51). They march behind the Ark of the Covenant, which later led them into battle (1 Sam. 4:3–4; cf. Num. 14:44), and when the Ark sets out Moses says, "Advance, O LORD! May your enemies be scattered" (Num. 10:33,35). Their camp is organized around standards and banners (Num. 2), and when censuses are taken, it is men "able to bear arms" who are counted (Num. 1:3; 26:2). Moses' appointment of military chiefs to assist him thus conforms with the way the tribes are already organized.[58]

    officials   Hebrew *shoterim*. In 16:18, too, *shoterim* are appointed along with the judges. The term cannot be defined precisely. The verb *sh-t-r* means "write" in Akkadian and Arabic, and the Septuagint and the Peshitta translate *shoterim* as "scribes." However, this etymology does not necessarily indicate the function of these officials in Israel,[59] for the verb is not known to have been used in Hebrew and the Bible never depicts *shoterim* as writing. The noun *shoter* was perhaps borrowed from another language in which it referred to an official whose duties involved writing and other activities, but was used in Hebrew only for those other activities. Traditional Jewish commentators see the *shoterim* as assistants enforcing the orders of higher officials, such as foremen of work forces (Exod. 5:6ff.), military adjutants (Deut. 20:5ff.; Josh. 1:10; 3:2), and police enforcing the decisions of judges.[60] However, there are few passages where the *shoterim* are clearly subordinate to other officials, and in a number of passages they are among the highest officials (see esp. Num. 11:16; Prov. 6:7).[61] The present verse also implies a high status, since the *shoterim* were chosen from among the tribal leaders. The translation "officials" suits the ambiguity of the evidence. Perhaps the verse means that Moses appointed miscellaneous officials in addition to the chiefs of thousands.

    16.   After appointing the chiefs and officials, Moses turned to those of the chiefs who were to serve as judges and charged them to carry out their role impartially and to bring difficult cases to him. It was traditional to address such charges to judges, either at the time of their appointment or in codes defining their responsibilities. King Jehoshaphat addressed a similar charge to the judges he appointed in Judah and Jerusalem (2 Chron. 19:6–11), and similar instructions are found in Egyptian and Hittite texts.[62]

    your magistrates   Rather, "judges" (Heb. *shofetim*). The translation "magistrates" reflects the view that the root *sh-f-t* refers to all types of governing authority, executive and legislative as well as judicial, like derivatives of the English "rule."[63] However, in the Bible the use of the noun in this broader sense seems to be limited to kings and national military rulers, as in the book of "Judges," whose title really means the book of "Chieftains."[64] In unambiguous contexts where the term refers to other kinds of officials, the meaning "judge" is clear.[65] The present verse is such a case.

    Hear out   Literally, "hear between." "Hear" is idiomatic for trying a case, as in English "hear a case."[66]

    fellow men   Literally, "brothers," meaning fellow Israelites. Deuteronomy regularly uses this term to emphasize the equality and fraternity of all Israelites, whether king or servant, prophet or priest (15:2 and passim; 17:15,20; 18:2,15,18; 22:1–4). The term is a precursor of *fraternité* in the motto of the French Revolution, *Liberté! Egalité! Fraternité!*[67]

    or a stranger   The "stranger" (*ger*) is the resident alien, the non-Israelite residing among Israelites. The strangers in the Israelite camp must have been the "mixed multitude" that joined the Israelites leaving Egypt, according to Exodus 12:38. When the Israelites settled in the promised land, the land was divided among the tribes and passed on by inheritance. Resident aliens did not normally own land and depended on others for their livelihood. Because of their dependency, *gerim* were often poor and exposed to exploitation, and the Torah regularly includes them along with widows, orphans, and the poor in appeals and laws designed to protect vulnerable groups.[68] The text reads

high alike. Fear no man, for judgment is God's. And any matter that is too difficult for you, you shall bring to me and I will hear it." [18]Thus I instructed you, at that time, about the various things that you should do.

מִפְּנֵי־אִישׁ כִּי הַמִּשְׁפָּט לֵאלֹהִים הוּא וְהַדָּבָר
אֲשֶׁר יִקְשֶׁה מִכֶּם תַּקְרִבוּן אֵלַי וּשְׁמַעְתִּיו:
[18] וָאֲצַוֶּה אֶתְכֶם בָּעֵת הַהִוא אֵת כָּל־הַדְּבָרִים
אֲשֶׁר תַּעֲשׂוּן:

literally "or *his* stranger," which implies that the *ger* was, at least in some cases, dependent on a specific individual.[69] The purpose of the present law is to protect the *ger*'s right to a fair trial even against an Israelite on whom he depends.

17. *Hear out low and high alike* Rather, "the low as well as the high."[70] The claims of the powerful will certainly be heard; the weak must be treated in the same way. This is usually understood to mean that both sides should be heard impartially when they come before the court. But it could also mean "give a hearing" to the low as well as the high, that is, allow the lowly to bring their lawsuits to the court. It was often difficult for the poor to get their day in court if they could not afford to pay the judge a fee for hearing their case. See Comment to 16:19.

for judgment is God's Judgment is a matter that concerns God, as lawgiver, and the judge acts as God's representative. The relationship of this clause to the preceding one, "fear no man," is ambiguous. It may mean that the judge ought to fear offending God more than he fears offending any human.[71] Alternatively, it means that the judge need not fear offending any human since God will protect him.

any matter that is too difficult for you, you shall bring to me and I will hear it Moses will not function as an appellate judge but will take over cases that lower judges find too difficult to decide. The high court was to function in the same way (see 17:8), as did the king in Hittite practice.[72]

To judge from Exodus 18:13–26, "difficult" cases are those in which the law is not known and Moses has to consult God to learn it (v. 19), as he does in Leviticus 24:10–23; Numbers 9:1–14; 15:32–36; 27:1–11; and 36:1–10. Here, Moses does not mention that he would consult God. Perhaps this is for the sake of brevity, since he is merely summarizing the narrative of Exodus. Perhaps, too, it was unnecessary to mention this aspect of his role in an address in which he is preparing Israel for the future, since Deuteronomy does not expect future prophets to reveal new laws. See introductory Comment to 18:9–22.

18. *Thus* Rather, "at that time," shortly before Israel left Sinai. This verse does not refer to the instructions Moses gave the judges in the preceding verses but to instructions addressed to the entire people. According to Exodus 18:20, Jethro advised Moses to minimize the number of disputes by instructing all the people in God's "laws and teachings and make known to them the way they are to go and the practices they are to follow." It is not clear what laws Moses is referring to here. The laws of chapters 12–26 were communicated to the people thirty-nine years later, after Israel left Sinai. However, the laws themselves indicate that the people were given some laws earlier, such as laws about slaughter and sacrifice, and the Levites were given laws about leprosy (see chap. 12 and 24:8). The other books of the Torah indicate that the people were given laws throughout their forty years in the wilderness (e.g., Exod. 21–24; 34:11–26; Lev. 25:1; Num. 9:1).

The practice of teaching the laws to the entire citizenry is virtually unparalleled. This was recognized by Josephus in his proud description of Judaism: "Most men, far from living in accordance with their own laws, hardly know what they are. . . . But, should anyone of our nation be questioned about the laws, he would repeat them all the more readily than his own name. The result, then, of our thorough grounding in the laws . . . is that we have them, as it were, engraven on our souls. A transgressor is a rarity; evasion of punishment by excuses an impossibility."[73]

Despite the hyperbole, Josephus accurately described the Torah's aim. Since Israel's primary duty to God is obedience to His laws, teaching them to every Israelite is imperative, and this is Moses' main aim in Deuteronomy. See 6:7; 31:10–13; introductory Comment to 16:18–18:22; and Excursus 28.

¹⁹We set out from Horeb and traveled the great and terrible wilderness that you saw, along the road to the hill country of the Amorites, as the LORD our God had commanded us. When we reached Kadesh-barnea, ²⁰I said to you, "You have come to the hill country of the Amorites which the LORD our God is giving to us. ²¹See, the LORD your God has placed the land at your disposal. Go up, take possession, as the LORD, the God of your fathers, promised you. Fear not and be not dismayed."

19 וַנִּסַּ֣ע מֵחֹרֵ֗ב וַנֵּ֜לֶךְ אֵ֣ת כָּל־הַמִּדְבָּ֣ר הַגָּד֣וֹל
וְהַנּוֹרָ֣א הַה֗וּא אֲשֶׁ֤ר רְאִיתֶם֙ דֶּ֚רֶךְ הַ֣ר הָֽאֱמֹרִ֔י
כַּאֲשֶׁ֥ר צִוָּ֛ה יְהֹוָ֥ה אֱלֹהֵ֖ינוּ אֹתָ֑נוּ וַנָּבֹ֖א עַ֥ד קָדֵ֥שׁ
בַּרְנֵֽעַ׃ 20 וָאֹמַ֖ר אֲלֵכֶ֑ם בָּאתֶם֙ עַד־הַ֣ר הָאֱמֹרִ֔י
אֲשֶׁר־יְהֹוָ֥ה אֱלֹהֵ֖ינוּ נֹתֵ֥ן לָֽנוּ׃ 21 רְאֵ֠ה נָתַ֨ן יְהֹוָ֧ה
אֱלֹהֶ֛יךָ לְפָנֶ֖יךָ אֶת־הָאָ֑רֶץ עֲלֵ֣ה רֵ֗שׁ כַּאֲשֶׁר֩ דִּבֶּ֨ר
יְהֹוָ֜ה אֱלֹהֵ֤י אֲבֹתֶ֙יךָ֙ לָ֔ךְ אַל־תִּירָ֖א וְאַל־
תֵּחָֽת׃ שלישי

ARRIVAL AT THE PROMISED LAND
AND THE PEOPLE'S REFUSAL TO PROCEED (vv. 19–33)

Moses now reminds the Israelites of their initial obedience to God's command, of their arrival at the border of the land, and of their loss of faith and their disobedience at the moment when they were to enter the land and take possession of it. This paragraph of Moses' address is framed by references to Israel's journey through the wilderness under the guidance of God (vv. 19, 31–33). That journey was Israel's latest experience of God's ability to meet their needs, and it should have sustained their faith in His ability to defeat the Amorites on their behalf.

19. The route taken through the wilderness is described in detail in Numbers (see Num. 10:33; 11:35; 12:16; 33:16ff.). Here Moses omits the details because they are not germane to the point he is making. The effect of the omission is to emphasize that the journey was without impediment.

the great and terrible wilderness that you saw The Sinai peninsula, a land "with *seraph* serpents and scorpions, a parched land with no water in it" (Deut. 8:15). By this allusion Moses reminds the Israelites that they were able to travel through the wilderness safely because God guided and provided for them. He states this explicitly in 8:15–16. Moses frequently reminds the people that they personally witnessed the events of which he speaks.[74] Their experience should enable them to fully appreciate the lessons of those events. See Comment to 11:1–9; compare 2:30.

the road to the hill country of the Amorites A road leading from Horeb to Kadesh-barnea. Its precise route is unknown.[75]

as the LORD our God had commanded us The initial response of the Israelites to God's command had been obedience, and as a result they reached their destination.

Kadesh-barnea On the southern border of the promised land (Num. 34:4).

20–21. When the Israelites arrived at the promised land, Moses instructed them to go take possession of it, and he exhorted them to have no fear. These words are not reported in the earlier account of the events in Numbers 13.[76] They serve to emphasize the people's effrontery in hesitating to proceed immediately.

20. **You have come to the hill country of the Amorites** Just as God commanded in verse 7. Here "the hill country of the Amorites" seems to refer to the promised land as a whole, just as the term "Amorites" sometimes designates its entire population.[77] This usage may be due to the fact that these highlands became the Israelite heartland. In Akkadian the entire Syro-Palestinian region was sometimes called the Land of Amurru and its inhabitants Amorites.[78]

the LORD our God is giving to us The participle is meant literally: God is in the process of giving us the land at the present moment.

21. Moses paraphrases God's command of verse 8 in terms designed to emphasize the certainty of success.

Go up, take possession The text consists of two short words (ʿaleh resh) with no conjunction, expressing by its brevity the intended ease of the conquest.

22Then all of you came to me and said, "Let us send men ahead to reconnoiter the land for us and bring back word on the route we shall follow and the cities we shall come to." 23I approved of the plan, and so I selected twelve of your men, one from each tribe. 24They made for the hill country, came to the wadi Eshcol, and spied it out.

22 וַתִּקְרְב֤וּן אֵלַי֙ כֻּלְּכֶ֔ם וַתֹּאמְר֗וּ נִשְׁלְחָ֤ה אֲנָשִׁים֙ לְפָנֵ֔ינוּ וְיַחְפְּרוּ־לָ֖נוּ אֶת־הָאָ֑רֶץ וְיָשִׁ֤בוּ אֹתָ֙נוּ֙ דָּבָ֔ר אֶת־הַדֶּ֙רֶךְ֙ אֲשֶׁ֣ר נַֽעֲלֶה־בָּ֔הּ וְאֵת֙ הֶֽעָרִ֔ים אֲשֶׁ֥ר נָבֹ֖א אֲלֵיהֶֽן: 23 וַיִּיטַ֥ב בְּעֵינַ֖י הַדָּבָ֑ר וָאֶקַּ֤ח מִכֶּם֙ שְׁנֵ֣ים עָשָׂ֣ר אֲנָשִׁ֔ים אִ֥ישׁ אֶחָ֖ד לַשָּֽׁבֶט: 24 וַיִּפְנוּ֙ וַיַּֽעֲל֣וּ הָהָ֔רָה וַיָּבֹ֖אוּ עַד־נַ֣חַל אֶשְׁכֹּ֑ל וַֽיְרַגְּל֖וּ אֹתָֽהּ:

as the LORD . . . **promised you**   This ensures you of success. God had promised that the same generation which experienced the Exodus would receive the land (Exod. 3:8,17; 6:8).

Fear not and be not dismayed   Though phrased as an imperative, this formula usually expresses assurance.[79] Here it is based on the promise to which Moses has just alluded. Israel's prior experience of God's protection should prepare the people to accept this assurance (see vv. 29–31). Their failure to be satisfied by it brings on the following turn of events.

The exhortation not to fear is one of the most characteristic expressions of religious feeling in the Bible and the ancient Near East. It is found in messages addressed by deities or their representatives to individuals facing battle or other trials, and it is accompanied explicitly or implicitly by promises of divine protection or victory. The patriarchs received such messages during difficult moments in their lives, as did Jeremiah and Ezekiel upon their initiation as prophets, and the Jews in Babylon during their exile.[80] The same assurance became a standard element in divine commands before battle: it is addressed to the Israelites in the days of Moses and Joshua, and the priest is to deliver the same encouragement to the Israelite army in future wars.[81] Ancient Near Eastern kings tell of receiving the same message in oracles from their deities.[82] This assurance of divine protection enabled people to face war and adversity with confidence. The hesitation of the Israelites in the face of this assurance reveals a serious flaw in their trust in God.

22. reconnoiter   In view of the scouts' assignment in Numbers 13:17–20, and their report in verse 25 of our chapter, this may mean to explore the land and its resources. Information about the land's natural resources is important both for strategic military purposes and for preparing to settle in it. The Danite scouts who sought a new home for their tribe obtained similar information along with intelligence about the defenses of the natives (Judg. 18:7–10).

bring back word on the route . . . and the cities   Literally, "report back to us the route . . . and the cities." The meaning is either that the scouts should themselves determine the best route and the order in which the cities should be attacked, or that they should obtain information about possible routes (such as which are narrow and dangerous) and the fortifications of the cities.[83]

The people's proposal to send out scouts contains the seeds of disaster. Some commentators argue that it reflects a lack of confidence in God's leadership, since choosing the route to follow is God's role. The description of God doing just that in verse 33 could be read as a pointed allusion to the people's effrontery in assigning this role to the scouts.[84] Verse 37 implies that Moses was blamed for his role in the affair, and it is hard to think of any act of Moses to which verse 37 might refer other than his approval of the people's proposal. Others, however, consider the proposal intrinsically reasonable as a preparation for war, and it must be admitted that the text does not portray the proposal in unfavorable terms.[85] The belief that the Lord fought for Israel did not require Israel to stand passively on the sidelines.[86] Since in Numbers 13:2 the plan to send out scouts is a command of God, and since Moses himself sent out scouts on another occasion (Num. 21:32), it is difficult to argue that their use is inherently inconsistent with faith. His approval of the plan (v. 23) certainly indicates that it was not obviously a sign of faithlessness at the time it was made.[87] He may well have taken it as indicating the people's determination to proceed into Canaan, just as Joshua later sent out scouts before leading the Israelites into the land (Josh. 2; cf. 7:2–3).

The account in this verse differs in several respects from that in Numbers 13. See Excursus 2.

23.   The twelve men are named in Numbers 13:2–16, where they are said to have been tribal chieftains.

24. the wadi Eshcol   A wadi is the channel of a river that is full in the rainy season and empty, or reduced to a brook, in the summer. Wadi Eshcol means "the wadi of the grape cluster(s)."

²⁵They took some of the fruit of the land with them and brought it down to us. And they gave us this report: "It is a good land that the LORD our God is giving to us."

²⁶Yet you refused to go up, and flouted the command of the LORD your God. ²⁷You sulked in your tents and said, "It is because the LORD hates us that He brought us out of the land of Egypt, to hand us over to the Amorites to wipe us out. ²⁸What kind of place are we going to? Our kinsmen have taken the heart out of us, saying, 'We saw there a people stronger and taller than we, large cities with walls sky-high, and even Anakites.'"

כה וַיִּקְח֤וּ בְיָדָם֙ מִפְּרִ֣י הָאָ֔רֶץ וַיּוֹרִ֖דוּ אֵלֵ֑ינוּ וַיָּשִׁ֤בוּ אֹתָ֨נוּ֙ דָבָ֣ר וַיֹּ֣אמְר֔וּ טוֹבָ֣ה הָאָ֔רֶץ אֲשֶׁר־יְהוָ֥ה אֱלֹהֵ֖ינוּ נֹתֵ֥ן לָֽנוּ׃ כו וְלֹ֥א אֲבִיתֶ֖ם לַעֲלֹ֑ת וַתַּמְר֕וּ אֶת־פִּ֥י יְהוָ֖ה אֱלֹהֵיכֶֽם׃ כז וַתֵּרָגְנ֣וּ בְאָהֳלֵיכֶ֒ם֒ וַתֹּ֣אמְר֔וּ בְּשִׂנְאַ֤ת יְהוָה֙ אֹתָ֔נוּ הוֹצִיאָ֖נוּ מֵאֶ֣רֶץ מִצְרָ֑יִם לָתֵ֥ת אֹתָ֛נוּ בְּיַ֥ד הָאֱמֹרִ֖י לְהַשְׁמִידֵֽנוּ׃ כח אָנָ֣ה | אֲנַ֣חְנוּ עֹלִ֗ים אַחֵ֩ינוּ֩ הֵמַ֨סּוּ אֶת־לְבָבֵ֜נוּ לֵאמֹ֗ר עַ֣ם גָּד֤וֹל וָרָם֙ מִמֶּ֔נּוּ עָרִ֛ים גְּדֹלֹ֥ת וּבְצוּרֹ֖ת בַּשָּׁמָ֑יִם וְגַם־בְּנֵ֥י עֲנָקִ֖ים רָאִ֥ינוּ שָֽׁם׃

According to Numbers 13:24 it was named for the grapes the scouts brought back from there. Numbers 13:22–23 suggests that it was near Hebron, in a region well known for its grapes.⁸⁸ Moses singles out this place because it is where the scouts found the grapes that exemplify the land's fertility and where they saw the giants who so terrified the people that they refused to enter the land.

*spied it out*⁸⁹

25. *some of the fruit of the land* The grapes, some pomegranates, and figs, which serve as evidence that the land is good (Num. 13:23,27). "Good" means rich in produce and other natural resources. See 8:7–9.

At this point Moses does not mention the rest of the scouts' report, to which the people reacted with fear. Mentioning it here would have suggested that it was the scouts who were responsible for what followed. By citing only the people's account of the report (v. 28), Moses implies that the real fault was in their reaction to what the scouts said. They should have realized that the size and strength of the enemy were irrelevant because God would fight for Israel. Assurance of the land's bounty should have sufficed for them; as the psalmist wrote, "They rejected the desirable land and put no faith in His promise" (Ps. 106:24). In 9:12–21 Moses summarizes the golden calf incident in similar fashion, alluding to Aaron's role only toward the end, so as not to divert attention from the people's responsibility.

27. *you sulked in your tents* Better translated as "you grumbled in your tents."⁹⁰ The people were in their tents because, according to Numbers 14:1, this happened at night.

because the LORD hates us "The people declared the greatest blessing conferred upon them by God, viz. their deliverance from Egypt, to have been an act of hatred on His part"⁹¹ instead of the act of love that it really was (7:9). In the Hebrew the word "hatred" appears at the beginning of the sentence ("because of the hatred of the LORD for us"), thereby prominently displaying the people's perversity and ingratitude.⁹²

28. *What kind of place* The expression suggests a flaw in the land, recalling Numbers 13:32: "The country . . . is one that devours its settlers." This aspersion is another illustration of the people's perversity, for the goodness of the land of Israel is practically an article of faith in the Bible.⁹³

our kinsmen The scouts. Referring to them as kinsmen emphasizes their credibility in the people's eyes.

a people stronger and taller than we, large cities with walls sky-high, and even Anakites Moses speaks of the land and its inhabitants in identical terms in 9:1–2, which indicates that the scouts did not lie. Their fault and that of the people was in believing that these facts made the Amorites unbeatable (see 9:2b; Num. 13:31).⁹⁴

stronger Rather, "more numerous."⁹⁵

taller than we The legendary height of the Amorites was later recalled by Amos, who describes them as having been as tall as cedars and as stout as oaks (Amos 2:9), a description that Maimonides cites as an example of biblical hyperbole.⁹⁶

walls sky-high Since Canaanite cities were built on tells, which themselves were often built on natural hills, their walls must indeed have looked sky-high, especially to people who had been

29I said to you, "Have no dread or fear of them. 30None other than the LORD your God, who goes before you, will fight for you, just as He did for you in Egypt before your very eyes, 31and in the wilderness, where you saw how the LORD your God carried you, as a man carries his son, all

29 וָאֹמַ֖ר אֲלֵכֶ֑ם לֹא־תַֽעַרְצ֥וּן וְלֹֽא־תִֽירְא֖וּן מֵהֶֽם׃

30 יְהוָ֤ה אֱלֹֽהֵיכֶם֙ הַהֹלֵ֣ךְ לִפְנֵיכֶ֔ם ה֖וּא יִלָּחֵ֣ם לָכֶ֑ם כְּכֹ֧ל אֲשֶׁ֛ר עָשָׂ֥ה אִתְּכֶ֖ם בְּמִצְרַ֣יִם לְעֵינֵיכֶֽם׃

31 וּבַמִּדְבָּר֙ אֲשֶׁ֣ר רָאִ֔יתָ אֲשֶׁ֤ר נְשָׂאֲךָ֙ יְהוָ֣ה אֱלֹהֶ֔יךָ כַּאֲשֶׁ֥ר יִשָּׂא־אִ֖ישׁ אֶת־בְּנ֑וֹ בְּכָל־הַדֶּ֙רֶךְ֙

living in the wilderness. An Assyrian inscription likewise describes an Israelite city as "reaching the sky."[97] As Maimonides notes, the rabbis considered this, too, a hyperbole.[98]

Anakites   In addition to the Amorites, who the scouts say were all tall, they report seeing a particularly gigantic group, the Anakites, next to whom the scouts felt like grasshoppers (Num. 13:32–33). In Numbers the scouts call them Nephilim, alluding to the "heroes of old" who were the offspring of the marriages between divine beings and human women before the flood (Gen. 6:1–4). The Anakites belonged to a race of giants known as Rephaim (Deut. 2:11). One of them, Og, King of Bashan, was said to have had an iron bedstead thirteen and a half feet long by six feet wide (Deut. 3:11). Anakim and Rephaim were also found in Philistia, particularly Gath, the hometown of the giant Goliath.[99] According to Numbers 13:22, the scouts encountered the Anakites at Hebron; other passages state that they were found throughout the southern and northern hill country and in Philistia (Josh. 11:21–22).

The exact meaning of "Anakites" is uncertain. Some take it as an epithet meaning "long-necked ones," based on Hebrew 'anak, "necklace," and its Arabic cognate meaning "neck."[100] Others relate it to names of people or places in Canaan or across the Mediterranean containing the element 'anak, or to Greek anax, "nobleman."[101]

Josephus (first century) and Benjamin of Tudela (twelfth century) tell of gigantic bones on display in Hebron and Damascus in their days, which were said to be the remains of Anakim. It is conceivable that there were some exceptionally tall people in the area, comparable to the Watusi of central Africa, who often exceed seven feet in height. A literary letter from Egypt, rich in information about Canaan, refers to unusually tall people there: "The narrow valley is dangerous with Bedouin, hidden under the bushes. Some of them are four or five cubits [seven to nine feet in the Egyptian system of measures] [from] their noses to the heel [the meaning of the latter phrase is uncertain], and fierce of face. Their hearts are not mild, and they do not listen to wheedling." The text dates from the reign of Raamses II in the thirteenth century B.C.E., shortly before the Israelites arrived in the promised land. Modern examination of skeletal remains from Canaan has revealed few of above-average size, but recently two seven-foot female skeletons were found in a twelfth-century-B.C.E. cemetery at Tell es-Sa'idiyeh on the east bank of the Jordan.[102]

29–31.   Moses repeats his assurance that the people have nothing to fear, explaining that the Lord will do the fighting for them. This assurance is reminiscent of his words encouraging the people at the Sea of Reeds (Exod. 14:29–30) and is a prototype for the priest's exhortation to the Israelite army before future wars (Deut. 20:3–4). Moses reminds the people that their own experience demonstrates the Lord's capacity to meet all their needs, and that they are ignoring what their experience teaches. This experience became the basis of Israelite faith in God. Wherever the Bible presents a credo explaining Israelite belief or practice, it consists of a summary of what God did for Israel rather than affirmations about His nature.[103] The events of the Exodus are the centerpiece of such summaries. In the present context the argument refers to God's ability to protect Israel in war. It is repeated for the same purpose in 7:17–21; 9:1–3; and 20:1.

30.   who goes before you   This refers to God's protective guidance of Israel on its journeys (v. 33). The one who "goes in front" is the vanguard (advance guard), protecting those who follow. According to Isaiah 52:12 and 58:8, God would both march before Israel and be its rear guard. According to the Babylonian *Gilgamesh Epic*, on a dangerous journey "the one who goes in front saves his companion."[104]

will fight for you, just as He did in Egypt   That is, at the Sea of Reeds (Exod. 14:14,25).

31.   and in the wilderness   God protected Israel from the Amalekites (Exod. 17:8–16) and from the natural dangers of the wilderness (8:15).

the LORD carried you, as a man carries his son   This refers to God's protection of Israel

the way that you traveled until you came to this place. [32]Yet for all that, you have no faith in the LORD your God, [33]who goes before you on your journeys—to scout the place where you are to encamp—in fire by night and in cloud by day, in order to guide you on the route you are to follow."

[34]When the LORD heard your loud complaint, He was angry. He vowed: [35]Not one of these men, this evil gen-

אֲשֶׁר הֲלַכְתֶּם עַד־בֹּאֲכֶם עַד־הַמָּקוֹם הַזֶּה:
32 וּבַדָּבָר הַזֶּה אֵינְכֶם מַאֲמִינִם בַּיהוָה אֱלֹהֵיכֶם:
33 הַהֹלֵךְ לִפְנֵיכֶם בַּדֶּרֶךְ לָתוּר לָכֶם מָקוֹם לַחֲנֹתְכֶם בָּאֵשׁ ׀ לַיְלָה לַרְאֹתְכֶם בַּדֶּרֶךְ אֲשֶׁר תֵּלְכוּ־בָהּ וּבֶעָנָן יוֹמָם:
34 וַיִּשְׁמַע יְהוָה אֶת־קוֹל דִּבְרֵיכֶם וַיִּקְצֹף וַיִּשָּׁבַע לֵאמֹר: 35 אִם־יִרְאֶה אִישׁ בָּאֲנָשִׁים הָאֵלֶּה הַדּוֹר

from danger (cf. Isa. 46:3–4; Ps. 91:11–12). Other passages, such as Exodus 19:4 and Deuteronomy 32:11, compare God's protection to the way an eagle carries its young. The comparison to a father adds a note of reassurance, since the compassion of a father for his offspring was proverbial (see Ps. 103:13 and elsewhere).[105]

until you came to this place   Kadesh-barnea. This clause indicates that the experience should have been fresh in the people's minds.

32. for all that   Despite the powerful evidence provided by the Exodus and by the experiences in the wilderness, Israel still doubted God's ability to give them victory over the Amorites. The theme of faithlessness has pervaded the narratives of Exodus and Numbers. Despite countless experiences that demonstrate God's ability to meet all their needs, the Israelites fail to remember this lesson from one experience to the next. Even after the Exodus and the crossing of the sea, at the first sign of trouble they acted as if their situation were hopeless (Exod. 14:10–12; 16:3; 17:3,7). In Deuteronomy, nothing motivates Moses more than the need to overcome the people's failure to recognize God's capacity to meet all their needs.

33.   The people ignore the evidence of God's care and guidance, although it is never out of their sight. The cloud and fire have been constant, visible signs of God's presence since the day they left Egypt.[106]

According to Numbers 10:33 the Ark traveled before the Israelites to seek out places for them to camp. It is clear from Numbers 10:35–37 that God was thought to be present above the Ark as it traveled, but that is not mentioned here. In Deuteronomy Moses never connects God's presence to physical objects, such as the Ark or the Temple.[107]

in fire by night and in cloud by day   Normally the cloud is mentioned first, as in Exodus 13:21 and Numbers 14:14. Perhaps Moses inverts the order because this incident took place at night (Num. 14:1) and the people could see the fire as he spoke.

GOD'S DECREE AND THE PEOPLE'S ABOUT-FACE   (vv. 34–41)

Moses' plea to the people fell on deaf ears. According to Numbers 14:11–20, God would have destroyed the entire generation and replaced them with Moses' descendants, had Moses not persuaded Him to be lenient. Here, Moses passes over these details and turns directly to God's final decision: this generation will die out in the wilderness, and only its children will enter the promised land. This decree prompts the people to further rebellion: now they insist that it is they, after all, who will enter the land, and they prepare to do so.

The solemnity of God's decree is emphasized by a series of alliterations and other types of repetition that are especially dramatic when the text is read aloud.[108]

34. your loud complaint   According to Numbers 14:11 and 22 it was the people's lack of faith in God that provoked His ire. In Abravanel's view the phrase "your loud complaint" implies that the people's accusatory words in verse 27a were their most inexcusable offense.

He vowed   That is, swore, echoing "the land that the LORD swore" in verse 8. This generation's rejection of the sworn land is met by a new swearing that now deprives them of it.

35.   God's decree fits the people's offense: since they refused to enter the land, they shall be banned from it.[109] The correspondences between the offense and the punishment are stated explicitly

eration, shall see the good land that I swore to give to your fathers—36none except Caleb son of Jephunneh; he shall see it, and to him and his descendants will I give the land on which he set foot, because he remained loyal to the LORD.—37Because of you the LORD was incensed with me

הָרָע הַזֶּה אֵת הָאָרֶץ הַטּוֹבָה אֲשֶׁר נִשְׁבַּעְתִּי לָתֵת לַאֲבֹתֵיכֶם: 36 זוּלָתִי כָּלֵב בֶּן־יְפֻנֶּה הוּא יִרְאֶנָּה וְלוֹ־אֶתֵּן אֶת־הָאָרֶץ אֲשֶׁר דָּרַךְ־בָּהּ וּלְבָנָיו יַעַן אֲשֶׁר מִלֵּא אַחֲרֵי יְהוָה: 37 גַּם־בִּי הִתְאַנַּף יְהוָה בִּגְלַלְכֶם לֵאמֹר גַּם־אַתָּה לֹא־

in Numbers 14: the people complained "if only we might die in this wilderness!" and God swore "I will do to you just as you have urged me: In this very wilderness shall your carcasses drop" (vv. 2, 28–29); similarly, the scouts toured the land for forty days and God swore, "You shall bear your punishment for forty years, corresponding to the number of days . . . that you scouted the land" (Num. 13:25; 14:34). Wherever possible the Bible seeks to show that the punishment reflects the offense, since that makes the justice of the punishment visible.

this evil generation Those aged twenty and older at the time of the incident (e.g., Num. 14:29; 32:11), referred to as warriors (that is, men of military age) in Deuteronomy 2:14,16. In Numbers 32:13 they are called "the generation which did evil in the sight of the LORD." The shorter phrase here contrasts with "the good land" and suggests the fitness of the decree: an evil generation may not enter a good land.

36. Caleb is exempted from the decree because he kept his faith that the Lord would enable Israel to overcome the Amorites and he pleaded with the people to remain faithful (Num. 13:30; 14:6–9). According to Numbers 14:6 and related passages, Joshua joined Caleb in this plea. For a discussion of those passages and the omission of Joshua from the present verse, see Excursus 2.

Caleb son of Jephunneh A leader of the tribe of Judah (Num. 13:6).[110]

the land on which he set foot Hebron (see, e.g., Josh. 14:6–14).

remained loyal[111]

37–38. In the middle of quoting God's oath about the people (vv. 35–36 and 39–40), Moses parenthetically quotes God's decree concerning him and Joshua. He does not necessarily mean that God told him at the time of this incident that he would be succeeded by Joshua. According to Numbers 27:12–23, Joshua was first chosen in the fortieth year, shortly before Moses' death; this date is also reflected in Deuteronomy 3:21 and 28. Moses mentions God's decree about himself and Joshua here because it was the outcome of the same incident that he is reviewing.

37. The Hebrew word order gives the verse the sense: "Even with me the LORD was incensed because of you, and He said: 'Even you shall not enter it.'"

because of you This apparently means because of the people's rebellion after the scouts' report, and not because of any other incident. Though Moses does not specify what provoked God's anger at him, its connection with that rebellion is implied by its mention here. A comparable passage is 9:20, where Moses refers to Aaron's punishment while recalling the golden calf incident: Moses does not identify Aaron's offense, but its connection with the golden calf incident is indicated, correctly, by the context (this is confirmed by Exod. 32).

The reason Moses was condemned for this incident is unclear. Abravanel holds that he sinned by changing the terms of the scouts' assignment. The people had asked only for information about the route to follow into the promised land (v. 21), but Moses added a request for information about the strength of the natives, their fortifications, and the quality of the land (Num. 13:17–20). It was the scouts' report on these subjects that discouraged the people and led to their rebellion. Moses had expected their answers to encourage the people, but although his motives were good, he was held responsible for the consequences of his initiative. However, if Moses has in mind a sin of his own, it is strange that he alludes to it three times, here and in 3:26 and 4:21, with phrases that mean "because of you," and is silent about his own actions. The plain sense of these phrases is that Moses was personally blameless but was caught up in God's anger at his contemporaries. Perhaps this was due to Moses' agreeing to the people's request for scouts. Even if that request did not initially imply a lack of faith in God, it eventually led to the people's loss of faith, and perhaps Moses was held accountable for the consequences of their initiative because he approved it.[112]

too, and He said: You shall not enter it either. 38Joshua son of Nun, who attends you, he shall enter it. Imbue him with strength, for he shall allot it to Israel.—39Moreover, your little ones who you said would be carried off, your children who do not yet know good from bad, they shall enter it; to them will I give it and they shall possess it. 40As for you, turn about and march into the wilderness by the way of the Sea of Reeds.

תָּבֹא שָׁם: 38 יְהוֹשֻׁעַ בִּן־נוּן הָעֹמֵד לְפָנֶיךָ הוּא יָבֹא שָׁמָּה אֹתוֹ חַזֵּק כִּי־הוּא יַנְחִלֶנָּה אֶת־יִשְׂרָאֵל: רביעי 39 וְטַפְּכֶם אֲשֶׁר אֲמַרְתֶּם לָבַז יִהְיֶה וּבְנֵיכֶם אֲשֶׁר לֹא־יָדְעוּ הַיּוֹם טוֹב וָרָע הֵמָּה יָבֹאוּ שָׁמָּה וְלָהֶם אֶתְּנֶנָּה וְהֵם יִירָשׁוּהָ: 40 וְאַתֶּם פְּנוּ לָכֶם וּסְעוּ הַמִּדְבָּרָה דֶּרֶךְ יַם־סוּף:

Numbers 20:12 and related passages give a different reason for Moses' exclusion from the promised land. For a discussion of this issue see Excursus 2.

38. Joshua, Moses' aide (see, e.g., Exod. 24:13), is his natural successor. His fitness is indicated in Numbers 27:18 where he is described as "an inspired man," that is, a man moved by the spirit of God. Joshua's prior military experience also prepares him to lead Israel in the upcoming wars (Exod. 17:8–13). As noted above, Numbers 14:6 and related passages indicate that Joshua was exempted from the decree that befell his contemporaries because of his role in the incident of the scouts; see the discussion of this subject in Excursus 2.

Joshua son of Nun Joshua (*yehoshuaʿ*) probably means "the LORD [*yeho*] is a noble [*shuaʿ*]." According to Numbers 13:16 Joshua was originally called Hoshea and was renamed by Moses. His original name (mentioned in Deuteronomy 32:44) is a short form of Hoshaiah, meaning "save, O LORD!"[113]

attends Literally, "stands before," an idiom for attending or serving.[114]

Imbue him with strength Rather, "say to him *ḥazak* [Be strong!]" (Heb. *ʾoto ḥazzek*). Likewise in 3:28, *ḥazzekehu ve-ʾammetsehu* means "say to him *ḥazak ve-ʾemats* [be strong and resolute!]," just as Moses does when he carries out this instruction in 31:7 (cf. 31:23 and Josh. 1:6–9,18). *Ḥazak* and *ḥazak ve-ʾemats* are formulas of encouragement, and the verbs used here mean to pronounce those formulas, just as the English verbs "to hail" and "to welcome" mean to say "hail!" and "welcome!"[115]

allot Rather, "apportion," as in 31:7. Joshua will assign each of the tribes and clans its territory. The process is described in Numbers 33:54 and Joshua 14–21.

39. Here God's address to the people is resumed.

who you said would be carried off See Numbers 14:3.

your children who do not yet know good from bad Therefore they cannot be held accountable for the rebellion. The parallel passages indicate that this refers to children below the age of twenty (see Comment to v. 35). According to talmudic literature, God does not punish those under twenty for crimes that are punishable only by Heaven and not by human courts. The same equation of knowing good and bad with the age of twenty is found in the Qumran "Manual of Discipline," which forbids a man to marry until that age, "when he knows [good] and bad." The idiom "knowing good and bad" has several different meanings in the Bible. Here it refers to moral judgment, as is clear from the context; this sense is paralleled by prophetic denunciations of "those who call evil good and good evil" in Isaiah 5:20 (cf. Mic. 3:2; Amos 5:14).[116]

40. **turn about and march into the wilderness** This command makes God's reversal of His promise palpable: from the border of the promised land the people are sent away from the land, back where they have just come from; their journey "through the great and terrible wilderness" was for naught. The wording of this command underscores the reversal with irony, for its first three words are identical to those with which the command to proceed *to* the land began in verse 7: *penu lakhem u-seʿu*, literally, "turn about and march."

by way of the Sea of Reeds That is, "on the Road to the Sea of Reeds," a road leading from Kadesh-barnea to the Gulf of Elath.[117] The "Sea of Reeds" refers both to the sea the Israelites crossed when leaving Egypt and to the Gulf of Elath (see Comment to Suph in v. 1). Hindsight indicates that

⁴¹You replied to me, saying, "We stand guilty before the LORD. We will go up now and fight, just as the LORD our God commanded us." And you all girded yourselves with war gear and recklessly started for the hill country. ⁴²But the LORD said to me, "Warn them: Do not go up and do not fight, since I am not in your midst; else you will be routed by your enemies." ⁴³I spoke to you, but you would not listen; you flouted the LORD's command and willfully marched into the hill country. ⁴⁴Then the Amorites who lived in those hills came out against you like so many bees

41 וַתַּעֲנוּ | וַתֹּאמְרוּ אֵלַי חָטָאנוּ לַיהוָה אֲנַחְנוּ
נַעֲלֶה וְנִלְחַמְנוּ כְּכֹל אֲשֶׁר־צִוָּנוּ יְהוָה אֱלֹהֵינוּ
וַתַּחְגְּרוּ אִישׁ אֶת־כְּלֵי מִלְחַמְתּוֹ וַתָּהִינוּ לַעֲלֹת
הָהָרָה: 42 וַיֹּאמֶר יְהוָה אֵלַי אֱמֹר לָהֶם לֹא תַעֲלוּ
וְלֹא־תִלָּחֲמוּ כִּי אֵינֶנִּי בְּקִרְבְּכֶם וְלֹא תִּנָּגְפוּ לִפְנֵי
אֹיְבֵיכֶם: 43 וָאֲדַבֵּר אֲלֵיכֶם וְלֹא שְׁמַעְתֶּם וַתַּמְרוּ
אֶת־פִּי יְהוָה וַתָּזִדוּ וַתַּעֲלוּ הָהָרָה: 44 וַיֵּצֵא
הָאֱמֹרִי הַיֹּשֵׁב בָּהָר הַהוּא לִקְרַאתְכֶם וַיִּרְדְּפוּ
אֶתְכֶם כַּאֲשֶׁר תַּעֲשֶׂינָה הַדְּבֹרִים וַיַּכְּתוּ אֶתְכֶם

the latter was meant here (see 2:8), since the Israelites never returned to the former. But to a generation that did not have the benefit of hindsight and, according to Numbers 14:4, had just declared, "Let us head back for Egypt," the command might well have sounded like an order to do just that.

41. The people's response to God's decree is ostensibly one of contrition, but in fact it is as rebellious as their response to His original command. When commanded to "turn about and march" and "go up" to the land (vv. 7,21) they "refused to go up" (v. 26). Now that they are commanded to "turn about and march" away from the land they respond "we will go up" to the land.

We will go up   Rather, "It is we who shall go up!"—that is, we and not the next generation, contrary to God's decree.

*recklessly*¹¹⁸

GOD FORBIDS THE PEOPLE TO ATTACK THE LAND AND MAKES THEM RETURN TO THE WILDERNESS   (1:42–2:1)

In this final section of Part 1, the undoing of God's original intentions for the Exodus generation reaches its climax. Now it is He who rules out an attack on the promised land, and they who insist on it. Only their defeat at the hands of the Amorites finally breaks their rebellious spirit and leads them to submit to God's decree. With the march back into the wilderness, their loss of what God had offered them at the beginning of Part 1 is complete. The stage is set for Part 2, where God starts over again.

42.   *Do not go up and do not fight*   From their preparations to attack the land it was clear that the people believed that God was as inconstant as they and would not enforce His decree if they would reverse themselves. Here God makes His intentions explicit, countermanding the people's declaration that they would go up and fight (v. 41) and His own earlier command (v. 21).

I am not in your midst   Israel's faith in their ability to overcome militarily superior enemies was based on the belief that God was present in their midst and fighting for them, as noted in Excursus 3 (see esp. 7:21 and Josh. 3:10). Moses had reminded the people of God's presence when they refused to go up and fight. Ironically, it is only after God withdraws His presence that they insist on going.

According to Numbers 14:42–44, God's absence from among those who went out to fight was expressed by the fact that the Ark did not leave the camp with them. Here Moses speaks directly of God's absence. See Comment to verse 33.

43.   *you flouted the LORD's command and willfully marched* (lit., "went up") *into the hill country*   An ironic contrast with verse 26: "you refused to go up, and flouted the command of the LORD." The similar wording highlights the people's contrariness.

44.   By their own action the Israelites brought about the disaster they had feared (v. 27): defeat at the hands of the Amorites.

Amorites   Here this name serves as a general designation for the natives of the promised land (see Comment on v. 20). In this case, according to Numbers 14:45, it was the Amalekites and Canaanites who attacked the Israelites.

and chased you, and they crushed you at Hormah in Seir. [45]Again you wept before the LORD; but the LORD would not heed your cry or give ear to you.

בְּשֵׂעִיר עַד־חָרְמָה: 45 וַתָּשֻׁבוּ וַתִּבְכּוּ לִפְנֵי יְהוָה וְלֹא־שָׁמַע יְהוָה בְּקֹלְכֶם וְלֹא הֶאֱזִין אֲלֵיכֶם:

2[46]Thus, after you had remained at Kadesh all that long time, [1]we marched back into the wilderness by the way of the Sea of Reeds, as the LORD had spoken to me, and we skirted the hill country of Seir a long time.

46 וַתֵּשְׁבוּ בְקָדֵשׁ יָמִים רַבִּים כַּיָּמִים אֲשֶׁר יְשַׁבְתֶּם: 1 וַנֵּפֶן וַנִּסַּע הַמִּדְבָּרָה דֶּרֶךְ יַם־סוּף כַּאֲשֶׁר דִּבֶּר יְהוָה אֵלָי וַנָּסָב אֶת־הַר־שֵׂעִיר יָמִים רַבִּים: ס

bees "Swarming about you as pertinaciously, as ferociously, and as numerously as bees"[119] (cf. Ps. 118:12). Wild honeybees that are unaccustomed to humans, especially the type of bees found in Israel, are said to be suspicious, irritable, and very prone to stinging.[120]

at Hormah in Seir[121]

45. *Again you wept* Literally, "you returned [*va-tashuvu*] and wept." Having swung from despair to overconfidence (vv. 27–28 and 41), the people's mood swung back to grief. Another possible translation is "you returned (from the defeat) and wept." The Septuagint and Peshitta read instead *va-teshevu*, "You sat (and wept)," a reading paralleled in Judges 20:26 and 21:2.

46. Literally this verse means "And you remained at Kadesh many days, like the days that you remained." Because of its imprecise terms its meaning is uncertain. "Many days" can refer to periods of a few days or many years.[122] Ibn Ezra holds that "like the days that you remained" means that after the defeat by the Amorites the Israelites stayed at Kadesh another forty days, matching the forty days they waited there for the scouts to return (Num. 13:25). Rashbam takes "like the days that you remained" to mean simply "as you know." The Israelites cannot have stayed at Kadesh for more than a few months, since the events of chapter 1 took place in the second year after the Exodus (see Num. 10:11) and, according to 2:14, the Israelites began the final phase of their wanderings thirty-eight years after leaving Kadesh-barnea.[123] Since 2:1 says that Israel left Kadesh "as God commanded," their stay must have been brief; a delay would have constituted another act of rebellion, and the text gives no hint of such. The present translation implies that "you remained at Kadesh" refers to the time up through the return from battle and that there was no further delay there at all.

The chronology implied by this verse and 2:1 is difficult to reconcile with that in Numbers. See Excursus 2.

CHAPTER 2   **2:1.** In their first act of obedience since leaving Horeb, the Israelites leave Kadesh-barnea and return to the wilderness, as commanded in 1:40. The passage echoes 1:19 but reverses its content: there the Israelites traveled through the wilderness *to* Kadesh-barnea.

skirted the hill country of Seir Their route skirted the southwestern edge of the Seir highlands (see Comment to v. 2).

many days Here, unlike 1:46, the phrase must refer to a long time, nearly thirty-eight years (see 2:14). The events of these years are passed over in complete silence. The aim of Moses' address is to illustrate the consequences of obedience and disobedience. Hence he concentrates on the failure of the first attempt to enter Canaan at the beginning of the period and on the successful battles against Sihon and Og at the end of that period.

The Second Command to Proceed to the Promised Land and Israel's Obedience   (2:2–3:29)

Themes and Structure

Part 2 opens as the thirty-eight-year sentence is about to end. God begins to move the Israelites into a position from which they can enter the promised land as soon as the previous generation has completely died out. This part resembles Part 1 and echoes it at many points, but it has the opposite outcome. It begins by echoing God's opening declaration in Part 1 (1:6), and it continues with the command that Israel "turn about" (*penu lakhem*) in the direction of the promised land (2:2) and with the statement that Israel did "turn about" and move on (*va-nefen* . . . , v. 8; cf. 1:7; see introduction to 1:6–3:29, Structure and Formulation). But unlike the situation in Part 1, the people do not refuse to proceed, and this part culminates in victory.

Instead of entering the promised land directly from the wilderness, as they could have done thirty-eight years earlier, the Israelites must now approach it from the east. This route requires them to pass five states which run the length of Transjordan: Edom, Moab, Ammon, and the Amorite kingdoms of Sihon and Og. The difference in routes is subtly expressed by the terminology of the text: in place of the verb *n-s-ʿ*, "travel," which describes the journeys of Part 1,[1] Part 2 uses the verb *ʿ-v-r*, "pass," "cross," which echoes the name of the region they are passing through, *ʿever ha-yarden*, "Across-the-Jordan," that is, "Transjordan."[2]

Dividing Part 2 as we did Part 1, we find six sections: (A) 2:2–8; (B) 2:9–16; (C) 2:17–30; (D) 2:31–3:1; (E) 3:2–26a; and (F) 3:26b–29. Sections A through E describe Israel's northward march through Transjordan, which consists of peaceful encounters with three nations and war with two others.[3] In Sections A through C God declares that Israel may not attack the lands of Edom, Moab, and the Ammonites because He will not give them these lands. Later in Section C, however, and in Section D, He promises to place the lands of two Amorite kings, Sihon and Og, "in the hands of Israel," the reverse of what the previous generation had claimed He intended (see 1:27). He commands Israel, "begin the occupation" (lit., "begin to take possession," 2:24,31; 3:2), echoing the aborted promises and commands in 1:8 and 21. Sihon and Og "take the field" (lit., "come out to war," 2:32; 3:1) against Israel, just as the Amorites "came out" a generation earlier (1:44), but this time Israel is victorious.

In Section E God exhorts Israel not to fear Og (3:2), echoing Moses' exhortations a generation earlier (1:21,29), and Moses addresses the same exhortation to Joshua regarding the forthcoming battles with the Amorites in the promised land (3:22). Moses describes the defeated cities of Og as "fortified with high walls, gates, and bars" and Og himself as a giant (3:5,11), pointedly recalling what the Israelites had previously believed made the Amorites and their cities invincible (1:28). After the conquest of these Transjordanian lands Moses tells the tribes who settle there that the Lord has given them that land to possess (3:18). This echoes the promise regarding the land west of the Jordan (1:8,21), but this is the first time such a gift to Israel is referred to as an accomplished fact. Moses then tells Joshua to have no fear in the coming battles for the promised land, for the Lord would fight for Israel as He had done in Transjordan (3:22). This section thus reiterates the assurance that the previous generation, to its ruin, refused to accept (1:29–33). The allusions to Part 1 thus underscore how the failures of the previous generation were reversed because the new generation trusted and obeyed God. With this lesson in mind, Israel is ready to advance to the promised land.

The successes of the new generation encourage Moses to hope for a reversal of his own fate, and he implores God to permit him to enter the land. But, in Section F, God rejects Moses' plea and ironically employs some of the same terms that have figured in the previous sections. God's first words, "Enough" (*rav lakh*, 3:26b), echo the phrases with which Parts 1 and 2 began, "You have . . . long enough" (*rav lakhem*, 1:6; 2:1), and His order that Moses "go up to the summit" (*ʿaleh rosh*, 3:27) echoes Moses' earlier command that Israel "go up, take possession" (*ʿaleh resh*, 1:21). Phrases that were used to encourage Israel to enter the promised land are used here to deny Moses' plea that

²Then the LORD said to me: ³You have been skirting this hill country long enough; now turn north. ⁴And charge the people as follows: You will be passing through the territory of your kinsmen, the descendants of Esau, who live in Seir. Though they will be afraid of you, be very careful ⁵not to provoke them. For I will not give you of their land so much

חמישי ² וַיֹּאמֶר יְהֹוָה אֵלַי לֵאמֹר: 3 רַב־לָכֶם סֹב אֶת־הָהָר הַזֶּה פְּנוּ לָכֶם צָפֹנָה: 4 וְאֶת־הָעָם צַו לֵאמֹר אַתֶּם עֹבְרִים בִּגְבוּל אֲחֵיכֶם בְּנֵי־עֵשָׂו הַיֹּשְׁבִים בְּשֵׂעִיר וְיִירְאוּ מִכֶּם וְנִשְׁמַרְתֶּם מְאֹד: 5 אַל־תִּתְגָּרוּ בָם כִּי לֹא־אֶתֵּן לָכֶם

he be allowed to do so. In this way the text underlines that Moses' lot is not with the new generation but with the old one that died out in the wilderness.

THE COMMAND TO PASS THROUGH SEIR (vv. 2–8)

The first stage of the northward march through Transjordan takes the Israelites through the territory of Seir-Edom east of the Negev highlands. The inhabitants of the region were seminomadic, as indicated by Egyptian inscriptions of the period and the paucity of archaeological evidence of a sedentary population there.[4]

2. This command was uttered near the end of the last year of the wanderings in the wilderness, as is evident from verse 7.

3. *You have been skirting this hill country long enough* As noted, this clause echoes the introduction to the command to leave Horeb a generation earlier, 1:6. See introductory Comment to 2:2–3:29.

turn north To judge from verse 8, the Israelites were now at the southern tip of Seir-Edom, near Elath and Ezion-geber.

4. *your kinsmen, the descendants of Esau* This refers to the Edomites, descendants of Jacob's brother Esau and hence the Israelites' kinsmen (see Gen. 36). Despite the hostility that developed between Israel and Edom in later times, their kinship was still remembered even in postexilic times, as Mal. 1:2–4 shows.[5] The reference to their kinship may be intended to back up the prohibition against provoking them, just as 23:8 commands Israel not to abhor Edomites because they are brothers.

Seir Since the territory about to be traversed is south of Moab (see vv. 3,8), Seir refers here to the eastern part of Seir-Edom, either the part in the Aravah (see Comments to 1:2 and 2:8) or the part in the highlands further east. Eastern Seir-Edom extended northward for 100 miles from the Gulf of Elath[6] to the southern end of the Dead Sea and Wadi Zered. To judge from Genesis 36:20, Seir bears the name of Seir the Horite, who dwelt in the area before the arrival of Esau and his family.[7]

they will be afraid of you The prospect of a huge population and its cattle traversing their territory would alarm the Edomites, as it would soon alarm the Moabites, who feared that the Israelites would "lick clean all that is about us as an ox licks up the grass of the field" (Num. 22:3–4). These concerns are reflected in Moses' assurances to the king of Edom and to Sihon that the Israelites would not enter their fields or vineyards or drink from their wells (Num. 20:17; 21:22). According to Exodus 15:14–16, the Edomites and Moabites were also terrified by reports of what the Lord had done to Egypt on Israel's behalf when they crossed the sea.

5. Here, God expresses one of the pervasive themes of this chapter: He has given the Edomites their land just as He is about to give the Israelites theirs. The same is said of the lands of the Moabites and Ammonites in verses 9 and 19. This theme indicates the universal dominion of God and His involvement in the history of all nations. The same idea is expressed poetically in 32:8, "When the Most High gave nations their homes." A close parallel to this idea is found in Amos 9:7: "To Me, O Israelites, you are just like the Ethiopians—declares the LORD. True, I brought Israel up from the land of Egypt, but also the Philistines from Caphtor and the Aramaeans from Kir." The idea is foreshadowed in Genesis in the blessings of Ishmael and the oracle about the future of the

as a foot can tread on; I have given the hill country of Seir as a possession to Esau. ⁶What food you eat you shall obtain from them for money; even the water you drink you shall procure from them for money. ⁷Indeed, the LORD your God has blessed you in all your undertakings. He has watched over your wanderings through this great wilderness; the LORD your God has been with you these past forty years: you have lacked nothing.

⁸We then moved on, away from our kinsmen, the descendants of Esau, who live in Seir, away from the road of the Arabah, away from Elath and Ezion-geber; and we marched on in the direction of the wilderness of Moab.

מֵאַרְצָ֑ם עַ֣ד מִדְרַ֣ךְ כַּף־רָ֔גֶל כִּֽי־יְרֻשָּׁ֥ה לְעֵשָׂ֖ו נָתַ֥תִּי אֶת־הַ֥ר שֵׂעִֽיר: 6 אֹ֣כֶל תִּשְׁבְּר֧וּ מֵֽאִתָּ֛ם בַּכֶּ֖סֶף וַאֲכַלְתֶּ֑ם וְגַם־מַ֜יִם תִּכְר֧וּ מֵאִתָּ֛ם בַּכֶּ֖סֶף וּשְׁתִיתֶֽם: 7 כִּי֩ יְהֹוָ֨ה אֱלֹהֶ֜יךָ בֵּֽרַכְךָ֗ בְּכֹל֙ מַעֲשֵׂ֣ה יָדֶ֔ךָ יָדַ֣ע לֶכְתְּךָ֔ אֶת־הַמִּדְבָּ֥ר הַגָּדֹ֖ל הַזֶּ֑ה | אַרְבָּעִ֣ים שָׁנָ֗ה יְהֹוָ֤ה אֱלֹהֶ֙יךָ֙ עִמָּ֔ךְ לֹ֥א חָסַ֖רְתָּ דָּבָֽר:

8 וַֽנַּעֲבֹ֞ר מֵאֵ֧ת אַחֵ֣ינוּ בְנֵי־עֵשָׂ֗ו הַיֹּֽשְׁבִים֙ בְּשֵׂעִ֔יר מִדֶּ֙רֶךְ֙ הָעֲרָבָ֔ה מֵאֵילַ֖ת וּמֵעֶצְי֣וֹן גָּ֑בֶר* ס וַנֵּ֗פֶן

v. 8. פיסקא באמצע פסוק

descendants of Jacob and Esau.⁸ Especially noteworthy is the moral obligation inherent in the fact that the Edomites, Moabites, and Ammonites received their lands from God: the Israelites have no right to any of those lands.⁹

This prohibition is a counterpart of 1:7–8, where the extent of the promised territory is described and the Israelites are told to take possession of it. The present verse reflects the concept of God as sovereign over all nations, granting territory to one of His vassals. Hittite documents recording such grants often include explicit warnings not to encroach on the territories given to other vassals.¹⁰

so much as a foot can tread on Not even a foot of their land.

6. That the seminomadic Edomites were able to supply produce and water is understandable. Abraham and Isaac, also seminomads, dug wells, and Isaac engaged in agriculture (Gen. 21:30; 26:12,18–22); seminomads in the Negev still engage in agriculture today.¹¹

7. Indeed Rather, "For." The Israelites' prosperity explains why they are able to pay the Edomites.¹²

blessed you in all your undertakings That is, He made you prosperous in every way; compare 30:9: "The LORD your God will grant you abounding prosperity in all your undertakings, in the issue of your womb, the offspring of your cattle, and the produce of your soil." "Blessing" often refers to prosperity, as in Genesis 24:35, "The LORD has greatly blessed my master, and he has become rich: He has given him sheep and cattle, silver and gold, male and female slaves, camels and asses."¹³

watched over Literally, "known." "Watch over" is one of the many meanings of "know." See, for example, Psalm 1:6.

8. The Israelites passed through and beyond Seir-Edom in the direction of Moab. According to Numbers 20:14–21 and Judges 11:17, the king of Seir-Edom—seemingly on a different occasion—denied Israel permission to pass through his territory from Kadesh, forcing them to turn away. The relationship between these passages is discussed in Excursus 2.

we marched on in the direction of the wilderness of Moab Literally, "we turned and passed on the road to the wilderness of Moab." Apparently the Israelites first traveled north thorough Seir-Edom along "the road of the Arabah"—presumably, a road running the length of the Aravah—to its northern end, and then turned east onto a road leading to the wilderness of Moab. According to this interpretation, the verse might be paraphrased, "After we passed our Edomite kinsmen . . . and left the road of the Aravah [which runs north] from Elath and Ezion-geber, we turned onto the road to the wilderness of Moab and passed along it."¹⁴

Elath and Ezion-geber Two cities at the northern end of the Gulf of Elath; their exact locations are not certain. See Excursus 1.

the wilderness of Moab The wilderness east of Moab (Num. 21:11).

9And the LORD said to me: Do not harass the Moabites or provoke them to war. For I will not give you any of their land as a possession; I have assigned Ar as a possession to the descendants of Lot.—

וַנַּעֲבֹר דֶּרֶךְ מִדְבַּר מוֹאָב: 9 וַיֹּאמֶר יְהוָה אֵלַי אַל־תָּצַר אֶת־מוֹאָב וְאַל־תִּתְגָּר בָּם מִלְחָמָה כִּי לֹא־אֶתֵּן לְךָ מֵאַרְצוֹ יְרֻשָּׁה כִּי לִבְנֵי־לוֹט נָתַתִּי אֶת־עָר יְרֻשָּׁה:

THE COMMAND TO PASS THROUGH MOAB
AND THE END OF THE EXODUS GENERATION (vv. 9–16)

The next stage of the march through Transjordan took the Israelites through Moab in the highlands east of the Dead Sea. Entering Moab marked a turning point, for by this time the last of the wilderness generation, those who had rebelled at Kadesh-barnea, had died out.

According to Judges 11:17, the king of Moab refused permission for Israel to pass through his territory. See Excursus 2.

9. *Moab* The territory of Moab at this time consisted of the southern half of the high tablelands east of the Dead Sea. Verses 13 and 24 indicate that it extended from Wadi Zered to Wadi Arnon (see Map 3).[15] Numbers 21:26–30 indicates that Moab had previously included territory north of the Arnon as well, but lost it to Sihon, king of the Amorites. Moabite territory must at one time have included all the territory east of the Dead Sea and the southern end of the Jordan. That explains why the eastern part of the Jordan valley just north of the Dead Sea was called "the steppes of Moab," as in Numbers 36:13 and Deuteronomy 34:1.

The earliest references to Moab are in Egyptian documents of the thirteenth century B.C.E. Archaeological investigation shows little evidence of sedentary population at this time, but, unlike the case in Edom, there are indications of some settlements.[16]

Ar A town or region in Moab. See Excursus 1.

the descendants of Lot The Moabites were also kin to the Israelites, though not as close as the Edomites. They were traced back to Abraham's nephew Lot, as were the Ammonites (v. 19; see Gen. 19:30–38).

10–12. These are the first of several parenthetic notes describing the prehistory of neighboring lands and explaining some of their ethnographic and geographic terminology. The others appear in verses 20–23 and in 3:9,11,13.

These notes indicate that Transjordan and Philistia had once been inhabited by earlier populations who were supplanted by the Edomites, Moabites, Ammonites, and Philistines, just as the land promised to the Israelites was inhabited by peoples whom they would supplant. The Transjordanian aborigines are already mentioned in Genesis 14:5–6, in a narrative about the days of Abraham. Verse 21 of the present chapter states that it was God who drove out the aborigines and gave the Ammonites and Edomites their lands, and verse 9 implies that He did the same for the Moabites.[17]

The purpose of these notes is apparently to underscore the reliability of God's promise to grant Israel victory over the inhabitants of the promised land by showing that He had already done the same thing for Israel's neighbors. The examples of the Moabites and Ammonites are particularly apt since the aborigines of their lands were giants like those in the promised land who had frightened the Israelites into rebellion against God.[18] There are clear allusions in 2:10 and 21 to verse 1:28, thereby rebutting the Israelites' earlier fears.

Since verse 12 speaks of the Israelites in the third person, these notes do not appear to have been part of Moses' speech to the Israelites, to whom he consistently refers in the second person. The notes are addressed instead to the readers of Deuteronomy. Hoffmann holds that these notes were added by Moses when he committed the Torah to writing (see 31:9). Since this would have been prior to the conquest of the promised land, this view implies that the notes were intended to bolster the Israelites' confidence in God as they approached the land for the second time. But since verse 12 refers to Israel's conquest of the promised land in the past tense, critical theory regards these notes as having been added to the text after the conquest (see the Introduction). In that case they are addressed to later generations, either in order to bolster their faith in the face of new dangers or to help them understand the role of God in history.

10It was formerly inhabited by the Emim, a people great and numerous, and as tall as the Anakites. 11Like the Anakites, they are counted as Rephaim; but the Moabites call them Emim. 12Similarly, Seir was formerly inhabited by the Horites; but the descendants of Esau dispossessed them, wiping them out and settling in their place, just as Israel did in the land they were to possess, which the LORD had given to them.—

13Up now! Cross the wadi Zered!

10 הָאֵמִים לְפָנִים יָשְׁבוּ בָהּ עַם גָּדוֹל וְרַב וָרָם
כָּעֲנָקִים: 11 רְפָאִים יֵחָשְׁבוּ אַף־הֵם כָּעֲנָקִים
וְהַמֹּאָבִים יִקְרְאוּ לָהֶם אֵמִים: 12 וּבְשֵׂעִיר
יָשְׁבוּ הַחֹרִים לְפָנִים וּבְנֵי עֵשָׂו יִירָשׁוּם
וַיַּשְׁמִידוּם מִפְּנֵיהֶם וַיֵּשְׁבוּ תַחְתָּם כַּאֲשֶׁר
עָשָׂה יִשְׂרָאֵל לְאֶרֶץ יְרֻשָּׁתוֹ אֲשֶׁר־נָתַן יְהוָה
לָהֶם:
13 עַתָּה קֻמוּ וְעִבְרוּ לָכֶם אֶת־נַחַל זָרֶד

10. It   The land of Moab, not only Ar; all of these notes refer to entire lands. In Genesis 14:5 the Emim were found in a second city in the (future) land of Moab.

Emim   The Targums and the midrash take this as an epithet meaning "the fearsome ones," from the root '-y-m, which refers to terror.[19] This may well be what the Moabites meant by the term, since the Emim were said to be gigantic.

as the Anakites   See Comment to 1:28.

11. Rephaim   From this verse, verse 20, and 3:11, it appears that "Rephaim" was the generic name or epithet of the gigantic aborigines, and that local peoples called them by different names or epithets: the Moabites called them Emim and the Ammonites called them Zamzummim. The Anakim west of the Jordan may also have been considered Rephaim, but our verse may mean merely that the Anakim were *comparable* to the Rephaim (cf. v. 21). The Rephaim are also listed among the pre-Israelite peoples living in the promised land (Gen. 15:20; Josh. 17:15). Their great height is indicated by the size of Og's bedstead (3:11) and of the weapons of their descendants in Philistia (2 Sam. 21:16–22).[20]

12.   This is a separate note, referring to the original inhabitants of Seir. The reason why this note appears here, rather than in the paragraph about Seir, may be suggested by verses 20–23, which also consist of a pair of notes. In each case the first note deals with gigantic aborigines, while the second does not. The fact that the Lord drove out giants in Transjordan is the strongest advance evidence of His ability to drive out the Amorites for Israel. While the notes about the Horites and the Avvim (2:22–3) also show how God controls the movement of peoples, they are less impressive than the notes about the gigantic Emim and Zamzummim. By appending these notes to those about the Emim and Zamzummim, the text gives prominence to the more impressive ones.

Horites   A people that preceded the Edomites in Seir and descended from Seir the Horite, according to Gen. 14:6 and 36:20–30. It is uncertain whether they are connected with the Hurrians, a non-Semitic people spread throughout the Near East in the third and second millennia B.C.E. Although "Horite" could mean "Hurrian," it would be strange for the Bible to explicitly mention the Hurrians in Seir-Edom and not in Canaan, since they were prominent in central Canaan in the Late Bronze Age but are not known to have been present ever in Seir-Edom. Hence the Horites of Seir-Edom may have been a people with a coincidentally similar name but unconnected with the Hurrians.[21]

the descendants of Esau dispossessed them, wiping them out   As verses 21–22 make clear, God made this happen. The Samaritan text of the Torah words the present verse so as to make this clear: "The LORD wiped them out before them [the descendants of Esau], so that they dispossessed them."

13. wadi Zered   The southern boundary of Moab. See Excursus 1.

14–16.   These verses mark the transition between the generation of the Exodus, which rebelled at Kadesh-barnea, and the generation that would enter the promised land. With the crossing of Wadi Zered, God's oath was fulfilled: all those of age when the Israelites refused to proceed to the land had died (1:35). Now the conquest would begin. The transition is noted at this point because when the Israelites crossed Wadi Zered they entered Moab, which would be the springboard for

So we crossed the wadi Zered. ¹⁴The time that we spent in travel from Kadesh-barnea until we crossed the wadi Zered was thirty-eight years, until that whole generation of warriors had perished from the camp, as the LORD had sworn concerning them. ¹⁵Indeed, the hand of the LORD struck them, to root them out from the camp to the last man.

¹⁶When all the warriors among the people had died off,

וַנַּעֲבֹר אֶת־נַחַל זָרֶד: 14 וְהַיָּמִים אֲשֶׁר־הָלַכְנוּ ׀
מִקָּדֵשׁ בַּרְנֵעַ עַד אֲשֶׁר־עָבַרְנוּ אֶת־נַחַל זֶרֶד
שְׁלֹשִׁים וּשְׁמֹנֶה שָׁנָה עַד־תֹּם כָּל־הַדּוֹר אַנְשֵׁי
הַמִּלְחָמָה מִקֶּרֶב הַמַּחֲנֶה כַּאֲשֶׁר נִשְׁבַּע יְהוָה
לָהֶם: 15 וְגַם יַד־יְהוָה הָיְתָה בָּם לְהֻמָּם מִקֶּרֶב
הַמַּחֲנֶה עַד תֻּמָּם:
16 וַיְהִי כַאֲשֶׁר־תַּמּוּ כָּל־אַנְשֵׁי הַמִּלְחָמָה לָמוּת

their conquests: from it they would march on the kingdoms of Sihon and Og and then on the promised land itself. The fulfillment of God's oath is a milestone whose importance is underscored by a number of literary devices calling attention to it. The action stops as Moses declares that the oath was fulfilled. The death of the rebellious generation is mentioned three times with the same sonorous verb for "perish," *tom*, *tummam*, and *tammu* (the effect is not noticeable in the translation, which renders each instance differently: "perished," "to the last man," "died off"). The central verse of the passage (v. 15), describing God's active role in finishing off the previous generation, is marked by the assonance of *ve-gam / bam / le-hummam / tummam*. Verse 15 repeats in chiastic order key words and phrases of verse 14 ("until perished . . . from the midst of the camp . . . the LORD // the LORD . . . from the midst of the camp . . . until perished"), while verse 16 repeats key elements of both verse 14 and verse 15 ("the warriors . . . perished . . . from the midst of").²²

14. *thirty-eight years* Since the Israelites left Kadesh-barnea during the second year after the Exodus, they must have crossed Wadi Zered in the fortieth year, before Moses began this address on the first day of the eleventh month (see 1:3).

warriors those of military age. The use of this term is perhaps ironic, since they at first refused to fight.²³

15. *Indeed, the hand of the LORD struck them* Better, "Even the hand of the LORD struck them." Not all of the previous generation died of natural causes; some were killed by "the hand of the LORD"—that is, destructive forces unleashed by God, such as pestilence.²⁴ The book of Numbers records several instances of people dying from pestilence and other divine actions because of various sins.²⁵

to root them out That is, to rout them, to wipe them out. *H-m-m* is usually used in military contexts to describe what God does to Israel's enemies, as in Exodus 14:24 (see also the variant form *hum* in Deut. 7:23). Here it implies that God's punishment of the rebellious generation amounted to a divine war against it,²⁶ and that God treated them as He would normally treat Israel's enemies. The phrase "to the last man" (*'ad tummam*, lit., "until they perished"), has the same connotations, for it, too, is used in descriptions of the defeat of Israel's enemies. Both idioms express the appropriateness of the punishment: the sinful generation had accused God of planning to "give them into the hand" of their enemies (1:28); as a punishment, He wiped them out instead of their enemies.²⁷

16. This verse links God's orders in verses 17–19 and 24–25 to the death of the rebels: no sooner had the rebels died off than the Lord directed Israel on a course that would lead to their first victory and territorial possession. The preceding thirty-eight years had been a deviation from God's plan, and He now returns to that plan as soon as possible.

THE COMMAND TO BYPASS THE AMMONITES
AND ATTACK THE KINGDOM OF SIHON (vv. 17–30)

The third section combines instructions concerning the territory of the Ammonites and that of Sihon, king of the Amorites. The chronological order of the instructions is reversed. Traveling north from the Arnon (v. 24), Israel entered Sihon's territory *before* approaching Ammonite territory (v. 19). His capital, Heshbon, and Jahaz, the battle site, are both south of Ammonite territory, and

17the LORD spoke to me, saying: 18You are now passing through the territory of Moab, through Ar. 19You will then be close to the Ammonites; do not harass them or start a fight with them. For I will not give any part of the land of the Ammonites to you as a possession; I have assigned it as a possession to the descendants of Lot.—

20It, too, is counted as Rephaim country. It was formerly inhabited by Rephaim, whom the Ammonites call Zamzummim, 21a people great and numerous and as tall as the Anakites. The LORD wiped them out, so that [the Ammonites] dispossessed them and settled in their place, 22as He did for the descendants of Esau who live in Seir, when He wiped out the Horites before them, so that they dispossessed them and settled in their place, as is still the case. 23So, too, with the Avvim who dwelt in villages

17 וַיְדַבֵּר יְהֹוָה אֵלַי לֵאמֹר: ס מִקֶּרֶב הָעָם:
18 אַתָּה עֹבֵר הַיּוֹם אֶת־גְּבוּל מוֹאָב אֶת־עָר:
19 וְקָרַבְתָּ מוּל בְּנֵי עַמּוֹן אַל־תְּצֻרֵם וְאַל־תִּתְגָּר בָּם כִּי לֹא־אֶתֵּן מֵאֶרֶץ בְּנֵי־עַמּוֹן לְךָ יְרֻשָּׁה כִּי לִבְנֵי־לוֹט נְתַתִּיהָ יְרֻשָּׁה:
20 אֶרֶץ־רְפָאִים תֵּחָשֵׁב אַף־הִוא רְפָאִים יָשְׁבוּ־בָהּ לְפָנִים וְהָעַמֹּנִים יִקְרְאוּ לָהֶם זַמְזֻמִּים:
21 עַם גָּדוֹל וְרַב וָרָם כָּעֲנָקִים וַיַּשְׁמִידֵם יְהֹוָה מִפְּנֵיהֶם וַיִּירָשֻׁם וַיֵּשְׁבוּ תַחְתָּם:
22 כַּאֲשֶׁר עָשָׂה לִבְנֵי עֵשָׂו הַיֹּשְׁבִים בְּשֵׂעִיר אֲשֶׁר הִשְׁמִיד אֶת־הַחֹרִי מִפְּנֵיהֶם וַיִּירָשֻׁם וַיֵּשְׁבוּ תַחְתָּם עַד הַיּוֹם הַזֶּה:
23 וְהָעַוִּים הַיֹּשְׁבִים בַּחֲצֵרִים עַד־עַזָּה כַּפְתֹּרִים

the battle must have taken place before Israel approached the latter (v. 19; cf. v. 37, after the battle with Sihon). Apparently Moses mentions God's instructions concerning the Ammonites first so that he can finish relaying the instructions about the three peaceful encounters before turning to the victories which are the climax of his narrative.[28]

*18. **passing through the territory of Moab, through Ar*** Rather, "passing beyond the territory of Moab, beyond Ar."[29] Verses 18–19 deal with what Israel is to do after leaving Moab; as verse 24 indicates, these instructions were given as they were about to do so.

19.   The territory of the Ammonites was centered around the capital city Rabbah (modern Amman), some twenty miles east of the Jordan. It was separated from the Jordan by Sihon's territory. Excavations in Amman have unearthed remains of this period (the Late Bronze Age).[30]

the Ammonites Literally, "the children [descendants] of Ammon" (benei 'ammon). The Bible refers to the Ammonites and their land as "the children of Ammon" and "the land of the children of Ammon," and almost never speaks simply of "Ammon," though it regularly speaks of "Moab." This distinction accurately reflects the names these peoples used to refer to themselves. An Ammonite inscription speaks of the "king of the children of Ammon," while a Moabite inscription speaks of the "king of Moab."[31]

the descendants of Lot The Ammonites were also traced back to Lot (see Comment on v. 9).

20–23.   Another pair of parenthetic notes, one about the prehistory of Ammonite territory (vv. 20–22) and the other about that of Philistia (v. 23). See Comment to verses 10–12.

*20. **Zamzummim*** The name "Zamzummim," by which the Ammonites called this people, looks like an imitation of their speech. It would mean, roughly, "the Buzz-buzzers," "the people whose speech sounds like buzzing."[32] The Zamzummim are presumably identical to "the Zuzim at Ham" who are mentioned in Genesis 14:5 alongside the Emim and the Rephaim, as the Zamzummim are here.[33]

23.   The second note digresses from the context of Transjordan to deal with the inhabitants of Philistia, near Gaza. The Israelites did not pass near Philistia on their way to Canaan and were not forbidden to conquer it. Nevertheless, this note, like the others, illustrates the supplanting of aboriginal populations by new ones. The Philistines, too, were said to have been brought to the region by God (Amos 9:7).

Avvim This people is mentioned again as living near Philistia in Joshua 13:3, and is not known from elsewhere.[34] They lived in unwalled villages (ḥatserim), which suggests that they may have been herders like the Ishmaelites and Kedarites, who also lived in such villages (see Gen. 25:16 and Isa. 42:11).[35]

in the vicinity of Gaza: the Caphtorim, who came from Crete, wiped them out and settled in their place.—

²⁴Up! Set out across the wadi Arnon! See, I give into your power Sihon the Amorite, king of Heshbon, and his land. Begin the occupation: engage him in battle. ²⁵This

הַיֹּצְאִים מִכַּפְתּוֹר הִשְׁמִידֻם וַיֵּשְׁבוּ תַחְתָּם:
²⁴ קוּמוּ סְּעוּ וְעִבְרוּ אֶת־נַחַל אַרְנֹן רְאֵה נָתַתִּי בְיָדְךָ אֶת־סִיחֹן מֶלֶךְ־חֶשְׁבּוֹן הָאֱמֹרִי וְאֶת־אַרְצוֹ הָחֵל רָשׁ וְהִתְגָּר בּוֹ מִלְחָמָה: ²⁵ הַיּוֹם הַזֶּה

Caphtorim, who came from Crete Literally, "Caphtorim who came from Caphtor." These are presumably the Philistines, who are said to come from Caphtor in Amos 9:7, Jeremiah 47:4, and apparently in Genesis 10:14. Caphtor is an island or coastland in the area of the Aegean Sea. Most scholars think that the evidence (such as Zeph. 2:5, where the Philistines are called "Cherethites," or "Cretans") points to Crete and the surrounding islands, though some think that it is an area on the coast of Asia Minor; a few think that it refers to both.[36]

The Philistines were one of the "Sea Peoples" from the Aegean region who invaded the eastern Mediterranean in the thirteenth and twelfth centuries B.C.E. They are first mentioned by name in an Egyptian inscription of the 1180s or 1170s. They settled along the southern Canaanite coast soon afterwards, perhaps shortly after the Israelites arrived in inland Canaan.[37] In later times they frequently clashed with the Israelites, and ruled them for a period, until they were subdued by David. It was military pressure from the Philistines and Ammonites that eventually led the Israelites to establish a monarchy.[38]

24–25. These verses resume the instructions of verses 18–19. The command to take possession of Sihon's land and the promise to give him into Israel's power are the counterpart, for the new generation, of the command and promise that the previous generation ignored. This time the Israelites obey without hesitation, God fulfills His promise, and Israel begins to experience the victories that the previous generation had forfeited.

24. *Set out across the wadi Arnon* Into Sihon's territory; see Comment to verse 9.

I give into your power Literally, "hand." This is another allusion to, and rebuttal of, the previous generation's charge that God intended "to hand us over to the Amorites" (lit., "to give us into the hand of the Amorites") in 1:27.

The Amorites of Sihon's kingdom were not kin to the Israelites and had not been promised territory by God, but the text does not explain why their territory was forfeit. This is in keeping with the schematic, noncircumstantial character of the narratives about Sihon and Og in Moses' speech (see introductory Comment to 2:31–3:1, below).[39] According to Numbers 21:21–23 Sihon refused Israel's request for peaceful passage through his territory and attacked the Israelites, which implicitly justifies the forfeiture of his land to the Israelites.[40] Here, however, Moses states that God planned in advance to give Israel Sihon's land and that it was He who caused Sihon to refuse passage, in order to lead to his defeat. Perhaps it was assumed that Sihon and his people shared in the guilt for which the Amorites west of the Jordan were to lose their land (see Gen. 15:16). Ramban holds that God gave Israel Sihon's land because, as Amorite territory, it was included in the land He promised to Abraham (Gen. 15:21). Although the Bible normally considers all of Transjordan to be outside the territory promised to the patriarchs, a few passages seem to reflect a view that the promise did include northern Transjordan, the territory here held by Sihon and Og.[41]

Sihon the Amorite, king of Heshbon, and his land Sihon is not mentioned outside of the Bible, though some scholars believe that his name may be preserved in the name of Tell Shihan, in Moab, south of the Arnon.[42] His territory, including the area he captured from Moab, was bordered by the Dead Sea and the Jordan on the west, Wadi Jabbok on the north, Ammon and the desert on the east, and Wadi Arnon on the south (see, e.g., v. 36; 3:12,16–17, and note Comment to 3:17). For his capital, Heshbon, see Excursus 1.

25. With the victory over Sihon, God would begin causing other peoples to fear Israel, as happened earlier when they crossed the sea (cf. Exod. 15:14–16). This was not merely for the glory of Israel but for the strategic effect of demoralizing potential enemies. The spies Joshua sent to Jericho learned that this victory had the desired effect, for reports about Israel's crossing the sea and defeating Sihon and Og had caused the Canaanites to lose heart (Josh. 2:9–11,24).

day I begin to put the dread and fear of you upon the peoples everywhere under heaven, so that they shall tremble and quake because of you whenever they hear you mentioned.

²⁶Then I sent messengers from the wilderness of Kedemoth to King Sihon of Heshbon with an offer of peace, as follows, ²⁷"Let me pass through your country. I will keep strictly to the highway, turning off neither to the right nor to the left. ²⁸What food I eat you will supply for money, and what water I drink you will furnish for money; just let me pass through—²⁹as the descendants of Esau who dwell in Seir did for me, and the Moabites who dwell in Ar—that I may cross the Jordan into the land that the LORD our God is giving us."

³⁰But King Sihon of Heshbon refused to let us pass through, because the LORD had stiffened his will and hard-

אָחֵל֙ תֵּ֣ת פַּחְדְּךָ֤ וְיִרְאָֽתְךָ֙ עַל־פְּנֵ֣י הָֽעַמִּ֔ים תַּ֖חַת כָּל־הַשָּׁמָ֑יִם אֲשֶׁ֤ר יִשְׁמְעוּן֙ שִׁמְעֲךָ֔ וְרָגְז֥וּ וְחָל֖וּ מִפָּנֶֽיךָ׃
²⁶ וָאֶשְׁלַ֤ח מַלְאָכִים֙ מִמִּדְבַּ֣ר קְדֵמ֔וֹת אֶל־סִיח֖וֹן מֶ֣לֶךְ חֶשְׁבּ֑וֹן דִּבְרֵ֥י שָׁל֖וֹם לֵאמֹֽר׃ ²⁷ אֶעְבְּרָ֣ה בְאַרְצֶ֗ךָ בַּדֶּ֤רֶךְ בַּדֶּ֙רֶךְ֙ אֵלֵ֔ךְ לֹ֥א אָס֖וּר יָמִ֥ין וּשְׂמֹֽאול׃* ²⁸ אֹ֣כֶל בַּכֶּ֤סֶף תַּשְׁבִּרֵ֙נִי֙ וְאָכַ֔לְתִּי וּמַ֛יִם בַּכֶּ֥סֶף תִּתֶּן־לִ֖י וְשָׁתִ֑יתִי רַ֖ק אֶעְבְּרָ֥ה בְרַגְלָֽי׃ ²⁹ כַּאֲשֶׁ֨ר עָֽשׂוּ־לִ֜י בְּנֵ֣י עֵשָׂ֗ו הַיֹּֽשְׁבִים֙ בְּשֵׂעִ֔יר וְהַמּ֣וֹאָבִ֔ים הַיֹּשְׁבִ֖ים בְּעָ֑ר עַ֤ד אֲשֶֽׁר־אֶֽעֱבֹר֙ אֶת־הַיַּרְדֵּ֔ן אֶל־הָאָ֕רֶץ אֲשֶׁר־יְהֹוָ֥ה אֱלֹהֵ֖ינוּ נֹתֵ֥ן לָֽנוּ׃
³⁰ וְלֹ֣א אָבָ֗ה סִיחֹן֙ מֶ֣לֶךְ חֶשְׁבּ֔וֹן הַעֲבִרֵ֖נוּ בּ֑וֹ כִּֽי־הִקְשָׁה֩ יְהֹוָ֨ה אֱלֹהֶ֜יךָ אֶת־רוּח֗וֹ וְאִמֵּץ֙ אֶת־לְבָב֔וֹ

v. 27. מלא וא״ו

---

everywhere under heaven   Everywhere on the whole earth.[43]

26–30.   These verses form a smaller unit within Section C,[44] indicating that before joining battle with Sihon, Moses requested permission to pass through his territory peacefully but was refused. This request is unexpected after Moses was told to attack Sihon. Ramban holds that this passage is a flashback and that the request was made prior to God's instruction to attack. However, the present order of the events is paralleled in Moses' negotiations with Pharaoh, when God told Moses to ask Pharaoh for permission to take the Israelites on a temporary pilgrimage, though He had already told Moses that He would free the Israelites for good.[45] The statement that God hardened Sihon's heart (v. 30) likens the negotiations with Sihon to those with Pharaoh, and it is likely that the two incidents have a similar explanation. The request addressed to Pharaoh was probably intended to deceive him, since he would never have agreed to release the Israelites outright, and Moses' request to Sihon may likewise have been intended to throw him off guard.[46] See further on v. 30. In any case, "Sihon would not trust Israel to pass through his territory" (Judg. 11:20).

26. ***the wilderness of Kedemoth***   This was probably near the city of Kedemoth in the formerly Moabite part of Sihon's territory (Josh. 13:18; see Excursus 1). If so, the Israelites had already crossed the Arnon and entered Sihon's territory when the messengers were sent.

offer of peace   Literally, "words of *shalom*," meaning either a statement of friendly intentions or a proposal of a nonaggression pact. The essence of Moses' message is his request for the peaceful use of a corridor through Sihon's territory under the terms stated in the next two verses.

27.   Moses anticipates that Sihon will fear that the huge Israelite population will ravage his land; this is clear from his assurances in Numbers 21:22: "We will not turn off into fields or vineyards, and we will not drink water from wells" (cf. Num. 20:17,19, and see Comment on v. 4).

strictly to the highway[47]

28. ***just let me pass through***   Literally, "just let me pass through on my feet." From the context here and in Numbers 20:19 the idiom seems comparable to English "stand on one's own two feet," "depend on oneself," here meaning "we will take nothing for free."[48]

29. ***as the descendants of Esau ... did***   See Comment to verse 8.

and the Moabites   As in the case of Edom, other passages state that when Moses made a similar request of Moab, from Kadesh, he was refused.[49] See Comment to 23:5 and Excursus 2.

30. ***stiffened his will and hardened his heart***   Although the Bible presupposes that God normally allows man free will (see Comment to 5:26), it records exceptional cases in which He

ened his heart in order to deliver him into your power—as is now the case. [31]And the LORD said to me: See, I begin by placing Sihon and his land at your disposal. Begin the occupation; take possession of his land.

[32]Sihon with all his men took the field against us at

לְמַעַן תִּתּוֹ בְיָדְךָ כַּיּוֹם הַזֶּה: ס   שׁשׁי
31 וַיֹּאמֶר יְהוָה אֵלַי רְאֵה הַחִלֹּתִי תֵּת לְפָנֶיךָ אֶת־סִיחֹן וְאֶת־אַרְצוֹ הָחֵל רָשׁ לָרֶשֶׁת אֶת־אַרְצוֹ:
32 וַיֵּצֵא סִיחֹן לִקְרָאתֵנוּ הוּא וְכָל־עַמּוֹ לַמִּלְחָמָה

punishes evildoers by causing them to act in a sinful or reckless way that will lead to their downfall. The best known case is that of Pharaoh, who hardens his own heart and refuses several times to free Israel, with the result that God then hardens his heart further. He does this in order to prevent Pharaoh from yielding before He can make an object lesson of him by means of further punishment (see, e.g., Exod. 7:3–5; 10:1–2). In cases similar to that of Sihon, God stiffens the heart of the Canaanites so that they do not surrender to Israel but do battle with them, in order that they be wiped out (Josh. 11:19–20); and He misleads Ahab into attacking Aram in order to cause his death in battle (1 Kings 22:19–23). In these and other cases God interferes with the free will of individuals only after they have sinned on their own initiative.[50]

as is now the case   Moses uses this phrase several times to remind his audience that they can see the effect of past events with their own eyes.[51] For other phrases with the same import see Comment to 1:19.

THE VICTORY OVER SIHON   (2:31–3:1)

The victory over Sihon, and that over Og which follows, are described in brief, schematic accounts that contrast with the detailed narratives about the major battles in the book of Joshua. Moses' brevity indicates that his focus is not on the battles themselves but on their paradigmatic quality and their consequences: God orders Israel to attack, urges courage, and promises victory; Israel obeys completely, defeats the enemy totally, and conquers all of its land. These battles are therefore models of how Israel should conduct itself in war, and of what they can expect when they do so. A leitmotif associated with this theme is the idea of totality: all the enemy is defeated in battle, all their territory is captured, all their cattle is taken as booty (the word *kol* ["all," "every," "whole"] appears fourteen times in fourteen verses), not a survivor escapes, not a city goes uncaptured. The contrast with the previous generation's disobedience is obvious.

31.   This verse recapitulates verses 24–25 because of the delay, or digression, related in verses 26–30. It may mean that God repeated His earlier statement to Moses right before the battle in order to remind Israel that victory is assured, so that they will not fear to proceed as their parents did. Or it could mean that Moses merely reminded his audience of God's earlier statement in order to remind them that the victory he is about to recall was due to their obedience to God's command.

I begin   See verse 25.

32.   *took to the field*   That is, went to war, unlike Edom, which made a show of force and was not challenged by Israel (Num. 20:20).

Jahaz   See Excursus 1.

33.   The two clauses of this verse represent two dimensions of the same event: the invisible, theological dimension, and the visible, mundane dimension. The second clause shows that the victory was not miraculous but involved normal human military action. The first clause reflects the conviction that the human action was successful because of God's control of the events. By mentioning God's role first, Moses implies that His action was decisive; Israel merely reaps the benefit. On this understanding of victory, see Excursus 3. This view of the two dimensions of human affairs is expressed by the psalmist in connection with other areas of endeavor: "Unless the LORD builds the house, its builders labor in vain on it; unless the LORD watches over the city, the watchman keeps vigil in vain" (Ps. 127:1).

Jahaz, ³³and the LORD our God delivered him to us and we defeated him and his sons and all his men. ³⁴At that time we captured all his towns, and we doomed every town—men, women, and children—leaving no survivor. ³⁵We retained as booty only the cattle and the spoil of the cities that we captured. ³⁶From Aroer on the edge of the Arnon valley, including the town in the valley itself, to Gilead, not a city was too mighty for us; the LORD our God delivered everything to us. ³⁷But you did not encroach upon the land of the Ammonites, all along the wadi Jabbok and the towns of the hill country, just as the LORD our God had commanded.

3 We made our way up the road toward Bashan, and King Og of Bashan with all his men took the field against us at Edrei. ²But the LORD said to me: Do not fear him, for I

וַֽיִּתְּנֵ֜הוּ יְהֹוָ֧ה אֱלֹהֵ֛ינוּ לְפָנֵ֖ינוּ וַנַּ֣ךְ אֹת֑וֹ יָ֑הְצָה: 33
וְאֶת־בָּנ֖וֹ וְאֶת־כָּל־עַמּֽוֹ: 34 וַנִּלְכֹּ֤ד אֶת־כָּל־עָרָיו֙
בָּעֵ֣ת הַהִ֔וא וַֽנַּחֲרֵ֗ם אֶת־כָּל־עִיר֙ מְתִ֣ם וְהַנָּשִׁ֔ים
וְהַטָּ֑ף לֹ֥א הִשְׁאַ֖רְנוּ שָׂרִֽיד: 35 רַ֥ק הַבְּהֵמָ֖ה בָּזַ֣זְנוּ
לָ֑נוּ וּשְׁלַ֖ל הֶעָרִ֖ים אֲשֶׁ֥ר לָכָֽדְנוּ: 36 מֵֽעֲרֹעֵ֡ר אֲשֶׁר֩
עַל־שְׂפַת־נַ֨חַל אַרְנֹ֜ן וְהָעִ֨יר אֲשֶׁ֤ר בַּנַּ֙חַל֙ וְעַד־
הַגִּלְעָ֔ד לֹ֤א הָֽיְתָה֙ קִרְיָ֔ה אֲשֶׁ֥ר שָׂגְבָ֖ה מִמֶּ֑נּוּ אֶת־
הַכֹּ֕ל נָתַ֛ן יְהֹוָ֥ה אֱלֹהֵ֖ינוּ לְפָנֵֽינוּ: 37 רַ֛ק אֶל־אֶ֥רֶץ
בְּנֵֽי־עַמּ֖וֹן לֹ֣א קָרָ֑בְתָּ כָּל־יַ֞ד נַ֤חַל יַבֹּק֙ וְעָרֵ֣י הָהָ֔ר
וְכֹ֥ל אֲשֶׁר־צִוָּ֖ה יְהֹוָ֥ה אֱלֹהֵֽינוּ:

ג וַנֵּ֣פֶן וַנַּ֔עַל דֶּ֖רֶךְ הַבָּשָׁ֑ן וַיֵּצֵ֣א עוֹג֩ מֶֽלֶךְ־הַבָּשָׁ֨ן
לִקְרָאתֵ֜נוּ ה֧וּא וְכָל־עַמּ֛וֹ לַמִּלְחָמָ֖ה אֶדְרֶֽעִי: 2 וַיֹּ֨אמֶר
יְהֹוָ֤ה אֵלַי֙ אַל־תִּירָ֣א אֹת֔וֹ כִּ֣י בְיָֽדְךָ֩

v. 33. בָּנָ֖יו ק'

the LORD . . . delivered him to us   Exactly as He had promised (vv. 24,31). This is an implicit rejoinder to the previous generation's doubt that God would fulfill His promises (see 1:27).

34–35.   The population of Sihon's territory was killed in accordance with the provisions of 20:16–17 for cities in the promised land. The same is done in Og's territory in 3:6. These instances, too, may reflect a view that northern Transjordan was part of the promised land. See Comment to verse 24.

36.   *Aroer . . . including the town in the valley itself*   See Excursus 1.

the Arnon valley   See Comment to verse 24.

to Gilead   The hill country extending eastward from the Jordan about twenty-five to thirty miles. Gilead was divided into northern and southern sections by the western leg of the Jabbok. According to Numbers 21:24 and Joshua 12:2, only southern Gilead was part of Sihon's territory (cf. Deut. 3:12). More precise details of the territory captured from Sihon are given in 3:16–17.[52]

not a city was too mighty for us   A pointed rejoinder to the previous generation's fears in 1:28.

37.   The territory of the Ammonites was a narrow strip abutting the northeastern corner of Sihon's territory. It was spread along the eastern Jabbok (which flows northward in an arc from near Amman) and extended eastward toward the wilderness. The Israelites obeyed God's command and did not encroach upon it.[53] The Jabbok was the wadi/river known today as the Zerka (called the Wadi Amman near Amman).

CHAPTER 3   *3:1.*   From Sihon's territory the Israelites headed north to the Amorite kingdom of Og, ruler of Bashan. For the territory of this kingdom, see Excursus 1 s.v. "Bashan."

Og   Hebrew ʿ-w-g. Og is not mentioned in sources outside the Bible, but similar names, such as ʿ-g-y and ʿ-g-w, are found in texts of the Late Bronze Age from the Canaanite city of Ugarit in northwest Syria.[54]

Edrei   See Comment to 1:4.

am delivering him and all his men and his country into your power, and you will do to him as you did to Sihon king of the Amorites, who lived in Heshbon.

נָתַתִּי אֹתוֹ וְאֶת־כָּל־עַמּוֹ וְאֶת־אַרְצוֹ וְעָשִׂיתָ לּוֹ כַּאֲשֶׁר עָשִׂיתָ לְסִיחֹן מֶלֶךְ הָאֱמֹרִי אֲשֶׁר יוֹשֵׁב בְּחֶשְׁבּוֹן׃

3So the LORD our God also delivered into our power King Og of Bashan, with all his men, and we dealt them such a blow that no survivor was left. 4At that time we captured all his towns; there was not a town that we did not take from them: sixty towns, the whole district of Argob, the kingdom of Og in Bashan 5—all those towns were fortified with high walls, gates, and bars—apart from a great number of unwalled towns. 6We doomed them as we had done in the case of King Sihon of Heshbon; we doomed every town—men, women, and children—7and retained as booty all the cattle and the spoil of the towns.

3 וַיִּתֵּן יְהוָה אֱלֹהֵינוּ בְּיָדֵנוּ גַּם אֶת־עוֹג מֶלֶךְ־הַבָּשָׁן וְאֶת־כָּל־עַמּוֹ וַנַּכֵּהוּ עַד־בִּלְתִּי הִשְׁאִיר־לוֹ שָׂרִיד׃ 4 וַנִּלְכֹּד אֶת־כָּל־עָרָיו בָּעֵת הַהִוא לֹא הָיְתָה קִרְיָה אֲשֶׁר לֹא־לָקַחְנוּ מֵאִתָּם שִׁשִּׁים עִיר כָּל־חֶבֶל אַרְגֹּב מַמְלֶכֶת עוֹג בַּבָּשָׁן׃ 5 כָּל־אֵלֶּה עָרִים בְּצֻרוֹת חוֹמָה גְבֹהָה דְּלָתַיִם וּבְרִיחַ לְבַד מֵעָרֵי הַפְּרָזִי הַרְבֵּה מְאֹד׃ 6 וַנַּחֲרֵם אוֹתָם כַּאֲשֶׁר עָשִׂינוּ לְסִיחֹן מֶלֶךְ חֶשְׁבּוֹן הַחֲרֵם כָּל־עִיר מְתִם הַנָּשִׁים וְהַטָּף׃ 7 וְכָל־הַבְּהֵמָה וּשְׁלַל הֶעָרִים בַּזּוֹנוּ לָנוּ׃

THE VICTORY OVER OG AND ITS SEQUEL (vv. 2–26a)

Victory over Og followed the defeat of Sihon, and Moses allotted their territory to the tribes of Reuben and Gad and half the tribe of Manasseh. He ordered the men of these tribes to accompany the remaining tribes in the battle for the rest of the promised land, and charged Joshua to take the lesson of these victories to heart and proceed to the coming battles without fear. Encouraged by these victories, Moses pleaded with God that he be allowed to enter the promised land, but was rebuffed.

3:2–7. The victory over Og is described in the same schematic form as the victory over Sihon.

2. God encourages Israel, using the same exhortation to have no fear with which Moses unsuccessfully encouraged the previous generation (1:21,29) and the same promise of victory which preceded the battle with Sihon (2:24). Now, however, he adds the precedent set by the recent victory over Sihon to remind the people that God's encouragement is reliable. Similar exhortations would become standard elements in preparing the people for war in the future (see Comments to 1:21 and 29–33); victories such as these gave them credibility.

3. See Comment to 2:33.

4. At that time we captured See Comment to verse 14.

sixty towns, the whole district of Argob For Argob, see Excursus 1. "Sixty" is probably meant as a round number; Argob of Solomon's day is said to consist of the same number of towns, and it is unlikely that the number of towns in Argob remained unchanged over more than two centuries. That there was a large number of cities in Bashan at this time is understandable in light of the region's well-known fertility (see, e.g., Isa. 2:13; Mic. 7:14); one Egyptian inscription of the fifteenth century B.C.E. lists eleven cities that are apparently in Bashan.[55]

5. The capture of cities fortified with high walls is another rejoinder to the doubts of the previous generation (1:28).

gates and bars The city gates (lit., "double doors") had two-leaf doors held closed by a bar running along their inner sides.

6–7. See Comment to 2:34–35.

6. as we had done in the case of King Sihon Just as God had promised (v. 2).

8–11. A summary of the territory conquered from Sihon and Og. Only verses 8 and 10 belong to the summary proper: verse 8 describes the southern and northern boundaries of the

8Thus we seized, at that time, from the two Amorite kings, the country beyond the Jordan, from the wadi Arnon to Mount Hermon—9Sidonians called Hermon Sirion, and the Amorites call it Senir—10all the towns of the Tableland and the whole of Gilead and Bashan as far as Salcah and Edrei, the towns of Og's kingdom in Bashan. 11Only King Og of Bashan was left of the remaining Rephaim. His bedstead, an iron bedstead, is now in Rabbah of the Ammonites; it is nine cubits long and four cubits wide, by the standard cubit!

ח וַנִּקַּח בָּעֵת הַהִוא אֶת־הָאָרֶץ מִיַּד שְׁנֵי מַלְכֵי הָאֱמֹרִי אֲשֶׁר בְּעֵבֶר הַיַּרְדֵּן מִנַּחַל אַרְנֹן עַד־הַר חֶרְמוֹן: 9 צִידֹנִים יִקְרְאוּ לְחֶרְמוֹן שִׂרְיֹן וְהָאֱמֹרִי יִקְרְאוּ־לוֹ שְׂנִיר: 10 כֹּל | עָרֵי הַמִּישֹׁר וְכָל־הַגִּלְעָד וְכָל־הַבָּשָׁן עַד־סַלְכָה וְאֶדְרֶעִי עָרֵי מַמְלֶכֶת עוֹג בַּבָּשָׁן: 11 כִּי רַק־עוֹג מֶלֶךְ הַבָּשָׁן נִשְׁאַר מִיֶּתֶר הָרְפָאִים הִנֵּה עַרְשׂוֹ עֶרֶשׂ בַּרְזֶל הֲלֹה הִוא בְּרַבַּת בְּנֵי עַמּוֹן תֵּשַׁע אַמּוֹת אָרְכָּהּ וְאַרְבַּע אַמּוֹת רָחְבָּהּ בְּאַמַּת־אִישׁ:

v. 11. כתיב בה״א

territory, and verse 10 identifies the regions it comprised.56 Verses 9 and 11 are parenthetic notes similar to 2:10–12 and 20–23. See Comment to 2:10–12.

8. to Mount Hermon on the north Mount Hermon is the southern section of the Antilebanon range, running northeast from above the Huleh Valley and today forming part of the border between Lebanon and Syria. In some passages Hermon may refer to the entire Antilebanon (see Comment to v. 9). According to Joshua 12:5 and 13:11, the territory captured from Og did not end at the southern slopes of Hermon but included all of Hermon.57

9. Sidonians The people of the Phoenician city Sidon; here, as frequently, the term probably refers to the Phoenicians in general.58

Amorites See Comment to 1:20.
The name Sirion and its variant Senir both appear elsewhere in the Bible and in ancient Near Eastern texts, though in these sources they do not seem to be used as exact synonyms of Hermon.59 Another term for Hermon is mentioned in 4:48.

10. the Tableland The plateau taken from Moab by Sihon. It stretches eastward from the Dead Sea to the desert, and from the Arnon north to Gilead.60

the whole of Gilead North and south of the Jabbok.

Salcah and Edrei Two towns on the southern boundary of Bashan, Salcah on the east (see Josh. 13:11) and Edrei on the west. See Excursus 1.61

11. The parenthetic comment about Og is another demonstration that the obstacles feared by the previous generation—in this case, giants (1:28)—could not prevent God from granting Israel victory. Og himself was a giant, as shown by the dimensions of his bedstead.

Only Og . . . was left of the remaining Rephaim The Moabites and the Ammonites had wiped out the others (see 2:10–11,20–22). According to Genesis 14:6, Rephaim were living in one of Og's capitals, Ashtaroth, as early as the days of Abraham.

an iron bedstead This may mean that Og's bed was decorated with iron. In the Late Bronze Age, when iron was still relatively uncommon, it was used for ceremonial objects, for jewelry, and for decoration.62

now in Rabbah of the Ammonites Present-day Amman, a name that reflects that of the Ammonites.

nine cubits long and four cubits wide Approximately thirteen and a half by six feet (a cubit is a foot and a half). The dimensions of Og's bed are naturally larger than Og himself, but they indicate how enormous he must have been.

by the standard cubit Literally, "by a man's cubit." This phrase distinguishes the cubit used in measuring Og's bedstead from some other type of cubit, probably a royal cubit. Royal cubits are known from Mesopotamia and Egypt, and special royal measurements for other weights and measures are mentioned in the Bible.63

35

12And this is the land which we apportioned at that time: The part from Aroer along the wadi Arnon, with part of the hill country of Gilead and its towns, I assigned to the Reubenites and the Gadites. 13The rest of Gilead, and all of Bashan under Og's rule—the whole Argob district, all that part of Bashan which is called Rephaim country—I assigned to the half-tribe of Manasseh. 14Jair son of Manasseh received the whole Argob district (that is, Bashan) as far as the boundary of the Geshurites and the Maacathites, and named it after himself: Havvoth-jair—as is still the case. 15To Machir I assigned Gilead. 16And to the Reubenites and the Gadites I assigned the part from

12 וְאֶת־הָאָרֶץ הַזֹּאת יָרַשְׁנוּ בָּעֵת הַהִוא מֵעֲרֹעֵר אֲשֶׁר־עַל־נַחַל אַרְנֹן וַחֲצִי הַר־הַגִּלְעָד וְעָרָיו נָתַתִּי לָרֵאוּבֵנִי וְלַגָּדִי: 13 וְיֶתֶר הַגִּלְעָד וְכָל־הַבָּשָׁן מַמְלֶכֶת עוֹג נָתַתִּי לַחֲצִי שֵׁבֶט הַמְנַשֶּׁה כֹּל חֶבֶל הָאַרְגֹּב לְכָל־הַבָּשָׁן הַהוּא יִקָּרֵא אֶרֶץ רְפָאִים: 14 יָאִיר בֶּן־מְנַשֶּׁה לָקַח אֶת־כָּל־חֶבֶל אַרְגֹּב עַד־גְּבוּל הַגְּשׁוּרִי וְהַמַּעֲכָתִי וַיִּקְרָא אֹתָם עַל־שְׁמוֹ אֶת־הַבָּשָׁן חַוֹּת יָאִיר עַד הַיּוֹם הַזֶּה: שביעי 15 וּלְמָכִיר נָתַתִּי אֶת־הַגִּלְעָד: 16 וְלָרֵאוּבֵנִי וְלַגָּדִי נָתַתִּי מִן־הַגִּלְעָד וְעַד־נַחַל

12–17. After summarizing the territory conquered, Moses describes its apportionment among two and a half of the tribes. In verses 12–13 he briefly indicates to whom he assigned each of the two areas conquered, and in verses 14–17 he describes in greater detail which tribes and clans received each part of these areas. This information is a prelude to the next section, in which Moses tells the two and a half tribes to leave their families and cattle behind in their cities while they accompany the remaining tribes across the Jordan.

Numbers 32 explains why these territories were given to Reuben, Gad, and half of Manasseh: they had requested them because they owned large amounts of livestock, for which northern Transjordan, especially Bashan, was well suited.[64] Moses alludes to this in verse 19.

13. All or part of the phrase between dashes is another parenthetic comment about the prehistory and terminology of the region. The phrase reads literally "the whole Argob district, the whole of Bashan—it is called Rephaim country."

14–17. The summary in verses 12–13 (like that in verses 8–10) lists areas in the order in which they were conquered, from south to north. Here Moses reverses the order: he begins with the area named last in verse 13 and proceeds southward, thus giving verses 12–17 a chiastic structure.

14. The half-tribe of Manasseh consists of two groups, those represented by Jair and those by Machir (v. 15).

Jair son of Manasseh "Son" means descendant here; according to 1 Chronicles 2:21–22, Jair was the great-great grandson of Manasseh. It is likely that "Jair" refers here to the clan that traced itself back to Jair, not to Jair himself, just as "Machir" refers to the descendants of Machir in verse 15. In biblical narratives, it is common for the names of individuals to stand for their descendants.

received Rather "captured," as *l-k-ḥ* is translated in verses 4 and 8. Numbers 32:41 also says that Jair "captured" (*l-k-d*) its territory. It is not clear how the present verse relates to verses 3–7, which imply that the Argob was conquered earlier. Conceivably it means that Jair constituted the unit that captured Argob earlier. Another possibility is that the conquest of the Argob was accomplished in two phases: a national one, in which Og's army was defeated by the entire Israelite army (vv. 3–5), and a local one in which Jair defeated the local defenders of the cities in its territory (v. 14). In that case, verse 3 has telescoped the two phases into a single summary that includes the phase mentioned in verse 14.[65]

the Geshurites and the Maacathites Geshur and Maaca were small states in the Golan Heights: Geshur was east of Lake Tiberias and Maaca was further north.[66]

Havvoth-jair See Excursus 1.

15. *Machir* That is, the descendants of Machir, as Numbers 32:39 states. As a grandson of Joseph, Machir himself could not have been alive at this time.

Gilead The northern part of Gilead (see v. 13).

36

Gilead down to the wadi Arnon, the middle of the wadi being the boundary, and up to the wadi Jabbok, the boundary of the Ammonites.

17[We also seized] the Arabah, from the foot of the slopes of Pisgah on the east, to the edge of the Jordan, and from Chinnereth down to the sea of the Arabah, the Dead Sea.

18At that time I charged you, saying, "The LORD your God has given you this country to possess. You must go as shock-troops, warriors all, at the head of your Israelite kinsmen. 19Only your wives, children, and livestock—I know that you have much livestock—shall be left in the towns I have assigned to you, 20until the LORD has granted your kinsmen a haven such as you have, and they too have taken possession of the land that the LORD your God is assigning them, beyond the Jordan. Then you may return each to the homestead that I have assigned to him."

אַרְנֹן תּוֹךְ הַנַּחַל וּגְבֻל וְעַד יַבֹּק הַנַּחַל גְּבוּל בְּנֵי עַמּוֹן:
17 וְהָעֲרָבָה וְהַיַּרְדֵּן וּגְבֻל מִכִּנֶּרֶת וְעַד יָם הָעֲרָבָה יָם הַמֶּלַח תַּחַת אַשְׁדֹּת הַפִּסְגָּה מִזְרָחָה:
18 וָאֲצַו אֶתְכֶם בָּעֵת הַהִוא לֵאמֹר יְהוָה אֱלֹהֵיכֶם נָתַן לָכֶם אֶת־הָאָרֶץ הַזֹּאת לְרִשְׁתָּהּ חֲלוּצִים תַּעַבְרוּ לִפְנֵי אֲחֵיכֶם בְּנֵי־יִשְׂרָאֵל כָּל־בְּנֵי־חָיִל:
19 רַק נְשֵׁיכֶם וְטַפְּכֶם וּמִקְנֵכֶם יָדַעְתִּי כִּי־מִקְנֶה רַב לָכֶם יֵשְׁבוּ בְּעָרֵיכֶם אֲשֶׁר נָתַתִּי לָכֶם:
20 מפטיר עַד אֲשֶׁר־יָנִיחַ יְהוָה | לַאֲחֵיכֶם כָּכֶם וְיָרְשׁוּ גַם־הֵם אֶת־הָאָרֶץ אֲשֶׁר יְהוָה אֱלֹהֵיכֶם נֹתֵן לָהֶם בְּעֵבֶר הַיַּרְדֵּן וְשַׁבְתֶּם אִישׁ לִירֻשָּׁתוֹ אֲשֶׁר נָתַתִּי לָכֶם:

16. *from Gilead*   The southern part of Gilead (see v. 12).

up to the wadi Jabbok   The eastern Jabbok, which flows northward, formed the eastern boundary of the Reubenite-Gadite territory (see Comment to 2:37).

17.   Literally this verse reads: "and the Arabah, with the Jordan as its [western] boundary: from Chinnereth down to the sea of the Arabah, the Salt Sea, at the foot of the slopes of Pisgah on the east." The verse seems to describe the western boundary of Reubenite-Gadite territory, indicating an exception to the picture given in verse 12: although the main part of these tribes' territory ended at the western Jabbok (which separates southern from northern Gilead), the western side of their territory, in the Aravah, extended further north all the way up to Lake Tiberias. That this extra arm of territory belonged to Sihon, and later to Gad, is also indicated by Joshua 12:3 and 13:27. Machir's territory, like Og's before it, was thus confined to the hill country and did not extend as far west as the Jordan.

the foot of the slopes of Pisgah   This mountain, or mountain chain, is the southeastern boundary of the Aravah. Pisgah overlooks the northeast corner of the Dead Sea and the southeastern end of the Jordan Valley. See Excursus 1.

Chinnereth   That is, the Sea of Kinneret (Lake Tiberias; see Josh. 12:3; 13:27).

the Dead Sea   Literally, "the Salt Sea," so-called because of its exceptionally high mineral content. The name "Dead Sea" is first attested in Greek and Latin authors of the last century B.C.E. and following. It is generally thought to refer to the sea's inability to support life because of its saltiness, but the earliest known explanation of the name says that it is due to the stillness of its waters.[67]

18–20.   Moses turns to the tribes of Reuben, Gad, and half of Manasseh and reiterates the condition he imposed for allowing them to settle in Transjordan (Num. 32:16–18).

18. *shock-troops*   The precise meaning of *ḥalutsim* is uncertain. "Shock-troops" (or "vanguard") seems a reasonable approximation, since the *ḥalutsim* often go in front of the rest of the army.[68] This understanding of the word underlies its use for "pioneers" in modern Hebrew.

20.   Joshua later declared that the condition stated here by Moses was satisfied (Josh. 22:4).

21–22.   Moses urges Joshua to recognize that the victories over Sihon and Og assure him of success in the coming battles.

²¹I also charged Joshua at that time, saying, "You have seen with your own eyes all that the LORD your God has done to these two kings; so shall the LORD do to all the kingdoms into which you shall cross over. ²²Do not fear them, for it is the LORD your God who will battle for you."

21 וְאֶת־יְהוֹשׁוּעַ צִוֵּיתִי בָּעֵת הַהִוא לֵאמֹר עֵינֶיךָ
הָרֹאֹת אֵת כָּל־אֲשֶׁר עָשָׂה יְהוָה אֱלֹהֵיכֶם לִשְׁנֵי
הַמְּלָכִים הָאֵלֶּה כֵּן־יַעֲשֶׂה יְהוָה לְכָל־הַמַּמְלָכוֹת
אֲשֶׁר אַתָּה עֹבֵר שָׁמָּה: 22 לֹא תִּירָאוּם כִּי יְהוָה
אֱלֹהֵיכֶם הוּא הַנִּלְחָם לָכֶם: ס

VA-'ETHANNAN

²³I pleaded with the LORD at that time, saying, ²⁴"O Lord GOD, You who let Your servant see the first works of

ואתחנן

23 וָאֶתְחַנַּן אֶל־יְהוָה בָּעֵת הַהִוא לֵאמֹר: 24 אֲדֹנָי
יְהוִה אַתָּה הַחִלּוֹתָ לְהַרְאוֹת אֶת־עַבְדְּךָ אֶת־

21. at that time   Some time after the victories, but not necessarily after the apportioning of the land to the two-and-a-half tribes.

You have seen with your own eyes   See Coment to 1:19. In the Hebrew "your eyes" is put first for emphasis: "It is your own eyes that saw"—you have no grounds for doubt, since you saw personally. The same emphatic word order appears in 4:3 and 11:7.

22.   This lesson, which the previous generation refused to believe, has been reconfirmed by the victories over Sihon and Og. See Comments to 1:21 and 29–30.

kingdoms   Canaan in the Late Bronze Age was not a nation-state but a land of separate city-states ruled by kings,[69] as indicated by Joshua 12:7–24 and the Amarna letters.

Va-'ethannan   **23–26a.**   A new weekly Torah portion begins here, highlighting the pathos of Moses' plea and God's refusal. In the overall structure of the narrative, however, this unit is part of the preceding section (E), since Moses' plea is prompted by the victories just narrated, as the phrase "at that time" makes clear.

God has allowed Moses to lead the conquest of Transjordan. This encourages him to hope that God might have relented in His decision to bar him from the promised land. Hence he turns to God with the plea that he be allowed to cross the Jordan into the land. Moses subtly relates his plea to what has just transpired by his use of the verb "begin" and derivatives of the root '-v-r, "cross," "pass." Since God had described the victories in Transjordan as a "beginning" (2:25,31), Moses suggests that God has merely "begun" to show Moses the mighty deeds of the conquest (3:24, literal translation). The root '-v-r was a leitmotif of chapters 2 and 3, where it appears fourteen times in a verb, usually rendered "pass" or "cross," and twice more in the phrase *'ever ha-yarden*, "beyond [across] the Jordan."[70] Moses uses both the verb and the phrase in his plea, as if to say "Let me, too, cross." God uses the verb twice more in His response. Even God's angry reaction to the plea is expressed by a verb derived from a homonym of this root, *va-yit'abber*, "was wrathful, cross" (v. 26). The effect of these terms is to suggest that Moses' hopes were raised as the Israelites crossed through Transjordan and prepared to cross into the promised land, and to underscore the poignancy of God's refusal to allow him to share in the future awaiting the people he led.

24–25.   Moses' prayer follows a standard form for petitions. Verses 24a and 25 are the heart of the prayer: He pleads to enter the promised land on the ground that God has already allowed him to see the beginning of the process that will lead there. Verse 24b is not an integral part of the plea but a formal element of prayer, which often has a statement of praise at or near the beginning. In prayers influenced by Deuteronomy these statements are often declarations of God's incomparability, similar to our verse. In later times the rabbis invoked this verse as the precedent for the rule that one should always begin petitions with the praise of God.[71]

24. Lord GOD   Literally, "my Lord YHVH," addressing God by His title and His name. See Excursus 4. This form of address is common in prayers, especially pleas, as in 9:26.[72]

You who let Your servant see the first works of Your greatness and your mighty hand   Literally, "You have begun to show Your servant Your greatness and Your mighty hand," echoing "begin" in 2:25 and 31.

Your greatness and Your mighty hand, You whose powerful deeds no god in heaven or on earth can equal! ²⁵Let
me, I pray, cross over and see the good land on the other
side of the Jordan, that good hill country, and the Lebanon." ²⁶But the Lord was wrathful with me on your
account and would not listen to me. The Lord said to me,
"Enough! Never speak to Me of this matter again! ²⁷Go

גׇּדְלְךָ וְאֶת־יָדְךָ הַחֲזָקָה אֲשֶׁר מִי־אֵל בַּשָּׁמַיִם
וּבָאָרֶץ אֲשֶׁר־יַעֲשֶׂה כְמַעֲשֶׂיךָ וְכִגְבוּרֹתֶךָ:
²⁵ אֶעְבְּרָה־נָּא וְאֶרְאֶה אֶת־הָאָרֶץ הַטּוֹבָה אֲשֶׁר
בְּעֵבֶר הַיַּרְדֵּן הָהָר הַטּוֹב הַזֶּה וְהַלְּבָנֹן:
²⁶ וַיִּתְעַבֵּר יְהוָה בִּי לְמַעַנְכֶם וְלֹא שָׁמַע אֵלָי
וַיֹּאמֶר יְהוָה אֵלַי רַב־לָךְ אַל־תּוֹסֶף דַּבֵּר אֵלַי

whose powerful deeds no god in heaven or on earth can equal The events Moses has
witnessed, from the Exodus up to the present moment, have shown him the Lord's incomparability
even among the beings known as "gods" (*'elim* or *'elohim*). He has in mind primarily the events of
the Exodus and Mount Sinai which, as 4:32–34 explain, no other deity has ever accomplished.

The phrase "no god in heaven or on earth can equal" is literally a rhetorical question, "who is a
god in heaven or on earth that can equal. . . ?" Similar declarations that none among the gods is
comparable to the Lord occur frequently in the Bible, often as rhetorical questions. Best known is
Exodus 15:11, "Who is like You, O Lord, among the *'elim*!"[73] Such declarations have polytheistic
prototypes: the first person to make one in the Bible is the Midianite priest Jethro (Exod. 18:11), and
similar passages are common in ancient Near Eastern literature.[74] But it is clear from passages like
Psalm 89:7 that in the Bible the "gods" referred to are the celestial or supernatural beings that
surround the Lord in the manner of a royal court—that is, the "host of heaven," including the sun,
moon, and stars, spirits, winds, fiery flames, seraphs, angels and the chief of God's heavenly army;
several of these also carry out missions for God on earth.[75] These are not what we would call "gods"
today. Biblical Hebrew, like other ancient Semitic languages, used words meaning "god" (*'el/'elim*
and *'elohim*) in several senses: God, angels, ghosts, and even idols and foreign gods.[76] The latter two
senses simply reflect customary ancient usage; in the biblical view the "gods" of the nations were
nothing but impotent statues or spirits, not gods (cf. 32:17). A modern writer might have put
quotation marks around the word "gods" in such passages, but since Hebrew-speaking audiences
knew that *'el/'elim* and *'elohim* did not necessarily refer to truly divine beings, a monotheistic text like
Deuteronomy (see 4:35–39) could use this motif to express the incomparability of God without fear
of being misunderstood.[77]

25. *the good land . . . that good hill country* These phrases express Moses' longing for
the promised land. The first is especially poignant: God had used it not only in His decree banning
the Exodus generation from the land (1:35), but in his very first words to Moses promising to take
Israel there (Exod. 3:8). All of Moses' efforts in the forty years since had been directed toward
reaching that destination.

26a. *on your account* See Comment to 1:37.

GOD'S RESPONSE TO MOSES' PLEA (vv. 26b–29)

God's response to Moses' plea is the final section of the retrospective in chapters 1–3. By using
phrases which duplicate or echo phrases in the first section (1:6–33), it joins with the latter to form a
frame around the entire retrospective. Those phrases are used ironically: in 1:6 and 21 they were used
to encourage Israel to proceed to the promised land; here they are part of God's refusal to let Moses
do so, making Moses' fate all the more poignant. In 1:6 God's command that Israel head for the
promised land began with *rav lakhem*, "You have stayed [at Horeb] long enough" (see also 2:3); here
the same phrase is used to silence Moses' plea to enter that land (*rav lakh*, "Enough!"). In 1:21 Moses
had urged the people to *'aleh resh*, "go up, take possession" of the land; that phrase is echoed here in
God's command that Moses' "go up to the summit of Pisgah" (*'aleh rosh ha-pisgah*), where he would
see the land that he could not enter.[78]

27. God tempers the severity of His decree by acceding to part of Moses' request: he may
not cross into the land, but he may see it.

up to the summit of Pisgah and gaze about, to the west, the north, the south, and the east. Look at it well, for you shall not go across yonder Jordan. 28Give Joshua his instructions, and imbue him with strength and courage, for he shall go across at the head of this people, and he shall allot to them the land that you may only see."

29Meanwhile we stayed on in the valley near Beth-peor.

עוֹד בַּדָּבָר הַזֶּה: 27 עֲלֵה | רֹאשׁ הַפִּסְגָּה וְשָׂא עֵינֶיךָ יָמָּה וְצָפֹנָה וְתֵימָנָה וּמִזְרָחָה וּרְאֵה בְעֵינֶיךָ כִּי־לֹא תַעֲבֹר אֶת־הַיַּרְדֵּן הַזֶּה: 28 וְצַו אֶת־יְהוֹשֻׁעַ וְחַזְּקֵהוּ וְאַמְּצֵהוּ כִּי־הוּא יַעֲבֹר לִפְנֵי הָעָם הַזֶּה וְהוּא יַנְחִיל אוֹתָם אֶת־הָאָרֶץ אֲשֶׁר תִּרְאֶה: 29 וַנֵּשֶׁב בַּגַּיְא מוּל בֵּית פְּעוֹר: פ

Complying with God's instructions in this verse is Moses' last act; see 34:1–5.

28. Give Joshua his instructions   Rather, "appoint Joshua."[79]

imbue him with strength and courage . . . he shall allot   Rather, "say to him, 'Be strong and resolute,' . . . he shall apportion" (see Comments to 1:38). Moses fulfills this command in 31:7–8.

29.   The abrupt end of the dialogue indicates that Moses was silent before God's decree.

in the valley near Beth-peor   A wadi in Moab, running into the Jordan or the northeastern corner of the Dead Sea. For the location of the valley and the town, see Map 5 and Comment on Beth-peor in Excursus 1. This is the valley where Moses delivered his final addresses and where he was buried, as indicated in 4:46 and 34:6. The name of the nearby town, Beth-peor, is probably short for Beth-Baal-peor, "the temple, or dwelling, of [the deity] Baal-peor." The deity's name presumably means "the lord of [Mount] Peor." The town was probably the center of the cult of this deity, whom the Israelites had worshiped in the scandalous incident at that site (4:3; see Num. 25:1–5).

The statement that the Israelites were encamped near this site brings the retrospective of chapters 1–3 up to the time of Moses' farewell addresses. It also serves as a transition to the coming chapters, which turn from the subject of faith and obedience to God in military affairs to faith and obedience in worshiping the Lord alone. That Moses' farewell addresses, which are filled with warnings against idolatry, are delivered in the shadow of the site where Israel had betrayed the Lord and incurred His wrath dramatically underscores the urgency of his warnings (see 4:3).

CHAPTER 4

EXHORTATIONS TO OBSERVE GOD'S LAWS (vv. 1–40)

Context

4:1–40 is the second division of Moses' first address. Having described how Israel reached the border of the promised land (1:6–3:29), Moses now addresses the people's future life inside the land. He had earlier reminded the people that their fate depended on obedience to God's *orders*. Now he teaches them that their future welfare will depend on obedience to God's *laws*.

This division of the address differs from the first in several respects. The first division is a historical narrative while the second is a sermon. It, too, is based on historical events, but it does not narrate them consecutively. Both divisions of the address stress obedience to God. The first speaks of obeying military directives while the second speaks of obeying permanent laws. In this respect chapter 4 is a précis of chapters 5–11, which contain the prologue and preamble of the second address, introducing the laws that Israel must obey in order to enter the promised land and to endure there. Together, chapters 4 and 5–11 present the historical experiences that establish the validity of the laws and the attitudes that are basic to their observance, and they appeal for obedience to the laws. They stress especially the duty of worshiping only the Lord (YHVH), which is the foundation of all the other laws. Chapter 4 explains the reasons for this duty. Chapter 5 (the prologue to the laws) validates Moses' role as mediator of the laws and thereby affirms their authenticity. In chapters 6–11 (the preamble) he begins to carry out this role by urging the general duties of love and reverence for God, exclusive loyalty to Him, and obedience to His commandments.

Chapter 4 also plays a role in the larger structure of Deuteronomy. Several of its themes are echoed in Moses' third address (chaps. 29–30), such as lessons based on the historical experiences that Israel saw (4:3–4,9–15,32–38; 29:1–2), the threat of exile (4:26–28; 29:27), and the possibility of repentance in exile (4:29–31; 30:10). There are clear terminological connections as well, such as being "lured" to worship deities whom the Lord did not "allot" to Israel (4:19; 29:25; 30:17) and invocation of heaven and earth as witnesses (4:26; 30:19). Together, then, chapters 4 and 29–30—the end of Moses' first address and his third address—serve as a frame to the second, and main, address of the book.[1]

In chapters 4–11 the first two commandments of the Decalogue (which is recapitulated in chap. 5) play a central role. Although Moses digresses to take up related topics, he consistently returns to the commandments of accepting the Lord alone as God and worshiping no idols. At times it seems that "the exhortation, the laws, and the norms" refers particularly to these commandments. These commandments are emphasized for their intrinsic meaning and also because they express the attitudes of love and reverence for God which are the fundamental premise of all the laws and the spirit in which they are to be observed. In introducing the laws this way, these chapters constitute a model for "The Book of Knowledge," Maimonides' introduction to his code of Jewish law (the *Mishneh Torah*), in which he summarizes the theological and ethical postulates of Judaism before presenting the laws.[2]

Structure and Themes

Chapter 4 is the theological heart of Deuteronomy, explaining its most fundamental precepts, monotheism and the prohibition of idolatry. It opens with an appeal to obey God's laws and rules. Moses develops this theme in four units.[3] The first (vv. 1–4) prohibits adding to the commandments or subtracting from them. This prohibition is backed by a reference to the present generation's recent worship of Baal-peor and its disastrous consequences. The second unit (vv. 5–8) appeals for obedience on the ground that this will earn Israel the admiration of its neighbors who will perceive the justice of the laws and the nearness of God that Israel enjoys because of obeying them. This unit refers to all the laws, not only the prohibition of worshiping other gods. The third unit (vv. 9–31) urges obedience to the prohibition of idolatry. It shows that this prohibition is based on the nature of Israel's encounter with God at Horeb (Mount Sinai), and it backs up the prohibition with the threat of exile. The fourth unit (vv. 32–40) argues on the basis of the two seminal experiences of Israelite history, the Exodus and the encounter with God at Horeb, that there is no other God but the Lord (YHVH) and that His laws should therefore be obeyed.

The four units of the chapter are arranged in reverse chronological order, based on their allusions to the past: the first alludes to the recent incident at Peor (v. 3), the third to the theophany at Horeb, the Exodus, and the division of nations (vv. 10–14, 19–20), and the fourth to the creation and the patriarchs as well as the Exodus and Horeb (vv. 32–34,36–37) (the order *within* each unit is not chronological). This arrangement contrasts with that in 1:6–3:29, which begins with the departure from Horeb and progresses chronologically up to the encampment at Peor (see 1:6; 3:29).[4]

Moses' address is not primarily a statement of the laws but an exhortation to obey them. He recognizes that the people may not be inclined to obey and must be persuaded. Like preachers in all ages, he advances various types of arguments for observance: history teaches the utility of observance; the laws are just; they secure God's closeness; they make Israel unique; observance will earn the admiration of others; the laws have logical reasons; they are the will of the only true God and a prerequisite for well-being. Especially noteworthy are the arguments that go beyond reward and punishment and emphasize the logic and justice of the laws. Such arguments show the Torah's aim of securing not merely mechanical observance of the laws but willing assent because of their inherent value. On this subject see also the comment regarding motive clauses in the Introduction.

Unity

The chapter is held together by a frame in which Moses urges obedience to God's laws so that Israel may live to occupy the land and remain in it indefinitely (vv. 1,40). This message is underscored within the chapter by a warning that failure to observe the law against idols will lead to banishment from the land (vv. 23–28). The four units of the chapter have numerous features in common, both thematic and verbal, which reflect the sermonic, didactic character of Deuteronomy. In all of them

4 And now, O Israel, give heed to the laws and rules that I   וְאֶל־ וְהַחֻקִּים אֶל־ שְׁמַע יִשְׂרָאֵל וְעַתָּה **ד**

Moses refers to the laws he is teaching or commanding and to the land Israel is about to enter.[5] In three of the units Moses bases his argument on history. In the first he argues that history shows the consequences of obeying or disobeying the commandments. In the third he argues that history justifies the prohibition of images. In the fourth he argues that history proves that the Lord is the only true God. Each unit opens with an appeal to the mind: "give heed" (lit., "hear"), "see," "do not forget," and "inquire" (vv. 1,5,9,32). The themes of seeing and hearing—the senses through which Israel experienced history—are mentioned throughout,[6] as are teaching and learning (*l-m-d*),[7] knowing and making known (*y-d-ʿ*),[8] forgetting,[9] wisdom, and understanding.[10] In each unit Moses lends immediacy to his words by referring to *ha-yom* ("today," "this day," "as is now the case").[11] The second and fourth show that Israel and its laws are unparalleled among the nations and the Lord is unparalleled among the gods.[12] The third and fourth refer to the theophany at Horeb and the Exodus, and both speak of heaven and earth.[13]

Relationship to First Division

The transitional "And now" at the beginning of this division of the address suggests that it is the continuation of the preceding one.[14] The first division tells how Israel arrived at the border of the promised land, and the second introduces the laws that must be obeyed in the land. The first division shows that those who did not obey God's orders died, and that Moses himself was condemned to die before entering the land, and the second divison begins by urging the people to obey God's commandments so that they may "live to enter and occupy the land" (4:1). The two divisions share a number of other thematic and verbal features. The incident of Baal-peor (4:3) took place near Beth-peor, where Israel encamped in 3:29. The argument in chapter 4 is based primarily on things that were *seen* or *not seen*. That theme echoes Moses' earlier references to Israel having *seen* the events to which he refers (1:19,30–31; 3:21) and God's decrees that Moses' contemporaries would never *see* the promised land (1:35–36) and that Moses would *see* it only from a distance (3:25,27,28). Moses' rhetorical question in 3:24, "What god in heaven or on earth can equal [the Lord's] mighty deeds?," is echoed in 4:6–7 ("what great nation is there?") and in the argument that no other god ever did the kinds of things the Lord did from the heavens and on earth (4:32–39). God's anger with Moses and His refusal to allow him to enter the promised land are mentioned in both chapters (4:21–22; 3:26–27). In Hebrew, "do not add anything . . . to what I command you" (*lo' tosifu ʿal ha-davar*, 4:2) is very similar to "Never speak to Me of this matter again" (*ʾal tosef . . . ba-davar*, 3:26). References to "the land you are about to cross into and occupy" (4:14,26) echo Moses' futile request to cross into the land (3:25; cf. 27,28, and 4:21–22). Nevertheless, as noted in the Introduction, the similarities and connections between the two divisions of this discourse do not necessarily mean that they are from the same author.

AN APPEAL TO OBSERVE GOD'S COMMANDMENTS, WITHOUT ADDING TO THEM OR SUBTRACTING FROM THEM, BASED ON THE EXPERIENCE AT PEOR (vv. 1–4)

The first unit appropriately begins with an appeal to observe God's commandments as the condition for being able to take possession of the promised land. The truth of this condition is demonstrated by the recent experience near Israel's camp at Beth-peor: those who worshiped the god of that place were wiped out, while those who remained loyal to the Lord survived. It is characteristic of Moses' addresses in Deuteronomy 4–11 that while calling repeatedly for obedience to all of God's laws, he focuses mainly on loyalty to Him, the duty which underlies all the others.

1. The appeal to "give heed" (lit., "hear"), like "see" in verse 5, is employed frequently in urging Israel to consider Moses' words carefully.[15] The verb "instruct" (often rendered "impart," as in v. 5) illustrates Moses' role as teacher of the laws.[16] This is the role for which he is best remembered in Jewish tradition, the role encapsulated in his epithet *Moshe Rabbenu*, "Moses our

am instructing you to observe, so that you may live to enter and occupy the land that the LORD, the God of your fathers, is giving you. ²You shall not add anything to what

הַמִּשְׁפָּטִים אֲשֶׁר אָנֹכִי מְלַמֵּד אֶתְכֶם לַעֲשׂוֹת לְמַעַן תִּחְיוּ וּבָאתֶם וִירִשְׁתֶּם אֶת־הָאָרֶץ אֲשֶׁר יְהֹוָה אֱלֹהֵי אֲבֹתֵיכֶם נֹתֵן לָכֶם: ² לֹא תֹסִפוּ עַל־הַדָּבָר

teacher." According to Deuteronomy, this role was assigned to him at Mount Sinai (see v. 14 and 5:28). The earlier books do not use "instruct" in describing Moses' role; it is characteristic of Deuteronomy's focus on wisdom and intellect.

laws and rules Hebrew *ḥukkim* and *mishpatim*. Moses refers to the commandments by several terms, usually two or more at a time. In addition to these two, he uses *mitsvah*, "commandment" (v. 2), and *ʿedot*, rendered "decrees" (v. 45). Etymologically, they all have distinct meanings. *Ḥukkim* is derived from the root *ḥ-k-k*, "engrave," and is thought to refer to engraved laws or decrees; it might well be rendered as "prescriptions." *Mishpatim* are rules issued by a judge (*shofet*) or a ruler (also *shofet*). *Mitsvah*, from *ts-v-h*, "command," is literally a "command(ment)" (the translation often renders it as "instruction"). *ʿEdot* refers to the terms or stipulations of a treaty (*ʿedut*) imposed by a suzerain on a vassal (the related term in Aramaic and Akkadian favors this interpretation over the view—homiletically attractive in its own right—that *ʿedot* means "testimonies" in the sense that the commandments are evidence of God's covenant with Israel). In actual usage, Moses employs the terms without distinction, just as English uses phrases like "rules and regulations" and "laws and ordinances."[17]

In traditional Jewish exegesis, *ḥukkim* and *mishpatim* are understood as referring to two broad categories of commandments. *Mishpatim* are thought to be laws whose purpose is evident and which people would have devised even if God had never commanded them, such as the prohibitions on murder and theft. *Ḥukkim* are understood to be commandments like the dietary laws, for which the reason is not obvious, and which people tend to question; these must be obeyed as expressions of divine sovereignty.[18]

to observe Literally, "to do." It is often stressed that the laws are not merely to be learned, but to be performed (see, e.g., vv. 5,6,13,14; 5:1; 6:1).

so that you may live This unit begins and ends by indicating that life itself depends on observance of the commandments (see v. 4). This belief is taken quite literally in the Bible. The commandments are "laws and rules, by the pursuit of which man shall live" (Lev. 18:5). "He who has regard for his life pays regard to the commandments; he who is heedless of his ways will die" (Prov. 19:16). God will put to the sword those who mistreat widows and orphans (Exod. 22:21–23), and the Israelites are cautioned to "be careful for your lives" not to make idols (see Comments to vv. 9,15). See 30:15–20.

2. This verse is generally taken as a blanket prohibition of abrogating any of the laws taught by Moses or adding new ones. As such, it would serve as a general introduction to the Instruction, expressing its completeness and immutability. Injunctions against adding and removing items appear in various genres of ancient literature, including treaties. Likewise, the Laws of Hammurabi conclude with exhortations against changing them.[19] This verse would also serve as a transition from chapters 1–3, which describe the consequences of Israel's refusal to follow God's directives.

However, this blanket interpretation is problematic. As noted in the Introduction, the laws of Deuteronomy, like those of the Torah as a whole, are not a complete code that could have sufficed to govern all areas of life. Important subjects, such as commerce, civil damages, and marriage, are covered insufficiently or not at all. Further laws were obviously necessary. In order to prevent paralysis and leave room for necessary legal innovations, Jewish legal exegesis had to subject this verse to very narrow interpretations, to the effect that no prophet may add laws claiming that they are in the Torah or that God has instructed him to do so, nor may private individuals add or subtract details in any of the commandments, nor may the total number of commandments recognized as biblical be changed. By restricting the scope of the present verse, these interpretations left wide parameters for legislation and innovative interpretation (see the Introduction and Comment to 17:11).[20]

Actually, the present verse does not seem intended to stymie legal innovation. In context, Moses

I command you or take anything away from it, but keep the commandments of the LORD your God that I enjoin upon you. ³You saw with your own eyes what the LORD did in the matter of Baal-peor, that the LORD your God wiped out from among you every person who followed Baal-peor; ⁴while you, who held fast to the LORD your God, are all alive today.

אֲשֶׁר אָנֹכִי מְצַוֶּה אֶתְכֶם וְלֹא תִגְרְעוּ מִמֶּנּוּ לִשְׁמֹר אֶת־מִצְוֹת יְהוָה אֱלֹהֵיכֶם אֲשֶׁר אָנֹכִי מְצַוֶּה אֶתְכֶם: 3 עֵינֵיכֶם הָרֹאֹת אֵת אֲשֶׁר־עָשָׂה יְהוָה בְּבַעַל פְּעוֹר כִּי כָל־הָאִישׁ אֲשֶׁר הָלַךְ אַחֲרֵי בַעַל־פְּעוֹר הִשְׁמִידוֹ יְהוָה אֱלֹהֶיךָ מִקִּרְבֶּךָ: 4 וְאַתֶּם הַדְּבֵקִים בַּיהוָה אֱלֹהֵיכֶם חַיִּים כֻּלְּכֶם הַיּוֹם: שני

seems to have but a single issue in mind. As noted above, when he speaks of "the exhortation, the laws, and the norms," he often seems to be referring particularly to the commandments of accepting the Lord alone as God and worshipping no idols. As noted by Ḥazzekuni, this seems to be the case with the prohibition of adding to or subtracting from the laws. This prohibition appears twice in biblical law and in each case it is connected with warnings against the worship of other gods and other pagan practices. In 13:1 it follows a warning not to imitate pagan practices and precedes a prohibition against following a prophet who claims that the Lord has commanded Israel to worship additional gods. Here it precedes a reminder that all who worshiped another god perished. Evidently, then, in both passages the prohibition is invoked to stress that one may not nullify the first commandment of the Decalogue by adding a commandment ordaining the worship of additional gods.[21]

That certain worshipers of the Lord might think it permissible to worship additional gods is not as strange as it might seem. Polytheists did not believe that their gods demanded exclusive worship. A polytheist who worshiped the Lord—even one who believed that He is the supreme deity—might think that He favored the worship of His "fellow gods" and lesser supernatural beings even by Israelites, as explained in the Comment to 13:2. One making such a claim might point to v. 19, which states that the Lord ordained the worship of the heavenly bodies by the other nations. The possibility of such a misunderstanding explains why the Torah so frequently repeats the prohibition of worshiping other gods. This interpretation of the verse is consistent with the fact that 4:1–40 are primarily concerned with preventing the worship of other gods, not simply with the integrity of Deuteronomy as a legal code. As noted above, throughout chapters 4–11 "the laws and rules" that Moses expounds are usually those against idolatry (note, e.g., v. 14 and the subject to which Moses turns after it). For this reason, the present unit is an appropriate beginning for chapters 4–11.

3. Moses demonstrates that life is contingent on obedience to the commandments by recalling an experience the present generation witnessed just a short time before.

in the matter of Baal-peor This refers to the god of Beth-peor, near the place where the Israelites are still encamped (3:29). Twenty-four thousand Israelites who joined in the worship of Baal-peor died in a plague (see Num. 25:1–9).

who followed Baal-peor "Following" (lit., "walking after") another god is a biblical idiom for apostasy, since Israel must follow only the Lord (13:5). The idiom is based on ancient Near Eastern political terminology in which "walking after" a king or a suzerain means giving them one's allegiance. Hence "walking after" another God means defecting from the Lord.[22]

4. ***held fast*** The verb *d-v-k*, "cling," "be (physically) close," expresses emotional attachment and loyalty. Deuteronomy uses it to express loyalty to God.[23]

AN APPEAL FOR OBSERVANCE BASED ON THE QUALITY AND EFFECT OF THE COMMANDMENTS (vv. 5–8)

Here Moses appeals for observance of the commandments because they are uniquely just and observing them brings about a closeness with God that is unparalleled among the other nations. By observing them Israel will earn admiration as a wise and discerning people.

5. ***I have imparted*** Rather, "I am imparting."[24]

5 See, I have imparted to you laws and rules, as the LORD my God has commanded me, for you to abide by in the land that you are about to enter and occupy. 6 Observe them faithfully, for that will be proof of your wisdom and discernment to other peoples, who on hearing of all these laws will say, "Surely, that great nation is a wise and discerning people." 7 For what great nation is there that has a god so close at hand as is the LORD our God whenever we call upon Him? 8 Or what great nation has laws and rules as perfect as all this Teaching that I set before you this day?

5 רְאֵה | לִמַּדְתִּי אֶתְכֶם חֻקִּים וּמִשְׁפָּטִים כַּאֲשֶׁר צִוַּנִי יְהוָה אֱלֹהָי לַעֲשׂוֹת כֵּן בְּקֶרֶב הָאָרֶץ אֲשֶׁר אַתֶּם בָּאִים שָׁמָּה לְרִשְׁתָּהּ: 6 וּשְׁמַרְתֶּם וַעֲשִׂיתֶם כִּי הִוא חָכְמַתְכֶם וּבִינַתְכֶם לְעֵינֵי הָעַמִּים אֲשֶׁר יִשְׁמְעוּן אֵת כָּל־הַחֻקִּים הָאֵלֶּה וְאָמְרוּ רַק עַם־חָכָם וְנָבוֹן הַגּוֹי הַגָּדוֹל הַזֶּה: 7 כִּי מִי־גוֹי גָּדוֹל אֲשֶׁר־לוֹ אֱלֹהִים קְרֹבִים אֵלָיו כַּיהוָה אֱלֹהֵינוּ בְּכָל־קָרְאֵנוּ אֵלָיו: 8 וּמִי גּוֹי גָּדוֹל אֲשֶׁר־לוֹ חֻקִּים וּמִשְׁפָּטִים צַדִּיקִם כְּכֹל הַתּוֹרָה הַזֹּאת אֲשֶׁר אָנֹכִי נֹתֵן לִפְנֵיכֶם הַיּוֹם:

as the LORD ... has commanded me   At Mount Sinai. See verse 14 and 5:24ff.

for you to abide by in the land   God's laws are to be the basis of the society Israel is about to establish in the land. This clause does not imply that the laws are inapplicable outside the land of Israel. Many have been in force since Israel left Egypt, such as the Sabbath and the prohibition of idolatry. There are, of course, specific laws whose performance is not possible outside of the land, such as those based on agriculture.[25] See also Comment to verse 28.

6.   *that*[26] *will be proof*   That Israel has the good sense to observe God's laws will be proof of its wisdom. The next two verses specify what will convince the nations that Israel is wise to observe the laws.

that great nation   "Great" is meant spiritually; numerically Israel will be the smallest of nations (7:7).[27]

7.   One effect of observing God's laws is that He is near whenever Israel calls upon Him, providing guidance, through prophecy, and deliverance in times of trouble.[28] No other nations enjoy such closeness from their gods[29] because their gods are mere idols, or heavenly bodies subordinate to the Lord, and incapable of independent action.[30] The nations do not know that the Lord is the only real God, but they will recognize that only Israel enjoys such divine aid.[31]

a god so close at hand   Or "gods so close at hand." Grammatically either translation is possible,[32] but since Moses refers here to the reaction of foreign nations, he may have phrased the question in accordance with their perception for the sake of comparison.

8.   *perfect*   Literally, "just." The other benefit which comes from observing God's laws is enjoyment of their justice, for "justice exalts a nation" (Prov. 14:34). The conviction that Israel's laws are uniquely just goes hand-in-hand with the Psalmist's declaration that God gave His laws only to Israel: "He issued His commands to Jacob, His statutes and rules to Israel. He did not do so for any other nation; of such rules they know nothing" (Ps. 147:19–20).

We have no information from biblical times about what impression Israel's laws made on other nations. In later times Jewish customs were often mocked by anti-Semites, but there are reports of proselytes to Judaism and even to Christianity being attracted by the Torah. According to Exodus Rabba, "Akilas the Proselyte" converted to Judaism because of the Torah, while Tatian, a Syrian of the second century, lists "the excellence of the precepts" of the Torah among the factors that induced him to become a Christian.[33] Modern scholars have compared biblical law to other legal systems of the ancient Near East and have shown a number of principles in biblical law that are unique in the ancient Near East, such as laws to ameliorate the treatment of aliens and bondservants, the prohibition of collective and vicarious punishment, and the absence of capital punishment for economic crimes.[34]

⁹But take utmost care and watch yourselves scrupulously, so that you do not forget the things that you saw with your own eyes and so that they do not fade from your mind as long as you live. And make them known to

9 רַ֣ק הִשָּׁ֣מֶר לְךָ֩ וּשְׁמֹ֨ר נַפְשְׁךָ֜ מְאֹ֗ד פֶּן־תִּשְׁכַּ֣ח אֶת־הַדְּבָרִ֣ים אֲשֶׁר־רָא֣וּ עֵינֶ֗יךָ וּפֶן־יָס֙וּרוּ֙ מִלְּבָ֣בְךָ֔ כֹּ֖ל יְמֵ֣י חַיֶּ֑יךָ וְהֽוֹדַעְתָּ֥ם לְבָנֶ֖יךָ וְלִבְנֵ֥י בָנֶֽיךָ: 10 י֗וֹם

A WARNING AGAINST IDOLATRY, BASED ON ISRAEL'S EXPERIENCES AT HOREB (vv. 9–31)

In this unit Moses returns to the subject of worship. In the first unit of the chapter He preached against violating the first commandment by worshiping foreign gods, represented by Baal-peor. Here he warns against two aspects of idolatry that might mistakenly be considered acceptable, making images of the Lord—violating the second commandment—and worshiping members of His retinue.

This unit consists of three main parts, all beginning with warnings to be careful. The first describes the people's encounter with God at Horeb (vv. 9–14). The second shows how the nature of that encounter demonstrates the illegitimacy of worshiping idols (vv. 15–18). It is followed by a parenthetic note including the heavenly bodies in the prohibition (vv. 19–20) and by a brief digression about Moses' fate (vv. 21–22). The third part warns about the consequences of violating the prohibition of idols (vv. 23–31).

9–14. Since Israel experienced God directly at Mount Sinai, without the mediation of any visual form, no visual form is to be used for securing His presence in worship.

9. This verse expresses clearly the fact that from biblical times on, Jewish faith has been based primarily on experience rather than speculative thought. "The essence of Jewish religious thinking does not lie in entertaining a concept of God but in the ability to articulate a memory of moments of illumination by His presence. Israel is not a people of definers but a people of witnesses" (Heschel).[35] In classical Jewish thought, the fact that the entire nation witnessed God speaking to Moses—and that their testimony was transmitted to later generations by reliable tradition—is *the* definitive evidence that the Torah is from God.[36]

Moses regularly speaks to the present generation as if *it* came out of Egypt and stood at Mount Sinai. Although most of those he is addressing were born later, something like a third of those now adults were probably present at those events as youngsters. Apparently he feels that his entire audience has an eyewitness's sense of the events since those now over thirty-nine *were* present and the younger ones undoubtedly heard about the events from their parents or others who were present.[37] In addition, the Bible often conceives of all generations of Israelites as a single corporate personality, so that later generations can be addressed as if they were part of earlier events, particularly the great formative events whose effects lasted ever afterwards.[38] This conception is expressed concisely in the Mishnah and the Haggadah of Passover: "In every generation one must view oneself as if he [personally] came out of Egypt. . . . It was not only our ancestors that the Holy One, Blessed be He, redeemed, but us, too, with them" (see introductory Comment to 26:1–11).

the things that you saw with your own eyes   That is, do not forget that you saw that certain things were invisible.

mind   Literally, "heart"; see Comment to 6:5.

make them known to your children and your children's children   Every parent is to be a teacher of religion. This obligation is the most pervasive expression of the biblical conviction that religion is not simply a personal, individual concern. Deuteronomy emphasizes repeatedly that the Israelites are not to keep to themselves the experiences they had and the responsibilities they were taught: they must transmit them to their children and grandchildren so that they, too, may share in the experiences, learn their responsibilities, and enjoy the benefits of faith and observance. See Comment to 6:7.

10.   The purpose of God's communication with the people at Horeb was as much to instill lifelong reverence for Him as it was to proclaim the commandments. Reverence is man's response to

your children and to your children's children: ¹⁰The day you stood before the LORD your God at Horeb, when the LORD said to me, "Gather the people to Me that I may let them hear My words, in order that they may learn to revere Me as long as they live on earth, and may so teach their children." ¹¹You came forward and stood at the foot of the mountain. The mountain was ablaze with flames to the very skies, dark with densest clouds. ¹²The LORD spoke to you out of the fire; you heard the sound of words but perceived no shape—nothing but a voice.

אֲשֶׁר עָמַדְתָּ לִפְנֵי יְהֹוָה אֱלֹהֶיךָ בְּחֹרֵב בֶּאֱמֹר יְהֹוָה אֵלַי הַקְהֶל־לִי אֶת־הָעָם וְאַשְׁמִעֵם אֶת־דְּבָרָי אֲשֶׁר יִלְמְדוּן לְיִרְאָה אֹתִי כָּל־הַיָּמִים אֲשֶׁר הֵם חַיִּים עַל־הָאֲדָמָה וְאֶת־בְּנֵיהֶם יְלַמֵּדוּן: ¹¹ וַתִּקְרְבוּן וַתַּעַמְדוּן תַּחַת הָהָר וְהָהָר בֹּעֵר בָּאֵשׁ עַד־לֵב הַשָּׁמַיִם חֹשֶׁךְ עָנָן וַעֲרָפֶל: ¹² וַיְדַבֵּר יְהֹוָה אֲלֵיכֶם מִתּוֹךְ הָאֵשׁ קוֹל דְּבָרִים אַתֶּם שֹׁמְעִים וּתְמוּנָה אֵינְכֶם רֹאִים זוּלָתִי קוֹל:

God's power. It consists of both respect and awe at His grandeur and dread of His power, which serves as a deterrent to disobeying Him. It is one of Moses' main aims in Deuteronomy to instill reverence for God as a guiding principle in the people's lives. As he explains here, this was both the purpose and the effect of the awesome, terrifying phenomena that accompanied God's communication with Israel—the quaking of the mountain, the thunder and lightning, the trumpets, the cloud and the darkness, the fire and smoke. The purpose of the experience is described similarly in Exodus 20:17: "God has come . . . in order that the fear of Him may be ever with you, so that you do not go astray."[39] Because of its deterrent effect, "reverence for God" is virtually a synonym for ethical behavior and fear of sin (see also Deut. 5:26; 25:18).[40]

11. The majestic, awesome presence of God is expressed by the natural phenomena that accompany His appearance. As the scene is described in Exodus 19:18, "Mount Sinai was all in smoke, for the LORD had come down upon it in fire." These phenomena are frequently mentioned in passages which describe the Lord appearing as a warrior, such as 2 Samuel 22:8–14:

> Then the earth rocked and quaked,
> The foundations of heaven shook—
> Rocked by His indignation.
>
> Smoke went up from His nostrils,
> From His mouth came devouring fire;
> Live coals blazed forth from Him.
>
> He bent the sky and came down,
> Thick cloud beneath His feet. . .
>
> He made pavilions of darkness about Him,
> Dripping clouds, huge thunderheads;
>
> In the brilliance before Him
> Blazed fiery coals.
>
> The LORD thundered forth from heaven,
> The Most High sent forth His voice.
>
> He let loose bolts, and scattered them [the enemies];
> Lightning, and put them to rout.

These motifs accompany theophanies in several other ancient literary traditions as well.[41]

12. During the course of His communication with Israel at Horeb the Lord was invisible; He spoke from the midst of fire and only His voice was heard. In the present address this aspect of the experience is emphasized over the content of what God said.

shape Hebrew *temunah*. English translations render this word as "shape" and "likeness."[42] A more precise translation would be "visage" in the sense of "aspect," "appearance." The

13He declared to you the covenant that He commanded you to observe, the Ten Commandments; and He inscribed them on two tablets of stone. 14At the same time the LORD commanded me to impart to you laws and rules for you to observe in the land that you are about to cross into and occupy.

15For your own sake, therefore, be most careful—since you saw no shape when the LORD your God spoke to you

וַיַּגֵּ֨ד לָכֶ֜ם אֶת־בְּרִית֗וֹ אֲשֶׁ֨ר צִוָּ֤ה אֶתְכֶם֙ לַעֲשׂ֔וֹת עֲשֶׂ֖רֶת הַדְּבָרִ֑ים וַֽיִּכְתְּבֵ֔ם עַל־שְׁנֵ֖י לֻח֥וֹת אֲבָנִֽים: 14 וְאֹתִ֞י צִוָּ֤ה יְהוָה֙ בָּעֵ֣ת הַהִ֔וא לְלַמֵּ֣ד אֶתְכֶ֔ם חֻקִּ֖ים וּמִשְׁפָּטִ֑ים לַעֲשֹׂתְכֶ֣ם אֹתָ֔ם בָּאָ֕רֶץ אֲשֶׁ֥ר אַתֶּ֛ם עֹבְרִ֥ים שָׁ֖מָּה לְרִשְׁתָּֽהּ: 15 וְנִשְׁמַרְתֶּ֥ם מְאֹ֖ד לְנַפְשֹׁתֵיכֶ֑ם כִּ֣י לֹ֤א רְאִיתֶם֙ כָּל־תְּמוּנָ֔ה בְּי֗וֹם דִּבֶּ֨ר יְהוָ֧ה אֲלֵיכֶ֛ם בְּחֹרֵ֖ב מִתּ֥וֹךְ

term does not mean a manufactured representation of something (as in modern Hebrew, where it means "picture") but the visible aspect of a being, as in the present verse.[43]

Moses does not argue here that God has no visible form. Other passages in the Bible show that God was thought to have a visual aspect. It was believed to normally be dangerous for humans to see God, but Moses, Aaron, and the elders of Israel were allowed to do so, and they were unharmed.[44] Although Deuteronomy avoids physical descriptions of God, the belief that He *has* no physical form developed only in postbiblical times, especially in the philosophical literature of the Middle Ages.

13-14. The reference to the laws proclaimed at Mount Sinai is brief since Moses' present focus is on the nonvisual aspect of God's revelation rather than on what He said. The laws themselves are reported in chapter 5.

13. the covenant that He commanded . . . the Ten Commandments In English "to command a covenant" sounds strange. In fact, the Hebrew term for covenant (*berit*) has three meanings, all based on the idea of obligation. It can refer to a promise (an obligation imposed on oneself), a stipulation (an obligation imposed on another), or a compact (reciprocal obligations accepted by two parties). All three senses of the word are operative in the formal relationship between God and Israel: the covenant (*compact*) consists of *stipulations* imposed by God upon Israel; Israel's *promise* to obey the stipulations; and God's *promise* to reward Israel. Here the term refers to the Ten Commandments as stipulations imposed by God upon Israel; in other words, as the obligation to which Israel must commit itself in its covenant with God. For the other senses see v. 31 (promise) and 5:2–3 and 29:11 (compact).[45] For the text of the Ten Commandments see 5:6–18.

two tablets of stone The tablets were made of stone because of their importance. Stone was normally used only for inscriptions that were intended to be permanent, such as royal and ceremonial inscriptions, boundary inscriptions, and treaties.[46] An impression of what the tablets may have looked like is given by an Aramaic decree of the seventh century B.C.E. written on a stone tablet about eleven inches square. It is inscribed on one side only, with thirty-two words covering eight lines. Two such tablets, fifteen or sixteen inches square and inscribed on both sides (as the tablets of the Decalogue were), could have held the 189 words of the Decalogue (172 according to Exodus).[47] This shape is consistent with Jewish tradition and early Christian art, which conceived of the tablets as rectangular. The tablets with curved tops, familiar today, were first introduced in Christian art around the eleventh century.[48]

14. God personally gave the people the Ten Commandments and commanded Moses to convey the rest of the laws to them. See 5:24ff.

15-18. Here Moses draws out the lesson of what he says in v. 12: Since Israel saw no visible form ("shape") when God spoke, it is to make no idols of any form. Since the immediate context does not refer to other gods, the prohibition must refer to images representing YHVH or members of His retinue (see Comment to 3:24).[49] This line of reasoning is spelled out more fully in Exodus 20:19–22: Israel has seen that God spoke directly to it from heaven; it is therefore to make no idols, but only an earthen altar, and wherever God causes His name to be mentioned, He will come and bless Israel. This sequence of ideas implies that idolaters used idols to bring deities near and thereby secure their blessings or receive communications from them, but that since God spoke to Israel directly from heaven, without the mediation of idols, it sees that idols are not necessary for these purposes.[50] In idolatry, the purpose of an idol was to draw the presence of a deity to the place

at Horeb out of the fire—¹⁶not to act wickedly and make for yourselves a sculptured image in any likeness whatever: the form of a man or a woman, ¹⁷the form of any beast on earth, the form of any winged bird that flies in the sky, ¹⁸the form of anything that creeps on the ground, the form of any fish that is in the waters below the earth.—¹⁹And when you look up to the sky and behold the sun and the moon and the stars, the whole heavenly

הָאֵשׁ: ¹⁶ פֶּן־תַּשְׁחִתוּן וַעֲשִׂיתֶם לָכֶם פֶּסֶל תְּמוּנַת כָּל־סָמֶל תַּבְנִית זָכָר אוֹ נְקֵבָה: ¹⁷ תַּבְנִית כָּל־בְּהֵמָה אֲשֶׁר בָּאָרֶץ תַּבְנִית כָּל־צִפּוֹר כָּנָף אֲשֶׁר תָּעוּף בַּשָּׁמָיִם: ¹⁸ תַּבְנִית כָּל־רֹמֵשׂ בָּאֲדָמָה תַּבְנִית כָּל־דָּגָה אֲשֶׁר־בַּמַּיִם מִתַּחַת לָאָרֶץ: ¹⁹ וּפֶן־תִּשָּׂא עֵינֶיךָ הַשָּׁמַיְמָה וְרָאִיתָ אֶת־הַשֶּׁמֶשׁ וְאֶת־הַיָּרֵחַ וְאֶת־הַכּוֹכָבִים כֹּל צְבָא

where the statue stood.⁵¹ It assumed that by a kind of sympathetic magic, like that connected with voodoo dolls, a being was somehow present in its representation. Here Moses forbids Israel to use idols to attract God: since no form was seen in the original contact with Him, none is to be made for future contacts.

16–18 These verses follow the second commandment (5:8) almost verbatim and elaborate on it.

16. A more likely translation of this verse would be "not to act wickedly and make for yourselves an idol [*pesel*] of the visage of anything [*temunat kol*], a statue [*semel*] which is the likeness [*tavnit*] of a man or a woman." *Pesel* is best rendered as "idol" since the noun is used for images of wood and metal as well as stone,⁵² and it is used only for images of gods. *Temunah* is explained in the Comment to v. 12. *Semel* is another term for statue; in its few biblical occurrences it refers to an idol, but in Phoenician it refers to a statue of a human as well as a deity⁵³ (in the present translation, it is reflected in "whatever" in the phrase "any likeness whatever"). *Tavnit* (rendered "form") refers to a copy, pattern, or model of something;⁵⁴ here the translation "likeness" would be best.⁵⁵

The final phrase ("a statue which is . . .") continues through verses 17–18, including in the prohibition likenesses of creatures on the land and in the skies and waters. This is probably not a separate prohibition but an explication of "idol." In other words, verses 16–18 mean: "Do not make *an idol* which is a statue that is the likeness of . . ." It does not rule out statues that are not idols. This inference is supported by the fact that individual prohibitions on images never begin with terms that can refer to nonreligious images (such as *tavnit*, *semel*, and *tselem*); when such terms appear in the prohibitions, they are always subordinated to terms that unambiguously denote idols. In fact, nonidolatrous statues of certain creatures were not considered violations of this commandment and were used in the Tabernacle and in Solomon's temple.⁵⁶

17–18. Nor may animal-like idols be made. These probably would not have been intended as representations of the Lord, who was thought to have a human appearance.⁵⁷ Rather, they might have represented His chariot or His mount. In ancient Near Eastern religious art animals served not only as images of a deity but as their mounts and as pedestals for their statues,⁵⁸ and as such they could symbolize the deities even when the latter were not represented explicitly. Since God was thought to travel on a chariot borne by hybrid creatures with the faces of men and animals, as we learn in Ezekiel 1, people might have thought it possible to attract His presence with an image of one or more of those animals. (It is possible that Aaron's golden calf and Jeroboam's calves were originally intended in this way, not as idols; see Excursus 12.)

18. **the waters below the earth** That is, in oceans, lakes, and rivers. The surface of the earth is conceived as standing or floating on a huge body of water that surrounds it in the form of oceans and breaks through to the earth's surface in the form of lakes, springs, and rivers.⁵⁹

19–20. Moses parenthetically reminds Israel that worship of the heavenly bodies is also forbidden. The fact that he mentions this prohibition here may imply that they are forbidden for the same reason that idols are: since the heavenly bodies were blotted out by the darkness and clouds at Mount Sinai and Israel did not see them, it must not worship them either.⁶⁰

19. **you must not be lured** A synonymous expression is used in 11:16, "Take care not to be lured away," and by Job in denying that he had committed this sin: "If I ever saw the light shining, the moon on its course in full glory, and I was secretly lured and my hand touched my

host, you must not be lured into bowing down to them or serving them. These the LORD your God allotted to other peoples everywhere under heaven; 20but you the LORD took and brought out of Egypt, that iron blast furnace, to be His very own people, as is now the case.

הַשָּׁמַיִם וְנִדַּחְתָּ וְהִשְׁתַּחֲוִיתָ לָהֶם וַעֲבַדְתָּם אֲשֶׁר חָלַק יְהֹוָה אֱלֹהֶיךָ אֹתָם לְכֹל הָעַמִּים תַּחַת כָּל־הַשָּׁמָיִם: 20 וְאֶתְכֶם לָקַח יְהֹוָה וַיּוֹצִא אֶתְכֶם מִכּוּר הַבַּרְזֶל מִמִּצְרָיִם לִהְיוֹת לוֹ לְעַם נַחֲלָה כַּיּוֹם הַזֶּה:

mouth in a kiss . . ." (Job 31:26–27). These passages express the seductiveness of idolatry, especially of the heavenly bodies. Their majestic position in the sky, their eternity, their movements, the light and warmth they provide, and their beneficial impact on agriculture suggest that they are powerful, and this moves people to worship them. The worship of celestial deities was common in the ancient Near East. The Bible itself personifies the heavenly bodies as God's servants; it includes them among the "divine beings" and speaks of them as "dominating" (lit., "ruling") the day and night.[61] The biblical context always makes it clear that these bodies are subordinate to the Lord and dependent on Him (see, e.g., Ps. 74:16), but people were not always so discriminating, and some Israelites did worship them, particularly in the eighth and seventh centuries B.C.E.[62] The reasoning which might lead even a loyal worshiper of the Lord to think that the worship of these objects is acceptable is spelled out by Maimonides:

> The essential principle in the precepts concerning idolatry is that we are not to worship anything created—neither angel, sphere, star, none of the four elements, nor whatever has been formed from them. Even if the worshiper is aware that the Eternal is God, and worships the created thing in the sense in which Enosh and his contemporaries did [i.e., as subordinates who manage the world under God's orders; see Comment to 13:6], he is an idolater. It is against this that the Torah warns us [in Deuteronomy 4:19]. The verse means that when your mind roams and you observe that the world is guided by these spheres and that God placed them in the world, as beings that live, endure permanently, and do not disintegrate like all other things, you might say that it is proper to bow down to these spheres, and worship them. Concerning this tendency, God commanded [us in Deuteronomy 11:16]; that is to say, do not be led astray by the fancies of your mind, to worship these beings as intermediaries between yourselves and the Creator.[63]

These the LORD allotted to other peoples He assigned these to other peoples as objects of worship but (v. 20 continues) He took Israel to be His own worshipers.[64] The concept that the Lord divided the peoples of the world between Himself and other heavenly beings is reminiscent of 32:8–9 according to the reading of a manuscript from Qumran and the Septuagint: when God divided mankind into separate nations, "He fixed the boundaries of the peoples equal to the number of divine beings," but took Israel to be His own people (see Excursus 31). That reading calls attention to a certain asymmetry here between verses 19 and 20: since verse 20 says that the Lord assigned Israel to Himself, one expects verse 19 to say that He assigned the other peoples to the heavenly bodies. Instead, it says the reverse: He assigned the heavenly bodies to the other peoples. This suggests that the text has intentionally skewed the motif of 32:8–9 in order to emphasize that the heavenly bodies are merely creations of the Lord, not divine beings that own or govern the other peoples.[65]

These passages seem to reflect a biblical view that the worship of idols and heavenly bodies began when God divided humanity into separate nations after it built the Tower of Babel. See Excursus 7.

20. This verse continues the thought of verse 19: Unlike the other nations, which were given inferior heavenly beings as objects of worship, Israel was taken by God Himself—in other words, to worship Him personally. This underscores the folly Israel would commit if it should worship the heavenly bodies.

but you the LORD took and brought out of Egypt Here Moses again alludes to the Decalogue (5:6).

to be His very own people Literally "to be a people that is His inheritance," His hereditary property (nahalah). Compare Leviticus 25:42: "They are My servants, whom I freed from the Land

21Now the LORD was angry with me on your account and swore that I should not cross the Jordan and enter the good land that the LORD your God is assigning you as a heritage. 22For I must die in this land; I shall not cross the Jordan. But you will cross and take possession of that good land.

23Take care, then, not to forget the covenant that the LORD your God concluded with you, and not to make for yourselves a sculptured image in any likeness, against which the LORD your God has enjoined you. 24For the LORD your God is a consuming fire, an impassioned God.

25When you have begotten children and children's children and are long established in the land, should you act

21 וַיהוָה הִתְאַנַּף־בִּי עַל־דִּבְרֵיכֶם וַיִּשָּׁבַע לְבִלְתִּי עָבְרִי אֶת־הַיַּרְדֵּן וּלְבִלְתִּי־בֹא אֶל־הָאָרֶץ הַטּוֹבָה אֲשֶׁר יְהוָה אֱלֹהֶיךָ נֹתֵן לְךָ נַחֲלָה: 22 כִּי אָנֹכִי מֵת בָּאָרֶץ הַזֹּאת אֵינֶנִּי עֹבֵר אֶת־הַיַּרְדֵּן וְאַתֶּם עֹבְרִים וִירִשְׁתֶּם אֶת־הָאָרֶץ הַטּוֹבָה הַזֹּאת: 23 הִשָּׁמְרוּ לָכֶם פֶּן־תִּשְׁכְּחוּ אֶת־בְּרִית יְהוָה אֱלֹהֵיכֶם אֲשֶׁר כָּרַת עִמָּכֶם וַעֲשִׂיתֶם לָכֶם פֶּסֶל תְּמוּנַת כֹּל אֲשֶׁר צִוְּךָ יְהוָה אֱלֹהֶיךָ: 24 כִּי יְהוָה אֱלֹהֶיךָ אֵשׁ אֹכְלָה הוּא אֵל קַנָּא: פ 25 כִּי־תוֹלִיד בָּנִים וּבְנֵי בָנִים וְנוֹשַׁנְתֶּם בָּאָרֶץ וְהִשְׁחַתֶּם וַעֲשִׂיתֶם פֶּסֶל תְּמוּנַת כֹּל וַעֲשִׂיתֶם

of Egypt." God acquired Israel by redeeming it from Egypt. The Exodus freed Israel from a human master and brought it under the authority of the Divine Master.[66] See also Exodus 6:6–7 and Numbers 15:41, "I the LORD am your God who brought you out of . . . Egypt to be your God."

The term *naḥalah* expresses not only God's sovereignty over the people of Israel but also His attachment to them, "since a person's personal property and his portion are dear to him" (Saadia; note how the phrase is used in 9:26,29). Inherited land was dear because it was normally inalienable. It was received from one's ancestors and passed on to one's descendants. 1 Kings 21:2–4 tells how Naboth even refused a king's request to exchange his vineyard for a better one because it was inherited from his fathers. The terms *segullah*, *ḥelek*, and *morashah*, likewise signify a person's attachment to personal property; see 7:6; 32:9; and 33:4.[67]

that iron blast furnace   A furnace for smelting iron, a metaphor for the severity of the Egyptian bondage (iron was smelted in ancient times at a temperature of about two thousand degrees Fahrenheit). Isaiah uses a similar metaphor for the Babylonian exile: "the furnace of affliction."[68]

as is now the case   As you see.

21–22.   Moses digresses to recall once again that he was barred from entering the promised land (cf. 1:37; 3:23–28). Why he brings this up here is not clear. Is his aim to strengthen the threat of exile (vv. 27–28) by showing that Israel cannot take its tenure in the land for granted, since even he was barred from it?[69] Another view, consistent with his warnings against illicit worship in the preceding verses, is that Moses wants to prevent posthumous worship of himself. By recalling that he is mortal and completely under God's control he shows that, despite all the supernatural deeds he performed, he is no more deserving of worship than idols or heavenly bodies.[70] See also Comment to 34:6.

23–31.   Moses now resumes the warning against worshiping idols, spelling out the consequences of violating it. The warning is framed by references to "forgetting the covenant" and to God's attributes of passion and compassion (vv. 23–24,31). It begins by echoing the command about idolatry in the Decalogue: "not to make for yourselves a sculptured image in any likeness. . . . For the LORD your God is . . . an impassioned God . . . [punishing] children and children's children . . ." (cf. 5:8–9).[71]

23. *a sculptured image in any likeness*   Better, "an idol of the visage of anything." See Comment to v. 16.

24. *a consuming fire*   God's fiery destructive power, which had struck the Exodus generation several times.[72] This metaphor is especially suitable here because it also alludes to God's fiery appearance at Mount Sinai, which so terrified the people (see 5:5,22–23; Exod. 24:17 describes God's appearance atop Mount Sinai with the same phrase).

an impassioned God   See Comment to 5:9. Note the contrasting divine quality described in v. 31.

wickedly and make for yourselves a sculptured image in any likeness, causing the LORD your God displeasure and vexation, 26I call heaven and earth this day to witness against you that you shall soon perish from the land that you are crossing the Jordan to possess; you shall not long endure in it, but shall be utterly wiped out. 27The LORD will scatter you among the peoples, and only a scant few of you shall be left among the nations to which the LORD will

הָרַע בְּעֵינֵי יְהוָה־אֱלֹהֶיךָ לְהַכְעִיסוֹ: 26 הַעִידֹתִי בָכֶם הַיּוֹם אֶת־הַשָּׁמַיִם וְאֶת־הָאָרֶץ כִּי־אָבֹד תֹּאבֵדוּן מַהֵר מֵעַל הָאָרֶץ אֲשֶׁר אַתֶּם עֹבְרִים אֶת־הַיַּרְדֵּן שָׁמָּה לְרִשְׁתָּהּ לֹא־תַאֲרִיכֻן יָמִים עָלֶיהָ כִּי הִשָּׁמֵד תִּשָּׁמֵדוּן: 27 וְהֵפִיץ יְהוָה אֶתְכֶם בָּעַמִּים וְנִשְׁאַרְתֶּם מְתֵי מִסְפָּר בַּגּוֹיִם אֲשֶׁר יְנַהֵג יְהוָה אֶתְכֶם שָׁמָּה: 28 וַעֲבַדְתֶּם־שָׁם אֱלֹהִים

25–28. The warning about God's fiery destructive power will lose effect as the people's memory fades and the comforts of the promised land lead future generations, with no personal recollection of that power, to forget their dependence on God (see Comment to 6:11–12). Moses therefore warns the people in terms more likely to be meaningful to future generations: they will be exiled from the land on which they have come to depend. He puts them on notice that tenure in the land, no less than entry into it, will always depend on obedience.

The conditional character of Israel's possession of the promised land has already been expressed several times: the Exodus generation was prevented from entering the land because of its rebellion; Moses was denied entry; and at the beginning of the present address Moses indicated that entry was dependent on obedience to God's commandments. In fact, Israel's possession of the land is the dominant theme of all the historical parts of the Bible, which tell how Israel received the land, was exiled from it, and returned to it. No other nation has devoted so much of its historical and religious thought to the possession of its land. Several facts led to this preoccupation: Israel's historical memory stretched back to the time when it had no land; much of Israel's effort was devoted to defending the land over the centuries; and much of Israel's population was eventually exiled. These factors prevented the Israelites from taking their possession of the land for granted and led them to view it as a special privilege that depended on their conduct.[73]

26. *I call heaven and earth to witness* To witness the following warning, as in 30:19 and 31:28; compare 32:1. The precise function of the witnesses is not spelled out. Traditional commentators suggest that they are called either to prevent Israel from later denying that it was warned[74] or to serve as instruments of reward or punishment if Israel does or does not heed the warnings (see Comment to 32:1). In ancient Near Eastern covenants, heaven and earth are called as witnesses along with the gods and other parts of nature (usually, but not always, in deified form) so that they will punish those who violate the agreement.[75] Since the present passage warns against violating a covenant, it is probable that they are invoked as instruments of punishment here, too. This is the role they play in 28:23 and especially 11:17: "He will shut up the heavens so that there will be no rain and the earth will not yield its produce; and you will soon perish from the good land that the LORD is assigning to you."[76] There is, however, an important difference between their role here and in ancient treaties. In the latter, heaven and earth, and the other gods, serve as witnesses because they were regarded as supreme authorities in the universe. In the Bible, however, the supreme authority is the Lord, who is Himself a party to the covenant. The heaven and earth are subordinate to Him and cannot act independently. They enforce the covenant only in the sense that they are the means by which God enforces it. Their role as "witnesses" is a vestigial motif that has lost its original significance.

shall be utterly wiped out This is a hyperbole meaning "be ruined." As verse 27 indicates, there will be survivors. See Comment to 28:20.

27. The punishments are the precise opposites of God's promises: instead of possessing the land (v. 1), Israel will be exiled from it; instead of being numerous (1:10–11), they will become few. This shows the conditionality of God's promises. See also 28:62–63.

For the punishment of exile see 28:36 and Excursus 27.

28. Exile will bring in its wake an additional punishment: worshiping artificial gods that can do nothing. The same punishment is threatened in 28:36,64, and Jeremiah 16:13. Worship of the true God is a privilege, and worship of statues is a punishment. It is one that fits the crime: if Israel

drive you. ²⁸There you will serve man-made gods of wood and stone, that cannot see or hear or eat or smell.

מַעֲשֵׂה יְדֵי אָדָם עֵץ וָאֶבֶן אֲשֶׁר לֹא־יִרְאוּן וְלֹא
יִשְׁמְעוּן וְלֹא יֹאכְלוּן וְלֹא יְרִיחֻן׃

worships statues, that is what it will be left with; if Israel ignores what it saw and heard, it will wind up worshiping objects which cannot see or hear.

Some commentators, viewing this verse through the prism of later Jewish history, assumed that it means that the Israelites in exile would be persecuted and forced to worship foreign gods.[77] However, religious coercion was not typical of the ancient Near East,[78] and it is more likely that Moses is thinking of religious assimilation. The likelihood of such assimilation might have been increased by the belief that it was impermissible to worship the Lord outside the land of Israel. Despite the fact that the Torah regards the Lord as accessible anywhere (see v. 29), it considers only the land of Israel as the "Holy Land" (Zech. 2:16) and considers other lands as impure to Him.[79] Therefore, it is impermissible to conduct normal, sacrificial worship of Him outside the land (an exception was the desert period when a portable sanctuary accompanied Israel in its wanderings). A person exiled from the land is therefore unable to worship the Lord. That is why the Israelites who arrived in Babylon lamented that they could not sing a song of the Lord on alien soil and David complained that those who forced him to flee from the land of Israel were telling him to "go worship other gods" (Ps. 137:4; 1 Sam. 26:19). The same viewpoint underlies Moses' warning.

(Presumably some exiled Israelites did adopt paganism, especially those from the northern tribes, most of whose descendants assimilated and disappeared. However, one of the most momentous achievements of the Jews living in the Babylonian exile was that they found acceptable ways to worship the Lord in foreign lands despite the prohibition on sacrificing there. They emphasized communal prayer and study as alternative modes of worship and made these into institutions that permitted Judaism to thrive outside the land of Israel. Most scholars believe that the synagogue originated in the Babylonian exile, though some think that its main components developed in Israel in the centuries preceding the exile [see Comment to 16:8].)[80]

man-made gods of wood and stone that cannot see or hear or eat or smell The Bible regards the worship of statues as the most absurd aspect of paganism and the most telling argument against it (cf. 27:15; 28:36,64; 29:16).[81] In pagan religions special ceremonies were believed to "quicken" the statues and give them all the powers that our verse denies them: sight, hearing, eating, and smelling.[82] Idolaters—certainly the more educated ones—did not think that the statue *was* the deity. They believed that the god was not present in the statue before the quickening ceremony and that it might abandon the statue at will. But the distinction between statue and deity was easily overlooked, and idolaters sometimes considered images as identical to the deity or as possessing powers of their own—in other words, as fetishes.[83] As Plutarch wrote: "Amongst the Greeks there were those who . . . through lack of knowledge and education, fell to calling . . . images 'gods' instead of saying 'images' or 'symbols' of the gods. One might hear men say that . . . Jupiter of the Capitol had been burnt [in a war]. . . . Men fail to observe that such incorrect ways of speaking lead actually to false notions."[84] The ease with which the distinction could be forgotten is illustrated by the case of the copper serpent that Moses made as a charm for healing snakebites; by the time of Hezekiah, people began to worship it (Num. 21:4–9; see 2 Kings 18:4).[85] This fetishistic level of idolatry is the one to which the Bible regularly refers, not the more sophisticated type to which verses 15–18 allude. It is possible that the Bible concentrates on fetishism for rhetorical effect, rebutting idolatry by focusing on its most implausible form. However, this picture of idolatry is pervasive in the Bible and it seems more likely that fetishistic idolatry was the type practiced by most Israelite idolaters,[86] and was emphasized for that reason. Apparently most Israelite idolaters saw pagans worshiping before images and calling them "gods," and concluded that the idols *were* the gods.

29–31. The futility of worshiping artificial gods will eventually drive the Israelites back to the Lord, and they will be accepted since the Lord is merciful and faithful to the covenant He made with the patriarchs. That they will be restored to the land of Israel is implied by the promise that they will "find" God and also by verse 31, since the covenant with the patriarchs was a promise to give the land of Israel to their descendants; see also 30:1–5.[87]

The idea that the punishment will not be permanent is inherent in God's covenant with the patriarchs (v. 31). God promised that He would give the land to Abraham's descendants forever

29But if you search there for the LORD your God, you will find Him, if only you seek Him with all your heart and soul—30when you are in distress because all these things have befallen you and, in the end, return to the LORD your God and obey Him. 31For the LORD your God

29 וּבִקַּשְׁתֶּם מִשָּׁם אֶת־יְהוָה אֱלֹהֶיךָ וּמָצָאתָ כִּי תִדְרְשֶׁנּוּ בְּכָל־לְבָבְךָ וּבְכָל־נַפְשֶׁךָ: 30 בַּצַּר לְךָ וּמְצָאוּךָ כֹּל הַדְּבָרִים הָאֵלֶּה בְּאַחֲרִית הַיָּמִים וְשַׁבְתָּ עַד־יְהוָה אֱלֹהֶיךָ וְשָׁמַעְתָּ בְּקֹלוֹ: 31 כִּי

(Gen. 13:15; 17:7–8; Exod. 32:13). As noted in the Introduction, God's relationship with Israel is embodied in two covenants, the reciprocal covenant established at Mount Sinai, with all of its detailed stipulations, and the earlier promissory covenant with the patriarchs (cited in v. 31), the main feature of which is God's commitments to the patriarchs concerning their descendants. The latter covenant is modeled on ancient Near Eastern promissory covenants in which a king grants land or some other gift to a servant in recognition of loyal service. Several such grants provide that the gift given would be passed on to the grantee's descendants in perpetuity. Even if one of his descendants should commit an offense against the king, only the offender would be punished; the grant itself would never be taken away from the grantee's descendants. The same stipulation appears in God's grant of a dynasty to David: even if a future king in the dynasty should sin, God would punish the sinner but would never take the kingship away from David's descendants (2 Sam. 7:11–16; Ps. 89:29–38). The land of Israel, promised by God to Abraham's descendants, is similarly inalienable, and while the guilty generation will suffer destruction and exile, Israel will not be banished from the land permanently.[88] (Moses also cites God's promises to the patriarchs in order to save Israel itself from extinction. See Comment to 9:27.)

Nevertheless, in the present context it is not clear why Moses mentions that God will accept the Israelites' repentance. His purpose in this address is not to summarize all the terms of the covenant but to deter the Israelites from violating it by warning them of the consequences. Some scholars hold that the promise of forgiveness, like that in 30:1–10, could weaken the effectiveness of the warning, and infer that these promises are interpolations added to the text during the Babylonian exile. See Excursus 5.

29. *with all your heart and soul*   See Comment to 6:5.

30.   The verse suggests a cause-and-effect relationship between distress and repentance: when the exiles see that worshiping idols brings them no relief in exile, they will return to the Lord and obey Him.

in the end   That is, afterwards, ultimately.[89] The idiom *'aḥarit ha-yamim* ("later days") does not have here the sense in which it is used by the prophets, "the culminating period of history," as in Isaiah 2:2.

return to the LORD . . . and obey Him   Shuv, "return," is the verb from which *teshuvah*, the Hebrew term for repentance, is derived. As the final phrase in the verse shows, the Hebrew term does not refer only to contrition but to a change of behavior, literally a "return" to God and to the behavior that He requires. The concept of returning to God in the Torah is not identical to its better-known form in the Prophets and in classical Judaism. In the Torah it is mentioned only as something that occurs after punishment has taken place: if the people take their punishment to heart and return to God, He will terminate their punishment.[90] The prophets developed the concept further. They called upon people to repent before it is too late, and to thereby avert punishment altogether. The concept of *teshuvah* in classical Judaism combines both ideas, with emphasis on the latter.[91]

31. *a compassionate God*   The Lord is not only impassioned (v. 24), but also compassionate. These are two aspects of God's personality in the Bible: He both punishes and forgives. In rabbinic literature these qualities are referred to as "the quality of justice" and "the quality of mercy" (*middat ha-din* and *middat ha-raḥamim*). Some scholars have spoken of these qualities as if they represent two stages in the history of religious thought: the "God of Wrath" supposedly representing a more primitive concept of God, and the "God of Mercy" a more advanced one. In reality these qualities appear side-by-side in the Bible and represent different aspects of God's response to human behavior.[92]

is a compassionate God: He will not fail you nor will He let you perish; He will not forget the covenant which He made on oath with your fathers.

אֵל רַחוּם יְהוָה אֱלֹהֶיךָ לֹא יַרְפְּךָ וְלֹא יַשְׁחִיתֶךָ וְלֹא יִשְׁכַּח אֶת־בְּרִית אֲבֹתֶיךָ אֲשֶׁר נִשְׁבַּע לָהֶם:

32 You have but to inquire about bygone ages that came before you, ever since God created man on earth, from one end of heaven to the other: has anything as grand as this ever happened, or has its like ever been known? 33 Has any people heard the voice of a god speaking out of a fire, as you have, and survived? 34 Or has any god ventured to go and take for himself one nation from the midst of another by prodigious acts, by signs and portents, by war,

32 כִּי שְׁאַל־נָא לְיָמִים רִאשֹׁנִים אֲשֶׁר־הָיוּ לְפָנֶיךָ לְמִן־הַיּוֹם אֲשֶׁר בָּרָא אֱלֹהִים | אָדָם עַל־הָאָרֶץ וּלְמִקְצֵה הַשָּׁמַיִם וְעַד־קְצֵה הַשָּׁמָיִם הֲנִהְיָה כַּדָּבָר הַגָּדוֹל הַזֶּה אוֹ הֲנִשְׁמַע כָּמֹהוּ: 33 הֲשָׁמַע עָם קוֹל אֱלֹהִים מְדַבֵּר מִתּוֹךְ־הָאֵשׁ כַּאֲשֶׁר־שָׁמַעְתָּ אַתָּה וַיֶּחִי: 34 אוֹ | הֲנִסָּה אֱלֹהִים לָבוֹא לָקַחַת לוֹ גוֹי מִקֶּרֶב גּוֹי בְּמַסֹּת בְּאֹתֹת וּבְמוֹפְתִים וּבְמִלְחָמָה

nor . . . let you perish (yashḥit) . . . will not forget the covenant   These promises echo Moses' earlier warnings that Israel should not *forget* the covenant or *act corruptly (tashḥitun,* vv. 16,23,25). God's actions are thus contrasted with Israel's: He will not act as they did.

AN APPEAL TO OBSERVE THE COMMANDMENTS BASED ON THE FACT THAT THE LORD (YHVH) IS THE ONLY GOD   (vv. 32–40)

Following the warning of exile Moses concludes with a final appeal to observe the commandments so that Israel may prosper and remain in the land forever.

32–35.   Moses argues that history demonstrates the truth of monotheism. No so-called god has ever done what YHVH did at the Exodus and at Mount Sinai. Such deeds are the true marks of divinity according to Moses, and since only YHVH has performed such deeds, it follows that He is the only true God. For Moses, the *sine qua non* of divinity is effectiveness. The same criterion is applied elsewhere in denying the divinity of foreign gods. In verse 28 Moses points out that foreign gods are merely wood and stone objects that can do nothing. Isaiah taunts the gods of Babylonia, "Foretell what is yet to happen, that we may know that you are gods! Do anything, good or bad, that we may be awed and see. Why, you are less than nothing, your effect is less than nullity" (Isa. 41:23–24; cf. 2 Chron. 25:15b). These texts do not argue that other beings called gods do not exist. As noted in Comment to 3:24, the words *'el* and *'elohim* were sometimes used for various types of supernatural beings and for idols, and the Bible does not deny the existence of such beings or of images. What is denied is that they are really gods. Other biblical texts make the same point. Jeremiah, for example, asks: "Has any nation changed its gods, even though they are no-gods [that is, non-gods]?" and "Can a man make gods for himself? No-gods are they!" (Jer. 2:11; 16:20). In Deuteronomy 32:17 Moses calls the gods worshiped by the Israelites in Canaan "demons, no-gods, gods they had never known, new ones, who came but lately." These passages say in effect that the common usage of the words *'el* and *'elohim* for supernatural beings and idols is loose and misleading, notwithstanding the fact that this usage is sometimes echoed in the Bible itself. Only YHVH deserves to be called God. (An argument from history is also employed in Exodus to show the Lord's superiority and uniqueness [cf. Deut. 3:24]; see Excursus 6.)

32. ever since God created man on earth   That is, as far back as human memory goes.[94]

from one end of heaven to the other   That is, from one end of earth to another. The heaven was pictured as a dome standing atop pillars situated at the ends of the earth; hence the ends of heaven and of earth were coterminous.[95]

33. and survived   Notwithstanding God's benevolent character, the belief is frequently expressed that a direct, visual encounter with Him would be too awesome to endure.[96] This passage and 5:21–23 imply that hearing Him was thought to be similarly dangerous.

34. by prodigious acts   These terms refer to the signs Moses and Aaron performed before

by a mighty hand and an outstretched arm and awesome power, as the LORD your God did for you in Egypt before your very eyes? [35]It has been clearly demonstrated to you that the LORD alone is God; there is none beside Him. [36]From the heavens He let you hear His voice to discipline you; on earth He let you see His great fire; and from amidst that fire you heard His words. [37]And because He

וּבְיָ֤ד חֲזָקָה֙ וּבִזְרֹ֣עַ נְטוּיָ֔ה וּבְמוֹרָאִ֖ים גְּדֹלִ֑ים כְּכֹ֧ל
אֲשֶׁר־עָשָׂ֨ה לָכֶ֜ם יְהוָ֧ה אֱלֹהֵיכֶ֛ם בְּמִצְרַ֖יִם לְעֵינֶֽיךָ׃
35 אַתָּה֙ הָרְאֵ֣תָ לָדַ֔עַת כִּ֥י יְהוָ֖ה ה֣וּא הָאֱלֹהִ֑ים אֵ֥ין
ע֖וֹד מִלְבַדּֽוֹ׃ 36 מִן־הַשָּׁמַ֛יִם הִשְׁמִֽיעֲךָ֥ אֶת־קֹל֖וֹ
לְיַסְּרֶ֑ךָ וְעַל־הָאָ֗רֶץ הֶרְאֲךָ֙ אֶת־אִשּׁ֣וֹ הַגְּדוֹלָ֔ה
וּדְבָרָ֥יו שָׁמַ֖עְתָּ מִתּ֥וֹךְ הָאֵֽשׁ׃ 37 וְתַ֗חַת כִּ֤י אָהַב֙

Pharaoh, the ten plagues, and the defeat of Egypt at the *Sea of Reeds*. Most of the terms occur in connection with those events in Exodus.[97] The first, *massot*, is usually rendered "trials" in the sense of "tests of the character and disposition of Pharaoh" (Driver); the translation "prodigious acts" is apparently based on another sense of the root *n-s-h*, "give experience."[98] *Mora'im gedolim* (translated as "awesome power") means literally "great fearsome acts."

take . . . one nation from the midst of another   This is the most telling point of Moses' argument: that the Lord took Israel out of Egypt shows the powerlessness of Egypt's gods, and that is what shows that He is the only true God (cf. Exod. 12:12).

35.   The events just described were witnessed by the entire nation and demonstrate that the Lord alone is God. This demonstration goes beyond the practical concern of the second commandment, which prohibits *worshiping* other gods. Here Moses states clearly that there *are* no others. For further discussion see Excursus 6.

Because this verse refers to the revelation at Mount Sinai (v. 33), it appears as the first in a collection of verses (*'Attah Hor'eita*) recited when the Torah scrolls are taken from the Ark on Simḥat Torah, according to Ashkenazic practice, and every Sabbath according to Sephardic practice.[100]

36–39.   Because of their seminal importance, the contents of verses 32–35 are repeated and explained in further detail.

36.   God's purpose in speaking to the people was to "discipline" them. The verb *y-s-r* denotes "the discipline or education of the moral nature: the spectacle was one adapted to quell waywardness and pride, to generate in Israel's heart a temper of submissiveness and reverence" (Driver). See Comment to verse 10.

From the heavens . . . on earth   The verse seems to resolve an inconsistency in Exodus. According to Exodus 19:11,18,20, God came down onto Mount Sinai before speaking, whereas Exodus 20:19 states that He spoke from heaven. Our verse states that there was indeed something on the earth when God spoke but it was not God: He spoke from heaven; only the fire and sound were on the earth. This verse is cited in midrashic literature as a classic case of how an inconsistency between two verses is resolved by a third.[101]

Showing that God remained in heaven is consistent with the rest of Deuteronomy. Unlike the previous books of the Torah, Deuteronomy avoids descriptions that might suggest that God is physical and human in nature. It never describes God as descending to earth or as dwelling in the sanctuary.[102]

37–38.   It was love for Israel's ancestors that led God to choose Israel, take them out of Egypt, and give them the promised land. Deuteronomy is the first book in the Torah to speak of God *loving* and *choosing* Israel.[103] In speaking of love it makes the emotional dimension of God's relationship with Israel explicit. This dimension is expressed in two of the metaphors that the Bible uses to describe the relationship, the bonds between father and son and between husband and wife. If Moses has one of these in mind here, it is probably the former, which is mentioned regularly in Deuteronomy.[104] The sequence of ideas in our passage—loving, choosing, assigning an inheritance (*nahalah*)—suggests the process of adoption by a loving father. Compare God's words in Jeremiah 3:19: "I had resolved to adopt you as a child, and I gave you a desirable land—the fairest inheritance of all the nations; and I thought you would surely call Me 'Father.'"[105] The metaphor of fatherly

loved your fathers, He chose their heirs after them; He Himself, in His great might, led you out of Egypt, [38]to drive from your path nations greater and more populous than you, to take you into their land and assign it to you as a heritage, as is still the case. [39]Know therefore this day and keep in mind that the LORD alone is God in heaven above and on earth below; there is no other. [40]Observe His laws and commandments, which I enjoin upon you this day, that it may go well with you and your children after you, and that you may long remain in the land that the LORD your God is assigning to you for all time.

אֶת־אֲבֹתֶיךָ וַיִּבְחַר בְּזַרְעוֹ אַחֲרָיו וַיּוֹצִאֲךָ בְּפָנָיו בְּכֹחוֹ הַגָּדֹל מִמִּצְרָיִם: 38 לְהוֹרִישׁ גּוֹיִם גְּדֹלִים וַעֲצֻמִים מִמְּךָ מִפָּנֶיךָ לַהֲבִיאֲךָ לָתֶת־לְךָ אֶת־אַרְצָם נַחֲלָה כַּיּוֹם הַזֶּה: 39 וְיָדַעְתָּ הַיּוֹם וַהֲשֵׁבֹתָ אֶל־לְבָבֶךָ כִּי יְהוָה הוּא הָאֱלֹהִים בַּשָּׁמַיִם מִמַּעַל וְעַל־הָאָרֶץ מִתָּחַת אֵין עוֹד: 40 וְשָׁמַרְתָּ אֶת־חֻקָּיו וְאֶת־מִצְוֺתָיו אֲשֶׁר אָנֹכִי מְצַוְּךָ הַיּוֹם אֲשֶׁר יִיטַב לְךָ וּלְבָנֶיךָ אַחֲרֶיךָ וּלְמַעַן תַּאֲרִיךְ יָמִים עַל־הָאֲדָמָה אֲשֶׁר יְהוָה אֱלֹהֶיךָ נֹתֵן לְךָ כָּל־הַיָּמִים: פ   שְׁלִישִׁי

love would explain why Deuteronomy is also the first book in the Torah to describe the promised land as Israel's "inheritance" from God.

How Israel's ancestors earned God's love is explained in Genesis, especially in the narratives that illustrate Abraham's obedience and trust in Him.

37. *He Himself* Literally "with His face," the Hebrew equivalent of "in person." The idiom emphasizes that God used no intermediary (such as an angel) in freeing Israel but, as a sign of His favor, freed them personally.[106] This passage supplements verses 19–20 and 32:8–9: God took Israel as His own people and did not assign them to one of His subordinates.

Numerous passages in the Bible speak of God's direct involvement in the Exodus, but there are others that speak of an angel acting as His agent during the Exodus, the journey through the wilderness, and the conquest of the promised land.[107] Most notable is Numbers 20:16 in which Moses says that when Israel cried out to God, He "sent a *mal'akh* who freed" Israel from Egypt. *Mal'akh*, literally "emissary," is the normal term for an angel. Deuteronomy, in contrast, never speaks of angels having any role in the events. Midrashic exegesis reconciles Numbers 20:16 with the passages speaking of God's direct involvement by taking the *mal'akh* as Moses. However, although prophets are sometimes called *mal'akh*, Moses never is, and several of the passages referring to angelic involvement cannot easily be explained as referring to prophets.[108] Critical theory sees the two sets of passages as reflecting competing traditions about the involvement of angels in the great events of Israelite history.[109] This difference of opinion about angels was still alive in talmudic times. The view of Deuteronomy is expressed in passages in talmudic literature which insist that in freeing Israel from Egypt, giving the Torah, providing rain for Israel, and even in punishing the people, God acted personally, "not by means of an angel, not by means of a seraph, and not by means of a messenger." The repeated denial that angels were involved in these events indicates that claims that they *were* involved must have remained a bone of contention and that the rabbis—like Deuteronomy—considered them incompatible with absolute monotheism.[110] See also Excursus 31.

39. *keep in mind* Rather, "take to heart."[111] Israel should reflect upon the fact that the Lord is the only God and draw the appropriate conclusion, which is stated in v. 40.

in heaven above and on earth below That God spoke from heaven and acted on earth shows His dominion in both realms. He is God everywhere. The midrash notes that this verse is the most thoroughgoing statement of monotheism in the entire Bible.[112] For this reason, this verse is cited as a proof text in the *Aleinu* prayer, recited three times daily, which expresses gratitude that the Jewish people were chosen to worship the true God instead of false ones, and prays that all humankind will one day be united in worshiping Him alone.

40. The fact that the Lord alone is God leads to the conclusion that observance of His commandmants is the prerequisite for prosperity and well-being. The address thus ends on the note with which it began, reminding the audience that observance is its central message. Moses' aim is not to teach belief alone, but belief with its behavioral implications.

and your children The promise that a reward will be enjoyed by one's descendants adds to its appeal (cf. 11:21; 12:28; 30:19).[113]

41Then Moses set aside three cities on the east side of the Jordan 42to which a manslayer could escape, one who unwittingly slew a fellow man without having been hostile to him in the past; he could flee to one of these cities and live: 43Bezer, in the wilderness in the Tableland, belonging to the Reubenites; Ramoth, in Gilead, belonging to the Gadites; and Golan, in Bashan, belonging to the Manassites.

41 אָז יַבְדִּיל מֹשֶׁה שָׁלֹשׁ עָרִים בְּעֵבֶר הַיַּרְדֵּן
מִזְרְחָה שָׁמֶשׁ: 42 לָנֻס שָׁמָּה רוֹצֵחַ אֲשֶׁר יִרְצַח
אֶת־רֵעֵהוּ בִּבְלִי־דַעַת וְהוּא לֹא־שֹׂנֵא לוֹ מִתְּמוֹל
שִׁלְשׁוֹם וְנָס אֶל־אַחַת מִן־הֶעָרִים הָאֵל וָחָי: 43
אֶת־בֶּצֶר בַּמִּדְבָּר בְּאֶרֶץ הַמִּישֹׁר לָרֻאוּבֵנִי
וְאֶת־רָאמֹת בַּגִּלְעָד לַגָּדִי וְאֶת־גּוֹלָן בַּבָּשָׁן
לַמְנַשִּׁי:

APPENDIX TO FIRST DISCOURSE: SELECTION OF ASYLUM CITIES IN TRANSJORDAN (vv. 41–43)

Verses 41–43 are not part of Moses' address but a narrative appendix, relating that Moses designated three cities in Transjordan to provide asylum for accidental manslayers.[114] The law establishing these cities appears in 19:1–13 (v. 42 is an abridgement of 19:3–5) and Numbers 35:9–34. According to Numbers 35:14, six such cities were to be chosen, three of them in Transjordan.

41. **Then** This adverb does not necessarily mean that Moses designated the cities after he delivered the address of 1:6–4:40. It could refer to any time after the conquest of Transjordan, which took place shortly *before* the address. It is possible that Moses selected the cities after the actions described in 3:18–29, but that since verses 41–43 are by the narrator, and not Moses, they were placed here to avoid interrupting his address. Nevertheless, the adverb does suggest that the timing of Moses' action was significant. It was not necessary for him to select these cities himself, since Numbers 35:10 stated that all six cities should be provided after Israel crosses the Jordan. According to Deuteronomy Rabba, Moses was reacting to God's denial of his appeal to enter the land (3:26–29): he had expected to designate all six cities himself, after crossing the Jordan, and after that was ruled out, he did what was still possible.[115] This interpretation is consistent with Moses' feelings at this time. As noted in the Comment to verses 21–22, his exclusion from Israel's future is very much on his mind. Here he does what little he can to be involved in that future.[116]

43. The three cities are listed in south-to-north order. For their identification, see Excursus 1.

Bezer, in the wilderness in the Tableland In Moab (for the Tableland see Comment to 3:10).

Ramoth in Gilead That is, upper Gilead (see Comment to 2:36).

Golan in Bashan The location of this city is uncertain. On Bashan see Comment to 3:1.

MOSES' SECOND DISCOURSE: THE COVENANT MADE IN MOAB (4:44–28:69)

Moses' second, and longest, discourse extends from 4:44 through 28:69. Its main subject is the laws that he communicates to the people in Moab, in preparation for Israel's entry into the promised land. They are presented in chapters 12–26. In 5:1–11:30 Moses introduces the laws with a prologue, describing the historical circumstances under which God gave them to him for transmission to the people (5), and a preamble, presenting their ideological basis and appealing for their observance (6:1–11:30). Following the laws Moses describes the mutual commitments made by God and Israel (26:16–19), prescribes ceremonies to reaffirm the covenant upon entering the promised land (27), and proclaims a series of promises and warnings about the consequences that will follow upon Israel's fulfilling or violating the covenant (28:1–68). The discourse concludes with a subscription (28:69).

⁴⁴This is the Teaching that Moses set before the Israelites: ⁴⁵these are the decrees, laws, and rules that Moses addressed to the people of Israel, after they had left Egypt, ⁴⁶beyond the Jordan, in the valley at Beth-peor, in the land of King Sihon of the Amorites, who dwelt in Heshbon, whom Moses and the Israelites defeated after they had left Egypt. ⁴⁷They had taken possession of his country and that of King Og of Bashan—the two kings of the Amorites—which were on the east side of the Jordan ⁴⁸from Aroer on the banks of the wadi Arnon, as far as Mount Sion, that is, Hermon; ⁴⁹also the whole Arabah on the east side of the Jordan, as far as the Sea of the Arabah, at the foot of the slopes of Pisgah.

44 וְזֹאת הַתּוֹרָה אֲשֶׁר־שָׂם מֹשֶׁה לִפְנֵי בְּנֵי
יִשְׂרָאֵל: 45 אֵלֶּה הָעֵדֹת וְהַחֻקִּים וְהַמִּשְׁפָּטִים
אֲשֶׁר דִּבֶּר מֹשֶׁה אֶל־בְּנֵי יִשְׂרָאֵל בְּצֵאתָם
מִמִּצְרָיִם: 46 בְּעֵבֶר הַיַּרְדֵּן בַּגַּיְא מוּל בֵּית פְּעוֹר
בְּאֶרֶץ סִיחֹן מֶלֶךְ הָאֱמֹרִי אֲשֶׁר יוֹשֵׁב בְּחֶשְׁבּוֹן
אֲשֶׁר הִכָּה מֹשֶׁה וּבְנֵי יִשְׂרָאֵל בְּצֵאתָם מִמִּצְרָיִם:
47 וַיִּירְשׁוּ אֶת־אַרְצוֹ וְאֶת־אֶרֶץ | עוֹג מֶלֶךְ־הַבָּשָׁן
שְׁנֵי מַלְכֵי הָאֱמֹרִי אֲשֶׁר בְּעֵבֶר הַיַּרְדֵּן מִזְרַח שָׁמֶשׁ:
48 מֵעֲרֹעֵר אֲשֶׁר עַל־שְׂפַת־נַחַל אַרְנֹן וְעַד־הַר
שִׂיאֹן הוּא חֶרְמוֹן: 49 וְכָל־הָעֲרָבָה עֵבֶר הַיַּרְדֵּן
מִזְרָחָה וְעַד יָם הָעֲרָבָה תַּחַת אַשְׁדֹּת הַפִּסְגָּה: פ

This discourse is framed by references to the earlier covenant made at Mount Sinai, appearing in Moses' opening words and in the concluding subscription (5:2 and 28:69). The core of the discourse, the laws, is also encompassed within framing passages. The laws are preceded and followed by instructions about the ceremonies reaffirming the covenant (11:29–30; chap. 27), and the immediate heading to the laws in 11:32–12:1 is echoed by Moses' remarks at their conclusion (26:16). The chiastic structure of these framing passages may be seen in the following diagram:

A. "The LORD our God made a covenant with us at Horeb" (5:2)
    B. Ceremony at Mounts Ebal and Gerizim (11:29–30)
        C. "Take care to observe all the laws and rules that I have set before you today. These are the laws and rules that you must carefully observe. . ." (11:32–12:1)
            D. The laws (12:2–26:15)
        C'. "The LORD your God commands you this day to observe these laws and rules; take care to observe them. . ." (26:16)
    B'. Ceremonies at Mounts Ebal and Gerizim (chap. 27)
A'. "The covenant which He had made with them at Horeb" (28:69)

HEADING   (vv. 44–49)

The heading describes the contents of this discourse, indicating when and where it was delivered. Since verses 44–46 essentially repeat the contents of 1:1–5, Abravanel holds that the second address is the Teaching to which 1:1–5 refers. In his view, the present recapitulation is necessary because the Teaching was delayed by the long digression of 1:6–4:40.[1] Verse 44 might then be paraphrased as "This, finally, is the Teaching. . . ."

45. *decrees* See Comment to 4:1.

after they had left Egypt Literally, "when they left Egypt." Like the victories mentioned in verse 46, these laws were given to the people forty years after the Exodus, but Deuteronomy refers to the entire period between the Exodus and the arrival in the promised land as "after they/you had left Egypt"; see 23:5; 24:9; 25:17.

48–49. Transjordan is described in terms of its two topographical regions, the highlands (v. 48) and the Jordan Valley (v. 49).

48. *Mount Sion* A third variant of the alternate name for the Hermon, along with Sirion and Senir (see Comment to 3:9). *Si'on* seems to be derived from *si'*, "loftiness," "top," and is not related to the other two names, despite the resemblance. Perhaps it originally referred to a different section of the Hermon.[2]

CHAPTER 5

PROLOGUE TO THE LAWS: THE THEOPHANY AND COVENANT AT HOREB (vv. 1–30)

In the prologue to the laws Moses tells the people how and why the laws were given to him. God began to give them laws forty years earlier, at Horeb (Mount Sinai). After they heard the Decalogue, they were so terrified that they asked Moses to receive God's further instructions on their behalf, promising to obey whatever he conveyed to them. The laws that Moses is about to convey to the people now, forty years later, are what God gave him then. Although first given to the people now, they are an authentic part of the covenant that was initiated with the Decalogue. This information is indispensable, for the validity of the laws rests firmly on their divine authorship and on Moses' legitimacy as the intermediary conveying them to the people. Everything else in Deuteronomy depends on the people's acceptance of these two premises.[3]

The belief that God is the author of the laws is a distinctive feature of Israelite law. Elsewhere in the ancient Near East the laws of society were believed to be the product of human minds. The source of law in Mesopotamia was the king. He claimed to have learned the principles of truth and justice from the gods, but to have turned those principles into specific laws himself. In the Bible not only the principles behind the laws but the laws themselves were believed to have been authored by God and revealed to Israel through His spokesmen, the prophets.[4] This belief reflects the conviction that God is Israel's king, hence its legislator. This belief elevated the status of law beyond matters of practicality and endowed it with sanctity. As a result, obedience to the law—civil no less than moral and ritual law—became a religious duty, not only an act of good citizenship. Obedience made one holy and crimes were sins, a flouting of God's authority.[5] In Deuteronomy Moses states repeatedly that obedience to the laws is the condition stipulated by God in return for the promised land.

Since Israel received God's laws from Moses, there must be no doubt in the people's mind that he is really acting on God's authority. This issue has concerned Moses since he first entered God's service. At the burning bush he was afraid the Israelites would not believe he had been sent by God, and one of the purposes of the ten plagues was to convince Pharaoh that God was really behind Moses. According to Exodus 19:9, God's purpose in speaking to Moses publicly at Sinai was to show the people that He indeed speaks to Moses, so that they would trust Moses. Here in chapter 5 Moses addresses this issue by reminding the people that they had heard God speaking, that his appointment as intermediary was made at *their* request, and that they had promised to obey whatever instructions he brought them from God.

The legitimacy of Moses' intermediation is thus the main thrust of this chapter. Since the people heard the Decalogue themselves, they could have no doubt of *its* divine origin. What needed to be emphasized was that the laws which they did not hear directly from God—those they were receiving now in Moab, forty years later—were also part of the covenant and really came from God.[6] Conceivably, Moses' remarks are made in response to a challenge to this belief. We know that in postbiblical times there was a sect that claimed that only the Decalogue was revealed at Sinai.[7] It is not known whether such a claim was voiced in the biblical period, but Moses' remarks seem designed to preclude challenges to the legitimacy of the remaining laws.

Chapter 5 follows chapter 4 naturally since its two main topics—the Decalogue and Moses' mission to teach the laws—are mentioned in 4:13–14. Both chapters are based on different, but literarily comparable, aspects of the experience at Mount Sinai. Chapter 4 is based primarily on the fact that Israel did not see God at Mount Sinai but heard His voice, from which it concludes that idols may not be used as intermediaries between God and Israel. Chapter 5 is based on the fact that God spoke to Israel "face to face" and that Israel was afraid to hear His voice, and it explains that Moses is God's authorized intermediary. Both chapters continue the practice of chapters 1–3: they teach on the basis of events that the Israelites witnessed personally.

The chapter consists of three parts: the scene at Mount Sinai (vv. 1–5); the Decalogue (vv. 6–18); and the appointment of Moses as intermediary (vv. 19–30). In some respects 6:1–3 are a continuation of the third part; see the introductory Comments to those verses.[8]

5 Moses summoned all the Israelites and said to them: Hear, O Israel, the laws and rules that I proclaim to you this day! Study them and observe them faithfully!

²The LORD our God made a covenant with us at Horeb. ³It was not with our fathers that the LORD made this covenant, but with us, the living, every one of us who is here today. ⁴Face to face the LORD spoke to you on the mountain out of the fire—⁵I stood between the LORD and you at that time to convey the LORD's words to you, for you were afraid of the fire and did not go up the mountain—saying:

ה   רביעי [שלישי לספרדים] וַיִּקְרָ֤א מֹשֶׁה֙ אֶל־
כָּל־יִשְׂרָאֵ֔ל וַיֹּ֥אמֶר אֲלֵהֶ֖ם שְׁמַ֣ע יִשְׂרָאֵ֗ל אֶת־
הַחֻקִּ֤ים וְאֶת־הַמִּשְׁפָּטִים֙ אֲשֶׁ֧ר אָנֹכִ֛י דֹּבֵ֥ר בְּאָזְנֵיכֶ֖ם
הַיֹּ֑ום וּלְמַדְתֶּ֣ם אֹתָ֔ם וּשְׁמַרְתֶּ֖ם לַעֲשֹׂתָֽם׃
² יְהוָ֣ה אֱלֹהֵ֗ינוּ כָּרַ֥ת עִמָּ֛נוּ בְּרִ֖ית בְּחֹרֵֽב׃ 3 לֹ֣א
אֶת־אֲבֹתֵ֔ינוּ כָּרַ֥ת יְהוָ֖ה אֶת־הַבְּרִ֣ית הַזֹּ֑את כִּ֣י
אִתָּ֗נוּ אֲנַ֜חְנוּ אֵ֧לֶּה פֹ֛ה הַיֹּ֖ום כֻּלָּ֥נוּ חַיִּֽים׃ 4 פָּנִ֣ים |
בְּפָנִ֗ים דִּבֶּ֨ר יְהוָ֧ה עִמָּכֶ֛ם בָּהָ֖ר מִתֹּ֥וךְ הָאֵֽשׁ׃
⁵ אָֽנֹכִ֞י עֹמֵ֧ד בֵּין־יְהוָ֛ה וּבֵֽינֵיכֶ֖ם בָּעֵ֣ת הַהִ֑וא
לְהַגִּ֥יד לָכֶ֖ם אֶת־דְּבַ֣ר יְהוָ֑ה כִּ֤י יְרֵאתֶם֙ מִפְּנֵ֣י
הָאֵ֔שׁ וְלֹֽא־עֲלִיתֶ֥ם בָּהָ֖ר לֵאמֹֽר׃   ס

THE SCENE AT HOREB   (vv. 1–5)

1. This introduction is virtually identical to 4:1, save that here the people's obligation to study the laws, so important to Deuteronomy, is made explicit (see Comments to 1:5,18). This passage is cited in halakhic sources as the basis of the law that one whose father failed to teach him Torah is obligated to learn it himself.[9]

the laws and rules   This refers to the laws Moses received from God after the people heard the Decalogue. The Decalogue itself is called "the covenant" or "the (ten) words" (4:13).

2. Since this verse is reminiscent of the beginning of the first discourse (1:6), it can be read as a reminder: you saw what happened when you violated one command given by God at Horeb (that in 1:7–8); do not violate the covenant He made with you there.

made a covenant   Here "covenant" does not refer to the Decalogue alone (as in 4:13) but to the relationship that God established with Israel at Horeb, where Israel agreed to do *all* that the Lord commanded,[10] including the laws that Moses would later give Israel in Moab (vv. 24, 28).

The Hebrew idiom, literally "cut a covenant," is apparently derived from a ceremony in which parties to a covenant would cut up an animal to signify their acceptance of a like fate in case they should violate the agreement.[11] The idiom was used even where a covenant was ratified by other ceremonies, as in the present case (see Exod. 24:1–8). See Comment to 29:9–20.

3–4. The covenant at Mount Sinai was not made in the distant past but with those whom Moses is addressing. They know from personal experience that God did speak to Israel directly and made the covenant with it. See Comment to 4:9 for Moses' audience's eyewitness sense of those events. Compare 11:2–7, where Moses says that he is not addressing his audience's children, who did not personally witness the Exodus and subsequent events that he cites.

It was not with our fathers   Abraham, Isaac, and Jacob. In Deuteronomy, "our/your fathers" always refers to the patriarchs.

4. Verse 5 states that the people sent Moses to hear God on their behalf because they were terrified by the fire on Mount Sinai. The present verse makes it clear that they nevertheless heard God directly long enough to know that it was really He speaking. What they heard, according to verse 19, was the Decalogue. This indicates that "saying" at the end of verse 5 is a continuation of verse 4 and that the rest of verse 5 is parenthetic.[12]

Face to face   That is, in person, without intermediation. "Face" is used in the same sense in 4:37.[13] The idiom does not mean that Israel literally saw God's face. That is ruled out by the fact that God spoke from within fire and clouds and that Israel saw no visual image (see vv. 4b,20–21; 4:12).

5. This verse seems to contradict verse 4 by indicating that Moses stood between God and the people in order to transmit the Decalogue to them. Perhaps the verse does not mean that Moses

actually did so, but that that had been his (and the people's) intention and that God had overruled it: in their fright the people sent Moses ahead to hear God for them, but God insisted on their hearing Him directly. Most commentators explain that the people heard God's voice but were too distant to hear His words distinctly and Moses had to repeat the words for them.[14] However, it is hard to believe that God could not speak audibly. Another possibility is that the verse reflects a variant tradition according to which the people did not hear God directly, or that it is an attempt to resolve the confusing picture in Exodus 19–20, which leaves unclear whether Moses was up on the mountain when God proclaimed the Decalogue, or down below with the people.[15] Talmudic exegesis resolves the inconsistency in Solomonic fashion by explaining that the people heard the first two commandments, in which God speaks in the first person, directly from God, and the remainder, in which God is spoken of in the third person, from Moses.[16]

THE DECALOGUE (vv. 6–18)[17]

Moses repeats the Decalogue, which was first presented in Exodus 20. He does not repeat the text verbatim. Most of the differences from the wording of Exodus are minor but some, especially in the Sabbath commandment, are substantial. Moses does not repeat the Decalogue here for its own sake but as evidence that God spoke to Israel and gave them laws, and that the subsequent laws, which he is now about to give the people, and which implement the principles of the Decalogue, are also from God.[18]

The Decalogue epitomizes God's requirements of the Israelites as individuals and as a nation. It is not formulated in the usual, impersonal style of laws but is addressed directly to the people, reflecting the biblical attitude that the law must be known by all, not only by specialists (see Comment to 1:18). The fact that the people are addressed in the singular emphasizes the responsibility of each individual, while their collective responsibility is indicated by the fact that the commandments were proclaimed in a public assembly to the entire nation.

The Decalogue consists of a series of prohibitions banning conduct unacceptable to God; even the two commandments formulated positively entail prohibitions. The commandments cover interpersonal as well as religious behavior: both are subject to God's will. Most laws in the Bible are stated in casuistic form ("If a person does X, then he/the authorities shall do Y") because their applicability depends on circumstances. The Ten Commandments are given as unconditional imperatives ("You shall not," "You shall") because they are applicable in all circumstances. Nor are specific punishments stated, as they are elsewhere in the Torah. Here the primary motivating factor for obedience is not fear of punishment but God's absolute authority and the people's desire to live in accordance with His will.

The commandments are arranged in two groups that deal respectively with conduct toward God and toward fellow humans. Within each group they are arranged in descending order, according to the gravity of the prohibited offense. Duties to God come first, since the commandments presuppose His authority and their very purpose is to serve as the terms of Israel's covenant with Him. Worshiping other gods or idols would be a direct repudiation of God's demand for exclusive loyalty; hence such worship is prohibited in the first two commandments. Swearing falsely in God's name would imply contempt for Him and His ability to punish (third commandment), while violation of God's Sabbath would constitute disrespect for matters sacred to Him (fourth commandment). Duties toward fellow humans begin with honoring one's parents (fifth commandment). It is the first to follow those having to do with honoring God because it is a counterpart to the honor due Him; it thus forms a bridge between duties toward God and toward man. The last five commandments begin with the prohibition of taking another's life (sixth commandment) and proceed to taking his wife (seventh commandment) and property (eighth commandment), then to an indirect means of acquiring another's property, by false testimony (ninth commandment), and finally to a prohibition of coveting another's property (tenth commandment).

The divine orientation of the first five commandments is reflected in the phrase "the LORD your God," which appears in each of them. All but the last of these five are uniquely Israelite duties. Because the reasons for them are not well known or self-understood, or because they are easy to violate, the entire group is accompanied by explanatory comments or by exhortations that encourage

their observance. The remaining five commandments are universally recognized ethical requirements and need no such support.

These Ten Commandments are the initial stipulations of the covenant made at Mount Sinai (4:13,23; 5:2–3).[19] Since the first century C.E. they have been viewed as a summary of biblical law or as headings for all its categories.[20] They do indeed relate to most of the categories of law governing conduct toward God and man. In so doing, they introduce the Israelites to the areas governed by God's legislation and provide an apt introduction to the detailed laws (*ḥukkim* and *mishpatim*) that Moses will subsequently communicate to them.

The reference to these commandments in 4:13 and 10:4 as "the ten words" (i.e., commandments or articles) makes it clear that there are ten of them. Because of the ambiguous role of the first sentence and the fact that there are more than ten imperative verbs in the commandments, there are different views about precisely how the ten commandments are to be divided. Here we follow the view of Philo and Josephus and some talmudic sources, which seems closest to the sense of the text.[21] It differs from the traditional enumeration found on tablets in synagogues and art primarily in the way it divides the first two commandments. For the two tablets on which the Decalogue was written, see Comment to 4:13.

There are two systems of cantillation of the Decalogue, known as the lower and the upper notes. The Leningrad Codex and many other Hebrew editions of the Torah combine both systems in their texts of the Decalogue. For greater clarity, this edition follows editions that present the lower notes in chapter 5 and a separate copy of the Decalogue, with the upper notes, immediately after Chapter 34. The significance of the two systems and the occasions on which each is used are discussed there as well.

THE FIRST COMMANDMENT:
ISRAEL MAY HAVE NO OTHER GODS BUT THE LORD (vv. 6–7)

Commentators have long debated whether verse 6 is an introduction to the entire Decalogue,[22] the beginning of the first commandment,[23] or a command in itself (such as to believe in God or to acknowledge Him exclusively).[24] The last view is unlikely since there is no imperative verb in the verse and the very notion of commanding beliefs is dubious.[25] The first two views seem correct: the verse appears to function both as a general introduction to the entire Decalogue and as an introduction to the first command in particular.

As an introduction to the entire Decalogue, which is an oracular utterance from God, this verse is paralleled in other oracles where God identifies Himself by name, usually at the beginning or the end, to solemnly indicate that His authority stands behind promises or commands.[26] By adding that it was He who freed the Israelites from bondage, God establishes the basis on which He expects them to accept His authority.[27]

The verse also serves as part of the first commandment, "you shall have no other gods beside Me." This is indicated by other passages in which God likewise identifies Himself as the God who freed Israel from Egypt and prohibits the worship of other gods, and which seem to allude to the present passage (Judg. 6:8–10; Ps. 81:9–11). In these passages, God stipulates that since He and no other deity freed Israel from Egypt, He alone is Israel's God, and the worship of other gods is prohibited. Seen in this light, verse 6 is an introductory motive clause that grounds the first commandment in moral obligation and good sense.[28] For a similarly positioned motive clause, see 14:1.

The obligation to worship YHVH alone because He alone freed Israel from Egypt is the central doctrine of biblical religion, which is based on the historical experience of the Israelites (see Comment to 4:9).[29] The logic is that of the covenant (Heb. *berit*), the term used in verse 2 to designate the relationship established at Horeb (cf. Exod. 19:3–8). As noted in the Introduction, the concept of a covenant between the Lord and Israel is modeled on ancient suzerainty treaties, in which a weaker king accepted a more powerful one as his suzerain, and possibly also on royal covenants in which a citizenry accepted someone as its king. Such covenants established relationships that were inherently exclusive: a subject population or king could have only one sovereign or suzerain, and ancient oaths of allegiance and treaties explicitly prohibit subjects and vassals from accepting another.[30] The basis on which subjects entered into such relationships was the past benefactions of the king or suzerain to the subject, often his delivering them from enemies.[31] The covenant was thus an apt metaphor for Israel's exclusive relationship with YHVH because of the Exodus.[32]

[6]I the LORD am your God who brought you out of the land of Egypt, the house of bondage: [7]You shall have no other gods beside Me.

6 אָנֹכִי יְהוָה אֱלֹהֶיךָ אֲשֶׁר הוֹצֵאתִיךָ מֵאֶרֶץ מִצְרַיִם מִבֵּית עֲבָדִים: 7 לֹא־יִהְיֶה לְךָ אֱלֹהִים אֲחֵרִים עַל־פָּנָי:

brought you out   That is, liberated. "Bring out" has more than a geographic meaning. As distinct from "take" or "bring up," it has the connotation of releasing or saving,[33] just as "go out" is used for going free from bondage (Exod. 21:1–11).

house of bondage   Literally, "house of slaves," perhaps a term for slave barracks.[34] This is a common biblical designation for Egypt, expressing vividly what God saved Israel from.[35] Ralbag's paraphrase, "a house that was shut up tight . . . like a house where slaves are kept, which is closed tight to prevent escape,"[36] recalls the walls and fortresses along the eastern frontier of Egypt that impeded the escape of both citizens and slaves.[37] Throughout the second millennium B.C.E., Egypt captured and bought large numbers of slaves from neighboring lands.[38] Much of the native Egyptian population was owned by the temples and dominated by a monarchy of unparalleled power.[39] The designation of Egypt as a slave barracks could refer to either of these phenomena.

7.   Unlike 4:35–39, this commandment is less a theological statement, denying the existence of other gods, than a practical, behavioral injunction ruling out relationships with any of the other beings and objects known as gods (see below). This prohibition, banning the worship of all but one deity, is unique in the history of religion. Polytheism was inherently tolerant of the worship of many gods since no single god was thought to control all the phenomena that are vital for human life. The gods themselves were believed to tolerate this pluralism, and several could be worshiped in the same sanctuary or addressed in the same prayer.[40] The biblical demand for monolatry (see Excursus 6) was consistently based on the argument that the worship of other gods would be unjustified and pointless, since the Lord alone liberated Israel and provides for all her needs.[41] This is the point of introducing the command with verse 6.[42]

you shall have no other gods   As in English, "have" means to be in a relationship with; it is the same idiom that is used for establishing family relationships, especially marriage.[43] In the Bible it is a fundamental idiom for the establishment of the covenant relationship between God and Israel, as in "I will take you to be My people, and I will be your God" (Exod. 6:7) and "I will be your God and you shall be My people" (Lev. 26:12). Compare Deuteronomy 26:17–18; 27:9.[44] In practical terms the commandment means that Israelites may have no relationship of any kind with other gods: they may not build altars, sanctuaries, or images to them, make offerings to them, consult them, prophesy or take oaths in their names, or even mention their names. This is made clear in verse 9 and elsewhere in the Torah.[45]

other gods   As noted in the Comment to 3:24, the Hebrew terms for "god" (*'el* and *'elohim*) can be used for angels, spirits, idols, and pagan deities as well as God Himself. All but the last are "other gods" and their worship is prohibited.[46] Commentators have sought to explain why these beings are called gods after 4:35 and 39 have stated that there are no other gods but YHVH. Some suggest that the text merely adopts the terminology of those who had worshiped those beings in order to be understood by them.[47] In any case, traditional language is slow to change even after it becomes theologically obsolete; for example, Exodus 15:11, "Who is like You among the gods, O LORD," remains part of the Jewish liturgy to this day, and Deuteronomy, like other monotheistic writings (e.g., Ps. 66:8), continued to use words meaning "gods" in their other senses, too (see Deut. 3:24; 10:17; 7:4,25; 21:23).[48]

beside me   Hebrew *'al panai*, "in addition to Me." Like the idiom "have no other god," the complementary phrase "beside Me" also echoes an idiom from marital relations, as in Laban's demand that Jacob not "take other wives beside [*'al*] my daughters" (Gen. 31:50).[49] This commandment recognizes that Israelites tempted to worship other gods would not abandon YHVH but would worship others *in addition* to Him. As noted above, polytheists do not choose one god to the exclusion of others, but worship many.[50] See Comments to 4:2,19; 13:6.

8You shall not make for yourself a sculptured image, any likeness of what is in the heavens above, or on the earth below, or in the waters below the earth. 9You shall not bow down to them or serve them. For I the LORD your God am an impassioned God, visiting the guilt of the

8 לֹא-תַעֲשֶׂה-לְךָ פֶסֶל כָּל-תְּמוּנָה אֲשֶׁר בַּשָּׁמַיִם מִמַּעַל וַאֲשֶׁר בָּאָרֶץ מִתָּחַת וַאֲשֶׁר בַּמַּיִם מִתַּחַת לָאָרֶץ: 9 לֹא-תִשְׁתַּחֲוֶה לָהֶם וְלֹא תָעָבְדֵם כִּי אָנֹכִי יְהוָה אֱלֹהֶיךָ אֵל קַנָּא פֹּקֵד

THE SECOND COMMANDMENT: PROHIBITION OF IDOLS (vv. 8–10)

8. The ban on idols immediately follows the command against worshiping other gods. The text does not distinguish between idols of the Lord and idols of other gods. Since idolaters often spoke of idols as if they were gods, not merely symbols of gods, and since the Bible insists that no statue can be the Lord, it considers any idol as de facto *another* god no matter whom or what the worshiper identifies it with.[51] The reference to God's jealousy thus applies to the second commandment as well as the first; this is why it comes only after the second.

For details of this commandment and the reasons for it see Comments to 4:15–19 and 28.

a sculptured image, any likeness of what is in the heavens   Better: "an idol of the visage of anything that is in the heavens"; see Comment to 4:16.[52] The language of this verse is more inclusive than that in 4:16–18, which prohibits idols of animate creatures only. "Anything that is in the heavens . . . on the earth", etc. would also include images of inanimate objects, such as stars, sacred trees, sacred garments, and the like.[53]

9-10.   These verses fuse the first two commandments into a single concept with a shared warning. Although these verses follow the ban on idols (v. 8), their warning of God's "jealousy" applies at least as well to the prohibition of other gods (v. 7), just as it does in 6:14–15, Exodus 34:14, and Joshua 24:19–20. Also pointing to a connection with verses 6–8 is the fact that God continues to speak in the first person through verse 10 (from v. 11 on He is referred to in the third person). Both commandments contain the phrase "I . . . the LORD your God," which appears in the first and last sentences of verses 6–10, forming a frame around them and delineating them as a unit.[54] These shared features are probably why rabbinic exegesis considered verses 7–10 a single commandment and why the Masoretic paragraphing treats all of verses 6–10 as a single unit.[55]

9. bow down . . . serve   Each of these verbs has a technical meaning. "Bowing" refers to prostration; "serving" often refers to making offerings. When the two are paired they refer more broadly to any form of worship or submission.[56]

them   The various types of idols mentioned in verse 8 and the other gods mentioned in verse 7.[57] The combination of idols and other gods reinforces the position of the commandments (and the Bible as a whole) that any idol is de facto another god.

an impassioned God   Hebrew *kanna'* combines the meanings of "jealous" and "zealous" (the two English words themselves have a common origin). Etymologically, *kanna'* is similar to "fervent" and "incensed," which come from words referring to heat and fire. The root *k-n-'* apparently means "become dark red." It is often associated with fire (see 4:24) and refers primarily to fiery passions such as love, anger, indignation, and jealousy,[58] particularly "the resentful rage of one whose prerogatives have been usurped by, or given to, another" (M. Greenberg).[59] In the Torah the Lord's *kin'ah* is provoked by the worship of idols and other gods.[60] In these contexts God's outrage includes jealousy: He does not tolerate the honor due Him being given to another (see Isa. 42:8, "I am the LORD . . . I will not yield My glory to another, nor My renown to idols"; similarly in Isa. 48:11).[61] The term reflects the emotional tie between God and Israel that was described metaphorically by the prophets as a marital bond in which the Lord is like a husband and Israel a wife.[62] This metaphor befits the exclusiveness of the relationship: Israel must restrict her fidelity to one God, just as a wife owes exclusive fidelity to her husband; worship of other gods is thus as repugnant as adultery (Exod. 34:15–16; Ezek. 16), and God's reaction to such an offense, like that of an aggrieved husband, is jealousy (cf. Num. 5:14 and Prov. 6:34, where *k-n-'* refers to a husband's jealousy over his unfaithful wife).[63]

parents upon the children, upon the third and upon the fourth generations of those who reject Me, ¹⁰but showing

עֲוֹן אָבֹת עַל־בָּנֶים וְעַל־שִׁלֵּשִׁים וְעַל־רִבֵּעֶים לְשֹׂנְאָי: ¹⁰ וְעֹשֶׂה חֶסֶד לַאֲלָפֶים לְאֹהֲבַי

Postbiblical commentators found the implications of divine jealousy troubling, since jealousy was considered a character defect tantamount to envy, as an emotion that controls one who experiences it, or as seeming to concede that there is substance to false gods.[64] Maimonides explained the Bible's use of terms like "jealous," which ascribe human feelings to God, as mere anthropopathisms based on the necessity of borrowing terms from human experience to describe God based on his actions: "Whenever any one of His actions is perceived by us, we ascribe to God that emotion which is the source of that act when performed by ourselves. . . . [In reality, his punitive actions] are in accordance with the guilt of those who are to be punished, and not the result of any emotion; for He is above all defect!"[65] In the biblical view, however, God's *kin'ah* is an aspect of His passionate involvement with man; it is no more considered a flaw than is jealousy over marital infidelity.[66] Nevertheless, His *kin'ah* was apparently thought to be of a different quality from that of humans; the adjectival forms *kanna'* and *kanno'* are used exclusively for God, never for jealous humans.

God's *kin'ah* not only explains why He forbids worship of other gods. References to His *kin'ah* are usually accompanied by a description of His punitive action or power, as in the remainder of this verse. The very mention of God's jealousy is therefore a warning against provoking it.[67]

visiting the guilt of the parents upon the children The warning implied by God's passionate jealousy is explicated by a description of its extent: the punishment will not be limited to the idolater alone, but will last for generations.[68] "Visiting the parents' guilt" means inflicting punishment for their guilt upon their descendants.[69] The next verse indicates that God likewise rewards descendants for their ancestors' loyalty and obedience to Him. This view of divine retribution as extending to descendants corresponds to the concept of family solidarity that was felt strongly in ancient societies, especially those with a tribal background. This view was progressively modified in the Bible in the direction of the principle that individuals should be rewarded and punished only for their own deeds. See Excursus 8 and Comments to "those who reject me" and "those who love Me" in verses 9–10.

upon the third and . . . fourth generations That is, upon grandchildren and great-grandchildren (or upon great- and great-great-grandchildren, if the parents are not counted as the first generation).[70] Living to see three or four generations of descendants is as long as one could naturally live.[71] Thus God extends punishment only to descendants the guilty are likely to see in their own lifetimes.[72] This indicates that the suffering of the descendants is intended as a deterrent to, and punishment of, their ancestors, not a transfer of guilt to the descendants in their own right.[73]

those who reject me Hebrew *sane'* means literally "hate." This verb and its counterpart in the next verse, *'ohev*, are often used in describing family relationships and, in a derived sense, political relationships. *Sane'* refers to types of disaffection that can arise in such relationships: a husband or father may disfavor one of his wives or children, members of a group may reject one of their number, and enemies are described literally as "haters." The verb *sane'* is also used of the disaffection that leads to divorce. It is unlikely that a polytheistic Israelite would literally hate, or even reject, the Lord; at worst one might worship Him together with other gods or ignore Him. However, since the Lord demands exclusive fidelity, the Bible views the worship of another god alongside of Him as tantamount to rejecting Him.[74]

The position of the phrase "those who reject Me" and the corresponding "those who love Me" (v. 10) at the end of their verses makes the verses culminate in descriptions of human behavior since that, and not God's attributes for their own sake, is what they seek to emphasize.[75] These two phrases apparently refer to descendants who act as their ancestors did, meaning that God "visits the guilt of the parents on future generations—that is, future generations that reject Him—and rewards the loyalty of ancestors to the thousandth generation of descendants—that is, descendants who are also loyal to Him." In other words, He punishes or rewards descendants for ancestral sins and virtues *along with their own*, but only if they "continue the deeds of their ancestors." Otherwise, descendants are not affected by their ancestors' behavior at all. For further discussion see Excursus 8.

kindness to the thousandth generation of those who love Me and keep My commandments.

¹¹You shall not swear falsely by the name of the LORD your God; for the LORD will not clear one who swears falsely by His name.

וּלְשֹׁמְרֵי מִצְוֺתוֹ: ס
11 לֹא תִשָּׂא אֶת־שֵׁם־יְהוָה אֱלֹהֶיךָ לַשָּׁוְא כִּי לֹא יְנַקֶּה יְהוָה אֵת אֲשֶׁר־יִשָּׂא אֶת־שְׁמוֹ לַשָּׁוְא: ס

v. 10. מִצְוֺתָי ק'

10. showing kindness Better "keeping faith" or "dealing faithfully," as in 1 Samuel 20:8 and 2 Samuel 9:1; 10:2; compare Deuteronomy 7:9. The basic meaning of *ḥesed* is acts of kindness of the type that can be expected between parties in a relationship—husband and wife, parents and children, relatives, and allies—and repayment of kindnesses. Thus Joseph asks the cupbearer, whose dream he had interpreted favorably, to "keep faith with me and mention me to Pharaoh" (Gen. 40:14) and David asks Jonathan to "deal faithfully with your servant, since you have taken your servant into a covenant of the LORD with you" (1 Sam. 20:8).[76] Our verse assures Israel that the Lord will faithfully reciprocate the devotion and obedience of the people whom He has taken into a covenant relationship.[77]

to the thousandth generation This indicates that God's kindness far exceeds His wrath, which extends only to the third and fourth generation.

of those who love Me and keep My commandments On the point of the phrase, see Comment on "those who reject Me" in verse 9. In biblical Hebrew, "love" includes friendship and loyalty, including the loyalty of allies and of a vassal toward his suzerain.[78] In Deuteronomy, love and loyalty toward God is virtually synonymous with keeping His commandments; it refers to an emotional attachment which is expressed in action (see, e.g., 10:12–13; 11:1,22). See Comment to 6:5.

THE THIRD COMMANDMENT: PROHIBITION OF FALSE OATHS (v. 11)

swear falsely by the name of the LORD[79] Assertions in court, in public affairs, and even in ordinary conversation were often backed up with oaths that included God's name.[80] These were conditional self-curses that would take effect if the swearer's assertion was not true or his promise was not fulfilled. The normal formulations were: "By the life of the LORD, I will [or will not] . . . ," or: "May the LORD do such and such to me if I did [or didn't] . . ." The swearer proved his sincerity by calling down punishment on himself from God, who cannot be deceived or evaded. A false oath would show contempt for God by implying that the swearer does not fear His punishment. Hence Leviticus 19:12 admonishes, "You shall not swear falsely by My name, profaning the name of your God."[81]

Literally, the commandment reads "Do not take the LORD's name for a vain thing." Since Leviticus 19:12 explicitly forbids swearing falsely in God's name, and since the rabbis believed that no two commandments have exactly the same meaning, they presumed that this commandment refers to something else, namely oaths that can make no difference, such as affirming a known fact or promising the impossible,[82] and other frivolous uses of God's name, such as uttering superfluous blessings and praying without devotion.[83] (The popular view that this commandment is the basis of the prohibition of pronouncing or writing God's name is groundless; see Excursus 4.)

will not clear Rather, "will not leave unpunished."[84] The translation "clear" implies an oath taken by someone accused of wrongdoing, but oaths were also taken in business, political affairs, and other situations. The point of this motive clause is that if one swears falsely, "even if he escapes human justice, he will not escape divine justice" (Shadal). This belief was taken seriously throughout the ancient world; in an Egyptian penitential prayer, a man confesses that his suffering is a punishment for taking a false oath in the name of a deity.[85]

THE FOURTH COMMANDMENT: OBSERVING THE SABBATH (vv. 12–15)

The first three commandments prohibit actions that show disrespect for the Lord. The fourth requires a positive act of honoring Him by observing a day sacred to Him. The positive formulation

12Observe the sabbath day and keep it holy, as the LORD your God has commanded you. 13Six days you shall labor and do all your work, 14but the seventh day is a sabbath of the LORD your God; you shall not do any work—you,

שָׁמ֛וֹר אֶת־י֥וֹם הַשַּׁבָּ֖ת לְקַדְּשׁ֑וֹ כַּאֲשֶׁ֥ר צִוְּךָ֖ ׀ יְהוָ֥ה אֱלֹהֶֽיךָ׃ 13 שֵׁ֤שֶׁת יָמִים֙ תַּֽעֲבֹ֔ד וְעָשִׂ֖יתָ כָּל־ מְלַאכְתֶּֽךָ׃ 14 וְי֙וֹם֙ הַשְּׁבִיעִ֔י שַׁבָּ֖ת ׀ לַיהוָ֣ה אֱלֹהֶ֑יךָ לֹ֣א תַעֲשֶׂ֣ה כָל־מְלָאכָ֡ה אַתָּ֣ה ׀ וּבִנְךָֽ־וּבִתֶּ֡ךָ

of the commandment expresses the fact that the Sabbath is sanctified not merely by acts of abstention but by ceremonies that foster contact with the divine (see below).[86]

12.   Observe   That is, celebrate the day by following its prescribed procedures;[87] the verb *shamar* is commonly used for keeping a holiday and fulfilling obligations (see, e.g., Exod. 12:17; 23:15; Deut. 29:8). The earlier version of the Decalogue (Exod. 20:8) uses the verb "remember," meaning "remember to observe the Sabbath."

the sabbath day   The seventh day of each week. The Bible understands the word "sabbath" (Heb. *shabbat*) as a derivative of the verb *sh-b-t*, "cease," "desist" (Exod. 23:12; Lev. 23:32).[88] "The sabbath day" thus means "the day of desistance (from labor)."

and keep it holy   "Holy" in biblical Hebrew means withdrawn from common use and reserved for a special purpose associated with God. The Sabbath day is withdrawn from common use by desisting from labor. Its dedication to God was expressed by visits to sanctuaries and prophets (2 Kings 4:23; Isa. 1:13; 66:23), by special sacrifices and other activities in the temple (Num. 28:9–10; Lev. 24:8), by the recitation of a special psalm for the day (Ps. 92), and by a joyous atmosphere (Hos. 2:13; Isa. 58:13; Lam. 2:6).

In the Exodus version of the Decalogue it is clear that keeping the Sabbath holy is an emulation of God's actions at the time of creation. Exodus states that God created the world in six days and rested on the seventh, and concludes: "Therefore the LORD blessed the sabbath day and made it holy" (Exod. 20:11; see Gen. 2:3). The fact that Sabbath observance is an emulation of God's activity and an acknowledgment of His creation of the world explains why observing it honors Him. It explains, too, why the Sabbath command is the longest in the Decalogue and why it is sometimes paired with the prohibition of idolatry:[89] like the latter commandment, observing the Sabbath is one of the quintessential expressions of loyalty to God. Deuteronomy explains the Sabbath differently; see verses 14–15.

as the LORD your God has commanded you   That is, as you were already commanded. This is a technical formula by which Deuteronomy refers to the sources that it relies on.[90] It appears in the Decalogue only here and in the next commandment. Since these two commandments are formulated positively, requiring more than simple avoidance of prohibited acts, the text assumes that they are more in need of cross-reference to detailed instructions than the eight negative commandments are. The Sabbath rules are abundantly attested earlier in the Torah (see the next two Comments).

14.   a sabbath of the LORD your God   The day belongs to the Lord, and it must therefore be used for the Lord's purposes, not one's own purposes (cf. Isa. 58:13). This explains why certain activities which may not be performed for human benefit on the Sabbath are permitted in the Temple, such as burning the sacrifices and kindling the lamps (Exod. 27:20–21; 29:38–42; Num. 28:9–10). (See also Comment to 15:2, "for the remission proclaimed is of the LORD.")

you shall not do any work   All kinds of work are prohibited. Examples of what constitutes work, such as agricultural labor, gathering food and firewood, kindling fire, and business activities, are mentioned elsewhere in the Bible.[91] Postbiblical exegesis worked out more precisely what kinds of work fell under this prohibition. From the juxtaposition of Exodus 25:1–31:11 and 31:12–17 the rabbis reasonably inferred that all categories of labor required in constructing the Tabernacle— thirty-nine in all—were prohibited on the Sabbath.[92]

The "you" addressed in this commandment must include both males and females, since both are specified in the following list of those covered by this law ("your son or your daughter, your male or female slave"). This implies that in general, biblical laws are addressed to males and females alike. See Comment to 12:7.

your son or your daughter, your male or female slave, your ox or your ass, or any of your cattle, or the stranger in your settlements, so that your male and female slave may rest as you do. [15]Remember that you were a slave in the land of Egypt and the LORD your God freed you from there with a mighty hand and an outstretched arm; therefore the LORD your God has commanded you to observe the sabbath day.

וְעַבְדְּךָ־וַאֲמָתֶךָ וְשׁוֹרְךָ וַחֲמֹרְךָ וְכָל־בְּהֶמְתֶּךָ וְגֵרְךָ אֲשֶׁר בִּשְׁעָרֶיךָ לְמַעַן יָנוּחַ עַבְדְּךָ וַאֲמָתְךָ כָּמוֹךָ: [15] וְזָכַרְתָּ כִּי־עֶבֶד הָיִיתָ בְּאֶרֶץ מִצְרַיִם וַיֹּצִאֲךָ יְהוָה אֱלֹהֶיךָ מִשָּׁם בְּיָד חֲזָקָה וּבִזְרֹעַ נְטוּיָה עַל־כֵּן צִוְּךָ יְהוָה אֱלֹהֶיךָ לַעֲשׂוֹת אֶת־יוֹם הַשַּׁבָּת: ס

your male or female slave   The term "slave" covers both outright slaves and bondservants or peons (see introductory Comment to 15:12). No distinction is made here between Israelite and foreign slaves.

your ox or your ass, or any of your cattle   Kindness to animals is the theme of several other laws in the Torah.[93]

the stranger in your settlements   The stranger is the *ger*, the resident alien. See Comment to 1:16. This reminder to include resident aliens in the Sabbath rest is comparable to Deuteronomy's exhortations to include them in religious celebrations (16:11,14; 26:11). Such reminders are necessary because of the aliens' vulnerability and the likelihood that their needs would be overlooked. The motive given for the Sabbath in Exodus 23:12 is indicative of the low status they might hold as well as the Torah's solicitude for their welfare: labor is forbidden "in order that your ox and your ass may rest, and that your bondman and the stranger [i.e., the resident alien] may be refreshed."

the stranger   Literally, "your stranger." See Comment to 1:16.

so that your male and female slave may rest as you do   This statement of the aim of the Sabbath is not found in Exodus 20, which explains only its origin. It is reminiscent of the motive stated in Exodus 23:12, just quoted. Here, however, only the benefit to servants, not cattle, is emphasized, since that benefit speaks to the Israelites' recent experience as slaves and is recalled in the motive clause of verse 15. Because of that experience, humane treatment of servants became a regular concern of biblical law.[94]

Although all must abstain from labor on the Sabbath, this explanation emphasizes only the benefit to servants. The law seems to assume that the householder will in any case find time for himself and his family to rest, but may neglect the servants' need to do so. It is as if the entire household is required to rest so that there can be no occasion to make the servants work. This one day a week the servant is treated as the master's equal.

15.   The experiences of servitude and redemption are recalled in order to motivate observance of several humanitarian laws in Deuteronomy (see 15:15; 16:12; 24:18,22). Commentators are divided over what this motive emphasizes. Some believe that it is the memory of servitude, in order to create empathy for the servant's need to rest. Others believe that it is God's redemption of Israel, in order either to remind Israel of His kindness, to establish His authority to issue such a command, or to encourage the Israelites to emulate Him by temporarily relieving their servants' bondage.

In place of Deuteronomy's statement of the aim of the Sabbath and its motivating reference to the redemption from Egypt, the Exodus Decalogue mentions the origin of the Sabbath in God's cessation from labor after the creation (see also Gen. 2:1–3; Exod. 31:17). These references are not mutually exclusive but serve different functions: Exodus explains the origin of the Sabbath, while Deuteronomy explains its aim and offers a motive for observing it. Perhaps Deuteronomy intentionally avoids explaining its origin because the concept of God resting was not compatible with the book's less anthropomorphic view of God (see the Introduction).

THE FIFTH COMMANDMENT: HONORING PARENTS (v. 16)

Honoring of parents is first among duties toward other human beings, just as it is first among the laws of holiness in Leviticus 19:3. One aspect of this duty is respect, which includes obedience to parents[95] and adherence to their teachings[96] and forbids hitting, insulting, and behaving disrespect-

16Honor your father and your mother, as the LORD your God has commanded you, that you may long endure, and that you may fare well, in the land that the LORD your God is assigning to you.

17You shall not murder.

16 כַּבֵּד אֶת־אָבִיךָ וְאֶת־אִמֶּךָ כַּאֲשֶׁר צִוְּךָ יְהוָה אֱלֹהֶיךָ לְמַעַן ׀ יַאֲרִיכֻן יָמֶיךָ וּלְמַעַן יִיטַב לָךְ עַל הָאֲדָמָה אֲשֶׁר־יְהוָה אֱלֹהֶיךָ נֹתֵן לָךְ: ס
17 לֹא תִרְצָח: ס

fully toward them[97] and misappropriating their property.[98] Another aspect is caring for parents when they require it (this commandment, like the Decalogue as a whole, is not addressed merely to youngsters; see v. 14). This aspect of the commandment is recognized in the Talmud: "What is honoring? Providing them food and drink, clothing and covers, and taking them in and out."[99] Care of one's aged parents is one of the fundamental duties spelled out in adoption contracts and other documents of the ancient Near East.[100] The Akkadian cognate of *kabbed*, "honor," is one of the verbs used to describe such care.[101]

The juxtaposition of this commandment with the Sabbath is paralleled in Leviticus 19:3, where they also appear side by side: "You shall each revere his mother and father, and keep My sabbaths: I the LORD am your God." These are also the only positive commandments in the Decalogue and the only ones containing the clause "as the LORD your God commanded you." The connection between these two commandments probably lies in the idea that observing the Sabbath is a means of honoring God and is thus a counterpart to honoring parents. (Note that Isa. 58:13 also calls for "honoring" the Sabbath.) The fact that honoring parents appears among the first five commandments, all of which deal with honoring God and mention His name, indicates how important this commandment was considered to be. Other ancient societies, too, ranked the honor of parents second only to the honor of the gods.[102]

your father and your mother Commands relating to honoring parents invariably name father and mother on an equal footing. The command to revere them in Leviticus 19:3 mentions the mother first, in contrast to the present commandment. Talmudic exegesis explained that the child naturally reveres his father more because he teaches him Torah, and he naturally honors his mother more because she sways him with persuasive words; accordingly, the Torah emphasized that it is also necessary to honor one's father and revere one's mother since both are equal.[103]

as the LORD your God has commanded you See Comment to verse 12. Earlier commands pertaining to honoring parents are mentioned in Exodus and Leviticus; see above.

that you may long endure on the land This is the only commandment in the Decalogue for which a reward is promised, though the promise can be read as a veiled threat ("otherwise your days will be shortened").[104] The promise of enduring in the promised land is attached elsewhere to other commandments (e.g., Deut. 4:40; 25:15). Yet there may be a reason that the Decalogue attaches this promise to this particular command. Some of the legal documents mentioned above make children's right to inherit their parents' property contingent on honoring their parents by providing and caring for them. Here God applies the same condition on a national scale: the right of future generations of Israelites to inherit the land of Israel from their parents is contingent upon honoring them.[105]

that you may fare well This reward does not appear in the Exodus version of this commandment (Exod. 20:12). It is characteristic of Deuteronomy (see, e.g., 4:40; 5:26; 12:25; 22:7).

THE SIXTH COMMANDMENT: PROHIBITION OF MURDER (v. 17)

You shall not murder Hebrew *ratsaḥ* refers to illicit killing, both intentional and accidental (see 1 Kings 21:19; Deut. 19:4). The translation "you shall not kill" (RSV) is too broad.[106] It implies that even capital punishment and war are prohibited, whereas the Torah sometimes mandates these.

Since biblical law recognizes intention as affecting the moral quality of an action, special provisions are made for dealing with accidental killing. See 19:1–13.

In Genesis 9:6 the prohibition of murder is grounded in the idea that humans are created in the

You shall not commit adultery.

You shall not steal.

You shall not bear false witness against your neighbor.

ס וְלֹא תִּנְאָף:

ס וְלֹא תִּגְנֹב:

ס וְלֹא־תַעֲנֶה בְרֵעֲךָ עֵד שָׁוְא:

image of God, a concept that confers supreme value on human life and makes taking it an offense not only against the victim and his family, but also against God Himself. This placed human life beyond monetary value and led to the provision in Numbers 35:31 that a murder victim's family could not accept reparations from the murderer in lieu of the death penalty, as was possible elsewhere in the Near East.[107] Since the author of the prohibition is God, no human authority could pardon a murderer.

THE SEVENTH COMMANDMENT: PROHIBITION OF ADULTERY (v. 17)

You shall not commit adultery In the Bible and the ancient Near East adultery meant voluntary sexual relations between a married or engaged woman and a man other than her husband or fiancé. It did not refer to the extramarital relations of a married man (unless, of course, the other woman was married). One reason for this distinction is that ancient Near Eastern society was polygamous. In such a context, although a husband had an exclusive right to his wife, a wife might share her husband with his other wives and did not have an exclusive right to him. Furthermore, in a patrilineal society, it was essential to be certain of the *paternity* of heirs, and it was the extramarital intercourse of the wife that made such certainty impossible.[108]

Adultery is viewed with abhorrence as an act that defiles its perpetrators (Lev. 18:20; Num. 5:13). It is termed the "great sin" by Abimelech in Genesis 20:9 and in texts from Egypt and Ugarit,[109] and is the subject of numerous admonitions in Proverbs.[110] It is punishable by stoning, a procedure that expresses public outrage over crimes that threaten the well-being of the entire nation (Deut. 22:24).

As in the case of murder, adultery is regarded as an offense against both God and man.[111] No option is offered for the husband or any human authority to waive or mitigate the punishment, as is possible in ancient Near Eastern law.[112] Provisions for dealing with adultery are found in Numbers 5:11–31 and Deuteronomy 22:22–27.

THE EIGHTH COMMANDMENT: PROHIBITION OF THEFT (v. 17)

You shall not steal The commandment prohibits all forms of theft. Talmudic exegesis construed the law more narrowly. Since theft of property is prohibited elsewhere (Lev. 19:11) and since the present commandment follows two capital crimes, talmudic exegesis took this commandment as a prohibition of kidnaping, which in biblical law is also a capital crime (Exod. 21:16, which uses the verb "steal").[113] However, this view implies that the text left its main point unexpressed, which is very unlikely. Since the Decalogue does not specify penalties, there is no reason to interpret its laws in light of the penalties. Nevertheless, the commandment way well *include* kidnapping as one form of theft.

THE NINTH COMMANDMENT: PROHIBITION OF FALSE TESTIMONY (v. 17)

You shall not bear false witness The commandment covers both false accusation and false testimony in court. Its location between theft and coveting reflects the fact that false accusation is a means of depriving one's fellow of what belongs to him (cf. Lev. 19:11). This can happen when a person claims ownership of something in another's possession, as in Exodus 22:8; if the claim is false, but the accused cannot disprove it, the false accuser would wind up acquiring his fellow's property. Similarly, Jezebel acquired Naboth's vineyard for Ahab by having false witnesses accuse Naboth of *lèse majesté* and blasphemy, so that his property would be awarded to the crown (1 Kings 21:1–16).[114]

The penalty for false testimony is described in 19:16–21.

18You shall not covet your neighbor's wife. You shall not crave your neighbor's house, or his field, or his male or female slave, or his ox, or his ass, or anything that is your neighbor's.

19The LORD spoke those words—those and no more—to your whole congregation at the mountain, with a

18 וְלֹא תַחְמֹד אֵשֶׁת רֵעֶךָ ס וְלֹא תִתְאַוֶּה בֵּית רֵעֶךָ שָׂדֵהוּ וְעַבְדּוֹ וַאֲמָתוֹ שׁוֹרוֹ וַחֲמֹרוֹ וְכֹל אֲשֶׁר לְרֵעֶךָ׃ ס חמישי [רביעי לספרדים]

19 אֶת־הַדְּבָרִים הָאֵלֶּה דִּבֶּר יְהֹוָה אֶל־כָּל־קְהַלְכֶם בָּהָר מִתּוֹךְ הָאֵשׁ הֶעָנָן וְהָעֲרָפֶל קוֹל

THE TENTH COMMANDMENT: PROHIBITION OF COVETING (v. 18)

You shall not covet . . . You shall not crave Both Hebrew verbs sometimes refer to actions that are not inherently wrong,[115] but here they describe states of mind wrongfully directed at things that belong to others. Commentators have wondered whether this Commandment forbids mere mental activity or refers to more concrete action. Since the Decalogue consists of fundamental principles and is not concerned with enforceability, some think that it is an ethical exhortation to master the kinds of impulses that would lead to violation of the preceding commandments. There is little evidence that the verbs refer to concrete action, but they do sometimes refer to mental states that go beyond simple, or passive, desire. *Ḥamad* sometimes refers to having designs on a desired object, perhaps even to scheming or maneuvering to acquire it (see esp. Exod. 34:24; for a possible example, see 19:14).[116] The grammatical form of *tit'avveh* implies continuous or repeated action; in other words, constant craving (cf. Prov. 21:26).[117] Hence, the commandment could be paraphrased as "do not scheme to acquire . . . do not long for."

Both Exodus and Deuteronomy divide the present commandment into two clauses. Exodus uses the verb *ḥamad* in both, suggesting that the second clause is simply an explanation of the first. Deuteronomy replaces *ḥamad* in the second clause with *hit'avvah*, which seems to imply a gradation within the commandment: "neither scheme nor even long for." This is compatible with the fact that the last five commandments are arranged in descending order of gravity, as noted above. The final commandment bans attempts on another's property at the stage of scheming, and, in Deuteronomy, even at the stage of longing.

your neighbor's wife. . . . your neighbor's house, or his field In Exodus, the first clause mentions only the neighbor's house, which the second clause explicates as consisting of his wife, servants, and livestock. This shows that in Exodus "house" means "household."[118] The version in Exodus resembles similar descriptions in patriarchal and wilderness times when the Israelites lived as nomadic herders without real estate.[119] Deuteronomy categorizes the neighbor's belongings more discriminatingly. It separates family from property by placing the wife in the first clause by herself. Then it places the house, servants, and cattle in the second clause and adds fields to the list. This shows that in Deuteronomy "house" has the narrower sense of a dwelling. By including houses and fields in the list, this version refers to the kinds of property people will own after settlement in Canaan, in keeping with Deuteronomy's aim of preparing the Israelites for life in the land.[120] Lists of possessions close to, and sometimes identical to, that in Deuteronomy's second clause are found in documents from the urban centers of Canaan and Mesopotamia.[121]

THE APPOINTMENT OF MOSES AS INTERMEDIARY (vv. 19–30)

The third section of the chapter indicates that the experience of God's revelation has the desired effect of teaching the people to fear Him (see 4:10). The people are frightened and ask that they be spared further direct contact with God and that Moses receive all future communications from Him. God approves of the spirit in which they make the request and tells Moses to stay with Him to receive the remaining laws and norms.

19. those words That is, those commandments (*devarim*).

congregation Hebrew *kahal*, "assembly." The present occasion is referred to as "the day of the Assembly" in 9:10; 10:4; 18:16.

mighty voice out of the fire and the dense clouds. He inscribed them on two tablets of stone, which He gave to me. 20When you heard the voice out of the darkness, while the mountain was ablaze with fire, you came up to me, all your tribal heads and elders, 21and said, "The LORD our God has just shown us His majestic Presence, and we have heard His voice out of the fire; we have seen this day that man may live though God has spoken to him. 22Let us not die, then, for this fearsome fire will consume us; if we hear the voice of the LORD our God any longer, we shall die. 23For what mortal ever heard the voice of the living God speak out of the fire, as we did, and lived? 24You go closer and hear all that the LORD our God says, and then you tell us everything that the LORD our God tells you, and we will willingly do it."

25The LORD heard the plea that you made to me, and the LORD said to me, "I have heard the plea that this people made to you; they did well to speak thus. 26May they always be of such mind, to revere Me and follow all My commandments, that it may go well with them and with

גָּדוֹל וְלֹא יָסָף וַיִּכְתְּבֵם עַל־שְׁנֵי לֻחֹת אֲבָנִים וַיִּתְּנֵם אֵלָי: 20 וַיְהִי כְּשָׁמְעֲכֶם אֶת־הַקּוֹל מִתּוֹךְ הַחֹשֶׁךְ וְהָהָר בֹּעֵר בָּאֵשׁ וַתִּקְרְבוּן אֵלַי כָּל־רָאשֵׁי שִׁבְטֵיכֶם וְזִקְנֵיכֶם: 21 וַתֹּאמְרוּ הֵן הֶרְאָנוּ יְהוָה אֱלֹהֵינוּ אֶת־כְּבֹדוֹ וְאֶת־גָּדְלוֹ וְאֶת־קֹלוֹ שָׁמַעְנוּ מִתּוֹךְ הָאֵשׁ הַיּוֹם הַזֶּה רָאִינוּ כִּי־יְדַבֵּר אֱלֹהִים אֶת־הָאָדָם וָחָי: 22 וְעַתָּה לָמָּה נָמוּת כִּי תֹאכְלֵנוּ הָאֵשׁ הַגְּדֹלָה הַזֹּאת אִם־יֹסְפִים | אֲנַחְנוּ לִשְׁמֹעַ אֶת־קוֹל יְהוָה אֱלֹהֵינוּ עוֹד וָמָתְנוּ: 23 כִּי מִי כָל־בָּשָׂר אֲשֶׁר שָׁמַע קוֹל אֱלֹהִים חַיִּים מְדַבֵּר מִתּוֹךְ־הָאֵשׁ כָּמֹנוּ וַיֶּחִי: 24 קְרַב אַתָּה וּשֲׁמָע אֵת כָּל־אֲשֶׁר יֹאמַר יְהוָה אֱלֹהֵינוּ וְאַתְּ | תְּדַבֵּר אֵלֵינוּ אֵת כָּל־אֲשֶׁר יְדַבֵּר יְהוָה אֱלֹהֵינוּ אֵלֶיךָ וְשָׁמַעְנוּ וְעָשִׂינוּ:

25 וַיִּשְׁמַע יְהוָה אֶת־קוֹל דִּבְרֵיכֶם בְּדַבֶּרְכֶם אֵלָי וַיֹּאמֶר יְהוָה אֵלַי שָׁמַעְתִּי אֶת־קוֹל דִּבְרֵי הָעָם הַזֶּה אֲשֶׁר דִּבְּרוּ אֵלֶיךָ הֵיטִיבוּ כָּל־אֲשֶׁר דִּבֵּרוּ: 26 מִי־יִתֵּן וְהָיָה לְבָבָם זֶה לָהֶם לְיִרְאָה אֹתִי

---

two tablets of stone　See Comment to 4:13.

which He gave to me　Forty days later (9:9).

21.　His majestic Presence　This refers to the fire and clouds on the mountain. God's Presence (Heb. *kavod*)—the physical form in which He appears to people—is usually described as fiery or as enveloped in cloud or fire. Compare Exodus 24:17: "Now the Presence of the LORD appeared in the sight of the Israelites as a consuming fire on the top of the mountain."[122]

though God has spoken to him　The meaning is probably "though God has spoken to him out of a fire." That is what verse 23 and 4:33 describe as unprecedented. That humans can survive simply hearing God speak is not new. The people were aware of earlier revelations to Moses.[123]

22.　Nevertheless, they fear hearing God speak further, since continued exposure to the fire might yet prove fatal.[124] After all, no mortal has ever survived such an experience before (v. 23).

23.　the living God　The demonstration of God's power has made the people conscious of His character as "the living God." This epithet expresses God's effectiveness in contrast to the lifelessness of false gods. The epithet is used similarly before another demonstration of God's power, the crossing of the Jordan on dry land, when Joshua announces: "By this you shall know that a living God is among you."[125]

24.　we will willingly do it　Literally, "we will hear [what you tell us] and do it." This is a key moment in the narrative: the people pledge to accept Moses' reports of what God commands and to perform whatever laws he transmits to them. They have voluntarily given up receiving the remaining laws from God personally, and they may not in the future disobey Moses or challenge what he reports to them.

25–26.　God appreciates the reverence that leads the people to make their request. He hopes that this reverence will remain with them and motivate them to observe the commandments. Implicit in His words is the concern that as the experience recedes from the people's memory, so will their reverence. On reverence, or fear, of God see Comment to 4:10.

That God hopes for reverence, but does not cause the people to be reverent, reflects the freedom that He gives man to choose whether or not to obey. It is a fundamental premise of the Bible that

their children forever! ²⁷Go, say to them, 'Return to your tents.' ²⁸But you remain here with Me, and I will give you the whole Instruction—the laws and the rules—that you shall impart to them, for them to observe in the land that I am giving them to possess."

²⁹Be careful, then, to do as the LORD your God has commanded you. Do not turn aside to the right or to the left: ³⁰follow only the path that the LORD your God has enjoined upon you, so that you may thrive and that it may go well with you, and that you may long endure in the land you are to possess.

וְלִשְׁמֹר אֶת־כָּל־מִצְוֹתַי כָּל־הַיָּמִים לְמַעַן יִיטַב לָהֶם וְלִבְנֵיהֶם לְעֹלָם: ²⁷ לֵךְ אֱמֹר לָהֶם שׁוּבוּ לָכֶם לְאָהֳלֵיכֶם: ²⁸ וְאַתָּה פֹּה עֲמֹד עִמָּדִי וַאֲדַבְּרָה אֵלֶיךָ אֵת כָּל־הַמִּצְוָה וְהַחֻקִּים וְהַמִּשְׁפָּטִים אֲשֶׁר תְּלַמְּדֵם וְעָשׂוּ בָאָרֶץ אֲשֶׁר אָנֹכִי נֹתֵן לָהֶם לְרִשְׁתָּהּ: ²⁹ וּשְׁמַרְתֶּם לַעֲשׂוֹת כַּאֲשֶׁר צִוָּה יְהוָה אֱלֹהֵיכֶם אֶתְכֶם לֹא תָסֻרוּ יָמִין וּשְׂמֹאל: ³⁰ בְּכָל־הַדֶּרֶךְ אֲשֶׁר צִוָּה יְהוָה אֱלֹהֵיכֶם אֶתְכֶם תֵּלֵכוּ לְמַעַן תִּחְיוּן וְטוֹב לָכֶם וְהַאֲרַכְתֶּם יָמִים בָּאָרֶץ אֲשֶׁר תִּירָשׁוּן:

the individual human being determines his own behavior and is not controlled by God. As R. Ḥanina put it in the Talmud, "All is under the control of Heaven except for the fear of Heaven."[126]

28. Moses' role as intermediary is now formalized. This episode is cited in 18:15–22 as the precedent for the institution of prophecy.

remain here with Me Moses stayed with God for forty days and nights (9:9–11; Exod. 24:18).

Instruction Mitsvah, literally "commandment," defined here as "the laws and the rules." Deuteronomy often uses this term, in the singular, to refer to its legal corpus.[127] It functions more or less as a synonym of "the Teaching [*torah*]" (for all these terms see Comments to 1:5; 4:1).

29-30. The lesson learned at Mount Sinai—and Moses' main point in this speech—is that the laws and rules that he is about to teach came from God and must therefore be observed. Their divine origin makes it clear that they are a prerequisite for well-being in the promised land.

CHAPTER 6

PREAMBLE TO THE LAWS GIVEN IN MOAB (6:1–11:30)

INTRODUCTION (vv. 1–3)

Moses now shifts his focus to the present and begins to transmit the remaining laws to the people—the main subject of Deuteronomy. He begins in chapters 6–11 with a preamble to the laws, urging the general duties of exclusive loyalty to God, love and reverence for Him, and obedience to His commandments. Verses 1–3 serve as an introduction to the preamble and the laws, expressing the hope that Israel will always revere God and follow His commandments, and reminding the people of the rewards of remaining and prospering in the land.

From a purely literary point of view, the shift of focus from the theophany at Mount Sinai (chap. 5) to the present, in Moab, indicates that 6:1 marks the beginning of a new section of the book. This is recognized in the fact that a new chapter begins here. However, the paragraph divisions in Hebrew texts do not recognize this beginning. The Masoretic text has no break until verse 4.[1] By treating 5:19–6:3 as a single paragraph, it emphasizes that "the Instruction—the laws and the rules" that Moses is about to transmit (6:1) are identical to the ones he was commissioned to receive at Mount Sinai (5:28), that they are a continuation of the commandments given there and not separate from them. This is a very important issue in Deuteronomy (see the introductory Comment to chap. 5).[2]

6 And this is the Instruction—the laws and the rules—that the LORD your God has commanded [me] to impart to you, to be observed in the land that you are about to cross into and occupy, [2] so that you, your children, and your children's children may revere the LORD your God and follow, as long as you live, all His laws and commandments that I enjoin upon you, to the end that you may long endure. [3] Obey, O Israel, willingly and faithfully, that it may go well with you and that you may increase greatly [in] a land flowing with milk and honey, as the LORD, the God of your fathers, spoke to you.

וְ זֹאת הַמִּצְוָה הַחֻקִּים וְהַמִּשְׁפָּטִים אֲשֶׁר צִוָּה
יְהוָה אֱלֹהֵיכֶם לְלַמֵּד אֶתְכֶם לַעֲשׂוֹת בָּאָרֶץ
אֲשֶׁר אַתֶּם עֹבְרִים שָׁמָּה לְרִשְׁתָּהּ: [2] לְמַעַן
תִּירָא אֶת־יְהוָה אֱלֹהֶיךָ לִשְׁמֹר אֶת־כָּל־חֻקֹּתָיו
וּמִצְוֹתָיו אֲשֶׁר אָנֹכִי מְצַוֶּךָ אַתָּה וּבִנְךָ וּבֶן־בִּנְךָ
כֹּל יְמֵי חַיֶּיךָ וּלְמַעַן יַאֲרִכֻן יָמֶיךָ: [3] וְשָׁמַעְתָּ
יִשְׂרָאֵל וְשָׁמַרְתָּ לַעֲשׂוֹת אֲשֶׁר יִיטַב לְךָ וַאֲשֶׁר
תִּרְבּוּן מְאֹד כַּאֲשֶׁר דִּבֶּר יְהוָה אֱלֹהֵי אֲבֹתֶיךָ לָךְ
אֶרֶץ זָבַת חָלָב וּדְבָשׁ: פ

שני   [חמישי לספרדים]

1. ***this is the Instruction—the laws and the rules*** By using the same terms that God used in 5:28, Moses shows that he is giving Israel exactly what He was commanded to give.

2. ***so that you . . . may revere the LORD your God and follow . . . all His commandments*** In keeping with the hope expressed by God in 5:26. Moses has a twofold purpose in teaching the laws: ensuring their performance and inculcating reverence for God. Thus the laws were not only an expression of reverence for God but also a means of *teaching* reverence,[3] like the theophany at Mount Sinai, the festivals, and reading the Teaching.[4] The idea that the habit of observing God's laws has the long-term effect of instilling reverence for him is expressed in the rabbinic statement that God would even tolerate Israel abandoning Him if it would observe His commandments, since that would lead Israel back to Him.[5]

revere . . . and follow Literally, "revere . . . by following." Following God's laws is the means of revering Him, the expression of reverence.[6]

The practice of explaining the aim, reason, or consequence of a law is one of the recurrent themes in Moses' attempts to persuade the people to observe them in the coming chapters.

3. ***Obey . . . willingly and faithfully*** Literally, "Obey . . . and faithfully do." Moses urges Israel to do as it promised in 5:24, which says literally "we will obey and do."

***that you may increase greatly [in] a land flowing with milk and honey, as the LORD, the God of your fathers spoke to you*[7]

a land flowing with milk and honey Rather, "a land oozing milk and honey." The Hebrew verb *z-w-v* refers to bodily organs leaking fluids and, in poetry, to water gushing (see Lev. 15 and Ps. 78:20). The phrase is a favorite one for describing the fertility of the land of Israel. See Excursus 9.

A SERMONIC ELABORATION OF THE FIRST COMMANDMENT (vv. 4-25)

As noted above, themes from the first two commandments of the Decalogue play a central role in chapters 6-11. Allusions to the Decalogue, especially the first commandment, appear throughout chapter 6. Verses 4 and 14 restate the first commandment, "you shall have no other gods beside Me," while verses 12, 21, and 23 echo its introduction, "I the LORD am your God who brought you out of the land of Egypt, the house of bondage." In verse 15 the injunction against worshiping other gods is backed with a warning about God's jealousy, just as we find after the first two commandments. The exhortations to love God and keep His commandments in verses 5 and 17 echo the Decalogue's description of God as showing kindness to "those who love Me and keep My commandments." Verse 18 echoes the reward promised for observing the fifth commandment, "that you may fare well" (lit., "that it may go well with you" [5:16]; vv. 2-3 also echo both rewards promised in 5:16).[8] In light of these allusions, the exhortations to love God, to remember Him, to teach children about His

⁴Hear, O Israel! The LORD is our God, the LORD alone.
⁵You shall love the LORD your God with all your heart and

4 שְׁמַע יִשְׂרָאֵל יְהוָה אֱלֹהֵינוּ יְהוָה | אֶחָֽד:*

5 וְאָהַבְתָּ אֵת יְהוָה אֱלֹהֶיךָ בְּכָל־לְבָבְךָ וּבְכָל־

ע׳ ד׳ רבתי v. 4.

words and deeds, and all the other themes of chapter 6 can be regarded as a sermonic reflection on the first commandment, explaining what must be done to carry it out.

The Masoretic text divides verses 4–25 into four paragraphs: (A) verses 4–9, (B) 10–15, (C) 16–19, and (D) 20–25. Thematically these paragraphs fall into a chiastic pattern: paragraphs A and D refer to teaching God's words and instructions to one's children; paragraphs B and C warn against forgetting God and His providence and testing his ability to provide. In addition, paragraphs C and D, emphasizing the rewards for obedience and the role of the laws in expressing and inculcating reverence for God, echo the introductory paragraph 6:1–3, thus creating with that paragraph a frame for the entire chapter.

THE DUTY OF UNDIVIDED LOYALTY TO THE LORD AND CONSTANT AWARENESS OF HIS TEACHINGS (vv. 4–9)

The position of this paragraph in Deuteronomy lends it special significance. As the first paragraph of the Instruction that God gave Moses on Mount Sinai it is, in a sense, the beginning of Deuteronomy proper. It concisely states the central themes of the book and the central demands of the covenant, paraphrasing the first commandment and explicating its meaning: Israel's love and loyalty to YHVH must be undivided and accompanied by constant efforts to remember His instructions and teach them to future generations. The significance of this paragraph is reflected in the fact that it became the centerpiece of Jewish daily worship, the *Keri'at Shema'* ("Recitation of the Shema"), named for its first word (see Excursus 10). Its significance is underscored in the Nash Papyrus and the Septuagint which preface it with an extra introductory verse, "These are the laws and the rules that Moses [Septuagint: the LORD] commanded Israel in the desert when they left Egypt."⁹

4. Hear, O Israel! Focus your attention and heed the following teaching:

the LORD is our God, the LORD alone Hebrew YHVH *'eloheinu* YHVH *'ehad*, literally, "YHVH our God YHVH one." For all of its familiarity, the precise meaning of the Shema is uncertain and it permits several possible renderings. The present translation indicates that the verse is a description of the proper relationship between YHVH and Israel: He alone is Israel's God. This is not a declaration of monotheism, meaning that there is only one God. That point was made in 4:35 and 39, which state that "YHVH alone is God." The present verse, by adding the word "our," focuses on the way Israel is to apply that truth: though other peoples worship various beings and things they consider divine (see Comment to 3:24), Israel is to recognize YHVH alone.

This understanding of the Shema as describing a relationship with God, rather than His nature, has the support of Zechariah 14:9. According to Zechariah, what is now true of Israel will, in the future, be true of all humanity: "the LORD will be king over all the earth; on that day *the LORD shall be one* and His name one," meaning that for all of humanity, YHVH and His name will stand alone, unrivaled; as Zechariah says earlier, "I will erase the very names of the idols from the land; they shall not be uttered any more" (13:2). YHVH will be recognized exclusively and His name alone will be invoked in prayer and oaths. In other words, Deuteronomy and Zechariah both use "one" in the sense of "alone," "exclusively."¹⁰ This understanding of the phrase is consistent with similar formulations of the same idea in Isaiah and Zephaniah: "The LORD alone shall be exalted in that day" (Isa. 2:11,17); "For then I will make the peoples pure of speech, so that they all invoke the LORD by name and serve Him with one accord" (Zeph. 3:9). This interpretation of the Shema is appropriate for the beginning of the speech in which Moses explicates the first commandment of the Decalogue, "You shall have no other gods beside Me" (5:7). It means, in essence, what 6:13–14 say: Israel must revere, worship, and swear by YHVH alone.

This interpretation is not without difficulty. For further discussion, see Excursus 10.

5. You shall love The idea of commanding a feeling is not foreign to the Torah, which assumes that people can cultivate proper attitudes. Thus Leviticus 19:17–18 commands, "You shall

with all your soul and with all your might. ⁶Take to heart   נַפְשְׁךָ וּבְכָל־מְאֹדֶךָ: 6 וְהָיוּ הַדְּבָרִים הָאֵלֶּה אֲשֶׁר

not hate your kinsfolk in your heart . . . you shall not bear a grudge against your countrymen" (see also Comment to Deut. 5:18). Nevertheless, love of God in Deuteronomy is not only an emotional attachment to Him, but something that expresses itself in action.[11] This is in keeping with the fact that Hebrew verbs for feelings sometimes refer as well to the actions that result from them.[12] When Deuteronomy describes God's love for man, it means a love expressed in benevolent acts, as in 10:18: God "loves [NJPS: befriends] the stranger, providing him with food and clothing" (see also 7:8, "favored," lit., "loved," and 23:6). Israel's duty to love God is likewise inseparable from action; it is regularly connected with the observance of His commandments, as in 10:12–13; 11:1,13; 19:9; 30:16. In such contexts "love" means "act lovingly." This usage is comparable to that of ancient Near Eastern political terminology where "love" refers to the loyalty of subjects, vassals, and allies (see Comment to 5:10). In fact, one of the striking parallels between political treaties and the covenant between God and Israel is the requirement that the vassal "love" the suzerain—that is, act loyally to him—with all his heart.[13] The command to love God may accordingly be understood as requiring one to *act* lovingly and loyally toward Him. How that should be done is spelled out in this paragraph and throughout Deuteronomy.

Deuteronomy is the first book in the Torah to speak of loving God. The previous books emphasize reverence (see Comment to 4:10). Deuteronomy speaks of both love and reverence (lit., "fear") as desirable attitudes that should motivate Israel to obey God's commandments. Both attitudes have the same practical effect, and Deuteronomy does not draw a distinction between them; they appear side by side in such passages as 10:12 and 13:4–5. For postbiblical writers love and fear represented two distinct motives for serving God. The dominant view in rabbinic thought is that love of God is superior since it is a more durable attitude.[14]

with all your heart and with all your soul   In Hebrew, "heart" (*lev* or *levav*) usually refers to the interior of the body, conceived of as the seat of thought, intention, and feeling,[15] and "soul" (*nefesh*) refers to the seat of the emotions, passions, and desires.[16] God's "heart and soul" refers to His wishes and purposes (1 Sam. 2:35). To do something with all the heart and soul means to do it with the totality of one's thoughts, feelings, intentions, and desires. The phrase is used to describe how Israel must love God, serve Him, observe His commandments, and return to Him (see 4:29; 10:12; 26:16; 30:2,10). In these exhortations the emphasis is on the word "all": Since YHVH *alone* is Israel's God, Israel must love and serve Him with *undivided* devotion. This is clear from 13:4 and 1 Samuel 7:3, where the phrase refers to serving the Lord alone without dividing one's loyalty between Him and other gods.[17]

with all your might   That is, "exceedingly." Hebrew *be-khol me'odekha* is comparable to the more common phrase *bi-me'od me'od*, "very, very much."[18] Elsewhere the requirement to love God is usually modified only by the first two phrases of this verse, "with all your heart and with all your soul." Perhaps "with all your might" was added here to give the strongest possible emphasis, since this is the very first time this requirement appears in the Bible. This full form of the formula appears again only in 2 Kings 23:25, describing King Josiah, who returned to God in a way unmatched by any other Israelite king.

Rabbinic exegesis, prompted by the observation that this commandment requires action and not only emotion, gave these three phrases specific behavioral application.[19] Since "heart" sometimes means "intentions," "with all your heart" was taken to mean "with all your inclinations," that is with the inclination to evil (*yetser ha-ra'*) as well as the inclination to good (*yetser ha-tov*), which are roughly equal to the id and the superego; in other words, even libidinal instincts are to be channeled to the service of God. Since another meaning of *nefesh* is "life" (see 19:6,11,21), "with all your *nefesh*" was interpreted as meaning "even at the cost of your life."[20] And since *me'od* can also means "property," "with all your might" was taken to mean "with all your wealth or possessions."[21]

6. *Take to heart*   Moses speaks here as a teacher. The father and teacher speak similarly in Proverbs, urging the son and disciple to internalize their teachings (Prov. 3:1; 4:4; 6:21; 7:3). Since the teachings Moses conveys here are ultimately those of God, it is worth noting that constant awareness of the sovereign's words is also the duty of a king's subject; in a letter to his Egyptian suzerain a

these instructions with which I charge you this day. 7Impress them upon your children. Recite them when you stay at home and when you are away, when you lie down and when you get up. 8Bind them as a sign on your hand

אָנֹכִי מְצַוְּךָ הַיּוֹם עַל־לְבָבֶךָ: 7 וְשִׁנַּנְתָּם לְבָנֶיךָ וְדִבַּרְתָּ בָּם בְּשִׁבְתְּךָ בְּבֵיתֶךָ וּבְלֶכְתְּךָ בַדֶּרֶךְ וּבְשָׁכְבְּךָ וּבְקוּמֶךָ: 8 וּקְשַׁרְתָּם לְאוֹת עַל־יָדֶךָ

Phoenician vassal wrote: "On my innards and on my back I carry the word of the king, my lord."[22] Inspired by the models of devotion to the instructions of a father and a teacher and to the words of a sovereign, constant awareness of God's teachings became an ideal of Israelite piety.[23]

these instructions with which I charge you this day This and similar phrases refer to the entire body of Deuteronomic law and teaching.[24] The present paragraph is the source for several *mitsvot* (commandments) that require reciting or writing the instructions in question, and halakhic exegesis defines the phrase more narrowly in a way that makes those *mitsvot* manageable. See Excursuses 10 and 11. Note the similar problem in connection with 17:18 and 27:3,8.

7. Essential to Deuteronomy's aim of disseminating knowledge of God's laws widely among the citizenry is that parents teach them to their children and speak of them constantly among themselves.

Impress them Rather, "teach them" (Heb. *ve-shinnantam*, lit., "repeat them"). This meaning is made clear by 11:19, where "teach" (*l-m-d*) is used in place of this verb. Hebrew *sh-n-n* is probably an alternate form of *sh-n-h*, "repeat," "teach."[25] It refers to oral teaching, which remained the primary means of instruction in Israel even after the spread of literacy (see Excursus 28). This verse, along with 5:1, is the source of the halakhic requirements that one must study the Torah and teach it to one's children.[26]

The idea of a sacred body of knowledge that must be transmitted from fathers to children is also mentioned in the Babylonian creation epic Enuma Elish: "Let the father repeat them and impart them to his son." There, however, it is not the laws or moral and religious teachings of the god Marduk that are to be taught, but his fifty names and their arcane interpretations.[27] Ancient Near Eastern treaties emphasize the vassal's duty to instruct his sons about the treaty and the duty of following it.[28] The provisions of the treaty deal, of course, with political loyalty to the suzerain, which is comparable to those provisions of God's covenant with Israel that deal with loyalty to God. They are not comparable to the covenant's demand for social justice and morality.

Recite them Rather, "speak about them" (*dabber be-*, as in 1 Sam. 19:3,4). The Psalmist, too, in describing his devotion to God's laws, tells of speaking about them (Ps. 119:13,46).

when you stay at home and when you are away, when you lie down and when you get up These pairs of contrasting phrases are merisms. Accordingly, our verse means "speak of these words wherever you are, and at all times" (cf. Prov. 6:21–22).[29]

Halakhic exegesis used this and the next two verses to shape the pattern of daily worship and observance. The present verse was taken to require the recitation, morning and evening, of verses 4–9 and certain other passages, together known as the *Keri'at Shemaʿ* ("Recitation of the Shema"), from the first word of verse 4. See Excursus 10.

8. Not only must God's commandments be remembered and spoken of constantly, but copies of them must also be worn on the body. A similar idea appears in Exodus 13:9,16, as well as Deuteronomy 11:18, but Deuteronomy modifies the idea in two ways. In Exodus it is the event of the Exodus, or some of its commemorative ceremonies, that must be "bound" to the body, which suggests that "binding" is meant metaphorically for remembering or cherishing them. In Deuteronomy, it is *words* that must be bound to the body, and the connection with writing the words on doorposts and gates in verse 9 seems to indicate that Deuteronomy means the injunction literally, although this is debated. Moreover, for Deuteronomy it is God's commandments in general that must be "bound" to the body, not only the Exodus or its commemorative rites. According to halakhic exegesis, selected commandments must be written on parchment and placed in leather capsules called *tefillin* that are fastened to the arm and forehead. See Excursus 11.

Bind them as a sign on your hand Bind "these words" (v. 6) on your hand the way that

and let them serve as a symbol on your forehead; [9]inscribe them on the doorposts of your house and on your gates.

וְהָיוּ לְטֹטָפֹת בֵּין עֵינֶיךָ: 9 וּכְתַבְתָּם עַל־מְזוּזֹת בֵּיתֶךָ וּבִשְׁעָרֶיךָ: ס   [ששי לספרדים]

[10]When the LORD your God brings you into the land that He swore to your fathers, Abraham, Isaac, and Jacob,

10 וְהָיָה כִּי יְבִיאֲךָ | יְהוָה אֱלֹהֶיךָ אֶל־הָאָרֶץ אֲשֶׁר נִשְׁבַּע לַאֲבֹתֶיךָ לְאַבְרָהָם לְיִצְחָק וּלְיַעֲקֹב

signs are placed on the hand. Many commentators suggest that the comparison refers to the practice of tying a string around the finger to remember something.

as a symbol   Rather, "as a frontlet," that is, a headband.[30] The headband was the characteristic headdress worn in the Syro-Palestinian area in biblical times, as shown by illustrations in Egyptian and Assyrian art depicting inhabitants of this area.[31]

forehead[32]

9.   *inscribe them on the doorposts of your house*   In this way people would be reminded of God's instructions every time they left their houses or returned to them (cf. v. 7).[33]

and on your gates   This refers to the gates of the cities (houses rarely had gates). This ensures constant public exposure for God's teachings because the city gate was the center of public activity.[34] It consisted of not only the doors to a city but the entire roofed structure that housed them, including several chambers (some up to ten meters wide), benches, and a long passageway. It functioned as the center of public activity because it was often the most open area in an otherwise crowded city, and people constantly passed through it on their way to and from the city. It was the most effective place to publicize matters of personal or public importance, and something well known was said to be known in the gate.[35] In it elders, and sometimes kings, judged and held court (Deut. 21:19; 22:15),[36] public affairs were deliberated, legal agreements concluded and witnessed, markets set up, and prophets addressed the people.[37] In Mesopotamia it was used for displaying royal inscriptions and charters guaranteeing the rights of temple cities. All of this shows that inscribing God's teachings on the walls of the gate would ensure them the widest visibility. Philo expressed the aim succinctly: it is "so that those who leave or remain at home, citizens and strangers alike, may read the inscriptions engraved on the face of the gates and keep in perpetual memory what they should say and do."[38]

The text implies that the words were to be inscribed directly on the doorposts and gate structures. We do not know how many people could actually read them—literacy was far from universal[39]—but seeing the inscriptions would remind nonreaders of the authority of God's commandments and the need to speak about them (v. 7). Those who could read would be reminded of their contents as well, and could even consult the laws in the course of legal proceedings in the gate.

At some point during the Second Temple period, Jewish law ruled that selected passages should be written on parchment and placed into containers affixed to the doorposts of a house; this is how the practice is carried out today. The inscription in its container is known as a *mezuzah*, from the word used for "doorpost" in our verse. See Excursus 11.

DO NOT ALLOW PROSPERITY TO MAKE YOU FORGET THE LORD AND TURN TO OTHER GODS (vv. 10–15)

Having prescribed steps to ensure that God's words will be remembered, Moses now warns against forgetting God Himself. Ironically, it is the gift of the promised land that may lead to forgetting Him. Deuteronomy and other books frequently point out that prosperity causes people to forget that they are dependent on God for all that they have.

As noted above, verses 12–15 echo parts of the Ten Commandments. They not only allude to the commandments but specify how they are to be carried out and relate them to the conditions of life in the promised land.

10–11.   *cities . . . houses . . . cisterns . . . vineyards . . . olive groves*   Basic possessions of a settled agricultural society, which the Israelites, after a generation of wandering in the wilderness, are about to become.

As this passage and 19:1 indicate, the cities of the Canaanites would not be destroyed but would

to assign to you—great and flourishing cities that you did not build, ¹¹houses full of all good things that you did not fill, hewn cisterns that you did not hew, vineyards and olive groves that you did not plant—and you eat your fill, ¹²take heed that you do not forget the LORD who freed you from the land of Egypt, the house of bondage. ¹³Revere only the LORD your God and worship Him

לָתֶת לְךָ עָרִים גְּדֹלֹת וְטֹבֹת אֲשֶׁר לֹא־בָנִיתָ: ¹¹ וּבָתִּים מְלֵאִים כָּל־טוּב אֲשֶׁר לֹא־מִלֵּאתָ וּבֹרֹת חֲצוּבִים אֲשֶׁר לֹא־חָצַבְתָּ כְּרָמִים וְזֵיתִים אֲשֶׁר לֹא־נָטַעְתָּ וְאָכַלְתָּ וְשָׂבָעְתָּ: ¹² הִשָּׁמֶר לְךָ פֶּן־תִּשְׁכַּח אֶת־יְהוָה אֲשֶׁר הוֹצִיאֲךָ מֵאֶרֶץ מִצְרַיִם מִבֵּית עֲבָדִים: ¹³ אֶת־יְהוָה אֱלֹהֶיךָ תִּירָא

be settled by the Israelites. The book of Joshua indeed indicates that only a few cities were destroyed and burned during the initial conquest.[40] This may help explain why it is difficult for archaeology to find signs of the Israelite conquest, since layers of destruction datable to the period of the conquest—the clearest evidence of conquest archaeology can provide—are rare.

10. that you did not build ... that you did not fill This reminder that the Israelites did not create the material wealth they are about to possess is an implicit warning against the attitude of self-sufficiency that prosperity can induce. That attitude is paraphrased in 8:17: "My own power and the might of my own hand have won this wealth for me."

12. cisterns Most Israelite population centers were in the highlands, which depend mainly on rain for their water. Since rain falls in Israel only between October and May, it was necessary to store rainwater for the dry season; otherwise, the highlands could not have supported many people. Water was stored in large jars and in communal cisterns and private ones located beneath houses or their inner courtyards. Archaeologists have found cisterns in a number of Canaanite and Israelite cities.[41]

vineyards and olive groves Among the agricultural staples of the land of Israel, grapes and olives were second in importance only to cereals (cf. 8:8; 28:51). Grapes were eaten fresh or dried, as raisins, or were made into grape juice and wine, which, after water, were the main drinks. Olive oil was used in eating, cooking, lighting, healing, and anointing (a necessity in hot, dry climates). (The omission of cereals from this list of the land's products could be due to the fact that grapes and olives were more symbolic of richness[42] and more characteristic of the highlands than were grains, which also grow in the lowlands. It could also be due to the fact that on their own the Israelites could grow cereals as soon as they entered the land, whereas olive groves and vineyards require years to develop; only existing ones would produce immediately.)

11-12. and you eat your fill—take heed that you do not forget the LORD The idea that material wealth and satiety can lead to pride and arrogance and forgetting one's dependence on God is a persistent concern in the Bible. It is repeated several times in Deuteronomy (8:12–14; 11:14–16; 31:20; 32:15) and elsewhere. Proverbs 30:8–9 sums up this concern as follows: "Give me neither poverty nor riches, but provide me with my daily bread, lest, being sated, I renounce, saying, 'Who is the LORD?'"[43] The Talmud quotes a popular proverb to similar effect: "Filled stomachs are a type of evil."[44]

take heed Rather, "be careful." As verse 15 shows, forgetting one's dependence on God is not only wrong but dangerous. See also 8:19–20; 11:17.

13-14. These verses give examples of how to observe the prohibition against having other gods beside the Lord (5:7).

13. Revere See Comments to verse 2 and 4:10.

Worship Literally, "serve," that is, worship and obey. This term was common in the ancient Near East for worshiping deities and obeying kings and suzerains.[45]

swear only by his name Swearing by the Lord's name is an expression of loyalty to Him, and swearing by the name of another god would indicate a belief that that god is effective and has authority (see Comment to 5:11). The Bible therefore considers it a test of fidelity that the Israelite swear by YHVH alone. When foreign nations in the future recognize the Lord exclusively, they too will swear by Him alone.[46] Like much else in biblical theology and law, this expression of loyalty to

alone, and swear only by His name. [14]Do not follow other gods, any gods of the peoples about you [15]—for the LORD your God in your midst is an impassioned God—lest the anger of the LORD your God blaze forth against you and He wipe you off the face of the earth.

[16]Do not try the LORD your God, as you did at Massah. [17]Be sure to keep the commandments, decrees, and laws that the LORD your God has enjoined upon you. [18]Do

וְאֹתֽוֹ תַעֲבֹ֖ד וּבִשְׁמ֥וֹ תִּשָּׁבֵֽעַ׃ 14 לֹ֣א תֵֽלְכ֔וּן אַֽחֲרֵ֖י אֱלֹהִ֣ים אֲחֵרִ֑ים מֵֽאֱלֹהֵי֙ הָֽעַמִּ֔ים אֲשֶׁ֖ר סְבִיבֽוֹתֵיכֶֽם׃ 15 כִּ֣י אֵ֥ל קַנָּ֛א יְהֹוָ֥ה אֱלֹהֶ֖יךָ בְּקִרְבֶּ֑ךָ פֶּן־יֶ֠חֱרֶ֠ה אַף־יְהֹוָ֤ה אֱלֹהֶ֨יךָ֙ בָּ֔ךְ וְהִשְׁמִ֣ידְךָ֔ מֵעַ֖ל פְּנֵ֥י הָֽאֲדָמָֽה׃ ס 16 לֹ֣א תְנַסּ֔וּ אֶת־יְהֹוָ֖ה אֱלֹֽהֵיכֶ֑ם כַּֽאֲשֶׁ֥ר נִסִּיתֶ֖ם בַּמַּסָּֽה׃ 17 שָׁמ֣וֹר תִּשְׁמְר֔וּן אֶת־מִצְוֺ֖ת יְהֹוָ֥ה

God is comparable to the ways of showing loyalty to a king; in a Sumerian prayer the writer denies that he has sworn an oath by a foreign king.[47]

14. *follow* Literally, "go after." This idiom seems to be a double-entendre here. In connection with the preceding verse it has the political connotation "give allegiance," while in connection with the following warning about God's passionate rage it has the pejorative sexual connotation of "traipse after."[48]

gods of the peoples about you All foreign deities are prohibited to Israel (5:7; 13:8), but Moses' immediate concern is with the temptations the people will encounter in the promised land, namely the temptation to worship the gods of the surrounding peoples.

15. *an impassioned God* See Comment to 5:9.

in your midst For the concept of God being "in the midst" of Israel, see Comment to verse 16. The recognition that God is present in Israel's midst, supervising their affairs, is a deterrent to sin; contrast the rationale of the sinning Jerusalemites in Ezekiel 8:12: "The LORD does not see us; the LORD has abandoned the country" (cf. 23:15).

DO NOT TEST GOD, BUT OBEY HIS COMMANDMENTS (vv. 16–19)

After indicating that God will meet all of Israel's needs, Moses recalls an incident in which the people challenged God's ability to do so and implicitly threatened to rebel against Him. He urges them not to do so again, but to observe the commandments so that all may go well with them.

16. *Do not try* That is, test. During the incident in question, the people complained because they lacked water to drink (Exod. 17:1–7). In the course of complaining they "tried the LORD, saying, 'Is the LORD present among us [lit., in our midst] or not?'" The Lord's presence among a people or within a land refers to His providential control of events affecting them.[49] The people saw their demand as a test of God's control of conditions in the desert, specifically His ability to supply water.[50] Tests of that sort imply a lack of confidence in God's ability. Such a lack of confidence was understandable at a time when there had been only a few demonstrations of that ability, and the Israelites were therefore not punished for their complaints in Exodus.[51] But after repeated demonstrations of His power their continued lack of confidence angered God and led to punishment because it was a sign of spiritual obtuseness.[52] This reasoning is spelled out in Psalms 78 and 106, which indicate that testing God is a consequence of forgetting His past marvels, especially those that took place during the Exodus.[53] For this reason, the present paragraph is a natural sequel to verses 10–15, which warn against forgetting God who brought Israel out of Egypt, and a natural introduction to verses 20–25, which urge that children be taught about the Exodus.[54]

Massah The incident referred to took place at Rephidim. After the incident, the Israelites named the place Massah and Meribah, "The Place of Testing and Quarreling" (Exod. 17:7).

17. The juxtaposition of testing God in verse 16 with this exhortation to obey His commandments implies that testing God is associated with disobedience. The people's intentions at Massah are explicitly paraphrased this way by R. Nehemiah in Exodus Rabbah 26:2: "If He supplies our food . . . we shall serve Him; otherwise we shall rebel against Him." That testing God carried an implicit threat of disobedience is reflected in passages that mention testing and disobedience together, such as Psalm 78:56: "Yet they defiantly tested God Most High, and did not observe His

what is right and good in the sight of the LORD, that it may go well with you and that you may be able to possess the good land that the LORD your God promised on oath to your fathers, [19]and that all your enemies may be driven out before you, as the LORD has spoken.

[20]When, in time to come, your children ask you, "What mean the decrees, laws, and rules that the LORD our God has enjoined upon you?" [21]you shall say to your children, "We were slaves to Pharaoh in Egypt and the LORD freed

אֱלֹהֵיכֶם וְעֵדֹתָיו וְחֻקָּיו אֲשֶׁר צִוָּךְ: [18] וְעָשִׂיתָ
הַיָּשָׁר וְהַטּוֹב בְּעֵינֵי יְהוָה לְמַעַן יִיטַב לָךְ וּבָאתָ
וְיָרַשְׁתָּ אֶת־הָאָרֶץ הַטֹּבָה אֲשֶׁר־נִשְׁבַּע יְהוָה
לַאֲבֹתֶיךָ: [19] לַהֲדֹף אֶת־כָּל־אֹיְבֶיךָ מִפָּנֶיךָ
כַּאֲשֶׁר דִּבֶּר יְהוָה: ס
[20] כִּי־יִשְׁאָלְךָ בִנְךָ מָחָר לֵאמֹר מָה הָעֵדֹת
וְהַחֻקִּים וְהַמִּשְׁפָּטִים אֲשֶׁר צִוָּה יְהוָה אֱלֹהֵינוּ
אֶתְכֶם: [21] וְאָמַרְתָּ לְבִנְךָ עֲבָדִים הָיִינוּ לְפַרְעֹה

decrees."[55] Accordingly, the exhortation not to test God means that the Israelites should not make their obedience conditional upon further miracles. The memory of His past wonders should suffice to establish His power and His claim on their obedience.[56]

18. *Do what is right and good in the sight of the LORD* "Doing what is right in the sight of the LORD" is associated elsewhere with obeying His commandments,[57] and that is undoubtedly the meaning of what is "right and good" in His sight here and in 12:28. However, since the phrase "the commandments, decrees, and laws that the LORD has enjoined upon you" in verse 17 seems to cover all the requirements of the law, Ramban inferred that "doing what is right and good" adds something extra, namely that the spirit of the Torah must be extended to cases of interpersonal conduct that the Torah did not mention; since the Torah could not mention all possible cases, it gives many examples and adds here the general rule that one should do what is right and good in every situation.[58] Talmudic exegesis went further, inferring that the additional clause in verse 18 meant that one must also go beyond the requirements of the law. According to this interpretation, doing what is right *and good* meant that in the interest of fairness, or to avoid the impression of impropriety, the law should require individuals to forgo certain rights afforded them by the law.[59] Rashi took it as requiring individuals to compromise in disputes and as urging them to act *li-fnim mi-shurat ha-din*, that is, to voluntarily waive certain privileges and exemptions that they enjoy under the law.

18b–19. *that it may go well with you and that you may be able to occupy the good land . . . and that your enemy may be driven out before you* A reminder that the injunctions of the present paragraph are a condition for the conquest of the promised land.[60]

EXPLAINING THE COMMANDMENTS TO ONE'S CHILDREN (vv. 20–25)

In this paragraph, Moses resumes the theme of verse 7, which calls for teaching children about God's instructions. Children will be curious about the instructions and ask about their meaning, just as the book of Exodus expected children to ask about the ceremonies commemorating the Exodus (Exod. 12:26–27; 13:14).[61] In answering, one is to go beyond the intrinsic value of the individual laws (cf. 4:6,8) and explain the reasons for obeying God altogether. The answer elaborates on the introduction to the Decalogue: obedience is Israel's response to its history. God gave the commandments after He freed Israel from Egypt. By these actions He showed His faithfulness and power and established His sovereign authority over Israel (see Comment to 4:20). Obedience expresses Israel's recognition of these benefactions and acceptance of God's sovereignty.[62]

This lesson is typical of Deuteronomy's practice of using laws as educative devices for theological and moral teachings. It builds on Exodus in much the same way that verse 8 develops Exodus 13's idea of binding God's commandments to the arm and forehead. Exodus expects children to ask about the ceremonies commemorating the Exodus. Here, Moses assumes that they will be curious about Israel's entire way of life. Deuteronomy sees all the commandments, civil as well as ceremonial, as opportunities for religious education.

20–21. These two verses play prominent roles in the Passover Haggadah. See the Introduction.

us from Egypt with a mighty hand. ²²The LORD wrought
before our eyes marvelous and destructive signs and portents in Egypt, against Pharaoh and all his household;
²³and us He freed from there, that He might take us and
give us the land that He had promised on oath to our
fathers. ²⁴Then the LORD commanded us to observe all
these laws, to revere the LORD our God, for our lasting
good and for our survival, as is now the case. ²⁵It will
be therefore to our merit before the LORD our God to
observe faithfully this whole Instruction, as He has
commanded us."

בְּמִצְרַיִם וַיּוֹצִאֵנוּ יְהֹוָה מִמִּצְרַיִם בְּיָד חֲזָקָה:
²² וַיִּתֵּן יְהֹוָה אוֹתֹת וּמֹפְתִים גְּדֹלִים וְרָעִים |
בְּמִצְרַיִם בְּפַרְעֹה וּבְכָל־בֵּיתוֹ לְעֵינֵינוּ: ²³ וְאוֹתָנוּ
הוֹצִיא מִשָּׁם לְמַעַן הָבִיא אֹתָנוּ לָתֶת לָנוּ
אֶת־הָאָרֶץ אֲשֶׁר נִשְׁבַּע לַאֲבֹתֵינוּ: ²⁴ וַיְצַוֵּנוּ
יְהֹוָה לַעֲשׂוֹת אֶת־כָּל־הַחֻקִּים הָאֵלֶּה לְיִרְאָה
אֶת־יְהֹוָה אֱלֹהֵינוּ לְטוֹב לָנוּ כָּל־הַיָּמִים לְחַיֹּתֵנוּ
כְּהַיּוֹם הַזֶּה: ²⁵ וּצְדָקָה תִּהְיֶה־לָּנוּ כִּי־נִשְׁמֹר
לַעֲשׂוֹת אֶת־כָּל־הַמִּצְוָה הַזֹּאת לִפְנֵי יְהֹוָה
אֱלֹהֵינוּ כַּאֲשֶׁר צִוָּנוּ: ס   שביעי

22. before our eyes The parents—that is, those over the age of thirty-nine—can assure
their children that they speak from personal experience, not hearsay. See Comment to 4:9.

24. to observe all these laws, to revere the LORD See Comment to verse 2. The absence of
a conjunction between these two phrases suggests that they are equivalents: observing the laws is
itself an act of reverence.

for our lasting good and for our survival Since these phrases consistently describe the
reward for observance, that is what they most likely mean here (cf. 4:1; 5:26; 6:2–3). This creates a
slight redundancy with verse 25, which also indicates that there is a reward for observance. Perhaps to
avoid the redundancy, Ramban takes this clause to refer to the social laws which by their very nature
benefit society (cf. 4:6,8 and Ezek. 20:11,25).

25. It will be therefore to our merit That is, "it will be to our credit," implying that one
accumulates credit for meritorious deeds (see also 24:13).[63] The concept is like that of acquiring
"principal" in the talmudic idea that "a good deed yields a principal and bears interest," as in the list
of "deeds whose interest one uses in this world while the principal remains for the hereafter"[64]—
except that in the Bible the concept refers only to this world. The idiom used in our verse was
employed by the Jews of Elephantine, Egypt, in the fifth century B.C.E. when they assured the Persian
governor of Judah that if he permitted them to rebuild their temple, he would "have a merit before . . .
the God of Heaven more than a man who offers to Him burnt offering and sacrifices worth a
thousand talents of silver . . . and gold."[65] The opposite idea, incurring guilt for sin, is mentioned in
15:9; 23:22–24; and 24:15.

AVOIDING DANGERS TO FAITH
AND OBEDIENCE AFTER THE CONQUEST
OF THE PROMISED LAND (7:1–10:22)

Moses now turns to specific laws, beginning with the first issue that Israel will face when it enters the
promised land: what to do with the Canaanites. The laws about this subject take up four verses
(7:1–3,5); they prompt four chapters of exhortation based on them. This is a characteristic feature of
Deuteronomy: laws are accompanied by explanation, reflection, and exhortation; the proper attitude
in observing the laws is as important as the laws themselves. See the introductory Comments to
chapter 4, "Structure and Themes."

The exhortations prompted by the opening laws deal with dangers to faith and obedience that
might arise during or after the conquest of the land: fear of a numerically superior enemy; the lure of
the Canaanites' idolatry (chap. 7); the sense of self-sufficiency that might result from prosperity and
might lead Israel to forget its dependence on God (chap. 8); and the mistaken feeling that the

7 When the LORD your God brings you to the land that you are about to enter and possess, and He dislodges many nations before you—the Hittites, Girgashites, Amorites,

זֹ כִּי יְבִיאֲךָ יְהוָה אֱלֹהֶיךָ אֶל־הָאָרֶץ אֲשֶׁר־אַתָּה בָא־שָׁמָּה לְרִשְׁתָּהּ וְנָשַׁל גּוֹיִם־רַבִּים | מִפָּנֶיךָ הַחִתִּי וְהַגִּרְגָּשִׁי וְהָאֱמֹרִי וְהַכְּנַעֲנִי וְהַפְּרִזִּי וְהַחִוִּי

conquest is proof of righteousness (chaps. 9–10). Moses argues against all of these possibilities and concludes with a call for reverence and love for God alone and for obedience to His commandments.

Literally these four chapters fall into two units, chapters 7–8 and chapters 9–10. Each deals with some erroneous idea that Israel might arrive at (see 7:17; 8:17; 9:4). Chapters 7–8, which focus on the danger of abandoning God or forgetting Him, are unified by the presence in almost every unit of the root *r-b-h*, which refers to numerousness. It is used to express the numerical superiority of the Canaanites, the Israelites' lack of numbers, God's promise to make the Israelites and their possessions numerous, and the proliferation of wild animals.[1] Chapters 9–10 are unified by the motifs of Israel's rebellion, stiff neck, and provocations.

EXHORTATIONS CONCERNING THE CONQUEST
OF THE PROMISED LAND   (7:1–8:20)

In seeking to prevent Israel from forgetting the Lord and turning to other gods, chapters 7–8 serve as further explications of the first two commandments of the Decalogue. Chapter 7 is concerned with the conquest. It is based on the covenant documents in Exodus 23:20–33 and 34:11–16, with expansions and omissions in keeping with Deuteronomy's sermonic approach and its main ideas.[2] The first section of the chapter states the requirement to eradicate the Canaanites and their religious artifacts; the final section concludes with that theme (7:1–6,17–26). The sequence of ideas in the chapter is prompted by verse 1, which refers to the Canaanites as more numerous than the Israelites. The second section uses this as the occasion to warn Israel against delusions of numerical importance (v. 7), but promises that if Israel obeys God's commandments, God will increase its numbers (v. 13). The last section urges Israel not to be discouraged by the Canaanites' numerical superiority (v. 17), since God will defeat them.[3] On chapter 8, see below.

CHAPTER 7   DESTROYING THE CANAANITES AND THEIR RELIGIOUS ARTIFACTS
                (vv. 1–6)

Moses repeats, with some variation, God's earlier instructions about destroying the Canaanites and their religious objects, and he explains the reasons for these actions. These instructions are based on Exodus 23:24,32–33 and 34:12–16.[4] See also Numbers 33:50–56 and Deuteronomy 12:2–3.

1. When the LORD your God brings you to the land   Although this passage depends on Exodus 23, it does not mention the angel referred to in Exodus 23:20: "When My angel goes before you and brings you to the Amorites." The omission of the angel accords with Deuteronomy's insistence on the exclusive role of God in Israel's history. See Comment to 4:37.

the Hittites,   etc. This list of the inhabitants of the promised land is not meant to be exhaustive. Other lists name as many as twelve nations, though many name six and some name fewer. They indicate the number and variety of the nations that will be conquered, some well known, and others obscure.[5]

Hittites   A people by this name, living in Hebron, Beth-el, and elsewhere in the central highlands of Canaan, is mentioned in Genesis. Outside the Bible "Hittites" refers to several groups, and it is not clear which, if any, is meant in Genesis or here. It refers to the population of Hatti in Asia Minor prior to ca. 2000 B.C.E.; to Indo-Europeans who conquered them and established the Hittite Empire that eventually controlled northern Syria and collapsed around 1200 B.C.E.; and to several small "Neo-Hittite" kingdoms that subsequently sprang up in Syria. The latter are mentioned later in the Bible, from the time of King David on; Assyrian scribes who were familiar with them called all of Syria-Palestine "Hittite land." Conceivably the Hittites in the promised land were settlers

Canaanites, Perizzites, Hivites, and Jebusites, seven na- tions much larger than you—2and the LORD your God delivers them to you and you defeat them, you must doom them to destruction: grant them no terms and give them no quarter. 3You shall not intermarry with them: do not give your daughters to their sons or take their daughters for your sons. 4For they will turn your children away from

וְהַיְבוּסִי שִׁבְעָה גוֹיִם רַבִּים וַעֲצוּמִים מִמֶּךָּ: 2 וּנְתָנָם יְהוָה אֱלֹהֶיךָ לְפָנֶיךָ וְהִכִּיתָם הַחֲרֵם תַּחֲרִים אֹתָם לֹא־תִכְרֹת לָהֶם בְּרִית וְלֹא תְחָנֵּם: 3 וְלֹא תִתְחַתֵּן בָּם בִּתְּךָ לֹא־תִתֵּן לִבְנוֹ וּבִתּוֹ לֹא־תִקַּח לִבְנֶךָ: 4 כִּי־יָסִיר אֶת־בִּנְךָ מֵאַחֲרַי וְעָבְדוּ אֱלֹהִים אֲחֵרִים וְחָרָה אַף־יְהוָה

descended from one of these groups, perhaps refugees fleeing the invasion of the "Sea Peoples" (see Comment to 2:23). Another possibility is that the Hittites here are the inhabitants of the northern extremity of the promised land, south of the Euphrates (see 1:7), in territory that was formerly occupied by the Hittite Empire and later by the Neo-Hittite kingdoms.[6]

Girgashites Virtually nothing is known of this people, although Girgish and similar names appear as names of persons in Ugaritic and Punic texts. There was a land of Kirkash in northern Syria or Asia Minor. Perhaps the Girgashites migrated to Canaan from there.[7]

Amorites, Canaanites Sometimes these terms refer to all the inhabitants of the promised land (see Comment to 1:6), but here they refer to specific groups or inhabitants of specific regions.

Perizzites Several passages mention the Perizzites in connection with the territory of Ephraim and Manasseh, in the north-central part of the land; that may be where they were concen- trated.[8]

Hivites The population of Shechem in the days of Jacob. In Joshua's time they made up the population of Gibeon and were also found in the far north, at the foot of Mount Hermon and in the Lebanon range.[9]

Jebusites The population of Jerusalem prior to its conquest by David. Nothing is known of them outside the Bible, but at Mari, in Syria, Yabasi appears as a clan and as a geographic name.[10]

much larger than you A detail not mentioned in Exodus. It is added here to serve as the basis for Moses' arguments later, in verses 7ff. and 17ff.

2. According to Exodus the Canaanites were to be expelled from the land; here they are to be killed. See Comment to 20:16–17 and Excursus 18. The rabbinic mitigation of this command is discussed in the excursus. (In this and the following comments "Canaanites" refers to all the nations of the promised land.)

grant them no terms That is, conditions, such as corvée labor, in return for which they would be spared (cf. 20:11).

3–4. The reason for the severe treatment of the Canaanites is to prevent the Israelites from intermarrying with them and being lured into the worship of their gods, in violation of the first two commandments. This is the same reason given for the Canaanites' expulsion in Exodus 23:32–33 and 34:15–16. Deuteronomy 20:17–18 explains that these steps are required because of the Canaanites' abominable religious rites, such as child sacrifice, necromancy, and other occult arts (see 12:31 and 18:9–14). The experience at Peor, recorded in Numbers 25:1–3, had already shown how sexual attraction leads to worship of foreign gods.[11]

According to Judges 3:5–6, the Israelites did not eliminate all the Canaanites and did intermarry with them and worship their gods. For further discussion see the commentary to chapter 20 and Excursus 18.

3. You shall not intermarry with them . . . For they will turn your children away from Me to worship other gods Halakhic exegesis, beginning with I Kings 11:1–2 and Ezra 9–10, extends the prohibition to intermarriage with all non-Jews, not only the Canaanites, since all intermarriages carry the danger of apostasy.[12] See Excursus 21.

4. from Me Moses, when transmitting God's commands, often shifts between speaking of God in the third person and quoting Him directly.[13]

Me to worship other gods, and the Lord's anger will blaze forth against you and He will promptly wipe you out. ⁵Instead, this is what you shall do to them: you shall tear down their altars, smash their pillars, cut down their sacred posts, and consign their images to the fire.

⁶For you are a people consecrated to the Lord your

בָּכֶם וְהִשְׁמִידְךָ מַהֵר: 5 כִּי־אִם־כֹּה תַעֲשׂוּ לָהֶם מִזְבְּחֹתֵיהֶם תִּתֹּצוּ וּמַצֵּבֹתָם תְּשַׁבֵּרוּ וַאֲשֵׁירֵהֶם תְּגַדֵּעוּן וּפְסִילֵיהֶם תִּשְׂרְפוּן בָּאֵשׁ: 6 כִּי עַם קָדוֹשׁ אַתָּה לַיהוָה אֱלֹהֶיךָ בְּךָ בָּחַר | יְהוָה אֱלֹהֶיךָ לִהְיוֹת לוֹ לְעַם סְגֻלָּה מִכֹּל הָעַמִּים

He will promptly wipe you out Leaving Canaanites who might lure the Israelites into idolatry was a matter of life and death, since the exclusive worship of YHVH was the fundamental condition for Israel's survival.

5. Even the physical objects of Canaanite religion must be eliminated. The common practice of taking them as booty or bringing them as offerings to the victor's god[14] is forbidden because anything associated with the religion of the Canaanites is repugnant to the Lord (see vv. 25–26).

altars These were structures on which offerings of food, drink, or incense were made to gods. They might be simple stones or mounds of dirt, tables plated with precious metal, or platforms large enough to be ascended by steps or ramps.

pillars This refers here to stones, either cut or uncut, that were erected for a cultic purpose. Some contained engravings or reliefs showing a deity or its symbols, while others were plain. Apparently they were thought to embody the presence of a deity, either by representing the deity or serving as its residence. Sacrifices were offered to them and they were treated as equivalents of idols. This is undoubtedly why the Torah bans the use of pillars in the sanctuaries of the Lord. See Comment to 16:22.[15]

sacred posts The 'asherah was a standing wooden object at a place of worship. According to 16:21, it was a tree planted by an altar. Other passages suggest that it might also be an image, an artificial tree or perhaps a tree trunk or a pole. Some passages suggest that it was regarded as a symbol of the Canaanite goddess Asherah, and it is indeed possible that all sacred trees or posts were called 'asherah because of those which symbolized the goddess. But other passages speak of trees, sometimes called 'asherim, at the cult places of other gods, and even at those of YHVH. In some cases they may have represented the consort of the deity, but perhaps they only symbolized the protection, fertility, or nourishment the worshiper hoped to receive from a deity. The association with the goddess may be the reason the Bible bans these objects at sanctuaries of the Lord (see 16:21).[16]

consign their images to the fire On images see Comments to 4:15–18 and 28. If burning is meant literally, the text must be referring to wooden images with metal plating; see verse 25. However, in 12:3 the verbs referring to the destruction of images and sacred posts are reversed, which may imply that all the verbs in these commands are used loosely to mean simply "destroy." In the excavations at Hazor a statue with its head deliberately chopped off was found in the remains of the stratum destroyed by the Israelites at the time of the conquest.[17]

6. Here Moses expands on the instructions from Exodus 23 and 34: the requirements of verses 2–5 are due to Israel's privileged status; because it is consecrated to the Lord, it must shun all activities that are incompatible with that relationship. This explanation alludes to Exodus 19:6, "you shall be to Me a kingdom of priests and a holy nation," but whereas that passage describes Israel's consecration as its reward for keeping the covenant, here it is cited as a source of its obligations to God.[18]

consecrated *Kadosh*, usually translated "holy," here has the sense of its cognate in talmudic Hebrew, *mekudeshet*, "betrothed," which expresses the idea that when a man betroths a woman she becomes "forbidden to others like something consecrated" (Kid. 2b). The term carries the same implication as the marital metaphor described in the Comment to 5:9: because Israel is the Lord's people, it may have no traffic with idolatry.

In Leviticus *kadosh* is used in a different sense. There it refers to the holiness to which individuals

God: of all the peoples on earth the LORD your God chose you to be His treasured people. 7It is not because you are the most numerous of peoples that the LORD set His heart on you and chose you—indeed, you are the smallest of peoples; 8but it was because the LORD favored you and kept the oath He made to your fathers that the LORD freed you with a mighty hand and rescued you from the house of bondage, from the power of Pharaoh king of Egypt.

אֲשֶׁר עַל־פְּנֵי הָאֲדָמָה: ס 7 לֹא מֵרֻבְּכֶם מִכָּל־הָעַמִּים חָשַׁק יְהֹוָה בָּכֶם וַיִּבְחַר בָּכֶם כִּי־ אַתֶּם הַמְעַט מִכָּל־הָעַמִּים: 8 כִּי מֵאַהֲבַת יְהֹוָה אֶתְכֶם וּמִשָּׁמְרוֹ אֶת־הַשְּׁבֻעָה אֲשֶׁר נִשְׁבַּע לַאֲבֹתֵיכֶם הוֹצִיא יְהֹוָה אֶתְכֶם בְּיָד חֲזָקָה וַיִּפְדְּךָ מִבֵּית עֲבָדִים מִיַּד פַּרְעֹה מֶלֶךְ־מִצְרָיִם:

מפטיר

must aspire. Here it refers to the consecrated status that God conferred on Israel as a whole by the act of election, and which Israel must not profane by repugnant behavior. See also 14:1–2 and 14:21.[19]

the LORD chose you Israel was the only people devoted to YHVH. The Bible considers this a special privilege for which He chose Israel. See Comments to 4:37–38 and 4:19. Moses is at pains to point out that this privilege was not due to Israel's own merits and that it was a source of obligations that are a precondition for its well-being.[20] Compare Amos 3:2: "You alone have I singled out of all the families of the earth—That is why I will call you to account for all your iniquities." On the concept of Israel as a chosen people, see the Introduction.

His treasured people Literally, "treasure [Heb. *segullah*] people." Hebrew *segullah* refers to accumulated property. It often denotes the private accumulation of a person who normally handles the property of others or is financially dependent on others, such as a wife's nest-egg or a slave's *peculium*. The owner's personal stake in his *segullah* gives it the connotation of something cherished, like "treasure." It is in this sense that the text can speak of God's *segullah*: although He owns all things, he cherishes Israel because of His personal stake in her (see also 14:2; 26:18). This use of the term is comparable to its use by a Hittite king who called his vassal, the king of Ugarit, his treasure, and to its use in a Syrian royal seal in which the king is described as the servant of one god, the beloved of another, and the treasure of a third.[21]

AN APPEAL TO AVOID COMPLACENCY AND OBSERVE THE COMMANDMENTS (vv. 7–16)

The concept of Israel's election carries the danger of complacency: Israel might think that God chose it because of some remarkable quality that it already possesses, and that it need do nothing further to earn His blessing. For example, the phenomenal growth of Israel's population (1:10; 10:22) might lead Israel to believe that it was chosen because of numbers. Moses therefore digresses from the instructions about the conquest to warn Israel against such delusions. This warning is prompted by the reference in verse 2 to "nations much larger than you."[22] Moses reminds Israel that, notwithstanding its present size, it is still the smallest of nations. It was not chosen on account of its own merits, but because of God's love for it and His faithfulness to His promise to Israel's ancestors; its future well-being depends on adherence to God's commandments. Another appeal against complacency appears in 9:4ff.

7. you are smallest of peoples This assertion contrasts with others which say that in Egypt Israel grew into "a great and very populous nation" (26:5) and that it is now as numerous as the stars (1:10; 10:22; 28:62). Unless the present assertion is a hyperbole for the sake of dismissing Israel's size as a factor, it may reflect the conditions of a different historical period than the other references.[23]

9–11. Not only does God keep faith with the descendants of those who are loyal to Him, as shown in verses 7–8; He also punishes those who are not. Observance of the commandments is therefore essential.

9. Know, therefore Know, from God's election and redemption of Israel, that He is reliable and steadfast. The terms used for these qualities are synonymous with those used in 5:10 in the Decalogue.

9Know, therefore, that only the LORD your God is God, the steadfast God who keeps His covenant faithfully to the thousandth generation of those who love Him and keep His commandments, 10but who instantly requites with destruction those who reject Him—never slow with those who reject Him, but requiting them instantly. 11Therefore, observe faithfully the Instruction—the laws and the rules—with which I charge you today.

ʿEKEV

12And if you do obey these rules and observe them carefully, the LORD your God will maintain faithfully for you the covenant that He made on oath with your fathers: 13He will favor you and bless you and multiply you; He will bless the

9 וְיָדַעְתָּ כִּי־יְהֹוָה אֱלֹהֶיךָ הוּא הָאֱלֹהִים הָאֵל הַנֶּאֱמָן שֹׁמֵר הַבְּרִית וְהַחֶסֶד לְאֹהֲבָיו וּלְשֹׁמְרֵי מִצְוֺתוֹ לְאֶלֶף דּוֹר: 10 וּמְשַׁלֵּם לְשֹׂנְאָיו אֶל־פָּנָיו לְהַאֲבִידוֹ לֹא יְאַחֵר לְשֹׂנְאוֹ אֶל־פָּנָיו יְשַׁלֶּם־לוֹ: 11 וְשָׁמַרְתָּ אֶת־הַמִּצְוָה וְאֶת־הַחֻקִּים וְאֶת־הַמִּשְׁפָּטִים אֲשֶׁר אָנֹכִי מְצַוְּךָ הַיּוֹם לַעֲשׂוֹתָם: פ

עקב

12 וְהָיָה | עֵקֶב תִּשְׁמְעוּן אֵת הַמִּשְׁפָּטִים הָאֵלֶּה וּשְׁמַרְתֶּם וַעֲשִׂיתֶם אֹתָם וְשָׁמַר יְהֹוָה אֱלֹהֶיךָ לְךָ אֶת־הַבְּרִית וְאֶת־הַחֶסֶד אֲשֶׁר נִשְׁבַּע לַאֲבֹתֶיךָ: 13 וַאֲהֵבְךָ וּבֵרַכְךָ וְהִרְבֶּךָ וּבֵרַךְ פְּרִי־בִטְנְךָ וּפְרִי־

v. 9. מִצְוֹתָיו ק׳

10. instantly requites . . . requites instantly Rather, "requites in person . . . but requiting them in person" (lit., "to his face"; see Comment to 4:37). Although punishment may extend to three or four generations of descendants (5:9), the offender himself cannot hope to escape punishment if he violates God's laws. The relationship between this idea and 5:9 is discussed in Excursus 8.

11. The lesson to be drawn from verses 9–10 is that Israel should obey the commandments. Similar lessons are drawn in 4:39–40; 8:5–6; 11:2–8.

observe The same verb (sh-m-r) describes Israel's obligation to "observe" and God's action of "keeping" the covenant (v. 9). This implies that there is a moral dimension to Moses' argument: Israel's motive should be to respond to God's faithfulness with its own faithfulness, not simply to avoid punishment and receive a reward. The same idea is expressed in reverse order in the next verse: "if you observe [sh-m-r] . . . the LORD will maintain [sh-m-r]."

ʿEkev **12–16.** Following the digression of verses 7–11, Moses resumes his paraphrase of the covenant documents in Exodus. He describes the blessings that obedience will bring. The description is based on Exodus 23:25–26, but in the present context these blessings are the reward for observing the totality of the law, not only the instructions about the conquest as in Exodus.

12. if Hebrew ʿekev, literally, "on the heels of," that is, "as a consequence of." The Masoretic Text begins a new paragraph (and a new weekly portion) here, perhaps because it sees this word as framing a literary unit that runs through 8:20, whose final clause begins with the same word (rendered "because"). Logically, however, verses 12–16 seem to be a continuation of verse 11.

for you By redeeming the Exodus generation God has fulfilled His oaths to the patriarchs. If the present generation obeys His commandments, He will fulfill those oaths on its behalf as well.

13–15. Moses specifies what is meant by the promise he has frequently made that "it will go well" with Israel in the promised land. The promise that God will provide fertility and health buttresses the command to shun the religion of the Canaanites (vv. 4–5): the Canaanites believed that fertility and health were under the control of their gods (see Comment to 11:16–17), but Moses teaches that they are controlled by the Lord.

Several of the blessings mentioned here are paralleled in 28:1–11.

13. favor Literally, "love." See Comment to 6:5.

bless you and multiply you These promises are not found in Exodus 23:25–26, but they are the main elements of God's oaths to the patriarchs, in addition to the land of Canaan.[24] By mentioning them, Moses makes plain that the reward in store for Israel is a fulfillment of the patriarchal covenant. The promise to multiply Israel also ties the promises in with verse 7: although Israel is a small people, God will increase its numbers.

issue of your womb and the produce of your soil, your new grain and wine and oil, the calving of your herd and the lambing of your flock, in the land that He swore to your fathers to assign to you. ¹⁴You shall be blessed above all other peoples: there shall be no sterile male or female among you or among your livestock. ¹⁵The LORD will ward off from you all sickness; He will not bring upon you any of the dreadful diseases of Egypt, about which you know, but will inflict them upon all your enemies.

¹⁶You shall destroy all the peoples that the LORD your God delivers to you, showing them no pity. And you shall not worship their gods, for that would be a snare to you.

אַדְמָתֶ֜ךָ דְּגָֽנְךָ֣ וְתִֽירֹֽשְׁךָ֣ וְיִצְהָרֶ֗ךָ שְׁגַר־אֲלָפֶ֙יךָ֙ וְעַשְׁתְּרֹ֣ת צֹאנֶ֔ךָ עַ֚ל הָ֣אֲדָמָ֔ה אֲשֶׁר־נִשְׁבַּ֥ע לַאֲבֹתֶ֖יךָ לָ֥תֶת לָֽךְ׃ 14 בָּר֥וּךְ תִּֽהְיֶ֖ה מִכָּל־הָעַמִּ֑ים לֹא־יִהְיֶ֥ה בְךָ֛ עָקָ֥ר וַֽעֲקָרָ֖ה וּבִבְהֶמְתֶּֽךָ׃ 15 וְהֵסִ֧יר יְהוָ֛ה מִמְּךָ֖ כָּל־חֹ֑לִי וְכָל־מַדְוֵי֩ מִצְרַ֨יִם הָרָעִ֜ים אֲשֶׁ֣ר יָדַ֗עְתָּ לֹ֤א יְשִׂימָם֙ בָּ֔ךְ וּנְתָנָ֖ם בְּכָל־שֹׂנְאֶֽיךָ׃ 16 וְאָכַלְתָּ֣ אֶת־כָּל־הָֽעַמִּ֗ים אֲשֶׁ֨ר יְהוָ֤ה אֱלֹהֶ֙יךָ֙ נֹתֵ֣ן לָ֔ךְ לֹא־תָחֹ֥ס עֵֽינְךָ֖ עֲלֵיהֶ֑ם וְלֹ֤א תַעֲבֹד֙ אֶת־אֱלֹ֣הֵיהֶ֔ם כִּֽי־מוֹקֵ֥שׁ ה֖וּא לָֽךְ׃ ס 17 כִּ֤י תֹאמַר֙

new grain and wine and oil These are the principal products of Israelite agriculture. Compare 6:12; 8:8; 28:51.

the calving of your herd and the lambing of your flock Rather, "the calves of your oxen and the lambs of your flocks."[25]

The terms for grain (*dagan*), wine (*tirosh*), calves (*sheger*), and lambs (*'ashtarot*, lit., "Astartes") are also names of Semitic deities. The use of the same word to refer to a deity and a phenomenon which that deity was thought to personify or control is comparable to the English use of "cereal," which is related to the name of the Greek goddess Ceres. Most Israelites were probably as unaware of the etymology of these terms as English speakers are when they speak of cereal.[26]

14. blessed See Comment to 2:7.

sterile male or female Human sterility was regarded as one of the greatest personal tragedies. Abraham felt that nothing God could give him would be meaningful if he died childless (Gen. 15:2), and Rachel cried out in frustration, "Give me children or I shall die" (Gen. 30:1). Archaeologists have found hundreds of fertility charms, which testify to the longing for children in the ancient Near East and Israel.[27] Male infertility is mentioned less frequently than that of females (it is not mentioned in Exod. 23:26), but, as the present passage shows, it was recognized.

15. the dreadful diseases of Egypt This could refer to the pestilence and skin inflammation that were part of the ten plagues.[28] More likely, it refers to diseases endemic to Egypt, such as elephantiasis, ophthalmia, and dysentery. The Roman natural historian Pliny (first century C.E.) called Egypt the mother of skin diseases and referred to elephantiasis as "the particular Egyptian disease"[29] (cf. 28:27,60).

16. Moses recapitulates the contents of verses 1–5 before resuming their theme, the conquest of the land. The first part of the verse can be read either as a command or as a promise. As a promise of victory over enemies, it is reminiscent of another of the promises that God made to the patriarchs.[30] That is probably why the Masoretic Text groups this verse with verses 12–15 instead of verses 17–26.

that would be a snare to you Worshiping the Canaanites' gods would lead to Israel's ruin. Compare verse 25 and 12:30–31. A similar warning also appears in Exodus 23 (see v. 33).[31]

ISRAEL NEED NOT FEAR THE CANAANITES DESPITE THEIR NUMBERS (vv. 17–26)

After disabusing the Israelites of any illusion of their own numerical grandeur, Moses wants to ensure that awareness of the Canaanites' numerical superiority does not panic them as it had the previous generation (1:18). He therefore reassures the Israelites that their small numbers will not prevent God from granting them victory. Then he returns to the main theme of the chapter: the

17Should you say to yourselves, "These nations are more numerous than we; how can we dispossess them?" 18You need have no fear of them. You have but to bear in mind what the LORD your God did to Pharaoh and all the Egyptians: 19the wondrous acts that you saw with your own eyes, the signs and the portents, the mighty hand, and the outstretched arm by which the LORD your God liberated you. Thus will the LORD your God do to all the peoples you now fear. 20The LORD your God will also send a plague against them, until those who are left in hiding perish before you. 21Do not stand in dread of them, for the LORD your God is in your midst, a great and awesome God.

22The LORD your God will dislodge those peoples before you little by little; you will not be able to put an end to them at once, else the wild beasts would multiply to your hurt. 23The LORD your God will deliver them up to you, throwing them into utter panic until they are wiped

בִּלְבָבְךָ֗ רַבִּ֛ים הַגּוֹיִ֥ם הָאֵ֖לֶּה מִמֶּ֑נִּי אֵיכָ֥ה אוּכַ֖ל לְהוֹרִישָֽׁם: 18 לֹ֥א תִירָ֖א מֵהֶ֑ם זָכֹ֣ר תִּזְכֹּ֗ר אֵ֤ת אֲשֶׁר־עָשָׂה֙ יְהוָ֣ה אֱלֹהֶ֔יךָ לְפַרְעֹ֖ה וּלְכָל־מִצְרָֽיִם: 19 הַמַּסֹּ֣ת הַגְּדֹלֹ֣ת אֲשֶׁר־רָא֣וּ עֵינֶ֗יךָ וְהָאֹתֹ֤ת וְהַמֹּֽפְתִים֙ וְהַיָּ֤ד הַחֲזָקָה֙ וְהַזְּרֹ֣עַ הַנְּטוּיָ֔ה אֲשֶׁ֥ר הוֹצִֽאֲךָ֖ יְהוָ֣ה אֱלֹהֶ֑יךָ כֵּֽן־יַעֲשֶׂ֞ה יְהוָ֤ה אֱלֹהֶ֨יךָ֙ לְכָל־הָ֣עַמִּ֔ים אֲשֶׁר־אַתָּ֥ה יָרֵ֖א מִפְּנֵיהֶֽם: 20 וְגַם֙ אֶת־הַצִּרְעָ֔ה יְשַׁלַּ֛ח יְהוָ֥ה אֱלֹהֶ֖יךָ בָּ֑ם עַד־אֲבֹ֗ד הַנִּשְׁאָרִ֛ים וְהַנִּסְתָּרִ֖ים מִפָּנֶֽיךָ: 21 לֹ֥א תַעֲרֹ֖ץ מִפְּנֵיהֶ֑ם כִּֽי־יְהוָ֤ה אֱלֹהֶ֨יךָ֙ בְּקִרְבֶּ֔ךָ אֵ֥ל גָּד֖וֹל וְנוֹרָֽא: 22 וְנָשַׁל֩ יְהוָ֨ה אֱלֹהֶ֜יךָ אֶת־הַגּוֹיִ֥ם הָאֵ֛ל מִפָּנֶ֖יךָ מְעַ֣ט מְעָ֑ט לֹ֤א תוּכַל֙ כַּלֹּתָ֣ם מַהֵ֔ר פֶּן־תִּרְבֶּ֥ה עָלֶ֖יךָ חַיַּ֥ת הַשָּׂדֶֽה: 23 וּנְתָנָ֛ם יְהוָ֥ה אֱלֹהֶ֖יךָ לְפָנֶ֑יךָ וְהָמָם֙ מְהוּמָ֣ה גְדֹלָ֔ה עַ֖ד הִשָּֽׁמְדָֽם: 24 וְנָתַ֣ן

destruction of the Canaanites and their religious objects. Like verses 1–6 and 12–16, this section, too, is based on the covenant document in Exodus 23 (see Exod. 23:27–30).

17-19. These verses reflect Moses' continuing concern in Deuteronomy to reassure the Israelites, as they prepare for battle, not to fear the Canaanites' numbers.[32] As usual, the experience of the Exodus is the basis of the reassurance. See Comments to 1:21 and 29–31. The form of his address—anticipating a thought that Israel might have and countering it with a reminder of experiences that prove otherwise—is one that he also uses in 8:17–18 and 9:4–7.

20. There will be no escape: even those who elude the Israelites will be overtaken.

plague Hebrew *tsir'ah*. A more likely translation is "hornets" or "wasps," as in rabbinic Hebrew, since that is the only actually attested meaning of the word.[33] Literally the text means that ferocious swarms of wasps will hunt down the remaining Canaanites and sting them to death. Some commentators compare this to instances of populations driven from their homes by swarms of ferocious insects.[34] Another possibility is that *tsir'ah* is a metonymy for panic or frenzy like that caused by wasps and means that God will cause the remaining Canaanites to panic and flee or be caught.[35]

21. *in your midst* See Comment to 6:15.

22. Because of their small numbers, there were too few Israelites to fill the entire land. If all the Canaanites were dislodged at once, some of the land would remain unoccupied and would be overrun by wild animals. Therefore God will give Israel only as much territory as it can occupy, and—if they obey His commandments (19:8–9)—will give them the rest when there are enough of them to fill the entire land. The same thing is said in Exodus 23:29–30, whereas Deuteronomy 9:3 says that the conquest will be quick; see Comment there.

23. *throwing them into utter panic* Rather, "throwing them into utter confusion," *ve-hamam mehumah gedolah*. The translation "panic" relates the idiom to the fear that God induces to incapacitate and overwhelm Israel's enemies.[36] However, the terms in question rarely, if ever, express the idea of fear, although fear is sometimes *part* of the situation they describe. The underlying root *hum* (a variant of the more common *h-m-m*) refers to noise; it is probably an onomatopoeia, like English "hum."[37] The noun *mehumah* means "confusion," "turmoil," "tumult." It is used in reference to war, to confusion that can cause soldiers to kill their comrades, to the pandemonium caused by a raging pestilence, and to social disorder.[38] Here it is comparable to Greek *kydoimos*, the

out. ²⁴He will deliver their kings into your hand, and you shall obliterate their name from under the heavens; no man shall stand up to you, until you have wiped them out.

²⁵You shall consign the images of their gods to the fire; you shall not covet the silver and gold on them and keep it for yourselves, lest you be ensnared thereby; for that is abhorrent to the LORD your God. ²⁶You must not bring an abhorrent thing into your house, or you will be proscribed like it; you must reject it as abominable and abhorrent, for it is proscribed.

מַלְכֵיהֶם֙ בְּיָדֶ֔ךָ וְהַאֲבַדְתָּ֣ אֶת־שְׁמָ֔ם מִתַּ֖חַת הַשָּׁמָ֑יִם לֹֽא־יִתְיַצֵּ֥ב אִישׁ֙ בְּפָנֶ֔יךָ עַ֥ד הִשְׁמִֽדְךָ֖ אֹתָֽם:
²⁵ פְּסִילֵ֤י אֱלֹֽהֵיהֶם֙ תִּשְׂרְפ֣וּן בָּאֵ֔שׁ לֹֽא־תַחְמֹד֩ כֶּ֨סֶף וְזָהָ֤ב עֲלֵיהֶם֙ וְלָקַחְתָּ֣ לָ֔ךְ פֶּ֚ן תִּוָּקֵ֣שׁ בּ֔וֹ כִּ֧י תוֹעֲבַ֛ת יְהֹוָ֥ה אֱלֹהֶ֖יךָ הֽוּא: ²⁶ וְלֹא־תָבִ֤יא תֽוֹעֵבָה֙ אֶל־בֵּיתֶ֔ךָ וְהָיִ֥יתָ חֵ֖רֶם כָּמֹ֑הוּ שַׁקֵּ֧ץ ׀ תְּשַׁקְּצֶ֛נּוּ וְתַעֵ֥ב ׀ תְּתַעֲבֶ֖נּוּ כִּי־חֵ֥רֶם הֽוּא: פ

confusion or tumult (sometimes personified) that the gods inflict on the enemies of their protégés in the Homeric epics.³⁹ The related verb *h-m-m*, when not accompanied by *mehumah*, means "rout," and frequently refers to the defeat that God inflicts on Israel's enemies. See Comment to 2:15.

24. ***their kings*** Canaan was not a unified country but a series of city-states ruled by individual kings. Thirty-one Canaanite kings conquered by the Israelites are listed in Joshua 12:7–24.

obliterate their name This is a frequent curse,⁴⁰ referring to total extinction. People's names are all that is left of them on earth after death, and the preservation of their names is considered vitally important for the well-being of their spirits in the afterlife (see Excursus 23). To obliterate one's name is to leave no oral or written trace of his name on earth, that is, to leave him no survivors or monuments.⁴¹

from under the heavens From the surface of the earth. See Comment to 2:25.

25. Moses returns to the theme with which the chapter began, obliterating idolatry (vv. 1–6). Since idols are abhorrent, even the reuse of their silver and gold plating for nonreligious purposes is prohibited (see Comment to v. 5). Such reuse might seem innocuous, but it would be a trap (see v. 16); God would punish Israel for keeping anything associated with idols.

abhorrent to the LORD *To'evah* refers to morally and religiously detestable practices and objects such as cheating, perverse sexual relations, impure foods, defective sacrifices, and especially idolatry and its rites, such as child sacrifice and occult practices. The phrase "abhorrent to the LORD" expresses God's revulsion at these things.⁴²

26. ***you will be proscribed . . . it is proscribed*** *Ḥerem*, "a proscribed thing," is the noun related to the verb *haḥarem*, "doom to destruction" (v. 2). Objects used in idolatry were to be destroyed together with the idolaters. This verse indicates that the proscribed status of such objects was quasi-contagious: one who appropriated them for himself became proscribed like them.⁴³ Retaining vestiges of idolatry would earn Israel the same fate as the Canaanites.

CHAPTER **8**   AN APPEAL TO REMEMBER ISRAEL'S DEPENDENCE ON GOD
                            AND TO OBSERVE THE COMMANDMENTS (vv. 1–20)

Chapter 8 continues to address dangers to faith that might arise in the promised land (see the introductory Comments to chap. 7). Prosperity may lead Israel to forget its dependence on God, a danger that was addressed briefly in 6:10–15.¹ Once again, Moses' argument is based on history: Israel's experience in the wilderness showed that man depends on God, not solely on natural forces, for sustenance. In the promised land Israel will no longer have to overcome hardships of the sort that made this clear in the wilderness, but if it forgets this lesson and turns to other gods, it will suffer the same fate as the nations whose land it is now receiving.

The chapter seems to constitute a single appeal.² It is based on the memory of God's provision of manna in the wilderness. It is held together by repeated calls to remember and not forget (vv. 2,11,14,18,19), by contrasts between the riches of the promised land and the rigors of the wilder-

8 You shall faithfully observe all the Instruction that I enjoin upon you today, that you may thrive and increase and be able to possess the land that the LORD promised on oath to your fathers.

²Remember the long way that the LORD your God has made you travel in the wilderness these past forty years, that He might test you by hardships to learn what was in your hearts: whether you would keep His commandments or not. ³He subjected you to the hardship of hunger and

ח כָּל־הַמִּצְוָה אֲשֶׁר אָנֹכִי מְצַוְּךָ הַיּוֹם תִּשְׁמְרוּן
לַעֲשׂוֹת לְמַעַן תִּחְיוּן וּרְבִיתֶם וּבָאתֶם וִירִשְׁתֶּם
אֶת־הָאָרֶץ אֲשֶׁר־נִשְׁבַּע יְהוָה לַאֲבֹתֵיכֶם:
² וְזָכַרְתָּ אֶת־כָּל־הַדֶּרֶךְ אֲשֶׁר הֹלִיכֲךָ יְהוָה
אֱלֹהֶיךָ זֶה אַרְבָּעִים שָׁנָה בַּמִּדְבָּר לְמַעַן עַנֹּתְךָ
לְנַסֹּתְךָ לָדַעַת אֶת־אֲשֶׁר בִּלְבָבְךָ הֲתִשְׁמֹר
מִצְוֹתָו אִם־לֹא: ³ וַיְעַנְּךָ וַיַּרְעִבֶךָ וַיַּאֲכִלְךָ אֶת־

מְצֹותָיו ק'   v. 2.

ness (vv. 7–10,12–13,15), and by derivatives of the root *r-b-h*, "be numerous, increase, multiply," as in chapter 7 (see vv. 1,12). The structure of the chapter is chiastic: appeals to observe the commandments and to remember and not forget appear at the beginning and end. Inside these are references to the desert and the manna. Inside these references, in turn, are appeals for observance and remembering under conditions of prosperity. This structure may be diagrammed as follows:

    A. Observe the commandments and prosper (v. 1)
      B. The wilderness and the manna (vv. 2–4)
        C. Observe the commandments in prosperity (vv. 6–10)
        C'. Do not forget the Lord in prosperity (vv. 11–14)
      B'. The wilderness and the manna (vv. 15–16)
    A'. Remember and do not forget the Lord or you will perish (vv. 18–20)

1.   Since his message is that Israel should always remember its dependence on God, it is noteworthy that Moses begins with an appeal to observe the commandments. This reflects the biblical view that awareness of God and obedience are not separate phenomena: the commandments are the practical expression of awareness of God and serve to foster it. Note verses 6 and 11 and see Comment to 6:2.

that you may . . . increase   So as to take control of the entire land; see Comment to 7:22.³

2-6.   These verses are the basis of Moses' appeal. The purpose of the hardships in the wilderness was to prepare Israel for the future. Although the reason that God kept Israel in the wilderness was to punish the rebellious Exodus generation, He used those years to teach Israel that it is dependent on Him, and to test whether it would obey His commandments.⁴ The achievement of those purposes will be indicated by Israel's continued observance and reverence. See also 29:4–5.

2. that He might test you by hardships   Literally, "that He might subject you to hardship so that He might test you." God made the Israelites hungry and then fed them manna (vv. 3,16), by which He tested their obedience and trust (Exod. 16:4). He instructed them not to hoard manna overnight and not to search for any on the Sabbath.⁵ Those who violated these instructions showed a lack of confidence that God would continue to provide food (Exod. 16:20,27).

to learn   Maimonides found it problematic that God would test Israel in order to learn something; that would imply that He did not know how they would act. Hence he took this verse to mean that the test was for *others* to learn the strength of Israel's obedience and to see how God provides for those who are devoted to Him. However, this interpretation is forced. The concept of divine foreknowledge is not a systematic doctrine in the Bible, for the Bible sometimes describes God as testing and discovering.⁶ Because humanity has free will, God does not know how people will act, and He therefore tests them.

3.   Israel's hunger in the wilderness was no accident: it was brought about by God to teach the people that nature alone could not be relied upon for food. Then He fed them manna, a previously unknown food, to show them that nourishment depends on Him: man does not live on natural foods alone but on whatever God decrees to be nourishing.⁷

then gave you manna to eat, which neither you nor your fathers had ever known, in order to teach you that man does not live on bread alone, but that man may live on anything that the LORD decrees. 4The clothes upon you did not wear out, nor did your feet swell these forty years. 5Bear in mind that the LORD your God disciplines you just as a man disciplines his son. 6Therefore keep the commandments of the LORD your God: walk in His ways and revere Him.

הַמָּן אֲשֶׁר לֹא־יָדַעְתָּ וְלֹא יָדְעוּן אֲבֹתֶיךָ לְמַעַן הוֹדִעֲךָ כִּי לֹא עַל־הַלֶּחֶם לְבַדּוֹ יִחְיֶה הָאָדָם כִּי עַל־כָּל־מוֹצָא פִי־יְהוָה יִחְיֶה הָאָדָם: 4 שִׂמְלָתְךָ לֹא בָלְתָה מֵעָלֶיךָ וְרַגְלְךָ לֹא בָצֵקָה זֶה אַרְבָּעִים שָׁנָה: 5 וְיָדַעְתָּ עִם־לְבָבֶךָ כִּי כַּאֲשֶׁר יְיַסֵּר אִישׁ אֶת־בְּנוֹ יְהוָה אֱלֹהֶיךָ מְיַסְּרֶךָּ: 6 וְשָׁמַרְתָּ אֶת־מִצְוֹת יְהוָה אֱלֹהֶיךָ לָלֶכֶת בִּדְרָכָיו וּלְיִרְאָה אֹתוֹ:

manna If the manna has a natural explanation, it was probably the sweet, edible honeydew found in parts of the Sinai in June and July. This substance comes from secretions that scale insects and plant lice deposit on tamarisk trees and that crystallize and fall to the ground as sticky solids. If this honeydew was the manna, what was miraculous about the Israelites' experience was that it arrived just when they needed it and that, contrary to its natural pattern, it was found throughout the Sinai, lasted year-round, and was produced in quantities sufficient to feed the entire people. The term "manna" (*man*) is used in Arabic for honeydew and for some of the insects that produce it.[8] According to Exodus, the term means essentially "whatch'macallit." The Israelites called it this because when they first saw it they asked "what [*man*] is it?" (see Exod. 16:15,31). The very name thus expresses its unprecedented character.

4. Another indication of Israel's dependence on God and His control of nature: Israel's clothing and feet were immune to the effects of nature during the years in the wilderness.

The clothes upon you did not wear out Better, "Your clothing did not wear out and fall off of you."[9]

5. The hardships in the desert are a paradigm for all of God's disciplinary actions with Israel: their aim is educational. The comparison to a father's discipline indicates that the discipline, whether punitive or not, is administered with love, as stated explicitly in Proverbs 3:11–12:

Do not reject the discipline of the LORD, my son;
Do not abhor His rebuke.
For whom the LORD loves He rebukes,
As a father the son whom he favors.

6. See introductory Comments to the chapter and to verses 2–6.

walk in His ways The ways He commanded (see 5:30).

7–18. The lessons taught in the wilderness will not be apparent in the promised land, where Israel will lack nothing. In prosperity Israel's dependence on God will be less obvious, and once its own efforts begin to succeed Israel might imagine that all its new wealth is due to those efforts. It must therefore keep in mind what it learned in the wilderness, always remembering that prosperity depends on God.

In describing the riches of the land in verses 7–9 Moses' style becomes elevated and quasi-poetic. The description consists of six parts, each beginning with "a land" followed by some of the land's features. In this way the text mentions only a few features at a time and lingers over them lovingly before going on to the next group. Several of these parts are formulated in parallelism (cf. 11:11–12). The laudatory description culminates in verse 10, where "land" is mentioned a seventh time in the phrase "the good land," which echoes the same phrase in verse 7 and, with it, forms a frame around the description. The description goes far beyond the terms of 6:10–11. It makes the contrast with the wilderness palpable (cf. vv. 7–8 to the description of the wilderness in Num. 20:5) and the likelihood of taking prosperity for granted more understandable.

7For the LORD your God is bringing you into a good land, a land with streams and springs and fountains issuing from plain and hill; 8a land of wheat and barley, of vines, figs, and pomegranates, a land of olive trees and honey; 9a land where you may eat food without stint, where you will lack nothing; a land whose rocks are iron and from whose hills you can mine copper. 10When you have eaten your fill, give thanks to the LORD your God for the good land which He has given you.

7 כִּי יְהוָה אֱלֹהֶיךָ מְבִיאֲךָ אֶל־אֶרֶץ טוֹבָה אֶרֶץ נַחֲלֵי מָיִם עֲיָנֹת וּתְהֹמֹת יֹצְאִים בַּבִּקְעָה וּבָהָר:
8 אֶרֶץ חִטָּה וּשְׂעֹרָה וְגֶפֶן וּתְאֵנָה וְרִמּוֹן אֶרֶץ־זֵית שֶׁמֶן וּדְבָשׁ: 9 אֶרֶץ אֲשֶׁר לֹא בְמִסְכֵּנֻת תֹּאכַל־בָּהּ לֶחֶם לֹא־תֶחְסַר כֹּל בָּהּ אֶרֶץ אֲשֶׁר אֲבָנֶיהָ בַרְזֶל וּמֵהֲרָרֶיהָ תַּחְצֹב נְחֹשֶׁת: 10 וְאָכַלְתָּ וְשָׂבָעְתָּ וּבֵרַכְתָּ אֶת־יְהוָה אֱלֹהֶיךָ עַל־הָאָרֶץ הַטֹּבָה אֲשֶׁר נָתַן־לָךְ: שני

7. *a good land* The goodness of the promised land is a leitmotif of Deuteronomy and is graphically illustrated by the following description. The phrase occurs no less than ten times in the book.[10]

8. The principal agricultural products of the land, known in halakhic literature as "the seven species for which the land of Israel is praised." The appeal of these products is reflected in 2 Kings 18:32, where an Assyrian official tries to convince the Judahites to surrender by promising that their place of exile will be a land like their own, described in virtually identical terms. Part of Syria-Palestine is described in similar terms in the Egyptian text quoted in Excursus 9.

wheat and barley The land's principal grains, from which bread, the staple of the Israelite diet, was made. See also Comment to 6:12.

vines Important as the source of grapes and of wine, the principal man-made drink. See Comment to 6:11.

figs A favorite fruit, eaten fresh or dried or baked into cakes.

pomegranates Another popular fruit, eaten fresh or dried. Their juice could be drunk or made into wine. They were also valued as objects of beauty and symbols of fertility, and were therefore used as decorations in Israelite religious and secular art.[11]

olive trees Rather, "oil-olives." In mishnaic Hebrew "oil-olive" refers to a kind of olive that retains its oil even under rainy conditions when other kinds lose it. The text uses this phrase advisedly since olives were valued chiefly for their oil; see Comment to 6:11.[12]

honey Since this verse is a list of agricultural products, "honey" must refer to the nectar of dates and figs. See Excursus 9.

9. *whose rocks are iron and from whose hills you can mine copper* The wording reflects the fact that iron is mined from the surface, while copper is mined underground.

Within the boundaries of the promised land the only known sources of iron and copper are small deposits in Galilee and in the Bekaa Valley. There are more significant deposits in Gilead (in Transjordan), in the Jordan Rift south of the Dead Sea, and in the southern Negev. If the text has some of these in mind, then these verses refer to territory controlled by Israel in later times, not only territory within the boundaries of 1:6. Some scholars believe that the reference to iron includes basalt, a volcanic stone containing about 20 percent iron, which is found in a number of places, especially in the Jezreel Valley and north of it.[13]

10. *give thanks* Literally, "bless." As Ehrlich notes, in blessings addressed to the Lord, *b-r-k* means "thank"; thus "blessed are You, O LORD" means "thank You, O LORD."

Grammatically *u-verakhta* could mean either "you *will* give thanks" or "you *shall* give thanks." In the first case it means that the land is so bountiful that it will move the Israelites to thank the Lord when they have eaten their fill.[14] In the second case it is a requirement that Israel thank the Lord when it has done so. Halakhic interpretation follows the second possibility and takes this verse as a commandment to recite the *Birkat Ha-Mazon*, the blessing after meals. This interpretation is favored by verses 12ff, which admonish Israel not to forget the Lord when it has eaten its fill. This would be

11Take care lest you forget the LORD your God and fail to keep His commandments, His rules, and His laws, which I enjoin upon you today. 12When you have eaten your fill, and have built fine houses to live in, 13and your herds and flocks have multiplied, and your silver and gold have increased, and everything you own has prospered, 14beware lest your heart grow haughty and you forget the LORD your God—who freed you from the land of Egypt, the house of bondage; 15who led you through the great and terrible wilderness with its *seraph* serpents and scorpions, a parched land with no water in it, who brought forth water for you from the flinty rock; 16who fed you in the wilderness with manna, which your fathers had never known, in order to test you by hardships only to benefit

וּ הִשָּׁ֣מֶר לְךָ֗ פֶּן־תִּשְׁכַּ֖ח אֶת־יְהוָ֣ה אֱלֹהֶ֑יךָ
לְבִלְתִּ֣י שְׁמֹ֤ר מִצְוֺתָיו֙ וּמִשְׁפָּטָ֣יו וְחֻקֹּתָ֔יו אֲשֶׁ֛ר
אָנֹכִ֥י מְצַוְּךָ֖ הַיּֽוֹם: 12 פֶּן־תֹּאכַ֖ל וְשָׂבָ֑עְתָּ וּבָתִּ֥ים
טוֹבִ֛ים תִּבְנֶ֖ה וְיָשָֽׁבְתָּ: 13 וּבְקָֽרְךָ֤ וְצֹֽאנְךָ֙ יִרְבְּיֻ֔ן
וְכֶ֥סֶף וְזָהָ֖ב יִרְבֶּה־לָּ֑ךְ וְכֹ֥ל אֲשֶׁר־לְךָ֖ יִרְבֶּֽה:
14 וְרָ֖ם לְבָבֶ֑ךָ וְשָֽׁכַחְתָּ֙ אֶת־יְהוָ֣ה אֱלֹהֶ֔יךָ
הַמּוֹצִֽיאֲךָ֛ מֵאֶ֥רֶץ מִצְרַ֖יִם מִבֵּ֥ית עֲבָדִֽים:
15 הַמּוֹלִֽיכֲךָ֗ בַּמִּדְבָּ֣ר | הַגָּדֹ֤ל וְהַנּוֹרָא֙ נָחָ֣שׁ |
שָׂרָ֣ף וְעַקְרָ֗ב וְצִמָּאוֹן֙ אֲשֶׁ֣ר אֵֽין־מָ֔יִם הַמּוֹצִ֥יא לְךָ֛
מַ֖יִם מִצּ֥וּר הַֽחַלָּמִֽישׁ: 16 הַמַּֽאֲכִֽלְךָ֥ מָן֙ בַּמִּדְבָּ֔ר
אֲשֶׁ֥ר לֹא־יָדְע֖וּן אֲבֹתֶ֑יךָ לְמַ֣עַן עַנֹּֽתְךָ֗ וּלְמַ֙עַן֙
נַסֹּתֶ֔ךָ לְהֵיטִֽבְךָ֖ בְּאַחֲרִיתֶֽךָ: 17 וְאָֽמַרְתָּ֖ בִּלְבָבֶ֑ךָ

superfluous if verse 10 means that Israel *will* bless the Lord, but it is understandable if verse 10 *requires* Israel to do so.

11–19. An admonition to remember the lessons taught by the hardships in the wilderness (vv. 2–4). The fear that prosperity can lead to complacency and forgetting one's dependence on God is discussed in the Comment to 6:11–12. Here Moses warns that the effects of satiety are liable to be exacerbated with the passage of time, when Israel's own labors yield further prosperity, and it credits that prosperity to its labors alone.

11. *forget the LORD and fail to keep His commandments* Literally, "forget the LORD by failing to keep His commandments." See Comment to verse 1.

13. *multiplied . . . increased . . . prospered* The same Hebrew verb, *r-b-h*, is used in all three cases. It is the leitmotif of chapters 7–8 (see introductory Comment preceding chap. 7). Although the increase of Israel's cattle and wealth, like the building of houses (v. 12), will naturally require effort on its part, Moses does not say "and you have multiplied your herds and flocks," but rather "your herds and flocks have multiplied." In this way he avoids giving the impression that this increase will be due to Israel's own activity. See Comment to verses 17–18.

14–16. All that Israel will have would be impossible were it not for God's benefactions. In listing these, the style again becomes elevated, as in verses 7–9. The list consists of four clauses beginning with participles.The first and the third are the same verb (*ha-motsi'*, lit., "who brought out/ forth"), and the second and fourth are assonant with each other (*ha-molikhakha / ha-ma'akhilkha*). The prevalence of the letter *mem* in these verses (twenty-two times) gives them a sonorous quality that calls attention to them.[15]

15. *seraph serpents and scorpions* The wilderness is described similarly in Isaiah 30:6, and Numbers 21:6–9 tells of serpents attacking the Israelites in the desert. *Seraph* serpents (lit., "fiery serpents") are apparently serpents whose bite causes a burning sensation.[16]

brought forth water for you from the flinty rock On two occasions when water was unavailable, God had Moses obtain water for the people from the inside of a rock (see Exod. 17:6 and Num. 20:7–11). In the Sinai there are limestone rocks from which small amounts of water drip and a blow to their soft surface can expose a porous inner layer containing water. On the occasions in question the rocks miraculously produced enough for the entire people. The description of the rock as "flinty" is undoubtedly a hyperbole emphasizing how unexpected it was as a source of water.[17]

16. *in order to test you by hardships, only to benefit you in the end* The translation, by its punctuation, implies that this part of the verse refers to the manna (v. 16a). If the word order is meant literally, it means that the manna itself was a form of hardship, apparently because it was monotonous (see Num. 11:4–6). However, it is possible that the verse is simply alluding to the

you in the end—[17]and you say to yourselves, "My own power and the might of my own hand have won this wealth for me." [18]Remember that it is the LORD your God who gives you the power to get wealth, in fulfillment of the covenant that He made on oath with your fathers, as is still the case.

[19]If you do forget the LORD your God and follow other gods to serve them or bow down to them, I warn you this day that you shall certainly perish; [20]like the nations that the LORD will cause to perish before you, so shall you perish—because you did not heed the LORD your God.

כֹּחִי֙ וְעֹ֣צֶם יָדִ֔י עָ֥שָׂה לִ֖י אֶת־הַחַ֥יִל הַזֶּֽה: 18 וְזָֽכַרְתָּ֙ אֶת־יְהֹוָ֣ה אֱלֹהֶ֔יךָ כִּ֣י ה֗וּא הַנֹּתֵ֥ן לְךָ֛ כֹּ֖חַ לַעֲשׂ֣וֹת חָ֑יִל לְמַ֨עַן הָקִ֧ים אֶת־בְּרִית֛וֹ אֲשֶׁר־נִשְׁבַּ֥ע לַאֲבֹתֶ֖יךָ כַּיּ֥וֹם הַזֶּֽה: פ

19 וְהָיָ֗ה אִם־שָׁכֹ֤חַ תִּשְׁכַּח֙ אֶת־יְהֹוָ֣ה אֱלֹהֶ֔יךָ וְהָֽלַכְתָּ֗ אַחֲרֵי֙ אֱלֹהִ֣ים אֲחֵרִ֔ים וַעֲבַדְתָּ֖ם וְהִשְׁתַּחֲוִ֣יתָ לָהֶ֑ם הַעִדֹ֤תִי בָכֶם֙ הַיּ֔וֹם כִּ֥י אָבֹ֖ד תֹּאבֵדֽוּן: 20 כַּגּוֹיִ֗ם אֲשֶׁ֤ר יְהֹוָה֙ מַאֲבִ֣יד מִפְּנֵיכֶ֔ם כֵּ֖ן תֹּאבֵד֑וּן עֵ֕קֶב לֹ֣א תִשְׁמְע֔וּן בְּק֖וֹל יְהֹוָ֥ה אֱלֹהֵיכֶֽם: פ

sequence of events in verse 3 in reverse (chiastic) order. Another possibility is that this part of the verse refers to everything mentioned in verses 15 and 16a, characterizing the entire wilderness period as a test by hardship and a preparation for the future.

to benefit you in the end Because the lesson of its dependence on God would lead Israel to obey Him and earn His continued benefactions. For the benefit that would come from being tested, see introductory Comment to verses 2–6.

17–18. If Israel forgets all that God did for it in the past, it is liable to think that all its prosperity is due to its own power. Moses reminds it that the very power which leads to prosperity is a gift of God.

18. *as is still the case* Better: "as He is now doing," that is, fulfilling His promise to the patriarchs to give you the promised land.

19–20. The consequences of forgetting the Lord and turning to other gods. The chapter division and some Hebrew manuscripts connect these verses with verses 1–18, which implies that turning to other gods is an inevitable result of forgetting one's dependence on God (v. 11). The Masoretic Text marks these two verses as a separate *parashah* and thereby makes verses 1–18 an independent unit.[18] This highlights the fact that forgetting God and aggrandizing oneself (vv. 11–17) is an independent evil even when it is not followed by idolatry.

19. *If you do forget* The Hebrew *ve-hayah 'im shakhoaḥ tishkaḥ* echoes, negatively, a formulation that appears several times in Deuteronomy to express the virtues for which Moses appeals. Compare *ve-hayah 'im shamoaʿ tishmaʿ* and *'im shamor tishmerun*.[19] This is the only passage where a sin is described in the same style.

20. If Israel acts like the Canaanites, it will suffer the same fate. Compare the similar warning in Leviticus 18:24–28.

CHAPTER 9   AN ARGUMENT AGAINST SELF-RIGHTEOUSNESS   (9:1–10:22)

In this sermon (9:1–10:22) Moses continues to address dangers to faith that might develop as a consequence of the conquest, a theme he began in chapters 7 and 8. Here he preaches against the feeling of self-righteousness that defeating the Canaanites might engender. He states that victory can be no proof of virtue, for Israel's history has been one of continuous provocation and rebellion. Nothing but the Canaanites' wickedness and God's oath to the patriarchs accounts for Israel's conquest of Canaan. Moses concludes by calling on Israel not to act rebelliously in the future but to serve God and obey His commandments.[1]

The outstanding example of rebelliousness is the incident of the golden calf, which Moses recalls at great length (9:8–21,25–29, and 10:1–11). This incident, in which Israel violated the Decalogue's commandment against idolatry, almost led to Israel's extinction. Moses saved Israel by imploring God to ignore its wickedness, arguing that other considerations should override its lack of merit.

9 Hear, O Israel! You are about to cross the Jordan to go in and dispossess nations greater and more populous than you: great cities with walls sky-high; [2]a people great and tall, the Anakites, of whom you have knowledge; for you have heard it said, "Who can stand up to the children of Anak?" [3]Know then this day that none other than the LORD your God is crossing at your head, a devouring fire; it is He who will wipe them out. He will subdue them before you, that you may quickly dispossess and destroy them, as the LORD promised you. [4]And when the LORD your God has thrust them from your path, say not to yourselves, "The LORD has enabled us to possess this land because of our virtues"; it is rather because of the wickedness of those nations that the LORD is dispossessing them

ט שְׁמַע יִשְׂרָאֵל אַתָּה עֹבֵר הַיּוֹם אֶת־הַיַּרְדֵּן לָבֹא לָרֶשֶׁת גּוֹיִם גְּדֹלִים וַעֲצֻמִים מִמֶּךָּ עָרִים גְּדֹלֹת וּבְצֻרֹת בַּשָּׁמָיִם: 2 עַם־גָּדוֹל וָרָם בְּנֵי עֲנָקִים אֲשֶׁר אַתָּה יָדַעְתָּ וְאַתָּה שָׁמַעְתָּ מִי יִתְיַצֵּב לִפְנֵי בְּנֵי עֲנָק: 3 וְיָדַעְתָּ הַיּוֹם כִּי יְהוָה אֱלֹהֶיךָ הוּא־הָעֹבֵר לְפָנֶיךָ אֵשׁ אֹכְלָה הוּא יַשְׁמִידֵם וְהוּא יַכְנִיעֵם לְפָנֶיךָ וְהוֹרַשְׁתָּם וְהַאֲבַדְתָּם מַהֵר כַּאֲשֶׁר דִּבֶּר יְהוָה לָךְ: שלישי 4 אַל־תֹּאמַר בִּלְבָבְךָ בַּהֲדֹף יְהוָה אֱלֹהֶיךָ אֹתָם | מִלְּפָנֶיךָ לֵאמֹר בְּצִדְקָתִי הֱבִיאַנִי יְהוָה לָרֶשֶׁת אֶת־הָאָרֶץ הַזֹּאת וּבְרִשְׁעַת הַגּוֹיִם הָאֵלֶּה יְהוָה מוֹרִישָׁם מִפָּנֶיךָ:

As in the case of chapters 1–3, Moses' recapitulation is based on earlier narratives of the same events (in this case, in Exod. 32–34), but it is modified in accordance with his aims in the present speech, as noted in the comments.

The themes and movement of the chapter are expressed in recurrent motifs: God's oath to the patriarchs; the danger that He would destroy Israel or Aaron; the Tablets of the Covenant; Israel's rebellion, provocation, and stiff neck; and Moses' forty-day fasts and prayers.[2]

THE THEME: VICTORY IS NO PROOF OF VIRTUE (vv. 1–5)

1–3. Moses sets the stage for his warning in verse 4: the Canaanites have advantages that would prevent Israel from defeating them on its own, but God will subdue the Canaanites for Israel. When Israel sees that it has won a victory with divine aid, it may mistakenly conclude that it *earned* God's help.

For the description of the Canaanites and their cities, see Comments to 1:28.

2. you have heard it said Either by the scouts (1:28; Num. 13:31) or by others describing the Anakites' reputation.[3]

3. See introductory Comment to 1:6–3:23 and Comment to 4:24.

quickly In 7:22 Moses states that Israel will not be able to put an end to the Canaanites quickly. Hoffmann argues that our verse refers to a quick rout of the main force of the Canaanites, whereas 7:22 refers to the survivors who will be left temporarily to prevent parts of the land from becoming barren.[4]

as the LORD promised you See Exodus 23:23–31; 34:11.

4. virtues Hebrew *tsedakah*, usually translated "righteousness." Here the term may refer specifically to loyalty or devotion, not to virtues in general. This meaning is attested in Hebrew and other Semitic languages,[5] and is suggested by the fact that the rest of the chapter is a demonstration of Israel's lack of loyalty (see vv. 7,24).

it is rather because of the wickedness Better: "as well as because of the wickedness."[6] This is a continuation of what the Israelites might think, though here it is represented by indirect speech instead of a quotation.[7] The Israelites realize that God would not drive out the Canaanites undeservedly. But they must not draw the conclusion that being chosen to replace the Canaanites proves that they, in contrast, are virtuous. The true reasons for their being chosen are stated in verse 5.

Moses' statement that the Israelites are undeserving is not incompatible with his frequent admonition that obedience to the commandments is a precondition for the conquest (see, e.g., 4:1; 6:18–19). That condition applies to their behavior *from now on* (see 10:16): future obedience is indispensable for the conquest, but it will not be the reason why God chose to give the land to Israel.

before you. ⁵It is not because of your virtues and your rectitude that you will be able to possess their country; but it is because of their wickedness that the LORD your God is dispossessing those nations before you, and in order to fulfill the oath that the LORD made to your fathers, Abraham, Isaac, and Jacob.

⁶Know, then, that it is not for any virtue of yours that the LORD your God is giving you this good land to possess; for you are a stiffnecked people. ⁷Remember, never forget, how you provoked the LORD your God to anger in the wilderness: from the day that you left the land of Egypt until you reached this place, you have continued defiant toward the LORD.

⁸At Horeb you so provoked the LORD that the LORD was angry enough with you to have destroyed you. ⁹I had

5 לֹא בְצִדְקָתְךָ וּבְיֹשֶׁר לְבָבְךָ אַתָּה בָא לָרֶשֶׁת אֶת־אַרְצָם כִּי בְּרִשְׁעַת ׀ הַגּוֹיִם הָאֵלֶּה יְהוָה אֱלֹהֶיךָ מוֹרִישָׁם מִפָּנֶיךָ וּלְמַעַן הָקִים אֶת־הַדָּבָר אֲשֶׁר נִשְׁבַּע יְהוָה לַאֲבֹתֶיךָ לְאַבְרָהָם לְיִצְחָק וּלְיַעֲקֹב:
6 וְיָדַעְתָּ כִּי לֹא בְצִדְקָתְךָ יְהוָה אֱלֹהֶיךָ נֹתֵן לְךָ אֶת־הָאָרֶץ הַטּוֹבָה הַזֹּאת לְרִשְׁתָּהּ כִּי עַם־קְשֵׁה־עֹרֶף אָתָּה: 7 זְכֹר אַל־תִּשְׁכַּח אֵת אֲשֶׁר־הִקְצַפְתָּ אֶת־יְהוָה אֱלֹהֶיךָ בַּמִּדְבָּר לְמִן־הַיּוֹם אֲשֶׁר־יָצָאתָ ׀ מֵאֶרֶץ מִצְרַיִם עַד־בֹּאֲכֶם עַד־הַמָּקוֹם הַזֶּה מַמְרִים הֱיִיתֶם עִם־יְהוָה:
8 וּבְחֹרֵב הִקְצַפְתֶּם אֶת־יְהוָה וַיִּתְאַנַּף יְהוָה בָּכֶם לְהַשְׁמִיד אֶתְכֶם: 9 בַּעֲלֹתִי הָהָרָה לָקַחַת לוּחֹת

5. As far as the Canaanites' defeat is concerned, the Israelites would be correct to attribute it to the Canaanites' wickedness. God's justice is a cardinal tenet in the Bible, and the point is made several times that God did not deprive the Canaanites of their land arbitrarily but because of their morally outrageous practices (see Comment to 7:3–4).⁸ But to date Israel has not *earned* the right to succeed them. God brings Israel into the promised land only to fulfill the oath He made to its ancestors, the oath that sustains it even when it is devoid of merits. See Comment to verse 27 and the introductory Comment to 4:29–31.

rectitude Literally, "uprightness of heart." This idiom, too, may refer to loyalty.⁹

A HISTORY OF PROVOCATIONS (vv. 6–24)¹⁰

This is the core of the chapter. Moses gathers the evidence of Israel's rebelliousness, particularly the golden calf incident. Following the introductory statement of his theme (v. 6), he frames this section with references to Israel's provocations and defiance/flouting (*m-r-h*) of God "from the day" it left Egypt and "from the day" that Moses came to know them (vv. 7–8,22–24). In accordance with this theme, in this section he focuses on Israel's sin and God's anger; he defers the subject of his successful intercession on Israel's behalf until the next section (9:25–10:5,10–11).

Moses' statement that these incidents typify the wilderness period as a whole is characteristic of Deuteronomy (see also 9:24; 29:3; 31:27). This evaluation of the period was shared by the prophet Ezekiel, whereas Hosea and Jeremiah, without necessarily denying the incidents of rebelliousness, viewed the period as one in which Israel also showed loyalty to God by following Him through the harsh wasteland.¹¹

6. *Know, then* From the following.

stiffnecked Obstinate. The Hebrew idiom is close in meaning to English "headstrong."¹²

7. *this place* The valley near Beth-peor (3:29), the site of their most recent rebellion (see Comment to 4:3).

8. Although the golden calf incident was not the first of Israel's provocations, it is mentioned first because it was the most outrageous. If there was one place above all others where the people should have been faithful, it was Horeb, where they had encountered God personally, had seen that He alone is God, and were commanded to worship no other gods.

9–10. The gravity of the offense is underscored by the fact that it took place while Moses was on the mountain to receive the tablets of the covenant that prohibited this very offense. Indeed, the people sinned "quickly" (v. 13)—the very day on which God gave Moses the tablets was the day on which Moses learned that the Israelites had made an image (vv. 11–12).

ascended the mountain to receive the tablets of stone, the Tablets of the Covenant that the LORD had made with you, and I stayed on the mountain forty days and forty nights, eating no bread and drinking no water. ¹⁰And the LORD gave me the two tablets of stone inscribed by the finger of God, with the exact words that the LORD had addressed to you on the mountain out of the fire on the day of the Assembly.

¹¹At the end of those forty days and forty nights, the LORD gave me the two tablets of stone, the Tablets of the Covenant. ¹²And the LORD said to me, "Hurry, go down from here at once, for the people whom you brought out of Egypt have acted wickedly; they have been quick to stray from the path that I enjoined upon them; they have made themselves a molten image." ¹³The LORD further said to me, "I see that this is a stiffnecked people. ¹⁴Let Me alone and I will destroy them and blot out their name from

הָאֲבָנִים לוּחֹת הַבְּרִית אֲשֶׁר־כָּרַת יְהוָה עִמָּכֶם
וָאֵשֵׁב בָּהָר אַרְבָּעִים יוֹם וְאַרְבָּעִים לַיְלָה לֶחֶם
לֹא אָכַלְתִּי וּמַיִם לֹא שָׁתִיתִי: 10 וַיִּתֵּן יְהוָה אֵלַי
אֶת־שְׁנֵי לוּחֹת הָאֲבָנִים כְּתֻבִים בְּאֶצְבַּע אֱלֹהִים
וַעֲלֵיהֶם כְּכָל־הַדְּבָרִים אֲשֶׁר דִּבֶּר יְהוָה עִמָּכֶם
בָּהָר מִתּוֹךְ הָאֵשׁ בְּיוֹם הַקָּהָל:
11 וַיְהִי מִקֵּץ אַרְבָּעִים יוֹם וְאַרְבָּעִים לַיְלָה נָתַן
יְהוָה אֵלַי אֶת־שְׁנֵי לֻחֹת הָאֲבָנִים לֻחוֹת הַבְּרִית:
12 וַיֹּאמֶר יְהוָה אֵלַי קוּם רֵד מַהֵר מִזֶּה כִּי שִׁחֵת
עַמְּךָ אֲשֶׁר הוֹצֵאתָ מִמִּצְרָיִם סָרוּ מַהֵר מִן־הַדֶּרֶךְ
אֲשֶׁר צִוִּיתִם עָשׂוּ לָהֶם מַסֵּכָה: 13 וַיֹּאמֶר יְהוָה
אֵלַי לֵאמֹר רָאִיתִי אֶת־הָעָם הַזֶּה וְהִנֵּה עַם־
קְשֵׁה־עֹרֶף הוּא: 14 הֶרֶף מִמֶּנִּי וְאַשְׁמִידֵם

9. *the Tablets of the Covenant*   Containing the Ten Commandments; see 4:13; 5:19.

forty days and forty nights   During this time Moses was learning the remainder of the laws (see 5:28). Forty-day periods are frequently encountered in the Bible and elsewhere. The present case seems to reflect the idea that forty days constitute the proper time for the completion of a lengthy process. Comparable periods are the cleansing of the earth by a forty-day flood, the forty days required for embalming, and the forty days given the Ninevites to repent.[13]

eating no bread and drinking no water   During his intimate encounter with God, inside the cloud, Moses was beyond human needs and concerns. This encounter surpasses the one that Moses shared with Aaron and the elders, when they all saw God and ate and drank (Exod. 24:9–11). Midrashic commentators see Moses' abstinence as raising him to the status of angels. His assumption of supernatural qualities while he was with God is also implied by the statement in Exodus 34:29–35 that, as a result of speaking with God, his face began to radiate an awesome light. Moses' ability to survive for so long a time without food or drink can only be due to divine support. According to R. Nathan, Moses had to wait six days before he was summoned into God's cloud (Exod. 24:15–18) "so that he might be purged of all food and drink in his bowels, before he was sanctified and became like the ministering angels." Perhaps this implies that the purpose of Moses' abstinence was to prevent him from having to attend to his bodily functions, which would be inappropriate in the presence of God. This would be similar to the requirement that the people avoid ritual impurity by abstaining from sexual relations before their encounter with God at Mount Sinai (Exod. 19:15).[14]

10. *inscribed with the finger of God*   According to Exodus 32:16 the tablets were also made by God.

the day of the Assembly   At Mount Sinai (Horeb).[15]

12. *Hurry, go down from here at once*   God's peremptory tone implies that He is annoyed with Moses because of the people's behavior.[16] So, too, does His reference to Israel as "the people whom you [Moses] brought out of Egypt"—literally, "*your* people whom you brought out of Egypt." God normally refers to Israel as "My people" "whom I brought out of Egypt."[17] Here He feels alienated from them and speaks of them as Moses' people, much as an exasperated parent may refer to a misbehaving child as the other spouse's child. Contrast Moses' language in verses 26 and 29.

a molten image   According to Exodus 32:2 and 24, the calf was made from melted gold ornaments.

14. *Let Me alone*   The phrase implies that Moses can, as it were, restrain God from

under heaven, and I will make you a nation far more numerous than they."

¹⁵I started down the mountain, a mountain ablaze with fire, the two Tablets of the Covenant in my two hands. ¹⁶I saw how you had sinned against the LORD your God: you had made yourselves a molten calf; you had been quick to stray from the path that the LORD had enjoined upon you. ¹⁷Thereupon I gripped the two tablets and flung them away with both my hands, smashing them before your

וָאֶמְחֶה אֶת־שְׁמָם מִתַּחַת הַשָּׁמָיִם וְאֶעֱשֶׂה אוֹתְךָ לְגוֹי־עָצוּם וָרָב מִמֶּנּוּ:

¹⁵ וָאֵפֶן וָאֵרֵד מִן־הָהָר וְהָהָר בֹּעֵר בָּאֵשׁ וּשְׁנֵי לֻחֹת הַבְּרִית עַל שְׁתֵּי יָדָי: ¹⁶ וָאֵרֶא וְהִנֵּה חֲטָאתֶם לַיהוָה אֱלֹהֵיכֶם עֲשִׂיתֶם לָכֶם עֵגֶל מַסֵּכָה סַרְתֶּם מַהֵר מִן־הַדֶּרֶךְ אֲשֶׁר־צִוָּה יְהוָה אֶתְכֶם: ¹⁷ וָאֶתְפֹּשׂ בִּשְׁנֵי הַלֻּחֹת וָאַשְׁלִכֵם מֵעַל שְׁתֵּי יָדָי וָאֲשַׁבְּרֵם לְעֵינֵיכֶם: ¹⁸ וָאֶתְנַפַּל לִפְנֵי

destroying Israel. Midrashic commentaries understand it as a hint for Moses to do just that by praying on Israel's behalf. In other words, God is saying that by right Israel ought to be destroyed, but that He wants the prophet to make the case for sparing them. Prophets frequently play this intercessory role in the Bible in addition to their role as God's messengers to man. This is part of what God wants them to do. Samuel says that he would sin against God if he failed to pray for the people, and Jeremiah implores God to protect him in return for his "plead[ing] in their behalf, to turn Your anger away from them" (1 Sam. 12:23; Jer. 18:20). God tells Ezekiel that sin causes a breach in Israel's defensive wall and that He sought a man "to repair the wall or stand in the breach before Me in behalf of this land, that I might not destroy it" (Ezek. 22:30–31). Psalm 106:23 describes Moses in similar terms: God "would have destroyed them had not Moses His chosen one confronted Him in the breach to avert His destructive wrath." This role is related to the concepts of divine anger and jealousy. God's emotional involvement with man is such that outrageous sin provokes Him to passionate anger, not merely detached disapproval. To balance this anger, the prophet is appointed to argue the case for mercy.[18]

blot out their name from under heaven As Israel was to do to the Canaanites and the Amalekites (7:24; 25:19).

I will make you a nation far more numerous than they Who are already as numerous as the stars (1:10; 10:22). The promise to the patriarchs would be continued through Moses and his descendants.[19]

15. The outrage is exacerbated by the fact that the idol was made in full view of the mountain that was still blazing with God's presence (see 4:11–12,36; 5:20), and violated the very commands written on the tablets that Moses carried. In modern terms, "the ink was not yet dry" on the covenant when the people violated it.

16. **a molten calf** What the calf represented is debated. The most likely view is that it did not represent another deity, but a pedestal or mount on which YHVH was thought to be invisibly present, much as the cherubs in the Holy of Holies were conceived as YHVH's throne (see Comment to 10:1–2). In any case, it is clear from Exodus 32:8 that even if the original motive for making the calf was nonidolatrous, the people immediately fell to worshiping it and violated the Decalogue's prohibition against worshiping idols. For further discussion see Excursus 12.

17. Breaking the tablets expresses Moses' rage. His act also has legal significance. In Mesopotamian law the cancellation of a contract is expressed by breaking the clay tablets on which it is written. This is the equivalent of ripping up legal documents written on tearable materials. By smashing the tablets, Moses indicated that the covenant was annulled because the people had violated one of its most fundamental conditions.[20] Relations between God and Israel were severed.

18. Moses mentions three times that he prayed to God for forty days and nights to spare the people. Here he mentions it briefly. In verses 25–29 he quotes what he said to God, and in 10:10–11 he reports God's favorable response. It is not clear precisely when in the course of the events he prayed. It is unlikely, despite the location of verse 18, that he did so between the time he broke the tablets (v. 17) and the time he destroyed the idol (v. 21); he would hardly have waited forty days to destroy it. According to Exodus 32–34 he pleaded with God three times: before coming down the

eyes. ¹⁸I threw myself down before the Lord—eating no
bread and drinking no water forty days and forty nights, as
before—because of the great wrong you had committed,
doing what displeased the Lord and vexing Him. ¹⁹For I
was in dread of the Lord's fierce anger against you, which
moved Him to wipe you out. And that time, too, the
Lord gave heed to me.—²⁰Moreover, the Lord was angry
enough with Aaron to have destroyed him; so I also interceded for Aaron at that time.—²¹As for that sinful thing
you had made, the calf, I took it and put it to the fire; I
broke it to bits and ground it thoroughly until it was fine
as dust, and I threw its dust into the brook that comes
down from the mountain.

יְהֹוָה כָּרִאשֹׁנָה אַרְבָּעִים יוֹם וְאַרְבָּעִים לַיְלָה לֶחֶם
לֹא אָכַלְתִּי וּמַיִם לֹא שָׁתִיתִי עַל כָּל־חַטַּאתְכֶם
אֲשֶׁר חֲטָאתֶם לַעֲשׂוֹת הָרַע בְּעֵינֵי יְהֹוָה
לְהַכְעִיסוֹ: ¹⁹ כִּי יָגֹרְתִּי מִפְּנֵי הָאַף וְהַחֵמָה אֲשֶׁר
קָצַף יְהֹוָה עֲלֵיכֶם לְהַשְׁמִיד אֶתְכֶם וַיִּשְׁמַע יְהֹוָה
אֵלַי גַּם בַּפַּעַם הַהִוא: ²⁰ וּבְאַהֲרֹן הִתְאַנַּף יְהֹוָה
מְאֹד לְהַשְׁמִידוֹ וָאֶתְפַּלֵּל גַּם־בְּעַד אַהֲרֹן בָּעֵת
הַהִוא: ²¹ וְאֶת־חַטַּאתְכֶם אֲשֶׁר־עֲשִׂיתֶם אֶת־
הָעֵגֶל לָקַחְתִּי וָאֶשְׂרֹף אֹתוֹ | בָּאֵשׁ וָאֶכֹּת אֹתוֹ
טָחוֹן הֵיטֵב עַד אֲשֶׁר־דַּק לְעָפָר וָאַשְׁלִךְ אֶת־
עֲפָרוֹ אֶל־הַנַּחַל הַיֹּרֵד מִן־הָהָר:

mountain with the first set of tablets, after punishing the sinners, and when he took the new tablets
up to God.²¹ Since the wording here in Deuteronomy is very close to that of Exodus and presupposes information found there (see Comments to vv. 20,22; 10:8), commentators have assumed
that Moses' three references to prayer here correspond to the three instances in Exodus.²² On the
other hand, the references here in Deuteronomy can be understood as three partial reports of one
prayer, and it is possible that Deuteronomy has condensed the three into a single instance.²³ In
either case, Deuteronomy is not interested in a chronological report but in presenting information
about Moses' prayer(s) at the points where it is most effective in illustrating Moses' theme. In the
present section (vv. 7–21), the contents of the narrative are determined by its focus on Israel's sin and
God's anger, and Moses' prayer(s) is mentioned only briefly. Details are deferred to the next section
(9:25–10:5,10–11).

eating no bread   Moses' second forty-day fast matches the first (v. 9) but has a different
purpose. Here it is an expression of grief over the people's sin and over the danger to their survival,
comparable both to the fast of the Day of Atonement and Esther's fast before approaching Ahasue-
rus.²⁴ In verse 19 Moses explains why he fasted and prayed for such an extraordinary length of time.

19.   that time, too   Since Moses is now speaking at the end of the Israelites' years in the
wilderness, the other times implied by "too" could be any of the other occasions when he interceded
with God during the preceding forty years.²⁵

20.   God was angry at Aaron because it was he who made the golden calf (Exod.
32:2–5,21–24). As noted in Excursus 12, Aaron's intentions in making the calf were probably not
idolatrous since he, at least, intended it only as the Lord's pedestal. If so, his intentions were
perverted by the people when they began to worship it. In any case, God held Aaron accountable for
the consequences of his actions, just as he held Moses accountable for the consequences of the scouts'
mission (Deut. 1:37). Moses' prayer for Aaron was only partly successful. He lived another forty
years (Num. 33:38), but the mention of his death later in the present context (10:6) indicates that his
death at that time was due to the present incident. In other words, Moses succeeded in postponing
Aaron's punishment but, because he made the calf, he died without entering the promised land.²⁶

angry enough   Literally, "very angry." The adverb—lacking in verse 8—indicates that
God was angrier with Aaron than with the people. Whatever his intentions, his guilt for making the
idol was greater even than the guilt of those who asked for it.

21.   Throwing the dust of the calf into the brook is a practical way of getting rid of an
impure object. Josiah did the same thing with pagan altars when he cleansed the temple (2 Kings
23:12), and the prayer that God "will hurl all our sins into the depths of the sea" is a metaphoric
allusion to the same practice (Mic. 7:19). According to Exodus 32:20 Moses threw the dust into water
in order to make the Israelites drink it. Ramban suggests that this was in order to degrade the idol
further by turning it into human waste. Rabbinic exegesis, followed by some modern scholars, takes

22Again you provoked the LORD at Taberah, and at Massah, and at Kibroth-hattaavah.

23And when the LORD sent you on from Kadesh-barnea, saying, "Go up and take possession of the land that I am giving you," you flouted the command of the LORD your God; you did not put your trust in Him and did not obey Him.

24As long as I have known you, you have been defiant toward the LORD.

25When I lay prostrate before the LORD those forty days and forty nights, because the LORD was determined to

כב וּבְתַבְעֵרָה וּבְמַסָּה וּבְקִבְרֹת הַתַּאֲוָה מַקְצִפִים הֱיִיתֶם אֶת־יְהֹוָה:

כג וּבִשְׁלֹחַ יְהֹוָה אֶתְכֶם מִקָּדֵשׁ בַּרְנֵעַ לֵאמֹר עֲלוּ וּרְשׁוּ אֶת־הָאָרֶץ אֲשֶׁר נָתַתִּי לָכֶם וַתַּמְרוּ אֶת־פִּי יְהֹוָה אֱלֹהֵיכֶם וְלֹא הֶאֱמַנְתֶּם לוֹ וְלֹא שְׁמַעְתֶּם בְּקֹלוֹ:

כד *מַמְרִים הֱיִיתֶם עִם־יְהֹוָה מִיּוֹם דַּעְתִּי אֶתְכֶם:

כה וָאֶתְנַפַּל לִפְנֵי יְהֹוָה אֵת אַרְבָּעִים הַיּוֹם וְאֶת־אַרְבָּעִים הַלַּיְלָה אֲשֶׁר הִתְנַפָּלְתִּי כִּי־אָמַר יְהֹוָה

מ' זעירא v. 24.

the forced drinking as a kind of ordeal designed to identify the guilty, comparable to the "waters of bitterness" ritual for testing the suspected adulteress (Num. 5:11–31).[27]

22–24. Four other provocations show that the golden calf incident was not an isolated one; rebelliousness has been the consistent pattern of Israel's behavior. Here, too, Moses relies on his audience's familiarity with the events; he alludes to three of them by no more than the place where they occurred (v. 22) and to the fourth by little more.

22. *Taberah* Where the people complained to the Lord for an unspecified reason and He caused a fire to ravage at the outskirts of the camp until Moses prayed to Him. See Numbers 11:1–3.

Massah Where the people, lacking water, complained that Moses had taken them out of Egypt to kill them with thirst. See Exodus 17:1–7 and Comment to Deuteronomy 6:16.

Kibroth-hattaavah Where the people angered the Lord by complaining that they were bored with the manna and wanted meat, and that they had eaten better in Egypt. He fed them quail, but also sent a plague against them. See Numbers 11:4–34.

23. See 1:26–43.

24. *As long as I have known you* Literally, "since the day I knew you." It is not clear what this refers to, since Israel's rebellious acts did not begin when Moses first came to them, but only in the wilderness. Bekhor Shor thinks the phrase refers to the Hebrew man who challenged Moses' right to intervene in a fight, but that was a challenge to Moses, not God (Exod. 2:13–14). The translation implies that the phrase is simply a hyperbole. The Septuagint and the Samaritan Pentateuch read "since the day He [God] knew you," corresponding to Hosea 13:4, "I knew you in the desert." In both passages "knew" can mean either "chose," "looked after," or "met." In any case, that reading means that Israel has been rebellious since the beginning of its relationship with God.[28]

THE AFTERMATH OF THE GOLDEN CALF INCIDENT (9:25–10:11)

Having made his point about Israel's history of provocations, Moses appends a more detailed account of how he persuaded God to spare the Israelites (9:25–29; 10:10–11). By devoting a special section to the prayer, he buttresses the lesson that Israel was not given the land because of its virtues.[29] Within this section he inserts accounts of how, as a result of his prayer, God commanded him to make the Ark, and how God appointed the Levites to carry the Ark and perform other priestly functions (10:1–5,8–10). Between these two accounts is a brief digression reporting the death, years later, of the first priest, Aaron.

Moses' Intercessory Prayer (vv. 25–29)

25. *those forty days and forty nights* That is, the period referred to in verses 18–19.

destroy you, ²⁶I prayed to the LORD and said, "O Lord GOD, do not annihilate Your very own people, whom You redeemed in Your majesty and whom You freed from Egypt with a mighty hand. ²⁷Give thought to Your servants, Abraham, Isaac, and Jacob, and pay no heed to the stubbornness of this people, its wickedness, and its sinfulness. ²⁸Else the country from which You freed us will say, 'It was because the LORD was powerless to bring them into

לְהַשְׁמִיד אֶתְכֶם: 26 וָאֶתְפַּלֵּל אֶל־יְהוָה וָאֹמַר אֲדֹנָי יְהוִה אַל־תַּשְׁחֵת עַמְּךָ וְנַחֲלָתְךָ אֲשֶׁר פָּדִיתָ בְּגָדְלֶךָ אֲשֶׁר־הוֹצֵאתָ מִמִּצְרַיִם בְּיָד חֲזָקָה: 27 זְכֹר לַעֲבָדֶיךָ לְאַבְרָהָם לְיִצְחָק וּלְיַעֲקֹב אַל־תֵּפֶן אֶל־קְשִׁי הָעָם הַזֶּה וְאֶל־רִשְׁעוֹ וְאֶל־חַטָּאתוֹ: 28 פֶּן־יֹאמְרוּ הָאָרֶץ אֲשֶׁר הוֹצֵאתָנוּ מִשָּׁם מִבְּלִי יְכֹלֶת יְהוָה לַהֲבִיאָם אֶל־הָאָרֶץ

26–29. Moses' plea for pardon is based on three arguments. The first is that Israel is God's own people on whose behalf He has invested much effort. This argument appears both at the beginning and end of the prayer, suggesting that it is the chief argument and the one Moses wishes to leave uppermost in God's mind (vv. 26,29). The second argument is a plea to spare the Israelites out of consideration for their ancestors, who were God's loyal servants (v. 27). The third is that destroying His own people will injure His reputation among other nations (v. 28).[30] The fact that three separate arguments are marshaled, none of which cites any virtue of the Israelites, illustrates Moses' point in verse 6. As verse 19 indicates, the prayer was successful.

*26. **O Lord GOD*** Literally, "O my Lord, YHVH." See Excursus 4.

do not annihilate Hebrew *tashḥet* is from *sh-ḥ-t*, the same root underlying "acted wickedly" (*shiḥet*) in verse 12. See Comment to 4:31.

Your very own people With this phrase Moses counters God's dissociation of Himself from Israel in verse 12, where He calls Israel "your [Moses'] people whom you brought out of Egypt." Moses uses the phrase to overcome God's feeling of estrangement from the people. His appeal, "do not annihilate your very own people" is an appeal to God's self-interest. Literally it means "do not destroy the people that is Your inheritance," Your cherished hereditary property (*naḥalah*; see 4:20). The idiom "do not annihilate . . . your inheritance" (*tashḥet . . . naḥalatekha*) is drawn from economic life, from the landowner's fear of taking actions that would impair his property. This is illustrated by Naomi's relative who declined to marry Ruth and redeem Elimelech's property, explaining that he was concerned "lest I impair my own estate" (*'ashḥit 'et naḥalati*, Ruth 4:6).

whom You redeemed All the effort that God has invested in Israel would be for naught if He were to destroy them.

27. Remembering the patriarchs means remembering the oath to make their descendants numerous and to give them the promised land (see Exod. 32:13). Destroying the Israelites would violate that oath. The argument is, in other words, that even a violation of the Sinai covenant would not justify God's destroying Israel, since the earlier covenant, with the patriarchs, was unconditional and irrevocable (see Comment to 4:29–31). Moses mentions the oath in verse 5 and in 10:11. Here he does not mention it explicitly, but simply asks God to "give thought to" the patriarchs. Perhaps this is to show that he has in mind more than a legal argument, but an emotional one as well, in that he invites God to remember everything about the patriarchs: not only the oath but also their loyal service (perhaps evoked by "Your servants") and His love for them (as in 4:37 and 10:15).

Moses' invocation of the patriarchs became the precedent for invoking the "merit of ancestors" (*zekhut 'avot*) in Jewish prayers. Going beyond the idea that God rewards later generations for their ancestors' merits (5:10; 7:9), this concept holds that even when Israel lacks merit—as in the present case—its ancestors' merits can sustain it and God may grant mercy for their sake.[31]

stubbornness . . . wickedness . . . sinfulness This acknowledgment of Israel's guilt is not mentioned in Exodus 32:11–13. Moses mentions it here in order to counter the delusion against which he warns Israel in verse 4: "it is because of our virtues . . . the wickedness of those nations."

28. Here Moses invokes the most daring argument against annihilating Israel: it would give a damaging impression of God. God is not indifferent to what humans think of Him. Moses

the land that He had promised them, and because He rejected them, that He brought them out to have them die in the wilderness.' ²⁹Yet they are Your very own people, whom You freed with Your great might and Your outstretched arm."

אֲשֶׁר־דִּבֶּר לָהֶם וּמִשִּׂנְאָתוֹ אוֹתָם הוֹצִיאָם לַהֲמִתָם בַּמִּדְבָּר: 29 וְהֵם עַמְּךָ וְנַחֲלָתֶךָ אֲשֶׁר הוֹצֵאתָ בְּכֹחֲךָ הַגָּדֹל וּבִזְרֹעֲךָ הַנְּטוּיָה:

פ רביעי

10 Thereupon the LORD said to me, "Carve out two tablets of stone like the first, and come up to Me on the mountain; and make an ark of wood. ²I will inscribe on the

י בָּעֵת הַהִוא אָמַר יְהוָה אֵלַי פְּסׇל־לְךָ שְׁנֵי־ לוּחֹת אֲבָנִים כָּרִאשֹׁנִים וַעֲלֵה אֵלַי הָהָרָה וְעָשִׂיתָ לְּךָ אֲרוֹן עֵץ: 2 וְאֶכְתֹּב עַל־הַלֻּחֹת אֶת־הַדְּבָרִים

knew that one of God's motives in His actions against Egypt was to show His incomparable power to the world,³² which is essential if the nations are to recognize Him voluntarily. Moses turns God's aim to Israel's advantage in arguing for pardon: if God should destroy Israel, He would appear powerless or diabolical and damage the stature that He had gained from the Exodus. Moses made the same appeal after the disastrous report of the scouts, and Joshua later made a similar one after Israel's defeat at Ai (Num. 14:15–16; Josh. 7:9).

The appeal to God to act for the sake of His name became a popular theme in prayers. In prophetic literature, the belief that He would do so became a source of hope for the end of the exile.³³

The invidious remarks of the Egyptians can be understood as separate alternatives or as complementary. If separate, the reasons are contradictory: either God wanted to bring them into Canaan but could not, or He was able but would not. In that case, the beginning of the second clause should be translated "*or* because He rejected them." If the reasons are complementary, the reasoning is: He knew all along that He would not able to bring them into Canaan, but out of hatred (the literal meaning of "rejected") He took them out to die in the wilderness.³⁴

The accusation of divine hatred was also made by the Israelites after the scouts frightened them (1:27).

29. Yet In contrast to what the Egyptians might say: the Egyptians might accuse You of weakness and of rejecting Israel, when in fact Israel is Your own beloved people whose redemption showed that you *are* strong.³⁵

CHAPTER 10　　　　***The New Tablets: Reaffirmation of the Sinai Covenant*** (vv. 1–5)

By promising to replace the broken Tablets of the Covenant, God agrees not only to spare Israel, but also to restore the special relationship governed by the tablets, the covenant established at Horeb that had been undermined by the people's conduct. According to Exodus, God had first agreed to spare Israel and allow it to settle in the promised land (cf. 10:10–11 here), but He did not agree to accompany Israel there personally (Exod. 32:14,34; 33:1–5). For Moses this was not enough. He insisted on more than what had been promised to the patriarchs. He insisted that Israel was God's very own people, and continued to plead until God agreed to reinstate His personal relationship with Israel and reestablish the covenant of Sinai as the terms of that relationship (Exod. 33:14–17; 34:1–4,9–28).³⁶

1-2. Although God would inscribe the new tablets, they would be man-made, unlike the first ones, which were made by God (Exod. 32:16). Sforno infers from the difference that God did not forgive Israel completely.

ark That is, a chest. Documents were sometimes stored in chests and other types of containers in the ancient world, protecting them against damage or loss. In the case of a contractual document this would help protect the evidence of the agreement. Placing a document in a sanctuary enhanced its safety and brought the agreement under the sponsorship of the deity. For this reason the texts of treaties were deposited in temples, sometimes "at the feet" of a deity.³⁷ This corresponds to what we know about the Ark from Exodus. According to Exodus, it was

tablets the commandments that were on the first tablets that you smashed, and you shall deposit them in the ark."

³I made an ark of acacia wood and carved out two tablets of stone like the first; I took the two tablets with me and went up the mountain. ⁴The LORD inscribed on the tablets the same text as on the first, the Ten Commandments that He addressed to you on the mountain out of the fire on the day of the Assembly; and the LORD gave them to me. ⁵Then I left and went down from the mountain, and I deposited the tablets in the ark that I had made, where they still are, as the LORD had commanded me.

⁶From Beeroth-bene-jaakan the Israelites marched to Moserah. Aaron died there and was buried there; and his son Eleazar became priest in his stead. ⁷From there they marched to Gudgod, and from Gudgod to Jotbath, a region of running brooks.

אֲשֶׁר הָיוּ עַל־הַלֻּחֹת הָרִאשֹׁנִים אֲשֶׁר שִׁבַּרְתָּ וְשַׂמְתָּם בָּאָרוֹן:

3 וָאַעַשׂ אֲרוֹן עֲצֵי שִׁטִּים וָאֶפְסֹל שְׁנֵי־לֻחֹת אֲבָנִים כָּרִאשֹׁנִים וָאַעַל הָהָרָה וּשְׁנֵי הַלֻּחֹת בְּיָדִי: 4 וַיִּכְתֹּב עַל־הַלֻּחֹת כַּמִּכְתָּב הָרִאשׁוֹן אֵת עֲשֶׂרֶת הַדְּבָרִים אֲשֶׁר דִּבֶּר יְהֹוָה אֲלֵיכֶם בָּהָר מִתּוֹךְ הָאֵשׁ בְּיוֹם הַקָּהָל וַיִּתְּנֵם יְהֹוָה אֵלָי: 5 וָאֵפֶן וָאֵרֵד מִן־הָהָר וָאָשִׂם אֶת־הַלֻּחֹת בָּאָרוֹן אֲשֶׁר עָשִׂיתִי וַיִּהְיוּ שָׁם כַּאֲשֶׁר צִוַּנִי יְהֹוָה:

6 וּבְנֵי יִשְׂרָאֵל נָסְעוּ מִבְּאֵרֹת בְּנֵי־יַעֲקָן מוֹסֵרָה שָׁם מֵת אַהֲרֹן וַיִּקָּבֵר שָׁם וַיְכַהֵן אֶלְעָזָר בְּנוֹ תַּחְתָּיו: 7 מִשָּׁם נָסְעוּ הַגֻּדְגֹּדָה וּמִן־הַגֻּדְגֹּדָה יָטְבָתָה אֶרֶץ נַחֲלֵי מָיִם:

covered by a lid adorned with two three-dimensional cherubs. It was kept in the Holy of Holies in the sanctuary and God would speak with Moses from above the cherubs. The Ark was regarded as God's footstool, and the cherubs were probably viewed as His throne. Placing the tablets in the Ark was thus to place them at God's feet and subject their contents to His enforcement. This conception of the Ark makes its mention in the context of the golden calf incident appropriate: as part of the sanctuary complex, the Ark, with its cherub cover, was a *legitimate* symbol of God's presence, in contrast to the calf.[38]

Unlike Exodus, however, Deuteronomy does not mention that the Ark is a symbol of God's presence, but only that it contains the tablets (see also 31:26, where "the book of this Teaching" is placed beside the Ark). This may be due to the fact that Deuteronomy's subject matter does not call for this information. However, as noted above, in 1:33 and 42 Moses omits references to the Ark where accounts of the same events in Numbers reflect the conception of God traveling above the Ark. Critical theory sees all of these differences as representing Deuteronomy's attempt to downplay anthropomorphic conceptions that localize God's presence in specific objects, just as it insists that the Temple is not God's dwelling but the place where His name is present (see 12:5).[39]

wood According to Exodus 25:11, the wood of the Ark was overlaid with gold.

3. In Exodus the Ark is built later, by Bezalel, along with the rest of the Tabernacle. Some commentators infer that there were two Arks and that the one built by Moses was used to house the tablets temporarily until Bezalel built the permanent one. Others hold that there was only the Ark built by Bezalel, and that Moses' "making" the Ark means that he *had* it made after he came down from the mountain. Critical theory assumes that the passage reflects a different tradition about the building of the Ark from that related in Exodus.[40]

The Death of Aaron (vv. 6–7)

At this point in Moses' narrative about the aftermath of the golden calf incident the text digresses to mention Aaron's death. This is not part of Moses' narrative. Since it refers to Israel in the third person, instead of the first person plural or the second person that Moses uses in Deuteronomy, it must be by a different narrator.[41] Since Aaron died forty years after the golden calf incident (Num. 33:37–39), the reason that his death is mentioned here must be to indicate that although he was spared at the time, he did not escape punishment for his role in Israel's idolatry.[42] Like Moses, he died in the wilderness and never reached the promised land. The note was probably placed before verses 8–9 because Aaron was the High Priest and those verses deal with the priestly functions of the Levites.

None of the places mentioned in these verses has been identified with certainty. See Excursus 1.

8At that time the LORD set apart the tribe of Levi to carry the Ark of the LORD's Covenant, to stand in attendance upon the LORD, and to bless in His name, as is still the case. 9That is why the Levites have received no hereditary portion along with their kinsmen: the LORD is their portion, as the LORD your God spoke concerning them.

8 בָּעֵת הַהִוא הִבְדִּיל יְהוָֹה אֶת־שֵׁבֶט הַלֵּוִי לָשֵׂאת אֶת־אֲרוֹן בְּרִית־יְהוָה לַעֲמֹד לִפְנֵי יְהוָה לְשָׁרְתוֹ וּלְבָרֵךְ בִּשְׁמוֹ עַד הַיּוֹם הַזֶּה: 9 עַל־כֵּן לֹא־הָיָה לְלֵוִי חֵלֶק וְנַחֲלָה עִם־אֶחָיו יְהוָֹה הוּא נַחֲלָתוֹ כַּאֲשֶׁר דִּבֶּר יְהוָֹה אֱלֹהֶיךָ לוֹ:

10I had stayed on the mountain, as I did the first time, forty days and forty nights; and the LORD heeded me once again: the LORD agreed not to destroy you. 11And the LORD said to me, "Up, resume the march at the head of

10 וְאָנֹכִי עָמַדְתִּי בָהָר כַּיָּמִים הָרִאשֹׁנִים אַרְבָּעִים יוֹם וְאַרְבָּעִים לַיְלָה וַיִּשְׁמַע יְהוָה אֵלַי גַּם בַּפַּעַם הַהִוא לֹא־אָבָה יְהוָה הַשְׁחִיתֶךָ: 11 וַיֹּאמֶר יְהוָה אֵלַי קוּם לֵךְ לְמַסַּע לִפְנֵי הָעָם וְיָבֹאוּ וְיִרְשׁוּ

The Election of the Levites and Permission to Continue on to the Promised Land (vv. 8–11)

8–9. Following the notice of Aaron's death, the text returns to the subject of the Ark and the Levites who are in charge of it.

8. At that time Not when Aaron died but at the time of the golden calf incident. The Levites were chosen for their priestly role at that time because it was they who rallied to Moses and punished the worshipers of the calf (see Exod. 32:26–29).[43] The priesthood is an appropriate reward for their devotion: having battled illegitimate worship, they are made the ministers of legitimate worship. See also 33:10.

the tribe of Levi According to Numbers, there was a hereditary hierarchy among the Levites. Only those descended from Aaron might serve as priests (*kohanim*), while the other Levites were subordinates who assisted them by performing menial tasks. This distinction is never mentioned in Deuteronomy. See the discussion in the Comments to 18:1–6.

to carry the Ark of the LORD's Covenant Whenever the Israelites traveled or the Ark had to be moved for some other reason. "The Ark of the LORD's Covenant" is Deuteronomy's standard term for the Ark, referring to the fact that it contained the Tablets of the Covenant.[44] According to 31:9 it was carried by "the priests, sons of Levi,"[45] while according to Numbers this task was assigned to the Kohathite branch of the Levites (Num. 4:1–15; 10:21). See Comments to 18:1–6 and 31:9.

to stand in attendance upon the LORD To offer sacrifices.[46]

to bless in His name To pronounce the priestly benediction (see 21:5; Num. 6:22–27; cf. Lev. 9:22). The high regard in which that blessing was held is illustrated by the discovery in Jerusalem of two silver amulets from the biblical period on which copies of the blessing were inscribed.[47]

9. The Levites received no tribal territory but were dispersed throughout the territories of the other tribes. They were supported by the income of the sanctuaries so that they might devote their time to their clerical duties. See 18:1–2.

10–11. Moses returns to the main subject of 9:26–10:11, his successful prayer to spare Israel (9:26–29). He begins in verse 10 by recapitulating 9:25 and 19b.

11. Although God had already agreed to spare Israel (9:19) and to renew the Sinai covenant (10:1–5), He might have punished the sinners by delaying Israel's entry into the land until the next generation, as He eventually did after the incident of the scouts. Instead, he agrees that the sinners themselves may go to the land, reaffirming for them another part of the patriarchal covenant. With this final reference to the patriarchs, Moses alludes to the main theme of chapters 9–10, that Israel was allowed to enter the land because of God's promise, not because of its virtues.

Up, resume God's final words of forgiveness, *kum lekh*, echo His first angry words about the sin, *kum red*, "hurry, go down!" (9:12).

resume the march at the head of the people In Exodus this was not God's final word. After

the people, that they may go in and possess the land that I swore to their fathers to give them."

אֶת־הָאָ֕רֶץ אֲשֶׁר־נִשְׁבַּ֥עְתִּי לַאֲבֹתָ֖ם לָתֵ֥ת
לָהֶֽם׃ פ חמישי

12And now, O Israel, what does the LORD your God demand of you? Only this: to revere the LORD your God, to walk only in His paths, to love Him, and to serve the LORD your God with all your heart and soul, 13keeping the LORD's commandments and laws, which I enjoin upon you today, for your good. 14Mark, the heavens to their uttermost reaches belong to the LORD your God, the earth and all that is on it! 15Yet it was to your fathers that the LORD was drawn in His love for them, so that He chose you, their lineal descendants, from among all peoples—as is now the case. 16Cut away, therefore, the thickening about your hearts and stiffen your necks no more. 17For the LORD

12 וְעַתָּה֙ יִשְׂרָאֵ֔ל מָ֚ה יְהוָ֣ה אֱלֹהֶ֔יךָ שֹׁאֵ֖ל מֵעִמָּ֑ךְ
כִּ֣י אִם־לְ֠יִרְאָה אֶת־יְהוָ֨ה אֱלֹהֶ֜יךָ לָלֶ֣כֶת בְּכָל־
דְּרָכָ֗יו וּלְאַהֲבָ֤ה אֹתוֹ֙ וְלַעֲבֹד֙ אֶת־יְהוָ֣ה אֱלֹהֶ֔יךָ
בְּכָל־לְבָבְךָ֖ וּבְכָל־נַפְשֶֽׁךָ׃ 13 לִשְׁמֹ֞ר אֶת־מִצְוֺ֤ת
יְהוָה֙ וְאֶת־חֻקֹּתָ֔יו אֲשֶׁ֛ר אָנֹכִ֥י מְצַוְּךָ֖ הַיּ֑וֹם לְט֖וֹב
לָֽךְ׃ 14 הֵ֚ן לַיהוָ֣ה אֱלֹהֶ֔יךָ הַשָּׁמַ֖יִם וּשְׁמֵ֣י הַשָּׁמָ֑יִם
הָאָ֖רֶץ וְכָל־אֲשֶׁר־בָּֽהּ׃ 15 רַ֧ק בַּאֲבֹתֶ֛יךָ חָשַׁ֥ק יְהוָ֖ה
לְאַהֲבָ֣ה אוֹתָ֑ם וַיִּבְחַ֞ר בְּזַרְעָ֤ם אַחֲרֵיהֶם֙ בָּכֶ֔ם
מִכָּל־הָעַמִּ֖ים כַּיּ֥וֹם הַזֶּֽה׃ 16 וּמַלְתֶּ֕ם אֵ֖ת עָרְלַ֣ת
לְבַבְכֶ֑ם וְעָ֨רְפְּכֶ֔ם לֹ֥א תַקְשׁ֖וּ עֽוֹד׃ 17 כִּ֚י יְהוָ֣ה

telling Moses that His angel would lead the people to the promised land, God responded to Moses' further entreaties and agreed to lead the people personally.[48]

GOD'S REQUIREMENTS (vv. 12–22)

Having shown through his account of Israel's rebelliousness that it has no cause to feel self-righteous, Moses appeals for total obedience to God in the future. He does not focus on obeying the rules of the renewed covenant that come at this point in Exodus (Exod. 34:12–26), but on underlying attitudes, as he does throughout this part of Deuteronomy. He summarizes the principles that must guide the people's behavior if they are to avoid further acts of rebellion. His appeal is premised on the preceding account of rebelliousness, as indicated by his call for Israel to cease stiffening its neck as it had done heretofore (v. 16; cf. 9:6,13,27), and by the transitional "And now," meaning "Now, then" (see 4:1).[49] In other words, "Your history of rebellion shows that you lack the following qualities, to which you must dedicate yourselves in the future."

The summary of God's requirements is composed in a quasi-poetic style which attracts the listener's attention and would have facilitated memorization.[50] Because of its aptness as a summary of God's basic requirements, this summary appears in some prayerbooks as "the paragraph on reverence" (*parashat ha-yir'ah*) and excerpts from it were used in *tefillin* and *mezuzah* texts at Qumran.[51]

12–13. Here God's requirements are summarized. These are the main principles expressed throughout Deuteronomy, and all have been expressed earlier. See Comments to 4:10,40; 6:5,13,24; 8:6.

revere Reverence—literally, "fear of God"—comes first, reflecting the lesson just taught: Israel's narrow escape from destruction should deter it from disobedience.

14–15. The argument for obedience is backed up with a reminder of the special privilege that God granted Israel in electing it, since the entire universe belongs to Him. The reminder echoes God's original proposal of the covenant (Exod. 19:5). See also Deuteronomy 4:35–40; Nehemiah 9:6–7.

the heavens to their uttermost reaches Literally, "the heavens and the heaven of heavens," the idea being that there are skies above the sky, and God is master of them all.

16. Since God chose Israel, it must cease to be stubborn.

Cut away ... the thickening about your hearts Literally, "circumcise the foreskin of your heart," the "cover" that blocks your heart and renders it inaccessible to God's teachings. "Foreskin"

your God is God supreme and Lord supreme, the great, the mighty, and the awesome God, who shows no favor and takes no bribe, [18]but upholds the cause of the fatherless and the widow, and befriends the stranger, providing him with food and clothing.—[19]You too must befriend the stranger, for you were strangers in the land of Egypt.

[20]You must revere the LORD your God: only Him shall you worship, to Him shall you hold fast, and by His name shall you swear. [21]He is your glory and He is your God,

אֱלֹהֵיכֶם הוּא אֱלֹהֵי הָאֱלֹהִים וַאֲדֹנֵי הָאֲדֹנִים
הָאֵל הַגָּדֹל הַגִּבֹּר וְהַנּוֹרָא אֲשֶׁר לֹא־יִשָּׂא פָנִים
וְלֹא יִקַּח שֹׁחַד: 18 עֹשֶׂה מִשְׁפַּט יָתוֹם וְאַלְמָנָה
וְאֹהֵב גֵּר לָתֶת לוֹ לֶחֶם וְשִׂמְלָה: 19 וַאֲהַבְתֶּם
אֶת־הַגֵּר כִּי־גֵרִים הֱיִיתֶם בְּאֶרֶץ מִצְרָיִם:
20 אֶת־יְהוָה אֱלֹהֶיךָ תִּירָא אֹתוֹ תַעֲבֹד וּבוֹ
תִדְבָּק וּבִשְׁמוֹ תִּשָּׁבֵעַ: 21 הוּא תְהִלָּתְךָ וְהוּא
אֱלֹהֶיךָ אֲשֶׁר־עָשָׂה אִתְּךָ אֶת־הַגְּדֹלֹת וְאֶת־

is a metaphor for a mental block that has made Israel stubborn.[52] Its use may have been prompted by the reference in verse 15 to the patriarchs, whom God commanded to practice circumcision as a sign of the covenant (Gen. 17:10–14,23–27; 21:4).

stiffen your necks no more   As you did in the wilderness (9:6,13,27).

17–18.   Another argument for obedience to God: He is the greatest authority, the mightiest power, and an impartial judge.

God supreme and Lord supreme   Literally, "the God of gods and Lord of lords," the greatest of all heavenly beings and of all rulers. "Lord of lords" and similar titles were used as epithets of kings in the ancient Near East.[53] On "gods" see Comment to 3:24.

the great, the mighty, and the awesome God   Since talmudic times this passage has formed part of the first paragraph of the Amidah prayer.

who shows no favor and takes no bribe   He exemplifies the qualities of the ideal judge (cf. 1:16–17; 16:19). It is not clear why these qualities are mentioned at this point. One possibility is that they are the practical consequence of God's supreme authority, because of which He cannot be influenced to overlook guilt in the ways that human authorities can.[54]

18.   God defends those who have no influence or standing. According to Hoffmann the point of this verse is to demonstrate that God is beyond influence and favoritism and that Israel cannot expect to sin and escape punishment because of its special relationship with Him. The juxtaposition of this verse with verse 17 led the Talmud to observe that when the Bible mentions God's power, it immediately mentions his kindness as well.[55]

the fatherless[56] and the widow   Those who have no man to protect and provide for them. They are frequently mentioned as examples of the impoverished and the powerless, subject to exploitation, and the Torah makes special provisions for their protection.[57] See Comment to 24:17. That God is their protector is mentioned in Exodus 22:21ff and elsewhere. This is another aspect of God's royalty, for protecting the fatherless, the widow, and the poor was a proverbial responsibility of ancient kings.

befriends   Literally, "loves." As the final clause of the verse indicates, the verb refers to affection expressed in action. See Comment to 6:5.[59]

the stranger   The resident alien; see Comments to 1:16; 5:14; and 24:17. God's concern for strangers is also mentioned in Psalm 146:9.

19.   This is a digression prompted by verse 18. It seems to be an almost instinctive reaction to that verse: no sooner are strangers mentioned than Israel's duty toward them enters the mind.

for you were strangers   Israel's own experience as aliens in a foreign land is regularly cited to encourage fair and kind treatment of strangers in its own land. Note especially Exodus 23:9, which adds: "for you know the feelings of the stranger."[60]

20.   See 6:13.

hold fast   See 4:4.

21.   *He is your glory*   That is, He and none other, continuing the thought of verse 20. The

who wrought for you those marvelous, awesome deeds that you saw with your own eyes. [22] Your ancestors went down to Egypt seventy persons in all; and now the LORD your God has made you as numerous as the stars of heaven.

בִּשְׁבְעִ֗ים [22] הַנּֽוֹרָאֹת֙ הָאֵ֔לֶּה אֲשֶׁ֥ר רָא֖וּ עֵינֶֽיךָ:
נֶ֗פֶשׁ יָרְד֤וּ אֲבֹתֶ֙יךָ֙ מִצְרָ֔יְמָה וְעַתָּ֗ה שָֽׂמְךָ֙ יְהֹוָ֣ה
אֱלֹהֶ֔יךָ כְּכוֹכְבֵ֥י הַשָּׁמַ֖יִם לָרֹֽב:

phrase has been taken to mean that God is the source of Israel's glory or pride. Saadia and Ramban take it to mean "He alone is the proper object of your glorification."[61]

marvelous, awesome deeds   The ten plagues and the crossing of the sea, and the theophany at Mount Sinai.[62]

22.   The astonishing multiplication of the Israelites is apparently cited as another of God's benefactions, in addition to the deeds mentioned in verse 21. In 26:5–9 it heads the list of God's benefactions.[63]

seventy persons   Jacob, his children, and his grandchildren.[64]

as numerous as the stars of heaven   See Comment to 1:10.[65]

The chapter division ends this section of the sermon abruptly. It seems that 11:1, the introduction to the following sermon, is transitional and serves simultaneously as the end of the present unit. It states God's requirements one final time and, with 10:12–13, forms a frame around the unit.[66]

CHAPTER 11   CONQUERING AND KEEPING THE PROMISED LAND
DEPEND ON LOYALTY AND OBEDIENCE TO THE LORD   (vv. 1–25)

In the preceding section, having reviewed Israel's history of faithlessness in the wilderness, Moses summed up God's demand for loyalty and obedience, the central theme of Deuteronomy (10:12–22). In the present section he urges Israel to realize that its future depends on compliance with this demand (11:1–25). He frequently refers to it, urging Israel "to walk in all His ways," "to love Him," "to serve Him with all your heart and soul," "to keep/obey all His commandment(s) which I enjoin upon you this day," and "to hold fast to Him" (11:1,8,13,22), echoing the same phrases in 10:12–13 and 20.

The argument for loyalty and obedience proceeds in three distinct paragraphs arranged in chiastic order.[1] In 11:1–9, after repeating God's demand, Moses argues that his audience should obey God's commands because, having witnessed His redemptive and punitive power, this generation is able to understand better than any future generation that success, both in conquering the land and remaining in it, depends on obedience. In the next two paragraphs, Moses explains these two conclusions in reverse order. In verses 10–21 he argues for obedience on the grounds that the promised land, unlike Egypt, depends on rain for irrigation, without which Israel would perish from the land, and that the rain is dispensed by God only if Israel is loyal and obedient. In verses 22–25 he promises that if Israel is loyal and obedient, God Himself will dislodge the Canaanites for Israel. These verses also complement the argument begun in 9:4–6: the conquest is not to be taken for granted as reward for past loyalty, which Israel has failed to display; rather, it depends, on future loyalty.

Though each paragraph makes a distinct point and is independent of the others, they complement one another and share many features. Each calls for "loving the LORD your God" (vv. 1,13,22), "keeping/obeying the commandment(s) which I command you (this day)" (vv. 1,8,13,22; the verbs *shamar*, "keep," and *shama*, "obey," sound alike). The first two paragraphs share the themes of "the land which you are about to cross into/invade and occupy" (vv. 8,10,11)[2] and "enduring long upon the soil which the LORD swore to your fathers to give to them" (vv. 9,21). The first and third section deal with God's power as manifested in historical events, while the second deals with His governance of nature. For the juxtaposition of these two themes, see the introductory Comment to the first fruits ceremony in 26:1–11.

11 Love, therefore, the Lord your God, and always keep His charge, His laws, His rules, and His commandments.

²Take thought this day that it was not your children, who neither experienced nor witnessed the lesson of the Lord your God—

His majesty, His mighty hand, His outstretched arm; ³the signs and the deeds that He performed in Egypt against Pharaoh king of Egypt and all his land; ⁴what He did to Egypt's army, its horses and chariots; how the Lord rolled back upon them the waters of the Sea of Reeds when they were pursuing you, thus destroying them once and for all; ⁵what He did for you in the

יא וְאָהַבְתָּ אֵת יְהֹוָה אֱלֹהֶיךָ וְשָׁמַרְתָּ
מִשְׁמַרְתּוֹ וְחֻקֹּתָיו וּמִשְׁפָּטָיו וּמִצְוֹתָיו כָּל־הַיָּמִים:
2 וִידַעְתֶּם הַיּוֹם כִּי | לֹא אֶת־בְּנֵיכֶם אֲשֶׁר לֹא־
יָדְעוּ וַאֲשֶׁר לֹא־רָאוּ אֶת־מוּסַר יְהֹוָה אֱלֹהֵיכֶם
אֶת־גָּדְלוֹ אֶת־יָדוֹ הַחֲזָקָה וּזְרֹעוֹ הַנְּטוּיָה:
3 וְאֶת־אֹתֹתָיו וְאֶת־מַעֲשָׂיו אֲשֶׁר עָשָׂה בְּתוֹךְ
מִצְרָיִם לְפַרְעֹה מֶלֶךְ־מִצְרַיִם וּלְכָל־אַרְצוֹ:
4 וַאֲשֶׁר עָשָׂה לְחֵיל מִצְרַיִם לְסוּסָיו וּלְרִכְבּוֹ
אֲשֶׁר הֵצִיף אֶת־מֵי יַם־סוּף עַל־פְּנֵיהֶם בְּרָדְפָם
אַחֲרֵיכֶם וַיְאַבְּדֵם יְהֹוָה עַד הַיּוֹם הַזֶּה: 5 וַאֲשֶׁר

LOVE AND OBEY GOD, FOR YOU HAVE SEEN THE CONSEQUENCES OF DISOBEYING HIM (vv. 1–9)

In this paragraph Moses refers again, as he had in 10:21, to the fact that his audience had personally witnessed God's "marvelous, awesome deeds." Here, however, this refers to God's punitive actions against Egypt and Israel, not to the benefactions mentioned in 10:21. This generation's personal experience of God's punitive power in the preceding forty years is something that no later generation will share. On this experience Moses bases the argument that Israel should obey God's commands in the future, so that it may be strong enough to conquer the promised land and keep it. Personal experience, he implies, puts this generation in a better position than any other to appreciate that its well-being is contingent upon obedience.

Deuteronomy regularly stresses the persuasiveness inherent in personal experience of God's actions (see Comment to 1:19). The converse of this—only hinted at here—is the assumption that those who know of these actions only second hand, from tradition, do not appreciate as fully the obligations these actions impose.³ This problem is spelled out in Judges 2:7ff.: "The people served the Lord during the lifetime of [those] who had witnessed all the marvelous deeds that the Lord had wrought for Israel. . . . Another generation arose after them, which had not experienced the Lord or the deeds that He had wrought for Israel. And the Israelites . . . forsook the Lord" (cf. Ps. 78:1–11). The Bible tries to overcome this problem by writing about these experiences, by instituting frequent occasions, such as holidays, for teaching new generations about them, and by displaying concrete reminders of them, such as unleavened bread.⁴ The generation addressed by Moses has less need of such reminders.⁵

1. This verse is transitional. It introduces 11:2–25 by stating their theme and calling for love of God, as do verses 13 and 22. Without it, 11:2–9 would begin abruptly with verse 2. However, as noted at the end of the Comments to chapter 10, it also serves as the conclusion to 10:12–22.

*2. that it was not your children*⁶ Compare 5:2–3: "It was not with our fathers that the Lord made this covenant, but with us . . . face to face." Moses stresses that he is not appealing to the people on the basis of another generation's experience, but of their own.⁷

lesson Hebrew *musar*, literally, "chastisement," referring to the redemptive and punitive actions listed in the next four and one half verses. The term *musar* encompasses both punishment and the lesson it teaches.⁸ Here God's actions in the past forty years are viewed in their punitive aspect, stressing the lesson they taught. See Comments to 4:36 and 8:5.

majesty Hebrew *godlo*, literally, "greatness," referring to God's power.⁹

4. once and for all Literally, "to this day," meaning that now, forty years later, Egypt still has not replaced the army, horses, and chariots that it lost at the Sea of Reeds.¹⁰ The phrase directs the audience's attention to an aspect of the event that is still visible,¹¹ thus emphasizing that Moses is speaking of evidence that his listeners know firsthand.

The present verse, though not intended as such, is an Israelite rejoinder to a claim made in an

wilderness before you arrived in this place; 6and what He did to Dathan and Abiram, sons of Eliab son of Reuben, when the earth opened her mouth and swallowed them, along with their households, their tents, and every living thing in their train, from amidst all Israel—

7but that it was you who saw with your own eyes all the marvelous deeds that the LORD performed.

8Keep, therefore, all the Instruction that I enjoin upon you today, so that you may have the strength to enter and take possession of the land that you are about to cross into and possess, 9and that you may long endure upon the soil that the LORD swore to your fathers to assign to them and to their heirs, a land flowing with milk and honey.

עָשָׂה לָכֶם בַּמִּדְבָּר עַד־בֹּאֲכֶם עַד־הַמָּקוֹם הַזֶּה: 6 וַאֲשֶׁר עָשָׂה לְדָתָן וְלַאֲבִירָם בְּנֵי אֱלִיאָב בֶּן־רְאוּבֵן אֲשֶׁר פָּצְתָה הָאָרֶץ אֶת־פִּיהָ וַתִּבְלָעֵם וְאֶת־בָּתֵּיהֶם וְאֶת־אָהֳלֵיהֶם וְאֵת כָּל־הַיְקוּם אֲשֶׁר בְּרַגְלֵיהֶם בְּקֶרֶב כָּל־יִשְׂרָאֵל: 7 כִּי עֵינֵיכֶם הָרֹאֹת אֶת־כָּל־מַעֲשֵׂה יְהוָה הַגָּדֹל אֲשֶׁר עָשָׂה:

8 וּשְׁמַרְתֶּם אֶת־כָּל־הַמִּצְוָה אֲשֶׁר אָנֹכִי מְצַוְּךָ הַיּוֹם לְמַעַן תֶּחֶזְקוּ וּבָאתֶם וִירִשְׁתֶּם אֶת־הָאָרֶץ אֲשֶׁר אַתֶּם עֹבְרִים שָׁמָּה לְרִשְׁתָּהּ: 9 וּלְמַעַן תַּאֲרִיכוּ יָמִים עַל־הָאֲדָמָה אֲשֶׁר נִשְׁבַּע יְהוָה לַאֲבֹתֵיכֶם לָתֵת לָהֶם וּלְזַרְעָם אֶרֶץ זָבַת חָלָב וּדְבָשׁ: ס

inscription of Merneptah (1208 B.C.E.), the Pharaoh many scholars think was the pharaoh of the Exodus. In celebrating a string of Merneptah's victories in the area of Canaan, the inscription declares: "Israel is laid waste, his seed is not!"[12]

5. *did for you* Rather "did *to* you" (Heb. *'asah lakhem*). The rest of the context refers only to punitive acts.[13] Moses must be referring to the punishments that God inflicted for Israel's insubordination upon hearing the scouts' report (1:22–45), for the golden calf (Exod. 32), and for sundry other acts of faithlessness (Deut. 2:15; 9:22).

6. *Dathan and Abiram* Korah's cohorts in the celebrated rebellion described in Numbers 16. The omission of Korah himself is conspicuous.[14] Traditional commentators explain that Moses passed over Korah to spare the feelings of Korah's sons.[15] Critical theory holds that Numbers 16 combines the stories of two separate rebellions, one led by Korah and the other led by Dathan and Abiram. According to this view, Deuteronomy knows only the Dathan and Abiram story because the two stories were not yet combined in their present form when Deuteronomy was composed.

along with their households On the divine punishment of an offender's entire family along with him, see Excursus 8.

in their train[16]

from amidst all Israel Rather, "in the midst of all Israel" (Heb. *be-kerev*). The point is either that it happened in full sight of all the people, who thus know of the event first-hand (v. 7), or that it was miraculous because the sinners alone fell into the earth although they were surrounded by the rest of the people.[17]

7–9. Here Moses drives home the lesson: this generation has seen what happens to those who thwart God (cf. Num. 14:34). The people should therefore realize that obedience to God's commands is the precondition for conquering the promised land and remaining in it.

8. *Instruction* Literally, "Commandment," as in verse 22. See Comment to 5:28.

9. *flowing with milk and honey* See Comment to 6:3 and Excursus 9. This phrase indicates that "enduring upon the soil" is to be viewed in the context of agriculture and the supply of food and serves as a transition to the next paragraph.

ENDURING IN THE PROMISED LAND DEPENDS ON
LOYALTY AND OBEDIENCE TO GOD (vv. 10–21)

In this paragraph Moses develops the second conclusion mentioned in the previous paragraph,

10For the land that you are about to enter and possess is not like the land of Egypt from which you have come. There the grain you sowed had to be watered by your own labors, like a vegetable garden; 11but the land you are about to cross into and possess, a land of hills and valleys, soaks up its water from the rains of heaven. 12It is a land which the LORD your God looks after, on which the LORD

שִׁשִׁי 10 כִּי הָאָרֶץ אֲשֶׁר אַתָּה בָא־שָׁמָּה
לְרִשְׁתָּהּ לֹא כְאֶרֶץ מִצְרַיִם הִוא אֲשֶׁר יְצָאתֶם
מִשָּׁם אֲשֶׁר תִּזְרַע אֶת־זַרְעֲךָ וְהִשְׁקִיתָ בְרַגְלְךָ כְּגַן
הַיָּרָק: 11 וְהָאָרֶץ אֲשֶׁר אַתֶּם עֹבְרִים שָׁמָּה
לְרִשְׁתָּהּ אֶרֶץ הָרִים וּבְקָעֹת לִמְטַר הַשָּׁמַיִם
תִּשְׁתֶּה־מָּיִם: 12 אֶרֶץ אֲשֶׁר־יְהוָה אֱלֹהֶיךָ דֹּרֵשׁ

arguing that Israel must observe God's commandments in order to survive and remain in the promised land (v. 9). The basis of his argument is the type of irrigation on which the land's agriculture depends. Unlike Egypt, where irrigation of the fields is a human activity, the land of Israel is watered by God directly, by means of rain.[18] But this benefit is conditional: God will provide rain only if Israel remains loyal and obedient; otherwise, he will withhold rain and Israel will ultimately perish from the land (vv. 12–21). Therefore, Israel should make constant efforts to remember these teachings and teach them to their children so that they, too, may obey them and live in the land forever.

10–12. The dependence of the land on God for irrigation is both an advantage and disadvantage, and the rabbis discussed whether verses 10–12 mean to praise the land or denigrate it.[19] In the end they decided that the passage is one of praise but, as Rashbam observed, "This land is better than Egypt and all other lands to those who observe God's commands, but worse than all other lands to those who do not observe them." As A. Dillmann put it: "The very land is suited to educating a pious, Godfearing people" because it makes their dependence on God obvious.[20]

10. In Egypt, you had to bring water to the fields (cf. Exod. 1:14) on your own, by a method normally used only in vegetable gardens, for which rainfall is insufficient; in the promised land the fields will be watered by God, by means of rain.

Since little rain falls in Egypt, irrigation depends completely on the annual flooding of the Nile, which is caused by melting snow and spring rains at its Ethiopian source. The river floods in the summer and fall, and its water flows into a system of canals and reservoirs, from which it is directed into the fields. Once it begins to sink below the level of the fields that are above river level, it is raised from the canals by artificial means so as to continue irrigating crops in the fields. "A single crop requires the lifting of 1,600 to 2,000 tons of water per acre in a hundred days."[21]

by your own labors Literally, "by your foot," referring to some aspect of the Egyptian irrigation system. It may refer to the use of the foot for opening and closing sluice gates, or to the more primitive method of making and breaking down ridges of dirt to control the flow of water into the irrigation channels in gardens and fields, as has been observed in Egypt and Israel. The phrase could also be translated "on your foot" (or feet) and refer to carrying water (in containers) to fields or gardens.[22]

11. a land of hills and valleys Which could not be irrigated by human effort but only by rain.[23]

The Egyptians were also aware of the difference between the sources of their irrigation and that of foreign lands. An Egyptian hymn speaks of the rain as a Nile in the sky:[24]

> For thou [the sun god] hast set a Nile in heaven,
> That it may descend for [distant foreign countries] and make waves upon the mountains,
> Like the great green sea,
> To water their fields in their towns.

A view similar to that of our chapter is attributed by Herodotus to Egyptian priests who, "on hearing that the whole land of Greece is watered by rain from heaven, and not, like their own, inundated by rivers," observed: "If God shall some day see fit not to grant the Greeks rain, but shall afflict them with a long drought, the Greeks will be swept away by a famine, since they have nothing to rely on but rain from Zeus, and have no other resource for water."[25]

your God always keeps His eye, from year's beginning to year's end.

13If, then, you obey the commandments that I enjoin upon you this day, loving the LORD your God and serving Him with all your heart and soul, 14I will grant the rain for your land in season, the early rain and the late. You shall

אַתָּה תָּמִיד עֵינֵי יְהוָה אֱלֹהֶיךָ* בָּהּ מֵרֵשִׁית הַשָּׁנָה וְעַד אַחֲרִית שָׁנָה׃ ס

13 וְהָיָה אִם־שָׁמֹעַ תִּשְׁמְעוּ אֶל־מִצְוֺתַי אֲשֶׁר אָנֹכִי מְצַוֶּה אֶתְכֶם הַיּוֹם לְאַהֲבָה אֶת־יְהוָה אֱלֹהֵיכֶם וּלְעָבְדוֹ בְּכָל־לְבַבְכֶם וּבְכָל־נַפְשְׁכֶם׃ 14 וְנָתַתִּי

v. 12. חסר אל״ף

12. always The translation, construing "always" as part of the second clause, follows the Masoretic cantillation. However, it is superfluous in the second clause, which contains a phrase meaning the same thing, "from the year's beginning to year's end." In the Hebrew text "always" follows "looks after" in the first clause, and it should be construed as part of that clause, modifying "looks after." Although this seems like a minor point, it indicates that the verse is constructed in synonymous parallelism, in other words, that it is quasi-poetic, like the description of the promised land in 8:7–9. These poetic descriptions show how much Deuteronomy cherishes the land.

on which the LORD . . . always keeps His eye On which God's attention is always focused.[26] Commentators disagree whether Moses is using this idiom to mean benevolent concern[27] or judgmental scrutiny.[28] In its benevolent sense, the idiom normally takes the preposition 'el or 'al. Our verse, however, uses the preposition be-, which is paralleled only in Amos 9:8, where the context is punitive: God's eyes are turned against the sinful kingdom. Here in Deuteronomy the meaning is undoubtedly favorable, as indicated by the poetic style of the verse. However, the preposition be- seems to alert the audience to the message of the coming verses: God's protection is conditional upon Israel's conduct (vv. 13–17).

from year's beginning to year's end God is attentive to the land in every season, "seedtime and harvest, cold and heat, summer and winter" (Gen. 8:22).

13–21. Here Moses draws the conclusion from the facts he describes in verses 10–12. Since the land of Israel is watered by God, rainfall is conditional upon obedience to Him. In verses 13–17 Moses describes the benefits that will follow upon obedience and the harmful consequences of disobedience. Then, in verses 18–20, he stresses the value of learning and teaching God's commands, and in verse 21 he concludes with a promise of long tenure in the land as a result of obedience. As Abravanel put it: "You will not prosper in that land by your own strength and ability, for the commandments are the sole method of cultivating it."[29] These nine verses express the effect of the commandments so concisely and clearly that they were later prescribed as part of the daily recitation of the Shema, expressing "acceptance of the yoke of the commandments." See Excursus 10.

13. serving Him with all your heart In halakhic exegesis this clause is taken to show that prayer is required by the Torah: "What service is with the heart? It is prayer."[30]

14. I will grant Compare verse 15, "I will provide." In both cases Moses is speaking in God's name. See Comment to 7:4, "from Me."[31]

rain . . . in season Promises of rainfall often indicate that it will come in the proper season, since for agricultural purposes rain in the wrong season is useless, at times even harmful.[32]

> Contrary to common belief, the amount of rainfall in agricultural areas in . . . Israel is no less than in agricultural countries in the temperate zones. The difference lies not in the annual amount of rain, but in the number of rainy days and in the intensity of rain per hour or per day. In . . . Israel the entire annual amount falls in 40 to 60 days in a season of seven to eight months. In temperate climates precipitation occurs on 180 days spread over 12 months.[33]

Hence timing is all-important. In Israel, the first showers, known as the *yoreh*, fall intermittently in October and November. They soften the soil, which is hardened and cracked from the summer, and permit farmers to begin plowing and sowing. The rain increases from December through February, with about seventy percent of the year's rain normally falling in these months. The final showers, or *malkosh* ("late rain"), come in April or early May, right before the final burst of growth of the grain

gather in your new grain and wine and oil—¹⁵I will also provide grass in the fields for your cattle—and thus you shall eat your fill. ¹⁶Take care not to be lured away to serve other gods and bow to them. ¹⁷For the LORD's anger will flare up against you, and He will shut up the skies so that there will be no rain and the ground will not yield its produce; and you will soon perish from the good land that the LORD is assigning to you.

¹⁸Therefore impress these My words upon your very heart: bind them as a sign on your hand and let them serve as a symbol on your forehead, ¹⁹and teach them to your children—reciting them when you stay at home and when you are away, when you lie down and when you get up;

מְטַר־אַרְצְכֶם בְּעִתּוֹ יוֹרֶה וּמַלְקוֹשׁ וְאָסַפְתָּ דְגָנֶךָ וְתִירֹשְׁךָ וְיִצְהָרֶךָ: ¹⁵ וְנָתַתִּי עֵשֶׂב בְּשָׂדְךָ לִבְהֶמְתֶּךָ וְאָכַלְתָּ וְשָׂבָעְתָּ: ¹⁶ הִשָּׁמְרוּ לָכֶם פֶּן יִפְתֶּה לְבַבְכֶם וְסַרְתֶּם וַעֲבַדְתֶּם אֱלֹהִים אֲחֵרִים וְהִשְׁתַּחֲוִיתֶם לָהֶם: ¹⁷ וְחָרָה אַף־יְהוָה בָּכֶם וְעָצַר אֶת־הַשָּׁמַיִם וְלֹא־יִהְיֶה מָטָר וְהָאֲדָמָה לֹא תִתֵּן אֶת־יְבוּלָהּ וַאֲבַדְתֶּם מְהֵרָה מֵעַל הָאָרֶץ הַטֹּבָה אֲשֶׁר יְהוָה נֹתֵן לָכֶם: ¹⁸ וְשַׂמְתֶּם אֶת־דְּבָרַי אֵלֶּה עַל־לְבַבְכֶם וְעַל־נַפְשְׁכֶם וּקְשַׁרְתֶּם אֹתָם לְאוֹת עַל־יֶדְכֶם וְהָיוּ לְטוֹטָפֹת בֵּין עֵינֵיכֶם: ¹⁹ וְלִמַּדְתֶּם אֹתָם אֶת־

and are crucial for its maturation. If the early or late rains come too soon or are delayed, this can unduly lengthen or shorten the growing season and stunt the growth of the grain, impede the harvest, or cause it to rot.[34] The talmudic treatise *Taʿanit* prescribes fasting if the rain is delayed, and it observes that rain falling after the normal rainy season was considered a curse.[35]

> *gather* This verb does not refer to harvesting but to bringing crops in from the field for processing, and to gathering in the processed products for storage.[36]

> **15. *I will provide grass . . . for your cattle—and thus you shall eat*** Commentators have speculated on how these two clauses are related. According to one approach, the point is that well-fed cattle will plow better, thus increasing the harvest, or will be fatter and provide more meat.[37] The hyphens in the translation imply that the two clauses are not related, but that "you shall eat" refers back to the produce mentioned in verse 15.[38] The talmudic sage Rav construed the conjunction *ve-* (here rendered "thus") in its sense of "then" and inferred from the sequence of the clauses that the verse is concerned with kindness to animals, indicating that one must feed one's cattle before feeding oneself.[39]

> **16-17.** As in 6:12 and 8:11, the promise "you shall eat your fill" is followed by a warning to "take care" not to be led astray by satiety to forget YHVH and worship other gods. The text must have in mind the Canaanite *baʿal*s. These were local forms of Hadad (his epithet "Baal" means "lord, master"),[40] the deity whom Canaanites believed responsible for rain and agricultural fertility.[41] The Israelites lived among peoples who saw the control of the world as divided among many independent divine powers. Gods of fertility were especially prominent and their lure was a recurrent challenge to monotheism. When the Israelites left the desert and settled in Canaan, some must have reasoned that the Canaanites' gods were responsible for the land's fertility, since the Canaanites had successfully practiced agriculture before the Israelites arrived. This thinking is vividly described—and rejected—in Hosea 2:4–19. One of the most celebrated episodes in the struggle against this temptation came in the days of Ahab, when YHVH first withheld rain and finally granted it when Elijah confronted the prophets of Baal on Mount Carmel. In this way He showed that only He, and not Baal, controls the rain (1 Kings 17–18; cf. Jer. 14:22). In our passage, as the Israelites prepare to settle in a land where they will adopt a new, agricultural way of life, Moses forewarns them that rain and fertility are given by God in return for obedience, and that if the Israelites should turn to false gods, He will withhold these gifts, causing the Israelites to perish from the land.

> **16. *be lured*** See Comment to 4:19.

> **18-21.** Consequently, the Israelites should remind themselves of God's teachings so as to obey them and avoid a disastrous fate. The reminders are those prescribed in 6:6–9.

> **18. *your very heart*** Rather, "your heart and soul." See Comment to 6:5.

> **bind them** See Comment to 6:8.

בְּנֶיכֶם לְדַבֵּר בֶּם בְּשִׁבְתְּךָ בְּבֵיתֶךָ וּבְלֶכְתְּךָ
בַדֶּרֶךְ וּבְשָׁכְבְּךָ וּבְקוּמֶךָ: 20 וּכְתַבְתָּם עַל־
מְזוּזוֹת בֵּיתֶךָ וּבִשְׁעָרֶיךָ: 21 לְמַעַן יִרְבּוּ יְמֵיכֶם
וִימֵי בְנֵיכֶם עַל הָאֲדָמָה אֲשֶׁר נִשְׁבַּע יְהֹוָה
לַאֲבֹתֵיכֶם לָתֵת לָהֶם כִּימֵי הַשָּׁמַיִם עַל־
הָאָרֶץ: ס   שביעי ומפטיר

22 כִּי אִם־שָׁמֹר תִּשְׁמְרוּן אֶת־כָּל־הַמִּצְוָה הַזֹּאת
אֲשֶׁר אָנֹכִי מְצַוֶּה אֶתְכֶם לַעֲשֹׂתָהּ לְאַהֲבָה אֶת־
יְהֹוָה אֱלֹהֵיכֶם לָלֶכֶת בְּכָל־דְּרָכָיו וּלְדָבְקָה־בוֹ:
23 וְהוֹרִישׁ יְהֹוָה אֶת־כָּל־הַגּוֹיִם הָאֵלֶּה מִלִּפְנֵיכֶם
וִירִשְׁתֶּם גּוֹיִם גְּדֹלִים וַעֲצֻמִים מִכֶּם: 24 כָּל־הַמָּקוֹם
אֲשֶׁר תִּדְרֹךְ כַּף־רַגְלְכֶם בּוֹ לָכֶם יִהְיֶה מִן־הַמִּדְבָּר
וְהַלְּבָנוֹן מִן־הַנָּהָר נְהַר־פְּרָת וְעַד הַיָּם הָאַחֲרוֹן
יִהְיֶה גְּבֻלְכֶם: 25 לֹא־יִתְיַצֵּב אִישׁ בִּפְנֵיכֶם פַּחְדְּכֶם
וּמוֹרַאֲכֶם יִתֵּן | יְהֹוָה אֱלֹהֵיכֶם עַל־פְּנֵי כָל־הָאָרֶץ
אֲשֶׁר תִּדְרְכוּ־בָהּ כַּאֲשֶׁר דִּבֶּר לָכֶם: ס

20and inscribe them on the doorposts of your house and on your gates—21to the end that you and your children may endure, in the land that the LORD swore to your fathers to assign to them, as long as there is a heaven over the earth.

22If, then, you faithfully keep all this Instruction that I command you, loving the LORD your God, walking in all His ways, and holding fast to Him, 23the LORD will dislodge before you all these nations: you will dispossess nations greater and more numerous than you. 24Every spot on which your foot treads shall be yours; your territory shall extend from the wilderness to the Lebanon and from the River—the Euphrates—to the Western Sea. 25No man shall stand up to you: the LORD your God will put the dread and the fear of you over the whole land in which you set foot, as He promised you.

20. *inscribe them*   See Comment to 6:9.

21. *as long as there is a heaven over the earth*   That is, forever. The sky and other heavenly bodies symbolize longevity and permanence.[42]

OBEDIENCE TO GOD WILL ENSURE A SUCCESSFUL CONQUEST OF THE PROMISED LAND (vv. 22–25)

In this paragraph Moses develops the first conclusion mentioned in the first paragraph (v. 8), promising that if Israel obeys and loves God, God Himself will dispossess the Canaanites and enable Israel to succeed them. This paragraph caps the argument of 11:1–21. It also casts a new light on the promise of victory uttered in 9:1–2 by making it clear that everything promised in chapters 9–11 is conditional.

24. *Every spot on which your foot treads shall be yours*   This wording may reflect the ancient practice of formally acquiring title to land by walking through it.[43]

your territory shall extend from . . .   Since the point of this verse is that God is giving Israel the entire promised land, from one end to the other, only its extremities are named: the deserts in the south, the Lebanon and the Euphrates in the north, and the Mediterranean on the west. The unmentioned eastern boundary, the Jordan, is implicit in the fact that the Israelites are about to cross it to enter the land (e.g., 11:8). For details on this conception of the boundaries see Comment to 1:7 (which also mentions the land's main internal divisions).

the Western Sea   Literally, the "hind" or "rear" sea. The geographic orientation of the ancient western Semites was not toward the north, as in modern cartography, but the east. Hence one set of terms for the four points of the compass expresses "east" by "forward" (*kedem*), "west" by "behind" (*'aḥor*), "north" by "left" (*semo'l*), and "south" by "right" (*yamin, teiman*).

25. *dread . . . and fear*   Compare 2:25; 7:23.

as He promised you   See Exodus 23:26–31; Deuteronomy 7:19–24.[44]

RE'EH

26See, this day I set before you blessing and curse:
27blessing, if you obey the commandments of the LORD
your God that I enjoin upon you this day; 28and curse, if
you do not obey the commandments of the LORD your
God, but turn away from the path that I enjoin upon you
this day and follow other gods, whom you have not experienced. 29When the LORD your God brings you into the
land that you are about to enter and possess, you shall
pronounce the blessing at Mount Gerizim and the curse at
Mount Ebal.—30Both are on the other side of the Jordan,
beyond the west road that is in the land of the Canaanites
who dwell in the Arabah—near Gilgal, by the terebinths of
Moreh.

ראה

26 רְאֵה אָנֹכִי נֹתֵן לִפְנֵיכֶם הַיּוֹם בְּרָכָה וּקְלָלָה:
27 אֶת־הַבְּרָכָה אֲשֶׁר תִּשְׁמְעוּ אֶל־מִצְוֺת יְהוָה
אֱלֹהֵיכֶם אֲשֶׁר אָנֹכִי מְצַוֶּה אֶתְכֶם הַיּוֹם:
28 וְהַקְּלָלָה אִם־לֹא תִשְׁמְעוּ אֶל־מִצְוֺת יְהוָה
אֱלֹהֵיכֶם וְסַרְתֶּם מִן־הַדֶּרֶךְ אֲשֶׁר אָנֹכִי מְצַוֶּה
אֶתְכֶם הַיּוֹם לָלֶכֶת אַחֲרֵי אֱלֹהִים אֲחֵרִים אֲשֶׁר
לֹא־יְדַעְתֶּם: ס 29 וְהָיָה כִּי יְבִיאֲךָ יְהוָה אֱלֹהֶיךָ
אֶל־הָאָרֶץ אֲשֶׁר־אַתָּה בָא־שָׁמָּה לְרִשְׁתָּהּ
וְנָתַתָּה אֶת־הַבְּרָכָה עַל־הַר גְּרִזִים וְאֶת־הַקְּלָלָה
עַל־הַר עֵיבָל: 30 הֲלֹא־הֵמָּה בְּעֵבֶר הַיַּרְדֵּן אַחֲרֵי
דֶּרֶךְ מְבוֹא הַשֶּׁמֶשׁ בְּאֶרֶץ הַכְּנַעֲנִי הַיֹּשֵׁב בָּעֲרָבָה
מוּל הַגִּלְגָּל אֵצֶל אֵלוֹנֵי מֹרֶה:

Re'eh   SUMMARY: BLESSING AND CURSE   (vv. 26–30)

ISRAEL'S CHOICE (vv. 26–28)

Moses sums up the preamble to the laws (5:1–11:28). All that he has said in the preceding chapters
culminates in a choice between two futures, a blessed one if the people obey the terms of their
covenant with God and an accursed one if they do not.

26. *I set before you blessing and curse*   That is, "I give you the choice between material
well-being and misfortune." The two possibilities are graphically illustrated in Deuteronomy 28.[45]

28. *other gods whom you have not experienced*   That is, "gods who have not proved
themselves to you."[46] The Lord's claim on Israel's loyalty is based on the fact that He alone has acted
on Israel's behalf (see 5:6). From other gods Israel has experienced nothing. Compare Hosea 13:4:
"Only I the LORD have been your God ever since the land of Egypt; you have never experienced a
God but Me, you have never had a helper but Me."

A CEREMONY OF BLESSING AND CURSING (vv. 29–30)

The covenant relationship with God is vital for Israel's existence in the promised land. Therefore,
upon entering the land Israel is to reaffirm its commitment to the covenant in a public ceremony
dramatically proclaiming the consequences of obeying or disobeying its terms. The ceremony is
described in chapter 27, immediately following the laws. Verses 29–30 and chapter 27 thus form a
frame around the laws.

29. *Mount Gerizim and Mount Ebal*   Mountains facing each other south and north of
Shechem, respectively. Shechem was located on the eastern approach to modern Nablus. See Map 4
and Comments to 27:4 and 12–13.

30. *the other side of the Jordan*   West of the Jordan, across from the side on which Moses
is addressing the people.

beyond the west road   Rather, "beyond the westward road," since roads are commonly
designated by their terminus (literally its name means "Sunset Boulevard" or, more precisely,
"Sunset Road"). The road in question must have led west from the Jordan to Shechem and perhaps
all the way to the Mediterranean. (See Maps 4 and 6 and Excursus 1, s.v. "the westward road.") The
precise force of the preposition *'aharei* ("beyond," "west of") is uncertain here. Perhaps the sense is
"down the westward road."

that is in the land of the Canaanites who dwell in the Arabah—near Gilgal   The mean-

ing of this part of the verse is uncertain. It seems to indicate that Mount Ebal and Mount Gerizim are in the Aravah (the Jordan valley, 1:7), near Gilgal, a city in the Aravah (see Map 6). This is geographically impossible since Ebal and Gerizim are in the highlands some thirty miles west of the valley and of that particular Gilgal. If the text is to make sense as it stands, we must take the phrase "that is in the land of the Canaanites who dwell in the Arabah" not as giving the location of the two mountains, but of part of the westward road.[47] This is how the translation understands it, meaning: "Both are on the other side of the Jordan—beyond the westward road [that is] in [i.e., traverses] the territory of the Canaanites who dwell in the Arabah—near Gilgal, by the terebinths of Moreh." In that case, "near Gilgal" refers to a lesser-known Gilgal, near Ebal and Gerizim. Since the name Gilgal (lit., "the *gilgal*") means a heap or circle of stones, it could refer to any such structure in the vicinity. A few different places in Israel, including one near Gerizim and Ebal, bore this name. See Map 4 and Excursus 1.[48]

However, this is not the smoothest way to read the verse, since it requires mentally inserting the bracketed words "that is," and some scholars believe that the verse really is internally contradictory. They consider this the result of editorial activity that sought to combine in this verse two different traditions about where the ceremony was to take place. One tradition located it on Mount Gerizim and Mount Ebal, by Shechem, and the other at the Gilgal in the Aravah, which was the Israelites' first camp when they entered the promised land (Josh. 5:10). This is a possible explanation, since something similar appears to have happened in 27:1–8. See Comments to 27:2–4 and Excursus 25.[49]

the terebinths of Moreh   Probably the same as "the terebinth of Moreh" at Shechem mentioned in Genesis 12:6. "Moreh" probably means "oracle giver" and may indicate that the place was named for Canaanite diviners who once gave oracles at the trees. Several other passages refer to sacred terebinths at Shechem, and the Arabic name of the site, Balatah, may be derived from the Arabic word for oak, *ballut*.[50]

THE LAWS GIVEN IN MOAB   (11:31–26:15)

Following the prologue and preamble in chapters 5–11, Moses turns to the laws themselves. They constitute the core of Deuteronomy and its lengthiest section, and continue on into chapter 26. The laws begin with regulations concerning the place of worship. The reasons underlying the arrangement of the laws are discussed in Excursus 13.

Moses does not present the laws in the style of a legal code. He devotes more attention to their basic provisions than to their practical details. The latter must have been provided by an oral interpretive tradition developed by courts, as they were in later times, and perhaps by administrative agencies. The most distinctive feature of Moses' presentation of the laws is the way he frequently devotes as much—or more—attention to exhorting the people to obey the laws as to presenting the laws themselves. He recognizes that people must be persuaded to obey the laws. On this subject see the Comment about motive clauses in the Introduction.

Chapter 12 is a good example of Deuteronomy's legal style. The core of the chapter, verses 2–28, contains three basic rules: Canaanite places of worship must be destroyed; Israel may perform sacrificial worship at only one place, chosen by God; and nonsacrificial slaughter is permitted to those living at a distance from the chosen place. The chapter requires twenty-seven verses to state these rules because it devotes much attention to repeating, clarifying, exhorting, cautioning, and explaining when the rules will come into effect. From a strictly legal point of view much of this is unnecessary, as shown by the fact that the Temple Scroll from Qumran conveys the essence of the chapter in eleven short lines. At the same time, the inattention to detail is reflected in the law that permits those living far from the chosen place to slaughter animals nonsacrificially but that does not define "far" (v. 21); the Temple Scroll defines this as living three days' journey from the Temple.[1]

³¹For you are about to cross the Jordan to enter and possess the land that the LORD your God is assigning to you. When you have occupied it and are settled in it, ³²take care to observe all the laws and rules that I have set before you this day.

12 These are the laws and rules that you must carefully observe in the land that the LORD, God of your fathers, is giving you to possess, as long as you live on earth.

כִּי אַתֶּם עֹבְרִים אֶת־הַיַּרְדֵּן לָבֹא לָרֶשֶׁת אֶת־ ‎31
הָאָרֶץ אֲשֶׁר־יְהוָה אֱלֹהֵיכֶם נֹתֵן לָכֶם וִירִשְׁתֶּם
אֹתָהּ וִישַׁבְתֶּם־בָּהּ: וּשְׁמַרְתֶּם לַעֲשׂוֹת אֵת כָּל־ ‎32
הַחֻקִּים וְאֶת־הַמִּשְׁפָּטִים אֲשֶׁר אָנֹכִי נֹתֵן לִפְנֵיכֶם
הַיּוֹם:

י״ב אֵלֶּה הַחֻקִּים וְהַמִּשְׁפָּטִים אֲשֶׁר תִּשְׁמְרוּן
לַעֲשׂוֹת בָּאָרֶץ אֲשֶׁר נָתַן יְהוָה אֱלֹהֵי אֲבֹתֶיךָ
לְךָ לְרִשְׁתָּהּ כָּל־הַיָּמִים אֲשֶׁר־אַתֶּם חַיִּים עַל־
הָאֲדָמָה:

Introduction and Heading to the Laws   (11:31–12:1)

11:31. *For you are about to cross* It is probably better to translate the verse: "*When* you cross the Jordan to enter and possess the land . . . and you have taken possession of it and settled in it." This is likely not an explanation of what was said in the preceding verse, but an introductory clause specifying when the laws are to be put into effect.[2] The immediate heading to the laws is 12:1. Verses 11:32–12:1 are echoed right after the laws in 26:16; together these verses form an inner frame around the laws, within the one noted in the introductory Comment to 11:29–30.

CHAPTER 12   **12:1. *as long as you live on earth*** Or: "as long as you live in the land." Compare 4:10 and 31:13.

The Sanctuary and Other Religious Matters   (12:2–16:17)

The first section of the laws focuses primarily on the sanctuary, the rites and festivals celebrated within it, and other religious matters, such as shunning Canaanite religious practices, punishing instigation to worship other gods, and holiness in mourning and diet.

THE PLACE OF WORSHIP   (12:2–13:1)

The Israelites may not take over and use places where the Canaanites worshiped their gods, but must destroy them. They must not sacrifice to the Lord wherever they please, as they have been permitted to do until now. Such worship may continue only until the Israelites achieve security, but then they must restrict sacrificial worship to a single place, chosen by God. Because traveling to this place will entail a lengthy journey for most Israelites, the existing law that even animals slaughtered purely for food must be sacrificed at a sanctuary will become impractical and will therefore be relaxed.

The chapter falls into three main parts. The first deals with the place of worship: the many sanctuaries of the Canaanites are to be destroyed, and the Israelites are to shun the Canaanite practice of worshiping at many places and limit their sacrificial worship to one place, chosen by God (vv. 2–7). The second part consists of five sections which clarify the restriction of sacrifice to a single place and spell out the ramifications of this restriction (vv. 8–28). The third part generalizes the principle of shunning Canaanite ways of worship and identifies the most horrendous of them, which is child sacrifice (12:29–13:1).[3]

The limitation of sacrificial worship to a single place is the most unique and far-reaching law in Deuteronomy. It affected the religious life of individuals, the sacrificial system, the way festivals were

2You must destroy all the sites at which the nations you are to dispossess worshiped their gods, whether on lofty mountains and on hills or under any luxuriant tree. 3Tear down their altars, smash their pillars, put their sacred posts to the fire, and cut down the images of their gods, obliterating their name from that site.

2 אַבֵּ֣ד תְּאַבְּד֞וּן אֶֽת־כָּל־הַמְּקֹמ֗וֹת אֲשֶׁ֣ר עָֽבְדוּ־
שָׁ֣ם הַגּוֹיִ֗ם אֲשֶׁ֨ר אַתֶּ֜ם יֹרְשִׁ֤ים אֹתָם֙ אֶת־אֱלֹ֣הֵיהֶ֔ם
עַל־הֶהָרִ֤ים הָֽרָמִים֙ וְעַל־הַגְּבָע֔וֹת וְתַ֖חַת כָּל־עֵ֥ץ
רַעֲנָֽן׃ 3 וְנִתַּצְתֶּ֣ם אֶת־מִזְבְּחֹתָ֗ם וְשִׁבַּרְתֶּם֙ אֶת־
מַצֵּבֹתָ֔ם וַאֲשֵֽׁרֵיהֶם֙ תִּשְׂרְפ֣וּן בָּאֵ֔שׁ וּפְסִילֵ֥י
אֱלֹֽהֵיהֶ֖ם תְּגַדֵּע֑וּן וְאִבַּדְתֶּ֣ם אֶת־שְׁמָ֔ם מִן־
הַמָּק֖וֹם הַהֽוּא׃

celebrated, the economic status of the Levites, and even the judicial system.[4] According to the Bible, the conditions under which Deuteronomy expects this limitation to be enforced were first met in the days of Joshua and again in the days of David and Solomon (see Comment to vv. 9–10). However, the only known attempts to enforce such a restriction occurred centuries later, during the eighth and seventh centuries, in the reigns of Kings Hezekiah and Josiah. This fact has played a major role in dating Deuteronomy. See the discussion in the Introduction and in Excursus 14.

The limitation also affected the personal religious lives of individuals. With sacrifice restricted to one location, distant from the homes of most people, it became difficult to give thanksgiving and sin offerings, to undergo purificatory ceremonies, and pay vows; and meat meals were deprived of their religious dimension (see Comments to vv. 15ff). Deuteronomy must have expected that some other religious activities would take the place of sacrifice in people's lives throughout the year. A book so concerned with the religious attitudes of all the people could not have intended to leave a religious vacuum in their lives, to be filled only during the three annual pilgrimage festivals. It is likely that prayer and study were expected to fill the gap. This is suggested by the fact that Deuteronomy emphasizes these more than the earlier books of the Torah do. Although it prohibits sacrificing at local sanctuaries, it places no limits on praying there.[5] It requires farmers to recite prayers when they bring first-fruits and the third-year tithe to the Temple, and it makes provisions for regular and periodic study of its own contents by individuals and by the public at large. It prescribes religious gatherings throughout the country on the last day of the Feast of Unleavened Bread (16:8), and an expiatory prayer to be recited as part of the ritual performed by the elders of a town near which an unsolved murder has taken place (21:7–8).[6]

DESTROYING CANAANITE SANCTUARIES (vv. 2–3)

The text implies that most Canaanite places of worship were open-air sanctuaries rather than temple buildings, and that those in the countryside outnumbered those in the cities. This is indicated by the fact that the text speaks of sanctuaries on hills and mountains and under trees, and that buildings are not mentioned in any of the passages dealing with this subject.[7] The term "sites" is broad enough to include temple buildings, but these were evidently not numerous enough to be mentioned separately.[8] The main appurtenances of the open-air sanctuaries were altars, sacred pillars, sacred posts, and images (v. 4; see Comment to 7:5).[9]

2. *sites* Not the geographic sites but the altars and other objects used in worship at them.[10]

3. See Comments to 7:5.

obliterating their name Wiping out all reminders of their existence.[11] Compare Zechariah 13:2: "I will erase the very names of the idols from the land; they shall not be uttered any more." See Comment to 7:24. The present command contrasts with the description of God's chosen sanctuary as "the place where He chooses to *establish* His name" (vv. 5,11,21).

According to Numbers 32:38, the Israelites changed the names of certain cities that they conquered when the cities' names included the names of pagan gods. Halakhic exegesis took "obliterating their name" as a command to replace the names of pagan places of worship with uncomplimentary distortions of their names.[12]

from that site Halakhic exegesis took this phrase as indicating that one is commanded to eradicate idolatry only in the promised land, not elsewhere.[13] The Torah does not require Israel to

4Do not worship the LORD your God in like manner, 5but look only to the site that the LORD your God will choose amidst all your tribes as His habitation, to establish His name there. There you are to go, 6and there you are to

4 לֹא־תַעֲשׂוּן כֵּן לַיהוָה אֱלֹהֵיכֶם: 5 כִּי אִם־אֶל־הַמָּקוֹם אֲשֶׁר־יִבְחַר יְהוָה אֱלֹהֵיכֶם מִכָּל־שִׁבְטֵיכֶם לָשׂוּם אֶת־שְׁמוֹ שָׁם לְשִׁכְנוֹ תִדְרְשׁוּ וּבָאתָ שָּׁמָּה: 6 וַהֲבֵאתֶם שָׁמָּה עֹלֹתֵיכֶם וְזִבְחֵיכֶם

engage in a world-wide campaign against idolatry, but only to eliminate it from the land of Israel where it might influence Israelites. This is consistent with the biblical view that for other nations idolatry is not a sin since it was ordained for them by God, and that it will be brought to an end by God, not by Israelite actions. See Excursus 7.

THE SINGLE PLACE OF SACRIFICE (vv. 4–7)

The reason for restricting sacrifice to a single place is not explained. From the wording of verses 4 and 31 it seems that using many places for sacrifice was objectionable because it was regarded as an inherently pagan way of worship (note that in 2 Kings 18:22 it is a pagan who disparages Hezekiah's enforcement of the restriction).[14] See Excursus 14.

4. **Do not worship the LORD your God in like manner** Literally, "You shall not act thus toward the LORD your God," as in verse 31. The prohibition means that Israel must not worship the Lord in the ways that Canaanites worshiped their gods, as indicated in verses 2–3: by sacrificing in many places, on hills and under trees, with pillars and idols and sacred posts.[15] This meaning is clear from the indictment of northern Israel in 2 Kings 17:9–11: "The Israelites . . . built for themselves shrines in all their settlements . . . they set up pillars and sacred posts for themselves on every lofty hill and under every luxuriant tree; and they offered sacrifices there, at all the shrines, like the nations whom the LORD had driven into exile before them." The prohibition is repeated below, and the warning not to adopt Canaanite religious practices even in honor of the Lord is made more explicit (vv. 30–31). Compare Exodus 23:24: "You shall not follow their [the Canaanites'] practices."[16]

5. **look** Rather, "resort," "make pilgrimages."[17]

the site The site is not named in the Torah. Eventually Jerusalem was chosen, but according to Jeremiah 7:12 it was preceded by Shiloh. See Comment to verses 9–10.

the LORD your God will choose The divine choice would presumably be communicated by a prophet. The site where Solomon built the Temple was originally chosen by David for an altar on the instructions of the prophet Gad.[18] Compare 17:15.

as His habitation, to establish His name there Rather, "to establish His name there, for it [His name] to dwell."[19] Deuteronomy regularly describes the chosen place as the one where God will "establish" His name. It expresses this idea with the verbs *s-w-m*, literally, "place," and *sh-k-n*, literally, "(make) dwell."[20] Other passages in the Bible paraphrase these expressions by stating that the place is *called* by God's name. This implies that God's name is *established* in the Temple because it is called "The Temple of YHVH," indicating that it is His possession.[21] That God's name is established at the Temple means that He is accessible there in worship, since it is the focus of His attention. Thus, when Solomon dedicates the Temple and prays that God will answer prayers uttered there, demonstrating that it is rightly called by His name, God assures him, "I consecrate this House which you have built and I set My name there forever. My eyes and My heart shall ever be there" (1 Kings 8:29,43; 9:3).[22] The expression "make His name dwell (*sh-k-n*) there" seems to allude to passages that speak of God Himself as dwelling in the sanctuary or among the Israelites.[23] By speaking instead of God's *name* as dwelling in the chosen place, Deuteronomy seeks to correct the impression that God Himself literally dwells there: only His name "dwells" there, whereas God Himself is in heaven.[24]

6. In choosing a single sanctuary, God limits all sacrificial worship to it. The offerings are summed up in four pairs of terms that represent, respectively, animal sacrifices, taxes on agricultural products, voluntary offerings, and firstlings of cattle. Subsequent verses in the chapter refer back to parts of this list.[25] The text does not say when these offerings are to be brought to the sanctuary. In

bring your burnt offerings and other sacrifices, your tithes and contributions, your votive and freewill offerings, and the firstlings of your herds and flocks. ⁷Together with your households, you shall feast there before the LORD your God, happy in all the undertakings in which the LORD your God has blessed you.

וְאֵת֙ מַעְשְׂרֹ֣תֵיכֶ֔ם וְאֵ֖ת תְּרוּמַ֣ת יֶדְכֶ֑ם וְנִדְרֵיכֶם֙
וְנִדְבֹ֣תֵיכֶ֔ם וּבְכֹרֹ֥ת בְּקַרְכֶ֖ם וְצֹאנְכֶֽם׃ 7 וַאֲכַלְתֶּם־
שָׁ֗ם לִפְנֵי֙ יְהֹוָ֣ה אֱלֹהֵיכֶ֔ם וּשְׂמַחְתֶּ֗ם בְּכֹל֙ מִשְׁלַ֣ח
יֶדְכֶ֔ם אַתֶּ֖ם וּבָתֵּיכֶ֑ם אֲשֶׁ֥ר בֵּרַכְךָ֖ יְהֹוָ֥ה אֱלֹהֶֽיךָ׃

most cases, the regular pilgrimage festivals were probably the most convenient occasion, but farmers probably made private pilgrimages at other times as well, as did Elkanah in the first chapter of 1 Samuel (see Comment to 23:22).

burnt offerings   Hebrew *'olah*, literally, "that which goes up" (the translation "burnt offering" is based on the Greek rendering *holokautoma*, "holocaust," "wholly burnt"). The flesh of the offering "goes up" completely in smoke, with nothing left for human consumption (see v. 27a). For this reason burnt offerings were, of all the sacrifices, the gift *par excellence*. They were the mainstay of the priestly service at the sanctuary, were offered every morning and evening, and were given on Sabbaths and holidays in addition to the basic offerings that were specific to those occasions. They were also part of purification rituals, and some votive and freewill offerings belonged to this category.[26]

other sacrifices   The term *zevaḥ* refers to sacrifices of the *shelamim* category, in which most of the meat was eaten by the offerer (see v. 27b). These included thanksgiving sacrifices, some votive and freewill offerings (see below), the passover offering, and annual family offerings (see Comment to 23:22).[27]

tithes   The tithe (lit., "a tenth") was a gift or payment of ten percent of agricultural products and cattle. Tithes were originally used to support temples and their personnel, but their function was changed when the local sanctuaries were abolished. See 14:22–29.[28]

contributions   Literally, "the contribution of your hands." The term *terumah* refers to something separated out of a larger amount and dedicated, such as tithes, first fruits, the priest's share of a sacrificial animal, and the portion of war spoils assigned to the sanctuary. Here the term likely refers to the first fruits. This interpretation is supported by Deuteronomy 26:4, according to which the first fruits are taken by the priest "from the hand" of the offerer.[29]

votive and freewill offerings   The votive offering was a gift that was promised to God on condition that He grant a benefaction, such as the birth of a son or safe return from a journey or battle. The freewill offering was one which the worshiper—usually with no prior obligation or commitment—promised to give as an expression of devotion or gratitude. Apparently, the personal offerings required on pilgrimage festivals were also considered freewill offerings. Both types might take the form of a sacrifice or a gift to the sanctuary.[30] See 23:22–24.

firstlings   First-born male oxen, sheep and goats, all of which had to be sacrificed to God.[31] See 15:19–23.

7.   A literal translation of the verse makes its similarity to verse 18 and to 14:26 and 16:11,14 clearer: "You shall eat [the offerings] there before the LORD your God and celebrate—you and your households—all the fruits of your labors with which the LORD your God has blessed you."

Together with your households   Literally, "you and your households," the members of which are listed in verses 12 and 18. According to 16:18, only males were required to attend pilgrimage festivals. However, since verses 12 and 18 indicate that daughters and female slaves were typically present, the text can hardly expect wives to remain at home; it must include them in the "you" to whom the law is addressed (halakhic exegesis takes "households" as an explicit reference to them). The story of Hannah and Peninah in 1 Samuel 1 indicates that it was common for wives to attend except under special circumstances, as when they were nursing.[32]

feast   This refers to the offerings listed in verse 6 (see vv. 17–18) and is a generalization, since some of the offerings, especially the burnt offerings, were not eaten.

⁸You shall not act at all as we now act here, every man as he pleases, ⁹because you have not yet come to the allotted haven that the LORD your God is giving you. ¹⁰When you cross the Jordan and settle in the land that the LORD your God is allotting to you, and He grants you safety from all

8 לֹא תַעֲשׂוּן כְּכֹל אֲשֶׁר אֲנַחְנוּ עֹשִׂים פֹּה הַיּוֹם אִישׁ כָּל־הַיָּשָׁר בְּעֵינָיו: 9 כִּי לֹא־בָּאתֶם עַד־עָתָּה אֶל־הַמְּנוּחָה וְאֶל־הַנַּחֲלָה אֲשֶׁר־יְהוָה אֱלֹהֶיךָ נֹתֵן לָךְ: 10 וַעֲבַרְתֶּם אֶת־הַיַּרְדֵּן וִישַׁבְתֶּם בָּאָרֶץ אֲשֶׁר־יְהוָה אֱלֹהֵיכֶם מַנְחִיל אֶתְכֶם

happy Literally, "you shall celebrate," with a sacrificial meal.[33] Although each type of offering has a specific purpose, Deuteronomy emphasizes their overall value in providing occasions for celebration over God's bounty, which is the principal ceremonial means recognized by the book for thanking Him. These occasions serve to inculcate love and reverence for God (see esp. 14:23).[34] Deuteronomy stresses the effect that the offerings have on people rather than any effect they may have on God. In keeping with this emphasis, Deuteronomy makes no explicit reference to the daily offerings by the priests, in which the public had no direct part, even though these were the principal services conducted at the chosen sanctuary. Likewise, only Deuteronomy indicates that firstlings, first fruits, and some of the tithes were the occasion for feasts by the laity and that at least some of them were eaten by the laity themselves.[35]

undertakings in which the LORD your God has blessed you Rather, "the fruits of your labors with which the LORD your God has blessed you." *Mishlaḥ yad* means both "labor" (lit., "that to which one sends one's hand") and the products of one's labor.[36] The latter meaning is favored here by 26:11, where the same idea is expressed by "you shall celebrate all the *bounty* that the LORD your God has bestowed upon you and your household."

EXPLICATION OF THE LAW OF CENTRALIZATION (vv. 8–28)

The next five sections of the chapter explicate the law restricting sacrifice to the chosen place, clarifying its details and adjusting other laws that are affected by it. Key points appear in alternating order in these five sections: centralization of sacrifice (8–12), secular slaughter (13–16), centralization of sacrifice (17–19), secular slaughter (20–25), and centralization of sacrifice (26–28). These sections are framed by clauses contrasting "every man doing what is right in his own sight" to "doing what is right in the sight of God" (vv. 8,28), which together indicate that sacrificing to God in the *place* that He chooses is part of the larger principle of worshiping Him in the *way* that He chooses. The principle that God, rather than man, chooses the way in which God is to be worshiped is also expressed in the fact that worship consists of prescribed ceremonies performed on prescribed dates and conducted by a chosen priesthood.[37]

When Centralization of Sacrifice Is to Take Effect (vv. 8–12)

This section explains why sacrifice is not yet limited to a single site and indicates when the limitation is to be put into effect.

8. every man as he pleases Literally, "every man [doing] what is right in his own sight." From the context and verse 13 it seems clear that this means sacrificing wherever one pleases, implying that at the time of Moses' address, individual Israelites could perform sacrifices wherever they wished.

This implication seems inconsistent with Leviticus 17:1–9, which states that a restriction of sacrifice to a single place—the Tent of Meeting—was already commanded in the wilderness. Hoffmann supposes that the rule of Leviticus 17 must have been relaxed once the Israelites entered the settled territory of Transjordan, since its purpose—to prevent the worship of satyrs that were thought to reside in the wilderness (Lev. 17:7)—no longer applied.[38] However, this explanation is undermined by Leviticus 17:7, which calls that rule "a law for all time, throughout the ages." Critical scholars, who assign Leviticus 17 to a different source, assume that Deuteronomy was not aware of Leviticus 17:1–9.[39]

9–10. The present situation is permitted because the Israelites are not yet settled in their "allotted haven" (Heb. *menuḥah ve-naḥalah*, lit., "haven and hereditary property"). As verse 10

122

your enemies around you and you live in security, [11]then you must bring everything that I command you to the site where the LORD your God will choose to establish His name: your burnt offerings and other sacrifices, your tithes and contributions, and all the choice votive offerings that you vow to the LORD. [12]And you shall rejoice before the LORD your God with your sons and daughters and with your male and female slaves, along with the Levite in your settlements, for he has no territorial allotment among you.

[13]Take care not to sacrifice your burnt offerings in any place you like, [14]but only in the place that the LORD will choose in one of your tribal territories. There you shall

וְהֵנִ֨יחַ לָכֶ֧ם מִכָּל־אֹיְבֵיכֶ֛ם מִסָּבִ֖יב וִֽישַׁבְתֶּם־
בֶּֽטַח: שני [11] וְהָיָ֣ה הַמָּק֗וֹם אֲשֶׁר־יִבְחַ֞ר
יְהוָ֧ה אֱלֹהֵיכֶ֛ם בּ֖וֹ לְשַׁכֵּ֤ן שְׁמוֹ֙ שָׁ֔ם שָׁ֣מָּה תָבִ֔יאוּ
אֵ֛ת כָּל־אֲשֶׁ֥ר אָנֹכִ֖י מְצַוֶּ֣ה אֶתְכֶ֑ם עוֹלֹתֵיכֶ֣ם
וְזִבְחֵיכֶ֗ם מַעְשְׂרֹֽתֵיכֶם֙ וּתְרֻמַ֣ת יֶדְכֶ֔ם וְכֹל֙ מִבְחַ֣ר
נִדְרֵיכֶ֔ם אֲשֶׁ֥ר תִּדְּר֖וּ לַֽיהוָֽה: [12] וּשְׂמַחְתֶּ֞ם לִפְנֵ֣י
יְהוָ֣ה אֱלֹֽהֵיכֶ֗ם אַתֶּ֤ם וּבְנֵיכֶם֙ וּבְנֹ֣תֵיכֶ֔ם וְעַבְדֵיכֶ֖ם
וְאַמְהֹֽתֵיכֶ֑ם וְהַלֵּוִי֙ אֲשֶׁ֣ר בְּשַֽׁעֲרֵיכֶ֔ם כִּ֣י אֵ֥ין ל֛וֹ
חֵ֥לֶק וְנַֽחֲלָ֖ה אִתְּכֶֽם: [13] הִשָּׁ֣מֶר לְךָ֔ פֶּֽן־תַּֽעֲלֶ֖ה עֹלֹתֶ֑יךָ בְּכָל־מָק֖וֹם אֲשֶׁ֥ר

indicates, the phrase refers to two conditions necessary for putting centralization into effect: the Israelites must enter their allotted territory, west of the Jordan, and must hold it securely. Security is necessary so that pilgrims may travel safely to the chosen place and will not fear that their homes may be attacked by enemies in their absence (see Exod. 23:24).

According to Joshua 21:42, these conditions were met when Joshua conquered the land, and Shiloh was considered the chosen place for a time. The later historical books imply that they were met once and for all in the days of David and Solomon, when the Canaanites in the promised land had been overcome and Israel ruled over the neighboring territories,[40] and Solomon built the Temple. It is from that point on that the book of Kings judges each king in accordance with whether or not he enforced centralization.

11. choice votive offerings That is, your votive offerings, which are of the choicest products.

12. rejoice Rather, "celebrate." See Comment to verse 7.

along with the Levite in your settlements Deuteronomy often mentions the Levites alongside the economically disadvantaged groups for whom special care must be taken. It must be concerned about the fact that once the local sanctuaries are abolished, most of the Levites will lose their positions and main source of income, portions of sacrificial animals and donations to the sanctuaries (18:1–5). They had no tribal lands from which to earn a living, as the verse notes, and the single chosen sanctuary could not possibly support all the Levites in the country despite the fact that they all had the right to come and serve there (18:6–8). Hence Deuteronomy frequently appeals to the people to remember the Levites and establishes a special tithe for them, along with the poor, every three years (14:28–29). Here, their participation in the sacrificial meals partly makes up for their former shares of sacrifices and donations.[41]

slaves Like the requirement that slaves rest on the Sabbath (5:14), the requirement to involve them in religious celebrations is part of the Torah's unique concern for their welfare. See Comments to 5:14 and 15:12–18.

The Prohibition of Sacrificing Elsewhere and Permission for Nonsacrificial Slaughter (vv. 13–16)

The rule of centralization is stated negatively to prevent the inference that there are exceptions, that one may sometimes offer sacrifices at places of one's own choosing. Because of the stringency of this rule, it is followed by a relaxation of the existing rule that all slaughter of domestic animals must be sacrificial.

13. burnt offerings This stands here for all types of offerings. After the list in verse 6, the text regularly refers to the offerings only by partial lists; see also verses 17,26–27.

like[42]

sacrifice your burnt offerings and there you shall observe all that I enjoin upon you. ¹⁵But whenever you desire, you may slaughter and eat meat in any of your settlements, according to the blessing that the LORD your God has granted you. The unclean and the clean alike may partake of it, as of the gazelle and the deer. ¹⁶But you must not partake of the blood; you shall pour it out on the ground like water.

¹⁷You may not partake in your settlements of the tithes

תִּרְאֶה: 14 כִּי אִם־בַּמָּקוֹם אֲשֶׁר־יִבְחַר יְהוָה בְּאַחַד שְׁבָטֶיךָ שָׁם תַּעֲלֶה עֹלֹתֶיךָ וְשָׁם תַּעֲשֶׂה כֹּל אֲשֶׁר אָנֹכִי מְצַוֶּךָּ: 15 רַק בְּכָל־אַוַּת נַפְשְׁךָ תִּזְבַּח | וְאָכַלְתָּ בָשָׂר כְּבִרְכַּת יְהוָה אֱלֹהֶיךָ אֲשֶׁר נָתַן־לְךָ בְּכָל־שְׁעָרֶיךָ הַטָּמֵא וְהַטָּהוֹר יֹאכְלֶנּוּ כַּצְּבִי וְכָאַיָּל: 16 רַק הַדָּם לֹא תֹאכֵלוּ עַל־הָאָרֶץ תִּשְׁפְּכֶנּוּ כַּמָּיִם: 17 לֹא־תוּכַל לֶאֱכֹל בִּשְׁעָרֶיךָ מַעְשַׂר דְּגָנְךָ

15. This verse establishes a major change in religious and dietary practice. Previously, only game animals could be slaughtered nonsacrificially (the rabbis called nonsacrificial slaughter *sheḥitat ḥullin,* "secular slaughter"). Domestic cattle (oxen, sheep, and goats) could only be slaughtered on altars, as sacrifices, even if the offerer's purpose was solely to use them for food. Only after the blood was dashed on the altar and certain of the innards burnt there could the remainder be eaten.[43] This rule was practical when all Israelites lived near a sanctuary, as when they lived in the wilderness. Even after they settled in Canaan and scattered across the land, it would remain practical as long as it was legitimate to have sanctuaries throughout the land. But once a single sanctuary was chosen the requirement would become impractical, since those who lived far from it would be able to eat meat only on the infrequent occasions when they visited there. To avoid this hardship, secular slaughter of domestic cattle, too, will be permitted, and people may eat meat whenever they want and can afford to. For further details see verses 20–22.

whenever you desire   Or, "*wherever* you desire."[44]

according to the blessing that the LORD *. . . has granted you*   That is, as much as the means that God gives you permit, as much as you can afford.[45] Meat was eaten less frequently in the ancient Near Eastern and Mediterranean world than in modern Western society, and this must have been due in part to economic factors. Domestic cattle were used primarily for their products and for labor, and only the wealthy could regularly spare some for slaughter. Furthermore, without modern refrigeration techniques, meat could only be consumed when there were enough people present to finish it before it spoiled. This would limit consumption to special occasions, such as sacrifices and festivals or the presence of an honored guest, or to large or fairly wealthy households. In talmudic literature the daily consumption of meat is regarded as an extravagance that could reduce all but the wealthy to poverty. Note that verse 20 refers to eating meat as the result of a special "urge," implying that it was not a daily expectation.[46]

The unclean and the clean   These categories do not refer to dirtiness and cleanliness but to ritual impurity and purity. Impurity is caused by such things as bodily discharges, leprosy, and contact with corpses and certain carcasses, and by eating forbidden food (see Lev. 11–15 and Num. 19). Those who were ritually unclean were not permitted to eat the meat of sacrifices, which would be defiled by contact with them (see Lev. 7:19–21). Therefore, as long as domestic cattle had to be slaughtered sacrificially, those who were ritually unclean could eat meat only from nonsacrificial animals, such as gazelle and deer. Once domestic cattle may be slaughtered secularly, they will be treated like game animals in that the ritually unclean may also eat their meat.

16. The prohibition on eating blood will remain in effect.[47] When domestic animals are slaughtered secularly, their blood is to be poured on the ground, unlike the blood of sacrifices (v. 27). This disposition of the blood is partly identical to that of the blood of game animals and birds, except that Leviticus requires that the blood of the latter groups be covered with earth.[48]

Sacrificial Food May Be Eaten Only at the Chosen Place (vv. 17–19)

Not only is sacrifice restricted to the chosen place; so is the eating of the sacrifice. The text states this explicitly in order to make clear that the new freedom to eat nonsacrificial meat at home will not mean that sacrificial food may be taken home and eaten there after undergoing the sacrificial

of your new grain or wine or oil, or of the firstlings of your herds and flocks, or of any of the votive offerings that you vow, or of your freewill offerings, or of your contributions. **18**These you must consume before the LORD your God in the place that the LORD your God will choose—you and your sons and your daughters, your male and female slaves, and the Levite in your settlements—happy before the LORD your God in all your undertakings. **19**Be sure not to neglect the Levite as long as you live in your land.

20When the LORD enlarges your territory, as He has promised you, and you say, "I shall eat some meat," for you have the urge to eat meat, you may eat meat whenever you wish. **21**If the place where the LORD has chosen to establish His name is too far from you, you may slaughter any of the cattle or sheep that the LORD gives you, as I have instructed you; and you may eat to your heart's content in your settlements. **22**Eat it, however, as the gazelle and the deer are eaten: the unclean may eat it

וְתִירֹשְׁךָ וְיִצְהָרֶ֔ךָ וּבְכֹרֹ֥ת בְּקָרְךָ֖ וְצֹאנֶ֑ךָ וְכָל־
נְדָרֶ֙יךָ֙ אֲשֶׁ֣ר תִּדֹּ֔ר וְנִדְבֹתֶ֖יךָ וּתְרוּמַ֥ת יָדֶֽךָ׃ 18 כִּ֡י
אִם־לִפְנֵי֩ יְהֹוָ֨ה אֱלֹהֶ֜יךָ תֹּאכְלֶ֗נּוּ בַּמָּקוֹם֙ אֲשֶׁ֣ר
יִבְחַ֞ר יְהֹוָ֣ה אֱלֹהֶ֮יךָ֮ בּוֹ֒ אַתָּ֣ה וּבִנְךָ֣ וּבִתֶּ֗ךָ וְעַבְדְּךָ֙
וַאֲמָתֶ֔ךָ וְהַלֵּוִ֖י אֲשֶׁ֣ר בִּשְׁעָרֶ֑יךָ וְשָׂמַחְתָּ֗ לִפְנֵי֙ יְהֹוָ֣ה
אֱלֹהֶ֔יךָ בְּכֹ֖ל מִשְׁלַ֥ח יָדֶֽךָ׃ 19 הִשָּׁ֣מֶר לְךָ֔ פֶּֽן־תַּעֲזֹ֖ב
אֶת־הַלֵּוִ֑י כָּל־יָמֶ֖יךָ עַל־אַדְמָתֶֽךָ׃ ס
20 כִּֽי־יַרְחִיב֩ יְהֹוָ֨ה אֱלֹהֶ֜יךָ אֶֽת־גְּבֻֽלְךָ֮ כַּאֲשֶׁ֣ר
דִּבֶּר־לָךְ֒ וְאָמַרְתָּ֙ אֹכְלָ֣ה בָשָׂ֔ר כִּֽי־תְאַוֶּ֥ה נַפְשְׁךָ֖
לֶאֱכֹ֣ל בָּשָׂ֑ר בְּכָל־אַוַּ֥ת נַפְשְׁךָ֖ תֹּאכַ֥ל בָּשָֽׂר׃
21 כִּֽי־יִרְחַ֨ק מִמְּךָ֜ הַמָּק֗וֹם אֲשֶׁ֣ר יִבְחַ֞ר יְהֹוָ֣ה
אֱלֹהֶ֘יךָ֘ לָשׂ֣וּם שְׁמ֣וֹ שָׁם֒ וְזָבַחְתָּ֞ מִבְּקָרְךָ֣ וּמִצֹּֽאנְךָ֗
אֲשֶׁ֨ר נָתַ֤ן יְהֹוָה֙ לְךָ֔ כַּאֲשֶׁ֖ר צִוִּיתִ֑ךָ וְאָ֣כַלְתָּ֗
בִּשְׁעָרֶ֔יךָ בְּכֹ֖ל אַוַּ֥ת נַפְשֶֽׁךָ׃ 22 אַ֗ךְ כַּאֲשֶׁ֨ר יֵֽאָכֵ֤ל
אֶֽת־הַצְּבִי֙ וְאֶת־הָ֣אַיָּ֔ל כֵּ֖ן תֹּאכְלֶ֑נּוּ הַטָּמֵא֙

v. 21. חסר יו"ד

procedure in the chosen place. The entire household must travel to the chosen place and eat the sacrificial food there, "before the LORD," so as to experience the religious influence of the place (see 14:23). For further details see below, verses 26–27.

    18. See Comments to verse 7.

Details about Secular Slaughter (vv. 20–25)

This section adds further details to verses 15–16, which permit secular slaughter, explaining why it will be permitted and spelling out rules of secular slaughter and eating.

    20. enlarges your territory And thereby gives you the entire promised land (see 19:8 and Exod. 34:24). Full possession of the land will come gradually (7:22). As long as some of it remains in the hands of the Canaanites, Israel will lack the security that is a prerequisite for centralization (see v. 10). By referring to the time of full possession and centralization as "when the LORD *enlarges*" Israel's territory, the text anticipates verse 21, which explains that it is because of the distance from the chosen place that God will permit secular slaughter.[49]

    as He has promised you In Exodus 34:24; compare Deuteronomy 7:22–23.

    21. If the place . . . is too far from you The text does not define what "too far" means. It may mean to leave this to the discretion of each individual (cf. 14:24). The Temple Scroll, as noted above, defines the distance as three days' journey. Rabbinic halakhah permits secular slaughter anywhere outside the Temple Court.[50] Verse 15, which permits secular slaughter "in any of your settlements," is favorable to the latter view.

    you may slaughter . . . as I have instructed you This clause implies a prescribed method of slaughter. The text's use of the verb *zavaḥ*, which refers to sacrificial slaughter, indicates that secular slaughter is to be performed by the method used in sacrificial slaughter, namely slitting the animal's throat.[51] This method of ritual slaughter minimizes the pain felt by the animal and facilitates maximal drainage of its blood, in keeping with verses 16 and 23–25. It is known as *shehitah* in the halakhah, which spells out its details on the basis of oral tradition. The clause "as I have instructed you" refers either to the oral tradition or to passages in the Torah that refer to this method, or to both.[52] (For further dietary laws see vv. 23–25,27, and 14:3–21.)

together with the clean. 23But make sure that you do not partake of the blood; for the blood is the life, and you must not consume the life with the flesh. 24You must not partake of it; you must pour it out on the ground like water: 25you must not partake of it, in order that it may go well with you and with your descendants to come, for you will be doing what is right in the sight of the LORD.

26But such sacred and votive donations as you may have shall be taken by you to the site that the LORD will choose.

וְהַטָּהוֹר יַחְדָּו יֹאכְלֶנּוּ: 23 רַק חֲזַק לְבִלְתִּי אֲכֹל הַדָּם כִּי הַדָּם הוּא הַנָּפֶשׁ וְלֹא־תֹאכַל הַנֶּפֶשׁ עִם־הַבָּשָׂר: 24 לֹא תֹּאכְלֶנּוּ עַל־הָאָרֶץ תִּשְׁפְּכֶנּוּ כַּמָּיִם: 25 לֹא תֹּאכְלֶנּוּ לְמַעַן יִיטַב לְךָ וּלְבָנֶיךָ אַחֲרֶיךָ כִּי־תַעֲשֶׂה הַיָּשָׁר בְּעֵינֵי יְהוָה: 26 רַק קֳדָשֶׁיךָ אֲשֶׁר־יִהְיוּ לְךָ וּנְדָרֶיךָ תִּשָּׂא וּבָאתָ אֶל־הַמָּקוֹם אֲשֶׁר־יִבְחַר יְהוָה: 27 וְעָשִׂיתָ עֹלֹתֶיךָ

22. together Not only may the impure eat secular meat, they may even share the meat that is eaten by those who are pure, eating "from the same bowl" (Sifrei). Since this meat is not sacrificial, defilement by contact with impure persons does not disqualify it, and there is no need to avoid sharing meat with them (see Comment to v. 15).[53]

23–25. The prohibition of blood is first mentioned in Genesis. According to Genesis 1:29–30, God originally assigned all creatures an exclusively vegetarian diet. After the flood He allowed humans to eat living creatures but prohibited eating meat with the blood still in it, since blood was considered to be the life force within the animal (Gen. 9:2–4). The blood prohibition is thus an expression of reverence for life, indicating that man is not granted unlimited ownership of life. It is the sole remaining trace of man's original vegetarianism and of the time when living creatures did not prey upon each other for food.[54]

The procedures developed by Jewish law for observing the prohibition of blood include *shehitah* (see Comment to v. 21) and the removal of residual blood from the meat by "kashering" it (rendering it kosher, or "fit") through salting, soaking, and rinsing.

23. make sure[55] This exhortation and the reiteration of the blood prohibition in verses 24–25 indicate a concern that people might not be careful to avoid the blood, either because they desired to consume it or because of the effort involved in removing it from the meat (see next Comment).[56]

partake . . . consume The Hebrew in both cases is literally "eat." The use of this verb instead of "drink" implies that the text is not dealing with the likelihood that people might drink blood but that they might eat it, either in the form of blood pudding or gravy, or simply while eating meat because of laxity in draining it.[57]

the blood is the life Blood is the life force in living creatures. This belief was probably based on the observation that loss of much blood leads to death. Homer speaks of "life running out" through a stab wound.[58]

you must not consume the life with the flesh Literally this clause paraphrases the first half of the verse, but halakhic exegesis saw it as an additional injunction prohibiting eating a limb severed from an animal while it is still living. This interpretation was based on the phrase "the life with the flesh," which was taken to mean "(you may not eat) any of the flesh while there is still life in the animal."[59] The time-consuming procedure of draining all the blood from the animal prevents one from tearing off a limb and eating it immediately.

Details about Sacrificial Slaughter (vv. 26–28)

This section adds further details to verses 17–19. It reiterates that the permission to slaughter animals locally for food does not apply to sacrifices, and indicates how sacrificial slaughter differs from secular slaughter.

26. sacred and votive donations Anything sacrificial in character, including votive offerings. The latter are probably singled out because they are voluntary, which might lead the worshiper to believe that he has greater discretion in where to present them. "Votive donations" may stand for all types of voluntary offerings, freewill as well as votive (see v. 6).[60]

27You shall offer your burnt offerings, both the flesh and the blood, on the altar of the LORD your God; and of your other sacrifices, the blood shall be poured out on the altar of the LORD your God, and you shall eat the flesh.

28Be careful to heed all these commandments that I enjoin upon you; thus it will go well with you and with your descendants after you forever, for you will be doing what is good and right in the sight of the LORD your God.

29When the LORD your God has cut down before you the nations that you are about to enter and dispossess, and you have dispossessed them and settled in their land, 30beware of being lured into their ways after they have been wiped out before you! Do not inquire about their gods, saying, "How did those nations worship their gods? I too will follow those practices." 31You shall not act thus toward the LORD your God, for they perform for their gods every abhorrent act that the LORD detests; they even offer up their sons and daughters in fire to their gods.

הַבָּשָׂר וְהַדָּם עַל־מִזְבַּח יְהוָה אֱלֹהֶיךָ וְדַם־זְבָחֶיךָ יִשָּׁפֵךְ עַל־מִזְבַּח יְהוָה אֱלֹהֶיךָ וְהַבָּשָׂר תֹּאכֵל: 28 שְׁמֹר וְשָׁמַעְתָּ אֵת כָּל־הַדְּבָרִים הָאֵלֶּה אֲשֶׁר אָנֹכִי מְצַוֶּךָּ לְמַעַן יִיטַב לְךָ וּלְבָנֶיךָ אַחֲרֶיךָ עַד־עוֹלָם כִּי תַעֲשֶׂה הַטּוֹב וְהַיָּשָׁר בְּעֵינֵי יְהוָה אֱלֹהֶיךָ: ס

שלישי

29 כִּי־יַכְרִית יְהוָה אֱלֹהֶיךָ אֶת־הַגּוֹיִם אֲשֶׁר אַתָּה בָא־שָׁמָּה לָרֶשֶׁת אוֹתָם מִפָּנֶיךָ וְיָרַשְׁתָּ אֹתָם וְיָשַׁבְתָּ בְּאַרְצָם: 30 הִשָּׁמֶר לְךָ פֶּן־תִּנָּקֵשׁ אַחֲרֵיהֶם אַחֲרֵי הִשָּׁמְדָם מִפָּנֶיךָ וּפֶן־תִּדְרֹשׁ לֵאלֹהֵיהֶם לֵאמֹר אֵיכָה יַעַבְדוּ הַגּוֹיִם הָאֵלֶּה אֶת־אֱלֹהֵיהֶם וְאֶעֱשֶׂה־כֵּן גַּם־אָנִי: 31 לֹא־תַעֲשֶׂה כֵן לַיהוָה אֱלֹהֶיךָ כִּי כָל־תּוֹעֲבַת יְהוָה אֲשֶׁר שָׂנֵא עָשׂוּ לֵאלֹהֵיהֶם כִּי גַם אֶת־בְּנֵיהֶם וְאֶת־בְּנֹתֵיהֶם יִשְׂרְפוּ בָאֵשׁ לֵאלֹהֵיהֶם: 1 אֵת כָּל־

27. The essential difference between the burnt offering and the other sacrifices is that the flesh of the former is burned while that of the latter is eaten by the offerer and the priests (18:3). In both cases the blood is poured on the altar.[61]

28. *you will be doing what is good and right in the sight of the* LORD   See Comment to verse 8.

SHUNNING CANAANITE RELIGIOUS PRACTICES (12:29–13:1)

These verses are a transitional unit between chapters 12 and 13, expressing two related principles: Israel may not worship the Lord in ways that the Canaanites worshiped their gods (12:29–31), and it may not add to God's commandments nor subtract from them (13:1; see 4:2). The chapter division emphasizes the connection of the first principle with chapter 12 (compare vv. 4 and 31a) and of the second with the theme of chapter 13 (resisting attempts to add other gods to Israelite religion). Hebrew manuscripts treat 12:28–13:1 as a single unit,[62] thereby recognizing that both principles relate to both chapters: the theme of chapter 13 is also an aspect of not worshiping God in Canaanite ways, that is, worshiping many gods; and the theme of chapter 12 is also an aspect of not adding to God's commandments, that is, adding sacrificial sites in addition to the chosen one.

30. *beware of being lured into their ways*   Rather: "beware lest you be ensnared as they were." This is a metaphor for punishment; being ensnared does not refer to being enticed to behave in a certain way, but to stumbling into a trap. Idolatry is often described as such a trap (cf. 7:25).[63]

The NJPS translation, "beware of being lured into their ways," corresponds to halakhic exegesis, which sees this verse as a warning not to follow foreign customs that are idolatrous or superstitious in nature. The principle was even extended to clothing and hair styles, and has at times been used as a precaution against assimilation, its precise application being debated.[64]

31. *You shall not act thus toward the* LORD *your God*   This injunction echoes verse 4, which implies that using many places for sacrifice is an inherently pagan practice. Here the principle of not imitating Canaanite practices is applied across the board and explained: none of their religious practices may be adopted because many were abominable, including even child sacrifice (see the more complete list in 18:10–11).

they even offer up their sons and daughters in fire to their gods   This is not a law prohibiting child sacrifice. Moses takes for granted that the people already know that child sacrifice is

13 Be careful to observe only that which I enjoin upon you: neither add to it nor take away from it.

י״ג הַדָּבָ֗ר אֲשֶׁ֤ר אָנֹכִי֙ מְצַוֶּ֣ה אֶתְכֶ֔ם אֹת֥וֹ תִשְׁמְר֖וּ לַעֲשׂ֑וֹת לֹא־תֹסֵ֣ף עָלָ֔יו וְלֹ֥א תִגְרַ֖ע מִמֶּֽנּוּ׃ פ

wrong, and he cites it as an extreme and shocking example of Canaanite abominations.[65] The literary and archaeological evidence about Canaanite child sacrifice is discussed in Excursus 15, along with the question of whether this practice is related to the cult of Molech and to the practice of passing children through fire mentioned in 18:10.

CHAPTER 13

13:1. This verse complements 12:31a: Israel may worship God only in the ways He commands, no less and no more. It may not abolish His commandments or add to them. It would do both of these if it adopted any of the Canaanites' abominable practices. For further discussion see Comment to 4:2.

INSTIGATION TO WORSHIP OTHER GODS (vv. 2–19)

This section deals with three cases in which individuals urge their fellow Israelites to worship other gods.[1] In the first case, the proposal is made publicly by one who claims prophetic authority and backs up his claim by a sign that seems to authenticate it (vv. 2–6). In the second, it is made in secret by a close relative or friend (vv. 7–12). In the third, the proposal has reportedly succeeded and an entire city has been led to worship another god (vv. 13–19).

These cases reflect the concept that God is Israel's king and that worshiping other gods is high treason. There are close parallels to these provisions in laws against sedition in ancient treaties and similar texts. These laws, which require that acts of agitation against the sovereign be reported and punished, correspond to this chapter in many details. For example, they deal with instigators who may be prophets or relatives of the witness; they paraphrase the instigators' proposal in terms such as "Come let us join another [king]"; they warn against concealing the instigators (cf. vv. 2–3,7,9); and they also deal with rebellious cities.[2]

The theme of the chapter is expressed in terminology that appears in all three units. Each proposal is paraphrased in virtually identical terms as "Come let us worship other gods," whom, the text comments, the Israelites have never "experienced" (vv. 3,7,14), and each is characterized as an attempt to make Israel stray from the Lord or His path (vv. 6,11,14 ["subverted" in v. 14 is literally "made stray"]). The verb *shamaʿ*, "hear," "heed," also appears in all three units. In the first two, it is part of the admonition not to heed the instigator (vv. 4,9), and it frames the third unit, beginning with "If you hear" a report of apostasy and ending with the promise of renewed favor for "heeding" God (vv. 13,19).

Each paragraph gives reasons for the prescribed punishment. The first two explain why the instigator is punished (vv. 6,11), and all three state the effect intended by the punishment (vv. 6,12,18). With these statements, Moses seeks to explain the laws and motivate the people to obey them, even when it might be painful for them to do so. Most of the reasons would be appropriate to all three cases, but the text makes do with one or two for each. Its aim was not to provide an encyclopedic justification for each punishment, but to present one or two reasons that would suffice to demonstrate its appropriateness in each case.[3] Together, the three reasons add up to a theory of punishment: to remove evil from the community, to deter wrongdoing, and to protect the community's relationship with God.

These cases are a natural sequel to chapter 12, which includes the command to uproot Canaanite polytheism as soon as Israel enters the promised land. Chapter 13 prescribes what is to be done if anybody tries to reestablish polytheism. Although 13:1 is the conclusion of chapter 12, it is also an apt introduction to the rest of chapter 13 (note the call to "obey *all* His commandments" at the end of chap. 13).[4] Those who would urge Israel to worship other gods in addition to the Lord would in effect be adding to His commandments or subtracting from them (see Comment to 4:2). In fact, the first case is apparently one in which the instigator falsely prophesies that the proposal is a new commandment from God (see v. 6). Clauses about not adding or subtracting often refer to prophets,

²If there appears among you a prophet or a dream-diviner and he gives you a sign or a portent, ³saying, "Let

כִּי־יָקוּם בְּקִרְבְּךָ נָבִיא אוֹ חֹלֵם חֲלוֹם וְנָתַן 2
אֵלֶיךָ אוֹת אוֹ מוֹפֵת: 3 וּבָא הָאוֹת וְהַמּוֹפֵת

scribes, and messengers who must faithfully report what they have been told.[5] The placement of 13:2–6 after 13:1 implies that 13:1 was also understood as a warning against the falsification of God's message by prophets who would claim that He has said more or less than He really said.

The simple case of individuals who worship other gods appears later, in 17:2–7. That case would fit well here, but, because it also contains rules of judicial procedure, it appears in a separate section dealing with that subject (16:18–17:12). See Excursus 13.

INSTIGATION BY A PROPHET OR A DREAMER (vv. 2–6)

The first case is one in which the instigator's proposal is hard to resist because he seems to have divine authority for what he proposes. Moreover, from verse 6 it appears that he even claims that the proposal comes from the Lord Himself, not another god. The law puts a rational limit on the authority of prophecy and miracles. It indicates that the prohibition against worshiping other gods is an absolute, eternally binding principle, and that even prophecies and seemingly miraculous proofs to the contrary are to be disregarded.[6] Keeping in mind that a prophet is God's envoy (see Comment to v. 2), it is noteworthy that in a Hittite treaty, the suzerain tells his vassal that when he sends him messages, if there is a discrepancy between the written text of a message and the oral version given by his envoy, the written message is authoritative and the envoy is not to be believed.[7] Here in Deuteronomy the discrepancy is between the written text of the Decalogue and the oral claims of the false prophets.

2–3. The clauses of these two verses should be understood in the following order: "If there appears among you a prophet or a dream-diviner saying, 'Let us follow and worship another god whom you have not experienced,' and he gives you a sign or a portent, even if the sign or portent that he named to you comes true . . ."[8]

2. Prophecy and dreams are two of the regular means by which God communicates with man in the Bible (see 1 Sam. 28:6).[9]

prophet   Hebrew *navi'*. The prophet is God's spokesman or envoy (see 18:18). This is indicated by the fact that prophetic speeches frequently begin with "Thus says the LORD," since "thus says so-and-so" is the standard formula with which messengers introduce the words of those who send them.[10] The prophet's role as spokesman is reflected in Exodus 4:16 and 7:1, where Aaron is alternately termed Moses' *navi'* and spokesman (lit., "mouth"). The cognate term *nabiu*, referring to a type of prophet or diviner, appears in a West-Semitic letter from Mari, Syria.[11] Literally, *navi'* probably means "proclaimer," to judge from Akkadian and Arabic cognates in which the root *n-b-'* means "call," "proclaim," and "announce."[12]

dream-diviner   A person—either a prophet or a lay person—who claims to have received a message from God in a dream.[13] The translation "dream-diviner" implies a functionary who regularly seeks and receives revelation through dreams. However, the Hebrew means simply "a dreamer" (lit., "one who dreams a dream") and does not necessarily have professional connotations.

It is not clear whether the prophet and dreamer here are people who had already performed these roles legitimately in the past and had now become corrupted, or new and false claimants to these roles. In practice the law would undoubtedly have been applied to both.[14]

gives you a sign or a portent   As Moses did in Exodus. Hebrew *'ot* and *mofet* refer to portentous signs shown by the prophet to demonstrate that his message really comes from God. The terms refer to marvels beyond human capability, such as a staff turning into a snake, which could only have been brought about by supernatural power (Exod. 4:1–9). As indicated by verse 3 ("comes true"), such signs are usually announced in advance. God armed Moses with such marvels to convince the Israelites and Pharaoh that He had really spoken to him. Similarly, the altar at Bethel broke apart to authenticate the words of a prophet, and the shadow on the steps of a sundial receded to authenticate a prophecy by Isaiah.[15] Such signs are used only when those addressed by the

us follow and worship another god"—whom you have not experienced—even if the sign or portent that he named to you comes true, [4]do not heed the words of that prophet or that dream-diviner. For the LORD your God is testing you to see whether you really love the LORD your God with all your heart and soul. [5]Follow none but the LORD your God, and revere none but Him; observe His commandments alone, and heed only His orders; worship none but Him, and hold fast to Him. [6]As for that prophet or dream-diviner, he shall be put to death; for he urged disloyalty to the LORD your God—who freed you from the land of Egypt and who redeemed you from the house of

אֲשֶׁר־דִּבֶּר אֵלֶיךָ לֵאמֹר נֵלְכָה אַחֲרֵי אֱלֹהִים
אֲחֵרִים אֲשֶׁר לֹא־יְדַעְתָּם וְנָעָבְדֵם: 4 לֹא
תִשְׁמַע אֶל־דִּבְרֵי הַנָּבִיא הַהוּא אוֹ אֶל־חוֹלֵם
הַחֲלוֹם הַהוּא כִּי מְנַסֶּה יְהוָה אֱלֹהֵיכֶם אֶתְכֶם
לָדַעַת הֲיִשְׁכֶם אֹהֲבִים אֶת־יְהוָה אֱלֹהֵיכֶם בְּכָל־
לְבַבְכֶם וּבְכָל־נַפְשְׁכֶם: 5 אַחֲרֵי יְהוָה אֱלֹהֵיכֶם
תֵּלֵכוּ וְאֹתוֹ תִירָאוּ וְאֶת־מִצְוֹתָיו תִּשְׁמֹרוּ וּבְקֹלוֹ
תִשְׁמָעוּ וְאֹתוֹ תַעֲבֹדוּ וּבוֹ תִדְבָּקוּן: 6 וְהַנָּבִיא
הַהוּא אוֹ חֹלֵם הַחֲלוֹם הַהוּא יוּמָת כִּי דִבֶּר־
סָרָה עַל־יְהוָה אֱלֹהֵיכֶם הַמּוֹצִיא אֶתְכֶם | מֵאֶרֶץ

prophet find it difficult to believe him or stubbornly refuse to do so. A prophecy calling for the worship of another god would, or should, meet such resistance, since it contradicts God's teachings; but if the prophet produced a sign which seemingly could not occur without God's help, the people might feel compelled to believe him.

The reliance on signs to authenticate a prophet corresponds to the way that messengers were tested in the ancient world. In an Akkadian letter, King Shamshi-Adad I of Assyria (1800 B.C.E.) says that he interrogated an envoy from the Gutians and trusted him on the basis of "signs" (Akk. *ittati*) in what he said. The signs in that case were not supernatural wonders but convincing information contained in the messenger's answers.[16]

3. saying What follows is not a literal quotation of the prophet's proposal but Moses' pejorative paraphrase of it. An instigator would not use the vague and disparaging phrases "another god, whom you have not experienced" but would identify a specific god. See also verses 7 and 14. For the meaning of "whom you have not experienced," see Comment to 11:28. For a similar pejorative paraphrase by Moses, see Comment to 29:18.[17]

let us follow Literally, "walk after." Since this idiom frequently expresses loyalty to a king, by paraphrasing the prophet's invitation as calling for "walking after" another god, Moses indicates that it is tantamount to proposing treason against the Lord. See Comment to 4:3.

4. the LORD . . . is testing you By allowing the sign to come true. Moses does not explain why God will test Israel, but counters the false prophet's argument that the sign proves his prophecy true. For the concept of God testing Israel, see Comment to 8:2; for the issue of false prophecy, see 18:20–22.

whether you really love the LORD . . . with all your heart and soul That is, whether your loyalty to Him is undivided. See Comments to 6:5.

5. Follow none but the LORD . . . worship none but Him In contrast to what the false prophet urges. Moses is reiterating God's basic demands, as in 6:13–14 and 10:20.

On the idiomatic meaning of "follow," see Comment to verse 3. In talmudic literature the exhortation to "follow the Lord" was interpreted midrashically to express one of the cardinal principles of Jewish ethics, "following in God's ways," doing as He does by performing acts of kindness such as clothing the naked, visiting the sick, comforting the bereaved, and burying the dead.[18]

6. This verse explains why the false prophet is executed and the effect intended by his death.

because he urged disloyalty to the LORD Rather, "because he uttered falsehood [Heb. *dibber sarah*] about the LORD."[19] The prophet is guilty of false prophecy, a capital crime (see 18:20). It is not certain that *dibber sarah* ever means "urge disloyalty" in the Bible. There are, however, several passages where it clearly means "utter falsehood." When describing the speech of prophets, it means to claim falsely that God said something.[20] Since the prophet in question has urged the worship of other gods, his falsehood "about the LORD" must have been a claim that He authorizes

bondage—to make you stray from the path that the LORD your God commanded you to follow. Thus you will sweep out evil from your midst.

מִצְרַיִם וְהִפֶּדְךָ מִבֵּית עֲבָדִים לְהַדִּיחֲךָ מִן־הַדֶּרֶךְ אֲשֶׁר צִוְּךָ יְהוָה אֱלֹהֶיךָ לָלֶכֶת בָּהּ וּבִעַרְתָּ הָרָע מִקִּרְבֶּךָ:

their worship.[21] That the Torah has such a claim in mind is also implied by 17:3, where God denies that He ever commanded Israel to worship the heavenly bodies; the need to deny that He made such a command seems to imply that someone might claim that He did.

The reasoning that might lead a worshiper of the Lord to think that He desires the worship of other beings in addition to Himself is explained by Maimonides in his theory of the origin of paganism:

> In the days of Enosh [Gen. 4:26], the people [reasoned]: "Since God created these stars and spheres to guide the world, set them on high and allotted to them honor, and since they are ministers who minister before Him [see Comment to 4:19], they deserve to be praised and glorified, and honor should be rendered them; and it is the will of God . . . that men should aggrandize and honor those whom He aggrandized and honored, just as a king desires that respect should be shown to the officers who serve Him, and thus honor is shown to the king." [The people then began to honor these objects in order] to obtain the Creator's favor. . . . Their error and folly consists in imagining that this vain worship is [God's] desire.[22]

Maimonides' comment refers to the worship of natural phenomena. Ramban suggests that even the worship of foreign gods might be rationalized in a similar way: "The prophet mentioned here utters prophecies in the name of the LORD saying, 'The LORD sent me to say that you are to worship [Baal] Peor since he was associated with Him in the work of creation, or he is the greatest of all the gods in His service, and He wants you to worship him.'" See also Comment to 4:2.

If our understanding of *dibber sarah* is correct, the law does not refer to a prophet of another god, but to a prophet of the Lord who advocates the worship of additional gods. Perhaps the text assumes that proposals made in the name of other gods would not be credible and were not a serious danger. The real danger would come from a prophet who seemed loyal to the Lord and argued in effect that worshiping other gods was compatible with loyalty to Him. This would remove the stigma from polytheism and pave the way for a polytheistic YHVH-ism like that practiced by Ahab and Manasseh, who worshiped the Lord and other gods simultaneously.[23] It goes without saying that prophets of other gods who advocated their worship by Israelites would be subject to execution, as were the prophets of Baal in the days of Elijah and Elisha.[24]

to make you stray   This is a second reason for executing the instigator. Urging apostasy, the religious equivalent of sedition, is also a capital crime (see v. 11).

who freed you from the land of Egypt and who redeemed you from the house of bondage   This allusion to the beginning of the Decalogue is the opposite of "whom you have not experienced" (v. 3): unlike false gods, the Lord *has* proved Himself to Israel. This underscores the gravity of the prophet's sin, since the Lord's redemption of Israel from bondage established its obligation to worship Him alone (see 5:6–7).

Thus you will sweep out evil from your midst   This expression appears several times at the close of instructions for punishing a criminal. In every case but one it refers to capital punishment. It expresses the view that the punishment removes a palpable evil from the people's midst.[25] The precise meaning of the verb rendered "sweep" (*ba'er*) is not certain ("burn," in a figurative sense, is a possibility), but its connotations are graphically illustrated in 1 Kings 14:10: "I will sweep away the house of Jeroboam utterly, as dung is swept away."

INSTIGATION BY A CLOSE RELATIVE OR A DEAR FRIEND (vv. 7–12)

In the second case, the proposal to worship another god is hard to resist because it comes from a close relative or a dear friend. Because of this, and because the proposal is made secretly, one may be tempted to cover it up and take no action against the instigator.

7If your brother, your own mother's son, or your son or daughter, or the wife of your bosom, or your closest friend entices you in secret, saying, "Come let us worship other gods"—whom neither you nor your fathers have experienced—8from among the gods of the peoples around you, either near to you or distant, anywhere from one end of the earth to the other: 9do not assent or give heed to him. Show him no pity or compassion, and do not shield him; 10but take his life. Let your hand be the first against him to

7 כִּי יְסִיתְךָ אָחִיךָ בֶן־אִמֶּךָ אוֹ־בִנְךָ אוֹ־בִתְּךָ
אוֹ | אֵשֶׁת חֵיקֶךָ אוֹ רֵעֲךָ אֲשֶׁר כְּנַפְשְׁךָ בַּסֵּתֶר
לֵאמֹר נֵלְכָה וְנַעַבְדָה אֱלֹהִים אֲחֵרִים אֲשֶׁר לֹא
יָדַעְתָּ אַתָּה וַאֲבֹתֶיךָ: 8 מֵאֱלֹהֵי הָעַמִּים אֲשֶׁר
סְבִיבֹתֵיכֶם הַקְּרֹבִים אֵלֶיךָ אוֹ הָרְחֹקִים מִמֶּךָּ
מִקְצֵה הָאָרֶץ וְעַד־קְצֵה הָאָרֶץ: 9 לֹא־תֹאבֶה לוֹ
וְלֹא תִשְׁמַע אֵלָיו וְלֹא־תָחוֹס עֵינְךָ עָלָיו וְלֹא־
תַחְמֹל וְלֹא־תְכַסֶּה עָלָיו: 10 כִּי הָרֹג תַּהַרְגֶנּוּ

7. The verse lists four categories of people, in descending order of kinship and closeness: brother, children, wife, and friend. "The text specifies those who are dear to you; others, all the more so" (Rashi).

your brother, your own mother's son This phrase refers to the most closely related brother, just as the fourth category is the closest friend. Therefore, it probably means "your full brother, who is the son of your mother as well as your father."[26]

the wife of your bosom That is, your wife, who lies in your bosom.[27] In other words, the instigator is someone toward whom one feels particularly affectionate and would be reluctant to prosecute. Cases in point are Solomon's foreign wives and Ahab's wife Jezebel, who enticed their husbands to worship other gods (see 1 Kings 11:3 and 21:25).

in secret Public instigation is not exempt but, as Rashi notes, "The text refers to what usually occurs." Given the stigma and punishment that were to befall those who worshiped other gods, it was expected that they would make their proposals secretly. Similarly, 27:15 refers to one who makes an idol and sets it up in secret.[28]

9. do not assent or give heed Verse 4 says only "do not give heed" to a prophet or dreamer. The additional verb here reflects the fact that family and friends can exert sustained pressure, and greater effort is required to resist their importunings.

show him no pity or compassion Do not spare him, as you might be tempted to do out of love.[29] The danger to public welfare posed by these instigators requires the stifling of normal feelings: "harshness toward these [instigators] . . . is compassion toward the world" (Torah Temimah).

do not shield him By keeping his proposal secret.

10. take his life On the face of it the text seems to be calling for summary execution of the instigator caught *in flagrante delicto*, much as Phinehas executed Zimri and Cozbi during the Baal-peor incident (Num. 25).[30] However, this is not consistent with verses 13–19 and 17:2–7, according to which even those who actually worshiped other gods are executed only after a thorough investigation. Presumably, then, our verse means "not only must you not protect your loved one [v. 9], but you, as witness, must take part in his execution" (cf. 17:7), or: "see to it that he is executed" by reporting the incident to the authorities and taking part in the stoning that will follow their investigation. The investigation is not mentioned here because the present paragraph does not focus on the role of the court but on the duty of the person approached by the instigator.[31]

In place of "take his life," the Septuagint reads "you must report him," contrasting with "do not shield him" in the preceding verse. This reading avoids the suggestion of summary execution and is consistent with clauses in ancient Near Eastern treaties that require people to report plots against the king.[32] However, since this clause introduces "Let your hand be the first against him to put him to death," the Masoretic text's "take his life" may be preferable. The requirement to report the instigator is implicit in "do not shield him" or in "take his life."

According to 17:6, at least two witnesses are required to convict a person of worshiping another god. The present law gives the impression that, in the case of secret instigation, the testimony of the person approached by the instigator would suffice. Conceivably instigation to idolatry was regarded as so serious a threat to public safety that normal judicial safeguards had to be set aside. It may be, however, that the text is elliptical, since, as noted, it focuses on the duty of the person approached by

put him to death, and the hand of the rest of the people thereafter. ¹¹Stone him to death, for he sought to make you stray from the LORD your God, who brought you out of the land of Egypt, out of the house of bondage. ¹²Thus all Israel will hear and be afraid, and such evil things will not be done again in your midst.

יָדְךָ֩ תִּֽהְיֶה־בּ֨וֹ בָרִֽאשׁוֹנָ֤ה לַהֲמִיתוֹ֙ וְיַ֣ד כָּל־הָעָ֔ם בָּאַחֲרֹנָ֑ה: ¹¹ וּסְקַלְתּ֥וֹ בָאֲבָנִ֖ים וָמֵ֑ת כִּ֣י בִקֵּ֗שׁ לְהַדִּֽיחֲךָ֙ מֵעַל֙ יְהוָ֣ה אֱלֹהֶ֔יךָ הַמּוֹצִיאֲךָ֖ מֵאֶ֥רֶץ מִצְרַ֖יִם מִבֵּ֥ית עֲבָדִֽים: ¹² וְכָל־יִשְׂרָאֵ֔ל יִשְׁמְע֖וּ וְיִרָא֑וּן וְלֹֽא־יוֹסִ֣פוּ לַעֲשׂ֗וֹת כַּדָּבָ֥ר הָרָ֛ע הַזֶּ֖ה בְּקִרְבֶּֽךָ: ס

the instigator and not on judicial procedure. Halakhic exegesis required the original witness to induce the instigator to repeat his proposal in the presence of two other witnesses before the case could be prosecuted.[33]

the rest of the people   Of his city; see 21:21.

11.   Stone him to death   Stoning is the most commonly prescribed form of capital punishment in the Bible. It normally took place outside the city. The witnesses to the crime cast the first stone, followed by the rest of the people.[34] It was used mostly for crimes that challenged God's authority or proper human authority: the worship of other gods or incitement to do so, blasphemy, divination by spirits, violation of the Sabbath, keeping the booty of idolatrous cities, insubordination against parents (including fornication by a daughter still under her father's authority), lèse majesté, and adultery.[35] Such crimes constituted acts of "high treason" against God or society. If ignored, they could cause the punishment of the entire community or undermine its stability; thus, they were viewed as threats to national safety.[36] Punishment of these crimes by stoning enabled the entire public to participate and thereby express its outrage against the crime and the threat it posed to society's welfare. Since Israel and parts of the Sinai wilderness are stony lands, stones are always at hand and pelting with them was a common expression of instinctive mass anger.[37]

12.   The participation of all the townspeople in the execution will deter them from committing the same crime, and news of the execution will have the same effect on the rest of the nation. Deuteronomy points out the deterrent effect of punishment in a few other cases as well, although not as often as it points out the cleansing effect (see v. 6).[38]

REPORTED SUBVERSION OF AN ENTIRE TOWN (vv. 13–19)

The third and most serious case is one in which the instigation has reportedly succeeded and an entire town has committed the crime. Notwithstanding the severity of the crime, a thorough and careful investigation must precede punishment. If the report is confirmed, the punishment is a mass application of 17:2–7, which prescribes the execution of individual Israelites who worship other gods, although the method of execution is different. Both laws are based on Exodus 22:19: "Whoever sacrifices to a god other than the LORD alone shall be proscribed" (that is, "doomed to destruction," as the same verb is translated below in v. 16).

The severe punishment accorded to Israelites who worship other gods reflects the severity with which the Bible regards the crime. Worshiping another god is high treason against Israel's Sovereign, the Lord, hence a capital crime. It threatens Israel's continued existence as a nation (see Comment to v. 10). Those who commit it are to be treated in the same manner as the Canaanites, who are doomed to destruction so that they may not influence the Israelites to adopt their ways. Only recently this punishment had been dealt out to those who worshiped Baal-peor.[39]

Talmudic exegesis of this law considered its severity more apparent than real. The rabbis subjected the law to a very narrow interpretation so that it applies in very few cases. They held that the subverters must be at least two adult males from the town itself and from the tribe to which the town belongs; the town must not be on the border; the majority of the population must have been subverted; its population must be at least one hundred persons but less than the majority of the tribe; every single individual must have been warned that the action was illegal and punishable by death; the townspeople are to be reasoned with and given a chance to reform; and the investigation must include all the procedural limitations which made executions rare in other capital cases. In the absence of any of these conditions the town as a whole is not destroyed, and those who worshiped

13If you hear it said, of one of the towns that the LORD your God is giving you to dwell in, 14that some scoundrels from among you have gone and subverted the inhabitants of their town, saying, "Come let us worship other gods"— whom you have not experienced—15you shall investigate and inquire and interrogate thoroughly. If it is true, the fact is established—that abhorrent thing was perpetrated in your midst—16put the inhabitants of that town to the

יג כִּי־תִשְׁמַע בְּאַחַת עָרֶיךָ אֲשֶׁר יְהֹוָה אֱלֹהֶיךָ
נֹתֵן לְךָ לָשֶׁבֶת שָׁם לֵאמֹר: 14 יָצְאוּ אֲנָשִׁים בְּנֵי־
בְלִיַּעַל מִקִּרְבֶּךָ וַיַּדִּיחוּ אֶת־יֹשְׁבֵי עִירָם לֵאמֹר
נֵלְכָה וְנַעַבְדָה אֱלֹהִים אֲחֵרִים אֲשֶׁר לֹא־יְדַעְתֶּם:
15 וְדָרַשְׁתָּ וְחָקַרְתָּ וְשָׁאַלְתָּ הֵיטֵב וְהִנֵּה אֱמֶת נָכוֹן
הַדָּבָר נֶעֶשְׂתָה הַתּוֹעֵבָה הַזֹּאת בְּקִרְבֶּךָ: 16 הַכֵּה
תַכֶּה אֶת־יֹשְׁבֵי הָעִיר הַהוּא לְפִי־חָרֶב הַחֲרֵם

v. 16. הַהִיא ק׳

other gods are judged individually and stoned to death (in any case, the innocent are spared). Because this interpretation makes it so unlikely that the total combination of circumstances required for applying the law would ever occur, the rabbis held that it was never expected to be applied, and that it was stated in the Torah only for educational purposes, to show the gravity of the crime.[40] The rabbis used the same type of narrow interpretation to limit capital punishment and the destruction of the Canaanites (see Comments to v. 15; 21:18–21; and Excursus 18).

13. **If you hear it said** Unlike the first two cases, in which there are witnesses to the instigation, in this case the authorities learn of it by rumor.[41] Hence the law stresses the necessity of carefully investigating the rumor, which is as important as prosecuting the crime. The Sifrei takes the opening phrase to mean that the authorities are required to investigate only if the crime is reported to them by others; they need not search for such cases on their own.[42]

that the LORD your God is giving you to dwell in This description of the town calls attention to the ingratitude of its inhabitants.

14. **scoundrels** Hebrew *benei beliyaʿal*. The precise meaning of *beliyaʿal* is uncertain. Various antisocial types are called *benei beliyaʿal*, such as murderers and rapists, false witnesses, rebels, corrupt priests, drunks, ingrates, boors, and the selfish. Many scholars think that *beliyaʿal* is a compound noun consisting of *beli*, "without," and a noun, *yaʿal*, which refers to some positive quality such as value[43] or honor.[44] Thus *benei beliyaʿal* may mean "useless" or "dishonorable" men. The question is complicated by the fact that *beliyaʿal* is also used as a term for death or the nether world, which calls for quite a different etymology, such as "(the land from which one) does not come up" (*bal yaʿal*) or "the swallower" (from *b-l-ʿ*, "swallow"). This meaning is reflected in "Belial," a name of Satan in the Dead Sea Scrolls, the Pseudepigrapha, and the Christian Scriptures. The two meanings of *beliyaʿal* may be unrelated and they may be homonyms, but it is conceivable that the term originally meant "the nether world" and that *benei beliyaʿal* meant "denizens of the nether world" or "demons," and then "evildoers," "scoundrels."[45]

subverted Literally, "made stray," the same verb used in verses 6 and 11.

15. The use of three verbs for investigating, instead of one as elsewhere (17:4; 19:18), and three phrases to indicate that the charge is confirmed, indicates the need for extreme care in the investigation and absolute certainty in the verdict. To ensure such care and certainty in all capital cases, halakhic exegesis required that witnesses answer seven questions about time and place in order to prove their presence at the scene of the crime, and that they all agree about other details, such as the identity of the deity worshiped and the rite that was performed or, in the case of a murder, the weapon used and the clothing worn by both victim and killer. Such procedures made a sentence of capital punishment virtually impossible.[46]

16. Although individual apostates are executed by stoning (17:5), it would be impossible to stone large numbers of people. Obviously, the apostate town would resist. Halakhic exegesis reasonably infers that the city is to be conquered militarily.[47]

the inhabitants There is no indication of what is to be done with innocent inhabitants if there are any. The text apparently deals only with the hypothetical case where the entire town is guilty. Halakhic exegesis presumes that the conduct of each adult in the town is investigated and that only those are executed against whom there is sufficient evidence of guilt.[48]

sword and put its cattle to the sword. Doom it and all that is in it to destruction: [17]gather all its spoil into the open square, and burn the town and all its spoil as a holocaust to the LORD your God. And it shall remain an everlasting ruin, never to be rebuilt. [18]Let nothing that has been doomed stick to your hand, in order that the LORD may turn from His blazing anger and show you compassion, and in His compassion increase you as He promised your fathers on oath—[19]for you will be heeding the LORD your God, obeying all His commandments that I enjoin upon you this day, doing what is right in the sight of the LORD your God.

אֹתָהּ וְאֶת־כָּל־אֲשֶׁר־בָּהּ וְאֶת־בְּהֶמְתָּהּ לְפִי־חָרֶב: 17 וְאֶת־כָּל־שְׁלָלָהּ תִּקְבֹּץ אֶל־תּוֹךְ רְחֹבָהּ וְשָׂרַפְתָּ בָאֵשׁ אֶת־הָעִיר וְאֶת־כָּל־שְׁלָלָהּ כָּלִיל לַיהוָה אֱלֹהֶיךָ וְהָיְתָה תֵּל עוֹלָם לֹא תִבָּנֶה עוֹד: 18 וְלֹא־יִדְבַּק בְּיָדְךָ מְאוּמָה מִן־הַחֵרֶם לְמַעַן יָשׁוּב יְהוָה מֵחֲרוֹן אַפּוֹ וְנָתַן־לְךָ רַחֲמִים וְרִחַמְךָ וְהִרְבֶּךָ כַּאֲשֶׁר נִשְׁבַּע לַאֲבֹתֶיךָ: 19 כִּי תִשְׁמַע בְּקוֹל יְהוָה אֱלֹהֶיךָ לִשְׁמֹר אֶת־כָּל־מִצְוֹתָיו אֲשֶׁר אָנֹכִי מְצַוְּךָ הַיּוֹם לַעֲשׂוֹת הַיָּשָׁר בְּעֵינֵי יְהוָה אֱלֹהֶיךָ: ס רביעי

Doom it . . . to destruction The apostate town is subjected to the *ḥerem* as the Canaanites were to be (see 7:2; 20:17), but this *ḥerem* is even more severe than that applied to the Canaanites, whose booty, except in the case of Jericho, was permitted.[49] Shunning the booty entirely expresses abhorrence at Israelites who apostasize.

17. open square Literally, "broad place," the large open space of the town where gatherings were held and public business was transacted. The square at Beer-sheba covered 216 square meters and could hold hundreds of people.[50]

as a holocaust Burn it totally, leaving nothing for human use,[51] as if it were a burnt offering.

ruin That is, a tell, the mound formed by the accumulated ruins of a city.

18. God's anger at the town's apostasy is such that His favor toward all of Israel is suspended until every trace of the offenders is removed. The situation is illustrated by Achan's violation of the *ḥerem* at Jericho. Achan took a garment and some silver and gold from the booty, and God, in His anger, allowed Israel to be defeated in the subsequent battles until Achan was identified and executed, along with his family, and his possessions and the booty were destroyed. Only then did the Lord "turn from His blazing anger" and enable Israel to defeat the Canaanites.[52]

show you compassion, and in His compassion Literally, "will give you compassion [*raḥamim*] and will be compassionate [*riḥam*] toward you." The verb *r-ḥ-m* sometimes means "acknowledge," "accept," "restore to favor."[53] If that is the meaning here, the verse means "He will have compassion on you and restore you to favor."

increase you as He promised your fathers This promise implies that the nation's continued growth will be jeopardized unless the apostate city is destroyed. Some commentators think that this promise also aims to reassure Israel that the loss of population caused by destroying the city would be compensated for by future growth. This view accords with the nation's concern when most of the tribe of Benjamin was wiped out after it refused to surrender a mob of murderers to the rest of the tribes for execution. The other tribes were grief-stricken over the loss of most of a tribe and took extraordinary steps to find wives for the surviving Benjaminites so that the tribe could replenish itself.[54]

19. obeying all His commandments Compare 13:1.

CHAPTER 14　　LAWS OF HOLINESS　(vv. 1–21)

14:1–21 consists of two sections, one dealing with mourning and the other with diet (vv. 1–2 and 3–21).[1] According to verses 2 and 21, only mourning and dietary practices that maintain holiness and purity are compatible with Israel's status as a people consecrated to the Lord. This explanation of the present laws is identical to that given the laws against idolatry in 7:6.

14 You are children of the LORD your God. You shall not gash yourselves or shave the front of your heads because of the dead. ²For you are a people consecrated to the LORD your God: the LORD your God chose you from among all other peoples on earth to be His treasured people.

י״ד בָּנִים אַתֶּם לַיהוָה אֱלֹהֵיכֶם לֹא תִתְגֹּדְדוּ וְלֹא־תָשִׂימוּ קָרְחָה בֵּין עֵינֵיכֶם לָמֵת: ² כִּי עַם קָדוֹשׁ אַתָּה לַיהוָה אֱלֹהֶיךָ וּבְךָ בָּחַר יְהוָה לִהְיוֹת לוֹ לְעַם סְגֻלָּה מִכֹּל הָעַמִּים אֲשֶׁר עַל־פְּנֵי הָאֲדָמָה: ס

Elsewhere in the Torah these laws appear in different contexts dealing with various subjects (see Exod. 22:30; 23:19; 34:20; Lev. 11; 19:27–28; 21:5). They are gathered together here, in a manner characteristic of Deuteronomy's method of organization, because, along with chapters 12 and 13, they share a common theme: Israel's obligation to maintain its holiness by avoiding pagan practices and "abhorrent things" (to'evot). The first of the forbidden practices, self-gashing, is identified as pagan in 1 Kings 18:28. Forbidden animals are called abhorrent (v. 3), like the rites of the Canaanites and the sin of the apostate city (12:31; 13:15), and eating the flesh of some of these animals is associated with pagan rites in Isaiah 65:3–4 and 66:3 and 17. That the actions forbidden in this chapter were regarded as pagan is also indicated by the fact that each section ends with a reminder of Israel's consecrated status, the same reminder that in 7:6 explains why Israel must avoid idolatry.

HOLINESS IN MOURNING (vv. 1–2)

1. ***You are children of the LORD your God*** The Israelites' relationship to God, with all the obligations and privileges that it entails, is like that of children to their father.² Hence, they may not disfigure themselves when mourning. The connection between these ideas is unexplained. To Rashi it means that the high station of the Israelites demands a dignified appearance: "because you are children of the LORD, it is appropriate for you to be comely, not gashed and baldened." In Abravanel's view, Israelites should not perform extreme rites of mourning when bereaved because, as God's children, they are never totally orphaned.³

shave the front of your heads Better, "make baldness in the front of your heads." The verb refers to any form of removing hair, cutting and plucking as well as shaving. For the translation "front of your heads" see Comment to 6:8.

Gashing the flesh until the blood runs and removing hair are known as mourning rites the world over. They were practiced by Israel's neighbors and by some Israelites.⁴ According to 1 Kings 18:28, the prophets of Baal practiced self-gashing, although in that context there is no obvious connection to mourning.⁵ These practices were probably understood differently in different cultures. Some scholars think that they were believed to have an effect on the ghost of the dead person, either as offerings of blood and hair to strengthen the ghost in the nether world or to assuage the ghost's jealousy of the living by showing it how grief-stricken they are. These rites could also be acts of self-punishment expressing feelings of guilt, which are often experienced by survivors after a death.⁶ Beating the breast is a mild and permitted way of expressing such feelings, while gashing and pulling out hair is extreme and, therefore, forbidden.

Similar laws against excessive manifestations of grief are found elsewhere. In Athens, Solon (sixth century B.C.E.) forbade "mourners tearing themselves to raise pity," and the Twelve Tables of Roman law (fifth century B.C.E.) forbade mourning women to lacerate their cheeks.⁷

2. This verse, which is virtually identical to 7:6, adds a second reason for prohibiting self-gashing and baldening: these rites are not compatible with Israel's status as a people consecrated ("holy") to God. This reason corresponds to that given in Leviticus 21:5–6 for prohibiting the priests from practicing these rites: "They shall be holy to their God and not profane the name of their God, for they offer the LORD's offerings . . . and so must be holy." According to verses 16–23 in the same chapter, priests who have bodily defects may not offer the Lord's offerings, lest they profane the sacred places (Lev. 21:16–23). This suggests that self-inflicted bald spots and gashes would profane those who are holy because they are comparable to bodily defects. Here Deuteronomy, like Leviticus 19:27–28, forbids the entire people to engage in these rites. This is because the entire people is

consecrated to God and all must maintain a quasi-priestly level of holiness (cf. Lev. 19:2 and Rashi's comment cited in Comment to v. 1 here).[8]

HOLINESS IN DIET (vv. 3–21)

Verses 3–21 contain several of the basic dietary laws: a list of animals whose flesh is permitted or forbidden, a law prohibiting the flesh of an animal that has died a natural death, and a law prohibiting boiling a kid in its mother's milk. These laws appear in several places earlier in the Torah and are brought together here in a single place (for other dietary laws in Deuteronomy see 12:16,21,23–25).[9] The list of permitted and forbidden animals is largely identical to that in Leviticus 11, but it is more concise and is tailored for practical use: it adds a list of the main types of permitted quadrupeds, which were the types of animals usually eaten, and it omits those less likely to be eaten: permitted winged insects, forbidden animals that walk on paws, and forbidden swarming land creatures (Lev. 11:20–21,27,29–31).

The identity of some of the animals is uncertain. Most of the Hebrew terms appear infrequently in the Bible, without enough information to identify the animals to which they refer. The ancient translations, cognate languages, and later Hebrew usage sometimes help but cannot always be relied upon, since the same name is sometimes used for different animals in different times and places. Some of the translations, therefore, are but educated guesses.

The Torah regards limitations on man's appetite as fundamental to a proper way of life. The very first statement by God to man in the Garden of Eden was that man might eat the fruit of all the trees in the garden except the fruit of the Tree of Knowledge of good and bad, though it was "good for eating and a delight to the eyes" (Gen. 2:16–17; 3:6). Whatever specific knowledge may have been conferred by that fruit, the command itself made humanity aware that it may not satisfy every desire, that there are prohibited as well as permitted actions. Distinguishing between these is God's first requirement of man. The new dietary rules established after the flood for all of humankind also included both a permission and a prohibition: man may eat the flesh of animals, but not their blood (Gen. 9:3; see Comment to 12:23–25).

The dietary code given to the Israelites is far more complex than the dietary laws addressed to Adam and the descendants of Noah. The Torah explains the Israelite code as a means of achieving and maintaining holiness, like the prohibition of pagan mourning practices in verses 1–2. Israel affirms its status as a people consecrated to God by avoiding what He declares impure. Eating such foods is incompatible with that status. Verse 21 and Exodus 22:30 show this by explaining that Israel's holiness to God is the reason for the prohibitions on eating animals that die a natural death or are torn by beasts. The dietary laws in Leviticus 11 conclude with the declaration that Israel must make itself holy because God Himself is holy. This is explained as meaning that Israel must not eat what God declares to be impure and abominable, since that would make Israel impure and abominable (Lev. 11:43–45).

Leviticus 20:24–26 adds a further dimension to the dietary laws by indicating that in separating the pure from the impure, Israel emulates God's act in separating Israel from the nations and making it His own people (cf. v. 21 here). The Torah sees "setting apart," or differentiation, as the characteristic activity by which God created and organized the world. According to the first chapter of Genesis, God separated light from darkness, the upper waters from the lower waters, the oceans from the dry land, and the day from the night. By these acts of separation He created an orderly world out of chaos. Later, He separated humanity into different nations, separated Israel from other peoples, and separated the Levites from the rest of Israel.[10] All of this indicates that God created order in the world by establishing distinctions, and that Israel emulates His acts as creator by respecting the distinctions He established between the pure and the impure.

The Torah devotes no attention to the question of why a particular animal or class of animals is pure or impure. The notion that the choice was made for hygienic reasons is groundless. It originated with Jewish writers in the Middle Ages, some of whom were physicians and thought in medical terms,[11] but was rebutted by others who observed that other peoples eat forbidden animals with no harm and that if the laws had a hygienic purpose they would have prohibited poisonous plants as well.[12] Many cultures prohibit the eating of certain foods. It is possible that some of the prohibitions in the Torah reflect ancient popular aversions to the appearance or habits of certain animals, such as swine or predators, or that some are due to the association of certain animals with

³You shall not eat anything abhorrent. ⁴These are the animals that you may eat: the ox, the sheep, and the goat; ⁵the deer, the gazelle, the roebuck, the wild goat, the ibex, the antelope, the mountain sheep, ⁶and any other animal that has true hoofs which are cleft in two and brings up the cud—such you may eat. ⁷But the following, which do bring up the cud or have true hoofs which are cleft through, you may not eat: the camel, the hare, and the daman—for although they bring up the cud, they have no

3 לֹא תֹאכַל כָּל־תּוֹעֵבָה: 4 זֹאת הַבְּהֵמָה אֲשֶׁר תֹּאכֵלוּ שׁוֹר שֵׂה כְשָׂבִים וְשֵׂה עִזִּים: 5 אַיָּל וּצְבִי וְיַחְמוּר וְאַקּוֹ וְדִישֹׁן וּתְאוֹ וָזָמֶר: 6 וְכָל־בְּהֵמָה מַפְרֶסֶת פַּרְסָה וְשֹׁסַעַת שֶׁסַע שְׁתֵּי פְרָסוֹת מַעֲלַת גֵּרָה בַּבְּהֵמָה אֹתָהּ תֹּאכֵלוּ: 7 אַךְ אֶת־זֶה לֹא תֹאכְלוּ מִמַּעֲלֵי הַגֵּרָה וּמִמַּפְרִיסֵי הַפַּרְסָה הַשְּׁסוּעָה אֶת־הַגָּמָל וְאֶת־הָאַרְנֶבֶת וְאֶת־הַשָּׁפָן כִּי־מַעֲלֵה גֵרָה הֵמָּה וּפַרְסָה לֹא הִפְרִיסוּ טְמֵאִים

pagan rites.¹³ Some passages in the flood narrative indicate that a distinction between pure and impure animals was recognized in pre-Israelite times, and some of the prohibitions or aversions to certain animals are indeed known from elsewhere in the ancient Near East.¹⁴ However, these factors carry no authority in the Torah. The language of the dietary codes indicates that what is impure for Israel is so because God declares it to be so: "they are unclean *for you*" (vv. 7,8,10,19). Thus, holiness is maintained by avoiding what is impure not by human standards, but by divine standards.

The reasons stated in the Torah for the dietary laws are only the first stage in the history of their interpretation. The effects they have on Jews go beyond the purposes stated in the Torah, and this has led to the view that they may have had additional purposes. Since they curb Israel's freedom of action, they are understood as an expression of submission to God's authority. Since they limit the right to take animal life and the method by which it is taken, they are understood as an expression of reverence for life and compassion for animals. Because of their effects, they are also understood as a regimen teaching self-discipline and as a force for Jewish distinctiveness and unity.¹⁵

In modern Hebrew permitted and forbidden animals are referred to, respectively, as *kasher* and *taref* (in English, from Yiddish, "kosher" and "treif"). *Kasher* means "fit," "proper," and refers to animals and meat that conform to all the dietary laws, including the rules of slaughter and preparation; *taref* refers to animals and meat that do not. The latter term is derived from *terefah*, which originally referred to one type of impure animal, one that was torn by beasts instead of being properly slaughtered (Exod. 22:30). The system of dietary laws as a whole is called *kashrut*, "fitness."

Land Animals (vv. 3–8)

The first section begins with a heading for the entire list (v. 3). As in Leviticus, a general rule is given for distinguishing between permitted and forbidden land animals (v. 6). Deuteronomy adds a list identifying the main types (vv. 4–5).

3. abhorrent Hebrew *to'evah*, "an abhorrent thing." See Comment to 7:25. This verse has no counterpart in Leviticus. By adding it as a heading, Deuteronomy places forbidden foods in the same category of abhorrence as idolatrous and immoral actions that would defile Israel's holiness.

4–5. The main categories of permitted land animals are the three types of domesticated bovids and seven types of wild animals of the deer family or undomesticated bovids (vv. 4–5). The males of each type stand for both sexes.¹⁶

ibex Or "bison."¹⁷

7–8. Four animals are listed to illustrate the principle that those which have only one of the required characteristics are forbidden.

7. camel Only the upper part of the camel's hoof is split, while the bottom is joined.

the hare and the daman—for although they bring up the cud These animals are not ruminants, but since they chew their food for a long time and sometimes move their jaws from side to side, they look as if they are chewing the cud.

unclean That is, ritually impure; see Comment to 12:15.

true hoofs—they are unclean for you; [8]also the swine—for although it has true hoofs, it does not bring up the cud—is unclean for you. You shall not eat of their flesh or touch their carcasses.

[9]These you may eat of all that live in water: you may eat anything that has fins and scales. [10]But you may not eat anything that has no fins and scales: it is unclean for you.

[11]You may eat any clean bird. [12]The following you may not eat: the eagle, the vulture, and the black vulture; [13]the kite, the falcon, and the buzzard of any variety; [14]every variety of raven; [15]the ostrich, the nighthawk, the sea gull, and the hawk of any variety; [16]the little owl, the great owl,

הֶם לָכֶם: 8 וְאֶת־הַחֲזִיר כִּי־מַפְרִיס פַּרְסָה הוּא וְלֹא גֵרָה טָמֵא הוּא לָכֶם מִבְּשָׂרָם לֹא תֹאכֵלוּ וּבְנִבְלָתָם לֹא תִגָּעוּ: ס 9 אֶת־זֶה תֹּאכְלוּ מִכֹּל אֲשֶׁר בַּמָּיִם כֹּל אֲשֶׁר־לוֹ סְנַפִּיר וְקַשְׂקֶשֶׂת תֹּאכֵלוּ: 10 וְכֹל אֲשֶׁר אֵין־לוֹ סְנַפִּיר וְקַשְׂקֶשֶׂת לֹא תֹאכֵלוּ טָמֵא הוּא לָכֶם: ס 11 כָּל־צִפּוֹר טְהֹרָה תֹּאכֵלוּ: 12 וְזֶה אֲשֶׁר לֹא־תֹאכְלוּ מֵהֶם הַנֶּשֶׁר וְהַפֶּרֶס וְהָעָזְנִיָּה: 13 וְהָרָאָה וְאֶת־הָאַיָּה וְהַדַּיָּה לְמִינָהּ: 14 וְאֵת כָּל־עֹרֵב לְמִינוֹ: 15 וְאֵת בַּת הַיַּעֲנָה וְאֶת־הַתַּחְמָס וְאֶת־הַשָּׁחַף וְאֶת־הַנֵּץ לְמִינֵהוּ: 16 אֶת־הַכּוֹס וְאֶת־

8. In the midrash the image of a reclining pig stretching out its cloven hooves and saying, "Look, I'm pure," while concealing the fact that it does not chew the cud, is used to characterize the hypocrisy of the Roman Empire, which posed as being dedicated to law and justice while actually oppressing the peoples it ruled.[18]

or touch their carcasses   Verse 21 also applies this prohibition to permissible animals if they die a natural death. Leviticus 11 applies it to other categories of forbidden animals as well.[19]

Water Animals (vv. 9–10)

As in Leviticus, only a general rule is given for distinguishing between permitted and forbidden aquatic animals.

Winged Animals and Other Restrictions (vv. 11–21)

The final section deals with winged animals. It concludes with restrictions based on the way in which animals die and the manner in which they are cooked.

All the winged animals listed here are birds except for the bat, which is a winged rodent. The permitted and forbidden winged animals are not distinguished by easily observable external characteristics. Hence no general rule is given for distinguishing among them, but only a list identifying the impure ones.

11. *You may eat any clean bird*   Other passages indicate that permitted birds included quail, certain types of doves and pigeons, and *barburim*, which are interpreted by different scholars as chickens, turkeys, ducks, geese, or guinea-fowl.[20]

It is generally presumed that all birds not listed as impure were permissible. Halakhic exegesis did not accept this presumption but identified characteristics common to all the forbidden birds and allowed only those that do not display these characteristics (see Comment to v. 12). In practice, only a limited number of birds (and their eggs) are considered permissible: chicken, capon, Cornish hen, turkey, domestic duck and goose, house sparrow, pigeon, squab, palm dove, turtledove, partridge, peacock, and, according to some authorities, guinea-fowl, quail, and what is today called pheasant.[21]

12. *The following you may not eat*   Virtually all the forbidden winged creatures are birds of prey or scavengers. Halakhic exegesis identified four characteristics as common to them all: they lack crops, they lack an extra toe on the back of the foot, the sac in their gizzards cannot be peeled off, and they tear their prey.[22]

eagle   Or griffon vulture. *Nesher* can refer to either.[23]

13. *the kite, the falcon, and the buzzard*[24]

and the white owl; ¹⁷the pelican, the bustard, and the cormorant; ¹⁸the stork, any variety of heron, the hoopoe, and the bat.

¹⁹All winged swarming things are unclean for you: they may not be eaten. ²⁰You may eat only clean winged creatures.

²¹You shall not eat anything that has died a natural

הַיַּנְשׁוּף וְהַתִּנְשָׁמֶת: 17 וְהַקָּאָת וְאֶת־הָרָחָמָה
וְאֶת־הַשָּׁלָךְ: 18 וְהַחֲסִידָה וְהָאֲנָפָה לְמִינָהּ
וְהַדּוּכִיפַת וְהָעֲטַלֵּף:
19 וְכֹל שֶׁרֶץ הָעוֹף טָמֵא הוּא לָכֶם לֹא יֵאָכֵלוּ:
20 כָּל־עוֹף טָהוֹר תֹּאכֵלוּ:
21 לֹא תֹאכְלוּ כָל־נְבֵלָה לַגֵּר אֲשֶׁר־בִּשְׁעָרֶיךָ

17. *pelican* Hebrew *ka'at* is more likely a type of owl.²⁵

19. *winged swarming things* Winged insects. *Sherets,* "swarming things," refers to creatures that swarm or crawl, such as insects, rodents, reptiles, and ambulatory marine animals.

20. *You may eat only clean winged creatures* "Clean" means ritually pure; see Comment to verse 7. This verse probably refers only to winged insects, the subject introduced in verse 19; otherwise, it is redundant with verse 11.²⁶ Leviticus, at this point in the list, identifies the clean winged insects as certain leaping locusts (Lev. 11:21–23).

21. *Anything that has died a natural death* Hebrew *nevelah.* This rule complements Exodus 22:30, which prohibits eating the flesh of an animal that was torn by another (*terefah*). The connection of these two prohibitions with holiness is underscored by Leviticus 22:8 and Ezekiel 44:31, where they are addressed to priests (see Comment to v. 2).

give it to the stranger . . . sell it to a foreigner According to Leviticus 17:15, eating the flesh of animals that die naturally or are torn renders both Israelites and "strangers" (resident aliens) impure. Deuteronomy does not require the latter to avoid impurity, since they are not subject to the requirements of holiness that are incumbent upon Israelites. Hence they may eat the flesh of animals that die naturally.

The distinction between *giving* the meat to strangers and *selling* it to foreigners reflects the differing economic statuses of the two classes. Resident aliens were often poor and objects of charity (see Comments to 1:16 and 5:14). Nonresident foreigners were normally present in Israel for purposes of trade and were able to support themselves.

You shall not boil a kid in its mother's milk This rule is listed with the food prohibitions because meat cooked this way may not be eaten. Meat boiled in sour milk (*leben*) was probably regarded as a delicacy, as it is by Arabs, since it is tastier and more tender than meat boiled in water. The point of this prohibition is that the animal's own mother's milk may not be used. It is similar to the rules against slaughtering cattle on the same day as their young and capturing a mother bird along with her fledglings or her eggs, and the requirement that newborn cattle remain with their mothers at least a week before they may be sacrificed.²⁷ All of these rules have the humanitarian aim of preventing acts of insensitivity against animals. It is likely, therefore, that the present rule also applied to lambs and calves, and that kids are mentioned only because goats were the most commonly owned type of cattle or because their meat is most in need of tenderizing and flavoring.²⁸

Maimonides reasoned that since this prohibition is mentioned twice in Exodus right after the pilgrimage festivals, boiling a kid in milk was probably a rite practiced at a pagan festival and prohibited for that reason (see Exod. 23:19; 34:26).²⁹ This is not a sufficient explanation, since the Torah does not oppose all pagan forms of worship; even sacrifice and prayer were practiced by pagans. The association of the rule with the harvest festivals is best explained by the fact that it seems to refer to something done at one of them. Meat was not eaten frequently (see Comment to 12:15), but it was part of festival meals. In Israel goats begin to give birth in the fall, so the fall harvest festival was probably the one at which kids were typically eaten.³⁰

The text specifies only boiling the flesh of a kid in its own mother's milk. Halakhic exegesis interpreted the rule more broadly, prohibiting the cooking or eating of any domestic cattle with the milk or milk products of any domestic cattle, or deriving any benefit from such mixtures. Supplementary regulations also prohibited eating fowl or game with milk and required the use of separate utensils for milk and meat, including their products.³¹ This broad interpretation is presumably based on the desire to prevent inadvertent violation of the original prohibition. In a society of small settlements

death; give it to the stranger in your community to eat, or you may sell it to a foreigner. For you are a people consecrated to the LORD your God.

    You shall not boil a kid in its mother's milk.

תִּתְּנֶנָּה וַאֲכָלָהּ אוֹ מָכֹר לְנָכְרִי כִּי עַם קָדוֹשׁ
אַתָּה לַיהוָה אֱלֹהֶיךָ
לֹא־תְבַשֵּׁל גְּדִי בַּחֲלֵב אִמּוֹ:   פ   חמישי

where dairy and cattle farming were not kept separate, there was considerable likelihood that if a young animal was boiled in milk, the milk would come from its own mother. Furthermore, milk and meat from different types of animals are similar in appearance, and small pieces of food can adhere to most types of utensils. The halakhah minimizes the possibility of errors due to these factors.

Periodic Duties   (14:22–16:17)

At this point the text introduces several laws that are performed at intervals of a certain number of years or a certain number of times each year: the annual and triennial tithes, the septennial remission of debts and manumission of bondsmen in the seventh year, annual sacrifices of firstlings, and the pilgrimage festivals that occur three times a year.

TITHES   (vv. 22–29)

Continuing the subject of foodstuffs, verses 22–29 deal with tithes of agricultural produce. The farmer must set aside a tithe of his produce each year and use it in one of two ways. In most years he is to take it to the chosen sanctuary and, along with his household and Levite guests, consume it there in festive sacral meals. But in the third and sixth year of each sabbatical cycle, he is to deposit it instead at his settlement where it is to be distributed to the Levites and the poor.

    Although tithing was a well-known practice in the ancient world and elsewhere in the Torah, the uses prescribed for tithes in Deuteronomy are innovative. Leviticus 27:30–33 speaks of tithes on both produce and cattle. Both are "holy to the LORD," a phrase which normally indicates that they belong to the priests or the Levites (cf. Lev. 27:21 and 22:10). The farmer may redeem the produce tithe from them by paying its value plus an extra fifth. Numbers 18:21–32 says that all tithes (probably of produce only) are given to the Levites and that they in turn must give a tithe of the tithe to the priests; they may then eat the rest anywhere. Some scholars believe that the tithes of Leviticus and Numbers are voluntary donations since neither book states that tithing is obligatory upon the public. It is clear that later, in Second Temple times, tithes in support of the Temple and clergy were obligatory (Neh. 10:38–39; 13:10–12). Within the Torah, only the tithes of Deuteronomy are explicitly said to be obligatory. These, however, are not given to the clergy or the sanctuary. They are eaten by their owners or given to the poor.

    Halakhic exegesis assumes that all the tithes are part of a single system consisting of three obligatory tithes. Numbers refers to a "first tithe" of produce given to the Levites, who give a tithe of that to the priests. Deuteronomy 14:21–27 and Leviticus 27:30–31 refer to a "second tithe," taken from the remaining ninety percent of produce, which is to be eaten by the owners at sacral feasts in Jerusalem, as is the tithe on cattle (Lev. 27:32–33). The "second tithe" on produce is replaced, in the third and sixth years of each sabbatical cycle (see 15:1), by a "third tithe" or "tithe for the poor," to which Deuteronomy 14:28–29 refers. It is given to the poor and Levites in the farmers' hometowns.[32]

    Since halakhic exegesis deals with the entire Torah as a consistent, authoritative code, this was a natural approach for it to take. Critical scholars, however, point out that the various tithe laws do not seem to assume the simultaneous existence of the others. The injunction to share the tithes with the Levites (vv. 27 and 29) seems superfluous if the Levites are already being given the tithe mentioned in Numbers; Deuteronomy 14:22 refers to a tithe on *"all* the yield of your sowing," not on ninety percent of the yield. That verses 22–27 and Leviticus 27:30–33 refer to the same tithe is unlikely: Leviticus does not say that its tithes are to be eaten by their owners at the sanctuary, and although

²²You shall set aside every year a tenth part of all the yield of your sowing that is brought from the field. ²³You shall consume the tithes of your new grain and wine and oil, and the firstlings of your herds and flocks, in the presence of the LORD your God, in the place where He will choose to establish His name, so that you may learn to revere the LORD your God forever. ²⁴Should the distance

22 עַשֵּׂר תְּעַשֵּׂר אֵת כָּל־תְּבוּאַת זַרְעֶךָ הַיֹּצֵא הַשָּׂדֶה שָׁנָה שָׁנָה: 23 וְאָכַלְתָּ לִפְנֵי ׀ יְהוָה אֱלֹהֶיךָ בַּמָּקוֹם אֲשֶׁר־יִבְחַר לְשַׁכֵּן שְׁמוֹ שָׁם מַעְשַׂר דְּגָנְךָ תִּירֹשְׁךָ וְיִצְהָרֶךָ וּבְכֹרֹת בְּקָרְךָ וְצֹאנֶךָ לְמַעַן תִּלְמַד לְיִרְאָה אֶת־יְהוָה אֱלֹהֶיךָ כָּל־הַיָּמִים: 24 וְכִי־יִרְבֶּה מִמְּךָ הַדֶּרֶךְ כִּי לֹא

Deuteronomy provides for exchanging the tithe for its cash value, it says nothing about paying a twenty percent premium in order to do so.

Because of these and other inconsistencies between the different tithe laws in the Torah, critical theory generally assumes that they were not originally parts of a single system but reflect the practices of different times or places, though there is not enough evidence to trace their development thoroughly. Abraham and Jacob gave voluntary tithes (Gen. 14:20; 28:22), and there were apparently voluntary tithes during the period of the First Temple, at least in the northern kingdom, since Amos 4:4–5 mentions tithes together with freewill offerings. As noted above, scholars disagree whether or not the tithes of Leviticus and Numbers were intended to be obligatory. Those in Deuteronomy are, but Deuteronomy modifies the uses to which they are put because of its special purposes and the conditions that it addresses. Once sacrificial worship at local sanctuaries was abolished in accordance with Deuteronomy 12, there would no longer be a need to support those sanctuaries and their clergy with tithes. Deuteronomy preserves the holy status of the tithes by requiring that in most years they be consumed in sacral meals at the sanctuary and by placing religious restrictions on how the tithe for the poor may be used (26:13–14). But it gave the tithes new functions. By requiring the owners to travel to the sanctuary and themselves eat the tithes, Deuteronomy turns the tithes into a means of linking the laity to the sanctuary and providing them with religious experience there. By giving the tithes to the poor in some years, it meets a humanitarian need as well.³³

THE ANNUAL TITHE (vv. 22–27)

In four years out of seven the tithe is to be consumed by the farmer and his household in the course of worship at the chosen sanctuary. This serves a religious purpose, as verse 23 states.

22. *every year* Rather, "year after year." This verse introduces only the first tithe, which is given only in the first, second, fourth, and fifth years. Verses 28–29 deal with the third and sixth years. In the seventh year no tithe can be given since neither planting nor harvest take place then (see Exod. 23:10–11; Lev. 25:2–7; and Comment to 15:1).

the yield of your sowing that is brought in from the field From verse 23 it is clear that this includes wine and oil as well as grains. 2 Chronicles 31:5 implies that tithes were brought from fruit honey and other types of produce as well. The halakhah requires that tithes be given from all foodstuffs grown in, or on stems rooted in, the soil.³⁴

23. The text does not say when these offerings are to be brought to the sanctuary. As noted in the Comment to 12:6, the regular pilgrimage festivals were probably the most convenient occasion, though farmers probably made private pilgrimages at other times, too.

grain and wine and oil See Comment to 11:14.

and the firstlings of your herds and flocks It is clear from 15:19–20 that all the firstlings are consumed, not merely a tenth of them. They are mentioned here because, like the tithe, they are eaten by their owners at the chosen sanctuary and are probably brought there at the same time.

so that you may learn to revere the LORD forever Reverence will be fostered by contact with the priests in the chosen city, who teach the people piety and law. This view is consistent with 31:10–13, which commands the reading of Deuteronomy in the chosen place every seventh year so that the people will learn reverence. Another possibility is that the festive celebration of God's

be too great for you, should you be unable to transport them, because the place where the LORD your God has chosen to establish His name is far from you and because the LORD your God has blessed you, 25you may convert them into money. Wrap up the money and take it with you to the place that the LORD your God has chosen, 26and spend the money on anything you want—cattle, sheep, wine, or other intoxicant, or anything you may desire. And you shall feast there, in the presence of the LORD your God, and rejoice with your household. 27But do not neglect the Levite in your community, for he has no hereditary portion as you have.

תוּכַל֙ שְׂאֵת֔וֹ כִּֽי־יִרְחַ֤ק מִמְּךָ֙ הַמָּק֔וֹם אֲשֶׁ֤ר יִבְחַר֙ יְהֹוָ֣ה אֱלֹהֶ֔יךָ לָשׂ֥וּם שְׁמ֖וֹ שָׁ֑ם כִּ֥י יְבָרֶכְךָ֖ יְהֹוָ֥ה אֱלֹהֶֽיךָ: 25 וְנָתַתָּ֖ה בַּכָּ֑סֶף וְצַרְתָּ֤ הַכֶּ֨סֶף֙ בְּיָ֣דְךָ֔ וְהָֽלַכְתָּ֙ אֶל־הַמָּק֔וֹם אֲשֶׁ֥ר יִבְחַ֛ר יְהֹוָ֥ה אֱלֹהֶ֖יךָ בּֽוֹ: 26 וְנָֽתַתָּ֣ה הַכֶּ֡סֶף בְּכֹל֩ אֲשֶׁר־תְּאַוֶּ֨ה נַפְשְׁךָ֜ בַּבָּקָ֣ר וּבַצֹּ֗אן וּבַיַּ֨יִן֙ וּבַשֵּׁכָ֔ר וּבְכֹ֛ל אֲשֶׁ֥ר תִּֽשְׁאָלְךָ֖ נַפְשֶׁ֑ךָ וְאָכַ֣לְתָּ שָּׁ֗ם לִפְנֵי֙ יְהֹוָ֣ה אֱלֹהֶ֔יךָ וְשָׂמַחְתָּ֖ אַתָּ֥ה וּבֵיתֶֽךָ: 27 וְהַלֵּוִ֥י אֲשֶׁר־בִּשְׁעָרֶ֖יךָ לֹ֣א תַֽעַזְבֶ֑נּוּ כִּ֣י אֵ֥ין ל֛וֹ חֵ֥לֶק וְנַֽחֲלָ֖ה עִמָּֽךְ: ס

bounty will teach people reverence by keeping them aware of their dependence on God and prevent them from taking their prosperity for granted.[35]

24. *because the LORD your God has blessed you* With abundant crops.[36] The tithe would therefore be too copious to transport a long distance. For "bless" referring to material gifts, see Comments to 2:7; 12:7; and 12:15.

25. *money* Literally, "silver." Money consisted of precious metal, such as gold or, most often, silver. The metal was shaped into rings, bracelets, ingots, and the like, the value of which was ascertained by weighing them at the time of each transaction. The standard unit of weight was the shekel, from the verb *shakal*, "weigh." (Coins, officially minted and stamped with marks guaranteeing their value, were not used in Israel until after the Babylonian exile.)[37]

wrap up the money Keep the entire sum intact in a moneybag, spending none of it along the way.[38]

26. *wine, or other intoxicant* Opinions differ as to whether this phrase refers to different types of grape wine, such as new and old or mixed and unmixed, or to grape wine and another intoxicant, such as date wine, pomegranate wine, or beer. There is no direct evidence that beer was drunk in Israel, but it was common elsewhere in the ancient Near East.[39] Although intoxication was deprecated, alcoholic beverages were valued as part of any celebration. Wine was appreciated for bringing joy and banishing sorrow, and complete abstinence was associated with mourning and turning away from civilization.[40]

anything you may desire To eat as part of the feast. According to the halakhah, it may not be spent on items that will not be consumed at the feast, such as clothing.[41]

rejoice with your household See Comments to 12:7.

It is not clear how the farmer and his household could consume the entire tithe during pilgrimages to the sanctuary. In the course of a 354-day lunar year, a household producing at subsistence level would theoretically require 35.4 days to consume ten percent of its produce. The three pilgrimage festivals require farmers and their households to be present in the chosen city for only nine days each year (16:1–17). In so short a time they could not consume thirty-five days worth of produce plus firstlings, festival offerings, and other sacrifices that would have to be consumed at the same time (see 12:6–7,17–18,26–27). Assuming that the farmers invited the Levites and poor to the meals, as required, even if they doubled their normal consumption at the festivals, they could not dispose of all the food involved unless there were as many Levites and poor as there were members of the farmers' households, which is unlikely. Conceivably the law aimed to encourage farmers to travel to the sanctuary more often, but it would have been extremely difficult for those living far away to do so. Shadal conjectures, on the basis of 26:12, that whatever was left over after three years had to be given to the poor. The halakhah requires that whatever is left over be destroyed.[42]

27. *the Levite in your community* Those residing in the various towns and cities. See Comment to 12:12.

28Every third year you shall bring out the full tithe of your yield of that year, but leave it within your settlements. 29Then the Levite, who has no hereditary portion as you have, and the stranger, the fatherless, and the widow in your settlements shall come and eat their fill, so that the LORD your God may bless you in all the enterprises you undertake.

28 מִקְצֵה ׀ שָׁלֹשׁ שָׁנִים תּוֹצִיא אֶת־כָּל־מַעְשַׂר תְּבוּאָתְךָ בַּשָּׁנָה הַהִוא וְהִנַּחְתָּ בִּשְׁעָרֶיךָ: 29 וּבָא הַלֵּוִי כִּי אֵין־לוֹ חֵלֶק וְנַחֲלָה עִמָּךְ וְהַגֵּר וְהַיָּתוֹם וְהָאַלְמָנָה אֲשֶׁר בִּשְׁעָרֶיךָ וְאָכְלוּ וְשָׂבֵעוּ לְמַעַן יְבָרֶכְךָ יְהוָה אֱלֹהֶיךָ בְּכָל־מַעֲשֵׂה יָדְךָ אֲשֶׁר תַּעֲשֶׂה: ס ששי

THE TRIENNIAL POOR TITHE (vv. 28–29)

In the third and sixth year of each seven-year cycle (see 15:1), the farmers shall not eat the tithe at the sanctuary but must deposit it in their hometowns to feed the Levites and the poor. Chapter 26:12–15 prescribes a declaration for them to make when they complete delivery of this tithe. Other gifts for the poor are prescribed in 24:19–22.

Presumably the produce collected in each of these two years was expected to suffice for three or four years until the next collection.[43] It seems unlikely that the poor were to be fed only two years out of seven.

28. *bring out* From your property.

the full tithe None is to be diverted to any other use. See 26:12.

leave it within your settlements Presumably certain public locations were designated for the deposit, distribution, and long-term storage of the produce. Storage facilities and public threshing floors near the city gate would have been natural locations.[44]

29. *the Levite . . . the stranger, the fatherless, and the widow* The poor. See Comments to 1:16; 5:14; and 10:18.

come and eat their fill This seems to imply that the recipients of the tithe would receive food daily as needed, rather than quantities to save for longer periods. The Mishnah understands the verse in this way and stipulates the minimum amounts that may be given of each commodity.[45]

so that the LORD your God may bless you in all the enterprises you undertake Such assurances are given in connection with laws that require economic sacrifice for the sake of the poor: freeing the indentured servant after six years, lending to fellow Israelites even close to the remission year and without interest, and leaving overlooked sheaves, olives, and grapes for the poor (see 15:10,18; 23:21; 24:19–21). Lest the Israelite fear that these sacrifices will cause economic hardship, he is assured that, on the contrary, they will ultimately lead to greater prosperity.[46]

CHAPTER 15 ## MEASURES TO PROTECT THE POOR (vv. 1–18)

Chapter 15:1–18 contains three provisions that are part of the Torah's program to alleviate the suffering of the poor. Here the concern is with extreme difficulties that can befall the poor: inability to pay off debts, inability to obtain loans, and indentured servitude. The first provision requires that every seven years creditors remit debts owed to them (vv. 1–6). The second, consequent upon the first, is an exhortation not to refuse loans to the poor because the debt would be remitted in the seventh year (vv. 7–11). The third puts a limit of six years on the time that a person may be required to work as an indentured servant (vv. 12–18).[1]

Certain aspects of these laws are paralleled elsewhere in the Torah and in other ancient societies. The parallels clarify details of the laws and illustrate how they may have been administered. The relationship between the present chapter and similar provisions elsewhere in the Torah is discussed in Excursus 16.

The thematic unity of these three provisions is expressed by terms that recur throughout: the phrases "seven years/seventh year" (vv. 1,9,12), the description of a fellow Israelite as one's "brother" (vv. 2,3,7,9,11,12), and references to God's blessing that make generosity possible and reward it (vv. 4,6,10,14,18).

15 Every seventh year you shall practice remission of debts. ²This shall be the nature of the remission: every creditor shall remit the due that he claims from his fellow;

ט״ז מִקֵּץ שֶׁבַע־שָׁנִים תַּעֲשֶׂה שְׁמִטָּה: ² וְזֶה דְּבַר הַשְּׁמִטָּה שָׁמוֹט כָּל־בַּעַל מַשֵּׁה יָדוֹ אֲשֶׁר יַשֶּׁה בְּרֵעֵהוּ לֹא־יִגֹּשׂ אֶת־רֵעֵהוּ וְאֶת־אָחִיו כִּי־

These provisions continue those that are performed at intervals of one or more years, starting with 14:22–29.

Verses 1–18 are another example of Deuteronomy's homiletic, hortatory style (see the Introduction and introductory Comment to chap. 12). Less than half of the chapter—verses 1–3,12–14,16–17—is devoted to legal details; more than half is devoted to explication and exhortation.

REMISSION OF DEBTS (vv. 1–6)

The first law enjoins the remission of debts every seventh year. The type of debt that concerns the Torah is that incurred by the poor and insolvent.[2] A farmer, for example, might need funds, seed, or supplies because of crop failure; or a city dweller might become impoverished because of unemployment.[3] Loans to individuals in such circumstances were acts of charity rather than commercial ventures, and the forgiving of such loans was an extension of the charity.

Some Mesopotamian kings proclaimed remissions of debt and release of debt servants, usually at the beginning of their reigns and, in some cases, again several years later. The act of remission was called *misharum* ("justice, equity") and the release of servants *andurarum* or *durarum*, related to Hebrew *deror*, "release," in Leviticus 25:10.[4] Similar proclamations were made by rulers in the Greek and Hellenistic worlds. The most famous of these was the *seisachtheia* ("shaking off of burdens") in which Solon, in sixth-century Athens, "canceled all debts for which land or liberty was the security . . . and so released the peasants from serfdom, restored their farms, and redeemed those who had been sold into slavery."[5] These practices rectified extreme and dangerous disparities between social classes and ingratiated the new ruler with certain elements of the public. Possibly some Israelite monarchs made similar proclamations.[6] The present law differs from such royal proclamations in the regularity of the remissions it requires. These do not depend on the accession of a new ruler or on political calculations, but aim to restore economic equilibrium on a regular, predictable basis.

Practical details of how the law was applied—such as the date on which the remission went into effect and the types of loans it covered—are not spelled out. Some of these may have been common knowledge, and others may have been worked out by courts and administrative agencies. The Torah's aim here is primarily to state the principle that indebtedness is not to continue indefinitely, and to identify the authorized legal remedy for long-term debt.

Observance of the law in the early Second Temple period and developments in talmudic times are discussed in Excursus 16.

The remission of debts and other provisions for the relief of debtors are part of the Torah's program for preserving a balanced distribution of resources across society.[7] See Exodus 22:24–26; Leviticus 25:36–37; Deuteronomy 23:20–21 and 24:6,10–13,17.

1. Every seventh year Literally, "after a term of seven years." According to the halakhah, debts were canceled at sunset on the last day of the seventh year.[8]

remission of debts Hebrew *shemittah* literally means "dropping, release," from the verb *sh-m-t*. That it refers to debts is clear from the next verse. The word may also imply that the agricultural "sabbatical" (Exod. 23:10–11; Lev. 25:2–6) is to be observed in the same year, for that is the context in which *sh-m-t* is used in Exodus 23:10–11, which states that fields, vineyards, and olive groves are to be "released"—that is, left uncultivated—in the seventh year. Nehemiah 10:32 indicates that in early Second Temple times the seventh year included both fallowing and debt remission. For further discussion, see Excursus 16.

2. every creditor shall remit the due that he claims from his fellow Since the remission is for the benefit of the poor, it probably does not cover all types of debts. According to the halakhah, it does not cancel unpaid wages, bills owed to shopkeepers for merchandise, and certain types of secured loans. Similarly, in the *misharum* act of the Babylonian King Ammitsaduka, business loans are not canceled.[9]

he shall not dun his fellow or kinsman, for the remission proclaimed is of the LORD. ³You may dun the foreigner; but you must remit whatever is due you from your kinsmen.

⁴There shall be no needy among you—since the LORD your God will bless you in the land that the LORD your God is giving you as a hereditary portion—⁵if only you heed the LORD your God and take care to keep all this Instruction that I enjoin upon you this day. ⁶For the LORD your God will bless you as He has promised you: you will extend loans to many nations, but require none yourself; you will dominate many nations, but they will not dominate you.

קְרָא שְׁמִטָּה לַיהֹוָה: 3 אֶת־הַנָּכְרִי תִּגֹּשׂ וַאֲשֶׁר יִהְיֶה לְךָ אֶת־אָחִיךָ תַּשְׁמֵט יָדֶךָ:
4 אֶפֶס כִּי לֹא יִהְיֶה־בְּךָ אֶבְיוֹן כִּי־בָרֵךְ יְבָרֶכְךָ יְהֹוָה בָּאָרֶץ אֲשֶׁר יְהֹוָה אֱלֹהֶיךָ נֹתֵן־לְךָ נַחֲלָה לְרִשְׁתָּהּ: 5 רַק אִם־שָׁמוֹעַ תִּשְׁמַע בְּקוֹל יְהֹוָה אֱלֹהֶיךָ לִשְׁמֹר לַעֲשׂוֹת אֶת־כָּל־הַמִּצְוָה הַזֹּאת אֲשֶׁר אָנֹכִי מְצַוְּךָ הַיּוֹם: 6 כִּי־יְהֹוָה אֱלֹהֶיךָ בֵּרַכְךָ כַּאֲשֶׁר דִּבֶּר־לָךְ וְהַעֲבַטְתָּ גּוֹיִם רַבִּים וְאַתָּה לֹא תַעֲבֹט וּמָשַׁלְתָּ בְּגוֹיִם רַבִּים וּבְךָ לֹא יִמְשֹׁלוּ: ס

he shall not dun his fellow or kinsman Rather, "his fellow, that is, his kinsman."[10] That the two terms refer to one and the same person is clear from the rest of the chapter, which speaks only of the kinsman. The repeated use of the term "kinsman" (lit., "brother") in this chapter emphasizes that those for whose sake so many sacrifices are demanded are, after all, one's kin (see esp. v. 12, where "fellow Hebrew" is literally "Hebrew kinsman").[11] See Comment to 1:16.

for the remission proclaimed is of the LORD[12] This seems to be the equivalent of the formula in the Mesopotamian *misharum* decrees explaining that debts may not be collected "because the king has established a remission for the land."[13] Here it is God—Israel's divine king—who establishes the remission.

3. The remission applies only to debts owed by fellow Israelites, not those owed by foreigners. Similarly, the *misharum* edict of the Babylonian king Ammitsaduka canceled only the debts of Akkadians and Amorites in Babylon. The distinction between citizens and foreigners may be due to the fact that forgiving debts is an extraordinary sacrifice. Collecting debts is a legitimate right that members of society are willing to forgo only on behalf of those who have a special familylike claim on their generosity. In practical terms, remission of debts aims to reestablish economic equilibrium within a society, and since foreigners are only temporary residents they are not members of that society. Indeed, since foreigners were normally present in a country for purposes of trade, goods or money given to them on credit were usually investments or advance payments on goods, not loans because of poverty.

4–6. Moses digresses from the details of the law to deal with its religious implications and to exhort the people to obey it.

In the Hebrew text, verse 4 begins with "However," which indicates that verses 4–6 are meant as a contrast to verses 1–3. Since verses 1–3 imply the presence of poverty, verses 4–6 counter with the assurance that there need be no poverty. If Israel will obey God's laws, the present law will be unnecessary. Note the contrasting statement in verse 11.[14]

will bless you With prosperity. See Comments to 2:7; 12:7,15; and 14:24.

6. If Israel will obey God's laws, not only will it have no poor who need loans, but it will be so prosperous that other nations will turn to it for loans. Compare the blessing promised in 28:12 and the curse threatened in 28:44.

as He has promised you See Exodus 23:22–25; Leviticus 26:3–13. As here, the promises are contingent on Israel's obedience.

you will dominate many nations Economically. Compare Proverbs 22:7, "The rich dominate the poor, and the borrower is subservient to the lender."

AN EXHORTATION TO LEND TO THE POOR (vv. 7–11)

Moses anticipates a complication arising from the preceding law. Even those who would normally be willing to lend to the poor might be reluctant to do so as the year of remission approaches, since they

7If, however, there is a needy person among you, one of your kinsmen in any of your settlements in the land that the LORD your God is giving you, do not harden your heart and shut your hand against your needy kinsman. 8Rather, you must open your hand and lend him sufficient for whatever he needs. 9Beware lest you harbor the base thought, "The seventh year, the year of remission, is approaching," so that you are mean to your needy kinsman and give him nothing. He will cry out to the LORD against you, and you will incur guilt. 10Give to him readily and have no regrets when you do so, for in return the LORD your God will bless you in all your efforts and in all your undertakings. 11For there will never cease to be needy ones in your land, which is why I command you: open your hand to the poor and needy kinsman in your land.

7 כִּי־יִהְיֶה֩ בְךָ֨ אֶבְי֜וֹן מֵאַחַ֤ד אַחֶ֙יךָ֙ בְּאַחַ֣ד שְׁעָרֶ֔יךָ בְּאַרְצְךָ֕ אֲשֶׁר־יְהוָ֥ה אֱלֹהֶ֖יךָ נֹתֵ֣ן לָ֑ךְ לֹ֧א תְאַמֵּ֣ץ אֶת־לְבָבְךָ֗ וְלֹ֤א תִקְפֹּץ֙ אֶת־יָ֣דְךָ֔ מֵאָחִ֖יךָ הָאֶבְיֽוֹן׃ 8 כִּֽי־פָתֹ֧חַ תִּפְתַּ֛ח אֶת־יָדְךָ֖ ל֑וֹ וְהַעֲבֵט֙ תַּעֲבִיטֶ֔נּוּ דֵּ֚י מַחְסֹר֔וֹ אֲשֶׁ֥ר יֶחְסַ֖ר לֽוֹ׃ 9 הִשָּׁ֣מֶר לְךָ֡ פֶּן־יִהְיֶ֣ה דָבָר֩ עִם־לְבָבְךָ֨ בְלִיַּ֜עַל לֵאמֹ֗ר קָֽרְבָ֣ה שְׁנַֽת־הַשֶּׁ֘בַע֮ שְׁנַ֣ת הַשְּׁמִטָּה֒ וְרָעָ֣ה עֵֽינְךָ֗ בְּאָחִ֙יךָ֙ הָֽאֶבְי֔וֹן וְלֹ֥א תִתֵּ֖ן ל֑וֹ וְקָרָ֤א עָלֶ֙יךָ֙ אֶל־יְהוָ֔ה וְהָיָ֥ה בְךָ֖ חֵֽטְא׃ 10 נָת֤וֹן תִּתֵּן֙ ל֔וֹ וְלֹא־יֵרַ֥ע לְבָבְךָ֖ בְּתִתְּךָ֣ ל֑וֹ כִּ֞י בִּגְלַ֣ל ׀ הַדָּבָ֣ר הַזֶּ֗ה יְבָרֶכְךָ֙ יְהוָ֣ה אֱלֹהֶ֔יךָ בְּכָֽל־מַעֲשֶׂ֔ךָ וּבְכֹ֖ל מִשְׁלַ֥ח יָדֶֽךָ׃ 11 כִּ֛י לֹא־יֶחְדַּ֥ל אֶבְי֖וֹן מִקֶּ֣רֶב הָאָ֑רֶץ עַל־כֵּ֞ן אָנֹכִ֤י מְצַוְּךָ֙ לֵאמֹ֔ר פָּ֠תֹחַ תִּפְתַּ֨ח אֶת־יָדְךָ֜ לְאָחִ֧יךָ לַעֲנִיֶּ֛ךָ וּלְאֶבְיֹנְךָ֖ בְּאַרְצֶֽךָ׃ ס

would very likely lose what they loaned. Moses urges the people to disregard such calculations, arguing that God would bless with further prosperity those who do lend to the poor and would punish those who refuse to lend. (In late Second Temple times this law did become a deterrent to lending, and a legal fiction was devised to remedy the problem. See Excursus 16.)

This section of the chapter is not a law but an ethical exhortation. Because there is no way for authorities to judge the true motives of persons who refuse to lend, the exhortation could hardly have been enforceable. That is why the only recourse of the poor who are denied loans is a plea to God (v. 9b). To add force to the exhortation, Moses uses several value-charged idioms—"hardening the heart," "base thought," and "mean"—to deprecate refusal to lend.

7. *If, however, there is a needy person among you* If the ideal promised in verse 4 is not achieved.

9. *base* See Comment to 13:13.

he will cry out to the LORD *against you and you will incur guilt*[15] Guilt builds up until it leads to punishment, just as merit builds up and leads to reward (see Comment to 6:25 and cf. 24:13,15). In 24:14–15 the same warning is addressed to those who delay paying the wages of poor laborers. Exodus 22:20–23 warns that the oppressed will cry out to God against those who mistreat them and describes the punishment explicitly. By making the same warning here, Moses implies that even the passive act of refusing to lend the poor what they need is as bad as outright abuse. By way of contrast, 24:13 promises that those who treat the poor compassionately will be blessed by them and gain merit before God.

10. The closer the year of remission, the more likely it is that the loan will end up as a gift. But any loss incurred will be more than made up by God. See Comment to 14:29, and compare Leviticus 25:20–21.

all your undertakings See Comment to 12:7.

11. The realism of this verse contrasts with the ideal described in verse 4. In Hoffmann's view this reflects the pessimism Moses expresses in 31:27–29. Since Israel will ultimately break faith with God, it will violate the conditions required for the elimination of poverty.

MANUMISSION OF INDENTURED SERVANTS (vv. 12–18)

Verses 12–18 enjoin that Israelites who have become indentured servants be freed after six years. This is one of several laws in the Torah that deal with servitude. There are two types of servants in biblical law: indentured servants and full slaves. Both are termed *'eved*, "servant." Servitude was an accepted

12If a fellow Hebrew, man or woman, is sold to you, he
shall serve you six years, and in the seventh year you shall

12 כִּי־יִמָּכֵ֨ר לְךָ֜ אָחִ֣יךָ הָֽעִבְרִ֗י א֚וֹ הָֽעִבְרִיָּ֔ה וַעֲבָֽדְךָ֖
שֵׁ֣שׁ שָׁנִ֑ים וּבַשָּׁנָה֙ הַשְּׁבִיעִ֔ת תְּשַׁלְּחֶ֥נּוּ חָפְשִׁ֖י

fact of life in Israel as it was everywhere in the ancient world. Biblical law and ethical teachings aimed
at securing humane treatment for servants. These aims are based on the Bible's recognition of the
shared humanity of master and servant and on the special empathy the Bible expects of Israelites
because their ancestors were slaves in Egypt.[16] The Torah, unique among ancient law codes, insists
that servants be given rest on the Sabbath, be included in the festivities of holidays, and be protected
from physical abuse and harm by their masters.[17] Furthermore, full lifelong slavery is in principle
limited to foreigners. Israelites may only become indentured servants and may not be held
indefinitely against their wishes.[18]

This subject is a natural sequel to verses 1–11, which deal with loans and poverty. Poverty is the
underlying cause of indentured servitude. A person with no means of support might indenture
himself or a member of his household in order to obtain food, clothing, lodging, and perhaps capital.
A convicted thief who lacked the means to make restitution was sold by the court to raise the money
to pay what he owed.[19]

In practice indenture might also result from default on a loan. This was the case, in law and in
practice, in Mesopotamia as well as Greece and Rome. Debtors and members of their households
were considered collateral for loans. In case of default, the debtor would have to surrender himself or
herself or a member of his or her household to the creditor (or to a third party who would cover the
debt), or else the creditor might seize ("distrain") one of them.[20] A few instances of this practice are
mentioned in the Bible.[21] It is questionable whether the Torah tolerates it.[22] It seems inconsistent
with the laws that forbid creditors to act like creditors and charge interest, to distrain the debtor's
handmill, or to enter his house.[23] Some scholars, however, think that Leviticus 25 presupposes the
practice.[24] Certainly the present law, whether or not it condones debt servitude, would have the
effect of limiting its duration. A similar Babylonian law, limiting the term of servitude, clearly has
reference to debt servitude (see Comment to v. 12).

Parallel laws appear in Exodus 21:2–6 and Leviticus 25:39–55. See Comments below and Excursus
16 for discussion. Observance of the law in the days of Jeremiah and in the early Second Temple
period are also discussed in Excursus 16.

12. fellow Hebrew That is, "Hebrew kinsman" (lit., "brother"). The law limits the
amount of time one Israelite may control another. Only foreigners may be owned in perpetuity and
passed on to heirs (Lev. 25:39–55). The phrase "Hebrew kinsman" reminds one of special, brotherly
obligations toward fellow Israelites.

"Hebrew" (*ivri*) is the oldest designation for Israelites, who could not be called "Israelites"
before the time of Israel (Jacob) himself. It appears mostly in narratives about the patriarchs and
Joseph, the Exodus, and the period before David became king. It seems largely to have fallen out of
common use after that time. It may be related to the word *apiru*, which is found in ancient Near
Eastern texts and refers to a social class of rootless, subservient individuals. Texts from Nuzi refer to
apiru people who indenture themselves in exchange for food and clothing. In the light of these texts,
some scholars have suggested that our passage and Exodus 21:2 refer only to servants who are
members of the *apiru* class, not to all Israelite servants. However, the terms *apiru* and *ivri* are not
necessarily related. There are phonetic differences between them, and in all other contexts "Hebrew"
clearly refers to an ethnic group, whereas *apiru* refers to a social class. Conceivably an older, different
meaning has survived in Exodus 21:2, but it is more likely that "Hebrew" is used there to indicate
that that law refers only to Israelite slaves, not non-Israelites. Here in Deuteronomy "Hebrew"
clearly means simply "Israelite": "fellow Hebrew" means literally "Hebrew kinsman," and in Jeremiah 34:9 it is paraphrased as "Judean kinsman."[25]

or woman According to Exodus 21:7–11, a daughter sold as a slave does not go free in the
same way male slaves do. She is sold back to her father or released if her master fails to fulfill certain
obligations, such as providing her with a husband. Some scholars view Deuteronomy's law as
superseding that of Exodus, by granting equal treatment to females instead of permitting their
manumission only in a limited number of circumstances.[26] This view assumes that the Hebrew
woman of Deuteronomy 15 is the same as the daughter in Exodus 21. However, it is possible that the

set him free. [13]When you set him free, do not let him go empty-handed: [14]Furnish him out of the flock, threshing floor, and vat, with which the LORD your God has blessed you. [15]Bear in mind that you were slaves in the land of Egypt and the LORD your God redeemed you; therefore I enjoin this commandment upon you today.

[16]But should he say to you, "I do not want to leave you"—for he loves you and your household and is happy

מֵעִמָּךְ: 13 וְכִי־תְשַׁלְּחֶנּוּ חָפְשִׁי מֵעִמָּךְ לֹא
תְשַׁלְּחֶנּוּ רֵיקָם: 14 הַעֲנֵיק תַּעֲנִיק לוֹ מִצֹּאנְךָ
וּמִגָּרְנְךָ וּמִיִּקְבֶךָ אֲשֶׁר בֵּרַכְךָ יְהוָה אֱלֹהֶיךָ
תִּתֶּן־לוֹ: 15 וְזָכַרְתָּ כִּי עֶבֶד הָיִיתָ בְּאֶרֶץ מִצְרַיִם
וַיִּפְדְּךָ יְהוָה אֱלֹהֶיךָ עַל־כֵּן אָנֹכִי מְצַוְּךָ אֶת־
הַדָּבָר הַזֶּה הַיּוֹם:
16 וְהָיָה כִּי־יֹאמַר אֵלֶיךָ לֹא אֵצֵא מֵעִמָּךְ כִּי

two laws refer to different cases. Exodus refers to a minor sold conditionally by her father for the purpose of marriage; such a sale would naturally not be terminated after six years. Sales of this type, by poor families, are known from the ancient Near East. Deuteronomy, on the other hand, may refer only to a girl or woman who becomes indentured because of insolvency or debt—her own or that of a husband or father—with no intention of marriage. Since both types of female servitude existed simultaneously in the ancient Near East, there is no need to assume that Deuteronomy is superseding Exodus's law about girls. It is quite possible that the manumission law of Exodus 21:2–6 regarding male bondsmen also applied to indentured women, as in Deuteronomy, and that Deuteronomy would have recognized the Exodus law about sale for marriage as a special case.[27]

is sold to you   Hebrew *yimmakher* could mean either "is sold" or "sells himself." In the former case, it might refer to the sale of a son or daughter by an indigent father or of a thief by the court. If it means "sells himself/herself," it would refer to self-sale by an indigent person for support of himself/herself and his/her family. If debt servitude is permitted, the aim in either case would be to satisfy a debt or raise the funds to do so.

six years . . . seventh   Six years is the standard term of indenture (see also v. 18 and Exod. 21:2). According to Leviticus 25:10 and 40–41, the servant goes free in the fiftieth year. These differences are discussed in Excursus 16. According to the Babylonian laws of Hammurabi, debt servants worked for three years and went free in the fourth;[28] this difference may be due to differences between the Israelite and Mesopotamian economies.

13–14.   Deuteronomy here goes beyond Exodus and requires that the newly freed servant be given capital and supplies to live on as he/she resumes independent life. The aim is to prevent him/her from starting off penniless and having to indenture himself/herself or borrow in order to eat, thus returning to the same condition that led to servitude in the first place.

Some medieval and modern authorities have used this rule as the basis of a moral or legal obligation to give severance pay to employees at the conclusion of their employment.[29]

14. furnish[30]

out of the flock, the threshing floor, and the vat   That is, give him some sheep or goats (for their products, such as milk or wool), some grain, and some wine. To the Sifrei, these are merely examples, and other items of the same types may be given.

with which the LORD your God has blessed you   Rather, "giving him according as the LORD your God has blessed you,"[31] giving him what you can afford. According to halakhic exegesis, the gift must be worth at least thirty shekels, the value of a slave according to Exodus 21:32.[32]

15.   The Israelites' own experience of servitude and redemption by God is cited, either as a reason why they should treat servants generously or to remind them of God's authority to make such a difficult demand of them. See Comment to 5:15 and compare 16:12; 24:18 and 22.

16.   The servant may consider the security gained through subservience preferable to the financial risks of independence. The fact that the law thinks it possible that the servant would love the master implies that the treatment of indentured servants was expected to be benign, as required by the other laws dealing with them (see the introductory Comment to this unit).

happy   Or "well off."

with you—[17]you shall take an awl and put it through his ear into the door, and he shall become your slave in perpetuity. Do the same with your female slave. [18]When you do set him free, do not feel aggrieved; for in the six years he has given you double the service of a hired man. Moreover, the LORD your God will bless you in all you do.

וְלָקַחְתָּ֣ 17 אֶהֳבְךָ֙ וְאֶת־בֵּיתֶ֔ךָ כִּי־ט֥וֹב ל֖וֹ עִמָּ֑ךְ
אֶת־הַמַּרְצֵ֗עַ וְנָתַתָּ֤ה בְאָזְנוֹ֙ וּבַדֶּ֔לֶת וְהָ֥יָה לְךָ֖ עֶ֣בֶד
עוֹלָ֑ם וְאַ֥ף לַאֲמָתְךָ֖ תַּעֲשֶׂה־כֵּֽן׃ 18 לֹא־יִקְשֶׁ֣ה
בְעֵינֶ֗ךָ בְּשַׁלֵּֽחֲךָ֙ אֹת֤וֹ חָפְשִׁי֙ מֵֽעִמָּ֔ךְ כִּ֗י מִשְׁנֶה֙
שְׂכַ֣ר שָׂכִ֔יר עֲבָֽדְךָ֖ שֵׁ֣שׁ שָׁנִ֑ים וּבֵֽרַכְךָ֙ יְהֹוָ֣ה
אֱלֹהֶ֔יךָ בְּכֹ֖ל אֲשֶׁ֥ר תַּעֲשֶֽׂה׃ פ   שביעי

17. The ceremony for making the servant's status permanent consists of driving the point of an awl through his or her ear into the door. The precise significance of this action is unclear. Hoffmann thinks that piercing the ear symbolizes the servant's obligation to have his or her ear always open to hear the master's orders (one Egyptian word for slave means literally "listener"). Another view is that a pierced ear was a slave mark or that it was used to hold an earring or some other object that served as a slave mark, although in that case the text has omitted the main point. In Exodus 21:6 the essence of the ceremony is piercing the ear; driving the awl into the door is not mentioned. This additional requirement in Deuteronomy seems to symbolize the servant's becoming permanently attached to the master's house. Later Jewish exegesis saw the ceremony as punitive: the ear, which heard God say at Mount Sinai that Israelites are *His* slaves and may not be sold into permanent servitude (Lev. 25:42), is punished for ignoring God's declaration by electing to remain a servant to a human master.[33]

door The door of the master's house. Exodus 21:6 states that the servant is brought "before God. He shall be brought to the door or the doorpost." "Before God" implies that in Exodus the ceremony has a religious dimension and takes place either at the door of a sanctuary near the master's home (which would explain why Deuteronomy, which abolishes local sanctuaries, omits the phrase) or in the presence of some symbol of God kept at the door of his home. The omission of the phrase "before God" probably implies that in Deuteronomy the ceremony is a completely secular one.[34]

slave in perpetuity[35] According to halakhic exegesis, "perpetuity" means for the rest of the master's life, unless a Jubilee year (as prescribed in Leviticus 25) comes first. Even if the servant chooses to remain with the master, he is not passed on to the master's heirs and does not remain beyond the Jubilee.[36]

18. do not feel aggrieved Deuteronomy is not only interested in compliance with the law but in the Israelite's feelings while carrying it out. The master, having grown accustomed to the servant's service, is liable to regard the Torah's demand to free him as an unreasonable hardship. The text reminds him that he has profited handsomely from the servant and has no reason to feel deprived.

double the service of a hired man The Hebrew is difficult. The sense seems to be that the servant has given twice the service that a hired man would have performed for the same cost. The point may be that the wages of a hired man would have been twice what the servant cost (room and board, and perhaps a loan on which he defaulted), or that a hired man would have worked only during the day, while the servant was available day and night.[37]

the LORD your God will bless you As in verse 10, this means that any loss incurred will be more than made up by God. See also 14:29.

THE SACRIFICE OF FIRSTBORN CATTLE (vv. 19–23)

The requirement to give animal firstlings to God is a counterpart, for herdsmen, of the requirement that farmers donate the first fruits of their crops to God before the rest may be eaten; so is the requirement that the first shearings of sheep be given to Him (see 18:4).[38] The first issue of all living things is considered holy and is reserved for the Lord. Only after these are given to God, thereby acknowledging Him as the source and owner of all life, are the remainder of the crop and subsequent

19You shall consecrate to the LORD your God all male firstlings that are born in your herd and in your flock: you must not work your firstling ox or shear your firstling sheep. 20You and your household shall eat it annually before the LORD your God in the place that the LORD will choose. 21But if it has a defect, lameness or blindness, any serious defect, you shall not sacrifice it to the LORD your

19 כָּל־הַבְּכוֹר אֲשֶׁר יִוָּלֵד בִּבְקָרְךָ וּבְצֹאנְךָ הַזָּכָר תַּקְדִּישׁ לַיהוָה אֱלֹהֶיךָ לֹא תַעֲבֹד בִּבְכֹר שׁוֹרֶךָ וְלֹא תָגֹז בְּכוֹר צֹאנֶךָ: 20 לִפְנֵי יְהוָה אֱלֹהֶיךָ תֹאכֲלֶנּוּ שָׁנָה בְשָׁנָה בַּמָּקוֹם אֲשֶׁר־יִבְחַר יְהוָה אַתָּה וּבֵיתֶךָ: 21 וְכִי־יִהְיֶה בוֹ מוּם פִּסֵּחַ אוֹ עִוֵּר כֹּל מוּם רָע לֹא תִזְבָּחֶנּוּ לַיהוָה אֱלֹהֶיךָ:

offspring of animals desacralized and freed for human use. Such practices were common in the ancient world.[39] According to Genesis 4:4, the sacrifice of firstlings goes back to the beginning of the human race when Abel brought "the choicest of the firstlings of his flock" as a gift to the Lord. According to Exodus 13:12–15, the first-born of Israelites and of cattle must be consecrated to the Lord, and those of humans and impure animals redeemed, in order to commemorate God's slaying the firstborn of Egypt and sparing those of Israel at the time of the Exodus.

This law recasts the one requiring sacrifice of first-born male cattle to God, previously stated in Exodus and Numbers, with Deuteronomy's characteristic modifications: the sacrifice may be offered only at the chosen sanctuary and is to be eaten by the worshiper in a sacrificial meal.[40] This differs from Numbers 18:15–18, according to which firstlings were eaten by the priests. Halakhic exegesis harmonized the present law with that in Numbers by taking verses 20–23 as addressed to the priests.[41] However, it is clear from verse 19 that this law is addressed to the farmers who own the cattle (see also 12:6,17; 14:23). It is probable, therefore, that the present law is a modification of that in Numbers, undoubtedly motivated by the same considerations that lie behind Deuteronomy's similar modification of the tithe law. With all sanctuaries but one closed, there would no longer be a need to support local sanctuaries and their clergy with firstlings. Deuteronomy preserves the firstlings' holy status by requiring their owners to consume them in a sacrificial meal at the chosen sanctuary, and in this way uses them as a means of linking the laity to the sanctuary and the religious experience it offers. See Comment to 12:6 and introductory Comment to 14:22–27.

The law of firstlings appears here because it is one of those that takes place at intervals of one or more years, like those which precede it. See Excursus 13. The procedures for observing this law are presented in the Mishnah, Tractate Bekhorot ("Firstlings").

19. *consecrate*[42]   Treat them as holy by not using them for any secular purpose and by eating them in a sacral meal. See Comment to "keep holy" in 5:12.

20. *you and your household shall eat it annually before the LORD*   As a *shelamim* sacrifice. See Comments to 12:6,7,27; 14:23; 27:7. According to 12:17–18, Levites were also invited to take part in the meal.

annually   The first-born cattle must be sacrificed within a year of their birth.[43] According to Exodus 22:29, the animal is to be sacrificed on the eighth day after its birth. This was possible when there were sanctuaries in every locality, but Deuteronomy's restriction of sacrifice to a single place necessitated a revision of that requirement. Under the present rule, the firstlings would presumably be sacrificed on one of the pilgrimage festivals (see Comment to 12:5). The prohibition of working or shearing the firstlings (v. 19) probably reflects this situation: now that a year might pass before the animal is sacrificed, the owner might be tempted to make use of it, especially since the softest, finest wool comes from lambs six to twelve months old. He is therefore warned that the animal's sacred status prohibits any such use.

21.   Only unblemished animals may be sacrificed to the Lord. The reason is expressed in Malachi 1:6–9: offering defective animals to God shows contempt; it is something one would never dare to do to a human governor. Hence sacrificing defective animals is called an abomination in 17:1 and is included among offenses that profane God's name in Leviticus, where the defects that disqualify an animal for sacrifice are listed (see Lev. 22:2,17–25,32).[44]

22.   A disqualified firstling may simply be eaten as food, and need not be replaced sacrificially by another animal, redeemed for money, or destroyed, as would the firstling of an impure animal.[45]

God. [22]Eat it in your settlements, the unclean among you no less than the clean, just like the gazelle and the deer. [23]Only you must not partake of its blood; you shall pour it out on the ground like water.

22 בִּשְׁעָרֶ֖יךָ תֹּאכֲלֶ֑נּוּ הַטָּמֵ֤א וְהַטָּהוֹר֙ יַחְדָּ֔ו כַּצְּבִ֖י וְכָאַיָּֽל׃ 23 רַ֥ק אֶת־דָּמ֖וֹ לֹ֣א תֹאכֵ֑ל עַל־הָאָ֛רֶץ תִּשְׁפְּכֶ֖נּוּ כַּמָּֽיִם׃ פ

16 Observe the month of Abib and offer a passover sacrifice to the LORD your God, for it was in the month of

ט״ז שָׁמוֹר֙ אֶת־חֹ֣דֶשׁ הָאָבִ֔יב וְעָשִׂ֣יתָ פֶּ֔סַח לַיהֹוָ֖ה אֱלֹהֶ֑יךָ כִּ֞י בְּחֹ֣דֶשׁ הָֽאָבִ֗יב הוֹצִֽיאֲךָ֛ יְהֹוָ֥ה

---

the unclean among you no less than the clean   See Comment to 12:15,22.

23.   See Comments to 12:16,23.

CHAPTER 16   THE PILGRIMAGE FESTIVALS   (vv. 1–17)

Chapter 16:1–17 describes the three pilgrimage festivals.[1] The first two form a pair framing the spring grain harvest: the Feast of Passover and Unleavened Bread precedes it and the Feast of Weeks follows it.[2] The third, the Feast of Booths, occurs in the fall when the new grain and wine are stored away for the winter. The reasons why this festival calendar follows the law of firstlings in 15:19–23 is discussed in Excursus 13.

The main themes of these festivals are commemoration of the Exodus and gratitude for the harvest. Deuteronomy's purpose in mentioning them is to make the point that they must be observed at the chosen sanctuary. For this reason it lists only the three festivals on which the people are required to be there. (Prior to the establishment of a single chosen sanctuary, the festivals would have been observed by a pilgrimage to any of the country's temple cities.) Further information about them appears in Exodus 12 and 13; 23:14–19; 34:18–26; Leviticus 23; and Numbers 9:1–14; 28–29. There are differences in practice among these passages. Halakhic exegesis harmonized the differences so as to create a unified, practicable system. This harmonization began during the biblical period and is reflected in the book of Chronicles. Critical theory holds that these differences reflect variations in practice over long periods, or in various places, or among diverse groups within ancient Israel.

THE *PESAḤ* SACRIFICE AND THE FEAST OF UNLEAVENED BREAD (vv. 1–8)

The first festival consists of two distinct institutions, the *pesaḥ* ("passover"), which refers only to the sacrifice offered at the end of the fourteenth day of the first month, and the Feast of Unleavened Bread, which technically refers only to the seven-day festival that begins on the fifteenth day (see Lev. 23:6; Num. 28:17). The *pesaḥ* sacrifice commemorates the sacrifice made by the Israelites on the night before the Exodus, while the Feast of Unleavened Bread commemorates the fact that the following morning they had to bake unleavened bread in their rush to leave Egypt. Nevertheless, since the two institutions occur on consecutive days, and since unleavened bread was also eaten along with the *pesaḥ* sacrifice, the latter could be spoken of as part of the Feast of Unleavened Bread, as in verses 4 and 16.[3] See also Comment to verse 3.

Since the Feast of *Pesaḥ* and Unleavened Bread commemorates the Exodus, it is known today as *zeman ḥerutenu*, "the time of our freedom." Although some think of it as a harvest festival, it actually falls before the harvest and does not celebrate God's bounty as do the other two feasts.[4] Nor does the Bible attribute to it any connection with the harvest. It is possible, however, that in the popular mind, eating primitive, unleavened bread was perceived as a type of abstinence expressing anxiety about the success of the coming harvest, as did the counting of weeks until its completion (see Comment on v. 9).[5]

1. Observe the month of Abib   Abib, or Aviv, is the old name or epithet of the month that falls in March and April. It means "new ears of grain," and refers to the fact that this month begins when immature ears of grain have begun to grow on the stalks.[6] Elsewhere in the Torah it is known as the first month. In books of the postexilic period, when Jews adopted the Babylonian month names still in use today, it is known as Nisan.[7]

Abib, at night, that the LORD your God freed you from Egypt. ²You shall slaughter the passover sacrifice for the LORD your God, from the flock and the herd, in the place where the LORD will choose to establish His name.

אֱלֹהֶיךָ מִמִּצְרַיִם לָיְלָה: ² וְזָבַחְתָּ פֶּסַח לַיהוָה
אֱלֹהֶיךָ צֹאן וּבָקָר בַּמָּקוֹם אֲשֶׁר־יִבְחַר יְהוָה
לְשַׁכֵּן שְׁמוֹ שָׁם: ³ לֹא־תֹאכַל עָלָיו חָמֵץ

The command to observe "the month of Abib" (ḥodesh ha-ʾaviv) may simply mean to observe the holiday during this month on a date that is well known and need not be specified, namely the fourteenth and fifteenth of the month, the dates given in the majority of passages in the Torah. Deuteronomy and some of the other festival calendars do not give specific dates for the festivals, but refer only to seasons, such as "at the end of the year."[8] These calendars may simply presume the same dates given in Leviticus 23. Another possibility is that "observe the month of Abib" means to observe all the ceremonies prescribed for the month of Aviv, including the selection of the sacrificial animal on the tenth day (Exod. 12:3), the first sheaf offering (Lev. 23:15), and the rites prescribed in the following verses.

However, ḥodesh can also be translated as "new moon," and in that case the command would mean "Observe the new moon of (the month of) Abib," referring to the first day of the month. Some scholars believe that this translation is favored by the second part of the verse, since "the LORD . . . took you out of Egypt in/on the ḥodesh of Abib, at night," seems to refer to a specific date. "The ḥodesh of Abib" also occurs in Exodus 13:4, where the context may imply that a specific date is meant. If "the new moon of (the month) of Abib" is the meaning intended here, the text may preserve a variant tradition that the Exodus occurred, and was to be celebrated, on the first day of the month rather than the fourteenth and fifteenth. That such a variant tradition is possible is suggested by a similar disagreement in the Mishnah between the schools of Hillel and Shammai over whether the "new year of trees" is on the fifteenth day of the month of Shevat or the first.[9]

In halakhic exegesis "observe the month of new ears of grain" serves as the Scriptural warrant for creating leap years by periodically adding an extra month to the year to coordinate the lunar year with the longer solar year (a system followed in ancient Mesopotamia). The verse was read as meaning: be sure that Passover falls in the month when new ears of grain have actually appeared, and if the grain will not reach that stage after the month of Adar, add an additional month (Adar II) to the year.[10]

passover sacrifice Or "protective sacrifice." This sacrifice, called *pesaḥ* in Hebrew, reenacts the original *pesaḥ* sacrifice that the Israelites performed on the eve of the Exodus right before the last of the ten plagues. The name is derived from the verb *pasaḥ*, which describes the manner in which God spared the firstborn in the houses of Israel after they smeared the blood of the sacrifice on their doorposts and lintels (see Exod. 12:13,23,27). The Vulgate translates the verb as "(the LORD) passed over" and the name of the sacrifice as "passover." However, the Hebrew verb does not mean "pass over." Most of the ancient translations and commentaries render the verb as "(the LORD) spared," "had compassion," or "protected," and the name of the sacrifice as "protective sacrifice," referring to the protection of Israel during the final plague. This rendering is supported by the way the verb is used in Isaiah 31:5.[11]

at night Although the Israelites themselves started to leave Egypt "on the morrow of the passover offering" (Num. 33:3), God's action—the slaying of Egypt's firstborn at night—is viewed as the essence of the event.[12] See also verse 6.

2. from the flock and from the herd According to Exodus 12:3–5 and 21, the *pesaḥ* offering was brought only from the flock. Since Exodus 12:24–25 states that the same rite is to be observed in the future, it presumably intends the offering to be limited to sheep and goats in the future as well, as the halakhah inferred. The present verse, which permits bovines as well, is inconsistent with that. Halakhic exegesis resolved the conflict in favor of Exodus, limiting the *pesaḥ* offering to sheep and goats and taking the large cattle of our verse as referring to extra offerings in honor of the festival. This view was already adopted in late biblical times, as can be seen from 2 Chronicles 35:7–13, where bovines are spoken of separately from the *pesaḥ* offerings and are used for "sacred offerings."[13]

The difference between Exodus and Deuteronomy may be due to the fact that the original *pesaḥ*, in Exodus, was offered by individual households, for which even a single head of small cattle might

³You shall not eat anything leavened with it; for seven days thereafter you shall eat unleavened bread, bread of distress—for you departed from the land of Egypt hurriedly—so that you may remember the day of your departure from the land of Egypt as long as you live. ⁴For seven days no leaven shall be found with you in all your territory,

שִׁבְעַת יָמִים תֹּאכַל־עָלָיו מַצּוֹת לֶחֶם עֹנִי כִּי בְחִפָּזוֹן יָצָאתָ מֵאֶרֶץ מִצְרַיִם לְמַעַן תִּזְכֹּר אֶת־יוֹם צֵאתְךָ מֵאֶרֶץ מִצְרַיִם כֹּל יְמֵי חַיֶּיךָ: 4 וְלֹא־יֵרָאֶה לְךָ שְׂאֹר בְּכָל־גְּבֻלְךָ שִׁבְעַת יָמִים וְלֹא־

have been too much to consume (Exod. 12:4), whereas Deuteronomy deals with a time when the sacrifice would be made at the central sanctuary and many households could share a larger animal. Another possibility is that the *pesaḥ* offering originated at a time when the Israelites owned primarily sheep and goats (cf. Gen. 46:32–47:4), and that Deuteronomy reflects later conditions when large cattle had also become important in their economy.

3.   *anything leavened*   Any food prepared from dough to which a leavening agent was added to make it rise. According to halakhic exegesis this means any leavened product of wheat, barley, spelt, rye, or oats. In Ashkenazic practice, rice, millet, corn, and legumes are also not permitted.[14]

unleavened bread   *Matsah*, bread made without yeast and not allowed to rise. Since it can be made quickly, it was commonly prepared for unexpected guests. It was probably similar to the flat unleavened bread that bedouins still bake on embers and that Arab peasants prepare for unexpected guests. Prior to modern times *matsah* was usually shaped like a disk and was not as thin or crisp as it now is.[15]

bread of distress   The *matsah* is primitive, unluxurious fare that one would not normally eat. "Bread of distress" can be understood as "bread of poverty" or "bread of affliction," suggesting that it is eaten by the poor or those intentionally deprived, such as prisoners.[16] Since the term distress (*'oni*) is sometimes used to describe Israel's affliction in Egypt, it has been assumed that this phrase means that the Israelites ate unleavened bread when they were slaves.[17] However, according to Exodus, eating unleavened bread recalls the haste of the Exodus, not the bondage (Exod. 12:39; 13:8–10).

so that you may remember the day of your departure from the land of Egypt   By reenacting the first *pesaḥ* sacrifice and by eating unleavened bread. The unleavened bread recalls the Exodus in two ways: it was eaten in conjunction with the first *pesaḥ* sacrifice (Exod. 12:8), and the Israelites had to bake unleavened bread while rushing to leave Egypt because there was no time to wait for it to become leavened (Exod. 12:39).

This verse combines two prohibitions into one: eating leavened food with the *pesaḥ* sacrifice, and eating leavened food on the following seven days. These began as separate prohibitions. Eating unleavened bread for seven days commemorates the hasty departure from Egypt when there was no time to bake leavened bread, but eating it with the *pesaḥ* sacrifice the night before the Exodus could not have been due to this. It must have been due to the general preference for unleavened food in connection with most sacrifices.[18] Our verse subtly combines these independent practices into one. By saying, literally, "You shall not eat anything leavened with it ['*alayv*]; for seven days you shall eat unleavened bread with it ['*alayv*]," it relates both prohibitions to the sacrifice and then explains, in the last part of the verse, that both commemorate the haste of the Exodus. This implies that the prohibition of eating leaven with the original *pesaḥ* sacrifice was a foreshadowing of the next day's hasty departure. In this way the text blends the *pesaḥ* sacrifice into the Feast of Unleavened Bread.[19]

4.   *no leaven shall be found with you*   "Leaven" (Heb. *se'or*) refers to leavening agents, such as sourdough or yeast. It differs from "anything leavened" (Heb. *ḥamets*, v. 3), which refers to foodstuffs that have been leavened by *se'or*.

Literally this clause means "no leaven shall be seen by you." Since "by you" (*lekha*) can also be translated "of yours," halakhic exegesis took the clause to mean that only leaven belonging to Jews had to be eliminated, not that belonging to gentiles. This interpretation serves as the warrant for temporarily selling leavened goods to gentiles so as to avoid the economic hardship that would result from the destruction of large quantities of leavened goods.[20]

and none of the flesh of what you slaughter on the evening of the first day shall be left until morning.

⁵You are not permitted to slaughter the passover sacrifice in any of the settlements that the LORD your God is giving you; ⁶but at the place where the LORD your God will choose to establish His name, there alone shall you slaughter the passover sacrifice, in the evening, at sundown, the time of day when you departed from Egypt. ⁷You shall cook and eat it at the place that the LORD your God will choose; and in the morning you may start back on your journey home. ⁸After eating unleavened bread six

יָלִין מִן־הַבָּשָׂר אֲשֶׁר תִּזְבַּח בָּעֶרֶב בַּיּוֹם הָרִאשׁוֹן לַבֹּקֶר:

5 לֹא תוּכַל לִזְבֹּחַ אֶת־הַפָּסַח בְּאַחַד שְׁעָרֶיךָ אֲשֶׁר־יְהוָה אֱלֹהֶיךָ נֹתֵן לָךְ: 6 כִּי אִם־אֶל־הַמָּקוֹם אֲשֶׁר־יִבְחַר יְהוָה אֱלֹהֶיךָ לְשַׁכֵּן שְׁמוֹ שָׁם תִּזְבַּח אֶת־הַפֶּסַח בָּעָרֶב כְּבוֹא הַשֶּׁמֶשׁ מוֹעֵד צֵאתְךָ מִמִּצְרָיִם: 7 וּבִשַּׁלְתָּ וְאָכַלְתָּ בַּמָּקוֹם אֲשֶׁר יִבְחַר יְהוָה אֱלֹהֶיךָ בּוֹ וּפָנִיתָ בַבֹּקֶר וְהָלַכְתָּ לְאֹהָלֶיךָ: 8 שֵׁשֶׁת יָמִים תֹּאכַל

none of the flesh . . . shall be left until morning   The sacrifice is made at sunset (v. 6). It has to be eaten through the night and finished by morning, in imitation of the original *pesah* sacrifice in Egypt (Exod. 12:8).²¹

5–6. Deuteronomy's characteristic requirement: once sacrificial worship is centralized in the chosen place, the *pesah* offering must be made there. According to the books of Kings and Chronicles, before Josiah enforced the law of centralization there had been no united celebration of the festival since the days of the chieftains and Samuel (2 Kings 23:22; 2 Chron. 35:18).

The text emphasizes that the *pesah* offering must be made at the chosen place by stating this three times (see also vv. 2 and 7). Some scholars believe that prior to the centralization of worship the *pesah* was offered at private homes, as it was in Egypt, rather than at sanctuaries, and that its new location had to be emphasized lest people think that they should continue offering it at home so as to faithfully reenact the original sacrifice.²²

6. ***the time of day when you departed from Egypt***   See Comment to verse 1, "at night." The original *pesah* sacrifice, which was indispensable in assuring the safety of the Israelites during the tenth plague, is here viewed as the beginning of the Exodus.

7. ***cook***   Hebrew *b-sh-l* normally means "boil."²³ If that is the meaning here, the verse contradicts Exodus 12:8–9, which requires that the *pesah* be roasted and not boiled (*b-sh-l*) in water. 2 Chronicles 35:13 says that King Josaiah's *pesah* offering was *b-sh-l* "in fire." Chronicles is probably alluding to our verse with the intention of indicating that *b-sh-l* can refer to any kind of cooking and that our verse does not contradict Exodus. Since *b-sh-l* refers to several kinds of cooking in Akkadian, it may well have had an equally broad meaning in Hebrew, and Chronicles' clarification may indeed represent the meaning intended by Deuteronomy. Otherwise, it is harmonizing the verses by means of halakhic midrash.

in the morning you may start on your journey back home²⁴   The entire seven days need not be spent at the chosen place, since it is necessary to return home in time to begin the harvest.

This provision has occasioned considerable discussion since it seems to imply, contrary to the halakhah, that travel was permitted on the first day of the Feast of Unleavened Bread, which according to Exodus 12:16 and Leviticus 23:7 is a sacred day on which no work may be done. Perhaps Deuteronomy does not regard travel as forbidden on festival days (according to the Tosafot, the prohibition of traveling on festivals is a rabbinic enactment).²⁵ It is also possible that Deuteronomy does not regard the second part of the day, following the *pesah* sacrifice and meal, as sacred. This could be an adjustment of the law due to the centralization of worship. Since the chosen place was far from the towns of many pilgrims, perhaps Deuteronomy treated the remainder of the day, after daybreak, as profane so that people could return home quickly in time for the harvest. Some traditional commentators hold that "in the morning" refers to the morning of the second day of the festival.²⁶

8. ***After eating unleavened bread six days***   That is, for the first six of the seven days on which it must be eaten (v. 3). Another possible interpretation is: After leaving for home on the first day (v. 7), you shall eat unleavened bread for six days more.²⁷ According to the halakhah, eating

days, you shall hold a solemn gathering for the LORD your God on the seventh day: you shall do no work.

⁹You shall count off seven weeks; start to count the seven weeks when the sickle is first put to the standing

מַצּוֹת וּבַיּוֹם הַשְּׁבִיעִי עֲצֶרֶת לַיהוָה אֱלֹהֶיךָ לֹא תַעֲשֶׂה מְלָאכָה: ס
9 שִׁבְעָה שָׁבֻעֹת תִּסְפָּר־לָךְ מֵהָחֵל חֶרְמֵשׁ בַּקָּמָה

unleavened bread is obligatory only on the first day; on the remaining days, as long as nothing leavened is eaten, it is not obligatory to eat unleavened bread.[28]

solemn gathering Hebrew *'atseret*.[29] Since this gathering occurs after the people have returned home, it must take place in their hometowns. This indicates that Deuteronomy intends nonsacrificial religious gatherings to take place throughout the country; only sacrifice is restricted to the chosen place. Such local gatherings may well have been the earliest forerunners of the synagogue. Indeed, the Targum renders *'atseret* as *kenish*, "gathering," which is related to the Aramaic and Hebrew terms for synagogue (Heb. *beit keneset*, lit., "house of gathering").

do no work According to Exodus 12:16, the preparation of food is not prohibited as it is on the Sabbath.

According to the preceding books of the Torah, this prohibition also applies to the Feast of Weeks and the first and last days of the Feast of Booths. Deuteronomy mentions it only here, probably because the last day of the Feast of Unleavened Bread is the only festival ceremony that people would celebrate at home, and the only one that might take place at the height of the harvest, when the need to work would seem pressing. For the other festivals they would be at the chosen sanctuary, where the prohibition would be obvious, and people would be far from their places of work.[30]

THE FEAST OF WEEKS (vv. 9–12)

The Feast of Weeks celebrates the grain harvest, as indicated by its other names and epithets, "the Feast of the Harvest" and "the day of the first fruits" of the grain harvest (see Exod. 23:16; 34:22; Num. 28:26).

The name of the festival is derived from the fact that it is observed exactly seven weeks after the onset of the harvest. The passage of seven weeks ("the weeks appointed for reaping," Jer. 5:24) is an essential aspect of the festival. Until seven weeks have passed, it is not known whether the harvest will be successfully completed and plentiful enough to sustain life and not be damaged by late rain or pests. As David Abudraham, the fourteenth-century commentator on the liturgy, noted: "Some explain [the counting of days and weeks] on the ground that the world is anxious between Pesah and Weeks about the crops and the fruit trees. . . . Therefore God commanded us to count these days, to keep the anxiety of the world in mind and to turn to Him in wholehearted repentance, to plead with Him to have mercy upon us, upon mankind and on the land, so that the crops should turn out well, for they are our life." The quasi-mourning character of the seven weeks of counting (*Sefirah*) in Jewish practice also expresses this anxiety.[31]

At least since Second Temple times the Feast of Weeks has served to commemorate the giving of the Torah, which began with the revelation of the Ten Commandments at Mount Sinai. For this reason it is known as *zeman mattan Toratenu*, "the time when our Torah was given." This function of the festival was based on the calculation that its date coincides with the date which Exodus 19 implies for the revelation.[32]

9. you shall count off That is, calculate. The halakhah gives concrete form to the calculation by prescribing a ceremonial oral counting daily.[33]

seven weeks This was the period of time required to complete the harvest. That approximately seven weeks were required is confirmed by a tenth-century-B.C.E. inscription found at Gezer that lists the characteristic agricultural activities of the year. According to the inscription, the barley harvest took place one month and "the harvest [of wheat] and measuring" took place the following month.[34] This is consistent with a period extending from early in one month to late in the next.

start to count the seven weeks when the sickle is first put to the standing grain That is, when the grain harvest begins, normally in April. The text gives no exact date. Leviticus 23:9–21

grain. ¹⁰Then you shall observe the Feast of Weeks for the LORD your God, offering your freewill contribution according as the LORD your God has blessed you. ¹¹You shall rejoice before the LORD your God with your son and daughter, your male and female slave, the Levite in your communities, and the stranger, the fatherless, and the widow in your midst, at the place where the LORD your God will choose to establish His name. ¹²Bear in mind that you were slaves in Egypt, and take care to obey these laws.

תָּחֵל לִסְפֹּר שִׁבְעָה שָׁבֻעֽוֹת: ¹⁰ וְעָשִׂ֜יתָ חַ֤ג
שָׁבֻעוֹת֙ לַיהֹוָ֣ה אֱלֹהֶ֔יךָ מִסַּ֛ת נִדְבַ֥ת יָֽדְךָ֖ אֲשֶׁ֣ר
תִּתֵּ֑ן כַּאֲשֶׁ֥ר יְבָרֶכְךָ֖ יְהֹוָ֥ה אֱלֹהֶֽיךָ: ¹¹ וְשָׂמַחְתָּ֞
לִפְנֵ֣י | יְהֹוָ֣ה אֱלֹהֶ֗יךָ אַתָּ֨ה וּבִנְךָ֣ וּבִתֶּ֣ךָ וְעַבְדְּךָ֣
וַאֲמָתֶ֗ךָ וְהַלֵּוִי֙ אֲשֶׁ֣ר בִּשְׁעָרֶ֔יךָ וְהַגֵּ֛ר וְהַיָּת֥וֹם
וְהָֽאַלְמָנָ֖ה אֲשֶׁ֣ר בְּקִרְבֶּ֑ךָ בַּמָּק֔וֹם אֲשֶׁ֣ר יִבְחַר֙
יְהֹוָ֣ה אֱלֹהֶ֔יךָ לְשַׁכֵּ֥ן שְׁמ֖וֹ שָֽׁם: ¹² וְזָכַרְתָּ֗ כִּי־עֶ֤בֶד
הָיִ֙יתָ֙ בְּמִצְרָ֔יִם וְשָׁמַרְתָּ֣ וְעָשִׂ֔יתָ אֶת־הַֽחֻקִּ֖ים
הָאֵֽלֶּה: פ מפטיר

likewise gives no fixed dates for beginning the counting or for the Feast of Weeks, although (unlike the present chapter) it gives exact dates for all other holidays. This is probably due to the fact that the harvest begins on different dates from year to year and, because of regional variations in climate, from place to place.³⁵ Perhaps, then, the counting would begin at different times in different places, and seven weeks later, after completing the harvest, farmers would travel to the sanctuary to observe the Feast of Weeks. This would mean that farmers from different places observe the feast at different times. The fact that the date was still debated in the Second Temple period (see the next paragraph) may also be due to the lack of a fixed date earlier.

According to Leviticus 23:11, the counting begins with an offering of the first sheaf of the harvest "on the day after the Sabbath." From the context this seems to refer to the Sunday after the first sheaf is cut, whenever that should occur, some time during or after the Feast of Unleavened Bread. In Second Temple times it was assumed that "on the day after the Sabbath" does refer to an exact date. There was controversy among various Jewish sects as to whether a Sabbath within the Feast of Unleavened Bread was meant or one following it. The Pharisees held that "the day after the Sabbath" does not mean a Sunday at all, but the day after a Sabbath-like holiday, namely the first day of the Feast of Unleavened Bread. This became the basis of the halakhic ruling that the first sheaf is brought, and the counting begins, on the second day of the feast, the sixteenth of Nisan, and that the Feast of Weeks falls on the sixth of Sivan (May-June).³⁶

10. As noted above, tithes and firstlings and freewill and obligatory offerings were presumably brought on the Feast of Weeks as on other festivals (see Comments to 12:6; 14:23; and 15:20). According to Leviticus 23:16–21, the Feast of Weeks is also a day of solemn gathering on which no work is permitted, and loaves made of new grain are offered as first fruits of the grain harvest. The ceremony prescribed for "every first fruit" in chapter 26 is not tied to this festival, and apparently first fruits of other products were brought at various times (see Comment to 26:2). According to the halakhah, they were brought between the Feast of Weeks and the Feast of Booths, whenever the farmer wished to bring them.³⁷

*offering*³⁸ *your freewill contribution according as the LORD has blessed you* That is, offering what you can afford as a result of the harvest (cf. v. 17; 12:15; 15:14). The contribution might be of produce, animals, or money. It is noteworthy that the present passage mentions only the freewill offering. Perhaps this is because the feeling of prosperity, and hence generosity, would be foremost in the farmer's mind after the harvest.

11. See Comments to 12:7,12 and below, verse 16.

12. As elsewhere in Deuteronomy, the memory of slavery is invoked to motivate extending the benefits of this prescription to servants and other poor individuals. See 5:15 and Comment to 15:15. This verse undoubtedly applies to verse 14 as well.

THE FEAST OF BOOTHS (vv. 13–17)

The third feast, at the end of the summer, celebrates the gathering of grain and new wine into storage for the coming year, the goal of all the preceding agricultural activities.³⁹ It is described

¹³After the ingathering from your threshing floor and your vat, you shall hold the Feast of Booths for seven days. ¹⁴You shall rejoice in your festival, with your son and daughter, your male and female slave, the Levite, the stranger, the fatherless, and the widow in your communities. ¹⁵You shall hold a festival for the LORD your God seven days, in the place that the LORD will choose; for the LORD your God will bless all your crops and all your undertakings, and you shall have nothing but joy.

13 חַג הַסֻּכֹּת תַּעֲשֶׂה לְךָ שִׁבְעַת יָמִים בְּאָסְפְּךָ מִגָּרְנְךָ וּמִיִּקְבֶךָ: 14 וְשָׂמַחְתָּ בְּחַגֶּךָ אַתָּה וּבִנְךָ וּבִתֶּךָ וְעַבְדְּךָ וַאֲמָתֶךָ וְהַלֵּוִי וְהַגֵּר וְהַיָּתוֹם וְהָאַלְמָנָה אֲשֶׁר בִּשְׁעָרֶיךָ: 15 שִׁבְעַת יָמִים תָּחֹג לַיהוָה אֱלֹהֶיךָ בַּמָּקוֹם אֲשֶׁר־יִבְחַר יְהוָה כִּי יְבָרֶכְךָ יְהוָה אֱלֹהֶיךָ בְּכֹל תְּבוּאָתְךָ וּבְכֹל מַעֲשֵׂה יָדֶיךָ וְהָיִיתָ אַךְ שָׂמֵחַ:

elsewhere as "the Feast of Ingathering at the end of the year, when you gather in the results of your work from the field" (Exod. 23:16; cf. 34:22 and Lev. 23:39). According to Leviticus 23:35–43, it begins on the fifteenth day of the seventh month (Tishri, or September–October) and its first and last day are sacred occasions on which no work is permitted. It is characterized by dwelling in booths and the ceremonial use of "the product of *hadar* trees, branches of palm trees, boughs of leafy trees, and willows of the brook." According to Numbers 29:12–38, it is marked by large numbers of sacrifices.

This is the most joyous of the festivals, for which reason it has come to be called *zeman simhatenu*, "the time of our rejoicing." It takes place when the bounty of the harvest is manifest and farmers have the leisure to remain at the sanctuary for all seven days of the festival, the longest stay of all the three pilgrimages. It is often called simply "the Feast," meaning "the festival *par excellence*,"[40] and its sacrifices are the most numerous of all the festivals. According to Deuteronomy 31:10–13, this is the festival on which "the Teaching" (*ha-torah*) is to be read to the entire nation every seventh year, perhaps because it is the festival that would attract the largest number of pilgrims to the chosen place.

Zechariah 14:17 implies that on this festival prayers were recited for rain during the coming winter months. This dimension of the festival is reflected in some of the prayers and ceremonies prescribed for it in talmudic literature, including the practice of praising God for giving rain in the Amidah prayer from Shemini ʿAtseret (the festival concluding Sukkot according to Lev. 23:36) until the first day of Passover.[41] To this day a prayer for rain (*tefillat geshem*) is recited on Shemini ʿAtseret.

13. *After the ingathering from your threshing floor and from the vat* That is, after the processed grain and the must (unfermented grape juice) are put in containers and stored away in advance of the autumn rains. These are the raw materials for the most important manmade foods, bread and wine (see Comments to 6:12 and 8:8). The processing of grain—threshing, winnowing, sifting, and measuring—can last through the summer. The grape harvest begins in late June or July, and the pressing of the grapes likewise continues until the end of the summer.[42]

Feast of Booths According to Leviticus 23:42, the festival is named for the practice of dwelling in booths, or bowers, during the seven-day festival. The meaning of this practice is discussed in Excursus 17.

14. *rejoice in your festival* Rather, "celebrate on your festival." See Comment to "happy" in 12:7. The harvest season and festivals were proverbial for celebration, as reflected in the similes "as they rejoice at reaping time" and "singing as on a night when a festival is hallowed . . . rejoicing as when they march to the Mount of the LORD" (Isa. 9:2; 30:29). The Psalmist, too, tells of "the festive throng [going] to the House of God with joyous shouts of praise" (Ps. 42:5).

with your son and daughter See Comments to 12:7,12.

15. *for the LORD will bless* Note the sweep of the promise: "*all* your crops . . . *all* your undertakings . . . *nothing but* joy." The totality of the blessing explains why the celebrating is to last a full seven days.

16Three times a year—on the Feast of Unleavened Bread, on the Feast of Weeks, and on the Feast of Booths—all your males shall appear before the LORD your God in the place that He will choose. They shall not appear before the LORD empty-handed, 17but each with his own gift, according to the blessing that the LORD your God has bestowed upon you.

שָׁלוֹשׁ פְּעָמִים ׀ בַּשָּׁנָה יֵרָאֶה כָל־זְכוּרְךָ֮ אֶת־ 16
פְּנֵי ׀ יְהוָה אֱלֹהֶיךָ בַּמָּקוֹם אֲשֶׁר יִבְחָר בְּחַג
הַמַּצּוֹת וּבְחַג הַשָּׁבֻעוֹת וּבְחַג הַסֻּכּוֹת וְלֹא יֵרָאֶה
אֶת־פְּנֵי יְהוָה רֵיקָם: 17 אִישׁ כְּמַתְּנַת יָדוֹ כְּבִרְכַּת
יְהוָה אֱלֹהֶיךָ אֲשֶׁר נָתַן־לָךְ: ס

SUMMARY (vv. 16–17)

Every male Israelite must present himself before God three times a year. The point of this duty is made clear in the earlier formulation of this commandment, where God is called "the Sovereign" (Exod. 23:17; 34:23; cf. Zech. 14:16). God is Israel's king, and His subjects must appear before Him regularly to acknowledge His sovereignty, just as subjects of a human suzerain were required to acknowledge his sovereignty by appearing before him regularly at his residence.[43]

16. *males*   Only the adult males are obligated to appear, probably because pregnant and nursing women and young children could not reasonably be required to make long trips. Nevertheless, women and children frequently did take part, as is clear from verses 11 and 14.[44]

on the Feast of Unleavened Bread   Here this term must refer to the night of the *pesaḥ* sacrifice (and not the following seven days), since that is the only time, according to verse 7, that worshipers are required to be at the chosen place. Note also the end of verse 4, where the sacrifice is said to take place on "the first day," that is, the first of the seven days of the Feast of Unleavened Bread. The term "Feast of Unleavened Bread" does not normally have this meaning, but see also Exodus 12:18, where the week of eating unleavened bread is said to begin on the fourteenth of the month—when the *pesaḥ* sacrifice takes place.[45]

appear before the LORD   The translation "appear before" conveys the meaning intended by the traditional vocalization of the Hebrew text, *yera'eh . . . 'et penei YHVH*, literally, "be seen at the face of the LORD." However, grammatically the simplest way to understand *'et penei YHVH* is as a direct object, suggesting that the first word was originally vocalized *yir'eh*, "shall see," and that the clause means "shall see the face of the LORD." Idiomatically the expression probably does not mean to literally see God, but to visit Him and pay homage to Him at His sanctuary. If this was indeed the original reading, the vocalization was probably changed because of the danger that the idiomatic meaning might be misunderstood to mean that God could literally be seen there.[46]

17. *each with his own gift*   Rather, "each according to his means," as in verse 10.[47]

Civil and Religious Authorities   (16:18–18:22)

Shofetim

The weekly portion *Shofetim* (Judges), which deals with the responsibilities of public officials, begins here and continues through 21:9. It introduces four main types of human authorities: judges, kings, priests, and prophets (nothing is said of the elders, perhaps because their authority was traditional and taken for granted). Unlike a constitution, the text does not give a thorough definition of their offices and duties, but emphasizes broad principles. Prominence is given to the limits established by God on the rights of each authority. By dispersing authority and prestige among various officials and limiting their powers, Deuteronomy seeks to prevent the development of a single, strong focus of prestige and power.

That these limitations are here made known to the public is an important and original feature of the Torah. It lays the ground for public supervision and criticism of human authorities, and prevents them from gaining absolute authority and prestige. Knowledge of these limitations empowers citizens to resist and protest abuses of authority. Prophets in particular exercised this power to admonish kings, officials, and priests as well as the people for moral and religious sins.[1]

For the reasons why this section appears here, see Excursus 13.

SHOFETIM

18You shall appoint magistrates and officials for your tribes, in all the settlements that the LORD your God is giving you, and they shall govern the people with due justice. **19**You shall not judge unfairly: you shall show no partiality; you shall not take bribes, for bribes blind the

שופטים
18 שֹׁפְטִים וְשֹׁטְרִים תִּתֶּן־לְךָ בְּכָל־שְׁעָרֶיךָ אֲשֶׁר
יְהוָה אֱלֹהֶיךָ נֹתֵן לְךָ לִשְׁבָטֶיךָ וְשָׁפְטוּ אֶת־הָעָם
מִשְׁפַּט־צֶדֶק: 19 לֹא־תַטֶּה מִשְׁפָּט לֹא תַכִּיר פָּנִים
וְלֹא־תִקַּח שֹׁחַד כִּי הַשֹּׁחַד יְעַוֵּר עֵינֵי חֲכָמִים

THE JUDICIARY (16:18–17:13)

First mentioned are judges and related officials. The paragraph assumes that the judicial system established in 1:13–17 will not continue in the promised land, presumably because it was tailored to the military requirements of the trek through the wilderness and the conquest of the land, but not suitable for conditions after settlement in the land.

The paragraph falls into four units: the appointment of local judges (16:18–20); a group of religious rules (16:21–17:1); the judicial procedure to be followed in cases of apostasy (17:2–7); and the high court of referral (17:8–13).[2]

APPOINTING JUDGES AND OFFICIALS (vv. 18–20)

Judges and officials are to be appointed to judge the people justly. The description of the judges as "discerning" in verse 19, and the qualifications listed in 1:13 (see Comment there) indicate that the judges should be chosen for their wisdom. Nothing more is said about their qualifications or the method of appointment. Characteristically, Deuteronomy devotes attention instead to the broad principles of judicial propriety that they are to follow.

18. *magistrates and officials . . . and they shall govern* Rather, "judges and officials . . . and they shall judge"; see Comments to 1:15–16. It is clear from the next verse that the context refers to adjudication, not to government in general. This is consistent with the fact that warnings against favoritism and bribes commonly appear in instructions to judges.[3]

The command to appoint judges and officials is addressed to the people (literally the text reads "appoint for yourselves"), implying that they, or the elders on their behalf, are to make the appointments. At first, judging was probably not separate from other aspects of leadership and was done by the elders of a tribe or village acting collectively, as in several cases mentioned later in Deuteronomy (see Comment to 19:12). It is not clear whom Deuteronomy has in mind when it speaks of "judges" (*shofetim*) as distinct from elders (see 17:9,12; 19:17–18; 21:2; and 25:2). It is possible that when a village chief was chosen from among the leading elders, he became the judge, just as a sheikh is chosen in traditional Arab society.[4] Deuteronomy also assigns priests a role in judging, although their precise role is unclear (see Comment to 17:9). In later times, judges were also appointed by national figures such as the prophet Samuel, who appointed his sons, and by kings.[5]

19. This and the next verse state the three fundamental rules of judicial propriety, all of which are reiterated frequently in the Bible. These rules are addressed to the entire people,[6] unlike 1:16–17, where the obligation to judge fairly is addressed only to the judges. Here, Moses may want to indicate that all Israelites are responsible to ensure that the judges act fairly. Or, he may address all Israelites because any of them might become a judge, either by virtue of being an elder or in some other way (Deborah, for example, was a judge by virtue of being a prophetess).[7]

You shall not judge unfairly By ruling in favor of the guilty and against the innocent. This injunction is often invoked in connection with cases involving the needy, who were most vulnerable to judicial mistreatment. Here, however, it is stated as a comprehensive rule: do not judge anyone unfairly.[8]

you shall show no partiality The principle is addressed to judges in 1:17 and stated more fully in Leviticus 19:15: "Do not favor the poor or show deference to the rich; judge your kinsman fairly."[9]

eyes of the discerning and upset the plea of the just. [20]Justice, justice shall you pursue, that you may thrive and occupy the land that the LORD your God is giving you.

[21]You shall not set up a sacred post—any kind of pole beside the altar of the LORD your God that you may make—[22]or erect a stone pillar; for such the LORD your God detests.

20 צֶדֶק צֶדֶק תִּרְדֹּף לְמַעַן תִּחְיֶה וְיָרַשְׁתָּ אֶת־הָאָרֶץ אֲשֶׁר־יְהוָה אֱלֹהֶיךָ נֹתֵן לָךְ: ס

21 לֹא־תִטַּע לְךָ אֲשֵׁרָה כָּל־עֵץ אֵצֶל מִזְבַּח יְהוָה אֱלֹהֶיךָ אֲשֶׁר תַּעֲשֶׂה־לָּךְ: ס 22 וְלֹא־תָקִים לְךָ מַצֵּבָה אֲשֶׁר שָׂנֵא יְהוָה אֱלֹהֶיךָ: ס

bribes   Rather, probably, "gifts."[10] Hebrew *shoḥad* refers to a gift for which something is expected in return. Although one of its common meanings is a payoff intended to influence judges (see 27:25; Isa. 5:23), it does not always refer to a gift given with dishonest intent. The prophets use it to refer to fees charged by judges merely for hearing cases.[11] If that is the meaning here, the point would be that judges may not accept fees since a fee paid by one party to a dispute would inevitably incline the judge in that party's favor. Had the text intended merely to prohibit a bribe, there would probably have been no need to add an explanation at the end of the verse.[12]

for bribes blind the eyes of the discerning   The same saying in Exodus 23:8 reads "blind the clear-sighted," a more natural idiom. Deuteronomy's choice of the word "discerning" (lit., "wise") is in keeping with its emphasis on the intellectual qualifications of judges. See Comment to 1:13. The explanation is in a poetic style resembling that of wisdom literature; compare Ecclesiastes 7:7: "for cheating may rob the wise man of reason and destroy the prudence of the cautious."

upset the plea of the just   That is, influence the judge against the claims of the innocent party.

20.   The injunctions of the previous verse have all been stated earlier in the Torah. Characteristically, Deuteronomy adds an exhortation pleading for the basic principle of justice and seeks to persuade its audience to follow it by emphasizing the benefits it will bring.

justice, justice   That is, justice alone, justice and only justice.[13]

that you may thrive and occupy the land   The pursuit of justice is an indispensable condition for God's enabling Israel to endure and thrive in the promised land.

THREE PROHIBITIONS REGARDING WORSHIP (16:21–17:1)

Three unacceptable religious practices are prohibited. Possible reasons why these verses follow those concerning the appointment of judges are discussed in Excursus 13.

21. sacred post   As noted in the Comment to 7:5, an *'asherah* was a standing wooden object at a place of worship, and its significance is uncertain. Not all objects of this type were inherently idolatrous. Abraham worshiped the Lord at a tamarisk, and there were trees in the sanctuary of the Lord at Shechem and in the Temple.[14] Trees may have symbolized the protection or fertility the worshiper hoped to receive from a deity. The reason Deuteronomy bans objects of this type from sanctuaries of the Lord is probably because they were associated with Canaanite deities[15] and might eventually have led the Israelites to blur the distinctions between Israelite and Canaanite religion. Compare Rashi's comment about pillars, quoted in the Comment to verse 22.

any kind of pole   Rather, "any treelike object," whether a natural tree, an artificial one, or a pole. This broad definition of a sacred post prevents anyone from claiming that the prohibition covers only certain objects of this type and that others are legitimate. Such a distinction could lead to confusion that can only be prevented by a comprehensive ban.[16]

beside the altar . . . that you may make   The prohibition applies to the many altars that would be legitimate prior to centralization, not only to the chosen sanctuary.[17]

22. stone pillar   See Comment to 7:5. Unadorned pillars, like sacred posts, were thought of as monuments or residences of God and were at one time considered legitimate in Israelite religion. Jacob erected one to the Lord at Bethel, Moses set up twelve at Mount Sinai, and Joshua set

17 You shall not sacrifice to the LORD your God an ox or a sheep that has any defect of a serious kind, for that is abhorrent to the LORD your God.

י"ז לֹא־תִזְבַּח לַיהֹוָה אֱלֹהֶיךָ שׁוֹר וָשֶׂה אֲשֶׁר יִהְיֶה בוֹ מוּם כֹּל דָּבָר רָע כִּי תוֹעֲבַת יְהֹוָה אֱלֹהֶיךָ הוּא: ס

²If there is found among you, in one of the settlements that the LORD your God is giving you, a man or woman who has affronted the LORD your God and transgressed His covenant—³turning to the worship of other gods and bowing down to them, to the sun or the moon or any of the heavenly host, something I never commanded—⁴and you

² כִּי־יִמָּצֵא בְקִרְבְּךָ בְּאַחַד שְׁעָרֶיךָ אֲשֶׁר־יְהֹוָה אֱלֹהֶיךָ נֹתֵן לָךְ אִישׁ אוֹ־אִשָּׁה אֲשֶׁר יַעֲשֶׂה אֶת־הָרַע בְּעֵינֵי יְהֹוָה־אֱלֹהֶיךָ לַעֲבֹר בְּרִיתוֹ: 3 וַיֵּלֶךְ וַיַּעֲבֹד אֱלֹהִים אֲחֵרִים וַיִּשְׁתַּחוּ לָהֶם וְלַשֶּׁמֶשׁ | אוֹ לַיָּרֵחַ אוֹ לְכָל־צְבָא הַשָּׁמַיִם אֲשֶׁר לֹא־צִוִּיתִי:

up one in the sanctuary at Shechem.¹⁸ However, the distinction between legitimate and idolatrous pillars was apparently too difficult to maintain, and all pillars were eventually outlawed. As Rashi explains, "Although [the pillar] was pleasing to Him in the days of the Patriarchs, now He hates it because it was made into an idolatrous practice."¹⁹

CHAPTER 17   *17:1.*   See Comment to 15:21.

PROSECUTION OF APOSTATES (vv. 2–7)

Worshiping other gods violates the first commandment, the most fundamental rule of the covenant. It is a crime that undermines the very existence of Israel as a nation, since its punishment, frequently stated, is destruction of the state and exile. The present law, requiring prosecution of individuals who violate the commandment, is an application of Exodus 22:19, "Whoever sacrifices to a god other than the LORD alone is to be proscribed." This case would fit well with those in chapter 13. On the reasons for its location here, see Excursus 13.

3. turning to the worship (lit., "service") *of other gods and bowing down to them*   The phrasing echoes that of the Decalogue: "You shall have no other gods . . . you shall not bow down to them or serve them" (5:9).

to the sun or the moon or any of the heavenly host   See Comment to 4:19. This phrase is in apposition to "other gods," implying that the heavenly bodies *are* other gods and a typical example of illicit worship.²⁰ Heavenly bodies were worshiped in Syria and Canaan before the Israelites settled in Canaan. The practice became especially prevalent in Judah during the seventh century B.C.E., during the reign of Manasseh, as a form of assimilation to the Assyrian-Aramaean culture of the Assyrian empire.²¹ Deuteronomy is the only book of the Torah to mention these practices. The implication of this fact for the dating of the book is discussed in the Introduction.

something I never commanded   Literally, "which I [God] did not command." Some commentators take this as a case of litotes, a figure of speech in which a positive idea is expressed by negating its contrary, meaning "which I commanded not to do" (compare "not a few" meaning "many").²² However, the same phrase appears several times in Jeremiah, where God describes child sacrifice as something "which I never commanded, never decreed, and which never came to My mind."²³ There the phrase does not seem to be a litotes but a denial of something that others claimed was true. It appears from Micah 6:7 and Ezekiel 20:25–26 that some people claimed that God did require child sacrifice, and apparently it is this view that Jeremiah is rejecting.²⁴ In the present context, therefore, "something I never commanded" is probably meant to reject any claim that God does authorize the worship of certain other gods along with Himself.²⁵ In the decades preceding the discovery of Deuteronomy, King Manasseh of Judah, who established the worship of other gods in the Temple of the Lord, must have claimed that he did so with the Lord's authorization, as must those behind the polytheistic practices that Ezekiel witnessed in the Temple.²⁶ The reasoning that might buttress such a claim is discussed in Comments to 4:19 and 13:6. (On child sacrifice, see Comment to 12:31, Excursus 13, and Comment to 18:10.)

have been informed or have learned of it, then you shall make a thorough inquiry. If it is true, the fact is established, that abhorrent thing was perpetrated in Israel, ⁵you shall take the man or the woman who did that wicked thing out to the public place, and you shall stone them, man or woman, to death.—⁶A person shall be put to death only on the testimony of two or more witnesses; he must not be put to death on the testimony of a single witness.—⁷Let the hands of the witnesses be the first against him to put him to death, and the hands of the rest of the people thereafter. Thus you will sweep out evil from your midst.

וְהֻגַּד־לְךָ וְשָׁמָעְתָּ וְדָרַשְׁתָּ הֵיטֵב וְהִנֵּה אֱמֶת 4
נָכוֹן הַדָּבָר נֶעֶשְׂתָה הַתּוֹעֵבָה הַזֹּאת בְּיִשְׂרָאֵל:
וְהוֹצֵאתָ אֶת־הָאִישׁ הַהוּא אוֹ אֶת־הָאִשָּׁה 5
הַהִוא אֲשֶׁר עָשׂוּ אֶת־הַדָּבָר הָרָע הַזֶּה אֶל־
שְׁעָרֶיךָ אֶת־הָאִישׁ אוֹ אֶת־הָאִשָּׁה וּסְקַלְתָּם
בָּאֲבָנִים וָמֵתוּ: עַל־פִּי | שְׁנַיִם עֵדִים אוֹ 6
שְׁלֹשָׁה עֵדִים יוּמַת הַמֵּת לֹא יוּמַת עַל־פִּי עֵד
אֶחָד: יַד הָעֵדִים תִּהְיֶה־בּוֹ בָרִאשֹׁנָה לַהֲמִיתוֹ 7
וְיַד כָּל־הָעָם בָּאַחֲרֹנָה וּבִעַרְתָּ הָרָע מִקִּרְבֶּךָ: פ

In some ancient manuscripts of the Torah, the meaning of this verse was made explicit by the addition of an extra word at the end, reading "which I never commanded *to worship*." This reading is apparently reflected in the Sifrei and, according to a tradition recorded in talmudic literature, it was reflected in the Septuagint, too, though it is not found in the existing copies of the Septuagint.²⁷ This reading was probably created to prevent readers from misunderstanding "which I never commanded" as if it meant "which I never commanded into existence," since "command" is sometimes used in that sense.²⁸

4. See Comments to 13:13 and 15.

5. *to the public place* Literally, "to your gates." See Comment to 6:9. This may mean just outside the city gate. Other passages indicate that stoning took place outside the camp or city.²⁹

stone them to death On stoning see Comment to 13:11.

6. *two or more*³⁰ As a safeguard against dishonest or mistaken testimony, at least two witnesses are required. "Two *or more*" indicates that two are the minimum but not the maximum. Ramban and Ehrlich explain that as many witnesses as are available must be heard so that the truth may be clear. See also Comment to 13:10. According to 19:15, this rule applies to all types of cases. It was followed in the trial of Naboth, although in that case the witnesses were false.³¹

7. Execution was performed by the people themselves; there were no appointed executioners. See Comment to 13:12.

Let the hands of the witnesses be the first This requirement would impress on the witnesses that by their testimony they are in effect executing the accused; if their testimony is incorrect, initiating the stoning would make them murderers. The Mishnah seeks to make the same impression by requiring that witnesses in capital cases be warned: "Know that capital cases are unlike monetary cases: in monetary cases a witness may pay money and make atonement [for harm caused the accused by wrongful testimony], but in capital cases the witness is answerable for the blood of him [that is wrongfully condemned] and for the blood of his posterity [that should have been born to him]" (Mish. Sanh. 4:5). Compare Leviticus 24:14, where all who heard the act of blasphemy place their hands on the blasphemer's head before he is stoned.

Thus you will sweep out evil from your midst See Comment to 13:6.

THE HIGH COURT OF REFERRAL (vv. 8–13)

When the local judges cannot reach a decision, they are to seek a ruling from the high court in the chosen place. This is not a court of appeals but a court of referral for difficult cases in which guilt or innocence cannot be determined or how to apply the law is unclear. The court's role is comparable to that of Moses in the wilderness and to that of the later court established by King Jehoshaphat in Jerusalem.³² The high court's decision is final, and disobeying it is punishable by death.

Halakhic exegesis sees the high court as the prototype of the Great Sanhedrin in Jerusalem, and

⁸If a case is too baffling for you to decide, be it a controversy over homicide, civil law, or assault—matters of dispute in your courts—you shall promptly repair to the place that the LORD your God will have chosen, ⁹and

8 כִּי יִפָּלֵא מִמְּךָ דָבָר לַמִּשְׁפָּט בֵּין־דָּם | לְדָם
בֵּין־דִּין לְדִין וּבֵין נֶגַע לָנֶגַע דִּבְרֵי רִיבֹת בִּשְׁעָרֶיךָ
וְקַמְתָּ וְעָלִיתָ אֶל־הַמָּקוֹם אֲשֶׁר יִבְחַר יְהוָה
אֱלֹהֶיךָ בּוֹ: 9 וּבָאתָ אֶל־הַכֹּהֲנִים הַלְוִיִּם וְאֶל־

accordingly attributes to it legislative, executive, and judicial powers. Some of these are pointed out in the comments below.³³

8. *If a case is too baffling for you to decide*   The judges in the local courts are addressed; they are to bring the case to the high court, just as the chiefs brought difficult cases to Moses (1:17).

homicide, civil law, or assault   The three Hebrew terms, meaning literally "blood," "legal case," and "affliction," are slightly ambiguous. Since they are summed up by the phrase "matters of dispute," that is, litigation, they likely all refer to matters of criminal and civil law.³⁴ Halakhic exegesis understands the high court's jurisdiction to include matters of ritual law as well. It understands "blood" as referring to laws of menstruation and related subjects, "affliction" as "leprosy" (see 24:8), and "legal case" as referring to all types of criminal and civil law.³⁵ This view seems to be influenced by the jurisdiction of Jehoshaphat's high court, which included "ritual" and "cases concerning the LORD." However, no matter what the competence of Jehoshaphat's court may have been, menstruation and "leprosy" are unlikely to have been subjects of litigation in the local courts to which the present verse refers.

homicide   That is, if you cannot decide whether a person accused of homicide is guilty or not, or whether a homicide was intentional or accidental.³⁶

civil law   Rather, civil or criminal law, such as theft or damage. For some examples see Exodus 22:6–14. The Hebrew term *din* means simply "case," "lawsuit." Its precise referent in the present passage is inferred by process of elimination from the accompanying terms.

assault   Cases of physical injury, as in Exodus 21:22–26; Leviticus 24:19–20.³⁷

matters of dispute   Matters of litigation.

in your courts   Literally, "gates," referring to the local courts that met at city gates. See Comment to 6:9. Another possible translation is "in your settlements," in contrast to the chosen place.

9.   Because of ambiguities in the Hebrew, it is not clear whether the high court has one lay judge or more; whether it must always include both priests and lay judges; and whether or not all cases are heard by both types of judge acting together. Jehoshaphat's court included lay judges, priests, and Levites. It was chaired by either a layman or a priest, depending on whether the case concerned secular or ritual law. According to halakhic exegesis, based on Numbers 11:16–17, the high court has seventy-one members; it should include some priests and Levites, but its rulings are valid even if it does not.³⁸

The previous books of the Torah—including Leviticus and Numbers, which deal with the priests in detail—do not assign priests a regular judicial role. Priests become involved only when insoluble cases must be referred to God by sacral means that they administer, namely oaths, the Urim and Thummim, and ritual ordeals.³⁹ According to Deuteronomy the priests also have a role in local civil and criminal cases (see 19:17; 21:5; and perhaps 33:10).⁴⁰ However, since none of the sacral methods is mentioned by Deuteronomy,⁴¹ it probably expects the priests to decide cases by secular means based on reasoning.⁴²

It is not clear why Deuteronomy assigns the priests a role in civil and criminal cases; nor do we understand why it gives them a role on the high court. Several factors may have contributed to their presence. Priests were educated, with civil and criminal law forming part of their knowledge. According to verse 18 and 31:9 and 24, they have charge of the scroll of God's teachings, and according to Leviticus 10:11, their tasks include teaching the people all of God's laws. In addition, by abolishing sacrifice at local sanctuaries, Deuteronomy may have created a need to make up for the priests' loss of duties and revenues and, at the same time, have made them available for new

appear before the levitical priests, or the magistrate in charge at the time, and present your problem. When they have announced to you the verdict in the case, [10]you shall carry out the verdict that is announced to you from that place that the LORD chose, observing scrupulously all their instructions to you. [11]You shall act in accordance with the instructions given you and the ruling handed down to you; you must not deviate from the verdict that they announce to you either to the right or to the left. [12]Should a man act presumptuously and disregard the priest charged with serving there the LORD your God, or the magistrate, that man

הַשֹּׁפֵט אֲשֶׁר יִהְיֶה בַּיָּמִים הָהֵם וְדָרַשְׁתָּ וְהִגִּידוּ לְךָ אֵת דְּבַר הַמִּשְׁפָּט: [10]וְעָשִׂיתָ עַל־פִּי הַדָּבָר אֲשֶׁר יַגִּידוּ לְךָ מִן־הַמָּקוֹם הַהוּא אֲשֶׁר יִבְחַר יְהוָה וְשָׁמַרְתָּ לַעֲשׂוֹת כְּכֹל אֲשֶׁר יוֹרוּךָ: [11]עַל־פִּי הַתּוֹרָה אֲשֶׁר יוֹרוּךָ וְעַל־הַמִּשְׁפָּט אֲשֶׁר־יֹאמְרוּ לְךָ תַּעֲשֶׂה לֹא תָסוּר מִן־הַדָּבָר אֲשֶׁר־יַגִּידוּ לְךָ יָמִין וּשְׂמֹאל: [12]וְהָאִישׁ אֲשֶׁר־יַעֲשֶׂה בְזָדוֹן לְבִלְתִּי שְׁמֹעַ אֶל־הַכֹּהֵן הָעֹמֵד לְשָׁרֶת שָׁם אֶת־

v. 10. חצי הספר בפסוקים

responsibilities. A third factor may be that the priests were already involved in legal matters as a result of helping to resolve insoluble cases, as noted above. Finally, their status as God's servants and representatives gave confidence that they would judge in accordance with God's will.

levitical priests Deuteronomy's normal way of referring to the priests; see Comment to 18:1.

magistrate Rather, "judge"; see Comment to 1:16. Grammatically, "judge" is singular. This could mean that the court has only one lay judge. But some commentators hold that the singular refers to all the lay judges collectively, or perhaps to the head of the lay judges.[43]

the levitical priests, or the magistrate The phrase can also be translated "the levitical priests *and* the magistrate" (that is, judge).[44]

in charge at the time Priests and judges are described this way several times in Deuteronomy and Joshua, perhaps to emphasize that the books are legislating for the future as well as the present. Since in this sense the phrase seems superfluous, rabbinic exegesis took it as emphasizing the authority of the judges of each generation: one should not hesitate to seek rulings from the judges of one's own generation because of an assumption that they are less expert or pious than those of previous generations; the judges of each generation are as authoritative as those of earlier ones.[45]

present your problem Literally, "inquire (of the court)." The Septuagint and the Samaritan Pentateuch read instead "*they* [the members of the court] shall inquire," that is, investigate the matter.

11. In rabbinic exegesis this verse does not refer only to judicial verdicts but serves also as the warrant for the legislative authority of the Sanhedrin and its successors, the Sages.[46] This interpretation was as important in the development of Jewish law as was Chief Justice John Marshall's assertion of the right of judicial review in American constitutional history.

12. *Should a man act presumptuously* Since the aim of the punishment is to deter all the people from acting presumptuously again (v. 13), "a man" probably refers to one of the parties to the case in question, not to one of the judges.[47]

Halakhic exegesis holds that the text continues to address the judges, and that it prescribes capital punishment for a judge who disregards the high court's ruling. Notably, the Mishnah prescribes this punishment only if a judge later decides a case contrary to the high court's ruling. If, in his teaching capacity, he merely *teaches* contrary to the ruling, he is not punished. As a teacher he has academic freedom.

the priest ... or the magistrate Whichever announces the court's decision.

the priests charged with serving there the LORD your God The same idiom is translated "stand in attendance upon the LORD" in 10:8. See Comment there and compare 18:5.

that man shall die Even though the case in question may not have been a capital case, disobeying the nation's highest tribunal threatens the entire social order and is dealt with severely as a deterrent (v. 13).[48] Compare the punishment of an insubordinate son in 21:18–21.

shall die. Thus you will sweep out evil from Israel: ¹³all the people will hear and be afraid and will not act presumptuously again.

¹⁴If, after you have entered the land that the LORD your God has assigned to you, and taken possession of it and settled in it, you decide, "I will set a king over me, as do all the nations about me," ¹⁵you shall be free to set a king over yourself, one chosen by the LORD your God. Be sure

יְהוָה אֱלֹהֶיךָ אוֹ אֶל־הַשֹּׁפֵט וּמֵת הָאִישׁ הַהוּא וּבִעַרְתָּ הָרָע מִיִּשְׂרָאֵל: ¹³ וְכָל־הָעָם יִשְׁמְעוּ וְיִרָאוּ וְלֹא יְזִידוּן עוֹד: ס　שני

¹⁴ כִּי־תָבֹא אֶל־הָאָרֶץ אֲשֶׁר יְהוָה אֱלֹהֶיךָ נֹתֵן לָךְ וִירִשְׁתָּהּ וְיָשַׁבְתָּה בָּהּ וְאָמַרְתָּ אָשִׂימָה עָלַי מֶלֶךְ כְּכָל־הַגּוֹיִם אֲשֶׁר סְבִיבֹתָי: ¹⁵ שׂוֹם תָּשִׂים עָלֶיךָ מֶלֶךְ אֲשֶׁר יִבְחַר יְהוָה אֱלֹהֶיךָ בּוֹ מִקֶּרֶב

sweep out evil　See Comment to 13:6.

13.　See Comment to 13:12.

THE KING　(vv. 14–20)

The law about the king continues Deuteronomy's policy of limiting the power and prestige of human authorities. The role of the king—the official likely to become the most powerful and prestigious—is deemphasized more than that of any other official. Whereas the laws about judges, priests, and prophets allude to their rights and authority as well as their duties, and require obedience to the high court and the prophets, the law about the king says nothing about his rights or authority or obeying him or about any governmental functions performed by him. When the people established the monarchy in the days of Samuel, they intended the king to be responsible for adjudication and national defense.[49] Deuteronomy, however, assigns him no role in these or any other areas of government and says nothing of the powers that were actually exercised by Israelite kings.[50] The only positive responsibility that Deuteronomy assigns the king is copying and studying God's Teaching. The aim of this law is to limit the king's power and to characterize him as essentially an optional figurehead who is as much subject to God's law as are the people as a whole.[51] These aspects of the law were very influential in the development of western constitutional monarchy.

Deuteronomy's view of the monarchy is not as negative as the view of those who originally opposed its establishment altogether,[52] but it seeks to prevent the excesses that the antimonarchists feared. Israelite kings and their supporters naturally held a more favorable view of the monarchy. As mentioned, they intended the king to be responsible for adjudication and national defense. Kings did gain real power and prestige, although their power never became absolute and never included the right to legislate.[53] This disparity of views often led to conflict, and throughout Israelite history prophets felt free to criticize the excesses of kings.[54] The relative impunity that prophets enjoyed in voicing these criticisms shows that the kings had to acknowledge their right to do so and shows how deeply rooted the concept of a limited monarchy was.

Deuteronomy's view of the monarchy contrasts even more strongly with the ideas of neighboring Mesopotamia and Egypt. In Mesopotamia the monarchy was viewed as an institution created by the gods early in human history and practically indispensable for the welfare of society. The king was the lawgiver. He was inspired by the gods with the wisdom to make laws, but the laws themselves were his. In Egypt, the king was believed to be a god, and he *was* the law.[55] These ideas had few echoes in Israel.[56]

14.　*as do all the nations about me*　Most of the neighboring states had monarchies before Israel did, and when the people demanded that Samuel establish a monarchy they stated that this would make them "like all the other nations" (1 Sam. 8:20). Deuteronomy, by mentioning only this motive for wanting a monarchy, characterizes the institution as unnecessary and unworthy.

15.　*you shall be free to set a king over yourself*　The appointment of a king is optional. The monarchy is the only office so characterized.

one chosen by the LORD your God　God's choice would be communicated by a prophet.[57] Saul, David, and the northern kings Jeroboam and Jehu were chosen in this way.[58]

to set as king over yourself one of your own people; you must not set a foreigner over you, one who is not your kinsman. 16Moreover, he shall not keep many horses or send people back to Egypt to add to his horses, since the LORD has warned you, "You must not go back that way again." 17And he shall not have many wives, lest his heart go astray; nor shall he amass silver and gold to excess.

אָחֶ֨יךָ תָּשִׂ֤ים עָלֶ֙יךָ֙ מֶ֔לֶךְ לֹ֥א תוּכַ֛ל לָתֵ֥ת עָלֶ֖יךָ אִ֣ישׁ נָכְרִ֔י אֲשֶׁ֥ר לֹֽא־אָחִ֖יךָ הֽוּא׃ 16 רַק֩ לֹא־ יַרְבֶּה־לּ֨וֹ סוּסִ֜ים וְלֹֽא־יָשִׁ֧יב אֶת־הָעָ֣ם מִצְרַ֗יְמָה לְמַ֙עַן֙ הַרְבּ֣וֹת ס֔וּס וַֽיהוָה֙ אָמַ֣ר לָכֶ֔ם לֹ֥א תֹסִפ֛וּן לָשׁ֥וּב בַּדֶּ֖רֶךְ הַזֶּ֥ה עֽוֹד׃ 17 וְלֹ֤א יַרְבֶּה־לּוֹ֙ נָשִׁ֔ים וְלֹ֥א יָס֖וּר לְבָב֑וֹ וְכֶ֣סֶף וְזָהָ֗ב לֹ֥א יַרְבֶּה־לּ֖וֹ מְאֹֽד׃

one of your own people   No reason is given for requiring that the king not be a foreigner. It may have been self-evident that the people would feel more secure with one of their own as king,[59] much as the United States Constitution requires that the President be a native-born citizen. However, given Deuteronomy's priorities, it is likely that the book objects to a foreigner because he would not be a loyal monotheistic worshiper of the Lord and would probably lead the people into apostasy. The likelihood of a foreigner becoming king was probably greatest in the case of coups d'état, since usurpers were often military officers and military officers were sometimes foreign mercenaries.

16–17.   A series of provisions aimed at curbing three types of excess to which kings are prone: horses, wives, and wealth (vv. 16,17a,17b). These clauses are not phrased like a law, setting specific limits, but as general principles, like the wisdom teachings addressed to kings in Proverbs 31:1–9 and wisdom manuals addressed to kings in the ancient world.[60] Halakhic exegesis gave these principles legal specificity by setting guidelines and limits, as noted below.[61]

he shall not keep many horses   For cavalry and chariots. In the king's personal entourage these represent royal self-aggrandizement, as indicated by the would-be kings Absalom's and Adonijah's use of them.[62] In war, reliance on them encourages the king to feel that he is self-sufficient and not dependent on God. The proper attitude toward them is expressed in 20:1 and Psalm 20:8, which indicate that Israel relies on God, not horses and chariots.[63] The aim of this rule is therefore to keep the king's escort modest, to prevent him from establishing cavalry and chariot forces in the army, or both. Halakhic exegesis, which assumes that the king is responsible for the army, holds that he may acquire only enough horses for military needs, but none for personal use or grandeur.

or send people back to Egypt to add to his horses   Egypt was an exporter of horses. The verse is generally thought to refer to sending trade delegations to Egypt, or perhaps establishing permanent trade missions there, to arrange for the purchase of horses. Another possibility is that it refers to sending Israelites to Egypt as slaves or mercenary troops in order to pay for horses.[64] The translation "*or* send people back" implies that this prohibition is separate from keeping many horses, but that makes it redundant. More likely, this clause explains the preceding one (meaning "lest he send people back to Egypt in order to do so") or qualifies it (meaning "especially not to the point where it involves sending people to Egypt for that purpose").[65]

since the LORD has warned (lit., "said to") *you, "You must not go back that way again"*   No warning about returning to Egypt is known. Before the Israelites crossed the Reed Sea, God promised that they would never see the Egyptians again (Exod. 14:13). In Deuteronomy 28:68, too, not returning to Egypt sounds more like a promise than a warning.[66] Perhaps the verse is an allusion to that promise and means that by returning people to Egypt, the king would be nullifying God's promise. If so, a better translation would be: "since the LORD has promised you, 'You will never go back that way again.'" Deuteronomy may be interpreting the promise as implying a command: If God promised that Israel would never return to Egypt, Israel may not choose to do so.[67]

17.   many wives   A large harem would distract the king from God's teachings and from performing his responsibilities. Solomon and Ahab tolerated and even indulged in idolatry to please the foreign wives they married to cement political alliances.[68] However, the text does not limit the prohibition to foreign wives or to straying from God, and it must have in mind other types of dereliction in addition to idolatry. A similar warning against distraction by the harem is found in the advice to a king in Proverbs 31:3. A case in point is reflected in a letter from the Assyrian King

18When he is seated on his royal throne, he shall have a
copy of this Teaching written for him on a scroll by the
levitical priests. 19Let it remain with him and let him read

18 וְהָיָה כְשִׁבְתּוֹ עַל כִּסֵּא מַמְלַכְתּוֹ וְכָתַב לוֹ אֶת־
מִשְׁנֵה הַתּוֹרָה הַזֹּאת עַל־סֵפֶר מִלִּפְנֵי הַכֹּהֲנִים
הַלְוִיִּם: 19 וְהָיְתָה עִמּוֹ וְקָרָא בוֹ כָּל־יְמֵי חַיָּיו

Shamshi-Adad I (1813–1781 B.C.E.) criticizing his son Yasmah-Addu, king of Mari, for sleeping with women and neglecting his military duties.[69]

Halakhic exegesis took this law to mean that the king may have no more than eighteen wives. According to the Qumran Temple Scroll, it limits him to one.[70]

silver and gold to excess   This clause would restrain the king from imposing heavy taxes, but in context its primary concern is probably the danger that wealth would induce the illusion of self-sufficiency, as indicated in 6:11–12 and especially 8:11–17 (see Comments on those passages). The injunction against excessive wealth is not followed directly by a motive clause. Conceivably its reason was considered self-evident, but it is possible that verse 20 is the motive clause to this injunction as well as those in verses 18–19. The reasoning would be the same as that in 8:13–14: "and your silver and gold have increased . . . beware lest your heart grow haughty" (the first clause of v. 20 means literally "so that his heart does not grow haughty").[71] According to the halakhah, the king may only acquire enough silver and gold to support the army, the government, and his personal needs.

18–20.   The king is to be a constitutional monarch, subject to the laws of God's Teaching (*torah*). Nothing expresses this more clearly than the requirement that he personally make a copy of the Teaching and study it constantly. The concept of texts studied by kings, in some cases expressly written for their guidance, is known from elsewhere in the ancient world.[72] A noteworthy feature of this concept in Deuteronomy is that the king must study the same law that is addressed to the entire people rather than one applicable to himself alone.[73]

18.   when he is seated on his throne   This probably means "as soon as he takes the throne."[74] The study of God's Teaching is a duty incumbent on every Israelite from childhood on (5:1; 6:6–8; 11:18–19). The king must continue to study it while in office. It is to be not only a past influence on him but a current one as well. Sefer Ha-Ḥinnukh explains that since the king is under his own authority and no one will rebuke him for his actions, and he has the power to harm the people, he must study God's Teaching as a safeguard and a constant reminder to subdue his inclinations and obey God.[75]

he shall have a copy of this Teaching written for him on a scroll by the levitical priests   Rather, "he shall write a copy of this Teaching for himself on a scroll from the one that is in the charge of the levitical priests." The king makes his copy from the original given to the priests by Moses after he finished writing it (31:9,24–26).[76] According to Philo, the king is required to make his own copy because writing makes a more lasting impression than does merely reading.[77]

a copy of this Teaching   A copy of certain parts of Deuteronomy, including the laws of chapters 12–16. See Comments to 1:5 and 27:3. The translation of *mishneh* (lit., "a double") as "copy" follows Targum Onkelos and is probably correct. Another interpretation of the term that was current in Second Temple and rabbinic times is "repetition." On the basis of that interpretation, the phrase *mishneh ha-torah ha-zo't* was taken to mean "this repetition of the Torah," an apt designation for Deuteronomy since it repeats law and history known from the earlier books of the Torah. Talmudic literature accordingly uses *mishneh torah*, "the repetition of the Torah," as the name of the book. This is also the meaning of the Septuagint's translation of the phrase, *Deuteronomion*, "a second Law," which became the Greek name of the book and, ultimately, its English name, "Deuteronomy." (In the Middle Ages, Maimonides adopted the same phrase as the name of his compendium of Jewish law, the *Mishneh Torah*.)

19.   let it remain with him   Halakhic exegesis took this to mean that the king is to carry a copy of the Torah on his person at all times. Various explanations have been suggested as to how this was physically possible. One view quoted in the Talmud is that he wore a miniature Torah on his arm like an amulet. Various post-talmudic commentators suggest that he carried a full-sized copy that contained only Deuteronomy or the Ten Commandments, or that an aide carried a complete, full-sized Torah scroll.[78]

in it all his life, so that he may learn to revere the LORD his God, to observe faithfully every word of this Teaching as well as these laws. [20]Thus he will not act haughtily toward his fellows or deviate from the Instruction to the right or to the left, to the end that he and his descendants may reign long in the midst of Israel.

לְמַ֣עַן יִלְמַ֗ד לְיִרְאָה֙ אֶת־יְהֹוָ֣ה אֱלֹהָ֔יו לִשְׁמֹ֞ר אֶֽת־כׇּל־דִּבְרֵ֞י הַתּוֹרָ֥ה הַזֹּ֛את וְאֶת־הַחֻקִּ֥ים הָאֵ֖לֶּה לַעֲשֹׂתָֽם: ²⁰ לְבִלְתִּ֤י רוּם־לְבָבוֹ֙ מֵֽאֶחָ֔יו וּלְבִלְתִּ֛י ס֥וּר מִן־הַמִּצְוָ֖ה יָמִ֣ין וּשְׂמֹ֑אול* לְמַ֨עַן֙ יַאֲרִ֤יךְ יָמִים֙ עַל־מַמְלַכְתּ֔וֹ ה֥וּא וּבָנָ֖יו בְּקֶ֥רֶב יִשְׂרָאֵֽל: ס   שלישי

18 The levitical priests, the whole tribe of Levi, shall have no territorial portion with Israel. They shall live only

י״ח לֹא־יִ֠הְיֶ֠ה לַכֹּהֲנִ֨ים הַלְוִיִּ֜ם כׇּל־שֵׁ֧בֶט לֵוִ֛י

v. 20. מלא ו"ו

---

let him read it   The same charge is addressed to Joshua: "Let not this Book of the Teaching depart from your lips, but recite it day and night." Since reading in ancient times was normally done audibly (the Hebrew term for read, *kara*ʾ, literally means "call out"), reading included reciting.[79]

so that he may learn to revere . . . to observe   The two aims of studying God's Teaching are to inculcate reverence for Him and to learn how to properly perform His commandments. See Comment to 6:2.

20. Thus   The paragraph division in the translation implies that this verse only describes the result of studying the Teaching. In the traditional Hebrew text, however, verses 18–20 are not separated from verses 16–17; thus the present verse may also describe the intended effect of curbing the king's acquisition of horses, wives, silver, and gold (see Comment to v. 17b).

not act haughtily toward his fellows   That is, so that he will not oppress them or engage in the excesses forbidden in vv. 16–17.

fellows   Literally, "brothers," underscoring the essential equality of the king and the other citizens. He is not their master. See Comment to 1:16. See also verse 15, where "one of your own people" is literally "one of your own brothers" or, as it is translated at the end of the verse, "kinsmen."

nor deviate from the Instruction   That is, violate God's laws and worship other gods (cf. 8:11–19).

CHAPTER 18   THE ENDOWMENTS OF THE CLERGY   (vv. 1–8)

Chapter 18:1–8 describes how the clergy are to be supported. Nothing is said of their appointment or their tasks, except, in verse 5, as an explanation of why support is due them. These subjects were already mentioned in 10:8–9. They are also treated at great length from Exodus through Numbers. This section consists of three parts: an introduction stating that the priests are to be supported by offerings made to God rather than by landed property (vv. 1–2); a list of the portions of the offerings to which they are entitled (vv. 3–5); and a statement of the right of any Levite to come from elsewhere to serve at the chosen sanctuary and share in the endowments (vv. 6–8).[1]

Deuteronomy differs significantly from the earlier books of the Torah with regard to who may be a priest and what the public is required to give the priests. It considers all Levites, not only descendants of Aaron, eligible for the priesthood, and it assigns them portions of sacrificial animals and first products that are different from those assigned by Leviticus and Numbers. Modern critical theory regards these differences as reflecting the practices of different times and places, though there is little consensus as to the exact time and place each view reflects.[2] For the traditional explanation of these differences, see the Comments on individual verses below.

1. The levitical priests, the whole tribe of Levi   "The levitical priests" and "the priests, sons of Levi" are Deuteronomy's standard way of referring to the priests, indicating that they are descended from Levi (see, e.g., 17:18 and 21:5). The second phrase, "the whole tribe of Levi,"

off the Lord's offerings by fire as their portion, ²and shall have no portion among their brother tribes: the Lord is their portion, as He promised them.

חֵלֶק וְנַחֲלָה עִם־יִשְׂרָאֵל אִשֵּׁי יְהוָה וְנַחֲלָתוֹ
יֹאכֵלוּן: ² וְנַחֲלָה לֹא־יִהְיֶה־לּוֹ בְּקֶרֶב אֶחָיו יְהוָה
הוּא נַחֲלָתוֹ כַּאֲשֶׁר דִּבֶּר־לוֹ: ס

emphasizes that *all* Levites are priests or are eligible to be priests. So does "fellow Levites"—literally, his brothers, the Levites—in verse 7. This emphasis seems designed to counter the view of Leviticus and Numbers that restricts the priesthood to Aaron's family.[3]

As noted in the Comment to 10:8, the book of Numbers distinguishes between descendants of Aaron, who have an exclusive right to the priesthood, and the other Levites, who merely assist the priests. Deuteronomy evidently does not recognize this distinction. It refers to the priests as "levitical" or "sons of Levi," never as sons of Aaron, indicating that descent from Levi is the qualification for priesthood. Without distinction, it assigns to the levitical priests tasks, income, and promises that Numbers assigns either to the Levites or the priests, but not to both. Verse 1 of this chapter states that the entire tribe of Levi is to live off "offerings by fire"; in Leviticus and Numbers these are assigned only to Aaron and his descendants (Lev. 7:28–36; Num. 18:9). Verse 2 mentions a promise previously made to the Levites; this can only refer to Numbers 18:20, which is addressed to Aaron. Similarly, in Deuteronomy 10:8, priestly tasks are said to have been assigned to "the tribe of Levi," with no indication that only Aaron's descendants are meant. On the other hand, Deuteronomy assigns the task of carrying the Ark to the priests, whereas Numbers assigns it to the Levites (see Deut. 31:9 and Comment to 10:8). The only distinction found in Deuteronomy is that between Levites currently serving as priests and others who are not, but who have the right to do so (vv. 6–8). Since the phrase "the *whole* tribe of Levi" in verse 1 seems to insist that the priesthood is not limited to descendants of Aaron, some scholars believe that it is intended to define "the levitical priests" in such a way as to abolish the hierarchy established by Numbers.[4]

Traditional exegesis considers the absence of a distinction between priests and Levites in Deuteronomy more apparent than real.[5] It assumes that Moses takes the distinction for granted but does not repeat it because it would be superfluous and because here he is not addressing the clergy, to whom the distinctions were most important, but the public as a whole.

territorial portion   Hereditary tribal territory, like those of the other tribes. Tribal territory is viewed here as a source of livelihood. The priests are given their sustenance directly so that they can devote their efforts to clerical duties instead of producing food and other necessities. Verses 3–5 make clear that only those Levites serving as priests are supported in this way. That is why other Levites are indigent and dependent on charity. See Comment to 12:12.

Although the Levites are given no territory as a tribe, other books mention that they are given their own cities, fields, cattle, and pasturelands within the territories of the other tribes.[6] Deuteronomy never mentions such cities, and since it regularly refers to the Levites as residing "in your settlements" (as in 12:12), it appears to assume that Levites normally live in cities belonging to the other tribes.

offerings by fire   Hebrew *'isheh* refers to offerings of which a part was burnt on the altar. These included meal offerings, sacrifices of well-being, guilt offerings, and the bread of display. The priests receive part of what is not burnt.[7] See verse 3.

as their portion[8]

2.   *no portion*   No territorial portion, as in verse 1.

the Lord is their portion   He is their source of livelihood, as the end of verse 1 explains.

as he promised them   See Numbers 18:20.

3–4.   The priests are given portions of the sacrifice of well-being and first products of produce and shearing. Since some of these endowments are from sacrificial animals, it is clear that they are given only to Levites serving as priests, not to all Levites.

The endowments fall into three categories: food and drink, oil, and material for clothing (wool from the first shearing). These categories are often mentioned in ancient Near Eastern legal texts as the basic necessities that people supported by others must receive.[9] On the use of oil see Comment to "vineyards and olive groves" in 6:11.

³This then shall be the priests' due from the people: Everyone who offers a sacrifice, whether an ox or a sheep, must give the shoulder, the cheeks, and the stomach to the priest. ⁴You shall also give him the first fruits of your new grain and wine and oil, and the first shearing of your sheep. ⁵For the LORD your God has chosen him and his descendants, out of all your tribes, to be in attendance for service in the name of the LORD for all time.

³ וְזֶ֡ה יִהְיֶה֩ מִשְׁפַּ֨ט הַכֹּהֲנִ֜ים מֵאֵ֣ת הָעָ֗ם מֵאֵ֛ת זֹבְחֵ֥י הַזֶּ֖בַח אִם־שׁ֣וֹר אִם־שֶׂ֑ה וְנָתַן֙ לַכֹּהֵ֔ן הַזְּרֹ֥עַ וְהַלְּחָיַ֖יִם וְהַקֵּבָֽה: ⁴ רֵאשִׁ֨ית דְּגָֽנְךָ֜ תִּירֹֽשְׁךָ֣ וְיִצְהָרֶ֗ךָ וְרֵאשִׁ֛ית גֵּ֥ז צֹאנְךָ֖ תִּתֶּן־לֽוֹ: ⁵ כִּ֣י ב֗וֹ בָּחַ֛ר יְהוָ֥ה אֱלֹהֶ֖יךָ מִכָּל־שְׁבָטֶ֑יךָ לַעֲמֹ֨ד לְשָׁרֵ֧ת בְּשֵׁם־יְהוָ֛ה ה֥וּא וּבָנָ֖יו כָּל־הַיָּמִֽים: ס

רביעי

⁶If a Levite would go, from any of the settlements throughout Israel where he has been residing, to the place that the LORD has chosen, he may do so whenever he

⁶ וְכִֽי־יָבֹ֨א הַלֵּוִ֜י מֵאַחַ֤ד שְׁעָרֶ֙יךָ֙ מִכָּל־יִשְׂרָאֵ֔ל אֲשֶׁר־ה֖וּא גָּ֣ר שָׁ֑ם וּבָא֙ בְּכָל־אַוַּ֣ת נַפְשׁ֔וֹ אֶל־

---

the priests' due   *Mishpat* is used here as a technical term for the portions legally assigned the priests as their entitlements. Leviticus uses *ḥok* the same way.[10] The comprehensive rabbinic term for such gifts is *mattenot kehunah*, "the endowments of the priesthood."

sacrifice   *Zevaḥ* refers strictly to the *zevaḥ shelamim*, "sacrifice of well-being." See Comment to "other sacrifices" in 12:5. This is the most typical animal sacrifice of which the priests would receive a share.

the shoulder, the cheeks, and the stomach   Halakhic exegesis defines these as the upper part of the right foreleg (from the shoulder to the knee), the jowls (including the tongue), and the maw (the fourth stomach). The maw was a favored dish at Athens, and large numbers of right forelegs of sacrificial animals have been found in a sanctuary at an ancient village in Israel and elsewhere.[11]

This list differs from Leviticus 7:32–34, which states that the priests receive the breast and the right thigh of the sacrifice of well-being. Critical theory sees the two passages as reflecting the practices of different times and places. Halakhic exegesis resolves the inconsistency by holding that Deuteronomy's list refers to animals slaughtered for food, not for sacrifice. However, the noun *zevaḥ* always refers to a sacrifice, and the notion of sending parts of every animal slaughtered for food, in every part of the country, to the priests at the central sanctuary is unrealistic.[12]

4.   The priests also receive the first products of the farmer and the herdsman, namely the first grain, wine, and oil[13] and the first wool. Giving the first products to the priests is tantamount to giving them to God (see Num. 18:12–13). For the religious meaning of first products, see introductory Comment to 15:19–23, and see 26:1–11. Presumably the first products were normally brought during the pilgrimage festivals, though other times might also be permissible; according to the halakhah, any time was permissible from the Feast of Weeks through the Feast of Booths, and if necessary, as late as Hanukkah. See Comments to 12:5,6; 14:22–27; 15:19–23.[14]

In halakhic literature these gifts of produce are known as *terumah gedolah*, "the larger *Terumah*" (gift). The halakhah rules that at least one sixtieth of the first fruits and of the first shearings must be given as *terumah gedolah*.[15]

5.   **to be in attendance for service in the name of the LORD**   That is, to stand in attendance on the Lord and minister to Him (by offering sacrifices) and to pronounce blessings in His name.[16] See 10:8 and 21:5; compare the list of the priests' tasks in 33:8–10.

him and his descendants . . . for all time   The priesthood is hereditary in the tribe of Levi.

6–8.   As noted above, only those Levites serving as priests receive the endowments listed in verses 3–6. Following the restriction of sacrifice to the chosen place, Levites living elsewhere would be unable to serve as priests and would therefore be cut off from their livelihood. The present paragraph remedies this situation by providing that any Levite who wishes to go to the chosen sanctuary and serve as a priest there is entitled to do so and to share in the endowments.[17]

In 2 Kings 23:8–9, when King Josiah abolished the provincial sanctuaries and centralized sacrificial worship in Jerusalem, the priests of those sanctuaries were brought to Jerusalem and

pleases. ⁷He may serve in the name of the LORD his God like all his fellow Levites who are there in attendance before the LORD. ⁸They shall receive equal shares of the dues, without regard to personal gifts or patrimonies.

הַמָּקוֹם אֲשֶׁר־יִבְחַר יְהֹוָה: 7 וְשֵׁרֵת בְּשֵׁם יְהֹוָה
אֱלֹהָיו כְּכָל־אֶחָיו הַלְוִיִּם הָעֹמְדִים שָׁם לִפְנֵי
יְהֹוָה: 8 חֵלֶק כְּחֵלֶק יֹאכֵלוּ לְבַד מִמְכָּרָיו עַל־
הָאָבוֹת: ס

⁹When you enter the land that the LORD your God is giving you, you shall not learn to imitate the abhorrent practices of those nations. ¹⁰Let no one be found among

9 כִּי אַתָּה בָּא אֶל־הָאָרֶץ אֲשֶׁר־יְהֹוָה אֱלֹהֶיךָ נֹתֵן
לָךְ לֹא־תִלְמַד לַעֲשׂוֹת כְּתוֹעֲבֹת הַגּוֹיִם הָהֵם:

allowed to share in the endowments (or at least part of them),[18] but were not allowed to serve at the altar. Their prior service at those sanctuaries was perhaps held to disqualify them from service at the legitimate sanctuary (cf. Lev. 21:21–23), or perhaps the Jerusalem priests simply refused to share their office with them.

    8.   Levites joining the priesthood at the chosen sanctuary and those already there are to receive equal shares of the endowments.

    without regard to personal gifts or patrimonies   This seems to mean that the share of individual priests is not to be reduced even though they may have other resources. The precise meaning of the awkward Hebrew phrase *levad m-m-k-r-y-v ʿal ha-ʾavot*—literally, "exclusive *m-m-k-r-y-v* on/plus the fathers"—is uncertain. The translation is based on 2 Kings 12:6,8, where individual priests receive contributions for the Temple from their *makkarim*, "acquaintances," and Numbers 5:9–10, according to which donations are kept by the priest who receives them. The phrase would then mean: "exclusive of (gifts from) their acquaintances plus (inheritances from) their fathers." Thus construed, however, the phrase is unusually elliptical. Furthermore, in the Hebrew text the second word is vocalized as *mimkarayv*, which implies that it is from *mimkar*, "price," "sale," "ware." Thus understood, the phrase could refer to property the Levites inherit from their ancestors or to proceeds they receive from selling ancestral property.[19] However, this vocalization, which makes both *mems* part of the noun, deprives the preceding *levad* of the *preposition mem* that it requires in order to mean "exclusive *of*," "without regard *to*."[20]

THE PROPHET (vv. 9–22)

The fourth type of authority is the prophet.[21] Prophets were among the leaders of society, along with priests, elders, and, in monarchic times, kings and royal officials. Some, in fact, were influential members of the royal court.[22] To Deuteronomy the prophet is the most important and authoritative leader. In contrast to the king, whose power it limits, Deuteronomy strengthens the authority of the prophet. It affirms that he is the successor of Moses, the highest authority during the desert period (v. 15). His word is God's word, and whoever disobeys it is threatened with divine punishment (v. 19). Prophecy is the only office whose legal basis Moses describes by quoting the words of God rather than using his own words (vv. 17–20).

    The law focuses on the authority of prophets as the only legitimate channel of communication with God. The nations that Israel is replacing "heed" diviners and sorcerers (see v. 14); that is, they conduct their affairs, both private and public, in accordance with the instructions of such functionaries. Israel, in contrast, is to conduct its affairs according to the instructions of prophets. The contrast, and the test mentioned in verses 21–22, indicate that this law focuses on the prophet's roles as oracle, foreteller, healer, and the like, giving instructions about such matters as selecting a king, going to war, building a temple, and curing illness.[23] It does not expect future prophets to continue Moses' role as lawgiver.[24] The reason Israel is to heed prophets is that they are God's messengers and spokesmen (vv. 16–18; see Comment to 13:2). Hence, following them is an expression of loyalty to God, whereas following diviners and sorcerers is an attempt to circumvent Him.

    9–11.   The forbidden practices are abhorrent, like other Canaanite practices prohibited earlier in Deuteronomy.[25] These practices are techniques for invoking occult powers. The eight

you who consigns his son or daughter to the fire, or who is an augur, a soothsayer, a diviner, a sorcerer, [11]one who casts spells, or one who consults ghosts or familiar spirits, or one who inquires of the dead. [12]For anyone who does such things is abhorrent to the LORD, and it is because of these abhorrent things that the LORD your God is dis-

10 לֹֽא־יִמָּצֵ֣א בְךָ֔ מַעֲבִ֥יר בְּנֽוֹ־וּבִתּ֖וֹ בָּאֵ֑שׁ קֹסֵ֣ם קְסָמִ֔ים מְעוֹנֵ֥ן וּמְנַחֵ֖שׁ וּמְכַשֵּֽׁף: 11 וְחֹבֵ֖ר חָ֑בֶר וְשֹׁאֵ֥ל אוֹב֙ וְיִדְּעֹנִ֔י וְדֹרֵ֖שׁ אֶל־הַמֵּתִֽים: 12 כִּֽי־ תוֹעֲבַ֥ת יְהוָ֖ה כָּל־עֹ֣שֵׂה אֵ֑לֶּה וּבִגְלַל֙ הַתּֽוֹעֵבֹ֣ת הָאֵ֔לֶּה יְהוָ֣ה אֱלֹהֶ֔יךָ מוֹרִ֥ישׁ אוֹתָ֖ם מִפָּנֶֽיךָ:

listed here constitute the longest list in the Torah of such practices.[26] The precise differences between some of them are not clear. It is possible that some of the terms are synonymous and were included so as to leave not the slightest room for thinking that some of these practices are permitted. The order of the individual terms is chiastic, based on their length in Hebrew. It begins with a term consisting of three phonetic units (*ma'avir beno-u-vito ba-'esh*) and continues with two- and one-word terms (v. 10), and then again (v. 11) a two-word term and two three-word terms.

10–11. *consigns his son or daughter to the fire*   It not clear whether this refers to child sacrifice, like 12:31, or to a nonlethal ceremony. See the discussion in Excursus 15.

an augur, a soothsayer, a diviner   The first term, *kosem kesamim*, is a general term for a diviner or soothsayer. It covers techniques as diverse as belomancy (interpreting the way arrows fall when shaken out of a quiver), hepatoscopy (interpreting the configurations of the liver of a sacrificial animal), and necromancy (consulting the spirits of the dead). The term is even used disparagingly of false prophecy.[27] There is no explicit evidence about the type of divination to which the second term, *me'onen*, refers, and all conjectures are based on etymology. Ibn Ezra, for example, thinks that it is derived from *'anan*, "cloud," and refers to those who draw omens from the appearance and movements of clouds. The third term, *menaḥesh*, also seems to be a general one. In Genesis 44:5 and 15 it refers to divination based on the patterns formed when liquids of different density are mixed in a goblet, such as drops of oil added to water or the reverse (oleomancy and hydromancy). In Numbers 24:1 the related noun refers to a type of divination practiced outdoors, such as observing the clouds or the flight patterns of birds.[28]

a sorcerer, one who casts spells   *Mekhashef* and *ḥover ḥaver* are practitioners of magic. In Exodus 22:17 the first term refers to a capital crime, hence to a practitioner of *black* magic.[29] Elsewhere, however, derivatives of the root *k-sh-f* are used for divination and magic tricks.[30] The second term, *ḥover ḥaver*, is less common. It appears in Psalm 58:6 with "charmers" (*melaḥashim*, lit., "whisperers"), referring to defensive magic used against a snake. In Isaiah 47:9 and 12 the plural form *ḥavarim* refers to a type of magic used against enemies in self-defense. Etymologically the term may refer to the act of "murmuring" a spell.[31]

one who consults ghosts or familiar spirits, or one who inquires of the dead   These are mediums, practitioners of necromancy, which rests on the assumption that the spirits of the dead know hidden things and the future and can reveal them to those who know how to contact them. "Ghost" is the normal meaning of *'ov*. Its etymology is uncertain. One current view derives it from a term referring to a hole in the ground through which offerings are made to entice the dead to communicate with the living. *Yide'oni*, "familiar spirit," probably refers to the ghost as knowing hidden things; it always appears following *'ov*, never alone, and it may function simply as an adjective to the first term. According to Isaiah 29:4, ghosts speak from underground. According to 1 Samuel 28:11–15, they ascend from the earth and are visible to the medium. Leviticus 20:11, "a man or a woman in whom there is a ghost or a familiar spirit," implies that the ghost resided (probably temporarily) in the necromancer. It is not known whether these passages represent different conceptions of the process or different stages in a single process. As Ramban notes, the final phrase, "or one who inquires of the dead," means "one who performs necromancy by any other means." Isaiah 65:4 refers to those "who sit inside tombs," which may be one such technique.[32]

12–13.   It is because of such abhorrent practices that God is driving out the Canaanites. For Israel to resort to such practices would violate its duty of wholehearted loyalty to God.

Sorcery and divination owe their prominence to the universal human desire to learn the future and in some way control it, especially in times of illness and war. The Torah does not deprecate this

possessing them before you. ¹³You must be wholehearted
with the LORD your God. ¹⁴Those nations that you are

desire but insists that it be pursued only by means chosen by God, particularly prophecy. Interestingly, magic and divination are not opposed because they are deemed ineffective. Indeed, the Bible records cases in which they work, such as the Egyptian magicians' ability to duplicate the first three plagues and Saul's learning the outcome of a battle from Samuel's ghost.³³ Nor is the objection due to the antisocial character of black magic, which led many societies to ban it. That may be the reason behind the prohibition of sorcery in Exodus 22:17, but the present law is more sweeping than anything known elsewhere, and most of the activities it prohibits are not antisocial. Although the reason divination and magic are unacceptable ways of learning God's will is nowhere explicitly stated, it is inferably because they rely, or seem to rely, on powers other than God, both human and supernatural. Magic is frequently predicated on the belief that there are powers independent of the gods, and even superior to them, that may be employed without their consent or even against their will.³⁴ Even where magic is assumed to rely on divine assistance, the spells uttered by pagan magicians leave room for the impression that it is their own power, not the gods', that is operating. A similar impression is given by divination. Although the information that diviners uncover is often thought to have been sent by the gods, the omens on which pagan diviners rely are usually ambiguous. The "science" of deciphering them requires such extensive learning as to give the impression that the prognostication owes more to the diviner's wisdom than to divine revelation.³⁵ Necromancy is especially objectionable because the spirits of the dead can potentially be thought of as other gods (as noted in the Comment to 3:24, they were even called ʾelohim).³⁶

Verse 15 indicates that for the services pagans seek at the hands of diviners and magicians, Israel is to turn to prophets. Prophets were believed to be capable of doing whatever magicians and diviners could do. The normative view in the Bible is that the prophets' mantic (that is, prognostic) and quasi-magical powers grow out of their role as God's spokesmen. The prophets perform these services in ways that avoid what seems objectionable in magic and divination. The role of spokesman includes the role of "seer," in which the prophet answers inquiries about personal or public affairs, such as the location of lost animals or the prognosis for a sick person, the outcome of a battle or the building of a temple.³⁷ In his response, the prophet either quotes God's answer directly or refers to information that God has imparted to him. In either case, he conveys a direct verbal message that requires no decipherment. Because of his intimacy with God, the prophet also has the power to assist those in need by such actions as healing the sick and securing victory in battle.³⁸ Sometimes he does this by means of intercessory prayer (see Comment to 9:14). Even where he does not directly call on God, he relies on simple gestures and not on spells, and it is usually clear that he is acting as God's agent and not relying on his own "science."³⁹ Both as a mantic and as a healer he employs methods which avoid giving the impression that he is relying on his own powers rather than God's. No doubt this distinction was sometimes lost on the ordinary folk. Nevertheless, it is probably the key to understanding why the Torah endorses prophecy while prohibiting divination and magic.⁴⁰

Verse 13 implies that the use of pagan techniques constitutes a deviation from wholehearted loyalty to God. This is because God has assigned prophets to communicate His will to Israel directly and unambiguously, that is, by means that do not require the esoteric methods of diviners to implement and interpret His words. As the pagan seer Balaam phrased it in Numbers 23:23: "There is no augury in Jacob, no divining in Israel: Jacob is told at once, yea Israel, what God has planned." Other means of invoking supernatural knowledge or power are therefore an attempt to circumvent Him, a rejection of His gift of direct and unambiguous communication. This is well illustrated by the case of Saul, who, after banning necromancy, resorted to it when God refused to answer him through prophets and other authorized means of communication.⁴¹ The rebellious character of divination was so self-evident that earlier, when Samuel castigated Saul for a different act of rebellion against God, he declared that "rebellion is like the sin of divination" (1 Sam. 15:23).

13. *wholehearted*   Hebrew *tamim*, meaning undivided in your loyalty to God, relying on Him alone. Compare Joshua 24:14: "revere the LORD and serve Him with undivided loyalty [*be-tamim u-ve-ʾemet*]; put away the gods that your forefathers served."⁴²

14. *Those nations ... do indeed resort to soothsayers and augurs*   Rather, "Those nations

about to dispossess do indeed resort to soothsayers and augurs; to you, however, the LORD your God has not assigned the like.

אוֹתָ֣ם אֶל־מְעֹנְנִ֥ים וְאֶל־קֹסְמִ֖ים יִשְׁמָ֑עוּ וְאַתָּ֕ה לֹ֣א כֵ֥ן נָ֥תַן לְךָ֖ יְהֹוָ֥ה אֱלֹהֶֽיךָ׃

15 The LORD your God will raise up for you a prophet from among your own people, like myself; him you shall

15 נָבִ֨יא מִקִּרְבְּךָ֤ מֵאַחֶ֙יךָ֙ כָּמֹ֔נִי יָקִ֥ים לְךָ֖ יְהֹוָ֣ה אֱלֹהֶ֑יךָ אֵלָ֖יו תִּשְׁמָעֽוּן׃ 16 כְּכֹ֨ל אֲשֶׁר־שָׁאַ֜לְתָּ

heed soothsayers and augurs." The same word appears in the next verse, "him [the prophet] you shall heed." The point is that the Canaanites conducted their affairs in accordance with the instructions of diviners and sorcerers, but Israel is to conduct its affairs in conformity with the instructions of prophets.

In the pagan societies of the ancient Near East the functionaries in question were exceedingly influential. They were regularly consulted by commoners and kings, who would often not make an important move without them.[43] In Israel, too, in periods when such functionaries were tolerated, they were accorded similar status. Their standing is reflected in Isaiah 3:2–4 where, in one and the same context, Isaiah foretells the downfall of prophets, augurs, and enchanters as well as magistrates, elders, and military leaders.

There is archaeological evidence of several practices of this type in pre-Israelite Canaan. A letter found at Taanach, in the Jezreel Valley, refers to consulting omens. Clay models of sheep livers, used to assist diviners in interpreting their configurations, have been found at Hazor, in the Upper Galilee, and at Ugarit. Texts containing spells against snakebite have also been found at Ugarit. Roughly contemporary with this evidence from Canaan is the case of Balak, King of Moab in Transjordan, seeking the services of Balaam son of Beor, "the augur," as told in Numbers 22–24 and mentioned in Joshua 13:22. If consigning children to the fire does refer to child sacrifice, the evidence cited at 12:31 is also pertinent.[44]

15. *The LORD your God will raise up for you a prophet*   That is, "Instead, the LORD your God will raise up for you a prophet." This is the direct continuation of verse 14, indicating that Israel is to turn to prophets for the services that pagans seek from diviners and magicians.[45] Since prophets are raised up by God, who will put His word in their mouths, they are His agents, and by turning to them one turns to God.

Although the prophet is contrasted with pagan functionaries, this does not mean that Israel's neighbors did not have prophets. Prophets are known from Syria and Phoenicia, as well as Mesopotamia, both before and after the Israelites entered the promised land, and prophets of Baal and Asherah were associated with Jezebel, Ahab's Phoenician wife (1 Kings 18:19). A recently discovered text from Deir-Alla in Jordan describes Balaam as a "seer of the gods."[46] The point of the contrast is not to reject all forms of divine-human communication that were used among Israel's neighbors, but those that were "abhorrent." Nevertheless, prophecy was developed to unique heights in Israel; see Comment to verse 16.

from among your own people   Literally, "from among your own brothers," as in 17:15.

like myself   As 34:10 indicates, no future prophet would ever be enough "like" Moses to be his equal. The comparison refers only to the prophetic *role* that Moses played as God's spokesman. Nevertheless, the Torah never directly calls Moses a prophet. Even 34:10, which says that there was never again a prophet like Moses, does not directly say that he was a prophet. Instead, the Torah calls Moses "the LORD's minister" (v. 5; Num. 12:7–8) and "man of God" (33:1). Apparently, despite the status of the prophet as God's messenger, the title "prophet" was felt to be too narrow and too restricted, at least in the popular mind, to oracular, divinatory, and magical functions (note the pagan analogues in vv. 10–11) to be applied to a figure as exalted and comprehensive as Moses.[47]

Since "prophet" is grammatically singular, Christian and Moslem writers took this verse as referring to a specific individual, namely, the founders of their respective religions, and argued that "like you" implies equality with Moses.[48] However, the singular is clearly meant collectively, referring to a succession of prophets, just as the singular "king" in 17:14–20 refers to any and all kings, and "the Levite" here in 18:6 refers to many Levites.

16.   The people's words at Horeb are quoted in paraphrase from 5:22. As Ramban notes,

heed. ¹⁶This is just what you asked of the Lord your God at Horeb, on the day of the Assembly, saying, "Let me not hear the voice of the Lord my God any longer or see this wondrous fire any more, lest I die." ¹⁷Whereupon the Lord said to me, "They have done well in speaking thus. ¹⁸I will raise up a prophet for them from among their own people, like yourself: I will put My words in his mouth and he will speak to them all that I command him; ¹⁹and if

מֵעִם יְהוָה אֱלֹהֶיךָ בְּחֹרֵב בְּיוֹם הַקָּהָל לֵאמֹר לֹא
אֹסֵף לִשְׁמֹעַ אֶת־קוֹל יְהוָה אֱלֹהָי וְאֶת־הָאֵשׁ
הַגְּדֹלָה הַזֹּאת לֹא־אֶרְאֶה עוֹד וְלֹא אָמוּת:
¹⁷ וַיֹּאמֶר יְהוָה אֵלָי הֵיטִיבוּ אֲשֶׁר דִּבֵּרוּ:
¹⁸ נָבִיא אָקִים לָהֶם מִקֶּרֶב אֲחֵיהֶם כָּמוֹךָ וְנָתַתִּי
דְבָרַי בְּפִיו וְדִבֶּר אֲלֵיהֶם אֵת כָּל־אֲשֶׁר אֲצַוֶּנּוּ:

only the introduction to their request for prophetic mediation is quoted; Moses' audience will remember the rest: "You go closer and hear all that the Lord our God says, and then you tell us everything that the Lord our God tells you, and we will willingly do it" (5:24). This method of quotation (common in the midrash) presumes that the audience is intimately familiar with the text.

According to verse 18, the role established for Moses as a result of the people's request is the precedent for making prophecy the permanent channel of God's communication with Israel. Since they requested it, obeying prophets is a commitment they cannot disregard. This precedent requires explanation. Since the law focuses on the mantic role of prophets, the reference to Moses' role at Horeb seems like a non sequitur, since he did not play a mantic role there. Apparently the precedent is cited to show that the prophets are not merely the counterpart of diviners and magicians. Their mantic and quasi-magical powers are an aspect of their broader role, established at Horeb, to serve as God's messengers, communicating His will in all areas of national life. On this broader role, see Comment to verse 18.⁴⁹

18–20. This statement by God is not found in chapter 5. The text must regard it either as a very free paraphrase of 5:25–28 or as something additional that God said to Moses at the time. The Samaritan Pentateuch implies the latter by inserting verses 18–22 into the text of chapter 5, between verses 29 and 30.

18. *from among their own people* See Comment to verse 15.

I will put my words in his mouth The same idiom is used in Jeremiah's commissioning as a prophet: "The Lord put out His hand and touched my mouth, and the Lord said to me: Herewith I put My words into your mouth" (Jer. 1:9). Compare Jeremiah 15:16 and Ezekiel 2:9–3:3.

all that I command him The prophet's role is not limited to mantic and quasi-magical activities, responding to pleas for information and assistance. His primary role is as God's messenger and spokesman (see Comment to 13:2), communicating God's will in all matters of national life, including religion and domestic and foreign affairs. He is, in essence, the envoy through whom God, the divine king, governs Israel. As such, he plays a political role. Moses proclaimed the laws by which Israelite society was to be governed and established its religious institutions. He and other prophets declared war on Israel's enemies. Samuel established Israel's monarchy and chose its first two kings. Nathan declared the Davidic dynasty to be elected in perpetuity and overruled David's plan to build a temple. In the northern kingdom of Israel, prophets legitimated and deposed dynasties. In both kingdoms they denounced the religious and moral offenses of kings, priests, and the public, and conveyed God's *demarche* when Israel violated the terms of His covenant.⁵⁰ The prophets served, in sum, as the monitors of Israel's fulfillment of its covenant obligations to God and as the primary bearers of Israel's religious and moral ideology.

This role is a unique development in the history of the messenger-prophet. Laypersons and cultic functionaries serving as messenger-prophets are known among the western Semites at Mari in the eighteenth century B.C.E. They carry messages from gods, usually to the king, about military activities or demanding cultic activity such as performance of a ceremony or a gift to a sanctuary, and sometimes promising something in return; in one case the god urges the king to provide justice for the oppressed. "Seers and prophets" conveyed to an eighth-century king of Hamath, in Syria, a message from his god, in response to his prayer, telling him not to fear the attacking armies of his enemies.⁵¹ Nowhere are these prophets or other types of mantic functionaries known to have been so independent of other political and religious institutions as were the prophets of Israel, and to have

anybody fails to heed the words he speaks in My name, I Myself will call him to account. ²⁰But any prophet who presumes to speak in My name an oracle that I did not command him to utter, or who speaks in the name of other gods—that prophet shall die." ²¹And should you ask yourselves, "How can we know that the oracle was not spoken by the LORD?"—²²if the prophet speaks in the

19 וְהָיָה הָאִישׁ אֲשֶׁר לֹא־יִשְׁמַע אֶל־דְּבָרַי אֲשֶׁר יְדַבֵּר בִּשְׁמִי אָנֹכִי אֶדְרֹשׁ מֵעִמּוֹ: 20 אַךְ הַנָּבִיא אֲשֶׁר יָזִיד לְדַבֵּר דָּבָר בִּשְׁמִי אֵת אֲשֶׁר לֹא־צִוִּיתִיו לְדַבֵּר וַאֲשֶׁר יְדַבֵּר בְּשֵׁם אֱלֹהִים אֲחֵרִים וּמֵת הַנָּבִיא הַהוּא: 21 וְכִי תֹאמַר בִּלְבָבֶךָ אֵיכָה נֵדַע אֶת־הַדָּבָר אֲשֶׁר לֹא־דִבְּרוֹ יְהוָה: 22 אֲשֶׁר

claimed the broad authority, or at least tolerance, from the public, as was enjoyed by prophets in Israel. Their role reflects the unprecedented seriousness with which Israelite religion believed that God and not the king was the true sovereign, and that human kingship was a man-made institution, established by prophetic mediation and hence subordinate to prophetic authority.

19. God will punish anyone who disobeys the instructions he sends by means of prophets. This declaration establishes the prophet as the highest authority in the land, higher even than the king, about whose orders no similar declaration is made. It was disregard of this hierarchy that led to the downfall of Israel's first king, Saul, who disobeyed the divine commands delivered to him by the prophet Samuel.⁵²

call him to account God will punish him. Talmudic exegesis took this to mean death, citing the example of a disciple of the prophets who disregarded an order given in the name of God in 1 Kings 20:35–36.⁵³ According to the book of Samuel, God caused Saul to be killed in battle for disobeying Samuel.⁵⁴

20. Two types of false prophecy are punishable by death.

who speaks in My name an oracle that I did not command him to utter The Bible records two cases in which proceedings were initiated, possibly on the basis of this law, against prophets accused of falsely attributing their prophecies to God; in both cases they were exonerated. When Micaiah son of Imlah prophesied that Ahab would fall in battle, Ahab had him taken into custody, assuming—wrongly—that he would return from battle safely and Micaiah's claim to divine authority would be proven false (1 Kings 22:17–28). Jeremiah was tried for false prophecy when he foretold the destruction of Jerusalem. His accusers called for the death penalty, but he was exonerated on the grounds that he truly spoke in the name of the Lord (Jer. 26).⁵⁵ The prophet mentioned in Deut. 13:2–6 would be covered by this clause.

who speaks in the name of other gods A prophet who claims to bring a message to Israelites, either to individuals or to the nation, from another god. That pagan gods in the region were believed to send messages by means of prophets is clear from the evidence cited in Comments to verses 15 and 18. Presumably such messages were proclaimed by the prophets of Baal and Asherah who were opposed by Elijah and Jehu and executed on their orders (1 Kings 18:19–40; 2 Kings 10:19), and by the prophets who prophesied by Baal, mentioned by Jeremiah (Jer. 2:8; 23:13). Note that this case is different from that of a prophet who claims in the name of the Lord that the worship of other gods is permitted (13:2–6).

shall die In Deuteronomy this phrase refers to execution by human hands, as in 17:12.⁵⁶ Ahab's seizure of Micaiah son of Imlah implies that he intended to have him executed for false prophecy (1 Kings 22:26–27). On the other hand, Jeremiah's opponent, Hananiah son of Azzur, died at the hands of God for his false prophecy (cf. Jer. 28:17).

21. "How can we know the oracle that was not spoken by the LORD?" Since the people will rely on the instructions of prophets for vital matters, they need a criterion for identifying oracles that are not truly from God. Verse 22 answers that the false oracle is one that does not come true. The oracles in question must have included predictions foretelling the consequences of obeying or disobeying the prophet's instructions. The failure of a prediction to materialize would show the oracle to be false. Understood literally, this answer is puzzling. It seems too obvious to need stating, and not very useful. The people could hardly suspend judgment about the authenticity of every prophecy until its outcome was clear. Those who receive instructions from a prophet must

name of the LORD and the oracle does not come true, that oracle was not spoken by the LORD; the prophet has uttered it presumptuously: do not stand in dread of him.

יְדַבֵּר הַנָּבִיא בְּשֵׁם יְהוָה וְלֹא־יִהְיֶה הַדָּבָר וְלֹא יָבוֹא הוּא הַדָּבָר אֲשֶׁר לֹא־דִבְּרוֹ יְהוָה בְּזָדוֹן דִּבְּרוֹ הַנָּבִיא לֹא תָגוּר מִמֶּנּוּ: ס

often decide immediately whether or not to follow them. In practice, the credibility of a prophet could only be tested in the long run, after he or she had established a record of accurate or inaccurate predictions. In the case of Samuel, "all Israel . . . knew that Samuel was trustworthy as a prophet of the LORD" because "the LORD did not leave any of Samuel's predictions unfulfilled" (1 Sam. 3:19–20).[57]

Because the stakes were sometimes vital, the concern about false prophecy was a serious one in the ancient world. Despite unanimous assurance of victory in war by a group of four hundred prophets, King Jehoshaphat of Judah insisted upon seeking an oracle from another, independent, prophet, perhaps suspecting collusion among those already consulted.[58] Similar concerns, and solutions, are mentioned in Mesopotamian literature.[59] See also the Comments to 13:2–6.

Apparently the predictions in question were of natural events, not "signs and portents," marvels unrelated to the content of the prophecy. Although Moses performed "signs and portents" to demonstrate that God had really spoken to him (Exod. 4:1–9), that phrase is conspicuously absent here. To judge from 1 Samuel 9:6, Samuel's credibility as a prophet was based on successful predictions about commonplace things, such as where to find lost animals. Similarly, Micaiah declared that his claim to speak for the Lord would be disproved if his prediction of Ahab's death in battle did not come true, and Jeremiah was convinced that a revelation "was indeed the word of the LORD" when his cousin asked him to redeem some land, just as the revelation had foretold.[60] That the test should consist of predicting commonplace events is understandable, since "signs and portents" would not normally be pertinent to the oracles that people requested from prophets.

The demand for fulfillment of predictions is a natural criterion for mantic prophecy, which replaces pagan divination and magic, since prediction is inherent in such prophecy. It was much less appropriate for classical prophecy as attested in the books of the latter prophets. The classical prophets' oracles focus on reforming people's behavior. Often they involve no explicit prediction, and hence cannot be tested by the criterion of fulfillment. Predictions of doom were often regarded as conditional, and ideally their nonfulfillment would be the result of the people repenting, not a sign that the prophecy was false.[61] Furthermore, since the classical prophets addressed the long-term effects of the people's conduct, which might cause disaster many years in the future, the fact that a prophecy of doom had not yet been fulfilled could not prove it false. Jeremiah therefore qualified the criterion of fulfillment by stating that it did not apply to prophecies of doom, but only to prophecies of well-being.[62] Nevertheless, it was expected that when prophecies of doom did come true, the authenticity of the prophet who uttered them would be recognized.[63]

do not stand in dread of him   Since he is a fraud, you need not be afraid to punish him. Such fear may have been based on the assumption that authentic prophets are able to harm their enemies, as did Elijah and Elisha.[64]

CHAPTER 19

Judicial and Military Matters   (19:1–21:9)

After introducing the four main types of human authorities, the text turns to matters under their direct jurisdiction: criminal cases, in which the judges and priests play a role; and war, in which the priests are again involved. The first three criminal cases deal with homicide, the movement of boundary markers, and perjury (chap. 19). These are followed by laws about mobilizing the army and the conduct of war (chap. 20). One additional criminal law, and another relating to war, appear in 21:1–9 and 10–14. All the criminal cases except 19:14 deal with the prevention and removal of guilt (19:10,13,19; 21:9), and the laws of war include steps to avoid incurring guilt (20:18).[1]

THREE LAWS PERTAINING TO THE COURTS   (vv. 1–21)

ASYLUM CITIES (vv. 1–13)[3]

Three cities are to be assigned as asylums where manslayers may be protected from retaliation until a trial can determine whether the killing was accidental or deliberate. These cities serve to control the ancient practice of blood vengeance. In tribally organized societies, where there is no strong central authority, the kinship group is the primary defender of the life of its members. When a person is killed, his or her kinsmen are obliged to "redeem" the blood by slaying the killer.[4] In its earliest form, blood vengeance was exacted whether or not the killing was intentional. However, biblical criminal law limits execution to cases of deliberate murder. Since the family of the victim, "in hot anger" (v. 6), may not be disposed to recognize that a killing might be accidental, the asylum cities are established to protect the killer until a court of law can determine whether or not he acted intentionally.

If the killing is found to have been accidental, the killer remains safe in the asylum; if deliberate, he is handed over to the victim's kin for execution. In Numbers 35:6,11 these cities are called "cities of *miklat*," conventionally translated "cities of refuge."[5] It is clear from verse 6 and Numbers 35 that a manslayer can gain refuge and receive a trial only if he reaches the city before the blood avenger catches him. This procedure, which leaves the killer's safety to chance instead of directly prohibiting the blood avenger from harming him before a trial is held, reflects the social conditions of the time. Biblical law developed at a period in Israelite history when communal authority was just beginning to replace that of kinship groups in matters pertaining to private interests. The obligation of blood vengeance was still deeply felt.[6] This situation was similar to what is encountered today in some modern states that are built on tribal societies; periodically wars still break out between tribes in the wake of vengeance for murder.[7] Had the Torah simply forbidden the blood avenger to slay the killer until a trial was held, the law might well have been ignored.[8] The cities of refuge were created to provide a realistic means of achieving the same aim to the extent possible under existing conditions.[9] At the same time, by allowing the victim's relative (the "blood avenger") to serve as the community's authorized executioner if the killing was found to have been intentional, the family's traditional right was respected.

Laws about asylum appear twice earlier in the Torah, each time with a different emphasis.[10] Exodus 21:13–14 establishes the distinction between accidental and intentional killing, stating that God will establish a place to which accidental killers may flee, but that intentional killers are to be denied even the time-honored asylum of the altar. This law revolutionizes the institutions of blood vengeance and asylum. Both, as originally practiced in the ancient world, were indiscriminate: blood vengeance did not distinguish between deliberate and accidental killings, and the innocent and guilty alike could claim asylum at altars and sanctuaries. Exodus establishes the principles that only deliberate homicide is a capital crime and that the sanctity of the altar cannot be invoked in such a case. Exodus does not specify what it means by a "place" of asylum. The cases of Adonijah and Joab show that altars were indeed used for this purpose, at least for temporary asylum.[11] But since Exodus refers to a "place" as distinct from "the altar," it likely has in mind one or more long-term asylums other than altars. Whether these "places" were at or near sanctuaries or at nonsacred sites is debated.[12]

Numbers 35:9–34 fleshes out the law. It identifies the places of refuge as six Levitical cities. It describes circumstances which create a prima facie case that the killing was intentional and then a smaller number of conditions establishing that it may not have been. It confines the accidental killer to the city until the death of the high priest, and warns that if he leaves earlier, the blood avenger may kill him with impunity.[13] These details indicate that confinement to the city not only protects the killer from vengeance but also plays a punitive and expiatory role, since even an unintentional killing, though not a capital crime, creates bloodguilt. (Rabbinic texts recognize these functions by terming the killer's stay in the city "exile" and explaining that the high priest's death serves as expiation for the killing.)[14] A supplementary paragraph (Num. 35:30–34) requires the testimony of two witnesses before capital punishment can be imposed, and it admonishes against allowing a murderer to buy his life, or an accidental killer to avoid confinement in the city, by indemnifying the victim's family. The law concludes with a warning that bloodshed pollutes the land, and that only the blood of the killer can expiate the victim's blood. The concluding admonitions, as well as the order

19 When the LORD your God has cut down the nations whose land the LORD your God is assigning to you, and you have dispossessed them and settled in their towns and homes, ²you shall set aside three cities in the land that the LORD your God is giving you to possess. ³You shall survey the distances, and divide into three parts the territory of the country that the LORD your God has allotted to you, so that any manslayer may have a place to flee to. ⁴—Now this is the case of the manslayer who may flee there and live: one who has killed another unwittingly, without hav-

י"ט כִּי־יַכְרִית יְהוָה אֱלֹהֶיךָ אֶת־הַגּוֹיִם אֲשֶׁר
יְהוָה אֱלֹהֶיךָ נֹתֵן לְךָ אֶת־אַרְצָם וִירִשְׁתָּם וְיָשַׁבְתָּ
בְעָרֵיהֶם וּבְבָתֵּיהֶם: 2 שָׁלוֹשׁ עָרִים תַּבְדִּיל לָךְ
בְּתוֹךְ אַרְצֶךָ אֲשֶׁר יְהוָה אֱלֹהֶיךָ נֹתֵן לְךָ לְרִשְׁתָּהּ:
3 תָּכִין לְךָ הַדֶּרֶךְ וְשִׁלַּשְׁתָּ אֶת־גְּבוּל אַרְצְךָ אֲשֶׁר
יַנְחִילְךָ יְהוָה אֱלֹהֶיךָ וְהָיָה לָנוּס שָׁמָּה כָּל־רֹצֵחַ:
4 וְזֶה דְּבַר הָרֹצֵחַ אֲשֶׁר־יָנוּס שָׁמָּה וָחָי וַאֲשֶׁר יַכֶּה
אֶת־רֵעֵהוּ בִּבְלִי־דַעַת וְהוּא לֹא־שֹׂנֵא לוֹ מִתְּמֹל

and number of the provisions, indicate that the main focus of the law in Numbers is to prevent avoidance of appropriate punishment by intentional or accidental killers.

Deuteronomy's main focus is the complementary principle that the innocent not be wrongly executed (the law about witnesses in vv. 15–21 likewise aims at preventing wrongful punishment). It explains that the number of cities is a means to prevent the execution of an accidental killer and indicates that his execution would also be a case of shedding innocent blood and would bring bloodguilt upon the nation. It only identifies circumstances that create a prima facie case that the killing was unintentional. It says nothing of the punitive and expiatory functions of the cities, and therefore says nothing about how long the killer stays in the city and under what circumstances he may safely leave.

Asylum cities are mentioned again in Joshua 20, which tells how the six cities were chosen and briefly describes their function, combining details from Numbers and Deuteronomy.[15] In talmudic literature the subject is treated in the second chapter of Tractate Makkot in the Mishnah, Tosefta, and Babylonian and Jerusalem Talmuds.[16]

The Three Original Cities in the Promised Land and their Function (vv. 1–7)

1. This is similar to other introductory verses in Deuteronomy, but the others rarely mention settling in the Canaanites' cities.[17] It is mentioned here because this law deals with cities.[18] The text may mean that the law must be implemented immediately, using existing cities and not waiting until new ones are built.

*2. **three cities in the land*** Literally, "in the midst of the land." The three cities Moses set aside earlier are east of the Jordan and therefore not "in the midst" of the promised land (4:41–43; see Comment to 2:24).[19] Those in the promised land are identified in Joshua 20:7 as Kedesh in Naphtali, Shechem in Ephraim, and Hebron in Judah. According to Numbers 35:6 and Joshua 21:13–36, these as well as the three transjordanian cities were Levitical cities.

*3. **survey**[20] **the distances, and divide into three parts*** Measuring the distances will ensure that the cities are centrally located in the regions they serve. The three cities listed in Joshua 20:7 are located in three sections of the land mentioned in Deuteronomy 34:2: Naphtali, Ephraim-Manasseh, and Judah; the present passage may refer to these sections.

any manslayer Any manslayer may flee there and have his case heard, though only some will be granted its protection, as verses 4ff explain.

4–5. The condition for receiving asylum is that the killing was unintentional. Verse 5 gives an example[21] of circumstances that create a prima facie case for lack of intention. Several other circumstances are described in Numbers 35:16–21.

*4. **and live*** That is, be granted protection in one of the cities. Deuteronomy, as noted, does not say how long the accidental killer stays in the asylum city. Taken by itself, the text could be interpreted as viewing the asylum as a temporary shelter until the "hot anger" of the victim's family

ing been his enemy in the past. ⁵For instance, a man goes with his neighbor into a grove to cut wood; as his hand swings the ax to cut down a tree, the ax-head flies off the handle and strikes the other so that he dies. That man shall flee to one of these cities and live.—⁶Otherwise, when the distance is great, the blood-avenger, pursuing the man-slayer in hot anger, may overtake him and kill him; yet he did not incur the death penalty, since he had never been the other's enemy. ⁷That is why I command you: set aside three cities.

⁸And when the LORD your God enlarges your territory, as He swore to your fathers, and gives you all the land that He promised to give your fathers—⁹if you faithfully observe all this Instruction that I enjoin upon you this day, to love the LORD your God and to walk in His ways at all times—then you shall add three more towns to those three. ¹⁰Thus blood of the innocent will not be shed,

שְׁלְשֹׁם: 5 וַאֲשֶׁר יָבֹא אֶת־רֵעֵהוּ בַיַּעַר לַחְטֹב
עֵצִים וְנִדְּחָה יָדוֹ בַגַּרְזֶן לִכְרֹת הָעֵץ וְנָשַׁל הַבַּרְזֶל
מִן־הָעֵץ וּמָצָא אֶת־רֵעֵהוּ וָמֵת הוּא יָנוּס אֶל־
אַחַת הֶעָרִים־הָאֵלֶּה וָחָי: 6 פֶּן־יִרְדֹּף גֹּאֵל הַדָּם
אַחֲרֵי הָרֹצֵחַ כִּי־יֵחַם לְבָבוֹ וְהִשִּׂיגוֹ כִּי־יִרְבֶּה
הַדֶּרֶךְ וְהִכָּהוּ נָפֶשׁ וְלוֹ אֵין מִשְׁפַּט־מָוֶת כִּי לֹא
שֹׂנֵא הוּא לוֹ מִתְּמוֹל שִׁלְשׁוֹם: 7 עַל־כֵּן אָנֹכִי
מְצַוְּךָ לֵאמֹר שָׁלֹשׁ עָרִים תַּבְדִּיל לָךְ: ס
8 וְאִם־יַרְחִיב יְהוָה אֱלֹהֶיךָ אֶת־גְּבֻלְךָ כַּאֲשֶׁר
נִשְׁבַּע לַאֲבֹתֶיךָ וְנָתַן לְךָ אֶת־כָּל־הָאָרֶץ אֲשֶׁר
דִּבֶּר לָתֵת לַאֲבֹתֶיךָ: 9 כִּי־תִשְׁמֹר אֶת־כָּל־
הַמִּצְוָה הַזֹּאת לַעֲשֹׂתָהּ אֲשֶׁר אָנֹכִי מְצַוְּךָ הַיּוֹם
לְאַהֲבָה אֶת־יְהוָה אֱלֹהֶיךָ וְלָלֶכֶת בִּדְרָכָיו כָּל־
הַיָּמִים וְיָסַפְתָּ לְךָ עוֹד שָׁלֹשׁ עָרִים עַל הַשָּׁלֹשׁ
הָאֵלֶּה: 10 וְלֹא יִשָּׁפֵךְ דָּם נָקִי בְּקֶרֶב אַרְצְךָ אֲשֶׁר

(v. 6) subsides,²² much as Adonijah sought asylum at the altar until Solomon swore not to harm him. According to Numbers 35, however, he must remain in the asylum until the death of the high priest, and may then return safely to his city.

unwittingly   That is, unintentionally.²³

6–7.   These verses explain the purpose of the law, beginning with the reason why there must be three cities of refuge: If there were only one, it might be too far to reach before the killer is overtaken by the avenger.²⁴ The explanation is concluded in verse 10.

*6. **blood avenger***   The relative who executes the killer, literally, "the redeemer of the blood." Blood vengeance is an aspect of the obligation of relatives to "redeem"—that is, rectify—vital losses suffered by their kin when the latter are unable to do so, such as redeeming an enslaved kinsman, redeeming his real estate, marrying his widow, or receiving reparations due his estate. Since Gideon and Joab avenge their brothers' killings,²⁵ it is generally assumed that in Israel this responsibility was exercised by the next of kin as defined in the laws of inheritance and other types of "redemption": these are, in order of precedence, one's child, brother, father's brothers, and the latter's children.²⁶

Additional Asylum Cities and the Purpose of the Cities (vv. 8–10)

Verses 8–9 are a parenthetic comment prompted by verses 6–7, which indicate that there must be three cities because of distance. They add that when the distances increase, three more cities will be needed.²⁷

To Deuteronomy, enlargement of territory to the extent promised to the patriarchs means reaching the Euphrates in the north (see 1:7–8; 11:24; Map 2). According to 7:22, full possession of the land was to come gradually. The book of Joshua states that Joshua conquered the land from the Negev in the south up to Mount Hermon in the north.²⁸ Our chapter indicates that conquest of the remaining territory, up to the Euphrates, was contingent on Israel fulfilling God's commandments (v. 9; see also 11:22–25). According to Judges 2:20–3:4, because of Israel's disobedience, God eventually canceled the promise of the remaining territory.²⁹

*9. **three more towns***   Along with the first three and the three previously assigned in Transjordan (4:41–43), there would be a total of nine.³⁰

10.   This verse continues the explanation of the law, starting where verse 7 left off. Accord-

bringing bloodguilt upon you in the land that the LORD your God is allotting to you.

¹¹If, however, a person who is the enemy of another lies in wait for him and sets upon him and strikes him a fatal blow and then flees to one of these towns, ¹²the elders of his town shall have him brought back from there and shall hand him over to the blood-avenger to be put to death; ¹³you must show him no pity. Thus you will purge Israel of the blood of the innocent, and it will go well with you.

יְהוָה אֱלֹהֶיךָ נֹתֵן לְךָ נַחֲלָה וְהָיָה עָלֶיךָ דָּמִים: ס ¹¹ וְכִי־יִהְיֶה אִישׁ שֹׂנֵא לְרֵעֵהוּ וְאָרַב לוֹ וְקָם עָלָיו וְהִכָּהוּ נֶפֶשׁ וָמֵת וְנָס אֶל־אַחַת הֶעָרִים הָאֵל: ¹² וְשָׁלְחוּ זִקְנֵי עִירוֹ וְלָקְחוּ אֹתוֹ מִשָּׁם וְנָתְנוּ אֹתוֹ בְּיַד גֹּאֵל הַדָּם וָמֵת: ¹³ לֹא־תָחוֹס עֵינְךָ עָלָיו וּבִעַרְתָּ דַם־הַנָּקִי מִיִּשְׂרָאֵל וְטוֹב לָךְ: ס

ing to the order of the phrases in Hebrew, it should be translated "Thus blood of the innocent will not be shed in the land that the LORD your God is allotting to you, bringing bloodguilt upon you."

Here, "blood of the innocent" refers to the blood of the accidental killer, since he does not deserve to die. If the community does not prevent his blood from being shed, it will bear the bloodguilt created by his death. The shedding of innocent blood brings guilt upon the entire community (cf. v. 13; 21:8–9). This guilt is regarded as a palpable, virtually physical stain (Greek *miasma*), comparable to the blood that Shakespeare's Lady Macbeth imagined to be staining her hands. If it is not eradicated, the welfare of the community is threatened, as when a famine befell Israel because Saul had killed the Gibeonites (2 Sam. 21:1).[31]

Intentional Murderers (vv. 11–13)

This section is the converse of verses 4–5: intentional murderers may not claim protection in the asylum. As noted above, asylums in the ancient world generally did not discriminate between the innocent and the guilty, the intentional and the accidental; they protected all who reached them. Tacitus, for example, writes that in the days of Tiberius, temples in the Greek cities were filled with felons as well as debtors, all enjoying sanctuary.[32] Biblical law institutes a revolutionary change in the concept of asylum; not even the sacred protection of the altar can be invoked amorally: "When a man schemes against another and kills him treacherously, you shall take him from My very altar to be put to death" (Exod. 21:14).

The text does not state where the trial takes place, but since the elders of the killer's town have him brought back for execution if he is convicted (v. 12), it seems likely that it is they who try the case, apparently in his absence.[33] Presumably the killer's town would be the one closest to the scene of the killing and the place where his prior relationship with the victim would be known. According to Numbers 35:12,24–25 and Joshua 20:6, the trial is conducted by "the assembly," but the identity of that body is debated.[34]

12. the elders The elders are the heads of the families, or at least the leading families, of the political units to which they belong, such as the nation, the tribe, the region, or the town. As such they represent the entire population and, except where limited by higher authority, direct its affairs. Nevertheless, in Deuteronomy, adjudication seems to be performed in most cases by "judges."[35] When the town *elders*, as a group, are specified as the judicial body, it is primarily in cases involving family law: the rebellious son, the husband who accuses his new wife of nonvirginity, and the refusal of levirate marriage.[36] Their role here may be due to the fact that blood vengeance is a concern of the victim's family. Note, in addition, that in 21:3–6 the elders represent their town in expiating an unsolved murder so as to protect it from incurring bloodguilt.

to be put to death Literally, "so that he dies" (*va-met*), echoing the same verb that describes the victim's fate in verse 11, which says literally "strikes him fatally so that he dies." The identical verbs underscore that the punishment matches the crime.

13. show him no pity See Comment to 13:9. Elsewhere this admonition appears in cases where one might be tempted to spare the offender out of love or a feeling that the penalty is too harsh for the crime.[37] No similar reason for such a temptation is obvious here. Perhaps some people were reluctant to impose capital punishment, or at least to be responsible for its imposition.[38]

14You shall not move your countryman's landmarks, set up by previous generations, in the property that will be allotted to you in the land that the LORD your God is giving you to possess.

15A single witness may not validate against a person any guilt or blame for any offense that may be committed; a

שְׁשִׁי 14 לֹא תַסִּיג גְּבוּל רֵעֲךָ אֲשֶׁר גָּבְלוּ
רִאשֹׁנִים בְּנַחֲלָתְךָ אֲשֶׁר תִּנְחַל בָּאָרֶץ אֲשֶׁר יְהוָה
אֱלֹהֶיךָ נֹתֵן לְךָ לְרִשְׁתָּהּ: ס
15 לֹא־יָקוּם עֵד אֶחָד בְּאִישׁ לְכָל־עָוֹן וּלְכָל־
חַטָּאת בְּכָל־חֵטְא אֲשֶׁר יֶחֱטָא עַל־פִּי | שְׁנֵי

Another possibility is suggested by Numbers 35:31, which warns against sparing the murderer in return for his indemnifying the family of the victim. The present verse may likewise be responding to the possibility that the victim's kin might prefer to forgo execution of the murderer in return for reimbursement of the economic loss the murder will cause them. Its point would be the same as that of Numbers 35:31: since life is infinitely precious, no economic value can be assigned to it, and a murderer may not escape execution by paying for the victim.

purge Israel of the blood of the innocent In this verse this refers to the blood of the murderer's victim. As noted above, the shedding of innocent blood creates guilt that lies on the entire community; it can only be eradicated by executing the murderer.

it will go well with you The community's welfare is assured only if the guilt is eradicated. For the procedure to be followed where the identity of the killer is not known, see 21:1–9.

THE INVIOLABILITY OF BOUNDARY MARKERS (v. 14)

Moving a landmark so as to encroach on a neighbor's property is a serious moral offense. One who commits it is cursed in 27:17. The same admonition appears in the book of Proverbs, ancient Near Eastern law and wisdom literature, and Plato's *Laws*.[39]

Possible reasons for the appearance of this law here are discussed in Excursus 13.

14. move Literally, "move back" the landmark into his property so as to extend your own.[40] This may be an example of the kind of machination against one's neighbor's property that is prohibited by the tenth commandment.[41] This crime was most easily committed in secret, like several of those associated with it in 27:15–25. However, halakhic sources also speak of its commission by force, as does Plato in his *Laws*.[42]

landmarks Objects, usually stones, marking property lines.[43]

set up by previous generations That is, ancestors.[44] Compare Proverbs 22:28, "Do not move the ancient boundary stone that your ancestors set up." The fact that the boundaries were established by earlier generations made their inviolability more than an objective matter of property rights. Landowners felt a deep attachment to the land they inherited from their ancestors. This is well illustrated by Naboth's reaction to King Ahab's offer of a better field in exchange for his: "The LORD forbid that I should give up to you what I have inherited from my fathers!" (1 Kings 21:3).

In halakhic literature this admonition against encroachment was widely expanded to encompass other types of misappropriation, such as wrong attributions of rabbinic dicta, and eventually to copyright violations. In Jewish law and ethics the phrase "moving landmarks" (*hassagat gevul*), in the sense of "violating boundaries," refers to unfair competition that encroaches on another's livelihood and other rights.[45]

LAWS ABOUT WITNESSES (vv. 15–21)

These two provisions are designed to prevent wrongful conviction on the basis of inadequate or false testimony: no conviction may be based on the testimony of a single witness (v. 15) and, to deter false testimony, a false witness is to receive the same punishment that his testimony would have brought upon the accused (vv. 16–21).

15. The basic principle that two or more witnesses are required is discussed in the Comment to 17:6.

case can be valid only on the testimony of two witnesses or more. ¹⁶If a man appears against another to testify maliciously and gives false testimony against him, ¹⁷the two parties to the dispute shall appear before the LORD, before the priests or magistrates in authority at the time, ¹⁸and the magistrates shall make a thorough investigation. If the man who testified is a false witness, if he has testified falsely against his fellow, ¹⁹you shall do to him as he schemed to do to his fellow. Thus you will sweep out evil from your midst; ²⁰others will hear and be afraid, and such evil things will not again be done in your midst. ²¹Nor must you

עֵדִים אוֹ עַל־פִּי שְׁלֹשָׁה־עֵדִים יָקוּם דָּבָר: 16 כִּי־
יָקוּם עֵד־חָמָס בְּאִישׁ לַעֲנוֹת בּוֹ סָרָה: 17 וְעָמְדוּ
שְׁנֵי־הָאֲנָשִׁים אֲשֶׁר־לָהֶם הָרִיב לִפְנֵי יְהוָה לִפְנֵי
הַכֹּהֲנִים וְהַשֹּׁפְטִים אֲשֶׁר יִהְיוּ בַּיָּמִים הָהֵם:
18 וְדָרְשׁוּ הַשֹּׁפְטִים הֵיטֵב וְהִנֵּה עֵד־שֶׁקֶר הָעֵד
שֶׁקֶר עָנָה בְאָחִיו: 19 וַעֲשִׂיתֶם לוֹ כַּאֲשֶׁר זָמַם
לַעֲשׂוֹת לְאָחִיו וּבִעַרְתָּ הָרָע מִקִּרְבֶּךָ:
20 וְהַנִּשְׁאָרִים יִשְׁמְעוּ וְיִרָאוּ וְלֹא־יֹסִפוּ לַעֲשׂוֹת
עוֹד כַּדָּבָר הָרָע הַזֶּה בְּקִרְבֶּךָ: 21 וְלֹא תָחוֹס עֵינֶךָ

any offense   Not only capital offenses, as 17:6 and Numbers 35:30 prescribe.

16–21.   The prohibition of false testimony appears in the Decalogue (see Comment to 5:17) and the Book of the Covenant (Exod. 23:1–2).

Verses 16–18 should be translated as follows: "If a felonious witness[46] appears against a man and gives false testimony[47] against him, and the two parties to the dispute appear before the LORD, before the priests or judges in authority at the time, the judges shall make a thorough investigation, and if the man who testified is a false witness, if he has testified falsely against his fellow, you shall do to him . . ."[48] The litigants' appearance before the judges (v. 17) is not a separate inquiry but part of the original trial (v. 16).

17.   **the two parties to the dispute**   The two original litigants in the case. Compare 25:1.

before the LORD   This phrase, which often implies a sanctuary, cannot mean that here. It would be impossible for trials to be held at sanctuaries once the local sanctuaries are destroyed, as they were when sacrifice was abolished in the provinces (2 Kings 23). Possibly the text intends trials to be held at local places of nonsacrificial worship such as those postulated in Comment to 16:8. Another possibility is that "before the LORD" does not refer to the location of the trial but to the fact that judges are God's representatives and He is with them when they adjudicate, since "judgment is God's" (1:17; 2 Chron. 19:6).[49]

before the priests or magistrates in authority at the time   For the judicial role of the priests, see Comment to 17:9. These priests must be ones who live in the town where the case is tried and have not moved to the central sanctuary (see also 21:5). Otherwise the text would have said "in the place that the LORD your God will have chosen," as it invariably does when referring to something that takes place there (see, e.g., 17:8,10).

18.   See 13:15 and 17:4.

19.   **you shall do to him as he schemed to do to his fellow**   This is the *lex talionis* or "law of punishment in kind." By this means the law strives to make the punishment fit the crime perfectly: whatever penalty would befall the accused if wrongly convicted—whether execution, flogging, a fine, or some other punishment—is to be imposed on the false witness.[50]

The phrase "you shall do to him" is addressed to the court. This is the only case in which the text states unambiguously that talionic punishment is carried out by the court; elsewhere (see the passages cited in Comment to v. 21) the wording leaves room for the possibility that the victim or his representatives execute the sentence. The court executes punishment in the case of false testimony because, from the point of view of the law, it is the aggrieved party, since the witness has threatened to subvert its ability to judge correctly.[51]

sweep out evil   See Comment to 13:6. This is the only instance where this phrase includes noncapital punishment.

20.   See Comments to 13:12.

21.   **Nor must you show pity**   See verse 13. In the present case, the court might be

show pity: life for life, eye for eye, tooth for tooth, hand for hand, foot for foot.

נֶפֶשׁ בְּנֶפֶשׁ עַיִן בְּעַיִן שֵׁן בְּשֵׁן יָד בְּיָד רֶגֶל בְּרָגֶל: ס

reluctant to impose punishment as severe as that which the law requires if the lie were discovered in time and no harm actually befell the slandered party.

life for life, eye for eye The penalty specified in verse 19 is here spelled out in the terms of the classic formula of the *lex talionis*. The meaning of the formula is not limited to what it says literally. Had the accused been charged with murder or maiming, the false witness would indeed pay with his life, eye, tooth, hand, or foot. In other cases, however, he would pay whatever other penalty would have been imposed on the accused.[52]

The talion formula appears in slightly varying forms in Exodus 21:23-24 and Leviticus 24:17-21, referring to the punishment for intentionally causing bodily injury or death. The latter passage expresses the basic principle: "If anyone maims his fellow, as he has done, so shall it be done to him: fracture for fracture, eye for eye, tooth for tooth. The injury he inflicted shall be inflicted on him." Talmudic exegesis holds that the formula is not to be taken literally, but means that the assailant is required to indemnify the victim with a sum of money that corresponds to the severity of the injury.[53] However, since the cases in Exodus and Leviticus are paired with and *contrasted* to cases in which the punishment is monetary, the formula itself must refer to corporal punishment. Nevertheless, one passage seems to imply that the victim of a nonlethal injury had the right to accept an indemnity in lieu of talion. Numbers 35:31 states: "You may not accept a ransom for the life of a murderer who is guilty of a capital crime; he must be put to death." This may well indicate that for all other injuries accepting an indemnity was permitted, though not required.[54] This shows that "an eye for an eye" is not a requirement for exacting vengeance in kind (as it is often popularly misunderstood), but a limitation of such vengeance: it may not exceed the original injury.

The penalty for intentionally causing bodily injury underwent a complex development in the ancient world. In the oldest Mesopotamian laws, perpetrators were required to pay monetary indemnities.[55] Later, talion was imposed when the victim was a member of the upper class. In the Bible, talion was imposed in all cases, no matter what the class of the victim. Halakhic exegesis reversed the process and imposed monetary fines in all instances. The rabbinic interpretation is an example of rabbinic loose construction of the law that has the effect of making it more just and humane.[56]

CHAPTER 20   LAWS ABOUT WARFARE   (vv. 1–20)

Chapter 20 consists of three laws about warfare: preparing the army for battle (vv. 1–9), treatment of defeated populations (vv. 10–18), and treatment of trees near besieged cities (vv. 19–20).[1] Further laws about war appear later, in 21:10–14; 23:10–15; and 24:5. Most of the laws about war limit the prerogatives of the military by defining who may be sent to war and what may be done to conquered cities and their populations. Harsh as some of them are in the light of modern ideals (though not modern practice), they limit wanton destruction of life and property and are the oldest known rules of war regulating the treatment of conquered people and territory.

These laws refer to all wars, not only the imminent conquest of the promised land. This is clear from v. 15, which refers to cities distant from the promised land; from the assumption that some of the soldiers will have planted vineyards and built houses shortly before the war (vv. 5–6), which was not the case before the war for the promised land;[2] and from the references to forced labor and siege warfare (vv. 17,19–20), which the Israelites did not practice until the monarchic period.[3]

PREPARING THE ARMY (vv. 1–9)

The laws are introduced by a statement of the fundamental principle underlying the biblical concept of war: God is with Israel in battle, therefore Israel is not to fear the enemy (see Excursus 3 and Comments to 1:21,29–31, and 7:17–21). The first law requires that two declarations be made before military officers assume command of the troops: the priest must remind the troops of God's presence and exhort them not to fear (vv. 3–4); and civilian officials must proclaim deferrals for those

20 When you take the field against your enemies, and see horses and chariots—forces larger than yours—have no fear of them, for the LORD your God, who brought you from the land of Egypt, is with you. ²Before you join battle, the priest shall come forward and address the

כ כִּי־תֵצֵא לַמִּלְחָמָה עַל־אֹיְבֶ֔יךָ וְרָאִיתָ סוּס
וָרֶ֗כֶב עַ֚ם רַ֣ב מִמְּךָ֔ לֹא תִירָ֖א מֵהֶ֑ם כִּי־יְהוָ֣ה
אֱלֹהֶ֗יךָ עִמָּ֔ךְ הַמַּעַלְךָ֖ מֵאֶ֣רֶץ מִצְרָֽיִם: ² וְהָיָ֕ה
כְּקָרָבְכֶ֖ם אֶל־הַמִּלְחָמָ֑ה וְנִגַּ֥שׁ הַכֹּהֵ֖ן וְדִבֶּ֥ר אֶל־

engaged in certain critical personal activities (vv. 5–7) and for those who do fear, lest the latter demoralize the rest of the army (v. 8). Although the priest's exhortation is mentioned first, the text probably intends it to be conveyed after the deferrals are announced, since it is delivered just before battle (v. 2 reads literally "As you approach battle . . .") and it is addressed only to those who are going into battle.[4] Perhaps it is mentioned first because it expresses the conviction on which all else depends and which Moses himself expresses in the previous verse.

This law refers to a civilian army, or militia, mobilized at times of need and commanded by officers appointed for the occasion. It seems that Deuteronomy does not intend Israel to maintain a standing army, at least not one of any significant size. The laws dealing with the king (17:13–20), who would be the commander of a standing army, assign him no military responsibility, though the reference to horses in 17:16–17 may imply some military role for him.[5] Reliance on a militia for military needs, rather than a standing army, is another example of Deuteronomy's dispersal of power among different officials, noted in the introductory Comment to 16:18–18:22.

In the second century B.C.E., according to the First Book of Maccabees, Judah Maccabee ordered deferrals for the reasons mentioned here before battling the Seleucid Syrian forces, and exhorted the troops before battle with a speech in the spirit of that prescribed in verses 2–4.[6]

Introduction (v. 1)

Moses encouraged the people before battle in similar terms in 1:21,29–31, and in his speeches in 7:17–21; 9:1–3; 31:2–6.

horses and chariots Horse-drawn war chariots were essentially mobile platforms for launching arrows and spears; their speed and maneuverability gave the army that possessed them a tremendous technological advantage. At the time when the Israelites invaded the promised land the Canaanites possessed chariots and they did not. They sometimes faced the same disparity against later enemies as well.[7]

forces larger than yours Rather, "and forces larger than yours." "Forces" (Heb. *ʿam*, lit., "people") refers to the enemy's army.[8] Compare Joshua 11:4: "They [the Canaanites] took the field with all their armies—an enormous host [*ʿam*] . . . *and* a vast multitude of horses and chariots."

have no fear . . . for the LORD your God, who brought you from the land of Egypt, is with you Chariotry has a great psychological value because of its ability to surprise and shock the enemy. Moses reminds the people that they have no cause to panic, since they enjoy the greater advantage of God's assistance. His reference to the Exodus reminds the people that Egypt's entire army, including its chariots and horsemen, were no match for God who destroyed them all at the Reed Sea (Exod. 14–15). The contrast between reliance on chariots and reliance on God is stated plainly in Psalms 20:8: "They [call] on chariots, they [call] on horses, but we call on the name of the LORD our GOD."

The Priest's Exhortation (vv. 2–4)

The priest, following the example of Moses (see Comment to v. 1), is to address the army with words of encouragement, reminding them that they are accompanied by God. Presumably verses 3–4 are but a précis of what he is to say.[9]

2. the priest shall come forward Narratives about wars in the times of Moses, Saul, and David indicate that priests sometimes accompanied the army, carrying sacred utensils, trumpets, and the Ark, and consulting God by means of the Urim and Thummim oracle. Deuteronomy appears to expect fewer religious practices to accompany war. The only military role it assigns to the priests is

troops. ³He shall say to them, "Hear, O Israel! You are about to join battle with your enemy. Let not your courage falter. Do not be in fear, or in panic, or in dread of them. ⁴For it is the LORD your God who marches with you to do battle for you against your enemy, to bring you victory."

⁵Then the officials shall address the troops, as follows: "Is there anyone who has built a new house but has not dedicated it? Let him go back to his home, lest he die in battle and another dedicate it. ⁶Is there anyone who has planted a vineyard but has never harvested it? Let him go back to his home, lest he die in battle and another harvest

הָעָם: 3 וְאָמַר אֲלֵהֶם שְׁמַע יִשְׂרָאֵל אַתֶּם קְרֵבִים הַיּוֹם לַמִּלְחָמָה עַל־אֹיְבֵיכֶם אַל־יֵרַךְ לְבַבְכֶם אַל־תִּירְאוּ וְאַל־תַּחְפְּזוּ וְאַל־תַּעַרְצוּ מִפְּנֵיהֶם: 4 כִּי יְהֹוָה אֱלֹהֵיכֶם הַהֹלֵךְ עִמָּכֶם לְהִלָּחֵם לָכֶם עִם־אֹיְבֵיכֶם לְהוֹשִׁיעַ אֶתְכֶם: 5 וְדִבְּרוּ הַשֹּׁטְרִים אֶל־הָעָם לֵאמֹר מִי־הָאִישׁ אֲשֶׁר בָּנָה בַיִת־חָדָשׁ וְלֹא חֲנָכוֹ יֵלֵךְ וְיָשֹׁב לְבֵיתוֹ פֶּן־יָמוּת בַּמִּלְחָמָה וְאִישׁ אַחֵר יַחְנְכֶנּוּ: 6 וּמִי־הָאִישׁ אֲשֶׁר־נָטַע כֶּרֶם וְלֹא חִלְּלוֹ יֵלֵךְ וְיָשֹׁב לְבֵיתוֹ פֶּן־יָמוּת בַּמִּלְחָמָה וְאִישׁ אַחֵר

the present speech, and it does not indicate that the Ark is to accompany the army into battle (see Comments to 1:33,42).¹⁰

3.   The heart of the priest's message is that the troops should not have the slightest fear. He emphasizes this by expressing it in four different ways.

4.   **to bring you victory**   Rather, "to deliver you," to protect you from the enemy.

Deferments from Battle (vv. 5–8)

The first three grounds for deferral ensure that young men, once they have initiated certain important personal activities, are able to complete them before risking their lives in war. Jeremiah 29:5–6 mentions the same activities, and the enjoyment of their results, as typical of a normal life. In Deuteronomy 28:30, deprivation of the opportunity to complete these activities is mentioned as a curse.¹¹ Here and in 28:30, Deuteronomy mentions an aspect of the tragedy that would be particularly painful for a man to contemplate, that the fruits of his labors would be taken by someone else.

Further regulations concerning the application of these laws were presumably known to the officials responsible for mobilization. Such regulations doubtless covered matters similar to those dealt with in halakhic exegesis: whether these are the only grounds for deferral or are examples of broader categories, how long the deferrals last, and whether they are granted in all circumstances.¹²

Something like a mirror image of this law is found in the Ugaritic *Legend of King Keret*, which describes a total mobilization in which new grooms, widows, and even the sick are called up.¹³ The participation of the sick indicates that this is an unusual situation; there must have been wars from which they, along with new grooms, widows, and others mentioned in the Ugaritic text were exempted. Halakhic interpretation of Deuteronomy likewise distinguishes between wars requiring total mobilization and those permitting deferrals. There is no clear evidence for such a distinction in the Bible itself.¹⁴

5.   **officials**   These are apparently civilian officials responsible for mobilization, perhaps in each town; there is no mention of military officers until verse 9.¹⁵ Placing civilian authorities in charge of mobilization prevents the military from ignoring the rights of those entitled to deferral.

dedicated it   Rather, "initiated it." The parallel phrase in 28:30 implies that this phrase may mean simply "started to live in it." It is possible, however, that ceremonies were involved, as in the initiation of the walls of Jerusalem in Nehemiah's time and the initiations of the sanctuary, the altar, and Solomon's temple.¹⁶

6.   **harvested**   Rather, "eaten." Literally, Hebrew *ḥillelo* means "desacralized it," "treated it as nonsacred."¹⁷ According to Leviticus 19:23–25, the fruit of a newly planted tree may not be eaten until the fifth year. It is dedicated to God in the fourth year, and the fifth year, when it is eaten, is the first time it is put to nonsacred use. If Deuteronomy has that law in mind, this would amount to a five-year deferral from the army. There is no way of knowing that this is really the case.

187

it. ⁷Is there anyone who has paid the bride-price for a wife, but who has not yet married her? Let him go back to his home, lest he die in battle and another marry her." ⁸The officials shall go on addressing the troops and say, "Is there anyone afraid and disheartened? Let him go back to his home, lest the courage of his comrades flag like his." ⁹When the officials have finished addressing the troops, army commanders shall assume command of the troops.

¹⁰When you approach a town to attack it, you shall offer it terms of peace. ¹¹If it responds peaceably and lets you in,

 יַחְלְּלֶנּוּ: 7 וּמִי־הָאִישׁ אֲשֶׁר־אֵרַשׂ אִשָּׁה וְלֹא
לְקָחָהּ יֵלֵךְ וְיָשֹׁב לְבֵיתוֹ פֶּן־יָמוּת בַּמִּלְחָמָה
וְאִישׁ אַחֵר יִקָּחֶנָּה: 8 וְיָסְפוּ הַשֹּׁטְרִים לְדַבֵּר
אֶל־הָעָם וְאָמְרוּ מִי־הָאִישׁ הַיָּרֵא וְרַךְ הַלֵּבָב
יֵלֵךְ וְיָשֹׁב לְבֵיתוֹ וְלֹא יִמַּס אֶת־לְבַב אֶחָיו
כִּלְבָבוֹ: 9 וְהָיָה כְּכַלֹּת הַשֹּׁטְרִים לְדַבֵּר אֶל־הָעָם
וּפָקְדוּ שָׂרֵי צְבָאוֹת בְּרֹאשׁ הָעָם: ס

שביעי 10 כִּי־תִקְרַב אֶל־עִיר לְהִלָּחֵם עָלֶיהָ
וְקָרָאתָ אֵלֶיהָ לְשָׁלוֹם: 11 וְהָיָה אִם־שָׁלוֹם תַּעַנְךָ

7.   The tragedy of dying before consummating a marriage is also mentioned in Babylonian texts, one of which states that young men and women who were denied this pleasure grieve in the netherworld.[18]

A related law, which defers a newly wed husband from military service for a year, appears in 24:5. Here, the deferments are given because of the feelings of the soldier. The reason cited in 24:5 is for the sake of the bride.

paid the bride-price   Literally, "betrothed," which was normally done by paying the bride-price (Heb. *mohar*) to the fiancée's father (see 22:23,29).[19] Once the bride-price is paid, the fiancée is considered legally married even though the wedding has not yet taken place (see Comment to 22:23). It is debated whether the *mohar* was considered a kind of "purchase" price or as compensation to the bride's family for the loss of her services. It is also not known whether in biblical times it was kept by the bride's father or used for her benefit, as it was in later times.[20]

8.   **The officials shall go on**   This separate introduction to the final deferral indicates that it is of a different type from the others. The first three were for the benefit of the individuals deferred; the last is for the benefit of the army as a whole, lest the fear of a few spread to others.[21]

disheartened   Literally, "soft-hearted," meaning cowardly, as in verse 3 ("courage falter"). Some tannaitic and medieval commentators took this idiom to mean "tender-hearted" in the sense of compassionate and unable to inflict harm on others.[22]

Military Officers Take Charge of the Troops (v. 9)

army commanders   Presumably chiefs of thousands, hundreds, fifties, and tens (see Comment to 1:15 and cf. Num. 31:14,48).[23]

army commanders shall assume command of the troops   A translation more in keeping with Hebrew idiom would be "they [the officials or some higher authority] shall appoint army commanders at the head of the people."[24] This would imply that there will be no permanent commanders, but ones appointed before each war. This procedure is compatible with the fact that the text deals with a militia mobilized for the occasion, not a standing army.

THE TREATMENT OF DEFEATED POPULATIONS (vv. 10–18)

The General Rule (vv. 10–14)

Cities attacked by Israel are to be offered an opportunity to surrender. If they agree, their populations are not to be harmed. If they insist on battle and are defeated, only their men are to be killed; women, children, and property are to be spared and taken captive. Compare 21:10–14.[25]

10.   **offer it terms of peace**   Offer it *shalom*, here meaning terms of surrender, a promise to spare the city and its inhabitants if they agree to serve you.[26] The same idiom appears in an Akkadian letter from Mari: "when he had besieged that city, he offered it terms of submission [*salimam*]." In

188

all the people present there shall serve you at forced labor. ¹²If it does not surrender to you, but would join battle with you, you shall lay siege to it; ¹³and when the LORD your God delivers it into your hand, you shall put all its males to the sword. ¹⁴You may, however, take as your booty the women, the children, the livestock, and everything in the town—all its spoil—and enjoy the use of the spoil of your enemy, which the LORD your God gives you.

¹⁵Thus you shall deal with all towns that lie very far from you, towns that do not belong to nations hereabout. ¹⁶In the towns of the latter peoples, however, which the LORD your God is giving you as a heritage, you shall not let a soul remain alive. ¹⁷No, you must proscribe them—

וּפָתְחָה לָךְ וְהָיָה כָּל־הָעָם הַנִּמְצָא־בָהּ יִהְיוּ לְךָ
לָמַס וַעֲבָדוּךָ: 12 וְאִם־לֹא תַשְׁלִים עִמָּךְ וְעָשְׂתָה
עִמְּךָ מִלְחָמָה וְצַרְתָּ עָלֶיהָ: 13 וּנְתָנָהּ יְהוָה אֱלֹהֶיךָ
בְּיָדֶךָ וְהִכִּיתָ אֶת־כָּל־זְכוּרָהּ לְפִי־חָרֶב: 14 רַק
הַנָּשִׁים וְהַטַּף וְהַבְּהֵמָה וְכֹל אֲשֶׁר יִהְיֶה בָעִיר
כָּל־שְׁלָלָהּ תָּבֹז לָךְ וְאָכַלְתָּ אֶת־שְׁלַל אֹיְבֶיךָ
אֲשֶׁר נָתַן יְהוָה אֱלֹהֶיךָ לָךְ:
15 כֵּן תַּעֲשֶׂה לְכָל־הֶעָרִים הָרְחֹקֹת מִמְּךָ מְאֹד
אֲשֶׁר לֹא־מֵעָרֵי הַגּוֹיִם־הָאֵלֶּה הֵנָּה: 16 רַק מֵעָרֵי
הָעַמִּים הָאֵלֶּה אֲשֶׁר יְהוָה אֱלֹהֶיךָ נֹתֵן לְךָ נַחֲלָה
לֹא תְחַיֶּה כָּל־נְשָׁמָה: 17 כִּי־הַחֲרֵם תַּחֲרִימֵם

an Egyptian inscription, the prostrate princes of Canaan say *shalom* when submitting to the Pharaoh. The same meaning is found in verse 11, which reads literally "If it responds '*shalom*' and lets you in," and in verse 12, where a verb derived from *shalom* (*hishlim*) is used for "surrender."[27]

11. *serve you at forced labor*   Literally, "as forced laborers." Hebrew *mas* refers to a contingent of forced laborers working for the state.[28] They were employed in agriculture and public works, such as construction. In monarchic times, David imposed labor on the Ammonites and Solomon subjected the remaining Canaanites to labor.[29]

12-14.   A town that refuses to submit peaceably, but chooses to fight, is dealt with more severely. The men, who constitute the city's capacity to rebel in the future, are killed. Women and children are taken as booty; Numbers 31 probably implies that they would be distributed among the army, the clergy, and the general population as domestic slaves, concubines and, in some cases, wives.[30] (For restrictions on how one may treat a captive taken as a wife, see 21:10–14.) The cattle and goods are taken as booty, too.

13. *males*   This probably refers only to adult males.[31] According to verse 14, children are spared, and there is no reason to assume that only girls are meant.

An Exception: Cities in the Promised Land (vv. 15–18)

Cities in the promised land are an exception to the preceding rule. They are not to be offered the option of surrender, and their entire population is to be destroyed (see also 7:1–2 and 16). According to verse 18, the aim of this harsh policy is to prevent Israel from being influenced by the Canaanites to adopt their abhorrent practices. The Torah regards preventing such influence as a matter of life and death since it teaches that Israel's security depends on exclusive loyalty to the Lord and eschewing Canaanite abominations (see 4:26; 7:4; 11:13–21). It views Israel as a small, impressionable nation living in a pagan world, with a record of susceptibility to the lure of paganism that made stringent precautions necessary (see Exod. 32 and Num. 25:1–3). To Deuteronomy, the Canaanites' guilt in practicing child sacrifice—that is, ritual murder—underscored the necessity of forestalling their influence and eliminated any doubt that they deserved annihilation. The frequency with which enemy populations were annihilated in the ancient world made this seem an acceptable way of eliminating the danger. The basis of this policy is not ethnic but behavioral; 13:16 requires that Israelite cities that lapse into paganism be treated the same way.

Postbiblical exegesis found the idea of unconditional condemnation of the Canaanites too harsh and reinterpreted the text more leniently. For different reasons, modern scholars also believe that at the time the Israelites took possession of the promised land the law did not require the unconditional destruction of the Canaanites. For further discussion, see Excursus 18.

17. *proscribe*   Hebrew *haharem taharim*, the same phrase translated as "doom to destruction" in 7:2.

the Hittites and the Amorites, the Canaanites and the Perizzites, the Hivites and the Jebusites—as the LORD your God has commanded you, [18]lest they lead you into doing all the abhorrent things that they have done for their gods and you stand guilty before the LORD your God.

[19]When in your war against a city you have to besiege it a long time in order to capture it, you must not destroy its trees, wielding the ax against them. You may eat of them, but you must not cut them down. Are trees of the field human to withdraw before you into the besieged city? [20]Only trees that you know do not yield food may be destroyed; you may cut them down for constructing siege-

הַחִתִּי֙ וְהָ֣אֱמֹרִ֔י הַֽכְּנַעֲנִי֙ וְהַפְּרִזִּ֔י הַחִוִּ֖י וְהַיְבוּסִ֑י כַּאֲשֶׁ֥ר צִוְּךָ֖ יְהוָ֥ה אֱלֹהֶֽיךָ׃ [18]לְמַ֗עַן אֲשֶׁ֨ר לֹֽא־יְלַמְּד֤וּ אֶתְכֶם֙ לַעֲשׂ֔וֹת כְּכֹל֙ תּֽוֹעֲבֹתָ֔ם אֲשֶׁ֥ר עָשׂ֖וּ לֵאלֹֽהֵיהֶ֑ם וַחֲטָאתֶ֖ם לַיהוָ֥ה אֱלֹהֵיכֶֽם׃ ס [19]כִּֽי־תָצ֣וּר אֶל־עִיר֩ יָמִ֨ים רַבִּ֜ים לְהִלָּחֵ֧ם עָלֶ֣יהָ לְתָפְשָׂ֗הּ לֹֽא־תַשְׁחִ֤ית אֶת־עֵצָהּ֙ לִנְדֹּ֤חַ עָלָיו֙ גַּרְזֶ֔ן כִּ֚י מִמֶּ֣נּוּ תֹאכֵ֔ל וְאֹת֖וֹ לֹ֣א תִכְרֹ֑ת כִּ֤י הָֽאָדָם֙ עֵ֣ץ הַשָּׂדֶ֔ה לָבֹ֥א מִפָּנֶ֖יךָ בַּמָּצֽוֹר׃ [20]רַ֣ק עֵ֞ץ אֲשֶׁר־תֵּדַ֗ע כִּ֣י־לֹא־עֵ֤ץ מַאֲכָל֙ ה֔וּא אֹת֥וֹ תַשְׁחִ֖ית וְכָרָ֑תָּ

---

the Hittites . . . and the Jebusites   The statement of this commandment in 7:1 includes a seventh nation, the Girgashites. Their omission is probably not significant; lists of the nations of Canaan often appear in varying forms.[32]

as the LORD your God has commanded you   See 7:1–2.[33]

18.   The danger that the Canaanites may—and did—influence the Israelites to adopt their religious practices, especially if the two peoples intermarry, is frequently stressed.[34] Relations with Midianite women had the same effect (Num. 25:1–3; 31:16).

abhorrent things   Child sacrifice is singled out as the Canaanites' most outrageous rite, in addition to necromancy and other occult practices (see 12:31 and 18:9–14). These are regarded as the Canaanites' own abominations, not part of the astral worship that the Lord ordained for nations other than Israel (4:19).

TREATMENT OF TREES NEAR BESIEGED CITIES (vv. 19–20)

It was common practice in ancient warfare to destroy the enemy's fruit trees and fields. This weakened its economic potential and hampered its ability to fight again in the near future. It may also have been intended to pressure besieged cities into surrendering before they suffered such long-term damage.[35] Deuteronomy forbids destroying trees for such purposes. An exception is made in the case of military necessity: non-fruit-bearing trees may be felled for the purpose of constructing siegeworks.[36]

19. ***a long time***   An attacking army would not necessarily resort to destruction of trees, from which it could itself benefit, unless the siege was protracted and additional pressure was necessary to force a surrender.

you must not destroy its trees   Rabbinic exegesis expanded this rule into a broad prohibition, not limited to wartime, of destroying anything useful, such as vessels, clothing, buildings, springs, or food. The prohibition is termed *bal tashḥit*, from the phrase of *lo' tashḥit*, "you must not destroy."[37]

Are trees of the field human to withdraw before you into the besieged city?   The syntax of the Hebrew is difficult and the translation uncertain. This translation suggests that trees are unable to protect themselves by taking refuge within the city, or that they are not like human enemies that they should have to take refuge. This is essentially a "humanitarian" rather than utilitarian reason for the prohibition.[38]

20. ***siegeworks***   Hebrew *matsor* refers primarily to the encirclement of a city. Here it probably means a siege wall, a series of fortifications built by an attacking army around a besieged city to blockade it so that it cannot be resupplied with food, weapons, and manpower, and to protect itself from raids by the city's defenders or its allies.[39] Fruit trees, among others, were often used for this purpose. An Egyptian inscription describing the siege of Megiddo by Thutmose III (ca. 1490–1436 B.C.E.) relates how his commanders "measured the town, surrounded it with a ditch,

works against the city that is waging war on you, until it
has been reduced.

21 If, in the land that the LORD your God is assigning
you to possess, someone slain is found lying in the open,
the identity of the slayer not being known, ²your elders
and magistrates shall go out and measure the distances
from the corpse to the nearby towns. ³The elders of the

וּבָנִיתָ מָצוֹר עַל־הָעִיר֙ אֲשֶׁר־הִוא עֹשָׂה עִמְּךָ
מִלְחָמָה עַד רִדְתָּהּ: פ

כ"א כִּי־יִמָּצֵא חָלָל֙ בָּאֲדָמָה֙ אֲשֶׁר֩ יְהוָה֙
אֱלֹהֶ֨יךָ נֹתֵ֤ן לְךָ֙ לְרִשְׁתָּ֔הּ נֹפֵ֖ל בַּשָּׂדֶ֑ה לֹ֥א נוֹדַ֖ע
מִ֥י הִכָּֽהוּ: ² וְיָצְא֥וּ זְקֵנֶ֖יךָ וְשֹׁפְטֶ֑יךָ וּמָדְד֖וּ אֶל־
הֶעָרִ֔ים אֲשֶׁ֖ר סְבִיבֹ֥ת הֶחָלָֽל: ³ וְהָיָ֣ה הָעִ֔יר

and walled it up with the fresh timber from their [the city's] fruit trees."⁴⁰ The present law prohibits
the use of fruit trees for this purpose. "Siegeworks" may also include equipment used in assaulting
the city; ladders, battering rams, and the ramps on which the rams were rolled up to the city wall all
contained wood.⁴¹

that is waging war on you   That is, resisting you.

CHAPTER 21　　UNSOLVED MURDER   (vv. 1–9)¹

This is the last of the laws dealing with public officials. Like 19:1–13, it seeks to protect the nation
from bloodguilt that would befall it because of an unpunished homicide (see Comments to 19:10,13).
According to Numbers 35:33, "the land can have no expiation for blood that is shed on it, except by
the blood of him who shed it." In the present case, since the killer has not been identified and
punishment is impossible, the law provides instead for ritual removal of the bloodguilt.²

The ceremony for removing bloodguilt is complex. The elders of the nearest town slaughter a
heifer in a wadi, wash their hands over the heifer, declare their innocence, and pray for absolution.
The meaning of the slaughter, the handwashing, and the elders' declaration is uncertain. Despite
Deuteronomy's predilection for explaining what it prescribes, it leaves these unexplained. The role of
the priests is also puzzling. They are present for only part of the ceremony and have no specific task
in it. On the other hand, the prayer in verse 8a is unambiguous and only after it does the text promise
the desired absolution (v. 9). The prayer is also the only element of the ceremony that is worded in
characteristically Deuteronomic language. All this suggests that the ambiguous elements are remnants of traditional practices that Deuteronomy has preserved, but that in its view prayer is the key
to absolution and only God can absolve.³ For further discussion, see Excursus 19.

1. *in the land*   Bloodguilt pollutes the land as well as the people of Israel.⁴

someone slain   A corpse bearing marks of human violence. *Halal* normally refers to a
corpse that is wounded, usually by stabbing, not to any dead body.⁵

in the open   Since a body found within a town would present the same problem, the
ceremony of verses 4–8 would presumably be performed in that case, too. It is probable that the law
(like the Hittite one cited below in the Comment to v. 3) focuses on a body found in the open
because, given the size and life patterns of ancient towns, unsolvable murders would most often take
place outside of towns; within a town the victim's cries would usually be heard and the killer detected
(cf. Deut. 22:23–27). This is therefore a case of the principle that the rabbis called *dibber ha-katuv ba-
hoveh*, "the Bible cites the typical circumstance" without meaning to exclude others.⁶

not being known   Rather, "not having become known." The verb is in the perfect (past)
tense, implying that the ceremony is performed some time after the discovery of the body. An
investigation was probably to be conducted first to determine whether anybody knew the identity of
the killer.⁷

2. *your elders and magistrates*   Rather, "your elders and judges"; see Comments to 19:12;
1:16; 16:18. The wording "Your elders and judges," rather than "the elders and judges of the nearest
town" (cf. v. 3), implies that elders and judges from all over the region supervise the measuring to
make sure that it is conducted fairly.⁸

town nearest to the corpse shall then take a heifer which has never been worked, which has never pulled in a yoke; [4]and the elders of that town shall bring the heifer down to an everflowing wadi, which is not tilled or sown. There, in the wadi, they shall break the heifer's neck. [5]The priests, sons of Levi, shall come forward; for the LORD your God has chosen them to minister to Him and to pronounce blessing in the name of the LORD, and every lawsuit and case of assault is subject to their ruling. [6]Then all the elders of the town nearest to the corpse shall wash their hands over the heifer whose neck was broken in the wadi. [7]And they shall make this declaration: "Our hands did not shed

הַקְּרֹבָ֖ה אֶל־הֶחָלָ֑ל וְלָקְח֡וּ זִקְנֵי֩ הָעִ֨יר הַהִ֜וא
עֶגְלַ֣ת בָּקָ֗ר אֲשֶׁ֤ר לֹֽא־עֻבַּד֙ בָּ֔הּ אֲשֶׁ֥ר לֹא־
מָשְׁכָ֖ה בְּעֹֽל׃ 4 וְהוֹרִ֡דוּ זִקְנֵי֩ הָעִ֨יר הַהִ֤וא אֶת־
הָֽעֶגְלָה֙ אֶל־נַ֣חַל אֵיתָ֔ן אֲשֶׁ֛ר לֹא־יֵעָבֵ֥ד בּ֖וֹ וְלֹ֣א
יִזָּרֵ֑עַ וְעָֽרְפוּ־שָׁ֥ם אֶת־הָעֶגְלָ֖ה בַּנָּֽחַל׃ 5 וְנִגְּשׁ֣וּ
הַכֹּֽהֲנִים֮ בְּנֵ֣י לֵוִי֒ כִּ֣י בָ֗ם בָּחַ֞ר יְהוָ֤ה אֱלֹהֶ֙יךָ֙
לְשָׁ֣רְת֔וֹ וּלְבָרֵ֖ךְ בְּשֵׁ֣ם יְהוָ֑ה וְעַל־פִּיהֶ֥ם יִהְיֶ֖ה כָּל־
רִ֥יב וְכָל־נָֽגַע׃ 6 וְכֹ֗ל זִקְנֵי֙ הָעִ֣יר הַהִ֔וא הַקְּרֹבִ֖ים
אֶל־הֶֽחָלָ֑ל יִרְחֲצוּ֙ אֶת־יְדֵיהֶ֔ם עַל־הָעֶגְלָ֖ה
הָעֲרוּפָ֥ה בַנָּֽחַל׃ מפטיר 7 וְעָנ֖וּ וְאָמְר֑וּ יָדֵ֗ינוּ

---

3. the town nearest to the corpse The nearest town has the responsibility to purge the bloodguilt. This reflects a practice, common in the ancient Near East, that the town in or near which a crime took place was required to indemnify the victim or his survivors, since the perpetrator most likely came from there.[9] Even in cases of murder, ancient Near Eastern law was more often concerned with financial responsibility than with purgation of the bloodguilt.[10] Biblical law, on the other hand, presumes that it is impossible to compensate for loss of life; hence, it makes no provisions for compensating the survivors. Its concern is with the jeopardy in which the nation is placed by the unrequited blood that was shed in its midst.[11]

a heifer Halakhic sources define 'egel (fem. 'eglah) for legal purposes as a calf in its first or second year, like those mentioned in Leviticus 9:3 and Micah 6:6.[12]

which has never been worked, which has never pulled in a yoke This gives the heifer a ritual character, though its slaughter is not actually a sacrifice (see Excursus 19). The same qualities are required of firstlings, the red cow, and the cows that the Philistines sent to pull the wagon on which they returned the Ark of the Lord to Israel.[13]

4. an everflowing wadi A wadi with a perennial stream, as distinct from one that is full only in the rainy season. The translation of 'eitan as "everflowing" is uncertain. Modern scholars base this translation on a rare Arabic word watana, found in medieval Arabic dictionaries which state that it meant "be constant, unfailing," and was used especially of water, such as a continuously flowing (watin) spring.[14] A problem with this interpretation is that since there are not many perennial wadis in Israel, it would be difficult to carry out this ceremony, and purge bloodguilt, in most parts of the country.[15] Earlier commentators take 'eitan as "strong," "hard," meaning either strongly flowing[16] or rugged and resistant to cultivation.[17] Strongly flowing wadis are found throughout the land, though they are weak or empty in the dry season and would present a similar problem then. If the meaning is "rugged wadi," the point would presumably be that it cannot be cultivated, but then it would not be clear what advantage the wadi would have over any other remote, uncultivable spot.

which is not tilled or sown Meaning either that it is never tilled or sown or cannot be.

break the heifer's neck[18] According to Exodus 13:13 and 34:20 this is a method of slaughter used on firstlings of impure animals that may not be sacrificed.

5. The priests are present because of their normal duties (on which see Comments to 10:8; 17:9; and 18:5). Their exact role in the ceremony is not indicated. See Excursus 19.

6. Hands full of blood are a well-known symbol of guilt, and washing the hands a sign of innocence.[19] The function of handwashing in this ceremony is discussed in Excursus 19.

over the heifer[20]

7. The elders, speaking for their town, declare their innocence. The nature of this declaration is discussed in Excursus 19.

this blood, nor did our eyes see it done. ⁸Absolve, O LORD, Your people Israel whom You redeemed, and do not let guilt for the blood of the innocent remain among Your people Israel." And they will be absolved of bloodguilt. ⁹Thus you will remove from your midst guilt for the blood of the innocent, for you will be doing what is right in the sight of the LORD.

לֹא שָׁפְכוּ אֶת־הַדָּם הַזֶּה וְעֵינֵינוּ לֹא רָאוּ: ⁸ כַּפֵּר לְעַמְּךָ יִשְׂרָאֵל אֲשֶׁר־פָּדִיתָ יְהוָה וְאַל־תִּתֵּן דָּם נָקִי בְּקֶרֶב עַמְּךָ יִשְׂרָאֵל וְנִכַּפֵּר לָהֶם הַדָּם: ⁹ וְאַתָּה תְּבַעֵר הַדָּם הַנָּקִי מִקִּרְבֶּךָ כִּי־תַעֲשֶׂה הַיָּשָׁר בְּעֵינֵי יְהוָה: ס

KI TETSE'

כי תצא

¹⁰When you take the field against your enemies, and the

¹⁰ כִּי־תֵצֵא לַמִּלְחָמָה עַל־אֹיְבֶיךָ וּנְתָנוֹ יְהוָה

v. 7. שָׁפְכוּ ק'

this blood   The blood of the murder victim, or the bloodguilt caused by his murder.

nor did our eyes see it done   This means either, "We do not know who the killer is (and are not protecting him)," or "We did not see it happening and stand idly by."[21]

Literally, the Hebrew of the second clause states simply "our eyes did not see," and does not specify what was not seen. The Mishnah, prompted by the ambiguity, read the elders' entire declaration as a broad denial of communal negligence, meaning "He is not someone who came to us and we sent him away; we did not see him and leave him." The Palestinian rabbis took this paraphrase as referring to the victim: "We did not see him and send him away without an escort, nor did we leave him without food, causing him to try to steal food, in the course of which he was killed." For the Babylonian rabbis it referred to the killer: "We did not see him [kill] and neglect to bring him to justice."[22]

8.   The final stage in the ceremony is the elders' prayer. Whatever may be the meaning of the earlier acts, to Deuteronomy this is the key to absolution.

Your people Israel   The twofold mention of the people emphasizes that the nation as a whole, not only the nearest city, requires absolution because of its collective responsibility for bloodshed. Compare 19:10,13, and the introductory Comment to the Decalogue in chapter 5. According to Ibn Ezra the nation needs absolution for its negligence in failing to keep the roads safe.

whom you redeemed   See Comment to 9:26.

9.   See Comments to 13:5; 19:13; and 6:18.

According to the halakhah, if the killer is later discovered, he must be executed despite the fact that the bloodguilt has been absolved by the present ceremony.[23]

Miscellaneous Laws, Mostly about Civil and Domestic Life   (21:10–25:19)

Ki Tetse'   The final group of laws in Deuteronomy is primarily concerned with private matters regarding individuals, their families and their neighbors, in contrast to the preceding group, which dealt with public officials and matters concerning the nation as a whole.

Several laws in this section reflect Deuteronomy's concern for the welfare of women. The first two limit the rights of husbands who dislike their wives: verses 10–14 deal with the husband's treatment of a captive wife and limit his rights in case he seeks to be rid of her, and verses 15–17 protect the rights of the firstborn son of a disliked wife. Verses 22:13–21 likewise limit a husband's right to be rid of a wife he dislikes. Verse 24:5 guarantees the new bride a year of spousal companionship before her husband is sent to war. Concern for the welfare of women is also reflected in passages that stress their participation in religious ceremonies (12:12,18; 16:11,14; 29:10; 31:12) and deal with their manumission (15:12,17).

The sequence of the laws in this section is discussed in Excursus 13.

LORD your God delivers them into your power and you take some of them captive, [11]and you see among the captives a beautiful woman and you desire her and would take her to wife, [12]you shall bring her into your house, and she shall trim her hair, pare her nails, [13]and discard her captive's garb. She shall spend a month's time in your house lamenting her father and mother; after that you may come to her and possess her, and she shall be your wife.

אֱלֹהֶיךָ בְּיָדֶךָ וְשָׁבִיתָ שִׁבְיוֹ: 11 וְרָאִיתָ בַּשִּׁבְיָה
אֵשֶׁת יְפַת־תֹּאַר וְחָשַׁקְתָּ בָהּ וְלָקַחְתָּ לְךָ לְאִשָּׁה:
12 וַהֲבֵאתָהּ אֶל־תּוֹךְ בֵּיתֶךָ וְגִלְּחָה אֶת־רֹאשָׁהּ
וְעָשְׂתָה אֶת־צִפָּרְנֶיהָ: 13 וְהֵסִירָה אֶת־שִׂמְלַת
שִׁבְיָהּ מֵעָלֶיהָ וְיָשְׁבָה בְּבֵיתֶךָ וּבָכְתָה אֶת־אָבִיהָ
וְאֶת־אִמָּהּ יֶרַח יָמִים וְאַחַר כֵּן תָּבוֹא אֵלֶיהָ
וּבְעַלְתָּהּ וְהָיְתָה לְךָ לְאִשָּׁה: 14 וְהָיָה אִם־לֹא

THREE FAMILY LAWS   (vv. 10–21)

MARRIAGE WITH A WOMAN CAPTURED IN WAR (vv. 10–14)

The law dealing with marriage to a woman captured in war appears here and not in chapter 20 because it focuses on marital relations, not the war in which she is captured. Most women captives in the ancient world became slaves (see 20:14 and Judg. 5:30), but in some cases a soldier found one whom he desired to take as a wife or concubine, a practice well known from Homeric Greece and early Arabia.[24] This law requires a soldier who wishes to marry a captive woman to show consideration for her feelings. He must allow her to adjust to all that has happened by bringing her back to his home and waiting a month before marrying her. In case he later becomes dissatisfied with her, he may not reduce her to slavery. A significant aspect of this law is its respect for the personhood of the captive woman and the moral obligations created by initiating a sexual relationship with her.[25]

In the light of 20:10–18, this law, permitting marriage with foreign women, must refer to non-Canaanite women. It apparently does not regard them as posing the same threat to Israel's religious integrity as would Canaanites. Perhaps it assumes that since they are separated from their own culture, they will quickly assimilate to Israelite ways and will not attract their husbands to their own native religion.

By talmudic times a formal procedure of religious conversion had been created and the halakhah permitted such marriages only if the woman agreed to convert to Judaism (on conversion, see Excursus 21). Even so, the rabbis took a dim view of marriage with captives. They regarded such unions as motivated by lust and considered the present law a concession to the likelihood that they would take place whether permitted or not. In their view, verses 12–13 are designed to delay and, ideally, discourage such a marriage by making the woman unattractive.[26]

11.   *a beautiful woman*   Since verse 13 does not mention a husband, for whom a married captive would surely mourn, the law possibly has only unmarried women in mind.[27]

12–13.   *she shall trim her hair, pare her nails, and discard her captive's garb*   Josephus and Ramban see these acts as part of the woman's mourning for her family and countrymen (see v. 13).[28] Rashi and Abravanel, following R. Akiba, see them as separate acts intended to make her unappealing so that her captor, who was attracted by her beauty, might change his mind about marrying this pagan woman.[29] Some commentators think that they signify her change of status: by discarding her old clothing and those parts of her body that are removable, she "sheds" her former life,[30] or even her former self, since hair, fingernails, and clothing are sometimes regarded as symbolizing the person.[31]

13.   *a month's time . . . lamenting her father and mother*   Because they died in the war (Ibn Ezra) or because she will never see them again (Ramban). In either case, the law recognizes her grief and requires respect for it: "It is not decent for you to take your pleasure in her while she is weeping" (Bekhor Shor; Ḥazzekuni). Thirty days are a normal period of mourning. The same period was observed for Aaron and Moses[32] and is part of Jewish mourning practice to this day.

14.   Establishing a sexual relationship imposes obligations on the husband. If he should later change his mind about the captive, he must treat her as a free woman and release her; he may not sell her or treat her as a slave (cf. Exod. 21:7–11). A similar provision is known from Arabia of the time of Mohammed: once a woman became pregnant by her captor it was not proper for her to be

¹⁴Then, should you no longer want her, you must release her outright. You must not sell her for money: since you had your will of her, you must not enslave her.

חֲפַצְתָּ בָּהּ וְשִׁלַּחְתָּהּ לְנַפְשָׁהּ וּמָכֹר לֹא־תִמְכְּרֶנָּה בַּכֶּסֶף לֹא־תִתְעַמֵּר בָּהּ תַּחַת אֲשֶׁר עִנִּיתָהּ: ס

¹⁵If a man has two wives, one loved and the other unloved, and both the loved and the unloved have borne him sons, but the first-born is the son of the unloved one—¹⁶when he wills his property to his sons, he may not treat as first-born the son of the loved one in disregard of

כִּי־תִהְיֶיןָ לְאִישׁ שְׁתֵּי נָשִׁים הָאַחַת אֲהוּבָה וְהָאַחַת שְׂנוּאָה וְיָלְדוּ־לוֹ בָנִים הָאֲהוּבָה וְהַשְּׂנוּאָה וְהָיָה הַבֵּן הַבְּכוֹר לַשְּׂנִיאָה: ¹⁶ וְהָיָה בְּיוֹם הַנְחִילוֹ אֶת־בָּנָיו אֵת אֲשֶׁר־יִהְיֶה לוֹ לֹא

sold in the market or even ransomed to her own people.[33] There, however, pregnancy was the determining factor; here it is the sexual relationship as such. This provision would have had the effect of causing a man to think twice before marrying a captive, since the marriage would diminish her potential economic value to him.[34]

should you no longer want her R. Meyuḥas interprets this condition homiletically as a warning: since such a marriage is undertaken because of attraction to the captive's beauty, this verse teaches that if one marries a woman (any woman, not only a captive) solely because of beauty, he will ultimately dislike her.

enslave The meaning of *tit'amer* is uncertain. This translation is an ancient conjecture based on the context here and in 24:7, the only other place in which it appears.[35]

THE RIGHT OF THE FIRSTBORN IN A POLYGAMOUS FAMILY (vv. 15–17)

In much of the ancient Near East, even before the time of the Torah, the firstborn son had the right to inherit a larger share of his father's estate than the other sons did. The present law seeks to protect this right in circumstances where it might be overridden by extraneous factors. The law envisages a situation where the father may be tempted to pass over the firstborn in favor of a younger son because he prefers the latter's mother. It forbids this because the right of the biological firstborn is inherent in his being the "first fruit of his [father's] vigor" (v. 17).

There were several varieties of firstborn inheritance rights in the ancient Near East.[36] In some places the firstborn received the entire estate; in others an extra ten percent or a double share; and in others he received an equal share but was entitled to choose his share first. It was not always the biological firstborn who was designated chief heir: in some cases it was the son of the first wife, no matter when he was born; in others it was whichever son the father chose.[37]

15. one loved and the other unloved As in the case of Jacob's wives Rachel and Leah, and Elkanah's wives Hannah and Peninah.[38] Literally the two Hebrew terms mean "loved" and "hated," but in describing a husband's feelings toward his wives, they mean his favorite wife and any other, whether she is simply unfavored, the object of indifference, or disliked.[39] The literal meaning of "hated," however, prompted Rabbi Ishmael to comment that the text's choice of words constitutes a warning that if one marries two wives, he will wind up hating one of them.[40]

first-born It is clear from verse 17 that here this refers to the firstborn of the father, not necessarily that of the mother. In contrast, the laws about sacrificing and redeeming the firstborn refer to the firstborn of the mother, but not necessarily of the father (see, for example, Exod. 13:2).[41]

16. when he wills his property to his sons From here it appears that the father could divide his property among his sons as he wished, so long as he did not violate the following prescription.[42]

17. double portion Hebrew *pi shenayim* means "a portion [lit., mouth] of two" or "two portions [mouths]." The ancient translations and halakhic exegesis understand this as meaning two shares of the estate.[43] This interpretation is consistent with the fact that in some parts of the ancient Near East a man's estate was divided into shares equal to one more than the number of his sons; his chief heir received two of these shares and the others each received one.[44] However, another

the son of the unloved one who is older. [17]Instead, he must accept the first-born, the son of the unloved one, and allot to him a double portion of all he possesses; since he is the first fruit of his vigor, the birthright is his due.

יוּכַל לְבַכֵּר אֶת־בֶּן־הָאֲהוּבָה עַל־פְּנֵי בֶן־הַשְּׂנוּאָה הַבְּכֹר: [17] כִּי אֶת־הַבְּכֹר בֶּן־הַשְּׂנוּאָה יַכִּיר לָתֶת לוֹ פִּי שְׁנַיִם בְּכֹל אֲשֶׁר־יִמָּצֵא לוֹ כִּי־הוּא רֵאשִׁית אֹנוֹ לוֹ מִשְׁפַּט הַבְּכֹרָה: ס

interpretation is also possible. In Zechariah 13:8, *pi shenayim* is an idiom for "two-thirds."[45] Hence, the present law may mean that the firstborn inherits two-thirds of the estate. Ibn Janaḥ argues that the text uses this idiom only because in the present, hypothetical case, there are only two heirs and a double share amounts to two-thirds of the estate; where there are more heirs, the firstborn would receive less than two-thirds—whatever a double share would amount to. However, an adoption contract from Mari stipulates that the chief heir would receive two-thirds of the estate no matter how many others there were.[46] This may seem excessive to the modern reader, but it is plausible in light of the fact that in some places the chief heir received the entire estate, as was the case in medieval England.

he is the first fruit of his vigor   This is a common description of the firstborn, who is proof of his father's potency and a token of future fertility.[47] Priority of birth was considered so important that when the twins Zerah and Perez were being delivered and the hand of the first emerged, the midwife tied a crimson thread to it so that there could be no mistake about whose birth began first (Gen. 38:27–28).[48]

To the Bible, the preferential share is so bound up with the firstborn that it is called the "birthright," *bekhorah*, which literally means "primogeniture," "first-bornship."[49] Nevertheless, the granting of a preferential share to one of the sons and the special status of the firstborn are separate issues and are not inherently connected. This is indicated by the fact that fathers might be tempted to grant the preferential share to some other son and that in some places they regularly did so, and by the fact that preferential shares were sometimes awarded to adopted sons. The purpose of granting one son a preferential share may have been to enable him to bear additional responsibilities as head of the family, such as managing the estate on behalf of all the survivors, providing for survivors who were minors, bearing the costs of burying and mourning for deceased parents, or simply to enable him to carry on his father's name in dignity. In societies where the father chose the chief heir, his choice may have been based on his estimation of who could best carry out these responsibilities.

THE PUNISHMENT OF AN INSUBORDINATE SON (vv. 18–21)

Verses 18–21 describe the procedure to be followed if a son is repeatedly insubordinate and his parents conclude that there is no hope of reforming him: they are to bring him before the town elders who will hear the case and, if they agree, order his execution. The law seeks to deter filial insubordination, but, by requiring that the case be judged by the elders, it also places limits on parental authority, as does the preceding law. Earlier, in the patriarchal period, it appears that the father's authority over his children was absolute, like the *patria potestas* of early Roman law, even to the point of his being able to have them executed for wrongdoing; this is implied by Judah's ability to order the execution of his daughter-in-law for adultery, with no trial (Gen. 38:24).[50] The present law respects the parents' right to discipline their son, but it prevents them from having him executed on their own authority. This may only be done by the community at large on the authority of the elders.

Ancient Near Eastern laws and documents also mention legal action by parents against misbehaving children. The grounds include such offenses against parents as disobedience, flight, repudiation, lawsuits against them, failure to respect and provide for them in their old age, and striking them. The punishments range from disinheritance to enslavement and mutilation.[51]

Filial insubordination is a grave offense because respect and obedience toward parents is regarded as the cornerstone of all order and authority, especially in a tribal, patriarchal society like ancient Israel. If the death penalty specified by the present law is meant literally, it implies that biblical law regards insubordination and the danger it poses to the stability of society more severely than do other known ancient Near Eastern laws. The fact that Exodus 21:15 requires the death penalty for striking one's parents, whereas the Laws of Hammurabi require only that the son's hand

¹⁸If a man has a wayward and defiant son, who does not heed his father or mother and does not obey them even after they discipline him, ¹⁹his father and mother shall take hold of him and bring him out to the elders of his town at the public place of his community. ²⁰They shall say to the elders of his town, "This son of ours is disloyal and defiant; he does not heed us. He is a glutton and a drunkard." ²¹Thereupon the men of his town shall stone him to death. Thus you will sweep out evil from your midst: all Israel will hear and be afraid.

18 כִּי־יִהְיֶ֣ה לְאִ֗ישׁ בֵּ֚ן סוֹרֵ֣ר וּמוֹרֶ֔ה אֵינֶ֣נּוּ שֹׁמֵ֔עַ בְּק֥וֹל אָבִ֖יו וּבְק֣וֹל אִמּ֑וֹ וְיִסְּר֣וּ אֹת֔וֹ וְלֹ֥א יִשְׁמַ֖ע אֲלֵיהֶֽם: 19 וְתָ֥פְשׂוּ ב֖וֹ אָבִ֣יו וְאִמּ֑וֹ וְהוֹצִ֧יאוּ אֹת֛וֹ אֶל־זִקְנֵ֥י עִיר֖וֹ וְאֶל־שַׁ֥עַר מְקֹמֽוֹ: 20 וְאָמְר֞וּ אֶל־זִקְנֵ֣י עִיר֗וֹ בְּנֵ֤נוּ זֶה֙ סוֹרֵ֣ר וּמֹרֶ֔ה אֵינֶ֥נּוּ שֹׁמֵ֖עַ בְּקֹלֵ֑נוּ זוֹלֵ֖ל וְסֹבֵֽא: 21 וּרְגָמֻ֠הוּ כָּל־אַנְשֵׁ֨י עִיר֤וֹ בָאֲבָנִים֙ וָמֵ֔ת וּבִֽעַרְתָּ֥ הָרָ֖ע מִקִּרְבֶּ֑ךָ וְכָל־יִשְׂרָאֵ֖ל יִשְׁמְע֥וּ וְיִרָֽאוּ: ס שני

be cut off, supports this inference. Nevertheless, some scholars, modern and ancient, believe that the death penalty stipulated in the present law is meant only rhetorically, *in terrorem*, to strengthen parental authority and deter the young from disobedience. As in the case of the apostate city (13:13–19), halakhic exegesis subjected the law to an exceedingly narrow reading, according to which it could hardly ever be carried out. Several rabbis held that it was never actually applied, but was stated in the Torah only for educational purposes.[52]

18. *his father or mother*   The Torah requires equal respect for both; see Comment to 5:16.

even after they discipline him   This indicates that the son is a repeated offender. The halakhah understands "discipline" (*y-s-r*) as flogging, as in 22:18 and elsewhere.[53] Flogging was regarded as a proper and effective means of deterring sons from evil and self-destructive behavior. As the book of Proverbs puts it, "Rod and reproof produce wisdom"; "Do not withhold discipline from a child. . . . Beat him with a rod and you will save him from the grave"; "He who spares the rod hates his son, / But he who loves him disciplines him early."[54]

19. *his father and mother shall . . . bring him*   The fact that both parents must agree deprives the father of unilateral authority even to prosecute his son. In view of the preceding law, the requirement that the mother concur in the charge would also prevent a father from falsely charging his firstborn from an unfavored wife as a pretext for depriving him of his inheritance rights.[55]

to the elders . . . at the public place   See Comments to 17:5 and 6:9.

20. *He is a glutton and a drunkard*   This is probably meant as a typical example of insubordination. As Proverbs 28:7 declares, "An intelligent son heeds instruction, / But he who keeps company with gluttons disgraces his father." The same offense is deprecated in Proverbs 23:20–21: "Do not be of those who guzzle wine, / Or glut themselves on meat; / For guzzlers and gluttons will be impoverished, / And drowsing will clothe you in tatters." The law's choice of this example implies that disobedience to parents is a capital crime even when the specific offense is not otherwise criminal. Essentially the same principle is involved in 17:12, where insubordination to the high court is punishable by death even if the original offense about which it ruled was not.

21. *thereupon*   The Hebrew is simply the conjunction and does not necessarily imply that an execution follows immediately upon the parents' declaration. Presumably the elders first conduct a hearing to determine whether the son really is guilty and incorrigible, or whether the parents are merely speaking out of frustration and anger. Perhaps they would seek to mediate between the parents and the son. According to the halakhah, they actually conduct a trial. They would probably order the son's execution only when all else failed.[57]

the men of his town shall stone him to death   Unlike the normal practice, where the accusers initiate the stoning (17:7), the parents are not said to participate. Perhaps this is out of sensitivity to their feelings, though it also indicates that they do not have the power of life and death over their children[58] and that the community as a whole is outraged by insubordination, since it threatens the community's stability.

On the penalty of stoning and its deterrent effect see Comment to 13:11,12.

sweep out evil   See Comment to 13:6.

²²If a man is guilty of a capital offense and is put to death, and you impale him on a stake, ²³you must not let his corpse remain on the stake overnight, but must bury him the same day. For an impaled body is an affront to God: you shall not defile the land that the LORD your God is giving you to possess.

כב וְכִי־יִהְיֶה בְאִישׁ חֵטְא מִשְׁפַּט־מָוֶת וְהוּמָת וְתָלִיתָ אֹתוֹ עַל־עֵץ: כג לֹא־תָלִין נִבְלָתוֹ עַל־הָעֵץ כִּי־קָבוֹר תִּקְבְּרֶנּוּ בַּיּוֹם הַהוּא כִּי־קִלְלַת אֱלֹהִים תָּלוּי וְלֹא תְטַמֵּא אֶת־אַדְמָתְךָ אֲשֶׁר יְהֹוָה אֱלֹהֶיךָ נֹתֵן לְךָ נַחֲלָה: ס

TREATMENT OF THE BODY OF AN EXECUTED CRIMINAL (vv. 22–23)

After execution, the body of a criminal might be hung and exposed. The law prohibits continuing the exposure beyond sunset; the body must be buried the same day.

22. *and is put to death and you impale him on a stake* The second phrase refers to exposing the criminal's body after execution, a practice mentioned elsewhere in the Bible.[59] The phrase is literally "hang on a tree" or "on wood" and does not necessarily mean impaling. According to the Mishnah a gibbet (a pole with a horizontal beam) was erected and the dead man's hands were bound and slung over the beam, leaving his body suspended. The translation "impale on a stake" is based on Assyrian practice.[60] Whatever the exact means, exposure served to degrade the criminal and warn others against similar conduct, and was perhaps originally intended as well to deprive him of proper burial. See first Comment to verse 23.

This verse does not *require* hanging the body, but merely reflects the existence of the practice. It was not necessarily common. In Mesopotamian law it was rare, and both in Israel and Mesopotamia it seems to have been applied in war more commonly than in criminal cases.[61]

23. *you must not let his corpse remain on the stake overnight, but must bury him the same day* In the Egyptian practice mentioned in Genesis 40:19, the impaled body of the offender is left unburied (as in the Middle Assyrian Laws) and its flesh is eaten by birds. Denial of burial and exposure of the body to predators is often mentioned in the Bible as a grievous curse, perhaps because of the folk belief that the unburied find no rest in the netherworld.[62] The present law forbids extension of the punishment in this way: exposure must not last beyond the day of execution.

The Talmud cites this passage as the basis of the requirement that all persons must be buried on the day of their death unless a delay is necessary for a suitably honorable burial.[63]

an impaled body is an affront to God This clause has occasioned considerable speculation because the meaning and syntax of the final phrase, *kilelat 'elohim*, are ambiguous. The present translation reflects a rabbinic explanation that the criminal's body may not be maltreated since that would be an offense against God in whose image even the criminal was created.[64] This is a homiletically attractive view but it is problematic in the context, because if impalement was an affront to God it should not be performed at all.

Since God is almost never referred to as *'elohim* in the laws of Deuteronomy, it is quite possible that Sforno's view is the correct one: *'elohim* here does not mean "God" but "spirit," and the clause means that an impaled body is an affront to the spirit of the dead man.[65] Tur Sinai speculates that the requirement of burial by nightfall reflects a popular belief that the spirits of the dead rise up to earth at night and that the spirit of the executed man would harm the living if it found his body still unburied. If this is the original reason for the prohibition, that may be why Deuteronomy saw fit to add a second reason, more in keeping with biblical law, in the next clause.

you shall not defile the land A dead body is the primary source of ritual impurity in the Bible, and if it were left to decompose, its parts would eventually be scattered by birds and animals, spreading the impurity. Ezekiel reflects the same concept when he describes burying the scattered corpses of Gog's army as a cleansing of the land (Ezek. 39:11–16).[66]

According to Joshua 8:29 and 10:27, the bodies of Canaanite kings were hung by Joshua and then buried by nightfall in conformity with the present law.

22 If you see your fellow's ox or sheep gone astray, do not ignore it; you must take it back to your fellow. ²If your fellow does not live near you or you do not know who he is, you shall bring it home and it shall remain with you until your fellow claims it; then you shall give it back to him. ³You shall do the same with his ass; you shall do the same with his garment; and so too shall you do with anything that your fellow loses and you find: you must not remain indifferent.

כ"ב לֹא־תִרְאֶה אֶת־שׁוֹר אָחִיךָ אוֹ אֶת־שֵׂיוֹ
נִדָּחִים וְהִתְעַלַּמְתָּ מֵהֶם הָשֵׁב תְּשִׁיבֵם לְאָחִיךָ:
2 וְאִם־לֹא קָרוֹב אָחִיךָ אֵלֶיךָ וְלֹא יְדַעְתּוֹ וַאֲסַפְתּוֹ
אֶל־תּוֹךְ בֵּיתֶךָ וְהָיָה עִמְּךָ עַד דְּרֹשׁ אָחִיךָ אֹתוֹ
וַהֲשֵׁבֹתוֹ לוֹ: 3 וְכֵן תַּעֲשֶׂה לַחֲמֹרוֹ וְכֵן תַּעֲשֶׂה
לְשִׂמְלָתוֹ וְכֵן תַּעֲשֶׂה לְכָל־אֲבֵדַת אָחִיךָ אֲשֶׁר־
תֹּאבַד מִמֶּנּוּ וּמְצָאתָהּ לֹא תוּכַל לְהִתְעַלֵּם: ס

CHAPTER **22**   MISCELLANEOUS DOMESTIC LAWS   (vv. 1–12)

This section consists of nine laws, dealing mostly with property: domestic animals, clothing, houses, and vineyards.[1] The connections between them are discussed in Excursus 13.

RETURNING LOST ANIMALS (vv. 1–4)

This law and that in v. 4 require assisting one's fellow in certain situations where he faces difficulty or possible economic loss. They paraphrase and supplement Exodus 23:4–5.[2]

1.   *your fellow's* Literally, "your brother's." See Comment to 1:16. These four verses use this designation five times. This reminder that the owner of the animal is one's kinsman counters the temptation to ignore his problem because it would be inconvenient or expensive to return, feed, or lift the animal. According to Exodus 23:4–5, one must help even when the owner of the animal is one's enemy.

gone astray Since much of the population owned livestock and animals were used for transport, it was common to come upon strays.[3]

do not ignore it The same admonition appears in verse 4, where it is translated "you must not remain indifferent." It is not present in the basic law in Exodus, but the following law there includes a similar condition, "and [if] you would refrain from raising [a fallen animal]" (Exod. 23:4), which may have suggested the idea to Deuteronomy. Anticipation of psychological reactions is common in Deuteronomy, with its sermonic approach to the law; compare, for example, 15:9,18.[4]

2–3.   These verses elaborate on the basic law, answering questions that must have arisen about implementing it: What is to be done if the owner is distant or unknown? Does this law apply only to the animals named or to other animals and inanimate objects as well? Questions and answers such as these initiated the legal discussion that is continued in the Talmud (particularly in Tractate Bava Metsia), which discusses the finder's and the owner's responsibilities and distinguishes between things that the finder must try to return and those he may keep.[5]

2.   *you shall bring it home* Literally, "bring it inside [*'el-tokh*] your house." In multistory homes, especially in villages, the ground floor often served as a stable for cattle. The practice is reflected in 1 Samuel 28:24, where a woman has a calf in her house. Houses of this type were still found in Palestinian villages in modern times.[6] The law means, therefore, that one must house the stray animal as if it were one's own.

until your fellow claims it According to the halakhah, the finder must publicize what he has found and the owner must prove it is his by describing its identifying marks.[7]

give it back to him The law had to anticipate attempts by people to keep what they found. Exodus 22:8 and Leviticus 5:20–26 deal with situations where the finder refuses to return the property, claiming that it is his or that he does not have it. Ancient Near Eastern law collections deal with similar attempts.[8]

3.   With this supplementary list the law covers the two main types of cattle (v. 1), the main

⁴If you see your fellow's ass or ox fallen on the road, do not ignore it; you must help him raise it.

⁵A woman must not put on man's apparel, nor shall a man wear woman's clothing; for whoever does these things is abhorrent to the LORD your God.

4 לֹא־תִרְאֶה֩ אֶת־חֲמ֨וֹר אָחִ֜יךָ א֤וֹ שׁוֹרוֹ֙ נֹֽפְלִ֣ים
בַּדֶּ֔רֶךְ וְהִתְעַלַּמְתָּ֖ מֵהֶ֑ם הָקֵ֥ם תָּקִ֖ים עִמּֽוֹ׃ ס
5 לֹא־יִהְיֶ֤ה כְלִי־גֶ֨בֶר֙ עַל־אִשָּׁ֔ה וְלֹא־יִלְבַּ֥שׁ גֶּ֖בֶר
שִׂמְלַ֣ת אִשָּׁ֑ה כִּ֧י תוֹעֲבַ֛ת יְהוָ֥ה אֱלֹהֶ֖יךָ כָּל־עֹ֥שֵׂה
אֵֽלֶּה׃ פ

beast of burden, clothing, and "anything else." This is the full range of lost property summarized in Exodus 22:8.

ASSISTING WITH FALLEN ANIMALS (v. 4)

4. *ass or ox* These are the usual beasts of burden. According to the halakhah the obligation applies to any animal.[9]

fallen . . . raise it The situation is clarified by the wording in Exodus 23:5, "lying under its burden": a pack animal might collapse or lose its balance under its load. The fastest way to raise it was for two people to lift the load simultaneously, one on each side of the animal; otherwise it had to be unpacked and repacked, which also might require two people.

Some talmudic sages hold that this commandment, specifically the version in Exodus 23:5, is meant to benefit the animal as well as its owner. They cite it as evidence that the obligation to prevent animals from suffering (called *tsaʿar baʿalei ḥayyim*) has its origin in the Torah.[10] The details of this commandment are elaborated in Tractate Bava Metsia.

NOT WEARING CLOTHING OF THE OPPOSITE SEX (v. 5)

Several plausible reasons have been suggested for this commandment. Some think that it is directed against disguising oneself as a member of the opposite sex since this would facilitate mingling with them and hence fornication. Others think that transvestism is inherently abhorrent, either because it blurs the sexual differences that God created (see Gen. 1:27 and compare the laws of forbidden mixtures below, vv. 9–11), because it is a perverse means of sexual stimulation or homosexual role-playing, or because it was a part of certain pagan rites and magical practices.[11] Pertinent to the suggestion that it was a pagan practice is a Babylonian adage, according to which a person who is apparently an Amorite says to his wife, "You be the man and I'll be the woman," but there is no indication of what act this refers to.[12]

put on a man's apparel Literally, "a man's *keli* may not be on a woman." The translation "apparel" makes this clause synonymous with the second part of the verse; it is based on the fact that the plural of *keli* means "clothing" in rabbinic Hebrew. However, it is not certain that it has this meaning in biblical Hebrew, where it normally means "implement, vessel," or—as Targum Onkelos and R. Eliezer b. Jacob take it here—"weapon."[13] This would not necessarily eliminate any of the possible explanations of the law listed above, since weapons, as symbols of masculinity, could have been used for any of the purposes mentioned. The halakhah combines both views: women may not wear armor or clothing, hairdos, or other adornments that are characteristic of men, nor may men wear what is characteristic of women (what is characteristic of each sex is defined by local practice).[14]

abhorrent See Comment to 7:25.

NOT CAPTURING A MOTHER BIRD ALONG WITH HER YOUNG (vv. 6–7)

This law is similar to Leviticus 22:28, "No animal from the herd or from the flock shall be slaughtered on the same day with its young." Both laws inculcate reverence for the parent-child relationship even among animals. This motive is suggested by the preceding law in Leviticus 22:27: "When an ox or a sheep or a goat is born, it shall stay seven days with its mother, and from the eighth day on it shall be acceptable as an offering." The prohibition of boiling a kid in its mother's milk (14:21) most likely has essentially the same motive. The halakhic details of the law, such as when and where it applies, are presented in Tractate Ḥullin, chapter 12.

⁶If, along the road, you chance upon a bird's nest, in any tree or on the ground, with fledglings or eggs and the mother sitting over the fledglings or on the eggs, do not take the mother together with her young. ⁷Let the mother go, and take only the young, in order that you may fare well and have a long life.

⁸When you build a new house, you shall make a parapet for your roof, so that you do not bring bloodguilt on your house if anyone should fall from it.

כִּי יִקָּרֵא קַן־צִפּוֹר ׀ לְפָנֶיךָ בַּדֶּרֶךְ בְּכָל־עֵץ ׀ 6
אוֹ עַל־הָאָרֶץ אֶפְרֹחִים אוֹ בֵיצִים וְהָאֵם רֹבֶצֶת
עַל־הָאֶפְרֹחִים אוֹ עַל־הַבֵּיצִים לֹא־תִקַּח הָאֵם
עַל־הַבָּנִים: 7 שַׁלֵּחַ תְּשַׁלַּח אֶת־הָאֵם וְאֶת־הַבָּנִים
תִּקַּח־לָךְ לְמַעַן יִיטַב לָךְ וְהַאֲרַכְתָּ יָמִים: ס
שלישי
כִּי תִבְנֶה בַּיִת חָדָשׁ וְעָשִׂיתָ מַעֲקֶה לְגַגֶּךָ וְלֹא־ 8
תָשִׂים דָּמִים בְּבֵיתֶךָ כִּי־יִפֹּל הַנֹּפֵל מִמֶּנּוּ: ס

6. _the mother together with her young_ Hebrew *'em 'al banim*. The same phrase, which also appears in descriptions of warfare,[15] was evidently a common expression denoting total, cruel extermination. Its use here may be an allusion to such descriptions, so as to indicate that taking the mother bird together with its offspring would mark one as ruthless.

7. _Let the mother go_ Hebrew *shalleah teshallah* can mean either "release" or "chase away."[16] Traditionally the latter interpretation has been preferred, and the law has been explained as sparing the mother the painful sight of seeing her offspring taken away.[17] However, it is not likely that chasing the mother away would spare her pain, since forcible separation from her young and finding them gone later would also be painful. Nor do the comparable laws prevent pain (the mother animal would not know if her calf or kid was sacrificed on the same day or boiled in her milk). What the text finds callous are the acts themselves, quite apart from any impact they may have on the mother.

in order that you may fare well and have a long life These clauses repeat, in reverse order, the reward promised for honoring parents in the Decalogue (5:16). Inversion of clauses often indicates an intentional allusion to earlier passages in biblical literature. This allusion calls attention to the fact that the present command is likewise an aspect of respecting a parent.[18]

To Abravanel the promise of a long life signals an additional aim of the law, conservation of natural resources: releasing the mother enables her to produce more offspring in the future and thus helps maintain the supply of food needed by humans. In a similar vein, Sefer Ha-Ḥinnukh holds that the aim of the law is to teach that God does not want any species to become extinct.[19]

BUILDING A PARAPET (v. 8)

The roofs of houses in the ancient Near East were flat and were regularly used for a variety of purposes: drying and storing produce, strolling and socializing, and sleeping in warm weather. Hence people were in constant danger of falling off unless a protective barrier was built.[20]

This law is comparable to Exodus 21:33–34, which holds a person responsible if an animal falls into a pit he has left uncovered. Halakhic literature sees it as an example of an obligation to block or remove anything on one's property that is capable of causing death, such as a pit, a faulty ladder, or a vicious dog; and to personally avoid potentially harmful food and drink and other risky practices. It has recently been argued that the principle underlying this obligation would support a ban against smoking.[21]

8. _When you build a new house_ According to the halakhah, one must also build a parapet if he acquires an old house that lacks one, and a blessing is to be recited when building it.[22]

parapet a low wall around the edge of the roof. According to the halakhah, it must be at least ten hand-breadths (thirty inches) high and strong enough not to collapse if someone leans on it.[23]

do not bring bloodguilt on your house Because a human life is involved, such criminal negligence would be tantamount to homicide.

9You shall not sow your vineyard with a second kind of seed, else the crop—from the seed you have sown—and the yield of the vineyard may not be used. 10You shall not plow with an ox and an ass together. 11You shall not wear cloth combining wool and linen.

9 לֹא־תִזְרַ֤ע כַּרְמְךָ֙ כִּלְאָ֔יִם פֶּן־תִּקְדַּ֗שׁ הַֽמְלֵאָ֛ה הַזֶּ֛רַע אֲשֶׁ֥ר תִּזְרָ֖ע וּתְבוּאַ֥ת הַכָּֽרֶם׃ ס 10 לֹא־תַחֲרֹ֥שׁ בְּשֽׁוֹר־וּבַחֲמֹ֖ר יַחְדָּֽו׃ ס 11 לֹ֤א תִלְבַּשׁ֙ שַֽׁעַטְנֵ֔ז צֶ֥מֶר וּפִשְׁתִּ֖ים יַחְדָּֽו׃ ס

FORBIDDEN COMBINATIONS OF SEED, PLOW ANIMALS, AND TEXTILES (vv. 9–11)

These three provisions supplement related ones in Leviticus 19:19: "You shall observe My laws. You shall not let your cattle mate with a different kind; you shall not sow your field with two kinds of seed; you shall not put on cloth from a mixture of two kinds of material." These mixtures are termed *kil'ayim*, "two kinds," "different/second kind."[24]

The reason for these laws is uncertain. To Rashi they are sovereign decrees of God, for which no reason need be given.[25] Many commentators believe that their aim is to preserve the species distinctions that God established at creation, as described in Genesis 1:11–12,21,24–25.[26]

Though all these laws deal with forbidden combinations, it is probable that each of them originally had its own specific purpose, as will be noted in Comments below. Precisely which practices and species are covered by these laws, where they apply, and what may or may not be done with the products of such mixtures is discussed in detail in Tractate Kil'ayim.

9. *You shall not sow your vineyard* In Leviticus 19:19 the wording is "you shall not sow your *field*." The present law indicates that vineyards are covered as well. To halakhic exegesis the juxtaposition of sowing and mating in Leviticus 19:19 implies that sowing includes plant grafting, but this is not the plain sense of the text.

with a second kind of seed Literally, "with two kinds of seed." The translation agrees with the view of Josephus and R. Jonathan, according to which "two kinds" means the grapes and one other crop.[27] The halakhah endorses the opposing view of R. Josiah that the verse refers to two kinds of seed *in addition* to the grapes.[28]

Mixing of crops in the same field ("mixed cropping" or "intercropping") is practiced in many places, especially in areas of subsistence farming and where arable land is scarce. Although mixed cropping is less efficient, for the purpose of harvesting, than growing each crop in a separate field, it enables different species of plants to benefit from the nutrients given off by each other and can thereby increase the yield of all species in the field. It also spreads the risk of crop failure in case of a shortage of water, since different plants require less water than others do. Also, because pests and diseases attack specific plants and not others, the entire field is not at risk in the case of these dangers. These protective benefits are not entirely eliminated by the present law: the replenishing of depleted nutrients can be accomplished by crop rotation, and the halakhah requires only enough space between species to prevent them from drawing sustenance from each other and to make their separation visible.[29]

The reason for the prohibition of mixed cropping is not clear. Since it is not a method of hybridization, the practice does not undermine the species distinctions established at creation. Nevertheless, mixing of plant seed may have been regarded as sufficiently similar to the mixing of animal seed that they seemed analogous. Ramban's explanation may well express the reasoning of the Torah: "The nature and form [of the mixed seeds] are modified by their drawing nourishment from each other, and it is as if each resultant grain is composed of two species."[30]

the crop[31]

may not be used Hebrew *tikdash*, literally, "become sacrosanct." This probably means that the crop will become forbidden for use. According to the halakhah, it must be burnt.[32]

10. The present law protects draught animals. Since the ox and the ass are of unequal strength, if they were yoked together the stronger one might exhaust the weaker (Varro, a Roman writer on agriculture, advises against pairing two oxen of unequal strength for this reason), or one might cause the other to stumble and be injured.[33]

¹²You shall make tassels on the four corners of the garment with which you cover yourself.

גְּדִלִים תַּעֲשֶׂה־לָּךְ עַל־אַרְבַּע כַּנְפוֹת כְּסוּתְךָ ¹²
אֲשֶׁר תְּכַסֶּה־בָּהּ: ס

11. This prohibition cannot be viewed as protecting the distinction between species. It does not prohibit combining wool and linen, but only wearing a cloth made from that combination. The rabbis could think of no explanation for this prohibition and considered it one of the commandments for which there is no apparent reason and which other nations and the "impulse for evil" challenge, like the ceremony of the broken-necked heifer in 21:1–9.[34] Josephus's conjecture is probably correct: the prohibition applies to the laity, because the priests, when they officiate, do wear garments made of such mixtures. The status of such garments is thus comparable to that of the sacred anointing oil and the incense that is used in the sanctuary and may not be made or used by laypersons, as stated in Exodus 30:22–37.[35]

Literally, the verse reads "You shall not wear *sha'atnez,* wool and linen together." The final phrase explains the meaning of *sha'atnez,* a term of non-Hebrew, possibly Egyptian, origin. In Leviticus 19:19 the term appears in apposition to *beged kil'ayim,* "cloth of two kinds of material." Pairing wool and linen made for a stronger fabric; fragments of such fabric have been unearthed at the site of Kuntillet Ajrud in the Sinai Peninsula, where religiously heterodox inscriptions in Hebrew were also found, along with inscriptions in other languages.[36]

TASSELS ON GARMENTS (v. 12)[37]

The requirement of tassels is stated more fully in Numbers 15:37–41, where they are called "fringes" (*tsitsit*) and designated as reminders to obey God's commandments and resist temptation, and thereby be holy to God. According to postbiblical tradition the fringes remind Israelites of the commandments because the number of threads (four folded double, hence eight) and double knots (five) required in the tassel, plus the numerical value of the word *tsitsit* (600), add up to 613, the traditional number of commandments. The halakhic details of this law are elaborated in Tractate Menaḥot.

Numbers 15:38 requires that a blue cord be attached to each fringe. According to early rabbinic sources, the blue cord is made of wool while the other cords are linen. In other words, the tassels are made of *sha'atnez,* the combination of fabrics forbidden in verse 11. This interpretation most likely stems from biblical times, since it is highly unlikely that the rabbis would have initiated a practice contradicting a biblical prohibition. It is, in other words, an exception to the general rule stated in verse 11. According to Jacob Milgrom, the purpose of this exception is suggested by the fact that *sha'atnez* characterized the priestly garments; hence, wearing these tassels reminds every Israelite of the duty to strive for holiness like the priests, to become "a kingdom of priests and a holy nation" (Exod. 19:6). The requirement of the blue cord was suspended in talmudic times. Milgrom holds that this was due to the general impoverishment of the Jews following the Roman wars, which made the dye prohibitively expensive for many.

12. tassels Hebrew *gedilim,* literally, "twists," "braids" (of thread), a meaning known from rabbinic Hebrew and cognates in other languages.[38]

four corners Ancient Near Eastern art shows people wearing closed skirts and robes, not rectangular poncho-like garments. The four corners (lit., "wings" or "extremities") were probably either the points on scalloped hems or the places at which vertical bands of embroidery met the hems. Both styles, sometimes with tassels attached, are visible in ancient Near Eastern murals.[39]

the garment with which you cover yourself The tassels are to be attached to everyday clothing and worn all day. In the Middle Ages, when this made Jews too easily identifiable to persecutors, the tassels were attached instead to a small rectangular inner garment with a hole for the head. This garment, which has become the normal means of fulfilling the commandment since then, is known as a *tallit katan* ("small *tallit*") or *'arba' kanfot* ("four corners," taken from this verse). An outer, fringed shawl, the *tallit,* is generally worn only during morning prayer.

There is nothing in the commandment to suggest that it is limited to men, and some of the early rabbis held that tassels are to be worn by women, too. Women were eventually exempted when the halakhah endorsed the view that this is one of the commandments from which women are exempt because it must be performed at a fixed time of day.[40]

13A man marries a woman and cohabits with her. Then he takes an aversion to her 14and makes up charges against her and defames her, saying, "I married this woman; but when I approached her, I found that she was not a virgin." 15In such a case, the girl's father and mother shall produce the evidence of the girl's virginity before the elders of the

13 כִּי־יִקַּח אִישׁ אִשָּׁה וּבָא אֵלֶיהָ וּשְׂנֵאָהּ: 14 וְשָׂם לָהּ עֲלִילֹת דְּבָרִים וְהוֹצִיא עָלֶיהָ שֵׁם רָע וְאָמַר אֶת־הָאִשָּׁה הַזֹּאת לָקַחְתִּי וָאֶקְרַב אֵלֶיהָ וְלֹא־מָצָאתִי לָהּ בְּתוּלִים: 15 וְלָקַח אֲבִי הַנַּעַר וְאִמָּהּ וְהוֹצִיאוּ אֶת־בְּתוּלֵי הַנַּעַר אֶל־זִקְנֵי הָעִיר

v. 15. הַנַּעֲרָה ק'

LAWS ABOUT MARITAL AND SEXUAL MISCONDUCT　(vv. 13–29)

Verses 13–29 deal with types of sexual misconduct: accusations of premarital unchastity, adultery, and rape. Accusations of premarital unchastity appear first (vv. 13–21), probably for the reasons that are suggested in Excursus 13. The remaining cases appear in decreasing order of gravity: clear-cut consensual adultery, cases in which the woman's consent is not certain, and nonadulterous rape (vv. 22–29).

ACCUSATIONS OF PREMARITAL UNCHASTITY (vv. 13–21)

These two paragraphs deal with a man who, following his wedding, spreads the charge that he found his wife not to have been a virgin. He probably does so in order to get out of the marriage—should he simply divorce her without cause, he would probably forfeit the bride-price[41]—or perhaps to get the bride-price reduced to that of a nonvirgin[42] (on the bride-price, see Comment to 20:7). The bride's parents produce physical evidence of her virginity, namely, a sheet or garment that was spotted with blood when the marriage was consummated. Upon this evidence the slandering husband is flogged, fined, and prohibited from ever divorcing the bride.

According to the second paragraph, if the charge proves true the bride is stoned to death for having sexual intercourse before marriage, "while under her father's authority" (v. 21). In this respect it may be viewed as the equivalent, for girls, of the law about the insubordinate son in 21:18–21.[43]

This law raises a number of procedural difficulties. These are discussed in Excursus 20.

The Case of a False Accusation (vv. 13–19)

13. *A man marries a woman . . . Then he takes an aversion to her*　The Hebrew is a single conditional sentence: "If a man marries a woman . . . and then takes an aversion to her." Such sudden changes of feeling are not unknown. David's son Amnon lusted for Tamar and then, after raping her, turned against her.[44] See also 21:14.

14. *makes up charges against her*　Rather, "accuses her of misconduct."[45]

defames her　Literally, "puts out a bad name about her," that is, he publicizes the charge. This seems to imply that the following procedure is invoked only if the husband makes the charge public. A similar condition was known among some Arabs in recent times: if a groom found his bride not to have been a virgin, he turned her out immediately and if her family refunded the bride-price, he was obligated to keep quiet. If, however, he spoke out, the girl was examined. If she was found guilty, irrespective of whether she lost her virginity long before or recently, she was executed, but if she was innocent, the groom was executed.[46] Perhaps the present verse similarly implies that the groom is expected to return the bride quietly and receive back the bride-price, in which case the girl would simply be dealt with by her family as they see fit. Only if he makes a public issue of the matter do the consequences become more serious: for the bride, perhaps because her conduct, once publicized, would serve as a bad example; for the groom because his public accusation defames the girl and her family and could lead to her death.

I found that she was not a virgin　Literally, "I did not find [evidence of] virginity in her," meaning that he did not find her hymen intact or that she did not bleed (see v. 17).

15. *the girl's father and mother shall produce the evidence of the girl's virginity*　The

204

town at the gate. ¹⁶And the girl's father shall say to the elders, "I gave this man my daughter to wife, but he has taken an aversion to her; ¹⁷so he has made up charges, saying, 'I did not find your daughter a virgin.' But here is the evidence of my daughter's virginity!" And they shall spread out the cloth before the elders of the town. ¹⁸The elders of that town shall then take the man and flog him, ¹⁹and they shall fine him a hundred [shekels of] silver and give it to the girl's father; for the man has defamed a virgin in Israel. Moreover, she shall remain his wife; he shall never have the right to divorce her.

הַשָּׁעְרָה: 16 וְאָמַר אֲבִי הנער אֶל־הַזְּקֵנִים אֶת־בִּתִּי נָתַתִּי לָאִישׁ הַזֶּה לְאִשָּׁה וַיִּשְׂנָאֶהָ: 17 וְהִנֵּה־הוּא שָׂם עֲלִילֹת דְּבָרִים לֵאמֹר לֹא־מָצָאתִי לְבִתְּךָ בְּתוּלִים וְאֵלֶּה בְּתוּלֵי בִתִּי וּפָרְשׂוּ הַשִּׂמְלָה לִפְנֵי זִקְנֵי הָעִיר: 18 וְלָקְחוּ זִקְנֵי הָעִיר־הַהִוא אֶת־הָאִישׁ וְיִסְּרוּ אֹתוֹ: 19 וְעָנְשׁוּ אֹתוֹ מֵאָה כֶסֶף וְנָתְנוּ לַאֲבִי הַנַּעֲרָה כִּי הוֹצִיא שֵׁם רָע עַל בְּתוּלַת יִשְׂרָאֵל וְלוֹ־תִהְיֶה לְאִשָּׁה לֹא־יוּכַל לְשַׁלְּחָהּ כָּל־יָמָיו: ס

v. 16. הַנַּעֲרָה ק׳

evidence, as indicated in verse 17, is a garment or cloth that was spotted with the girl's blood when her hymen was perforated on the wedding night. The bride's parents would save it as evidence of her virginity. This custom is well known in the Middle East and has been practiced among various Jewish and Arab communities until recent times; in some places the cloth is displayed by the proud parents. They save it because their daughter, their reputation, and the bride-price they receive all depend on it. As Ramban notes, the mother joins the father here, though only the father speaks, because it was women who kept the cloth after the consummation of the marriage.[47]

before the elders of the town at the gate This is another case where the elders retain jurisdiction in matters of family law (cf. 21:19). On the gate, see Comments to 17:5 and 6:9.[48]

16. I gave this man my daughter This is not merely a formal idiom as it is in modern times, but is meant literally. Marriages were arranged by the parents and a bride-price was paid to the bride's father (see Comment to 20:7).

17. the cloth Hebrew *simlah* and its variant *salmah* usually refer to an outer garment, one that was sometimes also used as a cover while sleeping.[49] Here it refers either to a garment worn by the bride on her wedding night or to part of the bedding.

18–19. The triple punishment is exceptional but, as noted by Maimonides and Abravanel, each element corresponds to a part of the husband's offense. He is flogged, and thereby degraded (see 25:3), because he defamed the girl and her family.[50] He is fined because his accusation would have forced her father to return the bride-price. He loses the right to divorce her, which was probably his aim in slandering her. In this way the father is compensated for the harm attempted against him and the girl is protected against divorce.

a hundred [shekels of] silver This is generally taken to be double the bride-price for a virgin, on the assumption that the fifty shekels of verse 29 are identical to the "bride-price for virgins" mentioned in Exodus 22:16.[51] However, it is not certain that fifty shekels was really the bride-price for virgins; see Comment to verse 29.

and give it to the girl's father; for the man has defamed a virgin Although the bride was disgraced, the fine is given to her father because the financial loss caused by the accusation would be his, and because the accusation disgraced him, too, since it implied that he did not raise a virtuous daughter. There would be no point in giving the fine to the bride since, as Abravanel observes, she is under her husband's authority and he would be able to take the fine back from her.

he has defamed a virgin in Israel The final phrase reflects the text's concern for the good name of Israelite girls in general; as the Sifrei indicates, his accusation would raise doubts about the character of all Israelite girls.

20But if the charge proves true, the girl was found not to have been a virgin, 21then the girl shall be brought out to the entrance of her father's house, and the men of her town shall stone her to death; for she did a shameful thing in Israel, committing fornication while under her father's authority. Thus you will sweep away evil from your midst.

22If a man is found lying with another man's wife, both of them—the man and the woman with whom he lay—shall die. Thus you will sweep away evil from Israel.

20 וְאִם־אֱמֶת הָיָה הַדָּבָר הַזֶּה לֹא־נִמְצְא֥וּ
בְתוּלִים לַנַּעַר: 21 וְהוֹצִ֙יאוּ אֶת־הַנַּעַר אֶל־פֶּ֜תַח
בֵּית־אָבִ֗יהָ וּסְקָל֙וּהָ֩ אַנְשֵׁ֙י עִירָ֥הּ בָּאֲבָנִים֮ וָמֵ֒תָה
כִּי־עָשְׂתָ֤ה נְבָלָה֙ בְּיִשְׂרָאֵ֔ל לִזְנ֖וֹת בֵּ֣ית אָבִ֑יהָ
וּבִעַרְתָּ֥ הָרָ֖ע מִקִּרְבֶּֽךָ: ס
22 כִּֽי־יִמָּצֵ֨א אִ֜ישׁ שֹׁכֵ֣ב ׀ עִם־אִשָּׁ֣ה בְעֻֽלַת־בַּ֗עַל
וּמֵ֙תוּ֙ גַּם־שְׁנֵיהֶ֔ם הָאִ֛ישׁ הַשֹּׁכֵ֥ב עִם־הָאִשָּׁ֖ה
וְהָאִשָּׁ֑ה וּבִעַרְתָּ֥ הָרָ֖ע מִיִּשְׂרָאֵֽל: ס

v. 21. לַנַּֽעֲרָ֖ה ק'   v. 20. הַנַּֽעֲרָ֖ה ק'

The Case of a Correct Accusation (vv. 20–21)

20. *the girl was found not to have been a virgin* Rather, "[evidence of] virginity was not found in the girl," referring to the evidence required by verses 15-17.

21. *at the entrance of her father's house* A fitting location for her punishment, since, as the final clause in this sentence literally says, "she committed fornication while [living] in her father's house." A similar principle is reflected in the Laws of Hammurabi, where a man who breaks into a house is to be executed in front of the breach that he made.[52] Executing the daughter at this location also expresses communal disapproval of the father who failed to raise a chaste daughter.[53]

the men of her town The execution takes place in the bride's town, even if she is from a different town than her husband, because it must take place before her father's house.

stone her As is done to the insubordinate son. For stoning as a punishment for offenses against proper human authority, see Comment to 13:11.

she did a shameful thing in Israel Hebrew *nevalah*, "outrage," "deplorable act," often refers to sexual crimes such as rape and adultery.[54] It is often followed by "in Israel," sometimes indicating indignation that the act happened among Israelites, and at other times characterizing the act as a violation of Israelite standards, "a thing not to be done in Israel" (2 Sam. 13:12). The phrase expresses the importance of sexual morality as a feature of Israel's national character.

committing fornication while under her father's authority In other words, prior to marriage. The use of the term "fornication" rather than "adultery" suggests that the law refers to intercourse at any time before marriage and is not limited to the period of engagement (contrast vv. 23–24).[55] This is consistent with verse 14, in which the husband does not claim that his bride lost her virginity *after* he betrothed her. The available evidence would not enable him to do so. This clause makes it clear that the girl's crime is the act of fornication, not merely concealing the fact from her husband. On the apparent inconsistency of this law with verses 28–29 and Exodus 22:15–16, see Excursus 20.

Thus you will sweep away evil from your midst See Comment to 13:6.

ADULTERY WITH A MARRIED WOMAN (v. 22)

The definition of adultery and its gravity in biblical law are discussed in the Comments to 5:17.

22. *is found* For cases where the couple are not discovered but the husband suspects his wife of infidelity, Numbers 5:11–31 prescribes a ritual procedure for settling the matter.

both of them ... shall die That adultery is a capital crime is indicated by Leviticus 20:10 as well as the present passage. Other ancient Near Eastern law collections likewise prescribe capital punishment for adultery. However, since they consider it an offense solely against the woman's husband, they add that the husband or the king may spare the wife and her lover or impose a lesser

23In the case of a virgin who is engaged to a man—if a man comes upon her in town and lies with her, 24you shall take the two of them out to the gate of that town and stone them to death: the girl because she did not cry for help in the town, and the man because he violated another man's wife. Thus you will sweep away evil from your midst. 25But if the man comes upon the engaged girl in the open country, and the man lies with her by force, only the

כג כִּי יִהְיֶה֩ נַעֲרָ֨ בְתוּלָ֜ה מְאֹרָשָׂ֣ה לְאִ֗ישׁ וּמְצָאָ֤הּ
אִישׁ֙ בָּעִ֔יר וְשָׁכַ֖ב עִמָּֽהּ: כד וְהֽוֹצֵאתֶ֨ם אֶת־שְׁנֵיהֶ֜ם
אֶל־שַׁ֣עַר ׀ הָעִ֣יר הַהִ֗וא וּסְקַלְתֶּ֨ם אֹתָ֥ם בָּֽאֲבָנִים֮
וָמֵתוּ֒ אֶת־הַֽנַּעֲרָ֗ עַל־דְּבַר֙ אֲשֶׁ֣ר לֹא־צָעֲקָ֣ה בָעִ֔יר
וְאֶ֨ת־הָאִ֔ישׁ עַל־דְּבַ֥ר אֲשֶׁר־עִנָּ֖ה אֶת־אֵ֣שֶׁת רֵעֵ֑הוּ
וּבִֽעַרְתָּ֥ הָרָ֖ע מִקִּרְבֶּֽךָ: ס כה וְֽאִם־בַּשָּׂדֶ֞ה
יִמְצָ֣א הָאִ֗ישׁ אֶת־הַֽנַּעֲרָ֙ הַמְאֹ֣רָשָׂ֔ה וְהֶחֱזִֽיק־בָּ֤הּ

v. 23. נַעֲרָה ק׳   v. 24. הַֽנַּעֲרָה ק׳   v. 25. הַֽנַּעֲרָה ק׳

punishment.[56] Biblical law does not provide for such leniency. This has been attributed to the biblical view that God is the author of the laws: since He has forbidden adultery, it is a sin against Him as well as the husband,[57] and therefore no human, not even the husband, has the right to commute the punishment. Although other ancient Near Eastern cultures likewise believed that adultery angers the gods, their belief that the laws are the product of human wisdom rather than divine authorship left room for human discretion in case of violation.

It is not known whether or not adulterers were indeed executed. In the patriarchal period, according to Genesis 38, Judah ordered the execution of his daughter-in-law Tamar for what he thought was adultery because she was "betrothed" at the time for levirate marriage, but he canceled the punishment when he found her action justified. Some prophetic passages show knowledge of a practice of stripping and expelling the adulterous wife, but they do not necessarily imply that this practice was generally followed in Israel. Proverbs 6:32–35, warning that an aggrieved husband will not accept a financial settlement from an adulterer, seems to imply that the husband had the right to do so. However, it is debated whether passages from Proverbs, with its strong international literary ties, reflect actual Israelite practice.[58]

sweep away evil   See Comment to 13:6. The community must act to remove the guilt because its welfare is endangered on account of God's anger over the crime. According to Leviticus 18:20,24ff., adultery defiles the land and leads to exile. Prophets likewise identify it as one of the major causes of disaster and exile.[59]

ADULTERY WITH AN ENGAGED VIRGIN (vv. 23–27)

Once a girl is betrothed by the payment of the bride-price to her family (see 20:7), she is considered her fiancé's wife (v. 24), and sexual relations with another man are considered adulterous; the same view is found in Mesopotamian law.[60]

23-25.   In assessing the girl's guilt it is necessary to ascertain whether or not she was a consensual partner. The text provides a rule of thumb: if the act took place in town, she is presumed to have been willing, since otherwise she would have called for help and been heard. In the open country, however, where there are few passersby,[61] a cry for help would probably have gone unheard; hence she is given the benefit of the doubt and presumed to have called for help.[62] Philo, Josephus, and halakhic sources hold that this guideline is not absolute: whether in town or in the country, evidence that there was no one who could have saved her, that she resisted, or that her life was threatened if she resisted, would establish innocence; evidence to the contrary would establish guilt.[63]

It is not clear why Deuteronomy deals with the possibility of rape only in the case of engaged and unmarried girls (see v. 29). Unquestionably, evidence that a married woman was raped would clear her, too, as the halakhah rules.[64] Indeed, the Hittite Laws prescribe a similar rule of thumb for cases involving married women.[65] In general, however, Near Eastern laws, like Deuteronomy, tend to deal with the issue of rape in connection with engaged and unmarried girls instead of married women. This choice may have been due to experience. Since girls married relatively young (many probably by their mid-teens), engaged and unmarried girls were usually minors and were less likely to have deliberately sought sexual experience than were married

man who lay with her shall die, 26but you shall do nothing to the girl. The girl did not incur the death penalty, for this case is like that of a man attacking another and murdering him. 27He came upon her in the open; though the engaged girl cried for help, there was no one to save her.

28If a man comes upon a virgin who is not engaged and he seizes her and lies with her, and they are discovered, 29the man who lay with her shall pay the girl's father fifty

הָאִישׁ וְשָׁכַב עִמָּהּ וּמֵת הָאִישׁ אֲשֶׁר־שָׁכַב עִמָּהּ
לְבַדּֽוֹ: 26 וְלַנַּעֲרָ לֹא־תַעֲשֶׂה דָבָר אֵין לַנַּעֲרָ חֵטְא
מָ֫וֶת כִּי כַּאֲשֶׁר יָקוּם אִישׁ עַל־רֵעֵהוּ וּרְצָחוֹ נֶפֶשׁ
כֵּן הַדָּבָר הַזֶּה: 27 כִּי בַשָּׂדֶה מְצָאָהּ צָעֲקָה הַנַּעֲרָ
הַמְאֹרָשָׂה וְאֵין מוֹשִׁיעַ לָֽהּ: ס
28 כִּֽי־יִמְצָא אִישׁ נַעֲרָ בְתוּלָה אֲשֶׁר לֹא־אֹרָשָׂה
וּתְפָשָׂהּ וְשָׁכַב עִמָּהּ וְנִמְצָֽאוּ: 29 וְנָתַן הָאִישׁ

v. 26. וְלַנַּעֲרָ לַנַּעֲרָה ק׳
v. 27. הַנַּעֲרָ הַנַּעֲרָה ק׳
v. 28. נַעֲרָ נַעֲרָה ק׳

women, who were more sexually mature. Hence, of those who had been involved in extramarital sex, it was the engaged and unmarried girls who were most likely to have been forced, and laws dealing with them were the more natural context in which to present the guidelines for deciding the issue of consent.[66]

26. *you shall do nothing to the girl* In the halakhah this clause is the basis for the principle that one who commits a wrong under compulsion is not liable.[67]

the case is like that of a man attacking another and murdering him That is, she was a victim, not a participant.

RAPE OF AN UNENGAGED VIRGIN (vv. 28–29)

Intercourse with an unengaged virgin is also disapproved, but it is not a capital crime since it is not adulterous. The main concern of the law in such cases is to protect the girl and her father from the harm they would suffer from her loss of virginity, namely, the girl's diminished chances of marriage and the father's loss of a full bride-price. Exodus 22:15–16, which deals with a case where intercourse is the result of seduction, requires the seducer to pay the girl's father the bride-price and, if her father agrees, to marry her. The present law deals with a more severe offense, where the girl is not a willing participant but a victim of rape.

28. *who is not engaged* Hebrew *lo' 'orasah* is in the perfect tense and means literally "*was not engaged*," in other words, has never been engaged. As noted by Rabbi Yose in the Mekhilta, this excludes a girl who was once engaged but whose fiancé died or broke the engagement. In such a case, her father had already received a bride-price for her and would not have suffered financial harm because of the rape, and the rapist's fine may have been adjusted accordingly. The present law, requiring a payment of fifty shekels, deals only with a girl for whom a bride-price had never been paid.[68]

29. *fifty [shekels of] silver* This is often taken to be identical to the "bride-price for virgins" mentioned in Exodus 22:16 that the seducer must pay to a virgin's father, but this is questionable. There is no other evidence that the bride-price for virgins was fifty shekels. Leviticus 27:5–6—although not necessarily a guide in the present case—states that the value of a woman between twenty and sixty years old, whose value is pledged to the sanctuary, is thirty shekels, and that of a girl aged between five and twenty, ten shekels. Furthermore, it seems unlikely that a rapist's penalty would be identical to that of a seducer, since his offense is graver. If the seducer of Exodus 22:16 is required to pay an average bride-price, the fifty shekels paid by the rapist probably represents a combination of an average bride-price plus punitive damages.[69]

she shall be his wife According to Exodus 22:16, a seducer must likewise marry the girl, unless her father refuses to give her to him. According to the halakhah, the father has the same right of refusal in the case of rape, and this is doubtless correct; it is inconceivable that he would be forced to give his daughter to her rapist.[70] According to the halakhah in cases of both seduction and rape, the girl as well as the father has the right to refuse the marriage.

[shekels of] silver, and she shall be his wife. Because he has violated her, he can never have the right to divorce her.

23 No man shall marry his father's former wife, so as to remove his father's garment.

הַשֹּׁכֵב עִמָּהּ לַאֲבִי הַנַּעַר חֲמִשִּׁים כָּסֶף וְלוֹ־תִהְיֶה
לְאִשָּׁה תַּחַת אֲשֶׁר עִנָּהּ לֹא־יוּכַל שַׁלְּחָהּ כָּל־
יָמָיו: ס

כ״ג לֹא־יִקַּח אִישׁ אֶת־אֵשֶׁת אָבִיו וְלֹא יְגַלֶּה
כְּנַף אָבִיו: ס

v. 29. הַנַּעֲרָה ק׳

he can never have the right to divorce her   Exodus does not impose this restriction on the seducer. The rapist's offense is graver and he is treated more stringently.

Several of these features are paralleled in the Middle Assyrian Laws: the rapist must pay triple the normal bride-price and marry the girl (if her father is willing) without right of divorce. If the rapist has a wife, a typically Mesopotamian measure-for-measure punishment is added: the girl's father can have the rapist's wife raped and then keep her.[71]

CHAPTER 23   **FORBIDDEN RELATIONSHIPS**   (vv. 1–9)[1]

Verses 1–9 comprise a series of prohibitions in categorical style ("No . . . shall . . ."). The first one, prohibiting marriage with one's father's wife, continues the marital laws of chapter 22 (the opening clause, "No man shall marry . . . wife," echoes 22:13, "If a man marries a wife . . ."). Marriage is also probably part of what verses 2–9 prohibit.

PROHIBITION OF MARRYING ONE'S FATHER'S FORMER WIFE (v. 1)

1. his father's former wife   This refers to a former wife who is not one's own mother; sexual relations with one's own mother are prohibited separately; see Leviticus 18:7–8. The word "former" is not in the Hebrew, but it is clearly what the text intends since it deals with marriage rather than incest; marriage with one's father's current wife would be legally impossible.

This law precludes a man from marrying a woman divorced by his father and from inheriting or marrying his father's wives and concubines after his death. In the Middle Assyrian Laws a man may marry his father's former wife. Among Arabs in pre-Islamic times, an heir, whether a father, brother, or son, inherited a man's wives and concubines along with his property.[2] The law would also ban actions such as that of King David's son Absalom who, during his *coup d'état*, publicly consorted with David's concubines in order to assert his claim to the throne.[3]

A broader prohibition, barring all sexual relations (not only marriage) with one's father's wife, appears in Leviticus 18:8 and 20:11, where it is a capital crime. Such relations are condemned in Deuteronomy 27:20 and are listed in Ezekiel 22:10 among the causes for Jerusalem's fall. All these references indicate that such relations were a real possibility. This is probably due to the young age at which girls married, which often resulted in a situation where a later wife of a man would be about the same age as his son by an earlier wife, if not younger.[4]

so as to remove his father's garment   "Removing someone's garment" is an equivalent of "seeing, or uncovering, someone's nakedness,"[5] an idiom used in Leviticus for sexual relations. In Leviticus, intercourse with the wife of one's father is condemned because it is tantamount to "seeing the father's nakedness." The point seems to be either that one sees nakedness that is reserved for his father or that the act is tantamount to having sexual relations with *him* (Lev. 18:7,8; 20:11).[6]

RESTRICTIONS ON ENTRY INTO THE ASSEMBLY OF THE LORD (vv. 2–9)

Verses 2–9 contain three regulations barring specific types or groups of people from entering the Assembly of the Lord (vv. 2,3, and 4–7) and a fourth one exempting two groups from this restriction (vv. 8–9).[7] "Assembly" is a more suitable translation than NJPS's "congregation." Hebrew *kahal*,

²No one whose testes are crushed or whose member is
cut off shall be admitted into the congregation of the
Lord.

2 לֹא־יָבֹא פְצֽוּעַ־דַּכָּא וּכְרוּת שָׁפְכָה בִּקְהַל
יְהוָה: ס

literally "gathering," sometimes refers to religious gatherings, but it is by no means limited to them
as English "congregation" might suggest. Sometimes it is used in a very broad sense meaning simply
"all Israelites."[8] But it also refers to the national governing Assembly of the Israelites, that is, the
entire people, or all the adult males, meeting in plenary session, and perhaps sometimes to their
representatives acting as an executive committee. This Assembly convenes to conduct public business
such as war, crowning a king, adjudicating legal cases, distributing land, and worship.[9] It is synonymous with 'edah, "community," which likewise refers to the entire nation, to the adult males
(especially those bearing arms), and perhaps to the tribal leaders acting as an executive on behalf of
the nation.[10] The fuller phrases kehal 'Adonai ("the Assembly of the Lord") and kehal 'am ha-'elohim
("the Assembly of God's people") function similarly.[11]

This Assembly seems to have been of a type similar to other popular assemblies in the ancient
world, such as the ekklesia in Athens and the puḥrum in Mesopotamian cities.[12] It existed before the
Exodus from Egypt[13] and likely antedated Moses. In the wilderness it functioned alongside of Moses
and usually under him,[14] and it is mentioned sporadically after the settlement in the promised land.[15]
The point of verses 2–9 is that certain types of people may not become members of this governing
Assembly.[16]

Eligibility for membership in the Assembly seems to have been tantamount to eligibility for full
citizenship.[17] Israel's concept of citizenship was not necessarily identical to that of the Greek polis,
but several factors indicate some similarity: (1) Most if not all of the groups excluded from the
Assembly are non-Israelites residing in Israel. In Athens, too, aliens could not be members of the
Assembly.[18] The same was true in Babylonia.[19] (2) One of the functions of the Assembly was to
allocate land. Land-ownership, too, was a privilege of citizenship. Aliens could not normally own
land in Israel, just as they could not own land or buildings in Athens without special permission.[20]
(3) Those barred from the Assembly were forbidden to marry Israelites. This is implied by the fact
that these rules immediately follow a marital prohibition (v. 1), and perhaps also by the fact that the
"misbegotten" (v. 3) may be the product of a forbidden marriage, and possibly by the additional fact
that verse 2 involves people of impaired fertility. The author of 1 Kings 11:1–2, the leaders of the Jews
who returned from exile in the Persian period, and rabbinic halakhah clearly took these rules as
banning intermarriage.[21] In Athens, citizens could only marry people whose mothers and fathers
were both citizens; foreigners, even resident aliens, could not marry Athenians.[22] The present law is
not as comprehensive. It does not ban all foreigners, but only those from certain nations. See,
further, the introductory Comment to verses 4–9.

The point of our law, then, seems to be that certain groups of aliens may never become citizens
or may become citizens only after a waiting period, and, further, if any of those mentioned in verses
2–3 are Israelites, that certain types of Israelites do not enjoy the full rights of citizens.

The historical background and later development of these prohibitions are discussed in
Excursus 21.

      2. whose testes are crushed or whose member is cut off   These are two types of emascula-
tion, the first accomplished by destroying the testes, the second by some type of castration.[23] It is
not clear whether this law applies to all who have these conditions or only to those who acquired
them voluntarily.

Intentional emasculation was performed for various purposes in the ancient Near East: at least
some royal officials of the saris ("eunuch") category were emasculated; castration is mentioned as a
punishment in the Middle Assyrian Laws; and self-castration was part of certain religious ceremonies
in Syria during the Hellenistic period.[24] It is not known whether emasculation was performed in
Israel. Some Israelite royal officials are called sarisim, but it is not entirely certain that they were
emasculated, nor even that they were native Israelites.[25] If no Israelites were castrated, the law may
refer to non-Israelites, as do verses 4–9.

Deuteronomy may exclude emasculated men from the Assembly because of the association of
emasculation with paganism or because of revulsion against mutilation.[26] Since emasculation also

3No one misbegotten shall be admitted into the congregation of the LORD; none of his descendants, even in the tenth generation, shall be admitted into the congregation of the LORD.

4No Ammonite or Moabite shall be admitted into the congregation of the LORD; none of their descendants, even in the tenth generation, shall ever be admitted into the congregation of the LORD, 5because they did not meet you with food and water on your journey after you left Egypt,

3 לֹא־יָבֹא מַמְזֵר בִּקְהַל יְהֹוָה גַּם דּוֹר עֲשִׂירִי לֹא־
יָבֹא לוֹ בִּקְהַל יְהֹוָה: ס

4 לֹא־יָבֹא עַמּוֹנִי וּמוֹאָבִי בִּקְהַל יְהֹוָה גַּם דּוֹר
עֲשִׂירִי לֹא־יָבֹא לָהֶם בִּקְהַל יְהֹוָה עַד־עוֹלָם:

5 עַל־דְּבַר אֲשֶׁר לֹא־קִדְּמוּ אֶתְכֶם בַּלֶּחֶם
וּבַמַּיִם בַּדֶּרֶךְ בְּצֵאתְכֶם מִמִּצְרָיִם וַאֲשֶׁר שָׂכַר
עָלֶיךָ אֶת־בִּלְעָם בֶּן־בְּעוֹר מִפְּתוֹר אֲרַם נַהֲרַיִם

disqualifies priests from officiating, and invalidates animals for sacrifice,[27] such defects may have been considered incompatible with the holiness demanded of Israelites.

3. *misbegotten* The meaning of Hebrew *mamzer* is not certain. Derivation from a root *m-z-r*, "rot," has been suggested. There is no evidence that the term refers to a bastard, a child born out of wedlock. Talmudic exegesis, noting the proximity of verse 1, holds that it refers to the offspring of incestuous or adulterous intercourse.[28] The Septuagint and Targum Jonathan understand the term as referring to the offspring of a prostitute, while others take it as a term for foreigners or the name of a particular foreign nation (cf. vv. 4–9 and possibly v. 2).[29]

the tenth generation Verse 4 supplements "the tenth generation" with "ever," and that is probably the meaning here as well: no descendant of a *mamzer* may ever enter the Assembly, no matter how many generations later.[30]

4–9. The remaining regulations deal with the admissibility of certain foreigners to the Assembly. The Ammonites, Moabites, Edomites, and Egyptians in question are those living in the land of Israel as resident aliens (*gerim*). The references to their third and tenth generations mean the third or tenth generation since they settled in the land, counting the generation that first arrived in the land as the first. Compare Comment to verse 9. In English, compare the term "third-generation American."

There is no blanket exclusion of foreigners as such, nor any racial objection to them. The Torah's general policy toward resident aliens is to grant them equal protection under civil law and to extend the benefits of many religious laws to them, such as Sabbath rest.[31] The four groups mentioned here are subject to permanent or temporary exclusion from the Assembly because of specific historic experiences Israel had with them. Presumably, other foreigners were eligible for membership after residing in the land and assimilating, perhaps after a number of years, or perhaps after a generation or two.[32] In the early postexilic period this law was construed as part of a prohibition of marriage with all foreigners. Later, once a formal procedure for conversion was created, this reading was modified and people from most foreign nations were permitted to marry Jews if they first became proselytes. See Excursus 21.[33]

4. *Ammonite or Moabite* On these Transjordanian neighbors of Israel, see Comments to 2:9 and 19. Despite their distant kinship with Israel and the respect Israel showed for their territorial rights, these peoples reacted with hostility and indifference when Israel passed near their territory on its way to the promised land. Israel suffered several attacks from them following its settlement in the promised land before Kings Saul and David subdued them.[34]

5. The first clause is problematic for two reasons: 2:28–29 state that the Moabites did provide the Israelites with food and water, and 2:37 states that Israel bypassed Ammonite territory and gives no indication that they even asked the Ammonites for supplies.[35] The verse may reflect a variant tradition about Israel's encounters in Transjordan, according to which Ammon and Moab were both asked for food, and refused to give it. We have already met variant traditions about these encounters in 2:29. See Excursus 2.

after you left Egypt See Comment to 4:45.

and because they hired Balaam son of Beor, from Pethor of Aram-naharaim, to curse you.—⁶But the LORD your God refused to heed Balaam; instead, the LORD your God turned the curse into a blessing for you, for the LORD your God loves you.—⁷You shall never concern yourself with their welfare or benefit as long as you live.

⁸You shall not abhor an Edomite, for he is your kinsman. You shall not abhor an Egyptian, for you were a

לְקַלְלֶֽךָ: 6 וְלֹֽא־אָבָ֞ה יְהוָ֤ה אֱלֹהֶ֙יךָ֙ לִשְׁמֹ֣עַ אֶל־
בִּלְעָ֔ם וַיַּהֲפֹךְ֩ יְהוָ֨ה אֱלֹהֶ֥יךָ לְּךָ֛ אֶת־הַקְּלָלָ֖ה
לִבְרָכָ֑ה כִּ֥י אֲהֵֽבְךָ֖ יְהוָ֥ה אֱלֹהֶֽיךָ: 7 לֹא־תִדְרֹ֥שׁ
שְׁלֹמָ֖ם וְטֹבָתָ֑ם כָּל־יָמֶ֖יךָ לְעוֹלָֽם: ס
רביעי 8 לֹֽא־תְתַעֵ֣ב אֲדֹמִ֔י כִּ֥י אָחִ֖יךָ ה֑וּא
ס לֹא־תְתַעֵ֣ב מִצְרִ֔י כִּי־גֵ֥ר הָיִ֖יתָ בְאַרְצֽוֹ:

they hired Literally, "he hired," referring to Balak, King of Moab. Frightened by the passing Israelites, who had just defeated Sihon and Og, Balak hired Balaam, a prominent diviner, to curse the Israelites and disable them so that they could be defeated. The incident is narrated in Numbers 22–24. A non-Israelite inscription about another incident involving Balaam was discovered at Deir ʿAlla in Transjordan. There he is called "a seer of the gods." The practice of engaging a foreign sorcerer, from a people known for its magical skills, to disable an enemy nation is also mentioned in a Sumerian narrative poem.[36]

Pethor of Aram-naharaim Pethor, a city in northern Syria. See Excursus 1. Aram-naharaim, which means "Aram alongside the River (Euphrates)," is the biblical term for eastern Syria and northern Iraq, the area from which the patriarchs migrated to the promised land.[37]

6. Balaam's attempts to utter curses were frustrated by the Lord, who transformed them into blessings (see Num. 23:7–11,18–26; 24:1–10). This recollection is not required by the context (the hyphens in the translation show that it is parenthetic), but the text is unwilling to miss the opportunity to show God's control of events and His loving protection of Israel.

Balaam's intentions are ambiguous in Numbers. His stated attitude toward Israel is neutral, and he insists that he can only say what God puts into his mouth. On the other hand, the account of his journey to Balak (Num. 22:22–35) indicates that he went, against God's will, after God told him not to curse Israel; this implies that he did intend to curse Israel. The present verse takes the position that Balaam indeed planned to curse Israel; the phrase "turned the curse" implies that he had already formulated the curse in his mind, but that God reversed it.[38]

7. *never concern yourself with their welfare or benefit* That is, do not seek their welfare, do nothing for their benefit.[39]

The terms translated "welfare" and "benefit" (*shalom* and *tovah*) mean literally "peace" and "good." Both of these terms can also refer to peaceful and friendly relations. In Akkadian, the cognate phrase *ṭubtu u sulummû* refers to such relations, especially when established by treaty. Accordingly, some commentators understand this verse as a ban on establishing friendly relations or treaties with the Ammonites and Moabites.[40]

According to either interpretation, the verse tells Israel to repay the Ammonites and Moabites in kind,[41] either for their indifference and hostility toward Israel's welfare or for displaying the opposite of peaceful and friendly relations.

8–9. Remarkably, Edomites and Egyptians are not permanently excluded from the Assembly. In spite of the rivalry of the Edomites and the terrible suffering Israel experienced at the hand of the Egyptians, the kinship of the former and the hospitality of the latter at a crucial time justified acceptance of their descendants.

8. *for he is your kinsman* The Edomites were traced back to Esau, brother of Israel's ancestor Jacob, as related in Genesis 36. Despite the struggle between the two peoples, reflected in the stories of Jacob and Esau in Genesis 25–27 and 32–33, the feeling of kinship between them persisted. It is mentioned in Deuteronomy 2:4, and Moses referred to Israel as Edom's brother in his message to the King of Edom (Num. 20:14). Even after centuries of hostile relations with Edom, the prophets Obadiah and Malachi still referred to the two nations as brothers.[42] On the Edomites, see Comment to 2:4.

stranger in his land. ⁹Children born to them may be admitted into the congregation of the LORD in the third
generation.

9 בָּנִ֛ים אֲשֶׁר־יִוָּלְד֥וּ לָהֶ֖ם דּ֣וֹר שְׁלִישִׁ֑י יָבֹ֥א לָהֶ֖ם
בִּקְהַ֥ל יְהֹוָֽה: ס

¹⁰When you go out as a troop against your enemies, be
on your guard against anything untoward. ¹¹If anyone

10 כִּֽי־תֵצֵ֥א מַחֲנֶ֖ה עַל־אֹיְבֶ֑יךָ וְנִ֨שְׁמַרְתָּ֔ מִכֹּ֖ל דָּבָ֥ר
רָ֑ע: 11 כִּֽי־יִהְיֶ֤ה בְךָ֙ אִ֔ישׁ אֲשֶׁ֛ר לֹא־יִהְיֶ֥ה טָה֖וֹר

for you were a stranger in his land   Despite all that the Egyptians eventually did to the
Israelites, they had provided a haven in a time of famine, for which Israel was to recognize a
continuing debt of gratitude.[43]

9. *in the third generation*   After two generations of living among Israelites. This implies
that all those banned from entering the Assembly may live in the land of Israel as resident aliens, and
that the grandchildren of Edomites and Egyptians who do so may be admitted to the Assembly.[44]

MISCELLANEOUS LAWS   (23:10–25:19)

The remaining laws in chapters 23–26 are the final group of laws in Deuteronomy. They consist of
rules about a variety of subjects that did not find a place earlier. The subjects that appear here most
frequently are marriage (24:1–4,5; 25:5–10), giving strangers some of the crops (23:25–26; 24:19–21; cf.
25:4; 26:12), and protecting and helping debtors, laborers, the poor, and the disadvantaged (23:20–21;
24:6,10–15,17–18). Some of the laws in these chapters seem to follow each other because of some
incidental phrase or theme that they share. See Excursus 13.

THE SANCTITY OF THE MILITARY CAMP (vv. 10–15)

A military camp, in which God is present to fight for Israel, is subject to an even stricter regimen
than the residential camp of Israel. One of the fundamental premises of the priestly legislation in
Leviticus and Numbers is that impurity is incompatible with the presence of God and must be kept
away from the residential camp, where His sanctuary is located: "You shall put the Israelites on
guard against their uncleanness, lest they die through their uncleanness by defiling My Tabernacle
which is among them."[45] For this reason, anyone suffering from an abnormal skin eruption or
genital discharge, or defiled by contact with a corpse, must leave the residential camp.[46] In the
military camp, even one who experiences a normal nocturnal emission must leave, and the routine
act of defecation must take place outside its boundaries. Conceivably, as Ibn Ezra suggests, these
enhanced requirements go back to the time when the Ark accompanied the army and was not
shielded from impurity by the sanctuary and the surrounding courtyard. However, Deuteronomy
never indicates that the Ark accompanies the army (see Comments to 1:33 and 20:2). Indeed, verse 15
states that God is directly present in the military camp;[47] that is why anything untoward must be
avoided. These extreme precautions must also owe something to the heightened danger faced by
the army.[48]

In a more rationalistic vein, Ramban and Shadal hold that these regulations, by requiring the
army to keep the camp permanently holy, aim to make the soldiers constantly aware of God's
presence (v. 15) and of their dependence on Him for victory.

10. *anything untoward*   "Anything" implies that the principle is more comprehensive
than the two examples cited (as does "anything unseemly" in v. 15). The same phrase, literally "any
bad thing," refers to bodily defects in sacrificial animals in 17:1. It can probably be inferred from
Numbers 5:1–4 (cited above) that those suffering abnormal skin eruptions or genital discharges also
had to leave the army camp (that those defiled by contact with corpses were to be removed from the
army camp seems impractical; to judge from Numbers 31:19, they were simply kept out of the
residential camp for a week after their return from war).

Later sources construe this admonition broadly. The Qumran War Scroll excludes those with
permanent bodily defects and defiling skin eruptions, and the Temple Scroll calls on the army to

among you has been rendered unclean by a nocturnal emission, he must leave the camp, and he must not reenter the camp. [12]Toward evening he shall bathe in water, and at sundown he may reenter the camp. [13]Further, there shall be an area for you outside the camp, where you may relieve yourself. [14]With your gear you shall have a spike, and when you have squatted you shall dig a hole with it and cover up your excrement. [15]Since the LORD your God moves about in your camp to protect you and to deliver your enemies to you, let your camp be holy; let Him not find anything unseemly among you and turn away from you.

מִקְרֵה־לָיְלָה וְיָצָא אֶל־מִחוּץ לַמַּחֲנֶה לֹא יָבֹא אֶל־תּוֹךְ הַמַּחֲנֶה: [12] וְהָיָה לִפְנוֹת־עֶרֶב יִרְחַץ בַּמָּיִם וּכְבֹא הַשֶּׁמֶשׁ יָבֹא אֶל־תּוֹךְ הַמַּחֲנֶה: [13] וְיָד תִּהְיֶה לְךָ מִחוּץ לַמַּחֲנֶה וְיָצָאתָ שָּׁמָּה חוּץ: [14] וְיָתֵד תִּהְיֶה לְךָ עַל־אֲזֵנֶךָ וְהָיָה בְּשִׁבְתְּךָ חוּץ וְחָפַרְתָּה בָהּ וְשַׁבְתָּ וְכִסִּיתָ אֶת־צֵאָתֶךָ: [15] כִּי יְהוָה אֱלֹהֶיךָ מִתְהַלֵּךְ | בְּקֶרֶב מַחֲנֶךָ לְהַצִּילְךָ וְלָתֵת אֹיְבֶיךָ לְפָנֶיךָ וְהָיָה מַחֲנֶיךָ קָדוֹשׁ וְלֹא־יִרְאֶה בְךָ עֶרְוַת דָּבָר וְשָׁב מֵאַחֲרֶיךָ: ס

avoid all types of impurity, sexual crimes, and every type of sin and guilt. To the Sifrei the admonition refers to idolatry, murder, sexual immorality, blasphemy, and all other sins for which the Canaanites were expelled and which would drive away God's presence. Ramban thinks that the warning includes these and all other forbidden actions, and that it is prompted by the fact that armies on campaign indulge in all kinds of unrestrained behavior that they would normally avoid.[49]

11-12. Apart from the removal of the man from the camp, this prescription essentially agrees with Leviticus 15:16: "When a man has an emission of semen, he shall bathe his whole body in water and remain unclean until evening." According to Leviticus 15:18, sexual intercourse also created impurity that required the same cleansing process. For that reason, in the time of David and Saul soldiers on campaign abstained, at least sometimes, from contact with women (1 Sam. 21:6 and perhaps 2 Sam. 11:11). It is not clear whether Deuteronomy ignores the subject because it takes such abstention for granted or because it regards it as unnecessary.[50]

11. nocturnal emission[51] An emission of semen. Undoubtedly an emission in the daytime would require the same procedure; as the Sifrei notes, the text mentions only the typical case (see Comment to 21:1).

13-14. Defecation must take place outside the camp. The Torah nowhere describes human excrement as impure, and it may be objectionable in God's presence simply because it is filthy and repugnant. However, Ezekiel's objection, as a priest, to eating food cooked over human excrement as fuel may indicate that it was regarded as impure in some contexts (Ezek. 4:12–15). Josephus thought it notable that although defecation is a natural function, the Essenes washed themselves afterward "as if defiled."[52]

13. area Hebrew *yad*, literally "hand," is thus understood by Targum Onkelos, the Septuagint, and the Sifrei. Another possibility is that the term means "marker," a sign indicating the latrine area. This interpretation is apparently reflected in the Qumran scrolls and is supported by several passages in which *yad* means "monument."[53]

outside the camp According to the Qumran War Scroll the latrine was to be two thousand cubits (ca. three thousand feet) from the camp.[54]

14. spike Hebrew *yated* usually refers to a tent peg. The text apparently has in mind a pointed digging tool like a dibble.[55]

15. moves about in your camp The point is not that He moves around within the camp but that He travels in the camp with Israel, as indicated in 20:4: "It is the LORD your God who marches with you to do battle for you."[56] For this concept, see Excursus 3.

anything unseemly This idiom (*'ervat davar*) is as broad as "anything untoward" in verse 10. Its use in 24:1 shows that it can refer to virtually anything offensive.

¹⁶You shall not turn over to his master a slave who seeks refuge with you from his master. ¹⁷He shall live with you in any place he may choose among the settlements in your midst, wherever he pleases; you must not ill-treat him.

¹⁸No Israelite woman shall be a cult prostitute, nor shall

לֹא־תַסְגִּיר עֶבֶד אֶל־אֲדֹנָיו אֲשֶׁר־יִנָּצֵל אֵלֶיךָ 16
מֵעִם אֲדֹנָיו: 17 עִמְּךָ יֵשֵׁב בְּקִרְבְּךָ בַּמָּקוֹם אֲשֶׁר־
יִבְחַר בְּאַחַד שְׁעָרֶיךָ בַּטּוֹב לוֹ לֹא תּוֹנֶנּוּ: ס
לֹא־תִהְיֶה קְדֵשָׁה מִבְּנוֹת יִשְׂרָאֵל וְלֹא־יִהְיֶה 18

ASYLUM FOR ESCAPED SLAVES (vv. 16–17)

Wherever slavery existed, there were slaves who escaped from their masters. Ancient Near Eastern law forbade harboring runaway slaves, and international treaties regularly required allied states to extradite them.[57] The present law, in contrast, permits escaped slaves to settle wherever they wish in the land of Israel and forbids returning them to their masters or enslaving them in Israel.

Virtually all commentators hold that this law refers to slaves who flee from foreign countries to Israel.[58] "He shall live with you among the settlements in your midst" (v. 17) seems to imply that previously the slave had been in a foreign land and not in Israelite territory. If the law referred to an Israelite slave it would probably have described him as "your kinsman." It would also have addressed the individual householder with whom the slave sought refuge, but the phrase "in your midst" and the stipulation that the fugitive may settle anywhere in the land imply that the law is addressed to the nation as a whole or to a national authority. What the law bans, then, is returning escaped slaves to other nations—the precise opposite of the provisions of ancient Near Eastern treaties mentioned above. The only thing remotely close to this biblical law in the ancient world is the practice at certain temples of granting asylum to slaves fleeing harsh treatment by their masters. Generally, such asylum was not permanent; it protected the slave until he could come to terms with his master or, as a last resort, was sold to another master.[59] By contrast, the biblical law is absolute and treats the whole land of Israel as a sanctuary offering permanent asylum.

If this law really is limited to slaves from abroad, the absence of a comparable law dealing with Israelite slaves is remarkable. There certainly were runaway Israelite slaves.[60] While some Israelites entered bondage voluntarily, to escape poverty, and might not be inclined to run away (15:16 expects some to decline freedom), some were enslaved involuntarily for debt or theft (see introductory Comment to 15:12–18), and even some who entered voluntarily must have been ill treated and fled.[61] We can only speculate on whether there was a comparable rule for Israelite slaves, or whether the six-year limit on bondage and the provisions for freeing slaves injured by their masters (see introductory Comment to 15:12–18) were regarded as sufficient protection.

17. *He shall live with you . . . wherever he pleases* This is the antithesis of the terms of an Aramaic treaty requiring extradition of escaped slaves: "You must not say to them: 'Live quietly in your place . . . live where you are.'"[62]

you must not ill-treat him Once settled in Israel he would be a resident alien and hence vulnerable to exploitation; see Comment to 1:16 and compare Exodus 22:20, "You must not ill-treat a resident alien."

PROHIBITION OF PROSTITUTION AND OTHER ABHORRENT PRACTICES (vv. 18–19)

No Israelite may be a *kedeshah* or a *kadesh*, and prostitutes' earnings and "the pay of a dog" are unacceptable in payment of vows to the Temple. At least part of what is prohibited has to do with sexual immorality, but the meaning of *kadesh* and "the pay of a dog" is uncertain in this context.

18. *no Israelite woman . . . any Israelite man* The law does not ban these abhorrent professions entirely, in the manner of 18:10–11, but prohibits *Israelites* from practicing them.[63] Perhaps the law assumes that "the world's oldest profession" cannot realistically be eliminated, and seeks to limit it to foreigners.

cult prostitute Rather, "prostitute." Hebrew *kedeshah* refers to a common prostitute elsewhere in the Bible, and that is probably its meaning here, synonymous with "whore" in the next verse.[64] This prohibition is similar to Leviticus 19:29, which prohibits a father from degrading his

any Israelite man be a cult prostitute. ¹⁹You shall not bring the fee of a whore or the pay of a dog into the house of the LORD your God in fulfillment of any vow, for both are abhorrent to the LORD your God.

קָדֵשׁ מִבְּנֵי יִשְׂרָאֵל: 19 לֹא־תָבִיא אֶתְנַן זוֹנָה וּמְחִיר כֶּלֶב בֵּית יְהוָה אֱלֹהֶיךָ לְכָל־נֶדֶר כִּי תוֹעֲבַת יְהוָה אֱלֹהֶיךָ גַּם־שְׁנֵיהֶם:

daughter by making her a harlot. There is scant justification for the translation "cult prostitute," a term used by modern scholars for a prostitute employed at a sanctuary. Although *kedeshah* means something like "holy woman," from the root *k-d-sh* ("holy," "set apart," "reserved"), etymology is not a reliable indication of meaning; in the present case it could simply be a euphemism like some other terms for prostitute.[65] It is questionable whether cultic prostitution existed at all in the ancient Near East. See Excursus 22.

The meaning of the masculine *kadesh* here is uncertain. In the book of Kings it refers to a type of abhorrent pagan cultic functionary, mentioned on a par with high places, sacred pillars and sacred posts, and in association with the goddess Asherah. In Ugaritic it refers to cultic personnel lower than priests.[66] There is reason to question whether the word has the same meaning here. A servant of a pagan deity would be banned by the general prohibition of paganism and would not require a separate law (there is no prohibition on *kemarim*, the other term for pagan priests).[67] Even if it did require a separate law, one would expect a practice involving the worship of another god to be banned absolutely, and the text to say "let no *kadesh* be found among you" at all (cf. 18:10–11), not "no *Israelite* shall be a *kadesh*." It seems, therefore, that the *kadesh* in this verse is not a pagan official. Since the *kedeshah* is a prostitute, perhaps the *kadesh* here is a male prostitute, either heterosexual or homosexual.[68] The term is not known to have this meaning elsewhere, but the order of the clauses in this verse may support this interpretation. Females are not usually listed before males;[69] and perhaps this was done here in order to clarify the theme of the verse and indicate that here *kadesh* is another type of prostitute and does not have its usual meaning.

In view of verses 2–9, it is notable that in Athens, although male prostitution was not forbidden, it was incompatible with Athenian citizenship and led to disfranchisement, including exclusion from the Assembly.[70]

19.   *the fee of a whore*   Hebrew *zonah*, the more common term for whore. Fees, including those of whores, were sometimes paid in kind, such as a kid, instead of cash (Gen. 38:17). Since income from other immoral sources, such as theft, was also offensive, the question arises why that of whores is singled out. Temples, with their throngs of festive travelers, must have been particularly attractive hangouts for prostitutes hoping to attract business from worshipers who were carried away by the festive mood of the holiday. This situation is reflected in Hosea 4:14, which criticizes worshipers who cavort with prostitutes.[71] It is easy to imagine prostitutes who ply their trade near temples vowing part of their income to the temple in return for success.[72] Indeed, Micah 1:7 states that the idols of Samaria were "amassed from fees for harlotry." Later Greek and Roman sources mention gifts given to temples by courtesans.[73] The present law, then, is based on revulsion at such perversion of sacred occasions. (There is no reason to believe that the prostitutes mentioned in this verse are employed by the temple or acting under religious obligation, as is the case with the temple prostitutes found in Greek and Roman sources; see Excursus 22.)

the pay of a dog   There is no fully convincing explanation of this phrase. Since the other clauses in verses 18–19 refer to humans, at least some of them prostitutes, it is often assumed that "dog" is an epithet of some human professional, perhaps a male prostitute, perhaps a homosexual one who performs in the stance of a dog.[74] Halakhic exegesis takes the phrase to mean that the price received for selling a dog may not be given to the temple. Dogs were valued as herding dogs and commanded a good purchase-price. Yet, they were regarded with some disgust: they were only semi-domesticated and, as scavengers and predators, were the only carnivores regularly encountered by Israelites. Hence, as the source of a gift to the Temple, even indirectly, they were objectionable.[75] The recent discovery of a huge dog cemetery at Phoenician Ashkelon, from the Persian period, has prompted the suggestion that dogs may have played a significant role in certain pagan cults, perhaps the cults of healing gods.[76] If such a practice was also known in or near Israel in preexilic times, this might account for the objection to "a dog's pay" here. In either case, the two parts of this verse would have in common the disallowance of gifts to the temple that come from objectionable sources.

abhorrent   See Comment to 7:25.

216

20 You shall not deduct interest from loans to your countrymen, whether in money or food or anything else that can be deducted as interest; 21 but you may deduct interest from loans to foreigners. Do not deduct interest from

20 לֹא־תַשִּׁיךְ לְאָחִיךָ נֶשֶׁךְ כֶּסֶף נֶשֶׁךְ אֹכֶל נֶשֶׁךְ
כָּל־דָּבָר אֲשֶׁר יִשָּׁךְ: 21 לַנָּכְרִי תַשִּׁיךְ וּלְאָחִיךָ לֹא
תַשִּׁיךְ לְמַעַן יְבָרֶכְךָ יְהֹוָה אֱלֹהֶיךָ בְּכֹל מִשְׁלַח

PROHIBITION ON LENDING AT INTEREST (vv. 20–21)

The laws about loans must be understood in the light of the simple agrarian economy of ancient Israel. There is no evidence that there was a money market of any significance, or that solvent Israelites commonly borrowed for commercial or other purposes, though a couple of passages imply that not all borrowers were poor (Exod. 22:24; Deut. 24:12).[77] As noted in the Comments to 15:1–6, the type of loans with which the Torah regularly deals is charitable loans to countrymen who have fallen on hard times. This is clear from the statements of the present law in Exodus 22:24 and Leviticus 25:36–37, which explicitly refer to the borrower as impoverished. Under these circumstances, lending is a moral obligation incumbent on those who can afford it, and it is to be done without further increasing the borrower's poverty by requiring interest, which could be ruinous (rates of 20 to 25 percent for silver and $33\frac{1}{3}$ to 50 percent for grain were common in the ancient Near East, and higher rates were known).[78] As Josephus puts it, "It is not just to draw a revenue from the misfortunes of a fellow-countryman. Rather, in succoring his distress, you should reckon as gain the gratitude of such persons and the recompense which God has in store for an act of generosity." Lending without interest is frequently listed among important virtues and praised as an act of generosity, and exacting interest is condemned.[79]

Although interest-free loans are sometimes mentioned in Mesopotamian texts, no prohibition on interest is known from the ancient Near East, possibly because the sites from which we have documentation had more developed commercial economies. There is an interesting letter from Ugarit in which the writer claims that gentlemen do not demand interest of each other.[80] Greek philosophers opposed interest, and it was periodically forbidden in early Rome.[81] As economies developed and money began to play a more important role, the prohibition of interest became impractical, and the halakhah devised legal means for circumventing it. Eventually the prohibition was restricted to the realm of charitable loans, in keeping with its original purpose.[82]

20. deduct interest Rather, "require interest." The translation "deduct" is based on the assumption that the term for interest, *neshekh*, refers to "advance interest," or "discount," which is deducted from the loan at the outset (the term is generally thought to derive from *n-sh-k*, "bite"). According to this interpretation, *neshekh* differs from *tarbit* and *marbit*, "increase," which refer to "accrued interest" paid during the term of the loan or at its end (Lev. 25:36–37). However, the argument for this interpretation, by Eliezer of Beaugency,[83] is weak, and although other distinctions between the Hebrew terms have been proposed,[84] it is not known whether there really is a difference between them. According to Rava in the Babylonian Talmud, there is none, and according to the commentary *Keli Yakar*, the terms merely describe interest from the differing perspectives of the borrower, to whom it is a "bite," and the lender, to whom it is an "increase."[85] A cognate of *neshekh*, *ntk* appears in Ugaritic as a term for interest, and *mrby(t)*, the Aramaic cognate of *tarbit* and *marbit*, appears in the Elephantine papyri.[86]

to your countrymen Since Exodus 22:24 and Leviticus 25:35–37 refer to loans to the poor, some scholars believe that interest was first prohibited only on loans to them, and that Deuteronomy is the first to protect all Israelite borrowers from interest. However, nonlegal passages consistently regard the taking of interest from one's countryman as wrong, without differentiating between solvent and poor borrowers, and it is unlikely that exacting interest from solvent people, on the rare occasion when they might borrow, was ever acceptable. Most likely Exodus and Leviticus specify the poor simply because it was they who normally borrowed.

or anything else Such as seed. Exodus and Leviticus mention only loans of money and food; this phrase makes it clear that the prohibition covers all types of loans. A similar generalization as compared to the earlier version of a law is found in 22:3.

21. loans to foreigners This exception is similar to 15:3, which exempts loans to foreigners

loans to your countrymen, so that the Lord your God may bless you in all your undertakings in the land that you are about to enter and possess.

²²When you make a vow to the Lord your God, do not put off fulfilling it, for the Lord your God will require it of

יָדֶ֔ךָ עַל־הָאָ֕רֶץ אֲשֶׁר־אַתָּ֥ה בָא־שָׁ֖מָּה
לְרִשְׁתָּֽהּ׃ ס
²² כִּֽי־תִדֹּ֣ר נֶ֙דֶר֙ לַיהֹוָ֣ה אֱלֹהֶ֔יךָ לֹ֥א תְאַחֵ֖ר
לְשַׁלְּמ֑וֹ כִּֽי־דָרֹ֨שׁ יִדְרְשֶׁ֜נּוּ יְהֹוָ֤ה אֱלֹהֶ֙יךָ֙ מֵֽעִמָּ֔ךְ

from remission. As Shadal notes, the foreigner is normally a businessman visiting the country for purposes of trade, and he borrows in order to invest in merchandise and make a profit, not to survive poverty. There is no moral imperative to remit loans made for such purposes or forgo interest on them. Furthermore, assuming the risk of lending and making the sacrifice that remission and interest-free loans entail are special obligations toward one's countrymen (Heb. ʾaḥim, lit. "brothers") and for the sake of maintaining equilibrium in Israelite society. The law does not require assuming the same risk and sacrifice toward others who do not share the same obligation.

so that the Lord your God may bless you in all your undertakings See Comments to 2:7 and 14:29.

TIMELY FULFILLMENT OF VOWS (vv. 22–24)

Petitions for divine assistance often took the form of vows. A person who sought God's aid in achieving a desired goal, or relief from trouble, might promise to do something pleasing to God afterwards in gratitude for His assistance. Examples of such desired goals include the birth of a child, victory in battle, recovery from illness, and escape from danger.[87] The vower frequently promised to perform an act of tribute to God: to offer a sacrifice (12:6) or give a gift to the sanctuary, such as money, cattle or produce; in one case, dedication of a child to service at the sanctuary is mentioned.[88] The Psalms mention vows frequently, including vows to utter prayers of thanksgiving.[89] Another type of vow was one of abstention: the nazirite vow, for example, included abstention from grape products.[90]

At first glance the vow looks like a bargain with God. The practice originates with pre-Israelite religions that regarded worship as a means of supporting the gods, providing them food and shelter. It was assumed that a request to the gods could be strengthened if the worshiper offered something in return that would be useful or pleasing to the god who granted the petition. This is a natural impulse, since worship is based on the forms of interaction, including petition, that people are familiar with in human society. Such forms of worship survived in the Bible, despite its view that God does not eat or have other physical needs, because they also expressed the worshiper's gratitude, devotion, and recognition of his dependence on God, attitudes the Bible values.[91] For this reason, there was no need to suppress people's instinctive urge to strengthen petitions to God by promising something in return. Even Psalm 50:1–14, which criticizes the popular notion that sacrifice is a benefit to God, approves of thanksgiving offerings and the payment of vows. Moshe Greenberg summarizes its message thus: "To turn to God for help in time of trouble, and when help comes, to praise God by thanksgiving sacrifice in payment of vows—that is true honoring of God . . . with [these sacrifices] alone there is no room for mistake as to who is doing for whom."[92] Nevertheless, the present passage and its parallels in wisdom literature reflect a remarkably reserved attitude toward the practice, as do several passages in rabbinic literature, where some sages prefer that people completely avoid making vows.[93]

Various laws pertaining to vows are detailed in Leviticus and Numbers, as well as in Deuteronomy 12:6 and verse 19 of the present chapter.[94] Numbers 30:3 states that a vow may not be broken. The present law complements the latter and warns against procrastination in fulfilling the vow once the desired goal has been achieved. Such warnings are typical of wisdom literature; essentially the same advice is found in Ecclesiastes 5:3–5.[95]

22. *do not put off fulfilling it* The text does not specify what constitutes an impermissible delay, perhaps because circumstances might differ in individual cases. Since most vows consisted of sacrifices and gifts to the sanctuary, they would presumably be due on the first occasion when the vower could travel to the sanctuary following the realization of his or her petition. It is reasonable to

you, and you will have incurred guilt; [23]whereas you incur no guilt if you refrain from vowing. [24]You must fulfill what has crossed your lips and perform what you have voluntarily vowed to the LORD your God, having made the promise with your own mouth.

וְהָיָה בְךָ חֵטְא: [23] וְכִי תֶחְדַּל לִנְדֹּר לֹא־יִהְיֶה בְךָ חֵטְא: [24] מוֹצָא שְׂפָתֶיךָ תִּשְׁמֹר וְעָשִׂיתָ כַּאֲשֶׁר נָדַרְתָּ לַיהוָה אֱלֹהֶיךָ נְדָבָה אֲשֶׁר דִּבַּרְתָּ בְּפִיךָ: ס

assume that people were normally expected to fulfill a vow during the next pilgrimage festival. Some people may have made special trips for the purpose (Absalom claimed to be doing so when he started his rebellion against David). In the period of the chieftains and the early monarchy there seems to have been a custom of an annual family pilgrimage to Shiloh, in addition to the three pilgrimage festivals, for the purpose of offering sacrifice and fulfilling vows. According to the halakhah, the vow should indeed be paid on the next pilgrimage festival, but it is not regarded as unacceptably late until all three festivals of a year have passed.[96]

the LORD will require it of you   He will hold you responsible and punish you for not fulfilling it. For the idiom see 18:19.

and you will have incurred guilt   See Comment to 15:9. In 24:14–15, too, this warning concerns delayed payment, in that case payment of wages. The approximate meaning of this warning is clarified by the parallel passage in Ecclesiastes 5:5, which warns that unfulfilled vows will anger God and He will destroy the offender's possessions.[97]

23.   Vowing is a purely voluntary activity, by no means required by God, and there is no penalty for not making vows; but once a vow is made, delay in fulfilling it is hypocritical and disrespectful. Implicit in this verse is a teaching that vows are not necessary for securing God's aid or remaining in His favor.

24.   *You must fulfill* . . .   Compare Numbers 30:3: "If a man makes a vow to the LORD . . . he shall not break his pledge; he must carry out all that has crossed his lips." A vow is unconditionally binding, and the Bible mentions no procedure for an individual to have his vow annulled, even if it is impossible to keep. Jephthah was unable to annul his vow even when it turned out to require the sacrifice of his daughter, as related in Judges 11:35–36. This is the reason for the Bible's warnings against vowing rashly. The rabbis eventually developed a system for annulling vows under the auspices of a court when necessary, as spelled out in Tractate Nedarim. The *Kol Nidrei* declaration recited on Yom Kippur is an example of such an annulment.[98]

what has crossed your lips   This is a standard idiom for a solemn promise.[99]

voluntarily[100]

THE RIGHT TO EAT FROM A NEIGHBOR'S UNHARVESTED CROPS
(vv. 25–26)

Apparently fields and vineyards were laid out in such a way that people often had to pass through those belonging to others. This was not considered trespass; to judge from Exodus 22:4–5, only damaging the field is trespass. When passing another's crops, if one is hungry he may pick enough grapes or ears of grain to satisfy his hunger, but he may not take more than he can eat on the spot. According to nineteenth-century travelers, this right was still recognized as a charitable obligation in the Middle East in recent times.[101] A similar regulation is proposed in Plato's *Laws*, according to which a foreign visitor traveling along the road should be allowed, out of hospitality, to pick enough grapes and figs of the type that are eaten fresh to feed himself and one attendant, but not of the types that are dried, stored, or used for wine. They may also pick less valuable fruits, such as apples and pomegranates.[102]

That the biblical laws apply to any passerby is the view of Josephus and R. Isi b. Yehudah. The practice is reflected in a story in the Christian scriptures in which Jesus's disciples pluck ears of grain while passing through grainfields; they are rebuked by the Pharisees, but only for doing so on the Sabbath.[103] However, the halakhah restricts the law to workers who are harvesting the field or

25When you enter another man's vineyard, you may eat as many grapes as you want, until you are full, but you must not put any in your vessel. 26When you enter another man's field of standing grain, you may pluck ears with your hand; but you must not put a sickle to your neighbor's grain.

חמישי 25 כִּי תָבֹא בְּכֶרֶם רֵעֶךָ וְאָכַלְתָּ עֲנָבִים כְּנַפְשְׁךָ שָׂבְעֶךָ וְאֶל־כֶּלְיְךָ לֹא תִתֵּן: ס 26 כִּי תָבֹא בְּקָמַת רֵעֶךָ וְקָטַפְתָּ מְלִילֹת בְּיָדֶךָ וְחֶרְמֵשׁ לֹא תָנִיף עַל קָמַת רֵעֶךָ: ס

vineyard for the owner because, according to Rav, granting all passersby the right to take some of the crop might well ruin the owner.[104] It is not known whether changed economic conditions or some other factor lies behind the halakhic position.

Related laws requiring farmers to share their crops with others are found in 24:19–22 and 25:4, as well as 14:28–29.

25. *vessel* Rather, "bag," referring to baggage carried by travelers in which they would keep food and other necessities.[105]

26. *standing grain . . . ears* Hebrew *melilot*, "ears," apparently means ears of soft, "rubbable" grain, from *m-l-l*, "rub." When barley and wheat are still standing in the field, not yet ready for harvest, their grains are soft and edible after husking. This is what is described in the aforementioned passage about Jesus's disciples, who "plucked and ate some ears of grain, [first] rubbing them in their hands" to husk them. The process is described in the Mishnah: "If a man peels the husks of barley . . . and eats. . . . If he rubs [*molel*] ears of wheat, sifting them from one hand to the other [to remove the chaff] and eating them. . . ."[106]

you must not put a sickle to your neighbor's grain Since a sickle cuts several stalks at once, this could easily yield more than one can eat on the spot, which is all one is entitled to take.[107]

CHAPTER **24**
The group of miscellaneous laws that began in 23:10 continues in chapter 24. Like chapter 23, chapter 24 begins with laws about marriage (vv. 1–5) and ends with laws providing for the sharing of crops with those in need (vv. 19–22). Interspersed among these laws, because of incidental verbal or thematic connections (see Excursus 13), are several others, mostly of a humanitarian character and intended to protect or benefit the disadvantaged (vv. 6,10–15,17–18).[1]

FORBIDDEN REMARRIAGE (vv. 1–4)

The laws of divorce are not prescribed in the Torah. They were undoubtedly the subject of customary law. What little we know about them comes from indirect references in prophecies, narratives, and laws like the present one. Talmudic texts subject the present law to a very close reading in order to extract as much guidance about divorce as possible. The results appear primarily in the Tractate Gittin ("Divorce Certificates").

This law—a marital prohibition, like 23:1–9—supplements the customary laws of marriage and divorce in one particular area: a man may not remarry his former wife if she has been married to another man in the interim. Verses 3–4 imply that there would be something adulterous about such an act. Ramban infers that the aim of the law is to prevent the use of divorce and marriage as a legal subterfuge for wife-swapping, whereby couples might divorce, marry their paramours temporarily, then divorce them and reestablish their original marriages. Such a practice would be the mirror image of *mut'a* ("enjoyment") marriage, a temporary marriage employed in some Islamic countries as a legal veneer for prostitution.[2] This explanation is unlikely, since verses 1 and 3 state explicitly that the reason for the divorce is the husband's dislike of his wife.[3] Perhaps, though, the law was prompted by a concern that if husbands take their wives back after they have had voluntary sexual relations with other men, adultery might begin to seem less objectionable.

This law was well-enough known that two prophets alluded to it as a metaphor.[4]

1–4. A better translation would be: "If a man takes a wife and possesses her, and she fails to please him because he discovers her doing something obnoxious . . . [v. 4] then the first husband

24 A man takes a wife and possesses her. She fails to please him because he finds something obnoxious about her, and he writes her a bill of divorcement, hands it to her, and sends her away from his house; ²she leaves his

כ״ד כִּי־יִקַּח אִישׁ אִשָּׁה וּבְעָלָהּ וְהָיָה אִם־לֹא תִמְצָא־חֵן בְּעֵינָיו כִּי־מָצָא בָהּ עֶרְוַת דָּבָר וְכָתַב לָהּ סֵפֶר כְּרִיתֻת וְנָתַן בְּיָדָהּ וְשִׁלְּחָהּ מִבֵּיתוֹ:

who divorced her shall not take her to wife again." These four verses constitute a single sentence. Verses 1–3 are the protasis, stating the conditions, and verse 4a is the apodosis, stating the law.

she fails to please him If she ceases to please him. By itself this clause implies that a husband could divorce his wife for any reason, however subjective. This is how the law was understood by Josephus, the School of Hillel, and Rabbi Akiba. Some commentators believe that the following clause ("because he finds something obnoxious about her") is intended to restrict this right to a single reason. However, this law was not written to present the rules for divorce, but to describe one of its consequences, and it is likely that the following clause simply refers to the most common type of reason, but not the only one permitted. The husband's latitude was eventually abolished for Ashkenazic Jewry by a *takkanah* (rabbinic enactment) issued by Rabbenu Gershom (ca. 960–1028), prohibiting the husband from divorcing his wife against her will except for a legally compelling reason such as apostasy or refusal of conjugal rights. (It was also Rabbenu Gershom who issued the *takkanah* prohibiting polygamy.)[5]

The suggested translation, "because he discovers her doing something obnoxious," is based on the meaning of the Hebrew "find something in [*matsa' be-*] somebody." This idiom means to catch a person doing something wrong,[6] and refers to conduct, not to an unpleasant quality or physical feature. "Something obnoxious" apparently refers to any kind of offensive conduct. In 23:15 the same Hebrew phrase, *'ervat davar*, refers to obnoxious bodily emissions. What the husband might find similarly offensive is obviously a subjective matter. According to ancient Near Eastern documents, typical motives for divorce included suspicious absences from home, wasting or embezzling the husband's property, humiliating him, denial of conjugal rights, and—when it was not punished with death—adultery.[7]

Since *'ervah* literally means "nakedness" or "genitals," and Leviticus describes incest as uncovering a relative's *'ervah*, the School of Shammai and some subsequent commentators inferred that *'ervat davar* refers to sexually indecent behavior—in the opinion of some, adultery.[8] However, in biblical law the punishment for adultery is execution, which would preclude the remarriage spoken of here.[9] Furthermore, "uncovering *'ervah*" is used only in cases of incest, which is unlikely to be the meaning here; adultery is described by other expressions.[10] Although the idiom could refer to indecent exposure in public (which may be what the School of Shammai meant), it seems best to be guided by its only other occurrence, here in Deuteronomy, and to take it as referring to any conduct the husband finds intolerable.

he writes her a bill of divorcement . . . and sends her away Divorce is initiated by the husband. This is the norm in the Bible and elsewhere in the ancient Near East, and is clearly the case in the present law. It is possible, however, that in certain circumstances the wife might initiate it. According to Exodus 21:7–11, a girl sold for the purpose of marriage must be given her freedom if her master does not provide her basic necessities. Assuming that the rights of free women were not less than those of such girls, this seems to imply that a wife could initiate the dissolution of the marriage on the grounds of nonsupport.[11] Furthermore, a number of ancient Near Eastern marriage contracts stipulate that either the husband or the wife may initiate divorce, and similar provisions are known in Palestinian Jewish marriage contracts down into the Middle Ages. So it is not out of the question that some women had this right in biblical Israel, too, at least if it was stipulated in the marriage agreement.[12] Halakhic sources recognize a number of cases in which a wife may petition the court to compel her husband to grant a divorce, such as nonsupport, beating, and fornication.[13]

a bill of divorcement A certificate of divorce, now known as a *get* (Aramaic for "legal document," from a Sumerian term meaning "oblong tablet"). Hebrew *keritut* literally means "severance," an apt term for the divorce. However, since "sever" (*karat*) is not the verb used for divorce in the Bible, it has been conjectured that the term did not originally refer to the severance of the marriage but to the act of cutting the wife's hem or garment, which is a ceremonial act of divorce

household and becomes the wife of another man; ³then this latter man rejects her, writes her a bill of divorcement, hands it to her, and sends her away from his house; or the man who married her last dies. ⁴Then the first husband who divorced her shall not take her to wife again, since she has been defiled—for that would be abhorrent to the LORD. You must not bring sin upon the land that the LORD your God is giving you as a heritage.

⁵When a man has taken a bride, he shall not go out with the army or be assigned to it for any purpose; he shall be

```
2  וְיָצְאָה מִבֵּיתוֹ וְהָלְכָה וְהָיְתָה לְאִישׁ־אַחֵר:
3  וּשְׂנֵאָהּ הָאִישׁ הָאַחֲרוֹן וְכָתַב לָהּ סֵפֶר
   כְּרִיתֻת וְנָתַן בְּיָדָהּ וְשִׁלְּחָהּ מִבֵּיתוֹ אוֹ כִי יָמוּת
   הָאִישׁ הָאַחֲרוֹן אֲשֶׁר־לְקָחָהּ לוֹ לְאִשָּׁה: 4 לֹא־
   יוּכַל בַּעְלָהּ הָרִאשׁוֹן אֲשֶׁר־שִׁלְּחָהּ לָשׁוּב
   לְקַחְתָּהּ לִהְיוֹת לוֹ לְאִשָּׁה אַחֲרֵי אֲשֶׁר הֻטַּמָּאָה
   כִּי־תוֹעֵבָה הִוא לִפְנֵי יְהוָה וְלֹא תַחֲטִיא אֶת־
   הָאָרֶץ אֲשֶׁר יְהוָה אֱלֹהֶיךָ נֹתֵן לְךָ נַחֲלָה: ס
שׁני 5 כִּי־יִקַּח אִישׁ אִשָּׁה חֲדָשָׁה לֹא יֵצֵא
```

known from Mesopotamia. Since *karat* is used in the Bible for cutting off the hem of a garment, this suggestion is plausible.[14]

To judge from various ancient Near Eastern documents referring to divorce, the certificate was probably a statement by the husband that the couple is no longer husband and wife (as in Hosea 2:4, which is quoted in Karaite divorce certificates) and that she is free to marry whomever she wishes. The latter provision is what the Mishnah terms "the essential clause" of the divorce certificate, its purpose being to provide the wife with proof of her freedom to remarry.[15]

3. rejects Hebrew *sane'*, literally, "hates," the same verb rendered "takes an aversion" in 22:13. The verb expresses the emotion of turning against one's spouse and sometimes the act of rejecting him or her, as in Judges 15:2.[16]

4. the first husband . . . shall not take her to wife again since she has been defiled That is, disqualified for him by virtue of her second marriage.[17] Had she not remarried, there would be no objection to the couple's reunion. A contract from the year 124 C.E. for the remarriage of a Jewish couple was found in a cave in the Wadi Murabbaat in the Judaean desert.[18]

Interestingly, Islamic law prescribes the opposite procedure: if a man has irrevocably divorced his wife, he may not remarry her unless she *has* been married in the interim. When a couple wishes to reunite, a beggar is hired to marry the woman and consort with her for one night, after which he divorces her and frees her to reunite with her husband. Wives understandably find this repulsive, and some Muslims permit a sacrifice to be offered in place of the intervening marriage.[19]

bring sin upon the land That is, lead its people to sin, as explained in the introductory Comment to this law. Leviticus 19:29 warns against a similar influence from prostitution: "Do not degrade your daughter and make her a harlot, lest the land fall into harlotry and the land be filled with depravity."

DEFERRAL OF THE NEW HUSBAND FROM MILITARY SERVICE (v. 5)

A newly married man is deferred from all types of military service for one year in order to give happiness to his wife. It is similar to the rules about draft deferral in 20:6–8, but because its concern is with the bride rather than the soldier, it appears here and not in chapter 20. According to the halakhah, this law does not apply in the case of an obligatory war, as noted in the Comment to 20:6–8. Support for this view is found in a Ugaritic legend in which even those normally exempt from war, such as the blind and the sick, are mobilized for an urgent military campaign, including new husbands.[20]

5. bride Literally, "a new wife." This deferral is granted only in the case of a new wife. Theoretically a new wife could mean only one who has never been married before. However, in the light of the preceding law, it probably means a wife who is not the former wife of the same man. In other words, a man who marries, whether or not his wife has been married previously, is deferred from military service unless he is marrying his own former wife.[21] This detail may be aimed at preventing men from gaining deferral by divorcing and remarrying their wives.

or be assigned to it for any other purpose[22] The deferral of the newlywed is total, excusing him even from noncombatant duties.

222

exempt one year for the sake of his household, to give happiness to the woman he has married.

⁶A handmill or an upper millstone shall not be taken in pawn, for that would be taking someone's life in pawn.

בַּצָּבָא וְלֹא־יַעֲבֹר עָלָיו לְכָל־דָּבָר נָקִי יִהְיֶה לְבֵיתוֹ שָׁנָה אֶחָת וְשִׂמַּח אֶת־אִשְׁתּוֹ אֲשֶׁר־לָקָח: ס

⁶ לֹא־יַחֲבֹל רֵחַיִם וָרָכֶב כִּי־נֶפֶשׁ הוּא חֹבֵל: ס

give happiness Hebrew *ve-simmaḥ* could also be translated "gratify, pleasure," meaning give her conjugal pleasure.[23] In either case, the aim of the law is to ensure that the bride enjoys a year of marital pleasure before her husband risks his life in war. This concern complements that of 20:7, where the reason given for an engaged man's deferment *before* marriage focuses on *his* fulfillment. Deuteronomy's interest in women's feelings is also expressed in 21:10–14. Some of the ancient Bible translations render the phrase as "he shall have happiness with his bride," as if the text read *ve-samaḥ* instead of *ve-simmaḥ*.[24] In that case, the text means either that the two rejoice equally, or that he rejoices over her.[25]

VITAL IMPLEMENTS MAY NOT BE DISTRAINED TO COMPEL REPAYMENT OF A LOAN (v. 6)

Verse 6, along with verses 10–13 and 17, limits the means by which creditors may pressure their debtors to repay. These laws are separated from each other by digressions in verses 7–9 and 16.

To increase the likelihood of repayment, in at least some cases lenders had a right to take property from their debtors to induce them to repay what they had borrowed. So far as is known, in Israel this property was not taken at the time of the loan, and the particular possession that would be taken may not even have been specified at that time. Rather, the lender had a lien on the debtor's possessions. If the debtor defaulted on the loan, the creditor would receive or seize ("distrain") some of his property, choosing what to take either in agreement with the debtor or at his own discretion. Because the property seized (the "distress") was sometimes of little value to the creditor (such as the upper millstone mentioned in v. 6), its function was evidently not to satisfy the debt but to pressure the creditor to repay by depriving him of something important.[26] Borrowers were usually impoverished and would often have few possessions left apart from clothing and necessary household items. This limited the creditor's choice of objects to distrain. The aim of the Torah's laws about distraint is to ensure that in such circumstances, the creditor's legitimate right to repayment is subordinated to the survival and dignity of the debtor, much like the laws about debts in 15:1–11 and 23:20–21. Accordingly, the creditor may not take a handmill, which is necessary for making food (v. 6); he may not take a widow's garment (v. 17); if he takes a poor man's night cover, he must return it every evening (vv. 12–13); and he may not invade the debtor's house to seize an object for distraint, but must wait outside while the debtor brings it to him (vv. 10–11). The restrictions considerably reduce the creditor's leverage in securing repayment, but they are consistent with the Bible's position that loans to the poor are acts of charity that may well turn into outright gifts (see introductory Comment to 15:1–6 and Comment to 15:10).

6. a handmill or an upper millstone That is, "a handmill set or even just its upper stone." The handmill was made of stone hard enough to withstand constant rubbing, normally basalt. It consisted of an oval or rectangular base on which grain was placed, and a much smaller upper stone that was rubbed back and forth over it to grind the grain. Such mills were used to prepare flour for baking bread, the staple of the common person's diet, and were probably found in every home. The lower stone was heavy, sometimes weighing as much as ninety pounds, and inconvenient to take away. In such cases, apparently, creditors sometimes took only the upper stone, which weighed only four or five pounds and could not easily be replaced since basalt was not found naturally in most parts of the country.[27] This would suffice to render the mill useless and induce the debtor to repay the debt as soon as possible.

taken in pawn Rather, "distrained," seized to compel repayment. As noted by Rashi, *ḥaval* refers to distraint of property after the debtor has defaulted on the loan.[28]

someone's life That is, something vital, a means of survival. Items necessary for producing

7If a man is found to have kidnapped a fellow Israelite, enslaving him or selling him, that kidnapper shall die; thus you will sweep out evil from your midst.

7 כִּי־יִמָּצֵא אִישׁ גֹּנֵב נֶפֶשׁ מֵאֶחָיו מִבְּנֵי יִשְׂרָאֵל וְהִתְעַמֶּר־בּוֹ וּמְכָרוֹ וּמֵת הַגַּנָּב הַהוּא וּבִעַרְתָּ הָרָע מִקִּרְבֶּךָ:

food, such as farming tools, as well as food itself and shelter, are often called "life" in Mesopotamian, Egyptian, and postbiblical Jewish literature.[29] Hence halakhic exegesis reasonably infers that the handmill here stands for anything with which the debtor prepares necessary food, such as pots, an oven, or a sieve; in some views, draught animals and the tools by which the debtor earns his livelihood are also not subject to distraint.[30] The Laws of Hammurabi similarly forbid the distraint of oxen and grain, and Job criticizes those who distrain the widow's ox.[31]

KIDNAPING (v. 7)

Essentially the same law appears in Exodus 21:16: "He who kidnaps a man—whether he has sold him or is still holding him—shall be put to death." It is clear from both passages that the primary purpose of kidnaping was to enslave the victim, either to the kidnaper or to others. Both versions of the law deal with the circumstances under which kidnaping is a capital crime. Here in Deuteronomy, it is a capital crime if the victim is an Israelite, but only if the victim has been enslaved or sold. In Exodus, it is a capital crime no matter who the victim is, and it apparently makes no difference whether the kidnaper has sold the victim or "is still holding him" (unless the latter phrase means the same thing as Deuteronomy's "enslaving him," which means that the kidnaper uses the victim as his own slave).

It is harder to harmonize the difference between Exodus and Deuteronomy regarding the nationality of the victim. The wording here, literally, "your fellow, one of the Israelites," explicitly restricts the law to Israelite victims. Presumably, it would punish the kidnapping of resident aliens and foreigners in some other way. This is the case in the Hittite Laws, where the penalty depends on the nationality of the victim.[32] Unless we assume, as halakhic exegesis does, that Exodus implicitly refers only to Israelite victims,[33] Deuteronomy seems to represent a modification of the law in Exodus. This is a puzzling variation, since Deuteronomy devotes more attention to the welfare of resident aliens than any other biblical book (see vv. 14–21).

On the location of this law, see Excursus 13.

7. enslaving him or selling him The translation agrees with the halakhic view that this is a necessary condition for capital punishment; kidnaping without enslavement or sale is not covered by this law.[34] On the translation "enslaving," and the possibility that the term could mean "ransom," see Comment to 21:14 and note thereon.

sweep out evil See Comment to 13:6.

DEALING WITH "LEPROSY" (vv. 8–9)

"Leprosy" is the conventional translation of *tsaraʿat*,[35] which refers to a variety of conditions affecting skin, clothing, and the walls of buildings. There is no single English term that covers all these conditions. When referring to a skin affliction the term probably refers to various different kinds of serious dermatological conditions, but probably not to what modern medicine calls leprosy (Hansen's disease). These conditions and the diagnostic and ritual procedures to be followed in case of their occurrence are described in Leviticus 13–14 for the benefit of the priests. It is they who observe and diagnose the symptoms.[36]

The present passage illustrates the difference between Deuteronomy, which is entirely addressed to the public, and Leviticus, much of which consists of professional lore addressed to the priests who specialize in its subject matter. The technical details of leprosy are too complicated for nonspecialists, but because leprous affections created ritual impurity, the public had to be reminded to scrupulously submit them to the judgment of those qualified to diagnose them correctly.

It is not clear why the text digresses to the subject of leprosy here. See Excursus 13.

8In cases of a skin affection be most careful to do exactly as the levitical priests instruct you. Take care to do as I have commanded them. 9Remember what the LORD your God did to Miriam on the journey after you left Egypt.

10When you make a loan of any sort to your countryman, you must not enter his house to seize his pledge. 11You must remain outside, while the man to whom you made the loan brings the pledge out to you. 12If he is a

8 הִשָּׁמֶר בְּנֶגַע־הַצָּרַעַת לִשְׁמֹר מְאֹד וְלַעֲשׂוֹת כְּכֹל אֲשֶׁר־יוֹרוּ אֶתְכֶם הַכֹּהֲנִים הַלְוִיִּם כַּאֲשֶׁר צִוִּיתִם תִּשְׁמְרוּ לַעֲשׂוֹת: ס 9 זָכוֹר אֵת אֲשֶׁר־עָשָׂה יְהוָה אֱלֹהֶיךָ לְמִרְיָם בַּדֶּרֶךְ בְּצֵאתְכֶם מִמִּצְרָיִם: ס

10 כִּי־תַשֶּׁה בְרֵעֲךָ מַשַּׁאת מְאוּמָה לֹא־תָבֹא אֶל־בֵּיתוֹ לַעֲבֹט עֲבֹטוֹ: 11 בַּחוּץ תַּעֲמֹד וְהָאִישׁ אֲשֶׁר אַתָּה נֹשֶׁה בוֹ יוֹצִיא אֵלֶיךָ אֶת־הַעֲבוֹט

8. *instruct* Hebrew *horah* is the characteristic verb for priestly instruction, especially in ritual matters. The corresponding noun, *torah*, refers to priestly instruction and to the regulations on which it is based, such as the "Instruction for Leprosy" in Leviticus 14:57.[37] For the term's full range of meanings see 17:10–11 and Comment to 1:5.

9. *what the LORD . . . did to Miriam* After Miriam and Aaron had spoken against Moses, Miriam was stricken with "leprosy" and was required to spend a week outside the camp, as related in Numbers 12:10–15. The purpose behind the mentioning of this incident is not clear. A traditional ethicizing interpretation takes this as a warning against gossip, since that is why Miriam was stricken; but the text could hardly expect many readers to get the point of a warning in which the dangerous conduct is not explicitly identified.[38] Many commentators believe that the point is to show that no one should receive special treatment from the priests and be excused from the required isolation, since not even Miriam was excused.[39] However, according to Jacob Milgrom, Miriam did receive special treatment; she was isolated only one week instead of the normal two.[40] Furthermore, "what the LORD did to Miriam" is most naturally understood as referring to the affliction itself, not the period of isolation that followed. So perhaps the point is to show that nobody is immune, so that people wouldn't assume "it can't happen to me" and fail to consult a priest regarding a potentially "leprous" skin affection.

after you left Egypt see Comment to 23:5.

TAKING AND HOLDING DISTRAINED PROPERTY (vv. 10–13)

These two laws return to the subject of distraint following default on a loan (v. 6). Here the verb for distraint is ʿavat, a synonym of ḥaval, which is used in vv. 6 and 17.[41] These laws limit the creditor's freedom in taking and holding the distrained object. The second law is essentially identical to Exodus 22:25–26. The first limits the creditor's discretion even further.

10–11. The creditor may not enter the debtor's home to distrain property. The debtor and his family would be humiliated by another man acting as master in the debtor's domain, and the confrontation could lead to a fight.

The halakhah construes this law broadly, understanding it to mean that the creditor may not distrain the debtor's possessions by force anywhere. To prevent that, it permits distraint only with permission of the court. In the same vein the Laws of Hammurabi penalize a creditor who distrains grain from a debtor without his consent.[42]

12–13. If the distrained object is the cloth that the debtor sleeps in at night for warmth, the creditor must return it to him every night (on this cloth, see Comment to 22:17). Here, too, the halakhah construes the law broadly, holding that all objects that are permissible to distrain but necessary to the debtor must be returned to him daily when he needs them, such as a pillow at night and a plow and tools of his trade by day.[43]

12. *If he is a needy man* This may imply that some borrowers were not needy (see Comment to 23:20–21), but it may simply mean if he is absolutely destitute, to the point where he owns nothing that can be distrained but the wrap he sleeps in at night. Apparently there were many borrowers in such straits. See next Comment.

needy man, you shall not go to sleep in his pledge; [13]you must return the pledge to him at sundown, that he may sleep in his cloth and bless you; and it will be to your merit before the LORD your God.

[14]You shall not abuse a needy and destitute laborer,

הַחוּצָה: 12 וְאִם־אִישׁ עָנִי הוּא לֹא תִשְׁכַּב בַּעֲבֹטוֹ: 13 הָשֵׁב תָּשִׁיב לוֹ אֶת־הָעֲבוֹט כְּבֹא הַשֶּׁמֶשׁ וְשָׁכַב בְּשַׂלְמָתוֹ וּבֵרֲכֶךָּ וּלְךָ תִּהְיֶה צְדָקָה לִפְנֵי יְהוָה אֱלֹהֶיךָ: ס
שביעי 14 לֹא־תַעֲשֹׁק שָׂכִיר עָנִי וְאֶבְיוֹן מֵאַחֶיךָ

go to sleep in his pledge Nightclothes were often the objects distrained from poor debtors, as indicated in Exodus 22:25–26. Distraint of clothing is mentioned in several other passages as well, including Amos's denunciation of those who are so heartless that they recline alongside altars on distrained garments.[44] In a Hebrew letter from the seventh century B.C.E., found near Kibbutz Palmaḥim, the writer appeals to an official, claiming that his garment was wrongfully seized and asking for its return. The reason for the seizure seems to be nonfulfillment of an obligation, either a work quota or some sort of required payment.[45]

sleep in his pledge The prohibition is not limited to its literal meaning, but means not to go to sleep at night with his pledge in one's possession.[46] Creditors probably did not normally actually sleep in garments distrained from the poor.

13. *you must return the pledge to him at sundown* That is, each day, and he will return it to you in the morning. The fact that the debtor has access to the pledge when needed seems to diminish his incentive to repay. The Tosafot explain that this is still an effective means of inducing him to repay since it prevents him from denying his debt and the embarrassment of facing the creditor daily would induce him to repay it as soon as possible.[47]

bless you He will express his gratitude by calling on God to bless you, that is, to reward you with prosperity (see Comment to 2:7). Such expressions of gratitude take the form *barukh 'atta* [or *peloni*] *la-'adonay* . . . , "Blessed may you [or so-and-so] be before, or by, the LORD, because you [or he] did. . . ."[48] The blessing itself comes from God; when a human is said to bless (*barekh*), it usually means "utter a prayer beginning with the word 'Blessed' [*barukh*]." On this use of the *pi'el* conjugation, see Comment to 1:38.

it will be to your merit See Comments to 6:25 and 23:22.

The promise of blessing for return of the cloth is a positive statement of the motive clause accompanying the same law in Exodus 22:26, which warns that the debtor whose cloth is not returned will cry out against the creditor and that God will hear the complaint. The promise and the warning (see also verse 15) rest upon the conviction that God is the ultimate patron of the powerless: although they cannot personally reward those who are kind to them or punish those who mistreat them, they have the recourse of God, who will heed their wishes. They may also imply that human government was not well-equipped to protect their rights and that God was virtually their only recourse.

TIMELY PAYMENT OF WAGES (vv. 14–15)

Wages of laborers must be paid on the day they do their work. Employers should be sensitive to the fact that poor laborers need their pay immediately; they do not have the wherewithal that an employer does that would enable them to wait for their pay.

Essentially the same law appears in Leviticus 19:13. There the law applies to all laborers. Here, in typical Deuteronomic fashion, the law focuses on poor laborers, both Israelites and aliens, and adds clauses appealing to the employer's conscience and warning him of the consequences of disregarding this moral obligation. Deuteronomy's version of the law is alluded to by the prophet Malachi, who excoriates those "who withhold the wages of the laborer, the widow, and the orphan, and subvert [the rights] of the stranger" (Mal. 3:5).

14. *You shall not abuse* The stem *'-sh-k* is a general term for maltreatment and cheating someone out of what belongs to them; it is frequently associated with robbing (*g-z-l*) and carries similar overtones. In fact, the version of this law in Leviticus 19:13 includes the exhortation "You shall

whether a fellow countryman or a stranger in one of the communities of your land. ¹⁵You must pay him his wages on the same day, before the sun sets, for he is needy and urgently depends on it; else he will cry to the LORD against you and you will incur guilt.

¹⁶Parents shall not be put to death for children, nor children be put to death for parents: a person shall be put to death only for his own crime.

not abuse [*'-sh-k*] your fellow, you shall not commit robbery [*g-z-l*]." This term stigmatizes even a temporary delay in paying wages as virtually a form of theft.⁴⁹

laborer Literally, "a hired man," one hired for a particular job, not a resident employee or servant who receives room and board from you.⁵⁰

15. urgently depends on it Rather, "he has his heart set on it," "he is counting on it," and it would be a cruel disappointment to make him wait.⁵¹

he will cry out to the LORD against you and you will incur guilt He may be powerless to compel you to pay him on time, but he can have recourse to God, who will punish you. Exodus 22:21–23 warns similarly against mistreatment of widows and orphans, as does Deuteronomy 15:9 regarding refusal of loans to the poor. See Comment on verse 13. Some of the prayers of Jeremiah, and a number of Psalms, are cries against mistreatment.⁵²

you will incur guilt Note the similar warning in 23:22 for late payment, there referring to payment of a vow to God.

TRANSGENERATIONAL PUNISHMENT FORBIDDEN (v. 16)

This is one of several laws in Deuteronomy that deal with judicial procedure rather than a specific crime.⁵³ Although it is recognized in 5:9 that God punishes descendants for their ancestors' wrongs, that is solely a divine prerogative: human authorities may not act likewise. That the verse here refers to execution by human judicial authorities is clear from the verb *yumat*, which always refers to judicial execution, not divine punishment.⁵⁴

Elsewhere in ancient Near Eastern law, the notion that members of a man's family were an extension of his own personality, rather than individuals in their own right, was sometimes taken to such an extreme that if a man harmed a member of another's family, he was punished by the same harm being done to a member of his own family, often the corresponding member. At other times, an offender's family might be punished along with him.⁵⁵ While these were not necessarily universal practices, no explicit prohibition of them is known prior to Deuteronomy.⁵⁶ There is, however, an implicit renunciation of the practice in Exodus 21:31, which rules that the owner of a goring ox is to be punished personally whether the ox gores an adult or a *child*; in other words, the owner's child is not to be punished if the victim was a child. The few instances where punishment of children was legally sanctioned were not criminal cases but those involving offenses against God, such as violations of the *ḥerem* and national oaths.⁵⁷ The Bible and other ancient sources mention cases of the execution of the entire family of those guilty of treason, as well as the families of kings whose dynasties were overthrown. This was probably done for tactical reasons, and in any case is not represented as legal. Indeed, we hear from time to time of kings who spared the families of traitors, and 2 Kings 14:6 reports that, in accordance with this law, King Amaziah spared the children of his father's murderers.⁵⁸

Halakhic exegesis reasons that since it is clear enough from the final clause of the verse that parents and children are not to be executed for each other's crimes, the first part of the verse must make a separate point: people may not be executed or even convicted on the strength of a relative's testimony, and hence relatives may not even testify about each other.⁵⁹

17You shall not subvert the rights of the stranger or the fatherless; you shall not take a widow's garment in pawn. 18Remember that you were a slave in Egypt and that the LORD your God redeemed you from there; therefore do I enjoin you to observe this commandment.

17 לֹא תַטֶּה מִשְׁפַּט גֵּר יָתוֹם וְלֹא תַחֲבֹל בֶּגֶד אַלְמָנָה: 18 וְזָכַרְתָּ כִּי עֶבֶד הָיִיתָ בְּמִצְרַיִם וַיִּפְדְּךָ יְהֹוָה אֱלֹהֶיךָ מִשָּׁם עַל־כֵּן אָנֹכִי מְצַוְּךָ לַעֲשׂוֹת אֶת־הַדָּבָר הַזֶּה: ס

PROTECTING ALIENS, THE FATHERLESS, AND WIDOWS (vv. 17–18)

Concern for the welfare of resident aliens, the fatherless, and widows is a recurrent theme in the Bible.[60] As explained in the Comments to 1:16 and 10:18, their economic and social disadvantages exposed them to exploitation. This is a universal problem, and concern for the welfare of the fatherless and widows is commonly mentioned in ancient Near Eastern wisdom literature and texts about the activities of kings, whose special duty it was to protect them (concern for the alien is not nearly so common outside the Bible).[61] Biblical law requires every Israelite to avoid wronging them and to be concerned with their welfare. Exodus and Leviticus warn against mistreating them economically and judicially, and earlier passages in Deuteronomy have focused on the obligation to include them in the triennial tithe for the poor (14:29), the Sabbath rest (5:14), and the celebration accompanying festivals (16:11,14).[62] Their economic needs are addressed again below in verses 19–21. Here the concern is with protecting them from mistreatment in court.

The second clause of this verse continues the subject of distraint (vv. 6,19–15).

17. *You shall not subvert the rights of the stranger or the fatherless* Rather, "You shall not judge the stranger or the fatherless unfairly," as the idiom is translated in 16:19. Although the fatherless and resident aliens are covered by the universal principle expressed there, the need to assure that they are treated fairly in court is often reiterated because their situation, like that of widows and the poor, exposes them to exploitation. In court the alien is at a disadvantage because he is neither a fully integrated member of society nor a peer of the judges or of his adversary, and the fatherless may have no adult male with the experience and eloquence to represent them capably.

you shall not take a widow's garment in pawn Rather, "you shall not distrain a widow's garment" (to compel repayment of a loan); see Comment to verse 6. Though other debtors' garments may be distrained, and must be returned at night if necessary, those of a widow may not be taken at all. In this respect the law shows greater solicitude for the widow than for aliens and orphans, about whom there is no such regulation.[63] Perhaps she is protected from this final inconvenience and indignity out of respect for her age, her bereavement, and the difficulties she faces living, and perhaps raising children, on her own.[64] Targum Jonathan and halakhic sources think the reason is that if a creditor held her garment and returned it to her each evening, it could lead to unchastity or to rumors harmful to her reputation.[65]

Distraint of a widow's ox is mentioned unfavorably in Job 24:3. 2 Kings 4:1ff. tells how Elisha miraculously enabled a widow to avoid distraint of her children. According to the halakhah, no possessions of a widow may be distrained.[66]

Just as the present verse separates the members of the common triad "stranger, orphan, and widow," mentioning two in the first clause and the third in the next, so does 10:18: "He upholds the cause of the orphan and widow, and befriends the stranger, providing him with food and clothing." These are examples of the breakup of stereotype phrases as an artistic device which is common in the Bible, especially in poetry.[67]

18. *remember that you were a slave . . . and that the LORD . . . redeemed you* See Comments to 5:15 and 15:15. According to this verse and verse 22, Israel's experience of slavery should lead to empathy not only with slaves, whose experience is identical to theirs, but with all the disadvantaged.

GLEANINGS FOR THE POOR (vv. 19–22)

This law contains further measures for the welfare of aliens, widows, and orphans. In harvesting, the farmer is not to double back to ensure that he has gathered up every last sheaf, olive, or grape. What

19When you reap the harvest in your field and overlook a sheaf in the field, do not turn back to get it; it shall go to the stranger, the fatherless, and the widow—in order that the LORD your God may bless you in all your undertakings.

20When you beat down the fruit of your olive trees, do not go over them again; that shall go to the stranger, the fatherless, and the widow. 21When you gather the grapes of your vineyard, do not pick it over again; that shall go to the stranger, the fatherless, and the widow. 22Always remember that you were a slave in the land of Egypt; therefore do I enjoin you to observe this commandment.

19 כִּי תִקְצֹר קְצִירְךָ בְשָׂדֶךָ וְשָׁכַחְתָּ עֹמֶר בַּשָּׂדֶה לֹא תָשׁוּב לְקַחְתּוֹ לַגֵּר לַיָּתוֹם וְלָאַלְמָנָה יִהְיֶה לְמַעַן יְבָרֶכְךָ יְהֹוָה אֱלֹהֶיךָ בְּכֹל מַעֲשֵׂה יָדֶיךָ: 20 כִּי תַחְבֹּט זֵיתְךָ לֹא תְפַאֵר אַחֲרֶיךָ לַגֵּר לַיָּתוֹם וְלָאַלְמָנָה יִהְיֶה: ס 21 כִּי תִבְצֹר כַּרְמְךָ לֹא תְעוֹלֵל אַחֲרֶיךָ לַגֵּר לַיָּתוֹם וְלָאַלְמָנָה יִהְיֶה: 22 וְזָכַרְתָּ כִּי־עֶבֶד הָיִיתָ בְּאֶרֶץ מִצְרָיִם עַל־כֵּן אָנֹכִי מְצַוְּךָ לַעֲשׂוֹת אֶת־הַדָּבָר הַזֶּה: ס

was forgotten should be left for the alien, the orphan, and the widow. This will enable them to harvest some crops for themselves, thereby sparing them the indignity of appealing to others for a handout.[68] The practice commanded here is illustrated in the book of Ruth, which describes how Ruth, who was both a widow and an alien, gleaned after Boaz's reapers.

Similar laws appear in Leviticus 19:9–10 and 23:22. Those passages include the present rule and another one requiring that an edge of the field and part of the vineyard not be reaped at all, but left uncut for the poor. Based on subtle differences between Leviticus and the present passage, halakhic exegesis inferred that there are four categories of what must be left for the poor: pe'ah (the edges of fields, vineyards, and groves, to be left unreaped), shikhehah (what is forgotten in fields, vineyards, and groves), leket and peret (grain and grapes that fall to the ground during reaping), and 'olelot (small, immature clusters of grapes). The details are spelled out in Tractate Pe'ah of the Mishnah.[69]

A related law appears in Deuteronomy 14:28–29, requiring that a tithe of produce be given the poor every third year. Exodus 23:10–11 and Leviticus 25:2–7 require that the poor be allowed to eat what grows of itself in the fields during the fallow seventh year.

There is some evidence that the poor may have been allowed to glean in ancient Egypt as well. Some parts of the practice have survived into modern times among Arab peasants in the Land of Israel.[70]

A number of scholars have compared this practice to the custom among some peoples of leaving the last sheaf in the field, burying it, or treating it in some other special way, in the belief that it contains the spirit of the crop and that this treatment can ensure the renewal of the crop the following year. If there is a connection, it is noteworthy that the Bible has abandoned the magical motive and preserved the practice for purely humanitarian reasons.[71]

19. *in order that the* LORD *your God may bless you*   For giving up that which is yours. See Comments to 2:7 and 14:29.

20. *beat down*   Olives were harvested by beating the branches with long poles, a method illustrated in Greek vase paintings and still used in recent times in the Land of Israel. According to Isaiah 17:6, this method only leaves a few olives on the tree.[72]

do not go over them again   To knock down any remaining olives.

21. *pick it over again*   To harvest the clusters that were immature the first time around.[73]

22. *always*   Not in the Hebrew; the translators apparently mean "in all these cases," and added this word to make it clear that this reminder refers to all three rules in verses 19–21, not only the last. The Septuagint does the same for the rule in verse 20 by adding the equivalent of this verse after that one as well.

remember   See Comment to verse 18.

CHAPTER 25   LIMITS ON FLOGGING (vv. 1–3)[1]

This is an additional law about judicial procedure (see Comment to 24:16). It prohibits excessive punishment of an offender who is sentenced to flogging. It requires that the flogging be carried out under the

25 When there is a dispute between men and they go to law, and a decision is rendered declaring the one in the right and the other in the wrong—²if the guilty one is to be flogged, the magistrate shall have him lie down and be given lashes in his presence, by count, as his guilt warrants. ³He may be given up to forty lashes, but not more, lest being flogged further, to excess, your brother be degraded before your eyes.

כ"ה כִּי־יִהְיֶה רִיב בֵּין אֲנָשִׁים וְנִגְּשׁוּ אֶל־הַמִּשְׁפָּט וּשְׁפָטוּם וְהִצְדִּיקוּ אֶת־הַצַּדִּיק וְהִרְשִׁיעוּ אֶת־הָרָשָׁע: ² וְהָיָה אִם־בִּן הַכּוֹת הָרָשָׁע וְהִפִּילוֹ הַשֹּׁפֵט וְהִכָּהוּ לְפָנָיו כְּדֵי רִשְׁעָתוֹ בְּמִסְפָּר: ³ אַרְבָּעִים יַכֶּנּוּ לֹא יֹסִיף פֶּן־יֹסִיף לְהַכֹּתוֹ עַל־אֵלֶּה מַכָּה רַבָּה וְנִקְלָה אָחִיךָ לְעֵינֶיךָ: ס

supervision of the judge, that the number of blows correspond to the severity of the offense, and that the number never exceed forty. For the reason why this law comes after 24:19–22, see Excursus 13.

1. dispute See 17:8.

a decision is rendered Literally, "they render a decision." Apparently, more than one judge was to hear the case.

2. if the guilty one is to be flogged Flogging was generally used as a means of disciplining workers and children. Here it is imposed by the court, as in 22:18, which prescribes flogging for a man who libels his bride. It is not known what other offenses the court might have punished this way. According to verse 1, flogging was used for matters that were subject to litigation between private individuals. In Mesopotamia, it was imposed—sometimes with additional punishments—for such offenses as destroying a neighbor's house, encroaching on a neighbor's land, selling persons whom one has distrained because of a debt, defrauding creditors, theft, and changing brands on sheep. In an Egyptian contract, one party agrees to be flogged if he fails to fulfill his contractual promise.[2] It is likely that Deuteronomy has offenses like these in mind.[3]

the magistrate The judge; see Comment to 1:16. Presumably the judge who supervises the flogging is one of those who hears the case, perhaps the head judge of the court.

given lashes Rather, "flogged," since Hebrew *hakkot* could refer either to whipping or beating with a staff.[4]

in his presence The judge supervises the flogging to make sure that the flogger delivers the correct number of strokes, neither too many nor too few. The Laws of Hammurabi also prescribe flogging in the presence of the court.[5]

by count Someone is to count each lash to make certain that the flogger does not lose count. It is possible, however, that "by count" goes with the following words and that the whole phrase means "in a number corresponding to his guilt."

as his guilt warrants Depending on the offense. In the Middle Assyrian Laws, different offenses merit differing numbers of blows, ranging from five to one hundred.[6]

3. In no case is the punishment to exceed forty blows. No other ancient Near Eastern source limits the number of strokes. An Egyptian mural that seems to show staffs used in flogging shows forty staffs; this might indicate that forty was the typical number of blows.[7]

but not more The halakhah limits the number to thirty-nine, apparently to avoid exceeding forty accidentally.[8] It also prescribes that all floggings, however severe the offense, consist in principle of thirty-nine lashes. The number is reduced only if the offender is judged to be physically incapable of bearing the full thirty-nine.[9]

your brother A pointed reminder: he is an offender, but he is nevertheless your brother. See Comment to 1:16.

be degraded Since the flogging itself is degrading, the concern must be that excessive flogging would lead to something even more degrading. Perhaps the person being flogged would humiliate himself further by crying or begging hysterically for mercy, or by soiling himself from fright or from the severity of the beating.[10]

before your eyes This would compound his humiliation.

⁴You shall not muzzle an ox while it is threshing.

⁵When brothers dwell together and one of them dies and leaves no son, the wife of the deceased shall not be

4 לֹא־תַחְסֹם שׁוֹר בְּדִישׁוֹ: ס

5 כִּי־יֵשְׁבוּ אַחִים יַחְדָּו וּמֵת אַחַד מֵהֶם וּבֵן אֵין־לוֹ

NOT MUZZLING AN OX WHEN IT THRESHES (v. 4)

Threshing was normally done by animals that either trampled the stalks with their hooves or pulled a threshing sledge—a board with sharp studs on the bottom—over the stalks. The animal would naturally stop and eat some of the grain when hungry (an Egyptian relief shows one doing so).[11] The farmer might seek to prevent this, either to save the grain or to keep the animal working. Deuteronomy forbids such pettiness. This rule is of the same humanitarian character as 22:10, reflecting the maxim that "a righteous man knows the needs of his beast" (Prov. 12:10). One view in the Talmud is that it would frustrate the animal to see the grain and be unable to eat any; according to Josephus and Sefer Ha-Ḥinnukh, it is simply unfair to deprive the animal of a share of what its own labor produces.[12] The rule has generally been followed in the Middle East down to modern times.

Threshing was usually done by oxen, though other animals were sometimes used. According to the halakhah, the rule applies to any animal that is threshing.[13] For the reason why this law follows that on flogging, see Excursus 13.

LEVIRATE MARRIAGE (vv. 5–10)

If a married man dies childless, his brother is to marry the widow and father a child who will be considered the son of the deceased man (vv. 5–6). This is known as "levirate marriage," from Latin *levir*, "husband's brother." In Hebrew it is called *yibbum*, from the noun *yavam*, which also means "husband's brother" (v. 5).[14] If the brother refuses, he must submit to a procedure that will stigmatize him (vv. 7–10).

According to verse 6, posthumously providing the dead man with a son prevents his name from being blotted out. This reflects the belief that death does not put an absolute end to an individual's existence, and that the living can assist the spirits of the dead by keeping their names present on earth, thus providing them with ongoing contact with the living. For discussion of this concept see Excursus 23.

Marriage of a widow to a member of her husband's family is mentioned in Genesis 38 and in the book of Ruth, and is known from various other places around the world. See the discussion in Excursus 23. An entire tractate of talmudic literature, Tractate Yevamot, is devoted to the explication of this law.

5. *together*   The precise force of this term here is uncertain. It could mean that the brothers are living on the same family estate, either because their father is still alive or because they have not yet divided the estate after his death. But it could also mean that they are living near each other, in the same vicinity.[15] In Genesis 13:6 and 36:7 "dwelling together" means dwelling close enough to use the same pasture land. In either case, this condition is perhaps related to the fact that the offspring of the levirate marriage will inherit the dead man's property. This may mean that in biblical times the marriage was obligatory only if the levir's home, where the widow and her future child would reside, was close to that property.

and he has no son   The halakhah and the Septuagint take *ben* to mean "offspring," whether male or female. Thus, levirate marriage takes place only if a man leaves no child of either sex. This view is based on reading the law in the light of Numbers 27:1–11, which implies that a sonless man's name can also be perpetuated if he has daughters to inherit his property, thus obviating the need for levirate marriage (see Excursus 23). However, in a legal passage like Deuteronomy 25, had the text meant to include daughters, it would probably have said so explicitly.[16]

wife   According to the halakhah, this includes the man's fiancée. The same is true in the Middle Assyrian Laws.[17] This reflects the view that legally the marriage takes effect at the time of engagement, as in 22:23–24.

married to a stranger, outside the family. Her husband's
brother shall unite with her: he shall take her as his wife
and perform the levir's duty. 6The first son that she bears
shall be accounted to the dead brother, that his name may
not be blotted out in Israel. 7But if the man does not want
to marry his brother's widow, his brother's widow shall

לֹא־תִהְיֶ֨ה אֵֽשֶׁת־הַמֵּ֧ת הַח֛וּצָה לְאִ֥ישׁ זָ֖ר יְבָמָ֑הּ
יָבֹ֣א עָלֶ֔יהָ וּלְקָחָ֥הּ ל֖וֹ לְאִשָּׁ֥ה וְיִבְּמָֽהּ: 6 וְהָיָ֗ה
הַבְּכוֹר֙ אֲשֶׁ֣ר תֵּלֵ֔ד יָק֕וּם עַל־שֵׁ֥ם אָחִ֖יו הַמֵּ֑ת
וְלֹֽא־יִמָּחֶ֥ה שְׁמ֖וֹ מִיִּשְׂרָאֵֽל: 7 וְאִם־לֹ֤א יַחְפֹּץ֙
הָאִ֔ישׁ לָקַ֖חַת אֶת־יְבִמְתּ֑וֹ וְעָלְתָה֩ יְבִמְתּ֨וֹ

Her husband's brother shall unite with her   Various attempts have been made to reconcile
this law with Leviticus 18:16 and 20:21, which prohibit sexual relations with one's brother's wife. The
Samaritans held that only a man's fiancée was subject to levirate marriage, not his wife. Some Karaite
commentators held that the "brothers" referred to in this law are relatives, not literally brothers. The
talmudic view is that the prohibition in Leviticus and the present levirate law are, respectively, a
generality and an exception. This view is supported by the Hittite Laws, which place the prohibition
of relations with one's brother's wife and the levirate law side-by-side, thus making it clear that the
latter is an exception to the former.[18] Nevertheless, a feeling of unease persisted and some talmudic
authorities held that levirate marriage was the preferred course of action only in the days when it was
performed out of a sense of duty, but since men had begun to perform it for the sake of sexual
gratification or money, it was preferable that they decline. This view was not widely accepted.[19]

take her as his wife   Although the purpose of the levirate could theoretically be satisfied by
a temporary sexual union, as in Hindu practice (see Excursus 23), such a possibility is out of the
question here. In the Bible a sexual union and the raising of children require a marital relationship
that is intended to be permanent. Compare Comment to 21:14.

6. ***be accounted to the dead brother***   That is, be considered the son of the deceased man
and inherit his property.[20] The Hebrew is literally "be established in the name [*yakum ʿal shem*] of
the dead brother" or "be transferred to the name of the dead brother."[21] A similar idiom is used in
Genesis 48:6. There, Jacob adopts Joseph's two oldest sons, Ephraim and Manasseh, giving them
inheritances like those of his own sons; he declares that future sons of Joseph will "be called in the
name of their older brothers [*ʿal shem ʾaheihem yikkareʾu*] in their inheritance," that is, for purposes
of inheritance they will be considered sons of their brothers, Ephraim and Manasseh. In these idioms
"name" refers to legal attribution, not to the personal name or patronym ("son of so-and-so") of the
adopted individuals. Similarly, the marriage of Ruth is intended "to establish the name [*lehakim
shem*] of the deceased upon his estate," that is, to perpetuate the deceased man's nominal ownership
of his estate. In essence, the son is posthumously adopted by the deceased brother.

Nevertheless, it seems likely that the son of the levirate marriage would indeed take the deceased
man's name as his patronym. There is, admittedly, no indication in the narratives of Genesis 38 and Ruth
4 that the offspring of the marriages described there did so. Indeed, later genealogies attribute them to
their biological fathers.[22] But in view of the importance attached to perpetuating the name of the
deceased, and in the light of the case described in Ezra-Nehemiah of a man who took the name of the
father-in-law whose estate he inherited, it still seems a reasonable conjecture that the offspring of levirate
marriages were referred to similarly during their lifetimes, though not in genealogies. See Excursus 23.

According to Sefer Ha-Ḥinnukh, the offspring of the levirate marriage can even be thought of as
the biological offspring of the deceased man, since when the child's mother married the deceased
man she had become "bone of his bones and flesh of his flesh" (Gen. 2:23), and since the husband's
brother is also partly his brother's flesh.[23]

that his name may not be blotted out in Israel   And thus deprive him of the posthumous
benefits that come from preserving his name. See introductory Comment and Excursus 23.

7. ***But if the man does not want to marry his brother's widow***   Notwithstanding its
importance for his deceased brother's welfare, many considerations might lead a man to refuse
levirate marriage: he might not care for his brother's wife; he might feel that she had brought his
brother bad luck; he might calculate that with his brother dead and heirless he could himself inherit a
larger share of their father's estate; if already married, he might not want to create a rival for his
present wife, or he might calculate that the expense of supporting an extra wife and a child who

appear before the elders in the gate and declare, "My husband's brother refuses to establish a name in Israel for his brother; he will not perform the duty of a levir." [8]The elders of his town shall then summon him and talk to him. If he insists, saying, "I do not want to marry her," [9]his brother's widow shall go up to him in the presence of the elders, pull the sandal off his foot, spit in his face, and make this declaration: Thus shall be done to the man who will not build up his brother's house! [10]And he shall go in Israel by the name of "the family of the unsandaled one."

הַשַּׁעְרָה אֶל־הַזְּקֵנִים וְאָמְרָה מֵאֵין יְבָמִי לְהָקִים לְאָחִיו שֵׁם בְּיִשְׂרָאֵל לֹא אָבָה יַבְּמִי: [8] וְקָרְאוּ־לוֹ זִקְנֵי־עִירוֹ וְדִבְּרוּ אֵלָיו וְעָמַד וְאָמַר לֹא חָפַצְתִּי לְקַחְתָּהּ: [9] וְנִגְּשָׁה יְבִמְתּוֹ אֵלָיו לְעֵינֵי הַזְּקֵנִים וְחָלְצָה נַעֲלוֹ מֵעַל רַגְלוֹ וְיָרְקָה בְּפָנָיו וְעָנְתָה וְאָמְרָה כָּכָה יֵעָשֶׂה לָאִישׁ אֲשֶׁר לֹא־יִבְנֶה אֶת־בֵּית אָחִיו: [10] וְנִקְרָא שְׁמוֹ בְּיִשְׂרָאֵל בֵּית חֲלוּץ הַנָּעַל: ס

would not be his own would diminish the estate that he could leave for his own children. According to Genesis 38:9, Onan was unwilling to father a son who would not count as his own.[24]

the elders in the gate Here again, as in 21:19 and 22:15, the elders have jurisdiction in matters concerning the family. See Comments to 17:5 and 6:9.

name Here "name" is virtually synonymous with "offspring," a child who would bear the dead man's name as a patronym (see Comment to v. 6 and Excursus 23); note the equivalent expression in Genesis 38:8: "establish offspring [*zera*ʿ] for your brother." Likewise, in Akkadian "name" sometimes means "heir."[25]

8. *talk to him* To discuss the matter with him.[26]

According to the halakhah, if the woman's husband leaves several brothers, they are all asked, starting with the oldest and proceeding in order of their age, if they will marry her. If they all refuse, the eldest undergoes the procedure described in verses 9–10.[27]

if he insists This rendition, going back to Saadia and favored by many translations, takes "stand" (ʿ*amad*) in its sense of "continue," "persist," "stand one's ground."[28]

9. *pull the sandal off his foot* The text does not explain the significance of removing the sandal, and talmudic sources list it among the biblical practices that other nations and the "impulse for evil" challenge because they have no obvious reason (see Excursus 19 and Comment to 22:11). It is actually very common for legal transactions to be accompanied by symbolic acts.[29] The present ceremony seems both to effectuate and symbolize the release of the widow from her husband's family. How it derives this meaning has been the subject of considerable speculation. In the Book of Ruth, the relative who transfers to Boaz his right to redeem Elimelekh's land and marry Ruth symbolizes the transfer by removing his sandal and handing it to Boaz. In Deuteronomy, the widow's removal of her brother-in-law's sandal, without handing it to another, may symbolize the cession to the widow of his (that is, his family's) claim on her. In other words, she is released to herself, the restriction stated in verse 5 being waived. A similar procedure was reportedly practiced among the ancient Germans, who symbolized the giving up of property and heritable rights by removing the shoe. Another possibility is suggested by a Bedouin formula used in divorce: "She was my slipper; I have cast her off." The present ceremony could likewise symbolize renunciation of marriage, in this case in advance.[30] If the sandal was removed by unfastening, the act could stand for release of the bond tying the widow to the levir.[31]

spit in his face Ancient authorities debated whether this means literally to spit in his face or to spit on the ground in front of him. Josephus and the Boethusians took the former view and the halakhah took the latter. The preposition translated "in" (*bi-fnei*) is ambiguous; it normally expresses the actor's hostile intent but is noncommital regarding the physical nature of the action.[32] In either case, it is clear that the purpose of this act is to humiliate the levir for refusing to perform a duty that is important for his dead brother.[33]

Thus shall be done to the man who will not build up his brother's house That is, "This is done because this man will not build up his brother's house"[34] (i.e., provide him with children).[35]

10. *family of the unsandaled one* Literally, "house of the unsandaled one," echoing the

11If two men get into a fight with each other, and the wife of one comes up to save her husband from his antagonist and puts out her hand and seizes him by his genitals, 12you shall cut off her hand; show no pity.

13You shall not have in your pouch alternate weights,

11 כִּי־יִנָּצוּ אֲנָשִׁים יַחְדָּו אִישׁ וְאָחִיו וְקָרְבָה אֵשֶׁת הָאֶחָד לְהַצִּיל אֶת־אִישָׁהּ מִיַּד מַכֵּהוּ וְשָׁלְחָה יָדָהּ וְהֶחֱזִיקָה בִּמְבֻשָׁיו: 12 וְקַצֹּתָה אֶת־כַּפָּהּ לֹא תָחוֹס עֵינֶךָ: ס

13 לֹא־יִהְיֶה לְךָ בְּכִיסְךָ אֶבֶן וָאָבֶן גְּדוֹלָה

preceding verse. The punishment suits the man's behavior: since he refused to build up his brother's house, the nickname degrades his own house; since he refused to protect his brother's name from obliteration, he acquires a pejorative nickname. [36]

IMPROPER INTERVENTION IN A FIGHT (vv. 11–12)

If a wife, to save her husband in a fight, seizes his opponent's genitals, her hand is to be cut off. This law complements Exodus 21:18–19,22–25, which have similar opening phrases and deal with injuries caused by men while fighting.

The punishment here seems remarkable since the woman's act is performed with legitimate intentions, and since the Bible nowhere else prescribes mutilation except as a talionic (measure-for-measure) punishment for mutilation (see Exod. 21:24–25; Lev. 24:19–20). In fact, talmudic exegesis took "cut off her hand" to mean that the woman should be fined the monetary value of her hand, as noted in Excursus 24, but that is not the plain sense of the text.

Some commentators explain the severity of the biblical law as reflecting abhorrence at the woman's immodesty. Others believe that it reflects a feeling that for a woman to seize a man's genitals is an intolerable humiliation for him. Still others hold that the danger of injuring the man's genitals, thereby threatening his ability to father children, is what makes the woman's act so objectionable.[37] See the discussion in Excursus 24.

12. cut off her hand It is common to inflict punishment on the part of the body with which an offense is committed.[38]

show no pity This clause is used in cases where one might be tempted to be lenient, in this case because the woman's motive, defending her husband, was honorable. Compare 13:9; 19:13,21.

HONEST WEIGHTS AND MEASURES (vv. 13–16)

Here the text turns to business ethics. Only honest weights and measures are permitted. The importance of this principle, so crucial for the justice and stability of commerce within a society, was widely emphasized in the ancient Near East. It is repeated frequently by the prophets and the book of Proverbs, who condemn its violation. In Egyptian religion the use of false weights and measures was thought to endanger one's safe passage to heaven, and a Babylonian magical text indicates that their use exposes one to a supernatural curse which must be warded off with a special ritual.[39] Here in Deuteronomy it is the final injunction dealing with civil law. Hoffmann notes that it is the final injunction in Leviticus 19 as well; he sees this as a climactic position reflecting the importance of honest dealings for all social order.

In the Bible, the principle of honest weights and measures is stated as a moral injunction, with no specifics about enforcement. Halakhic exegesis gives it practical force by inferring that the government is obligated to appoint inspectors of weights and measures and that merchants and private individuals must clean their weights at specified intervals.[40]

13. You shall not have Not only may one not use deceptive weights and measures, one may not even possess the means of deception.[41]

weights Literally, "stones." The weights in question were used on balance scales to determine the weight of money and commodities. The standard weight was the shekel (ca. 11.4 grams, or four-tenths of an ounce).[42]

in your pouch Where merchants carried their weights.[43]

234

larger and smaller. ¹⁴You shall not have in your house alternate measures, a larger and a smaller. ¹⁵You must have completely honest weights and completely honest measures, if you are to endure long on the soil that the LORD your God is giving you. ¹⁶For everyone who does those things, everyone who deals dishonestly, is abhorrent to the LORD your God.

וּקְטַנָּה: ס ‏14 לֹא־יִהְיֶה לְךָ בְּבֵיתְךָ אֵיפָה
וְאֵיפָה גְּדוֹלָה וּקְטַנָּה: ‏15 אֶבֶן שְׁלֵמָה וָצֶדֶק
יִהְיֶה־לָּךְ אֵיפָה שְׁלֵמָה וָצֶדֶק יִהְיֶה־לָּךְ לְמַעַן
יַאֲרִיכוּ יָמֶיךָ עַל הָאֲדָמָה אֲשֶׁר־יְהוָה אֱלֹהֶיךָ
נֹתֵן לָךְ: ‏16 כִּי תוֹעֲבַת יְהוָה אֱלֹהֶיךָ כָּל־עֹשֵׂה
אֵלֶּה כֹּל עֹשֵׂה עָוֶל: פ מפטיר

alternate weights, larger and smaller "So that one would not use the large one for receiving [so as to receive more] and the small one for dispensing [so as to give less]" (Sifrei). Formulations virtually identical to that in the Sifrei appear in Babylonian descriptions of the violation of this norm. The Laws of Hammurabi penalize the merchant who lends with a small stone or measure and receives with a large one, and a magical text refers to curses incurred for giving payment by small weights and measures and receiving payment by large ones. The prophet Amos criticizes merchants who use undersize 'eifah measures and overweight shekels (Amos 8:5).

Numerous stone and metal weights of the standard shekel and its fractions and multiples, as well as a few weights that may be based on a different standard, have been found in archaeological excavations; some have their denomination inscribed on them.[44] The examples of each denomination that have been found differ from one another in weight. This is probably due to the absence of technological and administrative means to maintain exact, uniform weights (ancient scales were not precise) and to normal wear and tear on the weights in antiquity. The more extreme differences are probably due to legally approved alternate standards, such as the sanctuary shekel.[45] Conceivably some of these weights were intentionally fraudulent, but this can hardly be true of most. No two examples of the same denomination weigh exactly the same, and it is hardly possible that nothing but fraudulent weights have been found.

14. *alternate measures* Literally, "alternate 'eifah-measures," here standing for all measures. The 'eifah was not a measuring device but a unit of capacity of pottery containers used for grain. Its exact modern equivalent is uncertain. Approximately twenty-two liters ($\frac{3}{5}$ bushel) is the most widely accepted estimate, but other estimates go as high as approximately forty-six liters.

The size and weight of large containers, such as 'eifah-jars, made it difficult for a buyer or seller of grain to carry his own jars from place to place in order to verify the amounts involved in a sale. As the text indicates, they were kept at home (cf. Mic. 6:10).

15. *completely honest* Literally, "complete (or full-sized) and honest." In the Hebrew, "completely honest weights and completely honest measures" appears at the beginning of the verse, giving the phrase an emphatic sense: "You must have *only* completely honest weights." This emphasizes the contrast to verse 14.

if you are to endure long Rather, "so that you may endure long." Long life, for the individual or the nation, is the reward granted by God for obedience to His laws.[46] In certain cases medieval commentators believe that there is an inherent connection between long life and the behavior prescribed. Here, for example, Ibn Ezra comments that only a just nation can endure, since justice is like a building, and injustice is like cracks that can cause a building to fall. See also Abravanel cited in Comment to 22:7.

16. *everyone who deals dishonestly is abhorrent to the LORD* A fitting conclusion to the civil and criminal laws of Deuteronomy.

abhorrent See Comment to 7:25. The use of false weights and measures is commonly described thus in Proverbs.

REMEMBERING THE AMALEKITE AGGRESSION (vv. 17–19)

The Amalekites were a nomadic group living in the Negev and Sinai, south of Israel.[47] Nothing is known of them from extrabiblical sources, though nomadic groups, called *Shasu* in Egyptian, are

17Remember what Amalek did to you on your journey, after you left Egypt—18how, undeterred by fear of God, he surprised you on the march, when you were famished

17 זָכוֹר אֵת אֲשֶׁר־עָשָׂה לְךָ עֲמָלֵק בַּדֶּרֶךְ בְּצֵאתְכֶם מִמִּצְרָיִם: 18 אֲשֶׁר קָרְךָ בַּדֶּרֶךְ וַיְזַנֵּב

known to have been present in the region, and some of them attacked travelers. Israelite tradition regarded the Amalekites as descended from Esau and hence distantly related to Israel, but also as invariably aggressive. In the periods of the chieftains (the "Judges") and Saul and David they periodically raided and pillaged Israel.[48] According to Psalm 83:4–9, they were among a group of aggressive nations that plotted to wipe out the Israelites, saying: "Let us wipe them out as a nation; Israel's name will be mentioned no more" (cf. v. 19 here). According to Exodus 17:8–16, they first attacked Israel at Rephidim, in the Sinai, shortly after the Exodus. The Israelites beat them off, and God declared that He would make war on Amalek throughout the ages and would ultimately wipe them out. Our passage refers to the same event, commanding Israel to carry out God's intention when they are secure enough to do so.

Israel's experience with the Amalekites must have been particularly bitter to have led to a determination to wipe them out. Acts of hostility by other nations did not elicit such a response, not even those of Egypt or of the nations that attacked and ruled Israel in the period of the Judges. The account in Exodus provides no explanation for this determination, but Deuteronomy does: this was a sneak attack on the defenseless weak lagging at the rear of the migrating Israelites, an attack which showed that Amalekites lacked even the most elementary decency.[49] Conceivably, the Israelites thought that the Amalekites had genocidal intentions, as in Psalm 83:4–9, and regarded the command to wipe them out as measure-for-measure punishment.

There is a Sumerian parallel to this command. An inscription of Utuhegal, king of the Sumerian city-state Uruk (Erech) in the twenty-second century B.C.E., states that the chief god, Enlil, commanded Utuhegal to "destroy the name" of the Gutians, the hated mountain folk who invaded Sumer, ruling cruelly and offending the gods before Utuhegal finally expelled them.[50]

17. *Remember* Exhortations to remember past events, and to take action on that basis, are more frequent in Deuteronomy than in any other book of the Torah.[51] They reflect the fact that Moses speaks here at the end of a long career during which Israel underwent many seminal exprinces, and that he seeks to persuade Israel to learn from its experience and act accordingly.

"Remember" is complemented by "Do not forget" at the end of the law, and it is clear from verse 19 that the point is to remember to wipe out the Amalekites. In Jewish practice, however, remembering what Amalek did became a separate obligation, carried out by reading this paragraph in the synagogue on the Sabbath before Purim. This is because Haman, the arch-anti-Semite in the book of Esther, is not only hostile like the Amalekites but is also referred to as an Agagite, implying that he is a descendant of Agag the Amalekite.[52]

18. As noted, the attack is described in Exodus 17:8–16. There is no indication of what prompted the Amalekites to attack. It has been conjectured that they saw the Israelites as a potential threat to their control of the oases and pasturelands in the Sinai and the Negev, much as the Moabites feared Israel later (Num. 22:2–4), and attacked them to forestall this possibility. However, in view of the Amalekites' later character as marauders, it is just as likely that their attack was a plundering raid on a target of opportunity.

undeterred by fear of God That is, showing a complete lack of conscience. "Fear of God" refers to the fear of divine punishment for killing innocent people. The Amalekites are not expected to fear the Lord, whom they do not recognize, and that is why the term used here is "fear of God," meaning fear of the divine. The Bible knows that pagan religions also teach that the gods punish sin, and when it refers to pagans who are or are not heedful of that belief, it uses the more general term "God." The point is that the Amalekites lacked the basic principles of morality common to all religions.[53] Interestingly the Gutians, mentioned in the Sumerian parallel cited above, were described elsewhere in Mesopotamian literature as a people "who were never shown how to worship a god, who do not know how to properly perform the rites and observances."[54]

surprised you Rather, "fell upon you," literally, "happened to you."[55] Hebrew *karah*

and weary, and cut down all the stragglers in your rear. [19]Therefore, when the LORD your God grants you safety from all your enemies around you, in the land that the LORD your God is giving you as a hereditary portion, you shall blot out the memory of Amalek from under heaven. Do not forget!

בְּךָ כָּל־הַנֶּחֱשָׁלִים אַחֲרֶיךָ וְאַתָּה עָיֵף וְיָגֵעַ וְלֹא יָרֵא אֱלֹהִים: 19 וְהָיָה בְּהָנִיחַ יְהוָה אֱלֹהֶיךָ | לְךָ מִכָּל־אֹיְבֶיךָ מִסָּבִיב בָּאָרֶץ אֲשֶׁר יְהוָה־אֱלֹהֶיךָ נֹתֵן לְךָ נַחֲלָה לְרִשְׁתָּהּ תִּמְחֶה אֶת־זֵכֶר עֲמָלֵק מִתַּחַת הַשָּׁמָיִם לֹא תִּשְׁכָּח: פ

"happen" often refers to a mishap. Its use here expresses the idea that the Amalekites constituted a misfortune.

famished[56]

stragglers[57]   Those traveling at the rear would include the sick and weak who could not keep up with the others—easy targets for marauders,[58] but people whom anyone with elementary decency would avoid attacking.

**19.   *when God grants you safety*   Once Israel is securely settled in the land, with no threat left to its existence, it is to turn its attention to Amalek. See Comment to 12:10 for discussion of when this degree of security was considered to have been achieved. According to the book of Samuel, the first attempt to eliminate the Amalekites was assigned to Saul, who lost his kingdom over his failure to implement the assignment completely. David later conquered the Amalekites, and they are not heard of again apart from a reference to "the last surviving Amalekites," living in Mount Seir, who were destroyed by five hundred men from the tribe of Simeon in the time of King Hezekiah.[59]

blot out the memory   Rather, "blot out the name," meaning "wipe them out."[60] The present clause echoes God's declaration in Exodus 17:14, "I will utterly blot out the name of Amalek from under heaven." Here, God's declaration has become a commandment.[61] The command does not mean to eradicate all recollection of the Amalekites; this is clear from the fact that Israel is commanded to remember what they did.

under heaven   See Comment to 2:25.

According to the halakhah, the Amalekites, like the Canaanites (see Excursus 18), were to be offered the option of surrender and were to be spared if they accepted.[62]

CHAPTER 26

Two Liturgical Declarations   (vv. 1–15)[1]

Ki Tavo'

Verses 1–15 prescribe liturgical declarations that the farmer is to recite when he brings the first fruits to the Temple (vv. 1–11) and after he gives the poor-tithe every third year (vv. 12–15). These prescriptions supplement the earlier laws that deal with these donations.[2] The declarations are the only addresses to God whose wording is prescribed in the Torah for the laity to recite, except for 21:7–9. They indicate the meaning that Deuteronomy sought to have the farmer find in these ceremonies.

Although these declarations vary according to the nature of the occasions on which they are recited, they have several features in common: each is to be recited "before the LORD your God"; each describes the land as one "flowing with milk and honey"; and each refers to the land as a gift from God in fulfillment of His promise to Israel's ancestors.[3]

For the reasons why these two ceremonies are mentioned here, see Excursus 13.

THE FIRST-FRUITS CEREMONY   (vv. 1–11)

Offerings of first products of the soil are a way of acknowledging God as the source of the land's fertility and the true owner of its produce (see Comments to 15:19–23 and 18:4). In the present

26 KI TAVO'

When you enter the land that the LORD your God is giving you as a heritage, and you possess it and settle in it, ²you shall take some of every first fruit of the soil, which

כ"ו וְהָיָה כִּי־תָבוֹא אֶל־הָאָרֶץ אֲשֶׁר יְהוָה
אֱלֹהֶיךָ נֹתֵן לְךָ נַחֲלָה וִירִשְׁתָּהּ וְיָשַׁבְתָּ בָּהּ:

כי תבוא

ceremony, however, the theme of fertility plays only a secondary role, as the farmer is led from his immediate situation to a recognition of the land's fertility as merely one aspect of a larger picture, namely God's guidance of Israel's history from its humble beginnings, freeing it from oppression and giving it the land. One may compare the way the biblical description of the pre-harvest rites of the *pesaḥ* sacrifice and the Festival of Unleavened Bread focus exclusively on the Exodus, not on the upcoming harvest (see introductory Comment to 16:1–8). This shift of the focus of a religious ceremony from exclusive attention to the role of God in nature to an emphasis on His role in history is one of the most important and original features of the Bible. Its effect on liturgy is this type of prescribed prayer, which leads the worshiper from the immediate experience to an understanding of the larger picture. This kind of prayer is an important one in Jewish liturgy. The Blessing after Meals (*birkat ha-mazon*) is of the same kind: thanksgiving for food is followed by thanksgiving for the gift of the land of Israel, for the covenant and the Torah, for God's other historical acts of kindness, and by a prayer for the rebuilding of Jerusalem.⁴ M. Kadushin termed this type of prayer "meditative," as distinct from "phenomenal" prayer, which refers only to the immediate experience or phenomenon.⁵

The ceremony consists of two parts, verses 3–4 and 5–10. In the first, the farmer declares that he has entered the land that God promised Israel's ancestors, and thereby acknowledges that God has fulfilled His promise (Ramban). In both parts the farmer speaks in the first person: "*I* have entered the land"; "the soil which You, O LORD, have given *me*" (vv. 3,10). In this way he identifies himself with the first generation of Israelites that entered the land. This is noteworthy since the ceremony is not a one-time occurrence⁶ but is to be recited throughout the generations (as implied by the reference to "the priest who shall be in charge at that time," v. 3). Indeed, the fact that the ceremony takes place at the chosen sanctuary, which would only be established several generations after Israel entered the land, means that it could not be performed by the generation that first entered the land. In other words, it is the farmer of later generations who acknowledges that he personally benefits from God's gift of the land made long before his own lifetime. This acknowledgment is similar to the exhortation in the Mishnah and the Passover Haggadah that "in every generation one must view oneself as if he [personally] came out of Egypt."⁷

In the second part of the ceremony the farmer recalls the landless beginnings of Israel's ancestors and their settlement in Egypt as aliens. Then, identifying himself with the Israelites who were enslaved, redeemed, and given the promised land, he acknowledges that the produce he has brought is the yield of the fertile land that God gave him. He thereby acknowledges that the same God who has guided his nation's history is the source of the land's fertility. This is a quintessential monotheistic prayer in which one God is acknowledged as the power behind all phenomena, historical and agricultural alike. Recited at a time when the fertility of the land is uppermost in the farmer's mind, it serves to rebut the claim of Canaanite religion that fertility is the sphere of *its* chief god, Baal (see Comment to 11:16–17). At the same time, the Recitation shows that the farmer has not, in his prosperity, succumbed to the forgetfulness against which 8:11–20 and 32:15–18 warn.

The main themes of the ceremony are underscored by the repetition of key words. The centrality of the Lord guiding history and fertility, and as the object of thanksgiving, is expressed by the appearance of His name fourteen (twice seven) times. The verb *natan*, "give," "assign," "impose," "bestow," appears seven times, six of them with reference to God's giving Israel the land and its bounty. As Abravanel notes, this emphasizes that the land was a gift from God, not something that Israel possessed naturally or by its own actions.⁸ Forms of the root *bo'*, "enter," "go," and (in the causative) "bring," "harvest" ("bring in") appear six times, expressing the idea that the farmer *goes* to the priest and *brings* the first fruits because God *brought* him into the land and enabled him to *harvest* his crops.

2. *you shall take . . . and go* The farmer, the typical Israelite, is addressed. The context suggests that farmers brought their first fruits individually. No date is specified for bringing them, and it probably varied for different farmers, depending on their work load, the species that each

you harvest from the land that the LORD your God is giving you, put it in a basket and go to the place where the LORD your God will choose to establish His name. ³You shall go to the priest in charge at that time and say to him, "I acknowledge this day before the LORD your God that I have entered the land that the LORD swore to our fathers to assign us."

² וְלָקַחְתָּ מֵרֵאשִׁית | כָּל־פְּרִי הָאֲדָמָה אֲשֶׁר תָּבִיא מֵאַרְצְךָ אֲשֶׁר יְהוָה אֱלֹהֶיךָ נֹתֵן לָךְ וְשַׂמְתָּ בַטֶּנֶא וְהָלַכְתָּ אֶל־הַמָּקוֹם אֲשֶׁר יִבְחַר יְהוָה אֱלֹהֶיךָ לְשַׁכֵּן שְׁמוֹ שָׁם: 3 וּבָאתָ אֶל־הַכֹּהֵן אֲשֶׁר יִהְיֶה בַּיָּמִים הָהֵם וְאָמַרְתָּ אֵלָיו הִגַּדְתִּי הַיּוֹם לַיהוָה אֱלֹהֶיךָ כִּי־בָאתִי אֶל־הָאָרֶץ אֲשֶׁר נִשְׁבַּע יְהוָה לַאֲבֹתֵינוּ לָתֶת לָנוּ:

grew, and the date of the harvest of each species in each part of the country. Conceivably, farmers living close enough to the temple brought each species in its own season. The Qumran Temple Scroll prescribes that the first barley, wheat, wine, and oil be brought on different dates, at fifty-day intervals. According to the halakhah, the first fruits could be brought from the Feast of Weeks through the Feast of Booths, the two festivals that followed the harvests and the processing of their products, or even as late as Hanukkah, though in that case without the present Recitation. Since this law is not connected to the festival calendar in chapter 16, the ceremony probably had no necessary connection with the festivals, but many farmers would have found it most convenient to bring the first fruits when they traveled to the Temple for those festivals.[9]

According to Tractate Bikkurim of the Mishnah, in the late Second Temple period farmers who did not bring first fruits on a festival would come in groups made up of people from towns in the same region. They traveled in a festive procession, led by a flute player and an ox with gilded horns and an olive wreath, and were welcomed by officials outside Jerusalem.[10]

some of every first fruit of the soil Literally, "some of the first of every fruit of the soil," meaning that some of every species must be brought, not only those that 18:4 assigns to the priests.[11] It is not clear how this gift of first fruits is related to that prescribed in 18:4. Perhaps the basket presented on this occasion contained a token amount of the three species listed there, plus token amounts of the remaining species, and the remainder of the three species of 18:4 were delivered to the priest on the same, or other, occasion(s).

some of The first fruits are a token gift and no specific amount is prescribed. As the Sifrei notes, even a single cluster of grapes or grain of wheat would suffice. The halakhah, however, holds that the minimum quantity is one-sixtieth of the crop, with no maximum.[12]

first fruit According to Tractate Bikkurim 3:1, when the farmer sees the first ripe fruit of each species he ties a cord or blade of grass on it for identification.

basket Philo states that the entire ceremony was called "the Basket," after this container. The Hebrew word *tene'* is borrowed from an Egyptian word for a basket used for fruit, corn, and the like, but in Hebrew it may mean "container" rather than basket.[13]

3–4. The first part of ceremony.

3. and say The words that the farmer utters in verses 3 and 5–10 are called "the First-Fruits Recitation" (*mikra' bikkurim*) in the Mishnah, which requires that it be said in Hebrew. According to the Mishnah, at first those who were able to recite it on their own did so, while those who could not were assisted by a prompter. When the latter group, out of embarrassment, ceased to bring the first fruits, the procedure was changed so that everybody was led by a prompter.[14]

I acknowledge The Hebrew can be understood in one of two ways: "By this declaration I acknowledge . . ." or "By bringing the first fruits I acknowledge . . ." In the latter case, the act of giving the first fruits constitutes an acknowledgment: tangible proof that the farmer has entered the land. "Tell" is used this way for actions that imply an idea.[15]

the LORD your God The farmer is addressing the priest. The Lord is, of course, the farmer's God as well, as the chapter states several times. People would often say "your God" or "so-and-so's God" when speaking to, or about, priests, prophets, and kings, because their offices were established by God and they were considered especially close to Him.[16]

4The priest shall take the basket from your hand and set it down in front of the altar of the LORD your God.

5You shall then recite as follows before the LORD your God: "My father was a fugitive Aramean. He went down

4 וְלָקַ֧ח הַכֹּהֵ֛ן הַטֶּ֖נֶא מִיָּדֶ֑ךָ וְהִ֨נִּיח֔וֹ לִפְנֵ֕י מִזְבַּ֖ח יְהוָ֥ה אֱלֹהֶֽיךָ׃

5 וְעָנִ֨יתָ וְאָמַרְתָּ֜ לִפְנֵ֣י ׀ יְהוָ֣ה אֱלֹהֶ֗יךָ אֲרַמִּי֙ אֹבֵ֣ד

5–10. The second part of the ceremony.

The main part of the Recitation is a brief epitome of Israel's history. Epitomes of this sort are prescribed for recitation, usually on religious occasions, in Exodus 12:27; 13:9,14–15 (all on the occasion of Passover), and Deuteronomy 6:20–25. Another one is found in a message from Moses to the king of Edom, in Numbers 20:15–16. In Psalms and in Nehemiah they appear, sometimes with much greater detail, in speeches by God or His spokesmen. They almost always focus on the Exodus, with other events added as the occasion requires. Their frequent appearance is occasioned by the fact that historical experience, especially the Exodus, forms the basis for Israel's religion. Because God's gift of the land is stressed on the present occasion, this epitome adds references to the landlessness of the patriarchs and Israel's entry into the promised land.[17]

The wording of this epitome is so similar to that of other passages in the Torah that either it must be based on them or all of them use vocabulary that had become standard in describing the events.[18] However, the epitome contains typically Deuteronomic language as well, as in verse 8; its omission of the angel, which is mentioned in Numbers 20:16, also reflects Deuteronomic ideas (see Comment to 4:37).[19] The description of Israel's prayer and God's response (v. 7–8) preceding the offering of the first fruits is reminiscent of inscriptions and psalms in which a worshiper states that he is dedicating a votive object or reciting a hymn of praise to the deity because he prayed to the deity and the latter heard his plea.[20]

Verses 5–8 are recited and interpreted midrashically as part of the Pesaḥ Seder (see the Introduction). This may be due to the fact that these verses were the best known epitome of Israel's origins since they were recited by every farmer at least once a year.

5. *my father was a fugitive Aramean* Hebrew *'arami 'oved 'avi*. The precise meaning of this phrase is uncertain. "My father" could refer to Jacob, who went down to Egypt, or it could be collective, referring to Jacob's entire family that went with him (note the very similar passage in Numbers 20:15–16, which begins "our ancestors went down to Egypt"). It could even refer to all the ancestors, Abraham and Isaac as well as Jacob and his sons. "Aramean" probably refers to the fact that the ancestors of Israel came from the region known as "Aram alongside the River" (*'Aram naharaim*) and *Paddan-aram* (Gen. 24:4,10; 25:20). The word rendered "fugitive," *'oved*, usually means "perish" or "stray." If it means "perishing" here, the phrase could refer to the danger posed by the famine that forced Jacob and his family to migrate to Egypt (*'oved* refers to perishing from starvation in Job 4:10). If it means "straying," it would refer to the unsettled, migratory life of Jacob or of all the patriarchs, or to their expatriate status. Abraham uses the synonymous verb *t-ʿ-h* when he refers to God's making him "wander" from his father's house (Gen. 20:13), and Ps. 105:13 describes the patriarchs as "wandering [*va-yit-hallekhu*] from nation to nation." If it means "fugitive," it would refer to Jacob's flight from Esau or from Laban (Gen. 27:43; 20–27). This translation is based on the cognate Akkadian verb *abātu*, one of whose nuances is "flee." Assyrian royal inscriptions of the eighth and seventh centuries B.C.E. refer to *Arame . . . munnabtu* (from *abātu*), "fugitive . . . Arameans." Whichever of these interpretations is correct, it is clear that the Recitation means to contrast the homeless, landless beginnings of the Israelites with their present possession of a fertile land.[21]

The Hebrew *'arami 'oved 'avi* is alliterative, which would facilitate memorization of this phrase. This would keep the memory of Israel's landless beginnings fresh in the farmer's memory.

This clause is probably very ancient, for it is unlikely that Israelite tradition would have chosen to describe Israel's ancestors as "Arameans" once the Arameans of Damascus became aggressive toward Israel in the ninth century B.C.E. The same consideration may underlie the fanciful interpretation of the clause as "[Laban the] Aramean sought to destroy my father." This interpretation, found in the Pesaḥ Haggadah and reflected in the Septuagint and the targums, is due, perhaps, to a disbelief that the Bible would describe one of Israel's ancestors as an Aramean.

240

to Egypt with meager numbers and sojourned there; but there he became a great and very populous nation. ⁶The Egyptians dealt harshly with us and oppressed us; they imposed heavy labor upon us. ⁷We cried to the LORD, the God of our fathers, and the LORD heard our plea and saw our plight, our misery, and our oppression. ⁸The LORD freed us from Egypt by a mighty hand, by an outstretched arm and awesome power, and by signs and portents. ⁹He brought us to this place and gave us this land, a land flowing with milk and honey. ¹⁰Wherefore I now bring the first fruits of the soil which You, O LORD, have given me."

You shall leave it before the LORD your God and bow

אָבִי וַיֵּרֶד מִצְרַיְמָה וַיָּגָר שָׁם בִּמְתֵי מְעָט וַיְהִי־שָׁם
לְגוֹי גָּדוֹל עָצוּם וָרָב: 6 וַיָּרֵעוּ אֹתָנוּ הַמִּצְרִים
וַיְעַנּוּנוּ וַיִּתְּנוּ עָלֵינוּ עֲבֹדָה קָשָׁה: 7 וַנִּצְעַק אֶל־
יְהוָה אֱלֹהֵי אֲבֹתֵינוּ וַיִּשְׁמַע יְהוָה אֶת־קֹלֵנוּ וַיַּרְא
אֶת־עָנְיֵנוּ וְאֶת־עֲמָלֵנוּ וְאֶת־לַחֲצֵנוּ: 8 וַיּוֹצִאֵנוּ
יְהוָה מִמִּצְרַיִם בְּיָד חֲזָקָה וּבִזְרֹעַ נְטוּיָה וּבְמֹרָא
גָּדֹל וּבְאֹתוֹת וּבְמֹפְתִים: 9 וַיְבִאֵנוּ אֶל־הַמָּקוֹם
הַזֶּה וַיִּתֶּן־לָנוּ אֶת־הָאָרֶץ הַזֹּאת אֶרֶץ זָבַת חָלָב
וּדְבָשׁ: 10 וְעַתָּה הִנֵּה הֵבֵאתִי אֶת־רֵאשִׁית פְּרִי
הָאֲדָמָה אֲשֶׁר־נָתַתָּה לִּי יְהוָה
וְהִנַּחְתּוֹ לִפְנֵי יְהוָה אֱלֹהֶיךָ וְהִשְׁתַּחֲוִיתָ לִפְנֵי יְהוָה

meager numbers   See 10:22.

sojourned   The ancestors' rootless life continued in Egypt. The verb *gur* means to reside temporarily in a place not one's own; thus it conveys as well the sense of living as a stranger.

6.   In Egypt, their rootlessness was further aggravated by oppression.

7.   The wording of this verse is similar to that of Exod. 2:23–24 and especially Num. 20:7.

the God of our fathers   The God of Abraham, Isaac, and Jacob, who had promised them that He would give this land to their descendants.[22]

plight   Rather, "affliction."

8.   *by a mighty hand*   See Comment to 4:34.

9.   *to this place*   The land of Israel.[23]

a land flowing with milk and honey   See Excursus 9.

10.   *which You, O LORD, have given me*   This refers to the soil, not the first fruits; compare verse 15.

This verse is marked by two significant grammatical shifts. After reciting the epitome of Israel's history and speaking *about* God, the farmer turns to God and speaks *to* Him. In this way he expresses his feeling that he stands directly in God's presence. And after speaking of Israel in the first person plural while describing the history of God's benefactions to Israel, he switches to the first person singular, expressing the feeling that he personally is participating in that history.[24]

leave it   The same verb, *hanniaḥ*, appears in verse 4, where it means "set it down." It is translated differently here, following the Septuagint and Abravanel, to avoid inconsistency with that verse. This is linguistically acceptable, since "leave" is another sense of *hanniaḥ*.[25] Hoffmann argues that this translation makes the prescription superfluous, but conceivably its point is to inform the worshiper that, unlike the tithe which is brought to the Temple and eaten by the worshiper, these fruits are not to be eaten by him in the festive meal to which verse 11 refers.

Another possibility is that the verb originally meant the same thing in both verses and that they are indeed inconsistent because verses 3–4 and 5–10 are alternative versions of the ceremony, both of which Deuteronomy accepted. Jewish liturgical practice frequently preserves alternative versions of a text or a rite, following both rather than eliminating one. For example, the Pesaḥ Haggadah contains two different answers to the Four Questions asked at the Seder; also, some Jews prayed with two different sets of *tefillin*, each made in accordance with a different view of how the texts in them should be arranged. In this case, we would have to assume either that the combined ceremony would require that the basket be set down twice (as the Sifrei holds), with the farmer picking it up at some unspecified point in between, or that in combining the two ceremonies Deuteronomy reconciled them by reinterpreting the second *hanniaḥ* as "leave it."[26]

low before the LORD your God. ¹¹And you shall enjoy, together with the Levite and the stranger in your midst, all the bounty that the LORD your God has bestowed upon you and your household.

¹²When you have set aside in full the tenth part of your yield—in the third year, the year of the tithe—and have given it to the Levite, the stranger, the fatherless, and the widow, that they may eat their fill in your settlements,

אֱלֹהֶֽיךָ׃ ¹¹ וְשָׂמַחְתָּ֣ בְכָל־הַטּ֗וֹב אֲשֶׁ֤ר נָֽתַן־לְךָ֙ יְהוָ֣ה אֱלֹהֶ֔יךָ וּלְבֵיתֶ֑ךָ אַתָּה֙ וְהַלֵּוִ֔י וְהַגֵּ֖ר אֲשֶׁ֥ר בְּקִרְבֶּֽךָ׃ ס

שני ¹² כִּ֣י תְכַלֶּ֞ה לַ֠עְשֵׂר אֶת־כָּל־מַעְשַׂ֧ר תְּבוּאָֽתְךָ֛ בַּשָּׁנָ֥ה הַשְּׁלִישִׁ֖ת שְׁנַ֣ת הַֽמַּעֲשֵׂ֑ר וְנָֽתַתָּ֣ה לַלֵּוִ֗י לַגֵּר֙ לַיָּת֣וֹם וְלָֽאַלְמָנָ֔ה וְאָֽכְל֥וּ בִשְׁעָרֶ֖יךָ

11. *you shall enjoy . . . all the bounty* Rather, "you shall celebrate all the bounty." See Comment to 12:7. The celebration takes the form of a festive meal at the sanctuary.[27]

and the stranger in your midst All other verses in Deuteronomy that require sharing the feast with the poor include the orphan and widow as well as the stranger, and it can hardly be otherwise in this case. Perhaps the verse singles out strangers because it is their situation that best corresponds to the Israelites' experience in Egypt mentioned in verse 5, "sojourned there" (*ger*, "stranger," echoes *gur*, "sojourn" in that verse; both words are from the same stem). The farmer, whose ancestors sojourned as strangers in Egypt and were oppressed, now provides generously for the strangers in his own land.[28]

THE TITHE DECLARATION   (vv. 12–15)

Every third year, when the farmer has removed all the tithe from his premises and given it to the Levites and other indigents (see 14:28–29), he is to make a formal declaration before God that he has divested himself of all the portions of the crop that must be donated and has not violated their sanctity by handling or using them improperly. Then he is to pray for God's continued blessing of the land and the people of Israel.

This declaration affirms that the poor-tithe is a religious duty like the tithe of the first and second years even though it is not taken to the Temple and eaten in a religious ceremony, as is the latter, but is distributed to the poor in the farmer's hometown.

The occasion of this Tithe Declaration (*viddui maʿaser* or *hodayat maʿaser* in rabbinic terminology)[29]—the donation of a tithe to the poor in the third year—is known only from Deuteronomy (14:28–29), and the declaration itself contains some Deuteronomic phrases. In some respects, however, its contents would suit the tithe of the first two years as well, and some scholars have conjectured that it is based on an older declaration that may have been recited every year when the tithe was still presented to the Levites around the country.[30] It is possible that even here the declaration refers to all the tithes of the three-year cycle at the end of which it is recited, and not only to the poor-tithe of the third year (see last Comment to verse 12).

The Mishnah reports that in late Second Temple times, the High Priest Yoḥanan Hyrcanus (135–104 B.C.E.) abolished this declaration. The reasons for his action are uncertain.[31]

12. *When you have set aside in full the tenth part of your yield* Literally, "When you have finished setting aside the full tithe of your yield" (cf. 14:28). Since each species may have been tithed in its own season, the declaration is not made until they have all been tithed.[32]

the third year, the year of the tithe The second phrase is puzzling, since tithes are given every year.[33] Hoffmann suggests two possibilities. The first is that the phrase reflects the farmer's perspective that only the third year is a tithe year, because only in that year must he give the tithe away, whereas in the first two years he keeps it and personally consumes it at the Temple; hence those are not really tithe years in his consciousness. (One might also suggest that the phrase reflects the perspective of the *recipients* of the poor-tithe: to them, the third year is the tithe year, since that is the only year in which it is given to them.) Hoffman's second suggestion is that the phrase means "that is, every third year of the years in which tithe is given." Since tithes are not given in the seventh year of a sabbatical cycle, four years elapse between the second poor-tithe of one sabbatical cycle and

13you shall declare before the LORD your God: "I have cleared out the consecrated portion from the house; and I have given it to the Levite, the stranger, the fatherless, and the widow, just as You commanded me; I have neither transgressed nor neglected any of Your commandments: 14I have not eaten of it while in mourning, I have not

וְשָׁבֵעוּ: 13 וְאָמַרְתָּ לִפְנֵי יְהֹוָה אֱלֹהֶיךָ בִּעַרְתִּי הַקֹּדֶשׁ מִן־הַבַּיִת וְגַם נְתַתִּיו לַלֵּוִי וְלַגֵּר לַיָּתוֹם וְלָאַלְמָנָה כְּכָל־מִצְוָתְךָ אֲשֶׁר צִוִּיתָנִי לֹא־עָבַרְתִּי מִמִּצְוֹתֶיךָ וְלֹא שָׁכָחְתִּי: 14 לֹא־אָכַלְתִּי בְאֹנִי מִמֶּנּוּ וְלֹא־בִעַרְתִּי מִמֶּנּוּ בְּטָמֵא וְלֹא־נָתַתִּי

the first poor-tithe of the next cycle, and the phrase means to correct the impression that "the third year" means exactly every three years.

13. ***before the LORD your God*** In the laws of Deuteronomy this phrase usually implies that something is done at the Temple. Conceivably, then, despite the fact that the farmer disposes of the poor-tithe in his hometown (14:28), Deuteronomy intends him to make this declaration about it at the Temple, when he takes the first fruits there and makes the declaration about them (vv. 1–11).[34] However, when Deuteronomy refers to the Temple, it normally adds the phrase "the place where the LORD will choose to establish His name" in the immediate context to make this explicit, as in verses 1–11. Deuteronomy is so careful to add this phrase in passages referring to worship that its absence here may be deliberate, implying that the declaration need not be made at the Temple, since the poor-tithe is not deposited there. In the present context, then, "before the LORD" may mean that the worshiper addresses God from his hometown, either at his home, or wherever he deposits the tithe (see Comment to 14:28), or at some place of prayer in the town (see Comment to 16:8). See also Comment to 19:17.[35]

cleared out This verb is normally used for purging sin from society. Here it seems to indicate total removal: the farmer has not held back even the slightest amount.

the consecrated portion Of the crop; that is, the poor-tithe. According to Leviticus 27:30, all tithes belong to God and are holy to Him. Here, this principle is applied to the poor-tithe: even though it is given up by God and is not brought to a sanctuary, it is treated as holy until it is handed over for distribution to the poor. Perhaps this treatment of the poor-tithe indicates that giving it to the poor is no less a sacred purpose than bringing it to a sanctuary or consuming it there.

I have neither transgressed nor neglected any of Your commandments This refers to the commandments about the tithe in 14:28–29. It is not a blanket claim of virtue, but a statement about the obligation that has just been discharged. The first clause, lo' 'avarti echoes bi'arti, "I have removed." The second means literally "I have not forgotten." In other words, "I have not retained any for myself either intentionally or accidentally."

just as You commanded me The same phrase appears again in verse 14. The first-person formulation expresses the idea that God commanded the farmer personally, and not only his ancestors. This wording is part of the liturgy's attempt to enhance the farmer's feeling of personal involvement in the history of his people. See introductory Comments to verses 1–11 and Comment to verse 10.

14. Here the farmer affirms that he has not handled or used the tithe in ways that would defile it. It is not clear why these types of misuse are singled out. Perhaps the text is concerned that people might be lax in protecting the poor-tithe from defilement since it did not have to be taken to a sanctuary and, since the farmer himself was not allowed to eat any of it, he would not be contaminated by its defilement.

The requirement to declare full compliance with the tithe obligation is reminiscent of a practice found in the Hittite "Instructions for Temple Officials." There, the herdsmen responsible for delivering cattle offerings to the temple must declare on oath, when they bring the cattle, that they have not misappropriated any of the cattle that were due.[36]

while in mourning This probably means that the farmer did not use any of the tithe for his meals while in mourning, which would defile what he ate and any other parts of the tithe he touched when taking it. A mourner, who becomes impure from being in the same tent as a dead body or from handling it during burial, or from contact with others who have become impure in one

cleared out any of it while I was unclean, and I have not deposited any of it with the dead. I have obeyed the LORD my God; I have done just as You commanded me. 15Look down from Your holy abode, from heaven, and bless Your people Israel and the soil You have given us, a land flowing with milk and honey, as You swore to our fathers."

מִמֶּנּוּ לְמֵת שָׁמַעְתִּי בְּקוֹל יְהוָה אֱלֹהָי עָשִׂיתִי
כְּכֹל אֲשֶׁר צִוִּיתָנִי: 15 הַשְׁקִיפָה מִמְּעוֹן קָדְשְׁךָ
מִן־הַשָּׁמַיִם וּבָרֵךְ אֶת־עַמְּךָ אֶת־יִשְׂרָאֵל וְאֵת
הָאֲדָמָה אֲשֶׁר נָתַתָּה לָנוּ כַּאֲשֶׁר נִשְׁבַּעְתָּ
לַאֲבֹתֵינוּ אֶרֶץ זָבַת חָלָב וּדְבָשׁ: ס

of these ways, would defile any food he touched.[37] Another possibility is that the declaration means that the farmer did not use any of the tithe for a funeral repast. Such repasts were part of the funeral ceremony in many ancient societies,[38] and the farmer might consider it a religious duty and think it legitimate to use the tithe in this way. However, we have no evidence that such repasts were part of funerals in Israel.

I have not cleared out any of it while I was unclean   Handling the tithe while unclean would defile it.[39]

deposited any of it with the dead   To feed their spirits. As noted in Excursus 23, the ancients believed that the living can assist the spirits of the dead in Sheol by providing them with food and drink. This practice was widespread in the ancient world, and it is also attested among some Jews in Second Temple times and later, as in Tobit 4:17: "Pour out your bread and wine on the tomb of the just, and give not to sinners." In some graves excavated at Samaria, the capital of the northern kingdom, holes were found in the floors, similar to holes found in tombs at Ugarit, which served as receptacles for food and drink offerings to the dead. The Torah does not forbid this practice, but because contact with the dead is ritually defiling, it prohibits the use of the tithe for it.[40]

I have obeyed . . . I have done just as you commanded me   Regarding the tithe.

15.   *Your holy abode, heaven*   In some biblical passages God's "abode" is the Temple. Here, the word "heaven" emphasizes the Deuteronomic idea that His abode is heaven, not the Temple.[41] Compare Comment to 12:5.

bless   With bountiful crops and prosperity. See Comment to 2:7.

your people Israel   The farmer is not to ask for his own prosperity but for that of the entire nation. This is typical of the prescribed prayers in Judaism: the individual does not pray on his own behalf but on behalf of the entire Jewish people or the whole human race.[42]

CONCLUSION TO THE LAWS   (26:16–28:68)

Mutual Commitments Between God and Israel   (26:16–19)

The laws in all their detail are now concluded. The present passage sums up Israel's duty to obey them wholeheartedly and underscores the fact that they are more than details of a legal code. They are the basis of the mutual relationship that God and Israel have established.[43] The relationship is not a purely emotional or spiritual association, but entails mutual obligations with consequences.

The main verbal link between this paragraph and the two that precede it is the term *he'emir*, "affirm," in verses 17 and 18. It is derived from the same root *'-m-r* that appears in verses 5 and 13, where it is rendered "recite" and "declare." At the same time, this paragraph plays a role in the structure of Deuteronomy as a whole, since the summary sentence in verse 16 echoes the introductory passage that immediately preceded the laws: "Take care to observe all the laws and rules that I have set before you this day. These are the laws and rules that you must carefully observe" (11:32–12:1). With the latter passage, the present paragraph forms a frame around the laws.[44] See

16The LORD your God commands you this day to observe these laws and rules; observe them faithfully with all your heart and soul. 17You have affirmed this day that the LORD is your God, that you will walk in His ways, that you will observe His laws and commandments and rules, and that you will obey Him. 18And the LORD has affirmed this day that you are, as He promised you, His treasured

שלישי 16 הַיּוֹם הַזֶּה יְהֹוָה אֱלֹהֶיךָ מְצַוְּךָ לַעֲשׂוֹת אֶת־הַחֻקִּים הָאֵלֶּה וְאֶת־הַמִּשְׁפָּטִים וְשָׁמַרְתָּ וְעָשִׂיתָ אוֹתָם בְּכָל־לְבָבְךָ וּבְכָל־נַפְשֶׁךָ: 17 אֶת־יְהֹוָה הֶאֱמַרְתָּ הַיּוֹם לִהְיוֹת לְךָ לֵאלֹהִים וְלָלֶכֶת בִּדְרָכָיו וְלִשְׁמֹר חֻקָּיו וּמִצְוֹתָיו וּמִשְׁפָּטָיו וְלִשְׁמֹעַ בְּקֹלוֹ: 18 וַיהֹוָה הֶאֱמִירְךָ הַיּוֹם לִהְיוֹת לוֹ

Comment to 11:31 and introductory Comment to 4:44–28:69. (For a frame encompassing this frame, see introductory Comments to chap. 27.)

16. This verse aptly sums up Israel's obligation to obey God's laws. Virtually identical terms are used in 2 Kings 23:3 to describe the people's covenantal commitment to obey God's laws—undoubtedly those of Deuteronomy—when they were discovered in the days of King Josiah (639–609 B.C.E.).

commands you this day Through this address, which Moses is delivering at God's command. Moses has referred to "this day" throughout (as in 4:8; 15:5; 19:9). According to 1:3, the address was delivered on the first day of the eleventh month (later known as Shevat) in the fortieth year after the Exodus.

these laws and rules Which Moses has just finished presenting, chapters 12:1–26:15.

with all your heart and soul See Comment to 6:5.

17–18. God and Israel have each proclaimed their acceptance of the other as parties to the covenant, and have proclaimed specific commitments to each other. The principles agreed to are strongly reminiscent of the earlier covenant at Horeb (Mount Sinai), of which this is a reaffirmation. There God stated that if Israel would obey Him and keep His covenant it would be His treasured possession among all the peoples, a kingdom of priests and a sacrosanct nation, and Israel agreed to do all that God commanded (Exod. 19:5–6,8; 24:3,7–8). The fact that the declarations of both Israel and God are described here with the same verb, "affirmed," highlights what was implicit at Sinai: the present covenant, like that at Sinai, was agreed to mutually and involved commitments on both sides; it was not an act of God alone.[45] Israel became God's people only when it agreed to follow His laws.

Precisely when God and Israel made the present declarations is not stated. The text alludes several times to the present covenant, made in the land of Moab (see also 27:9; 28:69; 29:9–14), but does not explicitly narrate the ceremony establishing it as it does in the case of other covenants, such as those in Exodus 24:1–8 (cf. 19:3–8) and 2 Kings 23:1–3. Perhaps the text assumes that the ceremony took place at the time of this speech.[46]

affirmed This rendering of *he'emir* is a conjecture based on the context. It takes *he'emir* (a *hiph'il* form of *'amar*, "say," "declare") as having a meaning similar to *'amar* in Hosea's description of the renewal of the covenant: God will declare to Israel, "you are my people," and Israel will declare, "[You are] my God" (Hos. 2:25). Apparently, then, the *hiph'il* form simply expresses a more intensive sense of the root, meaning something like "proclaim," "formally state."[47]

that the LORD is your God The counterpart to this phrase in verse 18 is "that you are . . . His . . . people." This pair of phrases is the classic expression of the covenant relationship, as in 29:12. It is rooted in the formulary used for establishing marriage and adoption, because the covenant creates a familylike relationship between Israel and God. See Comment to 5:7.

that you will walk in His ways This clause and the remainder of the verse are virtually a definition of what it means to accept the Lord as God: it consists of walking in His ways, observing His laws, and obeying Him—in short, it requires action as well as intellectual assent.[48]

18. ***as He promised you*** When He first proposed to enter into a covenant with you (Exod. 19:5).

people who shall observe all His commandments, [19]and that He will set you, in fame and renown and glory, high above all the nations that He has made; and that you shall be, as He promised, a holy people to the LORD your God.

לְעַם סְגֻלָּה כַּאֲשֶׁר דִּבֶּר־לָךְ וְלִשְׁמֹר כָּל־מִצְוֺתָיו: [19] וּלְתִתְּךָ עֶלְיוֹן עַל כָּל־הַגּוֹיִם אֲשֶׁר עָשָׂה לִתְהִלָּה וּלְשֵׁם וּלְתִפְאָרֶת וְלִהְיֹתְךָ עַם־קָדֹשׁ לַיהוָה אֱלֹהֶיךָ כַּאֲשֶׁר דִּבֵּר: ס

His treasured people   See Comment to 7:6.

who shall observe all His commandments   Rather, "and that [you] will observe all His commandments." Grammatically this clause is no different from those in verse 17, and it should be translated the same way. However, it is puzzling as part of a promise from God. To Ramban and Sforno, its presence in this verse reflects the fact that the commandments are not only an obligation, but an honor and a privilege conferred on Israel by God. While homiletically attractive, this is not the plain sense of the text. The clause is possibly a textual variant of one of the similar clauses in verse 17, mistakenly copied by a scribe here instead of there.[49]

19.   This verse defines what it means to be God's treasured people: He will exalt Israel and make it inviolable.

in fame and renown and glory, above all the nations   That is, He will make Israel more famous, praised, and glorified than any other nation. This will be due to the abundant prosperity and victory over enemies that Israel will enjoy. This is suggested by 28:1–14, where God's promise to set Israel high above all the nations is followed by blessings of these types.

that He has made   This clause emphasizes the honor that God's promise involves: He made *all* nations, but nevertheless Israel will be the most exalted. There is a similar emphasis in the passage to which this one alludes, Exodus 19:5–6: "Indeed, all the earth is Mine, but you shall be to Me a kingdom of priests and a sacrosanct nation."

as He promised, a holy people   See Exodus 19:6. Here "a holy people" means one that is sacrosanct, inviolable, a nation that others harm at their peril.[50] Compare 28:9–10: "The LORD will establish you as His holy people. . . . And all the peoples of the earth shall see that the LORD's name is proclaimed over you, and they shall stand in fear of you." Similarly, Jeremiah recalls a time when "Israel was holy to the LORD, the first fruits of His harvest. All who ate of it were held guilty; disaster befell them" (Jer. 2:3). For another implication of Israel's sanctity, see 7:6 and 14:1,21.

CHAPTER 27

Ceremonies to Mark Israel's Arrival in the Land   (vv. 1–26)

Chapter 27 consists of three sections, verses 1–8, 9–10, and 11–26.[1] Of these, only the middle section relates to the immediate concern of the preceding and following chapters, which is the covenant now being made in the land of Moab (see Comment to 26:17–18). In that section Moses and the priests reiterate the point made in 26:16–19: having entered into a covenant to become God's people, it is imperative that Israel obey His laws. Verses 9–10 thus serve as a transition to chapter 28, where Moses spells out in great detail the consequences of obedience and disobedience.

The remainder of chapter 27—verses 1–8 and 11–26—digresses from the covenant now being made in Moab and prescribes ceremonies to be performed later, when Israel arrives in the promised land. These constitute a third covenant, and it seems likely that they are interpolated here to make it clear that they are a reaffirmation of the one being made in Moab, and therefore of the earlier one concluded at Horeb as well.[2] The covenant relationship with God is so vital for Israel's existence in the promised land that it must be formally reaffirmed as soon as Israel arrives there.

Three ceremonies are to be performed in the land: on Mount Ebal, steles inscribed with the Teaching—the content of the covenant—are to be erected, an altar built, and sacrifices offered (vv. 2–8); at Mounts Gerizim and Ebal, the tribes are to proclaim the blessings and curses that the covenant entails (vv. 11–13); and the Levites are to invoke, and the people affirm, God's punishment

27 Moses and the elders of Israel charged the people, saying: Observe all the Instruction that I enjoin upon you

רביעי וַיְצַו מֹשֶׁה וְזִקְנֵי יִשְׂרָאֵל אֶת־ כ"ז
הָעָם לֵאמֹר שָׁמֹר אֶת־כָּל־הַמִּצְוָה אֲשֶׁר אָנֹכִי

on those who commit sins difficult for humans to prosecute (vv. 14–26). The purpose of these ceremonies is indicated by verse 1: to inaugurate Israel's life in the promised land with acts that dramatically express the message that its life must be based on obedience to God's Instruction.

That the ceremonies performed at Ebal and Gerizim constitute a covenant ceremony is suggested by the similarity of verses 1–8 to the covenant ceremony in Exodus 24 and by the proclamation of blessings and curses here in verses 11–13. The ceremony in Exodus 24:3–11 took place right after Moses gave the people God's laws and they formally agreed to obey them. The present ceremony takes place under comparable, though not identical, circumstances: Moses has just finished conveying God's laws, the people are in the process of accepting them, and he calls upon them to do so again formally as soon as they enter the land. The ceremony in Exodus included Moses' writing down God's laws, building an altar, offering sacrifices, and erecting twelve stones. Stones figure prominently in biblical covenants, though elsewhere they are uninscribed. In Exodus 24 they represent the twelve tribes of Israel, and stones "witness" Jacob's treaty with Laban (also accompanied by a sacrifice) (Gen. 31:44–54) and the covenant that Joshua established between God and Israel (Josh. 24:26–27). Treaty texts were sometimes inscribed on steles elsewhere in the ancient world (see Comment to 4:13). The component of the present ceremony that spells out blessings and curses—the consequences of fidelity or disloyalty to the covenant—is also an integral part of covenants known from ancient Near Eastern treaties (see Excursus 27). These ceremonies also constitute a foundation ceremony, establishing Israel as a nation as soon as it enters its land. They are comparable to ceremonies performed in the Greek world by settlers who founded colonies on divine command; such ceremonies included building altars and pronouncing blessings and curses.[3]

At some points the three sections of the chapter seem redundant and inconsistent, and their sequence is hard to follow. Traditional exegesis harmonizes these difficulties, while critical scholarship holds that the chapter contains material of disparate backgrounds as well as editorial revisions. For discussion of these issues see Comments below and Excursus 25.

The proclamation of blessings and curses at Mounts Ebal and Gerizim was mentioned briefly in 11:29, immediately before Deuteronomy's laws. That passage and the present chapter form a frame around the laws, consisting of proclamations and rites that remind the people, who are about to enter the land, that the laws have fateful consequences and that Israel's future in the land depends on observing them. See also the introductory Comment to 4:44–28:69.

WRITING THE TEACHING ON STELES
AND BUILDING AN ALTAR (vv. 1–8)

Israel is to erect steles, write God's Teaching on them, build an altar, and offer sacrifices. Erecting and inscribing the steles are each referred to twice, and critical scholars think that these repetitions reflect variant versions of the text or revisions of it (see Excursus 25). In its present form this section can be read as a general statement (*kelal*) in verses 2–3, followed by an itemization of specific steps (*perat*) in verses 4–8: the stones are to be erected on Mount Ebal and then plastered; an altar is to be built and sacrifices offered; and then the stones are to be inscribed with the words of the Teaching.[4]

1. Moses and the elders Only here is Moses joined by the elders in instructing the people. Similarly unusual are verses 9–10, where Moses is joined by the priests in charging the people to obey the commandments. In both passages the clause "that I enjoin upon you today" indicates that Moses is the primary speaker. Perhaps the elders and priests join Moses here because it is they to whom he gives the Teaching after he writes it down, and whom he commands to assemble the people every seven years to hear it read (31:9–13). These two groups would be the leaders of the people in their daily civil and religious affairs after Moses' death, and thus in the best position to ensure continued adherence to his teachings.

Observe all the Instruction That is, all the instructions given in Deuteronomy. The

this day. ²As soon as you have crossed the Jordan into the land that the LORD your God is giving you, you shall set up large stones. Coat them with plaster ³and inscribe upon them all the words of this Teaching. When you cross over to enter the land that the LORD your God is giving you, a land flowing with milk and honey, as the LORD, the God of

מְצַוֶּה אֶתְכֶם הַיּֽוֹם׃ ‏2‏ וְהָיָה בַּיּוֹם אֲשֶׁר תַּעַבְרוּ אֶת־הַיַּרְדֵּן אֶל־הָאָרֶץ אֲשֶׁר־יהוה אֱלֹהֶיךָ נֹתֵן לָךְ וַהֲקֵמֹתָ לְךָ אֲבָנִים גְּדֹלוֹת וְשַׂדְתָּ אֹתָם בַּשִּֽׂיד׃ ‏3‏ וְכָתַבְתָּ עֲלֵיהֶן אֶת־כָּל־דִּבְרֵי הַתּוֹרָה הַזֹּאת בְּעׇבְרֶךָ לְמַעַן אֲשֶׁר תָּבֹא אֶל־הָאָרֶץ אֲשֶׁר־ יהוה אֱלֹהֶיךָ ׀ נֹתֵן לְךָ אֶרֶץ זָבַת חָלָב וּדְבַשׁ

"Instruction" is synonymous with the "Teaching" (v. 3) and is not a reference to a specific law such as that which follows.[5]

2. As soon as you have crossed Literally, "on the day when you cross." According to verse 4, the instructions prescribed in this verse are to be carried out on Mount Ebal, which is some thirty miles, and over four thousand feet uphill, from where Israel would cross the Jordan—too distant to reach on the same day the Jordan is crossed. Read in the light of that verse, "on the day when you cross" must be understood loosely, meaning "once you have crossed"—not necessarily the same day. However, it is possible that verse 4 is reinterpreting verse 2 and understands the phrase more loosely than it was originally meant. Compare the Comment to verse 3 and see the discussion in Excursus 25.

Coat them with plaster If the text was engraved through the plaster into the stone, the white plaster would highlight the dark color of the letters.[6] Another possibility is that the plaster served as a clean surface for writing in ink or paint. Writing over plaster was common in Egypt where even outdoor inscriptions would last a long time because rain is infrequent. Semitic inscriptions on plaster have been found on the wall of a building at Kuntillet Ajrud, in the Sinai, and at Deir Alla in the eastern Jordan valley (in the latter inscription, the plaster may have been on a stele).[7] If Deuteronomy means that the text should be written over plaster, then the writing would eventually be washed away by rain, since the text does not require that a structure be built over the steles. This would mean that the inscription is only for use at this one-time ceremony.[8]

Since the stones would serve as a writing surface, they would be cut smooth, unlike those of the altar (vv. 5–6).[9]

3. inscribe upon them all the words of this Teaching. When you cross over to enter the land Rather, "inscribe upon them all the words of this Teaching upon crossing over, so that you may enter the land." This ceremony graphically dramatizes Israel's obligation to live by God's Teaching. Hence, its performance shortly after entering the land is a prerequisite for further penetration into the land. Similarly, obedience to the laws is the prerequisite for a successful occupation of the land in 4:1; 6:18; 8:1; 11:8; and 16:20.

Writing the Teaching on the stones is unique in biblical covenants. Although stones figure prominently in other biblical covenants, this is the only case where something is inscribed on them. This use of writing for didactic purposes is characteristic of Deuteronomy (cf. 6:7–8; 11:18–21; 17:18–19; 31:9).[10] The inscription also makes it clear that although these stones are placed near an altar, they are not cultic pillars (*matsevot*) such as those forbidden in 16:22.

The "Teaching" refers to part of Deuteronomy. At the least, it includes the laws (chaps. 12–26) framed by the instruction to ceremonially declare the consequences of obedience and disobedience (11:29–30 and here). It may also include some of Deuteronomy's introductory speeches and the concluding blessings and curses (chaps. 1–11 and 28, respectively). Some commentators have conjectured that the steles were to contain a shorter text, such as the Decalogue, a list of commandments, or the blessings and curses of chapter 28.[11] Such suggestions are based on the assumption that the steles had insufficient space for a long text, but there is no ground for this assumption. The text says that *all* the words of the Teaching—whatever that refers to—are to be inscribed, and places no limit on the size or number of steles to be used. In fact, two steles the size of that on which the laws of Hammurabi were written could easily contain more than Deuteronomy.

When you cross over Rather, "upon crossing over" (Heb. *be-ʿovrekha*), implying that the stones are to be set up immediately. As in the case of "on the day when you cross" in 2, this meaning is overridden by verse 4. In context, then, this phrase too must be understood loosely, meaning "once you have crossed," "shortly after you cross." See the discussion in Excursus 25.

your fathers, promised you—⁴upon crossing the Jordan, you shall set up these stones, about which I charge you this day, on Mount Ebal, and coat them with plaster. ⁵There, too, you shall build an altar to the LORD your God, an altar of stones. Do not wield an iron tool over them; ⁶you must

כַּאֲשֶׁר דִּבֶּר יְהוָה אֱלֹהֵי־אֲבֹתֶיךָ לָךְ: 4 וְהָיָה בְּעָבְרְכֶם אֶת־הַיַּרְדֵּן תָּקִימוּ אֶת־הָאֲבָנִים הָאֵלֶּה אֲשֶׁר אָנֹכִי מְצַוֶּה אֶתְכֶם הַיּוֹם בְּהַר עֵיבָל וְשַׂדְתָּ אוֹתָם בַּשִּׂיד: 5 וּבָנִיתָ שָּׁם מִזְבֵּחַ לַיהוָה אֱלֹהֶיךָ מִזְבַּח אֲבָנִים לֹא־תָנִיף עֲלֵיהֶם

4. *Mount Ebal*¹² Just north of Shechem (see Comment to 11:29), Mount Ebal is the highest mountain in the vicinity. It rises 3,083 feet (940 meters) above sea level, 1,200 feet (366 meters) above the valley in which it stands, and commands a view of most of the promised land: to Mount Hermon in the north, the Jordan and Gilead in the east, the hills around Jerusalem in the south, and the Mediterranean in the west. Perhaps it was this view, encompassing so much of the land, that made Mount Ebal an appropriate site for a ceremony solemnizing Israel's arrival in the land. The proximity of Shechem may have contributed to the choice of this site. Shechem was already an important city in Canaanite times. It is centrally located¹³ and was the natural capital of the central hill country, situated in the only east-west pass in the central mountain range, at the intersection of north-south and east-west roads.¹⁴ It was the site of Abraham's first stop in Canaan and the first place in Canaan where God spoke to him and identified the land as the one He would give to Abraham's descendants. It was there that Abraham first built an altar to God, Jacob first bought a plot within the promised land, and Joseph's bones were buried. Joshua led the Israelites in establishing a covenant with God there, and later it became the first capital of the independent kingdom of northern Israel. Interestingly, there is no record of Joshua having taken Shechem or the surrounding region by force. This has led to speculation that the Israelites took control of the area peacefully, and that its inhabitants were perhaps related to the Israelites and welcomed them.¹⁵

5–7. An altar is to be built, sacrifices offered, and the people are to celebrate the erecting of the steles inscribed with the Teaching. As Shadal notes, the celebration will express the people's joy over their covenant with God.¹⁶ The similarities to the covenant ceremony in Exodus 24 have been noted above.

These sacrifices are part of a one-time ceremony.¹⁷ Thus, there is no conflict with Deuteronomy's restriction of sacrificial worship to Jerusalem, because that was to take effect only later (see 12:8–12).

an altar of stones Stones in their natural state, unhewn, following the prescription of Exodus 20:22. An Israelite altar of uncut stones was found in excavations at Arad, and earlier ones have been found at Canaanite sites as well. When Solomon's Temple was built, the rule was extended to cover the entire edifice, but since it was impractical to construct everything of uncut stone, the extension was only partial: on the Temple grounds "no hammer or ax or any iron tool was heard in the Temple while it was being built," but the stones were cut at the quarry (1 Kings 6:7). Later sources indicate that the altar built in the Temple by Judah Maccabee was likewise of uncut stone, and that the altar in Herod's Temple was also never touched by iron.¹⁸

A structure found on Mount Ebal from the early Iron Age—when the Israelites were settling in the land—has been taken to be an altar, possibly the one Joshua built in fulfillment of this command. But whether it is really an altar, let alone an Israelite one, is debated.¹⁹

iron tool *Barzel*, literally "iron." The reason for the prohibition is uncertain. The Mishnah explains that "iron was created to shorten man's days [through its use in weapons], while the altar was created to lengthen man's days [by means of sacrifice]: what shortens may not rightly be lifted up against what lengthens."²⁰ Some modern scholars, noting that other ancient religions sometimes prohibited the use of iron in connection with religious ceremonies, maintain that this reflects a belief in the displeasure of the gods toward innovations such as iron.²¹ However, verse 6 indicates that the stones must be uncut no matter what the tool is made of. Similarly, Exodus 20:22 explains that cutting the stones with a *ḥerev*, "blade"—in other words, any kind of cutting tool²²—defiles them. Apparently, our verse says "iron" instead of "blade" because by the time of Deuteronomy iron was widely used for cutting tools,²³ and the word had acquired that meaning (cf. "steel" meaning a sword or dagger in English poetry). Here it refers to a chisel. Rashbam suggests that the prohibition on cutting the stones is to preclude the temptation to carve images on them.²⁴

build the altar of the LORD your God of unhewn stones. You shall offer on it burnt offerings to the LORD your God, [7]and you shall sacrifice there offerings of well-being and eat them, rejoicing before the LORD your God. [8]And on those stones you shall inscribe every word of this Teaching most distinctly.

בַּרְזֶל: 6 אֲבָנִים שְׁלֵמוֹת תִּבְנֶה אֶת־מִזְבַּח יְהוָה אֱלֹהֶיךָ וְהַעֲלִיתָ עָלָיו עוֹלֹת לַיהוָה אֱלֹהֶיךָ: 7 וְזָבַחְתָּ שְׁלָמִים וְאָכַלְתָּ שָּׁם וְשָׂמַחְתָּ לִפְנֵי יְהוָה אֱלֹהֶיךָ: 8 וְכָתַבְתָּ עַל־הָאֲבָנִים אֶת־כָּל־דִּבְרֵי הַתּוֹרָה הַזֹּאת בַּאֵר הֵיטֵב: ס

6. *burnt offerings* See Comment to 12:6. The two types of offerings mentioned in this verse and the next are the same as those offered at the conclusion of the covenant at Mount Sinai (Exod. 24:5).

7. The wording of this verse is very similar to that of 12:7 and 18, which describe the worship at the chosen sanctuary.

offerings of well-being Hebrew *shelamim*, a type of sacrifice in which most of the flesh was eaten by the worshiper and hence appropriate for a festive occasion. See Comment to "other sacrifices" in 12:6. *Shelamim* sacrifices were often offered, along with other types, on historic occasions inaugurating important institutions, such as the conclusion of the covenant at Mount Sinai, the inauguration of worship in the Tabernacle, King Saul's coronation, and the dedication of Solomon's Temple.[25]

The singular form of the name of this sacrifice, *shelem*, appears in Amos 5:22. The term is also known in Ugaritic and Punic texts. Its precise meaning is uncertain because of the wide range of nuances expressed by the root *sh-l-m*, the underlying meaning of which is "wholeness," "unimpaired condition." The translation "offerings of well-being" implies that the sacrifice expressed the worshiper's gratitude, or hope, for his welfare (from *shalem, shalom*, "full," "unimpaired," "safe"). The King James Version translated it as "peace offering," meaning that the sacrifice effects, or expresses, a harmony between the worshiper and God (from *shalom*, "peace"). Another possibility, based on the greeting *shalom*, is "sacrifice of greeting," that is, greeting God in worship. A promising recent theory holds that the term means "gift," "tribute," "token of submission." This is based on the fact that in Ugaritic the consonants *sh-l-m-m* refer both to a type of sacrifice and to tribute, or a gift, to a militarily superior king, a meaning perhaps originally based on the idea of greeting with a gift. This is very plausible as the name of a sacrifice, since other sacrifices, such as *minḥah* and *korban*, also have names that originate as types of gift or tribute.[26]

8. This verse recapitulates the requirement of verse 2 that the stones be inscribed with the Teaching. By making the point both before and after the provision about the altar, the text makes clear that the terms of the Teaching, and not the sacrifice, constitute the heart of the ceremony.

those stones Rather, as the text literally says, "the stones," referring to the stones of verses 2–4, not those of the altar. These two possibilities—whether the inscribed stones of verses 2–4 are separate stones or identical to the ones of which the altar is built—have been debated since antiquity. See the discussion in Excursus 25.

most distinctly Hebrew *ba'er heitev*, "very clearly," "setting it out well." For *ba'er*, see Comment to "expound" in 1:5.

Rabbinic exegesis took the requirement of making the Teaching clear to mean that it was to be written on the stones in seventy languages so that all nations might avail themselves of it and none would be able to evade the consequences for violating its precepts by claiming ignorance.[27]

AN APPEAL FOR OBEDIENCE, AS BEFITS A PEOPLE THAT HAS JUST BECOME GOD'S (vv. 9–10)

In verses 9–11 Moses reverts to the present situation and reminds the Israelites that this very day they had become God's people, referring to 26:17–18 (see also 29:12). In other words, Israel is now concluding the covenant that will be reaffirmed by the later ceremonies at Ebal and Gerizim. By

9Moses and the levitical priests spoke to all Israel, saying: Silence! Hear, O Israel! Today you have become the people of the LORD your God: 10Heed the LORD your God and observe His commandments and His laws, which I enjoin upon you this day.

9 וַיְדַבֵּר מֹשֶׁה וְהַכֹּהֲנִים הַלְוִיִּם אֶל כָּל־יִשְׂרָאֵל לֵאמֹר הַסְכֵּת | וּשְׁמַע יִשְׂרָאֵל הַיּוֹם הַזֶּה נִהְיֵיתָ לְעָם לַיהוָה אֱלֹהֶיךָ: 10 וְשָׁמַעְתָּ בְּקוֹל יְהוָה אֱלֹהֶיךָ וְעָשִׂיתָ אֶת־מִצְוֺתו וְאֶת־חֻקָּיו אֲשֶׁר אָנֹכִי מְצַוְּךָ הַיּוֹם: ס

v. 10. מִצְוֺתָיו ק׳

prescribing those ceremonies here, in the midst of the conclusion of the Moab covenant, Moses makes it clear that the later ceremonies will be a reaffirmation of the present covenant (itself a reaffirmation of the Horeb covenant) and not a new one.

9. Moses and the levitical priests See Comment to verse 1.

Silence! Hear This is the first time that the appeal to hear is preceded by a call for silence.[28] Absolute concentration[29] is required at the awesome moment when Israel becomes the people of God and in order for everyone to be prepared for the solemn promises and warnings they are about to hear (chap. 28; see Comment to v. 10).

Today See Comment to 26:17–18. The statement that Israel has just now become God's people is noteworthy, since other passages in the Torah suggest that this took place earlier, at the time of the Exodus or at Mount Sinai (see, e.g., Exod. 6:6–7; 19:5–6; Deut. 4:20,34). The statement here may be more rhetorical than historical. At Mount Sinai the people were frightened after hearing the Ten Commandments and asked Moses to receive the rest of God's commandments on their behalf (5:19–6:3). Now, forty years later, Moses is conveying to them the remaining commandments. Only now that they have received all of God's commandments—the full definition of their obligations to Him—are they fully His people.[30] There were varying views of when Israel actually became God's people; see Excursus 25.

become the people of the LORD This phrase echoes the formula that frequently describes the covenant between God and Israel: they become His people and He becomes their God (see, e.g., Lev. 26:12). The basic idiom involved is "to be someone's" (h-y-h le-someone). As in English, it means to be in a relationship with someone and is commonly used for establishing family relationships. See Comment to 5:7. Similar expressions are found in 26:16,17 and 29:12.[31] Here only half of the formula is used—Israel has become God's people—and only their responsibility under the covenant is addressed, in the next verse.

The verb for "become," nihyeita, is the passive form of h-y-h, "be."[32] Here it means "you were caused to become": Israel became God's people by an act of God.

10. This exhortation is continued in 28:1, which spells out its consequences and echoes it almost verbatim (this is clearer in the Hebrew, since "heed" here and "observe" there are the same word). Verse 11, in which the speaker is introduced again, indicates that the remainder of chapter 27 digresses.

CEREMONIAL PROCLAMATION OF BLESSINGS AND CURSES (vv. 11–26)

Verses 11–26, which consist of two sections, verses 11–13 and 14–26, have traditionally been considered a single section, since it was assumed that verses 14–26 are the curses to which verses 11–13 refer. As we shall see, this is not the case, and the two sections refer to different ceremonies.

PROCLAMATION OF BLESSINGS AND CURSES BY THE TRIBES (vv. 11–13)

Moses now describes the ceremony mentioned briefly in 11:29. When the twelve tribes of Israel arrive in the promised land, they are to proclaim the blessings and curses—the divinely imposed consequences of obeying or disobeying the terms of the covenant—at Mounts Gerizim and Ebal, the

11Thereupon Moses charged the people, saying: 12After you have crossed the Jordan, the following shall stand on Mount Gerizim when the blessing for the people is spoken: Simeon, Levi, Judah, Issachar, Joseph, and Benjamin. 13And for the curse, the following shall stand on Mount Ebal: Reuben, Gad, Asher, Zebulun, Dan, and Naphthali.

חמישי ‏‏11 וַיְצַו מֹשֶׁה אֶת־הָעָם בַּיּוֹם הַהוּא לֵאמֹר: ‏12 אֵלֶּה יַעַמְדוּ לְבָרֵךְ אֶת־הָעָם עַל־הַר גְּרִזִים בְּעָבְרְכֶם אֶת־הַיַּרְדֵּן שִׁמְעוֹן וְלֵוִי וִיהוּדָה וְיִשָּׂשכָר וְיוֹסֵף וּבִנְיָמִן: ‏13 וְאֵלֶּה יַעַמְדוּ עַל־הַקְּלָלָה בְּהַר עֵיבָל רְאוּבֵן גָּד וְאָשֵׁר וּזְבוּלֻן דָּן

latter being the site of the ceremony prescribed in verses 1–8. Such blessings and curses are an integral element of ancient covenants (see Excursus 27). The best known biblical examples are those in Leviticus 26 and Deuteronomy 28.

According to verses 12–13, six tribes are to stand on Mount Gerizim and pronounce the blessing, and the other six on Mount Ebal for the curse. According to Joshua 8:33, when Joshua carried out this command, "All Israel . . . stood on either side of the Ark, facing the levitical priests who carried the Ark. . . . Half of them faced Mount Gerizim and half of them faced Mount Ebal . . . in order to bless the people Israel."

Basing themselves on verses 14–26—which they presumed refers to the same ceremony—traditional commentators held that it was the Levites who actually recited the blessings and curses. In this view, the Levites first turned toward Mount Gerizim and recited a blessing that was the converse of the curse in verse 15 ("Blessed be the man who does not make a sculptured or molten image"), and then all twelve tribes would answer "Amen." Then the Levites would turn toward Mount Ebal and recite the curse of verse 15, and all the people would say "Amen." This would continue until all twelve curses of verses 14–26, each preceded by its corresponding blessing, were completed.[33] However, this reconstruction is unconvincing because it is unlikely that verses 14–26 are part of the ceremony to which verses 12–13 refer. Verse 12 clearly refers to a ceremony in which all twelve tribes proclaim the blessings and curses, six proclaiming the former and six the latter. In contrast, verses 14–26 describe a ceremony in which the Levites do all the speaking and all twelve tribes say "Amen" after the curses. Furthermore, verses 12–13 call for blessings as well as curses, whereas in 14–26 there are no blessings (the view that these verses do envision blessings is unconvincing; what conceivable reason could the text have had for omitting them?). And, finally, it is clear from 11:27–29 that the blessings and curses uttered on Mounts Gerizim and Ebal must be circumstantial descriptions of reward and punishment for obeying or disobeying the laws in general, not a list like that in verses 14–26 which anathematizes selected sins and focuses on the sins more than their consequences.[34] The latter type of proclamation, in which specific acts are interdicted and the people respond "Amen," was probably not even called a "curse" (kelalah) but rather an "oath" or "imprecation" (shevu'ah or 'alah).[35]

The blessings and curses called for in verses 12–13 are of the type found in chapter 28. Indeed, chapter 28, minus Moses' references to himself (28:1,13–15), could have served as the text of the ceremony, as Ibn Ezra proposed. Another possibility is that only the six brief blessings and six brief curses (28:3–6,16–19) were recited: the six tribes that proclaim blessings recited verse 1 (the contingency of obedience, minus Moses' reference to himself) and the six brief blessings—perhaps each one recited by a separate tribe; then, the other six tribes recited verse 15 (the contingency of disobedience, minus Moses' reference to himself) and the six brief curses in the same manner.[36]

12–13. *on Mount Gerizim . . . on Mount Ebal* The mountains north and south of Shechem. See Map 4. The precise location where the tribes should stand is not stated. Their pronouncements would be most audible if they stood on the slopes of the mountains rather than their peaks (which are 2.2 miles apart), and the text indeed says that the blessings and curses shall be recited "on," not "atop," the mountains. One plausible location would be a point at the eastern end of the valley where the mountains are only 1,676 feet apart. Another possibility is either of two spots a mile or so further west, at each of which the mountains are 4,920 feet apart. At each of the latter spots there are two facing bays in the mountains, forming natural amphitheaters (see Map 4). Acoustically, given the right temperature, humidity, and lack of air turbulence, the two groups of tribes could have heard each other across that distance.[37]

There is no explanation of why the tribes are divided as they are here. One reason may be geographic: of the six tribes that stand on the southern mountain (Gerizim), four settled south of the

14The Levites shall then proclaim in a loud voice to all the people of Israel:

וְנַפְתָּלִֽי: 14 וְעָנ֣וּ הַלְוִיִּ֗ם וְאָֽמְר֛וּ אֶל־כָּל־אִ֥ישׁ יִשְׂרָאֵ֖ל ק֥וֹל רָֽם: ס

Jezreel Valley, while all six that stand on the northern mountain (Ebal) settled north of the Jezreel Valley or east of the Jordan, a region that became part of the northen kingdom of Israel. Another reason may be genealogical: the tribes that proclaim blessings are descended from the sons of Rachel and four of Leah's sons, while those that proclaim curses are descended from the concubines Bilhah and Zilpah and Leah's two remaining sons: Reuben, the first-born, who was deposed because of his incest with Bilhah, and Zebulun, Leah's youngest son.[38]

when the blessing for the people is spoken . . . And for the curse   Literally, "to bless the people . . . And for the curse." The wording of the second clause is a circumlocution to avoid saying that the tribes would actually curse the people.

ANATHEMATIZATION OF CLANDESTINE SINS (vv. 14–26)

The people are to anathematize eleven specific sins and a twelfth, all-inclusive one. The eleven are all prohibited elsewhere, many on pain of death. They often escape detection because, as Ibn Ezra and Rashbam note, they are commonly committed in secret or are hard for their victims to publicize. The anathemas against idolatry and striking down a fellow explicitly refer to secret instances of those offenses (vv. 15,24). Disrespect toward parents often takes place in the privacy of the family circle (v. 16); moving a landmark is obviously done clandestinely (v. 17); the blind cannot identify those who mislead them (v. 18); strangers, orphans, and widows have no one to publicly defend their rights in court and the judge's motives are known only to himself (v. 19); and bribes and sexual offenses are obviously private acts (vv. 20–23,25).[39]

The present ceremony is designed to discourage such offenses and to provide for their punishment by God. An anathema is pronounced on those who commit them, and the people express their assent by responding "Amen," which constitutes an oath to avoid these acts. Procedures of this type were used to impose norms of conduct on groups of people. An inscription in a circa sixth-century C.E. synagogue at Ein Gedi declares that whoever violates certain ethical rules of that community or reveals its trade secrets will be wiped out, along with his family, by God. The inscription alludes to a ceremony in which this oath was imposed, stating: "Let all the people say, 'Amen.'" In a Hittite soldiers' oath ceremony from two millennia earlier, an official places various objects symbolic of disaster in the hands of the soldiers and declares that whoever breaks his oath of loyalty to the king shall suffer such a fate; the soldiers must declare, after taking each object, "So be it!"[40] In each of these cases, the disaster is described explicitly instead of being expressed by the declaration *'arur*, "Cursed be." In modern terms, the officials' words mean "Do you solemnly swear not to . . . ?" and the people's response means "We do," but the curse gives the ceremony more than moral or legal force.

Oaths of this type are used in the Bible to impose certain duties on people or to restrain them from performing certain acts. For example, the other tribes swore, "Cursed be anyone who gives a wife to Benjamin" after the tribe of Benjamin provoked a civil war (Judg. 21:18), and Saul declared, "Cursed be the man who eats any food before night falls and I take revenge on my enemies," making his army swear to fast all day during a battle (1 Sam. 14:24). Later, Nehemiah censured the nobles who foreclosed on their fellow Jews and made them swear to return their property; shaking out part of his garment, he said, "So may God shake free of his household and property any man who fails to keep this promise," and the nobles responded "Amen" (Neh. 5:13). In each case the oath effectively restrained all who knew of it from violating it; clearly, people feared the dire punishment the oath called for (see Comment to v. 15). Since punishment is handed over to God, such oaths are particularly well suited for discouraging acts whose would-be perpetrators might think they could escape detection or prosecution.[41]

The first and last of the anathemas are the longest of the twelve and are phrased in a different style than the rest: they are relative clauses ("Cursed be he who . . ."), whereas the others are participial (in Hebrew they read literally, "Cursed be the insulter . . . the mover . . ."; this is obscured in the translation). Perhaps their length and unique style are designed to call attention to them

15Cursed be anyone who makes a sculptured or molten image, abhorred by the LORD, a craftsman's handiwork,

אָר֣וּר הָאִ֡ישׁ אֲשֶׁ֣ר יַעֲשֶׂה֩ פֶ֨סֶל וּמַסֵּכָ֜ה תּוֹעֲבַ֣ת 15

because they are the most important of the twelve, dealing with the two sins emphasized most frequently in Deuteronomy. The first is about idolatry, the gravest sin and the one most fundamental to the others, since without loyalty to the Lord there is no commitment to His commandments and no fear of His power to carry out the curses. The last is the most comprehensive, dealing with violation of the Teaching.[42] The twelve sins are arranged in a concentric structure: the core of the list deals with sexual crimes (vv. 20–23); before and after these are social sins (vv. 16–19, 24–25); and before and after the latter are sins pertaining to relations with God.[43]

The twelve anathemas here have numerous parallels in other parts of the Bible, especially the Decalogue, the laws of Deuteronomy, the Book of the Covenant in Exodus 21–23, the Laws of Holiness in Leviticus 18–20, and the catalogue of Jerusalem's sins in Ezekiel 22. Each of these passages has several parallels to the present one.[44] The list of sins mentioned here is not comprehensive but representative. In scope and content it resembles epitomes of God's requirements, such as the Decalogue, Ezekiel 18, and Psalm 15.[45] These epitomes likewise present ten to twelve items, often selected from collections of God's laws or moral teachings, and deal mostly with social conduct. Those that include requirements dealing with relations with God always place that subject first. Such lists, appearing in the Torah, the prophets, and the Psalms, were apparently a popular pedagogic device for educating people in God's requirements. Their brevity and the fact that each item is formulated identically, or that they are often poetic and rhythmic, would have facilitated memorization.

As noted above, verses 14–26 are not the ceremony prescribed in verses 11–13. Conceivably they appear here simply because their theme is similar to that of verses 11–13, and because their twelve anathemas correspond to the twelve tribes mentioned there. However, their location strongly suggests that this ceremony is to take place on the same occasion as those of verses 1–8 and 11–13, when the covenant is reaffirmed upon entering the promised land. In that context vv. 14–26 may serve to warn those who, while publicly reaffirming the covenant, think that they can safely violate it in secret. Something similar is found in 29:17–28 where Moses, concluding the covenant made in Moab, warns those who may harbor the same illusion that secret sins will be detected by God and punished. Our passage may serve as a counterpart to that warning.[46] Conceivably the ceremony also serves to purge the community in advance of collective responsibility for sins committed in its midst that it is unable to prosecute, much as the ceremony in 21:1–9 does after the fact.[47]

14. *The Levites* In their priestly role. Although blessings and curses by any individual could be effective, priests' and prophets' curses were thought to be especially so. Hence Balak's choice of Balaam to curse Israel and, in contrast, the priests' duty of blessing Israel.[48]

15. *Cursed* Hebrew *'arur*, destined for divinely imposed misfortune. This invocation is the equivalent of more graphic descriptions of disaster in the oath imposed by Nehemiah, the inscription from Ein Gedi and the Hittite soldiers' oath (all cited above), the oath administered to the suspected adulteress (cited below), and in similar curses in the Bible, calling for such misfortunes as childlessness, the death of children, slavery, and all the misfortunes listed in Deuteronomy 28. A good illustration of this equivalence may be seen by comparing the curse "Cursed [*'arur*] be the man who opens this," inscribed on an eighth-century-B.C.E. sepulchre in Jerusalem, with the curses written on Phoenician sepulchres, which explicitly invoke upon anyone who would open them a miserable death, denial of burial and of acceptance among the spirits of the dead, and the death of his posterity.[49]

sculptured or molten image That is, any kind of idol, whether of the Lord or of another deity. On the first term, see Comment to 4:16; the second is used of the golden calf in 9:12.

abhorred by the LORD See Comment to 7:25.

a craftsman's handiwork The fact that idols are man-made is the Bible's most telling argument against their divinity. See Comment to 4:28.

and sets it up in secret To avoid detection. The anticipation that such attempts would be made in secret reflects the Torah's expectation that idolatry would be stigmatized and punished by

and sets it up in secret.—And all the people shall respond, Amen.

¹⁶Cursed be he who insults his father or mother.—And all the people shall say, Amen.

¹⁷Cursed be he who moves his fellow countryman's landmark.—And all the people shall say, Amen.

¹⁸Cursed be he who misdirects a blind person on his way.—And all the people shall say, Amen.

¹⁹Cursed be he who subverts the rights of the stranger, the fatherless, and the widow.—And all the people shall say, Amen.

יְהֹוָה מַעֲשֵׂה יְדֵי חָרָשׁ וְשָׂם בַּסֵּתֶר וְעָנוּ כָל־הָעָם
וְאָמְרוּ אָמֵן׃ ס

16 אָרוּר מַקְלֶה אָבִיו וְאִמּוֹ וְאָמַר כָּל־הָעָם
אָמֵן׃ ס

17 אָרוּר מַסִּיג גְּבוּל רֵעֵהוּ וְאָמַר כָּל־הָעָם
אָמֵן׃ ס

18 אָרוּר מַשְׁגֶּה עִוֵּר בַּדָּרֶךְ וְאָמַר כָּל־הָעָם
אָמֵן׃ ס

19 אָרוּר מַטֶּה מִשְׁפַּט גֵּר־יָתוֹם וְאַלְמָנָה וְאָמַר
כָּל־הָעָם אָמֵן׃ ס

the sinner's contemporaries. The same assumption is reflected in 13:7 and in Job's denial that he *secretly* worshiped the sun and moon (Job 31:27). The archaeological evidence indicates that idols were indeed rare. Very few have been found in ancient Israelite sites as compared to those of neighboring peoples.[50]

Amen "Let it be so" (Septuagint). The term is derived from the root '-*m*-*n*, "firm." Its meaning is explicated by Jeremiah, who expresses assent to what someone has just said by responding "Amen! May the LORD do so!" (Jer. 28:6). As in the case of Nehemiah cited above, it expresses the people's prayer that the punishment befall whoever commits the sin in question and acceptance of the punishment if they themselves commit it. The same usage is found in Numbers 5:22, where the suspected adulteress is adjured that the potion she drinks will harm her if she is guilty, and she must respond "Amen, amen!" As the Talmud puts it, "Answering 'Amen' after an oath is equivalent to pronouncing the oath with one's own mouth."[51]

16. insults That is, treats disrespectfully. The crime is not limited to verbal insults. Hebrew *makleh*, related to *kal*, "light," means literally to "slight," "make light of." It is the opposite of the verb used in the fifth commandment, to "honor" (*kabbed*, literally, treat as *kaved*, "heavy," "weighty") one's parents.[52] This crime would include the actions of the rebellious son (Deut. 21:18–21).

17. This curse is based on the prohibition against moving landmarks, 19:14. Since this crime is committed in secret, and fear of detection is not as effective a deterrent as in the case of other crimes, ancient literature is replete with curses and warnings of divine punishment against those who commit it. Babylonian boundary stones were inscribed with curses directed against those who would move them or alter their inscriptions.[53] The crime was a direct affront to God because property was assigned by lot, which was believed to be directed by God and expressive of His will.[54]

This curse is followed by those against harming the blind and strangers, orphans, and widows. This combination of subjects is also found in Proverbs 23:10 and Egyptian wisdom literature, which warn against encroaching on the property of widows and orphans. This association reflects the fact that the disadvantaged were especially vulnerable to boundary tampering because they lacked the means to defend their rights.

18. The same principle is expressed in Leviticus 19:14: "Do not place a stumbling block [an obstacle] before the blind." Similarly, Egyptian wisdom literature teaches: "Do not laugh at a blind man or tease a dwarf, nor injure the affairs of the lame."

Postbiblical authorities interpreted this principle more broadly. Combining this injunction with that in Leviticus, Josephus paraphrases: "One must point out the road to those who are ignorant of it, and not, for the pleasure of laughing oneself, impede another's business by misleading him." Halakhic exegesis took the prohibition to include misleading uninformed people with incorrect information or bad advice, or abetting sinners and criminals, who are blinded by their desires.[55]

19. subverts the rights of the stranger Rather, "judges the stranger . . . unfairly." See Comment to 24:17. Since these do not have power to prosecute and defend their rights, the Bible often points out that God is their protector, as in 10:18.

20Cursed be he who lies with his father's wife, for he has removed his father's garment.—And all the people shall say, Amen.

21Cursed be he who lies with any beast.—And all the people shall say, Amen.

22Cursed be he who lies with his sister, whether daughter of his father or of his mother.—And all the people shall say, Amen.

23Cursed be he who lies with his mother-in-law.—And all the people shall say, Amen.

24Cursed be he who strikes down his fellow countryman in secret.—And all the people shall say, Amen.

20 אָר֗וּר שֹׁכֵב֙ עִם־אֵ֣שֶׁת אָבִ֔יו כִּ֥י גִלָּ֖ה כְּנַ֣ף אָבִ֑יו
וְאָמַ֥ר כָּל־הָעָ֖ם אָמֵֽן: ס

21 אָר֗וּר שֹׁכֵ֖ב עִם־כָּל־בְּהֵמָ֑ה וְאָמַ֥ר כָּל־הָעָ֖ם
אָמֵֽן: ס

22 אָר֗וּר שֹׁכֵב֙ עִם־אֲחֹת֔וֹ בַּת־אָבִ֖יו א֣וֹ בַת־אִמּ֑וֹ
וְאָמַ֥ר כָּל־הָעָ֖ם אָמֵֽן: ס

23 אָר֗וּר שֹׁכֵ֖ב עִם־חֹתַנְתּ֑וֹ וְאָמַ֥ר כָּל־הָעָ֖ם
אָמֵֽן: ס

24 אָר֗וּר מַכֵּ֥ה רֵעֵ֖הוּ בַּסָּ֑תֶר וְאָמַ֥ר כָּל־הָעָ֖ם
אָמֵֽן: ס

20–23. These four anathemas cover the sexual crimes of incest and bestiality. They are forbidden in Exodus 22:18; Leviticus 18:6–23; 20:10–21; and Deuteronomy 23:1 and—with some exceptions—in other ancient Near Eastern laws.[56] The absence of adultery here is in keeping with the hard-to-detect character of the crimes listed: as Rashbam and Bekhor Shor observe, a man would arouse suspicion if seen in the company or home of another man's wife, but not if seen in the company of his stepmother, sister, mother-in-law, and cattle, since he is regularly with them. Even if an act of incest became known within a family, the family might hush it up to avoid disgrace. This is suggested by Absalom's advice to his full-sister Tamar to keep silent about her rape by her half-brother Amnon.[57]

20. *his father's wife*   Unlike 23:1, which refers only to his father's *former* wife, this could refer to his current wife and even the sinner's own mother. Note that here only sexual relations are mentioned; marriage, which is prohibited in 23:1, is inherently a public act and hence irrelevant here.

Elsewhere in Near Eastern law, the Laws of Hammurabi likewise oppose a man's having intercourse with his stepmother after his father's death; in the Hittite Laws, it is a crime only if the father is still alive.[58] For Near Eastern laws that permit marriage with one's father's former wife, see Comment to 23:1.

21.   Bestiality is not uncommon sexual behavior, especially in rural areas. The Hittite Laws prohibit it with certain animals but not others. Ancient Near Eastern myths sometimes describe sexual intercourse between gods and animals.[59] The story of Eve's creation, after Adam found all animals unacceptable as partners (Gen. 2:16–25), could have served as an implicit explanation for this prohibition.[60]

22. *his sister, whether daughter of his father or of his mother*   This explanatory phrase makes it clear that one may not marry (or have sexual relations with) even a half-sister. Marriage with a half-sister from a different mother was permitted at one time in Israel. Abraham told Abimelech that Sarah was his half-sister, and David's daughter Tamar told his son Amnon that David would permit them to marry (see Gen. 20:12; 2 Sam. 13:13). The practice was known in Greece and Arabia. In Egypt and Phoenicia, brother-sister marriages were practiced, mostly among the royalty.[61]

One version of the Septuagint reads "the sister of his father or of his mother."[62] This version may have been based on a Hebrew text that read *'aḥot 'aviv 'o 'immo*, in agreement with Leviticus 18:12–13; 20:19. The Masoretic text, *'aḥoto bat 'aviv 'o vat 'immo*, agrees with Leviticus 18:9; 20:17.

23.   Following this verse, two versions of the Septuagint have an additional anathema, "Cursed be he who lies with his wife's sister," in agreement with Leviticus 18:18.[63]

24. *strikes down*   Hebrew *makkeh*, "strike," can refer to lethal or nonlethal blows. Often, when murder is meant, more explicit idioms such as *makkeh nefesh*, "strike mortally," are used, as in the next verse. This verse may be intentionally equivocal so as to cover all types of clandestine assault.

256

25Cursed be he who accepts a bribe in the case of the murder of an innocent person.—And all the people shall say, Amen.

26Cursed be he who will not uphold the terms of this Teaching and observe them.—And all the people shall say, Amen.

25 אָרוּר לֹקֵחַ שֹׁחַד לְהַכּוֹת נֶפֶשׁ דָּם נָקִי וְאָמַר
כָּל־הָעָם אָמֵן: ס

26 אָרוּר אֲשֶׁר לֹא־יָקִים אֶת־דִּבְרֵי הַתּוֹרָה־
הַזֹּאת לַעֲשׂוֹת אוֹתָם וְאָמַר כָּל־הָעָם אָמֵן: פ

28 Now, if you obey the LORD your God, to observe faithfully all His commandments which I enjoin upon you this day, the LORD your God will set you high above all the

כ"ח וְהָיָה אִם־שָׁמוֹעַ תִּשְׁמַע בְּקוֹל יְהוָה
אֱלֹהֶיךָ לִשְׁמֹר לַעֲשׂוֹת אֶת־כָּל־מִצְוֹתָיו אֲשֶׁר
אָנֹכִי מְצַוְּךָ הַיּוֹם וּנְתָנְךָ יְהוָה אֱלֹהֶיךָ עֶלְיוֹן עַל

25. in the case of the murder of an innocent person Rather, "to mortally strike an innocent person." Conceivably this refers to a hired assassin or to a false witness whose testimony leads to the execution of an innocent defendant. However, since biblical laws about accepting bribes refer to judges, it more likely refers to a judge who accepts a bribe to condemn an innocent defendant to death. Compare Exodus 23:7–8, which is addressed to judges: "Do not bring death on those who are innocent and in the right. . . . Do not take bribes." See also Deuteronomy 16:22.[64]

26. The final anathema refers to all other provisions of the Teaching. As Rashi comments, this constitutes an oath to uphold the entire Teaching.

When Moses refers to "this Teaching," he means the Teaching he is currently expounding. Here, however, the phrase is part of what the Levites will say at a later date. If this ceremony was to be performed at Mount Ebal, at the same time as the others in this chapter, "this Teaching" may refer to the copy of the Teaching inscribed on the stones that stood nearby.

CHAPTER **28**

The Consequences of Obedience and Disobedience   (vv. 1–68)

This chapter is a detailed exposition of the consequences of Israel's obeying or disobeying the terms of the covenant that Moses has rehearsed in chapters 5–26. The chapter has two main parts; one describes the good fortune that will come upon Israel if it obeys God's laws (vv. 1–14), and the other tells of the disasters that will ensue if it disobeys (vv. 15–68). The second part consists of three subsections describing various groups of disasters (vv. 15–44, 45–57, and 58–68).[1]

For obedience God promises abundant crops and food, human and animal fertility, wealth, surplus, economic preeminence, and military success. Disobedience is threatened with the reverse: drought, diseases, crop failure, economic collapse and dependency, defeat in war, conquest, oppression, famine, cannibalism, and exile.

Promises and threats such as these are a very well known genre in the Bible and elsewhere in ancient Near Eastern literature. A few that illuminate the meaning of particular verses are cited here in the commentary. The genre is discussed, and representative parallels noted, in Excursus 27.

THE BLESSINGS FOR OBEDIENCE   (vv. 1–14)

Six concise blessings (vv. 3–6) and six promises expanding upon them (vv. 7–13a) are framed by an introductory and concluding statement reiterating that Israel's good fortune is contingent on faithful obedience to God's commandments (vv. 1–2, 13b–14). The relationship between the blessings and promises is explained in Excursus 26.

1. this day Following the digression in chapter 27, which looked ahead to the arrival in the promised land, Moses here turns his attention back to the present moment in the land of Moab.

nations of the earth. ²All these blessings shall come upon you and take effect, if you will but heed the word of the LORD your God:

³Blessed shall you be in the city and blessed shall you be in the country.

⁴Blessed shall be the issue of your womb, the produce of your soil, and the offspring of your cattle, the calving of your herd and the lambing of your flock.

⁵Blessed shall be your basket and your kneading bowl.

כָּל־גּוֹיֵי הָאָרֶץ: 2 וּבָאוּ עָלֶיךָ כָּל־הַבְּרָכוֹת הָאֵלֶּה וְהִשִּׂיגֻךָ כִּי תִשְׁמַע בְּקוֹל יְהוָה אֱלֹהֶיךָ:

3 בָּרוּךְ אַתָּה בָּעִיר וּבָרוּךְ אַתָּה בַּשָּׂדֶה:

4 בָּרוּךְ פְּרִי־בִטְנְךָ וּפְרִי אַדְמָתְךָ וּפְרִי בְהֶמְתֶּךָ שְׁגַר אֲלָפֶיךָ וְעַשְׁתְּרוֹת צֹאנֶךָ:

5 בָּרוּךְ טַנְאֲךָ וּמִשְׁאַרְתֶּךָ:

Briefly, he recapitulates the conditions and promises of 26:16–19 regarding the covenant now being made in Moab, and then spells out the consequences that will ensue if Israel is loyal or disloyal to it.

the LORD your God will set you high above all the nations The promise of 26:19 is conditional; Israel is not promised automatic special treatment but must earn it. To make this clear, the condition is repeated in verse 2.

2. *All these blessings* In this chapter the words "blessing" and "curse" do not refer to promises and threats but to the benign and destructive forces that blessings and curses call for.

shall come upon you and take effect The second verb is literally "overtake." Throughout the chapter the blessings and curses—that is, the benign and destructive forces—are almost personified by the verbs used of them: they "come," "pursue," and "overtake" (vv. 2,15,22,45), and God "commands" (translated "ordain") and "lets [them] loose" (vv. 8,20; cf. 32:24). See also 29:19, where sanctions (*'alah*, another term for "curse") "crouch" upon the sinner (the translation reads "come down"). This manner of speaking probably originated in personification of these forces as agents that God holds back or releases in accordance with Israel's behavior.[2] Such personification is also found in Exodus 12:23, where the agent of the tenth plague is called "the Destroyer," and in the book of Psalms, where destructive and protective forces are both pictured as "messengers" (*mal'akhim*, usually rendered "angels"). However, actual personification is absent in Deuteronomy, which avoids any suggestion of independent supernatural powers in addition to God, such as the Greek spirits of punishment, the Erinyes.[3] Instead, the blessings and curses are merely reified and treated as impersonal forces under God's absolute control, and the verbs express the idea that at God's command the blessings will come to Israel with no struggle on its part and the curses will ensue despite any effort on its part.

3–6. Six blessings, focusing on fertility and prosperity. They are arranged in three pairs, as are the curses in verses 16–19. The first and last pairs consist of opposites which together express totality, indicating that the blessings will cover every place and activity. The middle pair specifies, in list form, the abundance of fertility and food. The blessings are concise, rhythmic, and worded in a uniform pattern, with all but the third consisting of three Hebrew words. Their style is suitable for oral recitation. The six blessings and six curses correspond to the six tribes that bless and the six that curse in 27:11–13, and may have been intended for recitation at the ceremony prescribed there (see Comment to 27:11–13).

3. *Blessed* Prosperous. See Comment to 2:7.

in the city... in the country These opposites express the totality of places, meaning that wherever you live and work, your undertakings will prosper.[4] The elaboration of this verse in verses 12–13 focuses on the city and country, respectively, as the loci of trade and farming.[5]

4. *and the offspring of your cattle*[6]

the calving of your herd and the lambing of your flock See Comment to 7:13.

5. *your basket and your kneading bowl* The vessels used for gathering produce (see 26:2) and preparing bread. The blessing means that the harvest will be abundant and food plentiful.

⁶Blessed shall you be in your comings and blessed shall you be in your goings.

⁷The LORD will put to rout before you the enemies who attack you; they will march out against you by a single road, but flee from you by many roads. ⁸The LORD will ordain blessings for you upon your barns and upon all your undertakings: He will bless you in the land that the LORD your God is giving you. ⁹The LORD will establish you as His holy people, as He swore to you, if you keep the commandments of the LORD your God and walk in His ways. ¹⁰And all the peoples of the earth shall see that

6 בָּר֥וּךְ אַתָּ֖ה בְּבֹאֶ֑ךָ וּבָר֥וּךְ אַתָּ֖ה בְּצֵאתֶֽךָ:

ששי 7 יִתֵּ֨ן יְהוָ֤ה אֶת־אֹיְבֶ֙יךָ֙ הַקָּמִ֣ים עָלֶ֔יךָ נִגָּפִ֖ים לְפָנֶ֑יךָ בְּדֶ֤רֶךְ אֶחָד֙ יֵצְא֣וּ אֵלֶ֔יךָ וּבְשִׁבְעָ֥ה דְרָכִ֖ים יָנ֥וּסוּ לְפָנֶֽיךָ: 8 יְצַ֨ו יְהוָ֤ה אִתְּךָ֙ אֶת־הַבְּרָכָ֔ה בַּאֲסָמֶ֕יךָ וּבְכֹ֖ל מִשְׁלַ֣ח יָדֶ֑ךָ וּבֵ֣רַכְךָ֔ בָּאָ֕רֶץ אֲשֶׁר־יְהוָ֥ה אֱלֹהֶ֖יךָ נֹתֵ֥ן לָֽךְ: 9 יְקִֽימְךָ֨ יְהוָ֥ה לוֹ֙ לְעַ֣ם קָד֔וֹשׁ כַּאֲשֶׁ֖ר נִֽשְׁבַּֽע־לָ֑ךְ כִּ֣י תִשְׁמֹ֗ר אֶת־מִצְוֺת֙ יְהוָ֣ה אֱלֹהֶ֔יךָ וְהָלַכְתָּ֖ בִּדְרָכָֽיו: 10 וְרָאוּ֙ כָּל־עַמֵּ֣י הָאָ֔רֶץ כִּ֛י שֵׁ֥ם יְהוָ֖ה נִקְרָ֣א עָלֶ֑יךָ

6. *comings . . . goings* Literally "entering and going out." These opposites cover a range of activities. They may mean simply "wherever you go,"[7] but since the combination of "come" and "go" has a number of idiomatic meanings, there are several other possibilities: "in all your activities,"[8] "when you go to war" (the sense picked up in v. 7),[9] and "in traveling to and from the city."[10] Elsewhere these ideas are invariably expressed with the verbs in the order "going out and entering." It is possible that here the order is reversed in the light of verse 3, so that the text means "entering the city" and "going out to the country."[11] Abravanel takes blessedness in these activities to mean safety in traveling to and from the city, a common theme in descriptions of blessing and prosperity.[12]

7-14. This section consists of promises that elaborate on the concise blessings of verses 3–6. It highlights certain aspects of the blessings and repeats the all-important condition of obedience. Whereas verses 3–6 describe the results of the blessings, this section highlights the fact that God is their source: as verses 9–10 explain, Israel will be successful because God will make it sacrosanct, as He promised in 26:18–19. The order in which these promises are arranged is discussed in Excursus 26.

7. God will defeat Israel's enemies.

they will march out against you by a single road Too numerous and confident to bother separating their forces for safety.[13]

flee from you by many roads Literally, seven roads. Seven is often used to express a large number.[14] The point is that the enemy will scatter in every direction. Compare Numbers 10:35: "Advance, O LORD! / May Your enemies be scattered, / And may Your foes flee before You!" According to 1 Samuel 11:11, when Saul repulsed the invading Ammonites, no two were left together.

8. The LORD will ordain blessings for you upon your barns Compare Leviticus 25:21: "I will ordain My blessing for you . . . so that it shall yield a crop sufficient for three years."

"Blessings" is literally "the blessing." For the reification see Comment to verse 2 and contrast verse 20, "the curse."

barns That is, stores, granaries. Hebrew *'asam* is derived from the verb *'-s-m*, "store up," known from Syriac (*'-s-n*) and found in the seventh-century-B.C.E. Hebrew letter cited in the Comment to 24:12. Underground storage pits as well as storehouses or silos were used.[15]

9. See Comment to 26:19.

the LORD . . . the LORD your God These two ways of referring to God are used throughout the chapter. When God's acts of reward and punishment are described, He is called simply "the LORD." The full phrase "the LORD your/our God" appears more than three hundred times in Deuteronomy, but in this chapter it is reserved for passages that refer to Israel's duty of obeying God or to His gift of the land.[16] It has the connotation of "the LORD, who has kept His promises to you and whom you are obligated to obey."

if you keep Once again the conditional character of Israel's sacrosanctity is reiterated.

the Lord's name is proclaimed over you, and they shall stand in fear of you. [11]The Lord will give you abounding prosperity in the issue of your womb, the offspring of your cattle, and the produce of your soil in the land that the Lord swore to your fathers to assign to you. [12]The Lord will open for you His bounteous store, the heavens, to provide rain for your land in season and to bless all your undertakings. You will be creditor to many nations, but debtor to none.

[13]The Lord will make you the head, not the tail; you will always be at the top and never at the bottom—if only you obey and faithfully observe the commandments of the Lord your God that I enjoin upon you this day, [14]and do not deviate to the right or to the left from any of the commandments that I enjoin upon you this day and turn to the worship of other gods.

וְיָרְא֖וּ מִמֶּֽךָּ׃ [11] וְהוֹתִֽרְךָ֤ יְהוָה֙ לְטוֹבָ֔ה בִּפְרִ֧י בִטְנְךָ֛ וּבִפְרִ֥י בְהֶמְתְּךָ֖ וּבִפְרִ֣י אַדְמָתֶ֑ךָ עַ֚ל הָֽאֲדָמָ֔ה אֲשֶׁ֨ר נִשְׁבַּ֧ע יְהוָ֛ה לַאֲבֹתֶ֖יךָ לָ֥תֶת לָֽךְ׃ [12] יִפְתַּ֣ח יְהוָ֣ה ׀ לְךָ֡ אֶת־אוֹצָר֨וֹ הַטּ֜וֹב אֶת־הַשָּׁמַ֗יִם לָתֵ֤ת מְטַֽר־אַרְצְךָ֙ בְּעִתּ֔וֹ וּלְבָרֵ֕ךְ אֵ֖ת כָּל־מַעֲשֵׂ֣ה יָדֶ֑ךָ וְהִלְוִ֙יתָ֙ גּוֹיִ֣ם רַבִּ֔ים וְאַתָּ֖ה לֹ֥א תִלְוֶֽה׃ [13] וּנְתָֽנְךָ֙ יְהוָ֣ה לְרֹ֔אשׁ וְלֹ֣א לְזָנָ֔ב וְהָיִ֙יתָ֙ רַ֣ק לְמַ֔עְלָה וְלֹ֥א תִהְיֶ֖ה לְמָ֑טָּה כִּֽי־תִשְׁמַ֞ע אֶל־מִצְוֹ֣ת ׀ יְהוָ֣ה אֱלֹהֶ֗יךָ אֲשֶׁ֨ר אָנֹכִ֧י מְצַוְּךָ֛ הַיּ֖וֹם לִשְׁמֹ֥ר וְלַעֲשֽׂוֹת׃ [14] וְלֹ֣א תָס֗וּר מִכָּל־הַדְּבָרִ֗ים אֲשֶׁ֨ר אָנֹכִ֜י מְצַוֶּ֥ה אֶתְכֶ֛ם הַיּ֖וֹם יָמִ֣ין וּשְׂמֹ֑אול* לָלֶ֗כֶת אַחֲרֵ֛י אֱלֹהִ֥ים אֲחֵרִ֖ים לְעָבְדָֽם׃ ס

מלא ו"ו v. 14.

10. Prosperity and victory will show other nations that you are under the Lord's aegis, and they will be deterred from harming you. Earlier instances of such a reaction are related in Genesis, where Abimelech sees from the prosperity of Abraham and Isaac that God is with them and requests nonaggression treaties with them (Gen. 21:22–23; 26:26–31).

the Lord's name is proclaimed over you They will see that you are "the Lord's people" ('am 'adonai), that He is your lord and protector.[17] The linkage between God's name and protection is expressed in prayers that appeal to God for protection on the grounds that the supplicant is called by His name.[18] In a human context the same kind of linkage is expressed in an appeal from a Canaanite vassal to the Pharoah: "Behold, the king has set his name in the land of Jerusalem forever; so he cannot abandon the lands of Jerusalem!"[19]

11. abounding Rather, "surpassing." The verb *hotir* refers to giving more than enough. The same promise appears in 30:9. This surplus will enable Israel to lend to other nations and never to borrow (v. 12).

12. store The ancients pictured rain, snow, hail, wind, and other celestial phenomena as kept in storehouses that God opens as needed.[20]

in season See Comment to 11:14.

You will be creditor to many nations Because of your surplus wealth. Compare 15:6.

13a. the head, not the tail As a creditor you will be the leader among nations, not a follower. Compare 15:6: "you will extend loans to many nations, but require none yourself; you will dominate many nations, but they will not dominate you."

you will always be at the top and never at the bottom You will always thrive and never decline.

13b–14. The promises end with a final reminder that they are conditional. Verse 13b is practically identical to verse 1, while verse 14 reiterates the key condition on which the promises depend, shunning other gods.

THE CURSES FOR DISOBEDIENCE (vv. 15–68)

The remainder of the chapter, like the threats in Leviticus 26, is known as the *tokheḥah*, or "Warning," in postbiblical sources. It describes the curses that will befall Israel if it disobeys the terms of the

15But if you do not obey the Lord your God to observe faithfully all His commandments and laws which I enjoin upon you this day, all these curses shall come upon you and take effect:

16Cursed shall you be in the city and cursed shall you be in the country.

17Cursed shall be your basket and your kneading bowl.

18Cursed shall be the issue of your womb and the produce of your soil, the calving of your herd and the lambing of your flock.

19Cursed shall you be in your comings and cursed shall you be in your goings.

20The Lord will let loose against you calamity, panic,

15 וְהָיָ֗ה אִם־לֹ֤א תִשְׁמַע֙ בְּקוֹל֙ יְהוָ֣ה אֱלֹהֶ֔יךָ לִשְׁמֹ֤ר לַעֲשׂוֹת֙ אֶת־כָּל־מִצְוֺתָ֣יו וְחֻקֹּתָ֔יו אֲשֶׁ֛ר אָנֹכִ֥י מְצַוְּךָ֖ הַיּ֑וֹם וּבָ֧אוּ עָלֶ֛יךָ כָּל־הַקְּלָל֥וֹת הָאֵ֖לֶּה וְהִשִּׂיגֽוּךָ׃

16 אָר֥וּר אַתָּ֖ה בָּעִ֑יר וְאָר֥וּר אַתָּ֖ה בַּשָּׂדֶֽה׃

17 אָר֥וּר טַנְאֲךָ֖ וּמִשְׁאַרְתֶּֽךָ׃

18 אָר֥וּר פְּרִֽי־בִטְנְךָ֖ וּפְרִ֣י אַדְמָתֶ֑ךָ שְׁגַ֥ר אֲלָפֶ֖יךָ וְעַשְׁתְּרֹ֥ת צֹאנֶֽךָ׃

19 אָר֥וּר אַתָּ֖ה בְּבֹאֶ֑ךָ וְאָר֥וּר אַתָּ֖ה בְּצֵאתֶֽךָ׃

20 יִשְׁלַ֣ח יְהוָ֣ה ׀ בְּךָ֗ אֶת־הַמְּאֵרָ֤ה אֶת־הַמְּהוּמָה֙

---

covenant. Each section in this part of the chapter begins with an introduction, more or less comparable to that preceding the blessings in verse 1, stating that the curses will take effect in case of disobedience. The first section is structured like the blessings. It begins with six concise curses (vv. 16–19) that are practically verbatim counterparts to the blessings in verses 3–6, and then elaborates upon them (vv. 7–44). The second and third sections (vv. 45–57 and 58–68) are briefer and focus on a narrower range of themes.

The theme of the curses and threats is that God will turn nature and foreign nations against Israel, reversing all the blessings and, ultimately, reversing Israel's own history of deliverance from bondage. These warnings are presented in repeated, seemingly endless detail that aims to impress indelibly the consequences of disobdience on the mind and heart of the audience. Their desired effect is shown by the reaction of King Josiah, who tore his clothes in grief when he heard them, as related in 2 Kings 22:11,19. This list of curses and its companion in Leviticus were considered so frightening that in later times the custom developed of chanting them in an undertone during the Torah-reading service in the synagogue, and many people were reluctant to be called to the Torah when they were read.[21] To deter people from violating a tomb, a third-century Jewish tomb inscription invokes "all the curses written in Deuteronomy" on any person who does so.[22]

THE FIRST GROUP OF CURSES AND THREATS (vv. 15–44)

Verses 15–19 are the reverse of verses 1–6, matching them verbatim except for their negative formulation.[23] The identical wording highlights the choice being offered to Israel: obedience and disobedience have exactly opposite effects.

15. *overtake*   See Comment to verse 2.

20–44.   The first expanded description of disasters, dealing with natural calamities, disease, and military reverses. This section includes verses that identify God explicitly as the author of the conditions described in the curses (vv. 16–19), just as verses 7–14 did for the blessings of verses 3–6 (there are some exceptions that describe only the conditions themselves, such as vv. 23,26,29ff). This elaboration is far more expansive than that which accompanies the blessings (vv. 7–14). The individual threats are arranged in a chiastic pattern, as explained in Excursus 26.

20.   This verse sets the theme for the elaboration. Instead of the blessing (v. 8) God will send a triad of afflictions against all of Israel's undertakings: Curse, Confusion, and Cumbrance (the latter term, meaning "obstruction," is used to reproduce the alliteration of the Hebrew *ha-me'erah*, *ha-mehumah*, and *ha-mig'eret*; all three terms are reified with the definite article, which can be expressed in English by capitalization).

let loose   See Comment to verse 2.

and frustration in all the enterprises you undertake, so that you shall soon be utterly wiped out because of your evil-doing in forsaking Me. ²¹The LORD will make pestilence cling to you, until He has put an end to you in the land that you are entering to possess. ²²The LORD will strike you with consumption, fever, and inflammation, with scorching heat and drought, with blight and mildew; they shall hound you until you perish. ²³The skies above your

וְאֶת־הַמְּגְעֶרֶת בְּכָל־מִשְׁלַח יָדְךָ אֲשֶׁר תַּעֲשֶׂה עַד
הִשָּׁמֶדְךָ וְעַד־אֲבָדְךָ מַהֵר מִפְּנֵי רֹעַ מַעֲלָלֶיךָ
אֲשֶׁר עֲזַבְתָּנִי: 21 יַדְבֵּק יְהוָה בְּךָ אֶת־הַדָּבֶר עַד
כַּלֹּתוֹ אֹתְךָ מֵעַל הָאֲדָמָה אֲשֶׁר־אַתָּה בָא־שָׁמָּה
לְרִשְׁתָּהּ: 22 יַכְּכָה יְהוָה בַּשַּׁחֶפֶת וּבַקַּדַּחַת
וּבַדַּלֶּקֶת וּבַחַרְחֻר וּבַחֶרֶב וּבַשִּׁדָּפוֹן וּבַיֵּרָקוֹן
וּרְדָפוּךָ עַד אָבְדֶךָ: 23 וְהָיוּ שָׁמֶיךָ אֲשֶׁר עַל־

calamity Rather, "Curse," the antonym of *berakhah*, "blessing" (v. 8). The noun *me'erah* is from the same root as *'arur*, "cursed." In Malachi 3:9–11 it refers to the curses of drought and plant-destroying pests, both of which are mentioned in the catalogue of calamities below.

panic Rather, "Confusion," "Turmoil." *Mehumah* refers to the tumult and confusion caused by various types of phenomena, such as war, social disorder, and pestilence. See Comment to 7:23.²⁴ It could refer to several of the phenomena described in the following verses. In 7:23 God promised to strike Israel's enemies with *mehumah*; here, in contrast, He threatens to turn this affliction against Israel.

frustration That is, Cumbrance, Obstruction.²⁵ Hebrew *mig'eret* appears only here. Its meaning is inferred from the related verb *g-'-r*, "rebuke," which is often used in the sense of restraining, blowing back.²⁶ The use of the term in the present context is illuminated by Malachi 2:2–3 where, in referring to the Curse (*me'erah*), God threatens to restrain (*g-'-r*) the seed, meaning that He will prevent its growth or cause it to be destroyed (perhaps by pests; in Malachi 3:9–11 He promises to restrain [*g-'-r*] the locusts when He turns the curse into a blessing).²⁷ Here the term would refer to the drought of verses 23–24 and the crop failures of verses 38–42, though it may imply a wider range of obstacles, such as those in verses 30ff.

be utterly wiped out Literally "be destroyed and perish." These verbs are probably meant as hyperboles. The threat is real enough, but *'-v-d* and *sh-m-d* happen to Israel a total of eleven times in the chapter, and in verses 61ff, after Israel is "wiped out," there are still survivors to be exiled (see also 4:26–27). The verbs must mean what "wiped out" means in English slang, "ruined."²⁸

because of your evildoing Moses repeats regularly that the curse, like the blessing, is conditional.

forsaking Me Here Moses speaks in God's name, as sometimes happens in Deuteronomy; see verse 68 and Comment to 7:4, "from Me." On "forsake," see Comments to 4:2,19; 5:7; 13:6; 31:16.

21–26. Three main categories of punishment are introduced, disease (21–22), drought (23–24), and war (25–26). Compare the common triad "sword, famine, and pestilence."²⁹

21. pestilence A virulent epidemic.

22. Seven afflictions are listed, expressing the comprehensiveness of the harm. The exact nature of these afflictions is uncertain since ancient medical terminology was not as precise as modern nomenclature. The terms refer to symptoms that could stem from various causes.³⁰

consumption, fever, and inflammation *Shahefet*, *kaddahat*, and *dalleket*. Ibn Janah compares *shahefet* to Arabic *suhafun*, "consumption," "the disease that causes the body to waste away," perhaps tuberculosis. The meaning of *kaddahat* and *dalleket* is inferred from the fact that both derive from roots meaning "burn." In medieval Hebrew *kaddahat* was often used for malaria.³¹

scorching heat and drought Hebrew *harhur* and *herev* are ambiguous. The first, which appears only here, also stems from a root meaning "burn." Since the root is used of fever, charring of vines, and parched land, it is not certain whether the noun refers to an affliction of humans or of vegetation. *Herev*, as the Vulgate and Saadia recognized, is the equivalent of *horev*, "dryness," "heat," which is used of drought and the heat of the sun, but also of fever.³²

blight and mildew *Shiddafon* and *yerakon* (*yeraqon*) normally refer to crop afflictions. If

head shall be copper and the earth under you iron. ²⁴The
Lord will make the rain of your land dust, and sand shall
drop on you from the sky, until you are wiped out.

²⁵The Lord will put you to rout before your enemies;
you shall march out against them by a single road, but flee
from them by many roads; and you shall become a horror
to all the kingdoms of the earth. ²⁶Your carcasses shall
become food for all the birds of the sky and all the beasts
of the earth, with none to frighten them off.

²⁷The Lord will strike you with the Egyptian inflammation, with hemorrhoids, boil-scars, and itch, from which
you shall never recover.

רֹאשְׁךָ֖ נְחֹ֑שֶׁת וְהָאָ֥רֶץ אֲשֶׁר־תַּחְתֶּ֖יךָ בַּרְזֶֽל׃
²⁴ יִתֵּ֧ן יְהוָ֛ה אֶת־מְטַ֥ר אַרְצְךָ֖ אָבָ֣ק וְעָפָ֑ר מִן־
הַשָּׁמַ֙יִם֙ יֵרֵ֣ד עָלֶ֔יךָ עַ֖ד הִשָּׁמְדָֽךְ׃
²⁵ יִתֶּנְךָ֙ יְהוָ֜ה ׀ נִגָּף֮ לִפְנֵ֣י אֹיְבֶיךָ֒ בְּדֶ֤רֶךְ אֶחָד֙
תֵּצֵ֣א אֵלָ֔יו וּבְשִׁבְעָ֥ה דְרָכִ֖ים תָּנ֣וּס לְפָנָ֑יו וְהָיִ֣יתָ
לְזַעֲוָ֔ה לְכֹ֖ל מַמְלְכ֥וֹת הָאָֽרֶץ׃ ²⁶ וְהָיְתָ֤ה נִבְלָֽתְךָ֙
לְמַאֲכָ֔ל לְכָל־ע֥וֹף הַשָּׁמַ֖יִם וּלְבֶהֱמַ֣ת הָאָ֑רֶץ וְאֵ֖ין
מַחֲרִֽיד׃
²⁷ יַכְּכָ֙ה יְהוָ֜ה בִּשְׁחִ֤ין מִצְרַ֙יִם֙ ובעפלים וּבַגָּרָ֖ב
וּבֶחָ֑רֶס אֲשֶׁ֥ר לֹא־תוּכַ֖ל לְהֵרָפֵֽא׃

וּבַטְּחֹרִ֖ים ק׳　v. 27.

that is their meaning here, they serve as a transition to the theme of drought in the next verse. But
since the first five terms could all refer to human illness, it is possible that these do as well. In
Jeremiah 30:6 yerakon (yeraqon, lit. "yellowness," "greenness") refers to "pallor" or "sallowness" of
the human complexion. The cognate Akkadian amurriqānu means "jaundice," and Arabic yarqān
means both "mildew" and "jaundice." As an illness, shiddafon could refer to emaciation, since the
verb sh-d-f refers to the effect of hot winds on crops.³³

23–24. The theme of heat, and possibly of plant diseases, leads to drought, the reversal of
the promise of verse 12.

23. copper ... iron The sky will be too hard to yield rain and the soil too hard to plow.
Here nehoshet, "copper," probably means "bronze," a stronger alloy of copper and tin. The meaning
of these metaphors is clarified by a parallel Assyrian curse; see Excursus 27.³⁴ Virtually the same curse
appears in Leviticus 26:19.

24. In the absence of rain, the land will endure duststorms and sandstorms stirred up from
the waterless soil. The sirocco, or ḥamsin (the hot desert wind), "come[s] with a mist of fine sand,
veiling the sun, scorching vegetation, and bringing languor and fever to men" (Smith).³⁵

25–26. Horrifying military disaster, in contrast to the promises of verses 7 and 10.

25. horror Instead of respectful fear (v. 10), you will inspire horror in those who see
your rout.

26. Israel's fallen warriors will lie unburied and become food for scavenging animals. This
is a common threat in the Bible and elsewhere. Lack of burial was considered a fate worse than
death, since the spirits of the unburied would not be admitted to a resting place in the netherworld.
See Comment to 21:23.

with none to frighten them off To protect the corpses. The practice is poignantly illustrated by the case of Rizpah, daughter of Aiah, who camped for months by the bodies of her
children to protect them from scavengers.³⁶

27–28. Seven more human afflictions are listed, four physical, mostly affecting the skin,
and three psychological or psychosomatic.

27. Egyptian inflammation Sheḥin refers to skin inflammations of varying types and
degrees of severity; it appears again in verse 35. Conceivably the "Egyptian inflammation" is a type of
dermatitis characteristic of Egypt (see Comment to 7:15; in late antiquity diphtheria was referred to
as "Egyptian" or "Syrian ulcers," and elephantiasis was considered a peculiarly Egyptian disease,
though the present verse does not necessarily refer to either of these). More likely, it refers to the
type of inflammation that constituted the sixth of the ten plagues in Egypt, perhaps skin anthrax
(Exod. 9:8–12).³⁷ The "pestilence in the manner of Egypt" in Amos 4:10 is also ambiguous.

hemorrhoids This is the translation of the kere, teḥorim. The ketiv is ʿ-f-l-y-m (perhaps

²⁸The LORD will strike you with madness, blindness, and dismay. ²⁹You shall grope at noon as a blind man gropes in the dark; you shall not prosper in your ventures, but shall be constantly abused and robbed, with none to give help.

כח יַכְּכָה יְהֹוָה בְּשִׁגָּעוֹן וּבְעִוָּרוֹן וּבְתִמְהוֹן לֵבָב:
כט וְהָיִיתָ מְמַשֵּׁשׁ בַּצׇּהֳרַיִם כַּאֲשֶׁר יְמַשֵּׁשׁ הָעִוֵּר
בָּאֲפֵלָה וְלֹא תַצְלִיחַ אֶת־דְּרָכֶיךָ וְהָיִיתָ אַךְ עָשׁוּק
וְגָזוּל כׇּל־הַיָּמִים וְאֵין מוֹשִׁיעַ:

vocalized *ʿofalim*), "swellings," "tumors."[38] According to rabbinic tradition, *ʿ-f-l-y-m* also means "hemorrhoids," but was considered vulgar (like English "piles") and was therefore replaced with the more polite *teḥorim* when the Torah was read in the synagogue (another such substitution is found in v. 30).[39] Some modern scholars believe that *ʿ-f-l-y-m* originally referred to the swellings ("buboes") of bubonic plague, since the *ʿ-f-l-y-m/teḥorim* that plague the Philistines in 1 Samuel 5 are associated with mortality and, according to the Septuagint there, with mice.[40] In their view, the ancient interpretation as hemorrhoids, and hence the euphemism *teḥorim*, are due to misunderstanding. However, the interpretation "hemorrhoids" is supported by the paraphrases in the Septuagint and the Vulgate here ("in the seat," "in the part of your body from which excrement is cast out") and by Arabic *ʿafl/ʿafal*, which refers to swellings and other symptoms in the genital-anal area.

boil-scars and itch   *Garav* and *ḥeres* are also skin afflictions. To judge from Akkadian, Syriac, and Arabic cognates, they refer to types of dermatitis, possibly some serious ones.[41]

28-29.   Insanity, incomprehension, and bewilderment will incapacitate Israel and prevent it from acting sagaciously, causing failure and leaving it an easy prey for oppressors.

28.   **madness**   Ranting and carrying on wildly.

blindness   Since the other two afflictions in this verse are psychological, this probably refers metaphorically to incomprehension, stupefaction, or disorientation. Compare "bribes blind the eyes of the discerning" (16:19) and Lamentations 4:14, where the people of Jerusalem during the Babylonian conquest are described as wandering blindly through the streets. All three afflictions in the present verse appear in Zechariah 12:4, referring to panic and confusion affecting horse and rider in war. Similarly, in Babylonian texts, consternation in the face of battle and other situations is described as blurring of eyesight.[42] Another possibility is that this is real, psychosomatic blindness, induced by hysteria.[43]

dismay   Consternation, bewilderment.

29.   Psychological incapacitation will leave the people unable to act wisely; they will be as helpless as if they were blind. Compare Job 5:12–14: God "thwarts the designs of the crafty, / So that their hands cannot act wisely / . . . . The plans of the crafty go awry. / By day they encounter darkness, / At noon they grope as in the night."

in the dark   The point of this phrase is not quite clear, since blind people grope even in daylight.[44] The possibilities are (1) that "in the dark" means "in his darkness," (2) that the phrase refers to the first clause in the verse, "you will grope at noon [as if] in darkness, like a blind man does" (Ibn Janaḥ), or (3) that "a blind man" and "in the dark" are variant readings meaning, respectively, "as a blind man does" (with no reference to darkness) or "as one does in the dark" (with no reference to the blind).

abused and robbed   *ʿashuk ve-gazul.* The first term refers to maltreatment and being cheated out of one's property (see Comment to 24:14), the second to robbery and extortion. In the light of verses 30–33, they must refer to oppression by conquerors.[45]

with none to give help   *Moshiaʿ,* "reliever of distress," refers to kings, officials, or others who save the oppressed from their oppressors, and to military leaders who relieve the nation from foreign assailants. In the present context it could refer to either.[46]

30-34.   The Israelites will be helpless to resist oppression by their conquerors. Everything they have done will benefit only their assailants, who will rape their fiancées, deprive them of home and vineyard, seize their cattle, enslave their children, and consume their produce. The blessings of verses 4, 8, and 11 will be undone.

30If you pay the bride-price for a wife, another man shall enjoy her. If you build a house, you shall not live in it. If you plant a vineyard, you shall not harvest it. 31Your ox shall be slaughtered before your eyes, but you shall not eat of it; your ass shall be seized in front of you, and it shall not be returned to you; your flock shall be delivered to your enemies, with none to help you. 32Your sons and daughters shall be delivered to another people, while you look on; and your eyes shall strain for them constantly, but you shall be helpless. 33A people you do not know shall eat up the produce of your soil and all your gains; you shall be abused and downtrodden continually, 34until you are driven mad by what your eyes behold. 35The LORD will afflict you at the knees and thighs with a severe inflammation, from which you shall never recover—from the sole of your foot to the crown of your head.

30 אִשָּׁה תְאָרֵשׂ וְאִישׁ אַחֵר' יִשְׁגָּלֶנָּה בַּיִת תִּבְנֶה
וְלֹא־תֵשֵׁב בּוֹ כֶּרֶם תִּטַּע וְלֹא תְחַלְּלֶנּוּ: 31 שׁוֹרְךָ
טָבוּחַ לְעֵינֶיךָ וְלֹא תֹאכַל' מִמֶּנּוּ חֲמֹרְךָ גָּזוּל
מִלְּפָנֶיךָ וְלֹא יָשׁוּב לָךְ צֹאנְךָ' נְתֻנוֹת לְאֹיְבֶיךָ
וְאֵין לְךָ מוֹשִׁיעַ: 32 בָּנֶיךָ וּבְנֹתֶיךָ נְתֻנִים לְעַם
אַחֵר וְעֵינֶיךָ רֹאוֹת וְכָלוֹת אֲלֵיהֶם כָּל־הַיּוֹם וְאֵין
לְאֵל יָדֶךָ: 33 פְּרִי אַדְמָתְךָ וְכָל־יְגִיעֲךָ יֹאכַל עַם
אֲשֶׁר לֹא־יָדָעְתָּ וְהָיִיתָ רַק עָשׁוּק וְרָצוּץ כָּל־
הַיָּמִים: 34 וְהָיִיתָ מְשֻׁגָּע מִמַּרְאֵה עֵינֶיךָ אֲשֶׁר
תִּרְאֶה: 35 יַכְּכָה יְהֹוָה בִּשְׁחִין רָע עַל־הַבִּרְכַּיִם
וְעַל־הַשֹּׁקַיִם אֲשֶׁר לֹא־תוּכַל לְהֵרָפֵא מִכַּף רַגְלְךָ
וְעַד קָדְקֳדֶךָ:

v. 30. יִשְׁכָּבֶנָּה ק'

30. The most important personal endeavors, those that constitute grounds for draft deferment, will be made futile (see Comment to 20:5–7). The frustration of such efforts is so painful that the prophets often mention it as a threat, alongside violence, sometimes with the added indignity that a stranger or enemy will benefit from them in one's stead.[47]

another man will enjoy her Rather, "rape her," Hebrew y-sh-g-l-n-h (ketiv). The verb sh-g-l is used in this sense in prophetic threats; it is never used for legitimate sexual relations.[48] The kere reads yishkavennah, "lie with her,"[49] since sh-g-l was considered too vulgar for public reading in the synagogue (cf. v. 27).

harvest See Comment to 20:6.

31. Extortion of another's ox or ass is a proverbial example of oppression. Moses and Samuel, in defending their administration, deny these very acts, as does an earlier Canaanite ruler in the Amarna letters.[50]

32. ***delivered to another people*** Sold as slaves to a foreign land, so that their parents will never see them again.

your eyes shall strain for them Rather, "you shall cry your eyes out for them," literally, "your eyes shall run out [of tears] over them."[51] The same idiom appears in verse 65.

helpless To bring them back. 'ein le-'el yadekha is the negative form of the idiom yesh le-'el yad-. Although its meaning, "to have ability," is clear,[52] its etymology is not. Medieval Hebraists generally assumed that 'el comes from a stem '-y-l meaning "[have] power," and that the idiom stands for yesh 'el le-yad-, "[so-and-so's] hand has power."[53] Another possibility is "God/a god has [control of] so-and-so's hand, [enabling so-and-so] to. . . ."[54]

33. ***all your gains*** Yagia', literally, "toil," meaning all the products of your hard work. The use of this term, rather than "possessions," underscores the frustration of Israel's efforts.

34. Israel will not even be left with its sanity: its helpless suffering will drive its people mad, compounding the divinely sent madness of verse 28.

35. ***severe inflammation . . . from the sole of your foot to the crown of your head*** This may be a different ailment from the "Egyptian inflammation" of verse 27. Attempts to identify it are based on the fact that the knees and thighs are particularly involved (perhaps being affected first), that it extends from head to foot, and on other symptoms associated with it in the case of Job, who suffers the same affliction.[55] Suggested diagnoses include universalized eczema, smallpox, "joint leprosy," and psoriasis.[56]

³⁶The LORD will drive you, and the king you have set over you, to a nation unknown to you or your fathers, where you shall serve other gods, of wood and stone. ³⁷You shall be a consternation, a proverb, and a byword among all the peoples to which the LORD will drive you.

³⁸Though you take much seed out to the field, you shall gather in little, for the locust shall consume it. ³⁹Though

³⁶ יוֹלֵךְ יְהֹוָה אֹתְךָ וְאֶת־מַלְכְּךָ אֲשֶׁר תָּקִים עָלֶיךָ אֶל־גּוֹי אֲשֶׁר לֹא־יָדַעְתָּ אַתָּה וַאֲבֹתֶיךָ וְעָבַדְתָּ שָּׁם אֱלֹהִים אֲחֵרִים עֵץ וָאָבֶן: ³⁷ וְהָיִיתָ לְשַׁמָּה לְמָשָׁל וְלִשְׁנִינָה בְּכֹל הָעַמִּים אֲשֶׁר־יְנַהֶגְךָ יְהֹוָה שָׁמָּה: ³⁸ זֶרַע רַב תּוֹצִיא הַשָּׂדֶה וּמְעַט תֶּאֱסֹף כִּי

36–37. Israel will be exiled from its land. The deportation of defeated populations, partial or complete, was a common practice. It was done to provide population, manpower, or slaves for the conqueror, to enrich the conqueror through selling the deportees, or to break the resistance of rebellious peoples. Israel witnessed deportations of parts of its population and of some of its neighbors before its own final exiles in 720 B.C.E. and the 580's B.C.E.[57]

36. *and the king you have set over you* Literally, "your king whom you have set over you." The wording—it borders on saying, "the king whom you insisted on having"—reflects the same disparagement of the monarchy that is found in 17:14–20. Although Deuteronomy permits the establishment of a monarchy and insists that the king be chosen by God, it sees the very institution as an improperly motivated human innovation (17:14–15). The prophet Samuel, after establishing the monarchy, expresses the same attitude: "Well, the LORD has set a king over you! Here is the king that you have chosen, that you have asked for" (1 Sam. 12:13). The people had insisted on a monarchy in order to defend the nation, and the present verse shows how futile that hope will be if the people sin.[58]

Four Israelite kings were ultimately deported: Hoshea of northern Israel to Assyria, Jehoahaz of Judah to Egypt, and Jehoiachin and Zedekiah of Judah to Babylonia.[59]

unknown to you or your fathers Where you will feel completely alien.

where you shall serve other gods, of wood and stone See Comment to 4:28.

37. Israel's fate will shock other nations, a further reversal of the promise of verse 10. Compare verse 25.

consternation A source of consternation, or shock, to those who see your condition. Jeremiah describes this response graphically: it causes witnesses to hiss and shake their heads to ward off a like fate.[60]

a proverb An example to whom people will refer as an illustration of extreme misfortune.

a byword An object of repeated discussion. This interpretation derives Hebrew *sheninah* from *shannen*, "repeat." Another possibility is that the word means "the object of *sharp* or *cutting* remarks," from the more common *shanan*, "sharpen."[61]

all the peoples to which the LORD will drive you The northern Israelites and Judahites were exiled to various lands by their original captors, and migrated yet further afterward. The Bible mentions exiles and refugees in Phoenicia, Ammon, Moab, Edom, Syria, Assyria, Babylonia, Media, Persia, Elam, Asia Minor, Egypt, Nubia, and elsewhere.[62]

38–44. Destruction of crops by pests and the captivity of children will lead to economic dependence on resident aliens. These threats elaborate on the curse of "the issue of your womb and the produce of your soil" in verse 18; they are the converse of the promises in verses 11–13, where Israel's agricultural success leads to its economic domination of others.

38–40. All of Israel's hard work to produce the three staples of its agriculture—grain, wine, and oil—will be frustrated.

38. *the locust shall consume it* The crop. Locusts are types of grasshoppers that migrate in massive groups. They constitute one of the most devastating natural disasters. "The weight of a big swarm has been estimated at 15,000 tons, and its daily food consumption as equivalent to that of 1.5 million people. For days at a time, even for a week, locusts may darken the sky in a given region. . . .

you plant vineyards and till them, you shall have no wine to drink or store, for the worm shall devour them. ⁴⁰Though you have olive trees throughout your territory, you shall have no oil for anointment, for your olives shall drop off. ⁴¹Though you beget sons and daughters, they shall not remain with you, for they shall go into captivity. ⁴²The cricket shall take over all the trees and produce of your land.

⁴³The stranger in your midst shall rise above you higher and higher, while you sink lower and lower: ⁴⁴he shall be your creditor, but you shall not be his; he shall be the head and you the tail.

יַחְסְלֶ֖נּוּ הָאַרְבֶּֽה׃ 39 כְּרָמִ֥ים תִּטַּ֖ע וְעָבָ֑דְתָּ וְיַ֤יִן לֹֽא־תִשְׁתֶּה֙ וְלֹ֣א תֶאֱגֹ֔ר כִּ֥י תֹאכְלֶ֖נּוּ הַתֹּלָֽעַת׃ 40 זֵיתִ֛ים יִהְי֥וּ לְךָ֖ בְּכָל־גְּבוּלֶ֑ךָ וְשֶׁ֙מֶן֙ לֹ֣א תָס֔וּךְ כִּ֥י יִשַּׁ֖ל זֵיתֶֽךָ׃ 41 בָּנִ֥ים וּבָנ֖וֹת תּוֹלִ֑יד וְלֹא־יִהְי֣וּ לָ֔ךְ כִּ֥י יֵלְכ֖וּ בַּשֶּֽׁבִי׃ 42 כָּל־עֵצְךָ֖ וּפְרִ֣י אַדְמָתֶ֑ךָ יְיָרֵ֖שׁ הַצְּלָצַֽל׃ 43 הַגֵּר֙ אֲשֶׁ֣ר בְּקִרְבְּךָ֔ יַעֲלֶ֥ה עָלֶ֖יךָ מַ֣עְלָה מָּ֑עְלָה וְאַתָּ֥ה תֵרֵ֖ד מַ֥טָּה מָּֽטָּה׃ 44 ה֣וּא יַלְוְךָ֔ וְאַתָּ֖ה לֹ֣א תַלְוֶ֑נּוּ ה֚וּא יִהְיֶ֣ה לְרֹ֔אשׁ וְאַתָּ֖ה תִּהְיֶ֥ה לְזָנָֽב׃

Where they settle, almost nothing remains, not even the bark of trees less than two years old. . . . After a locust invasion . . . many animals starve to death. . . . Famine and destitution descend on the people."[63] Such an invasion is described in two chapters of exhaustive, graphic detail in the beginning of the Book of Joel: "Before them the land was like the Garden of Eden, behind them, a desolate waste." The eighth of the ten plagues in Egypt was an attack of locusts.

39. *worm* The larva of some type of moth such as the grape leaf folder, whose larvae defoliate grapevines, or the grape moth or berry moth, whose larvae eat the grapes.[64]

40. *no oil for anointment* In the hot, dry climate of the Middle East, one of the most important uses of olive oil was for anointing the skin, which was a necessary part of personal hygiene.[65]

41. The act of raising children will be frustrated just like the raising of crops. Children and crops are associated in the blessings of verse 4 and 7:13, as they are in the curses of verses 31–33.[66] For the analogy of children and crops, compare Psalm 128:3: "Your wife shall be like a fruitful vine within your house; your sons like olive saplings around your table."

42. *cricket* The onomatopoeic name *tselatsal* implies an animal that makes a chirping, or perhaps rasping sound. A common conjecture is that it is a variant of rabbinic Hebrew *tsartsur*, "cricket." If a destructive insect is meant, the grasshopper or katydid is likely.[67] However, "take over" could mean simply that after the captivity of the children (v. 41), there will be too few people to work the fields, which will then be overrun by insects.[68] In that case, the *tselatsal* could be the mole cricket, which eats roots and is quite injurious when abundant in crops and gardens but does not cause large-scale above-ground destruction.[69]

43–44. Just as agricultural bounty would bring economic superiority and creditor status (vv. 12–13), crop failure will cause impoverishment and debt. The economic collapse will be so calamitous that even the resident aliens (*gerim*), so often found among the poor, will become Israel's creditors and superiors. This is an extraordinary threat because the alien's economic dependence on Israelites would normally leave him worse off than they, even in hard times. However, Leviticus 25:47 shows that individual resident aliens might sometimes prosper more than some Israelites. The text apparently implies that Israel's economic collapse will be so great that whatever a few prosperous resident aliens have accumulated will put them in a position to make loans to Israelites and gain the upper hand economically.

THE SECOND GROUP OF THREATS (vv. 45–57)

This group of threats deals with conquest by other nations and its consequences. Verses 45–47 state the cause of the conquest and verse 48 summarizes its effect: starvation, poverty, and servitude. Verses 49–57 describe the course of the conquest and its gruesome climax: invasion, destruction of the food supply, siege, and cannibalism.

⁴⁵All these curses shall befall you; they shall pursue you and overtake you, until you are wiped out, because you did not heed the LORD your God and keep the commandments and laws that He enjoined upon you. ⁴⁶They shall serve as signs and proofs against you and your offspring for all time. ⁴⁷Because you would not serve the LORD your God in joy and gladness over the abundance of everything, ⁴⁸you shall have to serve—in hunger and thirst, naked and lacking everything—the enemies whom the LORD will let

וּבָ֣אוּ עָלֶ֗יךָ כָּל־הַקְּלָל֖וֹת הָאֵ֑לֶּה וּרְדָפ֙וּךָ֙ 45
וְהִשִּׂיג֔וּךָ עַ֖ד הִשָּֽׁמְדָ֑ךְ כִּי־לֹ֣א שָׁמַ֗עְתָּ בְּק֙וֹל֙ יְהֹוָ֣ה
אֱלֹהֶ֔יךָ לִשְׁמֹ֥ר מִצְוֺתָ֖יו וְחֻקֹּתָ֑יו אֲשֶׁ֖ר צִוָּֽךְ: 46 וְהָי֣וּ
בְךָ֔ לְא֖וֹת וּלְמוֹפֵ֑ת וּֽבְזַרְעֲךָ֖ עַד־עוֹלָֽם: 47 תַּ֗חַת
אֲשֶׁ֤ר לֹא־עָבַ֙דְתָּ֙ אֶת־יְהֹוָ֣ה אֱלֹהֶ֔יךָ בְּשִׂמְחָ֖ה
וּבְט֣וּב לֵבָ֑ב מֵרֹ֖ב כֹּֽל: 48 וְעָבַדְתָּ֣ אֶת־אֹֽיְבֶ֗יךָ
אֲשֶׁ֙ר יְשַׁלְּחֶ֤נּוּ יְהֹוָה֙ בָּ֔ךְ בְּרָעָ֧ב וּבְצָמָ֛א וּבְעֵירֹ֖ם

45.   This verse serves as a hinge joining verses 46–57 with verses 15–44. On the one hand, it serves as a conclusion to verses 15–44, joining with the nearly identical verse 15 to frame that entire section. Note how the order of the two main ideas in verses 15 and 45 is reversed, forming a chiasm (the following translation is literal to show the similarities):

> A. If you do not heed the LORD . . .
> > B. all these curses shall come upon you (15).
> > B'. All these curses shall come upon you . . .
> A'. because you did not heed the LORD (44).

On the other hand, by warning of the coming disasters and stating their cause, the verse serves as an introduction to verses 46–57, just as verses 15 and 58–59 introduce their sections.[70]

        pursue   See Comment to verse 15.

46.   *They shall serve as signs and proofs against you and your offspring for all time*   Rather, "They shall be signs and proofs, on you and your offspring, for all time."[71] "Signs and proofs" (Heb. 'ot and mofet) are the terms used for the ten plagues (4:34; 6:22; 34:11). Their befalling Israel is another example of the reversal of Israel's fate: because of its sins, Israel will be treated as Egypt was. Compare the Comment on "Egyptian inflammation" (v. 27), and the introductory Comment to verses 58–68; note also the Comment on "panic" (v. 20), about Israel being treated like its enemies.

    What the signs and proofs signify is not stated explicitly. It may be the guilt of the sinful generation,[72] as elaborated in 29:21–27: Israel's fate will cause people to ask what could have caused such a disaster, and they will be told that it was Israel's betrayal of God that led Him to do this. Another possibility is that the disasters will serve as a *warning*, demonstrating what happens to those who disobey God.[73]

        for all time   In this chapter Moses states the threats in their starkest and most effective form. He does not address the possibility of repentance and restoration, as he does in 4:29–31; 30:1–10.

47–48.   Israel's punishment will be the reverse of its prosperity: having refused to serve God when it enjoyed abundance, it will be forced to serve a conqueror in poverty.

        in joy and gladness over the abundance of everything   That is, when you were joyful and glad because of abundance.[74]

48.   This verse sums up the main themes of verses 49–57, conquest and utter privation (ḥoser kol, "lack of everything"; the phrase recurs in verse 57, where it is rendered "utter want").

        you shall have to serve—in hunger and thirst, naked and lacking everything—the enemies whom the LORD will let loose upon you   The translation obscures the way this verse corresponds to the preceding one. The Hebrew word order makes this clear: "Because you would not serve the LORD . . . in joy and gladness over the abundance of everything, you shall have to serve your enemy in hunger and thirst and nakedness and lack of everything." The exact reversal of Israel's fate will make the justice of its punishment manifest. The logic of a punishment that is the mirror image of

loose against you. He will put an iron yoke upon your neck until He has wiped you out.

⁴⁹The LORD will bring a nation against you from afar, from the end of the earth, which will swoop down like the eagle—a nation whose language you do not understand, ⁵⁰a ruthless nation, that will show the old no regard and the young no mercy. ⁵¹It shall devour the offspring of your cattle and the produce of your soil, until you have been wiped out, leaving you nothing of new grain, wine, or oil, of the calving of your herds and the lambing of your flocks, until it has brought you to ruin. ⁵²It shall shut you

וּבְחֹ֫סֶר כֹּ֑ל וְנָתַ֞ן עֹ֤ל בַּרְזֶל֙ עַל־צַוָּארֶ֔ךָ עַ֖ד הִשְׁמִיד֥וֹ אֹתָֽךְ׃

49 יִשָּׂ֣א יְהֹוָה֩ עָלֶ֨יךָ גּ֤וֹי מֵֽרָחֹק֙ מִקְצֵ֣ה הָאָ֔רֶץ כַּאֲשֶׁ֥ר יִדְאֶ֖ה הַנָּ֑שֶׁר גּ֕וֹי אֲשֶׁ֥ר לֹא־תִשְׁמַ֖ע לְשֹׁנֽוֹ׃ 50 גּ֖וֹי עַ֣ז פָּנִ֑ים אֲשֶׁ֨ר לֹא־יִשָּׂ֤א פָנִים֙ לְזָקֵ֔ן וְנַ֖עַר לֹ֥א יָחֹֽן׃ 51 וְ֠אָכַ֠ל פְּרִ֨י בְהֶמְתְּךָ֥ וּפְרִֽי־אַדְמָתְךָ֮ עַ֣ד הִשָּֽׁמְדָ֒ךְ֒ אֲשֶׁ֨ר לֹֽא־יַשְׁאִ֜יר לְךָ֗ דָּגָן֙ תִּיר֣וֹשׁ וְיִצְהָ֔ר שְׁגַ֥ר אֲלָפֶ֖יךָ וְעַשְׁתְּרֹ֣ת צֹאנֶ֑ךָ עַ֥ד הַאֲבִיד֖וֹ אֹתָֽךְ׃ 52 וְהֵצַ֨ר לְךָ֜ בְּכׇל־שְׁעָרֶ֗יךָ עַ֣ד רֶ֤דֶת חֹמֹתֶ֙יךָ֙

the prior situation is explained by Midrash Hagadol: "[It is] so that they may know what they have lost, just as in the verse: 'They will be subject to him [the king of Egypt], and they will know the difference between serving Me and serving earthly kingdoms' [2 Chron. 12:8]."⁷⁵

let loose   See Comment to verse 2.

iron yoke   The yoke is a familiar metaphor expressing submission to the rule of gods and kings in the ancient Near East. The metaphor is not always pejorative. It sometimes refers to loyal service to a legitimate ruler. It is used in that sense in the Jewish concept of *'ol malkhut shamayim*, "the yoke of the Kingdom of Heaven," meaning submission to the authority of God.⁷⁶ Here, however, the context is punitive. Since yokes were normally made of wood, an iron yoke implies exceptionally heavy, unbreakable servitude.

49. a nation . . . from afar, from the end of the earth . . . whose language you do not understand   The enemy will be utterly alien to Israel, even stranger than the "people you do not know" of verse 33, and Israel will be unable to communicate with it. It will come from so far away that its language will be unintelligible, unlike Israel's close neighbors who spoke languages similar to Hebrew. No specific nation is meant here. Similar terms are used by the prophets to describe Assyria and an unnamed nation that turned out to be Babylonia.⁷⁷

which will swoop down like the eagle   Or the griffon vulture; see Comment to 14:12. The simile refers to the suddenness, speed, and power of the attack. Habakkuk uses it to describe the Chaldeans: "Their steeds gallop . . . come flying from afar. Like vultures [the same word, *nesher*, is used] rushing toward food, they all come, bent on rapine. . . ."⁷⁸

50. ruthless   Hebrew *'az panim*, literally, "harsh of face." Elsewhere in the Bible this idiom refers to impudence, shamelessness.⁷⁹ Here, this would allude to the enemy's shamelessness in mistreating the elderly and the young. Other possible translations are "angry looking," "fierce looking,"⁸⁰ or "expressionless" (like Hebrew *kesheh-panim*).⁸¹ Whatever the precise sense, "harsh of face" is complemented by "show no regard"—literally, "not regard the face"—in the following clause.⁸²

will show the old no regard and the young no mercy   These are the ways of a brutal nation. The Medians and Babylonians are decribed thus in the books of Isaiah and Lamentations.⁸³

51.   The enemy will devastate the basis of Israel's economy: the three staple crops, the main draught animal, and the source of dairy products and wool. Compare verses 38–40.

the offspring of your cattle and the produce of your soil . . . the calving of your herds and the lambing of your flocks   The list of what the enemy will consume is the same as the list of blessings promised in verse 4, with one notable omission, "the issue of your womb." In the gruesome climax of the invasion, that blessing will be consumed by Israel itself (v. 53).

the calving of your herd and the lambing of your flock   See Comment to 7:13.

wiped out . . . to ruin   See Comment to verse 20.

52. shut you up   Literally, "press you," "distress you."⁸⁴

up in all your towns throughout your land until every mighty, towering wall in which you trust has come down. And when you are shut up in all your towns throughout your land that the LORD your God has assigned to you, 53you shall eat your own issue, the flesh of your sons and daughters that the LORD your God has assigned to you, because of the desperate straits to which your enemy shall reduce you. 54He who is most tender and fastidious among you shall be too mean to his brother and the wife of his bosom and the children he has spared 55to share

הַגְּבֹהוֹת וְהַבְּצֻרוֹת אֲשֶׁר אַתָּה בֹּטֵחַ בָּהֵן בְּכָל־
אַרְצֶךָ וְהֵצַר לְךָ בְּכָל־שְׁעָרֶיךָ בְּכָל־אַרְצְךָ אֲשֶׁר
נָתַן יְהוָה אֱלֹהֶיךָ לָךְ: 53 וְאָכַלְתָּ פְרִי־בִטְנְךָ בְּשַׂר
בָּנֶיךָ וּבְנֹתֶיךָ אֲשֶׁר נָתַן־לְךָ יְהוָה אֱלֹהֶיךָ בְּמָצוֹר
וּבְמָצוֹק אֲשֶׁר־יָצִיק לְךָ אֹיְבֶךָ: 54 הָאִישׁ הָרַךְ בְּךָ
וְהֶעָנֹג מְאֹד תֵּרַע עֵינוֹ בְאָחִיו וּבְאֵשֶׁת חֵיקוֹ
וּבְיֶתֶר בָּנָיו אֲשֶׁר יוֹתִיר: 55 מִתֵּת | לְאַחַד מֵהֶם

in all your towns throughout your land There will be no place to escape.

until every . . . wall . . . has come down Until the enemy has breached the walls with battering rams and razed them.

mighty Rather, "lofty."

in which you trust This phrase is a warning against misplaced trust. If the people disobey God, powerful fortifications will provide no more protection than they did for the Canaanites and the Amorites (see 1:28; 3:5; 9:1).

And when you are shut up, in all your towns throughout your land Literally, "It shall press you in all your towns in all your land."[85]

53–57. Besieged and starving, the people will turn to cannibalism. The famine will cause such desperation that even the most natural instincts of compassion will be destroyed: husbands and wives will turn against each other and their own children, refusing to share their meager supply of human flesh with anybody. Under such circumstances, cannibalism has taken place throughout history. Ancient cases are reported from Samaria, Jerusalem,[86] and elsewhere in the Near East.[87]

53. your own issue Literally, "the issue of your womb." The threat is made more painful by the use of the very phrase that appears in verse 4 as part of the blessings. The following phrase, literally, "that the LORD your God has given to you," has the same effect.

desperate straits Hebrew *be-matsor u-ve-matsok.* The phrase is a leitmotif of this section, recurring in verses 55 and 57. The second word, *matsok,* means "straits." The first, *matsor,* normally means "siege." The translation presumes that here it stands for *metsar,* "distress," which literally also means "straits." In that case, the phrase means "distress and straits," hence "desperate straits." If that is the sense intended here, the form *matsor* may have been chosen because it rhymes with *matsok.* The text may well intend both meanings as a double-entendre.

54–55. The most pampered of men will turn to the most disgusting of foods and will guard it so jealously that he will not share it with his dearest relatives.

54. fastidious Rather, "pampered," "indulged." For this sense note the habits of the woman described in the same terms in verse 56.

the wife of his bosom The wife who lies in his bosom, toward whom he would be expected to have the warmest feelings. The husband is described similarly in verse 56. The idiom is used in 13:7, where one must suppress his affection for his dearest relatives if they advocate idolatry.

spared Whom he has not slaughtered and eaten. The Hebrew could also mean "who are still left to him," who have survived the invasion and famine. This is another ironic use of a term from the promises, for in verse 11 the same verb (*hotir*) refers to God's giving Israel an abundance of children, cattle, and produce. There it refers to plenty, here to the barest survival.

56–57. The most pampered of women will likewise turn to the most disgusting of foods and guard it jealously. Newly delivered mothers will secretly consume their newborn and the afterbirth to avoid sharing them with their husbands and older children.

with any of them the flesh of the children that he eats, because he has nothing else left as a result of the desperate straits to which your enemy shall reduce you in all your towns. 56And she who is most tender and dainty among you, so tender and dainty that she would never venture to set a foot on the ground, shall begrudge the husband of her bosom, and her son and her daughter, 57the afterbirth that issues from between her legs and the babies she bears; she shall eat them secretly, because of utter want, in the desperate straits to which your enemy shall reduce you in your towns.

58If you fail to observe faithfully all the terms of this Teaching that are written in this book, to reverence this honored and awesome Name, the LORD your God, 59the

מִבְּשַׂר בָּנָיו אֲשֶׁר יֹאכֵל מִבְּלִי הִשְׁאִיר־לוֹ כֹּל בְּמָצוֹר וּבְמָצוֹק אֲשֶׁר יָצִיק לְךָ אֹיִבְךָ בְּכָל־ שְׁעָרֶיךָ: 56 הָרַכָּה בְךָ וְהָעֲנֻגָּה אֲשֶׁר לֹא־נִסְּתָה כַף־רַגְלָהּ הַצֵּג עַל־הָאָרֶץ מֵהִתְעַנֵּג וּמֵרֹךְ תֵּרַע עֵינָהּ בְּאִישׁ חֵיקָהּ וּבִבְנָהּ וּבְבִתָּהּ: 57 וּבְשִׁלְיָתָהּ הַיּוֹצֵת* | מִבֵּין רַגְלֶיהָ וּבְבָנֶיהָ אֲשֶׁר תֵּלֵד כִּי־ תֹאכְלֵם בְּחֹסֶר־כֹּל בַּסָּתֶר בְּמָצוֹר וּבְמָצוֹק אֲשֶׁר יָצִיק לְךָ אֹיִבְךָ בִּשְׁעָרֶיךָ: 58 אִם־לֹא תִשְׁמֹר לַעֲשׂוֹת אֶת־כָּל־דִּבְרֵי הַתּוֹרָה הַזֹּאת הַכְּתוּבִים בַּסֵּפֶר הַזֶּה לְיִרְאָה אֶת־הַשֵּׁם הַנִּכְבָּד וְהַנּוֹרָא הַזֶּה אֵת יְהוָה אֱלֹהֶיךָ: 59 וְהִפְלָא

v. 57. חסר אל״ף

56. dainty That is, "pampered," "indulged." See Comment to verse 54.

would never venture to set a foot on the ground But was accustomed to being carried on a litter or portable chair, or to riding in a carriage.[88]

shall begrudge . . . the afterbirth[89] The verb is the same idiom as that translated "be mean" in verse 54, namely "eye grudgingly."

THE THIRD GROUP OF THREATS (vv. 58–68)

58–68. The siege and starvation of verses 51–57 will lead to disease, and Israel will be decimated and forced into exile. These disasters will not only undo the blessings promised above, but will completely reverse Israel's history: God will inflict on Israel the sicknesses they feared in Egypt and think they have escaped; He will reverse the multiplication they enjoyed in Egypt, which He had promised to the patriarchs; He will remove Israel from the promised land that was the ultimate goal of the Exodus; they will be forced to worship false gods instead of the Lord; and He will return them to Egypt and they will *seek* to become slaves there.[90]

58. Lest the long catalogue of threats induce resignation, Moses repeats that they are conditional. This verse, like verse 45, serves as a hinge joining this section with the preceding one. Though it is clearly a conditional sentence introducing verse 59, by itself it can also be read as the conclusion to the preceding section: "[All this will happen] if you fail to observe. . . ." This equivocality is made possible by the fact that the verse does not begin with *ve-hayah*, "And it shall come to pass," as does verse 15.

all the terms of this Teaching that are written in this book Moses first writes down the Teaching in 31:9. The reference here to "*this*" book indicates that his attention is already focused primarily on later generations that will receive the Teaching only in its written form. See also verse 61 and 29:19.

to reverence . . . the LORD See Comments to 4:10 and 6:2. Moses chooses this term, rather than "serve" or "love," since the aim of this speech is to deter sin by inculcating fear of punishment.[91]

this Name God's name which, as the next phrase shows, is synonymous with God Himself. This is a common usage in the Bible, especially in poetry: one loves and fears God's name, blesses, thanks, and praises it, while sinners scorn and revile it.[92] Usually the expression "His name" or "Your name" is used. "*The* Name" (*Ha-Shem*), with no suffix, is found again only in Leviticus 24:11. The same term became a common way of referring to God in later times and is so used today, though it may not have developed directly from this biblical usage.[93]

LORD will inflict extraordinary plagues upon you and your offspring, strange and lasting plagues, malignant and chronic diseases. 60He will bring back upon you all the sicknesses of Egypt that you dreaded so, and they shall cling to you. 61Moreover, the LORD will bring upon you all the other diseases and plagues that are not mentioned in this book of Teaching, until you are wiped out. 62You shall be left a scant few, after having been as numerous as the stars in the skies, because you did not heed the command of the LORD your God. 63And as the LORD once delighted in making you prosperous and many, so will the LORD now delight in causing you to perish and in wiping you out; you shall be torn from the land that you are about to enter and possess.

64The LORD will scatter you among all the peoples from one end of the earth to the other, and there you shall serve

יְהוָה אֶת־מַכֹּתְךָ וְאֵת מַכּוֹת זַרְעֶךָ מַכּוֹת גְּדֹלוֹת
וְנֶאֱמָנוֹת וָחֳלָיִם רָעִים וְנֶאֱמָנִים: 60 וְהֵשִׁיב בְּךָ
אֵת כָּל־מַדְוֵה מִצְרַיִם אֲשֶׁר יָגֹרְתָּ מִפְּנֵיהֶם וְדָבְקוּ
בָּךְ: 61 גַּם כָּל־חֳלִי וְכָל־מַכָּה אֲשֶׁר לֹא כָתוּב
בְּסֵפֶר הַתּוֹרָה הַזֹּאת יַעְלֵם יְהוָה עָלֶיךָ עַד
הִשָּׁמְדָךְ: 62 וְנִשְׁאַרְתֶּם בִּמְתֵי מְעָט תַּחַת אֲשֶׁר
הֱיִיתֶם כְּכוֹכְבֵי הַשָּׁמַיִם לָרֹב כִּי־לֹא שָׁמַעְתָּ בְּקוֹל
יְהוָה אֱלֹהֶיךָ: 63 וְהָיָה כַּאֲשֶׁר־שָׂשׂ יְהוָה עֲלֵיכֶם
לְהֵיטִיב אֶתְכֶם וּלְהַרְבּוֹת אֶתְכֶם כֵּן יָשִׂישׂ יְהוָה
עֲלֵיכֶם לְהַאֲבִיד אֶתְכֶם וּלְהַשְׁמִיד אֶתְכֶם
וְנִסַּחְתֶּם מֵעַל הָאֲדָמָה אֲשֶׁר־אַתָּה בָא־שָׁמָּה
לְרִשְׁתָּהּ: 64 וֶהֱפִיצְךָ יְהוָה בְּכָל־הָעַמִּים מִקְצֵה הָאָרֶץ וְעַד־
קְצֵה הָאָרֶץ וְעָבַדְתָּ שָּׁם אֱלֹהִים אֲחֵרִים אֲשֶׁר

59–62. Israel will be decimated by disease. As Abravanel notes, this is a consequence of the siege described in the previous section. During a long siege, contagion is fostered by crowding, decaying corpses, and the flourishing of rats, lice, and fleas in the city. The inevitable starvation decreases resistance, causes deficiency diseases, and leads desperate people to ingest harmful or contaminated foods and other substances.[94] Epidemics of typhus, typhoid, scurvy, intestinal diseases, and dysentery are common results.[95]

59. *strange* Rather, "great," unusually severe.

lasting . . . chronic The Hebrew word in both cases is *ne'eman*, best known in the sense of "reliable, faithful, trusty." Here it means "long lasting,"[96] as in Proverbs 27:6, "Wounds by a loved one are long lasting." English "constant" has both senses of the word.

60. God will afflict Israel with the sicknesses of Egypt, from which He had promised to protect them if they would obey Him (7:15; Exod. 15:26).

bring back If *heshiv* is meant literally, it would imply that while in Egypt Israel suffered from the diseases endemic to that land. See Comment to 7:15. However, *heshiv bekha* could also mean "turn against you."[97] Perhaps this verb was chosen to echo *heshiv* in verse 68, in which Israel's return to its Egyptian experience is intensified: God will bring Israel itself back to Egypt.

61. Statements like this often appear in ancient Near Eastern documents at the end of lists to indicate that they stand for more than is mentioned.[98] In modern Hebrew the expression "a plague that is not written in the Torah" refers to a severe and unusual affliction.

62. Israel's population will revert to its original small size of the days prior to its multiplication in Egypt. The phrases "scant few" (*metei me'at*) and "as numerous as the stars in the skies" are the very terms that were used earlier to describe the beginning and culmination of that growth (see 1:9; 10:22; 26:5).

63–68. Exile and its terrors. The few who survive famine and disease will be deported and will be so distressed that they will seek relief by trying to sell themselves into bondage.

63. *delighted in . . . delight in* That is, "was determined to . . . will be determined to."[99]

making you perish and wiping you out See Comment to verse 20.

you shall be torn from the land That is, deported.[100]

64. *you shall serve other gods, wood and stone, whom neither you nor your ancestors have experienced* See verse 36 and Comments to 4:28 and 11:28.

272

other gods, wood and stone, whom neither you nor your ancestors have experienced. 65Yet even among those nations you shall find no peace, nor shall your foot find a place to rest. The LORD will give you there an anguished heart and eyes that pine and a despondent spirit. 66The life you face shall be precarious; you shall be in terror, night and day, with no assurance of survival. 67In the morning you shall say, "If only it were evening!" and in the evening you shall say, "If only it were morning!"—because of what your heart shall dread and your eyes shall see. 68The LORD will send you back to Egypt in galleys, by a route which I told you you should not see again. There you shall offer yourselves for sale to your enemies as male and female slaves, but none will buy.

65 וּבַגּוֹיִם הָהֵם לֹא תַרְגִּיעַ וְלֹא־יִהְיֶה מָנוֹחַ לְכַף־רַגְלֶךָ וְנָתַן יְהוָה לְךָ שָׁם לֵב רַגָּז וְכִלְיוֹן עֵינַיִם וְדַאֲבוֹן נָפֶשׁ: 66 וְהָיוּ חַיֶּיךָ תְּלֻאִים לְךָ מִנֶּגֶד וּפָחַדְתָּ לַיְלָה וְיוֹמָם וְלֹא תַאֲמִין בְּחַיֶּיךָ: 67 בַּבֹּקֶר תֹּאמַר מִי־יִתֵּן עֶרֶב וּבָעֶרֶב תֹּאמַר מִי־יִתֵּן בֹּקֶר מִפַּחַד לְבָבְךָ אֲשֶׁר תִּפְחָד וּמִמַּרְאֵה עֵינֶיךָ אֲשֶׁר תִּרְאֶה: 68 וֶהֱשִׁיבְךָ יְהוָה | מִצְרַיִם בָּאֳנִיּוֹת בַּדֶּרֶךְ אֲשֶׁר אָמַרְתִּי לְךָ לֹא־תֹסִיף עוֹד לִרְאֹתָהּ וְהִתְמַכַּרְתֶּם שָׁם לְאֹיְבֶיךָ לַעֲבָדִים וְלִשְׁפָחוֹת וְאֵין קֹנֶה: ס

65. Even in exile Israel will find no relief from the terrors left behind at home.

eyes that pine Rather, "cried-out eyes." See Comment to verse 32.

despondent spirit Rather, "a dry throat," a symptom of grief or depression.[101]

66. The exiles will live in constant suspense, unable to feel any confidence of survival.

67. Buffeted by the actual horrors of the day and the terrors they imagine in bed at night, they will find each segment of day so unbearable that they will long for the next. The verse is chiastic: the first and last clauses refer to the visible horrors of the day, and the middle two clauses refer to those imagined at night.[102]

68. The final reversal of history: Israel will be returned to Egypt and, what is even worse, they will seek to sell themselves as slaves to support themselves; the Egyptians, who once would not release them from slavery, will now refuse to have them back.

send you back to Egypt The Hebrew (*heshivekha*), Literally, "will bring you back to Egypt," echoes the threat of verse 60, "will bring back upon you all the sicknesses of Egypt." Their return may be for the purpose of escaping famine, as in the case of Israel's original descent to Egypt.[103]

in galleys Hebrew *'oniyyot* refers to ships in general; the translation "galleys" (ships manned by slaves) is an attempt to show a connection between ships and the punitive context, especially the reference to slavery in the second part of the verse. However, that reference shows that the Israelites will not be brought to Egypt as slaves, but will seek to enter slavery only after they arrive. Hence, Meklenburg and some modern commentators suggest translating *bo-'oniyyot* as "in mourning, in a lamentful condition." They understand *'oniyyot* as *'aniyyot*, an abstract plural of *'aniyah*, "mourning, lamenting."[104]

by a route which I told you you should not see again Rather, "a direction, or destination [*derekh*], I promised you would never see again." This verse seems to combine elements of 17:16, "the LORD has said to you, 'You must [or will] never go back that *route* [*derekh*] again,'" and Exodus 14:13, "The Egyptians whom you see today you will never *see* again." See Comment to 17:16. With this punishment, God will void His promise.

I told you Here Moses speaks in God's name, as in verse 20. According to 17:16, it was God who made this promise.

you shall offer yourselves for sale In Egypt they will experience poverty so bleak that in order to obtain food and shelter they will seek to become slaves.[105] For self-sale by impoverished people, see Leviticus 25:39 and the introductory Comment to 15:12–18.

none will buy Commentators suggest that so many Israelites will attempt to sell them-

⁶⁹These are the terms of the covenant which the LORD commanded Moses to conclude with the Israelites in the land of Moab, in addition to the covenant which He had made with them at Horeb.

69 אֵ֣לֶּה דִבְרֵ֣י הַבְּרִ֗ית אֲשֶׁר־צִוָּ֤ה יְהוָה֙ אֶת־מֹשֶׁ֔ה
לִכְרֹ֛ת אֶת־בְּנֵ֥י יִשְׂרָאֵ֖ל בְּאֶ֣רֶץ מוֹאָ֑ב מִלְּבַ֣ד
הַבְּרִ֔ית אֲשֶׁר־כָּרַ֥ת אִתָּ֖ם בְּחֹרֵֽב: פ

selves that the market will be glutted, that their suffering will have left them unfit for work, or that the Egyptians will not want to risk a repetition of what happened when their ancestors had Israelite slaves.[106] The text gives no reason for the refusal; the main thing is the refusal itself, which represents the ultimate irony and tragedy: those who once refused to free the Israelites from slavery will now refuse to take them back and relieve their poverty.

SUBSCRIPTION TO THE COVENANT (v. 69)

69. This subscription concludes the covenant made in the land of Moab, whose terms and consequences are presented in 4:44–26:19 and chapter 28. It is comparable to the subscriptions in Leviticus 27:34, Numbers 36:13, and elsewhere.[107] Abravanel and some modern scholars argue that the verse is really an introduction to the third discourse (chaps. 29–30), in which Moses prepares the people to enter the covenant and warns them about violating it.[108] However, the phrase "terms of the covenant" refers to specific legal obligations and their stated consequences, and applies to the laws, blessings, and curses of the preceding chapters much more readily than it does to the exhortations of chapters 29–30.[109] Literally, too, this verse belongs with the second discourse, since it echoes Moses' opening words there (5:2); together the two passages form a frame around that discourse (see introductory Comment to 4:44–28:69). The Masoretic and Samaritan *parashah* divisions agree that this verse refers to what precedes it.[110]

the covenant which He made with them at Horeb According to 4:13 and 5:2–19, the covenant at Horeb consisted of the Decalogue. The following laws and teachings, promises and warnings in chapters 6–26 and 28, which constitute the terms of the present covenant made in Moab, were given by God to Moses privately. Moses first communicated them to the people in Moab in the present long address (4:44–28:68) and then had the people commit themselves by covenant to observe them. But Deuteronomy regards these laws as also implicitly part of the Horeb covenant, since they are the direct continuation of God's words at Horeb and the people had pledged there to observe them (5:24). This means that the covenants of Horeb and Moab are virtually identical. This occasions no surprise, since the covenant that chapter 27 orders to be made at Shechem is also identical to the present one.

MOSES' THIRD DISCOURSE: EXHORTATIONS TO OBSERVE THE COVENANT MADE IN MOAB (chaps. 29–30)

Moses has presented all the terms of the second covenant to the people (4:44–26:19; 28). He now summons them to ratify it. First, he reviews the experiences that serve as its basis (29:1–8). Then he reminds the people of the purpose of their assembly: every man, woman, and child is to join the covenant, which is binding on all future generations as well (vv. 9–14). Once again he warns Israel of the consequences of disobeying the conditions of the covenant, even in secret (vv. 15–28). In 30:1–10 he digresses to assure Israel that if it sins and brings the punishment of exile upon itself, but sincerely repents while in exile, God will restore it to the land and His favor. Moses then resumes his

29

Moses summoned all Israel and said to them:

You have seen all that the LORD did before your very eyes in the land of Egypt, to Pharaoh and to all his courtiers and to his whole country: ²the wondrous feats that you saw with your own eyes, those prodigious signs and marvels. ³Yet to this day the LORD has not given you a mind to understand or eyes to see or ears to hear.

כ"ט שביעי וַיִּקְרָא מֹשֶׁה אֶל־כָּל־יִשְׂרָאֵל וַיֹּאמֶר אֲלֵהֶם אַתֶּם רְאִיתֶם אֵת כָּל־אֲשֶׁר עָשָׂה יְהוָה לְעֵינֵיכֶם בְּאֶרֶץ מִצְרַיִם לְפַרְעֹה וּלְכָל־עֲבָדָיו וּלְכָל־אַרְצוֹ: ² הַמַּסּוֹת הַגְּדֹלֹת אֲשֶׁר רָאוּ עֵינֶיךָ הָאֹתֹת וְהַמֹּפְתִים הַגְּדֹלִים הָהֵם: ³ וְלֹא־נָתַן יְהוָה לָכֶם לֵב לָדַעַת וְעֵינַיִם לִרְאוֹת וְאָזְנַיִם לִשְׁמֹעַ עַד הַיּוֹם הַזֶּה:

summons to the covenant and assures Israel that its terms are not too difficult to fulfill (30:11–14). He concludes by stating plainly that what he is offering Israel as a nation is the opportunity to choose between life and death (30:15–30).[1]

CHAPTER 29 THE BASIS OF THE COVENANT (vv. 1–8)

Moses first reminds the people of the Exodus, the basis of the covenant, just as he did when God originally proposed the covenant to Israel at Sinai. His opening words are similar to those God had used on that occasion: "You have seen what I did to the Egyptians" (Exod. 19:4). Moses states that although Israel saw the wonders that God performed against Egypt, it was not intellectually capable of learning the proper lessons from that experience, as shown by its rebellion at Kadesh and elsewhere. He then explains—reverting to the themes of his introductory speeches in 1:1–4:40 and 8:2–5—that that is why God led Israel through the wilderness for forty years, sustaining it by supernatural means to teach it His full power, and then granting it victory over Sihon and Og. These experiences should enable Israel, in renewing its covenant with God, to realize the wisdom of obeying Him and the folly of disobeying Him.[2] Moses' explanation of God's aim in leading Israel through the wilderness indicates that, as he looks back on the experience, he realizes that God had an educational purpose in mind in addition to the punitive one announced at the outset (1:34–35; Num. 14:20–35).

1. *summoned* This translation of Hebrew *kara'*, literally, "called," implies that Moses had dismissed the people after his previous address, perhaps to allow them time to reflect on it so that they could enter the covenant in full awareness of the solemnity of their action. "Called" could also mean that Moses simply continued proclaiming to the people on the same occasion as before.

You have seen . . . before your very eyes In Deuteronomy Moses frequently stresses that he is appealing to the people on the basis of their own personal experience. See verse 16 and Comments to 1:19; 4:9; 11:1–9. The earliest experience, what God did to Egypt, was witnessed only by those now forty and older, but the younger generation witnessed God's providence in the wilderness and the victory over Sihon and Og.[3]

2. *wondrous feats . . . prodigious signs and marvels* The plagues inflicted on Egypt. See Comment to 4:34 (there, *massot*, "feats," is translated as "prodigious acts").

3. Israel witnessed the events in Egypt, but could not understand what they implied about God's power and the obligation to obey Him. The people lacked the insight ("mind" [literally, "heart"], "eyes," and "ears")[4] to interpret the events properly. Moses must have inferred this obtuseness from Israel's refusal to trust and obey God at Kadesh and from its other provocations in the wilderness (1:26–43; 9:7–8,22–24).[5] It is characteristic of Deuteronomy that Moses sees these incidents as typifying the wilderness wanderings as a whole, as noted in the Comment to 9:7.

Yet to this day the LORD has not given you a mind to understand Rather, "But the LORD did not give you a mind to understand . . . until today."[6] The NJPS translation implies that even now Israel lacks the capacity to understand its experiences properly.[7] If that were Moses' meaning, his appeal that Israel observe the covenant would be hopeless. Verses 6–7 indicate that now, after forty years, Israel has shown that it finally does understand and trust in God's power (see Comment there).

Moses' statement that God had not given Israel the capacity to understand its experiences has

4I led you through the wilderness forty years; the clothes on your back did not wear out, nor did the sandals on your feet; 5you had no bread to eat and no wine or other intoxicant to drink—that you might know that I the LORD am your God.

6When you reached this place, King Sihon of Heshbon and King Og of Bashan came out to engage us in battle, but we defeated them. 7We took their land and gave it to the Reubenites, the Gadites, and the half-tribe of Manas-

4 וָאוֹלֵךְ אֶתְכֶם אַרְבָּעִים שָׁנָה בַּמִּדְבָּר לֹא־בָלוּ שַׂלְמֹתֵיכֶם מֵעֲלֵיכֶם וְנַעַלְךָ לֹא־בָלְתָה מֵעַל רַגְלֶךָ: 5 לֶחֶם לֹא אֲכַלְתֶּם וְיַיִן וְשֵׁכָר לֹא שְׁתִיתֶם לְמַעַן תֵּדְעוּ כִּי אֲנִי יְהוָה אֱלֹהֵיכֶם:

מפטיר 6 וַתָּבֹאוּ אֶל־הַמָּקוֹם הַזֶּה וַיֵּצֵא סִיחֹן מֶלֶךְ־חֶשְׁבּוֹן וְעוֹג מֶלֶךְ־הַבָּשָׁן לִקְרָאתֵנוּ לַמִּלְחָמָה וַנַּכֵּם: 7 וַנִּקַּח אֶת־אַרְצָם וַנִּתְּנָהּ לְנַחֲלָה לָראוּבֵנִי וְלַגָּדִי וְלַחֲצִי שֵׁבֶט הַמְנַשִּׁי:

puzzled commentators. If it means that the perception necessary to understand the religious meaning of historical experiences, even miraculous ones, comes only from God, how could God have held the rebellious Exodus generation responsible for its faithlessness? Such a view would seem to deny freedom of will and to conflict with verses which imply that the events of the Exodus at Horeb clearly taught Israel God's power (4:32–40). Some commentators hold that the reference to divine causality is not meant literally, but only in the sense that God is the ultimate cause of all things,[8] or as a pious figure of speech,[9] or even as a rhetorical question: "Didn't God give you a mind, eyes, and ears?"[10] However, a similar thought is expressed in 30:6, where Moses promises that after Israel repents in exile, God will open up the people's hearts and enable them to love Him. This seems to imply that God does give the heart the capacity for faith, but that He does so for those who seek it. Hoffmann explains the present verse similarly: Man must have the desire to obey God, and only then will God help him do so; as the Talmud says, "When a person seeks to purify himself, he receives help in doing so."[11] Another possibility is that this verse reflects a certain resignation on the part of the aged Moses.[12] Despite his—and God's—optimistic expectations after the Exodus and the theophany at Horeb (4:32–40; 5:26), all the miracles that the Exodus generation witnessed had no lasting effect on it. Only after forty years of providential acts by God was the new generation prepared for sustained faith and obedience to Him.

4–5. Here Moses speaks for God, as in 28:20 and elsewhere. As in 8:2–4, God reminds Israel that His providence in the wilderness had an educational purpose. Having seen that Israel was incapable of recognizing His power behind the events of the Exodus (v. 3), He fed them by supernatural means for forty years to overcome their spiritual obtuseness.

4. *the clothes on your back did not wear out* Rather, "your clothing did not wear out [and fall] off of you." See Comment to 8:4.

5. *you had no bread to eat and no wine or other intoxicant to drink* Rather, "it was not bread that you ate, and it was not wine or another intoxicant that you drank." This translation is suggested by the emphatic position of "bread" and "wine" at the beginning of their clauses. The point is that Israel ate something other than natural, or naturally obtained, food. It survived on manna, quail, and water provided directly by God, as described in Exodus and Numbers.[13] Cf. 8:3, "Man does not live on bread alone".

that you might know that I the LORD am your God In other words, "That you may know My power."[14] God's supernatural providence—His ability to make food out of any substance (8:3)—taught Israel that He controls all natural phenomena. This clause is probably a quotation from Exodus, where it appears frequently to explain the aim of God's actions. The use of Hebrew 'ani for "I" supports this conclusion, since Deuteronomy normally uses 'anokhi.[15]

6–7. As indicated in chapters 2–3, the willingness of this generation to wage war against Sihon and Og—in contrast to the previous generation's fear of fighting the Amorites—revealed that they had indeed gained a mature trust in God's power, and their victory showed them that their trust was justified.

6. *this place* Here "place" is used loosely for the territory of Transjordan. Sihon and Og battled with Israel at Jahaz and Edrei, respectively (2:32; 3:1), not in the Plains of Moab where Moses is speaking.

276

seh as their heritage. [8]Therefore observe faithfully all the terms of this covenant, that you may succeed in all that you undertake.

8 וּשְׁמַרְתֶּם אֶת־דִּבְרֵי הַבְּרִית הַזֹּאת וַעֲשִׂיתֶם אֹתָם לְמַעַן תַּשְׂכִּילוּ אֵת כָּל־אֲשֶׁר תַּעֲשׂוּן: פ

NITSAVIM

[9]You stand this day, all of you, before the LORD your God—your tribal heads, your elders and your officials, all the men of Israel, [10]your children, your wives, even the

נצבים

9 אַתֶּם נִצָּבִים הַיּוֹם כֻּלְּכֶם לִפְנֵי יְהוָה אֱלֹהֵיכֶם רָאשֵׁיכֶם שִׁבְטֵיכֶם זִקְנֵיכֶם וְשֹׁטְרֵיכֶם כֹּל אִישׁ יִשְׂרָאֵל: 10 טַפְּכֶם נְשֵׁיכֶם וְגֵרְךָ אֲשֶׁר בְּקֶרֶב

8. From the lessons of the past forty years Israel now knows that adherence to the covenant is required for success. Compare 4:34–40; 11:3–8.

THE COVENANT CEREMONY (vv. 9–20)

Nitsavim   Every single Israelite is taking part in the ceremony establishing the covenant with God. Moses has alluded to this ceremony before (see 26:17–18; 28:69; cf. 27:9), but we do not know precisely when it took place or of what it consisted, since the text never actually narrates it. Other covenant texts from the ancient Near East likewise allude to ceremonies without narrating the actual performances. They describe only the content of the agreement.[16] In modern times agreements are formally established when the parties sign a document. In ancient times covenants were established by ceremonies that involved the proclamation and writing of the terms, proclamation of blessings and curses, erecting of stelas, and sacrifice, such as the ceremonies described in Exodus 24 and Deuteronomy 27. They often included acts that symbolized the fate of violators.[17] In Genesis 15:9–18 and Jeremiah 34:18–20 the parties cut up (*k-r-t*) the body of an animal and then, to indicate that they call upon themselves a similar fate in case of violation, they pass (*ʿ-v-r*) between the pieces. The verbs *k-r-t*, "cut," and *ʿ-v-r*, "pass," in verses 11 and 13 (translated as "make" and "enter," respectively) must have originated in that type of ceremony, though the first, and perhaps both, eventually came to be used for making a covenant irrespective of the ceremony involved.[18]

Verses 9–14 are organized in a chiastic pattern with the covenant formula, its focal point, at the center (v. 12):[19]

     A. You [present generation] stand . . . this day before the LORD your God. . . (9–10)
       B. to enter the covenant . . . which the LORD . . . is concluding . . . with its sanctions (11)
         C. that He may establish you as His people and be your God. . . (12)
       B'. I am concluding this covenant . . . with its sanctions. . . (13)
     A'. those who are standing here . . . this day before the LORD our God
       and [future generations] (14)

9. You stand   That is, "You are presenting yourselves" before God. Hebrew *nitsav* has a more formal connotation than *ʿomed* (v. 14).[20]

    your tribal heads[21]   Moses lists those present in order of social standing. For the meaning of "heads," "elders," and "officials" see Comments to 1:15 and 19:12.

    10.   Not only the leaders and the adult males, but each individual member of the community takes part in the affirmation of the covenant. The responsibility is so important, and the consequences of disobedience so grave, that all must commit themselves personally, not through the action of a parent, husband, or superior. Full public participation is likewise required for the septennial reading of the Teaching (the *torah*, 31:10–13), and is mentioned in connection with the public commitments to live by the Teaching in the days of King Josiah and of Ezra and Nehemiah. In the ancient Near East, participation of all elements of the population involved is sometimes required for the swearing of loyalty oaths.[22] As in the case of festival celebrations (cf. 12:12,18; 16:11,14), this emphasis on full participation is typical of Deuteronomy; the other books of the Torah simply mention "the people."[23]

stranger within your camp, from woodchopper to water-drawer—[11]to enter into the covenant of the LORD your God, which the LORD your God is concluding with you this day, with its sanctions; [12]to the end that He may establish you this day as His people and be your God, as He promised you and as He swore to your fathers, Abraham, Isaac, and Jacob. [13]I make this covenant, with its sanctions, not with you alone, [14]but both with those who are standing here with us this day before the LORD our God and with those who are not with us here this day.

[15]Well you know that we dwelt in the land of Egypt and that we passed through the midst of various other nations;

מַחֲנֶיךָ מֵחֹטֵב עֵצֶיךָ עַד שֹׁאֵב מֵימֶיךָ: 11 לְעָבְרְךָ
בִּבְרִית יְהוָה אֱלֹהֶיךָ וּבְאָלָתוֹ אֲשֶׁר יְהוָה אֱלֹהֶיךָ
כֹּרֵת עִמְּךָ הַיּוֹם: שני 12 לְמַעַן הָקִים־אֹתְךָ
הַיּוֹם | לוֹ לְעָם וְהוּא יִהְיֶה־לְּךָ לֵאלֹהִים כַּאֲשֶׁר
דִּבֶּר־לָךְ וְכַאֲשֶׁר נִשְׁבַּע לַאֲבֹתֶיךָ לְאַבְרָהָם
לְיִצְחָק וּלְיַעֲקֹב: 13 וְלֹא אִתְּכֶם לְבַדְּכֶם אָנֹכִי
כֹּרֵת אֶת־הַבְּרִית הַזֹּאת וְאֶת־הָאָלָה הַזֹּאת:
14 כִּי אֶת־אֲשֶׁר יֶשְׁנוֹ פֹּה עִמָּנוּ עֹמֵד הַיּוֹם לִפְנֵי
יְהוָה אֱלֹהֵינוּ וְאֵת אֲשֶׁר אֵינֶנּוּ פֹּה עִמָּנוּ
הַיּוֹם: שלישי
15 כִּי־אַתֶּם יְדַעְתֶּם אֵת אֲשֶׁר־יָשַׁבְנוּ בְּאֶרֶץ

"The stranger within your camp" is the resident alien (see Comment to 1:16). While not Israelites (cf. 14:21), resident aliens are subject to the civil law and certain religious prohibitions, enjoy particular rights, and are permitted to participate in certain religious celebrations.[24] For this reason, they, too, take part in the covenant ceremony and must hear the Teaching read (31:12; Josh. 8:35).

from woodchopper to waterdrawer Since all categories of Israelites have already been listed, this phrase must refer to aliens who served as menial laborers. According to Joshua 9:21,23,27, the Gibeonites were later assigned these tasks. The wording "*from* woodchopper *to* waterdrawer" means that other types of menial laborers are also included, such as washermen, gardeners, and straw collectors who are often associated with these two in ancient Near Eastern texts.[25]

11-12. The purpose of the convocation is to establish the covenant and thereby create a mutual relationship between God and Israel. See introductory Comment to 26:16–19.

11. **the covenant . . . with its sanctions** Hebrew *berit ve-'alah*. The second word means literally an imprecation, or curse, on one who violates the law. The combination *berit ve-'alah*, here and in verse 13, is a hendiadys meaning "a covenant guarded by imprecations," referring to the curses detailed in chapter 28.[26]

12. **that He may establish you . . . as His people and be your God** The classic expression of the covenant relationship. See Comment to 26:17,18.

as He promised you and as He swore to your fathers The first clause refers to the mutual relationship God promised to the Exodus generation in Exodus 6:7 and Leviticus 26:12; the older people among those Moses is addressing here were alive then and received the promise, though they were then minors. The second clause refers to the Lord's promise that He would be God to Abraham and his descendants (Gen. 17:7–8).

14. **those who are not with us here this day** That is, future generations. The reference cannot be to absentees, since verses 9–10 indicate that all are present. According to Midrash Tanḥuma, the phrase refers to those who were spiritually present: the souls of all future generations of Jews (and, adds Bekhor Shor, of proselytes) were present and bound themselves to God by this covenant.[27] In any case, the point of the text is that the mutual commitments made here by God and Israel are binding for all future generations. Ancient Near Eastern treaties likewise stipulate that they are binding on the parties' descendants.[28]

15-20. Moses warns those who may harbor secret reservations about the covenant. Because Israel has not been sealed off from foreign influence, it has been exposed to other nations and their idolatry, and this may lead some to harbor thoughts of worshiping idols.

15. **various other nations** Literally, "the other nations through which you passed." The reference is to the nations of Transjordan, particularly Moab, which exposed Israel to the cult of Baal Peor (4:3; see Num. 25:1–3).

16and you have seen the detestable things and the fetishes of wood and stone, silver and gold, that they keep. 17Perchance there is among you some man or woman, or some clan or tribe, whose heart is even now turning away from the LORD our God to go and worship the gods of those nations—perchance there is among you a stock sprouting poison weed and wormwood. 18When such a one hears the words of these sanctions, he may fancy

מִצְרָיִם וְאֵת אֲשֶׁר־עָבַרְנוּ בְּקֶרֶב הַגּוֹיִם אֲשֶׁר
עֲבַרְתֶּם: 16 וַתִּרְאוּ אֶת־שִׁקּוּצֵיהֶם וְאֵת גִּלֻּלֵיהֶם
עֵץ וָאֶבֶן כֶּסֶף וְזָהָב אֲשֶׁר עִמָּהֶם: 17 פֶּן־יֵשׁ בָּכֶם
אִישׁ אוֹ־אִשָּׁה אוֹ מִשְׁפָּחָה אוֹ־שֵׁבֶט אֲשֶׁר לְבָבוֹ
פֹנֶה הַיּוֹם מֵעִם יְהוָה אֱלֹהֵינוּ לָלֶכֶת לַעֲבֹד אֶת־
אֱלֹהֵי הַגּוֹיִם הָהֵם פֶּן־יֵשׁ בָּכֶם שֹׁרֶשׁ פֹּרֶה רֹאשׁ
וְלַעֲנָה: 18 וְהָיָה בְּשָׁמְעוֹ אֶת־דִּבְרֵי הָאָלָה הַזֹּאת

    16. *you have seen* See Comment to verse 1. Perhaps this is a veiled allusion to the Israelites having worshiped foreign gods in Egypt and at Peor (4:2).[29] Or perhaps it means: you have seen how detestable and lifeless their idols are.

    detestable things Hebrew *shikkutsim*, a disparaging term regularly used in the Bible for idols. It comes from the verb *shakkets*, "spurn," "reject as abominable" (7:26), which is commonly employed in connection with rejecting impure foods.[30]

    fetishes Hebrew *gillulim* is another derisory term for idols. It may be based on a noun *gelal*.[31] An Aramaic form of this word is translated as "stela" in a bilingual Aramaic-Greek inscription from Syria.[32] The vocalization *gillulim*, which seems to echo *shikkutsim*, gives the term its disparaging connotation. So, perhaps, does its similarity to *gelalim*, "pieces of excrement," which medieval Hebraists think is the source of the term.[33]

    wood and stone See Comment to 4:28.

    silver and gold These were used as plating on the statues; see Comments to 7:5 and 25.

    17. *Perchance there is* Hebrew *pen yesh* is better translated both times in the verse as "Beware in case there is. . . ."

    some man or woman, or some clan or tribe Compare 17:2–7 and chapter 13, which provide for punishing idolaters and advocates of idolatry whether they are individuals, males or females, relatives, or entire cities. The concern to make the warning as comprehensive as possible is also found in other ancient treaties and oaths, such as a Greek oath that curses the violator "whether city, private man, or tribe."[34] No violator(s) of any number can hope to escape punishment. Here the list begins with individuals because, as verse 9 indicates, every single Israelite is entering the covenant individually.

    the gods of those nations The fetishes mentioned in verse 16. In the Bible's view there is no substance to foreign gods beyond their images; hence, pagans worship the images themselves, which they wrongly think have power. See Comment to 4:28. Moses fears, however, that Israel's exposure to those images may have left some people with a temptation to worship them, as happened at Peor (see 4:3).

    a stock sprouting poison weed and wormwood A person, clan, or tribe whose delusions would have bitter, deadly consequences. Hebrew *ro'sh* is poison, here a poisonous plant, often identified with hemlock, by which Socrates was put to death. *La'anah* is probably wormwood, a very bitter but nonpoisonous plant. These two plants serve as a metaphor for punishment, as again in 32:32.[35]

    stock[36]

    18. *such a one* Such a man or woman, clan or tribe. In the rest of the chapter Moses refers to the culprit, variously, as one or the other of these, or as the entire land.

    fancy himself immune Literally, "fancy himself blessed" instead of cursed as the sanction-imprecations provide.[37] The culprit may delude himself, thinking that by remaining silent while others swear allegiance to the covenant he will be exempted from its consequences.[38] This and the following clause could also be translated "bless himself in his heart, saying: 'May I be safe . . . ,'" meaning that he silently pronounces a blessing on himself as an antidote to the imprecations.[39]

himself immune, thinking, "I shall be safe, though I follow my own willful heart"—to the utter ruin of moist and dry alike. [19]The LORD will never forgive him; rather will the LORD's anger and passion rage against that man, till every sanction recorded in this book comes down upon him, and the LORD blots out his name from under heaven.

[20]The LORD will single them out from all the tribes of Israel for misfortune, in accordance with all the sanctions of the covenant recorded in this book of Teaching. [21]And

וְהִתְבָּרֵךְ בִּלְבָבוֹ לֵאמֹר שָׁלוֹם יִהְיֶה־לִּי כִּי בִּשְׁרִרוּת לִבִּי אֵלֵךְ לְמַעַן סְפוֹת הָרָוָה אֶת־הַצְּמֵאָה: 19 לֹא־יֹאבֶה יְהוָה סְלֹחַ לוֹ כִּי אָז יֶעְשַׁן אַף־יְהוָה וְקִנְאָתוֹ בָּאִישׁ הַהוּא וְרָבְצָה בּוֹ כָּל־הָאָלָה הַכְּתוּבָה בַּסֵּפֶר הַזֶּה וּמָחָה יְהוָה אֶת־שְׁמוֹ מִתַּחַת הַשָּׁמָיִם: 20 וְהִבְדִּילוֹ יְהוָה לְרָעָה מִכֹּל שִׁבְטֵי יִשְׂרָאֵל כְּכֹל אָלוֹת הַבְּרִית הַכְּתוּבָה בְּסֵפֶר הַתּוֹרָה הַזֶּה:

be safe Literally "have *shalom*," "safety, well-being." *Shalom* here has the sense of *shalem*, "complete, unimpaired," hence "well, safe."[40]

willful heart The general meaning of "*sherirut* of the heart" is clear from the fact that it is sometimes parallel to "counsels" and "plans."[41] More precise explanations have been suggested: "secret thought";[42] "sight," meaning, "I'll follow my own sights, do as I see fit";[43] or, "affirmation," or "stubbornness," of the heart.[44] In the latter case, this clause represents Moses' unfavorable view of the culprit's intentions.[45]

to the utter ruin [*sefot*] **of moist and dry alike** This difficult clause may reflect a lost idiom. It has called forth a host of interpretations. Most likely, the verb *sefot* is from the root *s-f-h*, "sweep away." Many commentators consider "moist and dry" a merism denoting "everything" and take the clause as Moses' comment on the consequences of the sinner's delusion: it will sweep away everything, either of the sinner or of the entire nation.[46] The terms could refer specifically to land, plants, or animals, meaning that the sinner's delusions will bring about a natural calamity that will sweep away not only what was parched or thirsty but even what was well watered. Others take "moist and dry" as referring to innocent and guilty people, perhaps inspired by Genesis 18:23 ("Will You sweep away the innocent along with the guilty?") and by Jeremiah's comparison of the righteous with a tree planted by water and the sinner with a bush in the desert.[47] Another approach holds that this clause expresses the sinner's intention. To Saadia, for example, the sinner means, "I'll sweep away my thirst with moisture," that is, "I'll indulge my cravings."[48]

19. The LORD will never forgive him Literally, "the LORD will never agree to forgive him," nothing he does will assuage God's anger.[49]

passion Hebrew *kin'ah*. This verse illustrates the Decalogue's warning that the Lord is an "impassioned God" in His reaction to the worship of other gods (see Comment to 5:9).

every sanction recorded in this book Such as those in Chapter 28. On the reference to the book see Comment to 28:58.

comes down upon him Literally, "crouches, or reclines, upon him." Hebrew *ravtsah* refers to the stretching out of an animal and practically personifies the curse (see Comment to 28:2). A variant reading *davkah*, "clings to him" (used of diseases in 28:60), is reflected in the Septuagint, Targum Onkelos, and some of the Dead Sea scrolls. That reading may be due either to a scribal error or to an attempt at softening the animal imagery.[50]

blots out his name from under heaven See Comments to 2:25; 7:24; 25:5–10; and Excursus 23. His fate will be the same as that which God threatened to impose on the worshipers of the golden calf (9:14) and which He commands Israel to impose on the Canaanites and the Amalekites (7:24; 25:19).

20. single . . . out This term is ironic here since it usually refers to choosing for a positive purpose, as in 10:8. Here Moses means that the would-be sinner should not imagine that God only deals with the community as a whole and that individuals can escape punishment so long as the community is virtuous.

later generations will ask—the children who succeed you, and foreigners who come from distant lands and see the plagues and diseases that the LORD has inflicted upon that land, 22all its soil devastated by sulfur and salt, beyond sowing and producing, no grass growing in it, just like the upheaval of Sodom and Gomorrah, Admah and Zeboiim, which the LORD overthrew in His fierce anger—23all

21 וְאָמַ֞ר הַדּ֣וֹר הָאַחֲר֗וֹן בְּנֵיכֶם֙ אֲשֶׁ֣ר יָק֣וּמוּ
מֵאַחֲרֵיכֶ֔ם וְהַ֨נָּכְרִ֔י אֲשֶׁ֥ר יָבֹ֖א מֵאֶ֣רֶץ רְחוֹקָ֑ה
וְרָא֞וּ אֶת־מַכּ֤וֹת הָאָ֨רֶץ֙ הַהִ֔וא וְאֶת־תַּ֣חֲלֻאֶ֔יהָ
אֲשֶׁר־חִלָּ֥ה יְהוָ֖ה בָּֽהּ׃ 22 גָּפְרִ֣ית וָמֶ֮לַח֮ שְׂרֵפָ֣ה
כָל־אַרְצָהּ֒ לֹ֤א תִזָּרַע֙ וְלֹ֣א תַצְמִ֔חַ וְלֹֽא־יַעֲלֶ֥ה בָ֖הּ
כָּל־עֵ֑שֶׂב כְּמַהְפֵּכַ֞ת סְדֹ֤ם וַעֲמֹרָה֙ אַדְמָ֣ה וּצְבֹייִ֔ם
אֲשֶׁר֙ הָפַ֣ךְ יְהוָ֔ה בְּאַפּ֖וֹ וּבַחֲמָת֑וֹ׃ 23 וְאָֽמְרוּ֙ כָּל־

v. 22. וּצְבוֹיִ֖ם ק׳

THE AFTERMATH OF PUNISHMENT   (vv. 21–27)

Moses dramatizes the folly of betraying the covenant by describing the reaction of future generations and foreigners who will ask what caused the disaster and give the answer themselves: it is because Israel violated the terms of God's covenant. Foreign nations, who would admire Israel's wisdom if it obeys God's laws (4:6), would recognize its folly if it disobeys.

The motif of asking about the reasons for disaster and learning that it was caused by violation of the covenant is echoed practically verbatim in the books of Jeremiah and Kings.[51] There is a close parallel in the inscriptions of King Ashurbanipal of Assyria (668–627 B.C.E.), describing his defeat of Arabia. Ashurbanipal records how the king of Arabia violated his treaty obligations and rebelled against Assyria, and how the gods afflicted Arabia with all the curses written in the treaty, so that whenever the inhabitants of Arabia asked each other:

> On account of what have these calamities befallen Arabia? [They themselves answered:] Because we did not keep the solemn oaths [sworn in the name of the god] Ashur, because we violated the pact of good relations with Ashurbanipal.[52]

In the Assyrian text, it is a political treaty that was violated, whereas Deuteronomy refers to Israel's covenant with God. This is another example of the way in which political treaties served as the model for Israel's understanding of its relationship with God. (See the Introduction.)

In this section, Moses speaks of the entire land being punished for its violation of the covenant. Reference to the entire land is unexpected, since verse 17 listed only an individual, a clan or a tribe as potential violators. Perhaps that list is merely suggestive, implying all units of society, from the smallest on up, and verses 19–28 are meant to be understood elliptically: verse 19 describes the punishment of the smallest unit, the individual, and Moses then skips over the fate of the intermediate-size units, which is in principle the same, so as to conclude with the climactic fate of the largest unit, the entire nation.[53]

21. *later generations*   Or, "the following generation." *Dor 'aharon* sometimes refers to a generation close enough that one can still communicate with it.[54]

plagues and diseases   A metaphoric reference to the natural disasters of verse 22.

that land   According to rabbinic exegesis, this paragraph foretells the fate of the northern kingdom, the ten tribes exiled to Assyria.[55]

22. *all its soil devastated by sulfur and salt*[56]   Because of the reference to Sodom and Gomorrah at the end of the verse, this curse is sometimes thought to refer to a conflagration like that which occurred when God rained down "sulfur and fire" on those cities (Gen. 19:24). However, the reference to salt and infertility suggests that this verse refers to soil sterilants. As a severe punishment, conquerors sometimes spread salt on the soil of conquered lands to render it infertile,[57] and an Aramaic treaty warns that the gods will sow salt on the city that violates its terms.[58] Sulfur can also sterilize soil. Though it is used as a fungicide and to reduce soil alkalinity, excessive amounts of it make soil too acidic to grow anything.[59] Apparently, this effect was known in antiquity.

grass   In the sense of vegetation, herbage.

just like the upheaval of Sodom and Gomorrah, Admah and Zeboiim   That is, just like

nations will ask, "Why did the LORD do thus to this land? Wherefore that awful wrath?" 24They will be told, "Because they forsook the covenant that the LORD, God of their fathers, made with them when He freed them from the land of Egypt; 25they turned to the service of other gods and worshiped them, gods whom they had not experienced and whom He had not allotted to them. 26So the LORD was incensed at that land and brought upon it all the curses recorded in this book. 27The LORD uprooted them from their soil in anger, fury, and great wrath, and cast them into another land, as is still the case."

הַגּוֹיִם עַל־מֶה עָשָׂה יְהוָה כָּכָה לָאָרֶץ הַזֹּאת מֶה חֳרִי הָאַף הַגָּדוֹל הַזֶּה: 24 וְאָמְרוּ עַל אֲשֶׁר עָזְבוּ אֶת־בְּרִית יְהוָה אֱלֹהֵי אֲבֹתָם אֲשֶׁר כָּרַת עִמָּם בְּהוֹצִיאוֹ אֹתָם מֵאֶרֶץ מִצְרָיִם: 25 וַיֵּלְכוּ וַיַּעַבְדוּ אֱלֹהִים אֲחֵרִים וַיִּשְׁתַּחֲווּ לָהֶם אֱלֹהִים אֲשֶׁר לֹא־יְדָעוּם וְלֹא חָלַק לָהֶם: 26 וַיִּחַר־אַף יְהוָה בָּאָרֶץ הַהִוא לְהָבִיא עָלֶיהָ אֶת־כָּל־הַקְּלָלָה הַכְּתוּבָה בַּסֵּפֶר הַזֶּה: 27 וַיִּתְּשֵׁם יְהוָה מֵעַל אַדְמָתָם בְּאַף וּבְחֵמָה וּבְקֶצֶף גָּדוֹל וַיַּשְׁלִכֵם* אֶל־אֶרֶץ אַחֶרֶת כַּיּוֹם הַזֶּה:

v. 27. ל׳ רבתי

Sodom and its sister cities, which were overturned. The comparison is not to the manner of destruction but to its consequences. Compare Isaiah 13:19: "Babylon . . . shall become like God's upheaval of Sodom and Gomorrah, nevermore shall it be settled," and Zephaniah 2:9: "Moab shall become like Sodom and the Ammonites like Gomorrah: thorn patches and salt mines, and desolation evermore."[60] Sodom and Gomorrah and their neighboring cities Admah and Zeboiim were destroyed in the days of Abraham.[61]

23. all nations The devastation will be so great that the entire world will learn of it and join future Israelites and passersby in asking about it. The wording of the question indicates that it will be obvious to all that the disaster was an act of God, not an accident of nature.

24. they will be told Or, "they will say" (*ve-'ameru*). It seems to be the nations themselves who will answer their own question. This is indicated by the reference to Israel and its ancestors in the third person in verses 24–27. In the inscription of Ashurbanipal, too, the question is answered by those who ask it, although in that case, the answer comes from the sinners themselves. How the nations will learn the answer is not said.

24–25. The answer indicates how foolish the sinners were: they offended the God of their own fathers, the God who had freed them from slavery, and worshiped gods who had never done a thing for them.

the covenant that the LORD . . . made . . . when He freed them from the land of Egypt After he freed them. See Comment to 23:5. This probably refers to the covenant at Sinai and the one being made now in Moab, essentially two forms of the same covenant (see Comment to 28:69).

25. gods whom they had not experienced Who had done nothing for them. See Comment to 11:28.

whom He had not allotted to them As objects of worship. They were to worship the Lord alone. See Comment to 4:19.

26. recorded in this book This phrase shows that this is not a precise quotation of what the nations will say, but a paraphrase addressed to those who would learn this Teaching in written form, that is, in the book of Deuteronomy. Compare 28:58.

27. cast Hebrew *va-yashlikhem*. Tractate Soferim 9:5 requires that the *lamed* in this word be written as a majuscule (a large letter) in Torah scrolls. Majuscules are sometimes used to highlight the first or middle letter of a book, but in most places where they appear no such purpose is obvious and midrashic commentators offer fanciful explanations.[62] One offered for the present verse is that a new word begins with the *lamed*, permitting the entire clause to be read as if it said *ve-yesh lakhem 'el 'erets 'aḥeret*, "but you [will] have God [in] another land."[63]

as is still the case In the days of the exile, when this question and answer will take place.

282

28Concealed acts concern the Lᴏʀᴅ our God; but with overt acts, it is for us and our children ever to apply all the provisions of this Teaching.

הַנִּסְתָּרֹת לַיהוָה אֱלֹהֵינוּ וְהַנִּגְלֹת לָֽנוּ 28 וּלְבָנֵינוּ עַד־עוֹלָם לַעֲשׂוֹת אֶת־כָּל־דִּבְרֵי הַתּוֹרָה הַזֹּאת: ס

י"א נקודות v. 28.

CONCLUSION TO MOSES' WARNING (v. 28)

Moses' meaning is most likely that expressed in Targum Jonathan: concealed acts (that is, concealed sins) are known to God, and He will punish them, but overt ones are our responsibility to punish ("to apply all the provisions of this Teaching"). Apparently Moses is here assuring the people, who have heard how the private schemes of one man (vv. 17–20) may lead to the destruction of the entire land (vv. 20–27), that this does not mean that they will be held collectively responsible for sins committed by individuals in secret. God will punish those and will hold the people responsible only if they fail to punish sins of whose commission they are aware.[64] This idea is referred to in rabbinic literature by the saying *kol yisra'el 'arevin zeh ba-zeh*, "all Israelites are surety for one another," meaning that the entire community is held accountable for the conduct of its individual members unless it restrains or punishes the sinners.[65] Compare 27:15–25, where those who commit secret crimes are anathematized, with divine punishment invoked upon them.

Another possible interpretation of the verse is that Moses is addressing those who might think that they can sin secretly. In that case his point is that although it is true that only overt sins can be punished by human authorities, God will detect and punish concealed ones.[66]

The Hebrew terms for concealed and overt acts, *nistarot* and *niglot*, are ambiguous, since they mean literally "concealed things" and "overt, revealed things." This ambiguity has invited numerous other suggestions as to Moses' meaning. According to Maimonides, "concealed things" refers to the reasons for the commandments, which are known to God, whereas "overt acts"—the physical performance of the commandments—are assigned to Israel. People may not exempt themselves from performing commandments even if they know their reasons and think that that makes their performance superfluous.[67] Several modern commentators believe that "concealed things" refers to the future, which only God knows. Humanity's role is not to speculate on the future but to concern itself with living according to the "revealed things," the terms of God's law.[68]

In Hebrew texts of the Torah, dots are placed over the words "for us and our children" and, in most texts, over the first letter of "ever" (literally, "until eternity"). There are fifteen places in the Bible where dots appear over letters or words. Ancient scribes commonly used such dots to indicate corrections, usually to delete the words thus marked, but there is nothing obviously questionable about the dotted words in this verse.[69] Rabbinic interpretation takes the dots as calling attention to midrashic explanations that limit the application of the words: it was not *until* ('*ad*, whose first letter is flagged by a dot) Israel entered the promised land that God held them collectively accountable ("us and our children") for concealed sins or, in another view, for overt ones.[70]

CHAPTER 30   ## THE POSSIBILITY OF RESTORATION (vv. 1–10)

Having warned of exile, Moses now digresses to offer assurance that if Israel should be exiled, God will nevertheless reinstate it if the people sincerely repent of their rebellion and return to Him and His Instruction. A similar digression appears in 4:29–31, although the promise of return to the land is not explicit there. For the question as to whether or not these assurances would undercut the effect of Moses' warnings, and whether or not they are an original part of the text, see Excursus 5.

The key term in this section is the Hebrew root *shuv*, "turn," "return," which expresses both Israel's return to God and God's return of Israel to its prior good fortune. It is also used in the idioms that express the idea of "taking to heart" and "doing something again." In all, the root is found in seven clauses in which acts of *shuv* by God and by Israel appear in a chiastic pattern (Israel acts [twice], God acts [twice], Israel, God, Israel), as follows:[1]

30 When all these things befall you—the blessing and the curse that I have set before you—and you take them to heart amidst the various nations to which the LORD your God has banished you, [2]and you return to the LORD your God, and you and your children heed His command with all your heart and soul, just as I enjoin upon you this day, [3]then the LORD your God will restore your fortunes and take you back in love. He will bring you together again from all the peoples where the LORD your God has

רביעי [שני כשהן מחוברות] וְהָיָה כִי־יָבֹאוּ
עָלֶיךָ כָּל־הַדְּבָרִים הָאֵלֶּה הַבְּרָכָה וְהַקְּלָלָה אֲשֶׁר
נָתַתִּי לְפָנֶיךָ וַהֲשֵׁבֹתָ אֶל־לְבָבֶךָ בְּכָל־הַגּוֹיִם
אֲשֶׁר הִדִּיחֲךָ יְהֹוָה אֱלֹהֶיךָ שָׁמָּה: [2] וְשַׁבְתָּ עַד־
יְהֹוָה אֱלֹהֶיךָ וְשָׁמַעְתָּ בְקֹלוֹ כְּכֹל אֲשֶׁר־אָנֹכִי
מְצַוְּךָ הַיּוֹם אַתָּה וּבָנֶיךָ בְּכָל־לְבָבְךָ וּבְכָל־
נַפְשֶׁךָ: [3] וְשָׁב יְהֹוָה אֱלֹהֶיךָ אֶת־שְׁבוּתְךָ וְרִחֲמֶךָ
וְשָׁב וְקִבֶּצְךָ מִכָּל־הָעַמִּים אֲשֶׁר הֱפִיצְךָ יְהֹוָה

A. you take [*hashevota*] them to heart . . . and you return [*shavta*] to the LORD . . . and heed His command (1–2)

B. then the LORD will restore your fortunes [*shav shevut*] . . . He will again [*shav*] bring you together. . . (3)

C. You will again [*tashuv*] heed the LORD. . . (8)

B'. the LORD will again [*yashuv*] delight in your well-being (9)

A'. since you will be heeding the LORD . . . once you return [*tashuv*] to the LORD . . . (10)

The chiasm shows how Israel's return to the Lord will lead to His returning them. Appropriately, this paragraph is part of the Torah portion read in the synagogue on the Sabbath preceding the Ten Days of Repentance (*teshuvah*, lit. "return") that extend from Rosh Hashanah to Yom Kippur.

Other leitmotifs in this section are the phrases "the LORD your God" (twelve times altogether, in almost every verse) and "with all your heart and soul" (vv. 2,6,10). Both phrases appear frequently in Deuteronomy.

1. the blessing and the curse   This phrase harks back to chapter 28, as do several others in this section (cf. 28:4,11,63–64), showing that Moses is not referring solely to the curse described in chapter 29, but to the blessings (and curses) of chapter 28 as well. This means that if Israel should bring disaster upon itself, the stock-taking that is a prerequisite for its restoration should include the recollection that obedience led to success, and not only that disobedience led to disaster.[2] Thus Moses is not entirely pessimistic; he expects that Israel will indeed remain faithful and prosper, at least for a time, after his death.

the blessing and the curse that I have set before you   That I have offered you as alternatives. This idiom, repeated in verses 15 and 19, harks back to Moses' preamble to the laws in 11:26.

2. return to the LORD   See Comment to 4:30.

with all your heart and soul   See Comment to 6:5. The repentance must be as thorough and sincere as the original duty.

3. restore your fortunes   Hebrew *shav 'et shevut*, literally, "return a return," is an idiom meaning "restore."[3] Midrashic exegesis takes it to mean "God will return with your captives," meaning that God himself, so to speak, returns from exile when Israel does. He accompanies Israel in exile, suffers along with them, and returns only when He brings them back.[4] This interpretation, homiletically attractive in itself, is reached by disregarding the idiomatic meaning of *shav 'et shevut* and assigning each of the three words a meaning which it has when it appears separately elsewhere: "return" (intransitive), "with," and "(your) captivity."[5]

take you back in love[6]

4.   This verse is quoted in the modern "Prayer for the Welfare of the State of Israel," urging God to continue gathering Jews from all corners of the Diaspora to Israel.

God's ability to retrieve people from anywhere was apparently proverbial. It is alluded to, with reference to fugitives, in Amos 9:2–3: "If they burrow down to Sheol, from there My hand shall take them, and if they ascend to heaven, from there I will bring them down; if they hide on the top of Carmel, there I will search them out and seize them."

scattered you. 4Even if your outcasts are at the ends of the world, from there the LORD your God will gather you, from there He will fetch you. 5And the LORD your God will bring you to the land that your fathers possessed, and you shall possess it; and He will make you more prosperous and more numerous than your fathers.

6Then the LORD your God will open up your heart and the hearts of your offspring to love the LORD your God with all your heart and soul, in order that you may live. 7The LORD your God will inflict all those curses upon the enemies and foes who persecuted you. 8You, however, will again heed the LORD and obey all His commandments that I enjoin upon you this day. 9And the LORD your God will grant you abounding prosperity in all your undertakings, in the issue of your womb, the offspring of your cattle, and the produce of your soil. For the LORD will again delight in your well-being, as He did in that of your fathers, 10since you will be heeding the LORD your God and

אֱלֹהֶיךָ שָׁמָּה: 4 אִם־יִהְיֶה נִדַּחֲךָ בִּקְצֵה הַשָּׁמָיִם מִשָּׁם יְקַבֶּצְךָ יְהֹוָה אֱלֹהֶיךָ וּמִשָּׁם יִקָּחֶךָ: 5 וֶהֱבִיאֲךָ יְהֹוָה אֱלֹהֶיךָ אֶל־הָאָרֶץ אֲשֶׁר־יָרְשׁוּ אֲבֹתֶיךָ וִירִשְׁתָּהּ וְהֵיטִבְךָ וְהִרְבְּךָ מֵאֲבֹתֶיךָ: 6 וּמָל יְהֹוָה אֱלֹהֶיךָ אֶת־לְבָבְךָ וְאֶת־לְבַב זַרְעֶךָ לְאַהֲבָה אֶת־יְהֹוָה אֱלֹהֶיךָ בְּכָל־לְבָבְךָ וּבְכָל־נַפְשְׁךָ לְמַעַן חַיֶּיךָ: חמישי [שלישי כשהן מחוברות] 7 וְנָתַן יְהֹוָה אֱלֹהֶיךָ אֵת כָּל־הָאָלוֹת הָאֵלֶּה עַל־אֹיְבֶיךָ וְעַל־שֹׂנְאֶיךָ אֲשֶׁר רְדָפוּךָ: 8 וְאַתָּה תָשׁוּב וְשָׁמַעְתָּ בְּקוֹל יְהֹוָה וְעָשִׂיתָ אֶת־כָּל־מִצְוֹתָיו אֲשֶׁר אָנֹכִי מְצַוְּךָ הַיּוֹם: 9 וְהוֹתִירְךָ יְהֹוָה אֱלֹהֶיךָ בְּכֹל | מַעֲשֵׂה יָדֶךָ בִּפְרִי בִטְנְךָ וּבִפְרִי בְהֶמְתְּךָ וּבִפְרִי אַדְמָתְךָ לְטוֹבָה כִּי | יָשׁוּב יְהֹוָה לָשׂוּשׂ עָלֶיךָ לְטוֹב כַּאֲשֶׁר־שָׂשׂ עַל־אֲבֹתֶיךָ: 10 כִּי תִשְׁמַע בְּקוֹל יְהֹוָה אֱלֹהֶיךָ לִשְׁמֹר מִצְוֹתָיו

outcasts Literally, "your banished ones," echoing the same root as in "banished" in verse 1.

the ends of the world Literally, "the end of the sky." See Comment to 4:32.

5. *your fathers* That is, the ancestors of the future, repentant generation—in other words, the present generation (the one about to enter the promised land) and its successors.

more prosperous and more numerous This promise is perhaps designed to encourage a future generation to return to God, assuring it that the nation's sinful past will not be held against it in any way.

6. *will open up your heart* Literally, "will circumcise your heart." In contrast to 10:16, where Moses exhorts Israel to circumcise its own heart, here he promises that once Israel returns to God, God Himself will remove the psychological impediments to wholehearted devotion. The rabbis described this process as follows: "When a person seeks to purify himself, he receives help in doing so."[7] Several of the prophets said that God would ultimately "program" Israel to be loyal and obedient to Him, so that they would obey Him instinctively and never again experience exile.[8] Moses stops short of saying that: the removal of the "foreskin" implies only that God would remove impediments that prevent Israel from voluntarily following God's teachings.

to love the LORD See Comment to 6:5.

9. The first half of the verse essentially reiterates the promise made in 28:11, while the second half promises the reverse of the punishment foretold in 28:63.

delight in your well-being That is, "be determined to grant you well-being." See Comment to 28:63.

your fathers See verse 5.

CONCLUSION OF THE SUMMONS TO THE COVENANT (vv. 11–20)

After the digression of verses 1–10, Moses resumes summoning Israel to the covenant. He assures the present generation that the terms of the covenant are not too difficult to know, understand, and fulfill (vv. 11–14). He concludes by stating plainly that he is offering Israel the opportunity to choose its own fate, life or death (vv. 15–30).

keeping His commandments and laws that are recorded in this book of the Teaching—once you return to the LORD your God with all your heart and soul.

11 Surely, this Instruction which I enjoin upon you this day is not too baffling for you, nor is it beyond reach. 12 It is not in the heavens, that you should say, "Who among us can go up to the heavens and get it for us and impart it to us, that we may observe it?" 13 Neither is it beyond the sea, that you should say, "Who among us can cross to the other side of the sea and get it for us and impart it to us, that we may observe it?" 14 No, the thing is very close to you, in your mouth and in your heart, to observe it.

וְחֻקֹּתָיו הַכְּתוּבָ֗ה בְּסֵ֙פֶר֙ הַתּוֹרָ֣ה הַזֶּ֔ה כִּ֤י תָשׁוּב֙
אֶל־יְהוָ֣ה אֱלֹהֶ֔יךָ בְּכָל־לְבָבְךָ֖ וּבְכָל־נַפְשֶֽׁךָ׃ פ
שׁשׁי 11 כִּ֚י הַמִּצְוָ֣ה הַזֹּ֔את אֲשֶׁ֛ר אָנֹכִ֥י מְצַוְּךָ֖
הַיּ֑וֹם לֹֽא־נִפְלֵ֥את הִוא֙ מִמְּךָ֔ וְלֹ֥א רְחֹקָ֖ה הִֽוא׃
12 לֹ֥א בַשָּׁמַ֖יִם הִ֑וא לֵאמֹ֗ר מִ֣י יַעֲלֶה־לָּ֤נוּ
הַשָּׁמַ֙יְמָה֙ וְיִקָּחֶ֣הָ לָּ֔נוּ וְיַשְׁמִעֵ֥נוּ אֹתָ֖הּ וְנַעֲשֶֽׂנָּה׃
13 וְלֹֽא־מֵעֵ֥בֶר לַיָּ֖ם הִ֑וא לֵאמֹ֗ר מִ֣י יַעֲבָר־לָ֜נוּ
אֶל־עֵ֤בֶר הַיָּם֙ וְיִקָּחֶ֣הָ לָּ֔נוּ וְיַשְׁמִעֵ֥נוּ אֹתָ֖הּ
וְנַעֲשֶֽׂנָּה׃ 14 כִּֽי־קָר֥וֹב אֵלֶ֛יךָ הַדָּבָ֖ר מְאֹ֑ד בְּפִ֥יךָ
וּבִלְבָבְךָ֖ לַעֲשֹׂתֽוֹ׃ ס   שביעי
[רביעי כשהן מחוברות]

11–14. God's Instruction is not unintelligible or esoteric (v. 11), nor is it inaccessible and unknown (vv. 12–14). It has already been imparted to Israel by Moses, permitting Israel to learn it, meditate on it, and carry it out.

Moses' declaration that God's requirements are known contrasts them implicitly with philosophical knowledge about the mysteries of the universe. According to the Wisdom Literature, only God possesses that kind of philosophical wisdom; for humans the only available wisdom is morality, that is, "fearing God and shunning evil." This is compatible with Moses' statement here that God's *requirements* are known.[9] Compare also 4:6 where Moses says that it is observing God's laws that will show Israel's wisdom. The view that law is the only revealed form of wisdom accounts for the fact that the classic focus of Jewish intellectual activity is law and ethics rather than philosophy.

11. Instruction The laws and teachings of Deuteronomy, the "Teaching" (*torah*). See Comments to 5:1,28.

not too baffling It is not beyond your ability to understand. The same root (*p-l-'*) refers in 17:8 to a legal case in which the judges do not know how to rule.

beyond reach Beyond your intellectual grasp.[10]

12–13. God's Instruction is not in an inaccessible place that humans cannot reach, which would prevent Israel from following it until it was communicated to them.[11]

12. not in the heavens Humans' inability to reach heaven was proverbial. Compare Proverbs 30:4: "Who has ascended heaven and come down?" and the Mesopotamian saying, "Who is tall enough to reach heaven, who is tall enough to encompass the earth?"

The pithy statement that God's Instruction is not in heaven is invoked in rabbinic literature to express fundamental concepts of Judaism. In the Talmud it is used to represent the idea that the authority for *interpreting* the Torah is not in God's hands. Once God gave the Torah to Israel, He gave the authority to decide how it is to be applied entirely to legal scholars, and retained none for Himself.[13] This is a halakhic counterpart of the idea that the intent of the original framers of the Constitution is not determinative for its interpretation. In the midrash the statement is also taken to mean that there is no further Torah in heaven waiting to be revealed in the future. This is a denial of the Christian claim to have superseded the Torah.[14]

13. beyond the sea The difficulty of crossing the sea was also proverbial. Mesopotamian literature describes it as something so difficult that only gods and heroes can do it.[15]

14. No, the Instruction is not beyond reach (v. 11) but nearby: it is known and understood, and therefore can be put into practice.[16]

in your mouth It is readily accessible to you, you know it by heart. Compare Hebrew *be-'al peh*, "by mouth," the equivalent of English "by heart," "from memory." This manner of speaking reflects a predominantly oral culture in which learning and review are accomplished primarily by oral recitation (see Comments to 6:7 and 31:9–13). Compare 31:19,21, "Write down this poem and teach it

286

15See, I set before you this day life and prosperity, death and adversity. 16For I command you this day, to love the Lord your God, to walk in His ways, and to keep His commandments, His laws, and His rules, that you may thrive and increase, and that the Lord your God may bless you in the land that you are about to enter and possess. 17But if your heart turns away and you give no heed, and are lured into the worship and service of other gods, 18I declare to you this day that you shall certainly perish; you shall not long endure on the soil that you are crossing the Jordan to enter and possess. 19I call heaven and earth to witness against you this day: I have put before you life and death, blessing and curse. Choose life—if you and your

15 רְאֵה נָתַתִּי לְפָנֶיךָ הַיּוֹם אֶת־הַחַיִּים וְאֶת־
הַטּוֹב וְאֶת־הַמָּוֶת וְאֶת־הָרָע: 16 אֲשֶׁר אָנֹכִי
מְצַוְּךָ הַיּוֹם לְאַהֲבָה אֶת־יְהוָה אֱלֹהֶיךָ לָלֶכֶת
בִּדְרָכָיו וְלִשְׁמֹר מִצְוֹתָיו וְחֻקֹּתָיו וּמִשְׁפָּטָיו וְחָיִיתָ
וְרָבִיתָ וּבֵרַכְךָ יְהוָה אֱלֹהֶיךָ בָּאָרֶץ אֲשֶׁר־אַתָּה
בָא־שָׁמָּה לְרִשְׁתָּהּ: 17 וְאִם־יִפְנֶה לְבָבְךָ וְלֹא
תִשְׁמָע וְנִדַּחְתָּ וְהִשְׁתַּחֲוִיתָ לֵאלֹהִים אֲחֵרִים
וַעֲבַדְתָּם: מפטיר 18 הִגַּדְתִּי לָכֶם הַיּוֹם כִּי
אָבֹד תֹּאבֵדוּן לֹא־תַאֲרִיכֻן יָמִים עַל־הָאֲדָמָה
אֲשֶׁר אַתָּה עֹבֵר אֶת־הַיַּרְדֵּן לָבֹא שָׁמָּה לְרִשְׁתָּהּ:
19 הַעִדֹתִי בָכֶם הַיּוֹם אֶת־הַשָּׁמַיִם וְאֶת־הָאָרֶץ
הַחַיִּים וְהַמָּוֶת נָתַתִּי לְפָנֶיךָ הַבְּרָכָה וְהַקְּלָלָה

to the people of Israel; put it in their mouths . . . it will never be lost from the mouth of their offspring," and Joshua 1:8, "Let not this Book of the Teaching cease from your mouth, but recite it day and night, so that you may observe faithfully all that is written in it."[17] Since Moses taught the Instruction to the people by heart, that—and not writing the copy that he gave to the priests and elders (31:9)—constituted its publication. For further discussion of the oral dissemination of the Teaching, see Excursus 28.

in your heart In your mind, known internally and not merely by rote. Compare 6:4; 11:18.

15–20. Here Moses concludes his summons to the covenant. He offers Israel the choice between life and death (v. 15). He reiterates the basic demands and consequences of the covenant, spelling out the path to each of these alternative futures (vv. 16 and 17–18, respectively).[18] He invokes heaven and earth to witness the fact that he has offered the choice (v. 19) and concludes by describing the path to life once more (v. 20). The words "life" and "live" appear no less than six times (there is a seventh occurrence in v. 6).[19] In concluding his summons to the covenant Moses harks back to the themes and style of his introductory words in chapters 4–11 (the end of the Prologue and the preamble to the laws), especially 11:26–28. The similarities are indicated in the Comments to the individual verses.

15. *I set before you* That is, "I give you the choice between . . ." This is not an invitation to *accept* the covenant—that Israel will accept it is a foregone conclusion; indeed, it had already done so earlier at Horeb. Here Moses urges Israel to *obey* the covenant, for that is the only way, under its terms, to survive. As noted, the theme and style of this verse echo 11:26–28.

prosperity . . . adversity This translation of *tov* and *ra*ʿ fits the context better than the literal "good" and "evil."[20] Hebrew *tov*, like English "prosperity," means all types of success and well being, not merely economic (Ibn Ezra: "wealth, bodily health, and honor").

16. The summary of God's requirements is the same as those presented in 10:12; 11:1,22; the promise is the same as those in 4:1; 7:13; 8:1.

For I command you[21]

to love For the meaning of commanding love, see Comment to 6:5.

His ways The ways that He commands (see 5:30).

17. The sins are described in terms echoing, for example, 4:19; 7:14.

18. *you shall not long endure on the soil* But shall go into exile. The warnings echo 4:26; 8:19.

19. *I call heaven and earth to witness against you* See 4:26 and Comment there.

I have put before you . . . blessing and curse Another echo of 11:26.

offspring would live—20by loving the LORD your God, heeding His commands, and holding fast to Him. For thereby you shall have life and shall long endure upon the soil that the LORD swore to your ancestors, Abraham, Isaac, and Jacob, to give to them.

וּבָחַרְתָּ֙ בַּֽחַיִּ֔ים לְמַ֥עַן תִּחְיֶ֖ה אַתָּ֥ה וְזַרְעֶֽךָ׃
20 לְאַֽהֲבָה֙ אֶת־יְהוָ֣ה אֱלֹהֶ֔יךָ לִשְׁמֹ֥עַ בְּקֹל֖וֹ
וּלְדָבְקָה־ב֑וֹ כִּ֣י ה֤וּא חַיֶּ֙יךָ֙ וְאֹ֣רֶךְ יָמֶ֔יךָ לָשֶׁ֣בֶת
עַל־הָֽאֲדָמָ֗ה אֲשֶׁר֩ נִשְׁבַּ֨ע יְהוָ֤ה לַאֲבֹתֶ֙יךָ֙
לְאַבְרָהָ֛ם לְיִצְחָ֥ק וּֽלְיַעֲקֹ֖ב לָתֵ֥ת לָהֶֽם׃ פ

20. The summary is similar to verse 16; compare 11:22.

For thereby you shall have life and shall long endure   Literally, "For that[22] is your life and the length of your days." In its literal form this phrase is adapted in the evening liturgy as "For they [God's commandments and the words of His Torah] are our life and the length of our days."

holding fast to Him   See Comment to 4:4.

EPILOGUE: MOSES' LAST DAYS (31:1–34:12)

Chapters 31–34 are the epilogue both to Deuteronomy and the entire Torah. They describe the steps taken by Moses, upon concluding his major addresses, to prepare Israel for the future, and conclude with his death and the people's mourning. Several actions are interwoven in this epilogue: Moses announces his imminent departure and appoints Joshua as his successor (31:1–8, 14–15,23); he writes a copy of the Teaching, places it in the care of the priests and elders, gives instructions for its regular public reading, and urges the people to observe it (31:9–13,24–26; 32:45–47); he teaches the people a prophetic poem orally and deposits a copy of it with the priests (31:16–22,27–30; 32:1–44); and he delivers a final blessing to the tribes (33). After all this, he ascends Mount Nebo and dies (32:48–52; 34).

MOSES' PREPARATION OF ISRAEL FOR THE FUTURE (chaps. 31–32)

CHAPTER 31

Preparatory Acts (vv. 1–30)

Va-yelekh

Chapter 31, the first part of the epilogue, consists of eight sections.[1] The first three are (1) Moses' announcement of his departure and identification of Joshua as his successor (vv. 1–6), (2) his appointment of Joshua (vv. 7–8), and (3) his writing down the Teaching and giving it to the priests and elders with instructions for its public reading (vv. 9–13). Before Moses continues with instructions about storing the text, the narrative unexpectedly digresses: (4) God summons Moses and Joshua so that He Himself may appoint Joshua (vv. 14–15); after Moses and Joshua appear before Him, (5) God tells Moses that the Israelites are sure to betray Him in the future and be punished severely, and He commands Moses to teach the people a poem that will serve as a witness, putting them on notice about their punishment and what will cause it (vv. 16–22); and then (6) God appoints Joshua (v. 23). After these digressions, (7) Moses tells the Levites where to store the Teaching, which he also characterizes as a witness in the event of Israel's future rebellion (vv. 24–26); and (8) he summons his audience to hear the poem (vv. 28–30).

31 VA-YELEKH

Moses went and spoke these things to all Israel. ²He said to them:

I am now one hundred and twenty years old, I can no longer be active. Moreover, the LORD has said to me, "You

ל"א וַיֵּ֖לֶךְ מֹשֶׁ֑ה וַיְדַבֵּ֛ר אֶת־הַדְּבָרִ֥ים הָאֵ֖לֶּה
אֶל־כָּל־יִשְׂרָאֵֽל׃ ² וַיֹּ֣אמֶר אֲלֵהֶ֗ם
בֶּן־מֵאָ֣ה וְעֶשְׂרִים֩ שָׁנָ֨ה אָנֹכִ֤י הַיּוֹם֙ לֹא־אוּכַ֥ל ע֖וֹד

Sections 5 and 7, and the poem they introduce (chapter 32), interject an unexpected note of pessimism. Throughout his addresses, Moses has warned the people against disobedience with the aim of deterring it, and never insinuated that they are more likely to sin than to obey. In verses 12–13 he is hopeful, even optimistic, that regular reading of the Teaching will convince future generations to remain loyal and obedient. All of this is overridden by the announcement from God and Moses that the people are certain to sin, that they are even now planning rebellion (vv. 16,20,27,29). This unexpected note of pessimism and the digressions from the anticipated order of events, along with other inconsistencies, suggest that the chapter has drawn upon material from disparate sources (see Excursus 29). Nevertheless, the present arrangement of the material shows evidence of careful literary design, for the themes of verses 9–27 are arranged in chiastic order:

A. (3) The Teaching (vv. 9–13)
   B. (4) Appointment of Joshua (vv. 14–15)
      C. (5) The poem (vv. 16–22)
   B'. (6) Appointment of Joshua (v. 23)
A'. (7) The Teaching (vv. 24–27)

MOSES ANNOUNCES HIS DEPARTURE
AND HIS REPLACEMENT BY JOSHUA (vv. 1–6)

After Israel had defeated Sihon and Og and reached the border of the promised land, God denied Moses' request to enter it (3:23–28). He instructed Moses to ascend the mountain where he would die and to appoint Joshua as his successor. Now Moses proceeds to carry out God's instructions. Urging Israel and Joshua not to fear the Canaanites, he encourages them with theological and historical reasons: God is their true leader, Joshua will be His earthly representative, and God's power is demonstrated by the recent victory over Sihon and Og.

Moses' remarks are similar to those often addressed to Israel's army and its leaders prior to battle.[2] See 20:2–4 and Comment there. Such exhortation is especially timely now, because Moses is about to die and the people, dependent on him for a whole generation, might lose their confidence as they prepare to do battle for the promised land.

1. Moses went and spoke these things The paragraphing in the translation is misleading because it implies that verse 1 and the first part of verse 2 are all introductory to this chapter. In the idiom of Hebrew narrative, "these things" refers to words previously spoken,[3] and verse 1 refers to the address of chapters 29–30. The statement that Moses "went" is unclear, since it does not indicate where he went from or to. But it is comparable to 32:44: "Moses came . . . and recited all the words of this poem . . . ," referring to the poem just recited. The verse also seems a bit superfluous in view of 29:1, though no more so than 32:44 is in view of 31:30. However, a smoother reading appears in a manuscript of Deuteronomy from Qumran: "When Moses had finished speaking these things."[4] This reading makes the verse identical to 32:45, which, like the present verse, is also followed by "He said to them."

2. After saying the "things" to which verse 1 refers, Moses turned to the matters at hand and explained that he could not continue as Israel's leader.

one hundred and twenty years old See Comment to 34:7.

be active Rather, "exercise military leadership"—literally, "come and go"—the task at hand. See Comment to 28:6 and Numbers 27:17.

the LORD has said to me A reference to 3:27; compare 1:37; 4:21–22.

shall not go across yonder Jordan." ³The LORD your God Himself will cross over before you; and He Himself will wipe out those nations from your path and you shall dispossess them.—Joshua is the one who shall cross before you, as the LORD has spoken.—⁴The LORD will do to them as He did to Sihon and Og, kings of the Amorites, and to their countries, when He wiped them out. ⁵The LORD will deliver them up to you, and you shall deal with them in full accordance with the Instruction that I have enjoined upon you. ⁶Be strong and resolute, be not in fear or in dread of them; for the LORD your God Himself marches with you: He will not fail you or forsake you.

⁷Then Moses called Joshua and said to him in the sight

לָצֵאת וְלָבוֹא וַיהוָה אָמַר אֵלַי לֹא תַעֲבֹר אֶת־
הַיַּרְדֵּן הַזֶּה: 3 יְהוָה אֱלֹהֶיךָ | עֹבֵר לְפָנֶיךָ
הוּא־יַשְׁמִיד אֶת־הַגּוֹיִם הָאֵלֶּה מִלְּפָנֶיךָ וִירִשְׁתָּם
יְהוֹשֻׁעַ הוּא עֹבֵר לְפָנֶיךָ כַּאֲשֶׁר דִּבֶּר יְהוָה:
שני 4 וְעָשָׂה יְהוָה לָהֶם כַּאֲשֶׁר עָשָׂה
לְסִיחוֹן וּלְעוֹג מַלְכֵי הָאֱמֹרִי וּלְאַרְצָם אֲשֶׁר
הִשְׁמִיד אֹתָם: 5 וּנְתָנָם יְהוָה לִפְנֵיכֶם וַעֲשִׂיתֶם
לָהֶם כְּכָל־הַמִּצְוָה אֲשֶׁר צִוִּיתִי אֶתְכֶם: 6 חִזְקוּ
וְאִמְצוּ אַל־תִּירְאוּ וְאַל־תַּעַרְצוּ מִפְּנֵיהֶם כִּי |
יְהוָה אֱלֹהֶיךָ הוּא הַהֹלֵךְ עִמָּךְ לֹא יַרְפְּךָ וְלֹא
יַעַזְבֶךָּ: פ   שלישי [חמישי כשהן מחוברות]
7 וַיִּקְרָא מֹשֶׁה לִיהוֹשֻׁעַ וַיֹּאמֶר אֵלָיו לְעֵינֵי כָל־

---

3. After Moses mentions his own inability to cross the Jordan, he might have been expected to continue immediately with the statement that Joshua will lead Israel across. Instead, he first mentions that God will lead Israel across and defeat the enemy. By saying this first, he makes clear that God's role, not Joshua's, is decisive. For this theological concept, see Excursus 3. Since there is no grammatical coordination between the two clauses of this verse, and the second clause is the natural sequel to verse 2, it has been suggested that the first is an interpolation made for the purpose of emphasizing the theological point.[5]

The LORD your God Himself Rather, "The LORD your God [and not I] is the one who shall cross over before you." The Hebrew is identical to the beginning of the clause about Joshua in the second part of the verse.

as the LORD has spoken To Moses, in 3:28.

4–6. These verses expand on the theological point made in verse 3a.[6]

4. To bolster the people's confidence, Moses reminds them of their recent victories (2:31–3:7), just as he encouraged Joshua in 3:21. The people's willingness to battle Sihon and Og showed that they were not beset by the faithlessness that had kept the previous generation out of the promised land, and their victory filled them with confidence.

5. For the instructions about the Canaanites see 7:1–5; 12:2–3; 20:16–17.

6. Be strong and resolute Trusting in God's strength, not their own, they may be fully confident of victory.

be not in fear or in dread See Comment to 1:21.

the LORD ... marches with you The promise that God will be, or go, with someone is a concise assurance of His assistance and protection.[7] It is often given by God or in His name when He charges a person with a mission, especially a military one. God made the same promise to Moses when He sent him to lead Israel out of Egypt; to Joshua in verse 8 and again after Moses' death; to Gideon when He charged him with delivering Israel from the Midianites; and to Jeremiah when commissioning him as a prophet.[8] Moses earlier offered the same assurance to the army and commanded that priests do so in the future each time the army prepares for battle (20:1,4).

MOSES APPOINTS JOSHUA (vv. 7–8)

Moses publicly appoints Joshua as his successor and encourages him, as God had instructed him earlier (1:38; 3:28).[9] According to 34:9 and Numbers 27:18–23, Moses laid his hands on Joshua in the course of appointing him, imparting to him a spirit of wisdom and a measure of his own authority.

of all Israel: "Be strong and resolute, for it is you who shall go with this people into the land that the LORD swore to their fathers to give them, and it is you who shall apportion it to them. 8And the LORD Himself will go before you. He will be with you; He will not fail you or forsake you. Fear not and be not dismayed!"

9Moses wrote down this Teaching and gave it to the priests, sons of Levi, who carried the Ark of the LORD's Covenant, and to all the elders of Israel.

10And Moses instructed them as follows: Every seventh year, the year set for remission, at the Feast of Booths, 11when all Israel comes to appear before the LORD your God in the place that He will choose, you shall read this

יִשְׂרָאֵל חֲזַק וֶאֱמָץ כִּי אַתָּה תָּבוֹא אֶת־הָעָם הַזֶּה
אֶל־הָאָרֶץ אֲשֶׁר נִשְׁבַּע יְהוָה לַאֲבֹתָם לָתֵת לָהֶם
וְאַתָּה תַּנְחִילֶנָּה אוֹתָם: 8 וַיהוָה הוּא | הַהֹלֵךְ
לְפָנֶיךָ הוּא יִהְיֶה עִמָּךְ לֹא יַרְפְּךָ וְלֹא יַעַזְבֶךָּ לֹא
תִירָא וְלֹא תֵחָת:
9 וַיִּכְתֹּב מֹשֶׁה אֶת־הַתּוֹרָה הַזֹּאת וַיִּתְּנָהּ אֶל־
הַכֹּהֲנִים בְּנֵי לֵוִי הַנֹּשְׂאִים אֶת־אֲרוֹן בְּרִית יְהוָה
וְאֶל־כָּל־זִקְנֵי יִשְׂרָאֵל: רביעי
10 וַיְצַו מֹשֶׁה אוֹתָם לֵאמֹר מִקֵּץ | שֶׁבַע שָׁנִים
בְּמֹעֵד שְׁנַת הַשְּׁמִטָּה בְּחַג הַסֻּכּוֹת: 11 בְּבוֹא כָל־
יִשְׂרָאֵל לֵרָאוֹת אֶת־פְּנֵי יְהוָה אֱלֹהֶיךָ בַּמָּקוֹם

it is you who shall go with In verse 23, God says to Joshua, "it is you who shall *bring*." Moses, speaking to Joshua in the hearing of the people, may want to emphasize that Joshua is one of them so as to avoid any implication that Joshua rather than God is the real leader. God, speaking privately to Joshua in verse 23, is at less pains to avoid the implication.[10]

7. apportion See Comment to 1:38, "allot."

8. Fear not and be not dismayed See Comment to 1:21. The same encouragement that Moses addressed to Joshua privately in 3:22 he now addresses to him publicly, making his appointment known to all.

THE WRITING AND READING OF THE TEACHING (vv. 9–13)

Now that Moses has finished expounding the Teaching (see 1:5), which he has imparted orally until now, he writes it down and arranges for its regular public reading so that the people may be reminded regularly of its contents and future generations may learn it. These were steps of far-reaching significance. The writing of the Teaching was part of the process that eventually led to the creation of sacred Scripture—that is, the Bible—which is the heart of Judaism. The public reading of the Teaching is part of the "democratic" character of biblical religion, which addresses its teachings and demands to all its adherents, with few distinctions between priests and laity, and calls for universal education of the citizenry in law and religion. These phenomena are discussed in Excursus 28.

9. Moses wrote down this Teaching The laws and other parts of Deuteronomy. See Comments to 1:5; 17:18; and 27:3.

gave it to the priests . . . and to all the elders The religious and civil leaders of the people, who would be responsible for guiding the nation's affairs in accordance with the Teaching, and for having it read to the public every seven years. The priests were to keep the text in the Ark that was in their charge (see vv. 25–26 and 10:8).

the priests, sons of Levi who carried the Ark See Comments to 10:8 and 18:1.

10. at the Feast of Booths See 16:13–15. This festival was the most propitious occasion for the reading because it attracted the largest number of pilgrims and was the lengthiest of the festivals, lasting for seven days. Since it came after the harvest was processed and stored, the people could feel secure about their food supply for the coming year and could absorb the lessons of the reading with minds free of concern.

11. to appear before the LORD See Comment to 16:16.

in the place that He will choose Where the Feast of Booths was celebrated (16:16) and

Teaching aloud in the presence of all Israel. ¹²Gather the people—men, women, children, and the strangers in your communities—that they may hear and so learn to revere the LORD your God and to observe faithfully every word of this Teaching. ¹³Their children, too, who have not had the experience, shall hear and learn to revere the LORD your God as long as they live in the land that you are about to cross the Jordan to possess.

אֲשֶׁ֥ר יִבְחַ֣ר תִּקְרָ֞א אֶת־הַתּוֹרָ֥ה הַזֹּ֛את נֶ֥גֶד כָּל־
יִשְׂרָאֵ֖ל בְּאָזְנֵיהֶֽם: ¹² הַקְהֵ֣ל אֶת־הָעָ֗ם הָֽאֲנָשִׁ֤ים
וְהַנָּשִׁים֙ וְהַטַּ֔ף וְגֵרְךָ֖ אֲשֶׁ֣ר בִּשְׁעָרֶ֑יךָ לְמַ֨עַן יִשְׁמְע֜וּ
וּלְמַ֣עַן יִלְמְד֗וּ וְיָֽרְאוּ֙ אֶת־יְהוָ֣ה אֱלֹֽהֵיכֶ֔ם וְשָֽׁמְר֣וּ
לַֽעֲשׂ֔וֹת אֶת־כָּל־דִּבְרֵ֖י הַתּוֹרָ֥ה הַזֹּֽאת: ¹³ וּבְנֵיהֶ֞ם
אֲשֶׁ֣ר לֹֽא־יָֽדְעוּ֮ יִשְׁמְעוּ֒ וְלָ֣מְד֔וּ לְיִרְאָ֖ה אֶת־יְהוָ֣ה
אֱלֹֽהֵיכֶ֑ם כָּל־הַיָּמִ֗ים אֲשֶׁ֨ר אַתֶּ֤ם חַיִּים֙ עַל־
הָ֣אֲדָמָ֔ה אֲשֶׁ֨ר אַתֶּ֜ם עֹבְרִ֧ים אֶת־הַיַּרְדֵּ֛ן שָׁ֖מָּה
לְרִשְׁתָּֽהּ: פ חמישי [ששי כשהן מחוברות]

where, according to 1 Kings 8:1–9, the Ark was kept. Learning to revere the Lord—the aim of the reading (vv. 12–13)—is one of the regular aims of visits to the chosen place (14:23).

you shall read Since Moses is addressing the priests and elders (v. 9) he presumably means that it is they who must read it or arrange for its reading. The singular form of "read" (*tikra'*) led early interpreters to presume that a single individual was meant, either Joshua and, later, the king,[11] or the high priest.[12] However, Moses often addresses even the entire people in the singular, so the grammar does not necessarily imply a single individual.[13]

this Teaching See Comment to verse 9. All of Deuteronomy can be read aloud in three to four hours. According to talmudic sources, the reading, termed "the king's lection" (*parashat ha-melekh*), consisted of a few selections from the book, but there is no reason to so limit the meaning.[14]

12. Gather Hebrew *hakhel* (pronounced *hak-hel*), from which the traditional name of this commandment, *mitsvat hakhel*, is derived. The same verb is used in 4:10 when God commands Moses to assemble the people at Horeb to hear the Decalogue for the same purpose as is specified here: "that they may learn to revere Me as long as they live on earth, and may so teach their children." See also Comment to verse 28, below.

men, women, children, and the strangers Although normally only adult male Israelites are obligated to appear at the festival, on this occasion women, children, and strangers must also attend so that all may hear their duties and rights read to them and be inspired with reverence for God. Compare 29:9–10. The verse makes no distinction between the need for men and women to learn the Teaching. Some authorities in the Talmud contend that there is no obligation to teach Torah to women; Rabbi Elazar ben Azariah states that men come to learn but women only to hear. But such opinions are products of the Greco-Roman view of women as intellectually weak, which began to appear in Jewish sources in the Hellenistic period.[15] By way of contrast, the talmudic sage Simeon ben Azzai held that a man is obligated to teach his daughter Torah.[16]

strangers See Comment to 29:10.

that they may hear and so learn to revere the LORD . . . and observe The Teaching's account of God's mighty deeds on behalf of Israel and its presentation of His commandments will inspire the people to revere Him and obey the commandments. See 4:32–40; 6:2–3; 11:2–9; and the introductory Comments to 1:6–3:29.

13. Their children, too, who have not had the experience That is, especially their children,[17] who have not had the experiences of the present generation, need to hear of those experiences and the lessons they taught. See introductory Comment to 11:1–9. Singling out the effect of the reading on the children reflects Deuteronomy's repeated concern with shaping their character and Moses' present concern with preparing for the future. Conducting the impressive public reading every seven years would mean that no generation would need to wait until reaching adulthood before having the experience; every child would have it soon after reaching an educable age.

14The LORD said to Moses: The time is drawing near for you to die. Call Joshua and present yourselves in the Tent of Meeting, that I may instruct him. Moses and Joshua went and presented themselves in the Tent of Meeting. 15The LORD appeared in the Tent, in a pillar of cloud, the pillar of cloud having come to rest at the entrance of the tent.

16The LORD said to Moses: You are soon to lie with your fathers. This people will thereupon go astray after the

14 וַיֹּאמֶר יְהֹוָה אֶל־מֹשֶׁה הֵן קָרְבוּ יָמֶיךָ לָמוּת קְרָא אֶת־יְהוֹשֻׁעַ וְהִתְיַצְּבוּ בְּאֹהֶל מוֹעֵד וַאֲצַוֶּנּוּ וַיֵּלֶךְ מֹשֶׁה וִיהוֹשֻׁעַ וַיִּתְיַצְּבוּ בְּאֹהֶל מוֹעֵד: 15 וַיֵּרָא יְהֹוָה בָּאֹהֶל בְּעַמּוּד עָנָן וַיַּעֲמֹד עַמּוּד הֶעָנָן עַל־פֶּתַח הָאֹהֶל: ס

16 וַיֹּאמֶר יְהֹוָה אֶל־מֹשֶׁה הִנְּךָ שֹׁכֵב עִם־אֲבֹתֶיךָ וְקָם הָעָם הַזֶּה וְזָנָה ׀ אַחֲרֵי ׀ אֱלֹהֵי נֵכַר־הָאָרֶץ

PREPARATIONS FOR GOD'S APPOINTMENT OF JOSHUA (vv. 14–15)

God informs Moses that He Himself will appoint Joshua as successor. This will confirm Moses' action in verses 1–8 and remove any doubt that the appointment is divinely authorized.

14. the Tent of Meeting The place where God speaks with Moses. There are two different conceptions of the Tent in the Torah. Most passages give the impression that it is identical to the Tabernacle sanctuary (the *mishkan*) in the middle of the camp, mentioned frequently in Exodus, Leviticus, and Numbers. According to those passages, the Tabernacle is God's residence. Inside, in the Holy of Holies, God meets with Moses, and speaks to him from within a cloud between the cherubs on the lid of the Ark. The Tabernacle is attended by priests and Levites.[18] On the other hand, Exodus 33:7–11 and other passages imply that the Tent of Meeting is a separate oracular tent *outside* the camp. It is constantly attended by Joshua. God comes to it, in a *pillar* of cloud, only to communicate with people, which He does while standing at its entrance.[19] As verse 15 indicates, Deuteronomy shares the latter conception of the Tent.

instruct him Rather, "appoint him." See Comment to 3:28.

15. The two parts of the verse seem inconsistent: was the cloud inside the Tent or did it remain outside at the entrance? The first possibility is consistent with the passages that equate the Tent with the sanctuary and have God speak in a cloud within its Holy of Holies. The second is consistent with the passages that describe it as a separate oracular tent; according to those passages, the cloud would always remain at the entrance and God would speak from there (see Exod. 33:9–11; Num. 12:4–5). Seen in that light, the first part of the present verse could perhaps mean "The LORD appeared *at* the Tent."[20] In the Septuagint, which is closer to the second view, the first half of the verse reads: "The LORD came down in a cloud and stopped at the entrance of the Tent of Meeting." For further discussion, see Excursus 29.

pillar of cloud The cloud is the vehicle by which God descends to earth.[21] In Psalm 68:5 God is called *rokhev ba-ʿaravot*, "He who rides the clouds."

GOD HAS MOSES COPY DOWN A POEM DESCRIBING ISRAEL'S FUTURE APOSTASY AND ITS CONSEQUENCES (vv. 16–22)

God tells Moses that after he dies the Israelites will betray Him and serve other gods; then, when disaster comes, they will not acknowledge the true reason (vv. 16–18). To counter their false explanation, He has Moses write down a poem (chapter 32) which will testify that betrayal of God is the cause of Israel's punishment (vv. 19–22).

ISRAEL'S FUTURE APOSTASY AND ITS CONSEQUENCES (vv. 16–18)

16. lie with your fathers That is, die; the idiom stands for "die and lie with one's fathers." It refers specifically to the reunion of one's spirit after death with those of one's ancestors in Sheol, as in the phrase "be gathered to one's kin" in 32:50.[22]

293

alien gods in their midst, in the land that they are about to enter; they will forsake Me and break My covenant that I made with them. [17]Then My anger will flare up against them, and I will abandon them and hide My countenance from them. They shall be ready prey; and many evils and troubles shall befall them. And they shall say on that day, "Surely it is because our God is not in our midst that these evils have befallen us." [18]Yet I will keep My countenance hidden on that day, because of all the evil they have done in turning to other gods. [19]Therefore, write down this poem and teach it to the people of Israel; put it in their mouths, in order that this poem may be My witness

אֲשֶׁר הוּא בָא־שָׁמָּה בְּקִרְבּוֹ וַעֲזָבַנִי וְהֵפֵר אֶת־בְּרִיתִי אֲשֶׁר כָּרַתִּי אִתּוֹ: 17 וְחָרָה אַפִּי בוֹ בַיּוֹם־הַהוּא וַעֲזַבְתִּים וְהִסְתַּרְתִּי פָנַי מֵהֶם וְהָיָה לֶאֱכֹל וּמְצָאֻהוּ רָעוֹת רַבּוֹת וְצָרוֹת וְאָמַר בַּיּוֹם הַהוּא הֲלֹא עַל כִּי־אֵין אֱלֹהַי בְּקִרְבִּי מְצָאוּנִי הָרָעוֹת הָאֵלֶּה: 18 וְאָנֹכִי הַסְתֵּר אַסְתִּיר פָּנַי בַּיּוֹם הַהוּא עַל כָּל־הָרָעָה אֲשֶׁר עָשָׂה כִּי פָנָה אֶל־אֱלֹהִים אֲחֵרִים: 19 וְעַתָּה כִּתְבוּ לָכֶם אֶת־הַשִּׁירָה הַזֹּאת וְלַמְּדָהּ אֶת־בְּנֵי־יִשְׂרָאֵל שִׂימָהּ בְּפִיהֶם לְמַעַן תִּהְיֶה־לִּי הַשִּׁירָה הַזֹּאת לְעֵד בִּבְנֵי יִשְׂרָאֵל:

go astray Literally, "fornicate," "go whoring." This metaphor for apostasy reflects the marriagelike bond between God and Israel, referred to in Comments to 5:9 and 7:6. Worship of other gods is an act of betrayal as repugnant as adultery.[23]

alien gods This is the expression used in the poem (32:12), instead of Deuteronomy's usual "other gods." In introducing the poem, God and Moses use several expressions and images from it (see vv. 17–18,20,28–29).

the alien gods in their midst, in the land That is, Canaanite gods that will be in Israel's midst after it enters the land.[24] Joshua later refers to these as "the gods . . . of the Amorites in whose land you are settled" (Josh. 24:15).[25]

forsake Me Israelite idolaters did not literally cease worshiping the Lord; they worshiped Him along with other gods, as was common in polytheism (see Comments to 4:2,19; 5:7; 13:6). But the exclusive, monotheistic character of the relationship between God and Israel is so integral to biblical religion that the worship of other gods is regarded as virtual abandonment of the Lord. Any relation the idolater continues to maintain with the Lord is meaningless. This is why the conception of the covenant as a marriagelike relationship is psychologically so apt.

17. I will abandon them Punishing them in kind for abandoning Me (v. 16). The same logic is expressed in 32:15–20, but here, by using the same verb that describes the sin in verse 16 (ʿ-z-v), Moses makes the justice of the punishment more obvious. See also 32:21 and, for the concept of "measure for measure" punishment, see Comment to 1:35.

hide My countenance from them Withdraw My favor and protection, abandon them and ignore their pleas for help.[26] God's "face" is His attentive presence, as in the Priestly Blessing: "May the LORD make His face shine on you and be gracious to you, / May the LORD lift up His face to you and grant you peace" (Num. 6:25–26). When God hides His countenance, Israel is exposed and unprotected. The same idea is expressed in the poem: "I will hide My countenance from them, / And see how they fare in the end" (32:20).

because our God is not in our midst Israel will realize from its troubles that it has lost divine protection (cf. 32:27–30; for the meaning of "not in our midst" see Comments to 1:42 and 6:16), but it will not admit guilt. It is clear from God's response in the next verse that Israel's reaction in this verse only compounds the sin. What, specifically, is wrong with its reaction depends on the meaning intended by *'elohai*, which can mean either "our God" or "our gods."[27] If the people mean "*our God* is not in our midst," they are most likely referring to the Lord, complaining that He is not involved, controlling events, or protecting Israel, but has broken His promise of verse 6 and abandoned them.[28] However, if that were the people's meaning, it would be strange for them to use so equivocal a term as *'elohai*. Whenever the Torah refers to God's presence or absence "in the midst" of the people, it refers to Him by name,[29] and whenever it refers to Him as *'elohai* it adds His name ("YHVH *'elohai*," "the LORD My God").[30] In this context, therefore, *'elohai* alone likely means "our gods" and implies that in their ignorance the people will think that they have been abandoned

against the people of Israel. ²⁰When I bring them into the land flowing with milk and honey that I promised on oath to their fathers, and they eat their fill and grow fat and turn to other gods and serve them, spurning Me and breaking

שׁשׁי [שׁביעי כשׁהן מחוברות] 20 כִּי־אֲבִיאֶנּוּ
אֶל־הָאֲדָמָה | אֲשֶׁר־נִשְׁבַּעְתִּי לַאֲבֹתָיו זָבַת
חָלָב וּדְבַשׁ וְאָכַל וְשָׂבַע וְדָשֵׁן וּפָנָה אֶל־אֱלֹהִים
אֲחֵרִים וַעֲבָדוּם וְנִאֲצוּנִי וְהֵפֵר אֶת־בְּרִיתִי:

by their (false) gods.[31] Even in distress they will cling to their error. Interestingly, a Qumran manuscript and the Septuagint read "the LORD our God" in this verse;[32] this is probably not an original reading but an attempt to resolve the ambiguity in favor of the first interpretation.

18. *Yet I will keep My countenance hidden* The Hebrew is simply "I will surely hide My countenance."[33] The meaning of the verse depends on that of the previous verse. If the people there mean that their gods have abandoned them, God's meaning here is: "But it is I—and not their false gods—who will abandon them . . . ," thus pointing out the people's error. The emphatic position of "I" at the beginning of the verse may favor this interpretation. If, on the other hand, the people are complaining in verse 17 of abandonment by God, then in the present verse God means to say, "But it is because of all the evil they have done . . . that I will hide My countenance," thus explaining that He was justified in abandoning them.

turning to other gods That is, relying on them or giving allegiance to them. The first sense of the idiom is attested elsewhere in the Bible, and both senses are found in Akkadian.[34]

WRITING THE POEM (vv. 19–22)

19. *write* The phrase is plural, literally, "write yourselves," referring to Moses and Joshua (see 32:44), though the remaining verbs in the verse are singular. Verse 22 mentions only Moses, who has the main responsibility. Possibly Moses was to dictate the poem to Joshua. Forty years earlier Moses wrote down a record of the defeat of Amalek and taught it orally to Joshua (Exod. 17:14). The simultaneous "recording" of the poem in two ways is notable: as in the case of the Teaching (vv. 9–13), a written copy is made, but the intended audience receives it orally.[35]

teach it . . . put it in their mouths Have them memorize it.[36] See Comment to 30:14. The idiom "put in the mouth," meaning "teach by heart," has recently been identified in Akkadian and Sumerian.[37] The poetic form would facilitate memorizing it.

be My witness against the people of Israel A witness proving that events were foretold prevents their misinterpretation.[38] The poem will testify that God had treated Israel with justice and kindness, but that Israel betrayed Him (see 32:1–18, esp. vv. 4–5). If the people's words in verse 17 represent a complaint that God had violated His promise to remain with them, the poem will rebut their charge, showing that God abandoned them for just cause.[39]

The idea of preserving a record of a prophecy as a "witness" for the future is also mentioned by the prophets Isaiah and Habakkuk, whom God tells to write down prophecies of punishment to serve in the future as witnesses that the disaster was foretold.[40] Their meaning is perhaps clarified by the "Second Isaiah," who tells the exiled Israelites that *they* are God's witnesses. Because they had heard God's earlier prophecies (*ri'shonot*), which have now come true, they can attest to the fact that He predicted the events, proving that He (and not false gods) controls the events:

> Long ago, I foretold things that happened, . . .
> Because I know how stubborn you are . . .
> Therefore I told you long beforehand,
> Announced to you things ere they happened—
> That you might not say, "My idol caused them,
> My carved and molten images ordained them."[41]

In verse 26 below, the Teaching is also described as a witness, probably in a different sense.

20. *flowing with milk and honey* See 6:3 and Excursus 9.

they eat . . . and turn to other gods Their prosperity and comfort will lead them to forget

My covenant, 21and the many evils and troubles befall them—then this poem shall confront them as a witness, since it will never be lost from the mouth of their off-spring. For I know what plans they are devising even now, before I bring them into the land that I promised on oath.

22That day, Moses wrote down this poem and taught it to the Israelites.

23And He charged Joshua son of Nun: "Be strong and resolute: for you shall bring the Israelites into the land that I promised them on oath, and I will be with you."

24When Moses had put down in writing the words of

21 וְהָיָ֡ה כִּֽי־תִמְצֶ֩אןָ֩ אֹת֨וֹ רָע֤וֹת רַבּוֹת֙ וְצָר֔וֹת וְ֠עָנְתָה הַשִּׁירָ֨ה הַזֹּ֤את לְפָנָיו֙ לְעֵ֔ד כִּ֛י לֹ֥א תִשָּׁכַ֖ח מִפִּ֣י זַרְע֑וֹ כִּ֣י יָדַ֗עְתִּי אֶת־יִצְרוֹ֙ אֲשֶׁ֨ר ה֤וּא עֹשֶׂה֙ הַיּ֔וֹם בְּטֶ֣רֶם אֲבִיאֶ֔נּוּ אֶל־הָאָ֖רֶץ אֲשֶׁ֥ר נִשְׁבָּֽעְתִּי:

22 וַיִּכְתֹּ֥ב מֹשֶׁ֛ה אֶת־הַשִּׁירָ֥ה הַזֹּ֖את בַּיּ֣וֹם הַה֑וּא וַֽיְלַמְּדָ֖הּ אֶת־בְּנֵ֥י יִשְׂרָאֵֽל:

23 וַיְצַ֞ו אֶת־יְהוֹשֻׁ֣עַ בִּן־נ֗וּן וַיֹּאמֶר֮ חֲזַ֣ק וֶֽאֱמָץ֒ כִּ֣י אַתָּ֗ה תָּבִיא֙ אֶת־בְּנֵ֣י יִשְׂרָאֵ֔ל אֶל־הָאָ֖רֶץ אֲשֶׁר־נִשְׁבַּ֣עְתִּי לָהֶ֑ם וְאָנֹכִ֖י אֶֽהְיֶ֥ה עִמָּֽךְ:

24 וַיְהִ֣י | כְּכַלּ֣וֹת מֹשֶׁ֗ה לִכְתֹּ֛ב אֶת־דִּבְרֵ֥י הַתּוֹרָֽה־

the true source of their well-being, which they will attribute to false gods the Canaanites believe responsible for fertility. Moses expresses this concern in similar terms in 6:10–13; 8:12–20; and 11:16, and again in the poem (32:13–18).

     21. *shall confront them ... since it will never be lost* Literally, "shall speak up ... since it will never be forgotten." Since the poem will be known by heart, it will virtually speak up by itself. When the predicted disasters materialize and the people recognize them, the poem, with its description of their sin (32:15ff), will irresistibly spring to their lips and witness their guilt to them.

     For I know what plans they are devising even now God concludes by repeating the point He made at the beginning, explaining why He expects the people to sin. Past experience—the incidents of the golden calf and Baal Peor (4:3; 9:12–29)—has shown Him how susceptible they are to idolatry. He is certain that they are taking the attitude warned against in 29:17–18. Moses is similarly pessimistic in verse 27.

     22. *and taught it to the Israelites* As related in verses 28ff.

GOD APPOINTS JOSHUA (v. 23)

The action announced in verses 14–15 resumes.

     He charged Rather, "He appointed"; see Comment to verse 14. This is the first time that God has spoken directly to Joshua.[42]

     I will be with you God confirms what Moses had promised Joshua in verse 8.

MOSES GIVES THE TEACHING TO THE PRIESTS AND ASSEMBLES THE PEOPLE TO HEAR THE POEM (vv. 24–30)

     24. *When Moses had put down in writing the words of this Teaching to the very end* As reported in verse 9. The text may mean that Moses gave the following instructions at that time, and not after the events of verses 14–23.

     put down in writing Literally, "wrote in a document." In the Bible *sefer*, used today for "book," means any kind of written document—even one as brief as a letter, a legal document, or an inscription—whether written on a sheet or scroll of papyrus or parchment, on stone, plaster, or pottery.[43] The word is thought to have developed from Akkadian *shipru*, "missive," "message" (from *shaparu*, "send"). The book in the modern sense—a collection of pages bound together in a volume—was not invented until early Christian times. In the present verse a leather scroll is undoubtedly meant.[44]

this Teaching to the very end, ²⁵Moses charged the Levites who carried the Ark of the Covenant of the LORD,
saying: ²⁶Take this book of Teaching and place it beside
the Ark of the Covenant of the LORD your God, and let it
remain there as a witness against you. ²⁷Well I know how
defiant and stiffnecked you are: even now, while I am still
alive in your midst, you have been defiant toward the

הַזֹּאת עַל־סֵפֶר עַד תֻּמָּם: שביעי ²⁵ וַיְצַו
מֹשֶׁה אֶת־הַלְוִיִּם נֹשְׂאֵי אֲרוֹן בְּרִית־יְהוָה לֵאמֹר:
²⁶ לָקֹחַ אֵת סֵפֶר הַתּוֹרָה הַזֶּה וְשַׂמְתֶּם אֹתוֹ מִצַּד
אֲרוֹן בְּרִית־יְהוָה אֱלֹהֵיכֶם וְהָיָה־שָׁם בְּךָ לְעֵד:
²⁷ כִּי אָנֹכִי יָדַעְתִּי אֶת־מֶרְיְךָ וְאֶת־עָרְפְּךָ הַקָּשֶׁה
הֵן בְּעוֹדֶנִּי חַי עִמָּכֶם הַיּוֹם מַמְרִים הֱיִתֶם עִם־

this Teaching   Since the immediate antecedent of this paragraph speaks about the poem, and "these words" in verse 28 refers to the poem, some scholars take "this Teaching," and "this document of Teaching" in verse 26, as references to the poem, meaning that the poem should be placed in the Ark.[45] However, everywhere else in the book "Teaching" refers to Deuteronomy itself, and it is virtually inconceivable that Deuteronomy would use *this* Teaching for something other than itself.[46]

25.   The Levites   See verse 9.

26.   place it beside the Ark of the Covenant   The Ark containing the two tablets of the covenant on which the Decalogue was written (4:13; 10:1–5). As noted in the Comment to 10:1–2, ancient treaties were commonly deposited in sanctuaries. Keeping the Teaching next to the Ark of the Covenant indicates that it embodies the principles of the Covenant and is as binding as the Decalogue itself because it comes from the same Divine source (see introductory Comment to chapter 5). The scroll with the Teaching was undoubtedly to be kept in a container, such as a jar or a box, to protect it against damage from moisture or worms.[47]

as a witness against you   Against Israel, whom the Levites here represent. Moses assigns the Teaching a new function, as a witness, like the poem (v. 19). Unlike the poem, it does not testify to Israel's betrayal of God after settling in Canaan. He probably means that the Teaching will serve as evidence that Israel accepted the terms and conditions of the covenant, which will enable the people to understand their future misfortunes.[48] Since the Teaching is not personified in this paragraph, as the poem is in verse 21, it is possible that 'ed, "witness," is used here in the related sense of "evidence" (of the covenant).[49]

A Hittite text tells of something similar: in the course of a persistent plague, the Hittite King Mursilis (fourteenth century B.C.E.) was led by an oracle to two old tablets describing oaths made by the Hittites to the gods, one of them part of a treaty; he learned that the violation of these oaths had caused the plague.[50] Many centuries later the Teaching played a similar role in Israel when it was discovered in the days of King Josiah of Judah (639–609 B.C.E.): it convinced the king of Israel's guilt and he instituted major religious reforms. After the Babylonian exile, the public reading of the Teaching convinced the people that violation of its tenets had caused the exile, and they organized themselves to obey its provisions.[51]

27.   Like God in verse 21, Moses explains that there must be a witness since the people will violate the covenant in the future.

Well I know   Rather, "I in particular know well," meaning, "no one knows better than I," having experienced your defiance so often. This sense is indicated by the emphatic position of "I" in the Hebrew.

defiant and stiffnecked   Moses used these terms to characterize Israel's behavior earlier, particularly its refusal to advance on the promised land and the golden calf incident.[52]

even now ... how much more, then   Literally, "Since even now ... how much more, then" (hen ... 'af ki). This is a biblical formula for expressing an *a fortiori* proposition (the talmudic kal va-ḥomer).[53] Since Moses, despite his authority, could not restrain Israel while alive, the people are even more likely to rebel after his death.

28–30.   Having explained the Teaching's function as a witness, Moses asks that the leaders be gathered to hear the poem. The transition to the poem is logical since it, too, will serve that

LORD; how much more, then, when I am dead! ²⁸Gather to me all the elders of your tribes and your officials, that I may speak all these words to them and that I may call heaven and earth to witness against them. ²⁹For I know that, when I am dead, you will act wickedly and turn away from the path that I enjoined upon you, and that in time to come misfortune will befall you for having done evil in the sight of the LORD and vexed Him by your deeds.

³⁰Then Moses recited the words of this poem to the very end, in the hearing of the whole congregation of Israel:

מַפְטִיר 28 הַקְהִילוּ אֵלַי אֶת־כָּל־זִקְנֵי שִׁבְטֵיכֶם וְשֹׁטְרֵיכֶם וַאֲדַבְּרָה בְאָזְנֵיהֶם אֵת הַדְּבָרִים הָאֵלֶּה וְאָעִידָה בָּם אֶת־הַשָּׁמַיִם וְאֶת־הָאָרֶץ: 29 כִּי יָדַעְתִּי אַחֲרֵי מוֹתִי כִּי־הַשְׁחֵת תַּשְׁחִתוּן וְסַרְתֶּם מִן־הַדֶּרֶךְ אֲשֶׁר צִוִּיתִי אֶתְכֶם וְקָרָאת אֶתְכֶם הָרָעָה בְּאַחֲרִית הַיָּמִים כִּי־תַעֲשׂוּ אֶת־הָרַע בְּעֵינֵי יְהֹוָה לְהַכְעִיסוֹ בְּמַעֲשֵׂה יְדֵיכֶם: 30 וַיְדַבֵּר מֹשֶׁה בְּאָזְנֵי כָּל־קְהַל יִשְׂרָאֵל אֶת־דִּבְרֵי הַשִּׁירָה הַזֹּאת עַד תֻּמָּם: פ

function (note the similarity of verse 27, in the context of the Teaching, and verse 29, in the context of the poem).

28. Gather This instruction implies another similarity between the poem and the Teaching: as the people are to be gathered to hear the Teaching (v. 12), their leaders are to be gathered to hear the poem. The prototype of both instructions is God's command to gather the people at Horeb (4:10).

the elders of your tribes The expression "elders of your tribes" never occurs elsewhere. The Septuagint and apparently a scroll from Qumran have a longer reading, "the heads of your tribes, your elders, judges, and officials."[54] This reading mentions four categories of officials, like 29:9 and Joshua 23:2 and 24:1. Since verse 30 indicates that Moses addressed the entire people, one would have expected the text to include a statement referring to *all* of Israel, as these other passages do. See Excursus 29.

all these words In the present context this refers to the poem,[55] but see Excursus 29.

that I may call heaven and earth to witness against them Heaven and earth will be the third "witness," attesting to the fact that Israel was warned. On the invocation of heaven and earth as witnesses, see 30:19 and Comment to 4:26. They are summoned for a different purpose in 32:1.

29. in time to come On this phrase see Comment to 4:30, "in the end." The situation described in the poem fits several periods in Israel's later history, starting with the period of the "Judges" following the death of Joshua. See Excursus 30.

30. This verse is the immediate introduction to the poem in chapter 32.

the whole congregation of Israel That is, the entire nation, formally convened for the occasion.[56] Earlier in Deuteronomy *kahal* refers to the assembly at Mount Sinai (5:19; 9:10; 10:4; 18:16) and to the national governing Assembly of the Israelites (23:2–9).

CHAPTER 32

Moses' Poem (Ha'azinu)   (vv. 1–43)

Ha'azinu   The poem of Moses, known from its first Hebrew word as *Shirat Ha'azinu*, describes the consequences of Israel's anticipated betrayal of God. The style is typical of biblical poetry. Each line consists of at least two phrases or clauses that are "parallel"—synonymous, antithetic, or complementary—to each other (see Excursus 30). Scholars refer to the phrases or clauses as "colons," and to pairs and trios of colons as "bicolons" and "tricolons." The poem is usually laid out in explicitly poetic form. This and other poetic characteristics of *Ha'azinu*, and its background, are discussed in Excursus 30. The outline of the poem is as follows:

32 HA'AZINU

Give ear, O heavens, let me speak;
Let the earth hear the words I utter!
[2]May my discourse come down as the rain,
My speech distill as the dew,

הַאֲזִינוּ הַשָּׁמַיִם וַאֲדַבֵּרָה   וְתִשְׁמַע הָאָרֶץ אִמְרֵי־פִי:
[2] יַעֲרֹף כַּמָּטָר לִקְחִי   תִּזַּל כַּטַּל אִמְרָתִי

I.   Exordium, inviting heaven and earth to pay attention as the poet declares God's qualities (vv. 1–3)
II. History of God's Relations with Israel (vv. 4–18)
    A. Thesis: God's justice and Israel's disloyalty (vv. 4–6)
    B. History of God's benefactions to Israel (vv. 7–14)
    C. Israel's disloyalty (vv. 15–18)
III. God's decisions (vv. 19–42)
    A. To punish Israel (vv. 19–25)
    B. To limit Israel's punishment and punish the enemy (vv. 26–42)
       1. God's reason for limiting Israel's punishment (vv. 26–31)
       2. His decision to punish the enemy, lest it draw the wrong inferences from its success (vv. 32–35)
       3. His plan to deliver Israel and punish the enemy (vv. 36–42)
IV. Coda: Celebration of God's deliverance of Israel (v. 43)

Section II, showing God's faithfulness and Israel's betrayal of Him, is the core of the poem and the basis for its earlier personification as a "witness" indicting Israel for its sin (31:19 and 21).

EXORDIUM   (vv. 1–3)

The poem opens with a call to heaven and earth to pay attention to a valuable lesson and a discourse on the nature of God. According to a variant reading in verse 43, heaven is called upon again at the end of the poem.

1.   Heaven and earth are also addressed in similar prophetic speeches that censure Israel for faithlessness to God after all His benefactions.[1] Earlier in Deuteronomy they are invoked, apparently as witnesses to the covenant and the poem and as instruments of punishment for violation of the covenant (see 4:26; 30:19; and 31:28). According to the Sifrei, Moses invoked them as witnesses because they are eternal and could refute Israel if, after his death, it should deny having accepted the covenant.[2] According to the Midrash Tanḥuma, Moses summoned them to punish Israel with drought and crop failure if it should violate the covenant, on the principle that the hand of the witnesses should be the first to act against the violator (17:7).[3] Modern scholars have made similar suggestions. In this poem, however, heaven and earth play no such role (see Excursus 30). They are summoned only to hear, and it seems that they are employed as a literary device, functioning as objective onlookers who witness the justice of the poem's charges and the fairness of Israel's punishment.[4] This is similar to their use in a speech by Jeremiah, who describes Israel's faithlessness to God and exclaims, "Be appalled, O heavens, at this; / Be horrified, utterly dazed!" (Jer. 2:12).

2.   The poem expresses the hope and expectation that its words—its demonstration of God's justice in all His dealings with Israel[5]—will be received as eagerly as the rain is welcomed and have the same life-giving effect.[6] The order of the similes in this verse matches the order of clauses in verse 1: the first two refer to the rain falling from heaven; the second two, to their effect on earth.[7]

discourse   Hebrew *lekaḥ*, "teaching," is derived from *lakaḥ*, "take"; its basic sense may be "what is grasped by the mind."[8] It is commonly used in the Book of Proverbs to describe the sage's teaching and the wisdom gained by those who heed it. Here it indicates that the poem has a didactic purpose beyond its forensic one of demonstrating God's justice and Israel's guilt.

distill   That is, precipitate.

Like showers on young growth,   וְכִרְבִיבִים עֲלֵי־עֵשֶׂב: כִּשְׂעִירִם עֲלֵי־דֶשֶׁא
Like droplets on the grass.
3 For the name of the LORD I proclaim;   הָבוּ גֹדֶל לֵאלֹהֵינוּ:   3 כִּי שֵׁם יְהוָה אֶקְרָא
Give glory to our God!

4 The Rock!—His deeds are perfect,   כִּי כָל־דְּרָכָיו מִשְׁפָּט   4 הַצּוּר תָּמִים פָּעֳלוֹ
Yea, all His ways are just;

---

the dew Rather, "moisture." Hebrew *tal* can refer to rain or dew, both of which were thought to fall from the sky.[9]

showers Hebrew *se'irim* appears only here. It is probably related to Ugaritic *s-r-ʻ*, which refers to the rising of rivers or fountains as a source of irrigation.[10]

3. the name of the LORD I proclaim Proclaiming God's name means declaring His qualities, recounting His deeds. See Exodus 33:19 and especially 34:5: "The LORD . . . proclaimed the name LORD . . . : 'The LORD! The LORD! a God compassionate and gracious'" and Psalm 105:1–2: "Proclaim His name, Proclaim His deeds . . . speak of all His wondrous acts." Proclaiming God's qualities is a major theme of *Ha'azinu*: His justice is epitomized in verse 4 and explicated throughout the poem.[11]

give glory Rather, "acknowledge God's greatness" (*godel*).[12] Usually God's "greatness" refers to His great power.[13] Here it seems to point to His great kindness and justice in dealing with Israel.[14]

The summons to praise God lends the poem a hymnic quality; similar invitations appear in the psalms.[15]

HISTORY OF GOD'S RELATIONS WITH ISRAEL (vv. 4–18)

In this section the poem begins to proclaim God's qualities, as promised in verse 3. It states the thesis that God is entirely just and faithful while Israel is faithless, foolish, and ungrateful (vv. 4–6).[16] The poem proceeds to elaborate on these two themes. It recalls God's fatherly kindness to Israel from the beginning: He divided the earth among many nations but took only Israel as His own people. He alone provided for Israel's needs in the wilderness, brought it safely to the promised land, and provided it with plenty (vv. 7–14). But prosperity turned Israel's head, causing it to forget God and turn to pagan deities, "non-gods," who had done nothing for it or its ancestors (vv. 15–18).

THE THESIS OF THE POEM (vv. 4–6)

4. This verse states the first main theme of the poem: God has treated Israel with complete justice. The adjectives used to describe God express the qualities of reliability and faithfulness.

The Rock "Rock," in the sense of mountain or cliff, appears as a term for "god" several times in the poem, referring both to the Lord and pagan gods (see vv. 15,18,30,31,37).[17] It expresses the idea that the deity is a source of refuge, a protector, as in verse 37, "the rock in whom they sought refuge."[18] From the Bible's viewpoint, the Lord is "*The* Rock," the only one deserving of the appellation.[19] The poem uses it of pagan gods only ironically, when pointing out their inferiority or complete inability as protectors (vv. 31, 37).

His deeds are perfect That is, reliable, faithful. Literally Hebrew *tamim* means "whole," "unimpaired," "flawless." It frequently expresses the idea of unimpaired loyalty, as in 18:13.[20]

just A quality often mentioned in the context of God's faithfulness and steadfastness.[21]

never false Never faithless.[22] In Jeremiah 2:5 *ʻavel* refers to a fault that might justify defection: "What wrong [*ʻavel*] did your fathers find in Me that they abandoned Me and went after delusion [idols] . . . ?"

A faithful God, never false,   צַדִּיק וְיָשָׁר הוּא: אֵל אֱמוּנָה וְאֵין עָוֶל

True and upright is He.   דּוֹר עִקֵּשׁ וּפְתַלְתֹּל: 5 שִׁחֵת לוֹ לֹא בָּנָיו מוּמָם

5Children unworthy of Him—

That crooked, perverse generation—   עַם נָבָל וְלֹא חָכָם   6 *הַ*-לַיהוָה תִּגְמְלוּ-זֹאת

Their baseness has played Him false.

6Do you thus requite the LORD,   v. 6. ה' רבתי

True *Tsaddik*, used here in the sense of "faithful," as in Isaiah 26:2, where it is parallel to "one who keeps faith."[23]

and upright That is, unswervingly trustworthy, reliable.[24]

5. This verse states the second main theme of the poem: Israel, in contrast to God, is faithless and perfidious, a "crooked, perverse generation."

Children unworthy of Him . . . Their baseness has played Him false Hebrew *shiḥet lo loʾ banayv mumam*. In the Hebrew text, these five words are not the first and third colons of the verse; they all appear together at the beginning of the verse. Their syntactic connection is unclear, as can be seen from a literal translation: "He has dealt corruptly with Him not His children their blemish."[25] Various paraphrases have been suggested for this awkward string of words, such as "They have dealt corruptly with Him, they are not His children, it is their blemish";[26] "Is corruption His? No; His children's is the blemish";[27] or "Their blemish corrupted them, His non-sons."[28]

Individually these words and phrases have meanings that suit the context. *Shiḥet*, "acted corruptly," describes the perfidy of worshiping the golden calf in 9:12 ("acted wickedly") and of violating a covenant in Malachi 2:8 ("corrupted the covenant"); its *hiphʿil* form is used for apostasy in 31:29. *Loʾ banayv* could be rendered "his non-children," conforming to the dismissive phrases that are characteristic of the poem (such as "witless" [lit., "not-wise"] in v. 6; "no-gods" in vv. 17,21; and "a no-folk" in v. 21).[29] It would mean that Israel has acted in an unfilial way (hence the emphasis in verse 6b that God is Israel's father). "Blemish" (*mum*), which normally refers to a physical blemish on an animal, is used occasionally for a moral blemish.[30] It is an apt antonym to "perfect" (*tamim*) (v. 4), for in their literal senses "perfect" and "blemish(ed)" are used to designate sacrificial animals as acceptable or unacceptable for sacrifice.[31]

The awkward syntax of the Hebrew suggests that the text has suffered from scribal error. Quite possibly, the text originally read *shiḥatu lo banayv ʾemun*, "His children violated, against Him, loyalty" or *shiḥatu loʾ-banayv ʾemun*, "His non-children violated loyalty."[32] If one of these emendations is correct, the two clauses of verse 20b are chiastically parallel to verse 5 (cf. Comment to 22:7 on inversion of clauses).

The reference to Israel as God's children (cf. "sons and daughters," v. 19) is part of the father-child metaphor that expresses God's relationship with Israel in the poem. God "creates" Israel (v. 6), nurtures, guides, and protects it (vv. 10–12), and expects filial loyalty in return (cf. v. 20). Elsewhere, Deuteronomy compares God's carrying of Israel through the wilderness (1:31) and His disciplinary acts (8:5) to those of a father, and prescribes standards of conduct that He expects of Israel as His children (14:1; see Comment there). The metaphor is fleshed out by the prophets, who speak of Israel's filial duties to God: God assigned Israel its land as a father assigns land to his children, and expected that Israel would acknowledge His fatherhood and remain loyal, and not "play false."[33] They often describe Israel's sins as the misbehavior of rebellious sons and daughters.[34] The present verse aptly expresses the ignominy of Israel's conduct and the frustration of God's expectations.

crooked, perverse *ʿIkkesh* and *petaltol*, the opposite of God, who is "true and upright" (v. 4). Derivatives of the same roots are also used as antonyms of *tamim*, "perfect, reliable, faithful."[35]

6. The poem now addresses Israel directly, charging it with answering God's fatherly benefactions with ingratitude and rebellion.

Do you thus requite the LORD The word order in Hebrew ("Is it the LORD you requite thus") underscores the shocking nature of Israel's unfilial behavior: Do you treat *even Him* this way? In Torah scrolls the interrogative prefix *ha* ("Is it . . . ?") is written in larger script and, anomalously,

O dull and witless people?
Is not He the Father who created you,
Fashioned you and made you endure!

הֲלוֹא־הוּא אָבִיךָ קָּנֶךָ
שני
הוּא עָשְׂךָ וַיְכֹנְנֶךָ:

7 זְכֹר יְמוֹת עוֹלָם
שְׁאַל אָבִיךָ וְיַגֵּדְךָ
בִּינוּ שְׁנוֹת דֹּר־וָדֹר
זְקֵנֶיךָ וְיֹאמְרוּ לָךְ:

7Remember the days of old,
Consider the years of ages past;
Ask your father, he will inform you,
Your elders, they will tell you:

as a separate word. The reason for this is unknown, but it has the effect of heightening the shock expressed by the rhetorical question.

dull Hebrew *naval*, "villain(ous)." As reflected in its combination with "witless" here, this word sometimes refers to the foolish attitudes of the villain (comparably, Eng. "villain" sometimes means "boor"). The villain feels safe because he is contemptuous of God, believing that He is inattentive to human events or powerless to affect them. Israel acts as if it shares this attitude.[36]

witless That is, "unwise." On obedience to God, and recognition of His guidance, as wisdom, see 4:6; 29:3; and 30:11–14.

created[37]

made you endure Rather, "brought you into existence."[38]

In all, four terms describe God as Israel's father and creator in this verse and verse 15, and two more appear in verse 18. The Bible is quite conscious of the fact that Israel had not existed from time immemorial but owed its national existence to God. The poem does not specify when God created Israel, but verse 8 suggests that it was when He divided the human race into separate nations (see Gen. 10–11).

THE HISTORY OF GOD'S BENEFACTIONS TO ISRAEL (vv. 7–14)

Summaries of God's benefactions to Israel are common. They are used in liturgy (see 26:5–9) as a means of expressing gratitude to God, and in prophetic speeches, such as the present one, as the basis for rebuking the nation for its sins against God.[39]

7. Israel should consider its history in order to be reminded of all that God did for it. Compare 4:32, where Moses again urges the consideration of ancient history to show the truth of his message.

Ask your father . . . your elders If the audience has any doubt about the truth of what is said, it can turn to its elders—the custodians of historical tradition in a predominantly oral culture[40]—for confirmation. The challenge to consult the elders was apparently a traditional element in ancient rhetoric; examples appear in the Book of Job and in a Mesopotamian royal inscription.[41]

8–9. God's benefactions to Israel began when He divided the human race into separate nations and chose Israel as His own. According to Genesis, the division of humanity into nations took place after the Flood, in the aftermath of the Tower of Babel (Gen. 10 and 11:1–9).[42]

According to the Masoretic text, the last colon in verse 8 reads "in relation [i.e., equal] to Israel's numbers" (*le-mispar benei yisra'el*). This reading implies that God created the same number of nations as there were Israelites.[43] He assigned territories to each nation, but took Israel to be His own people (cf. 7:6; 10:15).[44] Since Genesis 10 lists seventy nations,[45] the verse must mean that God created seventy nations, equal to the seventy members of Jacob's (Israel's) family who migrated to Egypt (see Deut. 10:22; Exod. 1:1–5).

This reading raises a number of difficulties. Why would God base the number of nations on the number of Israelites? According to Genesis, Israel did not exist at the time. And why would He have based the division on their number at the time they went to Egypt, an event not mentioned in the poem?[46] In addition, verse 9, which states that God's portion was Israel, implies a contrast: Israel was God's share while the other peoples were somebody else's share, but verse 8 fails to indicate whose share they were.

8 When the Most High gave nations their homes
And set the divisions of man,
He fixed the boundaries of peoples
In relation to Israel's numbers.
9 For the LORD's portion is His people,
Jacob His own allotment.

בְּהַנְחֵל עֶלְיוֹן גּוֹיִם 8
יַצֵּב גְּבֻלֹת עַמִּים
כִּי חֵלֶק יְהֹוָה עַמּוֹ 9

בְּהַפְרִידוֹ בְּנֵי אָדָם
לְמִסְפַּר בְּנֵי יִשְׂרָאֵל:
יַעֲקֹב חֶבֶל נַחֲלָתוֹ:

These problems are eliminated if we adopt a reading found in one of the Qumran scrolls, the Septuagint, and other texts (see Excursus 31). In place of "equal to Israel's numbers" (*le-mispar benei yisra'el*) these texts read "equal to the number of divine beings" (*le-mispar benei 'elohim*). Verses 8–9 would then be translated as follows:

> When the Most High allotted the nations,[47]
> and set the divisions of man,
> He fixed the boundaries [or territories][48] of peoples
> Equal to the number of divine beings,
> And lo, His people became the LORD's portion,
> Jacob His own allotment.

This means that when God was allotting nations to the divine beings, he made the same number of nations and territories as there were such beings. Verse 9 implies that He then assigned the other nations to those divine beings, and states explicitly that He kept Israel for Himself. This seems to be part of a concept hinted at elsewhere in the Bible and in postbiblical literature. When God organized the government of the world, He established two tiers: at the top, He Himself, "God of gods (*'elohei ha-'elohim*) and Lord of lords" (10:17), who reserved Israel for Himself, to govern personally; below Him, seventy angelic "divine beings" (*benei 'elohim*), to whom He allotted the other peoples.[49] The conception is like that of a king or emperor governing the capital or heartland of his realm personally and assigning the provinces to subordinates.[50]

These angelic "divine beings" are also mentioned in a variant reading of verse 43. For further discussion about them, see Excursus 31.

When the Most High gave nations their homes   Rather, "When the Most High allotted the nations." As noted, this and the next clause, "And set the divisions of man," refer to the division of the human race after the Flood and the Tower of Babel. When the reading "equal to the number of divine beings" is adopted in the final colon of verse 8, the verse reflects the Bible's assumption that the nations' worship of other divine beings began then. See Excursus 7.

the Most High   Hebrew *'elyon* is a common title of God in the Bible, primarily in poetry. It is sometimes combined with *'el*, "God," in the phrase *'el 'elyon*, "God Most High."[51] It is used by Israelites and non-Israelites, and also appears in non-Israelite sources.[52] "Most High" is an ideal epithet for God. In the present verse it emphasizes His supremacy over the other divine beings, and since it does not have exclusively Israelite associations it suits the context of God's organizing the human race as a whole. Verse 9, relating God's selection of Israel, reverts to the specifically Israelite name YHVH ("LORD").[53]

9.   In taking Israel for Himself, God granted it a privilege He gave no other nation. This exclusive personal relationship was valued so highly that after the golden calf incident, after God agreed to spare Israel but threatened to end His personal relationship with them, Moses insisted on its continuation, arguing "For how shall it be known that I have gained your favor, I and your people, unless *You* [and not an angel] go with us, so that we may be distinguished from every people on the face of the earth" (Exod. 33:16; cf. 32:34; 33:2). See Comment to 4:37 for further discussion.

For the LORD's portion is His people   Rather, "And lo, His people became the LORD's portion." *Ki* can hardly mean "for" here, since the verse does not explain the preceding one. Sometimes it has an emphatic meaning such as "yea," "indeed," "lo" (see also v. 32).[54] The particle highlights the magnitude of what God did for Israel in choosing it as His portion.

10 יְמְצָאֵ֙הוּ֙ בְּאֶ֣רֶץ מִדְבָּ֔ר　　וּבְתֹ֖הוּ יְלֵ֣ל יְשִׁמֹ֑ן

סְבֹבֶנְהוּ֙ יְב֣וֹנְנֵ֔הוּ　　יִצְּרֶ֖נְהוּ כְּאִישׁ֥וֹן עֵינֽוֹ׃

11 כְּנֶ֙שֶׁר֙ יָעִ֣יר קִנּ֔וֹ　　עַל־גּוֹזָלָ֖יו יְרַחֵ֑ף

יִפְרֹ֤שׂ כְּנָפָיו֙ יִקָּחֵ֔הוּ　　יִשָּׂאֵ֖הוּ עַל־אֶבְרָתֽוֹ׃

12 יְהוָ֖ה בָּדָ֣ד יַנְחֶ֑נּוּ　　וְאֵ֥ין עִמּ֖וֹ אֵ֥ל נֵכָֽר׃

שלישי

10 He found him in a desert region,
In an empty howling waste.
He engirded him, watched over him,
Guarded him as the pupil of His eye.
11 Like an eagle who rouses his nestlings,
Gliding down to his young,
So did He spread His wings and take him,
Bear him along on His pinions;
12 The LORD alone did guide him,
No alien god at His side.

"His people" refers, obviously, to Jacob, a synonym of Israel both as an individual and as a nation (see, e.g., Num. 23:7).[55]

allotment　As God's "allotment" (*naḥalah*)[56] Israel was cherished and protected by Him. See Comments to 4:20; 9:26.

10. He found him in a desert region　In the Sinai, where Israel roamed before entering the promised land. The statement that God "found" Israel implies that it was like a foundling or a desert wanderer, in danger of starvation and exposure. This metaphor shows how parlous Israel's situation was previously and how indebted it is to God for its survival. The use of this metaphor here is puzzling because it is inconsistent with the statements that God fathered Israel (v. 6) and chose it in primordial times (vv. 8–9).[57] However, Hosea likewise refers to God's "finding" Israel in the desert, and delighting in it as would one who discovered grapes in the desert, and Ezekiel pictures God as coming upon Israel "in the field" like a rejected, exposed child, and providing for its needs.[58] Both of these prophets are well aware of God's earlier relationship with Israel, in the days of the patriarchs and the Exodus, but they ignore it for the purposes of the metaphors they are using in the passages in question. Biblical poetry sometimes adopts metaphors because of their effectiveness in a specific context without regard for their consistency with the larger context.[59] The present poem speaks of God as Israel's father, but also speaks of its human fathers (v. 7); it calls Israel God's children (vv. 5–6,18–19,21) but also His servants (vv. 36,43); it compares God to an eagle and Israel to its young (v. 11), but it also compares Israel to an unruly animal (v. 15).

howling waste　A wasteland in which the howling of winds[60] or wild animals[61] is heard.

engirded　God encircled Israel protectingly. Rashbam sees this sense of the verb in Psalm 34:8: "The angel of the LORD camps around those who fear Him and rescues them."

guarded him　From snakes, scorpions, and marauders like the Amalekites.[62]

as the pupil of his eye　Since protecting the eye is a reflexive action, the pupil is an effective simile for an object of protective care.[63]

11.　God led Israel safely through the desert in the manner of an eagle training its young to fly, catching them on its back when they tire or fall.[64] Exodus 19:4 alludes to the same image.

rouses　In the present context, Hebrew *ya'ir* may mean "protects."[65]

12.　Here the poem leaves the similes about the Lord's protection and emphasizes the reason that Israel's worship of other gods is so grievous: no deity but the Lord helped Israel (cf. v. 39). The Bible repeatedly makes this point to show that for Israel to turn to other gods is groundless as well as ungrateful. This is the reasoning that underlies the beginning of the Decalogue (5:6–7) and the repeated reference to other gods as "gods whom you have not experienced" (11:28). Compare Hosea 13:4: "Only I the LORD have been your God ever since the land of Egypt; you have never experienced a God but Me, you have never had a helper but Me. I looked after you in the desert, in a thirsty land."

guide him　Through the desert to the promised land. The same expression is used in the Song at the Sea (Exod. 15:13).

13He set him atop the highlands,
To feast on the yield of the earth;
He fed him honey from the crag,
And oil from the flinty rock,
14Curd of kine and milk of flocks;
With the best of lambs,
And rams of Bashan, and he-goats;
With the very finest wheat—
And foaming grape-blood was your drink.

וַיֹּאכַל תְּנוּבֹת שָׂדָי   יַרְכִּבֵהוּ עַל־במותי אֶרֶץ 13
וְשֶׁמֶן מֵחַלְמִישׁ צוּר׃   וַיֵּנִקֵהוּ דְבַשׁ מִסֶּלַע
עִם־חֵלֶב כָּרִים   חֶמְאַת בָּקָר וַחֲלֵב צֹאן 14
עִם־חֵלֶב כִּלְיוֹת חִטָּה   וְאֵילִים בְּנֵי־בָשָׁן וְעַתּוּדִים
וְדַם־עֵנָב תִּשְׁתֶּה־חָמֶר׃

בָּמֳתֵי ק׳ v. 13.

13–14. God's benefactions continued beyond the desert. He brought Israel to the promised land and fed it honey and olive oil, dairy products and meat, grain and wine. These are the characteristic products of the region. They are all mentioned in an ancient Egyptian description of the land of "Yaa" located somewhere in Syria or Canaan.[66] Compare 8:8.

13. *set him atop the highlands* The mountainous heartland of Israel, "the hill country of the Amorites" (1:7).[67]

earth Rather, "field."[68]

He fed him honey from the crag and oil from the flinty rock "Fed" is, literally, "suckled," implying that God fed Israel with virtually no effort on its part. Even places that one would expect to be barren yielded abundant foodstuffs: honeycombs, found in the land's countless caves and fissures,[69] and oil-producing olive trees that flourish in its rocky limestone soils.[70]

14. The land's rich pastures sustain cattle that produce dairy products and meat, while its soil yields wheat and wine.

curd *Ḥem'ah* refers to some milk product. The suggested meanings include butter, cream, *leben* (coagulated sour milk), and "ghee" (a semifluid clarified butter known nowadays from India).[71]

with the best of lambs, / And rams of Bashan, and he-goats It is preferable to follow the way the text is divided in the Aleppo Codex of the Bible: "with the best of lambs and rams, / Cattle [lit., offspring] of Bashan, and he-goats."[72]

best of lambs Literally, "fat of lambs." Fat is often used figuratively to refer to the best, as in the idiom "the fat of the land."[73] The phrase could mean "the best parts of lambs," or could even be meant literally, "the fat of lambs."[74]

Bashan The mountain range in northern Transjordan (see Comment to 3:1). Bashan was the best pastureland in the region, and its herds were famed for their strength and size.[75]

very finest wheat Literally, "fat of the kidneys of wheat." "Fat of wheat" is mentioned elsewhere[76] and presumably means "the best of wheat" (see above), but "kidneys of wheat" is not otherwise found. Some commentators take "kidneys" to mean the kernel of the wheat; the full phrase would then mean "the finest grains of wheat."[77] Others hold that it is a hyperbole meaning wheat with grains as thick as kidneys.[78]

Since Isaiah 34:6 refers to "fat of the kidneys *of rams*," it has been conjectured that the word "kidneys" here belongs earlier in the verse, in the phrase translated "the best of lambs" (*ḥelev karim*), literally "the fat of lambs." If so, the original reading there was "kidney fat of lambs" (*ḥelev kilyot karim*) and the original reading here simply "the best of wheat" (*ḥelev ḥittah*).[79]

grape-blood A poetic metaphor for wine.[80]

ISRAEL'S DISLOYALTY (vv. 15–18)

Having grown fat on God's bounty, Israel forgot the source of its well-being and turned to alien gods. See Comment to 6:11–12.

15 So Jeshurun grew fat and kicked—
You grew fat and gross and coarse—
He forsook the God who made him
And spurned the Rock of his support.
16 They incensed Him with alien things,
Vexed Him with abominations.
17 They sacrificed to demons, no-gods,
Gods they had never known,
New ones, who came but lately,
Who stirred not your fathers' fears.

שָׁמַנְתָּ עָבִיתָ כָּשִׂיתָ
וַיִּנַבֵּל צוּר יְשֻׁעָתוֹ:
בְּתוֹעֵבֹת יַכְעִיסֻהוּ:
אֱלֹהִים לֹא יְדָעוּם
לֹא שְׂעָרוּם אֲבֹתֵיכֶם:

15 וַיִּשְׁמַן יְשֻׁרוּן וַיִּבְעָט
וַיִּטֹּשׁ אֱלוֹהַּ עָשָׂהוּ
16 יַקְנִאֻהוּ בְּזָרִים
17 יִזְבְּחוּ לַשֵּׁדִים לֹא אֱלֹהַּ
חֲדָשִׁים מִקָּרֹב בָּאוּ

15. So Jeshurun grew fat and kicked[81]　The epithet "Jeshurun" (Heb. *yeshurun*, "the Upright," from *yashar*, "upright") alludes to "Israel" (*yisra'el*) and sounds something like it. Although normally used honorifically (God Himself is called *yashar* in v. 4),[82] here it is used ironically, underscoring how Israel has failed to live up to its expected character.

kicked　Like an unruly, rebellious animal.[83] Instead of being satisfied and docile from being fed, Israel rejected Him who fed it.

you grew fat and gross and coarse　Here the poet addresses Israel directly. The precise meaning of the word rendered "coarse" (*kasita*) is uncertain.[84]

spurned[85]　Although the meaning is different, this verb (*n-v-l*) echoes *naval*, "villainous," in verse 6. Perhaps a double-entendre is intended: "you spurned/acted villainously toward God."[86]

rock of his support　Rather, "the Rock who delivered him," who protected him from danger.[87]

16.　By worshiping other gods Israel provoked the indignant rage that God warned about in the Decalogue. "Incensed" is derived from the root *k-n-'*, the same root underlying *kanna'*, "impassioned" in 4:24 and 5:9. See Comment to 5:9.

alien things . . . abominations　Alien gods (v. 12)[88] and idols.[89]

17.　This verse disparages the gods Israel worshiped. It does not argue that Israel worshiped nonexistent beings, mere statues, but that it worshiped nondivine beings, beings that lack effective power and are unworthy of worship.[90]

demons　Rather, "spirits." *Shed* is used in Akkadian for minor protective spirits.[91] The point is that the beings Israel worshiped are mere spirits, not gods.[92] Compare Psalm 106:36–38.

no-gods　Beings called "gods" (see the next colon) but undeservedly, pseudo-gods.[93] Compare "non-sons," "no-gods," "no-folk" in verses 5 and 21.

gods they had never known　See 11:28. Although the poem has just denied their divinity, it continues to use the word *'elohim* for these beings. This is due to the ambiguity of the word, discussed in the Comment to 3:24 and in Excursus 6. Possibly *'elohim* is used for "spirits" here, or else the word is used as if in quotation marks, meaning "so-called gods."

new ones　Compare Judges 5:8: "When they chose new gods. . . ." The term is dismissive: these are deities-come-lately. Unlike the Lord, who has acted on behalf of Israel since its beginning, these beings have no record of achievement or reliability. In the ancient world antiquity was a hallmark of authenticity,[94] and these new beings lacked it. The Lord, in contrast, is "the ancient God" (33:27) whose benefactions to Israel are "from of old."[95]

stirred not your fathers' fears　The meaning of the verb *se'arum*, which the translation renders as "stirred fears," is uncertain.[96] The Septuagint renders it as "whom your fathers did not know," synonymous with the second colon in the verse. This rendering can be supported by Arabic *sha'ara*, "know, be cognizant."[97] The Sifrei cites a view that *se'arum* should be interpreted as if it read *sha'um*, "[whom your fathers did not] turn to," a verb used elsewhere for reliance on a deity.[98]

18 You neglected the Rock that begot you,
Forgot the God who brought you forth.

19 The LORD saw and was vexed
And spurned His sons and His daughters.
20 He said:
I will hide My countenance from them,
And see how they fare in the end.

18 צ֤וּר יְלָֽדְךָ֙ תֶּ֔שִׁי*
רביעי
וַתִּשְׁכַּ֖ח אֵ֥ל מְחֹלְלֶֽךָ׃

19 וַיַּ֥רְא יְהוָ֖ה וַיִּנְאָ֑ץ
מִכַּ֥עַס בָּנָ֖יו וּבְנֹתָֽיו׃
20 וַיֹּ֗אמֶר
אַסְתִּ֤ירָה פָנַי֙ מֵהֶ֔ם
אֶרְאֶ֖ה מָ֥ה אַחֲרִיתָ֑ם

v. 18. י' זעירא

18. Again the poem turns directly to Israel and exclaims that it is guilty of the most unnatural behavior, forgetting its own parent. Compare the reverse image in Isaiah 49:15: "Can a woman forget her baby, or disown the child of her womb?"

begot . . . brought forth Although verse 6 describes God as Israel's father, the verbs *yalad* and *ḥolel* may have been chosen to suggest the image of a mother. The first is used far more often for giving birth than for fathering,[99] and the second refers literally to the mother's labor pains.[100] The image of forgetting one's *mother* would cast Israel's behavior in the most unnatural light and, combined with the father image, would suggest that Israel owes its existence *totally* to God, its father *and* mother. A similar combination of metaphors appears in ancient Syrian inscriptions which describe kings as father and mother to their people.[101]

GOD'S DECISIONS   (vv. 19–42)

God resolves to punish Israel by withdrawing His protection and exposing it to war and natural disasters (vv. 21–25). He would obliterate Israel entirely were it not that the triumphant enemy would misinterpret its success as a sign of its own power (26–31). Hence God will punish the enemy as well (32–35) and deliver Israel, showing that He alone controls the destiny of nations (36–42).

The punishment of Israel is emphatically just. Verse 21 shows that Israel is requited measure for measure, that is, its punishments match its sins. Verses 22–30 describe a justified reversal of the benefactions God had conferred on Israel: famine and other disasters undo the blessings conferred in verses 10–14; God nearly destroys Israel, which He had created (v. 6); and He "sells" and "gives up" Israel (v. 30) after having taken possession of it (v. 9).

GOD'S DECISION TO PUNISH ISRAEL (vv. 19–25)

19. *was vexed, and spurned His sons and His daughters* Rather, "The LORD saw and spurned[102] / Because of vexation by His sons and daughters," or, perhaps, "The LORD saw and spurned, because of vexation, his sons and daughters."[103] "Vexation" refers to the vexatious behavior described in verse 16.

sons and daughters The involvement of both men and women in the worship of foreign gods is also mentioned in 17:2 and 29:17 as well as Jeremiah 7:18. Both sexes are mentioned in favorable contexts as well: The Israelites are called God's "sons and daughters" in Isaiah 43:6 too (cf. Num. 21:29, which calls the Moabites the sons and daughters of their deity Kemosh).

20. *I will hide My countenance from them* See 31:17–18.

and see how they fare in the end Literally, "and see what their end will be." God's words are ironic, since He intends to determine the outcome Himself.

a treacherous brood Literally, "a turnabout generation" that broke faith with God. The expression is synonymous with the following colon and with "crooked, perverse generation" in verse 5. Hebrew *tahappukhot*, literally "overturning, turnabout," refers to treachery, unfaithfulness, and falsehood, a meaning confirmed by its Syriac and Akkadian cognates.[104]

For they are a treacherous breed,
Children with no loyalty in them.
²¹They incensed Me with no-gods,
Vexed Me with their futilities;
I'll incense them with a no-folk,
Vex them with a nation of fools.
²²For a fire has flared in My wrath
And burned to the bottom of Sheol,
Has consumed the earth and its increase,
Eaten down to the base of the hills.
²³I will sweep misfortunes on them,
Use up My arrows on them:

כִּי דוֹר תַּהְפֻּכֹת הֵמָּה בָּנִים לֹא־אֵמֻן בָּם׃
²¹ הֵם קִנְאוּנִי בְלֹא־אֵל כְּעִסוּנִי בְּהַבְלֵיהֶם
וַאֲנִי אַקְנִיאֵם בְּלֹא־עָם בְּגוֹי נָבָל אַכְעִיסֵם׃
²² כִּי־אֵשׁ קָדְחָה בְאַפִּי וַתִּיקַד עַד־שְׁאוֹל תַּחְתִּית
וַתֹּאכַל אֶרֶץ וִיבֻלָהּ וַתְּלַהֵט מוֹסְדֵי הָרִים׃
²³ אַסְפֶּה עָלֵימוֹ רָעוֹת חִצַּי אֲכַלֶּה־בָּם׃

no loyalty   Lo'-'emun, in contrast to God who is 'el 'emunah, "a faithful God" (v. 4).

21.   God will punish Israel measure for measure, treating it as it treated Him. As Israel incensed Him by favoring non-gods (lo'-'el), futilities (havalim), He will "incense" it by favoring a non-people (lo'-'am), a nation of fools (goy naval), sending it to invade Israel. The poetic justice of the punishment is highlighted by the use of identical verbs ("incense") and the assonance of the terms describing the sin and punishment. On measure-for-measure punishment, see Comment to 1:35.

futilities   Hebrew havalim, one of the Bible's pejorative terms for idols.[105] Literally it means "puffs of breath," "vapor"; in other words, insubstantial, evanescent things.

I'll incense them   For the meaning of the verb k-n-', see verse 16.

a no-folk ... a nation of fools   The second phrase means "a nation of dullards, villains" (goy naval). Israel is characterized similarly ('am naval) in verse 6. The description of the enemy as a no-folk and a nation of fools is reminiscent of stereotypical Mesopotamian characterizations of nomadic, "uncivilized" outlanders, particularly the Gutians, as "not classed among people, not reckoned as part of the [civilized] land ... people who know no inhibitions, with human instinct but canine intelligence ...," "stupid people," "who were never shown how to worship a god, who do not know how to properly perform the rites and observances."[106] It is impossible to identify the enemy described in Deuteronomy with certainty, but unless its characterization as barbarian is purely rhetorical, it is likely to be a nomadic or seminomadic invader such as the Midianites, Amalekites, or Kedemites (Judg. 6:2–6).

22.   For a fire has flared in My wrath / And burned to the bottom of Sheol   Sheol is the netherworld. The use of the past tense implies that once God has resolved upon the punishment it is as good as done. Fire is a metaphor for God's anger (cf. 4:24), and burning to the bottom of Sheol and to the foundations of the mountains is a picturesque description of its power.[107]

its increase   The earth's yield, its produce (11:17).

23–25.   God resolves to bring all of His destructive forces against Israel. The attack by the enemy (v. 21) will be followed by war's natural consequences: famine, disease, and wild animals overrunning devastated territory. In verses 23–24 the disasters are described by seven phrases, a number that expresses their comprehensiveness (compare the lists of seven disasters in 28:22,27–28). Ibn Ezra notes that the disasters fall into the four categories described by Ezekiel as God's "four terrible punishments—the sword, famine, wild beasts, and pestilence" (Ezek. 14:21).[108]

23.   I will sweep ... on them   This translation is based on the masoretic vocalization of '-s-p-h as 'aspeh, which implies that it is from the root s-p-h; but this root means "sweep away" rather than "sweep onto," and does not suit the context. It is likely that '-s-p-h is from a different root and was originally vocalized as either 'osefah, "I will gather,"[109] 'osifah, "I will multiply,"[110] or 'asifah, "I will expend," synonymous with "use up" in the next clause.[111]

use up My arrows   That is, use all My arrows, a metaphor for the calamities of verse 24 and used again in verse 42.[112]

24Wasting famine, ravaging plague,
Deadly pestilence, and fanged beasts
Will I let loose against them,
With venomous creepers in dust.
25The sword shall deal death without,
As shall the terror within,
To youth and maiden alike,
The suckling as well as the aged.

26I might have reduced them to naught,
Made their memory cease among men,

וְקֶטֶב מְרִירִי
עִם־חֲמַת זֹחֲלֵי עָפָר:
וּמֵחֲדָרִים אֵימָה
יוֹנֵק עִם־אִישׁ שֵׂיבָה:
אַשְׁבִּיתָה מֵאֱנוֹשׁ זִכְרָם:

מְזֵי רָעָב וּלְחֻמֵי רֶשֶׁף 24
וְשֶׁן־בְּהֵמֹת אֲשַׁלַּח־בָּם
מִחוּץ תְּשַׁכֶּל־חֶרֶב 25
גַּם־בָּחוּר גַּם־בְּתוּלָה
אָמַרְתִּי אַפְאֵיהֶם 26

24. Wasting famine Famine that will waste[113] their bodies.

Ravaging plague[114] Hebrew *reshef*, "plague," was used as the name of a Syro-Canaanite deity associated with plague, but it is not regarded as a deity in the Bible. A trace of personification appears in some biblical poems, one of which has *reshef* as a member of God's retinue. Personification is barely detectable in the present passage, where *reshef* is simply one of God's "arrows." On personification of disasters, see Comment to 28:2.[115]

deadly[116] pestilence In some Arabic dialects *ketev* refers to smallpox.[117] It is personified in Psalm 91:5, but here there is no sign of personification.[118]

fanged beasts . . . venomous creepers in dust Wild animals, such as lions or bears,[119] and poisonous snakes.[120] Settled territory was often in danger of being overrun by wild animals; the threat of that is one of the curses in Leviticus 26:22.[121]

25. Here the theme of war, implied in verse 21, is resumed. It will reach every place (inside and out), both sexes (not only the young men, who are the warriors), and people of every age.[122] Neither shelter, noncombatant status, nor age will provide protection.

as shall the terror Even those taking refuge indoors will die of fright. According to the Sifrei, fright would cause the heart to pound so hard that the victim dies; in medical terms, palpitations would trigger a fatal heart attack.[123] People with heart conditions conducive to such a reaction would likely be noncombatants and hence indoors taking refuge rather than outdoors doing battle.

GOD'S DECISION TO LIMIT ISRAEL'S PUNISHMENT AND TO PUNISH THE ENEMY (vv. 26–42)

God's Reason for Limiting Israel's Punishment (vv. 26–31)

Israel will be saved from total destruction only by God's concern that the enemy He sends will claim credit for itself. The Bible frequently expresses the idea that God would spare Israel to protect His own reputation. "For the sake of His great name, the LORD will never abandon His people" (1 Sam. 12:22). His aim of securing the universal recognition of humanity (see Comment to v. 8) would be undermined because the other nations, in their foolishness, would not recognize that Israel's defeat is an expression of God's power, not His weakness. Hence He stops short of total punishment and rescues Israel although it is undeserving. See Comment to 9:25ff.

26. I might have Literally, "I said," "I thought to myself," "I had intended." God decided at the outset only to "incense" Israel, not to destroy it entirely, for the reasons He explains.

reduced them to naught Rather, "obliterated them." The verb *'af'eh* (from the root p-'-h), not found elsewhere in Hebrew, has an Arabic cognate meaning "cut" that is used for effacing an inscription.[124]

Made their memory cease among men Rather, "Made their name cease among men," wiped them out entirely. See Comments to 7:24; 25:19; and Excursus 23.

27But for fear of the taunts of the foe,
Their enemies who might misjudge
And say, "Our own hand has prevailed;
None of this was wrought by the LORD!"
28For they are a folk void of sense,
Lacking in all discernment.
29Were they wise, they would think upon this,
Gain insight into their future:
30"How could one have routed a thousand,
Or two put ten thousand to flight,
Unless their Rock had sold them,
The LORD had given them up?"
31For their rock is not like our Rock,
In our enemies' own estimation.

לוּלֵי כַּעַס אוֹיֵב אָגוּר 27
פֶּן־יְנַכְּרוּ צָרֵימוֹ
פֶּן־יֹאמְרוּ יָדֵינוּ רָמָה
וְלֹא יְהוָה פָּעַל כָּל־זֹאת:
כִּי־גוֹי אֹבַד עֵצוֹת הֵמָּה 28
וְאֵין בָּהֶם תְּבוּנָה:
חמישי
לוּ חָכְמוּ יַשְׂכִּילוּ זֹאת 29
יָבִינוּ לְאַחֲרִיתָם:
אֵיכָה יִרְדֹּף אֶחָד אֶלֶף 30
וּשְׁנַיִם יָנִיסוּ רְבָבָה
אִם־לֹא כִּי־צוּרָם מְכָרָם
וַיהוָה הִסְגִּירָם:
כִּי לֹא כְצוּרֵנוּ צוּרָם 31
וְאֹיְבֵינוּ פְּלִילִים:

27. **taunts** Hebrew *ka'as*, literally, "vexation," as in verses 16, 18, and 21. The enemy, like Israel, would vex God by falsely claiming credit for the defeat of Israel. "Vexation" is certainly a plausible term in this context, but the parallel verb *yenakkeru* raises another possibility. Although translated "misjudge," *yenakkeru* actually means "dissemble," "misrepresent,"[125] and it has therefore been suggested that the parallel *ka'as* is a scribal error for *kahash*, "denial."[126] "Deny" is used in contexts very much like the present one, such as: "Lest . . . I deny, saying, 'Who is the LORD'?" (Prov. 30:9), and "They have denied the LORD, saying 'Not He'" (Jer. 5:12).

Our own hand has prevailed; / None of this was wrought by the LORD After its victory, this nation of dullards will reason exactly as Moses warns Israel not to reason when it prospers (8:17).

28–31. The poem interrupts God's words to explain the flawed reasoning that would lead the enemy to misrepresent the facts.

28. **They** The enemy.[127]

29. **gain insight into their future** Rather, "reflect on what happened to them," on the circumstances or cause behind their victory. The proper reasoning for the enemy, described in verse 36, has nothing to do with their future, but with understanding what made their victory possible. Here, therefore, *'aharit*, "end," must not mean "future" but "circumstances, cause," as its Akkadian synonym *arkatu* does in idioms meaning "look into, investigate the circumstances or cause [*arkatu*]" of someone or something.[128]

30. If the enemy were wise it would realize that its victory was not due to its own power: its small numbers could not have defeated thousands of Israelites without the Lord's help. The rout of Israel will be so great as to be explicable only by supernatural causes.[129] The motif of a few chasing thousands is a traditional way of describing a divinely determined rout.[130]

sold them . . . given them up Rather, "turned them over, delivered them."[131] Mere abandonment wouldn't have produced a rout of such proportions; God must have actively aided the enemy.

31. Nor could the enemy—if it were wise—credit its victory to its own god's power, because its gods are no equal for Israel's.

their rock Here the epithet is used ironically of the enemy's god, as if the text said "their so-called rock"; see verse 37.

in our enemies' own estimation The meaning of Hebrew *ve-'oyeveinu pelilim* is uncertain, but this translation is unlikely. It is based on an uncertain explanation of the root *p-l-l* as "assess"[132] and, in any case, does not fit the context: it is implausible that the enemy, having just routed Israel, would consider its own gods unequal to Israel's.[133] The parallel phrase "their rock" suggests that this phrase means something like "our enemies' gods." If so, perhaps *pelilim* here is cognate to Akkadian *palilu*, meaning something like "guardian," "leader," used as an epithet of deities,[134] and the phrase

32 Ah! The vine for them is from Sodom,
From the vineyards of Gomorrah;
The grapes for them are poison,
A bitter growth their clusters.
33 Their wine is the venom of asps,
The pitiless poison of vipers.
34 Lo, I have it all put away,
Sealed up in My storehouses,
35 To be My vengeance and recompense,
At the time that their foot falters.
Yea, their day of disaster is near,
And destiny rushes upon them.

כִּי־מִגֶּ֤פֶן סְדֹם֙ גַּפְנָ֔ם 32
עֲנָבֵ֖מוֹ עִנְּבֵי־ר֑וֹשׁ
חֲמַ֥ת תַּנִּינִ֖ם יֵינָ֑ם 33
הֲלֹא־ה֖וּא כָּמֻ֣ס עִמָּדִ֑י 34
לִ֤י נָקָם֙ וְשִׁלֵּ֔ם 35
כִּ֥י קָר֖וֹב י֣וֹם אֵידָ֑ם

וּמִשַּׁדְמֹ֖ת עֲמֹרָ֑ה
אַשְׁכְּלֹ֥ת מְרֹרֹ֖ת לָֽמוֹ׃
וְרֹ֖אשׁ פְּתָנִ֥ים אַכְזָֽר׃
חָתֻ֖ם בְּאוֹצְרֹתָֽי׃
לְעֵ֖ת תָּמ֣וּט רַגְלָ֑ם
וְחָ֖שׁ עֲתִדֹ֥ת לָֽמוֹ׃

should be interpreted as, or emended to read, *u-felilei 'oyeveinu*, "nor are our enemies' guardians [equal to our Rock]."[135]

God's Decision to Punish the Enemy, *Lest It Draw the Wrong Inferences from Its Success* (vv. 32–35)

The poem resumes God's words.

32–33. The enemy will suffer the same fate as did the people of Sodom and Gomorrah. They will drink the same wine—from the same vines—that was served to the people of those devastated cities. The metaphor of poisonous drink for a disastrous fate is also used by Jeremiah and Ezekiel.[136]

32. *Ah* Hebrew *ki*, used in its emphatic sense, as in verse 9.

vineyards Hebrew *shadmot* is often parallel to "vine," but its precise meaning is uncertain. Other possibilities are "fields" or "terraces."[137] It is assonant with Sodom.

a bitter growth their clusters Rather, "the clusters for them venomous."[138]

33. *pitiless poison of vipers* Meaning, apparently, painful or incurable poison[139]. The Aramaic Targums render, essentially, "poison of pitiless vipers"; they presume that "pitiless," although singular, more naturally modifies "vipers" than "poison."[140]

34. *sealed up in My storehouses* The poison wine[141] is stored up securely, waiting for the day when God will serve it to the enemy. Describing the wine as "sealed up" is based on the practice of sealing the latches to storerooms with clay, stamped with the signet of the king or the official in charge of them, so as to detect whether an unauthorized person had opened the room.[142]

35. *To be My vengeance* Hebrew *li nakam*, literally, "Vengeance is Mine." Translated thus this phrase has become proverbial in English based on its use in the Christian scriptures as a warning against taking vengeance on one's own.[143] However, that interpretation does not fit its original context here, since Israel is in no condition to avenge itself on the enemy. The phrase is simply a continuation of verse 34.

In place of *li* (spelled *l-y*) *nakam*, "to be My vengeance," the Samaritan Pentateuch and the Septuagint read *le-yom* (spelled *l-y-v-m*) *nakam*, "for the day of vengeance," which forms a better parallel with the following colon, "*At the time that* their foot falters."[144]

"Vengeance" (Heb. *nakam*), as the accompanying "recompense" makes clear, refers to just retribution, not to revenge.[145]

at the time that their foot falters Rather, "for the time that their foot falters." This is a regular biblical idiom for misfortune.[146]

destiny Hebrew *'atidot*, literally, "what is prepared," perhaps referring to the punishment sealed up in God's storehouses (v. 34; in Isa. 10:13 *'atidot* [or *'atudot*] refers to stored treasures).[147]

36 For the LORD will vindicate His people
And take revenge for His servants,
When He sees that their might is gone,
And neither bond nor free is left.
37 He will say: Where are their gods,
The rock in whom they sought refuge,

36 כִּי־יָדִין יְהֹוָה עַמּוֹ
כִּי יִרְאֶה כִּי־אָזְלַת יָד
37 וְאָמַר אֵי אֱלֹהֵימוֹ

וְעַל־עֲבָדָיו יִתְנֶחָם
וְאֶפֶס עָצוּר וְעָזוּב:
צוּר חָסָיוּ בוֹ:

God's Plan to Deliver Israel and Punish the Enemy (vv. 36–42)

36. **vindicate** *Yadin*, literally "judge," here meaning "judge in favor of"[148] Israel. This explanation agrees with the way the verse is used in Psalm 135:14, which quotes it: "For the LORD will champion [*yadin*] His people and obtain satisfaction for His servants."

take revenge for That is, avenge them, get satisfaction for the way the enemy treated them. Hebrew *hitnaḥem* does not have the negative connotations of English "revenge." Its meaning is to change one's mind or mood, to assuage one's feelings.[149] The usage here is comparable to that in Isaiah 1:24, where the similar form *'ennaḥem* is parallel to "wreak vengeance" and is therefore translated "get satisfaction," meaning that God will satisfy His outrage by punishing the guilty.[150] Another possible translation, also based on the sense "change one's mind," is "relent concerning His servants," meaning that God will relent from punishing Israel after all that it has suffered.[151]

When He sees that their might is gone When they have become totally powerless, so that they could not possibly attribute their salvation to themselves, He will intervene to save them.

neither bond nor free The alliterative Hebrew idiom *'atsur ve-'azuv* is of uncertain meaning.[152] Many explanations have been proposed. The present translation derives the terms from the roots *'-ts-r*, "restrain," and *'-z-v*, "leave," and implies that neither slaves nor freemen remain. That would, however, mean that no one at all is left, which would leave no one for God to deliver. Other speculative suggestions include: "kept in by legal impurity or at large," "under taboo and free," and "under parental restraint and free from it."

These interpretations are conjectures based on etymology; none shows a demonstrable relationship to the contexts in which the idiom appears. In the present verse the idiom is preceded by "their might is gone," and the context describes Israel's suffering. In 2 Kings 14:26 it appears in a similar context and is accompanied by the phrase "with none to help ['ozer] Israel." These two contexts suggest that the idiom has to do with power or help and means "neither supporter nor helper," as the Peshitta and the Talmud render it.[153] In its other three occurrences the idiom is part of a prophecy about the extirpation of a dynasty in which God says "I will cut off every male [and] *'atsur ve-'azuv* in Israel" (1 Kings 14:10; 21:21; 2 Kings 9:8). In those passages, too, it could refer to helpers, but in the context of destroying a dynasty it could also refer to rulers. Together, these contexts suggest that the idiom is a hendiadys meaning something like "ruler and helper."[154] It would be the equivalent of the two terms used in the book of Judges for Israel's early leaders, *shofet* and *moshia'*, "chieftain" and "champion, deliverer."[155] The verse would then mean that God will act when He, or Israel, sees that Israel is without a ruler and helper to deliver it.

37–39. When Israel reaches the point of total helplessness, God will point out how the gods in whom it trusted proved unworthy of its trust. God addresses Israel similarly in Judges 10:14, at the nadir of its oppression by the Ammonites. In both cases, God's address is probably conveyed to Israel by a prophet, as are similar remarks in Jeremiah 2:28.

37. **He will say** God will point out the nullity of Israel's false gods in contrast to His own power, which He describes in verse 39.[156]

rock As in verse 31, this epithet is used ironically, since its false gods will have proven unable to shield Israel from the enemy.

³⁸Who ate the fat of their offerings
And drank their libation wine?
Let them rise up to your help,
And let them be a shield unto you!
³⁹See, then, that I, I am He;
There is no god beside Me.
I deal death and give life;
I wounded and I will heal:
None can deliver from My hand.
⁴⁰Lo, I raise My hand to heaven
And say: As I live forever,
⁴¹When I whet My flashing blade
And My hand lays hold on judgment,
Vengeance will I wreak on My foes,
Will I deal to those who reject Me.

38 אֲשֶׁ֨ר חֵ֤לֶב זְבָחֵ֙ימוֹ֙ יֹאכֵ֔לוּ יִשְׁתּ֖וּ יֵ֣ין נְסִיכָ֑ם
יָק֙וּמוּ֙ וְיַעְזְרֻכֶ֔ם יְהִ֥י עֲלֵיכֶ֖ם סִתְרָֽה׃
39 רְא֣וּ ׀ עַתָּ֗ה כִּ֣י אֲנִ֤י אֲנִי֙ ה֔וּא וְאֵ֥ין אֱלֹהִ֖ים עִמָּדִ֑י
אֲנִ֧י אָמִ֣ית וַאֲחַיֶּ֗ה מָחַ֙צְתִּי֙ וַאֲנִ֣י אֶרְפָּ֔א
וְאֵ֥ין מִיָּדִ֖י מַצִּֽיל׃   ששי
40 כִּֽי־אֶשָּׂ֥א אֶל־שָׁמַ֖יִם יָדִ֑י וְאָמַ֕רְתִּי חַ֥י אָנֹכִ֖י לְעֹלָֽם׃
41 אִם־שַׁנּוֹתִי֙ בְּרַ֣ק חַרְבִּ֔י וְתֹאחֵ֥ז בְּמִשְׁפָּ֖ט יָדִ֑י
אָשִׁ֤יב נָקָם֙ לְצָרָ֔י וְלִמְשַׂנְאַ֖י אֲשַׁלֵּֽם׃

38. Who ate . . . and drank The pseudo-gods who were the objects of Israel's illicit cult. The poem—if it is not being merely sarcastic—can represent these beings as actually eating and drinking the offerings because it does not deny their existence, only their divinity (see Comment to v. 17).

39. See, then Israel's punishment by the Lord and the inability of its pseudo-gods to protect it should finally make it realize that the Lord alone is the only effective divine being, the only true God.[157] He brought all this about, and He alone can change it.

I, I am He That is, "I alone am He,"[158] I alone control events.[159]

There is no god beside Me Literally, "There is no god with me," no other god has been involved in the events (cf. v. 12).[160]

I deal death and give life, I wounded and I will heal The first clause is a general assertion, meaning that God alone determines people's welfare. The second means that it is He who is doing so in this particular case. The ability to deal death or life (to kill or cure) is a trait of divinity; compare 2 Kings 5:7, "am I God [or: a god] to deal death or give life?"[161] Here the statement that He will heal (future tense) resumes the promise God made in verse 36.

None can deliver from My hand None of your false gods could protect you from My punishment, and none will be able to save the enemy from Me.

40. I raise my hand to heaven Raising the hand heavenward is a gesture that accompanies invoking God in an oath.[162] Here, with God Himself the speaker, it is simply an idiom meaning "I swear."

as I live forever In human oaths, declaring "As the LORD lives" (*ḥai 'adonai*) is a verbal counterpart to raising the hand heavenward. When God swears, He says *ḥai 'anokhi* (or *'ani*), using the pronoun "I" instead of His own name.[163]

41. whet My flashing blade God is pictured as a warrior preparing for battle.[164]

judgment In the light of the parallel term "blade" (lit., "sword") and the parallelism "arrows . . . sword" in the next verse, *mishpat* must mean a weapon of judgment, an instrument of punishment. The Mekhilta interprets it as an arrow, serving as a metaphor for a decree of punishment.[165]

My foes The enemy, although used by God as an agent for punishing Israel, is His foe. The Bible implicitly assumes that God uses evil nations to punish Israel and that they, too, will ultimately be punished.[166]

wreak . . . deal Literally, "return . . . pay back." The enemy's punishment will be merited.

42 I will make My arrows drunk with blood—
As My sword devours flesh—
Blood of the slain and the captive
From the long-haired enemy chiefs.

וְחַרְבִּי תֹּאכַל בָּשָׂר
מֵרֹאשׁ פַּרְעוֹת אוֹיֵב׃

42 אַשְׁכִּיר חִצַּי מִדָּם
מִדַּם חָלָל וְשִׁבְיָה

42. The enemy will go down to a bloody defeat. The image of the devouring sword is a common one; that of arrows drinking is unique.[167]

As My sword devours flesh[168]

blood of the . . . captive   This refers either to the blood of wounded captives or to prisoners killed after capture.

long-haired . . . chiefs   The meaning of Hebrew *ro'sh par'ot* is uncertain. Since *pera'* means head-hair (possibly uncut or disheveled) the phrase could mean "the hairy heads of the enemy," with "heads" meant either literally or as "chiefs." *Par'ot* also appears in the opening phrase of the Song of Deborah, *bi-froa' pera'ot*, which the NJPS renders "When locks go untrimmed" (Judg. 5:1). Both passages have been explained as referring to a practice of warriors like Samson letting their hair grow long, either out of a belief that the strength resides in their hair or as a mark of nazirite dedication to the deity (see Num. 6:1–21). However, there is little evidence that warriors normally did this in the ancient Near East.[169]

CODA: CELEBRATION OF GOD'S DELIVERANCE OF ISRAEL   (v. 43)

According to the Masoretic Text, the poem concludes with a final invocation calling upon the nations to acclaim God's deliverance of Israel and punishment of the enemy. This invitation implies that God's salvation of Israel has importance for the world at large.[170] Rashbam explains that this is implicitly an invitation to the nations to revere the Lord as Israel does and a promise that if they do so, He will treat them as He does Israel (when it is meritorious). This explanation brings us back to God's original purpose in electing Israel: to make it a model nation so that all can see how He treats those who acknowledge Him (see Excursus 7).

The Masoretic text of this verse seems incomplete since the first and fourth colons, unlike any others in the poem, lack parallel colons. The missing colons are supplied in a Qumran manuscript of the poem and in the Septuagint. The Qumran manuscript is probably the closest to the original text, although it is possible that none of the three versions reflects the original exactly. The Qumran text reads as follows (the main segments of the verse are designated by letters and their component colons by numbers):

a1. O heavens, rejoice with Him,
a2. Bow to Him, all divinities
b1. For He'll avenge the blood of His sons,
b2. and wreak vengeance on His foes,
c1. Requite those who reject Him,
c2. And will cleanse His people's land.

In place of the first bicolon in the Qumran text, the Septuagint has two bicolons:

a1. O heavens, rejoice with Him.
a2. Bow to Him, all sons of the divine
a3. O nations, rejoice with His people
a4. And let all angels of the divine
      strengthen themselves in Him.

In the following comments we will note the variant readings briefly. Fuller discussion is found in Excursus 31.

43O nations, acclaim His people!
For He'll avenge the blood of His servants,
Wreak vengeance on His foes,
And cleanse the land of His people.

כִּי דַם־עֲבָדָיו יִקּוֹם
וְכִפֶּר אַדְמָתוֹ עַמּוֹ:

43 הַרְנִינוּ גוֹיִם עַמּוֹ
וְנָקָם יָשִׁיב לְצָרָיו
פ   שביעי

44Moses came, together with Hosea son of Nun, and recited all the words of this poem in the hearing of the people.

44 וַיָּבֹא מֹשֶׁה וַיְדַבֵּר אֶת־כָּל־דִּבְרֵי הַשִּׁירָה־הַזֹּאת בְּאָזְנֵי הָעָם הוּא וְהוֹשֵׁעַ בִּן־נוּן:

acclaim   Literally, "gladden," meaning congratulate[171] Israel on its deliverance and on having such a God.[172] Expressions of such congratulations are found in 33:29, "O happy Israel! Who is like you, a people delivered by the LORD, your protecting Shield, your Sword triumphant" and Psalm 144:15, "Happy is the people who have it so, happy is the people whose God is the LORD." A promise of congratulations by the nations is found in Malachi 3:12: "And all nations shall account [or declare] you happy, for you shall be the most desired of lands." The Qumran reading, "O heavens, rejoice with Him, / Bow to Him, all divinities," is probably closer to the original (see Excursus 31). If so, the final verse of the poem echoes the first verse by addressing the heavens once again.

He'll avenge the blood of His servants   The use of the verb "avenge" may be due to the fact that in this part of the poem Israel is no longer described as God's children but as His "servants" (v. 36). "Redeem" is used when the avenger is a relative (see Comments to 19:1–13), whereas "avenge" is used when it is God or human authorities.[173] The Qumran text and the Septuagint read "sons" here; see Excursus 31.

cleanse the land of His people   That is, cleanse His people's land.[174] According to Rashbam, by spilling the enemy's blood God will cleanse the land of the Israelite blood shed by the enemy. Compare Numbers 35:33: "the land can have no expiation [cleansing] for blood that is shed on it, except by the blood of him who shed it."[175] But the poem has not previously hinted at pollution of the land, and in the context of praising God for avenging the wrongs done to Israel, cleansing the *land* of pollution seems beside the point.[176] The NJPS translators imply that 'admato may be a scribal error for 'udma'ot, "tears," a variant (known from Ugaritic) of the Hebrew word for tears, dema'ot, and that the clause means that God "will wipe away His people's tears."[177] They compare Isaiah 25:8: "My Lord GOD will wipe the tears away from all faces and will put an end to the reproach of His people over all the earth."

Conclusion to the Poem   (vv. 44–52)

SUBSCRIPTION   (v. 44)

44. Moses came   This verse recapitulates the contents of 31:22b and 30. It probably means, "So Moses came, from the place where he received the instructions to teach the poem, or from where he wrote it, and taught it to the people."[178]

Hosea   That is, Joshua.[179] See Comment to 1:38. Joshua's involvement is consistent with the plural command in 31:19.

45And when Moses finished reciting all these words to
all Israel, 46he said to them: Take to heart all the words
with which I have warned you this day. Enjoin them
upon your children, that they may observe faithfully all
the terms of this Teaching. 47For this is not a trifling
thing for you: it is your very life; through it you shall
long endure on the land that you are to possess upon
crossing the Jordan.

48That very day the LORD spoke to Moses: 49Ascend
these heights of Abarim to Mount Nebo, which is in the

45 וַיְכַל מֹשֶׁה לְדַבֵּר אֶת־כָּל־הַדְּבָרִים הָאֵלֶּה
אֶל־כָּל־יִשְׂרָאֵל: 46 וַיֹּאמֶר אֲלֵהֶם שִׂימוּ
לְבַבְכֶם לְכָל־הַדְּבָרִים אֲשֶׁר אָנֹכִי מֵעִיד בָּכֶם
הַיּוֹם אֲשֶׁר תְּצַוֻּם אֶת־בְּנֵיכֶם לִשְׁמֹר לַעֲשׂוֹת
אֶת־כָּל־דִּבְרֵי הַתּוֹרָה הַזֹּאת: 47 כִּי לֹא־דָבָר
רֵק הוּא מִכֶּם כִּי־הוּא חַיֵּיכֶם וּבַדָּבָר הַזֶּה תַּאֲרִיכוּ
יָמִים עַל־הָאֲדָמָה אֲשֶׁר אַתֶּם עֹבְרִים אֶת־הַיַּרְדֵּן
שָׁמָּה לְרִשְׁתָּהּ: פ

מפטיר 48 וַיְדַבֵּר יְהוָה אֶל־מֹשֶׁה בְּעֶצֶם הַיּוֹם

MOSES' FINAL EXHORTATION TO OBSERVE
THE TEACHING   (vv. 45–47)

45. *all these words*   The entire Teaching, including the poem. See verse 46.

46. *all the words with which I have warned you*   Rather, "with which I have charged
you."[180] It is clear from the rest of the verse that the words in question include commands, and since
the poem contains none, "the words" must be those of the Teaching as a whole.[181] As noted in
Excursus 29, the phrase "these words" is a virtual synonym for the Teaching.

this day   See verse 48.

47. *trifling*   The teaching is not inconsequential,[182] for Israel's survival as a nation
depends on it.[183] The Hebrew adjective is *reik*, literally, "empty." Hammurabi uses the same term
when praising his laws and achievements: "My words are choice, my deeds have no equal; it is only
to the fool that they are empty; to the wise they stand forth as an object of wonder."[184]

In Hebrew this clause is literally "for it is not an empty thing *from* you." The unusual use of
"from" prompted a midrashic explanation: there is nothing empty in the Torah, and if it is empty
(unclear, meaningless)—(it is) from you; it is due to your own failure to study it thoroughly.[185]

it is your very life   Compare 4:1; 30:20.

GOD SUMMONS MOSES TO HIS DEATH   (vv. 48–52)

Now that Moses has transmitted the poem to the people, preparations for his departure resume. God
repeats His instructions of 3:27 that Moses should ascend a nearby mountain and look across the
Jordan to the promised land.

The same instructions are also given in Numbers 27:12–14, before the commissioning of Joshua
as Moses' successor. They are repeated here almost verbatim but with some expansion. Critical
scholarship assigns most, if not all, of this paragraph to the priestly source of the Torah. See
Excursus 32.

48. *That very day*   The day on which Moses concluded the activities just described. The
only specific date previously mentioned in the book is the first day of the eleventh month in the
fortieth year after the Exodus (1:3), but according to 1:5, Moses only began to expound the Teaching
on that date; he did not necessarily finish it then. The context implies that God said this to Moses on
the day he died, or perhaps the preceding day. On the date, see Comment to 34:5.

49. *Ascend these heights of Abarim to Mount Nebo*[186]   See Excursus 1 and Maps 5 and 6.
The "heights of Abarim" is probably the mountain range east of the Dead Sea.[187] Mount Nebo was
one of its prominent peaks. To reach it, Moses would have doubled back on the Israelites' route by
the distance of one day's march since, according to Numbers 33:47–48, "the heights of Abarim,
before [the city] Nebo," was the Israelites' last encampment before reaching their current one.

land of Moab facing Jericho, and view the land of Canaan, which I am giving the Israelites as their holding. 50You shall die on the mountain that you are about to ascend, and shall be gathered to your kin, as your brother Aaron died on Mount Hor and was gathered to his kin; 51for you both broke faith with Me among the Israelite people, at the waters of Meribath-kadesh in the wilderness of Zin, by failing to uphold My sanctity among the Israelite people. 52You may view the land from a distance, but you shall not enter it—the land that I am giving to the Israelite people.

הַזֶּה לֵאמֹר: 49 עֲלֵה אֶל־הַר הָעֲבָרִים הַזֶּה הַר־
נְבוֹ אֲשֶׁר בְּאֶרֶץ מוֹאָב אֲשֶׁר עַל־פְּנֵי יְרֵחוֹ וּרְאֵה
אֶת־אֶרֶץ כְּנַעַן אֲשֶׁר אֲנִי נֹתֵן לִבְנֵי יִשְׂרָאֵל
לַאֲחֻזָּה: 50 וּמֻת בָּהָר אֲשֶׁר אַתָּה עֹלֶה שָׁמָּה
וְהֵאָסֵף אֶל־עַמֶּיךָ כַּאֲשֶׁר־מֵת אַהֲרֹן אָחִיךָ בְּהֹר
הָהָר וַיֵּאָסֶף אֶל־עַמָּיו: 51 עַל אֲשֶׁר מְעַלְתֶּם בִּי
בְּתוֹךְ בְּנֵי יִשְׂרָאֵל בְּמֵי־מְרִיבַת קָדֵשׁ מִדְבַּר־צִן
עַל אֲשֶׁר לֹא־קִדַּשְׁתֶּם אוֹתִי בְּתוֹךְ בְּנֵי יִשְׂרָאֵל:
52 כִּי מִנֶּגֶד תִּרְאֶה אֶת־הָאָרֶץ וְשָׁמָּה לֹא תָבוֹא
אֶל־הָאָרֶץ אֲשֶׁר־אֲנִי נֹתֵן לִבְנֵי יִשְׂרָאֵל: פ

which is in the land of Moab facing Jericho   That is, east of Jericho, across the Jordan.[188]

view the land   This is a minor concession to Moses' plea in 3:25, "Let me, I pray, cross over and see the good land."[189] Moses complies in 34:1ff.

Canaan   See Comment to 1:8.

50. die . . . and be gathered to your kin   This refers to the reunion of the spirit with those of one's kin in Sheol after death.[190] (Cf. 31:16.)

as . . . Aaron died on Mount Hor   This happened six months earlier. See Numbers 20:23–28; 33:38; and Excursus 1. Deuteronomy 10:6 gives a different place for Aaron's death. See Comment there.

51. for you both broke faith with Me . . . failing to uphold My sanctity   This refers to the incident in Numbers 20:1–13 in which the people quarreled with Moses and Aaron because of a lack of water. God told Moses and Aaron to command a rock to produce water. Instead, Moses said to the people, "Listen, you rebels, shall we get water for you out of this rock?" and he then hit the rock with his rod. Although it produced water, God condemned Moses and Aaron for failing to affirm His sanctity before the people and declared that they would not be allowed to lead the people into the promised land. Why this infraction was considered grave enough to deserve so severe a punishment has exercised commentators for centuries.[191] This verse reflects the view of the priestly source (P) as to why Moses and Aaron were prevented from entering the promised land. Other passages in Deuteronomy hold that Moses was prevented because of the incident of the scouts and Aaron because of the golden calf. See 1:37; 3:26; 4:21; 9:20; and Excursus 2.

Meribath-kadesh   That is, "Meribah-at-Kadesh." The place at Kadesh where the incident in question occurred was called *Meribah*, "Quarrel-Place," commemorating the quarrel that touched it off (Num. 20:12). See also Comment to 33:8.

wilderness of Zin   The section of the Wilderness of Paran (the wilderness of the Negev and the Sinai) that formed the southern boundary of the promised land.

CHAPTER 33

MOSES' FAREWELL BLESSINGS OF ISRAEL   (vv. 1–29)

Ve-zo't Ha-berakhah   Moses bids Israel farewell with blessings of a happy future. These parting words reveal a side of Moses that the people have never seen. After a lifetime of instructing, rebuking, and admonishing Israel, he now gives expression to what he hopes will happen in place of the warnings he has uttered in chapters 31–32.

As in chapter 32, Moses views Israel's history from the perspective of later times, after the people have settled in the promised land. The blessings describe the lives of the individual tribes in their

VE-ZO'T HA-BERAKHAH

וזאת הברכה

33 This is the blessing with which Moses, the man of God, bade the Israelites farewell before he died. ²He said:

ל"ג וְזֹאת הַבְּרָכָה אֲשֶׁר בֵּרַךְ מֹשֶׁה אִישׁ הָאֱלֹהִים אֶת־בְּנֵי יִשְׂרָאֵל לִפְנֵי מוֹתוֹ: ² וַיֹּאמַר

territories, focusing primarily on the resources and abundance they enjoy, and their security and military prowess.

Like chapter 32 and Genesis 49, this chapter is poetic in form. Verse 1 characterizes it as a blessing. It combines features of several genres and employs a variety of styles. Some blessings are phrased as wishes or petitions addressed to God, one blesses God for His benefaction to the tribe (v. 20a), and others are addressed to the tribes themselves. Several are descriptions of the tribes or their territories, though in this context they are meant as petitions. For details see Excursus 33.

The poem consists of three sections. Its core is the blessings of the individual tribes (vv. 6–25). Framing them are an exordium (vv. 2–5) and a coda (vv. 26–29), both of which refer to God's benefactions to Israel as a whole.[1] The frame emphasizes the ideal unity of the tribes as a single people and places their security and prosperity in the broader context of God's benefactions to Israel (cf. introductory Comment to 26:1–11 regarding "meditative" prayer). The unity of the people and their indebtedness to the Lord are highlighted by the chiastic repetition of key words that form an *inclusio* around the poem: the names "LORD" (YHVH), "Jacob," and "Jeshurun" appear in the exordium (vv. 2,4,5) and then in reverse order in the coda (vv. 26,28,29). Likewise, "people" and "Israel" appear in the exordium and coda in chiastic order (vv. 5,28,29).

With the exception of a verse and a half in the blessing of Levi, the tribes are spoken of in the singular, as if they were individuals. A few of the tribes—Joseph, Gad, Dan—are compared to animals whose qualities symbolize fighting skill. Some parts of the blessings, like those in Genesis 49, are word plays, inspired by the tribes' names or, in one case, the name of a tribe's city (see Comments to the names of Judah, Benjamin, Joseph, Zebulun and Issachar, Gad, Dan, and Asher). Word-play on names—which are often intended by their bestowers as blessings—is common in the Bible and is frequent in blessings and curses,[2] as if to draw out the potential inherent in the name.[3] These word-plays are based on the sound of the names, not their etymologies.

This poem is one of the most difficult texts in all of ancient literature. It is full of rare words, syntactic difficulties, grammatical inconsistencies, and opaque allusions. Some of these difficulties are probably due to its rare vocabulary and poetic forms; others, to the poem's aphoristic style, which expresses things in a terse, symbolic way and is filled with allusions no longer understandable to us. Another possible source of confusion is that the first copy of the poem was probably written in the early Hebrew spelling system, which had no vowel signs and did not even use the letters *aleph*, *heh*, *vav*, and *yod* as vowels. This would have made it very easy for the scribe who transcribed it into the later, standard biblical spelling to misconstrue certain words. Some difficulties were doubtless caused by scribal errors.

The order in which the tribes are listed, the omission of Simeon, the historical background, and other aspects of the poem are discussed in Excursus 33.

Introduction   (v. 1)

1. **bade...farewell**   Rather, "blessed."

   man of god   That is, a prophet.[4] This designation suggests that Moses' remarks about the tribes have the power of prophetic predictions and prayers.[5]

The Lord came from Sinai;

He shone upon them from Seir;

יְהֹוָה מִסִּינַי בָּא

וְזָרַח מִשֵּׂעִיר לָמוֹ

The Poem (vv. 2–29)

EXORDIUM (vv. 2–5)

The exordium describes the Lord's coming to the Israelites and subsequent events. Related passages elsewhere in the Bible suggest that it refers to His coming to *deliver* Israel. Moses may be citing this as a precedent for the benefactions he is about to request for the tribes. This explanation is not certain because the exordium is extraordinarily difficult to understand. Ibn Ezra takes it as a blessing for all Israel, asking God to be a wall of fire surrounding Israel and to take Israel as His chosen people.[6] Shadal takes it as a statement informing Israel that God has come to them at their present location in Moab so that Moses may confer His blessing on them.

2–3.   These verses describe the approach of the Lord from the wilderness region south of the promised land. The text bristles with difficulties, but similar descriptions in other biblical poems show its approximate meaning.[7] These picture the Lord coming from the southern wildernesses and mountains (Sinai, Seir-Edom, Teiman, Mount Paran) to deliver His people. Leading His heavenly army, He rides on a chariot in a tempest, weapons flashing like lightning. He is surrounded by a brilliant radiance and accompanied by supernatural holy beings and by pestilence and plague. In His path the earth quakes, the heavens rain, and fire blazes. He treads the earth and tramples nations. These descriptions do not refer to the covenant and lawgiving that took place *at* Mount Sinai, but to God's coming *from* the Sinai region to aid Israel against its enemies (cf. vv. 26–29).[8] Here in Deuteronomy 33 only vv. 4–5 (and possibly the last clause in v. 3) refer to covenant and lawgiving, as a sequel to the events related in vv. 2–3.

The places mentioned in verse 2 are not synonymous, but are all located in the areas known today as the Sinai Peninsula and the Negev (see Map 1). The location of Mount Sinai and Seir is discussed in the Comments to 1:2 and in Excursus 1. Mount Paran must be a mountain or highland in the Wilderness of Paran, discussed in the Comment to 1:1. Ribeboth-kodesh (see below) must be in the same area and may be connected to Kadesh-barnea, also discussed at 1:2. Teiman, mentioned in some of the parallel passages, is the name of a place in Seir-Edom, just east of the Aravah in southern Transjordan, but since it literally means "south" it could refer to any southern area. The verse means that the Lord came to Israel's aid from this region, and implies that He was in some sense based there.

Other evidence also suggests that the Lord's base was in the southern wilderness in the period preceding the Exodus in the thirteenth century B.C.E. The Bible refers to Sinai-Horeb several times as "the mountain of God" or "the mountain of the Lord,"[9] once even before His appearance to Moses there at the Burning Bush, implying that the site was already a holy place. Egyptian inscriptions of the fourteenth century refer to a "land of the nomads, Yahwe," apparently in the same region (it is mentioned in the same context as, apparently, Seir and Laban [see 1:1]).[10] "Yahwe" could be an Egyptian transcription of Hebrew YHVH, "The Lord," and the Egyptian phrase means either "the land of the nomads of the place called Yahwe" or "land of the nomads who worship Yahwe." One of the later, ninth-century Hebrew inscriptions from Kuntillet Ajrud, in eastern Sinai near Kadesh-barnea, refers to "YHVH of the Teiman,"[11] which is the name of one of the places from which God comes to Israel's aid in the passages cited above. All of this suggests that there were sanctuaries and worshipers (not necessarily Israelite) of YHVH in the Sinai-Negev wilderness, perhaps as early as the fourteenth or fifteenth century B.C.E., that this region may have been the main center of His worship at that time, and that He was still worshiped there as late as the ninth century.[12]

2.   *The Lord came*   He came to the people of Israel.

He shone   The Bible describes God as surrounded by a brilliant radiance. Compare, for

He appeared from Mount Paran,
And approached from Ribeboth-kodesh,
Lightning flashing at them from His right.
[3] Lover, indeed, of the people,
Their hallowed are all in Your hand.

הוֹפִ֙יעַ֙ מֵהַ֣ר פָּארָ֔ן
וְאָתָ֖ה מֵרִבְבֹ֣ת קֹ֑דֶשׁ
מִֽימִינ֕וֹ אשׁדת לָֽמוֹ׃
3 אַ֚ף חֹבֵ֣ב עַמִּ֔ים
כָּל־קְדֹשָׁ֖יו בְּיָדֶ֑ךָ

v. 2. אֵשׁ דָּת ק׳

example, Psalm 104:2–3: "You are clothed in glory and majesty, wrapped in a robe of light." Ancient Near Eastern texts likewise describe deities as enveloped in light.[13]

　　upon them　Upon Israel.[14]

　　appeared　Or "beamed." Hebrew *hofiaʿ* sometimes has the sense of "shine."[15] It is used elsewhere of God coming to battle on Israel's behalf or to punish evildoers.[16]

　　approached from Ribeboth-kodesh　Ribeboth-kodesh, literally, "Myriads of Kodesh," must be the name of a place in the Negev or Sinai, like all the terms parallel to it. It may mean "Ribeboth at, or near, Kadesh" (the vocalization Kadesh appears in the Septuagint here). The name could be a variant form, or misrendering, of Meribat-kadesh mentioned in 32:51. A reference to Kadesh would suit the context, since Kadesh was located in the wilderness of Paran at the border of Seir-Edom (Num. 13:26; 20:14,16).

　　Lightning flashing　The meaning of *ʾeshdat* is uncertain. The traditional interpretation, reading it as two words, *ʾesh dat*, "a law of, or from, fire" (cf. 4:33)[17] is midrashic; *dat*, "law," is a Persian word that did not enter Hebrew before the fifth century B.C.E.[18] The translation "lightning flashing" reflects an implicit emendation of *ʾeshdat* to *ʾesh*, "fire," plus a second word of which only two letters have survived, such as *d[oleke]t*, "blazing."[19] This reading is suggested by the motif of God surrounded by radiance in the poetic passages mentioned above.[20] Lightning flashing from God's right could reflect the conception of the deity brandishing a lightning bolt in his right hand, ready to hurl at his people's enemies.[21] In that case, *lamo* would probably mean "for them" rather than "at them."

　　Another possibility is to interpret *ʾeshdat* as "slope," the singular of *ʾash(e)dot*, as in *ʾashdot ha-Pisgah*, "the slopes of Pisgah," mentioned in 3:17; 4:49.[22] In that case, "right" means "south"[23] and the clause means "From south of the slope [of Pisgah] [He came] to them," or "From the south [He came] to them at the slope [of Pisgah]," referring to the nearby mountain (see 34:1). The clause would then refer to God coming to Israel at its encampment in Moab, perhaps in anticipation of the coming conquest of the promised land.

　　Finally, it has been suggested that the text originally read "From the southland You *proceeded* [*ʾisharta*] to them."[24] This emendation would make the clause parallel to the preceding ones.

　　3.　The meaning of this verse cannot be determined, and the text may well be damaged. A literal translation might be: "Even the lover of peoples, all its/His hallowed ones [are] in your hand, and it is they who *tukku* at your feet, he bears/utters your pronouncements." The main difficulty is the unknown verb *tukku*. NJPS's "followed" is a surmise based on the next word *le-raglekha*, "in your steps."[25] Since *le-raglekha* could also mean "at your feet," *tukku* might also mean "they bowed."[26] The phrase translated "accepting Your pronouncements" is also problematic, since Hebrew *nasaʾ* does not normally mean "accept." A more likely translation is "bearing Your pronouncements," in which case this clause would be comparable to an expression in the Amarna letters in which a vassal declares that he bows at the feet of the suzerain (cf. the preceding clause in this verse) and that he carries his suzerain's words on his front and back, meaning that he is constantly attentive to the suzerain's commands.[27] Yet another possible translation is "uttering Your pronouncements."[28]

　　Despite the fact that verse 2 speaks of God in the third person, it seems likely that He is the one addressed in this verse, although the different pronouns and inconsistent grammatical number of the verbs make this uncertain. The main question is whether the last three clauses in the verse refer to Israel or to God's angels.[29]

　　Lover . . . of the people　Literally, "Lover[30] of peoples [*ʿammim*]." If this refers to God, it is

They followed in Your steps,
Accepting Your pronouncements,
⁴When Moses charged us with the Teaching
As the heritage of the congregation of Jacob.

וְהֵם֙ תֻּכּ֣וּ לְרַגְלֶ֔ךָ
יִשָּׂ֖א מִדַּבְּרֹתֶֽיךָ׃
4 תּוֹרָ֥ה צִוָּה־לָ֖נוּ מֹשֶׁ֑ה
מוֹרָשָׁ֖ה קְהִלַּ֥ת יַעֲקֹֽב׃

a surprisingly universalistic statement for a poem about His protection of Israel. The targums and medieval commentators understand "peoples" as the tribes of Israel, as in Genesis 28:3 and possibly here in verse 19.[31] The Septuagint has the singular, "His people," possibly reflecting a reading ʿammo. If the reference is to Israel, the phrase is comparable to the description of God as ʾohev ʿammo yisraʾel, "who loves His people Israel," in the Jewish liturgy, as well as ancient Near Eastern references to gods and kings as "lover of his people."[32]

If the last three clauses of the verse refer to Israel, then kedoshayv, literally either "its" or "His hallowed ones," refers to Israel's holy ones, the members of the holy people.[33] In that case, the basic idea is that God took Israel protectively in His hand because they followed Him and accepted His authority.[34] The last clause could mean "uttering Your pronouncements" and introduce verse 4, in which Israel is the speaker.[35]

If the "hallowed" are the "holy beings" of God's angelic entourage (in which case, translate "*His* hallowed ones"),[36] the verse continues the description of God's approach from the southland accompanied by holy beings. In that case, note the similarity of verses 2 and 3 to Zechariah 14:5, "And the LORD My God, with all the holy beings [kedoshim], will come to you." Then it would be these beings to whom the third and fourth clauses refer as following or bowing to God and bearing or uttering His pronouncements. The last clause might then be comparable to Psalm 103:20, "His angels, who fulfill His word."[37]

4. It is not clear how this verse fits into its context. The NJPS translation construes it as the continuation of verse 3b, indicating *when* the people followed in God's steps and accepted his pronouncements: it was at the time when Moses conveyed God's Teaching to them. Another possibility is to view the verse in the context of verse 5: after God came from the southland to assist Israel (vv. 2–3), He became Israel's king at an assembly of its tribes (v. 5) and at that time Moses, His emissary, charged Israel with His Teaching. A similar sequence of events is described in Joshua 24:1–28: after God granted Israel victory over the Canaanites, Joshua convened the tribes to reaffirm their acceptance of God's suzerainty and he then gave them laws.

Moses The reference to Moses by other speakers ("us") is puzzling since, according to verse 1, he is the speaker. According to some of the medieval commentators, it is the people who are speaking at this point: Having accepted, or uttered, God's pronouncements (commandments) in verse 3, they declare about them: "This Teaching with which Moses charged us is the heritage of the congregation of Jacob."[38]

Some modern scholars believe that the text did not originally mention Moses, but read "When He [God] charged us with the Teaching." In this view "Moses" [m-sh-h] is a partial dittography of the following word, m-v-r-sh-h, "heritage," originally spelled m-r-sh-h.[39] If so, the subject of the verse, like the following one, is God.

the Teaching In Deuteronomy "the Teaching" (Heb. *torah*) refers to the teachings of Deuteronomy. However, since the poem seems to have originated independently of Deuteronomy, the term may not have so specific a reference here, and may simply mean divine Teaching. See Comment to 1:5 and Excursus 33.

As the heritage of the congregation of Jacob "Heritage" (*morashah*) refers literally to property, particularly land, transmitted by inheritance. Here it is a metaphor for a spiritual possession. It connotes something vital and cherished, like its synonym *naḥalah*. Compare Psalm 119:111: "Your decrees are my eternal heritage, they are my heart's delight." See also Comments to 4:20 and 32:9. That the Teaching is the heritage of the entire people accords with the ideals discussed in Excursus 28.

Because this verse is such a pithy expression of fundamental Jewish beliefs—that the Teaching was commanded by Moses, that it is a heritage, and that it belongs to the entire people, not just to an

⁵Then He became King in Jeshurun,
When the heads of the people assembled,
The tribes of Israel together.

⁶May Reuben live and not die,
Though few be his numbers.

5 וַיְהִי בִישֻׁרוּן מֶלֶךְ
בְּהִתְאַסֵּף רָאשֵׁי עָם
יַחַד שִׁבְטֵי יִשְׂרָאֵל:

6 יְחִי רְאוּבֵן וְאַל־יָמֹת
וִיהִי מְתָיו מִסְפָּר: ס

elite group—the rabbis selected it and the first verse of the Shema (Deut. 6:4) as the first biblical verses to be taught to a child when it is able to speak.[40] It appears in Ashkenazic prayerbooks as part of a brief morning prayer for young children. In the Sephardic and Middle Eastern liturgy it is one of the verses recited when the Torah is lifted during the Torah-Reading Service.

5. *He became king* This probably refers to God:[41] He became Israel's king after coming to them from the south and delivering them from their enemies. Similarly, after God saved Israel from Egypt, Israel acclaimed God's kingship and accepted His sovereignty in Exodus 15:18 and 19:3–8, respectively. Compare also Joshua 24:1–28, cited above. This is a natural sequence of events, paralleled in human political affairs in Judges 8:23, where the people offer the kingship to Gideon after he leads them to victory and saves them from Midian.[42]

In light of verse 4, several commentators think that verse 5 refers to Moses.[43] In the larger context of Deuteronomy, which sees kingship as a later institution (17:14–20), the verse could not have been understood this way. It would also seem pointless to refer to Moses as king here, since the remainder of the poem describes God as the source of Israel's welfare. Furthermore, Moses is nowhere else called a king, whereas God is in numerous passages, including Exodus 15:18 and Numbers 23:21.[44] However, the possibility that this refers to Moses cannot be entirely excluded. It would be enhanced if, as some scholars believe, the last three clauses of verse 21 were originally found here. See the discussion below.

Jeshurun Israel. See Comment to 32:15.

When the heads of the people assembled As in the coronation of a human king, it is the people or their leaders whose acclamation legitimates the king's sovereignty.[45]

The tribes of Israel In view of the parallel "heads of the people," it has been suggested that *shivtei* means "rulers" rather than "tribes" here.[46] If so, a double-entendre may be intended, since this phrase is followed by the blessings of the individual *tribes*.

THE TRIBAL BLESSINGS (vv. 6–25)

Moses blesses the tribes individually, mentioning them in geographic order beginning with Reuben, in whose territory the Israelites are encamped. For details see Excursus 33 and Map 6.

REUBEN (v. 6)

6. The tribe of Reuben was allotted territory in Transjordan (see 3:12–17 and Num. 32). It is mentioned first, as in Jacob's last words (Gen. 49:3–4). The tradition that the tribe's eponymous ancestor was Jacob's first-born implies that Reuben was at one time a strong tribe and leader of the others. Its preeminence must have ended prior to settlement in the promised land or soon afterwards, because it later became a tribe of marginal importance. Its decline is reflected in Jacob's words which depose the tribe's ancestor from his first-born status because of his incestuous affair with Jacob's concubine Bilhah.[47]

The prayer that Reuben may live, though its population be small, must anticipate a situation in which the tribe's existence was threatened and survival was as much as it could hope for. We have no sure information about this. Reuben's population is not notably small in the censuses of Numbers 1 and 26. Although it lost its leading status early, it survived as a tribe after the period

7And this he said of Judah:
> Hear, O LORD the voice of Judah
> And restore him to his people.
> Though his own hands strive for him,
> Help him against his foes.

וְזֹאת לִיהוּדָה֮ וַיֹּאמַר֒ 7
שְׁמַ֤ע יְהֹוָה֙ ק֣וֹל יְהוּדָ֔ה
וְאֶל־עַמּ֖וֹ תְּבִיאֶ֑נּוּ
יָדָיו֙ רָ֣ב ל֔וֹ
וְעֵ֥זֶר מִצָּרָ֖יו תִּהְיֶֽה׃ ס   שני

of the "Judges." In the days of King Saul it defeated pastoral nomads in eastern Transjordan, and it still existed as a tribe, headed by a chieftain, until the 730s when it was exiled by the Assyrians.[48] However, texts about the period of Saul and later that refer to Transjordan only as the land of Gad and Gilead, not of Reuben, point to the tribe's decline.[49] One school of thought holds that Reuben's survival as a distinct tribe was threatened because its population and territory were assimilated by Gad, whose flourishing is reflected in vv. 20–21. Others think that its physical survival was threatened because it was slow to become sedentary. During the period of the Judges its people remained seminomadic pastoralists along the fringe of the desert in eastern Transjordan, leaving them poorly organized and exposed to attack by neighboring non-Israelite tribes.[50]

The phrase "though few be his numbers" could also be translated "and/but let his numbers become few." This would imply the same negative attitude as that expressed toward Reuben in Genesis 49. The phrase could even be taken as an interpretation of Jacob's words in verse 4 there, "you shall excel no longer," construing "excel" as "exceed, abound."

JUDAH (v. 7)

The tribe of Judah dominated the southern part of the land and, in the days of David and Solomon, the entire country. Its territory was centered in the southern highlands, reaching the Dead Sea on the east and including the Shephelah on the west and the Negev on the south (see Comments to 1:7 and Map 2). The blessing anticipates a time when the tribe will be at war. Moses prays that God will hear Judah's prayer, aid it in battle, and bring it home safely.

7. Hear, O LORD, the voice of Judah Targum Onkelos aptly paraphrases: "Accept, O LORD, the prayer of Judah when he goes forth in battle."[51]

restore him Targum Onkelos paraphrases "bring him back safely to his people." Similar language appears in the *Gilgamesh Epic* when the elders of Gilgamesh's city urge his companion Enkidu to bring him back safely from his expedition to destroy the monster Huwawa.[52]

to his people If this refers to Judah's fellow tribesmen, it means "bring the tribe's warriors home safely from battle." "His people" could also refer to the whole people of Israel, implying that the tribe of Judah is fighting apart from the rest of Israel and perhaps on its behalf, as in Judges 1:1–20. There, Judah (accompanied by Simeon) is the first to undertake battle for the unconquered parts of the promised land.

Though his own hands strive for him The precise translation of this clause is uncertain,[53] but it seems clear that the blessing is a play on the name of the tribe, since *yadav*, "his hands," sounds like *Yehudah* (Judah). (In biblical times, the two words were probably pronounced even more similarly: *yadayu* and *Yahuda*.) The blessing of Judah in Genesis 49:8 likewise plays on the tribe's name: "You, O Judah [*Yehudah*], your brothers shall praise [*yodukha*], your hand [*yadekha*] shall be on the nape of your foes."

LEVI (vv. 8–11)

Moses prays that the Levites enjoy the privilege of serving as Israel's priests and that God grant them prosperity and protection. As noted in the Comments to 18:1–8, Deuteronomy regards all Levites, not only descendants of Aaron, as potential priests.

⁸And of Levi he said:

Let Your Thummim and Urim
Be with Your faithful one,
Whom You tested at Massah,
Challenged at the waters of Meribah;
⁹Who said of his father and mother,
"I consider them not."
His brothers he disregarded,
Ignored his own children.
Your precepts alone they observed,
And kept Your covenant.

8 וּלְלֵוִ֣י אָמַ֔ר
תֻּמֶּ֥יךָ וְאוּרֶ֖יךָ
לְאִ֣ישׁ חֲסִידֶ֑ךָ
אֲשֶׁ֤ר נִסִּיתוֹ֙ בְּמַסָּ֔ה
תְּרִיבֵ֖הוּ עַל־מֵ֥י מְרִיבָֽה׃
9 הָאֹמֵ֞ר לְאָבִ֤יו וּלְאִמּוֹ֙
לֹ֣א רְאִיתִ֔יו
וְאֶת־אֶחָיו֙ לֹ֣א הִכִּ֔יר
וְאֶת־בנו לֹ֣א יָדָ֑ע
כִּ֤י שָֽׁמְרוּ֙ אִמְרָתֶ֔ךָ
וּבְרִֽיתְךָ֖ יִנְצֹֽרוּ׃

v. 9. בָּנָיו ק׳

8. **Thummim and Urim** The Urim and Thummim (the reverse order of the terms is found only here) were a device for obtaining God's decision on important questions. It was kept by the priest who administered it on behalf of the leader or the public for such matters as military decisions, allocation of land, and identifying those chosen by God for an office or convicted by Him of an offense. It apparently consisted of a pouch, attached to the priest's breastplate, containing lots which the priest drew out and interpreted as signifying one of two or more alternative answers to a question, or as indicating a particular message. *Urim* and *tummim* may have been the names of the lots. Derivation of these terms from '*or*, "light," and *tom*, "completeness, perfection, integrity," is suggestive but far from certain.[54]

Your faithful one That is, the Levites (note the plurals in vv. 9b–10), personified as a single individual. "Faithful," meaning "devoted" or "loyal," is the original meaning of Hebrew *ḥasid*.[55]

Whom You tested at Massah, / Challenged at the waters of Meribah The Hebrew is a word play: "Whom You tested [*nissito*] at Testing-Place [*Massah*] and challenged [*terivehu*] at Challenge-Place [*Merivah*]."[56] The context implies that this refers to an occasion when the Levites or their representative(s) remained loyal to God and were rewarded with the priesthood. The final bicolon, "Your precepts alone they observed, and kept Your covenant," implies an occasion when the covenant was seriously breached, perhaps involving idolatry. Several such instances are known. At the golden calf incident, the Levites rallied to the Lord and punished the calf-worshipers, including relatives, and were awarded the priesthood.[57] In the Baal-peor incident, Aaron's grandson Phinehas acted on behalf of the Lord, and was rewarded with the high priesthood.[58] According to Ezekiel, the Zadokites were later promised the priesthood because they alone of the Levites remained loyal to God.[59] All of these incidents took place at other locations and cannot be the one intended here; nor can any of the incidents at Massah and Meribah, as related in Exodus 17 and Numbers 20.[60] Those do not involve a breach of the covenant, and in neither does God test the Levites; it is the people who test Moses, Aaron, and God, and God condemns Moses and Aaron. Apparently, the present verse refers to an unknown incident at Massah and Meribah or to a different version of those related in Exodus 17 and Numbers 20.[61] According to this passage, it was then, and not at the golden calf incident, that the Levites were awarded the priesthood.[62]

9. By loyally carrying out God's laws, the Levites showed no favoritism even to their own families. It is not clear whether this refers to the occasion mentioned in verse 8 or to the golden calf incident, when the Levites followed Moses' order to execute the guilty, whether son, brother, neighbor, or kin (Exod. 32:27–29). For the principle itself, compare the commandment to turn in enticers to idolatry, even close relatives and neighbors (13:7).

10. Because of the devotion they showed to God's precepts, the Levites shall have the privilege of transmitting His laws to Israel (essentially a measure-for-measure reward) as well as conducting His worship.[63]

¹⁰They shall teach Your laws to Jacob
And Your instructions to Israel.
They shall offer You incense to savor
And whole-offerings on Your altar.
¹¹Bless, O LORD, his substance,
And favor his undertakings.
Smite the loins of his foes;
Let his enemies rise no more.

יוֹרוּ מִשְׁפָּטֶ֙יךָ֙ לְיַעֲקֹב 10
וְתוֹרָתְךָ֖ לְיִשְׂרָאֵ֑ל
יָשִׂ֤ימוּ קְטוֹרָה֙ בְּאַפֶּ֔ךָ
וְכָלִ֖יל עַל־מִזְבְּחֶֽךָ׃
בָּרֵ֤ךְ יְהוָה֙ חֵיל֔וֹ 11
וּפֹ֥עַל יָדָ֖יו תִּרְצֶ֑ה
מְחַ֨ץ מָתְנַ֧יִם קָמָ֛יו
וּמְשַׂנְאָ֖יו מִן־יְקוּמֽוּן׃ ס

They shall teach Your laws . . . Your instructions   This refers to the full range of priestly instruction in ritual, judicial, and civil matters, such as worship, distinction between sacred and profane, clean and unclean, judicial decisions, and division of territory.[64] For the priests' judicial role, see 17:9 and Comment and 21:5; for instructions concerning leprosy see 24:8. Priests gave some of their instructions as ad hoc rulings, sometimes probably obtained from the Urim and Thummim, in response to specific inquiries.[65] We do not know what further institutional form their instruction took, such as teaching in schools or at festivals or other gatherings.

incense . . . whole-offerings   These are two of the regular components of the sacrificial service. According to the books of Numbers and Chronicles, only the priests could offer them.[66] These responsibilities are referred to as "ministering" or "standing in attendance for service" to God in 10:8; 18:5; and 21:5.

They shall offer You incense to savor   This expression focuses on the pleasing aroma produced by the incense. Incense offerings of spices were burnt in the sanctuary as part of the daily morning and evening sacrifices and on the Day of Atonement,[67] and were performed in propitiatory rites as well.[68] Incense altars and censers are attested archaeologically.[69]

whole-offerings   Whole-offerings (Heb. *kalil*, a synonym of *'olah*) are mentioned because they were the mainstay of the priestly service, as noted in the Comment to 12:6.

11.   The final part of the Levites' blessing, like those of the other tribes, refers to their material welfare and security.

his substance   That is, their wealth.[70] Although the Levites are not given a tribal territory, they receive income in return for their priestly services and they are given cities, real estate, fields, pastureland, and cattle (see Comments to 18:1–8). Hence their wealth is potentially considerable. On the relationship of this idea to the rest of Deuteronomy, see Excursus 33.

favor his undertakings   This idiom is synonymous with "bless his undertakings"[71] (meaning "grant him prosperity"), a common idiom in Deuteronomy (see Comment to 2:7).[72]

Smite the loins of his foes; / Let his enemies rise no more   Moses does not ask God to grant the Levites military prowess but to defend them against attackers. As a clerical tribe the Levites had no military force and, unlike the other tribes, they were defenseless against military attacks, as when King Saul had the priests of the city of Nob slaughtered for helping David[73] and King Josiah wiped out the priests of the shrines in north Israel.[74] But the verse does not necessarily refer to physical assault. The psalms often describe verbal attacks and false accusations hyperbolically as physical danger.[75] The Levites' enemies could be those who would challenge their exclusive right to priesthood, as Korah and the tribal chieftains challenged Aaron's right.[76] Similar challenges are known from later times when Eli's family was replaced as priests by Zadok's and when King Jeroboam appointed non-Levitical priests.[77]

Smite the loins   Render them powerless. The loins are used figuratively as the seat of one's strength.[78]

rise no more[79]

12Of Benjamin he said:
Beloved of the LORD,
He rests securely beside Him;
Ever does He protect him,
As he rests between His shoulders.

12 לְבִנְיָמִן אָמַר
יְדִיד יְהֹוָה
יִשְׁכֹּן לָבֶטַח עָלָיו
חֹפֵף עָלָיו כָּל־הַיּוֹם
וּבֵין כְּתֵיפָיו שָׁכֵן: ס   שלישי

BENJAMIN (v. 12)

The tribe of Benjamin occupied a small but strategic territory between those of Judah and Ephraim, at one time encompassing, on its southern border, at least part of Jerusalem. Its blessing characterizes the tribe as God's beloved and describes the security it will enjoy. Its belovedness is reminiscent of Jacob's doting on the tribe's eponymous ancestor Benjamin (see Gen. 42:20).[80] Parts of the blessing may be based on its name *Binyamin*, literally, "son of the right." Although "right" is usually taken to mean south (see Comment to v. 2), in Psalm 110:1 sitting on God's right is a sign of favor or protection: "Sit at My right hand, while I make your enemies your footstool." The final clause of the blessing, "As he rests between [*bein*] his shoulders," may have been inspired by the first syllable of Benjamin.

12. Beloved of the LORD If this means that God favored Benjamin politically, it could reflect the tribe's prestige when Ehud the Benjaminite was chieftain, when Samuel's leadership was centered in Benjaminite territory,[81] or the choice of the Benjaminite Saul as Israel's first king (note that the future King Solomon was called Yedidiah, "Beloved of the LORD" [2 Sam. 12:25]).[82] Since Jerusalem and the Temple are also called "beloved,"[83] God's love might be manifest in the location of a sanctuary in Benjamin's territory.[84] Perhaps, then, our verse alludes to one or more of the older sanctuaries in Benjamin's territory, such as those in Nob, Ramah, or Bethel; at one time the Ark, and hence the Lord, resided at the latter.[85]

He rests securely The tribe dwells securely in its territory.[86]

beside Him Hebrew *'alayv*. This would seem to mean that Benjamin dwells alongside of the Lord's sanctuary.[87] However, *'alayv* usually means "over him" and rarely "beside somebody."[88] Since the remainder of the clause, "He rests securely," forms a complete idea without *'alayv*, and has the same number of stress units as the preceding clause, the word may not belong here. It is missing in the Samaritan Pentateuch and the Peshitta.[89]

Ever does He protect him The verse has changed subjects and is now referring to God (see v. 20 for a similar midverse change of subject without the new subject being identified). The verb *ḥofef* does not appear elsewhere in the Bible. The translation "protect" relates it to *ḥuppah*, "canopy," and Arabic *ḥaffa*, "surround."[90] The verb would thus mean "form a protective canopy." Compare Isaiah 4:5–6: "The LORD will create over . . . Mount Zion cloud by day and smoke . . . by night . . . a canopy, which shall serve as a cover for shade from heat by day and as a shelter for protection against drenching rain."

As he rests between His shoulders This translation implies that the verse is once more referring to Benjamin. This would be consistent with the fact that "rests" (*shakhen*) is always used of the tribes in this poem (see the preceding clause and vv. 20 and 28, where it is translated "poised" and "dwells"). If Benjamin is the subject, resting between God's shoulders would express the security that the tribe enjoys under His protection. The image could be that of a child carried on its parent's back.[91]

However, it seems preferable to construe God as the subject, as in the preceding clause, so that it is He who rests between Benjamin's "shoulders." "Shoulders" could be meant in the topographical sense of "sides, flanks," meaning that God dwells in His sanctuary "within its [Benjamin's] borders."[92] It could also be taken in an anatomical sense, "on or behind his back."[93] That would mean that God is guarding Benjamin from behind, from Benjamin's blind spot; compare the request "may my protective spirit not cease being behind me" in an Akkadian prayer.[94] The thought would parallel "protecting him ever" in the preceding clause.

13 And of Joseph he said:

Blessed of the LORD be his land
With the bounty of dew from heaven,
And of the deep that couches below;
14 With the bounteous yield of the sun,
And the bounteous crop of the moons;

13 וּלְיוֹסֵף אָמַר
מְבֹרֶכֶת יְהוָֹה אַרְצוֹ
מִמֶּגֶד שָׁמַיִם מִטָּל
וּמִתְּהוֹם רֹבֶצֶת תָּחַת׃
14 וּמִמֶּגֶד תְּבוּאֹת שָׁמֶשׁ
וּמִמֶּגֶד גֶּרֶשׁ יְרָחִים׃

JOSEPH (vv. 13–17)

The tribes of Ephraim and Manasseh are personified in their eponymous ancestor Joseph. Historically Ephraim, occupying the southern part of the central highlands, was the more prominent of the two, though its territory was smaller. Part of Manasseh occupied the northern part of the central highlands, while another part inhabited Bashan and Gilead in Transjordan. The blessings focus on the fertility of their territory and on their military prowess. The emphasis on fertility may be inspired by the names of Joseph and Ephraim. Joseph (Heb. *yosef*) means "May He increase," and Genesis 41:52 explains Ephraim's name as meaning "God has made me fertile," implying that it is derived from *p-r-h*, "be fertile."

More than any of the other blessings, that of Joseph resembles its counterpart in Jacob's blessing, Genesis 49:22–26.

13. The blessing begins with the prerequisite for fertility, abundant water. In Israel the main sources of water are rain and springs. Compare verse 28 and 8:7; 11:11–12; and 32:2.

bounty The word *meged* is the leitmotif of this blessing, appearing five times. It may be a double entendre. It has the sense of "gift," "blessing," like Hebrew *migdanot*, "presents," "precious objects"[95] (in its place Gen. 49:25 reads "blessings"), and of *megadim*, "choice fruits."[96] The double entendre depicts the rain and water as both the "fruit" of heaven and earth and as their gifts.[97]

bounty of dew from heaven A few medieval manuscripts of the Bible[98] read "bounty from heaven *above*" (Heb. *me-ʿal* instead of *mi-tal*, reading an *ʿayin* instead of the similar *tet*), as in the equivalent blessing in Genesis 49:25.[99] Such late manuscripts are not usually reliable, and the reading could have arisen simply to harmonize our text with that in Genesis. However, the Masoretic reading makes the word order awkward[100] and "above" is a more natural parallel to "below" in the next clause.

the deep that couches below The subterranean waters that issue from springs and wells, mentioned in 8:7. Here they are pictured as an animal—female, from the gender of the verb—couching (crouching) below the earth. The Hebrew word for "the deep," *tehom*, always lacks a definite article in the singular, suggesting that it is a proper name. The name and the imagery probably go back to a time when the subterranean waters were conceived mythologically as a sea monster like the Babylonian Tiamat, whose name (originally *tihamat*, with a feminine ending) is an Akkadian cognate of *tehom*. Here it is only a figure of speech. Originally mythological terms, such as Sol, Luna, and the like are used similarly in English. Compare Comment to 7:13 for common nouns derived from names of deities where the personification has entirely disappeared.

14. **yield of the sun** The crops warmed and lighted by the sun.

crop Hebrew *geresh*, appears only here and the translation is a surmise based on the parallel "yield."[101]

crops of the moons The parallel "sun" suggests that "moons" is meant literally; if so, perhaps the plural refers to the moon's various phases. Rashi explains that some fruits, such as cucumbers and melons, are ripened by the moon. A similar idea is expressed by the Roman author Apuleius, who addresses the moon goddess as "You who . . . nourish the joyous seeds with your moist fires."[102] Normally, however, the plural "moons" refers to months. If that is the meaning here, the translation would be "the bounteous crops of the months," referring to the different months in which various crops ripen.[103]

15With the best from the ancient mountains,
And the bounty of hills immemorial;
16With the bounty of earth and its fullness,
And the favor of the Presence in the Bush.
May these rest on the head of Joseph,
On the crown of the elect of his brothers.

15 וּמֵרֹאשׁ הַרְרֵי־קֶדֶם
וּמִמֶּגֶד גִּבְעוֹת עוֹלָם:
16 וּמִמֶּגֶד אֶרֶץ וּמְלֹאָהּ
וּרְצוֹן שֹׁכְנִי סְנֶה
תָּבוֹאתָה לְרֹאשׁ יוֹסֵף
וּלְקָדְקֹד נְזִיר אֶחָיו:

15. The bountiful products of the mountains, mentioned frequently in ancient Near Eastern literature, include wood, stone, precious and nonprecious metals, and foodstuffs.[104] Compare 8:9. The mountain regions in the territory of the Joseph tribes were richly forested when the tribes first arrived. Later, land was cleared for planting grains, olive trees, and vineyards.[105] The highlands of Bashan and Gilead, where half of Manasseh lived, were also rich in forests and pastures, and their balm was famous.[106]

best Hebrew *ro'sh*, literally "head." The translation "best" is suggested by the parallel "bounty." *Ro'sh* has this meaning in the idiom *ro'sh besamim*, "finest spices," but it is not a common usage.[107] More often it means "(mountain) top,"[108] and it may have been chosen here to form a double entendre. Some think that the clause is elliptical for "with the bounty of the tops of the ancient mountains."[109]

ancient mountains . . . hills immemorial[110] If the hills of Joseph's territory are meant, these adjectives may refer to the proverbial antiquity of hills (cf. the expression "as old as the hills"). Or this might be an allusion to a motif of ancient fertile mountains that played a significant role in myths about primordial times, such as the mountains where the Sumerians believed that the gods of cattle and grain came into existence.[111] The point would be that Joseph enjoys fertility like that of those ancient mountains.

16. **the bounty of earth and its fullness** This is perhaps a summary of the preceding blessings.[112] However, in the phrase "the earth/land and its fullness," "fullness" usually refers to inhabitants.[113] Therefore, this phrase may refer to gifts or tribute from all the inhabitants of the earth. Similar blessings are promised by the prophet of the Babylonian exile: "For the wealth of the sea [or coastlands] shall pass on to you, / The riches of nations shall flow to you."[114]

the favor of the Presence in the Bush That is, God's favor, in the sense of blessing (see Comment to v. 11). This is the climactic blessing and the ultimate source of all the others.

By calling God "the Presence in the Bush" (*shokheni seneh*) in this, his final speech, Moses alludes back to his first encounter with Him at the burning bush on Horeb, the Mountain of God (see Exod. 3:1–6). The Hebrew word for bush, *seneh*, sounds like, and calls to mind, Sinai, the other name of Horeb (see Comment to 1:2).[115] "Presence in the Bush" is literally "He who stays, or dwells, in the Bush." It is comparable to later descriptions of God as staying in the Israelite camp and dwelling in Jerusalem.[116] It seems to imply that He was in the bush longer than the few minutes of His revelation to Moses. Perhaps this is just a poetic image implying that the Lord also had a dwelling on Mount Sinai, "the Mountain of God," near the bush.[117] Conceivably this epithet was chosen here as a play on the name Manasseh (Heb. *menasheh*, echoed by *seneh*, "bush").[118]

May these rest[119]

On the crown of the elect of his brothers That is, on the head of the chief brother. This characterization corresponds both to the position of Joseph as ruler of his brothers in Egypt and to the later status of the Joseph tribes, particularly Ephraim, as preeminent among the ten northern tribes.[120] According to 1 Chronicles 5:1–2: "Reuben . . . was the first-born, but when he defiled his father's bed, his birthright was given to the sons of Joseph . . . though [later, in David's time] Judah became more powerful than his brothers and a leader came from him, yet the birthright belonged to Joseph." Whether this verse has a specific period of preeminence in mind is discussed in Excursus 33.

elect Hebrew *nazir* normally means "nazirite," a sense unsuitable here. The translation "elect" is based on the assumption that the underlying root *n-z-r* means "separate" (hence Nazirite,

17Like a firstling bull in his majesty,
He has horns like the horns of the wild-ox;
With them he gores the peoples,
The ends of the earth one and all.
These are the myriads of Ephraim,
Those are the thousands of Manasseh.

18And of Zebulun he said:

Rejoice, O Zebulun, on your journeys,
And Issachar, in your tents.

17 בְּכוֹר שׁוֹרוֹ הָדָר לוֹ
וְקַרְנֵי רְאֵם קַרְנָיו
בָּהֶם עַמִּים יְנַגַּח
יַחְדָּו אַפְסֵי־אָרֶץ
וְהֵם רִבְבוֹת אֶפְרַיִם
וְהֵם אַלְפֵי מְנַשֶּׁה: ס   רביעי

18 וְלִזְבוּלֻן אָמַר
שְׂמַח זְבוּלֻן בְּצֵאתֶךָ
וְיִשָּׂשכָר בְּאֹהָלֶיךָ:

"abstainer") and can also yield a meaning "single out," hence "elect." Another possibility is that here *nazir* means "prince," literally, "the crowned one," one who wears the *nezer*, "diadem." In either case, the word calls to mind the Nazirite, who is distinguished by his uncut hair, and thus suggests a word-play with "head" and "crown" (Heb. *kodkod*, the crown, or top, of the head).[121]

17. Like a firstling bull[122]   Compare 1 Chronicles 5:1–2, cited above, referring to Joseph acquiring the birthright (lit., "first-bornship"). Ibn Ezra supposes that the firstling is mentioned here to connote great strength; compare 21:17 and especially Genesis 49:3, where Jacob's first-born is "my might and first fruit of my vigor, exceeding in rank and exceeding in strength."

He has horns like the horns of the wild-ox   The wild ox goring its foes is a common metaphor for strength. Balaam compares God or Israel to one in Numbers 23:22, and Mesopotamian texts use the same metaphor for heroes and kings.[123]

The ends of the earth   That is, the most distant enemies.[124]

These . . . Those   Rather, "Those [horns] are the myriads of Ephraim, they are the thousands of Manasseh," meaning that Joseph's horns stand for the troops of Ephraim and Manasseh.[125] Ephraim is mentioned first, as in Jacob's blessing (Gen. 48:19), and its numbers (myriads, that is, tens of thousands) are larger.[126]

ZEBULUN AND ISSACHAR (vv. 18–19)

The heading names only Zebulun, but the blessing includes Issachar as well, reflecting the close association between these neighboring tribes. According to Genesis 30:17–20, Issachar and Zebulun were, respectively, the fifth and sixth sons of Leah, and they are mentioned side-by-side in the blessing of Jacob and in the Song of Deborah.[127] The two are generally listed in order of birth, but here the geographic order of the blessings dictates that Zebulun come first (see Excursus 33).

According to the Book of Joshua, Zebulun and Issachar were assigned neighboring inland territories in the lower Galilee and the Jezreel Valley, Zebulun in the central part of the region and Issachar to its southeast. On the other hand, Genesis 49:13 locates Zebulun on the Mediterranean coast, extending north to Phoenicia: "Zebulun shall dwell by the seashore and be a haven for ships." A coastal location is also indicated by verse 19b here. These passages seem to imply that Zebulun once controlled territory as far west as the Mediterranean in the Haifa bay area.[128]

The blessing wishes Zebulun and Issachar success in their endeavors and wealth from maritime resources. Much of it is ambiguous. Part of it may have been suggested by the sound of the names of the tribes. The sounds *z-b* of Zebulun may have inspired *yiZBeḥu ZiVeḥei* (originally pronounced *ZiBeḥei*), "offer sacrifices," while the sounds *s-s* or *sas* in "Issachar" (*yiSSakhar* or *yiSaSkhar*) may have inspired "rejoice" (*semaḥ*, a synonym of *sas*, "rejoice").

18. Rejoice, O Zebulun, on your journeys, / And Issachar, in your tents   Zebulun's journeys are most likely maritime trade journeys[129] or fishing excursions,[130] in view of the coastal location implied by verse 19b and Genesis 49:13.[131] Issachar's "tents" are probably herdsmen's dwellings,[132] in view of Genesis 49:14, "Issachar . . . crouching among the sheepfolds."[133]

19They invite their kin to the mountain,
Where they offer sacrifices of success.
For they draw from the riches of the sea
And the hidden hoards of the sand.

19 עַמִּים֙ הַר־יִקְרָ֔אוּ
שָׁ֖ם יִזְבְּח֣וּ זִבְחֵי־צֶ֑דֶק
כִּ֣י שֶׁ֤פַע יַמִּים֙ יִינָ֔קוּ
וּשְׂפֻנֵ֖י טְמ֥וּנֵי חֽוֹל׃ ס

It is conceivable, in view of the fact that the heading names only Zebulun, that "in your tents" is also addressed to Zebulun, and that the clause means that Zebulun should also rejoice over having Issachar in its tents. This would imply that Issachar lives in Zebulun's territory (like Simeon in Judah's),[134] under its protection or in its service,[135] and is too insignificant to rate a blessing in its own right. This would be consistent with verse 19b, which implies that the tribe addressed occupies a maritime territory since there is such evidence, as noted above, concerning Zebulun but none concerning Issachar. The plural verbs in verse 19 are no impediment to the possibility that only Zebulun is being addressed, since plural verbs are also used in addressing Levi in vv. 9b–10.

Traditional Jewish exegesis saw the association of Issachar and Zebulun here as a partnership in which the Zebulunites engaged in trade and supported the Issacharites so that they could remain in the academies and occupy themselves with the Torah. Hence Zebulun is mentioned before the elder Issachar, since the latter's learning is to Zebulun's credit.[136]

19. The meaning of this verse depends on the meaning of "kin," the identification of the mountain, and the kind of sacrifices it refers to.

their kin Literally "peoples," with no pronoun. Hebrew *'am* is a kindred group, a people. The verse could mean that the two tribes invite their own kin (fellow Israelites) or members of some other kinship group, that is, other peoples. In view of Zebulun's maritime location, other peoples might include Phoenicians, Egyptians, and others from Mediterranean islands and coastlands.[137]

to the mountain The reference to sacrifices in the next clause suggests that the mountain is one with a sanctuary. It could be Mount Tabor, where the territories of Zebulun, Issachar, and Naphtali met, or Mount Carmel above the Mediterranean coast.

sacrifices of success "Sacrifices of *tsedek*." *Tsedek* commonly means "righteousness," but it has many other nuances and its precise meaning here is unknown. It could refer to a thanksgiving offering,[139] in which case the verse could mean that Zebulun and Issachar will invite others to join them in thanking God for their maritime wealth.[140] Alternatively, they will invite other tribes and peoples to combined sacrificial festivals and fairs at which maritime goods will be traded.[141] Other suggestions include: sacrifices offered in a state of righteousness, or in the right spirit,[142] the sacrifices rightfully due to God,[143] or sacrifices of victory or salvation.[144]

For they draw from the riches of the sea / And the hidden hoards of the sand Only Zebulun is connected to the seacoast in Genesis 49:13. Perhaps members of Issachar worked for Zebulun in maritime commerce, or perhaps Issachar profited from the resources of Lake Tiberias, which was not far from its territory.

riches of the sea Riches drawn from the sea[145] and/or imported by sea.[146] Riches from the sea would include fish, shells, and murex snails. Shells were used for lamps, vessels, and ornaments. Murex snails were the source of the reddish and purple dyes[147] that gave the coast north of Acco its ancient name, "Phoenicia," related to Greek *phoinix*, "purple," "crimson."[148] Riches imported by sea might include timber from Phoenicia, gold, silver, and linen from Egypt, copper from Cyprus, and pottery vessels (or their contents) from Cyprus and eastern Greece.[149]

hidden Hebrew *sefunei* is not found elsewhere and the translation is uncertain.[150] Saadia translates "*they shall collect* the hidden hoards of the sand," as if the text read *ya'asfun*. Some modern scholars suggest emending the text to read thus, or to read *yahsefun*, "they shall uncover."[151]

hoards of the sand Literally, "things concealed in sand," perhaps shells and murex snails that wash up on the sand.[152]

20 And of Gad he said:

    Blessed be He who enlarges Gad!

    Poised is he like a lion

    To tear off arm and scalp.

21 He chose for himself the best,

    For there is the portion of the revered chieftain,

20 וּלְגָד אָמַר

בָּרוּךְ מַרְחִיב גָּד

כְּלָבִיא שָׁכֵן

וְטָרַף זְרוֹעַ אַף־קָדְקֹד:

21 וַיַּרְא רֵאשִׁית לוֹ

כִּי־שָׁם חֶלְקַת מְחֹקֵק סָפוּן

GAD (vv. 20–21)

Some parts of the blessing of Gad seem to allude to the fact that the tribe (along with Reuben and half of Manasseh) requested the fertile Transjordan pastureland that was Israel's first conquest. Moses had agreed to the request on condition that Gad and its partners march in Israel's vanguard in the battles for the land west of the Jordan (3:18–20).[153] But some parts of verse 21 are strikingly similar to verses 4–5 and may belong with them.

20. ***Blessed is He who enlarges Gad*** This probably refers to enlarging Gad's population.[154] Contrast the blessing of Gad's neighbor, Reuben, in verse 6. This is the only blessing in the chapter phrased as a blessing of God for helping the tribe. There is a parallel in Genesis 9:26, where Noah blesses Shem by blessing the Lord as Shem's God.

The use of *barukh*, "blessed," plays on the meaning of Gad's name, explained in Genesis 30:11 as "good luck." That the text intends this play is shown by the fact that it uses *barukh* again only in the blessing of Asher, which means "good fortune." Compare Comment on Joseph's name in verse 13.

Poised is he like a lion / To tear off arm and scalp Similar expressions of strength and prowess as a warrior are applied by Jacob to Judah and by Balaam to all of Israel.[155]

21. ***He chose***[156] ***for himself the best*** Literally, "the first" (*re'shit*), in the sense of prime, best,[157] referring to Gad's choice of fertile pasturelands in Transjordan as its territory. The clause could also mean that Gad chose the first-conquered portion of land.[158]

For there is the portion of the revered chieftain Hebrew *ki sham ḥelkat meḥokek safun*. This is an extremely difficult clause and the word rendered "revered" (Heb. *safun*) may belong with the next clause (see below). *Ḥelkah* is a portion of land. *Meḥokek*, "chieftain,"[159] comes from the verb *ḥ-k-k*, "dig/engrave in stone," which is used for writing laws and decrees.[160] Several ancient translations and medieval commentators understood the *meḥokek* as Moses, the "scribe" or lawgiver, and "the *meḥokek*'s portion" as his burial plot in Transjordan.[161] However, the implication that Gad chose its territory because it anticipated that Moses would later be buried there is implausible and contradicts the reason given in Numbers 32. Other interpretations are that "portion of the *meḥokek*" refers to a portion *worthy* of a chieftain,[162] or that it should be understood as "[Gad's] portion *from* the lawgiver," meaning the portion assigned to Gad *by* the lawgiver.[163]

Meḥokek also means a type of digging tool,[164] which is suggestive in the light of the following clause, "Where the heads of the people come." In Numbers 21:18 the people sing about a well in Moab (apparently in future Reubenite [and later Gadite?] territory) where God gave them water. They sing of "the well which the chieftains dug, which the nobles of the people started, with digging tools [*meḥokek*], with their own staffs." Conceivably, then, our verse means something like: "for there was the parcel of land where the digging tool [was used], where the heads of the people gathered [to dig the well]."

revered Hebrew *safun*, spelled *s-p-w-n*. The translation is based on rabbinic Hebrew where *safun* means "esteemed."[165] The Septuagint reflects a Hebrew text in which *s-p-w-n* is part of the next clause (see below). In that case the present clause reads simply "For there is the portion of the *meḥokek*." This is the least problematic solution and it has the advantage of reducing the clause to three stress-units, the dominant pattern in the poem.

Where the heads of the people come Literally, "came [*v-y-t-'*, singular] the heads of the people." This has been explained as meaning "he went *at* the head of the people," alluding to Gad marching in the vanguard of the Israelite forces (3:18–20).[166] However, this explanation is forced.

Where the heads of the people come.
He executed the LORD's judgments
And His decisions for Israel.

וַיֵּתֵא֙ רָ֣אשֵׁי עָ֔ם
צִדְקַ֤ת יְהוָה֙ עָשָׂ֔ה
וּמִשְׁפָּטָ֖יו עִם־יִשְׂרָאֵֽל׃ ס   חמישי

22 And of Dan he said:
Dan is a lion's whelp
That leaps forth from Bashan.

22 וּלְדָ֣ן אָמַ֔ר
דָּ֖ן גּ֣וּר אַרְיֵ֑ה
יְזַנֵּ֖ק מִן־הַבָּשָֽׁן׃

The Septuagint reflects a different Hebrew text: "when they [the heads of the people] gathered" (*v-y-t-ʾ-s-p-w-n*).[167] This could allude to the fact that the Gadites and Reubenites presented their special request for territory to Moses and the assembled chieftains of the community (Num. 32:2 and 28). Some scholars note that this clause, as emended, resembles the second clause in verse 5 and consider it a misplaced variant of the latter.[168]

He executed the LORD's judgments / And His decisions for Israel   It is not obvious how this sentence relates to Gad. Some explain that it refers to Gad carrying out its promise to fight in the vanguard.[169] Since "the LORD's *tsedakot*" refers to His benefactions and acts of deliverance, particularly the Exodus and Israel's victories in the promised land, and *sh-p-t* also means "deliver,"[170] Gad's *doing* the Lord's *tsedakah* and *mishpatim* could mean not that the tribe fulfilled its promise but that, by fighting in the vanguard, it was instrumental in effecting one of these benefactions, the conquest of the land.

Some commentators believe that this sentence refers to Moses, either as the leader who taught and enforced God's just laws,[171] or who was God's agent in effecting His benefactions for Israel, particularly the Exodus and the conquest of northern Transjordan. If this does refer to Moses, it is not integral to the blessing of Gad. Even assuming that "the chieftain's portion" is Moses' gravesite, that is only mentioned because it is in Gad's territory; it hardly calls for further elaboration of Moses' virtues. A number of modern commentators therefore believe that this sentence (as well as one or more of the preceding clauses) was originally located somewhere in verses 4–5, one or both of which they believe refer to Moses.[172]

DAN (v. 22)

Dan, like Gad, is blessed with lionlike strength and prowess. Dan was originally assigned territory in the Shephelah and the coastal plain, near Philistia. Later, it migrated to the northern extremity of the land where it destroyed and rebuilt the city of Laish, settled, and called the city Dan.[173] The geographic order of the tribes in this poem indicates that it pictures the tribe of Dan in its northern location (see Excursus 33). Contrast Numbers 34:22, where Dan is listed in accordance with its earlier, southern location.

22. a lion's whelp   Compare the comparison of Gad to a lion in verse 20. The simile "lion's whelp" does not imply something weaker than a lion; it is used of the powerful tribe of Judah in Genesis 49:9. The comparison to a lion could have been inspired by *Laish*, the former name of the northern town where Dan settled, since *layish* is another term for lion.

leaps forth[174]

from Bashan   The mountain range in northern Transjordan, assigned to Manasseh (3:13–14). This phrase is part of the metaphor: the lion of the metaphor, not Dan, leaps from Bashan (Dan did not control Bashan or attack Laish from there).

NAPHTALI (v. 23)

Naphtali is blessed with fertile territory. Its domain in upper Galilee was well watered and rich in woods, fruit trees, and many varieties of vegetation. It included the luxuriant western and southern shores of Lake Tiberias.[175] Doubtless, Naphtali also fished the lake, as indicated by Targum Jonathan and talmudic sources.[176]

23 And of Naphtali he said:

    O Naphtali, sated with favor

    And full of the LORD's blessing,

    Take possession on the west and south.

24 And of Asher he said:

    Most blessed of sons be Asher;

    May he be the favorite of his brothers,

    May he dip his foot in oil.

25 May your doorbolts be iron and copper,

    And your security last all your days.

23 וּלְנַפְתָּלִי אָמַר

נַפְתָּלִי שְׂבַע רָצוֹן

וּמָלֵא בִּרְכַּת יְהֹוָה

יָם וְדָרוֹם יְרָשָׁה: ס

24 וּלְאָשֵׁר אָמַר

בָּרוּךְ מִבָּנִים אָשֵׁר

יְהִי רְצוּי אֶחָיו

וְטֹבֵל בַּשֶּׁמֶן רַגְלוֹ:

25 בַּרְזֶל וּנְחֹשֶׁת מִנְעָלֶיךָ

וּכְיָמֶיךָ דָּבְאֶךָ:

---

23. *sated with favor*   With God's favor.[177]

on the west and south   On the western and southern shores of Lake Tiberias.[178]

ASHER (vv. 24–25)

Asher is blessed with fertility and security. Situated in the fecund hills of upper Galilee, between Naphtali and the Mediterranean, its fertility is also mentioned in Genesis 49:20: "Asher's bread shall be rich, And he shall yield royal dainties." But as a border tribe it needed strong defenses. Its territory was traversed by one of the international roads by which invaders from the north and northeast entered the land.[179]

24. *Most blessed of sons*[180]   The focus on Asher's blessedness was probably inspired by its name, which is connected in Genesis 30:13 with '-*sh-r*, "good fortune." Related terms, such as 'ashrei (cf. 'ashreikha in v. 29) and *me'ushar*, "happy" (in the sense of "fortunate"), are close in meaning to "blessed."[181]

the favorite of his brothers   Rather, "the most favored of his brothers," meaning the most blessed of the brothers.[182]

May he dip his foot in oil   The highlands of Galilee were famous for abundant olive oil,[183] and this could be a hyperbole to indicate how abundant the oil will be. It could also be simply a metaphor for prosperity and luxury, not necessarily based on the nature of Asher's territory.[184] Compare the hyperboles in Genesis 49:11, "[Judah] washes his garment in wine, his robe in blood of grapes," and Job 29:5–6 and 11: "When Shaddai was still with me. . . . When my feet were bathed in cream, and rocks poured out streams of oil for me. . . . The ear that heard [of it] acclaimed me fortunate" (*te'ashereni*, from the root '-*sh-r*).

It has been suggested that this clause is inspired by another play on the name of Asher, since 'ashur means "foot."[185]

25. *doorbolts*   Rather, "gate bolts," referring to the bolts on city gates.[186] As usual, *neḥoshet*, "copper," probably refers to copper's stronger alloy, bronze. The blessing may be metaphoric, meaning "may your land be as secure as if it were locked with bolts of iron or bronze."[187]

security   Hebrew *d-b-'* is a hapax legomenon. The translation is based on the parallel "bolts." The ancient translations render it as "strength."[188] Scholars once considered this word a textual error, but its existence has been confirmed by its discovery in Ugaritic, though in a passage that gives no clue to its meaning; "strength" would be suitable.[189]

CODA   (vv. 26–29)

Having blessed the tribes individually, Moses concludes with a coda celebrating the good fortune of Israel as a whole under the protection of God. He declares that Israel enjoys unparalleled

²⁶O Jeshurun, there is none like God,
Riding through the heavens to help you,
Through the skies in His majesty.
²⁷The ancient God is a refuge,
A support are the arms everlasting.

26אֵין כָּאֵל יְשֻׁרֻון
רֹכֵב שָׁמַיִם בְּעֶזְרֶךָ
וּבְגַאֲוָתוֹ שְׁחָקִים: ששי

27 מְעֹנָה אֱלֹהֵי קֶדֶם
וּמִתַּחַת זְרֹעֹת עוֹלָם

welfare because its God is unparalleled. He continues the theme of the exordium, God's coming to Israel's aid, and sums up the main themes of the blessings, divine protection and fertile territory.

The coda is framed by similar and assonant language in its opening and closing verses: "there is none like God," "Jeshurun," and the pair *'ezrekha* (or *'uzzo*) // *ga'avato* in verse 26, and "who is like you," "Israel," and the pair *'ezrekha* // *ga'avatekha* in verse 29.

26. This verse resumes the theme of verses 2–5 describing God's coming to the aid of Israel, called Jeshurun as in verse 5.

O Jeshurun, there is none like God Israel's protector is incomparable, a point often made in Scripture (see Comment to 3:24).

Riding through the heavens to help you, Through the skies in His majesty God's riding to Israel's aid is mentioned in a number of passages, including those similar to verses 2–3.[190] His "vehicle" is variously said to be a cherub, a cloud, wind, or a horse-drawn chariot. The same motif appears in Babylonian and Canaanite literature, particularly with reference to storm gods, whose power is associated with prowess in warfare.[191] It is natural for the Bible to appropriate such imagery for the Lord, not only because He incorporates the powers of all the pagan deities, but because Israel's geography made it so dependent on rain that it was one of the primary media for the exercise of His providence. Compare Psalm 29 and see Comments to 11:10–21.

to help you Be-*'ezrekha* (spelled *b-'-z-r-k*), literally, "as your help."[192] Some scholars emend this word so that this and the next clause would be entirely synonymous. They compare Psalm 68:34–35, "[God] who rides the ancient highest heavens . . . whose majesty is over Israel, whose *might* [*'uzzo*] is in the skies." Based on that passage, they suggest that the present verse originally read "Riding through the heavens in His might [*be'uzzo*], riding in His majesty through the skies."[193]

27. *The ancient God* Hebrew *'elohei kedem*. This epithet is synonymous with *'el 'olam*, "the everlasting God" (Gen. 21:33). It is consistent with descriptions of God as being "from everlasting" and as acting in primordial times, at the beginning (*mi-kedem, yemei kedem*).[194]

refuge Hebrew *me'onah*, literally, "dwelling." Compare Psalm 90:1, which likewise connects the idea of God as a refuge with His eternity: "O Lord, You have been our refuge [*ma'on*] in every generation. Before the mountains came into being, before You brought forth the earth and the world, from eternity to eternity You are God."

A support Hebrew *mi-tahat*, literally, "underneath," meaning "beneath you." In other words, God's arms are Israel's "underpinnings"; He carries Israel protectively on His arms.[195]

the arms everlasting Rather, "the arms of the Eternal [*'olam*]." In view of the parallel "ancient God," *'olam* is probably short for *'el 'olam*, "the everlasting God," or the synonymous *'elohei 'olam* of Isaiah 40:28. The epithet is an old one; "El the eternal one" (*'l d-'lm*) is mentioned in a Canaanite inscription of about the fifteenth century B.C.E. from the Sinai. A late account of Phoenician religion, written in Greek, also refers to a primordial deity *Oulomos*, evidently *'olam*.[196]

"Arms beneath" is an awkward parallel to "refuge" and a most unusual way to express protection. Some scholars assume that the text is damaged. One possibility is that the second clause originally read "and *a shelter* are the arms of the Everlasting."[197] But in the context of God riding to Israel's aid and expelling the Canaanites, something more dynamic may be called for. Some scholars suggest a simple emendation of the first two clauses, reading "Who humbled the divine beings of old and subdued the ancient powers,"[198] referring to God's rout of the rebel-

He drove out the enemy before you
By His command: Destroy!
28Thus Israel dwells in safety,
Untroubled is Jacob's abode,
In a land of grain and wine,
Under heavens dripping dew.
29O happy Israel! Who is like you,
A people delivered by the LORD,
Your protecting Shield, your Sword triumphant!
Your enemies shall come cringing before you,
And you shall tread on their backs.

וַיְגָרֶשׁ מִפָּנֶיךָ אוֹיֵב
וַיֹּאמֶר הַשְׁמֵד:
28 וַיִּשְׁכֹּן יִשְׂרָאֵל בֶּטַח
בָּדָד עֵין יַעֲקֹב
אֶל־אֶרֶץ דָּגָן וְתִירוֹשׁ
אַף־שָׁמָיו יַעַרְפוּ־טָל:
29 אַשְׁרֶיךָ יִשְׂרָאֵל מִי כָמוֹךָ
עַם נוֹשַׁע בַּיהֹוָה
מָגֵן עֶזְרֶךָ וַאֲשֶׁר־חֶרֶב גַּאֲוָתֶךָ
וְיִכָּחֲשׁוּ אֹיְבֶיךָ לָךְ
וְאַתָּה עַל־בָּמוֹתֵימוֹ תִדְרֹךְ: ס

lious powers of the sea in primordial times. This motif, mentioned elsewhere in biblical poetry as an example of God's incomparability, is often cited as a precedent for His defeat of Israel's enemies, particularly Egypt.[199] Here it would serve as a precedent for His defeat of the Canaanites.[200]

drove out . . . destroy   The relationship of this clause to other passages about the fate of the Canaanites is discussed in Excursus 33.

By His command: Destroy!   Whereas the previous clause describes God's role in the defeat of the Canaanites, this one refers to Israel's. See Comment to 2:33. Some scholars assume that this clause originally read "and the Amorites He destroyed," synonymous with the preceding clause.[201]

28.   Once the enemy was defeated Israel enjoyed security and prosperity in the promised land.

Israel dwells in safety   This echoes the blessing of Benjamin, verse 12.

Untroubled[202]

abode[203]

In a land of grain and wine, / Under heavens dripping dew   This description of the land is similar to that of Joseph's territory in verses 13–16 and nearly identical to Isaac's blessing of Jacob in Genesis 27:28: "May God give you of the dew [moisture] of heaven and the fat of the earth, abundance of grain and wine."[204] *Tal* means "moisture" rather than "dew"; see Comment to 32:2.

29. **happy**   Hebrew *'ashreikha*, "fortunate are you." See Comment to verse 24. The Psalms contain similar declarations in contexts referring to Israel's security and prosperity, such as: "Our storehouses are full . . . our flocks number thousands. . . . There is no breaching and no sortie. . . . Happy ['*ashrei*] the people who have it so; happy the people whose God is the LORD" (Ps. 144:13–15).[205]

Who is like you, / A people delivered by the LORD   Israel's uniqueness in enjoying God's protection is also mentioned in 4:7. The declaration "who is like you," normally addressed to God,[206] is here applied to Israel: the people of the incomparable God (v. 26) enjoys incomparable protection.

Your protecting Shield   A metaphor often applied to God.[207]

your Sword triumphant[208]

you shall tread on their backs   Placing one's foot on the back of a defeated foe, a ceremonial gesture of triumph, is mentioned in the Bible and ancient Near Eastern literature and illustrated in ancient Near Eastern art.[209]

34 Moses went up from the steppes of Moab to Mount Nebo, to the summit of Pisgah, opposite Jericho, and the

ל״ד שביעי וַיַּעַל מֹשֶׁה מֵעַרְבֹת מוֹאָב אֶל־הַר נְבוֹ רֹאשׁ הַפִּסְגָּה אֲשֶׁר עַל־פְּנֵי יְרֵחוֹ

CHAPTER **34**

THE DEATH OF MOSES (vv. 1–12)

After addressing his farewell blessing to Israel, Moses goes up to the top of Mount Nebo. There, before he dies, he is shown Israel's future territory. God buries Moses in the valley below, and the Israelites mourn him for thirty days and give their allegiance to Joshua. The narrative is followed by a brief eulogy about Moses' incomparable stature and deeds.[1]

As noted in the Comment to 3:26, by showing Moses the promised land God accedes to part of Moses' plea to let him enter the land and see it (3:25). The severity of God's decree banning Moses from the land is also somewhat softened by His caring act of personally burying Moses.

The narrative includes several themes that Deuteronomy regularly highlights. It opens with Moses' visual experience of the promised land (vv. 1,4) and concludes by referring to the visual experiences by which all Israel knew of his superiority as a prophet (v. 12, "in the eyes of [translated "before"] Israel"); Joshua is granted the wisdom to lead Israel (v. 9); and Moses' incomparability is emphasized (v. 10). Compare especially 1:9; 4:3,6–8,9–19,32–40; 16:19.

MOSES ASCENDS MOUNT NEBO
AND SEES THE PROMISED LAND (vv. 1–4)

1–3. God shows Moses Israel's future territory from Mount Nebo. Standing at three o'clock, Moses views representative regions of the land counterclockwise. Looking north in Transjordan, he sees the Gilead range (already conquered) and beyond it, about one hundred miles away and slightly to the northwest, as far as Dan, which would become the northern extremity of Israelite territory.[2] From there his eyes move west of the Jordan and southward, from Naphtali down through Manasseh, Ephraim, and Judah; the latter territory extended to Israel's western boundary, the Mediterranean, about sixty-five miles from where Moses stands. Finally, he sees the southern part of the land, the Negev and, closest to him, the Plain of the Jordan, as far south as Zoar, on the southeastern boundary, some fifty miles away.

Some parts of this panorama cannot be seen by the human eye from Mount Nebo. Dan, the Mediterranean, and Zoar are blocked by intervening mountains.[3] Since verse 1 says "the LORD showed him," perhaps the text means that God enabled Moses to see what would otherwise have been impossible. Alternatively, perhaps "as far as Dan" (v. 1) means "as far as the latitude of Dan," meaning that Moses saw Mount Hermon, visible above Dan,[4] while "as far as the Western Sea" and "as far as Zoar" (vv. 2–3) mean that Moses saw "Judah, which reaches as far as the Western Sea" (see Josh. 15:11–12) and "the Plain . . . which extends as far as Zoar."

1. *Moses went up* As commanded in 32:49 and earlier in 3:27.

the steppes of Moab The eastern part of the lower Jordan Valley, just north of the Dead Sea. This plain extends about nine miles from north to south and five to seven miles from the river to the mountains of Moab. This is the plain where the Israelites were encamped while Moses addressed them.[5] The corresponding plain west of the Jordan was sometimes called the Steppes of Jericho.[6] See Map 5.

Mount Nebo See Excursus 1, Maps 5 and 6, and Comment to 32:49.

the summit of Pisgah Pisgah was a mountain, or mountain chain, in Moab overlooking the southern end of the Jordan Valley and commanding a view of the promised land across the Jordan. See Excursus 1 and Maps 5 and 6.

LORD showed him the whole land: Gilead as far as Dan; [2]all Naphtali; the land of Ephraim and Manasseh; the whole land of Judah as far as the Western Sea; [3]the Negeb; and the Plain—the Valley of Jericho, the city of palm trees—as far as Zoar. [4]And the LORD said to him, "This is the land of which I swore to Abraham, Isaac, and Jacob, 'I will assign it to your offspring.' I have let you see it with your own eyes, but you shall not cross there."

[5]So Moses the servant of the LORD died there, in the

וַיַּרְאֵהוּ יְהוָה אֶת־כָּל־הָאָרֶץ אֶת־הַגִּלְעָד עַד־דָּן׃
2 וְאֵת כָּל־נַפְתָּלִי וְאֶת־אֶרֶץ אֶפְרַיִם וּמְנַשֶּׁה וְאֵת
כָּל־אֶרֶץ יְהוּדָה עַד הַיָּם הָאַחֲרוֹן׃ 3 וְאֶת־הַנֶּגֶב
וְאֶת־הַכִּכָּר בִּקְעַת יְרֵחוֹ עִיר הַתְּמָרִים עַד־צֹעַר׃
4 וַיֹּאמֶר יְהוָה אֵלָיו זֹאת הָאָרֶץ אֲשֶׁר נִשְׁבַּעְתִּי
לְאַבְרָהָם לְיִצְחָק וּלְיַעֲקֹב לֵאמֹר לְזַרְעֲךָ אֶתְּנֶנָּה
הֶרְאִיתִיךָ בְעֵינֶיךָ וְשָׁמָּה לֹא תַעֲבֹר׃
5 וַיָּמָת שָׁם מֹשֶׁה עֶבֶד־יְהוָה בְּאֶרֶץ מוֹאָב עַל־פִּי

opposite Jericho   East of Jericho. See Comment to 32:49.

Gilead   The Transjordanian hill country captured from Sihon and Og. See Comments to 2:36 and 3:1. This verse may reflect a view that Gilead was part of the promised land (see v. 4 and Comment to 2:24).

as far as Dan   That is, "[and beyond Gilead] as far as Dan" (Gilead itself does not reach as far as Dan).[7] Dan is the city of the Danites at the northern end of the Galilee, at the foot of Mount Hermon (see Comment to 33:22, Map 6, and Excursus 1).

2.   For the three sections of the land mentioned in this verse, see Comment to 19:3.

Naphtali   In upper Galilee, north and northwest of Lake Tiberias. See Comment to 33:23.

the Western Sea   The Mediterranean.

3.   *the Negev*   The northern part of today's Negev. See Comment to 1:7.

the Plain   The Plain of the Jordan.[8] This may be synonymous with what Josephus calls "the great plain," referring to the entire Jordan Valley and, apparently, the Dead Sea and Lake Tiberias as well.[9] Parts of it were easily visible from Mount Nebo.

the Valley of Jericho, the city of palm trees   Jericho became the first city that Israel conquered in the promised land. It was celebrated for its palms, which are depicted in the famed sixth-century mosaic map from Madaba in Jordan. Despite Jericho's desert location and climate, abundant sources of water make it like an oasis to this day.[10]

as far as Zoar   The Plain extended as far south as Zoar, which was probably located south or southeast of the Dead Sea, where there was a city called Zoar in Second Temple and talmudic times (see Map 6 and Excursus 1). It may therefore stand here for the southern tip of the Dead Sea, which is the southeastern limit of the promised land according to Numbers 34:3 and Joshua 15:2. As such, it would be the counterpart of Dan and the Western Sea in verses 1 and 2.

4.   *of which I swore*   See Comment to 1:8.

but you shall not cross there   As God decreed in 1:37 and reminded Moses on several occasions (see 3:27; 4:21–22; 32:52; Num. 20:12).

MOSES' DEATH AND BURIAL   (vv. 5–7)

5.   *Moses . . . died*   Biblical tradition assumes that Moses died early in the twelfth month, the month later called Adar. Postbiblical tradition fixes the date on the seventh day of the month.[11]

servant of the LORD   As a title, 'eved YHVH means "the LORD's minister," in Moses' case, His representative and agent in governing Israel. "Minister" is a title of high government officials in the Bible and in inscriptions.[12] It connotes high status and implies that its bearer is loyal, trusted, and intimate with his master.[13]

land of Moab, at the command of the LORD. ⁶He buried him in the valley in the land of Moab, near Beth-peor; and no one knows his burial place to this day. ⁷Moses was a hundred and twenty years old when he died; his eyes were undimmed and his vigor unabated. ⁸And the Israelites bewailed Moses in the steppes of Moab for thirty days.

The period of wailing and mourning for Moses came to an end. ⁹Now Joshua son of Nun was filled with the spirit

יְהֹוָה: 6 וַיִּקְבֹּר אֹתוֹ בַגַּיְ בְּאֶרֶץ מוֹאָב מוּל בֵּית
פְּעוֹר וְלֹא־יָדַע אִישׁ אֶת־קְבֻרָתוֹ עַד הַיּוֹם הַזֶּה:
7 וּמֹשֶׁה בֶּן־מֵאָה וְעֶשְׂרִים שָׁנָה בְּמֹתוֹ לֹא־כָהֲתָה
עֵינוֹ וְלֹא־נָס לֵחֹה: 8 וַיִּבְכּוּ בְנֵי יִשְׂרָאֵל אֶת־
מֹשֶׁה בְּעַרְבֹת מוֹאָב שְׁלֹשִׁים יוֹם
וַיִּתְּמוּ יְמֵי בְכִי אֵבֶל מֹשֶׁה: 9 וִיהוֹשֻׁעַ בִּן־נוּן מָלֵא
רוּחַ חָכְמָה כִּי־סָמַךְ מֹשֶׁה אֶת־יָדָיו עָלָיו וַיִּשְׁמְעוּ

at the command of the LORD   He died at God's command,[14] not from old age or illness (see v. 7).[15] The same idiom is used of Aaron's death.[16] Since it means literally "He died at God's mouth," it was interpreted midrashically to mean that Moses died at a kiss from God.[17] Hence the Hebrew idiom *mitat neshikah*, "death by a kiss," meaning sudden, painless death in old age.[18]

6. **He buried him in the valley**   The valley below Mount Nebo. Perhaps God removed Moses' body from the mountain, where everybody knew he had gone to die, in order to keep his grave site secret. See below.

in the valley in the Land of Moab, near Beth-peor   The valley where Israel was then encamped (see 3:29 and Comment; 4:46).

no one knows his burial place   Because God buried him. Many commentators have conjectured that Moses' grave site was kept secret to prevent people from making it a shrine and even worshiping Moses' spirit. It is known that descendants often brought food offerings to graves in order to sustain their ancestors' spirits and that, although forbidden, mediums consulted the spirits of the dead (see Comments to 18:10–11; 26:14; and Excursus 23). Perhaps there was concern that, because of Moses' stature and his intimacy with God, if his grave site were accessible, offerings to his spirit might turn into outright worship or that people might find consulting his spirit irresistible, just as Saul consulted·the spirit of the prophet Samuel, despite the ban on necromancy.[19] The statement that "no one knows his burial place to this day" could be polemical, intended to undermine claims that a particular site *is* Moses' grave.[20]

7. **one hundred and twenty years**   As mentioned in 31:2. Moses died forty years after the Exodus, which took place when he was eighty (Exod. 7:7; cf. Deut. 1:3). Genesis 6:3 mentions 120 years as the maximum human lifespan, a notion found in Sumerian literature as well. This figure was probably based on a combination of empirical observation and ancient Near Eastern mathematics. Exceptionally long-lived individuals have been known to live to the age of 110–140 years. In the sexagesimal mathematical system of ancient Mesopotamia, which was based on sixty instead of ten, 120 (2 x 60) was the only round typological number within these parameters.[21] The biblical concept is the basis of the Jewish idiom for wishing somebody a long life: "[May you live] to 120!"

his eyes were undimmed   Biblical and other ancient texts commonly describe the eyesight and other faculties of the aged to indicate whether they have remained healthy or become feeble.[22]

his vigor unabated   Rather, as recognized by Ibn Ezra, "he had not become wrinkled" (lit., "his moisture had not departed," or "dried up").[23] Moses' *vigor* had, in fact, abated (31:2), but despite his years he did not look aged. The Talmud describes the rejuvenation of Sarah and Jochebed in similar terms: their flesh became smooth and their wrinkles straightened.[24]

THE PEOPLE'S MOURNING AND
JOSHUA'S SUCCESSION TO LEADERSHIP   (vv. 8–9)

8. **thirty days**   On this period of mourning see Comment to 21:13.

9. **was filled with the spirit of wisdom**   A divine gift of wisdom to govern Israel.[25] Solomon asked God for such a gift to enable him to govern justly, and Isaiah promised Israel a future

of wisdom because Moses had laid his hands upon him; and the Israelites heeded him, doing as the LORD had commanded Moses.

אֵלָיו בְּנֵי־יִשְׂרָאֵל וַיַּעֲשׂוּ כַּאֲשֶׁר צִוָּה יְהוָה אֶת־מֹשֶׁה:

10Never again did there arise in Israel a prophet like Moses—whom the LORD singled out face to face—11for

10 וְלֹא־קָם נָבִיא עוֹד בְּיִשְׂרָאֵל כְּמֹשֶׁה אֲשֶׁר יְדָעוֹ יְהוָה פָּנִים אֶל־פָּנִים: 11 לְכָל־הָאֹתוֹת

king who would be graced with the same gift (see 1 Kings 3:7–12; Isa. 11:1–5). It is characteristic of Deuteronomy that it identifies the qualities given to Joshua as intellectual ones (see the Introduction, Comment to 1:9, and Excursus 2).[26] In contrast, according to Numbers 27:15–23, Joshua already possessed "spirit" of an unspecified type when God chose him to succeed Moses, and Moses transferred some of his *hod* ("authority"? "majesty"?) to Joshua.

    laid his hands upon him   A rite of investiture, as in Numbers 27:18,23. The precise meaning of the rite is not certain. It may serve to identify Joshua as the subject of the investiture or to transfer some of Moses' spirit of wisdom to him.[27] The same gesture became part of the ceremony of rabbinic ordination, which for that reason is known as *semikhah*, "laying [of hands]."

    the Israelites heeded him, doing as the LORD had commanded Moses   Thenceforth the people began to obey Joshua. See Numbers 27:20.

CONCLUDING EULOGY   (vv. 10–12)

Moses was never equaled by any other prophet, either in the directness of his communication with God or in the signs and portents which demonstrated that he was really sent by God. Since these verses are the final sentence of Deuteronomy, they are undoubtedly meant as more than a eulogy on Moses.[28] Medieval Jewish writers understood them as asserting the supreme authority of Moses' Torah, forestalling future claims to prophetic authority that might attempt to contradict or supersede it,[29] as was done by Christianity and Islam. For this reason Maimonides held that belief in Moses' incomparability as a prophet is a dogma of Judaism.[30] In the present context, Moses' incomparability would have buttressed the authority of Deuteronomy against versions of God's Teaching that were inconsistent with the book.[31] There is evidence, in Deuteronomy and in books describing conditions in the seventh century B.C.E., when Deuteronomy was discovered,[32] that some parties claimed that God authorized practices radically inconsistent with the fundamental principles of the Torah, particularly of Deuteronomy. These included claims that God commanded Israelites to worship the heavenly bodies and other gods in addition to Himself, and to offer child sacrifices (see Comments to 13:6 and 17:3). It is likely that various other practices forbidden by Deuteronomy were defended with similar claims. For example, the priests of the local sanctuaries, which are forbidden in chapter 12, undoubtedly claimed that their sanctuaries, and the sacred posts and pillars erected there (forbidden in 16:21–22), had been erected on the basis of divine commands. The present passage would nullify the authenticity of claims such as these, and others that are inconsistent with Deuteronomy.[33]

    In its own way, the epilogue of the *Laws of Hammurabi* concludes with a similar declaration. There, the Babylonian lawgiver boasts of the incomparability of his deeds and of his laws, and calls down curses on any future king who would change his laws or efface the monument on which they are written.[34] A notable difference between the passages is that Deuteronomy's argument is not something said by Moses about himself but the narrator's statement, citing historical evidence publicly witnessed by all of Israel.

    10. Never again did there arise   Rather, "But never again . . ." The verse contrasts Joshua to Moses: although Joshua succeeded Moses, neither he nor any subsequent prophet was Moses' equal.[35]

    a prophet like Moses   The role of prophets is discussed in Comments to 13:2; 18:15,18. Although Moses was far more than a prophet, and is never directly called that elsewhere in the Torah, prophecy was one of his roles, and the term is invoked here for the purpose of declaring that he is superior to all other prophets. The same is true of Numbers 12:1–8.

the various signs and portents that the LORD sent him to display in the land of Egypt, against Pharaoh and all his courtiers and his whole country, [12]and for all the great might and awesome power that Moses displayed before all Israel.

וְהַמּוֹפְתִים אֲשֶׁר שְׁלָחוֹ יְהֹוָה לַעֲשׂוֹת בְּאֶרֶץ מִצְרָיִם לְפַרְעֹה וּלְכָל־עֲבָדָיו וּלְכָל־אַרְצוֹ: 12 וּלְכֹל הַיָּד הַחֲזָקָה וּלְכֹל הַמּוֹרָא הַגָּדוֹל אֲשֶׁר עָשָׂה מֹשֶׁה לְעֵינֵי כָּל־יִשְׂרָאֵל:

singled out, face to face   Hebrew *yada'*, literally, "know," often means "choose."[36] This clause is probably elliptical, meaning "singled out by speaking to him face to face."[37] That God spoke to Moses face to face is stated in Exodus 33:11, which adds "as one man speaks to another," and Numbers 12:8 states that God spoke to Moses "mouth to mouth, plainly [lit., "(in) appearance"] and not in riddles, and he beholds the likeness of the LORD." The verse in Numbers is part of a narrative which, like the present passage, contrasts Moses to all other prophets and shows that his perception of God is superior. But whereas Numbers 12:8 states that Moses actually saw God, Deuteronomy does not use "face to face" literally. This is clear from 5:4, which says that God spoke to Israel "face to face . . . out of the fire," after having made it clear in 4:12,15 that the people did not in fact *see* God, who was hidden by cloud and fire (see also 5:19–21). In Deuteronomy, then, the phrase is an idiom meaning "in person," "directly," "without mediation" (cf. 4:37, where "with His face" means "in person").[38] The point of the text is that Moses had the most direct contact with God of any prophet, and hence had the clearest knowledge of Him and His will.

11–12.   Moses was also incomparable in the "signs and portents" that God performed through him, particularly those accompanying the Exodus. The uniqueness of those wonders is invoked in 4:32–40 to demonstrate God's uniqueness and exclusive divinity. Here, with reference to the uniqueness of the prophet, the text must have in mind the use of signs and portents by a prophet to demonstrate that his message really comes from God (see Comment to 13:2).[39] No prophet so thoroughly proved his authenticity as Moses did.

11.   the various   Literally, "all," as in verse 12. It was the large number of wonders executed by Moses that was unparalleled.[40] A few other prophets did execute wonders qualitatively as great, such as Joshua, for whom God stopped the flow of the Jordan and made the sun stand still.[41]

signs and portents . . . great might (lit., "mighty hand") **and awesome power**   These terms refer primarily to the wonders accompanying the Exodus, as explained in the Comment to 4:34.[42]

the LORD sent him to display   The Torah consistently reiterates that all the wonders Moses executed were by means of God's power and at His command, not by means of any personal power or occult skills possessed by Moses. See Comment to 18:12–13. Here and in the next verse, however, Moses' role is emphasized, since it was by such means that he first proved his authenticity as God's emissary.

12.   This verse is essentially parallel to verse 11. That is, "the great might [lit., "mighty hand"] and awesome power that Moses displayed before all Israel" refers to "all the signs and portents that the LORD sent Him to display in the land of Egypt." This is clear from 4:34.

before all Israel   Literally, "in the sight of all Israel." Deuteronomy concludes with a theme that it has frequently stressed: Israel saw these wonders firsthand (see 4:34; 6:22; and 29:1–2). The Israelites do not have to rely on secondhand reports. They witnessed the events and are certain of the truth they prove: the indisputable authenticity of Moses.

חזק

סכום הפסוקים של ספר
תשע מאות
וחמשים וחמשה
הֱנ֔ץ

וחציו ועשית על־פי
וסדרים ל֔א

סכום הפסוקים של תורה
חמשת אלפים
ושמונה מאות
וארבעים
וחמשה
הֱף מֱה

כל סדרי התורה
מאה וששים ושבעה
קֱסֱז

סכום התיבות של תורה
תשעה ושבעים אלף
ושמונה מאות
וחמשים
וששה

סכום האותיות של תורה ארבע מאות אלף
ותשע מאות וארבעים וחמשה

תם ונשלם תהלה לאל בורא עולם
חזק חזק ונתחזק

APPENDIX

The Decalogue with "Upper" Accents (Ta'am 'Elyon)

There are two different versions of the verse division and cantillation of the Decalogue. These are indicated by superlinear and sublinear "accent" signs (Heb. *te'amim*, Yiddish *trop*)[1] that accompany the text in manuscripts and printed Bibles (they do not appear in Torah scrolls). These signs serve simultaneously as a system of punctuation and of musical notation for cantillation of the text. In the Decalogue, one set of signs (printed with the text of the Decalogue in Exod. 20 and Deut. 5),[2] known as the "lower accents" (*ta'am taḥton*)[3] divides the commandments into thirteen verses of standard length. Because the verses are of standard length, long commandments are divided into several verses (vv. 6–10 and 12–15), while short commandments—the sixth through ninth—are conjoined in a single verse (v. 17). The other set of signs, the "upper accents" (*ta'am 'elyon*), printed here, divides the Decalogue so that each commandment, whether long or short, constitutes a single verse. There is one exception: what rabbinic tradition regards as the first two commandments, vv. 6 and 7–10, are combined in a single verse. This corresponds to the midrashic tradition that these two commandments, in which God refers to Himself in the first person, were spoken by God Himself to the people in a single, uninterrupted statement, whereas the rest, which speak of God in the third person, were transmitted to the people by Moses.[4]

The lower and upper sets of accents seem to have originated in Palestine and Babylonia, respectively. Since the lower set corresponds to the normal way of versifying the Torah, it is probably the older of the two.[5] There are varying practices in using the two sets.[6] Ashkenazic custom is to use the lower accents when the Decalogue is read in the Sabbath Torah portions during the year, and to use the upper accents when it is read on Shavuot (the Feast of Weeks). In this way, the reading on Shavuot reenacts the original proclamation of the Decalogue on Mount Sinai, when the people heard the first two commandments from God in a single utterance, as the upper accents render them.[7] Sephardic custom is to use the lower accents only for private study of the Torah, perhaps because of their punctuational value; the upper accents are used for all public Torah readings, which are regarded as a reenactment of the revelation at Sinai.[8]

6 אָנֹכִי יְהוָה אֱלֹהֶיךָ אֲשֶׁר הוֹצֵאתִיךָ מֵאֶרֶץ מִצְרַיִם מִבֵּית עֲבָדִים
7 לֹא־יִהְיֶה לְךָ אֱלֹהִים אֲחֵרִים עַל־פָּנָי 8 לֹא־תַעֲשֶׂה־לְךָ פֶסֶל | כָּל־
תְּמוּנָה אֲשֶׁר בַּשָּׁמַיִם | מִמַּעַל וַאֲשֶׁר בָּאָרֶץ מִתַּחַת וַאֲשֶׁר בַּמַּיִם |
מִתַּחַת לָאָרֶץ 9 לֹא־תִשְׁתַּחֲוֶה לָהֶם וְלֹא תָעָבְדֵם כִּי אָנֹכִי יְהוָה
אֱלֹהֶיךָ אֵל קַנָּא פֹּקֵד עֲוֹן אָבֹת עַל־בָּנִים וְעַל־שִׁלֵּשִׁים וְעַל־רִבֵּעִים
לְשֹׂנְאָי 10 וְעֹשֶׂה חֶסֶד לַאֲלָפִים לְאֹהֲבַי וּלְשֹׁמְרֵי מצותו: ס
11 לֹא תִשָּׂא אֶת־שֵׁם־יְהוָה אֱלֹהֶיךָ לַשָּׁוְא כִּי לֹא יְנַקֶּה יְהוָה אֵת
אֲשֶׁר־יִשָּׂא אֶת־שְׁמוֹ לַשָּׁוְא: ס   12 שָׁמוֹר אֶת־יוֹם הַשַּׁבָּת לְקַדְּשׁוֹ
כַּאֲשֶׁר צִוְּךָ | יְהוָה אֱלֹהֶיךָ 13 שֵׁשֶׁת יָמִים תַּעֲבֹד וְעָשִׂיתָ כָּל־
מְלַאכְתֶּךָ 14 וְיוֹם הַשְּׁבִיעִי שַׁבָּת | לַיהוָה אֱלֹהֶיךָ לֹא תַעֲשֶׂה כָל־
מְלָאכָה אַתָּה וּבִנְךָ־וּבִתֶּךָ וְעַבְדְּךָ־וַאֲמָתֶךָ וְשׁוֹרְךָ וַחֲמֹרְךָ וְכָל־
בְּהֶמְתֶּךָ וְגֵרְךָ אֲשֶׁר בִּשְׁעָרֶיךָ לְמַעַן יָנוּחַ עַבְדְּךָ וַאֲמָתְךָ כָּמוֹךָ
15 וְזָכַרְתָּ כִּי־עֶבֶד הָיִיתָ | בְּאֶרֶץ מִצְרַיִם וַיֹּצִאֲךָ יְהוָה אֱלֹהֶיךָ מִשָּׁם
בְּיָד חֲזָקָה וּבִזְרֹעַ נְטוּיָה עַל־כֵּן צִוְּךָ יְהוָה אֱלֹהֶיךָ לַעֲשׂוֹת אֶת־יוֹם
הַשַּׁבָּת: ס   16 כַּבֵּד אֶת־אָבִיךָ וְאֶת־אִמֶּךָ כַּאֲשֶׁר צִוְּךָ יְהוָה אֱלֹהֶיךָ
לְמַעַן | יַאֲרִיכֻן יָמֶיךָ וּלְמַעַן יִיטַב לָךְ עַל הָאֲדָמָה אֲשֶׁר־יְהוָה אֱלֹהֶיךָ
נֹתֵן לָךְ: ס   17 לֹא תִּרְצָח: ס   וְלֹא תִּנְאָף: ס   וְלֹא
תִּגְנֹב: ס   וְלֹא־תַעֲנֶה בְרֵעֲךָ עֵד שָׁוְא: ס   18 וְלֹא תַחְמֹד
אֵשֶׁת רֵעֶךָ   ס   וְלֹא תִתְאַוֶּה בֵּית רֵעֶךָ שָׂדֵהוּ וְעַבְדּוֹ וַאֲמָתוֹ שׁוֹרוֹ
וַחֲמֹרוֹ וְכֹל אֲשֶׁר לְרֵעֶךָ: ס

v. 10. מצותי ק׳

NOTES TO THE COMMENTARY

Chapter 1

1. See 1:1–5; 4:41 through the beginning of 5:1; 27:1,9,11; 29:1; chaps. 31,32,34.

2. Valedictory speeches are likewise delivered by Joshua, Samuel, and David. See Weinfeld, DDS, 10–14.

3. NJPS seeks to resolve the inconsistency between vv. 1 and 3 by taking only "on the other side of the Jordan" as the site of Moses' addresses. It construes the remainder of the verse and v. 2 as a parenthetic remark which has nothing to do with where the addresses were delivered. Understood thus, 1b must somehow define v. 2's "Mount Seir route," but it does so very awkwardly; normal biblical style would have been "by the Mount Seir route: the latter runs through the wilderness, in the Arabah . . . and Di-zahab," as in 11:29–30 and Judg. 21:19.

4. Deut. 3:29; 4:46; 28:69; 29:6; 32:49; 34:1,6,8.

5. See Ibn Ezra and Ramban. According to Ibn Ezra, the places listed in v. 1 were either unmentioned previously or had been called by other names in the earlier books. It is unlikely that this was the original meaning of these verses; the text could have employed the adverbs "originally" and "a second time," which this explanation requires the reader to supply mentally. But if vv. 1 and 3 stem from different writers who had different conceptions of where the addresses were delivered, a conservative redactor might have assumed that this is how the two were to be reconciled, but did not permit himself to supply the necessary adverbs. In other words, the approach of Ibn Ezra and Ramban makes the best sense of the text as it now stands.

6. Cf. Abravanel. In this way v. 1 is comparable to the beginning of the Book of Jubilees, which explains when and where God revealed that book's previously unreported contents to Moses (Jubilees, Prologue and 1:1ff).

7. Hoffmann.

8. This rules out sites in Moab, such as Khirbet Sufe, southeast of Medeba, or Suphah in Num. 21:14, which may be a place name.

9. Targs. Onk., Jon., Neofiti, taking "eleven days" as elliptical for "eleven days' *journey*" (with *derekh* or *mahalakh*, as in Gen. 30:36; Jonah 3:3).

10. Sifrei 2; Targs. Jon., Yer., Neofiti; Rashbam; the disciple of R. Eliezer of Beaugency whose comment is interpolated in the margin of Rashbam, *Peirush Ha-Torah 'asher Katav Rashbam*, ed. D. Rosin (New York: Om, 1949), 199.

11. See Rashbam on Gen. 1:1; N. M. Sarna, "The Anticipatory Use of Information as a Literary Feature of the Genesis Narratives," in R. E. Friedman, ed., *The Creation of Sacred Literature* (Berkeley: University of California Press, 1981), 76–82; Y. Zakovitch, "Foreshadowing in Biblical Narrative," *Beer-Sheva* 2 (1985): 85–105.

12. Aharoni, LOB, 45; cf. Gen. 3:24; perhaps 2 Kings 25:4. For *derekh* referring to a specific road, see Gen. 38:14; Num. 20:17; Deut. 11:30; 1 Sam. 6:12. There are several roads designated this way in Deut. 1–3; see 1:19,40; 2:1,8; 3:1. Although Heb. *derekh*, "way, road," sometimes functions as a preposition meaning "in the direction of" (see 1 Kings 8:44,48; Ezek. 40:20,24), when it is followed by the name of a place it refers to a specific road. When the biblical text expresses the idea of "via" a certain road or traveling on a certain road, *derekh* is usually not preceded by a preposition; cf. Num. 21:22 to the more common form in 20:17.

13. Cf. Exod. 16:1; 19:1; 40:17; Num. 1:1; 9:1; 10:11; 33:38. The Hebrew term flor "eleven" ('ashtei-'asar; contrast 'ahad 'asar in v. 2) and the practice of referring to months by number

are, in the Torah, characteristic of the priestly texts, whereas Deuteronomy uses a month *name* or epithet in 16:1. For this reason some critics assume that the verse is from a different source than vv. 1–2. In any case the verse agrees with the conception throughout Deuteronomy that the addresses were given at the end of the wanderings, right before the death of Moses.

14. SOR 10 (41).

15. "[And]" is found in Josh. 12:4; 13:12, and is read here by LXX, Pesh, and Vulg.

16. Taking *ho'il* from *y-'-l*, a presumed variant form of *'-w-l*. See Weinfeld, Commentary.

17. *Be'er* also means "clarify" in rabbinic Hebrew and Aramaic. Some commentators infer from 27:8 and Hab. 2:2 that *be'er* means "write," and that our verse means that Moses wrote down the Torah at this time. But in the other verses the act of writing is expressed by *katav*; in Hab. 2:2, *be'er* indicates that the writing is to be clear ("so that it can be read easily"), and that is probably what the verb adds in Deut. 27:8 as well.

18. Targ. Onk., LXX, Vulg., Pesh.

19. Exod. 18:16; Lev. 6:2.

20. Isa. 1:10.

21. Prov. 1:8; 2:1.

22. Ps. 78:1.

23. E.g., Deut. 4:8,44; 27:26; 28:58; 31:9,11,24.

24. Exod. 13:9; Josh. 1:8; Pss. 1:2; 94:12; Job 22:22.

25. See Weinfeld, DDS, Part 3. On *torah* in Deuteronomy see B. Lindars, "Torah in Deuteronomy," in P. R. Ackroyd and B. Lindars, eds., *Words and Meanings* (Cambridge: Cambridge University Press, 1968), 117–136; S. D. McBride, "Polity of the Covenant People: The Book of Deuteronomy," *Interpretation* 41 (1987): 231–233.

26. Pre-modern Hebrew texts divide the narrative before the following verses: 1:1 (all texts), 9 (SP and possibly 2Q10), 19,23b,29,34,42 (SP); 2:2 (M, SP, and presumably 4QDeut^h), either 8,8b, or 9 (in, respectively, SP after an interpolation, M, and MT variants), 17 (M and SP), 26 (SP), 31 (SP and M); 3:2,8,12, (SP), 18 (MT variants, SP, and possibly 4QDeut^d), 23 (M and SP; not 4QDeut^d), 26b (SP); 4:1 (M, SP, and 4QDeut^d). None of these texts has a break before v. 6. It is common for Hebrew manuscripts to make no separation between introductory verses and the first of several units that they precede. See 14:3,22. The Masoretic text distinguishes between major and minor breaks, but the manuscripts often disagree with each other in this regard. For present purposes it is not necessary to record these distinctions.

27. The most telling differences are at 1:42; 2:9,17,31; and 3:2, where Hebrew texts start new units at "the LORD said/spoke to me saying." NJPS, in contrast, marks paragraphs one verse before or after those statements by God.

28. See Weinfeld, DDS, 70,78.

29. Cf. Gen. 14:7; Num. 13:29; Josh. 10:5–6,12; 11:2.

30. "Neighbors" is used this way in Jer. 49:18; 50:40.

31. Num. 13:29; 14:45; Josh. 11:3.

32. Josh. 15:33–44.

33. Num. 13:21; 34:3.

34. Josh. 11:17; 12:7.

35. Josh. 9:1; Jer. 47:7.

36. On "Canaan" see B. Mazar, s.v. *'erets yisra'el*, EM 1:609–611; W. F. Albright and J. Liver, s.v. *kena'an, kena'ani*, EM 4:196–204; R. de Vaux, "Le pays de Canaan," JAOS 88 (1968): 23–30; Aharoni, LOB, 67–68.

37. Gen. 15:18; Exod. 23:31; Josh. 1:4.

38. For *li-fnei* meaning "at one's disposal," see Gen. 13:9; 20:15; 24:51; 34:10; 47:6; Jer. 40:4; for *natan li-fnei* see, e.g., Deut. 2:31; 7:2,23.

39. See, e.g., 2:31; Josh. 6:2; 8:1; Judg. 1:2; 7:9. In military contexts, "Give into your hand" is more common than "give before you," but the passages cited in this and the preceding note suggest that the two phrases are interchangeable (note esp. Deut. 2:31,33,36).

40. For such "performative" declarations (D. R. Hillers) see GKC §106m (cf. §106i); S. R. Driver, *A Treatise on the Use of the Tenses in Hebrew* (Oxford: Clarendon, 1892), sec. 13; Y. Muffs, *Studies in the Aramaic Legal Papyri from Elephantine* (Leiden: Brill, 1969), 32 n. 2; D. R. Hillers, "Some Performative Utterances in the Bible," in *Pomegranates and Golden Bells: Studies . . . Milgrom*, ed. D.P. Wright et al. (Winona Lake, IN: Eisenbraun's, 1995), 762. This usage is especially common with "give," as in Gen. 23:11 (see Rashbam there); for other verbs see Rashi at Gen. 14:22. For the legal connotations see Gen. 23:11 and the Elephantine papyri, such as AP 8:8; 13:2. Weinfeld, Commentary, points out that declarations of gifts and appointments are often preceded by "See" and "Behold."

41. Abravanel.

42. Weinfeld, DDS, 72, 78.

43. See, e.g., 11:13–14; Gen. 18:17–19; Exod. 24:1; 1 Sam. 12:11; Dan. 9:17. There is similar variation, between singular and plural, in referring to the people; see below, vv. 20–21, and Lev. 19:9,12,15,27,34; Judg. 20:22,23,28; 21:2,14; 2 Sam. 19:43. For ancient Near Eastern literature, see R. Sonsino, *Motive Clauses in Hebrew Law: Biblical Forms and Near Eastern Parallels* (Chico, Calif.: Scholars Press, 1980), 197–198; M. Weinfeld, "The Origin of the Apodictic Law: An Overlooked Source," VT 23 (1973), 68. Hebrew manuscripts and ancient translations often "correct" such readings for the sake of grammatical consistency (as do LXX and SP here).

44. See Ramban, Abravanel, Hoffmann.

45. See Zev. 116a; Av. Zar. 24a–24b with Tosafot; Rashi at Exod. 18:13; Ibn Ezra and Ramban at Exod. 18:1; Radak at Judg. 1:16; and Driver, *Exodus* (Cambridge: Cambridge University Press, 1953), 162.

46. See Exod. 12:37; 38:26; Num. 1:45–47; 3:39; N. M. Sarna, *Exploring Exodus* (New York: Schocken, 1986), 94–102. If, as Sarna suggests, the number reflects the population of Israel in the time of David and Solomon (ca. 960 B.C.E.), assuming that the Exodus took place ca. 1220 B.C.E. and that the Israelites' natural increase had been 1.5 percent, their population in 1220 would have been approximately 62,500. But a rate of increase 0.5 percent higher or lower would affect the result drastically (1 percent would imply 226,000; 2 percent would imply 17,421 [based on calculations by Eytan Tigay]). For comparison, statistics given in M. von Oppenheim, *Die Beduinen* (Leipzig: Harrassowitz, 1939) imply that the nomadic population of the Sinai ca. 1940 was approximately 20,000. However, according to Frank Stewart, given the possibility of undercounting, it could have been twice that high.

47. Hoffmann; Ehrlich thinks that Moses' statement (and Joab's in 2 Sam. 24:3) reflect the folk belief that when referring to good fortune, such as the growth of the Israelites, one must add a blessing or an apotropaic formula (such as *kayn 'eyn horeh* [Yiddish] or "knock on wood") to ward off the evil eye.

48. See Deut. 1:21; 4:1; 6:3; 12:1; 26:7; 27:3; 29:24.

49. Both nouns or their associated verbs appear in narratives about such incidents (Exod. 17:2,7; Num. 11:11,17; 20:3,13), and "burden" is used elsewhere to describe people who must be provided for or brought along in an entourage (2 Sam. 15:33; 19:36). The third noun in the verse, "trouble" (*torah*), is simply a synonym of "burden" (Isa. 1:14).

50. See Sanh. 18a and Tosafot there; Sifrei 13.

51. Mid. Hag. to 1:15; cf. Maimonides, Hilkhot Sanhedrin 2:7.

52. See Prov. 31:10,26 (for use of "capable"); Ps. 111:10 and Prov. 1:7 ("fear of the Lord"); Prov. 23:23–24 ("truth"); Prov. 28:16 ("spurning ill-gotten gain"). That morality is a form of wisdom is one of several concepts which Deuteronomy shares with wisdom literature; see the Introduction and Weinfeld, DDS, 244–281.

53. This translation takes *yedu'im* as a *pa'ul* active participle (as in *yedua' holi*, "familiar with disease," Isa. 53:3). This fits the preceding "wise and experienced" better than the translation "well known" (cf. Eccl. 9:11, where the vocalization *yode'im* makes the sense "knowing" clear; see also Job 34:2). See Hoffmann, following the targums and LXX; cf. GKC §§50–51; E. Y. Kutscher, *The Language and Linguistic Background of the Isaiah Scroll* (Hebrew) (Jerusalem: Magnes Press, 1959), 268; H. Yalon, *Pirkei Lashon* (Jerusalem: Mosad Bialik, 1971), 323–324.

54. See, e.g., Exod. 35:31; 1 Kings 7:14; Prov. 2:6.

55. For "head" see Judg. 10:18; 11:8,9,11; Mic. 3:9–11; Job 29:25; 1 Chron. 11:6,10,11,20,42. For officers of thousands, etc., see Num. 31:14; 1 Sam. 8:12; 17:18; 18:13; 2 Kings 1:9; Isa. 3:3; these ranks are also known in the organization of armies and work squads (where we would call them "foremen") in Canaan, Mesopotamia, and Persia; see M. Weinfeld, "Judge and Officer in Israel and in the Ancient Near East," IOS 7 (1977): 73–74.

56. ANET, 210–211; AP 1:3; 16:7; 20:4,5; 25:2,3; cf. Weinfeld, "The Origin of the Apodictic Law: An Overlooked Source," VT 23 (1973): 67 n. 2; idem, "Judge and Officer," 71–76.

57. 1 Sam. 8:6,20.

58. In paraphrasing this episode Josephus refers to the people as an "army" (Ant. 3.70,72).

59. Since offices often evolve into something considerably different from the functions from which they derived their names, etymology is a poor guide to their functions. "Secretary" originally meant "one entrusted with secrets," "clerk" meant "clergyman," and "constable" meant "count of the stable."

60. See Sifrei 15 and further sources cited by Rofé, *Mavo'*, 77–78 n. 13 (note also the exceptions cited there); Rashbam at Exod. 5:6; Rashi and Rashbam at Deut. 16:18; Weinfeld, "Judge and Officer," 83–86.

61. Exod. 5:6ff. is not necessarily an exception; the Israelite *shoterim* (translated "foremen") there may be leaders through whom the Egyptian taskmasters communicate with the Israelites. In Deut. 20:5ff there is no official commanding the *shoterim* ("officials"), and those in Josh. 1:10 and 3:2 take orders directly from Joshua, the commander-in-chief. There is no indication that the *shoterim* ("officials") in Deut. 16:18 are assistants to the "magistrates" (lit., "judges") there; both govern (or judge) the people. The book of Chronicles, a product of the Persian period, calls subordinate officials of the monarchic period *shoterim* (1 Chron. 27:1, "clerks"; 2 Chron. 19:11 "officials"). Since none of the earlier works dealing with that period uses the term, however, the use in Chronicles may be a revival of an old, premonarchic term, based on an interpretation of the usage in Deuteronomy, and not a reflex of the original meaning. The same may be true of the rabbinic usage cited by Weinfeld, "Judge and Officer," 85–86. For *shoterim* as high officials note also the cognate noun *mishtar*, "authority," in Job 38:33. For the nonspecific meaning of the term see s.v. *shoter*, EM 7:534–535.

62. See Weinfeld, "Judge and Officer," 76–81. As Weinfeld notes, Exod. 23:1–3,6–9; Lev. 19:15; and Deut. 16:19 are also addressed to judges. They are embedded in laws addressed to the public as a whole, probably because any Israelite man, upon becoming an elder, might serve in a judicial capacity.

63. Derivatives of *sh-f-t* have several of these nuances in the west Semitic dialect of Mari, in Syria. In Punic it refers to the ruler of a city. The root unquestionably refers to governing in passages where the verb *shafat* describes the normal activity of a king (2 Kings 15:5; Dan. 9:12) and where the noun *shofet* appears

in poetic parallelism with king and other terms for rulers (Ps. 2:10; 148:11; Prov. 8:16).

64. Ralbag paraphrases *shafat* in Judg. 3:9–10 as *hinhig*.

65. See Deut. 16:18; 17:9,12; 19:17–18; 25:2; Mic. 7:3. In Num. 25:5, Moses tells the *shofetim* to slay those of their own men who were guilty. The fact that the *shofetim* execute punishment, and that each has his own men, seems to favor NJPS's translation "officials." But the verse may simply mean that each judge is to have the men under his jurisdiction punished; cf. Deut. 25:2, where the text literally says that the judge is to cause the guilty party to lie down and is to flog him, though the flogging is actually done by others.

66. Cf. 2 Sam. 15:3; 1 Kings 3:11, and see Weinfeld, DDS, 244–245; idem, "Judge and Officer," 69 n. 20; 80 n. 90; 86 n. 134.

67. M. Weinfeld, "The Awakening of National Consciousness in Israel in the Seventh Century B.C.," in Y. Kaufmann et al., eds., *'Oz leDawid: Studies . . . Ben Gurion* (Hebrew) (Jerusalem: Kiryat Sefer, 1964), 416–418.

68. E.g., Exod. 22:20; Lev. 19:33–34; 23:22; Deut. 24:17,19; 27:19. Concern for the protection of strangers was not nearly so common elsewhere in the ancient Near East. The only passages I have noticed are the Egyptian wisdom text Amenemopet, chap. 28 (ANET, 424c), and the Hittite text cited by Weinfeld, Commentary, at 10:18.

69. "Your *ger*," as in 5:14 and 31:12, may imply the same thing. Cf. Neufeld, "The Prohibitions Against Loans at Interest in Ancient Hebrew Laws," HUCA 26 (1955): 391–392. In this respect the *ger* is comparable to the metic in Greece; cf. L. Whibley, *A Companion to Greek Studies*, 4th ed. (New York: Hafner, 1968), 448; J.A.O. Larsen, s.v. "Metics," OCD, 679; D. Whitehead, *The Ideology of the Athenian Metic* (Cambridge: Cambridge Philological Society, 1977; ref. courtesy Martin Ostwald). Gen. 23:4 (Canaan) and Ezek. 47:22–23 (future) refer to *gerim* buying land; the possibility of a *ger* buying an Israelite in Lev. 25:47 implies circumstances in which he could buy land, too.

70. The Hebrew idiom "like A like B" means that one thing, whose status may be uncertain, is or should be like another whose status is known. See GKC §161c; A. B. Davidson, *Hebrew Syntax*, 3rd ed. (Edinburgh: T. and T. Clark, 1942), §151 Rem. 2.

71. Cf. Jehoshaphat's injunction to the judges that he appointed (2 Chron. 19:6–7).

72. See ANET, 211; for further examples see Weinfeld, "Judge and Officer," 75–76.

73. Josephus, Apion, 2.177–178.

74. See 1:30–33; 3:21; 4:3,9,34; 6:22; 7:19; 9:17; 11:2–7; 29:1–2.

75. Kadesh-barnea was, as noted in Comment to v. 2, the gateway to the promised land, "the hill country of the Amorites," hence the road to the latter led to Kadesh (see n. 12).

76. In SP, Moses' statement in vv. 20–23a is quoted virtually verbatim before Num. 13:1, but this is not an original reading.

77. Cf. v. 44 to the account of the same event in Num. 14:45; see also Gen. 15:16; Josh. 24:15; Amos 2:9–10; the land is called a "hill country" in 3:25 and Exod. 15:17 as well.

78. See B. Mazar, s.v. *'Emori*, EM 1:440–446; A. Altmann, "On the Question of the Designation of the Land of Israel as *MAT AMMURI* ('The Land of the Emorites')," *Tarbiz* 51 (1981–82): 3–22.

79. See, e.g., Judg. 4:18; 6:23; 1 Sam. 22:23; 23:17; 2 Sam. 9:7; Prov. 3:25; Job 5:22. For this use of the imperative (including the negative jussive, by which the negative imperative is expressed), see GKC §§110c and f; Davidson, *Hebrew Syntax*, §60 Rem. 2.

80. See Gen. 15:1; 26:24; 46:3; Jer. 1:8; Ezek. 2:6; 3:9; Isa. 41:10–14; 44:2.

81. See Num. 21:34; Deut. 3:2; 7:18; 20:1; Josh. 8:1; 10:8; 11:6; cf. Isa. 7:4; 10:24.

82. See, e.g., ANET, 449–451, 605–606, 655. See the discussion and further examples cited by J. C. Greenfield, "The Zakir Inscription and the Danklied," Fifth World Congress of Jewish Studies, *Proceedings*, 1:181–190.

83. Abravanel.

84. See Tanh. Shelah Lekha, 7; Num. R. 16:7 (see M. Mirkin, *Midrash Rabbah* [Tel Aviv: Yavneh, 1956], ad loc.); Mid. Hag. to Num. 13:2; Ramban at Num. 13:2; Hoffmann at Deut. 1:22; M. Noth, *The Deuteronomistic History* (Sheffield: JSOT Press, University of Sheffield, 1981), 29. Rashi at Num. 13:2, following Tanh., thinks the people were guilty for assigning the scouts to see whether the land was good or bad (Num. 13:19; cf. Deut. 1:25), since God had already told them that it was good (e.g., Exod. 3:8).

85. Some commentators find guilt in the manner in which the people made their proposal; contrasting the orderly approach of the people's representatives with another proposal in 5:20, they take the phrase *"all of you came to me"* in our verse to imply an unruly mob, anxious because they lack confidence in God (Sifrei 20; Abravanel; Hoffman).

86. Ramban and Radak argue that the Bible does not require the faithful to go into danger relying on a miracle, but that God Himself generally protects the faithful by natural means and often gives them stratagems to use (see Ramban at Lev. 21:17; Num. 1:45; 13:1; and Deut. 20:8; Radak at 1 Sam. 16:2). Experiences like the crossing of the sea left room for the belief that God delivers the faithful miraculously with no effort on their part (Exod. 14:13–14; cf. 2 Kings 7:6–7; 19:35; Isa. 31:8; 2 Chron. 20:1–25). Nowhere, however, is human action forbidden. See, however, Rofé, "Ephraimite versus Deuteronomistic History," in D. Garrone and F. Israel, eds., *Storia e Tradizioni di Israele: Scritti in Onore de J. Alberto Soggin* (Brescia: Paideia Editrice Brescia, 1991), 230–231.

87. Seforno and Hoffmann hold that Moses took the proposal as innocent when it was first made, and only realized after its disastrous outcome that the people were motivated by doubts.

88. A connection with Hebron is also suggested by the fact that Abraham's ally Mamre, who lived at Hebron, had a brother named Eshcol (Gen. 14:13; for the location of Mamre at Hebron see Gen. 13:18; 23:19). B. Mazar thinks that "wadi of grape cluster(s)" is a folk etymology and that the wadi was originally named for Mamre's brother Eshcol, just as the places named Mamre and The Terebinths of Mamre were named for Mamre himself (Gen. 13:18; 23:19). See B. Mazar, *Cities and Districts* (Hebrew) (Jerusalem: Mosad Bialik, 1975), 57–58. There are also other cases in which the Bible gives one explanation for a name and implies another. See Y. Zakovitch, "Explicit and Implicit Name-Derivations," HAR 4 (1980): 167–181; idem s.v. *shem, midreshei shemot*, EM 8:65–67.

89. The translation implies that the scouts reconnoitered the wadi or the hill country. However, the pronoun for "it," *'otah*, is feminine, whereas the words for wadi and hill country are masculine. Conceivably *'otah* is a misreading of *'otoh*, the old spelling of the masculine form of "it." In place of "it" some texts read "the land" ([*'et*] *ha-'arets*, 1QDeut[a] [1Q4/1, in DJD 1 pl. IX]; Vulg.; Pesh.), a reading virtually identical to that in Num. 32:9. It could be original, but it could also represent a scribe's attempt to resolve the grammatical problem. The MT reading (spelled *'-t-h*) could go back to a text in which *'et ha-'arets* was abbreviated *'et ha—*, or the scribe responsible for the variant may have assumed that it did. For abbreviations in biblical manuscripts, see G. R. Driver, "Abbreviations in the Massoretic Text," *Textus* 1 (1960): 112–131; M. Fishbane, s.v. "Abbreviations, Hebrew Texts," IDBS, 3–4.

90. NJPS at Ps. 106:25. The meaning of this rare verb is indicated by Prov. 26:20, where its nominal form is used: "For lack of wood a fire goes out, and without a querulous man [*nirgan*] contention is stilled."

91. Keil-Delitzsch.

92. On the beginning of the verse as the emphatic position see GKC §§142–143. For the people's argument, cf. Deut. 9:28 and Exod. 32:12.

93. Exod. 3:8; 14:7; Deut. 1:35; 3:25; 4:21,22; 6:18; 8:7,10; 9:6; 11:17; Josh. 23: 13,15,16; 1 Kings 14:15; 1 Chron. 28:8. Cf. the similar expressions in Jer. 3:19; Ezek. 20:6,15; Zech. 7:14; Ps. 106:24 and "a land flowing with milk and honey" (references cited in Excursus 9).

94. The scouts "spoke the truth and perished from both this world and the next" (Pirkei Rabbenu Ha-Kadosh, cited by Ramban at Gen. 2:9). "Sky-high" is recognized as a hyperbole in the Talmud (Ḥul. 90b). Cf. Weinfeld, DDS, 358 n. 1, for a similar description in an Assyrian royal inscription.

95. See Jer. 31:7; Ezek. 17:17; Dan. 10:1; Neh. 5:7; 1 Chron. 12:22.

96. Ḥul. 90b; Tamid 29a; followed by Maimonides, Guide 2.47; Abravanel, 93.

97. N. Na'aman, "Sennacherib's 'Letter to God' on His Campaign to Judah," BASOR 214 (1974): 26–27 (cited by Weinfeld, Commentary).

98. Maimonides, Guide 2.47.

99. See Josh. 11:22; 1 Sam. 17:4–7; 2 Sam. 21:16,20.

100. Gen. R. 26:16; BDB.

101. Ugaritic texts mention people called 'nkt ("the Anakitess"?) and Thub-Anak (see UT 1101.10; PTU 416); there is a Hurrian personal name Khanakka; and Egyptian texts of the nineteenth and eighteenth centuries B.C.E. mention several places called Iy-Anaq in Syria-Palestine (see ANET, 328–329). An Assyrian text mentions a place Anaku across the Mediterranean (M. Weippert, s.v. "Kreta," RLA 6:227). None of these is certainly connected with the biblical Anakites. See the discussion by S. Ahituv, s.v. 'anak, EM 6:312–313; O. Margalit, "Benei ha-'anak u-motsa'am," Beth Mikra' 25 (1979–80): 359–364.

102. See Josephus, Ant. 5.125; M. N. Adler, The Itinerary of Benjamin of Tudela (London, 1907; reprint, New York: Feldheim, n.d.), 31 (Hebrew version), 30 (English version); ANET, 477–478 (an Egyptian cubit was 20.6 inches); G. E. Wright, "Troglodytes and Giants in Palestine," JBL 57 (1938): 305–309. The discovery in Jordan was reported by Jonathan Tubb of the British Museum in a lecture at the University of Pennsylvania in 1995; see the British Museum's forthcoming Excavations at Tell es-Sa'idiyeh III/2. Some think that the belief that giants inhabited pre-Israelite Palestine is a legend prompted by the sight of huge city walls and megaliths. See Wright; T. H. Gaster, Myth, Legend and Custom in the Old Testament (New York: Harper and Row, 1969), 311–312. Herodotus 1.68 says that Orestes' coffin and the body inside it were said to be ten feet long.

103. See, e.g., 4:32–40; 6:20–25; 11:2–9; 26:1–11; Josh. 24:2–14; Judg. 2:2–4; 6:7–10; 1 Sam. 12:6–11; Ps. 136. The classic description of the role of these events in Jewish faith is that of Judah Halevi, The Kuzari, 1:11–25.

104. ANET, 80, col. 5, l. 27; 81, col. 1, l. 4. For the same nuance elsewhere in the Bible see Deut. 31:8; Isa. 45:2. For the same idiom in an inscription of an Aramaean king, see A. Biran and J. Naveh, "An Aramaic Stele Fragment from Tel Dan," IEJ 43 (1993): 81–98.

105. See also Jer. 31:19; Job 29:16; 31:18. For the compassion of a father in Akk. texts, see CAD A1, 69d.

106. See Exod. 13:21; Num. 10:33–34; and esp. 14:14, where Moses reminds God of this in pleading with Him to forgive the people.

107. See also v. 42 and Comments to 10:1–5; 23:10–15.

108. The banning of the people from the land is expressed in v. 35 by five consecutive words containing alephs ('im yir'eh 'ish ba-'anashim ha-'elleh) followed by three short words beginning with ha- characterizing the generation as evil (ha-dor ha-ra' ha-zeh). The banning of Moses is expressed by two consecutive clauses beginning with gam (v. 37). The exemptions from the decree are highlighted by a series of pronouns at the beginning of clauses in vv. 36 and 38. They culminate in v. 39 with three clauses beginning with forms of hem, referring to the children (hemmah, la-hem, hem), and containing suffixes with the sound ah referring to the promised land (shammah, 'ettenennah, yirashuhah). The emphatic position of the pronouns at the beginning of each clause gives them the meaning "only he, only they—not you," underscoring for the parents and Moses their own exclusion from the land, a point made clear by the contrasting pronoun at the beginning of v. 40: ve-'attem, "[But] as for you. . . ." The people's reaction to the decree is phrased in the same style, with the pronoun at the beginning of a clause: "It is we who shall go up!"—that is, we and not the next generation (v. 41). Similar literary devices accompany the fulfillment of this decree in 2:14–16. For similar alliterative sequences of alephs, see Exod. 15:9 and Lev. 19:3.

109. Bekhor Shor.

110. The name Caleb is probably a form of kelev, "dog." In the light of Akkadian names meaning "dog of the god so-and-so," Caleb's name could be short for "dog of God" in the sense of "loyal servant of God." The meaning of Jephunneh is unknown.

111. The idiom "fill [mille'] after the LORD" is synonymous with "be wholehearted [lit., whole] with the LORD" and is the antonym of "turn away from following the LORD." This is clear from comparing the idiom with phrases that serve as its equivalents in parallel passages: cf. 1 Kings 15:3 with 11:6,9, and Num. 14:43 with 32:11; cf. Gen. 17:1; Deut. 18:13. See Weinfeld, "The Covenant of Grant in the Old Testament and in the Ancient Near East," JAOS 90 (1970): 186, 290.

112. Some midrashim express the view that Moses was blameless. One represents him as protesting to God in the words of Job 9:22, "It is all one; therefore I say, 'He destroys the blameless and the guilty'" (Tanḥ. B., Deut. 8–9; Deut. R. ed. Liebermann, 34–35). See also Mid. Ḥag. to Deut. 3:26 and 4:21; Num. R. 19:13; ARN² 25, 51). Others list several offenses of Moses not mentioned in the Torah, or other reasons why he had to die in the wilderness; these are a clear indication that the authors of these midrashim found insufficient ground in the Torah itself for Moses' punishment. See the texts paraphrased by Ginzberg, Legends, 3:417–428, esp. 424–425; S. E. Loewenstamm, From Babylon to Canaan (Jerusalem: Magnes Press, 1992), 136–166; J. Goldin, Studies in Midrash and Related Literature (Philadelphia: Jewish Publication Society, 1988), 175–186.

113. Midrashic exegesis took Joshua to mean "may the Lord save (yah yoshia') you" and inferred that Moses meant "may the LORD save you from the counsel of the other scouts" (Sot. 34b; Mid. Ag. to Num. 13:16; Num. R. 16:9). It is unlikely that the name originally meant that, since the vowel u in shua' does not favor a derivation from hoshia', "save." However, it is possible that this is how the Bible understood Moses' intention in changing Joshua's name, since it frequently explains names and name changes midrashically, as in Gen. 17:4–5. For the meaning of Joshua, cf. S. Loewenstamm, s.v. 'elishua', EM 1:353; on shua' see s.v. shua', EM 7:568 and J. C. Greenfield, "Some Glosses on the Keret Epic," EI 9 (1969): 60–61; cf. Ecclus. 46:1 (see Charles, 1:490); the midrashic interpretation may be reflected in a play on the name in Josh. 10:6 (see Y. Zakovitch, Kefel Midreshei Shem [M.A. thesis, Hebrew University, 1971], 177–178). "Nun" probably means "fish"; see S. Ahituv, s.v. nun, EM 5:794.

114. See 10:8; 18:7; 1 Sam. 16:21,22; 1 Kings 10:8; 12:6,8.

115. The formula is common; see, e.g., 2 Sam. 10:12; Isa. 41:6; Ḥag. 2:4; Ps. 27:14; Ezra 10:4. Pi'el forms of words used in formulas often mean to recite the corresponding formula. Thus le'asher means "say 'How fortunate ['ashrei] is so-and-so!'" and in talmudic Hebrew lekalles, "praise," literally means "say 'Beautiful!'" (kalos, Gk. loan-word). See D. R. Hillers, "Delo-

cutive Verbs in Biblical Hebrew," JBL 86 (1967): 320–324; S. Lieberman, *Kalles Killusin*, in *'Alei 'Ayin: Festschrift for Salman Schocken* (Jerusalem: n.p., 1951–52), 75–81.

116. For the talmudic concept see Mid. Hag. to Deut. 24:16; Shab. 89b; TJ Bik. 2:1, 64c; TJ Sanh. 11:7, 30b. T. H. Gaster paraphrases "knowing good and bad" in the Qumran text (1QSᵃ 1:10–11) as "the age of discretion" (*The Dead Sea Scriptures*, 3rd ed. [Garden City, N.Y.: Doubleday, 1976], 439). For the senses of "knowing good and bad" see Tigay, s.v. "Paradise," EncJud 13: 78–80.

117. See M. Avi-Yonah, s.v. *derekh, derakhim*, EM 2:715 and map between cols. 712–713. See n. 12 above.

118. The verb *va-tahinu* is not found elsewhere in the Bible. The translation assumes that it modifies "started" (lit., "went up") and is related to Arabic *h-w-n* which, in the comparable conjugation, means "slight, treat with disdain" (Driver; BDB, 223; HALAT, 232). Hence the clause means "you acted recklessly and went up" and illustrates the abrupt swing of the people's mood from panic to heedless overconfidence. Medieval commentators treat the verb as a delocutive (see n. 115). Rashi assumed that the two verbs in our clause are equivalent to "we are prepared [*hinnennu*] to go up" in Num. 14:40 and that *va-tahinu* is therefore the verbal counterpart of *hinnennu*, meaning either "you were prepared" or "you declared, 'We are prepared.'" In this view the people's fickleness is emphasized: When commanded to go up, they refused; when commanded not to go, they said they were prepared. After quoting *hinnennu* of Num. 14:40, Rashi adds that the people said *hen*, "yes!," which seems to reflect a different derivation of the verb; the latter derivation alone is cited by Ibn Ezra, Bekhor Shor, and Radak, *Sefer Ha-Shorashim*, 79; cf. Aq. (cited by Weinfeld, Commentary).

119. Driver.

120. J. Palmoni, s.v. *devorah*, EM 2:587. Since there is no evidence for beekeeping in Israel in biblical times, the metaphor undoubtedly refers to wild bees.

121. Heb. *be-se'ir 'ad hormah*, lit. "in Seir at [or as far as] Hormah." The phrase is puzzling because Hormah, though on the border with Seir, was in Canaan, near Arad (Num. 21:1–3; Josh. 12:14; 15:30; Judg. 1:17). The parallel passage in Num. 14:45 says simply *'ad ha-hormah*, lit. "at/as far as the *hormah*" (meaning "the Proscribed Place"). An alternative rendering, "*from* Seir to Hormah" (LXX, Pesh., Vulg., Saadia), implies that the Amorites hammered the Israelites while pursuing them from Seir to Hormah, but it is unclear why the Israelite attackers would have been in Seir (could it mean "from the border of Seir"?) and why the Amorites would chase them from there into, instead of away from, Canaan (Hormah). Furthermore the name "Hormah" ("the proscribed place") was given to the place only later, when it was destroyed by the Israelites (in the days of Moses, according to Num. 21:3, and [again?] in the days of Joshua, according to Judg. 1:17). Targs. Jon. and Yer. obviate the problem by construing *hormah* as a common noun here and in Numbers, translating "unto destruction" (cf. 4QDeutʰ, which reads *hhrmh* here, as does Num. 14:45). It implies that the Israelite troops fled from the Amorites into Seir, where they were caught and crushed. For the historical problems associated with this verse see Milgrom, *Numbers*, Excursus 51. For *'ad* meaning "at, near," cf. 2:23; Gen. 13:12; 38:1; Shadal at Gen. 13:12; H. L. Ginsberg, "A Preposition of Interest to Historical Geographers," BASOR 122 (1951): 12–14. In connection with the rendition "from Seir" note that *be-* sometimes appears for *mi(n)*, "from"; see S. R. Driver, *Notes on the Hebrew Text and the Topography of the Books of Samuel* (Oxford: Clarendon, 1913), lxvii; N. M. Sarna, "The Interchange of the Prepositions *beth* and *min* in Biblical Hebrew," JBL 78 (1959): 310–316.

122. For "many days" see Lev. 15:25; Est. 1:4; 1 Kings 18:1; 1 Kings 2:38–39; Num. 20:15; Josh. 24:7.

123. Hoffman.

Chapters 2–3

1. See 1:7,19,40; 2:1. The translation renders the verb as "make your way," "travel," and "march."

2. For the verb (sometimes rendered "move on," "march on," "set out across") see 2:4,8,13,14,18,24,27–30; 3:18,21. For *'ever ha-yarden* see 3:8; in 3:20 the phrase refers to the promised land as "beyond the Jordan" from where the Israelites were situated at the time.

3. For an analysis of 2:1–3:11 see W. A. Sumner, "Israel's Encounters with Edom, Moab, Ammon, Sihon, and Og According to the Deuteronomist," VT 18 (1968): 216–228.

4. For the Egyptian texts see ANET, 243, 259, 262; J. R. Bartlett, "The Land of Seir and the Brotherhood of Edom," JTS 20 (1969): 1–2; J. M. Miller in J. H. Hayes and J. M. Miller, *Israelite and Judaean History* (Philadelphia: Westminster Press, 1977), 250; S. Ahituv, *Canaanite Toponyms in Ancient Egyptian Documents* (Jerusalem: Magnes Press; Leiden: Brill, 1984), 90, 169; for the archaeological evidence see J. A. Sauer, "Transjordan in the Bronze and Iron Ages," BASOR 263 (1986): 8; M. Weippert, "Remarks on the History of Settlement in Southern Jordan during the Early Iron Age," in A. Hadidi, *Studies in the History and Archaeology of Jordan* (Amman: Department of Antiquities, 1982–87), 1:153–163; M. Haran, "The Historical Framework of the Exodus," in Y. Avishur and J. Blau, eds., *Studies in the Bible and the Ancient Near East* (Jerusalem: Rubinstein, 1978), 1:164–167. The "kings" of Edom and Moab in Num. 20:14 and 22:4 must have been sheikhs of tribal groups; see Sarna, *Genesis*, Excursus 28; Milgrom, *Numbers*, at Num. 20:14.

5. For the hostility see, e.g., Jer. 49:7–22; Obadiah; Ps. 137:7–9.

6. 1 Kings 9:26.

7. Gen. 14:6 and Deut. 2:12 likewise indicate that the Horites preceded the descendants of Esau in Seir.

8. Gen. 16:10–12; 17:20; 21:18,20; 25:23. See also 1 Kings 19:15; 2 Kings 5:1; 8:7–15; Amos 2:1–2. In Judg. 11:24, Jephthah implies that the deity of the Ammonites, not the Lord, gave them their land, but this is part of his attempt to dissuade the Ammonites from making war; he probably means to speak in the only terms they would accept.

9. According to Gen. R. 74:15, Edom and Moab later cited these chapters as evidence that David had no right to conquer them, but were overruled since they had previously voided the law by attacking Israel.

10. Weinfeld, DDS, 72.

11. S. Yeivin, "The Patriarchs in the Land of Canaan," in WHJP, 1:202. The Israelites would not have needed to buy meat or animal products from the Edomites, since they themselves had cattle (e.g., Exod. 12:38; 7:3,15–16).

12. NJPS's translation of *ki* as "indeed," rather than "for, because," leaves v. 7 as a non sequitur.

13. See also Gen. 30:27; 39:5. Elsewhere in Deuteronomy "blessing Israel's undertakings" refers to agricultural prosperity (14:29; 16:15; 24:19; 26:15; 28:12). "Blessing" means "gift" in Gen. 33:11; Josh. 15:19; 2 Kings 5:15; cf. Prov. 10:22, "It is the blessing of the LORD that enriches." See Weinfeld, DDS, 312–313; Y. Muffs, *Love and Joy* (New York: Jewish Theological Seminary, 1992), 188 n. 1.

14. See M. Haran, *Ages and Institutions in the Bible* (Tel Aviv: Am Oved, 1972), 64. Some commentators think that Israel skirted Edom on its east, but 2:4 says that they passed through Edom.

15. See also Num. 21:13 and Judg. 11:18.

16. See ANET, 243; Ahituv, *Canaanite Toponyms*, 82, 143; Hayes and Miller, *Israelite and Judaean History*, 250–251; J. M. Miller, "Archaeological Survey of Central Moab: 1978," BASOR 234 (1979): 51.

17. Amos 9:7 (quoted in Comment to 2:5) implies the same thing about the Philistines, but since the Israelites did not pass

by their land, that is not germane to Moses' speech and it is not mentioned here.

18. See Abravanel.

19. Targs. Onk., Jon., Neofiti; Gen. R. 26:7.

20. Cf. Josh. 11:22. In 2 Samuel the Rephaim (*r-p-ʾ-y-m*) are referred to by the collective form "the Raphah" (*r-p-h*, presumably equivalent to *r-p-ʾ*, as in 2 Chron. 20:6,8). *Repha'im* also refers to the shades of the dead in the Bible and Canaanite literature (see, e.g., Isa. 14:9; Isa. 26:14,19). Whether this sense is related to the name of the Rephaim is the subject of considerable speculation; see R. F. Schnell, s.v. "Rephaim," IDB 3:35; S. D. Sperling, s.v. "Rephaim," EncJud 14: 79–80; S. B. Parker s.v. "Rephaim," IDBS, 739; Loewenstamm, s.v. *Refa'im*, EM 7:404–407; Weinfeld, Commentary.

21. See E. A. Speiser, *Genesis* (Garden City, N.Y.: Doubleday, 1964), 282–283; R. de Vaux, *The Early History of Israel* (Philadelphia: Westminster Press, 1978), 136–137; E. A. Knauf, s.v. "Horites," ABD 3:288. For a contrary view see H. L. Ginsberg and B. Maisler, "Semitised Hurrians in Syria and Palestine," JPOS 14 (1934): 256–265 (arguing that several names in Gen. 36 are Hurrian). Note also Y. Aharoni's observation that Midianite pottery resembles that from Nuzi, suggesting the presence of Hurrians in the region (LOB, 205).

22. These observations are based on W. L. Moran, "The End of the Unholy War and the Anti-Exodus," *Biblica* 44 (1963): 333–342. Since these literary devices extend from v. 14 to v. 16, they show that literarily v. 16 belongs with vv. 9–15, as the Masoretic and Samaritan text divisions indicate, even though logically and grammatically v. 16 belongs with the next section, as the translation shows.

23. Weinfeld, DDS, 48–49, notes that the use of this term is part of Deuteronomy's more explicitly military view of the conquest.

24. Targs. Onk. and Jon. For "the hand of the LORD" in this sense, see Exod. 9:3,15; 1 Sam. 5:6–11, 6:3–9; 2 Sam. 24:16–17. For synonymous idioms in Akkadian and Ugaritic see J.J.M. Roberts, "The Hand of Yahweh," VT 21 (1971): 244–251.

25. Num. 16:31–35; 17:6–15; 21:6; 25:8–9; cf. 14:12.

26. In 1 Chron. 21:12 pestilence is "the sword of the LORD."

27. For *h-m-m* see, e.g., Exod. 14:24; 23:27; Josh. 10:10; Judg. 4:15; 1 Sam. 7:10; Est. 9:24. For *'ad tummam* see Josh. 8:24; 10:20. For further details see Moran, "End of the Unholy War." The related noun *mehumah* (from the variant form of the verb, *hum*), is associated with the hand of the Lord (meaning a plague) in 1 Sam. 5:6–11 (cf. MdRY Be-Shallaḥ 5 [Lauterbach 1:241]: "rout [*hmmh*, in Deut. 7:23 and Exod. 14:24] means by pestilence").

28. See Sumner, "Israel's Encounters with Edom," 217.

29. Passing *through* territory is *'avar bi-gevul* (v. 4); for *'avar* plus accusative, "pass beyond," vs. *'avar be-*, "pass through," see Num. 20:17 and 21:22.

30. R. W. Younker, s.v. "Rabbah," ABD 5:599.

31. See Gen. 19:37–38; Num. 21:11,13,15,24; Judg. 11:15; 1 Kings 11:7; KAI 181 (ANET, 320); K. Jackson, *The Ammonite Language of the Iron Age* (Chico, Calif.: Scholars Press, 1983), 36, 45.

32. In Arabic and Syriac *z-m-z-m* refers to noises such as buzzing, rumbling, roaring, and murmuring; onomatopoeic forms like *zamzum-*, with two virtually identical syllables, commonly designate speakers of foreign languages; cf. Gk. *barbaros* and Arabic *timtimmiyun*. Cf. the use of *kav-kav*, *kav-lakav*, and *tsav-tsav* to imitate the "gibberish" of foreign tongues in Isa. 18:2,7 and 28:10,13 (note 28:11). See J. Tigay, "'Heavy of Mouth' and 'Heavy of Tongue': On Moses' Speech Difficulty," BASOR 231 (1978): 57–67; cf. S. Lieberman, *Texts and Studies* (New York: Ktav, 1974), 240. Cf. modern Hebrew slang *vusvusim* (or *vuzvuzim*), originally used by Oriental Jews in Israel to refer to speakers of Yiddish, probably in imitation of Yiddish *vus*, "what?"

33. *Genesis Apocryphon* 21:29 renders the phrase in Gen. 14:5 as "the Zumzammim who were in Ammon" (J. Fitzmyer, *The Genesis Apocryphon of Qumran Cave I* [Rome: Pontifical Biblical Institute, 1966], 62–63). "Zuzim" is conceivably reflected in the name of Ziza, an Arab village in central Transjordan, south of the former Ammonite territory. See G. A. Smith and J. G. Bartholomew, *Atlas of the Historical Geography of the Holy Land* (London: Hodder and Stoughton, 1915), pl. 29, sec. E-1.

34. The Avvim here have no apparent connection with those of a later date (2 Kings 17:31) or with the city of that name in Josh. 18:23.

35. Lev. 25:31 explains that *hatserim* "have no encircling walls," unlike walled cities (v. 29). A document from Mari (in Syria) mentions the *hasirātum* (*hatserim*) of the Banu-yamina tribesmen; see CAD Ḥ, 131, and A. Malamat, "Mari and the Bible," JAOS 82 (1962): 143–150; idem, "Ḥaserim in the Bible and Mari" (Hebrew), *Yed'iot* 27 (1963): 181–184.

36. Caphtor is mentioned in Akkadian and Ugaritic texts, and is presumably identical to Keftiu in Egyptian texts. See B. Mazar, s.v. "Caphtor," EM 4: 216–218; de Vaux, *Early History of Israel*, 504–507.

37. See ANET, 262–263; H. J. Katzenstein and T. Dothan, s.v. "Philistines," ABD 5:326, 328–329.

38. See Judg. 13–16; 1 Sam. 4–2 Sam. 5.

39. In schematic narratives characters often stand for types, such as saints or sinners, without the text describing the behavior on which such characterization is based. For example, the virtues for which God saved Noah are not described; all that matters is that he was a *tsaddik*, a righteous man (Gen. 6:9).

40. Tactical considerations may have gone into the decision to attack Sihon and Og. These two kingdoms controlled all of northern Transjordan and were huge compared to the city-states west of the Jordan. Since Israel was planning to launch its attack from Sihon's territory, it may have taken his and Og's territory in order to protect its flank from these powerful, potentially hostile kings who were kin to the Amorites west of the Jordan. Awareness of tactical considerations is reflected in Tanḥ. B. Ḥukkat 52, according to which the kings in Canaan paid tribute to Sihon so that he would guard the approach to their land from the east. Smith, 46, notes that Pompey tried, and the first Moslem invaders succeeded, in taking Transjordan before crossing the Jordan. Such considerations are never discussed by the Torah, which focuses on the moral or religious grounds for such decisions.

41. See Ramban at Num. 21:21; Weinfeld, Commentary, 173–178. Maimonides infers from God's hardening of Sihon's heart that he was guilty of unnamed sins before Israel ever came into his orbit; see below, n. 50.

42. Ahituv, s.v. *Sihon*, EM 5: 1018; for the site see Smith and Bartholomew, *Atlas*, pls. 29–30, sec. D-3 (Kari'at Shiḥan) (cf. other sites incorporating the name Shiḥan in pls. 22, sec. G-2, and 26, sec. G-3). On this Amorite kingdom see B. Mazar, "The Exodus and the Conquest," in WHJP 3, 72–73.

43. Cf. Gen. 6:17 with 7:4 and 19; see Comment to Deut. 4:32.

44. Indicated by the fact that the following section begins in v. 31 with a recapitulation of vv. 24–25. Such "resumptive repetitions" are a common practice when a text returns to its main subject following a digression. See Ibn Janah, *Sefer Ha-Rikmah*, 296–297, 365–366; H. Wiener, *The Composition of Judges 2:11 to I Kings 2:46* (Leipzig: Hinrichs, 1929), 2; C. Kuhl, "Die Wiederaufnahme," ZAW 65 (1952): 1–11; I. L. Seeligmann, *Studies in Biblical Literature*, ed. A. Hurvitz et al. (Jerusalem: Magnes Press, 1992), 53–60; S. Talmon, *Literary Studies in the Hebrew Bible* (Jerusalem: Magnes Press; Leiden: Brill, 1993), 118–120; J. Tigay, ed., *Empirical Models for Biblical Criticism* (Philadelphia: University of Pennsylvania Press, 1985), 48–49, 74; E. Tov, in Tigay, ed., *Empirical Models*, 235–236; A. Toeg, *Lawgiving at Sinai* (Jerusalem: Magnes Press, 1977), 129 n. 82.

45. Exod. 3:16–20; 5:1–3; 8:23–25; 10:7–11,24–27.

46. Ehrlich. On the negotiations with Pharaoh see Loewenstamm, *The Tradition of the Exodus and Its Development* (Hebrew) (Jerusalem: Magnes Press, 1965), 48–49; M. Greenberg, *Understanding Exodus* (New York: Behrman House, 1969), 84–85; N. M. Sarna, *Exploring Exodus* (New York: Schocken, 1986), 55–56. The midrash gives this passage an ethical turn: after receiving God's order to attack Sihon, Moses offered Sihon peace and, accepting Moses' reasoning, God ordained that in the future Israel should always offer the possibility of peaceful surrender before attacking a city (Deut. 20:10; see Deut. R. 5:13; Ginzberg, *Legends*, 6:117–118 n. 672).

47. Heb. *ba-derekh ba-derekh*, lit., "on the highway, on the highway"; cf. "justice, justice," meaning "justice alone" (16:20); cf. GKC §123e. In Num. 21:22 the wording is *be-derekh ha-melekh*, "on the king's highway."

48. Thus, in essence, Shadal. Cf. "with your feet," which may mean "by your own efforts" (11:10).

49. Judg. 11:17; cf. Deut. 23:5.

50. Pharaoh hardened his own heart after the first five plagues (Exod. 7:22; 8:11,15,28; 9:7) and his heart was hardened by God after the next four (9:12,35 [see 10:1]; 10:20,27) and before he pursued Israel to the sea (14:4,8,17). God's earlier declarations that He would harden Pharaoh's heart refer to the final set of plagues (4:21, where it is mentioned together with the last plague; 7:3). See Exod. R. 11:6 and 13:3, where God's hardening of Pharaoh's heart is seen as matching Pharaoh's own behavior. On the subject in general see Maimonides, Hilkhot Teshuvah 6:3; idem, Introduction to Commentary on Avot, chap. 8; Y. Kaufmann, *The Religion of Israel*, trans. M. Greenberg (Chicago: University of Chicago Press, 1960), 75–76 and the extra comments in *Toledot Ha-'Emunah Ha-Yisre'elit* (Tel Aviv: Bialik Institute-Dvir, 1937–56), 1/2: 454; W. Eichrodt, *Theology of the Old Testament* (Philadelphia: Westminster Press, 1961–67), 2:177–180; M. Greenberg, *Ezekiel 1–20* (Garden City, N.Y.: Doubleday, 1983), 254, 369.

51. See 4:20,38; 6:24; 8:18; 10:15; Weinfeld, DDS, 175, 350; see also Seeligmann, *Studies in Biblical Literature*, 23–28.

52. For different conceptions of the territory captured from Sihon and Og see the comment of Weinfeld to 2:36.

53. Josh. 13:25, which says that part of Ammonite territory was conquered, may reflect the Ammonite claim quoted in Judg. 11:13. B. Oded holds that the text of that verse should be corrected to "and all the towns of part [lit., half] of Gilead up to the land of the Ammonites" (s.v. 'Ammon, Benei 'Ammon, EM 6:256–257).

54. Gordon, UT §§19.1809–1810.

55. For sixty as a round number in rabbinic literature see L. Ginzberg, *Legends*, 7:444. For the Egyptian list of cities see B. Mazar, *Cities and Districts in Eretz-Israel* (Jerusalem: Mosad Bialik and Israel Exploration Society, 1975), 182–189.

56. Chap. 3 describes the conquered territory, in greater or lesser detail, three times in succession, in addition to the summaries in 2:36 and 3:4. This amount of attention—especially when contrasted with the almost skeletal narratives that tell how the territory was won—indicates that these descriptions must have been very important, though Moses gives no indication of why. Perhaps it is because of the practical value of descriptions of territory in resolving territorial disputes (cf. Judg. 11). This would imply that chaps. 2–3 are a monotheistic version of what Jephthah said to the Ammonites: Israel may keep what God gave to it, and its neighbors may keep what He gave to them.

57. Y. Aharoni, s.v. *ḥermon*, EM 3: 294–297; Mazar, *Cities and Districts*, 173 n. 35.

58. C. Schmitz, s.v. "Sidon," ABD 6:17.

59. See Ps. 29:6 (Sirion); Ezek. 27:5 (Senir); for Ugaritic, Hittite, Hurrian, Akkadian, and Egyptian references, see Y. Aharoni, s.v. *Hermon*, EM 3:294–297; Mazar, *Cities and Districts*, 173 n. 35; and Y. Ikeda, "Hermon, Sirion, and Senir," AJBI 4 (1978): 32–44. In many sources the terms are parallel to Lebanon and may refer to the entire Antilebanon range, not only its southern section. However, in Song 4:8 and 1 Chron. 5:23 Senir is distinct from Hermon, and in Arabic sources, and possibly the Akkadian ones, it may refer to the northern section of the Antilebanon. These names may have been used in narrower and broader senses, and may been used for different parts of the Antilebanon in different periods.

60. See Josh. 13:9, 16–21; Jer. 48:21–24; EM 4:920.

61. The phrase "Bashan as far as Salcah and Edrei, the towns of Og's kingdom in Bashan" is puzzling. Since vv. 8–10 list places in geographical order from south to north, it should culminate with a point on the northern border or conceivably the eastern border, not in the south of Bashan where Edrei was. It seems likely that the text originally read: "Bashan as far as Salcah, *and (including) Ashtaroth* and Edrei, the royal cities of Og in Bashan"; in other words, the list culminated with Salcah—as descriptions of Bashan regularly do—and then added the capital cities; cf. Josh. 13:30–31. This emendation is supported by two other considerations: (1) in other descriptions of Bashan, "as far as Salcah" is never followed by another place (see Josh. 13:11; 1 Chron. 5:11); therefore Salcah in our verse should be followed by a comma and Edrei should be taken as part of what follows; (2) the phrase 'arei mamlakhah means "royal cities," not "towns of the kingdom"; it is synonymous with 'arei mamlekhut in Josh. 13:31 (see Josh. 10:2; 1 Sam. 27:5; cf. 2 Sam. 12:26). Salcah was not a royal city, but Ashtaroth and Edrei were, and we expect to find both of those cities described as Og's 'arei mamlakhah.

62. See A. R. Millard, "King Og's bed and Other Ancient Ironmongery," in L. Eslinger and G. Taylor, eds., *Ascribe to the Lord: Biblical and Other Studies in Memory of Peter C. Craigie* (Sheffield: Sheffield Academic Press, 1988), 481–492. Contrast J. D. Muhly review of P. McNutt, *The Forging of Israel* (1991), in JAOS 112 (1992): 698.

63. See R. de Vaux, *Ancient Israel* (New York: McGraw-Hill, 1961), 195–206.

64. See Ps. 22:12; Amos 4:1. For a different view of why these tribes were given this territory see Weinfeld, Commentary, 177.

65. It is possible that vv. 3–7 and v. 14 stem from different traditions about the capture of Transjordan, one which reported it as a unified action of the entire army and another which reported separate actions by individual tribes and clans. The same problem exists in relating the earlier accounts of these events in Num. 21:21–35 and Num. 32. The translation of *l-k-ḥ* as (Jair) "received" is an attempt to obviate the problem in Deuteronomy. See B. Mazar, s.v. *ḥavvot ya'ir*, EM 3: 66–67.

66. For possible extrabiblical references, see Mazar, *Canaan and Israel* (Jerusalem: Mosad Bialik and Israel Exploration Society, 1974), 32, 39, and Mazar, *Cities and Districts*, 195–196; Ahituv, *Canaanite Toponyms*, 132.

67. See M. Stern, *Greek and Latin Authors on Jews and Judaism* (Jerusalem: Israel Academy of Sciences and Humanities, 1974), 1:338, 341; 2:681.

68. See Num. 32:17,20,21,27,29,32; Josh. 4:13; 6:7,9,13. *Halutsim* may mean literally "the separated ones," from *ḥ-l-ts*, "remove," "separate," "withdraw," but only the usage indicates its approximate meaning. For the reasoning of the NJPS translators see H. M. Orlinsky, *Notes on the New Translation of the Torah* (Philadelphia: Jewish Publication Society, 1969), on Num. 32:17 and 31:3.

69. Weinfeld, Commentary. For the Amarna letters see ANET, 483–490.

70. See n. 2 above.

71. See 2 Sam. 7:22b–24; 1 Kings 8:23; 2 Kings 19:15–19; Jer. 32:17–23; for the rabbinic rule see Ber. 32a. See the discussions by Weinfeld, DDS, 37–45, and M. Greenberg, "On the

Refinement of the Conception of Prayer in Hebrew Scriptures," AJSR 1 (1976): 71–72.

72. Weinfeld, *Commentary.* See Gen. 15:2,8; Josh. 7:7; Judg. 6:22; 16:28; 2 Sam. 7:18,19.

73. In Exod. 15:11 and several other passages quoted below, NJPS renders "god(s)" and "sons of god(s)" as "celestials" and "divine beings."

74. See ANET, 71 no. 39; 383; 386 l. 23; BWL, 128 ll. 45–46.

75. See 1 Kings 22:19–21 (cf. Deut. 4:19); Pss. 103:20–21; 104:4; Zech. 6:5; Isa. 6:1–2; Josh. 5:14 (cf. Isa. 40:26 and Judg. 5:20). Some of these creatures are also termed "sons of god(s)" (e.g., Pss. 29:1 [referring to the stars, according to Ibn Ezra at v. 2]; 89:7; Job 1:6; 38:7 [cf. Ugar. *bn 'l // phr kkbm*, UT 76,i,3–4]; Dan. 3:25 [note v. 28; see also Comment to Deut. 32:8]) and "holy beings" (Pss. 16:2; 89:8; Job 15:15 [see 4:18]). They are often called upon to pay homage to God and sing His praises (see the passages just cited and Pss. 97:7; 148:1–3; Job 38:7; Neh. 9:6). That some of them also act on earth is indicated in Gen. 6:1–4; 32:2–3,25–31; Josh. 5:14; 1 Kings 22:2–23; Zech. 6:5; Ps. 16:3; Job 1:6–7. Passages like Ps. 96:4b–5, Isa. 40:18–25, and Jer. 10:6 leave open the possibility that the "god(s) . . . on earth" that are incomparable to the Lord include idols. On the divine retinue see G. E. Wright, *The Old Testament Against Its Environment* (London: SCM, 1957), 30–41.

76. See Judg. 13:20–22; Hos. 12:4–5 (angel; cf. Gen. 32:31); 1 Sam. 28:13; Isa. 8:19 (ghosts; see Deut. 21:23 and Comment there); Gen. 31:30; Judg. 18:24 (idols); Exod. 12:12; 1 Kings 11:5 (foreign gods). For similar usage in Akkadian and Canaanite texts see KAI 27, ll. 1,3; CAD I/J, 91–103 and passages cited in Comment to 21:23. For the biblical attitude toward foreign gods see Kaufmann, *Religion*, 7–20. The irony of using the term "gods" for beings whose divinity was denied is reflected in such statements as "the kings of Assyria . . . have committed the gods of the nations to flames for they are not gods, but man's handiwork" (2 Kings 19:17–18) and "Has any nation changed its gods, even though they are no-gods?" (Jer. 2:11; cf. 16:20). See Excursus 6.

77. See also 10:17 and Ps. 86:8,10b. On the other hand, the author of Ps. 96 apparently considered "gods" to be subject to misunderstanding; in borrowing parts of Ps. 29 he rephrased "sons of gods" (29:1); see Excursus 31.

78. Other phrases in God's response that seem to ironically recall terminology of the earlier sections are *ba-davar ha-zeh* (v. 26; cf. 1:32) and *re'eh be-'eineikha* (v. 27; cf. 1:19, 30; 3:21). On the verb *'-v-r* in vv. 27 and 28 see introductory Comment to vv. 23–26a.

79. See Num. 27:19 (see Ramban, Hoffmann, and Milgrom, *Numbers*, n. 42 ad loc.); Deut. 31:14 (see Saadia), 31:23 (Sforno); 1 Sam. 13:14; 2 Sam. 7:11; 25:30; Neh. 5:14; Sforno at Exod. 6:13; BDB, 845, sec. 1d.

Chapter 4:1–43

A.D.H. Mayes, "Deuteronomy 4 and the Literary Criticism of Deuteronomy," JBL 100 (1981): 23–51; A. Toeg, *Lawgiving at Sinai* (Jerusalem: Magnes Press, 1977), 89–90, 119–120, 131–136.

1. See J. Levenson, "Who Inserted the Book of the Torah?" HTR 68 (1975): 203–233; Weinfeld, *Commentary*, 214–221.

2. Cf. Maimonides, "The Essay on Resurrection," in A. Halkin and D. Hartman, *Crisis and Leadership: Epistles of Maimonides* (Philadelphia: Jewish Publication Society, 1985), 211–213. Note also Philo's and Josephus's explanations of why the Torah begins with narratives: Philo, Op. 1–3; Abr. 3–6; 2 Mos. 46–51; Josephus, Ant. 1.18–26.

3. Hebrew texts divide 4:1–40 before vv. 1 (M, SP, 4QDeut^d), 5,9,12, and 21 (SP), 25 (M, SP), 32 and 35 (SP), and after v. 40 (M, SP).

4. N. Lohfink cited by Levenson, "Who Inserted," 203, 204.

5. Vv. 1,5,14,21,26,40.

6. What Israel saw, or did not see, with its own eyes (vv. 3,9,12,15,34–36); the impression observance will make in the eyes of the nations (v. 6; see also vv. 5,19,28); hearing (vv. 1,6,10,12, 28,30,32,33,36).

7. Vv. 1,5,10,14.

8. Vv. 9,35,39.

9. Vv. 9,23,31.

10. V. 6.

11. Vv. 4,8,20,38–40.

12. Vv. 7–8,33–34. Both of these units refer to "great" things (vv. 6–8,32,38).

13. See vv. 10–12,26,32–33,36,39.

14. For *ve-'attah*, "and now," as a transition after a historical review see 10:12; 1 Sam. 12:13. The term functions more generally to introduce a practical conclusion based on something that has just been stated, as in Gen. 3:22; 21:23.

15. Cf. 5:1; 6:4; 9:1; 20:3; 27:9. See Weinfeld, *Commentary*; DDS, 305.

16. Cf. v. 5; 6:1; 31:19,22.

17. For *hukkim* see Isa. 10:1; 30:8 (for an Aramaic decree engraved on stone see A. Caquot, "Une Inscription Araméene d'époque assyrienne," in *Hommages . . . Dupont Sommer*, 9–16); for *shofet* see Comment to 1:16, "magistrates"; for *mitsvah* see 1 Kings 2:43; Est. 3:3; for *'edot* see J. Fitzmyer, *The Aramaic Inscriptions of Sefire* (Rome: Pontifical Biblical Institute, 1967), 23–24; H. Tadmor, "The Aramaization of Assyria," in H.-J. Nissen and J. Renger, eds., *Mesopotamien und seine Nachbarn* (Berlin: Reimer, 1982), 455–458.

18. See Sifra (Weiss, 86a par. 10); Yoma 67b; Rashi at Lev. 18:4; Maimonides, Guide 3.26.

19. See Weinfeld, *Commentary*; DDS, 262 n 3. Cf. ANET, 178cd; N. Lewis and M. Reinhold, *Roman Civilization* (New York: Columbia University Press, 1951), 1:169. For other genres, see Comment to 13:2.

20. Ramban; Maimonides, Hilkhot Yesodei Ha-Torah 8:3; 9:1; idem, Mamrim 2:9; J. D. Eisenstein, *Ozar Dinim U-Minhagim* (New York: Hebrew Publishing Company, 1938), 44–45; cf. Torah Temimah at Lev. 27:34, par. 216. Contrast the Karaite view in Keter Torah here.

21. Hazzekuni at 4:2 (cf. Seforno at 13:1); Ramban to 13:2 envisions a prophet who says in the name of the Lord that Israel should also worship Baal-peor, implying a connection between 13:2 and 4:1–4. See also Maimonides, Hilkhot Yesodei Ha-Torah 8:3; 9:1.

22. See Weinfeld, DDS, 83, 332. For examples see S. N. Kramer, *The Sumerians* (Chicago: University of Chicago Press, 1963), 333 no. 4; E. A. Speiser, *Oriental and Biblical Studies* (Philadelphia: University of Pennsylvania Press, 1967), 187; CAD A1, 320; ANET, 487 (EA no. 280). For some examples in the Bible see Jer. 2:2 (following the Lord); Deut. 6:14; 8:19; 13:3 (other gods).

23. See Gen. 2:24; 34:3 (emotional attachment); Prov. 18:24; Ruth 1:14 (devotion). See also Deut. 10:20; 11:22; 13:5; 30:20; 2 Kings 18:6 (contrasted with turning away from God).

24. Weinfeld, *Commentary.*

25. For laws in force in the wilderness see Exod. 16 and 32; Lev. 17 and 24:10–23; Num. 15:32–36. For laws dependent on the land of Israel see Lev. 23:9–22; 25:2; Num. 15:18–21; 35:9–34; Deut. 7:1–5; 26:1–11.

26. For *hi'* meaning "the aforementioned action(s)" see Num. 14:41; Judg. 14:4; GKC §135p. It is not the laws themselves that will show Israel's wisdom; they are the product of God's wisdom, not Israel's (though admittedly the nations might not realize that); see introductory Comment to chap. 5.

27. Weinfeld, *Commentary.*

28. See Isa. 58; Pss. 22:12,20; 34:16–19; 145:18.

29. See Deut. 18:14–22; 33:29. See also Exod. 33:16.

30. Isa. 44:9–20; 46:6–7; Zech. 10:2; Hab. 2:18–19.

31. See Exod. 14:25; Deut. 28:10; Josh. 2:8–11 (here the foreigner does recognize that YHVH is the only God); 1 Sam. 4:6–8; Isa. 2:3b (note Isaiah's hope for the future, 2:2–4; 19:19–21).

32. Although 'elohim is singular in meaning when it refers to "God" or "a god," its form is plural, and it can therefore mean "gods" as well (see Excursus 4, n. 13). The accompanying adjective "close," in the plural, may favor taking 'elohim as plural here, but this is not decisive since 'elohim is sometimes accompanied by plural adjectives and verbs when its meaning is unquestionably singular (cf. Gen. 20:13; 35:7; Josh. 24:19; 1 Sam. 17:26). See the discussion in Sanh. 38b. Pesh., LXX, and the targums take it as singular here.

33. See Exod. R. 30:12; M. Whittaker, Tatian: Oratio ad Graecos and Fragments (Oxford: Clarendon, 1982), 55.

34. See, e.g., Exod. 21:20–21,26–27; Deut. 24:16–22. See M. Greenberg, "Some Postulates of Biblical Criminal Law"; S. M. Paul, Studies in the Book of the Covenant (Leiden: Brill, 1970), 69, 78.

35. A. J. Heschel, God in Search of Man (Philadelphia: Jewish Publication Society, 1959), 140; see also 213ff; cf. Judah Halevi, Kuzari, 1: 11–25.

36. See MdRY Ba-Hodesh 9 (Lauterbach 2:275); Maimonides, Hilkhot Yesodei Ha-Torah 8:1; idem, "Epistle to Yemen," in Halkin and Hartman, Crisis and Leadership, 113; Judah Halevi, Kuzari, 1:87–88; cf. 25; M. Mendelssohn, Gesammelte Schriften (Stuttgart-Bad Cannstatt, 1971), 7:86–89 (ref. courtesy Devorah Janssens).

37. See Driver, lxix, 1:30, and 5:3. Cf. 1:26; 29:1,15.

38. See Judg. 2:1; 6:8–10; 10:11–12; Amos 2:10.

39. M. Greenberg argues that Exod. 20:17 (20) should be translated "God has come only in order to give you an experience (of Him)." See "N-s-h in Exod. 20:20 and the Purpose of the Sinaitic Theophany," JBL 79 (1960): 273–276; see also Abravanel at Exod. 20:17; Maimonides, Guide 3.24 on Deut. 8:16.

40. See Gen. 20:11; 42:18; Exod. 1:17; Lev. 19:14,32; 25:17,36,43; Deut. 25:18; Ps. 34:12–15; Prov. 3:7; Job 28:28. For the concept see Abravanel, 103–108; I. Heinemann, s.v. Yir'ah, yir'at ha-shem, EM 3:768–770; Weinfeld, DDS, 274–281; N. M. Sarna, Exploring Exodus (New York: Schocken, 1986), 120–121. Cf. R. F. Harper, Assyrian and Babylonian Letters (Chicago: University of Chicago Press, 1892–1914), 614:9, "fear of the gods creates kindness."

41. See also 1 Kings 19:11–12; Hab. 3; Ps. 104:1–4. Outside of the Bible these motifs appear especially in theophanies of storm gods and appear to be rooted in the phenomena of thunderstorms. In Israelite tradition the Lord is no mere storm god, but the literary motif was taken over as an apt expression of His majesty. See S. E. Loewenstamm, "The Trembling of Nature during the Theophany," in Loewenstamm, Comparative Studies in Biblical and Ancient Oriental Literatures (Neukirchen-Vluyn: Neukirchener Verlag, 1980), 173–189; F. M. Cross, Canaanite Myth and Hebrew Epic (Cambridge: Harvard University Press, 1973), 156–169; Weinfeld, "Divine Intervention in War," in H. Tadmor and M. Weinfeld, eds., History, Historiography, and Interpretation (Jerusalem: Magnes Press, 1983), 120–147; Sarna, Exploring Exodus, 132–134.

42. See vv. 15,16,23,25, and 5:8.

43. See A. Dillmann, Die Bücher Exodus und Leviticus, ed. V. Ryssel (Leipzig: Hirzel, 1897); A. Kahana, Sefer Shemot (reprint; Jerusalem: Makor, 1969); and the view retracted by Shadal at Exod. 20:4. Examples are Num. 12:8; Ps. 17:15 (parallel to "face"); Job 4:16 (parallel to "appearance"). Cf. the possibly cognate tmn in Ugaritic [UT §19.2565]). The MT of Exod. 20:4 reads "you shall not make for yourself a sculptured image or [ve-] any temunah," and the conjunction ("or") requires taking temunah as a direct object of "make," and hence as a manufac-

tured object. However, since this is inconsistent with the usage of temunah everywhere else in the Bible, and the conjunction is absent in Deut. 5:8 and related phrases in 4:23 and 25, it seems more likely that the three passages which lack the conjunction, not the one that has it, contain the original reading. The insertion of the conjunction may have been facilitated by the loss of the original meaning of temunah due to its disuse in postbiblical Hebrew.

44. See Exod. 24:9–11; 33:20–23; Num. 12:8. Visions of the Lord are also described by some of the prophets, and the Psalmist hopes for the experience; see 1 Kings 22:19; Isa. 6:1–5; Ezek. 1:26–28; Amos 9:1; Ps. 17:15.

45. See Weinfeld, "Berit—Covenant vs. Obligation," Biblica 56 (1975): 120–128. The etymology of berit is debated. The most attractive suggestions derive it (1) from a word meaning "bond," "fetter," cognate to Akk. biritu and mishnaic birit; in this case the term refers to the obligation as something binding; or (2) from the root b-r-h, "cut"; in this case the term refers to cutting up an animal, a ceremony by which acceptance of the obligation was signified (see Comment to 5:2). See Weinfeld, Biblica 56:123 and s.v. berit in TDOT 2:255; H. Tadmor, "Treaty and Oath in the Ancient Near East," in G. M. Tucker and D. Knight, eds., Humanizing America's Iconic Book (Chico, Calif.: Scholars Press, 1982), 137–138.

46. E.g., the Aramaic Sefire steles (ANET, 659) and the Greek Treaty of Nicias (Thucydides 5:18). See W. W. Hallo and W. K. Simpson, The Ancient Near East: A History (New York: Harcourt Brace Jovanovich, 1971), 155–156.

47. For the Aramaic decree see Caquot, "Inscription Araméene." The tablets of the Decalogue were inscribed on both sides (Exod. 33:15–16). Since the outer dimensions of the Ark of the Covenant were forty-five by twenty-seven inches (Exod. 25:10), it could have held tablets of about twenty-one by twenty-four side-by-side.

48. G. B. Sarfatti, "The Tablets of the Law as a Symbol of Judaism," in Ben-Zion Segal and G. Levi, eds., The Ten Commandments in History and Tradition (Jerusalem: Magnes Press, 1990), 383–418.

49. It is true that to the Bible, any image—even one of the Lord—is ipso facto another god (see Comment to 5:8); here, however, that is not the point being stressed.

50. Ibn Ezra at Exod. 20:20; Abravanel at Exod. 20:15–23, answers 4 and 5. For the gods communicating through their idols see Ezek. 21:26; Hab. 2:18–19; Zech. 10:2; 1 Macc. 3:48 in The Jerusalem Bible and NEB; A. L. Oppenheim, "Sumerian inim.gar, Akk. egirru = Gk. kleidon," AfO 17 (1954–56): 54; E. Bevan, Holy Images (London: George Allen and Unwin, 1940), 25–26.

51. This function was known to medieval Jewish writers; see Maimonides, Guide 1.36,63; 3.29; Ibn Ezra at Exod. 20:5; Radak at Isa. 40:21; 1 Sam. 19:13.

52. For pesel see Deut. 7:25; Isa. 30:22; 40:19–20; 44:15–17; Jer. 10:14; Dillmann at Exod. 20:24.

53. For semel see Ezek. 8:3,5; 2 Chron. 33:7,15; for Phoenician see DISO, 194–195; KAI 41:1.

54. For tavnit see Josh. 22:8; Exod. 25:9, 1 Chron. 28:11–19; see further M. Greenberg, Ezekiel 1–20 (Garden City, N.Y.: Doubleday, 1983), 167.

55. These four terms do not refer to separate kinds of images. Since temunah is not a type of image, the word must be part of a construct chain with pesel; the chain pesel temunat kol means "an idol of the visage of any. . . ." The Masoretic punctuation joins semel to the same chain, yielding "an idol of the visage of any statue," but this seems tautologous and overloaded (though "the idol of the statue" [pesel hasemel] in 2 Chron. 33:7,15 may be analogous). It seems best to take semel as part of the following phrase. This leaves pesel temunat kol as an independent unit, as in v. 25.

56. The copper serpent (Num. 21:8–9), the cherubs (e.g.,

Exod. 25:18–20), and the oxen supporting the water tank in Solomon's temple (1 Kings 7:25). The copper serpent was unobjectionable at first because its purely apotropaic function was obvious but, perhaps because it was visible to the public, it eventually became an object of worship and was destroyed by King Hezekiah (2 Kings 18:4). The cherubs represented God's throne (Exod. 25:22; see J. M. Grintz, s.v. "Ark of the Covenant," EncJud 3:459–465; S. M. Paul, s.v. "Cherub," EncJud 5:397–399). It is possible that they were unobjectionable because, unlike the golden calves, they were normally hidden from public view in the Holy of Holies and not prone to public veneration, hence were not idols (for a different view see U. M. D. Cassuto, *A Commentary on the Book of Exodus* [reprint; Jerusalem: Magnes Press, 1967], 407–408). The oxen were obviously functional and therefore in no danger of attracting worship (1 Kings 7:25). Some hold that there is no rational reason for the distinction between licit and illicit images, but that it is either an arbitrary expression of the sovereign divine will or an accident of history. See J. Faur, "The Biblical Idea of Idolatry," JQR 69 (1978): 2; Y. Kaufmann, *The Religion of Israel*, trans. M. Greenberg (Chicago: University of Chicago Press, 1960), 136.

57. See Gen. 1:26–27; 5:1–3; Ezek. 1:26–28. It is admittedly not out of the question that some might have attempted to represent the Lord as an animal, since animals were used to picture or symbolize deities elsewhere in the ancient Near East, and the text may be concerned about unreflecting imitation of foreign practices. See, e.g., ANEP, figs. 548–573; W. F. Albright, *The Proto-Sinaitic Inscriptions and Their Decipherment* (Cambridge: Harvard University Press, 1969), 19–22, 24–25; H. Ringgren, *Religions of the Ancient Near East* (Philadelphia: Westminster Press, 1974), 157; R. A. Oden, "The Persistence of Canaanite Religion," BA 39 (1976): 34. On images of bulls and calves, see Excursus 12.

58. See Excursus 12.

59. Pss. 24:2; 136:6; Gen. 49:25.

60. Weinfeld, Commentary, 213.

61. See Gen. 1:16,18; Pss. 19:2–6; 103:20–21; 104:4; 136:8–9; 148:2–3; Job 38:7.

62. 2 Kings 21:3,5; 23:4–5,12; Jer. 7:18; 8:2; 19:13; Ezek. 8:16; Zeph. 1:5; for earlier cases see Amos 5:26; 2 Kings 17:16. See M. Greenberg, "Religion: Stability and Ferment," in WHJP 4/2, 104; M. Cogan, *Imperialism and Religion* (Missoula, Mont.: Society of Biblical Literature and Scholars Press, 1974), 84–87; J. McKay, *Religion in Judah under the Assyrians* (Naperville, Ill.: Allenson, 1973), 45–59; J. Tigay, *You Shall Have No Other Gods* (Atlanta: Scholars Press, 1986), 95–96.

63. Maimonides, Hilkhot 'Avodah Zarah 2:1 (translation, slightly modified, from M. Hyamson, *The Mishneh Torah by Maimonides*, Book I [New York, 1937], 67a–b). Cf. Recanati cited by C. B. Chavel, *Perushei Ha-Torah le-Rabbenu Moshe Ben Naḥman* (Jerusalem: Mosad Ha-Rav Kook, 1962–63), 1:391, comment to *sod millat 'aḥerim*. On Enosh, cf. Comment to 13:6.

64. Rashbam; cf. Sifrei to 17:3; Meg. 9b. Some commentators think that the verse refers to the "princes" (*sarim*), the angels appointed over each nation, who are referred to in Daniel and in apocalyptic literature (see Excursus 31); see Ibn Ezra; Ramban (at v. 15 and at Exod. 20:3; Lev. 18:25; and Num. 11:16). For other interpretations of this verse, see Excursus 7.

65. See A. Rofé, *Israelite Belief in Angels in the Pre-Exilic Period* (Hebrew) (Ph.D. diss., Hebrew University, 1969), 98–101. For idols as the portion of others, not Israel, see Jer. 10:6.

66. See Milgrom, *Numbers*, at 15:41; cf. W. W. Hallo, *The Book of the People* (Atlanta: Scholars Press, 1991), 55. The sequence of ideas is reminiscent of the Cretan law of Gortyn, according to which a person ransomed from slavery became the servant of his ransomer until he paid him back (W. Westermann, *The Slave Systems of Greek and Roman Antiquity* [Phila-

delphia: American Philosophical Society, 1955], 44–45). See Weinfeld, Commentary, at 6:24.

67. See Saadia, *Book of Beliefs and Opinions*, 2:11. For the inalienability of inherited land see Lev. 25:14–28; Ezek. 46:16–18; cf. Ps. 94:14.

68. See Isa. 48:10. I owe information on the smelting of iron to James D. Muhly.

69. Cf. Abravanel, 45 col. i, question 12.

70. Meir Simḥah Ha-Kohen of Dvinsk (1843–1926), *Meshekh Ḥokhmah* (ref. courtesy Moshe Garfein); Ehrlich, *Randglossen* and *Mikra*.

71. For the connection of vv. 23–24 and 25–31, see Weinfeld, Commentary, 207. The Masoretic and Samaritan texts consider verse 25 to be the beginning of a new unit, apparently because verses 25–31 deal with the distant future instead of the present. Although the framing effect of v. 31 is literarily impressive, vv. 29–31 are probably a late interpolation; see the final introductory Comment there and Excursus 5.

72. See Lev. 10:2; Num. 11:1–3; 16:35. Fire also represents God's destructive power in Deut. 9:3; 32:22; 2 Kings 1:10–14; Amos 1:4; Ps. 79:5. It represents His presence for benign purposes in Gen. 15:17; Exod. 3:2–6; 24:17. For fire as a divine symbol see M. Greenberg, *Understanding Exodus* (New York: Behrman House, 1969), 71.

73. See M. Weinfeld, "Possession of the Land" (Hebrew), *Zion* 49 (1983–84): 115–137.

74. Rashi at 30:19 and 32:1.

75. See the treaties translated in ANET, 200–201, 205–206, 534–535, 538–541, 659–660.

76. Ibn Ezra; Rashbam; Rashi at 32:1 (prevent later denial, and execute punishment); Ḥazzekuni at Deut. 30:19 (execute reward and punishment). Cf. also Lev. 18:24–28.

77. Abravanel; Shadal.

78. There is, for example, no evidence that the Babylonians attempted to force the Jewish exiles to worship Babylonian gods (the incidents described in Dan. 3 and 6 are not deliberate attempts to do so; see Y. Kaufmann, *History of the Religion of Israel*, trans. C. W. Efroymson [New York: Ktav, 1977], 4:498).

79. See Hos. 9:3,4; Amos 7:17. Even the altar built by the tribes settled in Transjordan was regarded as illegitimate by the other tribes who thought that it would be used for sacrifice (see Josh. 22).

80. See the views summarized by L. I. Rabinowitz, s.v. "Synagogue," EncJud 15:579–581; L. I. Levine, *Ancient Synagogues Revealed* (Jerusalem: Israel Exploration Society, 1981), 1–4; L. Finkelstein, *Pharisaism in the Making* (New York: Ktav, 1972), 1–11; N. M. Sarna, "The Psalm Superscriptions and the Guilds," in S. Stein and R. Loewe, eds., *Studies . . . Alexander Altmann* (University, Ala.: University of Alabama Press, 1979), 281–300. In Elephantine, Egypt, during the Persian period and in Leontopolis, Egypt, in the Hellenistic period Jews actually offered sacrifices.

81. See, e.g., 2 Kings 19:18; Isa. 2:8; 44:9–20; 46:6–7; Jer. 10:3–5; 16:20; Pss. 115:4–7; 135:15–17; Dan. 5:23.

82. Cf. Av. Zar. 41b and S. Lieberman, HJP, 126. See W. G. Lambert, review of F. Gössmann, *Das Era-Epos*, in AfO 18 (1957–58): 398–400; Karl-Heinz Bernhardt, *Gott und Bild* (Berlin: Evangelische Verlagsanstalt, 1956); G. von Rad, *Theology of the Old Testament* (New York: Harper and Row, 1962), 1:214; E. M. Curtis, *Man as the Image of God in Genesis in the Light of Ancient Near Eastern Parallels*, Ph.D. diss., University of Pennsylvania (Ann Arbor, Mich.: University Microfilms, 1985), 97–142.

83. Fetish is used here in the sense of "an inanimate object worshiped . . . on account of its supposed inherent magical powers" (*Oxford English Dictionary*; cf. Kaufmann, *Religion*, 9, 14), like a rabbit's foot. On the image as a living being see further H. Frankfort, *Kingship and the Gods* (Chicago: Univer-

sity of Chicago Press, 1948), 302–306; J. Faur, "The Biblical Idea of Idolatry," JQR 69 (1978): 1–15.

84. Plutarch, *Isis and Osiris*, 71, quoted by Bevan, *Holy Images*, 22. The term "god" was used to mean the idol in Hebrew and other Semitic languages, too (see Comment to 3:24), and as in the cases reported by Plutarch, what was done to the image was said to be done to the god; see Gen. 35:2,4; Judg. 18:24; 2 Kings 19:17–18; CAD I/J, 102–103.

85. As noted above, this may be what happened in the case of the golden calves of Jeroboam, too. See Comment to 9:16 and Excursus 12.

86. See Kaufmann, *Religion*, 9–20.

87. On "finding" God see Jer. 29:13–14; on the covenant with the patriarchs see also Lev. 26:39–45.

88. See, e.g., Lev. 26:39–45; Deut. 29:21–30:5; Amos 9:8–12. For examples of inalienable grants see Weinfeld, DDS, 78–79, 81; idem, "The Covenant of Grant in the Old Testament and in the Ancient Near East," JAOS 90 (1970): 189–196, 199. McCarthy compares the fact that ancient kings sometimes forgave repentant vassals who had been unfaithful (D. J. McCarthy, *Treaty and Covenant*, rev. ed. [Rome: Biblical Institute Press, 1981], 205 n. 39).

89. H. Z. Hirschberg, s.v. *'aharit ha-yamim*, EM 1:230–234; G. Buchanan, "Eschatology and the 'End of Days,'" JNES 20 (61): 188–193; cf. Akk. *arkiat umi* (CAD A2, 282–283). As Weinfeld notes, "in the end" should probably precede "and."

90. Lev. 26:40–42; Deut. 4:29–31; 30:1–10. See J. Milgrom, *Cult and Conscience* (Leiden: Brill, 1976), §§71–72; s.v. "Repentance," IDBS, 736–738; cf. sources cited in S. Liebermann, *Midrash Devarim Rabbah*, 2nd ed. (Jerusalem: Wahrmann, 1965), 16 and 58.

91. See, e.g., Jer. 18:7–11; cf. Jonah 3:8–10; Isa. 1:16–20.

92. See esp. Exod. 34:6–7 and 14; Nah. 1:2–3.

93. See also Deut. 32:17; Jer. 5:7; Hos. 8:6; 2 Chron. 13:9.

94. Rabbinic literature cites this verse as discouraging speculation about events that preceded the creation of the world. This is because the mystical-philosophical doctrines associated with such speculation in rabbinic times were conducive to theological confusion and heresy. See, e.g., Ḥag. 11b; Gen. R. 1:10; cf. Loewenstamm, *Comparative Studies*, 122–136). This is not the plain sense of the verse, but it is consistent with the Torah's lack of interest in events that preceded creation. This is in striking contrast to ancient mythology, which tells of events preceding even the birth of the gods. For this subject see Sarna, *Genesis*, introduction to chap. 1.

95. Cf. Isa. 13:5 with Deut. 28:49, and see Comment to 2:25.

96. Gen. 32:31; Exod. 3:6; 19:21; 33:20–23; Judg. 13:22; Isa. 6:5 (exceptions are usually described as such; see, in addition to some of the verses just listed, Exod. 24:10–11; Num. 12:8; Deut. 34:10; Ezek. 1:26–28).

97. See, e.g., Exod. 6:1,6; 7:3; 14:14 (the verbal form of "war").

98. See Greenberg, cited in the endnote to v. 10.

99. A. Rofé, "The Monotheistic Argumentation in Deuteronomy 4:32–40: Contents, Composition and Text," VT 35 (1985): 434–445. Similarly, as in Elijah's confrontation with the prophets of Baal, when Baal did not respond to his prophets' entreaties the people declared that the Lord is the only true God (1 Kings 18:19–39).

100. For other aspects of vv. 32–40 reflected in Jewish liturgy see Weinfeld, Commentary, 210–211, 223–230.

101. Sifra (Weiss, 3a); A. Steinsaltz, ed., *Midrash Ha-Gadol . . . Sefer Va-Yikra'* (Jerusalem: Mossad Harav Kook, 1975), 28; MdRY Ba-Ḥodesh 9 (Lauterbach 2:275–276). See A. J. Heschel, *The Theology of Ancient Judaism* 2 (Hebrew) (London: Soncino, 1965), 58–60. Neh. 9:13 seems to represent a slightly different way of resolving the inconsistency: "You came down on Mount Sinai and spoke to them from heaven" seems to imply that God did come down, but returned to heaven before speaking.

102. Weinfeld, DDS, 190–209. Contrast Gen. 11:5,7; 18:21; Exod. 3:8; 34:5; Num. 11:17,25; 12:5 (descending to earth) and Exod. 25:8; 29:45 and Deut. 12:5,11,21; 16:2 (dwelling in the sanctuary). On Deut. 23:15 see chap. 23, n. 47.

103. See also Deut. 7:6–8,13; 10:15; 14:2; 23:6.

104. See Deut. 8:5; 14:1; 32:5,19,20 (cf. Exod. 4:22; Jer. 3:19; 31:8,19; Hos. 11:1; Prov. 3:12). For the metaphor of husband and wife see the passages cited in the endnotes to the Comment to 5:9–10 and cf. Weinfeld, DDS, 328. It has been suggested that the metaphor of love between God and Israel is based on ancient Near Eastern texts in which love refers to the political loyalty of a vassal to his suzerain or a subject toward a king. See Comment to 6:5.

105. See also Ps. 2:6–8 where the coronation of the king is described as his adoption by God, in the course of which an inheritance is assigned to him (see J. Tigay, s.v. "Adoption," EncJud 2:300).

106. See Exod. 33:14–15 (contrast v. 2 and 32:34); 2 Sam. 17:11; Baḥya at Exod. 20:3; Dillmann at Exod. 33:14. See also Isa. 63:8–9 and the note of NJPS there.

107. Exod. 12:23 (cf. Ps. 78:49); 14:19; 23:20–23; Josh. 5:13–15; Judg. 2:1–5. Note also the plan announced by God in Exod. 32:34 and 33:2 (withdrawn in 33:14).

108. The view that Num. 20:16 refers to Moses is cited by Rashi from Tanḥuma and relies on such verses as Hag. 1:13 and 2 Chron. 36:16; it is rejected by Ibn Ezra.

109. See Licht in EM 4:982–984; Weinfeld, DDS, 34; S. E. Loewenstamm, *The Tradition of the Exodus* (Hebrew) (Jerusalem: Magnes Press, 1965), 56–57, 92–93; Rofé, *Israelite Belief in Angels*, 255ff.

110. See J. Goldin, *Studies in Midrash* (Philadelphia: Jewish Publication Society, 1988), 163–173; Finkelstein, *Pharisaism in the Making*, 306–309; B. J. Bamberberger et al., s.v. "Angels and Angelology," EncJud 2: 956–972.

111. See 30:1; 1 Kings 8:47; Isa. 44:19; 46:8; Lam. 3:21.

112. Deut. R. 2:28. "Heaven and earth" may function as a merism.

113. Cf. Pss. 25:13; 112:2; Prov. 13:22; 14:26.

114. Hebrew texts have breaks before v. 41 and after v. 49 (M and SP). In separating vv. 41–49 both from what precedes and what follows them, these texts seem to imply that their relationship to their context is unclear. The chapter division apparently considers all of vv. 41–49 as supplementary to chap. 4 and not introductory to chap. 5.

115. See Liebermann, *Midrash Devarim Rabbah*, 57–58; Deut. R. 2:26–27.

116. According to Josh. 20, all six cities were designated by Joshua. Hoffman resolves this inconsistency by presuming that Moses told Joshua which cities to choose in Transjordan and Joshua formally designated them later. According to A. Rofé, the plural verbs in the Hebrew text of Josh. 20:7–8 imply that Moses as well as Joshua had a hand in choosing the cities (Rofé in J. Tigay, ed., *Empirical Models for Biblical Criticism* [Philadelphia: University of Pennsylvania Press, 1985], 135, 143). The fact that in Deut. 19 Moses does not refer to his designation of the Transjordanian cities has suggested to some scholars that our passage was added to the text at a later date. See Driver; Mayes; Rofé, "The History of the Cities of Refuge," in S. Japhet, ed., *Studies in Bible* (Jerusalem: Magnes Press, 1986), 227. The fact that v. 41 uses *'az*, "then," instead of Deuteronomy's usual "at that time," may support the view that the note is non-Deuteronomic.

Chapters 4:44–5:30

1. See chaps. 2–3, n. 44.

2. See Y. Ikeda, "Hermon, Sirion, and Senir," AJBI 4 (1978): 44 n. 58.

3. See A. Toeg, *Lawgiving at Sinai* (Hebrew) (Jerusalem: Magnes Press, 1977), 130–131.

4. See Y. Kaufmann, *The Religion of Israel*, trans. M. Greenberg (Chicago: University of Chicago Press, 1960), 171–172; R. de Vaux, *Ancient Israel* (New York: McGraw-Hill, 1961), 147–151; M. Greenberg, "Some Postulates of Biblical Criminal Law," in M. Haran, ed., *Yehezkel Kaufmann Jubilee Volume* (Jerusalem: Magnes Press, 1960), 9–13. In the Bible, laws are given by Moses and Ezekiel, and "the rule of the monarchy" by Samuel (1 Sam. 10:25).

5. See Lev. 19; Pss. 15; 24:3–5; contrast Lev. 5.

6. Abravanel, 61, 71.

7. See TJ Ber. 1:8, 3c; cf. the view attributed to Korah in Yal., Num. 752, 502b (cited in Ginzberg, *Legends*, 6: 101 n. 568). See A. J. Heschel, *The Theology of Ancient Judaism* (Hebrew) (London: Soncino, 1965), 2:108–110. That this view was held by a Christian sect is noted by Heschel, 110, and S. D. McBride, "The Yoke of the Kingdom," *Interpretation* 27 (1973): 276 n. 3.

8. The chapter is divided as follows: before vv. 1 (M, SP, chapters), 6 and 19 (M, SP); 25b (SP); after 30 (SP, chapters). On the end of the chapter see introductory Comments to 6:1–3. The Decalogue is subdivided before vv. 11 (M), 12 and 16 (M, SP), all four commandments in v. 17 (M), and both sentences in v. 18 (M).

9. Kid. 29a; Maimonides, Hilkhot Talmud Torah 1:3.

10. See Exod. 19:5,8; 24:3,7,8.

11. See Jer. 34:18 and cf. the Assyrian treaty in ANET, 532–533. See J. G. Frazer, *Folklore in the Old Testament*, abridged ed. (New York: Tudor, 1923), 153–172, supplemented by T. H. Gaster, *Myth, Legend, and Custom* (New York: Harper and Row, 1969), §53; Sarna, *Genesis*, at 15:9–17.

12. Rashi.

13. Mid. Hag.; Ibn Ezra; Maimonides, Guide 1.37 (citing Job 1:11 and 2 Kings 14:8 for the sense "in person"); Abravanel at Deut. 34:10 (354–360).

14. Hoffmann; Driver.

15. The inconsistency between vv. 4 and 5 is matched by inconsistencies within Exod. 19–20 and between Exodus and Deuteronomy. Critical theory holds that "the accounts apparently combine different versions of the event: (a) God spoke with Moses, and the people overheard; (b) He spoke with Moses and then Moses transmitted His words to the people; (c) God spoke to the people directly" (M. Greenberg, s.v. "Decalogue," EncJud 5:1436). See also J. Licht, "The Sinai Theophany" (Hebrew), in Y. Avishur and J. Blau, eds., *Studies in Bible and the Ancient Near East* (Jerusalem: Rubinstein, 1978), 1: 266–267; Toeg, *Lawgiving at Sinai* 58, 136; B. S. Childs, *The Book of Exodus* (Philadelphia: Westminster Press, 1974), 351–360; R. R. Wilson, *Prophecy and Society in Ancient Israel* (Philadelphia: Fortress Press, 1989), 163.

16. Mak. 24a; Hor. 8a.

17. See Greenberg, s.v. "Decalogue," EncJud 5:1435–1446; N. M. Sarna, *Exploring Exodus* (New York: Schocken, 1986), 134–148.

18. Abravanel, 73.

19. Hence the tablets on which the commandments are written are called the Tablets of the Covenant (9:9,11,15) and the Ark in which they are kept is called the Ark of the Covenant (10:1–8).

20. Philo, Decal., 154; for rabbinic sources see E. E. Urbach, *The Sages* (Cambridge: Harvard University Press, 1987), 360–364; cf. Greenberg, s.v. "Decalogue," EncJud 5:1446.

21. Philo, Decal., 52–174; Josephus, Ant. 3.91–92; Sifrei Num. 112, p. 121; Sanh. 99a; Hor. 8b.

22. MdRY Baḥodesh 6 (Lauterbach 2:237–238); SP; Ibn Ezra at Deut. 5:16 (contrast n. 24 below); Abravanel; Driver; M. Noth, *Exodus* (Philadelphia: Westminster Press, 1962), 161–162.

23. MT parashah division; Josephus, Ant. 3.91; Philo, Decal., 52–65; R. Ishmael in Sifrei Num. 112, p. 121; AT; Greenberg, s.v. "Decalogue," EncJud 5:1442.

24. Targ. Jon.; Targ. Neof.; MdRY Ba-Ḥodesh 8 (Lauterbach 2:262); R. Hamnuna in Mak. 24a; R. Levi in TJ Ber. 1:8, 3c; Maimonides, Hilkhot Yesodei Ha-Torah 1:6; idem, Sefer Ha-Mitsvot, positive no. 1; Ramban; Hoffmann; cf. Ibn Ezra's comments on Exodus in A. Weiser, ed., *Perushei Ha-Torah le-Rabbenu 'Avraham 'ibn 'Ezra* (Jerusalem: Mosad Ha-Rav Kook, 1976), 2:128, 131, 281, 282.

25. Abravanel notes that the Decalogue consists of practical commandments, since beliefs are not subject to legislation. See his question 7 and answers 2, 4, and 7–9.

26. Note esp. Gen. 15:7; Lev. 18:1–2 and throughout chaps. 18–22; Num. 15:41. See also Gen. 17:1–2; 26:24; 28:13; 31:13; 35:11–12; 46:3–4; Exod. 6:2–8,29; 12:12; for ancient Near Eastern parallels see ANET, 605.

27. Rashi; cf. Lev. 25:55; Deut. 6:20–25.

28. Cf. Hos. 13:1–5; Josh. 24:16–18; 2 Kings 17:35–39; in Deut. 13:6 and 11 the Exodus is cited in motive clauses explaining the punishment of inciters to apostasy (the language is nearly identical to that in our verse). The notion that Israel is obligated to God because He freed it from Egypt constitutes the logic behind the NJPS translation of v. 6, which takes YHVH ("the LORD") as appositive and "your God" as predicative (following Ibn Ezra; Weisel, cited by Luzzatto; and Ehrlich). Thus understood, the point of the clause is that "I, YHVH, *and no other*, am your God who liberated you from Egypt." However, in every other occurrence of *YHVH 'eloheikha* in Deuteronomy, the two words constitute a single phrase meaning "the LORD your God" (regarding 6:4, see Excursus 10). Furthermore, there are similar verses where YHVH or other names are predicative (cf. Gen. 15:7; 45:4; and Lev. 18–22, where *'ani YHVH 'eloheikhem* alternates with *'ani YHVH*). Thus, the ancient rendering "I am YHVH your God" is also possible (LXX, Targ. Jon., Vulg., Pesh.). In that case, the point of the clause is to identify the Lord in advance as the referent of "Me" in the first commandment, v. 7.

29. This concept is expressed often; see, e.g., Deut. 6:10–15; 32:12; 2 Kings 17:35–39. Ibn Ezra and Shadal hold that the Decalogue cites the Exodus rather than the creation because belief in the creation requires philosophical demonstration, since it is not an observable experience, and because it could not serve as the basis for obligations unique to Israel since it applies to all other nations as well.

30. M. Weinfeld, "The Loyalty Oath in the Ancient Near East," *Shnaton* 1 (1975): 60.

31. See Judg. 8:22; 11:8–11; 1 Sam. 11; 2 Sam. 5:1–3. Cf. MdRY Ba-Ḥodesh 5 (Lauterbach 2:229–230); M. Greenberg, "On the Refinement of the Conception of Prayer in Hebrew Scriptures," AJSR 1 (1976): 64–66.

32. Weinfeld, DDS, 81–82.

33. Exod. 6:6–7; Isa. 42:7; Jer. 52:31; for "save" see 2 Sam. 22:49; Ps. 18:20.

34. R. Boling, *Judges* (Garden City, N.Y.: Doubleday, 1975), at Judg. 6:8; cf. Moffatt here ("that slave-pen"). Cf. "house of prisoners" = prison (Judg. 16:21) and "house of women" = harem (Est. 2:9).

35. See Exod. 13:3,14; Deut. 6:12; Judg. 6:8; Mic. 6:4.

36. Ralbag at Exod. 20:2 (ed. Venice [1547], 75d); similarly Abravanel on Exodus, 186.

37. See ANET, 19, 259.

38. See ANET, 234–264 and 553–554; Abd al-Muhsin Bakir, *Slavery in Pharaonic Egypt* (Cairo: Institute français d'archeologie orientale, 1952); J. Vergote, *Joseph en Égypte* (Louvaine, 1959), 16–19.

39. See Gen. 47:13–26, esp. v. 25. Cf. J. Wilson, *The Culture of Ancient Egypt* (Chicago: University of Chicago Press, 1959), 201, 271; M. Greenberg, *Understanding Exodus* (New York: Behrman House, 1969), 198; W. F. Edgerton, "The Government

and the Governed in the Egyptian Empire," *JNES* 6 (1947): 152–160.

40. Not even the so-called monotheism of the Egyptian Pharaoh Akhenaton (1369–1353) was completely monolatrous, since it entailed worship of the king in addition to the sun god. See Wilson, *Culture of Ancient Egypt*, 223–225.

41. Ḥazzekuni.

42. See also chap. 8; 32:12–18; Josh. 24:16–18; Hos. 13:1–6.

43. Exod. 2:10; Deut. 24:2; Judg. 14:20; 15:2; 2 Sam. 7:14; Ezek. 16:8 (parallel to "enter a covenant"); Hos. 3:3. In Neh. 6:6 the idiom is used for becoming a nation's king. The relational connotations of the idiom are confirmed by the fact that it alternates with "taking" or "establishing" someone as a wife or a people (cf. Deut. 24:2 with 24:1; Judg. 15:2 with 14:2–3,8; 1 Kings 4:11 with v. 16; Lev. 26:12b with Exod. 6:7; Deut. 9:12; and 2 Sam. 7:24a). A violation of our commandment is described in Judg. 8:33 as "they adopted [*va-yasimu*] Baal-berith as a god."

44. See also Gen. 17:7–8; Weinfeld, DDS, 80–81, 327, 6; Y. Muffs, *Love and Joy* (New York: Jewish Theological Seminary, 1992), 49–51; Sarna, *Exodus*, at 6:7; Levine, *Leviticus*, at 26:12.

45. See, e.g., Exod. 22:19; 23:13; Num. 25:2–3; Deut. 6:13; 18:20; 1 Kings 11:7–10; 2 Kings 1:2–6. For "having a deity as one's god" see Gen. 28:20–22 [cf. 35:1–7]; cf. ANET, 350b: "he will make these into his personal god. He will make vows to thee." Halakhic exegesis took this verse as forbidding the possession of idols, as distinct from v. 8, which forbids their manufacture (MdRY Ba-Ḥodesh 4 [Lauterbach 2:223]; Rashi).

46. See Ramban.

47. MdRY Ba-Ḥodesh 5 (Lauterbach 2:239); Rashi; Ibn Ezra. Some critical commentators think that this usage indicates that the prohibition on worshiping other gods was established at a time when the existence of other gods was not yet denied. It is true that no such denial is reported in the Torah earlier than Moses' farewell speech forty years after the proclamation of the Decalogue. However, it is not certain that the Decalogue is premonotheistic—or, to put it in other words, that monotheism is later than the Decalogue. See Excursus 6.

48. See also the first clause of Deut. 32:17 compared with the second and with v. 39, as well as the extra clause in some versions of 32:43, "let all divinities bow to Him" (see Excursus 31). For Jeremiah, see above. The second part of the book of Isaiah avoids this usage almost completely, but cf. end of 45:20 with 22b.

49. The translation construes *ʿal panai* as *ʿal*, "in addition to" (see also Gen. 28:9; Num. 28:10,15,24; 11QTemple 57:17; BDB, 755, secs. 2, 4a–b) plus *panim* in its sense of "oneself" (Ralbag; see Comment to 4:37). Others explain it as the compound preposition *ʿal-penei* with pronominal suffix (see BDB, 818–819, sec. 7; HALAT, 890). Apposite usages of the compound preposition include "in front of," perhaps extended here to mean "in preference to (Me)" (cf. possibly Deut. 21:16), and "to one's face," defiantly (e.g., Job 1:11). However, *ʿal-penei* probably carries these nuances only in the company of particular verbs; it is not clear whether it carries them when used with *hayah*, as here. In Job 16:14, the compound preposition is used in the sense of "in addition to" (cf. Punic *ʿlt pn* in KAI 69:3, 5–6, 9–10; Akkadian *ana pan* in EA 189:4; Gurney, "The Cuthean Legend of Naram-Sin," *Anatolian Studies* 5 (1955): 104–105, l. 109). However, this usage is not common. For further discussion see Weinfeld, Commentary, 276–277.

50. Ibn Ezra, introduction to Exod. 20 (ed. Weiser, 133). Cases in point are the idolatrous kings of Judah who introduced the worship of several other gods into the temple of YHVH (2 Kings 23:4,11).

51. See Comment to 4:28 and Kaufmann, *Religion*, 9–20, 236–237.

52. Some ancient and modern translations, along with 4QDeut[n] and SP, read *pesel vekhol temunah*, which would affect this interpretation (see chap. 4, n. 43); however, this reading is a secondary attempt to harmonize the text with Exod. 20:4. The reading in the MT of Deuteronomy seems to be the original one (H. Holzinger, *Exodus* [Tübingen: J.C.B. Mohr (P. Siebeck), 1900], 20:4).

53. Amos 5:26; Deut. 16:21–22; Judg. 8:27. See the illustrations of cultic objects in ANEP, figs. 869–872, 874; Y. Yadin et al., *Hazor* I (Jerusalem: Magnes Press, 1958), pl. 155; R. Hestrin and M. Dayagi-Mendels, *Inscribed Seals* (Jerusalem: Israel Museum, 1979), no. 97. On sacred trees and pillars, see Comments to 7:5, 16:21–22.

54. For a thorough discussion of vv. 9–10 see M. Weiss, "Some Problems of the Biblical 'Doctrine of Retribution,'" part 2, *Tarbiz* 32 (1962–63): 1–18.

55. MdRY Baḥodesh 8 (Lauterbach 2:262–263).

56. For "bow" meaning prostrate oneself see LXX; Hor. 4a; Neh. 8:6; 2 Chron. 20:18; for "serve" referring to sacrifice see Ibn Ezra; Exod. 10:26; Isa. 19:21. Together the two verbs stand for the full gamut of ritual observances (Maimonides, Sefer Ha-Mitsvot, negative nos. 5–6) such as "fear, bow down, serve, and sacrifice" (2 Kings 17:35); see Deut. 30:16–17; Judg. 2:12–13; 1 Kings 9:9. They are also used with reference to serving kings/suzerains, as in Gen. 27:29; Ps. 72:11, where "serve" must mean "pay tribute."

57. Abravanel; Shadal; Hoffmann; Cassuto.

58. Rashi at Exod. 20:5 and Num. 11:29 and at Git. 7a; H. M. Orlinsky, *Notes on the New Translation of the Torah* (Philadelphia: Jewish Publication Society, 1969), 175; Shadal; H. A. Brongers, "Der Eifer des Herrn Zebaoth," VT 13 (1963): 269–284. For the connection with fire see also Zeph. 3:8; Ps. 79:5. For love see Song 8:6.

59. M. Greenberg, *Ezekiel 1–20* (Garden City, N.Y.: Doubleday, 1983), 115.

60. Exod. 34:14; Deut. 4:24; 6:15; 32:16,21; cf. Josh. 24:19; 1 Kings 14:22; Ezek. 8:3; Ps. 78:58. See Maimonides, Guide 1.36; Ramban to Exod. 20:5; the prophets use the term more broadly (Nah. 1:2; Zech. 1:14).

61. Bekhor Shor; Ramban; Sforno; for the meaning "jealous" see Gen. 37:11; Num. 5:11–31; Prov. 6:34.

62. Hos. 1–3; Jer. 2:2,23–25,32; 3:1–13,20; Isa. 50:1; 54:4–7; 62:4–5; Lam. 1:1–2,19.

63. Bekhor Shor; Ramban; Abravanel; Ehrlich, *Mikra*; see Gerson D. Cohen, *Studies in the Variety of Rabbinic Cultures* (Philadelphia: Jewish Publication Society, 1991), 3–17.

64. MdRY Ba-Ḥodesh 6 (Lauterbach 2:244–246); MdRSbY to Exod. 20:5, 147–148.

65. Maimonides, Guide 1.54.

66. See A. J. Heschel, *The Prophets* (New York: Harper and Row, 1962), chaps. 12–18. esp. p. 283.

67. Targ. Jon.; MdRSbY to Exod. 20:5, p. 147: 21–22; Rashi; see Deut. 4:24; 6:15; 32:16; Josh. 24:19; Nah. 1:2; Zeph. 3:8. See also Prov. 27:4 and 14:30 (*kin'ah* is irresistible and unrelenting, the antithesis of "a heart which relents"; see H. L. Ginsberg, *Koheleth* [Tel Aviv and Jerusalem: M. Newman, 1961], 119–120). Cf. Prov. 6:34–35: "The fury of the [betrayed] husband will be passionate" (*kin'ah*, lit., "jealousy") and he will insist on punishment.

68. Abravanel; Hoffmann.

69. Ramban; cf. Exod. 32:34; Isa. 27:1; Amos 3:14.

70. The first meaning seems implied in our verse, Gen. 50:23, and Num. 14:18. The second is clear in Exod. 34:7. See Ramban at Exod. 20:5; Hoffmann at Deut. 5:10; Dillmann at Gen. 50:23; Buhl, 839; Weinfeld, Commentary.

71. The phrase is attested frequently as an expression of a long life; see Gen. 50:23; Job 42:16; ANET, 561c, 661d; A. Malamat, "Longevity: Biblical Concepts and Some Ancient Near Eastern Parallels," in *AfO Beiheft* 19 (1982): 216–218.

72. Maimonides, Guide 1.54, followed by many others.

73. Hoffmann.

74. On *sane'* see Gen. 26:27; 29:30–31; Exod. 23:5; Deut. 21:15; 24:3; Judg. 11:7; 15:2; and Orlinsky, *Notes*, on most of those passages. Akkadian *zêru*, "hate," has the same range of meanings.

75. See M. Weiss, *Tarbiz* 32:14–15.

76. See also Gen. 20:13; 24:49; 47:29; 2 Sam. 10:2; 1 Kings 2:7.

77. On the meaning of *hesed* see N. Glueck, *The Word Hesed*; N. Snaith, *Distinctive Ideas of the Old Testament* (New York: Schocken, 1964), 94–130; K. D. Sakenfeld, *The Meaning of Hesed in the Hebrew Bible* (Missoula, Mont.: Scholars Press, 1978).

78. See 1 Sam. 18:1,3; 20:17; 1 Kings 5:15; cf. ANET, 483d ll. 47–48; 537 par. 24. See discussion by W. L. Moran, "The Ancient Near Eastern Background of the Love of God in Deuteronomy," CBQ 25 (1963): 77–87; M. Fishbane, "The Treaty Background of Amos 1:11 and Related Matters," JBL 89 (1970): 316; idem, "Additional Remarks on *rhmyw* (Amos 1:11)," JBL 91 (1972): 393; Weinfeld, DDS, 82 n. 6; Greenberg, "Conception of Prayer," 67–68.

79. That the commandment refers to swearing is understood in the apparent allusions to it in Jer. 7:9, Hos. 4:2, and by Philo, Decal., 82–95; Josephus, Ant. 3.91; Targums; Pesh.; Saadia; MdRY Ba-Hodesh 7 (Lauterbach 2:248); Shab. 120a and other talmudic sources; Rashi; Bekhor Shor; Ibn Ezra; Ramban; Shadal. "Taking the name" is elliptical for taking it *upon one's lips or mouth*, that is, uttering it (cf. Pss. 16:4; 50:16; cf. KAI 224:14–15). Similar expressions refer to taking oaths. Cf. "utter God's life" (that is, say "by the life of the LORD") and "invoke the God of Israel/the LORD" (Ps. 24:4; Isa. 48:1; 2 Sam. 14:11). For "a vain thing" meaning "falsehood," see v. 17 (Exod. 20:13 explicitly reads "falsehood"); Ezek. 13:8; Ps. 144:8,11.

80. Exod. 22:7,10; Judg. 21:1,5; 1 Kings 17:12; for similar oaths in ancient Hebrew letters, see Lachish ostraca nos. 3 and 6 in ANET, 322.

81. "For an oath is an appeal to God as a witness on matters in dispute, and to call him as witness to a lie is the height of profanity" (Philo, Decal., 86). "The practice in Egypt to this day is that if a man swears by the head of the king, and does not keep his word, he is doomed to die . . . because he has insulted the king publicly" (Ibn Ezra at Exod. 20:7).

82. Maimonides, Hilkhot Shevuot 1:4–7; cf. Josephus, Ant. 3.91.

83. See Ber. 33a; M. M. Kasher, *Torah Shelemah* 16 (New York: American Biblical Encyclopedia Society, 1954), 187–199; Ramban; Abravanel; cf. Josephus, Ant. 3.91; Philo, Decal., 92. Several Akkadian texts speak of the sin of swearing by one's god "lightly, frivolously" (ANET, 597c; cf. BWL, 38; W. G. Lambert, "DINGIR ŠÀ.DIB.BA Incantations," JNES 33 (1974): 274 l. 24, 278 l. 87, and 289 l. 12).

84. See 1 Kings 2:9; Exod. 34:7; Jer. 30:11; Ps. 19:13; the *niph'al hinnakeh* usually means "go unpunished, escape punishment"; see Jer. 25:29; Prov. 19:5,9.

85. W. Beyerlin, *Near Eastern Religious Texts Relating to the Old Testament* (Philadelphia: Westminster Press, 1978), 36.

86. Weinfeld, Commentary.

87. Ibn Ezra; Shadal. On the Sabbath see M. Greenberg, s.v. "Sabbath," EncJud 14:558–562; J. Tigay, s.v. *Shabbat*, EM 7:504–517.

88. See Gen. 8:22; Josh. 5:12; Isa. 14:4; Neh. 6:3.

89. See Lev. 19:3–4; 26:2; Ezek. 20:16–24.

90. These phrases are discussed by J. Milgrom, "Profane Slaughter and a Formulaic Key to the Composition of Deuteronomy," HUCA 47 (1976): 1–17.

91. Exod. 16:23–30; 34:21; 35:3; Num. 15:32–36; Amos 8:5; Jer. 17:21–22; Neh. 13:15–21.

92. Mish. Shab. 7:2–4; Shab. 49b; MdRY Shabbata 2 (Lauterbach 2:205–206).

93. See Exod. 22:29; Lev. 22:27–28; Deut. 22:6–7,10; 25:4.

94. See Exod. 21:20–21,26–27; Deut. 15:13–15,18; 16:11–12; 23:16.

95. Deut. 21:18–21; Prov. 23:22.

96. Prov. 1:8–9.

97. Exod. 21:15,17; Lev. 20:9; Deut. 27:16; Prov. 30:17.

98. Prov. 28:24.

99. Kid. 31b.

100. See Gen. 45:11; Ruth 4:14–15; Tob. 4:3; 14:13; ANET, 219–220 (Nuzi-Akkadian adoption contracts; note that "revere" in text no. 3 = "provide food and clothing" in text no. 2); Plato, *Laws*, 4:717 (ministering to aged parents part of honoring them); Josephus, Ant. 4.261; R. Albertz, "Hintergrund und Bedeutung des Elterngebots im Dekalog," ZAW 90 (1978): 348–374; J. C. Greenfield, "*adi baltu*—Care for the Elderly and Its Rewards," in *AfO Beiheft* 19 (1982): 309–316; idem, "Two Biblical Passages in Light of their Near Eastern Background," EI 16 (1982): 57–59. Note that Ruth 4:14–15 is connected with the naming of the child Oved ("Minister"); cf. the use of *'oved* in Mal. 3:17.

101. See Greenfield, "*adi baltu*." The verb "honor" (*kabbed*) and its Ugaritic and Akkadian cognates are used for honoring with gifts, usually of food (e.g. Num. 22:17–18; Isa. 43:23; Mal. 1:6–8; Prov. 3:9); see UT 2 Aqht v, 20, 30; PRU 3:109, l. 12; BWL, 102: 62; CAD K, 17b; Ben Yehudah, 2225; Jastrow, 606; J. Naveh, "*Lemakhbiram* or *Lammekhabedim*?" EI 15 (1981): 301–302.

102. Plato, *Laws*, 4:717; a Sumero-Akkadian lexical text lists in order "one who respects the god, one who respects his father, one who reveres his mother" (CAD A1, 108). On the equivalence between honoring God and parents see also Philo, Decal., 106–107, 119–120; Josephus, Ant. 4.262, and other sources cited by Weinfeld, Commentary, 311.

103. MdRY Ba-Hodesh 8 (Lauterbach 2:259).

104. Ibid.; cf. Prov. 20:20.

105. Sifrei sec. 309 mentions disinheritance for failure to honor (in the sense of disrespect).

106. That translation goes back to the Vulgate, where it may be due to the fact that Latin (like Aramaic) lacks a verb that unambiguously means "murder." It is true that the Hebrew verb does not always refer to murder in the strict sense of the term; sometimes it refers to manslaughter (as in Deut. 19:4) and in one context it refers to the nonculpable execution of an accidental manslayer (Num. 25:27,30). The translation "kill" seems broad enough to include all these usages. However, the use of *ratsah* for executing a manslayer is exceptional, and is probably simply a literary device for showing that his death corresponds to his own deed. The term *ratsah* is never used elsewhere for killing (*harag* and *hemit* are used instead). Since *ratsah* refers to intentional and accidental killing, and the latter, being unintentional, cannot be prohibited, the command must refer to the former, and "you shall not murder" remains the best translation.

107. See HL §§1–5; Qur'an, 2:178; discussion by Greenberg, "Some Postulates of Biblical Criminal Law."

108. Abravanel, 219; cf. Fustel de Coulanges, *The Ancient City* (Garden City, N.Y.: Doubleday, n.d.), 97.

109. See ANET, 24b; J. J. Rabinowitz, "The 'Great Sin' in Ancient Egyptian Marriage Contracts," JNES 18 (1959): 73; W. L. Moran, "The Scandal of the 'Great Sin' at Ugarit," JNES 18 (1959): 280–281; cf. Fustel de Coulanges, *The Ancient City*, 97.

110. E.g., Prov. 2:16–19; 5:1–20; 6:24–35; 7:5–27.

111. Gen. 20:6; 39:9; Ps. 51:6; Prov. 2:17.

112. See LH §129; MAL §§14–16; and HL §§197–198; contrast Fustel de Coulanges, *The Ancient City*, 97. Whether biblical law permitted pardon of adultery is debated, primarily on the basis of Prov. 6:32–35; see M. Greenberg, "More Reflections on Biblical Criminal Law," in S. Japhet, ed., *Studies in Bible* (Jerusalem: Magnes Press, 1986), 1–4, and the earlier studies by Loewen-

stamm, Weinfeld, and Jackson cited there, n. 2; Rofé, *Mavo'*, 152–153; H. McKeating, "Sanctions Against Adultery in Ancient Israelite Society," JSOT 11 (1979): 57–72; A. Phillips "Another look at Adultery," JSOT 20 (1981): 3–26; R. Westbrook, "Adultery in Ancient Near Eastern Law," RB 97 (1990): 542–580. For the subject of adultery in the Bible in general see further J. Tigay, s.v. "Adultery," EncJud 2:313–315.

113. MdRY Ba-Ḥodesh 8 (Lauterbach 2:260–261). The same interpretation was advocated in modern times by A. Alt, *Kleine Schriften* (Munich: C. H. Beck, 1959), 1:333–340.

114. Cf. MdRSbY, 153. There are also cases in which the accuser is rewarded with the property of the accused if he is convicted. See LH §2; see J. J. Finkelstein in ANET, 252 n. 25; T. Frymer-Kensky, "Tit for Tat: The Principle of Equal Retribution in Near Eastern and Biblical Law," BA 43 (1980): 231.

115. *Ḥamad* is used of God in Ps. 68:17; *hit'avvah* describes the legitimate desire of a king for his bride in Ps. 45:12.

116. Cf. Mic. 2:2 in light of Prov. 31:16. See MdRY Ba-Ḥodesh 8 (Lauterbach 2:266); MdRSbY, 153, to Exod. 20:18; Maimonides, *Sefer Ha-Mitsvot*, negative nos. 265–266 ("scheming"); a Phoenician inscription uses the verb in the same way Exod. 34:24 does; see KAI 26 A 3, 14–15; C 4, 16–17. For discussion of the verbs in this commandment see Hoffmann, *Sefer Devarim*, vol. 1, Appendix; W. L. Moran, "The Conclusion of the Decalogue," CBQ 29 (1967): 543–548; Rofé, in Ben-Zion Segal and G. Levi, eds., *The Ten Commandments in History and Tradition* (Jerusalem: Magnes Press, 1990), 45–65; Greenberg, in Segal and Levi, *Ten Commandments*, 106–109.

117. On the grammatical form (durative *hitpa'el*) see Speiser, *Oriental and Biblical Studies* (Philadelphia: University of Pennsylvania Press, 1967), 506–514, esp. 508. Admittedly, this sense is often not clear from the context.

118. For this meaning see Gen. 7:1; 35:2; Lev. 16:6; Num. 16:32; Deut. 11:6.

119. See Gen. 12:5,16; 26:14; Num. 16:30,32; Deut. 11:6.

120. Cf. Greenberg, s.v. "Decalogue," EncJud 5:1441.

121. See Moran, "Conclusion of the Decalogue," 548–554; R. Westbrook, *Old Babylonian Marriage Law*, AfO Beiheft 23 (Horn, Austria: F. Berger, 1988), 115.

122. See also Exod. 19:18 and 16:10 and Deut. 1:33.

123. Such as Exod. 4:29–31; 16:16,32. If the people ever knew that God spoke to Moses out of the burning bush (Exod. 3:2–4), they have overlooked it.

124. Shadal; Ehrlich.

125. For the contrast with false gods see 2 Kings 19:16; Jer. 10:10; Dan. 6:21,27. The epithet is studied by A. Rofé, "David's Battle with Goliath," *Eshel Beer-Sheva* 3 (1986): 77–81.

126. Ber. 33b (see G. F. Moore, *Judaism* [Cambridge: Harvard University Press, 1958], 1:453–459). That God *can* control human behavior is indicated by the case of His hardening Pharaoh's heart, but such instances are exceptional; see Comment to 2:30. In contrast to our verse, Ecclesiastes, which challenges much of biblical doctrine, states that God does cause people to fear Him (Eccl. 3:14).

127. Deut. 6:1,25; 7:11; 8:1; 11:8,22; 15:5; 17:20; 19:9; 27:1; 30:11; 31:5.

Chapter 6

1. Hebrew texts have breaks before vv. 4 (XQphyl2 and 4Qphylʲ [but not 4Qphylʰ], M, SP), 10 (M, SP), 16 (M), 20 (M, SP), and after 25 (M, SP). For the Qumran texts, see Y. Yadin, *Tefillin from Qumran* (Jerusalem: Israel Exploration Society and The Shrine of the Book, 1969), 22, on slip no. 2. For the transition between chaps. 5 and 6 see also Rofé, *Mavo'*, chap. 23.

2. This difference in emphasis may be related to a doctrinal dispute; see chap. 5 n. 7.

3. Maimonides, Guide 3.52; Baḥya, Deut. 28:58.

4. See 4:10; 6:24; 14:23; 17:19; 31:12–13.

5. Lam. Rabbati, Petiḥta 2; TJ Ḥag. 1:7.

6. Abravanel, 73; cf. v. 24. For the translation of *lishmor* cf. *ledabber* in 11:19.

7. Literally the text reads "that you may increase greatly as the LORD, the God of your fathers, spoke to you—a land flowing with milk and honey." The translation, following Ibn Ezra, construes the last phrase as if it were preceded by "in" (the preposition could have dropped out by haplography after the preceding *lakh*). However, "a land flowing with milk and honey" is usually appositional, referring back to an antecedent such as "the land which the LORD is giving us" (see the list of passages in Excursus 9). This suggests that the phrase continues the thought of v. 1 (Ibn Ezra, alternate suggestion). Another possibility is that the entire second half of v. 3 refers back to the end of v. 1: "the land that you are about to cross into and occupy . . . as the LORD, the God of your fathers, spoke to you, a land flowing with milk and honey" (cf. 26:15; Ibn Janah, *Sefer Ha-Rikmah*, chap. 34, p. 366, ll. 22ff). In either case, there is ample precedent for a phrase to be separated from its antecedent by one or more verses; see esp. Exod. 33:3, as well as 22:2b; Deut. 5:5; Judg. 20:27–28; 1 Kings 6:1.

8. For further details on allusions to the Decalogue in chap. 6, see W. L. Moran, "The Ancient Near Eastern Background of the Love of God in Deuteronomy," CBQ 25 (1963): 85–87.

9. The verse is modeled on 4:45 and 6:1.

10. "One" (*'eḥad*) seems to mean "alone" in 1 Chron. 29:1 and possibly Josh. 22:20; cf. Job 23:13. For a similar usage in Ugaritic (*'ḥdy* = "I alone") see UT 51 vii, 49–50 (ANET, 135, col. vii, 50). For further examples of this usage see M. Weinfeld, "The Loyalty Oath in the Ancient Near East," UF 8 (1976): 409 n. 226.

11. See, e.g., Sifrei 32; Maimonides, Hilkhot Yesodei Ha-Torah 2:2; Abravanel, 106.

12. See W. L. Moran, "The Conclusion of the Decalogue," CBQ 29 (1967): 543–548; G. A. Anderson, *A Time to Mourn, A Time to Dance* (University Park: Pennsylvania State University Press, 1991), 9–13.

13. E.g., ANET, 538a. See R. Frankena, "The Vassal-Treaties of Esarhaddon and the Dating of Deuteronomy," OTS 14 (1965): 140–141.

14. Sifrei 32; Sot. 31a. Some sages considered fear of God to be a higher degree of piety, perhaps because they considered it a more effective deterrent to sin. See L. Finkelstein, *Introduction to the Treatises of Abot and Abot of Rabbi Nathan* (Hebrew) (New York: Jewish Theological Seminary, 1950), 33–35.

15. As in 8:2,5; 15:9–10; 19:6; 28:47; and 29:3; see also Num. 15:39; 2 Kings 5:26; Jer. 3:15; 1 Chron. 12:38.

16. As in 12:20; 23:25; 24:15; Gen. 23:8; 34:3; 44:30.

17. Sifrei 32, second interpretation of "with all your heart"; Shadal, end of comment on v. 4. Cf. Jer. 32:41 where the phrase means "with full resolve."

18. The unusual form "with all your plenty" conforms the phrase to the preceding ones, "with all your heart and with all your soul." The idiom cannot mean "with all your possessions" (see below); since it follows idioms that express completeness and depth of love, it must have a comparable meaning.

19. See Targ. Jon.; Sifrei 32; Mish. Ber. 9:5.

20. Cf. 1 Kings 2:23.

21. Linguistically this is possible. In Akkadian *ma'ādu* means "be plentiful, increase," and in the Hebrew of the Second Temple period there is a noun *me'od*, "property" (CD IX, 11; XII, 10; Ecclus. 7:30).

22. ANET, 484c. See also the Hittite treaty cited by Weinfeld, Commentary.

23. See Pss. 1:2; 40:9; 119:11,16.

24. See, e.g., 4:2,40; 6:1–2; 19:9; 28:1,14,15.

25. *Shanah*, meaning "teach," "repeat for the sake of teach-

ing" is common in rabbinic Hebrew; its Akkadian cognate *shunnû* has the same meaning in Enuma Elish VII, 147, quoted below in the commentary. For *sh-n-n* as an alternate form of *sh-n-h* see G. R. Driver, "Problems of the Hebrew Text and Language," in *Alttestamentliche Studien Friedrich Noetscher . . . Gewidmet* (Bonn: Peter Hanstein Verlag, 1950), 48; M. Tsevat, "Alalakhiana," *HUCA* 29 (1959): 125 n. 112. In Ecclus. (Ben Sira) 42:15 the Masada manuscript reads '-*sh-n-n-h*, "let me tell" (parallel to '-*z-k-r-h*, "let me recall"), which is replaced by '-*s-p-r-h* in the Genizah manuscript; it could be an imitation of our verse. Note also that the Ugaritic equivalent of *sh-n-h*, "do again" (1 Kings 18:34) is *th-n-n* (UT Krt v,8).

26. Maimonides, Sefer Ha-Mitsvot, positive no. 11; Kid. 29a.

27. Enuma Elish VII, 147; see ANET, 72c; cf. ANET, 380c.

28. ANET, 537b, 538a; Weinfeld, "Loyalty Oath," 392.

29. Bekhor Shor. Cf. 17:19; Josh. 1:8; Ps. 1:2.

30. Aramaic *totefta'* renders "armband" and "turban" in Targ. Jon. at 2 Sam. 1:10 and Ezek. 24:17,23. Tannaitic texts mention a woman's headdress called *totefet*, explained in the Gemara as a frontlet or "something which encompasses her [head] from ear to ear" (Mish. Shab. 6:1; Tosef. Shab. 4:6; Shab. 57b). These usages are compatible with an etymology deriving *totefet* (earlier *tawtefet*, originally *taftefet*) from a root *tuf*, known from Arabic *tāfa*, "encircle, encompass." The spelling of the final syllable of *totafot* without a *vav* in almost all biblical manuscripts indicates that it must originally have been intended as a singular noun, like the tannaitic *totefet*. See J. Tigay, "On the Meaning of *T(W)TPT*," JBL 101 (1982): 321–331.

31. See ANEP, nos. 52–54; Tigay, "On the Meaning of *T(W)TPT*."

32. The idiom "between your eyes" cannot be meant literally. Deut. 14:1 shows that it refers to a place where one can make a bald spot—in other words, the hairline. This was recognized in rabbinic sources and has since been confirmed from other Semitic languages. See Menah. 37b; MdRY Bo 17 (Lauterbach 1:152–153); H. L. Ginsberg, *Kitvei Ugarit* (Jerusalem: Mosad Bialik, 1936), 73; other sources cited by Tigay, "On the Meaning of *T(W)TPT*," 326 n. 30.

33. Sefer Ha-Hinnukh, no. 422.

34. Dillmann; Shalag (cf. Isaac Arama, cited by M. M. Kasher, *Sefer Shema' Yisra'el* [Jerusalem: Beth Torah Shelemah, 1980], 154, no. 155); cf. Targ. Neof. On city gates see M. Cogan and Z. Herzog, s.v. *sha'ar*, EM 8:231–243; E. F. Campbell, *Ruth* (Garden City, N.Y.: Doubleday, 1955), 154–155.

35. Prov. 31:31; Ruth 3:11.

36. See also 2 Sam. 19:9; Jer. 38:7; Prov. 31:23.

37. Gen. 23:10,18; 34:20; 2 Kings 7:1,18; Amos 5:10; Ruth 4:1–12.

38. Philo, Spec. 4.142.

39. See Isa. 29:11–12; Lachish ostracon 3 (ANET, 322b). The relatively small number of letters in the Hebrew and other Canaanite alphabets facilitated literacy, but we are unable to say how widespread it actually became in the First Temple period. See J. Naveh, "A Paleographic Note on the Distribution of the Hebrew Script," HTR 61 (1968): 68–74; idem, *Early History of the Alphabet* (Jerusalem: Magnes Press; Leiden: Brill, 1982), 65–76; M. Haran, "On the Diffusion of Literacy and Schools in Ancient Israel," in *Congress Volume: Jerusalem, 1986*, SVT 40 (Leiden: Brill, 1988), 81–95, and earlier studies cited on 82 n. 3. Dissemination of religious teaching remained primarily oral throughout the First Temple period (see v. 7 and Excursus 28).

40. Cf. Josh. 24:12–13. Only Jericho, Ai, and Hazor are clearly said to have been destroyed (Josh. 6:24; 8:28; 11:11). A few other cities are said to have been "proscribed" (*heherim*; Josh. 10:28,37; 11:12), but to judge from Josh. 11:12–14, this refers only to their populations (see also Mesha Inscription, ll. 15–17 [ANET, 320d]; but cf. Num. 21:2–3; Josh. 10:21).

41. See 2 Kings 18:31; 1 Sam. 19:22; 2 Sam. 23:15–16;

Isa. 36:16; Mesha Inscription, ll. 24–25 (ANET, 320d); M. Avi-Yonah, s.v. *bor*, EM 2:41–43 and L. Stager, "The Archaeology of the Family in Ancient Israel," BASOR 260 (1985): 9–10; Aharoni and Rainey, LOB, 240, 281. According to A. Zertal, most of the earliest Israelite settlements in the Manassite highlands did not have cisterns but stored water in large jars ("Israel Enters Canaan," BAR 17/5 [September-October, 1991]: 34–36).

42. Cf. Judg. 9:7–13; Ps. 104:15.

43. Cf. Hos. 13:6; Prov. 30:22b; Job 1:4–5.

44. Ber. 32a; see Sifrei 43; Weinfeld, DDS, 280–281.

45. See Comment to 5:9 and accompanying endnote; Weinfeld, DDS, 332.

46. Cf. 10:20; Josh. 23:7; Isa. 19:18; 45:23; Jer. 5:7; 12:16; Amos 8:14; Zeph. 1:5. See M. Greenberg, s.v. "Oaths," EncJud 12:1297–1298.

47. See W. W. Hallo, "Individual Prayer in Sumerian," JAOS 88 (1968): 79. For other instances where God is treated like a king see M. Greenberg, "On the Refinement of the Concept of Prayer in Hebrew Scriptures," AJSR 1 (1976): 64–67; J. Tigay, "On Some Aspects of Prayer in the Bible," AJSR 1 (1976): 363–372.

48. For these two senses see Weinfeld, Commentary, 295; DDS, 83 nn. 1,2, and 320, 332.

49. See Exod. 8:18 (see Shadal there; cf. also Deut. 7:21; 31:17; Josh. 3:10).

50. Rashi, Exod. 17:2.

51. See Exod. 14:10–14; 15:22–25; 16; 17:1–7.

52. Num. 11; 14, esp. vv. 11,22.

53. Pss. 78:7,11–20,41–42; 106:11–14.

54. On testing God, see J. Licht, *Testing in the Hebrew Scriptures and in Post-Biblical Judaism* (Jerusalem: Magnes Press, 1973).

55. Cf. Num. 14:22; Mal. 3:15.

56. Ramban.

57. Exod. 15:26; 1 Kings 11:38.

58. On the talmudic concepts discussed here see M. Silberg, *Principia Talmudica* (Jerusalem: Hebrew University Students' Press, 1964), chap. 7; Eliezer Berkovits, *Not in Heaven* (New York: Ktav, 1983), 26–28.

59. See BM 16b,35a,108a; Tosef. Shek. 3:1–2.

60. Ps. 78:54ff describe how the northern Israelites continued to test God even after He gave them the land of Canaan, as a result of which He abandoned the northern kingdom.

61. For similar question-and-answer prescriptions see Josh. 4:6–7,21–24.

62. See M. Greenberg, *'Al Ha-Mikra' Ve-'al Ha-Yahadut* (Tel Aviv: Am Oved, 1984), 77–84.

63. Cf. Gen. 15:6; Ps. 106:31.

64. Tosef. Pe'ah 1:2; Mish. Pe'ah 1:1.

65. ANET, 492c.

Chapter 7

1. See 7:1 (twice), 7,13,17,22; 8:1,12 (3 times). Note also the opposite, *me'at*, "few," "little by little" (7:7,22).

2. See A. Rofé, *Israelite Belief in Angels in the Pre-Exilic Period* (Hebrew) (Ph.D. diss., Hebrew University, 1969), 289–297; Weinfeld, DDS, 34, 46.

3. Subdivisions of the chapter are before vv. 1 (M, SP, chapter division), 7 (MT variants but not M; SP), 9 (MT variants), 12 (SP and M), 17 (M and SP; not 5Q1); after v. 26 (M, SP, chapter division).

4. See Weinfeld, Commentary, 379–382.

5. See T. Ishida, "The Structure and Historical Implications of the Lists of Pre-Israelite Nations," *Biblica* 60 (1979): 461–490.

6. See Gen. 10:15; 15:20; 23; 26:34; 27:46; 36:2; Num. 13:29; 1 Sam. 26:6; 2 Sam. 11; 1 Kings 10:29; 2 Kings 7:6. For discussion

see B. Mazar, s.v. *Ha-Ḥittim ba-Mikra*', EM 3:355–357; H. A. Hoffner, Jr., "Some Contributions of Hittitology," *Tyndale Bulletin* 20 (1969): 28–37; Ishida, "Structure and Implications," 467–469.

7. For the names see F. Gröndahl, *Die Personennamen der Texte aus Ugarit* (Rome: Pontifical Biblical Institute, 1967) and F. L. Benz, *Personal Names in the Phoenician and Punic Inscriptions* (Rome: Biblical Institute Press, 1972); for the land of Kirkash see M. Lichtheim, *Ancient Egyptian Literature* (Berkeley: University of California Press, 1975–80), 2:61ff; O. Margalith, "The Girgashi" (Hebrew), *Shnaton* 8–9 (1983–84): 259–263 and XI.

8. See Gen. 13:7; 34:30; Josh. 15:17; Judg. 1:4–5.

9. See Gen. 34:2; Josh. 9:7; 11:3,19; Judg. 3:3. Identification of this people is complicated by the fact that different manuscripts of the Bible frequently interchange "Hivite" with "Horite" or "Hittite"; the three terms differ from each other only in their middle consonants. Cf. Gen. 36:2 with v. 20.

10. See Josh. 15:63; 2 Sam. 5:6; 24:18–25 (it was from Arauna the Jebusite that David bought the land on which the Temple was eventually built). For the names at Mari, including a personal name Yabusum, see H. B. Huffmon, *Amorite Personal Names in the Mari Texts* (Baltimore: Johns Hopkins Press, 1965), 177.

11. The marriages of Solomon, Rehoboam, and Ahab with foreign princesses had similar results, according to 1 Kings 11:1–5; 15:13; 16:31–33.

12. Philo, *Spec.* 3.29; Josephus, *Ant.* 8.190–196; Kid. 68b; Yev. 23a; Maimonides, Yad, Issurei Bi'ah 12.1. See S.J.D. Cohen, "From the Bible to the Talmud: The Prohibition of Intermarriage," HAR 7 (1983): 23–39.

13. See also 11:13–17; 17:3; 28:20; 29:4–5.

14. See 2 Sam. 5:21 (note the rewording in 1 Chron. 14:12); Ezra 1:7; ANET, 320 (what Mesha dragged before Chemosh was probably the vessels of the Lord); M. Cogan, *Imperialism and Religion* (Missoula, Mont.: Society of Biblical Literature and Scholars Press, 1974). In some cases the idols or symbols of defeated peoples' gods were even worshiped alongside the victors' gods, on the assumption that they had helped the victors by abandoning the defeated peoples; see 2 Chron. 25:14 and cf. 1 Sam. 5:2 (see Rabbi Yohanan in Mid. Sam. 11:4 and H. P. Smith, *A Critical and Exegetical Commentary on the Books of Samuel* [Edinburgh: T. and T. Clark, 1899], 39).

15. The function of the pillar as an abode of the deity is stated explicitly by Jacob (Gen. 28:16–22; on the use of sacred pillars in early Israel see Comment to 16:22). For sacrifices to pillars see ANET, 211a, 350b; H. W. Attridge and R. A. Oden, *Philo of Byblos: The Phoenician History* (Washington, D.C.: Catholic Biblical Association, 1981), 43. For idolatrous pillars see, e.g., 2 Kings 3:2; 10:27. Some pillars had other functions. See W. Robertson Smith, *The Religion of the Semites* (London: A. and C. Black, 1914), 201–206; T. H. Gaster, *Myth, Legend and Custom in the Old Testament* (New York: Harper and Row, 1969), 187–193; M. Burrows, *What Mean These Stones?* (New Haven: American Schools of Oriental Research, 1941), 210–212; G. A. Barrois, s.v. "Pillar," IDB 3:815–817; C. Graesser, s.v. "Pillar," IDBS 668–669. For pillars found in archaeological excavations see ANEP, sec. 6 and figs. 871, 872.

16. See M. Av. Zar. 3:7; Radak, *Sefer Ha-Shorashim*, 30. Passages like 2 Kings 21:3 speak of "making" an 'asherah, and v. 7 indicates that the reference is to an image, presumably of the goddess. In Judg. 6:25–32 there is an 'asherah at the altar of Baal, but no indication that the goddess was worshiped there. For a recent discussion of the 'asherah see J. Day, "Asherah in the Hebrew Bible and Northwest Semitic Literature," JBL 105 (1986): 385–408; R. Hestrin, "Understanding Asherah: Exploring Semitic Iconography," BAR 17/5 (September-October 1991): 50–59; E. Bloch-Smith, "The Cult of the Dead in Judah," JBL 111 (1992): 218 n. 16. See further at 16:21.

17. Y. Yadin, *Hazor* (New York: Random House, 1975),

43–46; other examples were found in earlier strata; see 84, 94, 102.

18. See Weinfeld, Commentary, and idem, DDS, 227 n. 2; M. Fishbane, *Biblical Interpretation in Ancient Israel* (Oxford: Clarendon, 1985), 121–123.

19. Weinfeld, DDS, 225–227. See also Exod. 22:30. For another sense of *kadosh* in Deuteronomy see 26:19; 28:9.

20. See, e.g., 4:37; 9:4–6; 10:15; 14:1–2.

21. Cf. Mal. 3:17; Eccles. 2:8; 1 Chron. 29:3. See MdRY, Ba-Ḥodesh 2 (Lauterbach 2:204); M. Greenberg, "Hebrew *segulla*: Akkadian *sikiltu*," JAOS 71 (1951): 172–174; Weinfeld, DDS, 69 n. 1, 226 n. 2; S. E. Loewenstamm, *From Babylon to Canaan* (Jerusalem: Magnes Press, 1992), 268–279.

22. Unlike the Leningrad codex and SP, M has no break between vv. 1–6 and 7ff, suggesting that the tradition on which M is based recognized the connection of vv. 7ff to vv. 1–6.

23. See, e.g., Gen. 12:2; 22:17; 26:3–4.

24. Weinfeld, Commentary, thinks that this reflects the sixth century, before the destruction of Judah, whereas references to Israel's being as numerous as the stars reflect the period of the united kingdom.

25. Note how the same promise is phrased in 30:9.

26. See Driver; W. F. Albright, *Yahweh and the Gods of Canaan* (Garden City, N.Y.: Doubleday, 1968), 185–186; Benz, *Personal Names*, 413–414; HALAT, 851; J. Pedersen, *Israel: Its Life and Culture*, III–IV (London: Oxford University Press, 1940), 510–511; Deir Alla inscription, combination 1 l.14 (see Milgrom, *Numbers*, 474); Weinfeld, Commentary; S. Dalley and B. Teissier, "Tablets from the Vicinity of Emar and Elsewhere," *Iraq* 54 (1992): 90–91 (ref. courtesy Avigdor Hurowitz); M. Astour, "Some New Divine Names from Ugarit," JAOS 86 (1966): 284. For the vocalization of *Sheger* see Exod. 13:12 (it may be derived from *sh-g-r*, "throw," "cast," hence, "offspring").

27. See Excursus 6 n. 14.

28. Ps. 78:50; Exod. 9:10. See Exod. 15:26.

29. Pliny, *Natural History* 26.3,4 and 26.5,8.

30. See Gen. 22:17.

31. See also Exod. 34:12; Josh. 23:12–13; Judg. 2:3; 8:27; Ps. 106:36.

32. See 1:21,29–31; 9:1–3; 20:1; 31:6,8.

33. Targums; LXX; Sot. 36a; Ben Yehudah, 5647 n. 2. See also Exod. 23:28; Josh. 24:12; cf. Deut. 1:44. The translation "plague" follows the medieval Hebrew grammarians; Ibn Ezra derives it from *tsara'at*, "leprosy" (see 24:8). See also Saadia and Ibn Janaḥ; cf. Ehrlich.

34. Keil-Delitzsch at Exod. 23:28; E. Neufeld, "Insects as Warfare Agents in the Ancient Near East," *Orientalia* 49 (1980): 30–57.

35. Wright. An apt parallel to the present case is Gk. *oistros*, which means both "horsefly" and "vehement passion," "madness," "frenzy" (Mayes and others); cf. *Odyssey* 22:297–300, where Athena causes Odysseus's foes to panic and stampede like a herd of cattle driven wild by a horsefly (ref. courtesy Deborah Roberts). In this case the meaning of *tsir'ah* is similar to *mehumah*, "turmoil," in v. 23 or *'eimah*, "terror," in Exod. 23:27 and elsewhere (see the next note).

36. Gen. 35:5; Exod. 23:27; 1 Sam. 14:15.

37. Mishnat Rabbi Eliezer sees "thunder" as the basic meaning (cited by Rashi at Exod. 14:24; cf. Ibn Ezra and Rashbam; Bekhor Shor and Ḥazzekuni there see the noise as the shouting of the Egyptians themselves). In Deut. 7:23 *ve-hamam* is to be analyzed as *ve-ham* (from *hum*) + *am* (accusative pronominal suffix).

38. 1 Sam. 5:9, 11 (note the role of "God's hand," meaning pestilence, as in Deut. 2:15); 14:20; Ezek. 22:5; Amos 3:9; Zech. 14:13 (note vv. 12–15); 2 Chron. 15:5–6. The targums usually render with *shiggushya*' or *'irburya*', "confusion," "tumult" (cf. Syriac *sh-g-sh*); cf. MdRY Be-Shallah 5 (Horovitz 108:14–15;

Lauterbach 1:241 ll. 123–124). See also Targ. Jon. and Rashi at Exod. 14:24; Targ. Yer. at Isa. 22:5; 28:28; Ezek. 7:7; 22:5.

39. *Iliad* 5:593; 18:217–231 (Lattimore's "terror" is really "confusion"), 535; cf. *Odyssey* 22:298. See M. Weinfeld, "Divine Intervention in War," in H. Tadmor and M. Weinfeld, eds., *History, Historiography, and Interpretation* (Jerusalem: Hebrew University, Institute of Advanced Studies, and Magnes Press, 1983), 135.

40. See, e.g., 9:14; 29:19; for Akkadian examples see CAD N2, 259c.

41. See 1 Sam. 24:22; Isa. 66:22; Ps. 83:5.

42. See, e.g., Deut. 12:21; 14:3; 17:1; 18:12; 22:5; 23:19; 25:16; 32:16; as well as Gen. 43:32; Lev. 18:22; 20:13; Isa. 1:13. For discussion see J. Milgrom, s.v. "Abomination," EncJud 2:96–98; idem, s.v. *to'evah*, EM 8:466–468; M. H. Lovelace, s.v. "Abomination," IDB 1:12–13; Weinfeld, DDS, 267–269; Rofé, *Mavo'*, 316. For ancient Near Eastern parallels see KAI no. 13:6 (ANET, 662a); W. W. Hallo, "Biblical Abominations and Sumerian Taboos," JQR 76 (1985): 21–40; J. Klein and Y. Safati, "To'evah and Abominations in Mesopotamian Literature and the Bible," *Beer-Sheva* 3 (1978): 131–148.

43. Cf. Josh. 6:17–18 and chap. 7; Deut. 13:16–18.

Chapter 8

1. For a comparison of 6:10–15 with chap. 8, see Weinfeld, Commentary, 396–397.

2. See Craigie, 184. The unity of the chapter is also expressed in recurrent terms associated with the contrast between the wilderness and the promised land, such as testing and hardship (vv. 2,3,16), feeding and eating (vv. 3,10,12,16), bread (vv. 3,9), and water (vv. 7,15). For the chiastic structure, cf. Moran and Craigie, following Lohfink. MT recognizes the unity of vv. 1–18 by having *parashah* breaks only before vv. 1 and 19 and after v. 20. SP, one MT variant, and 5Q1 frag. 1 have no break before v. 19 (C. D. Ginsburg, *Introduction to the Masoretico-Critical Edition of the Hebrew Bible* [reprint; New York: Ktav, 1966], 607). Whether vv. 19–20 belong with vv. 1–18 is discussed in the introductory Comment to vv. 19–20. SP also has breaks before vv. 1,5, and 11, but these mark logical transitions rather than new units. 4QDeut^n col. i presents vv. 5–10 as a unit by itself, with internal breaks before vv. 7,9, and 10. See Weinfeld, Commentary, 386, 393.

3. Shadal.

4. On the aims of the wilderness wanderings see MdRY Be-Shallah 1 (Lauterbach 2:171–172); MdRSbY, 45; Maimonides, Guide 3.24,32; Shadal at Num. 13:2 and here. The reason for the test is not stated; perhaps it was intended to determine whether Israel was ready to enter the promised land.

5. Rashi at Exod. 16:7.

6. Maimonides, Guide 3.24. See Gen. 3:19; 22:1,12; Deut. 13:4.

7. R. Meyuhas; *Da'at Soferim*. The translation of "the utterance of the mouth" of God as "decree" follows Ibn Ezra, who cites Est. 7:8 (in Akkadian "the utterance of the mouth" of a deity [*šit pî*] usually refers to an order). The phrase is equivalent to "the utterance of the lips," which usually refers to a vow or an oath, in other words, a binding utterance (23:24; Num. 30:13; Ps. 89:35). For an Egyptian parallel to food as the "utterance of the mouth" of God see H. Brunner, "Was aus dem Munde Gottes geht," VT 8 (1958): 428–429. Many commentators favor a spiritual interpretation to the effect that man needs not only food to survive but also spiritual sustenance, such as the words and commandments of God (see Matt. 4:4; Ibn Ezra; Bekhor Shor; Hatam Sofer, quoted by Plaut, 1392). This is homiletically attractive but far from the plain sense of the verse, since the manna did not show that man has spiritual needs.

8. See F. S. Bodenheimer, "The Manna of Sinai," BA 10

(1947): 2–6; N. M. Sarna, *Exploring Exodus* (New York: Schocken, 1986), 116–120.

9. This translation is suggested by the preposition *min*, "from"; cf. NAB. The targums render the next clause "nor did your feet go bare," essentially harmonizing with 29:3, "nor did the sandals on your feet (wear out and fall off)." Cf. Ibn Janah; J. Blau, "Zum Hebräisch der Übersetzer des AT," VT 6 (1956): 98–99.

10. In addition to the present verse see Deut. 1:25,35; 3:25; 4:21,22; 6:18; 8:10; 9:6; 11:17.

11. See Exod. 28:33–34; 1 Kings 7:18,20,42; Song 4:3,13; S. Moscati, *L'epigrafia ebraica antica* (Rome: Pontifical Biblical Institute, 1951), pl. 15 no. 4; A. Lemaire, "Probable Head of Priestly Scepter from Solomon's Temple Surfaces in Jerusalem," BAR 10/1 (1984): 24–29; cf. ANEP, 589.

12. See Sifrei 297; TJ Bik. 1:3, 63d; Lieberman, TK *Zera'im*, 332; cf. Keter Torah. A synonymous phrase for oil-olives appears in 2 Kings 18:32. Olives may not have been eaten in the biblical period; see M. Haran, s.v. *ma'akhalim u-mashka'ot*, EM 4:546–547.

13. J. Muhly, "How Iron Technology Changed the Ancient World," BAR 8/6 (1982): 44–45; M. Noth, *The Old Testament World* (Philadelphia: Fortress Press, 1966), 44–45; E. Orni and E. Efrat, *Geography of Israel*, 3rd ed. (Jerusalem: Israel Universities Press, 1973), maps on 12, 475; F. V. Winnet, s.v. "Mining," IDB 3:384–385; U. S. Würzberger, s.v. "Metals and Mining," EncJud 11:1431–1433; Driver; Josephus, War 4.454, mentions an "iron mountain" in Moab. Dillmann quotes Burckhardt as saying that nineteenth-century Arabs considered basalt to be iron. For evidence of a broader definition of the promised land see Comment to 2:24.

14. See Shadal; Ehrlich; cf. NEB; Jerusalem Bible.

15. Note also the sequence *'ayin-nun* in four of five consecutive words in v. 16.

16. Rashi at Num. 21:6. For similar descriptions in Assyrian literature and Herodotus, see Weinfeld, Commentary.

17. See EM 5:57. See also Pss. 78:15–16; 114:8.

18. If so, note the chiastic framework of vv. 1–18: "oath to/ with your fathers" (vv. 1,18b), "Remember" (vv. 2,18a).

19. See 11:13,22; 15:5; 28:1.

Chapters 9–10

1. M divides the text into three units: chap. 9; 10:1–11; and 10:12–11:9. MT variants and SP add breaks before 9:5 and 9 (SP), 12 (MT variants), 13 (MT variants and SP), 18 and 25 (SP); 10:6 (SP), 8 (MT variant and SP). Strangely, no Hebrew texts have a break before 10:10–11. Conceivably, the Levites' "standing before" God and Moses' "standing" on the mountain to intercede with God were seen as complementary roles ("standing before" God is sometimes used in connection with intercessory prayer; see Jer. 15:1; 18:20; 2 Chron. 20:9).

2. For these leitmotifs see (a) 9:5; 10:11; cf. 9:27; (b) 9:8,14,19, 20,25,26; 10:10; (c) 9:9–11,15,17; 10:1–5,8; (d) 9:6–8,13,22–23,27; 10:16; (e) 9:9,18,25; 10:10; cf. 9:11.

3. For reputations of invincibility and the like see 2 Sam. 5:6; ANET, 477d.

4. "Quickly" is missing in the Vatican Codex of LXX, but it may have been omitted intentionally to avoid the inconsistency.

5. See, e.g., 1 Kings 3:6; Isa. 26:2; Zech. 8:8. For further evidence see M. Weinfeld, "The Covenant of Grant in the Old Testament and in the Ancient Near East," JAOS 90 (1970): 186; J. Tigay, "Psalm 7:5 and Ancient Near Eastern Treaties," JBL 89 (1970): 184.

6. Abravanel, 93. "It is rather" would probably have been expressed by *ki* (as in v. 5) or *ki 'im*, rather than *u-*.

7. According to Ehrlich the last clause of the verse was

originally part of the direct quotation. He emends this clause and the beginning of the next verse to read: "as well as because of the wickedness of those nations that the LORD is dispossessing them before *me* [*mi-panai*].' For [*ki*] it is not. . . ."

8. See also Lev. 18:3,24–30; 20:23; Deut. 12:31; 18:12; 20:18. In Gen. 15:16 Abraham was told that since the Amorites' guilt was not yet complete, his descendants would have to wait several generations before receiving the land. See also Comment to Deut. 7:3–4.

9. See 1 Kings 3:6; 9:4; 1 Chron. 29:17.

10. Various Hebrew manuscripts subdivide this unit further (see n. 1). The break at v. 9 calls attention to the main example, at Horeb; those at vv. 12 and 13 single out God's statements, and that at v. 18 highlights Moses' intercession.

11. Weinfeld, DDS, 31.

12. See esp. Jer. 7:26; 17:23; 2 Chron. 36:13.

13. See Gen. 7:4,17; 50:2; Jonah 3:4.

14. See Exod. 24:18; ARN[1] 1:1; 37:109; cf. Philo, 2 Mos. 68. For radiance as a divine quality see Ps. 104:1–2; Weinfeld, s.v. "*Kabod*," TWAT 4:23–39. For defecation and sexual relations causing ritual impurity see Deut. 23:11–15; Lev. 15:16–18; 1 Sam. 21:5. Dan. 9:3; 10:2–3,12 and some postbiblical texts mention fasting in preparation for receiving divine revelation. However, in most of these examples the fasting expresses mourning and penitence, and it precedes rather than accompanies the revelation as it does in Moses' case.

15. The phrase *yom ha-kahal*, as in 10:4; 18:16, alludes to *h-k-h-l*, "gather," in 4:10 (cf. *kahal*, translated "congregation," in 5:19).

16. See Exod. R. 42:1–3.

17. E.g., Exod. 3:7; 29:46.

18. See Exod. R. 42:9 and parallels, and Y. Muffs, *Love and Joy* (New York: Jewish Theological Seminary, 1992), chap. 1. For prophets as intercessors see Gen. 20:7,17 (cf. 18:23–32); Num. 14:13–20; 1 Sam. 7:7–10; 12:23; Ps. 99:6.

19. In Exod. 32:10 the echo of Gen. 12:2 is clearer. See also Num. 14:12.

20. See Ibn Ezra at Exod. 32:19; N. M. Sarna, *Exploring Exodus* (New York: Schocken, 1986), 219. For tearing legal documents see BB 168b.

21. See Exod. 32:11–14; 32:30ff.; 34:4–28.

22. Abravanel, 95, 96–98, 101; Shadal at 9:18; Hoffmann at 9:25–29 and 10:10; Driver; and Weinfeld, DDS, at 9:18–20, 25–29, and 10:10.

23. If so, "as I did the first time" in 10:10 recapitulates "as before" in 9:18, and "the LORD heeded me once again" (10:10) recapitulates "at that time too the LORD gave heed to me" in 9:19b.

24. Lev. 16:29,31; 23:27,29,32; Est. 4:16; cf. 1 Sam. 7:6.

25. See Num. 11:2; 12:13–15; 14:13–20; 21:7–9.

26. According to Num. 20:12 and Deut. 32:50–51, Aaron died because of the incident at Meribah. This difference is similar to that between Deuteronomy and Numbers regarding the reason for Moses' punishment. See Excursus 2.

27. See Av. Zar. 44a; Rashi, Ibn Ezra, Rashbam, and Ramban at Exod. 32:20; Weinfeld, Commentary and DDS, 234 n. 2; Mayes; S. E. Loewenstamm, *Comparative Studies in Biblical and Ancient Oriental Literatures* (Kevelaer: Butzon and Bercker, and Neukirchen-Vluyn: Neukirchener Verlag, 1980), 240 n. 13; Sarna, *Exploring Exodus*, 219–220. Hoffmann thinks that Deuteronomy omits the drinking because the book means to recall only how Moses saved the people, not how he punished them. Weinfeld thinks it is because ritual means of establishing guilt and innocence were abandoned following the Deuteronomic centralization of worship.

28. For "chose" see Amos 3:2; for "looked after" see Nah. 1:7. For the idea that God first met Israel in the wilderness see Deut. 32:10. For another attempt to understand "I knew" see *Neveh Shalom* on Saadia's translation here.

29. Cf. Abravanel, 100.

30. On the prayer see Abravanel, 98–99; M. Greenberg, "Moses' Intercessory Prayer," *Tantur Yearbook* (1977–78): 21–36; Muffs, *Love and Joy*, 12–14.

31. See J. Ben-Shlomo, s.v. "Zekhut Avot," EncJud 16:976–978; Weinfeld, Commentary, at v. 27.

32. See esp. Exod. 9:14–16; 10:1–2; 14:4,18.

33. See, e.g., Pss. 23:3; 25:11; 79:9–10; 115:1–2; Isa. 48:9–11; Jer. 14:7, 21; Ezek. 20:9,22,44. A Hittite prayer appeals to the god, "bring not thy name into disrepute" (ANET, 396c). An argument similar to that used by Moses is found in a letter from the king of Byblos to the king of Egypt: "Why do you keep silent while your land is taken? Let it not be said, 'In the days of the commissioners the Ḥapiru took all the lands . . . and you were not able to take them back'" (EA 83:15–20, in M. Greenberg, *The Ḥab/piru* [New Haven: American Oriental Society, 1955], 36).

34. See Bekhor Shor; Abravanel, 84, Question 12, and 98, s.v. "the third argument."

35. Abravanel, 99.

36. See R. A. Hammer, "The New Covenant of Moses," *Judaism* 27 (1978): 345–350.

37. For "ark" (*'aron*) meaning "chest" see KAI 29:1; 2 Kings 12:10–11. For depositing documents in containers see Comment to 31:26. For placing something *by* the Ark for safekeeping, cf. Exod. 16:32–34; Num. 18:25. For depositing treaty texts in temples, see ANET, 205; D. D. Luckenbill, "Hittite Treaties and Letters," AJSL 37 (1920–21): 197; D. J. McCarthy, *Treaty and Covenant*, 2nd ed. (Rome: Biblical Institute Press, 1981), 304; J. C. Greenfield, "Some Glosses on the Sfire Inscriptions," *Maarav* 7 (1991): 147. For placing legal documents and agreements under the sponsorship of the deity, cf. 1 Sam. 10:25; Judg. 11:11 (see Weinfeld, DDS, 93 n. 1); Gen. 31:47–53; J. A. Montgomery, *Arabia and the Bible* (1934; reprint, New York: Ktav, 1969), 130; J. Cantineau, *Le Nabatéen* (Paris: Ernest Leroux, 1930–32), 2:34 l. 9.

38. For the Ark in Exodus see Exod. 25:10–22; 40:20 (cf. 1 Chron. 28:2); Sarna, *Exploring Exodus*, 209–211, 217–219. Note also Exod. 20:20–21, where the altar is contrasted with idols as the legitimate means of drawing God close for blessing; see Comment to Deut. 4:15–18. For cherubs flanking thrones see ANEP, figs. 332, 458 (royal thrones) and J. R. Davila and B. Zuckerman, "The Throne of 'Ashtart Inscription," BASOR 289 (1993): 67–68 (throne of a deity).

39. See Weinfeld, DDS, 191–209, esp. 208–209; R. E. Clements, "The Ark in Deuteronomy," CBQ 30 (1968): 1–14.

40. Two Arks: R. Judah b. Lakish in TJ Shek. 6:1, 49c; Tosef. Sot. 7:18 and parallels; Rashi; R. Meyuhas. One Ark: rabbis in TJ Shek. 6:1, 49c; Ibn Ezra; Ramban; Abravanel at Num. 10:33 (42–46) and at 1 Sam. 4 (189–192); Hoffmann. Critical theory: Driver.

41. For other passages spoken by a narrator other than Moses in Deuteronomy, see 1:1–5; 2:12; 4:41–5:1; 27:1,9,11; 28:69; 29:1; 31-34 passim. The phrase "Israelites" (lit., "children of Israel"), which is not Deuteronomic, suggests that the passage is from another source, perhaps an itinerary of the type found in Num. 33. It is not, however, based on the latter since the direction of the route and the place of Aaron's death differ (see Num. 33:31,37–39; cf. 20:22–28 and Deut. 32:50). These differences are discussed in Excursus 2. Driver and Weinfeld assign the passage to the Elohistic (E) source.

42. Abravanel, 100.

43. For a different view of the reason for their election here see S. E. Loewenstamm, *From Babylon to Canaan* (Jerusalem: Magnes Press, 1992), 55–65.

44. See Weinfeld, Commentary, for details.

45. See also Josh. 3:3; 6:6.

46. Cf. 21:5. For standing in attendance on God to offer sacrifices see Ezek. 44:15; 2 Chron. 29:11.

47. See G. Barkay, *Ketef Hinnom* (Jerusalem: Israel Museum, 1986), 29–31. A similar blessing, perhaps imitating the priestly one, is part of an inscription found in the Sinai; see Z. Meshel, *Kuntillet Ajrud* (Jerusalem: Israel Museum, 1978), 20.

48. Exod. 33:12–16.

49. Only the chapter division recognizes the connection between vv. 12ff. and the preceding narrative. Hebrew texts connect this unit instead with chap. 11 (see n. 66, below), as does Weinfeld. Perhaps its didactic content suggested that this unit is separate from the narrative of 9:6–10:11.

50. Note the series of matching phrases in vv. 12–13,17,20; the parallel clauses in vv. 14,16,18; the alliteration in vv. 17 and 20a (alephs) and 20b (beths); and the rhyme in v. 18.

51. *Siddur 'Otsar Ha-Tefillot* 1 (following *Parashat Ha-Man* and *Tefillah 'al Ha-Parnasah*); Y. Yadin, *Tefillin from Qumran* (Jerusalem: Israel Exploration Society and the Shrine of the Book, 1969), 13–36; DJD 3, 152–155; DJD 6 (4Q128, 4Q138, and 8Qmez).

52. Cf. 30:6; Lev. 26:41; Jer. 4:4 (cf. 6:10). See Rashi; NJPS at Lev. 26:41 note; J. Tigay, "On Moses' Speech Difficulty," BASOR 231 (1978): 63 n. 6.

53. See Weinfeld, Commentary; KAI 14:18 (ANET, 662d); 266:1,6. Cf. Ps. 136:2,3; Dan. 2:37,47. In similar manner, deities were sometimes praised as being preeminent among the gods; cf. "[Ishtar,] the goddess among the Igigi gods" (CAD I/J, 89, s.v. *iltu* A, sec. a, end).

54. Abravanel suggests that "showing favor" refers to forgiving Israel as a favor to a prophet who intercedes for it, as God did in the case of the golden calf (cf. 1 Sam. 25:35; Job 42:8). Moses is warning Israel that in the future it cannot count on escaping punishment through prophetic intercession.

55. Meg. 31a, alluded to by Rashi. Isa. 57:15 and Ps. 68:5–6 are also cited.

56. For *yatom* meaning "fatherless" rather than "orphan" see Exod. 22:23; Ps. 109:9; Lam. 5:3.

57. See 14:29; 16:11,14; 24:17–21; 26:12–13; 27:19; Exod. 22:21–22; Jer. 22:3.

58. See ANET, 149a and b, 151a; F. C. Fensham, "Widow, Orphan, and the Poor in Ancient Near Eastern Legal and Wisdom Literature," JNES 21 (1962): 129–139; Weinfeld, Commentary; Jer. 22:16. Cf. Ps. 68:6; Prov. 23:11.

59. See Y. Kaufmann, *Toledot Ha-'Emunah Ha-Yisre'elit* (Tel Aviv: Bialik Institute-Dvir, 1937–56), 2:568; A. Malamat, "You Shall Love Your Neighbor as Yourself," in E. Blum et al., eds., *Die Hebräische Bibel und ihre zweifache Nachgeschichte* (Neukirchen-Vluyn: Neukirchener Verlag, 1990), 113 n. 8.

60. Exod. 22:20; 23:9; Lev. 19:34.

61. See also Jer. 17:14 and Ps. 109:1. The various possibilities are reflected in the use of *tehillah* and its verbal form *h-l-l* in 26:19; Isa. 42:8; Jer. 9:22–23; Zeph. 3:19–20; Ps. 97:7. See Ramban; Hazzekuni; Saadia (ed. J. Kafih, *Perushei Rabbenu Sa'adiah Ga'on 'al Ha-Torah* [Jerusalem: Mosad Harav Kook, 1963]), 140 n. 4.

62. See 4:9,34; 7:19; 29:2; 2 Sam. 7:21; 1 Chron. 17:21; and esp. Ps. 106:21–22.

63. Abravanel, 111.

64. See Gen. 46:8–27; Exod. 1:1–5.

65. The population at the time of Moses' address was essentially identical to that in 1:10, forty years earlier, according to Num. 1:46; 3:39 (625,550 [603,550 Israelites plus 22,000 Levites]) and Num. 26:51,62 (624,730 [601,730 Israelites plus 23,000 Levites]).

66. SP indeed ends the present unit after 11:1, whereas MT ends it after 11:9.

Chapter 11:1–30

1. As observed in the endnotes to chaps. 9–10, Hebrew texts do not mark 11:1 as the beginning of a new unit; only the chapter division does. In Hebrew texts the units begin at 11:2 (SP), 10 (M, SP), 13 (M, SP, 4QDeut^j, and 4QDeut^k), 22 and 26 (M, SP), 29 (M), and 31 (SP).

2. *Yarash*, "occupy," is also echoed in the third paragraph, where it and its derivative are rendered "dislodge" and "dispossess" (v. 23), and in the assonant noun *tirosh*, "wine" (v. 14).

3. Bekhor Shor and Da'at Zekenim note that this does not exempt later generations from responsibility for these obligations.

4. Exod. 12:25–27; 13:5–16; 16:32; 17:14; Lev. 23:42–43; Num. 17:5,25; Deut. 6:20–25; 31:10–13; Judg. 6:13; 2 Sam. 7:22; Pss. 44:2; 78:3.

5. Abravanel, 111.

6. The syntax of Hebrew *ki lo' 'et beneikhem* is unusual. *'Et* cannot be the accusative particle here, since there is no verb governing it (some scholars have sought to restore one by textual emendation). One approach is to take *'et* as the preposition "with" and construe the phrase as elliptical for "for it is not with your children that I speak" (Rashi; Driver; OJPS; cf. GKC §117). The present translation takes *'et* in its looser sense as an emphatic particle, as in Ezek. 44:3 (see HALAT, 97; BDB, 85). This yields a more pronounced contrast with v. 7, the end of this long sentence: "it was not your *children*, but you who saw with your own eyes." For another view see Hoffman; for emendations see Ehrlich, *Randglossen*; Tur Sinai.

7. See Comment to 4:9.

8. Note the usage of the term in synonymous parallelism or conjunction with "strike" (Jer. 2:30; 30:14) and "rod" (Prov. 22:15), as well as "words," "wisdom," and "counsel" (Ps. 50:17; Prov. 1:2).

9. In 3:24 and 9:26 this is the quality by which God defeated Sihon and Og and Pharaoh. In all three passages it is associated with God's "mighty hand."

10. Ramban; Seforno. Cf. Jer. 32:20, where NJPS renders "with lasting effect."

11. Cf. Deut. 2:22; Josh. 7:25–26. See B. S. Childs, "A Study of the Formula 'Until This Day,'" JBL 82 (1963): 283.

12. ANET, 378.

13. Ramban at v. 2. Note that *'asah le-* means "did to" in the rest of vv. 3–6.

14. SP, 4QPhyl^a and 4QPhyl^k, and 8Qmez (DJD 6:50,68; DJD 3:159) add "and all Korah's people." Given ancient scribes' penchant for harmonizing discrepancies by filling in such gaps with phrases borrowed from parallel passages, this is probably an interpolation copied from Num. 16:32, not an original reading. Favoring this assumption are the facts that the phrase appears at different places in the verse in SP and in the Qumran texts, and the fact that only this phrase is worded identically in Deuteronomy and Numbers; the rest of the verse resembles Num. 16:32 only in content, not wording.

15. Rashi; Abravanel, 111; Hoffmann. Korah's children, unlike those of Dathan and Abiram, did not die with their father and would have been present when Moses delivered this address (see Num. 26:11; cf. Ps. 106:17).

16. Literally, "at their feet." See 2 Kings 3:9.

17. See Bekhor Shor and Weinfeld, Commentary.

18. The ground water mentioned in 8:7 is not sufficient for irrigation of fields (Sforno; Bekhor Shor; Driver). Cf. Ps. 104:10–11 and contrast vv. 13–16.

19. Sifrei 37–38; Yalqut 857–859; Rashi.

20. Cf. G. A. Smith, *The Historical Geography of the Holy Land* (reprint; New York: Harper and Row, 1966), 68. Cf. Gen. R. 13:9: dependence on rain teaches people to look to heaven.

21. J. Breasted, *A History of Egypt* (New York: Bantam, 1964), 5–6.

22. Rashi; Driver; Smith; Dalman, 2:219–241; P. Montet, *Everyday Life in Egypt* (Philadelphia: University of Pennsylvania Press, 1981), 104–105; J. Feliks, *Agriculture in Palestine in the*

Period of the Mishna and Talmud (Jerusalem: Magnes Press; Tel Aviv: Dvir, 1963), 318, 339. The mechanical devices used for lifting water in Egypt were not normally operated by foot, and in any case were either not used in fields, or were not known in Egypt, until later times. For the translation "by your own labors," cf. Speiser, *Genesis* (Garden City, N.Y.: Doubleday, 1964), comment to 30:30.

23. Bekhor Shor; Shadal.

24. ANET, 371.

25. Herodotus 2:13; cf. ANET, 257c.

26. Maimonides, Guide 2.12.

27. As in Pss. 33:18; 34:16; Jer. 24:6 (Rashbam). Note the use of the parallel verb *darash* in the sense of "care for" in Isa. 62:12; Ps. 142:5.

28. As in Prov. 5:21; 15:3 (Bekhor Shor). Rashi seems to allude to both senses.

29. Abravanel, 52.

30. Taʿan. 2a; Sefer Ha-Ḥinnukh, no. 431; Maimonides, Hilkhot Tefillah 1:1.

31. SP, 8Qmez (DJD 3:159) and LXX read here and in v. 15 "He will grant," as does 4QPhylᵃ (DJD 6:48) in v. 15.

32. Cf. 28:12; Lev. 26:4; Jer. 5:24; Ezek. 34:26.

33. D. Ashbel, s.v. "Israel, Land of. Climate," EncJud 9:185–186. Cf. Deut. 28:12; Lev. 26:4; Jer. 5:24; Ezek. 34:26.

34. Dalman, 1:115–130; C. F. Arden-Close, "The Rainfall of Palestine," PEQ 73 (1941): 122–128; Smith, *Historical Geography*, 62–70; Sifrei 42; Lev. R. 35:12; Targ. Jon.; Taʿan. 19b.

35. M. Taʿan. 1:7.

36. See 16:13; Exod. 23:16; Jer. 40:10,12; Job 39:12; Ruth 2:7.

37. Ramban; Sifrei 43.

38. Ibn Ezra.

39. Ber. 40a.

40. The title *baʿal* as an epithet for the rain god survived vestigially in Hebrew and Arabic idioms such as "field of *baʿal*," meaning a field watered by rain rather than artificial irrigation. See E. Y. Kutscher, *Millim Ve-Toldoteihem* (Jerusalem: Kiryat Sefer, 1965), 13; T. H. Gaster, *Thespis* (Garden City, N.Y.: Doubleday, 1961), 130 n. 13; Felix, 302–306. In this idiom, *baʿal* may have been understood in its sense of "husband," reflecting a metaphoric view of the rain, or the power behind it, as a husband impregnating his wife (the field). This metaphor is expressed explicitly in the talmudic statement that rainfall is called *reviʿah*, which appears to mean "copulation," because "the rain is the husband [*baʿal*] of the soil" (Taʿan. 6b).

41. See M. H. Pope, s.v. "Baal Worship," EncJud 4:7–12.

42. See, e.g., Ps. 89:30; KAI 266:3; J. Tigay, "What Is Man That You Have Been Mindful of Him?," in J. Marks and R. Good, eds., *Love and Death in the Ancient Near East* (Guilford, Conn.: Four Quarters Press, 1987), 169–171.

43. Cf. Gen. 13:17 (see Sarna, *Genesis*, there); Josh. 1:3–4; 24:3.

44. See J. Milgrom, "Profane Slaughter and a Formulaic Key to the Composition of Deuteronomy," HUCA 47 (1976): 3–9.

45. For the meaning of "bless" see Comment to 2:7; for "curse" see Gen. 8:21 (where it is translated "doom"). See H. C. Brichto, *The Problem of "Curse" in the Hebrew Bible* (Philadelphia: Society of Biblical Literature and Exegesis, 1963).

46. NJPS, translators' note; cf. Rashi at 29:25; H. L. Ginsberg, s.v. "Hosea, Book of," EncJud 8:1023–1024. The phrase also appears in 13:3,7,14; 28:64; 29:25; 32:17.

47. Y. Kaufmann, *Sefer Yehoshuaʿ*, 2nd ed. (Jerusalem: Kiryat Sepher, 1963), 131–132; Weinfeld, Commentary. For Canaanites in the Aravah see Num. 13:29; Josh. 11:3.

48. Driver's view that, looking west from Nebo, Gerizim and Ebal would appear to face Gilgal, is unconvincing: from Nebo they would appear to be *to the right* of any Gilgal near Jericho.

49. O. Eissfeldt, "Gilgal or Shechem," in J. Durham and J. R. Porter, eds., *Proclamation and Presence* (Richmond: John Knox, 1970), 90–101; Rofé, *Mavoʾ*, 24; cf. Weinfeld, Commentary.

50. E. Hoad, *Guide to the Holy Land*, 4th ed. (Jerusalem: Franciscan Printing Press, 1971), 522. For other terebinths in or near Shechem see Gen. 35:4; Josh. 24:26; Judg. 9:6,36.

Chapter 11:31–13:1

1. E. Tov, "Deut. 12 and 11QTemple LII–LIII: A Contrastive Analysis," RQ 15 (1991): 169–173.

2. Cf. 18:9; Num. 33:51; 34:2; 35:10. The text division in SP recognizes v. 31 as the introduction to what follows. See A. Rofé, "The Strata of the Law about the Centralization of Worship in Deuteronomy and the History of the Deuteronomic Movement," SVT 22 (1972): 221–226. The connection of 11:31–32 with 12:1 is also supported by the chiastic order of their elements (Mayes, 222). Weinfeld, Commentary, 453, suggests that vv. 31–32 play a dual role as the conclusion to chaps. 1–11 and the introduction to chaps. 12–26; cf. 11:1.

3. Hebrew texts have breaks before the following verses: 11:31 (SP; see n. 2), 12:8,13,17 (SP), 20 (M and SP), 26 (SP), 29 (M and SP), and after 13:1 (M and SP). Many scholars take the numerous repetitions in the chapter and the change from second person plural to singular after v. 7 to indicate that different strata were combined in composing it. Others question the significance of these criteria. See discussion and bibliography by A. Rofé, "The Strata of the Law about the Centralization of Worship," SVT 22 (1972): 221–226; R. Sonsino, *Motive Clauses in Hebrew Law* (Chico, Calif.: Scholars Press, 1980), 197; S. Kaufman, "The Structure of the Deuteronomic Law," *Maarav* 1 (1978–79): 121–122 and 153 n. 62; Hertz, 941; cf. H. Cazelles, "Passages in the Singular Within Discourses in the Plural of Dt. 1–4," CBQ 29 (1967): 207–219; Weinfeld, DDS, 97 n. 12. Rofé, "Strata," argues on the basis of content as well that 11:31–12:7 expect centralization to take place as soon as the Israelites enter the land, whereas 12:8ff expect it to take place later. Our concern in the Comments will be to indicate the significance of each section in the chapter as we have it.

4. See 14:22–29; 15:19–23; 16:1–17; 17:8–13; 18:6–8; 26:1–11.

5. See 1 Sam. 1:3,10–15; 7:9; 1 Kings 8:5,12–64; Isa. 1:13–15; Amos 5:21–23. See N. M. Sarna, "The Psalm Superscriptions and the Guilds," in S. Stein and R. Loewe, eds., *Studies in Jewish Religious and Intellectual History* (Tuscaloosa: University of Alabama Press, 1979), 282–283.

6. For prayer and study see 6:6–9; 11:18–20; 17:18–20; 26:2–15; 31:10–13; cf. 4:1; 5:1; 6:1. It may be significant that Deuteronomy does not include meal and incense offerings among those that are restricted to the chosen place. These two types of sacrifice were often accompanied by prayer, and conceivably they were permitted to continue elsewhere along with prayer. See Sarna, "Psalm Superscriptions," 291–294. Evidence for the continuation of prayer outside of the Temple may also be found in Solomon's prayer when he dedicated the Temple. The prayer, which is full of allusions to Deuteronomy, describes the Temple not only as a place *in* which people will pray, but as a place *toward* which they will pray, implying that prayer need not take place in the Temple (1 Kings 8:22–53; for the allusions to Deuteronomy see Weinfeld, DDS, 36 n. 2).

7. See Exod. 23:24; 34:13; Num. 33:52; Deut. 7:5.

8. This was also the case in Israel following the conquest. Prior to the centralization of sacrifice in Jerusalem there were only about a dozen temples, but many open-air sanctuaries. See M. Haran, *Temples and Temple Service in Ancient Israel* (Oxford: Clarendon, 1978), 13–57.

9. See 2 Kings 17:10–11. These objects are also mentioned in conjunction with Israelite open-air sanctuaries (*bamot*); see 1 Kings 14:23; Jer. 17:2; Ezek. 6:13. An illustration of such a

sanctuary at Tyre appears on a later Greek coin from that city; it shows a fire-altar and two sacred pillars under a tree (see H. Gese et al., *Die Religionen Altsyriens, Altarabiens und der Mandäer* [Stuttgart: Kohlhammer, 1970], 197). A figurine of a bull was found at an Israelite open-air sanctuary from the period of the Judges; see A. Mazar, "The 'Bull Site'—An Iron Age I Open Cult Place," BASOR 247 (1982): 27–42.

10. Abravanel, 120.

11. See Exod. 17:14; Deut. 7:24; 25:19; 29:19. Cf. BMAP 12: "Yaho [YHVH], the God who dwells in the fortress of Elephantine."

12. Sifrei 61, which also implies that "obliterating their name" includes effacing the names of the gods from inscriptions found at those sites, much as the name of the deity Amon was obliterated from Egyptian inscriptions during the religious revolution of the Amarna period (J. Wilson, *The Culture of Ancient Egypt* [Chicago: University of Chicago Press, 1951], 221).

13. Sifrei 61.

14. M. Greenberg, "Religion: Stability and Ferment," in WHJP 4/2, 119.

15. 11QTemple 51:19–20; Ibn Janaḥ; Rashi; Ibn Ezra.

16. According to M. Greenberg, in the context of Exod. 23:24, "You shall not follow their [the Canaanites'] practices" prohibits only the worship of foreign gods, and Deuteronomy's "You shall not act thus toward the LORD your God," prohibiting multiple cult sites, is a reinterpretation and extension of that principle (Greenberg, "Religion: Stability and Ferment," 119).

17. Heb. *darash*, when its object is a sacred place, means to visit that place for a religious purpose. See Hoffmann; Amos 5:5; 2 Chron. 1:5. Akk. *še'u*, "seek," is used the same way; see CAD A2, 459b; AHw, 1223, sec. Gtn 2; Atrahasis I, 380.

18. 2 Sam. 24:18–25; 2 Chron. 3:1; Sifrei 62.

19. For the vocalization of *leshikhno*, see GKC §61b. Some scholars vocalize the verb as *leshakkeno*, "to make it dwell," in conformity with the idiom in verse 11 and elsewhere in Deuteronomy (see n. 20). Others read it as *leshakken* (as in v. 11) and consider it merely a doublet of *lasum* earlier in the verse. "Double" or "conflate" readings occur when scribes, copying manuscripts with variant readings, preserve both readings. Another possibility is that, since this is the first of several passages that speak of God establishing His name in the Temple, the Author chose to introduce both verbs that would be used henceforth. The translation, following the Masoretic accents, construes *shikhno* as a noun *shekhen*, meaning "(His) habitation, dwelling." This is theoretically possible but no such noun is known in biblical Hebrew (it may appear in Ecclus. 14:25). See Driver; BHK; Z. Ben-Hayyim, *The Literary and Oral Tradition of Hebrew and Aramaic Amongst the Samaritans* (Hebrew) (Jerusalem: Mosad Bialik and the Academy of the Hebrew Language, 1957–1967), 3/1:117–118 (cf. targums); R. Weiss, *Studies in the Text and Language of the Bible* (Hebrew) (Jerusalem: Magnes Press, 1981), 131; S. Talmon, s.v. "Conflate Readings (OT)," IDBS, 173; Y. Zakovitch, "To Cause His Name to Dwell There—To Put His Name There," *Tarbiz* 41 (1972): 338–340.

20. These two idioms appear interchangeably throughout Deuteronomy. "To place His name" appears in v. 21 and 14:24; "to make His name dwell" appears in 14:23; 16:2,6,11; 26:2. In Isa. 18:7, Mount Zion is called "the place of the LORD's name."

21. R. de Vaux, "Le lieu que Yahvé a choisi pour y établir son nom," in F. Maass, ed., *Das Ferne und Nahe Wort* (Berlin: Töpelmann, 1967), 219–229; Weinfeld, DDS, 193–195; Greenberg, "Religion: Stability and Ferment," 90. Note the interchange of idioms in 1 Kings 8:16,29,43 and 2 Chron. 6:20, and then in Jer. 7:10,12 (for a full list of equivalent idioms, see Weinfeld, DDS, 325). For "being called by someone's name" indicating ownership and authority, see Isa. 63:19; Amos 9:12 (see also 2 Sam. 12:28 and the Akkadian letters from Jerusalem

translated in ANET, 488c, 488d). Cf. ANET, 261a (Ramses III builds Amon a temple "as the vested property of thy name").

22. For protective attention to the place where one sets his name, or to that which bears one's name, see ANET, 488c, and Deut. 28:10.

23. E.g., Exod. 25:8; 29:45; Isa. 8:18. The sanctuary was called God's *mishkan*, "dwelling place" (Exod. 25:9).

24. Cf. Deut. 26:15; 1 Kings 8:27–30. See von Rad, *Studies in Deuteronomy* (London: SCM Press, 1961), 37–44; Weinfeld, DDS, 191–209.

25. The first pair of terms often stands for all types of animal sacrifices, as in Josh. 22:26; 2 Kings 5:17; Jer. 6:20; 7:22; Ezek. 40:42.

26. For regular burnt offerings, see Exod. 29:42; Num. 28–29; for burnt offerings as purification offerings, see Lev. 12:6–8; 15:15,30; Num. 6:11; as votive and freewill offerings, see Lev. 22:17–24. The procedures for the burnt offering are described in Lev. 1:3–17; 6:1–6. See Levine, *Leviticus*, and Milgrom, *Numbers*.

27. See Lev. 3; 7:11–34; Exod. 12:27; 1 Sam. 1:21; 20:29.

28. See Lev. 27:30–33; Num. 18:21–32. For discussion of the institution see Weinfeld, s.v. "Tithe," EncJud 15:1156–1162. Opinions differ on whether or not this verse refers to all types of tithe; see Hoffmann.

29. Sifrei 63; Rashi. For *terumah* referring to the first fruits, see Num. 18:8–13 (cf. 15:19–21); for other offerings, see Lev. 7:32,34; Num. 18:24–29; 31:29,41. See the discussion by J. Milgrom, s.v. "Heave Offering," IDBS, 391–392.

30. For votive offerings, see Gen. 28:20–22; Judg. 11:30–31; 1 Sam. 1:11; 2 Sam. 15:7–8. For freewill offerings, see Exod. 25:2–8; 35:5–9,21–29; 36:3–7; Deut. 16:10,16–17; Ezra 1:4; 2:68–69; 3:5. As sacrifices, both types might take the form of burnt offerings or *shelamim* offerings; see Lev. 22:17–24 and below, Comment to Deut. 27:7.

31. See also Exod. 13:2,12–13; 22:29; 34:19–20; Num. 18:15–18.

32. Cf. 14:26; 16:11,14; 31:10–12; see Sifrei 64; Tosef. Ḥag. 1:4; Ḥag. 6b; Maimonides, Hil. Ḥag. 1:1; Sefer Ha-Ḥinnukh, sec. 451; Weinfeld, DDS, 291; Haran, *Temples and Temple Service*, 293, 301–303. On the inclusion of women among those addressed in Biblical laws, see also 13:7–11 and M. Greenberg, *Studies in the Bible and Jewish Thought* (Philadelphia: Jewish Publication Society, 1995), 434.

33. Sifrei to verses 7,12; G. A. Anderson, *A Time to Mourn, A Time to Dance* (University Park: Pennsylvania State University Press, 1991), 19–26. See vv. 12,18; 14:26; 16:11, 14–15; 26:11.

34. See also 12:12,18–19; 14:23–27; 15:20; 16:11,14; 26:11; 27:7. See Weinfeld, DDS, 190, 210–214. Keil-Delitzsch and Driver (144) refer to the "holy joy" of these occasions. For Deuteronomy's attitude toward sacrifices, see Excursus 14.

35. Weinfeld, DDS, 214–216. See Comments to 14:22–27; 15:19–23; 26:1–11.

36. Keil-Delitzsch; Hoffmann; Ehrlich; Moffatt; cf. *mishloaḥ yad* in Isa. 11:14. The same semantic development is seen in *mela'khah*, which means both "labor" and "property," derived from *l-'-kh*, "send." Other terms also refer both to labor and its fruits; see Levine, *Leviticus*, at Lev. 19:13; H. L. Ginsberg, *Studies in Koheleth* (New York: Jewish Theological Seminary, 1950), 1–6; idem, *Koheleth* (Hebrew) (Tel Aviv and Jerusalem: M. Newman, 1961), 13–15; cf. R. Gordis, *Koheleth—The Man and His World*, 3rd ed. (New York: Schocken, 1968), 418–419.

37. For insistence on prescribed ceremonies see the sin described in Lev. 10:1; for prescribed dates and chosen priesthood note the sinfulness of Jeroboam's actions in 1 Kings 12:31 and 33; 13:33. Note also the divine design of the Tabernacle and, according to Chronicles, of the first Temple (Exod. 25:9; 1 Chron. 28:11–19). This principle is summed up by Judah Hale-

vi: "One cannot approach God except through His commands" (*Kuzari*, 3:23).

38. Cf. Maimonides, Guide 3.46.

39. See Smith.

40. For Jerusalem see 2 Sam. 7:1, 11; 1 Kings 5:17–19; 8:16,56; 9:3; 2 Kings 21:7; Ps. 78:68–69; 132:13–14; 1 Chron. 22:9–10,18; 23:25. For Shiloh, see Josh. 18:1; 22:19,29 (cf. Josh. 9:27); 1 Sam. 2:14,22 (note: "all Israel"); cf. Ps. 78:60. This is the view of the halakhic sources as well; see Sifrei 66; Mish. Meg. 1:11; Zev. 14:4–8.

41. See also vv. 18–19; 14:27–29; 16:11,14; 26:11–12. See Weinfeld, DDS, 55; Rofé, *Mavo'*, 14. For Levites in provincial sanctuaries, see Judg. 17:7–12. Contrast the picture of the Levites in 33:11.

42. Lit., "see," which often has the connotation "approve," "choose" (33:21; 1 Sam. 16:1; 2 Kings 10:3; Lam. 3:36; see Bekhor Shor; Shadal; Buhl, 735, definition 2e; Jastrow, 1435, definition 3 of *kal* and *niph'al*. V. 8 uses the synonymous "see fit." Akk. *amāru*, "see," likewise has the nuance "select" (CAD A2, 12c, 25c).

43. See Lev. 17 and cf. 1 Sam. 14:31–35. This view of Lev. 17 follows Rabbi Ishmael (Sifrei 75; Sifra [Weiss, 83b.6]). According to Rabbi Akiba, however, Lev. 17 does not forbid secular slaughter; his view is adopted by Levine, *Leviticus*, 112–113. The evolution of profane slaughter is a much-debated question; see Levine, *Leviticus*; and J. Milgrom, *Leviticus 1–16* (Garden City, N.Y.: Doubleday, 1991); and H. C. Brichto, "On Slaughter and Sacrifice, Blood and Atonement," HUCA 47 (1976): 19–55.

44. See Rashi, Bekhor Shor.

45. Abravanel, 122; Driver; Y. Muffs, *Love and Joy* (New York: Jewish Theological Seminary, 1992), 178.

46. Driver at v. 20; Sifrei 75; Ḥul. 84a and Rashi there; Rashi at Lev. 17:13 and Deut. 12:20. Lists of normal foodstuffs often lack meat; see, e.g., Deut. 11:14–15; Joel 2:19–26; Ecclus. 39:26.

47. See Lev. 3:17; 7:26–27; 17:11–14 and, for further details, see below, vv. 23–25.

48. Weinfeld, DDS, 214, sees the difference as part of Deuteronomy's more secular orientation, denying the sacral value of the animal's blood and the need to make amends, by ceremonial means, for shedding it (Lev. 17:4,6,11). For another suggestion see Sefer Ha-Ḥinnukh, no. 185. The ancient Arabs also poured blood of slaughtered animals on the ground, and Islam prohibits eating blood altogether (W. Robertson Smith, *The Religion of the Semites* [London: A. and C. Black, 1914], 235).

49. Abravanel, 123.

50. See Sifrei 75; Kid. 57b; Maimonides, Hilkhot Sheḥitah 2:1; Ramban; Abravanel, 123; Hoffmann; Da'at Soferim.

51. The method is indicated by the regular use of *shaḥat* for sacrificial slaughter (Exod. 12:6; 29:11; Lev. 1:5; 3:8; Num. 19:3; cf. Gen. 22:10, which mentions the use of a knife). That *shaḥat* means "slit the throat" is recognized by LXX and confirmed by Arabic, in which the cognate verb has that meaning. See the discussion by Milgrom, *Leviticus 1–16*, 713–718. The use of this method in ancient Egypt is shown by murals and models of slaughterhouse scenes. See A. S. Gilbert, "Zooarchaeological Observations on the Slaughterhouse of Meketre," *Journal of Egyptian Archaeology* 74 (1988): 79, 83–86; W. J. Darby et al., *Food: The Gift of Osiris* (New York: Academic Press, 1977), 1:146; cf. *Iliad* 2:422–423 (but cf. *Odyssey* 14:425ff.).

52. See Sifrei 75; Ḥul. 28a; Rashi; Ramban; Abravanel, 123; Sefer Ha-Ḥinnukh, no. 440; Hoffmann; J. Milgrom, "Profane Slaughter and a Formulaic Key to the Composition of Deuteronomy," HUCA 47 (1976): 13–15; EM 7:620–621, s.v. *shehitah*.

53. See Sifrei 75.

54. See also Lev. 3:17; 7:26–27; 17:10–14; Deut. 15:23. See the discussions by Milgrom, s.v. "Blood," EncJud 4:1115–1116; idem, "A Prolegomenon to Leviticus 17:11," JBL 90 (1971):

149–156; idem, *Leviticus 1–16*, 704–706; C. Westermann, *Genesis 1–11: A Commentary* (Minneapolis: Augsburg, 1984), 464–465.

55. For the meaning of *ḥazak*, see 1 Chron. 28:7; cf. *hithazek* in Num. 13:20. See Ehrlich; for rabbinic Hebrew, see Tanḥ. B. Gen., 23a and S. Lieberman, "Three Notes," *Leshonenu* 33 (1968): 77.

56. Rashbam; Bekhor Shor.

57. See Milgrom, "Prolegomenon to Leviticus 17:11," 152; idem, *Leviticus 1–16*, 708–709. For blood pudding see A. S. Gilbert, *Journal of Egyptian Archaeology* 74:79; H. G. Fischer, *Varia* (New York: Metropolitan Museum of Art, 1976), 99 n. 14; Darby et al., *Food: The Gift of Osiris*, 1:146; A. Soyer, *The Pantropheon, or A History of Food* (reprint; New York: Paddington Press, 1977), 138; Smith, *Religion of the Semites*, 234. For meat cooked with blood see *Odyssey* 18:45,118–119; 20:25–26.

58. *Iliad* 14:518; cf. 17:86; for the same concept among the Arabs see Smith, *Religion of the Semites*, 40 n. 1.

59. See Torah Temimah, no. 88, citing Ḥul. 102b; Sefer Ha-Ḥinnukh, no. 587; H. Gevaryahu, s.v. *'ever min ha-ḥai*, EM 1:60–61.

60. See Sifrei 77; Hoffmann; Da'at Soferim.

61. The text says nothing about what to do with the entrail fat of the animal, whether slaughtered sacrificially or secularly. According to Leviticus, it is burnt as part of the sacrifice, and eating it is a serious offense (Lev. 3:17; 7:23, 25; 17:6; cf. 1 Samuel 2:12–17). The halakhah assumes that Deuteronomy prohibits its consumption in the case of secular slaughter as well. See Hoffmann, 184–185. The matter is debated by Haran, s.v. *ma'akhalim u-mashka'ot*, EM 4:557; Weinfeld, DDS, 212–213; idem, "On 'Demythologization and Secularization' in Deuteronomy," IEJ 23 (1973): 232; J. Milgrom, "The Alleged 'Demythologization and Secularization' in Deuteronomy," IEJ 23:157; and idem, *Numbers*, 401.

62. M and SP. Some translations number 13:1 as 12:32 (KJV; printed editions of Vulg., Pesh., and some editions of LXX). That a new unit begins with 12:29 is clear from the context and formulation. The subject of the place of sacrifice has been completed, and v. 29 resembles other introductions in 11:31, as explained above, and in 17:14; 18:9; 19:1; and 26:1. See Rofé, *Mavo'*, 26.

63. Hoffmann. For the metaphor see esp. Exod. 23:3; Josh. 23:13; Judg. 2:3. The verb *n-k-sh* is evidently a variant of *y-k-sh*, "trap, snare."

64. See Sifrei 81; Sefer Ha-Ḥinnukh, no. 262; Maimonides, Sefer Ha-Mitsvot, negative no. 30; M. Ydit, s.v. "Ḥukkat Ha-Goi," EncJud 8:1061–1062.

65. Rofé, *Mavo'*, 57.

Chapter 13:2–19

M. Weinfeld, DDS, 91–100; idem, "The Loyalty Oath in the Ancient Near East," UF 8 (1976): 389–390; P. E. Dion, "Deuteronomy 13: The Suppression of Alien Religious Propaganda in Israel during the Late Monarchical Era," in B. Halpern and D. W. Hobson, eds., *Law and Ideology in Monarchic Israel* (Sheffield: Sheffield Academic Press, 1991), 147–216.

1. These three cases are marked as separate units in M, SP, and 11QTemple cols. 54–55, which have breaks before vv. 2,7, and 13, and after v. 19. The break before v. 7 is also found in 1Q4/9.

2. See S. Mendelsohn, *The Criminal Jurisprudence of the Ancient Hebrews*, 2nd ed. (reprint; New York: Hermon Press, 1968), 47 n. 89; Weinfeld, DDS, 91–100; ANET, 535–537. Dion, "Deuteronomy 13," 196–204.

3. R. Sonsino, *Motive Clauses in Hebrew Law* (Chico, Calif.: Scholars Press, 1980), 116.

4. See Maimonides, Hilkhot Yesodei Ha-Torah 8:3; 9:1.

5. See Jer. 26:2; Revelations 22:18–19; Josephus, Ant. 1.17;

Erra Epic 5.43–44 (W. G. Lambert, "The Fifth Tablet of the Era Epic," *Iraq* 24 [1962]: 122–123); ANET, 413a, 434b.

6. Cf. Maimonides, Hilkhot Yesodei Ha-Torah 8:1–3; idem, "Epistle to Yemen," in A. Halkin and D. Hartman, *Crisis and Leadership: Epistles of Maimonides* (Philadelphia: Jewish Publication Society, 1985), 112–113.

7. S. A. Meier, *The Messenger in the Ancient Semitic World* (Atlanta: Scholars Press, 1988), 171.

8. Cf. Shalag.

9. S. Paul, s.v. "Prophets and Prophecy," EncJud 13:1150–1175; M. Greenberg, s.v. "Prophecy in Hebrew Scripture," *Dictionary of the History of Ideas* (New York: Scribner's, 1973), 657–664.

10. See, e.g., Exod. 5:1 and Ezek. 2:4, and cf. Gen. 32:4–5; 45:9; Judg. 11:14–15. For the prophet as envoy, see Hag. 1:13; Isa. 44:26; 2 Chron. 36:15–16 (cf. Jer. 29:19); Josephus, Ant. 15.136 (see W. D. Davies, "A Note on Josephus, Antiquities 15:136," HTR 47 [1954]: 135–140); Lev. R. 1:1; J. S. Holladay, "Assyrian Statecraft and the Prophets of Israel," HTR 63 (1970): 29–51; J. Ross, "The Prophet as Yahweh's Messenger," in B. W. Anderson and W. Harrelson, eds., *Israel's Prophetic Heritage* (London: SCM Press, 1962), 98–107.

11. J.-M. Durand, *Archives Épistolaires de Mari* I/1 (Paris: Éditions Recherche sur les Civilisations, 1988), 377–378, 444–445 (ref. courtesy of Avigdor Hurowitz); cf. H. M. Huffmon, s.v. "Prophecy," ABD 5:479.

12. Eng. "prophet" comes from Gk. *prophētēs*, which also means approximately "spokesman" (lit., "one who speaks for or forth"). For the prophet as "mouth"/"spokesman" see also Jer. 15:19. Some believe that *navi* means "one who is called," like the Akk. adjective *nabiu* (see CAD N1, 31c). This is less likely, since in that sense the word could refer to a person "summoned" for any task.

13. Revelatory dreams were experienced by prophets and lay persons. See Gen. 20:6; 28:12; 31:24; Num. 12:6; 1 Kings 3:5; Jer. 23:25–32; 27:9 (MT: "dreams," LXX: "dreamers"); 29:8; Joel 3:1; Job 33:14–16; ANET, 449, 606, 623, 624, 631. See also S. Ahituv, s.v. *'atid, haggadat 'atidot*, EM 6:418; Rofé, *Mavo'*, 61–62; R. R. Wilson, *Prophecy and Society in Ancient Israel* (Philadelphia: Fortress Press, 1980), 113; A. Malamat, "A Forerunner of Biblical Prophecy: The Mari Documents," in P. D. Miller et al., eds., *Ancient Israelite Religion* (Philadelphia: Fortress Press, 1987), 43–45.

14. See Sifrei 84; Sanh. 90a; Saadia; Ramban; Hoffmann.

15. For the synonymity of *'ot* and *mofet*, cf. Exod. 4:1–9 to 7:9; cf. Sifrei Num. 23. For the prophetic signs cf. Exod. 4:1–9,30–31; 7:8–13; 1 Kings 13:3,5; Isa. 38:7–8; see also Num. 16:28–29; 1 Kings 18:36; and Isa. 7:11.

16. Meier, *Messenger*, 170–171.

17. Dion, "Deuteronomy 13," 163.

18. Sot. 14a.

19. See Saadia; Rashi; Shadal here and at Isa. 1:5; *The Torah* (Philadelphia: Jewish Publication Society, 1962); Ehrlich, *Randglossen*; E. Jenni, "Dtn 19,16: *sarā* 'Falschheit,'" in A. Caquot and M. Delcor, eds., *Mélanges bibliques et orientaux en l'honneur de M. Henri Cazelles* (Kevelaer: Butzon and Bercker and Neukirchen-Vluyn: Neukirchener Verlag, 1981), 201–211.

20. As Shadal notes, *dibber sarah* unquestionably means "lie" in Jer. 28:16; 29:32; and probably in Isa. 59:13b, as does "testify *sarah*" in Deut. 19:16 (cf. v. 18). The cognate Akkadian expression, "to speak *sartu* [or *sarratu, surratu*]" means both to tell lies and to propose disloyalty. In biblical Hebrew, however, there are no convincing cases with the second meaning; in Jeremiah, the prophets are clearly not proposing rebellion against the Lord. If it meant that in Deut. 13:6, it could have been used in v. 11, too. Notably, the Akkadian term for a lying messenger is *mar shipri sarrati* (Meier, *Messenger*, 171 n. 23).

21. Sforno; Ramban, paraphrasing Sanh. 90a, top (see Rashi there); Maimonides, Hilkhot Yesodei Ha-Torah 9:5. Cf.

B. Goff, "Syncretism in the Religion of Israel," JBL 58 (1939): 154: "Even some prophets of Yahweh encouraged a syncretistic cult."

22. Maimonides, Hilkhot 'Avodah Zarah 1:1 (translation from I. Twersky, ed., *A Maimonides Reader* [New York: Behrman House, 1972], 71–72, slightly modified). For other commentators writing similarly see S. Fraade, *Enosh and His Generation* (Chico, Calif.: Scholars Press, 1984), 129 n. 53. For examples of pagan gods ordaining the worship of other gods or spirits, see Enuma Elish VI, 110–120 (ANET, 69); ANET, 624, letters e and g.

23. Ahab gave his children names that contained the name of YHVH (see 1 Kings 22:40; 2 Kings 3:1), but he worshiped Baal as well (1 Kings 16:32; 2 Kings 10:18); 1 Kings 18:21 implies that Elijah's audience was worshiping YHVH and Baal simultaneously. Since Manasseh established the worship of other gods in the temple of the Lord, he presumably claimed that this was done with the Lord's authorization (see 2 Kings 21:3–7; cf. 23:4,11; similar claims must have been made by those behind the practices described in Ezek. 8).

24. 1 Kings 18:40; 2 Kings 10:19.

25. See also 17:7,12; 19:19; 21:21; 22:21,22,24; 24:7; cf. Judg. 20:13. See discussion by Shadal at 19:19.

26. Cf. Gen. 43:29. The variant reading "your brother, the son of your father or the son of your mother," misses the point (LXX; SP; 11QTemple 54:19). In poetry "mother's son" is simply a synonym of "brother." See Gen. 27:29; Ps. 50:20; and, for Ugaritic, ANET, 141, col. 6, ll. 14–15; 143 col. i, l. 9.

27. See Mic. 7:5. Cf. Deut. 28:54 and 56 where the phrases "the husband/wife of her/his bosom" highlight the fact that one is normally particularly concerned about the welfare of one's spouse.

28. The secret worship of other gods is also mentioned in Ezek. 8:7–12 and Job 31:26–28.

29. *Hus* and *ḥamal* are not limited to emotions but to emotions which lead to action, or to the action itself, such as sparing. See Gen. 45:20; 1 Sam. 15:9,15; 2 Sam. 12:4; Jonah 4:10.

30. See Philo, Spec. 1.316 (cf. 1.55–57) and F. H. Colson, *Philo* 7 (1937; reprint, Cambridge: Harvard University Press, 1968), 616–618; cf. Spec. 3.94–98 and Mish. Sanh. 9:6 for other cases where summary execution was permitted in later times. This understanding of the text is defended by B. M. Levinson, "But You Shall Surely Kill Him!" in G. Braulik, ed., *Bundesdokument und Gesetz. Studien zum Deuteronomium* (Freiburg: Herder, 1995), 37–63.

31. Ramban.

32. See Weinfeld, DDS, 94–96; Dion, "Deuteronomy 13," 154. LXX presumably reads *h-g-d t-g-d-n-v* (*hagged taggidennu*) in place of MT's *h-r-g t-h-r-g-n-v* (*harog taharegennu*). For *hagged* meaning "report," "inform" see 17:4 (in a related case); Lev. 5:1; Jer. 20:10; cf. Ezek. 43:10. The two readings could easily have been confused since they use the same or similarly shaped letters.

33. Mish. Sanh. 7:10. According to the Mishnah, if the instigator refused to repeat his proposal in the presence of others, witnesses could be placed in hiding; this is the only capital case in which this is permitted. In the view of Rofé, the requirement of two witnesses in 17:6 is part of a later revision of the law, and our passage reflects a stage of the law prior to that revision (Rofé, *Mavo'*, 72).

34. See Deut. 17:7; Lev. 24:14; Num. 15:35–36; 1 Kings 21:13. Stoning at the gate in Deut. 17:5 and 22:24 may mean outside the gate. For an exception, see Deut. 22:21. According to Lev. 24:14, the witnesses placed their hands on the head of the offender before the stoning began.

35. See, in order of the crimes listed above: Deut. 17:2–7 and Lev. 20:2–5; the present law; Lev. 24:15–16; 20:27; Num. 15:32–36; Josh. 7:25; Deut. 21:18–21; 22:20–21; 1 Kings 21:13; and Deut. 22:22–23. The ox who gores a human to death was also

stoned (Exod. 21:28–32), the case apparently being viewed as treason "against the divinely ordained hierarchy of creation, wherein man is the lord of terrestrial life" (J. J. Finkelstein, "The Goring Ox," *Temple Law Quarterly* 46 [1973]: 180–181); cf. Gen. 1:26,28; 9:2,5–6. See also M. Greenberg, s.v. "Stoning," IDB 4:447.

36. See, e.g., Lev. 18:24–30; 20:22; Deut. 4:25–27; Josh. 7:1–12; 2 Kings 17:7–23; Jer. 17:21–27.

37. See Exod. 17:4; Num. 14:10; 1 Sam. 30:6; 1 Kings 12:18.

38. See 17:13; 19:20; 21:21.

39. Num. 25:4–8. The punishment of those who worshiped the golden calf is similar (Exod. 32:27–28), although, as noted in the Comments to 9:16 and Excursus 12, this appears to be a case of idolatry but not of the worship of another god.

40. See Mish. Sanh. 10:4–5; Sanh. 71a and 111b–112a; Tosef. Sanh. 14:1; Sifrei 92–94; Maimonides, Hilkhot ʿAvodah Zarah, 4; Torah Temimah. A forerunner of this narrow, ameliorating exegesis may be reflected in LXX and 11QTemple 50:3 and 6, according to which *all* the inhabitants of the city must be guilty and be punished (see L. Schiffman, "The Deuteronomic Paraphrase of the Temple Scroll," RQ 15 [1992]: 557; contrast Dion, "Deuteronomy 13," 154–155).

41. Ramban. The same is true of the charge in 17:4.

42. Sifrei 92; Mid. Hag.; cf. the latter at 17:4; Shadal at 27:15, end.

43. If related to the verb *hoʿil*, "profit," "benefit," from the root *y-ʿ-l*.

44. If related to Arabic *waʿala*, "honor," "good lineage."

45. For references to antisocial people and qualities, see Deut. 15:9; Judg. 20:13; 1 Sam. 1:16; 2:12; 25:25; 30:22; 2 Sam. 16:7; 20:1; 1 Kings 21:10; Prov. 19:28; for the nether world and Satan, see 2 Sam. 22:5; 2 Cor. 6:15. See the articles on *beliyaʿal* in HALAT; EM 2:132–133 (by N. H. Tur-Sinai); TDOT 2:131–136 (by B. Otzen).

46. Sifrei 93; Sanh. 40a; Maimonides, Hilkhot ʿEdut 1:4–6. On capital punishment see Mish. Mak. 1:10; EncJud 5:145–147.

47. Maimonides, Hilkhot ʿAvodah Zarah 4:6; Bekhor Shor; cf. Dion, "Deuteronomy 13," 165.

48. Whether or not the children of the guilty are to be executed—in other words, whether or not Deut. 24:16 applies in such a case—is debated by halakhic authorities. See Hoffmann. That the *ḥerem* may supersede Deut. 24:16 is suggested by the case of Achan (Josh. 7:24–25). Rofé, *Mavoʾ*, 72–73, holds that the present law reflects a stratum of Deuteronomy that is older than 24:16.

49. See 6:11; 7:2 and 20:10–16; Josh. 6:17–24; 7:1, 11–26; 8:2,27; 11:14. The differing degrees of *ḥerem* are described by M. Greenberg, s.v. "Ḥerem," EncJud 8:344–350.

50. 2 Sam. 21:12; Job 29:7; Est. 6:9,11; Neh. 8:1,16; 2 Chron. 32:6. On the square at Beer-sheba, see Y. Aharoni, s.v. "Beer-sheba, Tel," EAEHL 1:165; Herzog, s.v. *shaʿar*, EM 8:242.

51. *Kalil*, "totality," is used both as an adjective and adverb meaning "total(ly)" and as a synonym of *ʿolah*, "(totally) burnt offering." Although some think that it is an adverb here ("burn totally"; cf. Judg. 20:40), most prefer the present translation. The meaning is the same in either case: since the city is totally burnt, it is like a burnt offering in which nothing is left for human use (see Comment to 12:6). The burning of the city is not literally considered a sacrifice; it does not take place at an altar, let alone at the chosen place.

52. See Josh. 6:18–19 and chap. 7.

53. See NJPS at Isa. 14:1; Jer. 31:19; Hos. 1:6; 2:3,6,25; the cognate verb in Aramaic may have this sense in Aḥikar, l. 11 (DISO, 277, ll. 16–17).

54. Judg. 21; see Ehrlich; Hoffmann.

Chapter 14

J. Milgrom, "Ethics and Ritual: The Foundations of the Biblical Dietary Laws," in E. R. Firmage et al., eds., *Religion and Law: Biblical-Judaic and Islamic Perspectives* (Winona Lake, Ind.: Eisenbrauns, 1990), 159–191; D. P. Wright, "Observations on the Ethical Foundations of the Biblical Dietary Laws: A Response to Jacob Milgrom," ibid., 193–198.

1. Subdivisions of the chapter are as follows: before vv. 1 (M, SP), 3 (M; 4QpaleoDeutʳ frag. 20 [DJD 9:140]), 9 (M, SP), 11 (M), 22, 28, and after 29 (M, SP). It is unclear why v. 21 is treated as part of vv. 11–20. Perhaps the aim was to avoid giving the impression that the motive clause "Because you are a people consecrated to the LORD" applies only to that verse and not to the laws in vv. 3–20.

2. Other passages that refer to Israel as God's children speak of the filial duties of honor, loyalty, and service (Jer. 3:19; Mal. 1:6; 3:17). The metaphor is used negatively to describe faithlessness and rebellion in 32:5,19,20; Isa. 1:2,4; 30:1,9; 63:8; Jer. 3:14,22. Elsewhere Deuteronomy speaks of God as a father to illustrate the way He cares for and disciplines Israel; see 1:31; 8:5; and Comment to 4:37–38.

3. Abravanel, 132.

4. Isa. 15:2; 22:12; Jer. 16:6; 41:5; 47:5; 48:37; Ezek. 7:18; 27:31; Amos 8:10; Mic. 1:16. For talmudic sources see Sanh. 68a; Lam. R. Proem 24; Semaḥot 9. For foreign parallels see Syriac Aḥikar 4:13 (Charles 2:748–749); ANET, 88a, 139bc; T. H. Gaster, *Myth, Legend, and Custom in the Old Testament* (New York: Harper and Row, 1969), sec. 202; W. Robertson Smith, *The Religion of the Semites* (London: A. and C. Black, 1914), 322ff, 336, 433.

5. See R. de Vaux, *The Bible and the Ancient Near East* (Garden City, N.Y.: Doubleday, 1971), 242–243.

6. M. Ostow and B. Scharfstein, *The Need to Believe: The Psychology of Religion* (New York: International Universities Press, 1969), 54.

7. Plutarch, *The Lives of the Noble Grecians and Romans* (New York: Modern Library, n.d.), 110; N. Lewis and M. Reinhold, *Roman Civilization* (New York: Columbia University Press, 1959), 1.108. For rabbinic attempts to limit excessive mourning, cf. MK 27b.

8. Ramban, v. 1; M. Fishbane, *Biblical Interpretation in Ancient Israel* (Oxford: Clarendon, 1985), 121–123; M. Greenberg, "Three Conceptions of the Torah in Hebrew Scriptures," in E. Blum et al., eds., *Die Hebräische Bibel und ihre zweifache Nachgeschichte* (Neukirchen-Vluyn: Neukirchener Verlag, 1990), 370–371.

9. See Exod. 22:30; 23:19; 34:26; Lev. 11; 17:15; 22:8.

10. Nations: Deut. 32:8; Israel: Lev. 20:24; 26; 1 Kings 8:53; Levites: Num. 8:14; 16:9, Deut. 10:8.

11. Rashbam at Lev. 11:3; Maimonides, Guide 3.48; Ramban at Lev. 11:11.

12. Abravanel at Lev. 11, p. 65; Shadal, cited by Hoffmann, *Sefer Devarim*, 204; Hoffmann, *Sefer Vayikraʾ*, 216.

13. A Babylonian text describes pigs as filthy and abhorrent to the gods (BWL, 215). For eating pigs, reptiles, and mice in pagan rites see Isa. 65:4; 66:3; on pigs in such rites see also ANET, 351a; de Vaux, *The Bible and the Ancient Near East*, 252–269.

14. For clean and unclean animals in the flood narrative, see Gen. 7:2,8; 8:20. For pork prohibited in other ancient cultures see ANET, 110; de Vaux, *The Bible and the Ancient Near East*, 252–269.

15. See H. Rabinowicz, s.v. "Dietary Laws," EncJud 6:42–45.

16. That both sexes could be eaten is clear from the fact that both could be offered as *shelamim* sacrifices, which were almost completely eaten (see Lev. 3:1,6 and Deut. 12:27).

17. H. R. Cohen, *Biblical Hapax Legomena in the Light of*

Akkadian and Ugaritic (Missoula, Mont.: Scholars Press, 1978), 111.

18. Lev. R. 13:5. Bones of domestic pigs found at a few Israelite sites indicate that pigs were domesticated and that some people ate pork. It is not known how extensively this was done and under what circumstances. See G. W. Ahlström, *An Archaeological Picture of Iron Age Religions in Palestine* (Helsinki: Finnish Oriental Society, 1984), 13–14.

19. See Lev. 11:8,11,24–25,27–28,31–40.

20. See Exod. 16:13; Lev. 5:7; Num. 11:31–32; 1 Kings 5:3. On *barburim* see E. Bilik, s.v. *barbur, barburim*, EM 2:335–337.

21. Isaac Klein, *A Guide to Jewish Religious Practice* (New York: Jewish Theological Seminary, 1979), 304–305; S. H. Dresner and S. Siegel, *The Jewish Dietary Laws* (New York: Burning Bush Press, 1959), 65; Y. Lipschutz, *Kashruth* (New York: Mesorah, 1988), 19.

22. Sifrei 103. Some suggest that most of these birds are prohibited because they eat carrion or tear the flesh of their victims and eat it along with the blood. They were therefore unfit to be eaten by Israelites, who may not eat blood or carrion, or animals torn by preying creatures (see Comment to v. 21). See Mayes, 241; Levine, *Leviticus*, Excursus 6; Bodenheimer, cited by M. Haran, s.v. *ma'akhalim u-mashka'ot*, EM 4:556; contrast the view of Haran himself there.

23. The description of the *nesher* carrying its young on its wings in 32:11 and Exod. 19:4 fits an eagle, but in Mic. 1:16 the *nesher* is bald and must be a vulture ("bald" eagles are not bald and are found only in North America). See Y. Ahituv and S. Ahituv, s.v. *nesher*, EM 5:976–978.

24. Heb. *ra'ah*, *'ayyah*, and *dayyah*. For the first, Lev. 11:14 reads *da'ah*. In the Talmud, Abaye takes *ra'ah* and *da'ah* as synonyms (Ḥul. 63a–63b). Since *resh* and *dalet* are similar, the reading *ra'ah* may be a scribal error (it does not appear elsewhere, whereas *da'ah* does, in Isa. 34:15). The third bird, *dayyah*, is absent in Leviticus, and some scholars, following Abaye, think it is simply a variant form of *da'ah*. SP has only two birds here, *da'ah* and *'ayyah*; cf. LXX.

25. According to Isa. 34:11; Zeph. 2:14; Ps. 102:7, the *ka'at* dwells in ruins and in the wilderness, whereas pelicans are water birds.

26. Sifrei 103.

27. Exod. 22:29; Lev. 22:27–28; Deut. 22:6–7.

28. The humanitarian explanation of this law goes back to Philo, *Virt.* 143–144; see also Ibn Ezra and Rashbam at Exod. 23:19 and the thorough review of the entire subject by M. Haran, "Seething a Kid in Its Mother's Milk," JJS 30 (1979): 23–39. Cooking meat in milk may be attested in Syria in the early second millennium B.C.E.; see ANET, 20a, and H. G. Fischer, *Varia* (New York: Metropolitan Museum of Art, 1976), 99 n. 14.

29. Maimonides, *Guide* 3.48. A damaged Ugaritic text has been thought to mention a Canaanite custom of this sort, but its reading and interpretation are questionable. See T. H. Gaster, *Thespis*, 2nd ed. (Garden City, N.Y.: Doubleday, 1961), 422–423; P. C. Craigie, "Deuteronomy and Ugaritic Studies," *Tyndale Bulletin* 28 (1977): 156–159; S. E. Loewenstamm, *Comparative Studies in Biblical and Ancient Oriental Literatures* (Kevelaer: Butzon and Bercker; Neukirchen-Vluyn: Neukirchener Verlag, 1980), 449–450; Haran, "Seething a Kid in Its Mother's Milk," 25–27; R. Ratner and B. Zuckerman, "'A Kid in Milk?,'" HUCA 57 (1986): 15–60.

30. See Haran, 34–35; cf. Sarna, *Exodus*, at 23:19.

31. See J. H. Greenstone, s.v. "Milk," JE 8:591–592; Maimonides, Hilkhot Ma'akhalot 'Asurot, 9.

32. See A. Oppenheimer, s.v. "Terumot and Ma'aserot," EncJud 15:1025–1028. The essentials of this view are already reflected, with some variations, in LXX to Deut. 26:12; Tob. 1:6–8; Jub. 32:11–15; Josephus, Ant. 4.68,205,240.

33. For various views on the history of tithes see M. Wein-

feld, s.v. "Tithe," EncJud 15:1156–1162 and bibliography cited there; Rofé, *Mavo'*, chap. 5.

34. Mish. Ma'as. 1:1.

35. For the first view see Ramban; Seforno; cf. Rashbam; cf. R. P. Merendino, *Das Deuteronomische Gesetz* (Bonn: Peter Hanstein, 1969), 98, 104. Cf. 4:10 and 17:19. For the second view, see Hertz; Craigie.

36. NJPS translators' note.

37. R. de Vaux, *Ancient Israel* (New York: McGraw-Hill, 1961), 206–209; Z. Yeivin, "The Mysterious Silver Hoard from Eshtemoa," BAR 13/6 (November-December, 1987): 38–44; A. Kindler, s.v. "Coins and Currency," EncJud 5:696; H. Hamburger, s.v. "Money, Coins," IDB 3:423–425.

38. Ehrlich, *Randglossen*. For moneybags see Gen. 42:35; 2 Kings 5:23; Prov. 7:20.

39. See Targums; Sifrei Num. 203; Ibn Ezra, and Levine, *Leviticus*, at Lev. 10:9; E. Stern, s.v. *shekhar*, EM 7:677–680.

40. See Exod. 30:40–41; Judg. 9:13; Jer. 35; Ps. 104:15; Prov. 9:1–6; 31:6–7; Eccles. 10:19; Dan. 10:3; ANET, 492b. See J. Tigay, s.v. "Drunkenness," EncJud 6:237–238.

41. Mish. Ma'as. Sh., 1:5–2:1; Sifrei 107.

42. Shadal here and at 26:12; Maimonides, Hilkhot Ma'aser Sheni 11:8. Essentially the same solution is required by 11QTemple 43:10–12 and Jub. 32:13. O. Eissfeldt opines that the surplus would be given to the priests (Eissfeldt, *Erstlinge und Zehnten* [Leipzig: Hinrichsche Buchhandlung, 1917], 49–51), while W. E. Claburn implies that it would be given to the king (see Excursus 14 n. 11).

43. Grain and wine could be stored for several years (see Gen. 41:47–57; Lev. 25:20–22; Mish. BB 6:3). The shelf life of olive oil today is a year, but Milgrom cites an experiment that showed that flour mixed with oil lasted at least three and a half years unrefrigerated ("The Chieftains' Gifts," HAR 9 [1986]: 223–224).

44. Sifrei 109; Finkelstein, 170, note to line 10; Mish. Pe'ah 8:5. For storage facilities see O. Borowski, *Agriculture in Iron Age Israel* (Winona Lake, Ind.: Eisenbrauns, 1987), 71–83. For threshing floors near city gates, see 1 Kings 22:10; Jer. 15:7; ANET, 151, col. 5, ll. 6–7; cf. J. Feliks, *Agriculture in Palestine in the Period of the Mishna and Talmud* (Jerusalem: Magnes Press; Tel Aviv: Dvir, 1963), 235–236.

45. Mish. Pe'ah 8:5.

46. See Midrash Tannaim, 87 (to 15:18), cited by Hoffmann, 255, end; cf. Josephus, Ant. 4.266, end.

Chapter 15

1. M and SP have breaks before vv. 1,7,12, and 19, and after 23.

2. See Exod. 22:24; Lev. 25:36–37; Pss. 37:26; 112:5. It is not known whether and to what extent there were other types of debts in ancient Israel, such as business investments or selling on credit. The paucity of business laws in the Torah suggests a simple economy with minimal commerce; see the Introduction.

3. Small loans of money or grain to families, recorded in Old Assyrian documents from Anatolia, were probably made to individuals in economic difficulty. See K. R. Veenhof, "An Ancient Anatolian Money-Lender: His Loans, Securities, and Debt-Slaves," in B. Hruška and G. Komoróczy, eds., *Festschrift Lubor Matouš* (Budapest: Eotvos Lorand University, 1978), 279–311.

4. See "The Edict of Ammiṣaduqa," ANET, 526–528, with bibliography; N. P. Lemche, "*Andurārum* and *Mišarum*: Comments on the Problem of Social Edicts and Their Application in the Ancient Near East," JNES 38 (1979): 11–22; idem, "The Manumission of Slaves—The Fallow Year—The Sabbatical Year—The Jobel Year," VT 26 (1976): 38–59; J. Lewy, "The Biblical Institution of DeRÔR in the Light of Akkadian Docu-

ments," EI 5 (1958): 21–31; S. J. Lieberman, "Royal 'Reforms' of the Amurrite Dynasty," *Bibliotheca Orientalis* 46 (1989): 240–259; Weinfeld, DDS, 152–155; idem, "Sabbatical Year and Jubilee in the Pentateuchal Laws and Their Ancient Near Eastern Background," in T. Veijola, ed., *The Bible and Its Environment* (Göttingen: Vandenhoeck and Ruprecht, 1990), 39–62; idem, *Justice and Righteousness in Israel and the Nations* (Jerusalem: Magnes Press, 1985); S. Kaufman, "A Reconstruction of the Social Welfare Systems of Ancient Israel," in *In the Shelter of Elyon* (Sheffield: JSOT Press, 1984), 277–286.

5. A. W. Gomme and T. J. Cadoux, s.v. "Solon," in OCD, 999.

6. Weinfeld, DDS, 152–155; idem, *Justice and Righteousness*.

7. See M. Greenberg, "Biblical Attitudes Toward Power: Ideal and Reality in the Law and Prophets," in E. R. Firmage et al., eds., *Religion and Law: Biblical-Judaic and Islamic Perspectives* (Winona Lake, Ind.: Eisenbrauns, 1990), 101–112.

8. Maimonides, Hilkhot Shemittah ve-Yovel 9:4.

9. Mish. Shev. 10; "Edict of Ammiṣaduqa," §8 (ANET, 527).

10. S. Talmon argues that the two terms are a conflation of variant readings (Talmon, "Double Readings in the Massoretic Text," *Textus* 1 [1960]: 168).

11. See also Jer. 34:14–15,17.

12. This means either "for the LORD's remission has been proclaimed" (cf. "the sabbath of the LORD," used of the Sabbath day and the sabbatical year [5:14; Lev. 23:3 (note "proclaim" in v. 2); 25:2]) or "a remission has been proclaimed by the LORD" (taking *kara'* as standing for the passive *kora'* and the *lamed* as indicating the agent of the passive verb; see Ezek. 10:13 and Jüon, 132–133), or "by the LORD's authority."

13. See ANET, 526–528.

14. Since the idea in vv. 4–6 that "there shall be no needy" conflicts with the assumption of vv. 1–3 and 7–11 that there will always be needy, as stated explicitly in v. 11, it seems possible that vv. 4–6 were not originally part of the same context as the rest of vv. 1–11. Some scholars assume that vv. 4–6 are from a different author (see, e.g., Mayes at v. 4). Whatever the case, in the present context the function of vv. 4–6 is to counter the realism of vv. 1–3 and 7–11 with a vision of what could be.

15. "Incur guilt" (Heb. *ve-hayah bekha ḥet*') is Deuteronomy's equivalent of *nasa' 'avon* in priestly literature (Weinfeld, DDS, 356 no. 5).

16. Deut. 5:15; 15:15; 16:12; 24:18,22; Job 31:13–15.

17. See Exod. 20:10; 21:2–11,20–21,26–27; 23:12; Deut. 5:14; 12:18; 15:12–18; 16:11,14; and 23:16–17.

18. Exod. 21:2–6; Lev. 25:39–55; Deut. 15:12–18.

19. Exod. 22:2; Lev. 25:39,47; cf. Deut. 28:68. On self-sale by indigents see I. Mendelsohn, *Slavery in the Ancient Near East* (New York: Oxford University Press, 1949), 18–19, 88–90; B. L. Eichler, s.v. "Slavery," in P. Achtemeier et al., eds., *Harper's Bible Dictionary* (San Francisco: Harper and Row, 1985), 959.

20. For parallels to debt servitude from Mesopotamia, see LH §117; "Edict of Ammiṣaduqa," §20; Driver and Miles, BL 1:217–221; B. L. Eichler, *Indenture at Nuzi* (New Haven: Yale University Press, 1973); Mendelsohn, *Slavery in the Ancient Near East*, 26–32; for Ptolemaic Egypt, W. L. Westermann, *The Slave Systems of Greek and Roman Antiquity* (Philadelphia: American Philosophical Society, 1955), 50. The presence of the practice in Egypt, Greece, and Rome is implied by the sources cited below, n. 23.

21. 2 Kings 4:1; Neh. 5:1–6; cf. 1 Sam. 22:2; Isa. 50:1; perhaps Prov. 22:7. The distrainee may have been expected to work off the debt, but this is not necessarily so. At Nuzi a debt servant's labor covered only the interest on the debt, not the principal. In Babylonia the distrainee served primarily as a hostage for repayment. See Eichler, *Indenture at Nuzi*; Mendelsohn, *Slavery in the Ancient Near East*, 26–32; A. Goetze, *The Laws of Eshnunna* (New Haven: American Schools of Oriental Research, 1956), 69–73.

22. See E. A. Speiser, *Oriental and Biblical Studies* (Philadelphia: University of Pennsylvania Press, 1967), 131–135; M. Elon, *Freedom of the Debtor's Person in Jewish Law* (Hebrew) (Jerusalem: Magnes Press, 1964), 1–10; Y. Kaufmann, *Toledot Ha-'Emunah Ha-Yisre'elit* (Tel Aviv: Bialik Institute-Dvir, 1937–1956), 4:321–322 n. 24; M. Greenberg, "More Reflections on Biblical Criminal Law," in S. Japhet, ed., *Studies in Bible* (Jerusalem: Magnes Press, 1986), 5–7.

23. Exod. 22:24–26; Lev. 25:36–37; Deut. 23:20–21; 24:6,10–13. The halakhah does not permit distraint of persons for debt (M. Elon, s.v. "Execution [Civil]," EncJud 6:1007–1020). According to halakhic exegesis, the present law refers only to indentured thieves and minor daughters sold as slaves (Rashi), and indigents may voluntarily sell themselves for terms longer than six years (Maimonides, Hilkhot Avadim 2:3). Precisely when debt servitude was abandoned in practice is not known; Weinfeld suggests that both Zedekiah and Nehemiah intended to abolish it permanently (Weinfeld, *Justice and Righteousness*, 93–94, 101), and it is not found in the fifth-century-B.C.E. Aramaic papyri from Elephantine. It was abolished in Egypt, Athens, and Rome as well. See Diodorus of Sicily 1:79, 3 (Egypt, eighth century B.C.E.); A. W. Gomme and T. J. Cadoux, s.v. "Solon," OCD, 999, and Westermann, *Slave Systems*, 44 (Athens, early sixth century B.C.E.); N. Lewis and M. Reinhold, *Roman Civilization* (New York: Columbia University Press, 1951), 1:120–122 (Rome, fourth century B.C.E.).

24. The sequence of Lev. 25:35–38 and 39–40 (a loan to an indigent followed by his sale or self-sale) may imply that vv. 39–40 refer to debt servitude (see Isa. 50:1 for this use of "sell"). Vv. 47–48 may mean "If a resident alien among you has prospered and your kinsman has become impoverished (in his dealings with him) and comes under his authority," which may mean that he has become indebted, and then indentured, to the alien. This is suggested by "with him," which must mean "in his dealings with him"; it cannot mean "living in his community," as it does in vv. 35 and 39, since the alien is said to live among Israelites. In this case, the "purchase price" of the Israelite (v. 50) is the debt for which he became indentured. If this is the meaning of vv. 47–48, the same would be true of vv. 39–40, which use the same terminology. However, it is highly unlikely that v. 35 refers to distraint of a debt slave. Although *heḥezik be-* normally means "seize, take hold of," in the context of vv. 35–37, it refers to something that is done before any loan has taken place. See further M. Greenberg, "More Reflections," 5–7.

25. For a summary of the evidence on *'apiru*, see Sarna, *Genesis*, Excursus 4; M. Greenberg, *The Ḥab/piru* (New Haven: American Oriental Society, 1955). For a discussion of Exod. 21:2, see S. M. Paul, *Studies in the Book of the Covenant in the Light of Cuneiform and Biblical Law* (Leiden: Brill, 1970), 45–48; contrast Greenberg, *Ḥab/piru*, 92.

26. See Driver; Mayes.

27. See Mendelsohn, *Slavery in the Ancient Near East*, 5–14, 87–89; idem, "Slavery in the Ancient Near East," in E. F. Campbell and D. N. Freedman, eds., *Biblical Archaeologist Reader* 3 (Garden City, N.Y.: Doubleday, 1970), 128–131, 138; Paul, *Studies*, 52–53. Cases of daughters sold for marriage are cited by Mendelsohn, *Slavery*, and "Slavery." For females indentured for insolvency and debt, see LH §117; "Edict of Ammiṣaduqa," §20; MAL §48; Eichler, *Indenture at Nuzi*, 131–132 (no. 39).

28. LH §117.

29. Sefer Ha-Ḥinnukh, no. 450; M. Tamari, *With all Your Possessions* (New York: Free Press, 1987), 144.

30. The verb *ha'anek* appears only here. If it is related to the noun *'anak*, "necklace," the meaning would be "adorn," "bedeck," in other words, "endow generously" (Rashi; Ibn Ezra).

31. R. Meyuḥas. Cf. 16:10, "giving . . . according as [ka'asher] the LORD your God has blessed you," in the light of which 'asher here must be equivalent to ka'asher (see BDB, 83d,

s.v. *'asher*, sec. 8e). This interpretation is supported by the Masoretic punctuation. SP and LXX actually read *ka'asher* here. Since the preceding word ends with a kaph, *'asher* might be an error due to haplography, though *ka'asher* could be an error due to dittography.

32. Kid. 17a, where other amounts are considered. On the value of slaves see H. Cazelles, *Études sur le code de l'alliance* (Paris: Letouzey et Ané, 1946), 59; Paul, *Studies*, 83 n. 4; B. Porten, *Archives from Elephantine* (Berkeley: University of California Press, 1968), 75.

33. TJ Kid. 1:2, 59d. For the Egyptian word see P. Montet, *Everyday Life in Egypt* (Philadelphia: University of Pennsylvania Press, 1981), 61. For a recent discussion of the subject see V. Hurowitz, "His Master Shall Pierce His Ear with an Awl (Exodus 21:6)," *PAAJR* 58 (1992): 47–77.

34. Weinfeld, DDS, 233.

35. Heb. *'eved 'olam*, "a lifelong slave" (NJPS, Job 40:28), apparently a technical term referring to one who remains a slave permanently rather than temporarily. See 1 Sam. 27:12; Job 40:28; and Ugaritic parallels cited in ANET, 143bc (see H. L. Ginsberg, *The Legend of King Keret* [New Haven: American Schools of Oriental Research, 1946], 36, note to line 55).

36. Sifrei 122; MdRY Nezikin 2 (Lauterbach 3:17–18); Kid. 21b; TJ Kid. 1:2, 59d; Rashi; R. Meyuhas.

37. See Sifrei 123; Driver; R. de Vaux, *Ancient Israel* (New York: McGraw-Hill, 1961), 76. Ibn Ezra's suggestion that the meaning is clarified by Isa. 16:14 was refuted by Rashbam (cf. Isa. 21:16 and see S. Japhet, "The Laws of Manumission of Slaves," in Y. Avishur and J. Blau, eds., *Studies in the Bible and the Ancient Near East* [Jerusalem: Rubinstein, 1978], 1:245 n. 59). Contrast Y. Zakovitch, "Some Remnants of Ancient Law in the Deuteronomic Code," *Israel Law Review* 9 (1974): 349–351.

38. Exod. 23:19; 34:26; Lev. 19:23–35; 23:9–14; Num. 18:12–13; Deut. 18:4; 26:1–10; Jer. 2:3.

39. See W. Robertson Smith, *The Religion of the Semites* (London: A. and C. Black, 1914), 241, 462–463; M. P. Nilsson, s.v. "First Fruits," OCD, 439; E. S. Hartum, s.v. *bikkurim*, EM 2:127.

40. See Exod. 13:2,12–16; 22:29; 34:19–20; Lev. 27:26; Num. 18:15–18. The present law has been stated briefly in 12:6–7,17–18; and 14:23.

41. Rashi; Ibn Ezra; Neh. 10:37; Mish. Zev. 5:8.

42. According to Weinfeld and Rofé, Deuteronomy means that the farmer must *declare* the firstling holy because—in contradistinction to the JE and P sources—Deuteronomy does not regard sanctity as an inborn quality of firstlings. That is why blemished firstlings need not be killed or desacralized by a special ceremony such as redemption. See Weinfeld, DDS, 215–217, and Rofé, *Mavo'*, 43.

43. Sifrei 124.

44. See also Lev. 1:3; 3:1. For ancient parallels to the requirement that sacrificial animals be unblemished, see J. Leibovitz and J. Licht, s.v. *mum*, EM 4:725; Lieberman, HJP, 155–157.

45. Cf. Exod. 34:20; Lev. 27:27; Num. 18:15–17.

Chapter 16:1–17

1. Hebrew manuscripts divide the text before 16:1,9,13, and after v. 17 (M and SP). 1Q4/13 (in DJD 1) may have a break before v. 5.

2. Cf. Hoffmann, 263. The connection between the two spring festivals is reflected in the Masoretic paragraphing, which has a minor (*setumah*) break between them but a major (*petuhah*) break before the Feast of Booths. This implies that the two spring festivals are subdivisions of the same unit. This connection is reflected in rabbinic sources by the practice of beginning the countdown to the Feast of Weeks during the Festival of Unleavened Bread (see Comment to v. 9) and by the designation of the latter as "the *'atseret* of *Pesah*," a spring counterpart of the fall *'atseret* (*Shemini 'Atseret*) that concludes the Feast of Booths in Lev. 23:36 (Mish. Ḥag. 2:4; Bek. 9:5; Pesikta de-Rav Kahana (ed. B. Mandelbaum), 68:8, 428:8; 431:1 variant reading; cf. Targ. Neof. here; Targs. Onk. and Jon. at Num. 28:26; Josephus, Ant. 3.252).

3. On the separateness of the two festivals see J. Licht, s.v. *pesah*, EM 6:523–524; Rofé, *Mavo'*, 38–40; Sarna, *Exodus*, at 12:14–20. Note 2 Chron. 35:17.

4. The beginning of the harvest, and the offering marking it, are mentioned only *after* the Feast of Unleavened Bread is completed (16:9; Lev. 23:10–14). See further on v. 9.

5. Yal. 654.

6. See Exod. 9:31; Lev. 2:14; Mish. Kil. 5:7. *'Abib* refers specifically to the phase of growth when the grain is still green and the seeds are full of milky liquid (H. L. Ginsberg, *The Israelian Heritage in Judaism* [New York: Jewish Theological Seminary, 1982], 44). On the ancient month names, see Excursus 17.

7. See Exod. 12:2; Lev. 23:5; Est. 3:7; Neh. 2:1. See Sarna, *Exodus*, at Exod. 12:2.

8. See Exod. 23:15–16 and 34:18,22.

9. Mish. RH 1:1.

10. Sifrei 127; Rashi; Maimonides, Hilkhot Kiddush Ha-Ḥodesh 4:1.

11. NJPS notes to Exod. 12:11,23; LXX (at v. 27; at v. 13: pass over); Targums; Hebrew commentaries starting with MdRY Bo' 7 (Lauterbach 1:57–58); Sarna, *Exodus*, at 12:11; Levine, *Leviticus*, at 23:5; contrast J. B. Segal, *The Hebrew Passover* (Oxford: Oxford University Press, 1963), 95–101.

12. See Exod. 12:6–13,29–32,42; Sifrei 128; cf. Rashi; Ibn Ezra.

13. For variations on this interpretation see Sifrei 129; Rashi; Ramban; Shadal; Ibn Ezra; Plaut; Hoffmann, 266; M. Haran, *Temples and Temple Service in Ancient Israel* (Oxford: Clarendon, 1978), 322 n. 11.

14. MdRY Bo' 8 (Lauterbach 1:60–61, 67); Isaac Klein, *A Guide to Jewish Religious Practice* (New York: Jewish Theological Seminary, 1979), 110.

15. See Gen. 19:3; Judg. 6:19–22; 1 Sam. 28:24; J. Licht, s.v. *matsah*, EM 5:225–228; H. Schauss, *Guide to Jewish Holy Days* (New York: Schocken, 1964), 77; P. Goodman, *Passover Anthology* (Philadelphia: Jewish Publication Society, 1973), 86–88. Babylonian sources mention that shepherds and soldiers eat "ash-bread" (*Gilgamesh Epic* 6:59 [ANET, 84c]; CAD A1, 242a; K, 110–111).

16. Ibn Ezra reportedly said that he was fed unleavened bread while a captive in India (M. M. Kasher, *Haggadah Shelemah* [Jerusalem: Makhon Torah Shelemah, 1955], 5).

17. Rashi; Seforno; the paragraph *ha' lahma' 'anya'* in the Passover Haggadah ("this is the bread of affliction that our forefathers ate in the land of Egypt"; some manuscripts, however, read "when they left the land of Egypt"). *'Oni* is used for Israel's servitude in Egypt in Exod. 3:7,17; 4:31; Deut. 26:7; and Neh. 9:9.

18. Cf. Lev. 2:11; 6:9,10; and perhaps Amos 4:5; see J. Licht, s.v. *matsah*, EM 5:225–228. The independence of the prohibition in connection with the *pesah* sacrifice is also indicated in Num. 9:11, where it applies even when the sacrifice is offered a month late and is not followed by a Feast of Unleavened Bread.

19. Critical analysis of the text suggests that it consists of a *pesah* law (vv. 1–3a1, followed by 4b–7) that has been combined with a law about the Feast of Unleavened Bread (vv. 3b2–4a and v. 8). In the *pesah* law vv. 3a1 and 4b are based on Exod. 23:18 and 34:25, while vv. 2b and 5–7 are their Deuteronomic supplement. See Rofé, *Mavo'*, 39–40, following Steuernagel; cf. Licht, s.v. *Pesah*, EM 6:524.

20. Sifrei 131; J. D. Eisenstein, *Ozar Dinim U-Minhagim* (New York: Hebrew Publishing Company, 1938), 137.

21. See also Exod. 23:18b; 34:25b, and the discussion by Haran, *Temples*, 329–332.

22. Hertz; Rofé, *Mavo'*, 41; contrast Mish. Meg. 1:10; Jub. 49:16–18; Haran, *Temples*, 341ff.; Segal, *Hebrew Passover*, 133, 211 n. 5.

23. See 14:21; Exod. 23:19; 2 Kings 4:38; Ezek. 24:4–5.

24. Lit., "to your tents." Josh. 22:4 and 1 Kings 8:66 indicate that "return to one's tent" means "go back home" (for "tent" meaning "home" see also BDB, 13d, end). Some hold that the "tents" are the pilgrims' temporary lodgings in the chosen city and infer that they would spend the night in the temple and in the morning return to their tents; they would only return home on the second day (cited by Ibn Ezra and Hoffmann, *Sefer Vayikra'* [Jerusalem: Mosad Harav Kook, 1954], 2:122 n. 45). However, even the large Herodian Second Temple could not hold more than about six thousand people at a time (S. Safrai, *Pilgrimage at the Time of the Second Temple* [Tel Aviv: Am Hassefer, 1965], 73–74).

25. Tosafot to Ḥag. 17b; cf. supercommentaries to Rashi on the present verse. 2 Kings 4:22–23 may imply that travel was permitted even on the Sabbath, but this is not certain.

26. Rashi; Ḥag. 17a–b; Hoffmann, *Sefer Vayikra'*, 2:122–123 n. 45.

27. For the first interpretation see Ehrlich, *Mikra*; for the second see Ḥazzekuni; Abravanel, 146.

28. MdRY Bo' 8 (Lauterbach 1:62–63); Pes. 120a.

29. For *'atseret* as a gathering see Jer. 9:1; 2 Kings 10:20–21; Haran, *Temples*, 296–297; contrast Hoffmann, 264, 269 and *Sefer Vayikra'*, 2:160–161, 191–192; Segal, *Hebrew Passover*, 208–209. The special status of the seventh day is also mentioned in Exod. 12:16 and 13:6; Lev. 23:8; Num. 28:25.

30. Hoffmann, *Sefer Vayikra'*, 2:110.

31. *Sefer Abudraham Ha-Shalem* (Jerusalem: Usha, 1959), 241; Yal. 654; T. H. Gaster, *Festivals of the Jewish Year* (New York: William Sloane, 1964), 52; M. Greenberg, "Religion: Stability and Ferment," in WHJP 4/2, 88 and 297–298 nn. 22–24, and more fully in the Hebrew edition *Historiyah shel 'Am Yisra'el* 4/2 (Tel Aviv: Am Oved, 1982), 66 and 221–222 nn. 22, 25.

32. See Targ. Jon. to Exod. 19:16; MdRY Va-Yassa' 2 and Ba-Ḥodesh 3 (Lauterbach 2:99, 210); and Shab. 86b–87a, which all date it on the sixth day of the third month (Sivan), which is when it has been celebrated since talmudic times (a variant view dates it on the seventh). See Hoffmann, *Sefer Vayikra'*, 2:158–168; R. de Vaux, *Ancient Israel* (New York: McGraw-Hill, 1961), 494; J. Licht, s.v. *shavu'ot*, EM 7:494. The connection of the festival with the revelation at Sinai may be implied in earlier sources, such as Jub. 1:1 and 6:17–22; see Weinfeld, Commentary, 267–275.

33. As Hoffmann notes, audible counting is part of the Oral Tradition, not the plain sense of the text (Hoffmann, *Sefer Vayikra'*, 2:152–153). Cf. the fifth-century-B.C.E. Aramaic letter to the Jews of Elephantine, which tells them to "count four[teen days of the month of Nisan and] ob[serve the Passover], and from the fifteenth to the twenty-first day" (ANET, 491a).

34. See the translation in IR, no. 8, and O. Borowski, *Agriculture in Iron Age Israel* (Winona Lake, Ind.: Eisenbrauns, 1987), 36, 38; cf. Hesiod, *Works and Days*, l. 600.

35. See Dalman I/2, 415 for harvest dates in various places.

36. Hoffmann, *Sefer Vayikra'*, 2:112ff.; J. Licht, s.v. *'omer*, EM 6:302; Haran, s.v. *shabbat, mi-maḥarat ha-shabbat*, EM 7:517–521.

37. Mish. Bik. 1:3, 10. See Licht, s.v. *shavu'ot*, EM 7:493–494.

38. On *missat* see Rofé, *Mavo'*, 44 n. 29; contrast Rashi, Rashbam, and Hoffman.

39. See Comment to "gather" in 11:14; J. Licht, s.v. *sukkot*, EM 5:1039; Tur-Sinai, *Ha-Lashon Ve-ha-Sefer* (Jerusalem: Mosad

Bialik, 1948–55), 3:78–83. The entire grape harvest season leading up to the Feast of Booths is a joyous time; see Judg. 9:27; Isa. 16:10; Jer. 25:30.

40. 1 Kings 8:2,65; 12:32–33; Ezek. 45:25; Neh. 8:14.

41. Mish. Ta'an. 1:1–2; Tosef. Sukkah 3:18; Tosef. RH 1:12 (see RH 16a); cf. Mish. RH 1:2.

42. J. Feliks, *Agriculture in Palestine in the Period of the Mishna and Talmud* (Jerusalem: Magnes Press; Tel Aviv: Dvir, 1963), 238; Dalman 3:74–78.

43. Haran, *Temples*, 290; Shadal at Exod. 23:17 compares the practice of tenant farmers visiting landlords. For parallels in ancient Near Eastern treaty relationships see D. J. McCarthy, *Treaty and Covenant* (Rome: Pontifical Biblical Institute, 1963), 182 l. 10; A. L. Oppenheim, *Letters from Mesopotamia* (Chicago: University of Chicago Press, 1967), 137; ANET, 297d; M. Cogan, *Imperialism and Religion* (Missoula, Mont.: Scholars Press, 1974), 124–125; J. Tigay, "On Some Aspects of Prayer in the Bible," AJSR 1 (1976): 364 n. 13.

44. See also 12:7,12,18; 14:26; 31:10–12; 1 Sam. 1:2–7 (but note vv. 22–24) and see Ibn Ezra at 14:26. See also Haran, *Temples*, 293, 301–303, and Hoffmann. According to 20:13–14, "males" (*zekhur*) does not necessarily include children.

45. Some scholars believe that v. 16, requiring a pilgrimage for the Feast of Unleavened Bread, simply contradicts vv. 5–7, which require it only for the *pesah* sacrifice, and that these represent separate sources combined in the text. But in the present form of the text, "the Feast of Unleavened Bread" must refer to the *pesah* observance, and Exod. 12:18 makes that plausible.

46. See Shadal at Isa. 1:12; A. Geiger, *Ha-Mikra Ve-Targumav* (Jerusalem: Bialik Foundation, 1972), 337ff.; Driver; contrast Hoffmann, 275. The same idiom appears in Exod. 34:23 (cf. 23:17); Deut. 31:11 and 1 Sam. 1:22 (Isa. 1:12 and Ps. 42:3, which omit *'et*, confirm that *'et penei* is accusative and does not mean "before" as it does in other contexts [Gen. 33:18; 1 Sam. 22:4; Est. 1:10]). Since the vocalization implying the translation "appear" is found only in passages that refer to a sanctuary, perhaps its intention is to avoid giving the impression that God is physically visible there in the form of a statue. It does not seem likely that the vocalization is intended to avoid the implication that God is visible at all, since many passages that imply that He is visible have been left unaltered, such as Exod. 24:10–11 and Num. 12:8.

47. Saadia; Rashi; R. Meyuḥas; Hoffmann; Driver; Ehrlich, *Mikra*; Y. Muffs, *Love and Joy* (New York: Jewish Theological Seminary, 1992), 178–179.

Chapter 16:18–17:20

1. M. Greenberg, "Biblical Attitudes Toward Power: Ideal and Reality in the Law and Prophets," in E. R. Firmage et al., eds., *Religion and Law: Biblical-Judaic and Islamic Perspectives* (Winona Lake, Ind.: Eisenbrauns, 1990), 101–112.

2. M and SP recognize breaks before 16:18; 17:2; 17:8; and after 17:13 (2Q11 [DJD III] also has a break after 17:13). M also has breaks before 16:21 and 17:1. (MT variants also separate 16:21 and 22 [4QDeut^c does not]).

3. Cf. Lev. 19:15; Prov. 18:5; 24:23; 2 Chron. 19:7; cf. also Isa. 1:23; Ps. 82:2; ANET, 213; BWL, 113 l. 11; M. Weinfeld, "Judge and Officer in Israel and in the Ancient Near East," IOS 7 (1977): 76–80.

4. See Palgrave, cited by Driver, 199–200: the village judge (*kadi*), assisted by a few other leading citizens, judges local cases, with cases being referred to a higher tribunal when necessary; P. Ponafidine, *Life in the Muslim East* (New York: Dodd, Mead, 1911), 133 (on sheikhs); D. Peretz, *The Middle East Today*, 4th ed. (New York: Praeger, 1983), 467–468 (ref. courtesy Eytan Tigay); further information from Hamzah el-Mahasneh. The

office of sheikh is sometimes elective and sometimes hereditary. See also Weinfeld, "Judge and Officer," 87–88; Thompson, *Deuteronomy*, ad loc.

5. See 1 Sam. 8:1–3; 2 Chron. 19:5–11. Many scholars believe that Deuteronomy is also thinking of judges and officials appointed by the king (see, e.g., J. Milgrom, "The Ideological and Historical Importance of the Judge in Deuteronomy," in *Isac Leo Seeligmann Volume* (ed. Y. Zakovitch and A. Rofé [Jerusalem: Rubinstein, 1983], 3:129–139). This is questionable since, apart from Chronicles' narrative about Jehoshaphat appointing judges throughout Judah (2 Chron. 19:5), royally appointed judges are attested only in the capital, Jerusalem (2 Sam. 15:3; Isa. 1:26; 3:2; Mic. 7:3; Zeph. 3:3), and possibly in Jezreel, where King Ahab lived (1 Kings 21:8,11, if the *horim* are royal officers [see J. Liver, s.v. *horim*, EM 3:288–289]). If developments of the monarchic period do underlie Deuteronomy's concept of specialized judges, Deuteronomy has completely transformed the office. It commands *the people* to appoint both the judges and the king (16:18; 17:15), and it tells them to appoint judges before it even discusses the king, whose appointment is only optional and who in any case is not given authority to appoint *any* officials.

6. LXX words v. 19 in the third person: "*they* shall not judge unfairly . . . *they* shall show no partiality" (cf. 19:15–21, where the judges are referred to in the third person).

7. Judg. 4:4.

8. Cf. Exod. 23:2,6; Deut. 24:17; 27:19; Isa. 10:2; Amos 5:12; Prov. 17:23.

9. See also Exod. 23:3; Deut. 10:17; Mal. 2:9; Ps. 82:2; Prov. 18:5; 24:23; 28:21; 2 Chron. 19:7.

10. See Prov. 21:14 and perhaps 17:8.

11. Isa. 1:23; Mic. 3:11; 7:3. The term has the neutral sense of tribute (to induce a stronger power to intercede in one's behalf) in 1 Kings 15:19; 2 Kings 16:8; Isa. 45:13; see J. C. Greenfield, "Some Aspects of Treaty Terminology in the Bible," WCJS 4 (1967): 119.

12. See M. Greenberg, s.v. "Bribery, Bribe," IDB 1:465; J. J. Finkelstein, "The Middle Assyrian Šulmānu Texts," JAOS 72 (1952): 77–80; cf. Lambert, BWL, 320:98–99. For a contrary view, see S. E. Loewenstamm, s.v. *šohad*, EM 7:617–619; M. Cogan and H. Tadmor, "Ahaz and Tiglath-Pileser in the Book of Kings" (Hebrew), EI 14 (1978): 58–59. The halakhah prohibits charging a fee for judging (Mish. Bek. 4:6). Islamic "law forbids the *kadi* [judge] to take presents from people who are appearing in his court" (H.J.R. Gibb and J. H. Kramers, *Shorter Encyclopaedia of Islam* [Leiden: Brill and London: Luzac, 1961], s.v. "Kadi," 201), but judges in the Ottoman empire "gained their remuneration by charging litigants a fee" (Peretz, *Middle East Today*, 57).

13. See n. 47 to Comment to 2:27.

14. Gen. 21:33; Josh. 24:26; Ps. 52:10; cf. 92:13–15. The Inscriptions from Kuntillet 'Ajrud in the Sinai include blessings in the name of "YHVH of Samaria and His [or its, namely Samaria's] *'asherah*" and "YHVH of Teman and His [or its, Teman's] *'asherah*," which may also imply a sanctuary of YHVH containing a sacred post. See J. Tigay, *You Shall Have No Other Gods* (Atlanta: Scholars Press, 1986), 26–29; idem, "A Second Temple Parallel to the Blessings from Kuntillet Ajrud," IEJ 40 (1990): 218. Some scholars, however, believe that the inscriptions refer to the Canaanite goddess Asherah.

15. Note, e.g., the sacred post at the altar of Baal in Judg. 6:25.

16. At Lachish the remains of an olive tree trunk were found next to a sacred stone in a sanctuary, and an ivory box from Hazor shows a man kneeling in adoration toward a stylized tree that stands in front of a cherub; see Y. Aharoni, s.v. "Lachish," in EAEHL 3:749; Y. Yadin in *Hazor I* (Jerusalem: Magnes Press, 1958), 41–43 and pl. CLV. See further discussion in Comment to 7:5.

17. Sifrei 145; Mayes.

18. Gen. 28:16–22; Exod. 24:4; Josh. 24:26. Hos. 3:4 also seems to imply that pillars are legitimate, at least in northern Israel.

19. Following Sifrei 146.

20. The translation takes the *vav* preceding the phrase as the explicative *vav*, meaning "that is, to the sun." It is also possible that the conjunction means "or" and that the text is identifying two kinds of illicit worship, the heavenly bodies and other "other gods," such as idols (Ibn Ezra). See Y. Kaufmann, *The Religion of Israel*, trans. M. Greenberg (Chicago: University of Chicago Press, 1960), 10. This is less likely, since the passage uses *'o* for "or" when it means that.

21. See chap. 4, n. 62.

22. For litotes cf. Num. 11:11; Isa. 10:7 (Ehrlich, *Mikra*; Driver).

23. Jer. 7:31; 19:5; 32:35.

24. See M. Greenberg, *Ezekiel 1–20* (Garden City, N.Y.: Doubleday, 1983), 369–370.

25. Cf. Sifrei 148: this commandment "includes one who joins (God's name to idols)," that is, who worships the Lord along with other gods (Hoffmann, 300).

26. See 2 Kings 21:3–7 (cf. 23:4, 11); Ezek. 8.

27. See Sifrei 148 and Geiger, *Ha-Mikra Ve-Targumav* (Jerusalem: Mosad Bialik, 1972), 286 (contrast R. A. Hammer, *Sifre: A Tannaitic Commentary on Deuteronomy* (New Haven: Yale University Press, 1986), 451, Piska 148 n. 9, and Hoffmann, 300n.); E. Tov, "The Rabbinic Tradition Concerning the 'Alterations' Inserted into the Greek Pentateuch and their Relation to the Original Text of the LXX," JSJ 15 (1984): 84.

28. See Ps. 148:5 and perhaps Isa. 45:12 and Ps. 33:9.

29. See Lev. 24:14; Num. 15:25–36; 1 Kings 21:13. For an exception see Deut. 22:21.

30. Literally, "two or three"; cf. "a day or two" meaning "a day or more," Exod. 21:21.

31. 1 Kings 21:10, 13.

32. See Exod. 18:13–26; Deut. 1:13–18; 2 Chron. 19:8–11.

33. See Hoffmann.

34. Ibn Ezra; Ramban; Shadal.

35. Sifrei 152.

36. For some examples of such cases see Exod. 21:12–14,18–25; Num. 35:9–34; Deut. 19:1–13; Josh. 20.

37. The halakhic interpretation of "affliction" (Heb. *nega'*) as "leprosy" is based on the way the term is normally used, as in 24:8. However, *nega'* is sometimes used for injuries, which better fits the present context; see 21:5 and Prov. 6:33, and the verb *n-g-'* in Gen. 32:26,33.

38. Mish. Sanh. 1:6; 11:2; Sifrei 153. Some scholars question whether priests were part of the original text (they are missing in Codex Vaticanus of LXX), while others doubt that the lay judges were. See Weinfeld, DDS, 235; Rofé, *Mavo'*, 50–52, 68–69; Mayes. According to Ehrlich, *Randglossen*, vv. 10–11 interweave terms for decisions of lay judges ("ruling" [*mishpat*]) and priestly judges ("instruction" [*torah, yorukha*]; cf. 24:8), with "verdict" (*davar*) serving as a general term covering both.

39. See Exod. 22:7–10; 28:29–30 [see 1 Sam. 14:38–42]; Num. 5:11–31.

40. The judicial role of priests is also reflected in Ezek. 44:24 and possibly in Isa. 28:7 and 1 Kings 8:31–32.

41. An exception is the reference to Urim and Thummim in 33:8, but that chapter is older than Deuteronomy. Since Deuteronomy does not mention them in its lists of the priests' duties in 10:8 and 21:5, it probably does not intend their use to continue. See Excursus 33.

42. This issue is debated by Weinfeld, DDS, 233–236, and J. Milgrom, "The Alleged 'Demythologization and Secularization' in Deuteronomy," IEJ 23 (1973): 158–159.

43. The second possibility is compatible with v. 12, where

"priest" and "magistrate" are both singular and could refer, collectively, to the chief judges of each group, like the lay and clerical chief judges on Jehoshaphat's court. However, there would be no obvious reason for Deuteronomy's judges to split into two groups since, as noted above, it is questionable whether Deuteronomy's high court heard cases having to do with religious law. The difficulty of deciding how many lay judges there are is paralleled by the fact that 19:17 refers to the "judges" in a particular case whereas 25:1 has a plural verb and 25:2 has a singular "judge." See Rofé, *Mavo'*, 75–76.

44. The Hebrew conjunction *ve-* can mean "and" or "or." The present translation may be influenced by "the priest . . . or ('o) the magistrate" in v. 11. The translation *"or the magistrate"* implies one of two possibilities: (1) that the composition of the court is optional, and the judges may be either priests or laymen; or (2) that it consists of both, with the lay judges hearing cases that involve civil law and the priests hearing cases having to do with ritual law (however, as noted above, it is unlikely that the court heard cases having to do with ritual law).

45. Deut. 19:17; 26:3; Josh. 20:6; Rashi here; Sifrei 153; RH 25b; Torah Temimah.

46. Ber. 19b; Maimonides, Sefer Ha-Mitsvot, Root 1; Sefer Ha-Ḥinnukh, no. 108; Torah Temimah; Ramban; N. Leibowitz, *Studies in Devarim* (Jerusalem: World Zionist Organization, 1980), 158–174.

47. Ehrlich, *Randglossen* and *Mikra'*.

48. Contempt of court is also a capital crime in Plato's *Laws*, 958C.

49. 1 Sam. 8:5–6,20 (the term translated by NJPS as "rule" and "govern" means "judge"); cf. 1 Kings 3:9.

50. 1 Sam. 8:11–17.

51. This is not to deny that some aspects of the laws dealing with the judiciary and war may reflect practices of monarchic times in which the king played a role. The point is that the law deemphasizes those aspects.

52. Judg. 8:22–23; 1 Sam. 8.

53. A. Alt, *Essays on Old Testament History and Religion* (Garden City, N.Y.: Doubleday, 1967), 313.

54. 1 Sam. 13 and 15; 2 Sam. 12:1–15; 1 Kings 21:17–27; Jer. 22:13–19.

55. W. F. Edgerton, "The Government and the Governed in the Egyptian Empire," JNES 6 (1947): 154; M. Greenberg, "Some Postulates of Biblical Criminal Law," in M. Haran, ed., *Yehezkel Kaufmann Jubilee Volume* (Jerusalem: Magnes Press, 1960), 9–10; ANET, 43c, 265c, 594c (cf. 147b for a Canaanite text); J. Van Seters, "The Creation of Man and the Creation of the King," ZAW 101 (1989): 333–342; Lambert, BWL, 232: iv, 14–15.

56. Echoes were not entirely lacking in some circles; see J. Tigay, "On Some Aspects of Prayer in the Bible," AJSR 1 (1976): 370–371.

57. Sifrei 157.

58. 1 Sam. 9:16–17; 10:20–24; 16:1–13; 1 Kings 11:29–39; 2 Kings 9:1–13. Contrast Hos. 8:4.

59. See Judg. 9:2 and 2 Sam. 5:1.

60. See Weinfeld, "'Temple Scroll' or 'King's Law,'" *Shnaton* 3 (1978–79): 214–237; idem, "The Emergence of the Deuteronomic Movement," in N. Lohfink, ed., *Das Deuteronomium* (Leuven: Leuven University Press, 1985), 95–98. For an example, see Lambert, BWL, 112–115.

61. Sifrei 158–159; Mish. Sanh. 2:4; Sanh. 21b.

62. 2 Sam. 15:1; 1 Kings 1:5. See Y. Yadin, *The Art of Warfare in Biblical Lands* (New York: McGraw-Hill, 1963), 2:284–285; Y. Ikeda, "Solomon's Trade in Horses and Chariots in Its International Setting," in T. Ishida, ed., *Studies in the Period of David and Solomon* (Winona Lake, Ind.: Eisenbrauns, 1982), 215–238.

63. See also Isa. 31:1; Hos. 14:4; Ps. 33:16–17; Prov. 21:31; cf. Ramban; Weinfeld, DDS, 281.

64. For the first view see Rashi; Ramban; Driver; for the second see Liver, s.v. *melekh, melukhah*, EM 4:1103. For Egypt as an exporter of horses see 1 Kings 10:28–29; Isa. 31:1–3; and Ikeda, "Solomon's Trade."

65. The translation of *ve-lo'* as "or" follows Ramban; "lest" (which it certainly means in v. 17) follows Rashi.

66. Hoffmann; Torah Temimah at Exod. 14:13.

67. A. Rofé, who compares 25:19, in which God's promise to wipe out Amalek (Exod. 17:14) has become a commandment.

68. 1 Kings 3:1; 11:1–10; 16:31–33.

69. ARM 1:69, reverse l. 13.

70. Halakhic sources as cited above; 11QTemple 57:17–18.

71. Some scholars think that vv. 18–19 are an interpolation and that v. 20 was the original sequel to v. 17. See Weinfeld, DDS 5 n. 1; contrast Z. Ben-Barak, "The Religious-Prophetic Background of the 'Law of the King' in Deuteronomy," *Shnaton* 1 (1975): 36.

72. ANET, 414–420; BWL, 112–115. See Weinfeld, "'Temple Scroll,'" 224–232; idem, "Emergence of the Deuteronomic Movement," 96–97. Cf. Josh. 1:8.

73. R. Sonsino, "Characteristics of Biblical Law," *Judaism* 33 (1984): 203–204.

74. Ibn Ezra; Mayes. Cf. 27:2–8: Israel must copy the Teaching on steles as soon as it enters the land.

75. Sefer Ha-Ḥinnukh, no. 494.

76. A reading "they shall write for him" is found in 11QTemple and reflected in Targ. Jon. Grammatically, even the Masoretic reading "he shall write" could mean "he shall have written." But there is no compelling reason to doubt that the king was expected to make his own copy.

77. Philo, Spec. 4.160.

78. Sanh. 21b (see Steinsaltz, 93) and 22a; Lieberman, HJP, 108 n. 50; Philo, Spec. 4.160; Z. Leiter, *Hagahot Kevod Melakhim*, in *Mishneh Torah* (New York: Shulsinger, 1947), Hilkhot Melakhim, 3:1; Y. Yadin, *Megillat Ha-Mikdash* (Jerusalem: Israel Exploration Society, 1977) 1:264–265. Cf., perhaps, 2 Kings 11:12 (see the views of Gersonides and moderns summarized, though rejected, by Cogan and Tadmor, *II Kings* [New York: Doubleday, 1988]).

79. E. S. McCartney, "Notes on Reading and Praying Audibly," *Classical Philology* 43 (1948): 184–187; J. Tigay, *The Evolution of the Gilgamesh Epic* (Philadelphia: University of Pennsylvania Press, 1982), 102 n. 72; N. M. Sarna, *Songs of the Heart* (New York: Schocken, 1993), 38–39.

Chapter 18

1. M and SP have breaks before vv. 1 and 9 and after v. 22; M subdivides vv. 1–8 further with breaks before vv. 3 and 6. In vv. 9–22, an MT variant separates the forbidden practices of divination and magic (vv. 9–13) from prophecy, which is given to Israel in place of them (vv. 14ff). SP subdivides the section before v. 17, highlighting the direct quotation of God's words institutionalizing prophecy (vv. 17–20; on parashah breaks before statements by God, see introductory Comments to chap. 1).

2. See Y. Kaufmann, *The Religion of Israel*, trans. M. Greenberg (Chicago: University of Chicago Press, 1960), 193–200; M. Greenberg, "A New Approach to the History of the Israelite Priesthood," JAOS 70 (1950): 41–47; A. Cody, *A History of the Old Testament Priesthood* (Rome: Pontifical Biblical Institute, 1969); M. Haran, *Ages and Institutions in the Bible* (Hebrew) (Tel Aviv: Am Oved, 1972), 137–200; idem, s.v. "Priests and Priesthood," EncJud 13:1069–1086; Rofé, *Mavo'*, 243–249.

3. Weinfeld notes that Deuteronomy agrees with Korah's contention that all Levites are of equal status (DDS, 228). R. K. Duke disputes the view that Deuteronomy considers all Levites

eligible for priesthood; see "The Portion of the Levite: Another Reading of Deuteronomy 18:6–8," JBL 106 (1987): 193–201.

4. J. Milgrom, "Profane Slaughter and a Formulaic Key to the Composition of Deuteronomy," HUCA 47 (1976): 11–12.

5. Some ancient translations introduce a distinction in v. 1 by rendering "the levitical priests" (lit., "the priests the Levites") as "the priests *and* the Levites" or the like (Pesh.; Vulg.; see also Saadia). This translation is forced since the phrase never has the conjunction "and" in Deuteronomy and it clearly refers to the priests alone (see esp. 24:8; cf. M. Haran, *Temples and Temple Service* [Oxford: Clarendon, 1978], 63). Furthermore, Deuteronomy is not only silent about Numbers' distinctions but contradicts them by stating that the priests carry the Ark (31:9).

6. Lev. 25:32–34; 27:14–28; Num. 18:14; 35:1–8; Josh. 14:4; 21; 1 Sam. 22:19; 1 Kings 2:26; Jer. 32:6–9.

7. See Lev. 2:3; 3:3; 7:5; 24:7. The term '*isheh* also refers to burnt offerings (Lev. 1:9), but they are not intended here since no part of the burnt offering is eaten. Cf. Levine, *Leviticus*, at Lev. 1, n. 24. For a different understanding of '*isheh*, see Mayes.

8. Heb. *ve-naḥalato*, lit. "and His portion" or "and its [the tribe's] portion." Either translation implies something in addition to the offerings by fire. The word could be an awkward way of referring to the first products of v. 4. Perhaps it is simply a dittography of *hu' naḥalato* in v. 2 (perhaps copied from a manuscript in which the phrase had been omitted from v. 2 and then inserted above the line). Another possibility is to read something like "the LORD's offerings by fire are their portion, them they shall eat" ('*ishei YHVH hu' naḥalato 'oto yo'khelun*), following LXX and Josh. 13:14, which is certainly related to the present verse.

9. See S. Paul, *Studies in the Book of the Covenant* (Leiden: Brill, 1970), 56–61; *CAD* L, 234–235.

10. Lev. 6:11; cf. Gen. 47:22; Prov. 30:8. Note the similar use of *manah* and *mishḥah* in Lev. 7:33,35; Num. 18:8 (see commentaries of Levine and Milgrom). For this meaning of *mishpat* see P. K. McCarter, *1 Samuel* (Garden City, N.Y.: Doubleday, 1980), 78 and 82–83. The English equivalent of these terms is "prebend."

11. On the maw at Athens see Driver. On right forelegs see A. Ben Tor, "Tell Qiri: A Look at Village Life," BA 42/2 (Spring 1979): 113; O. Tufnell, "Lachish," in D. W. Thomas, ed., *Archaeology and Old Testament Study* (Oxford: Clarendon, 1967), 301.

12. For the halakhic view see M. Ḥul. 10:1; Josephus, Ant. 4.74; Philo, Spec. 1.147. Other attempts at harmonization are summarized by Driver. See also 1 Sam. 2:12–17. Deuteronomy does use the verb *zavaḥ* for secular slaughter (12:15,21), but not the noun *zevaḥ*.

13. According to Milgrom, with reference to these commodities "first fruits" means "first processed," not the first ripe or first harvested crops in their natural state (J. Milgrom, s.v. "First Fruits, OT," IDBS 336; idem, *Numbers* at 18:12).

14. See s.v. "First Fruits" in HDB, IDBS, and EncJud; Albeck, *Zera'im*, 308.

15. Rashi; Mish. Ter. 4:3. The phrase "larger *Terumah*" distinguishes this gift from the *terumat ma'aser*, the "*Terumah* from the Tithe," that the Levites give the priests, consisting of 10 percent of the tithe that they receive from the public.

16. With minor variations, LXX, SP, and 11QTemple 60:11 explicitly read thus.

17. Sifrei 168 takes this as referring to temporary service, permitting provincial priests to come and officiate at the Temple on festivals.

18. See Haran, *Temples*, 100 n. 20.

19. This interpretation accords with the use of the related Akkadian phrase *makkur bit abim*, "goods of the father's estate," in LH §166, etc., but it leaves unclear how the preposition *'al*, "on," is used. See G. R. Driver, "Two Problems in the Old Testament Examined in the Light of Assyriology," *Syria* 33 (1956): 77–78.

20. Cf. the summary of views by Hoffmann.

21. On prophecy see Kaufmann, *Religion*, 93–101; S. Paul, s.v. "Prophets and Prophecy," EncJud 13:1150–1175; M. Greenberg, "Religion: Stability and Ferment," in WHJP 4/2, 98–102, 106; idem, s.v. "Prophecy in Hebrew Scripture," *Dictionary of the History of Ideas* (New York: Macmillan, 1973), 3:657–661; R. Wilson, *Prophecy and Society in Ancient Israel* (Philadelphia: Fortress Press, 1980).

22. See 2 Sam. 24:11; 1 Kings 1; Isa. 3:2–4; Jer. 8:1; 13:13; 32:32; Mic. 3.

23. E.g., 1 Sam. 8–12; 15; 2 Sam. 7; 1 Kings 22:5–28; 2 Kings 5; 6:22. See Maimonides' *Commentary on the Mishnah*, introduction, in Y. Kafiḥ, *Mishnah 'im Perush Rabbenu Moshe ben Maimon: Seder Zera'im* (Jerusalem: Mosad Harav Kook, 1976), 4–5. For the influence of astrologers in Mesopotamia, see A. L. Oppenheim, "Divination and Celestial Observation in the Last Assyrian Empire," *Centaurus* 14 (1969): 120.

24. See Shab. 104a; Maimonides, Hilkhot Yesodei Ha-Torah 9:1–2; idem, Guide 2.39; idem, "Epistle to Yemen," in A. S. Halkin and Boaz Cohen, eds., *Moses Maimonides' Epistle to Yemen* (New York: American Academy for Jewish Research, 1952), 50–51 and x (translation in A. Halkin and D. Hartman, *Crisis and Leadership: Epistles of Maimonides* [Philadelphia: Jewish Publication Society, 1985], 111).

25. See 12:4,30–31; 16:21–17:1; see also 23:18–19. Several of these practices were employed at various times in Israel. See, e.g., 1 Sam. 28:3–19; 2 Kings 16:3; 17:17; 21:6; Isa. 3:2; 8:19; Jer. 27:9; Mic. 5:11; Mal. 3:5; Zech. 10:2.

26. See Exod. 22:17; Lev. 18:21; 19:26,31; and 20:2–6,27.

27. See Ezek. 21:26–28; 1 Sam. 28:8; Jer. 14:14; Mic. 3:6–7,11.

28. On belomancy and hepatoscopy see Gaster, *Myth, Legend and Custom in the Old Testament* (New York: Harper and Row, 1969), 620–621; Oppenheim, *Ancient Mesopotamia* (Chicago: University of Chicago Press, 1964), 213–215. On *me'onen* see Ibn Ezra at Lev. 19:26 (for other interpretations see Sifrei 171; Sanh. 65b–66a; and HALAT, 811). On divination from drinking vessels see Oppenheim, *Ancient Mesopotamia*, 208, 212; L. Y. Rahmani, s.v. *gavia'*, EM 2:401–402.

29. This is the meaning of the cognate term in Akkadian as well; see also Nah. 3:4 and Isa. 47:9,12. See Z. Abusch, "The Demonic Image of the Witch in Standard Babylonian Literature," in J. Neusner et al., eds., *Religion, Science, and Magic in Concert and Conflict* (New York: Oxford University Press, 1989), 31ff.

30. Jer. 27:9; Dan. 2:2; Exod. 7:11.

31. Targ. Onk.; J. J. Finkelstein compared Akkadian *Ḥabaru*, "be noisy" ("Hebrew *ḥbr* and Semitic *ḤBR*," JBL 75 [1956]: 328–331). Another view derives the term from *ḥ-b-r*, "unite," "join," and takes it to refer to the "binding" effect the act has on its target (Targ. Jon.). For a different view, see M. Held, "Studies in Biblical Lexicography in the Light of Akkadian," EI 16 (1982): 78–79.

32. In a few passages '*ov* seems to refer to the necromancer or the practice of necromancy rather than the ghost (1 Sam. 28:3,9; 2 Kings 21:6; 23:24). For the etymology see Ben Yehudah, s.v. '*ov*, and H. A. Hoffner, Jr., "Second Millennium Antecedents to the Hebrew '*ob*," JBL 86 (1967): 385–401. For "inquiring of the dead" as including "consulting ghosts and familiar spirits" see Isa. 8:19. For other types of necromancy see Sifrei and Rashi here; Tosef. Sanh. 10. '*Ov ve-yide'oni* may be a hendiadys; see E. Z. Melamed, *Biblical Studies in Texts, Translations, and Commentators* (Jerusalem: Magnes Press, 1984), 145.

33. Exod. 7:10–8:3; 1 Sam. 28.

34. As the talmudic sage R. Yoḥanan expressed it, sorcerers seek to "lessen the power of the divine agencies," thus contra-

dicting the biblical dictum "there is none beside Him" (Deut. 4:35; see Sanh. 67b).

35. Isa. 47:9–15 describes sorcery and divination as a "skill and science" and an "art" that gave Babylon the illusion of self-sufficient invincibility.

36. See Kaufmann, *Religion*, 78–93; Milgrom, *Numbers*, Excursus 50. For ancient societies banning black magic, see P. Artzi, s.v. *keshafim*, EM 4:361ff.

37. 1 Sam. 9:6; 28:6; 2 Sam. 7:2–17; 1 Kings 14:1–3; 22:5–17; 2 Kings 1:2–6; 3:11–19; 8:9; Jer. 37:17.

38. Num. 12:13–15; 1 Sam. 7:7–13; 2 Kings 2:19–22; 4:22–41; 5:1–15; 20:1–11; Isa. 38:1–8,21–22.

39. Cf. 1 Sam. 9:15–20; 1 Kings 14:5; 2 Kings 4:27; Amos 3:7.

40. As noted, this is the standard view in the Bible. The paradigm of this view is Moses, whose quasi-magical curative powers are explicitly said to depend on God (see Num. 21:5–9 and cf. Exod. 15:23–26 with 2 Kings 15:19–22; this is not explicit in Exod. 17:11; see Sarna, *Exodus*). However, it is common everywhere for the folk to attribute magical powers to holy men, and a number of passages in the Bible reflect such an evaluation of the prophets' powers. Elisha sometimes knows things not said to have been told to him by God, and he performs a number of wonders without explicitly calling on God (see 2 Kings 2:23–25; 4:1–7,38–41; 5:26; 6:1–7,9,12,17). These are probably folk tales that have not been recast in accordance with the standard viewpoint of the Bible. Other tales about Elisha have been so recast, and these are undoubtedly meant by the biblical writers to indicate how all the tales are to be understood (see 2 Kings 2:19–22; 4:8–37,42–44). For discussion see Greenberg, "Religion: Stability and Ferment," 100; A. Rofé, *The Prophetical Stories* (Jerusalem: Magnes Press, 1988), 13–22; Kaufmann, *Religion*, 276–277.

41. 1 Sam. 28.

42. For *tamim* as a term for loyalty see Comment to 32:4.

43. For the status of diviners throughout the ancient Near East, see Wilson, *Prophecy and Society*, 96–98. For Israel, see 1 Sam. 28; 1 Kings 22:6ff.; Isa. 8:19–20.

44. ANET, 490d; Landsberger and Tadmor, "Fragments of Clay Liver Models from Hazor," IEJ 14 (1964): 201–218; M. Dietrich and O. Loretz, "The Syntax of Omens in Ugaritic," *Maarav* 5–6 (1990): 89–109; M. Astour, "Two Ugaritic Serpent Charms," JNES 27 (1968): 13–36.

45. "Instead" is suggested by the Hebrew word order: "a prophet" is the first word in the verse, indicating a contrast with the preceding verses (the position of "him" as the first word in the second clause indicates the same thing).

46. For Phoenicia see ANET, 26 (Byblos, ca. 1100 B.C.E.); for Syria see below, n. 51. For the text about Balaam see Milgrom, *Numbers*, Excursus 60. For Mesopotamia, see ANET, 605–606 and the summary by Wilson, *Prophecy and Society*, 90–124.

47. Thus M. Greenberg, s.v. "Moses," EncJud 12:387 (only Hos. 12:14 explicitly calls Moses a prophet).

48. Acts 3:22; M. Perlmann, "Samau'al Al-Maghribi: Ifham Al-Yahud," PAAJR 32 (1964): 45, 81–82.

49. In the biblical conception, the prophet's mantic and quasi-magical powers stem from his role as messenger (his apostolic role). All of the wonders performed by Moses followed his appointment as God's messenger, and some are explicitly given him to further that role (Exod. 4:1–9). See Kaufmann, *Religion*, 276–277; Greenberg, "Prophecy," 660.

50. See, e.g., Exod. 21–23; 25–30; Num. 31; 1 Sam. 8–12; 16; 2 Sam. 7; 12; 1 Kings 11:29; 14:7–11; 21:17–24; 2 Kings 9:1–10; as well as the classical prophets.

51. For the messenger-prophets at Mari, see the texts in ANET, 623–625, 629–632, and the text cited by M. Weinfeld, "The Primacy of Morality in Ancient Near Eastern Prophecies," *Shnaton* 5–6 (1982): 233–234; discussions by Malamat, "Prophetic Revelations in New Documents from Mari and the Bible," SVT 15 (1966): 207–227; J. Ross, "Prophecy in Hamath, Israel, and Mari," HTR 63 (1970): 1–28; M. Weinfeld, "Ancient Near Eastern Patterns in Prophetic Literature," VT 27 (1977): 178–179. For the inscription of Zakir, King of Hamath, see ANET, 501; J. C. Greenfield, "Aspects of Aramean Religion," in P. D. Miller et al., eds., *Ancient Israelite Religion* (Philadelphia: Fortress Press, 1987), 72–73. See also M. de J. Ellis, "Observations on Mesopotamian Oracles and Prophetic Texts," JCS 41 (1989): 127–186.

52. 1 Sam. 15:18–26; cf. 13:13.

53. Sanh. 89b; Mish. Sanh. 11:5; Sifrei. Cf. 2 Kings 7:1–2, 16–20.

54. 1 Sam. 28:17–18.

55. On Micaiah see Ehrlich, *Mikra*, at 1 Kings 22:27; S. Yeivin, "The Patriarchs in the Land of Canaan," in WHJP 4/1, 142, and in greater detail in his *Studies in the History of Israel and His Country* (Tel Aviv: M. Newman, 1959–60), 240–244. On Jeremiah see S. D. Goitein, *'Iyyunim Ba-Mikra'*, 2nd ed. (Tel Aviv: Yavneh Publishing House, 1963), 130–141. A fragmentary list of false prophets from biblical times has been found among the texts from Qumran. See M. Broshi and A. Yardeni, "On *Netinim* and False Prophets," in *Solving Riddles and Untying Knots . . . Studies . . . Greenfield*, ed. Z. Zevit et al., (Winona Lake, IN: Eisenbrauns), pp. 33–37. A. Rofé, "The List of False Prophets from Qumran—Two Riddles and their Solution" (Hebrew), *Ha-'Arets*, April 13, 1994, B11.

56. See also 19:12; 22:22–25; 24:7. In 11QTemple 61:2 this meaning is made explicit by the reading *ve-humat*. Elsewhere the phrase sometimes refers to death at the hands of God, as in Lev. 22:9; Num. 4:15,20.

57. Cf. Maimonides, Hilkhot Yesodei Ha-Torah 7:7; 10; idem, *Commentary on the Mishnah*, introduction, 4–5; cf. Sanh. 89b. Moses established his credentials with supernatural signs at the outset and again when challenged by Korah and his cohorts (Exod. 4:1–9,30–31; 7:8ff.; Num. 16:28–30). The wonders performed by Elijah and Elisha are not offered as proof of their authenticity, but Elijah's first recorded act was the successful prediction of a drought (1 Kings 17:1–7), and Elisha's first independent act was to part the waters of the Jordan, proving that he had inherited Elijah's spirit (2 Kings 2:13–15). The signs that befall Saul in 1 Sam. 10:2–8 could be regarded as confirming Samuel's prophecy to him. Supernatural signs confirm that it is really God speaking to Gideon through an angel (Judg. 6:17–22; cf. 6:36–40) and back up prophecies in 1 Kings 13:1–6 and Isa. 38:7–8 (cf. the request in v. 22). A prediction of a natural event is offered in support of a prophecy in 1 Sam. 2:34. In Isa. 7:10–16, Isaiah seems to offer to produce a supernatural sign, but ultimately predicts a natural event. For the problem of false prophets see S. Paul, s.v. "Prophets and Prophecy," EncJud 13:1168–1169.

58. 1 Kings 22:7.

59. Weinfeld, "Ancient Near Eastern Patterns," 184–185; H. Tadmor, "The 'Sin of Sargon,'" EI 5 (1958): 150–163; Oppenheim, "Divination and Celestial Observation," 119–120.

60. 1 Kings 22:28; Jer. 32:8. See also 2 Kings 5:8; Ezek. 2:5.

61. Jer. 18:5–11; 26:17–19; Ezek. 33:13–20.

62. Jer. 28:7–9.

63. Ezek. 2:5; 33:33.

64. 2 Kings 1:9–12; 3:22–24; cf. 1 Kings 20:36. See Sifrei 178; Maimonides, Sefer Ha-Mitsvot, negative no. 29; idem, Hilkhot 'Avodah Zarah 5:9; idem, *Commentary on the Mishnah*, introduction, 6a. Another possible translation is "do not revere him" (as a prophet); cf. the use of *gur* in Pss. 22:24; 33:8. However, that may be a meaning restricted to poetry and coined because of the needs of parallelism.

Chapter 19

1. See Abravanel at 19:1; 20:1,10; 21:1,10; Sforno at 19:2; Rofé, *Mavo'*, 75, 130, 165, 176.

2. Hebrew manuscripts divide the text before vv. 8 (SP and MT vars.), 11 (M), 14 (M, SP), 15 (M), and 16 (MT var.), and after v. 21 (M, SP). The break before v. 8 separates the additional three cities from the main body of the law. The break before v. 11 separates intentional homicide (vv. 11–13) from the main body of the law, which focuses on preventing the killing of the accidental killer.

3. See M. Greenberg, "The Biblical Conception of Asylum," JBL 67 (1959): 125–132; idem, s.v. "Avenger of Blood," "Bloodguilt," and "City of Refuge," IDB 1:321, 449–450, 638–639; idem, s.v. *'arei miklat*, EM 6:383–388; Y. Kaufmann, *Sefer Yehoshua'*, 2nd ed. (Jerusalem: Kiryat Sefer, 1963), 259–270; A. Rofé, "The History of the Cities of Refuge in Biblical Law," S. Japhet, ed., in *Studies in Bible* (Jerusalem: Magnes Press, 1986), 205–239; Milgrom, *Numbers*, Excursuses 75–76; Weinfeld, DDS, 236–237. For asylum at Aleppo and elsewhere in the ancient world, see J. C. Greenfield, "Asylum at Aleppo: A Note on Sfire III, 4–7," in M. Cogan and I. Ephal, eds., *Ah, Assyria: Studies . . . Hayim Tadmor* (Jerusalem: Magnes Press, 1991), 272–278.

4. See 2 Sam. 3:27–30 (cf. 1 Kings 2:5–6,28–34); 14:7; 21:1–9; cf. MAL A §10; B §2; "Proclamation of Telepinus," §49, in E. H. Sturtevant and G. Bechtel, *A Hittite Chrestomathy* (Philadelphia: Linguistic Society of America, University of Pennsylvania, 1935), 193; LFM, 144. But see n. 6 below.

5. On the basis of rabbinic Hebrew *miklat* seems to mean "receiving," "absorbing," but there is also evidence for a meaning "rescue." See M. Greenberg, *'arei miklat*, 383.

6. Several cases in which blood vengeance was carried out or attempted are related in the narratives about King David; see the examples cited in n. 4 above. None is a perfect case: Abner also had political motives; the (fictional) Tekoite case is within the same clan, which may not be the same thing as blood feud (see W. Robertson Smith, *Kinship and Marriage in Early Arabia* [Boston: Beacon, 1903], 23); the Gibeonite case involves the violation of an oath, not only murder, and the Gibeonites didn't seek vengeance until David approached them. Kaufmann, *Sefer Yehoshua'*, argues that there is no case of actual blood vengeance for accidental killing in any biblical narrative, and that the practice was obsolete by the time of the monarchy.

7. See *New York Times*, October 12, 1962 (ref. courtesy M. Greenberg).

8. Shadal at Num. 35:12.

9. Kaufmann argues that the asylum cities are a phenomenon of the period of the judges and that the practice of blood vengeance for accidental killing was suppressed by the monarchy, starting with David, which led to the demise of asylum cities. He holds that vv. 8–9, which still expect the remaining territory to be conquered, indicate that the present law was formulated prior to the cancellation of the promise in Judg. 2:20–3:4 (Kaufmann, *Sefer Yehoshua'*, 262, 268–269). Ahituv argues that the cities presuppose a centralized government and hence cannot antedate the monarchy, and that the formulation of Deut. 19 and Num. 35 reflects the Persian period (S. Ahituv, "The Law of the Cities of Refuge," *Shnaton* 10 [1986–89]: 11–16). Rofé holds that Deut. 19 and Num. 35 presuppose the Josianic reformation. He argues, comparing 14:24, that "when the distance is great" (19:6) refers to the distance from the only sanctuary; once worship is restricted to that site, it would be the only asylum left unless more were established, which Deuteronomy and Numbers do (Rofé, "History of the Cities of Refuge," 214–218). It is true that the number of cities seems to be an important emphasis of Deut. 19. However, if the chapter were concerned with the effects of Josiah's reformation, one would have expected it to say "when the distance is great . . .

because the place where the Lord has chosen to establish His name is far," as does 14:24.

10. For the differences among the three, see Greenberg, *'arei miklat*, 385; Rofé, "History of the Cities of Refuge."

11. 1 Kings 1:50–53; 2:28–34. For discussion of Exod. 21:12–13, see Kaufmann, *Sefer Yehoshua'*, 263.

12. "Place" is often used of sanctuaries in Hebrew and other Semitic languages; see Sarna, *Exodus*, at 21:13. Tacitus indicates that the asylum of Greek temples was extended to their neighborhoods for 2 miles around (Tacitus, *Annals*, 3.62; cf. 1 Macc. 10:31,43). Contrast Kaufmann, *Sefer Yehoshua'*, 263; Milgrom, *Numbers*, 505.

13. Cf. the confinement of Shimei ben Gera to his house (1 Kings 2:36–37).

14. Josephus likewise uses the term "exile" (Ant. 4.172). Cf. the banishment of Cain for murdering Abel (Gen. 4). In Greece, the punishment for murder was banishment of the killer from his city or country. On expiation by the death of the high priest, see Greenberg, "Biblical Conception of Asylum," 125–132.

15. See A. Rofé, "Joshua 20: Historico-Literary Criticism Illustrated," in J. Tigay, ed., *Empirical Models for Biblical Criticism* (Philadelphia: University of Pennsylvania Press, 1985), 135–141; cf. Keil-Delitzsch, *Numbers*, 263. The cities are mentioned once again in 1 Chron. 6:42ff, 52ff.

16. See also Maimonides, Hilkhot Rotseah 5–8; L. Ginzberg, s.v. "Asylum—In Rabbinical Literature," JE 2:257–259.

17. See 11:29,31; 12:10,29; 17:14; and 26:1. An exception is 6:10.

18. Hoffmann, following Sifrei Zutta (H. S. Horovitz, *Sifrei de-Vei Rav . . . Be-Midbar* [Jerusalem: Wahrmann, 1966], 180).

19. Many scholars hold that 4:41–43 was added to the book later and that chap. 19 is unaware of it. See also Greenberg, *'arei miklat*, 386–387; Rofé, "History of the Cities of Refuge," 222; and idem, "Joshua 20," 135.

20. LXX. For *hekhin* meaning "measure," see Exod. 16:17 (see Rashi and Ehrlich there). The tripartite division of the land mentioned in the Comment makes no allowance for the Negev and the Plain, listed as a fourth section in 34:3. Since the Negev was sparsely populated, it probably did not constitute a separate section of the land for present purposes.

21. V. 5 is clearly an illustration of v. 4, not a separate case. Accordingly, the *vav* at the beginning of v. 5 must be the explicative *vav*.

22. Rofé, "History of the Cities of Refuge," 235.

23. *Bi-vli da'at = bi-shegagah*, "unintentionally," of Num. 35:11,15; Josh. 20:3,9. *Da'at* is used for "intention" in rabbinic Hebrew (Yev. 37b; Sanh. 104a).

24. Rashbam.

25. Judg. 8:18–21; 2 Sam. 3:26–30.

26. See Lev. 25:25,48; Num. 5:8; 27:8–11; Deut. 25:5–9; Jer. 32:7–12; Ruth 3–4 (see also 1 Kings 16:11, "kinsman," lit., "redeemers"). Cf. Milgrom, *Numbers*, at Num. 35:12; Keil-Delitzsch, *Numbers*, 263; J. Pedersen, *Israel* 1–2 (London: Oxford University Press, 1963–64), 390; R. de Vaux, *Ancient Israel* (New York: McGraw-Hill, 1961), 11, 21–22. Cf. Oppenheim, *Letters from Mesopotamia*. In Arabia, "the slain man may be avenged by any member of his own group" (Smith, *Kinship and Marriage*, 25–26). In the fictitious case described in 1 Sam. 14:6–11, the entire clan of the victim wants the killer (his brother) handed over to them for execution, though a single "blood avenger" is also mentioned. According to the halakhah, the avenger is the closest heir (Maimonides, Hilkhot Rotseah 1:2).

27. Hoffmann. Rofé argues that vv. 8–9 are an interpolation ("History of the Cities of Refuge," 222–223).

28. Josh. 11:17, 13:1–6.

29. Although David later extended his empire north to the Euphrates (2 Sam. 10:19; 1 Kings 5:1–5), Israelites did not settle

in the newly conquered territory, and the empire was not regarded as the fulfillment of the territorial promises to the patriarchs.

30. TJ Mak. 2:7, 31d–32a; cf. Tosef. Mak. 3 (2): 10. See also n. 19 above.

31. See Gen. 4:10–12; Num. 35:33–34; 2 Sam. 3:28–29; 21:1–6; Isa. 26:21; Jer. 26:15; Jonah 1:14; Shakespeare, *Macbeth*, V,i. In Greece even killings that were unintentional or in self-defense were thought to create a contagious stain. The Bible agrees that bloodshed, even when unintentional, defiles, though cases of self-defense, judicial execution, and war are excepted (see Exod. 22:1; Lev. 20:9–16; 1 Kings 2:5–6). See Greenberg, "City of Refuge," 638; Milgrom, *Numbers*, at Num. 35:33 and Excursus 76.

32. Greenberg, *'arei miklat*, 387. See Tacitus, *Annals*, 3:60; W. Robertson Smith, *The Religion of the Semites* (London: A. and C. Black, 1914), 148–149.

33. See Shadal; Rofé, "History of the Cities of Refuge," 228–229. For other views, see Mish. Mak. 2:6; Maimonides, Hilkhot Rotseah 5:7; J. Milgrom, "The Ideological Importance of the Office of the Judge in Deuteronomy," in A. Rofé and Y. Zakovitch, eds., *Isac Leo Seeligmann Volume* (Jerusalem: Rubinstein, 1983), 3:135–136.

34. The "assembly" has been identified as that of the killer's town, of the town where the killing took place, or as a national assembly.

35. Deut. 16:18; 17:9,12; 19:17–18; 25:2.

36. Deut. 21:19–20; 22:15–18; 25:8–9; cf. Ruth 4:2,4,9; Ezra 10:14. The elders' role in the criminal case in 1 Kings 21 could be due to the fact that the defendant's hereditary property was at stake in case of conviction (cf. ANET, 546c). Their jurisdiction in cases involving family law seems to be the remainder of a once-wider jurisdiction. See Rofé, *Mavo'*, 76–77.

37. See 13:9; 19:21; 25:12; cf. Weinfeld, DDS, 2.

38. Sifrei 186–187.

39. See Prov. 22:28; 23:10–11; also Hos. 5:10; Job 24:2; HL §§168–169; *Shurpu* 2:44–45 (Beyerlin, 132); "Wisdom of Amenemopet," chap. 6 (ANET, 422c); Plato, *Laws*, 8:842E. For the subject in general see Driver; E. S. Hartum and J. J. Rabinowitz, s.v. *gevul, hassagat gevul*, EM 2:395–397; Weinfeld, DDS, 265–267. The Romans considered moving landmarks a crime serious enough to permit killing those who attempted it (biblical law does not permit capital punishment for any offenses against property).

40. Rashi.

41. Rofé, *Mavo'*, 118–119; cf. Mic. 5:2.

42. Maimonides, Hilkhot Genevah 7:11; Plato, *Laws* 8:842E.

43. Gen. 31:51–52; E. Hull, s.v. "Landmark," HDB 3:24; Plato refers to them as stones, Josephus as pebbles. For inscribed Mesopotamian boundary stones see VBW 1:153, 274; Oppenheim, *Ancient Mesopotamia*, 123, 159.

44. Heb. *ri'shonim*, "previous generations," lit. "the first ones," may refer to the first generation that settled in the promised land, to whom the original allotments of territory were made (see Weinfeld, DDS, 267).

45. Sifrei; M. Elon, s.v. "Hassagat Gevul," EncJud 7:1460–1466.

46. *Hamas* ("crime," "injustice") characterizes the witness's act, not the crime of which he accuses the defendant; cf. Exod. 23:1. For *hamas* meaning "crime," "injustice" see Isa. 53:9; Ezek. 9:9 (note the telling variant *damim*, "bloodshed"); Ps. 35:11; Job 19:7; T. Frymer-Kensky, "The Atrahasis Epic and Its Significance for Our Understanding of Genesis 1–9," BA 40/4 (1977): 153. Some argue that *'ed* means "accuser" or "plaintiff," not simply "witness." However, in Exod. 23:1 it may refer to one who testifies *on behalf* of another, and in Lev. 5:1 it refers to one possessing knowledge about a case.

47. Saadia. For *sarah* meaning "falsehood" cf. v. 18 and Comment to 13:6.

48. This translation is suggested by 13:13–16 and 17:2–5, which have a similar structure: a lengthy protasis (conditional clause) describing the offense, followed by a compound apodosis (result clause); the apodosis begins with the requirement that the judges investigate carefully, and is followed by the condition: "and if" (*vehinneh*) the offense is discovered or confirmed by the investigation, and then by the punishment of the offender. In all three cases the protasis describes an offense that is only verified by a subsequent investigation. In chaps. 13 and 17 the offense is alleged before the trial and then verified by a trial. In the present case, it takes place during the judicial proceedings and is verified during their course. Cf. chap. 22, n. 61.

49. Sifrei; Keter Torah; cf. 11QTemple 61:8, where Y. Yadin finds the same interpretation. Some commentators believe that the phrase "before the LORD" and the presence of priests on the court imply that this is a baffling case that has been taken to the central sanctuary (17:8–12; see Driver; on "before the LORD" see M. Haran, *Temples and Temple Service* [Oxford: Clarendon, 1978], 26 n. 24; Ian Wilson, "Divine Presence in Deuteronomy" [Ph.D. diss., Cambridge University, 1992], 167–168; N. Rabban, "*lifnei YHVH*," *Tarbiz* 23 [1952]: 1–8). However, since the original trial would surely take place in a local court, this would imply that the charge of perjury was tried separately elsewhere, which is inconsistent with the translation proposed here. If the text meant the trial to take place at the central sanctuary, it would most likely have used the phrase "the place that the LORD your God will choose."

50. The Sadducees held that talion was to be imposed only if the falsely accused defendant had actually been punished (see also the Karaite Keter Torah), but the Pharisees noted that the text prescribes talion in return for the witness's "scheming" and ruled that once a *verdict* had been reached, he was subject to punishment if his testimony was found to be false (Mish. Mak. 1:6; thus also Josephus, Ant. 4.219). The plain sense of the text is that even if the false testimony never leads to a conviction, once it has been given the witness is subject to punishment, as in Mesopotamian law. (The earliest Mesopotamian laws generally punished false witnesses with standard monetary fines. The later laws imposed talion, which made the punishment match the severity of the crime more exactly and rendered false testimony far less palatable to those wealthy enough to afford a mere fine. See LUN §§10–11, 25; contrast §26]; LH §§1–4; and the discussion by T. Frymer-Kensky, "Tit for Tat," BA 43 [1980]: 230–234.)

51. M. Greenberg.

52. In Exod. 21:23–25 the full formula cannot be applied literally to the case at hand since several of the injuries in the formula would not occur as the result of pushing a pregnant woman and causing premature parturition. However, this does not imply that the formula loses all of its meaning and refers instead to monetary compensation (N. M. Sarna, *Exploring Exodus* [New York: Schocken, 1986], 187); the penalty expressed by this formula is explicitly *contrasted* to a monetary one (v. 22). Rather, the formula refers to punishment in kind by citing typical examples of it, not all of which apply to the case at hand. In other words, both in Exod. 21:23–25 and Deut. 19:21 the formula expresses a general policy, not only the punishment imposed in a specific case; in Exod. 21 it mentions more than necessary for the case at hand, whereas in Deut. 19 it mentions only some of the punishments that might apply in the case at hand.

53. MdRY Nezikin 8 (Lauterbach 3:67–69); Mish. BK 8:1 and BK 83b–84a; Sifra to Lev. 24:17 (ed. I. H. Weiss), 104b–105a.

54. Josephus, Ant. 4.280; talion was interpreted corporally, with no discretion allowed the victim, by the Boethusians, a

Sadducean sect (*Megillat Ta'anit*, ed. H. Lichtenstein, "Die Fastenrolle," HUCA 8–9 [1931–32]: 331).

55. LH §§196ff.

56. See discussions by Sarna, *Exodus*, at Exod. 21:23–25; Levine, *Leviticus*, Excursus 10; Frymer-Kensky, "Tit for Tat," 230–234.

Chapter 20

1. These are the divisions marked in M and SP.

2. The Transjordanian tribes did build cities before the war for Cisjordan, but they were not deferred from battle because of that; see Num. 32.

3. I. Eph'al argues that siege tactics (vv. 19–20) imply a professional army; see his "*Darkhei leḥimah u-mishtar ḥevrati bitekufat ha-mikra*'," in *Hagut Ba-Mikra' Le-Zekher Yishai Ron* (Israel: 'Am 'Oved and Israel Society for Biblical Research, 1974), 54–59. The fact that so much of Deut. 20 refers to later wars implies that it may contain material from different periods. For literary analyses reaching the same conclusion, see von Rad; G. Seitz, *Redaktionsgeschichtliche Studien zum Deuteronomium* (Stuttgart: Kohlhammer, 1971), 155–165; Mayes; Rofé, *Mavo'*, chap. 15.

4. The order proposed here is the same as that followed in 1 Macc. 3:56; 4:8–11, cited below.

5. See Craigie, 57; H. L. Ginsberg, *The Israelian Heritage in Judaism* (New York: Jewish Theological Seminary, 1982), 22–23; Rofé, *Mavo'*, 139–140; J. Milgrom, "The Ideological and Historical Importance of the Judge in Deuteronomy," in Y. Zakovitch and A. Rofé, eds., *Isac Leo Seeligmann Volume* (Jerusalem: Rubinstein, 1983), 3:132–133. In contrast, 11QTemple 57:3 makes this passage part of the king's authority; its scribe wrote "they shall appoint" and then corrected it to "he shall appoint," referring to the king, a correction which shows that by itself our text does *not* imply royal appointment (see Milgrom, "Ideological and Historical Importance," 133 n. 18).

6. 1 Macc. 3:56; 4:8–11.

7. See, e.g., Josh. 11:4; 17:16; Judg. 1:19; 4:3. Horses and chariots were first acquired by Israel under David and especially Solomon. See Ahituv, s.v. *merkavah*, EM 5:462ff.; Y. Ikeda, "Solomon's Trade in Horses and Chariots," cited in chap. 17, n. 62. Horses were not commonly ridden by cavalry until the end of the second or the start of the first millennium B.C.E. (A. Kempinski, s.v. *sus*, EM 5:1007), although horseback riding was known earlier.

8. For '*am* meaning "army," see vv. 2,8,9; Num. 20:20; 31:32; Judg. 5:2; Ps. 3:7. MT lacks the conjunction "and," but it is probably to be understood (it is supplied in SP, 11QTemple 61:13, and some ancient translations).

9. See Hezekiah's pre-battle speech in 2 Chron. 32:6–8. For an analysis of the pre-battle speeches in Deuteronomy and related literature, see Weinfeld, DDS, 45–51.

10. Num. 31:6 (see Milgrom, *Numbers*); 1 Sam. 4:11; 14:3,18,36ff; 23:2–12; 28:6. Pre-battle sacrifice is mentioned in 1 Sam. 13:9–12, though it is not offered by a priest. On the Urim and Thummim, see Comment to 33:8. Cf. J. M. Sasson, *The Military Establishments at Mari* (Rome: Pontifical Biblical Institute, 1969), 36–37. For pre-battle exhortations, not by priests, see Judg. 4:14; 7:15; 2 Sam. 10:12. On Deuteronomy's more secular view of warfare, see Rofé, *Mavo'*, 129–130; Weinfeld, DDS, 238–239. Rabbinic sources debate whether "the LORD your God marches with you" means that the Ark accompanied the army; see Hoffmann at v. 4.

11. Cf. Hesiod, *Works and Days*, ll. 405–406.

12. See Sifrei 192–198; Mish. Sot. 8:2–4 and parallels; Maimonides, Hilkhot Melakhim 7; cf. Josephus, Ant. 4.298. According to the halakhah these grounds stand for broader categories: the first two, for example, apply to *acquiring* houses

and vineyards in any legal way, and they cover as well certain other types of structures and other kinds of trees and plants. The deferrals are from combat duty only; those deferred serve in the quartermaster corps until they have completed their undertakings, and they are then exempt even from noncombat duties for one additional year.

13. *Keret* A, ii, 100ff (ANET, 143–144). The text states that "even the new-wed groom goes forth, he drives [trans. uncertain] to another his wife, to a stranger his well beloved," perhaps comparable to the end of Deut. 20:7. A letter from Mari states, "If the king goes on an expedition, everybody down to the youngsters should immediately assemble" (A. L. Oppenheim, *Letters from Mesopotamia* [Chicago: University of Chicago, 1967], no. 35).

14. Cf., in nonmilitary contexts, 1 Kings 15:22; Joel 2:15–16. According to the halakhah, the deferments of Deut. 20 are granted only during non-obligatory wars, those undertaken to deter or preempt attack by enemies or to expand Israelite territory. In obligatory wars—those for the conquest of the promised land and against the Amalekites, and defensive wars to repulse an attack—there are no deferrals. That deferrals were granted only during a non-obligatory war may be supported by the fact that the book of Joshua makes no reference to them during the conquest of the promised land. However, it is unlikely that Deuteronomy would have failed to mention the distinction between these two types of wars had it intended to make one. The chapter does mention other differences between the two types in vv. 15–16. For these two types of war in halakhic sources, see Mish. Sot. 8:7 (see S. Lieberman, *The Tosefta . . . Nashim*, 202, at Tosef. Sot. 7, end, and TK *Nashim* [New York: Jewish Theological Seminary, 1973], 696); Maimonides, Hilkhot Melakhim 5:1; M. Seligsohn, s.v. "War," JE 12:466. According to 1 Macc. 3:56, Judah Maccabee ordered these deferrals during a defensive war.

15. Rofé, *Mavo'*, 135; cf. 78. For a contrasting procedure at Mari, see Sasson, *Military Establishments*, 8–9.

16. For the meaning "initiate" see Rashi at Gen. 14:14; Radak, *Sefer Ha-Shorashim*, s.v. ḥ-n-k; Milgrom, *Numbers*, at Num. 7:10; cf. Josephus, Ant. 4.298. For ceremonial initiations see Num. 7:10,84–88; 1 Kings 8:63; Dan. 3:2–7; Ezra 6:16–18; Neh. 12:27–43; T. Canaan, "The Palestinian Arab House," JPOS 13 (1933): 64; Ps. 30:1 indicates the use of a psalm for initiating a house or temple. For fuller discussion see S. Reif, "Dedicated to ḥnk," VT 22 (1972): 495–501; W. Dommershausen, s.v. "ḥanak," TDOT 5:19–21. Targ. Jon. takes the initiation as affixing a *mezuzah*.

17. The Hebrew verb is used in the same sense in Jer. 31:5 (cf. 29:5: "plant gardens and eat their fruit").

18. A. Shaffer, *Sumerian Sources of Tablet XII of the Epic of Gilgamesh* (Ph.D. diss., University of Pennsylvania, 1963), 118, ll. 275–278, and 151–152; cf. J. J. Finkelstein, "*Ana bit emim sasû*," RA 61 (1967): 132; cf. Judg. 11:27.

19. Cf. Gen. 34:12; 1 Sam. 18:25,27; 2 Sam. 3:14.

20. R. de Vaux, *Ancient Israel* (New York: McGraw-Hill, 1961), 26–28; S. E. Loewenstamm, s.v. *mohar*, EM 4:702–706.

21. A deferral of the fainthearted is also mentioned in Judg. 7:3; its purpose there is to reduce the fighting force to a mere three hundred men and make it obvious that the victory comes from God, not from Israel's own power. For a suggestion that a similar rule is reflected in the *Iliad*, see R. Knox and J. Russo, "Agamemnon's Test: *Iliad* 2.73–75," *Classical Antiquity* 8 (1989): 351–358 (ref. courtesy R. Westbrook).

22. Coward: Sifrei 192, 197; Mish. Sot. 8:5; Rashi, Ramban; compassionate: Tosef. Sot. 7:22 (see Lieberman, TK *Nashim*, 693–694); cf. Ibn Ezra, Ḥazzekuni.

23. Thus 1 Macc. 3:55.

24. So LXX, Targs. Onk. and Jon., and most English translations, including OJPS. Cf. the usage of *pakad* in Num. 27:16 and "at the head" in the synonymous idiom in 1:13. Cf. 2

Chron. 32:6a; 1 Macc. 3:55; 11QTemple 57:3, cited above, n. 5. See also Milgrom, "Ideological and Historical Importance," 132–133. Driver argues that someone other than the local officials must have appointed the commanders. NJPS here follows Ehrlich, who thinks it implausible that officers would only be appointed at the last minute.

25. The Athenians treated Melos similarly in the Peloponnesian War. They called upon the Melians to surrender and become tributaries, but the latter resisted. After defeating them, the Athenians killed all the men and enslaved the women and children (Thucydides, 5:84–116, cited by Richard L. Rubinstein, "The Besieged Community in Ancient and Modern Times," *Michigan Quarterly Review* 22/3 [Summer 1983]: 447–451).

26. Sefer Ha-Ḥinnukh, no. 503.

27. See ARM 2, 42:8 (*salī[m]am iṣṣiṣumma*); ANET, 378b. See also Judg. 21:13 and 1 Kings 20:18. Treaties of submission are described in Josh. 9; 1 Sam. 11:1; and 2 Sam. 10:19. The superior party's *granting* terms of submission is expressed by *karat berit le-* (Josh. 9:6,7,11,15,16), whereas the defeated party's *submitting* to terms is described as *hishlim* (Josh. 10:1,4; 11:19); see also Exod. 23:32; 34:12,15; Josh. 24:25; Judg. 2:2; 1 Kings 20:34; 2 Kings 11:4; cf. 2 Sam. 5:3.

28. The term and the practice are known from Syria and Canaan; see A. Rainey, "Compulsory Labour Gangs in Ancient Israel," IEJ 20 (1970): 191–202; A. Biram, "*Mas 'oved*," *Tarbiz* 23 (1952): 137–142. For the seal of an Israelite supervisor of compulsory labor see N. Avigad, "The Chief of the Corvée," IEJ 30 (1980): 170–173. The term *mas* is never applied to the Gibeonites, who had a similar, but apparently not identical, status: after deceiving the Israelites into believing they were from a distant land (to which Deut. 20:15 implies that our law applies), they secured a non-aggression treaty with the Israelites; once the ruse was discovered, the Israelites, bound by the treaty, could not destroy them but compelled them to become servants to the community and the sanctuary (Josh. 9).

29. 2 Sam. 12:31; 1 Kings 9:15, 20–22; cf. Judg. 1:28–35. When imposed on citizens, such service took the form of periodic corvée labor. Solomon, for example, drafted Israelites to fell timber in Lebanon; each group served one month out of three (1 Kings 5:27–28). It is not known whether foreign populations subjected to forced labor served part-time or permanently. So far as known, *mas* service was first instituted in Israel by David and Solomon (outside the Bible, too, it is only attested under monarchic rule).

30. The insistence on killing nonvirgin women in Num. 31:17–18 (and Judg. 21:11–12) is due to special circumstances, not a general rule followed by those sources. For captive women see also Judg. 5:30; cf. *Iliad* 9:128–131, 592–594; 6:455; 16:830–832; *Odyssey* 8:527–529; 9:40; 24:278–279; I. Eph'al, "Lexical Notes on Some Ancient Military Terms," EI 20 (1989), 115.

31. Sifrei 200.

32. For varying forms of the list see Driver, 97. The Girgashites are added here by LXX, SP, and 11QTemple 62:14. Midrashic sources hold that the Girgashites were not destroyed because Joshua offered the Canaanites the option of emigrating and the Girgashites emigrated to Africa (Lev. R. 17:6; Ginzberg, *Legends*, 4:10 and 6:177 n. 34).

33. For a different view of what this phrase refers to, see J. Milgrom, "Profane Slaughter and a Formulaic Key to the Composition of Deuteronomy," HUCA 47 (1976): 6–9; idem, *Numbers*, 429–430.

34. Deut. 7:3–4; Exod. 23:33; 34:15–16; Judg. 3:5–6; Ps. 106:34–39.

35. See Driver; H. W. Parke, s.v. "War, Art of," OCD, 1136a; Herodotus 1:17; Thucydides 1:107; ANET, 228b, 239ab, 241d, 280c; examples in CAD K, 414a; CAD N 1, 172c–173b; I. Eph'al, "On Warfare and Military Control in the Ancient Near Eastern Empires," in H. Tadmor and M. Weinfeld, eds., *His-*

tory, Historiography and Interpretation (Jerusalem: Magnes Press, 1983), 97; and idem, *Ke-'ir Netsurah* (Jerusalem: Magnes Press, forthcoming), paragraph on *massa' u-mattan*; M. Cogan and H. Tadmor, *2 Kings* (Garden City, N.Y.: Doubleday, 1988), 238. For an illustration see the Egyptian relief in Y. Yadin, *The Art of Warfare in Biblical Lands* (New York: McGraw-Hill, 1963), 2:346, upper right.

36. According to 2 Kings 3:19,25 God, through the prophet Elisha, commanded Israel to destroy the trees of Moab and to stop up its springs and ruin its fields (cf. also 2 Sam. 11:1). Traditional commentators harmonize that incident with the present law: some argue that the law only applies when there is a siege; others, that God made an ad hoc exception in the case of Moab, in keeping with Deut. 23:7. See Num. R. 21:6; Rashi; Radak; Ralbag; Ramban at 23:7.

37. Maimonides, Hilkhot Melakhim 6:10; Sefer Ha-Ḥinnukh, no. 530; for details see J. D. Eisenstein, *Ozar Dinim U-Minhagim* (New York: Hebrew Publishing Co., 1938), 45.

38. See Shadal; as Hoffman notes, the ancient translations, which render "a tree is *not*," also imply that the clause is interrogative (see LXX; Vulg.; Targums; Pesh.; Mekhilta, cited by Hoffmann). This does not require emending the vocalization of *ha'adam*; the interrogative particle is frequently vocalized like the definite article as here (see, e.g., Gen. 17:17 and, before an *aleph*, Gen. 19:9; Num. 16:22). On the translation "You may eat of them," see I. Eph'al, "The Assyrian Siege Ramp at Lachish: Military and Lexical Aspects," *Zion* 49 (1974): 343–344 n. 28.

39. See LXX and the Targums; Buhl, 453; Yadin, *Art of Warfare*, 1:18, 98. The plural *metsurot* is apparently used with the same meaning in Isa. 29:3. See also 29:7 and Eccl. 9:14, according to H. L. Ginsberg, *Koheleth* (Tel Aviv and Jerusalem: Newman, 1961), 117.

40. M. Lichtheim, *Ancient Egyptian Literature* (Berkeley: University of California Press, 1976), 2:33. For the same practice among the Greeks and Romans, see Thucydides 2:75, 77–78; 3:21; 5:114–116; Josephus, War 5.499–510. On the nature of siege walls, see Eph'al, *Ke-'ir Netsurah*.

41. Philo, Spec. 4.229; Mayes. On siege ramps, see Eph'al, "The Assyrian Siege Ramp," *Zion* 49:340–343 (English translation in TA 11 [1984]: 63–66), who notes the use of trees and branches in building them; cf. Jer. 6:6; Thucydides 2:75; Josephus, War 5.522–523; 6:6. On the other items see Yadin, *Art of Warfare*, 1:16–18, 55–56, 69–71, 97, 314–316. Although etymologically *tsar* and *matsor* refer to the encirclement of the city (see 2 Kings 16:5), the ramp is built and the assault takes place during the encirclement; hence, these do not constitute fully distinct phases; see 2 Sam. 11:1,15ff; 1 Kings 16:17–18; Jer. 21:4; 32:2,24.

Chapter 21

1. Hebrew manuscripts have breaks before 21:1,10,15,18, and 22 (M, SP) and after v. 23 (M). All but those before vv. 15 and 18 are also indicated in 11QTemple 63:9; 64:6,9,13.

2. Mid. Hag. to v. 1.

3. Cf. "Your people Israel whom You redeemed" to 7:8; 9:26; 13:6; 15:15; 24:18; 26:15. The presence of the priests may also be part of the Deuteronomic adaptation of the ceremony; see Comment to v. 5 and the parallel Deuteronomic passages cited there. Part of v. 1 and all of v. 9, which do not describe parts of the ceremony, are also written in Deuteronomic style; see Weinfeld, DDS, 341 no. 1 (add 21:1 to the list); A. Roifer (Rofé), "*Eglah 'arufah*," *Tarbiz* 31 (1962): 142 n. 90.

4. Cf. 21:23 and 24:4. On the basis of this verse the halakhah rules that the present law is applicable only within the land of Israel (Sifrei 205; Mid. Hag.; Sefer Ha-Ḥinnukh, no. 504). For pollution of both people and land, see also Lev. 18:24–30 and T. Frymer-Kensky, "Pollution, Purification, and Purgation in

Biblical Israel," in C. L. Meyers and M. P. O'Connor, eds., *The Word of the Lord Shall Go Forth* (Winona Lake, Ind.: Eisenbrauns, 1983), 399–414.

5. Sot. 45b; see, e.g., Num. 19:16.

6. Sifrei 255; see Keter Torah; S. E. Loewenstamm, s.v. *'eglah 'arufah*, EM 6:77; J. J. Finkelstein, "The Goring Ox," *Temple Law Quarterly* 46 (1973): 276; cf. also Gen. 4:8. Deut. 23:11 is another case of this principle. Naturally, unsolved crimes took place within cities, too, and there were laws to deal with them, such as LH §§23–24.

7. Josephus, Ant. 4.220.

8. Cf. Mish. Sot. 9:5. In light of the Comment to 16:18, "your elders and judges" would mean "your elders, including those who are judges." SP reads "your elders and officials [*shoterim*]"; cf. Num. 11:16.

9. See LH §§23–24; HL §6; HSS 15:1 (E. R. Lacheman, "Nuziana II," RA 36 [1939]: 113ff; for more on Nuzi see Driver and Miles, BL 1:110–111; C. Gordon, "An Akkadian Parallel to Deuteronomy 21:1ff," RA 33 [1936]: 1–6, Text I only); J. Nougayrol et al., *Ugaritica* 5 (Paris: Imprimerie Nationale and Librairie Orientaliste Paul Geuthner, 1968), 94–97; PRU 4:106, 153–157; ANET 26b, 547a; Driver, 241; W. Robertson Smith, *The Religion of the Semites* (London: A. and C. Black, 1914), 420 n. 1 and cited by Driver, 241; E. Neufeld, *The Hittite Laws* (London: Luzac, 1951), 135 n. 41. Cf. the Ugaritic king Daniel's curse of, apparently, nearby cities after the murder of his son (ANET, 154–159). Many of the parallels are discussed by Roifer, "*'Eglah 'arufah*." For medieval and later English parallels see Driver and Miles, BL, 111 n. 3.

10. There are, however, Hittite rites for purifying a city after murder and other crimes; see Excursus 19.

11. The point is made by Roifer, "*'Eglah 'arufah*," 121–126; Finkelstein, "Goring Ox," 46:193, 277–278. In Hittite law, only a town located within three leagues of the body is responsible for indemnifying survivors; otherwise none is. Beyond three leagues the presumption that the killer came from the nearest town must not have seemed strong enough to impose financial responsibility on it. Since the aim of the biblical law is to determine who must take the steps to remove bloodguilt from the entire nation, and this need is absolute, the nearest town is chosen no matter how far it is from the body.

12. RH 10a; Mish. Parah 1:1; Maimonides, Hilkhot Rotseah 10:2. A cow can give birth at two years old, but it still grows until age three (information courtesy Richard Bartholomew, D.V.M.). However, some passages use *'eglah* for a mature cow; see Gen. 15:9; Isa. 7:21–22; cf. Exod. 32:4 and Ps. 106:19a with Ps. 106:20b, though this is poetry, which uses terms less precisely.

13. Deut. 15:19; Num. 19:2; 1 Sam. 6:7.

14. See Driver; G. A. Smith, *The Historical Geography of the Holy Land* (reprint; New York: Harper and Row, 1966), 439, both following Schultens, *Origines Hebraeae* (1724). Cf. perhaps Jer. 5:15 (NJPS: "enduring"), Prov. 13:15 (NJPS: "unchanging" or "harsh"); Job 33:19 (NJPS: "constant"). The Arabic word is notably not mentioned by the medieval Hebrew grammarians who lived in Arabic-speaking lands, and according to Y. Aharoni and S. E. Loewenstamm, in early Arabic *watana* meant "strong," not "permanent" (s.v. "*musagim ge'ografiyim ba-mikra*'," EM 4:747).

15. A. Weiser, "*nahal 'eitan*," *Beth Mikra*' 1 (1956): 14–15. It is not clear how many perennial wadis there are in Israel. There seem to be about eighteen west of the Jordan. However, more than half are perennial for only a few miles of their course, and most are on the periphery of Israelite territory or outside of it, such as the sources of the Jordan in upper Galilee and wadis along the Mediterranean coast. There are almost none in Judah and Samaria. (*Israel—Sites and Places*, 9th ed. [Jerusalem: Ministry of Defense and Carta, 1987]; H. Bar Deroma, *Nahal Aithan* [Yeruham's Library, no. 5; Jerusalem: B.E.R. Publish-

ers, 1968]: 8–12; E. Orni and E. Efrat, *Geography of Israel*, 3rd ed. [Jerusalem: Israel Universities Press, 1973]; *Atlas of Israel*, 2nd ed. [Jerusalem: Survey of Israel, Ministry of Labour, 1970]; S. Avitsur, "On the History of the Exploitation of Water Power in Eretz-Israel," IEJ 10 [1960]: 37; letter of Prof. David Amiran, 19 November 1989).

16. See Maimonides, Hilkhot Rotseah 9:2, followed by Mid. Hag.; cf. Torah Temimah at Deut. 21:4, note 31; Aharoni and Loewenstamm, "*musagim ge'ografiyim ba-mikra*'," 747; Weiser, "*nahal 'eitan*," 14–15. *'Eitan* is used with reference to strongly flowing water in Exod. 14:27; Amos 5:24; Ps. 74:15; Ecclus. 40:13–14; and perhaps 1 Kings 8:2.

17. See LXX; translation attributed to Aquila by Field, *Hexapla* 1:303; Josephus, Ant. 4.221; Sifrei; Mish. Sot. 9:5; Rashi; Shadal ("a stony valley"). This sense may be found in Num. 24:21 where *'eitan* is parallel to "cliff"; NJPS there translates as "secure," perhaps supposing the basic sense to be "strong," as possibly in Mic. 6:2 (there NJPS renders "firm" but suggests the possibility of an emendation) and Prov. 13:15 (NJPS: "unchanging" or "harsh").

18. This interpretation of *'-r-f* (from *'oref*, "back of the neck"), rather than traditional "behead," is supported by Isa. 66:3 which refers to a pagan rite of sacrificing a dog in this manner, since the bodies of dogs with broken necks have been discovered buried near an altar at Tel Haror (information courtesy of Eliezer Oren). Breaking the neck is a method that can be used on small animals such as dogs, calves, and young animals (Exod. 13:13; 34:20). Herodotus 4:188 mentions its use among the Libyans. It is not used for sacrifice in the Bible. As noted in the Comment, it is used on firstlings of animals that may not be sacrificed; its sacrificial use in Isa. 66:3 is part of an illicit rite.

19. See Isa. 1:15–16; Pss. 26:6; 73:13.

20. LXX and 11QTemple 63:5 read "over the head of the heifer." This reading highlights the resemblance of the ceremony to sacrifices, including sin offerings and the goat that is sent to Azazel, in which the offerer lays his hands on the head of the offering (Lev. 1:4; 4:4,15; 16:21). If the ceremony is viewed as a symbolic execution of the murderer, one might also compare the practice of witnesses laying their hands on a criminal's head before stoning him (Lev. 24:14).

21. For the first view see Abravanel, 197.

22. Mish. Sot. 9:6, following the text in TJ Sot. 9:6, 23d, and Maimonides' commentary (see Hoffmann, and J. N. Epstein, *Mavo' le-Nusah Ha-Mishnah*, 2nd ed. [Jerusalem: Magnes Press; Tel Aviv: Dvir, 1964], 955–956); cf. Sot. 38b, 46b; Targ. Jon. and Targ. Yer.; Sifrei 210 and Finkelstein's note on 244.

23. Mish. Sot. 9:7; Maimonides, Hilkhot Rotseah 10:8; cf. Torah Temimah at v. 9, n. 67.

24. W. Roberston Smith, *Kinship and Marriage in Early Arabia* (Boston: Beacon, 1903), 89–92; *Iliad* 1:30–31, 112–114; 2:689–693; 19:297–299; *Odyssey* 9:40–41; OCD, 63. At Mari the king is known to have taken captives as concubines; see B. F. Batto, *Studies on Women at Mari* (Baltimore: Johns Hopkins University Press, 1974), 83–84.

25. See M. Walzer, *Just and Unjust Wars* (New York: Basic Books, 1977), 134–135.

26. See Sifrei 213 and parallels; Rashi at vv. 12, 13; Maimonides, Hilkhot Melakhim 8:5; cf. Ramban. Cf. the homiletic explanation of the sequence of this and the following three laws cited in Excursus 13.

27. Keter Torah. Josephus and rabbinic sources presume that married women were also permitted, as in Homeric Greece; see Josephus, Ant. 4.257; Sifrei 211 (cf. Da'at Soferim here); *Iliad* 19:295–299.

28. Josephus, Ant. 4.257; Ramban ad loc.

29. Rashi ad loc.; Abravanel, 202; R. Akiba in Sifrei 212.

30. Hazzekuni at v. 13.

31. Moran; W. W. Hallo, *The Book of the People* (Atlanta: Scholars Press, 1991), 97; cf. T. H. Gaster, *Myth, Legend, and*

Custom in the Old Testament (New York: Harper and Row, 1969), 438.

32. Num. 20:29; Deut. 34:8.

33. Smith, *Kinship*, 90. Cf. LH §171; contrast ANET, 543, no. 4. Contrast the sale of a pregnant concubine captured in war, in I. Eph'al, "Lexical Notes on Some Ancient Military Terms," EI 20 (1989), 115 (it is not certain that the owner was the one who impregnated her).

34. Abravanel, 202.

35. Josephus, Ant. 4.259; Philo, Virt. 115; Sifrei 214 (cf. R. Judah in sec. 273); Rashi; Ramban. Cf. LH §141 which speaks of punishing an offending wife by divorcing her or keeping her as a slave-girl. Others take the verb to mean "treat as merchandise," "engage in trade with" (Targums here and at 24:7; Ibn Janaḥ). In the similar Muslim law cited above, the pregnant captive may not be sold in the market or ransomed back to her people for money, suggesting that *hit'amer* could mean "ransom for money."

36. See I. Mendelsohn, "On the Preferential Status of the Eldest Son," BASOR 156 (1959): 38–40; R. de Vaux, *The Early History of Israel* (Philadelphia: Westminster Press, 1978), 250–251; J. Milgrom, s.v. "Firstborn," IDBS, 337–338; E. R. Goodenough, *The Jurisprudence of the Jewish Courts in Egypt* (1929; reprint, Amsterdam: Philo Press, 1968), 56–57; A. R. Harmon, "Egyptian Property Returns," in *Yale Classical Studies* 4 (1934): 138–143.

37. Some scholars believe that such discretion was permitted among the Hebrews in the patriarchal period, as when Esau and Reuben lost their birthrights, and that the present law is a reform of that situation. However, neither case proves that the father could exercise arbitrary discretion. Jacob transferred Reuben's birthright because Reuben committed a serious offense against him (see Gen. 35:22; 49:3–4; 1 Chron. 5:1–2; Sforno; Rofé, *Mavo'*, 156 n. 54, comparing LH §§168–169). Esau bartered away his own birthright (Gen. 25:29–34).

38. Gen. 29:30–31; 1 Sam. 1:5.

39. See 5:9; Radak, *Sefer Ha-Shorashim*, s.v. *ś-n-'*; Sarna, *Genesis*, at 29:31 (see also Josephus, Ant. 4.249 and Ehrlich at Gen. 29:31 and 38:23). Arabic also terms the favorite and nonfavorite wives, respectively, "beloved" and "hated" (H. Granqvist, *Marriage Conditions in a Palestinian Village* [Helsinki: Akademische Buchhandlung, 1931–1935], 2:194), and Egyptian likewise terms the secondary wife "the hated one" (*mśddt*; A. Erman, cited by J. J. Rabinowitz, "Marriage Contracts in Ancient Egypt in the Light of Jewish Sources," HTR 46 [1953]: 94 n. 12). On the other hand, Akkadian sources also use "love" and "hate" to refer to wives (and sons) whom a man likes and dislikes; see *Gilgamesh Epic* 12:23–26, 42–45.

40. Sifrei; Mid. Hag.

41. Mish. Bek. 8:1.

42. R. Yohanan b. Barokah in Mish. BB 8:5; BB 130a; Mid. Hag. Nevertheless, BB 133b discourages giving one son's share to another.

43. LXX; Vulg.; Pesh.; Targ. Onk.; Targ. Jon.; Philo, Spec. 2, 133; Josephus, Ant. 4.249; Sifrei 217; BB 122b–123a (see Rashbam there). Ben Sira clearly uses *pi shenayim* in the sense of "double portion" (Ecclus. 12:5; 18:32), but this may reflect postbiblical exegesis of Deut. 21:17.

44. For this practice, in such places as Assyria, Nuzi, and Ptolemaic Egypt, see n. 36, above, and MAL B, §1, and O, §4; ANET, 220 no. 3. This is also consistent with the apparent meaning of Gen. 48:22, according to which Jacob gave Joseph one share more than each of his brothers (see Sarna, *Genesis*).

45. The phrase may also mean that in 2 Kings 2:9, the only other place it appears. See Ehrlich here and at 2 Kings 2:9; A. Goetze, "Number Idioms in Old Babylonian," JNES 5 (1946): 202; F. Rundgren, "Parallelen zu Akk. *Sinepum*, '2/3,'" JCS 9 (1955): 29–30; E. A. Speiser, *Oriental and Biblical Studies* (Philadelphia: University of Pennsylvania Press, 1967), 156–159; Z.

Zevit, *Matres Lectionis in Ancient Hebrew Epigraphs* (Cambridge, Mass.: American Schools of Oriental Research, 1980), 22–23. In Egyptian, too, "two mouths" means "two-thirds" (Albright, cited in Speiser, *Oriental and Biblical Studies*, 159n.; A. Gardiner, *Egyptian Grammar*, 3rd ed. [Oxford: Oxford University Press, 1957], 197, 452). All of the idioms in question may have originally meant "two parts," with the sense "two-thirds" developing from contexts in which two parties divide something and one of them takes two parts, which in such cases equals two-thirds of it (suggestion of Jonathan Paradise). Note the etymology of Akkadian *šittin*, "two-thirds," cited by W. von Soden, *Grundriss der Akkadischen Grammatik* (Rome: Pontifical Biblical Institute, 1952), §70i, and English "two parts," *Oxford English Dictionary* 7:498.

46. ARM 8:1 (the text uses Akk. *šittin*, although J. J. Finkelstein translates "double share" in ANET, 545 no. 13). In the neo-Babylonian laws the sons of a man's first wife inherit two-thirds of his estate and the sons of his second wife inherit one-third (ANET, 198).

47. Gen. 49:3; Pss. 78:51; 105:36; cf. Job 18:12.

48. Reasons for the special status of the first-born are suggested by Philo, Spec. 2.133; Abravanel, 203.

49. On responsibilities of the chief heir cf. Mendelsohn, "On the Preferential Status of the Eldest Son," 38–40; E. Neufeld, *Ancient Hebrew Marriage Laws* (London and New York: Longmans, Green, 1944), 263; N. Rubin, "On the Social Significance of the *bekhor* in the Bible" (Hebrew), *Beth Mikra'* 33 (1988): 162–163.

50. See also Gen. 42:37; Judg. 11:34–40. Zech. 13:3 may be only a hyperbole (Rofé, *Mavo'*, 150).

51. D. Marcus, "Juvenile Delinquency in the Bible and the Ancient Near East," JANES 13 (1981): 31–52. One text cited by Marcus likewise uses the Akkadian cognate of *sorer*, "wayward," with reference to a rebellious son (37, text a).

52. In the halakhic reading the law applies for only the three months after a son turns thirteen and only if he has ravenously eaten semi-cooked meat and drunk partially mixed wine, in the company of a group that does not include one decent person, and not on a religious occasion; paying for the food with money misappropriated from his father; only if both parents are living and are not deaf, mute, blind, lame, or maimed in the hand; and only if both agree to prosecute him. See Mish. Sanh. 8:1–4; Sanh. 71a; Maimonides, Hilkhot Mamrim 7. Prov. 30:17 may imply that in practice the ultimate punishment of disrespectful children was left to God, not to human authorities, though it could also mean that the body will be exposed after execution, or that the rebellious son who escapes human punishment will not escape divine punishment: "The eye that mocks a father and disdains the homage due to a mother—the ravens of the brook will gouge it out, young eagles will devour it."

53. Cf. 1 Kings 12:11. See Sifrei; Mish. Sanh. 8:4. In contrast, the targums, LXX, and Josephus, Ant. 4.260, hold that the parents are to admonish the son orally.

54. Prov. 29:15; 23:13–14; 13:24.

55. A. H. Freimann, s.v. *ben sorer u-moreh*, EM 2:161–162, comparing LH §§168–169. Herod I used this law as a pretext for killing two of his sons (Josephus, Ant. 16.365–366).

56. To the rabbis it is not insubordination by itself that merits such severe punishment, but the son's gluttony, which points to a criminal future: in their view the law refers to a son who misappropriates his father's property to pay for his gluttony, and they are convinced that when he uses up his father's property he will eventually turn to robbery and kill someone in the process; hence, they hold, he is to be executed before he begins his life of crime (Midrash Tannaim, 131).

57. Mish. Sanh. 8:4; Maimonides, Hilkhot Mamrim 7:7.

58. Thompson, 231.

59. Gen. 40:19; Josh. 10:26; Est. 9:6–14.

60. See Mish. Sanh. 6:4; Assyrian inscriptions and reliefs in ANET, 276b, 288a, 295b, 300c; ANEP, nos. 362, 368, 373; V. H. Kooy, s.v. "Impalement," IDB 2:690. The text does not mean that the criminal is executed by hanging, a method unknown in biblical and ancient Near Eastern law. The earliest possible reference to death by hanging is Est. 2:23; 5:14; 7:9–10; 9:13–14, though these may well refer to death by impaling. See M. Greenberg, s.v. "Hanging," IDB 1:522; note the similar expressions, referring to impaling, in CAD s.v. *alālu, gašišu, šulû* (CAD E, 128c), *zaqāpu,* and *zaqīpu.* See also Ezra 6:11. On Num. 25:4 and 2 Sam. 21 see S. E. Loewenstamm, s.v. *hokaʿah,* EM 2:798–800; Milgrom, *Numbers,* and McCarter, *2 Samuel* (Garden City, N.Y.: Doubleday, 1984); on the antiquity of the practice reflected there, see G. E. Mendenhall, *The Tenth Generation* (Baltimore: Johns Hopkins University Press, 1974), 113–121. Halakhic exegesis reads the verse as a prohibition of the Roman method of execution by crucifixion (Sifrei 221; Sanh. 46b). In contrast, 11QTemple, Pesh. and some manuscripts of LXX invert the verbs in our verse and read: "hang him on wood so that he dies," thus justifying crucifixion (11QTemple 64:8, 10–11; see Y. Yadin, *Megillat Hamikdash* [Jerusalem: Israel Exploration Society, 1977], 1:286–288).

61. Not obligatory: Bekhor Shor, contrary to the halakhah (Mish. Sanh. 6:4). According to Josephus and a minority view in the Mishnah it followed all executions; the majority view restricts the practice to blasphemers and idolaters (see Josephus, Ant. 4.265; cf. Ant. 4.202; Mish. Sanh. 6:4). Philo, Spec. 3.150–152 seems to apply it only to murder. 11QTemple 64:7–10 applies it to those guilty of treason (see Yadin, *Megillat Ha-Mikdash,* 1:286–288).

The only certain cases of impaling in Mesopotamian law are LH §153 and MAL A §53; some think that it also appears in LH §§21 and 227. For impaling in war see Josh. 8:29; 10:26; 1 Sam. 31:10; 2 Sam. 4:12; Lam. 5:12; Judith 14:1, 11; 2 Macc. 15:33; Assyrian examples cited above (on displaying bodies of rebel leaders for deterrent purposes see H.W.F. Saggs, "Assyrian Warfare in the Sargonid Period," *Iraq* 25 [1963]: 149–150; cf. Weinfeld, DDS, 51 n. 4).

62. Curse or threat: Deut. 28:26; 1 Sam. 17:44,46; Jer. 8:2; 16:4,6; 25:33; intentional denial of burial: 2 Sam. 21:1–14; 1 Kings 14:11; 21:23–24; 2 Kings 9:10; Ps. 79:2–3; feeding corpses to predators: ANET, 288d; suffering of the unburied: Isa. 14:15,19; *Gilgamesh Epic,* 12:151–152 (ANET, 99b); A. Heidel, *The Gilgamesh Epic and Old Testament Parallels* (Chicago: University of Chicago Press, 1963), 155, 166; Eshmunazar inscription, ANET, 662c; *Iliad* 23:72–74; *Aeneid* 6:324–330; Fustel de Coulanges, *The Ancient City* (Garden City, N.Y.: Doubleday, n.d.), 17–19.

63. Sanh. 46a.

64. See Tosef. Sanh. 9:7; Targ. Jon.; Rashi. For *kelalah* meaning "affront" see Rashi; H. C. Brichto, *The Problem of "Curse" in the Hebrew Bible* (Philadelphia: Society of Biblical Literature, 1963). The idea that an unburied body is an offense to the eyes of the gods, and must be buried by sunrise, is found in Greece; see H. Nettleship and J. E. Sandys, eds., *Dictionary of Classical Antiquities* (Cleveland: World Publishing Co., 1963), 101b, 101d; OCD 314b.

65. For *ʾelohim* = "spirit of the dead" see 1 Sam. 28:13; Isa. 8:19; N. H. Tur Sinai, *The Language and the Book* (Hebrew) (Jerusalem: Mosad Bialik, 1955), 3:163. For similar usage in Akkadian and Canaanite see A. Heidel, *Gilgamesh Epic,* 153, 190; T. J. Lewis, *Cults of the Dead in Ancient Israel and Ugarit* (Atlanta: Scholars Press, 1989), 49–51; KAI no. 27:1, 3; no. 117:1; CAD I/J, 91–103; UT 1 Aqht 112:141 and 62:45–47 (ANET, 154 and 141b). The only prescriptive passage to call God *ʾelohim* in Deut. is 25:18, where the reference to the attitude of non-Israelites requires a general term for deity.

66. See Targ. Jon.; Radak; Shadal.

Chapter 22

1. Hebrew manuscripts divide the text before vv. 1,4,5,6, 8,10,12,13,20,22,23,25,28, and after 29 (M; the Leningrad codex adds breaks before vv. 9 and 11). SP has breaks only before certain laws beginning with *(w)ky:* vv. 6,13,23,28. 11QTemple col. 65, to the extent that it covers the same ground, has breaks before 22:1,8, between 8 and 13 (it omits vv. 9–12), and not before v. 25.

2. See H. B. Huffmon, "Exodus 23:4–5: A Comparative Study," in H. N. Bream et al., eds., *A Light unto My Path: Old Testament Studies in Honor of Jacob M. Myers* (Philadelphia: Temple University Press, 1974), 271–278.

3. Cf. the story of Saul searching for lost asses (1 Sam. 9:3,20) and the frequent poetic comparisons of people to stray animals (Isa. 53:6; Jer. 23:1–4; 50:6,17; Ezek. 34:4,16; Mic. 4:6; Zeph. 3:19; Ps. 119:176).

4. See also 7:17; 12:20; 13:9; 18:21; 20:1.

5. For the way in which the basic law is supplemented by legal reflection see M. Fishbane, *Biblical Interpretation in Ancient Israel* (Oxford: Clarendon, 1985), 177–179. For the talmudic discussion see BM chap. 2.

6. L. Stager, "The Archaeology of the Family in Ancient Israel," BASOR 260 (1985): 12–15; T. Canaan, "The Palestinian Arab House," JPOS 13 (1933): 41–42, 70; J. H. Tigay, "Some Archaeological Notes on Deuteronomy," in D. P. Wright et al., eds., *Pomegranates and Golden Bells: Studies . . . Milgrom* (Winona Lake, Ind.: Eisenbrauns, 1994); cf. ARN¹, chap. 8.

7. Mish. BM 2:1–7; BM 27a–28b; cf. Josephus, Ant. 4.274. According to HL §45, the finder must publicize matters, but it is not clear whether he publicizes what he found or his attempt to locate the owner (recent practice in Transjordan was that the finding must be confirmed by two witnesses to protect the finder from charge of theft; Smith, 259). According to HL §71, the lost animal is first taken to the authorities; see also §79.

8. LH §9 and MAL C + G.

9. Mish. BK 5:7; BK 54b. SP adds "or any (other types) of his cattle" after the animals specified in vv. 1 and 4.

10. BM 32a–b; Maimonides, Sefer Ha-Mitsvot, positive nos. 202–203; idem, Hilkhot Rotseaḥ 13:1–2,13.

11. Sifrei 226; Ibn Ezra; Maimonides, Guide 3.37; idem, Sefer Ha-Mitsvot, negative nos. 39–40; Abravanel; Sefer Ha-Hinnukh. For parallels see Driver; H. Licht, *Sexual Life in Ancient Greece* (Routledge and Kegan Paul, 1932), 124, 125, 128, 500; H. A. Hoffner, Jr., "Symbols for Masculinity and Femininity," JBL 85 (1966): 326–334; idem, "Some Contributions of Hittitology to Old Testament Study," *Tyndale Bulletin* 20 (1969): 48–51; T. H. Gaster, *Myth, Legend, and Custom in the Old Testament* (New York: Harper and Row, 1969), 316–318; Lucian, *The Syrian Goddess (De Dea Syria),* ed. H. W. Attridge and R. Oden (Missoula, Mont.: Scholars Press, 1976), §§26–27, 51.

12. Lambert, BWL, 230.

13. Sifrei 226; Naz. 59a. *Keli* could mean "garment" in 1 Sam. 21:6 (the Qumran text reads differently) and "adornments" in Isa. 61:10; Gen. 24:53; Exod. 3:22; Ezek. 16:17. For women carrying weapons in magic and rituals see Hoffner, "Symbols"; Maimonides, Guide, 3.37; idem, Sefer Ha-Mitsvot, negative no. 40.

14. Maimonides, Hilkhot ʿAvodah Zarah 12:10; idem, Sefer Ha-Mitsvot, negative nos. 39–40; Shulḥan ʿArukh, Yoreh Deʿah 182.

15. Gen. 32:12; Hos. 10:14.

16. For "release" see Exod. 4:23; 5:12; for "chase away" see Deut. 22:19; 2 Sam. 13:16.

17. Maimonides, Guide 3.48

18. Ehrlich, *Mikra.* On inversion of clauses in allusions see M. Seidel, "Parallels between the Book of Isaiah and the Book of Psalms" (Hebrew), *Sinai* 38 (1956): 149–172, 229–240,

272–280, 333–354; R. Weiss, *Studies in the Text and Language of the Bible* (Jerusalem: Magnes Press, 1981), 259–273; M. Greenberg, *Ezekiel 1–20* (Garden City, N.Y.: Doubleday, 1983), 198, 333.

19. Abravanel, 207; Sefer Ha-Ḥinnukh, no. 537.

20. Josh. 2:6; 1 Sam. 9:25; 2 Sam. 11:2; 16:22; Isa. 22:1; Jer. 19:13; 48:38; Zeph. 1:5. See also Dalman, 1:473–474; 7:58–60, 82–87; Canaan, JPOS 13:69.

21. Sifrei 229; BK 15b, 46a; Maimonides, Hilkhot Rotseaḥ 11–12; F. Rosner, *Modern Medicine and Jewish Law* (New York: Bloch/Yeshiva University Press, 1972), 25–31.

22. Maimonides, Hilkhot Berakhot 11:8.

23. Maimonides, Hilkhot Rotseaḥ 11:3.

24. *Kil'ayim* is apparently something like a dual form of *kol*, "all," and literally means "both." Ugaritic, Akkadian, Arabic, and Ethiopic cognates are cited in UT §19.1231 and HALAT, 453.

25. Rashi at Lev. 19:19.

26. M. Douglas, *Purity and Danger* (London: Routledge and Kegan Paul, 1980), 53; C. Houtman, "Another Look at Forbidden Mixtures," VT 34 (1984): 226–228. Talmudic sources explain the forbidden combinations of Lev. 19:19 thus, basing their view on the beginning of the verse, "You shall observe My laws," which they understand as referring to the laws of nature. See TJ Kil. 1:7, 27b; Sifra to Lev. 19:19; Kid. 39a; Lev. R. 35:4; Ramban at Lev. 19:19.

27. Josephus, Ant. 4.228; TJ Kil. 8:1, 31b.

28. Ber. 22a; TJ Kil. 8:1, 31b; Maimonides, Hilkhot Kil'ayim 5:2; Shulḥan ʿArukh, Yoreh Deʿah 296:1.

29. On mixed cropping, see Arthur J. Dommen, *Innovation in African Agriculture* (Boulder, Colo.: Westview Press, 1988), index, s.v. "intercropping"; David C. Hopkins, *Highlands of Canaan* (Sheffield: Almond, 1985), 284–285 n. 38. On spaces between species see Mish. Kil. and Sefer Ha-Ḥinnukh, no. 250. Other sources cited in Sefer Ha-Ḥinnukh.

30. Ramban at Lev. 19:19.

31. The meaning of Heb. *meleʾah* is uncertain; see M. Haran, s.v. *meleʾah*, EM 4:975.

32. Maimonides, Hilkhot Kil'ayim 5:7. "Becoming sacrosanct" would normally imply that the crop would have to be forfeited for use in the sanctuary; this is unlikely in the present context because no hybrid crops are known to have been used in the sanctuary.

33. Philo, Spec. 4.205; Virt. 146; Ibn Ezra; W. D. Hooper and H. B. Ash, *Marcus Porcius Cato: On Agriculture; Marcus Terentius Varro: On Agriculture* (Cambridge: Harvard University Press, 1934), 235. Although Lev. 19:19 might suggest that the present law is a precaution to prevent the ox and ass from mating (Maimonides, Guide 3.49; Ramban here and at Lev. 19:19; Hoffmann), these two animals cannot crossbreed and are highly unlikely to mate. Were that the aim, one might expect the species to be kept apart after work as well.

34. Tanḥ. Mishpatim 7, end; Yoma 67b.

35. Josephus, Ant. 4.208; so also Daʿat Zekenim; Ḥazzekuni; Bekhor Shor at Lev. 19:19. Some of the priestly garments and parts of the Tabernacle also contain mixed species; see Exod. 26:31; 28:6,15; 39:2,5,8,29; M. Haran, *Temples and Temple Service* (Oxford: Clarendon, 1978), 160–162, 212.

36. The etymology of *shaʿatnez* is discussed by S. Ahituv, s.v. *shaʿatnez*, EM 8:228–229. On Ajrud see A. Sheffer, "The Textiles," in Z. Meshel, *Kuntillet Ajrud* (Jerusalem: Israel Museum, 1978).

37. For much of what follows see Milgrom, *Numbers*, Comments to chap. 15 and Excursus 38.

38. See Driver; HALAT, 172; Lieberman, TK *Moʿed*, 845; idem, *Nashim*, 175; cf. Aramaic *gedilta'*, Akkadian *gidlu*, and Arabic *jadila*.

39. See ANEP, nos. 6, 7, 45–48, 52.

40. The phrase "look at it," referring to the fringe, in Num. 15:39, was taken to mean that the commandment must be performed during daylight hours. See Sifrei Num. 115; Tosef. Kid. 1:10; Men. 43a; cf. Isserles in Shulḥan ʿArukh, 'Oraḥ Ḥayyim 17:2. Interestingly, Targ. Jon. translates v. 5 as "A woman may not wear a cloak with *tsitsit* [tassels] or *tefillin*, since these are men's appurtenances," but no halakhic source cites v. 5 in objecting to the practice.

41. Cf. Maimonides, Guide 3.49; Abravanel, 209. The halakhah requires a husband to pay his wife her *ketubbah* settlement (the halakhic equivalent of the bride-price) if he divorces her arbitrarily. MAL §38 and Cowley, AP 15:27 (ANET, 223c) likewise indicate that he forfeits the bride-price.

42. This is the practice among some tribes in Morocco; see E. Westermarck, *Marriage Ceremonies in Morocco* (London: Macmillan, 1914), 246. According to the halakhah, if the husband discovers after the wedding that his wife had already lost her virginity prior to their engagement, and that she had deceived him, he may divorce her, reduce her *ketubbah* settlement by half or entirely, depending on the circumstances; if he is willing to keep her, he writes her a new *ketubbah* for the amount due nonvirgins (Mish. Ket. 1:2–7; Maimonides, Hilkhot 'Ishut, 11).

43. Louis M. Epstein, *Sex Laws and Customs in Judaism* (reprint; New York: Ktav, 1967), 165, 206.

44. 2 Sam. 13:15.

45. For *sam lah . . . devarim* meaning "accuse her of . . . things" see Job 4:18 and 1 Sam. 22:15 (cf. the use of *natan* in 1 Sam. 1:16); for *ʿalilot* as "misconduct" see Ezek. 14:22–23; 20:43–44; 21:29; for the syntax of *ʿalilot devarim* (=*divrei ʿalilot*) cf. *ʿervat davar*, 23:15; 24:1.

46. A. Musil, *Arabia Petraea* (Vienna: Hoelder, 1908), 3:208 (other cases of the groom returning the bride are cited by H. Granqvist, *Marriage Conditions in a Palestinian Village* [Helsingfors: Akademische Buchhandlung, 1931–35], 2:128–130). For the parents punishing their daughter as they see fit, see MAL A, §12 regarding the consensual fornication of an unengaged virgin. On examination of the accused bride, see J. Tigay, "Examination of the Accused Bride in 4Q159: Forensic Medicine at Qumran," in E. L. Greenstein and D. Marcus, eds., *Comparative Studies in Honor of Yohanan Muffs*, JANES 22 (1993): 129–134; cf. Maimonides, Hilkhot 'Ishut 11:12.

47. Driver, 255; Westermarck, *Marriage Ceremonies*, 159, 228 (see index, s.v. "Virginity, marks of the bride's"); Granqvist, *Marriage Conditions*, 2:127–130; P. H. Williams, *South Italian Folkways in Europe and America* (New Haven: Yale University Press, 1938), 82 (ref. courtesy of Claudia Suter); J. J. Meyer, *Sexual Life in Ancient India* (New York: Dutton, 1930), 1:43 n. 1. For the practice among Jews in talmudic through modern times, see Ket. 16b (*mappah shel betulim*); Tanhuma, Korah, sec. 9; Karaite sources cited by M. Malul, "SUSAPINNU: The Mesopotamian Paranymph and His Role," JESHO 32 (1989): 264; I. Ben-Ami and D. Noy, eds., *Studies in Marriage Customs* (Jerusalem: Magnes Press, 1974), 54, 174, 260, 262 (ref. courtesy of Dan Ben-Amos).

48. According to talmudic sources, the custom that virgins wed on Wednesdays arose because courts held session on Thursdays; thus a man who suspected his bride of premarital unchastity could press charges immediately (Mish. Ket. 1:1; Tosef. Ket. 1:1).

49. Gen. 9:23; Exod. 22:25; Deut. 24:13; cf. Odyssey 14:457-533.

50. In Morocco, too, a man who falsely accuses his bride of nonvirginity is flogged (Westermarck, 229). MAL A §17–18 prescribes flogging as (part of) the punishment for falsely accusing another man's wife of adultery. Cf. also LH §127; MAL N §§1, 2.

51. If so, the fine is double what the bride's father would have had to refund to her accuser. This would accord with the principle that the false accuser is subjected to whatever would have been done to the accused (19:19) and the principle that a

convicted thief must pay double what he stole (Exod. 22:6,8; false claims are likewise punished with a fine equal to twice the value of the claim in LH §§120, 124, 126, and 160–161).

52. LH §21.

53. Rashi; Ket. 45a; TJ Ket. 4:5, end, 28d; A. Phillips, "Another Look at Adultery," JSOT 20 (1981): 10. Cf. Syriac Ahikar 4:4.

54. Gen. 34:7; Judg. 20:6,10; 2 Sam. 13:12; Jer. 29:23.

55. Shadal; "fornicate" (*zanah*) is used of both unbetrothed and betrothed girls; for the former see Lev. 19:29; 21:9; Ezek. 23:3; Hos. 4:13–14.

56. LH §129; MAL A §§14–16; HL §§197–198.

57. Gen. 20:6; 39:8; Ps. 51:6.

58. For the prophetic passages, see Hos. 2:5; Ezek. 16:37,39; 23:26; Jer. 13:26–27; see J. Tigay, s.v. "Adultery," EncJud 2:313–315. Stoning is also mentioned in Ezek. 16:38–40. For discussion of the punishment of adultery, see the studies of Greenberg and others cited in chap. 5, n. 112.

59. Hos. 4:2–3; Jer. 5:7–9; 7:9–15.

60. LE §26; LH §130; cf. Philo, Spec. 3.72; contrast Epstein, *Sex Laws*, 197.

61. 11QTemple 66:4–5 reads: "But if in the open country a man meets her [text adds above line: the woman,] in a far-away place, hidden from the city. . . ."

62. The two paragraphs of this law are worded in accordance with this rule of thumb: in v. 23 the man is said to simply "lie with her," while in v. 25 he is said to "lie with her by force." The wording of the protasis presupposes the conclusion drawn from the rule of thumb (cf. chap. 19, n. 48).

63. Philo, Spec. 3.77–78; Josephus, Ant. 4.252; Sifrei 243; Ramban to v. 22; Maimonides, Hilkhot Na'arah Betulah 1:2. Cf. Epstein, *Sex Laws*, 198ff. In MAL §12, the wife's resistance establishes her innocence.

64. Epstein, *Sex Laws*, 210.

65. HL §197. Cf. MAL A, §12, which specifies force against a resisting married woman; MAL A, §16 combines both.

66. LE §26; LH §§129–130. See J. J. Finkelstein, "Sex Offenses in Sumerian Laws," JAOS 86 (1966): 368–369; idem, "The Laws of Ur-Nammu," JCS 22 (1968–69): 73; cf. Abravanel, 210–211. On age at marriage see M. Roth, "Age at Marriage and the Household: A Study of Neo-Babylonian and Neo-Assyrian Forms," *Comparative Studies in Society and History* 29 (1987): 715–747; B. Schereschewsky, s.v. "Child Marriage," EncJud 5:423–426; Granqvist, *Marriage Conditions* 1:33–39.

67. Ned. 27a; Sefer Ha-Hinnukh, no. 573.

68. MdRY Nezikin 17 (Lauterbach 3:130); see Hoffmann; D. Halivni Weiss, "A Note on 'asher lo' 'orasah," JBL 81 (1962): 67–69.

69. Weinfeld, DDS, 285–286, notes that there was no standard bride-price, but that it varied with the economic circumstances of the families involved.

70. MdRY Nezikin 17 (Lauterbach 3:131–132); Maimonides, Hilkhot Na'arah Betulah 1:3 (contra 11QTemple 66:10–11; see Yadin, *Megillat Ha-Mikdash* [Jerusalem: Israel Exploration Society, 1977], 1:283).

71. MAL A, §55.

Chapter 23

1. Hebrew texts have breaks in this chapter before vv. 1,2,3,4, and 8 (M), 10 and 16 (M, SP), 22 (M, SP, 4QDeut^f), 25 (M, 4QDeut^i, not 4QDeut^k), 26 (M), and after 26 (M, SP, possibly 4QDeut^i). SP and 11QTemple 66:11, have no break before v. 1; this implies a connection with 22:29 (see Excursus 13); Vulg. and some English translations likewise count 23:1 as the last verse of chap. 22. The breaks before and after 23:1 in M and other Masoretic manuscripts do not indicate a view of which group of laws the verse belongs to since these manuscripts have breaks before each of the individual laws.

2. See MAL A, §46 (cf., perhaps, HL §190); W. Robertson Smith, *Kinship and Marriage in Early Arabia* (Boston: Beacon: 1903), 104–111; 1 Chron. 2:24 may be a similar case (see BHS; Driver); this is prohibited in the Qur'an 4:26 (22); cf. Ahikar 4:16. Reuben's act in Gen. 35:22 may have been a premature attempt to do the same thing (see Sarna, *Genesis*, at 35:22).

3. This was part of a practice of a usurper or an irregular successor taking over his predecessor's harem as a way of asserting or strengthening his claim to the throne; see 2 Sam. 16:21–22; cf. 2 Sam. 12:8 and see M. Tsevat, "Marriage and Monarchical Legitimacy in Ugarit and Israel," JSS 3 (1958): 237–243. In my opinion, this is also what Saul refers to at the end of 1 Sam. 20:30. People's actions were at least interpreted in the same way by their opponents in 1 Kings 2:13–25 and possibly 2 Sam. 3:7.

4. If men married at a somewhat later age than women, that would increase the likelihood that a man would have still-unmarried sons older than his later wife. Their presence in the house would facilitate regular contact with her and create enticing situations. For age at marriage see chap. 22, n. 66; note that Abraham was ten years older than Sarah (Gen. 17:17).

5. See Nah. 3:5, where lifting up a skirt is parallel to exposing nakedness.

6. Lev. 18:7,8; 20:11; see also 18:10,14,16; 20:20,21, where the same idiom is used for relations with the wife of one's uncle or brother and with one's own granddaughter. Note that in Gen. 9:22–27, seeing one's father's nakedness is itself an offense. Cf. Herodotus 1:10, end, and Thucydides 1:6, on the barbarian (non-Greek, particularly Asian) feeling of disgrace at being seen naked.

7. For the order of these regulations, see Excursus 13.

8. Exod. 16:3; Lev. 16:17; Num. 19:20; Deut. 31:30.

9. Judg. 21:5,8 (arms-bearing adult males); 1 Kings 12:3 (choosing king); Jer. 26:17; Ezek. 16:40; 23:45–47 (adjudication); Joel 2:16 (entire nation for prayer and fast); Mic. 2:5 (lots are cast in "the Assembly of the LORD" for acquiring property).

10. On the composition of the *'edah* see Exod. 12:19; 16:1 (entire nation); Num. 14:1–4 (all adult males); Num. 27:17–21; Josh. 22:16; Judg. 20:1 (those bearing arms); Exod. 12:3,21 (elders acting as executive). For its functions see Judg. 20:1 (military); Num. 31:26 (dividing spoils of war); Josh. 9:15 (making treaties); Num. 27:2; 35:12, 24–25 (judicial); Num. 32:2 (allocating land); 1 Kings 12:20; 2 Chron. 23:2–3 (electing and crowning king). According to Josh. 8:35, Num. 15:26, and 2 Chron. 30:25, the resident alien is not part of the *kahal*/*'edah* (see also Milgrom, *Numbers*, at 15:15).

11. See Num. 16:3; 20:4; Judg. 20:2; Mic. 2:5; 1 Chron. 28:8.

12. See R. Gordis, *Poets, Prophets, and Sages* (Bloomington: Indiana University Press, 1971), 45–60; M. Weinfeld, s.v. "Congregation," EncJud 5:893–896; J. Milgrom, "Religious Conversion and the Revolt Model for the Formation of Israel," JBL 101 (1982): 173 n. 20; idem, *Studies in Cultic Theology and Terminology* (Leiden: Brill, 1983), 1–17; idem, *Numbers*, Excursus 1; Levine, *Leviticus*, 241–243; J. Liver, s.v. *kahal*, EM 7:68–69. Etymologically, Gk. *ekklesia* (from *ekkalein*, "call out") is equivalant to "those called to the Assembly" (*keri'ei mo'ed*) in Num. 16:2, while Akk. *puhrum*, lit. "gathering," is equivalent to Heb. *kahal*.

13. Exod. 12:3.

14. See references to Exod. and Num. in nn. 10,11.

15. See references to Josh. and subsequent books in nn. 9–11.

16. Gen. 49:6 has, in poetic parallelism, the phrases "not enter the council of" and "be counted in the assembly of." There, however, both idioms may refer simply to associating with people, not literally to participating in their deliberations.

17. G. von Rad, *Studies in Deuteronomy* (London: SCM, 1961), 21; Uffenheimer.

18. See D. Whitehead, *The Ideology of the Athenian Metic* (Cambridge: Cambridge Philological Society, 1977), 70; D. M. MacDowell, *The Law in Classical Athens* (Ithaca: Cornell University Press, 1978), 75 (refs. courtesy of Martin Ostwald).

19. M. Dandamayev.

20. See I. L. Seeligmann, s.v. *ger*, EM 2:546–549. The possibility of a resident alien buying an Israelite in Lev. 25:47 may imply circumstances in which he could buy land, too. According to Ezek. 47:21–23, in the future resident aliens who have borne children in Israel will be allowed to acquire land. For Athens, see Whitehead, *Ideology*, 70; MacDowell, *Law in Classical Athens*, 75–78. Gen. 23:4 implies that in pre-Israelite Hebron aliens could acquire land only with special permission. Note also Hamor's offer in Gen. 34:10.

21. Neh. 13:1–3,23–26. On 1 Kings 11:1–2 see M. Fishbane, *Biblical Interpretation in Ancient Israel* (Oxford: Clarendon, 1988), 125–126.

22. MacDowell, *Law in Classical Athens*, 76, 87.

23. It is not known which part of the genitals the noun *shofkha*, from a root meaning "pour," refers to; the translation "member" agrees with the halakhah. See Sifrei 247; Mish. Yev. 8:2; Maimonides, Hilkhot 'Issurei Bi'ah 16.

24. On eunuchs, see T. L. Fenton, s.v. *saris*, EM 5:1126–1127; A. L. Oppenheim, "A Note on Ša rēši," JANES 5 (1973): 267–279; H. Tadmor, "Rab-saris and Rab-shakeh in 2 Kings 18," in C. L. Meyers and M. P. O'Connor, eds., *The Word of the Lord Shall Go Forth* (Winona Lake, Ind.: Eisenbrauns, 1983), 279–285; idem, "Was the Biblical *saris* a Eunuch?" in ed. Z. Zevit et al., eds., *Solving Riddles and Untying Knots: . . . Semitic Studies . . . Greenfield* (Winona Lake, Ind.: Eisenbrauns, 1995); on ritual self-castration, see Lucian, *The Syrian Goddess (De Dea Syria)*, ed. H. W. Attridge and R. Oden (Missoula, Mont.: Scholars Press, 1976), p. 55, §51; Driver; on emasculation as a punishment, see MAL §§15, 20 (the translation "castrate" in §§18 and 19, in ANET, 181, is doubtful).

25. For *sarisim* in Israel, see, e.g., 1 Sam. 8:15; 1 Kings 22:9; 2 Kings 8:6, etc. In Mesopotamia some *sarisim* were certainly emasculated (Tadmor, "Rab-saris," 281 n. 10). During the Babylonian exile, some Jews became eunuchs, apparently in the course of being taken into the service of the Babylonian court (Isa. 56:3–5; the context makes clear that they were infertile, hence emasculated).

26. For the first reason, see Josephus, Ant. 4.290; Bekhor Shor; Shadal; for the second see Driver.

27. Lev. 21:20; 22:24.

28. Sifrei 248; Mish. Yev. 4:13; Yev. 49a; Bekhor Shor; cf. Rashbam at v. 1; S. E. Loewenstamm, s.v. *mamzer*, EM 5:1–3; E. Neufeld, *Ancient Hebrew Marriage Laws* (London: Longmans, Green, 1944), 224–227. This view is consistent with the fact that the next verse deals with the Ammonites and Moabites, for according to Gen. 19:30–38 these two nations are the offspring of incest.

29. See Judg. 11:1–3,7 (rejecting the son of a prostitute); LXX at Zech. 9:6 ("foreigner"); Ibn Ezra and Keter Torah (name of a foreign nation).

30. Sifrei 248; Rashi at Bek. 17a, top; Keter Torah. Similarly, the idiom "ten times" means "countless times." See Gen. 31:7; Num. 14:22; Job 19:3; Neh. 4:6; Akk. *ešrišu*.

31. See, e.g., Exod. 22:20; 23:9,12; Lev. 19:10,33–34; 23:22; Deut. 1:16; 5:14; 10:18; 14:21,29; 16:11,14; 24:14,17,19–21; 26:11–13; 27:19. See Milgrom, *Numbers*, Excursus 34.

32. This would not include Canaanites or Amalekites, who were excluded on religious and historical grounds. See 7:2–4; 20:16–18; 25:17–19.

33. Y. Kaufmann, *The Religion of Israel*, trans. M. Greenberg (Chicago: University of Chicago Press, 1960), 300–301; idem, *History of the Religion of Israel*, trans. C. W. Efroymson

(New York: Ktav, 1977), 4:338, 384–385; Fishbane, *Biblical Interpretation*, 114–143.

34. Judg. 3; 10:6ff.; 11; 1 Sam. 11; 2 Sam. 8:2; 10. Cf. Gen. 19; Num. 25.

35. According to Ramban, the two clauses of this verse have different subjects: "because the one [Ammon] did not meet you with food and water . . . and the other [Moab] hired Balaam" (so, too, Keter Torah; Ehrlich; Craigie). He infers that since Israel did pass near Ammon (2:17–18), Moses' silence about Ammon in 2:29 implies that it did refuse. (This is not out of the question; the new information imparted by 2:29 implies that 2:2–13 was incomplete.) Apart from the difficulty that this is an argument from silence, the fact that the verb in the first clause of our verse is plural while that in the second is not may indicate that the first clause refers to both peoples (Abravanel 212a, end; Z. Falk, "Ha-'Asurim Lavo' Ba-Kahal," *Beth Mikra'* 62 [1975]: 350).

36. On the Deir 'Alla inscription, see Milgrom, *Numbers*, Excursus 60. For the Sumerian tale see Adele Berlin, *Enmerkar and Ensuḥkešdanna* (Philadelphia: University Museum, 1979).

37. Gen. 24:4,10. See Targs. Onk. and Jon. (*'aram de'al perat*); S. E. Loewenstamm, s.v. *'Aram Naharayim*, EM 1:581; J. J. Finkelstein, "Mesopotamia," JNES 21:85 n. 42; R. de Vaux, *The Early History of Israel* (Philadelphia: Westminster Press, 1978), 193–194; Sarna, *Genesis*, at 24:10. The ending -*aim* is not a dual signifying two rivers (the Tigris and Euphrates) but a locative.

38. Rofé, *Sefer Bil'am* (Jerusalem: Simor, 1980), 45–49; Milgrom, *Numbers*, Excursus 58. Cf. Josh. 24:9–10 (contrast LXX) and contrast Mic. 6:5.

39. For the same idiom see Jer. 29:7; Neh. 2:10; Est. 10:3.

40. Hoffmann; D. R. Hillers, "A Note on Some Treaty Terminology in the Old Testament," BASOR 176 (1964): 46–47; W. L. Moran, "A Note on the Treaty Terminology of the Sefire Stelas," JNES 22 (1963): 173–176. On the wording "do not seek their peace and good relations" (instead of "peace and good relations with them"), cf. GKC §135m.

41. Bekhor Shor.

42. Obad. 10; Mal. 1:2.

43. Philo, Virt. 105–108; Rashi; Ramban.

44. Yev. 78a; Driver; Ramban; Shalag.

45. Lev. 15:31. See Milgrom, *Numbers*, Excursus 49.

46. Num. 5:1–4.

47. See Weinfeld, DDS, 209. The very idea that God is present within the camp is unusual for Deuteronomy, which avoids suggesting that God is physically on earth or in the sanctuary (see Comments to 4:36 and 12:5). This suggests that the present law, including the explanation given in v. 14, is pre-Deuteronomic.

48. Cf. Rashi at v. 10 and TJ Shab. 2:6 (3), 5a, near top: the "accuser" only accuses at times of danger. For taboos of a similar nature among other peoples see J. G. Frazer, *The New Golden Bough*, ed. T. H. Gaster (Garden City, N.Y.: Doubleday, 1961), 75, 97–98; W. Robertson Smith, *The Religion of the Semites* (London: A. and C. Black, 1914), 455. That the regulation applies only to the military camp, not the residential one, is noted by Ibn Ezra and Maimonides, Sefer Ha-Mitsvot, positive no. 193. Shadal notes that these requirements are not due to the presence of the Ark, since it did not usually go out to war.

49. 1QWar 7:4–6; cf. 10:1; 11QTemple 58:17; Sifrei 254.

50. Rofé, *Mavo'*, 129–130; cf. Weinfeld, DDS, 238. On the passages in Samuel see J. Licht, s.v. *milḥamah*, EM 4:1058. On the need for purification after intercourse cf. Herodotus 1:198; 2:64.

51. Heb. *kareh* (in rabbinic Hebrew the form *keri* is used) is usually understood to mean "accident," "incident," but this is not certain.

52. Josephus, War 2.149.

53. 1QWar 7:7 and 11QTemple 46:13; see Y. Yadin, *The*

Scroll of the War of the Sons of Light Against the Sons of Darkness, trans. B. and C. Rabin (Oxford: Oxford University Press, 1962), 73 n. 3. *Yad* may take place in Num. 2:17; Jer. 6:3; and Ezek. 21:24. It means "monument" in 1 Sam. 15:12; 2 Sam. 8:3; 18:18; Isa. 56:5; 1 Chron. 18:3. NEB translates "sign."

54. 1QWar 7:6-7. In contrast, 11QTemple 46:13-16 requires latrines to be three thousand cubits outside of Jerusalem.

55. Smith.

56. For *mit-halekh* as "traveling" see 1 Sam. 30:31; 2 Sam. 7:6-7; Ps. 105:13. This meaning, and not "moves about the camp," is indicated by the remainder of the clause: "to protect you and deliver your enemies to you."

57. See LU §14; LLI §§12-13; LE §§49-51; LH §§16-20; HL §§22-24; for treaties see the Alalakh tablets in ANET, 531 (§5) and 532 (§2) and the treaty implied in 1 Kings 2:39-40. See H. Reviv, "The Escaped Slaves of Shimei ben Gera," in A. Mirsky et al., eds., *Galut 'Aḥar Golah: Studies . . . Beinart* (Jerusalem: Makhon Ben-Zvi, 1988), 32-39.

58. E.g., Targ. Onk.; Maimonides, Sefer Ha-Mitsvot, negative no. 254; Hilkhot 'Avadim 8:10; Driver; Craigie; R. de Vaux, *Ancient Israel* (New York: McGraw-Hill, 1961), 87. Only Philo, Virt. 124, takes this law as referring to fellow Israelite slaves; he sees it as describing a kind of asylum like that conferred by temples (see below).

59. See J. C. Greenfield, "Asylum at Aleppo: A Note on Sfire III, 4-7," in M. Cogan and I. Eph'al, eds., *Ah, Assyria: Studies . . . Tadmor* (Jerusalem: Magnes Press, 1991), 272-278; W. Westermann, *The Slave Systems of Greek and Roman Antiquity* (Philadelphia: American Philosophical Society, 1955), 17-18, 38-39, 40-41; cf. Herodotus 2:113. Cf. the Arab practice of temporary private asylum reported from Musil by Smith.

60. See Gen. 16:6; 2 Sam. 25:20; 1 Kings 2:39-40. For a case in Egypt, see ANET, 259.

61. Ehrlich argues, on the basis of *yinnatsel*, "seeks refuge" (lit. "saves himself"), that the present law is limited to such circumstances (Ehrlich, *Randglossen* 7:391).

62. Sefire III, 4-7 (KAI 224; ANET, 660d).

63. Cf. Sifrei 260. Cf. Prov. 23:27, where the harlot is called an alien woman. In some countries, most prostitutes have been foreigners. For condemnations of prostitution, see Jer. 5:7; Prov. 6:26; 7:10; etc., cf. Gen. 34:31.

64. Cf. Gen. 38:21-22 (cf. 15); Hos. 4:14 (despite the reference to sacrifice, the *kedeshah* here is not part of the temple personnel; see Excursus 22).

65. As a euphemism *kedeshah* would literally be the opposite of *ḥalalah*, "defiled," used of prostitutes in Lev. 21:7,14; Gk. *hetaira*, "courtesan," is also a euphemism, meaning literally "comrade" (cf. also English "hussy," from "housewife"; the Akkadian term for prostitute, *ḥarimtu*, may also be a euphemism: the root means "devote," "set aside," and is the root underlying Arabic *ḥarim*, "harem"). Note also that Judah privately considered Tamar a *zonah* (Gen. 38:15), but Hirah, asking for her publicly, called her a *kedeshah* (v. 21), implying that the latter is a more refined term. Akk. *kadištu* (*qadištu*) has been cited in support of interpreting *kedeshah* as a cult prostitute, but there is no evidence that the *kadištu*'s role was sexual; she was a temple singer and performed other tasks in temples and outside of them. See CAD Q; S. E. Loewenstamm, s.v. *kadesh* and *kedeshah*, EM 7:35-36, 62-66; M. Gruber, "The Qadesh in the Book of Kings and in Other Sources," *Tarbiz* 52 (1983): 167-176; idem, "Hebrew Qedešah and Her Canaanite and Akkadian Cognates," UF 18:133-148; idem, "The *qedešah*: What Was Her Function?" *Beer-Sheva* 3 (1988): 45-51.

66. 1 Kings 14:24; 15:12; 22:47; 2 Kings 23:7, Gordon, UT, 477, no. 2210; W. von Soden, "Zur Stellung des 'Geweihten' (*qdš*) in Ugarit," UF 2 (1970): 329; CAD Q, 50a.

67. See 2 Kings 23:5; Hos. 10:5; Zeph. 1:4.

68. Heterosexual: Ramban; Ralbag (cited by Abravanel); Bekhor Shor. Homosexual: Sanh. 54b (cf. Torah Temimah);

Rashi; Abravanel; Shadal. On homosexual prostitution see H. Licht, *Sexual Life in Ancient Greece* (London: Routledge and Kegan Paul, 1932), 436-440.

69. For the normal, male-first order, see Exod. 21:1-11,28-29; Lev. 13:29; Num. 5:6; Deut. 5:14; 15:12.

70. MacDowell, *Law in Classical Athens*, 126.

71. See, perhaps, Amos 2:7-8 as well, and cf. A. H. Godbey, *The Lost Tribes: A Myth* (reprint; New York: Ktav, 1974), 518-521 (ref. courtesy Sol Cohen).

72. Cf. Shadal; Lucian, *The Syrian Goddess*, §6.

73. H. Licht, *Sexual Life*, 350, 356, 404.

74. Cf. the slang idiom "dog fashion" for heterosexual intercourse in that stance (H. Wentworth and S. B. Flexner, *Dictionary of American Slang* [New York: Thomas Crowell, 1967], 154). For male prostitution, see CAD K, 315b, and the treaty curse cited in CAD Ḥ, 101c. Note the association of dogs and prostitutes in 1 Kings 22:38.

75. See Sifrei 261 and the discussion by E. A. Goodfriend, "Could *keleb* in Deut. 23:19 Actually Refer to a Canine?" in D. P. Wright et al., eds., *Pomegranates and Golden Bells: Studies . . . Milgrom* (Winona Lake, IN: Eisenbrauns, 1995), 381-397.

76. L. E. Stager, "Why Were Hundreds of Dogs Buried at Ashkelon?" BAR 17/3 (May-June 1991): 26-42.

77. MdRY Kaspa 1 (Exod. 22:24) (Lauterbach 3:148) says one *may* act like a creditor toward the rich! M. Silver, *Prophets and Markets* (Boston: Kluwer-Nijhoff, 1983), 65ff, 237, argues for the existence of interest-bearing commercial loans.

78. Driver and Miles, BL 1:173-177; B. Porten, *Archives from Elephantine* (Berkeley: University of California Press, 1968), 77. Rates were considerably lower in Greece and Rome; see F. M. Heichelheim, s.v. "Interest, Rate of," OCD 548-549.

79. Josephus, Ant. 4.266 (cf. Philo, Spec. 2.74-78; Virt. 82-87); Ezek. 18:8,13,27; 22:12; Pss. 15:5; 37:26; 112:5; Prov. 28:8. On Exod. 22:24 see Fishbane, *Biblical Interpretation*, 174-177.

80. ANET, 629.

81. Aristotle, *Politics*, 1:10, 1258b; Plato, *Laws*, 5:12, 742c; s.v. "Genucius," "Interest, Rate of," and "Usury," OCD 462, 548, 1104; I. L. Seeligmann, *Studies in Biblical Literature*, ed. A. Hurvitz et al. (Jerusalem: Magnes Press, 1992), 290-291.

82. H. H. Cohn, s.v. "Usury," EncJud 16:30-32.

83. Commentary to Ezek. 18:8. Eliezer assumes that since Ezekiel speaks of "lending for *neshekh*" and "collecting *tarbit*," the two terms must refer, respectively, to interest collected at the time of the loan and at the time of collection. However, other passages use both terms in connection with both lending and collecting. For the question whether advance interest was known in the ancient Near East, see B. L. Eichler, *Indenture at Nuzi* (New Haven: Yale University Press, 1973), 88; CAD Ḥ, 222a; S. E. Loewenstamm, "*neshekh* and *m/tarbit*," JBL 88 (1969): 78 n. 2; K. R. Veenhof, "An Ancient Anatolian Money-Lender: His Loans, Securities, and Debt-Slaves," in B. Hruška and G. Komoróczy, eds., *Festschrift Lubor Matouš* (Budapest: Eotvos Lorand University, 1978), 282, 284; E. Lipinski, "*Nešek* and *Tarbit* in the Light of Epigraphic Evidence," *Orientalia Lovaniensia Periodica* 10 (1979): 133-141.

84. See Mish. BM 5:1; Ramban at Lev. 25:36 and the Karaite commentary cited in Ben Yehudah, 7895 n. 1; de Vaux, *Ancient Israel*, 170; S. E. Loewenstamm, "*neshekh* and *m/tarbit*," 78-80, and idem, s.v. *neshekh ve-tarbit*, EM 5: 929-930; E. Neufeld, "The Prohibition Against Loans at Interest in Ancient Hebrew Laws," HUCA 26 (1955): 355-357.

85. BM 60b; *Keli Yakar* at Lev. 25:36.

86. UT 1146: 10,12; PRU 5:153; Cowley, AP 10 and 11, *passim*. See Lipinski, "*Nešek* and *Tarbit* in the Light of Epigraphic Evidence."

87. See 1 Sam. 1:11 (cf. Prov. 31:2); Num. 21:2; Judg. 11:30-31; Jonah 1:16; 2:10. On the subject of vows see Milgrom, *Numbers*, Excursus 66; M. Haran, s.v. *neder*, EM 5:786-790; L. I. Rabinowitz, s.v. "Vows and Vowing," EncJud 16:227-228;

Hertz, 730–731; H. L. Ginsberg, "Psalms and Inscriptions of Petition and Acknowledgement," in A. Marx et al., eds., *Louis Ginzberg Jubilee Volume* (New York: American Academy for Jewish Research, 1945), 163–164.

88. See Comment to 12:6.

89. Pss. 22:20–23; 27:6; 69:30–32; see M. Greenberg, "On the Refinement of the Conception of Prayer in Hebrew Scriptures," AJSR 1 (1976): 78–81.

90. Num. 6; 30.

91. See Greenberg, "On the Refinement," 69–70; Tigay, "On Some Aspects of Prayer in the Bible," AJSR 1 (1976): 372.

92. M. Greenberg, "Religion: Stability and Ferment," in WHJP 4/2, 91; cf. idem, "Conception of Prayer," 76–78.

93. See Ḥul. 2a; Ned. 22a, 77b; Shab. 32b.

94. Lev. 7:16; 22:17–24 (cf. Mal. 1:14); 27; Num. 15:3–12; 29:39; 30.

95. See also Prov. 20:25; Ecclus. 18:21–22; Weinfeld, DDS, 270–272.

96. 2 Sam. 15:7–8; 1 Sam. 1:3,21. M. Haran, *Temples and Temple Service* (Oxford: Clarendon, 1978), 304–316. For the halakhah see Sifrei 63; RH 4a; Hoffmann, 158; Ehrlich, *Randglossen*, at 12:12. For vows and pilgrimage festivals, see also Nah. 2:1.

97. A Babylonian medical text states that certain infant diseases are caused by unpaid vows (see K. van der Toorn, "Female Prostitution in Payment of Vows in Ancient Israel," JBL 108 [1989]: 196).

98. See Milgrom, *Numbers*, Excursus 66; Rabinowitz, s.v. "Vows and Vowing," EncJud 16:227–228; H. Kieval, s.v. "*Kol Nidrei*," EncJud 10:1166–1167.

99. See Num. 30:13; Ps. 89:35; cf. the verbal expression in Num. 30:3; 32:34; Judg. 11:36; Isa. 45:23.

100. For *nedavah* as an adverb, see Hos. 14:5.

101. Smith; Edward Robinson, *Biblical Researches in Palestine . . . 1838 and 1852* (London: J. Murray, 1867), 1:493; C. M. Doughty, *Travels in Arabia Deserta* (New York: Boni and Liveright, 1923), 1:520–521; Dalman, 4:297, 306.

102. Plato, *Laws*, 8:844e–845d.

103. Josephus, Ant., 4.234–237; BM 92a; Matthew 12:1; Mark 2:23; Luke 6:1; the same view is cited unfavorably by Ibn Ezra at v. 26.

104. Sifrei 266–267; Mish. BM 7:2; BM 87b.

105. 1 Sam. 9:7; 17:22 (cf. 17–18), 40,49.

106. Luke 6:1; Mish. Maʿas. 4:5. Cf. H. L. Ginsberg, *The Israelian Heritage of Judaism* (New York: Jewish Theological Seminary, 1982), 44 n. 60; Dalman, 1/2:455–456.

107. O. Borowski, *Agriculture in Iron Age Israel* (Winona Lake, Ind.: Eisenbrauns, 1987), 58–59.

Chapter 24

1. Hebrew text divisions: before 24:1 (M, SP, 4QDeutᵃ), 5 (M, 4QDeutᵃ), 6 (MT var.), 7 (M, SP, 4QDeutᵃ), 8 (M), 9 (MT Var.), 10 and 14 (M, SP), 16, 17 (M), 19 (M, SP), 20 (M, 4QDeutᵃ), 21 (MT Var., 4QDeutᵃ), 25:1 (M, SP, 4QDeutᵍ), 4 (MT var.), and after 4 (M, SP). Regarding the MT variant that treats v. 9 as a separate verse, see Baḥya and *Sefer Keter Torah: Ha-"Taj" Ha-Gadol*, ed. Yosef Ḥasid (Jerusalem, 1970), 173, s.v. *Taʿam ʿal zekhirat ʿonesh Miriam*. Regarding texts that do not separate vv. 5 and 6 (M 4QDeutᵃ), cf. the view dismissed by Ibn Ezra.

2. R. Levy, *The Social Structure of Islam* (Cambridge: Cambridge University Press, 1957), 113–117 (ref. courtesy Samuel Z. Klausner). See also Sforno; Abravanel, 220; Rofé, *Mavo'*, 154–157; cf. Craigie, 306.

3. See M. A. Friedman, "*Ha-maḥazir gerushato mi-she-niseʾt*," in Shamma Friedman, ed., *Saul Lieberman Memorial*

Volume (New York and Jerusalem: Jewish Theological Seminary, 1993), 189–195.

4. Isa. 50:1; Jer. 3:1,8. See M. Fishbane, *Biblical Interpretation in Ancient Israel* (Oxford: Clarendon, 1988), 307–312.

5. Josephus, Ant. 4.253; Mish. Giṭ. 9:10 (see the discussion by J. Goldin, *Studies in Midrash and Related Literature* [Philadelphia: Jewish Publication Society, 1988], 310–318); M. Elon, s.v. "Takkanot," EncJud 15:724–725; D. W. Amram, s.v. "Divorce," JE 4:625; Isserles in Shulḥan ʿArukh, 'Even Ha-ʿEzer 119:6. On the grounds for divorce see A. Gulak, *Yesodei Ha-Mishpat Ha-ʿIvri* (Berlin: Devir, 1922) 3:25–26; Isaac Klein, *A Guide to Jewish Religious Practice* (New York: Jewish Theological Seminary, 1979), 469–470.

6. 1 Sam. 29:3,6,8; 2 Kings 17:4; cf. 1 Sam. 12:5.

7. Cf. LH §§141,143; J. J. Finkelstein, "Sex Offenses in Sumerian Laws," JAOS 86 (1966): 362–363 (cf. S. Greengus, "A Textbook Case of Adultery in Ancient Mesopotamia," HUCA 40–41 [1969–70]: 33–44); M. J. Geller, "The Elephantine Papyri and Hosea 2:3," JSJ 8 (1977): 142; B. Porten, *Archives from Elephantine* (Berkeley: University of California Press, 1968), 224.

8. Mish. Giṭ. 9:10 (see Albeck, *Nashim*, 407); cf. Matt. 5:32. For modern advocates of this view, see J. J. Rabinowitz, "The Great Sin in Ancient Egyptian Marriage Contracts," JNES 18 (1959): 73; A. Toeg, "Does Deuteronomy 24:1–4 Incorporate a General Law on Divorce?" Dine Israel 2 (1970): v–xxiv. Cf. Jer. 3:8.

9. Driver; Smith; E. Neufeld, *Ancient Hebrew Marriage Laws* (London: Longmans, Green, 1944), 179; Mayes; Craigie; Thompson.

10. See Lev. 18:6–19; 20:11,17–21, and note 18:20; 20:10.

11. Driver and Miles, BL, 1:293; Y. Zakovitch, "The Woman's Rights in the Biblical Law of Divorce," JLA 4 (81): 35–36. Zakovitch also mentions cases where the wife's father presumes that the marriage is dissolved after the husband deserts his wife (36–40; cf. Neufeld, *Ancient Hebrew Marriage Laws*, 183–187).

12. For the norm, see Zakovitch, "Women's Rights," 34–35; note Josephus's statement that it is not the norm in Judaism for women to divorce (Ant. 15.259; contrast Mark 10:12). For contracts mentioning initiation of divorce by the wife, see AP 15 (ANET, 223); BMAP 2; BMAP 7 (ANET, 549); ANET, 219 (§F, no. 2) and 543 (no. 4); see also E. Lipinski, "The Wife's Right to Divorce in the Light of an Ancient Near Eastern Tradition," JLA 4:9–27; M. Friedman, "Divorce upon the Wife's Demand as Reflected in Manuscripts from the Cairo Geniza," JLA 4:103–127; idem, "Termination of the Marriage upon the Wife's Request: A Palestinian Ketubba Stipulation," PAAJR 37 (1969): 29–55.

13. See Mish. Ket. 7:1–5,10; Gulak, *Yesodei Ha-Mishpat Ha-ʿIvri* 3:25–26; Klein, *Guide*, 470–472; Boaz Cohen, *Law and Tradition in Judaism* (New York: Jewish Theological Seminary, 1959), 102–107.

14. 1 Sam. 24:4,5,11. On cutting the hem, see J. J. Rabinowitz, s.v. *gerushin*, EM 2:552; cf. S. Greengus, "The Old Babylonian Marriage Contract," JAOS 89:515 n. 44; CAD S, 322; J. J. Finkelstein, "Cutting the *sissiktu* in Divorce Proceedings," WO 8 (1976): 236–240; M. Malul, "'Sissiktu' and 'sikku'—Their Meaning and Function," *Bibliothecha Orientalis* 43 (1986): 19–36. Contrast R. Elazar b. Azariah, "something that severs them from each other" (Giṭ. 83b; Tosef. Giṭ. 7:3). See also Zakovitch, "Women's Rights," 35, 43. The divorce certificate is mentioned again in Isa. 50:1; Jer. 3:8.

15. Mish. Giṭ. 9:3; Geller, "The Elephantine Papyri and Hosea 2:3," 139–148; cf. M. Friedman, "Israel's Response in Hosea 2:17b: 'You Are My Husband,'" JBL 99 (1980): 199–204 (see 199 n. 1); Greengus, "Old Babylonian Marriage Contract," 517; Rabinowitz, s.v. *gerushin*, EM 2:551–552. On the divorce certificate as evidence, see Maimonides, Guide 3.49.

16. *Sane'* serves as a technical term for divorce in the Aramaic legal documents of the fifth century B.C.E. from the

Jewish and Aramaic garrison at Elephantine, Egypt (AP 9:8; 15:23; 18:1). See J. J. Rabinowitz, "Marriage Contracts in Ancient Egypt in the Light of Jewish Sources," HTR 46 (1953): 91–97; idem, s.v. *gerushin*, EM 2:552. Note, however, that "hate" (Heb. and Aram. *sane'*, Akk. *zerú*) does not commonly mean divorce; see R. Westbrook, "The Prohibition on Restoration of Marriage in Deuteronomy 24:1–4," in S. Japhet, ed., *Studies in Bible* (Jerusalem: Magnes Press, 1986), 399–403 (however, Westbrook's suggestion, that "hate" indicates that the divorce is for purely subjective reasons, is unconvincing; in LH §142 and Judg. 15:2 the spouse who initiates divorce has objective reasons, and in later Palestinian Jewish documents, when the "hatred" is gratuitous, "hate" is insufficient to express the idea; it is supplemented by "gratuitous" or an equivalent phrase; see Friedman, "Termination of the Marriage," 37:38–39, 46ff, 50).

17. Ibn Ezra; Ramban; Hoffmann. Ehrlich, *Mikra*, suggests that the unusual form *huttamma'ah* is used here because she is not defiled absolutely, or literally (a state expressed by the *pi'el* and *hitpa'el* forms, as in Num. 5:13; Ezek. 18:6), but only for her former husband.

18. DJD 2:243ff. For a later contract for remarriage, see A. Gulak, *'Otsar Ha-Shetarot* (Jerusalem: Defus Ha-Po'alim, 1926), 42, no. 37 (ref. courtesy J. C. Greenfield).

19. Qur'an 2:229–230, with commentary of Abdullah Yusuf Ali, *The Holy Qur'an* (Washington, D.C.: American International Printing Co., 1946); H. Granqvist, *Marriage Conditions in a Palestinian Village* (Helsinki: Akademische Buchhandlung, 1931–35), 2:281–282; Neufeld, *Ancient Hebrew Marriage Laws*, 244n.; Smith, 277.

20. See Chap. 20, n. 13.

21. Sifrei 271; Ehrlich. That the wife was never before married is the view of Keter Torah.

22. For the translation, see Ehrlich on the basis of Exod. 30:13; cf. Ramban.

23. Ehrlich, *Randglossen*; G. Anderson, *A Time to Mourn, A Time to Dance* (University Park, Penn.: Pennsylvania State University Press, 1991), 27–37, 55–57.

24. Targ. Jon.; Vulg.; and Pesh., but not LXX or Targ. Onk.

25. See Rashi; Ehrlich, *Randglossen*; cf. Isa. 62:5; Prov. 5:18; Eccl. 9:9; contrast the wording in *Gilgamesh Epic* 10:3, 13 (ANET, 90b).

26. See Josephus, Ant. 4.268–270; J. Milgrom, *Cult and Conscience* (Leiden: Brill, 1976), 94–104; I. L. Seeligmann, *Studies in Biblical Literature* (Hebrew), ed. A. Hurvitz et al. (Jerusalem: Magnes Press, 1992), 269–291; E. Neufeld, "Inalienability of Mobile and Immobile Pledges in the Laws of the Bible," *Revue Internationale des Droits de l'Antiquité* 9 (1962); J. J. Rabinowitz, s.v. *halva'ah*, EM 2:813–816; B. L. Eichler, *Indenture at Nuzi* (New Haven: Yale University Press, 1973), 88–89; idem, s.v. "Loan," *Harper's Bible Dictionary*, 571–572; S. E. Loewenstamm, "*bt = 'rb*?," *Leshonenu* 25 (1961): 111–114; Z. Falk, *Hebrew Law in Biblical Times* (Jerusalem: Wahrmann, 1964), 101; S. Paul, *Amos* (Minneapolis: Fortress Press, 1991), 84–85.

27. See R.A.S. Macalister, *The Excavation of Gezer 1902–1905 and 1907–1909* (London: Murray, 1912), 2:35–36; Dalman 3:207–212; ANEP, no. 149; VBW 1:281; R. Amiran, "The Millstone and the Potter's Wheel" (Hebrew), EI 4 (1956): 46–49; H. N. Richardson, s.v. "Mill, Millstone," IDB 3:380–381. The heaviness of millstones is reflected in Lam. 5:13. For information on their weight and on the provenance of basalt (mostly around lake Tiberias and in Syria and Transjordan), see J. Tigay, "Some Archaeological Notes on Deuteronomy," in D. P. Wright et al., eds., *Pomegranates and Golden Bells: Studies . . . Milgrom* (Winona Lake, Ind.: Eisenbrauns, 1994).

28. Rashi at Exod. 22:25; Milgrom, *Cult and Conscience*, 95–98.

29. J. Tigay, *The Evolution of the Gilgamesh Epic* (Phila-

delphia: University of Pennsylvania Press, 1982), 205 n. 28, 207 n. 42.

30. Mish. BM 9:13; Tosef. BM 10:11; Mish. Arakh. 6:3; M. Elon, s.v. "Pledge," EncJud 13:638. Cf. Josephus, Ant. 4.270.

31. Job 24:3; LH §§113 and 241 (see BL 1:210, 214–215). Cf. A. Goetze, *The Laws of Eshnunna* (New Haven: American Schools of Oriental Research, 1956), 71 with n. 23.

32. HL §§19–21.

33. Sifrei 273; Mish. Sanh. 11:1; Maimonides, Hilkhot Genevah 9:1–2. In Exod. 21:16 LXX achieves the same effect by reading "He who kidnaps a man *of the Israelites—whether he has enslaved him or* whether he has sold him or is still holding him—shall be put to death," borrowing the italicized words from Deuteronomy. In Josephus, on the other hand, the victim is simply "a person" (Ant. 4.271). In LH §14, kidnaping the young son of a man is a capital crime.

34. R. Judah in Sifrei 273; Mish. Sanh. 11:1; Maimonides, Hilkhot Genevah 11:9–2.

35. The form of Heb. *tsara'at* is one used for medical conditions (such as *kaddahat*, 28:22), in which the root indicates one of the obvious symptoms of the disease. The root *ts-r-'* could be related to Akkadian *sarāhu*, "heat, scorch, be feverish," which yields a noun *sirhtu*, "inflammation." Possibly, the similarity to Heb. *tsir'ah*, "hornet," implies that *tsara'at* refers to a skin condition in which the patient looks or feels as if he has been bitten by wasps; cf. *urticaria*, a skin condition in which the patient looks as if he has been stung by nettles (Latin *urtica*), and modern Hebrew *sirpedet*, "nettle rash," from Heb. *sirpad*, "nettle." See J.F.A. Sawyer, "A Note on the Etymology of *Sara'at*," VT 26 (1976): 241–245.

36. See D. P. Wright and R. N. Jones, s.v. "Leprosy," ABD 4:277–282.

37. In Leviticus, NJPS often translates *torah* loosely as "procedure" or "ritual."

38. Sifrei 275; Rashi; Ibn Ezra; Hoffmann.

39. Rashbam; Abravanel.

40. Milgrom, *Numbers* at 12:14.

41. Loewenstamm, "*bt = 'rb*?," 111–114; Milgrom, *Cult and Conscience*, 102–104, suggests that the use of two different verbs may be the result of conflation (cf. J. Tigay, ed., *Empirical Models for Biblical Criticism* [Philadelphia: University of Pennsylvania Press, 1985], 168).

42. Mish. BM 9:13 (see Albeck, *Nezikin*, 430); Maimonides, Sefer Ha-Mitsvot, negative no. 239; Sefer Ha-Hinnukh, no. 594; Shulhan 'Arukh, Hoshen Mishpat 97:6; LH §113.

43. Sifrei; Mish. BM 9:13; Maimonides, Sefer Ha-Mitsvot, positive no. 199, negative no. 240; Sefer Ha-Hinnukh, nos. 550, 595.

44. Amos 2:8; Prov. 20:16; 27:13; Job 22:6. Cf. BMAP 11:11 and Jewish marriage contracts which mention clothing among objects that may be seized in satisfaction of a debt (in marriage contracts it is as a last resort). In these cases, as in Amos 2:6, the clothing is not necessarily a night wrap of relatively little value.

45. See ANET, 568; J. Tigay, "A Talmudic Parallel to the Petition from Yavneh-Yam," in M. Brettler and M. Fishbane, eds., *Minhah le-Nahum: . . . Studies . . . Sarna* (Sheffield: JSOT Press, 1993), 328–333.

46. Sifrei 277; BM 114b; Saadia; Rashi; Rashbam; Keter Torah.

47. Tosafot, BM 115a, s.v. *lamah*.

48. On the formula see M. Greenberg, *Biblical Prose Prayer* (Berkeley: University of California Press, 1983), 30–36, 63 n. 4.

49. Milgrom, *Cult and Conscience*, 95–96, 98–102, argues that *'-sh-k* refers to withholding what is due, that is, illegally depriving a person of something that, unlike the case of theft, first came into the offender's hand legally; cf. Ehrlich, Hoffmann, and Levine at Lev. 5:21,23. The term does refer to this in our verse, in Lev. 19:13, and Ezek. 18:18 (see Milgrom, *Cult and Conscience*), but there are too few passages where this is clearly

the case to confirm that the term by itself, without assistance from context, would suffice to indicate this meaning. See, e.g., 1 Sam. 12:3–4; Mic. 2:2; Hos. 12:8; Ps. 105:14; Job 10:3; KAI 224:20; 226:8, where various types of abuse are implied.

50. See Levine, *Leviticus*, at 19:13. Theoretically the reading "wages of a laborer" (*sekhar sakhir*), reflected in the Targs. Jon. and Yer. and in Mal. 3:5, could be an original paraphrase of Deuteronomy of Leviticus's *pe'ulat sakhir*. However, *sekhar* probably originated as a scribal error, since the verb '-sh-k, used in Deuteronomy and Malachi, usually takes a person, not property, as its direct object (see Lev. 19:13a). The reading probably originated in the misreading of the defectively spelled *sakhir* as *sekhar* (reflected in LXX, Vulg., Pesh., and 1Q5, fragment 8, in DJD 1:58), followed by a conflation with the original reading. See S. Talmon, "Double Readings in the Massoretic Text," *Textus* 1 (1960): 154.

51. See Pss. 25:1; 143:8; and cf. Jer. 22:27; 44:14.

52. Cf. Jer. 11:20; 20:12; Ps. 109; Porten, *Archives from Elephantine*, 157–158, 315–316.

53. See also 17:8–11; 19:15; 21:22–23; 25:1–3 (Rofé, *Mavo'*, 69, 85).

54. Midrash Tannaim; Ibn Ezra; Rashbam; Driver; M. Greenberg, "Some Postulates of Biblical Criminal Law," in M. Haran, ed., *Yehezkel Kaufmann Jubilee Volume* (Jerusalem: Magnes Press, 1960), 21–22.

55. LH §§116, 209–210, 230; MAL §§50, 55; Hittite Instructions, ANET, 207–208.

56. Two cases which are sometimes said to be precedents to Deut. 24:16 are superficially similar to it, but neither reflects a general principle that only the guilty should be punished for crimes. See MAL §2 and the Hittite *Proclamation of Telepinus* in E. H. Sturtevant and G. Bechtel, *A Hittite Chrestomathy* (Philadelphia: Linguistic Society of America, University of Pennsylvania, 1935), 191 §§31–32.

57. Deut. 13:16; Josh. 7:24–25; Judg. 21:5,8–10; 2 Sam. 21:1–9.

58. Cf. Seforno, and see 1 Sam. 22:16–19; 1 Kings 15:29–30; 16:11–12; 2 Kings 9:26; 10:6–7; Herodotus 3:119; Josephus, Ant. 13.380–391; G. Furlani, s.v. "Familienhaftung," RLA 3:19. Dan. 6:25 and Est. 9:13–14 refer to Persian practice, not Israelite. Only the purges of dynastic families are said to have been sanctioned by God, and this is due to the kings' offenses against God directly (1 Kings 14:7–11; 16:1–14; 2 Kings 9:7–9). Conceivably, our verse means "parents shall not be put to death along with [their guilty] children, nor children together with [their guilty] parents," a possibility contemplated by M. Greenberg (letter of May 31, 1990; for this use of 'al, see 22:6; Gen. 32:12; Exod. 35:22; Hos. 10:14). In this case, the law is exclusively concerned with the collective punishment of entire families. For a suggestion regarding the point of the first clause in the law, see M. Greenberg, *Ezekiel 1–20* (Garden City, N.Y.: Doubleday, 1983), 332–333.

59. Sanh. 27b; Sefer Ha-Ḥinnukh, no. 596; Maimonides, Sefer Ha-Mitsvot, negative no. 287. See N. Leibowitz, *Studies in Devarim* (Jerusalem: World Zionist Organization, 1986), 238–239.

60. See, e.g., Exod. 22:20–23; 23:6; Lev. 19:33–34; Isa. 1:17,23; Jer. 7:6; Prov. 22:22; Job 29:12–13; 31:16–17.

61. See ANET, 151a, 178a, 408d, 415c, 424c; F. C. Fensham, "Widow, Orphan, and the Poor in Ancient Near Eastern Legal and Wisdom Literature," JNES 21 (1962): 129–139.

62. Exod. 22:20–23; 23:9; Lev. 19:33–34; see also Deut. 1:16; 10:18; 27:19.

63. Some halakhic sources hold that what applies to the widow here also applies to divorcees and, in some views, to all unmarried women. See Hoffmann; Lieberman, TK *Nezikin*, 302, ll. 28–29; A. Steinsaltz, *Bava' Metsi'a'* (Jerusalem: Israel Institute for Talmudic Publications, 1981), 2:497, *'Oraḥ Ha-Halakhah*.

64. 1 Kings 17:12; 2 Kings 4:7.

65. Targ. Jon.; Sifrei 281; Mish. BM 9:13 (see commentary of Maimonides); BM 115a; Sefer Ha-Ḥinnukh, no. 598; Abravanel, 225–226; Hoffmann.

66. Mish. BM 9:13; Shulhan 'Arukh, Hoshen Mishpat 97:14.

67. See E. Z. Melamed, "Break-up of Stereotype Phrases as an Artistic Device in Biblical Poetry," in C. Rabin, ed., *Studies in the Bible* (Jerusalem: Magnes Press, 1961), 115–153. In the present verse, LXX and some manuscripts of Targ. Jon. and of the Sifrei read the full triad, "the stranger, the fatherless, and the widow" in the first clause, as does 27:19, which alludes to this verse. LXX and some Qumran texts do the same in 10:18a (see Weinfeld, Commentary, at 10:18). These readings are probably due simply to harmonization with the full triad, which appears frequently (see, e.g., vv. 19–21; 14:29). But since the Hebrew text in v. 17a here reads literally "the stranger, the fatherless" (without "or" [BHS cites texts which add it]), it is indeed possible that "and the widow" was originally present there and was dropped by accident. Another possibility is that the absence of the conjunction means that the first clause originally mentioned *only* the fatherless (as in other verses where these are the only two mentioned, such as Isa. 1:17,23 and Ps. 68:6), and that the stranger was added to achieve the full triad.

68. Craigie.

69. See also Sifrei; Maimonides, Hilkhot Mattenot 'Aniyim, chaps. 1–5; idem, Sefer Ha-Mitsvot, positive nos. 120–124, negative nos. 210–214; Sefer Ha-Ḥinnukh, nos. 552, 599.

70. ANET, 424c (chap. 28); P. Montet, *Everyday Life in Egypt* (Philadelphia: University of Pennsylvania Press, 1981), 116; Smith; Dalman 1/2:573; 3:60–62; 4:281–282, 408.

71. See J. G. Frazer, *The Golden Bough*, 3rd ed. (London: Macmillan, 1912), 1/5:214–269; T. Canaan, "Plant-Lore in Palestinian Superstition," JPOS 8 (1928): 140–141; P. Bourdieu, *Outline of a Theory of Practice* (Cambridge: Cambridge University Press, 1977), 133–135 (ref. courtesy of Harvey Goldberg).

72. Sifrei 284; Dalman 4:194. See Isa. 17:6; 24:13.

73. See Dalman 4:304.

Chapter 25

1. Hebrew texts divide the chapter before vv. 1 (M, SP), 4 (MT var.), 5 and 11 (M, SP), 13 (M), 14 (MT var.), 17 (M), and after v. 19 (M, SP).

2. See LH §127, 202; MAL A, §§7, 18, 19, 21, 40, 57; B, §§7, 8–10, 14, 15, 18; C+G, §§2–3, 8, 11; E, §1; F, §1; N, §§1–2; E. Seidl, "Law," in S.R.K. Glanville, *The Legacy of Egypt* (Oxford: Clarendon, 1942), 204; cf. ANET, 213d. For illustrations from Egypt see VBW 1:283; John G. Wilkinson, *The Manners and Customs of the Ancient Egyptians*, ed. S. Birch (London: John Murray, 1878), 1:305–308.

3. The traditional view is that flogging is imposed for violations of negative commandments that are not punishable by death (such as that in v. 4, the laws of purity, and the laws banning incest and perjury). See Sifrei 286; Mish. Mak. 3:1–9; similarly Josephus, Ant. 4.231–239; Philo, Spec. 2.27–28; see also H. H. Cohn, s.v. "Flogging," EncJud 6:1348–1349; S. Loewenstamm, s.v. *malkot*, EM 4:1160–1161. This view is ruled out by v. 1, which, as noted, refers to litigation between two parties.

4. Both methods are mentioned in the Bible and ancient Near Eastern texts (Exod. 21:20; Prov. 10:13; 26:3; MAL as cited in n. 2; 1 Kings 12:11; LH §202; and probably ANET, 213d). According to Mish. Mak. 3:12–13, a whip of calfskin and ass-hide straps was used.

5. LH §§127, 202. For the translation "the magistrate shall have him lie down and be given lashes" see Ibn Ezra.

6. See the texts cited in n. 2.

7. See N. Davies, *The Tomb of Rekh-Mi-Re' at Thebes* (New York: Metropolitan Museum of Art, 1943), pl. 25 and pp. 31–32.

8. Mish. Mak. 3:13,14.

9. Ibid., 3:10–11.

10. Cf. ibid., 3:14 ("if he befouled himself with excrement or urine," which Mak. 23a derives from this verse). LXX's *aschēmonései*, which could mean "act unseemly, indecorously," may imply something like this (suggestion of Michael J. Williams). LXX uses this verb for *niklah* only here. It uses the related noun, *aschēmosunē*, for "excrement" and "anything unseemly" in 23:14–15.

11. See Dalman 3:78–116 and illustrations 13–24; M. S. and J. L. Miller, *Encyclopedia of Bible Life* (New York: Harper, 1955), 19 and illus. 7–8; ANEP, figs. 89, 122 row 6; S. Yeivin, s.v. *mela'khah*, EM 4:1015–1016; H. Weippert, s.v. "Dreschen und Worfeln," BRL 63–64; O. Borowski, *Agriculture in Iron Age Israel* (Winona Lake, Ind.: Eisenbrauns, 1987), 63–65; Driver, 380.

12. BM 90a; Josephus, Ant. 4.233; Sefer Ha-Ḥinnukh, no. 601.

13. See Hos. 10:11; Jer. 50:11; Isa. 28:28; LH §§268–270 (see Driver and Miles, BL 1:469); CAD D, 121b; ANEP, figs. 89, 122; *Iliad* 20:495–497; Dalman 3:104, 107; Sifrei 287; Mish. BK 5:7.

14. Cf. *yevamah*, "sister-in-law," in Ruth 1:15.

15. See Driver; Smith; Z. W. Falk, *Hebrew Law in Biblical Times* (Jerusalem: Wahrmann, 1964), 88. For the "redeemer's" refusal in Ruth 4:6, see the footnote in NJPS ad loc.

16. See LXX; Josephus, Ant. 4.254; Sifrei 288; BB 109a; Rashi; Driver.

17. Yev. 13b; Maimonides, Hilkhot Yibbum 1:1; MAL §43.

18. See L. I. Rabinowitz, s.v. "Levirate Marriage and Ḥalizah," EncJud 11:125; Kid. 75b–76a; TJ Yev. 1:6, 3a; Keter Torah; Sifrei 233; Hoffmann; HL §§193, 195; T. and D. Thompson, "Some Legal Problems in the Book of Ruth," VT 18 (1968): 95–96.

19. See Mish. Bek. 1:7; Albeck, *Nashim*, 9–10; Maimonides, Hilkhot Yibbum 1:2; Shulḥan 'Arukh, 'Even Ha-'Ezer 165:1; M. A. Friedman, "But now they have said that the duty of ḥalitsah is preferable to the duty of levirate marriage," in *Te'udah* (Hebrew) (forthcoming).

20. Targ. Jon.; Josephus, Ant. 4.254; Yev. 24a; Hoffmann; Driver.

21. For *kam* in the sense of "be established" (sometimes under new ownership) see Gen. 23:17,20; Lev. 25:30; 27:14,19; Num. 30:5; 1 Sam. 24:21.

22. See Gen. 46:12; Ruth 4:12,21 (but see v. 17, and E. F. Campbell, *Ruth* [Garden City, N.Y.: Doubleday, 1975], 160–161); 1 Chron. 2:3–5,9–12.

23. Sefer Ha-Ḥinnukh, no. 554.

24. See H. H. Rowley, "The Marriage of Ruth," in *The Servant of the Lord and Other Essays* (Oxford: Blackwell, 1952), 185–186; T. and D. Thompson, "Some Legal Problems in the Book of Ruth," 98; H. C. Brichto, "Kin, Land, Cult, and Afterlife—A Biblical Complex," HUCA 44 (1973): 16, 20. The unnamed relative in Ruth 4:6 was unwilling to redeem Elimelech's property and marry Ruth, fearing that to do so would impair his own estate; there, however, the expense of the redemption and the ultimate need to turn the redeemed property over to Ruth's future son was the decisive factor.

25. See Excursus 23 n. 4; cf. Brichto, "Kin, Land, Cult, and Afterlife," 22.

26. Sifrei 290; Mish. Yev. 12:6; Bekhor Shor; Da'at Soferim.

27. Mish. Yev. 4:5.

28. Saadia; KJV; Ehrlich; BDB, 764 left, sub. 3e; AT; NAB; NEB.

29. See M. Malul, *Studies in Mesopotamian Legal Symbolism* (Neukirchen-Vluyn: Neukirchener Verlag, 1988).

30. Cf. Smith; Hoffmann; Brichto, "Kin, Land, Cult, and Afterlife," 18–19; T. and D. Thompson, "Some Legal Problems in the Book of Ruth," 92–93; R. de Vaux, *Ancient Israel* (New York: McGraw-Hill, 1961), 169; W. Robertson Smith, *Kinship and Marriage in Early Arabia* (Boston: Beacon, 1903), 105 n. 1; H. A. Hoffner, Jr., "Some Contributions of Hittitology to Old Testament Study," *Tyndale Bulletin* 20 (1969): 43–44. Cf. also M. de J. Ellis, "The Goddess Kititum Speaks to King Ibalpiel," *Mari: Annales de Recherches Interdisciplinaires* 5 (1987): 235–266, esp. 261–263.

31. Some sandals, however, were slipped off like shoes. In fact, it is not always certain whether Heb. *na'al* means "sandal" or "shoe." Both types of footwear were used in the ancient Near East. See J. M. Myers, s.v. "Sandals and Shoes," IDB 4:213–214.

32. Josephus, Ant. 4.256; Midrash Tannaim 167; *Megillat Ta'anit*, ed. H. Lichtenstein, "Die Fastenrolle," HUCA 8–9 (1931–32): 331. LXX may reflect this dispute: most manuscripts translate *bifnei* as *eis*, "into," but a few read *kata*, which could mean "opposite," "facing" (L. I. Rabinowitz, s.v. "Levirate Marriage and Halizah," EncJud 11:126). For *bifnei* cf. Num. 12:14; Deut. 7:24; Hos. 5:5. For spitting as humiliation see Num. 12:14; Isa. 50:6.

33. Brichto, "Kin, Land, Cult, and Afterlife," 20.

34. Cf. Esther 6:9,11: "This is what is done for the man whom the king desires to honor."

35. Cf. Gen. 16:2; 30:3; Ruth 4:11.

36. Rofé, *Mavo'*, 155.

37. Mayes, 328; Craigie, citing Philips; cf. Sifrei 292; BK 27a; Maimonides, Hilkhot Rotseaḥ 1:7–8; Abravanel, 236d; Philo, Spec. 3.175–177.

38. Prov. 30:17; Lam. R. 1:22; Philo, Spec. 2.244; 3.175; Rofé, *Mavo'*, 155; S. Lieberman, *Texts and Studies* (New York: Ktav, 1974), 37–43; J. Heinemann, *Darkhei Ha-Aggadah*, 3rd ed. (Jerusalem: Magnes Press, 1970), 67; J. J. Finkelstein, in ANET, 525 n. 24.

39. Lev. 19:35–36; Ezek. 45:10; Mic. 6:10–11; Prov. 11:1; 16:11; 20:10,23; (cf. Amos 8:5; Hos. 12:8); LH §94; Babylonian "Hymn to the Sun-god" (ANET, 388d, ii, 52); E. Reiner, *Šurpu, A Collection of Sumerian and Akkadian Incantations (AfO Beiheft* 11; Graz, 1958), 8:64–67; cf. 2:37; "Wisdom of Amenemopet" §§16, 17 in M. Lichtheim, *Ancient Egyptian Literature* (Berkeley: University of California Press, 1973–80), 2:156–157; "Protestation of Guiltlessness" (ANET, 34c, A22–26); Weinfeld, DDS, 265, 267; J. Klein and Y. Safati, "*To'evah* and Abominations in Mesopotamian Literature and the Bible," *Beer-Sheva* 3 (1978): 147 n. 79.

40. Sifrei 294.

41. Ibid.

42. A weight of uncertain provenience, presumably from Israel, has the inscription "four shekels" and a drawing of a man holding a small balance-scale; see J. Briend, "Bible et archéologie," in *Le Monde du Bible* 75 (1992): 38 fig. 34 (ref. courtesy of Raz Kletter; the weight is cited, without a source, by R.B.Y. Scott, s.v. "Balance," EncJud 4:128).

43. Mic. 6:11; Prov. 16:11; BWL 132:108 (ANET, 388d, ii, 52), and 319 n. 69; CAD s.v. *kisu*.

44. ANEP, nos. 111, 117, 133, 350; W.M.F. Petrie, s.v. "Balance," HDB 1:234; O. R. Sellers, s.v. "Balances," IDB 1:342–343. For the value of weights and measures see R.B.Y. Scott, "Weights and Measures in the Bible," BA 22 (1959): 22–40; E. Stern, s.v. "Weights and Measures," EncJud 16:376–388; *midot u-mishkalot*, EM 4:846–878; M. A. Powell, s.v. "Weights and Measures," ABD 6:897–908.

45. E.g., Exod. 30:13,24. See also 2 Sam. 14:26 ("the royal weight") and 2 Chron. 3:3 ("the former measure"). See D. Diringer, "The Early Hebrew Weights Found at Lachish," PEQ (1942–43): 85–86.

46. See, e.g., 4:26,40; 5:16,30; 6:2.

47. S. Abramsky, s.v. "Amalekites," EncJud 2:787–791; Y. Aharoni, s.v. "Amalek," EM 6:289–292; N. M. Sarna, *Exploring Exodus* (New York: Schocken, 1986), 120–126. On the *Shasu* see R. Giveon, *Les Bédouins Shosu des Documents Égyptiens* (Leiden: Brill, 1971), nos. 11, 36; W. A. Ward, s.v. "Shasu," ABD

5:1165–1167; S. Ahituv, "*Nodedim ba-negev ba-mekorot ha-mitsriyyim*," in a forthcoming Festschrift in honor of Baruch A. Levine (ed. R. Chazan et al.).

48. Judg. 3:13; 6:3,33; 7:12; 10:12; 1 Sam. 14:48; 30:1. An earlier encounter is mentioned in Num. 14:45.

49. Weinfeld, DDS, 275; cf. Dillmann, cited by Driver.

50. See S. N. Kramer, *The Sumerians* (Chicago: University of Chicago Press, 1963), 325; W. H. Ph. Römer, "Zur Siegesinschrift des Königs Utuhegal von Unug," *Orientalia* NS 54 (1985): 274–288. The parallel is pointed out by Philip D. Stern, "A Window on Ancient Israel's Religious Experience: The Herem Re-investigated and Re-interpreted" (Ph.D. diss., New York University, 1989), 102–103.

51. See 5:15; 7:18; 8:2; 9:7; 15:15; 16:3,12; 24:9,18,22; 32:7.

52. Maimonides, Sefer Ha-Mitsvot, positive no. 189, negative no. 59; Est. 3:1; 1 Sam. 15:8.

53. Gen. 20:11; 42:18 (Joseph pretending to be an Egyptian); see also Exod. 1:17,21, if the midwives are Egyptian. See M. Greenberg, *Understanding Exodus* (New York: Behrman House, 1969), 30–31; Hoffmann; Ehrlich, *Mikra*, citing *Odyssey* 1:263.

54. See Comment to 32:21.

55. Gen. 42:29; 44:29; Est. 4:7; 6:13; Smith.

56. Heb. *'ayef*, which in biblical Hebrew means "thirsty" or "hungry" more often than "tired" (see esp. Isa. 29:8; Job 22:7; Gen. 25:29–30; Judg. 8:4–5). "Tired" is usually expressed by *ya'ef* (see, e.g., Judg. 4:21; Isa. 40:28–31). However, *'ayef* and *ya'ef* are sometimes used for each other, and *'ayef* could mean "tired" here, as in 2 Sam. 16:14; Isa. 5:27; 28:12; 46:1.

57. Heb. *neheshalim* appears only here. The translation is a conjecture based on the fact that the *neheshalim* travel at the rear. Medieval Hebrew grammarians took the term to mean either "broken," based on Aramaic *h-sh-l*, "crush" (the verb is now known in Akkadian, too), or "weakened," taking the root *h-sh-l* as a metathesized form of *h-l-sh*, "be weak." See Ibn Janah, Radak, Bekhor Shor, and Ibn Ezra; cf. Driver. HALAT compares an Arabic *hasala*, "drive straggling cattle (*hasil*)."

58. Smith compares attacks on stragglers in Arabia, cited by C. M. Doughty, *Travels in Arabia Deserta* (Cambridge: Cambridge University Press, 1888), 2:153.

59. 1 Sam. 14:48; chap. 15; 27:8; 30:18; 2 Sam. 1:1; 8:12; 1 Chron. 4:43.

60. See LXX and compare the similar expressions in 7:24; 9:14 and 29:19. "Name" is the most common meaning of Heb. *zekher*, like Akkadian *zikru*; see Exod. 3:15; Ps. 135:13; Prov. 10:7; Job 18:7.

61. A. Rofé (see chap. 17, n. 67).

62. Maimonides, Hilkhot Melakhim 6:1,4.

Chapter 26

Rofé, *Mavo'*, chap. 8; M. Buber, *On the Bible*, ed. N. Glatzer (New York: Schocken, 1968), chap. "The Prayer of the First Fruits"; Y. Gutmann, "The Ceremony of Bringing the First Fruits" (Hebrew), in M. Haran, ed., *Yehezkel Kaufmann Jubilee Volume* (Jerusalem: Magnes Press, 1960), 43–53; M. A. Beek, "Das Problem des Aramäischen Stammvaters (Deut. XXVI 5)," OTS 8 (1950): 193–212; G. von Rad, *The Problem of the Hexateuch* (New York: McGraw-Hill, 1966), chap. 1; Weinfeld, DDS, 32–34. On first fruits, see the articles with that title in HDB, IDBS, and EncJud; J. Pedersen, *Israel* (London: Oxford University Press, 1963–64), 3–4:299–307; Y. Kaufmann, *The Religion of Israel* (Chicago: University of Chicago Press, 1960), 188; Levine, *Leviticus*, at Lev. 2:12; Milgrom, *Numbers*, at 18:12 and Excursus 43; Albeck, *Zera'im*, 307–309.

1. Hebrew manuscripts divide the chapter before vv. 1 and 12 and after v. 15 (M; SP).

2. Exod. 23:19; 34:26; Num. 18:12–13; Deut. 12:6; 14:28–29; 18:4.

3. For other liturgical orations in Deuteronomy, including 6:21–25, end, see Weinfeld, DDS, 32–43. Weinfeld argues that teaching monotheism is one of the goals of these orations. On p. 213 he argues that prayers are one of Deuteronomy's means of subordinating sacrificial acts.

4. Gutmann, 53.

5. M. Kadushin, *Worship and Ethics* (Evanston: Northwestern University Press, 1964), 71–81. For another example in the Bible, see J. Tigay, "On Some Aspects of Prayer in the Bible," AJSR 1 (1976): 377–378.

6. As claimed by Craigie.

7. Mish. Pes. 10:5; N. Glatzer, *The Passover Haggadah* (New York: Schocken, 1969), 48–49. Cf. Deut. 29:13–14. Rofé, *Mavo'*, compares Exod. 13:8,14–15; Deut. 6:20–25.

8. Abravanel, 243–244.

9. Mish. Bik. 1:3,6,10; Yadin, 11QTemple 1:81–99; J. Licht, s.v. *Shavu'ot*, EM 7:494. See also Comments to 12:5–6; 14:22–27; 15:19–23; 16:10.

10. Mish. Bik. 3:2–7; Tosef. Bik. 2:8; S. Lieberman, HJP, 144–146; cf. Philo, Spec. 2.215–222.

11. Nevertheless, halakhic exegesis understands the phrase to mean "the first products of some of the fruits of the soil," and holds that first fruits are brought only from the species listed in 8:8 (Sifrei 297, construing the partitive *mem* in *me-re'shit* as applying to the entire phrase). This is unnatural and ignores "all." LXX, SP, and some manuscripts lack "all." One wonders whether the Sifrei is based on such a manuscript and whether MT's "all" is an interpolation to make clear that all species of fruit are covered.

12. Mish. Pe'ah 1:1 (see Bertinoro); TJ Bik. 3:1, 65c; Maimonides, Hilkhot Bikkurim 2:17.

13. T. O. Lambdin, "Egyptian Loan Words in the OT," JAOS 73 (1953): 151. According to Mish. Bik. 3:8, some used metal vessels (cf. Tosef. Bik., chap. 8). The Greek and Syriac of Ecclus. 34 (31): 14 render *tene'* as "bowl," and in talmudic sources the word seems sometimes to refer to metal containers.

14. Mish. Sot. 7:2–3; Mish. Bik. 3:7.

15. For the first view see Joüon, §112f (ref. courtesy D. R. Hillers); for the second, see Sforno and cf. 1 Sam. 24:19 (18); 2 Sam. 19:7; Pss. 19:2; 97:6; cf. Ehrlich, *Mikra*.

16. Lev. 21:7; 18:7; 1 Sam. 15:15; 2 Sam. 14:17; 1 Kings 2:3; 2 Kings 19:4. LXX reads "my God." Either LXX reflects a haplography or MT reflects a dittography.

17. Pss. 78; 105; 135; 136; Neh. 9:6–37; Josh. 24:2–13; Judg. 2:1; 6:8–9; 1 Sam. 12:7–12; Amos 2:9–11; Mic. 6:4–5. The Exodus is omitted in Josh. 4:22 and Ps. 106.

18. See esp. Exod. 1:9,14; 3:7,9,17; and Num. 20:15,16.

19. Weinfeld, DDS, 33–34, 329–330.

20. See H. L. Ginsberg, "Psalms and Inscriptions of Petition and Acknowledgment," in A. Marx et al., eds., *Louis Ginzberg Jubilee Volume* (New York: American Academy for Jewish Research, 1945), 159–171.

21. Rashbam; Bekhor Shor; Shadal; Ehrlich, *Mikra* and *Randglossen*; Buber, *On the Bible*; Torah Temimah; D. D. Luckenbill, "The 'Wandering Aramaean,'" AJSL 36 (1919–20): 244–245; C. J. Gadd, "Inscribed Prisms of Sargon II from Nimrud," *Iraq* 16 (1954): 192–193 (cited by A. Malamat, "The Aramaeans," in D. J. Wiseman, ed., *Peoples of Old Testament Times* [Oxford: Clarendon, 1973], 154 n. 40).

22. LXX reads "our God," not "God of our fathers"; see Rofé, *Mavo'*, 52.

23. See 1 Sam. 12:8; cf. Exod. 23:20; Num. 10:29. Sifrei 301 takes this as a reference to the Temple, but this would be chronologically misplaced since the phrase precedes "and gave us this land."

24. Rofé, *Mavo'*, 54.

25. See Gen. 39:16; 42:33; 2 Sam. 16:21; Vulg.; Ehrlich.

26. J. Tigay, ed., *Empirical Models for Biblical Criticism* (Philadelphia: University of Pennsylvania Press, 1985), 83–85. Some scholars hold that vv. 3–4 are an interpolation that aims to give a role to the priest, who would otherwise be absent from the ceremony, and to add the reference to God's promise to the patriarchs, which vv. 5–10 lack (see Smith; Rofé, *Mavo'*). However, that could have been accomplished more simply by adding "as He promised to our ancestors" at the end of v. 9 and the priest in v. 10.

27. See Deut. 12:7,12,18; 14:26–27; 16:11,14.

28. See Deut. 14:29; 16:11,14; 24:19–21; 26:12–13; cf. Buber, *On the Bible*.

29. Mish. Sot. 7:1; cf. Lieberman, HJP, 140n.

30. Von Rad; Rofé, *Mavo'*, 30, 32; Weinfeld, DDS, 198, 213. For the Deuteronomic phrases see Weinfeld, DDS, 326, 328, 345, 356.

31. Mish. Sot. 9:10; see Albeck, *Nashim*, ad loc. and 393; Lieberman, HJP, 139–143; S. Lieberman, *Texts and Studies* (New York: Ktav, 1974), 25 n. 34; Yadin, *Megillat Ha-Mikdash* (Jerusalem: Israel Exploration Society, Hebrew University Institute of Archaeology, and the Shrine of the Book, 1977), 1:126, 178ff, 297n.

32. According to Sifrei 302 and Mish. Maʿas. Sh. 5:6,10, this declaration is made at the end of the Festival of Unleavened Bread in the fourth and seventh years, since the farmer is given until then to finish disposing of all the sacred dues of the preceding three years.

33. Some scholars have suggested that the phrase is a relic of a time when tithes were obligatory only every third year, but there is no independent evidence that such was ever the case. W. Robertson Smith, *The Religion of the Semites* (London: A. and C. Black, 1914), 249; Rofé, *Mavo'*, chap. 8; Mayes; Y. Zakovitch, "Some Remnants of Ancient Laws in the Deuteronomic Code," *Israel Law Review* 9 (1974): 346–349.

34. Josephus, Ant. 4.240–243.

35. See Deut. 12:7,12,18; 14:23,26; 15:20; 16:11; 26:5,10; cf. 27:7; contrast Gen. 27:7 and see BDB, 817 sub 4 (h). See the discussion by Ian Wilson, "Divine Presence in Deuteronomy" (Ph.D. diss., Cambridge University, 1992), 169–170; N. Rabban, "*lifnei YHVH*," *Tarbiz* 23 (1952): 1–8.

36. ANET, 210bc, cited by Milgrom, *Cult and Conscience* (Leiden: Brill, 1976), 23 n. 75; 27–29; 30 n. 111.

37. Lev. 22:4; Num. 19. This must be why, according to Hos. 9:4, the food of mourners defiles (that is, others, besides the mourner) who eat it. Halakhic exegesis takes "mourning" (*'on*) as the period between death and burial (*'aninah*; Sifrei 303; Mish. Maʿas. Sh. 5:12). In 11QTemple 43:15–16 it is interpreted as workdays (see Yadin, *Megillat Ha-Mikdash* [Jerusalem: Israel Exploration Society, Hebrew University Institute of Archaeology, and The Shrine of the Book, 1977], 1:67,94).

38. Cf. T. H. Gaster, *Myth, Legend and Custom in the Old Testament* (New York: Harper and Row, 1969), 602–604. Cf. also the *marzeah* ceremony, which combined eating and memorial rites (Jer. 16:5–9 and evidence summarized by S. Paul, *Amos* [Minneapolis: Fortress Press, 1991], 210–212).

39. Num. 19:22.

40. Cf. Ecclus. 7:33; 30:18 (Gk. text); Charles, 1:198, 212–213, 342, 414; 2:730; KAI 214:17,21–22. For the practice see M. Bayliss, "The Cult of Dead Kin in Assyria and Babylonia," *Iraq* 35 (1973): 115–125; T. J. Lewis, *Cults of the Dead in Ancient Israel and Ugarit* (Atlanta: Scholars Press, 1989), esp. 97, 102–103; H. A. Hoffner, Jr., "Second Millennium Antecedents to the Hebrew *'ob*," *JBL* 86 (1967): 385–401; J. Gray, "Ugarit," in D. Winton Thomas, ed., *Archaeology and Old Testament Study* (Oxford: Clarendon, 1967), 149–150; E. L. Sukenik, "Arrangements for the Cult of the Dead in Ugarit and Samaria," in *Memorial Lagrange* (Paris: Gabalda, 1940), 59–65.

41. Pss. 26:8; 76:3 (*meʿonah*); 2 Chron. 36:15. In Jer. 25:30

(contrast Amos 1:2) and 2 Chron. 30:27, God's "holy abode" is "heaven." See Weinfeld, DDS, 198.

42. Weinfeld, DDS, 43–44.

43. Wright.

44. Rofé, *Mavo'*, 169.

45. For mutual oaths see ANET, 628b; McCarthy, *Treaty and Covenant*, 2nd ed. (Rome: Pontifical Biblical Institute, 1981), 182–185.

46. Ramban at 29:9; Abravanel, 278a-b.

47. Abravanel, 250; Git. 57b and Mid. Hag. at 28:50 ("swear"); KJV; Torah Temimah; M. Friedman, "Israel's Response to Hosea 2:17b, 'You are my Husband,'" JBL 99 (1980): 202; J. Licht, "The Biblical Claim of Establishment," *Shnaton* 4 (1980): 107–108. The *hiph'il* of *'amar*, not found elsewhere, is probably not causative here (as held by Ibn Ezra, Rashbam, and others). It would not make sense to say that Israel caused *God* to say that Israel will accept Him as their God and walk in His ways and obey Him (v. 17), or that God induced *Israel* to say that it would be His treasured people and that He will elevate it above the nations (v. 18). Clearly, Israel makes the promises in v. 17 and God makes those in v. 18. For noncausative *hiph'ils* that are intensive of *kal*, cf. *hazʿek* (Job 35:9), *harnen* (Ps. 32:11), and see GKC §53d. Other interpretations of *he'emir* are: (1) "betroth," "speak for" (as in the rabbinic use of *ma'amar* for espousal; thus Targ. Onk.; Malbim; Ehrlich, *Mikra*; Torah Temimah; Falk, *Hebrew Law in Biblical Times* [Jerusalem: Wahrmann, 1964], 135; cf. Ber. 6a and S. A. Wertheimer, *Sefer Perush Rav Saadia Gaon ʿal Massekhet Berakhot* [Jerusalem, 1908; reprint, Jerusalem: Tsiyon, 1927], 2a-b; M. Levanon, "*he'emarta, he'emirkha*," *Sinai* 51 [1962]: 238–240 [ref. courtesy of Jonas Greenfield]); (2) "declare allegiance" (A. Kaplan, *The Living Torah* [New York: Maznaim, 1981]); (3) "exalt," "elevate," from *'-m-r*, "be high" (Saadia and others; Ben Yehudah 1:297a, n. 1; J. Barth, *Wurzeluntersuchungen* [Leipzig: Hinrichs, 1902], 5–6 [ref. courtesy of Sol Cohen]).

48. Pesh. (see Smith); Moffatt; Licht, "Biblical Claim," 107.

49. According to BHS, the clause is missing in some MSS of LXX; its absence may reflect a sense that it is superfluous in view of the same clause at the end of v. 19. It is even possible that v. 19, likewise, is a textual variant of all or some of God's promises in v. 18a. This is suggested by the appearance of the clause "as He promised" both at the end of v. 18a and in v. 19. Such clauses are Deuteronomy's way of referring back to earlier parts of the Torah, but they never appear twice in the same context, not even when they accompany a series of promises (see 6:3,19; 9:3; 31:3; see J. Milgrom, "Profane Slaughter and a Formulaic Key to the Composition of Deuteronomy," HUCA 47 (1976): 3–4. Possibly, then, vv. 17–18a represent one version of God's and Israel's declarations, and vv. 18b–19 variants of that version.

50. Cf. Y. Muffs, *Love and Joy* (New York: Jewish Theological Seminary, 1992), 51. "Profane" (*hullin/hullim*), the antonym of "holy," is used in the sense of "abandoned," "vulnerable," in Sifra (Weiss, 88c, 2:7); Gen. R. 23:6 (ed. Theodor-Albeck, 227).

Chapter 27

1. Hebrew texts divide the text before vv. 1 (M, SP, 4QDeutᶜ), 9 (M, SP), 11 (M), and after 26 (M, SP, and 4QDeutᶜ). Within the third section, M also has breaks before vv. 15,16,17,18,19,21,22,23,24,25, and 26.

2. See rabbinic sources collected by S. Lieberman, TK 8:707–709; Ralbag at v. 4; Abravanel, 251 at v. 1; Shadal at v. 10; Rofé, *Mavo'*, 26; M. Weinfeld, "The Emergence of the Deuteronomic Movement: The Historical Antecedents," in N. Lohfink, ed., *Das Deuteronomium* (Leuven: Leuven University Press, 1985), 83.

3. Weinfeld, "Emergence," 79.

4. Hoffmann, 494–496; cf. Baḥya at v. 1.

5. See 5:28; 6:2; 8:1; 11:8,22; 19:9; 30:11.

6. M. D. Cassuto and N. Avigad, s.v. *ketovot*, EM 4:380–381. Note that some scholars believe that *b-'-r* originally meant "engrave" (e.g., Ben Yehuda, 455).

7. See Dan. 5:5; Driver; Z. Meshel, *Kuntillet Ajrud* (Jerusalem: Israel Museum, 1978), 12–13 (Eng. section); J. Hoftijzer and G. van der Kooij, *Aramaic Texts from Deir ʿAlla* (Leiden: Brill, 1976), 17–28; cf. A. Rofé, *The Book of Balaam* (Jerusalem: Simor, 1979), 60.

8. Cf. Shadal at v. 2.

9. Cf. Malbim at v. 5.

10. Weinfeld, DDS, 164.

11. Mekhilta to Deuteronomy quoted by Lieberman, TK 8:700; Josephus, Ant. 4.307–308; cf. Ralbag at Josh. 8:32; the view attributed to Saadia (see J. Kafiḥ, ed., *Perushei Rabbenu Saʿadiah Gaʾon ʿal Ha-Torah* [Jerusalem: Mossad Harav Kook, 1963] and citations in Ibn Ezra here and by Radak at Josh. 8:32; but see M. Zucker, *ʿAl Targum Rasaʾg la-Torah* [New York: Feldheim, 1959], 254–255); ibn Kaspi (I. Last, *Mishneh Kesef* [Pressburg: Alakalai, 1905; Cracow: Fischer, 1906]). See also Meklenburg at v. 8; Hoffmann, 337–340; Ramban thinks it was the whole Torah. Cf. Keter Torah.

12. SP reads "Mount Gerizim" instead of "Mount Ebal." Gerizim lies across the valley of Shechem from Ebal and is the sacred mountain of the Samaritans; it was the site of their temple in the Second Temple period. (An open-air sanctuary is in use by them there today.) The Samaritans, who regard themselves as the descendants of the tribes of Ephraim and Manasseh, consider their sanctuary and not the Temple in Jerusalem to be the authentic site chosen by God. They claim that the Jews altered the text of the Torah to remove all evidence of the sanctity of Gerizim (see J. MacDonald et al., s.v. "Samaritans," EncJud 14:726–758). However, had a Jewish scribe removed Gerizim from v. 4, he would also have removed it from v. 12, or switched it with Ebal in v. 13 so as to make Gerizim the mountain on which the curses and not the blessings were recited. It is more likely that the reading of the Samaritan text is a tendentious revision by the Samaritans to support their doctrine of Mount Gerizim's sanctity. On the reading in v. 4 see J. Tigay, ed., *Empirical Models for Biblical Criticism* (Philadelphia: University of Pennsylvania Press, 1985), 81 n. 64.

13. Shechem is the centermost of the three cities of refuge prescribed in 19:3 (see Josh. 20:7).

14. A. Zertal, "Has Joshua's Altar Been Found on Mt. Ebal?" BAR 11/1 (1985): 29; G. A. Smith, *The Historical Geography of the Holy Land* (New York: Harper and Row, 1966), 171; s.v. "Ebal," HDB 1:636; G. E. Wright, *Shechem: The Biography of a Biblical City* (New York: McGraw-Hill, 1965), 9.

15. Gen. 12:6–7; 33:19; Josh. 24:32; 1 Kings 12:25; John Bright, *A History of Israel*, 3rd ed. (Philadelphia: Westminster Press, 1981), 136; Y. Aharoni and M. Avi-Yonah, *The Macmillan Bible Atlas*, rev. ed. (New York: Macmillan, 1977), 43.

16. Comment to v. 10.

17. Josephus, Ant. 4.308; Lieberman, TK 8:701.

18. See D. Winton Thomas, ed., *Archaeology and Old Testament Study* (Oxford: Clarendon, 1967), 300, 313, 395; M. Fishbane, *Biblical Interpretation in Ancient Israel* (Oxford: Clarendon, 1988), 159–162; R. Panitz, *Textual Exegesis and Other Kinds of Interpretation in Scripture* (Ph.D. diss., University of Pennsylvania, 1983), 171–174; 1 Macc. 4:47; Josephus, War 5.225.

19. A. Zertal, "Has Joshua's Altar Been Found," BAR 11/1 (1985): 26–43; A. Kempinski, "Joshua's Altar—An Iron Age I Watchtower," and A. Zertal, "How Can Kempinski Be So Wrong!" BAR 12/1 (1986): 42–53; M. D. Coogan, "Of Cults and Cultures: Reflections on the Interpretation of Archaeological Information," PEQ 119 (1987): 1–8; H. Shanks, "Two Israelite Cult Sites Now Questioned," BAR 14/1 (1988): 48–52.

20. Mish. Middot 3:4.

21. L. Vincent, "Essai sur le sacrifice de communion des rois Atlantes," in L. H. Vincent, ed., *Mémorial Lagrange* (Paris: Gabalda, 1940), 88. He cites Plato, *Critias*, 119.

22. In addition to the meaning "sword," *ḥerev* refers to a circumcision knife, a dagger, a razor, and something like a pickax (Josh. 5:2–3; Judg. 3:16; Ezek. 5:1–2; 26:9). Cognates refer to a type of plow (Akk. *ḥarbu*), a sword or large knife for carving meat (Ugar. *ḥrb*), and a dart or spear (Arab. *ḥarbatu*).

23. See J. Muhly, "How Iron Technology Changed the Ancient World," BAR 8/6 (1982): 46.

24. Rashbam at Exod. 20:21; cf. E. Nielsen, *Shechem: A Traditio-Historical Investigation* (Copenhagen: Gad, 1955), 59–61.

25. Exod. 24:5; Lev. 9:4,18,22; Num. 7:17 etc.; 1 Sam. 11:15; 1 Kings 8:63–64; see also 2 Sam. 6:17 and 2 Kings 16:13. See B. A. Levine, *In the Presence of the Lord* (Leiden: Brill, 1974), 46, 50, 52.

26. Levine, *Leviticus*, at 3:1; idem, *In the Presence of the Lord*, 3–52, 118–122; see also Hoffmann, *Sefer Vayikra'*, 115–116; J. Milgrom, s.v. "Sacrifices and Offerings, OT," IDBS, 769; NJPS at Amos 5:22 ("gifts").

27. See Mish. Soṭ. 7:5; Tosef. Soṭ. 8:6; Targs. Jon. and Yer.; Lieberman, HJP, 200–202.

28. *Hasket*, "be silent," appears nowhere else in the Bible, but it appears in Ecclus. 13:23. The meaning is known from Akkadian and Arabic cognates (P. Wechter, *Ibn Barun's Arabic Works on Hebrew Grammar and Lexicography* [Philadelphia: Dropsie College, 1964], 106, 220 n. 691; HALAT, 714; H. R. Cohen, *Biblical Hapax Legomena in the Light of Akkadian and Ugaritic* [Missoula, Mont.: Scholars Press, 1978], 111).

29. Meklenburg, citing Ber. 16a; Zohar 1, Noah, 72a.

30. Cf. Malbim; Rofé, *Mavo'*, 26.

31. Driver; Weinfeld, DDS, 80, 181n.; J. Licht, "The Biblical Claim of Establishment," *Shnaton* 4 (1980): 105–106.

32. For *nihyeh* expressing the causality behind an action see 1 Kings 1:27; 12:24; BDB, 227d, §2.

33. Sifrei 55; Mish. Soṭ. 7:5; Tosef. Soṭ. 8:9; Shadal at v. 15; Radak at Josh. 8:34. The Masoretic *parashiyot*, in which vv. 11–26 are a single section, also reflect the assumption that these verses describe the same ceremony.

34. Rofé, *Mavo'*, 22.

35. Cf. Josh. 6:26; Judg. 21:18; 1 Sam. 14:24,28. See P. Buis, "Deuteronome XXVII 15–26, Malédictions ou Exigences de l'Alliance?" VT 17 (1967): 478–479.

36. See Ibn Ezra at 27:14; Shadal; Hoffmann, 501, 504–505, 506–507; Rofé, *Mavo'*, 22ff; Weinfeld, "Emergence," 79–80.

37. The first site is suggested by Rofé, *Mavo'*, 21. The amphitheaters are suggested by C. W. Wilson, "Ebal and Gerizim, 1866," PEQ (April 1873): 69–70. (Acoustical information courtesy Christopher Brooks of Artec Consultants, an acoustic consulting firm in New York [letter of November 18, 1991].)

38. Mayes; Nielsen, *Shechem*, 70–72; Driver. For a survey of views, see M. J. Broyde and S. S. Weiner, "A Mathematical Analysis of the Division of the Tribes and the Role of the Levites on Grizim and Aval in Deuteronomy 27," *Tradition* 27 (1992): 48–57.

39. Ibn Ezra; Rashbam; Malbim; Ehrlich, *Randglossen*; A. Alt, *Essays on Old Testament History and Religion* (Garden City, N.Y.: Doubleday, 1967), 148, 155; Weinfeld, DDS, 276–278.

40. ANET, 353–354; IR no. 185, Eng. section, 85; cf. 1QS 2:11–18, cited below, n. 47; parallels noted by Weinfeld, "The Secret of the En-Gedi Community," *Tarbiz* 51 (1981–82): 125–129 (Hebrew).

41. For the form-critical background of the curses, see Mayes; Alt, *Essays*, 147–148, 156–157, 161–168; G. von Rad, *Studies in Deuteronomy* (London: SCM Press, 1953), 25–36; Weinfeld, DDS, 276–279; idem, "Emergence," 81; D. J. McCarthy, *Treaty and Covenant*, rev. ed. (Rome: Biblical Institute Press, 1981), 198–199; R. Sonsino, *Motive Clauses in Hebrew Law* (Chico, Calif.: Scholars Press, 1980), 22–23.

42. Ibn Ezra at v. 14; Nielsen, *Shechem*, 82.

43. Nielsen, *Shechem*, 82.

44. There are two or three parallels in the Decalogue (Deut. 5:8,16, perhaps 17); five in the Book of the Covenant (Exod. 20:23; 21:17; 22:18, 21–24; 23:8,9; 22:18); three in Lev. 19 (vv. 4,14,33–34); four in Lev. 18 (vv. 8,9,17,23); five in Lev. 20 (vv. 9,11,14,15,17); and seven in Ezekiel 22 (vv. 3–4,6–7,10–12). See the tables in Driver, 299; Alt, *Essays*, 156.

45. For these see M. Greenberg, *Ezekiel 1–20* (Garden City, N.Y.: Doubleday, 1983), 342–347; *Ha-Segullah Ve-Ha-Koah* (Tel Aviv: Ha-Kibbutz Ha-Meʾuḥad and Sifriyat Poʿalim, 1986), 57–64.

46. Cf. Shadal.

47. Cf. Sforno; von Rad; Weinfeld, DDS, 147; idem, "Zion as a Religious and Political Capital," in R. E. Friedman, ed., *The Poet and the Historian* (Chico, Calif.: Scholars Press, 1983), 82ff; idem, Commentary, 253–254. This is how 29:17–28 was apparently understood by the Qumran sect, which modeled its annual covenant reaffirmation ceremony on that passage plus 27:14–26. According to 1QS 2:11–18, the ceremony ends with the Priests and Levites declaring accursed any man who enters the covenant while planning to defect from it, and calling down upon him God's unforgiving wrath, all based on 29:18–20; following this declaration, all those admitted to the covenant are to respond "Amen and amen."

48. Num. 6:22–27; 22:6; Deut. 10:8; 21:5; 23:5; Josh. 13:22. See M. Weinfeld, s.v. *kelalah*, EM 7:187–188; idem, "Emergence," 81.

49. See Gen. 9:25–26; 49:7; see also Deut. 28:16ff; Josh. 6:26; Jer. 20:15–16; IR no. 14; ANET, 661–662; cf. H. C. Brichto, *The Problem of "Curse" in the Hebrew Bible* (Philadelphia: Society of Biblical Literature, 1963), 77ff; W. Robertson Smith, *The Religion of the Semites* (London: A. and C. Black, 1914), 164 n. 1.

50. See J. Tigay, *You Shall Have No Other Gods* (Atlanta: Scholars Press, 1986), 91–96.

51. Shevuot 29b; cf. Shevuot 36a; Num. R. 9:35; Deut. R. 7:1; Sot. 17a ("assents" meaning "Amens"); Radak, *Sefer Ha-Shorashim*, s.v. ʾ-m-n; see Weinfeld, "Secret of the Ein-Gedi Community," 126 n. 4. Whether "Amen" in the Hebrew letter from Metsad Hashavyahu (IR no. 33:11) goes with what precedes it or follows it is debated.

52. See Isa. 3:5; Hos. 4:7; Hab. 2:16; Prov. 12:9. It is debated whether Exod. 21:17 and Lev. 20:9, which use the related term *kallel*, refer to the same crime; see Ehrlich, *Randglossen*, at Exod. 21:17; Brichto, *Problem of "Curse"*, 132–135; B. Epstein, *Tosefet Berakhah* (Pinsk, 1937; reprint, Tel Aviv: Moreshet, 1981), 198; Weinfeld, DDS, 241 n. 2, 277–278. According to BHS, two medieval Hebrew manuscripts read *mekallel* here.

53. See ANET, 422c; Shurpu 2:46 (in W. Beyerlin, *Near Eastern Religious Texts Relating to the Old Testament* [Philadelphia: Westminster Press, 1978], 132); A. L. Oppenheim, *Ancient Mesopotamia* (Chicago: University of Chicago Press, 1964), 287; CAD s.v. *kudurru, nakāru, nasāhu*; E. S. Hartum and J. J. Rabinowitz, s.v. *gevul, hassagat gevul*, EM 2:395–397.

54. H. M. Gevaryahu and S. E. Loewenstamm, s.v. *goral, goralot*, EM 2:460–461; cf. Milgrom, *Numbers*, at 26:52–56 and Excursus 62. For division of land by lot in Assyria, see MAL B, §§1,9. Likewise, the Egyptian sage Amenemopet says that by respecting boundaries one satisfies the Lord who determines boundaries (ANET, 422c). The Babylonian god Ninurta was called "Lord of Boundary Stones," and to the Greeks and Romans, boundaries were under the protection of Zeus, "Lord of Boundaries"/"Jupiter Terminus" (CAD K, 495a; Driver at 19:14).

55. Josephus, *Ant.* 4.276; Maimonides, Sefer Ha-Mitsvot, negative no. 299; Sefer Ha-Ḥinnukh, no. 240.

56. Cf. Ezek. 22:10–11. Cf. LH §§154–158; HL §§187–200.

57. Ehrlich, *Randglossen*.

58. LH §158; HL §190.

59. HL §§187–188, 199–200; the Ugaritic Baal myth (ANET, 139a); *Gilgamesh Epic* 6, 48ff. (ANET, 84b). See H. A. Hoffner, Jr., "Incest, Sodomy, and Bestiality in the Ancient Near East," in Hoffner, ed., *Orient and Occident* (Kevelaer: Butzon and Bercker; Neukirchen-Vluyn: Neukirchener Verlag, 1973), 81–90; for Greek tales see H. Licht, *Sexual Life in Ancient Greece* (London: Routledge and Kegan Paul, 1932), 504. On bestiality among rural populations see W. B. Pomeroy and P. H. Gebhard, s.v. "Human Sexual Behavior," *Encyclopedia Britannica* (Chicago: Encyclopedia Britannica, 1966), 20:426ad, 427d (cf. Hoffner, "Incest," 82).

60. According to Yev. 63a, Adam tried all the animals sexually before Eve was created (see Rashi ad loc.).

61. See W. Robertson Smith, *Kinship and Marriage in Early Arabia* (Boston: Beacon, 1903), 191–198; KAI no. 14:13–15 (ANET, 662c; see KAI 2:22); J. Černý, "Consanguineous Marriages in Pharaonic Egypt," JEA 40 (1954): 23–29.

62. LXX B (BHS).

63. LXX B and S.

64. See Ibn Ezra; Ehrlich, *Mikra*; Weinfeld, DDS, 278.

Chapter 28

1. Hebrew texts have breaks before vv. 1 (M, SP, 4QDeutᶜ), 12 (SP), 15 (SP, M), 22,27,36,49,54,56,58, and 64 (SP), 69 (M [*setumah*]), and after 69 (M [*petuhah*], SP).

2. Abravanel; Mid. Hag. at v. 46; cf. Pss. 78:49; 91:5,11; Zech. 5:1–4; also 2 Sam. 24:16–17; 2 Kings 19:35. For "letting loose" plagues, cf. Lev. 26:25b; Ezek. 5:17; Amos 1 passim; Mal. 2:2; Sefire IA, 30 (see H. Tawil, "A Curse Concerning Crop-Consuming Insects in the Sefire Treaty and in Akkadian: A New Interpretation," BASOR 225 [1977]: 61).

3. Cf. H. J. Rose, "Erinyes," OCD, 406–407; S. Eitrem, s.v. "Curses," OCD, 302–303; cf. Herodotus 6:86; note the personification implied by the verbs used in curses in the cuneiform passages cited by Weinfeld, DDS, 108–109; CAD A2, 304cd, s.v. *arratu*; D. J. McCarthy, *Treaty and Covenant*, 2nd ed. (Rome: Biblical Institute Press, 1981), 2.

4. Mayes. Cf. Gen. 34:28; 1 Kings 14:11; Jer. 14:18.

5. Cf. Rashbam and Abravanel.

6. This phrase is redundant with the remainder of the verse. Since it is missing in LXX and in the parallel curse in v. 18, it could be an addition to harmonize the first half of the verse with v. 11 and 30:9. Some scribes tended to homogenize texts in this way (SP and a medieval manuscript have it in v. 18; see BHK to v. 4), though the MT of the Torah usually avoids such readings.

7. See 2 Kings 11:8; Jer. 37:4.

8. See 1 Kings 3:7; 2 Kings 19:27; Deut. 31:2.

9. Bekhor Shor; Keter Torah. See Num. 27:17,21; 1 Sam. 18:13,16; 29:6; cf. ANET, 482c.

10. See Josh. 6:1; 1 Kings 15:17; Zech. 8:10; and 2 Chron. 15:5.

11. Cf. Schottroff cited by G. Seitz, *Redaktionsgeschichtliche Studien zum Deuteronomium* (Stuttgart: Kohlhammer, 1971), 269.

12. Zech. 8:10–13 (see C. and E. Meyers, *Haggai, Zechariah 1–8* [Garden City, N.Y.: Doubleday, 1987], 421); LXX Esther, Addition B, 2; ANET, 378a, 654a; Streck, Asb. 260 ii 21 (CAD B, 180a); ARM 2, 112:8 (CAD E, 355d); A. L. Oppenheim, "Zur Keilschriftlichen Omenliteratur," *Orientalia* 5 (1936): 215 (text to n. 6). Contrast Judg. 5:6.

13. Ehrlich, *Mikra*.

14. Lekaḥ Tov; Rashi; Bekhor Shor; Siftei Hakhamim; Keter Torah. Cf. 1 Sam. 2:5; Isa. 4:1; 11:15; Prov. 24:16.

15. See Prov. 3:10; KAI 200, ll. 5,7; ANET, 568 n. 5; H. Weippert, s.v. "Speicher," BRL, 308–309; cf. R. Meyuḥas.

16. See Smith, 307, end; Driver, lxxix.

17. NJPS footnote; R. Meyuḥas; Ralbag; cf. 2 Sam. 12:28; Isa. 4:1. For Israel as "the LORD's people," see, e.g., Num. 11:29; 17:6; Judg. 5:11.

18. Jer. 14:9; Dan. 9:19.

19. ANET, 488c.

20. Job 37:9; 38:22; Jer. 10:13; Ps. 135:7; Enoch 41:4; 60:11–21; cf. M. H. Pope and J. H. Tigay, "A Description of Baal," UF 3 (1971): 118,124.

21. A. Rothkoff, s.v. "Tokheḥah," EncJud 15:1192.

22. J. B. Frey, *Corpus Inscriptionum Judaicarum* 2 (Rome: Pontificio Istituto di Archeologia Cristiana, 1952), 24, no. 760 (cf. 34, no. 774).

23. In vv. 4–5, the offspring of humans and cattle precede the basket and the kneading bowl, whereas in vv. 17–18 the order is reversed. There is no obvious reason for this; Hoffmann explains it by citing a midrash based on the experience of Job: "The Merciful One does not strike living things first" (Lev. R. 17:4).

24. Targ. Onk. (*shiggushayya*'; cf. Syriac *š-g-š*); Targ. Jon. *'irbuva*', "confusion," "tumult"; MdRY Be-Shallaḥ 5 (Lauterbach 1:241).

25. Saadia; R. Meyuḥas; Ḥazzekuni.

26. For restraining and forcing back by a blast of wind, and sometimes perhaps verbally, see Isa. 17:13; 50:2; Jer. 29:27; Nah. 2:4; Mal. 2:3; 3:11; Pss. 18:16; 104:7; 106:9. Rebuke and restraint are expressed by the same word in several languages. Saadia renders *mig'eret* with Arabic *zajra*, which has both meanings. Etymologically, English "rebuke" means "force back" while "reprimand" means "repress," "restrain."

27. The text of Mal. 2:3 differs in LXX. See BHS; A. Caquot, s.v. *ga'ar*, TDOT 3:53; A. A. Macintosh, "A Consideration of Hebrew *g-'-r*," VT 19 (1969): 477.

28. Cf. Levine, *Leviticus*, at 26:41.

29. See, e.g., Jer. 21:7; 32:24; 38:2; 43:17; Ezek. 5:12; 7:15; cf. Lev. 26:25.

30. For identification of the diseases in the chapter see J. Leibovitch and J. S. Licht, s.v. *maḥalot u-nega'im*, EM 4:794–795; J. Leibovitch, s.v. *refu'ah*, EM 7:421–423.

31. Ben Yehuda, 5745.

32. For *ḥarḥur* see Job 30:30; Ps. 102:4; Ezek. 15:4,5; Jer. 17:6. For *ḥerev/ḥorev* see Hag. 1:11; Gen. 31:40; Job 30:30; note the vocalization *ḥerev* in Zech. 11:17 (see BDB, 351b); Lam. 5:9. Vulg., Ibn Ezra, Bekhor Shor, and Abravanel recognize the meaning.

33. For crop afflictions, see Amos 4:9; for human afflictions, see Bekhor Shor; Leibovitch and Licht, s.v. *maḥalot u-nega'im*, EM 4:795. For *yerakon* see LXX; Ibn Ezra; Ibn Barun (P. Wechter, *Ibn Barun's Arabic Works on Hebrew Grammar and Lexicography* [Philadelphia: Dropsie College, 1964], 98); Ralbag; J. Preuss, *Biblical and Talmudic Medicine*, trans. F. Rosner (New York: Sanhedrin Press, 1978), 164–166; CAD A2, 91–92; cf. AHw, 1465d. For *shiddafon* cf. Gen. 41:6; 2 Kings 19:26; and see Abravanel.

34. For *neḥoshet* meaning bronze see S. Abramsky, s.v. *mattakhot*, EM 5:645.

35. G. A. Smith, *Historical Geography of the Holy Land* (New York: Harper and Row, 1966), 65; cf. Rashbam; R. Meyuḥas; Driver; Shalag. According to the MT punctuation, the verse should be translated: "The LORD will make the rain of your land dust and sand, they shall drop on you. . . ."

36. 2 Sam. 21:10.

37. G. Hort, "The Plagues of Egypt," ZAW 69 (57–58): 101–102.

38. HALAT, 814, s.v. II *'-p-l*, citing Arabic cognates (see G. R. Driver, "The Plague of the Philistines," JRAS 1950:51; cf. Wechter, *Ibn Barun's Arabic Works*, 130 n. 33; 211 n. 571). For *teḥorim* (*teḥorim*) cf. Syr. *teḥora*' and see Wechter, 211 n. 571. See also Targ. and Rashi at Ps. 78:66. Other occurrences of *'-f-l-y-m* are 1 Sam. 5:6,9,12; 6:4,5.

39. Meg. 25b; Soferim 9:8.

40. A. Macalister, s.v. "Medicine," HDB 3:324–325; Preuss, *Biblical and Talmudic Medicine*, 154–157; Smith, *Historical Geography*, 118–120; P. K. McCarter, *1 Samuel* (Garden City, N.Y.: Doubleday, 1980), 119–120, 123; O. Neustätter, "Where Did the Identification of the Philistine Plague (1 Samuel, 5 and 6) as Bubonic Plague Originate?" *Bulletin of the History of Medicine* 11 (1942): 36–47. This view is based partly on the seeming association of *'-f-l-y-m* with fatality in 1 Sam. 5, but v. 12 there states that those who did *not* die were stricken with *'-f-l-y-m*; hence the latter and the cause of death must have two separate phenomena. See also Driver, "Plague of the Philistines," 50–51.

41. See LXX; Vulg.; Saadia. The cognates, and their definitions in the standard dictionaries, are Arab. *jarab*, "mange," "itch," "scabies," "eczema"; Akk. *garabu*, "leprosy" (?), "scab," "pellagra"; Syr. *garba*, "leprosy"; and Syr. *ḥersa*', "mange," "scabies."

42. Cf. Isa. 29:9,10,18; Zeph. 1:17; Job 5:12–14; *Enuma Elish* 4:70 (ANET, 66d); LH epilogue xxvii, §§5–6 (see M. Held, "A Faithful Lover in an Old Babylonian Dialogue," JCS 15 [1961]: 15). See Targ. Jon.; Ibn Ezra; Ralbag.

43. Abravanel, 265 col. 2; Leibovitch and Licht in EM 4:795. According to an Italian proverb, "The eye is blind if the mind is troubled."

44. Cf. Meg. 24b.

45. For *g-z-l* see R. Westbrook, *Studies in Biblical and Cuneiform Law* (Paris: Gabalda, 1988), chap. 1; J. C. Greenfield, "Some Phoenician Words," *Semitica* 38 (1990): 156. Conceivably the paragraph refers to the acts of raiders (see the use of *g-z-l* and *'-sh-k* in Judg. 9:25; 21:23; Jer. 50:33).

46. Exod. 2:17; 2 Sam. 14:4; 2 Kings. 6:26; Ps. 72:4; Judg. 3:9,15; 6:36; 1 Sam. 9:16.

47. Amos 5:11; Mic. 6:15; Zeph. 1:13; cf. Jer. 6:12; 8:10; Hag. 1:6; see also the promises in Isa. 62:8–9; 65:21–22.

48. Isa. 13:16; Zech. 14:2; cf. Lam. 5:11 (different verb: *'innu*).

49. SP reads *yishkav 'immah*.

50. Num. 16:15; 1 Sam. 12:3; ANET, 280b; cf. Job 24:3.

51. M. Gruber, *Aspects of Nonverbal Communication* (Rome: Biblical Institute Press, 1980), 386–400. See esp. Lam. 2:11 and, for the use of *k-l-h*, 1 Kings 17:14,16.

52. See Gen. 31:29; Mic. 2:1; Prov. 3:27; Neh. 5:5.

53. Ibn Janah, *Sefer Ha-Shorashim*, and Radak, *Sefer Ha-Shorashim*, s.v. *'-y-l*; Rashi and Ibn Ezra at Gen. 31:29 (see comment of A. Weiser, *Perushei Ha-Torah le-Rabbenu 'Avraham 'ibn 'Ezra* [Jerusalem: Mosad Harav Kook, 1976] on Ibn Ezra ad loc.); Shadal at Gen. 31:29.

54. Cf. Isa. 45:1, in which divine assistance is expressed by God "holding one's hand to" do something (see also 41:13). Some modern scholars believe that the key phrase in the idiom is *'el yad*, "the god of the hand" or "the god (who stands or goes) at one's side," meaning the spirit behind one's ability, or one's protective deity (Akk. *il idi* [see CAD I/J, 100d]). If so, the full idiom means "the god of so-and-so's hand/at so-and-so's side has (the power) to . . ." (C. Brockelmann, "'el yadi," ZAW 26 [1906]: 29ff.; Weinfeld, in *Entsiklopedia 'Olam Ha-Tanakh: Bere'shit* [Tel Aviv: Revivim, 1982], 186). In that case, the idiom would be a survival from a pre-monotheistic stage of Hebrew (cf. Comment to 7:13). However, construing *'el yad* as a construct phrase is contrary to the MT punctuation, and in three of five cases there is no complementary infinitive verb.

55. Job 2:7. The first phrase also appears in Aramaic in 4QPrNab; see J. Fitzmyer and D. J. Harrington, *A Manual of Palestinian Aramaic Texts* (Rome: Biblical Institute Press, 1978), 2–3, no. 2; F. M. Cross, "Fragments of the Prayer of Nabonidus," IEJ 34 (1984): 260–264.

56. See Preuss, *Biblical and Talmudic Medicine*, 339–343;

Smith; Driver; Hoffmann; the possibility of psoriasis was suggested by Frank Kern, M.D., a dermatologist.

57. 1 Chron. 5:6,22,26; 8:6–7; 2 Kings 15:29; 16:9; 17:6; 24:15–16; 25:7,11,21; Amos 1:6,9; Nah. 3:10; Joel 4:4–8; ANET, 283c, 284a and d, 285a, 288a, 308c. On deportation, see B. Oded, *Mass Deportations and Deportees in the Neo-Assyrian Empire* (Wiesbaden: Reichert, 1979).

58. See also Lam. 4:20; Hos. 13:10–11. Conceivably, but less likely, the phrase reflects the human, rather than divine, appointment of kings, against which Hosea complains in Hos. 8:4.

59. See 2 Kings 17:4; 23:33; 24:8–16; 25:6–7; Jer. 22:10–12; 52:11; ANET, 308c.

60. Jer. 18:16; Jer. 49:17.

61. For the first view see Comment to 6:7; Ibn Janaḥ, *Sefer Ha-Shorashim*; Radak, *Sefer Ha-Shorashim*; Rashbam. For the second view see Driver.

62. 2 Kings 17:6; 25:11; Isa. 11:11; Jer. 40:11; 41:16–chap. 44; Obad. 20; Est. 3:8.

63. W. Linsenmaier, *Insects of the World* (New York: McGraw-Hill, 1972), 78–79. See Exod. 10:1–20; Joel 1–2; Y. Palmoni, s.v. "Locust," IDB 3:144–148.

64. Desmia funeralis, Eudemis botrana, or Polychrosis botrana. See Dalman 4:296, 304–305; A. J. Winckler, s.v. "Pests and Diseases," EB 10 (1966): 691; Driver. Heb. *toleʿah*, "worm" = Akk. *túltu*, which is listed along with other pests; see AHw, s.v. *túltu*; CAD, s.v. *mubattiru*; cf. Tawil, "Curse," 59–62.

65. 2 Sam. 12:20; 14:2; Ruth 3:3; Eccl. 9:8.

66. See also Jer. 5:17.

67. Suggestion of Dr. Daniel Otte, Philadelphia Academy of Natural Sciences.

68. The *piʿel* form of the verb (*yeyaresh*) is unparalleled (possibly excepting Judg. 14:15), but the *kal* form is used to express the idea that abandoned land will be taken over by birds and weeds (Isa. 34:11; Hos. 9:6).

69. For identification as the mole-cricket (Gryllotalpa), see I. Aharoni, "Animals Mentioned in the Bible," *Osiris* 5 (1938): 478; cf. R. D. Alexander, s.v. "Cricket," EB (1966 edition) 6:753.

70. Cf. Dillmann; McCarthy, *Treaty and Covenant*, 178; Mayes; Seitz, *Redaktionsgeschichtliche Studien*, 263–264.

71. Hoffmann; Abravanel. The NJPS translation implies that the disasters would mark all future generations as guilty, which would not be true. They are rather signs that will be carried by the guilty and their descendants.

72. Rashbam; R. Meyuḥas; Abravanel.

73. Cf. *'ot* meaning "warning," "lesson," in Num. 17:3,25; cf. Ezek. 14:8.

74. Abravanel, 267c; Ehrlich, *Randglossen*.

75. Mid. Hag.; cf. Abravanel; Hoffmann.

76. See Gen. 27:40; Lev. 26:13; 1 Kings 12:9,11; Jer. 2:20; 5:5; 27:8,11,12; 28:2,4,11,14; C. U. Wolf, s.v. "Yoke," IDB 4:924–925; CAD N2, 262–263; Weinfeld, DDS, 84 n. 4; idem, "The Loyalty Oath in the Ancient Near East," UF 8 (1976): 406.

77. Isa. 5:26; 33:19; Jer. 5:15.

78. Hab. 1:8; cf. Jer. 48:40; 49:22; Job 9:26; 39:29–30. See Abravanel; Hoffmann; Driver; Craigie; M. Greenberg, *Ezekiel 1–20* (Garden City, N.Y.: Doubleday, 1983), at 17:3.

79. Dan. 8:23; cf. Prov. 7:13; 21:29.

80. For *'oz* meaning "anger" see Eccl. 8:1; Ezra 8:22; Y. Muffs, *Love and Joy* (New York: Jewish Theological Seminary, 1992), 103–105; cf. Akk. *uzzat pani* in BWL 200–201, IV, 4.

81. Ezek. 2:4 (see Greenberg, *Ezekiel 1–20*, ad loc.); cf. Smith.

82. Craigie.

83. Isa. 13:18; 47:6; Lam. 4:16; 5:12–13.

84. Root *ts-r-r*, "restrict," "be restricted." The verb is not from *ts-w-r*, "besiege," although in this case it amounts to the same thing.

85. This clause duplicates parts of the first half of the verse.

Possibly, a scribe copied these words over by accident; or, it may be a variant version of part of the first half of the verse. It joins the two phrases "in all your towns" and "in all your land," which are separated in the first half of the verse (this is not visible in the translation). Without this clause the verse would read: "It shall press you in all your towns until every mighty, towering wall in which you trust has come down in all your land that the LORD your God has assigned to you."

86. Cannibalism in Jerusalem and Samaria: 2 Kings 6:28–29; Isa. 9:19; Lam. 2:20; 4:10; from the final siege of Second Temple Jerusalem: Josephus, War 6.201–213; Lam. R. 1:51 (to 1:16); and Sifra Be-Ḥukotai 6:3 (Weiss, 112a).

87. For cannibalism see ANET, 298c, 300a; D. D. Luckenbill, *Ancient Records of Assyria and Babylonia* (Chicago: University of Chicago Press, 1926–27), 2:794; treaty curses and predictions cited in Excursus 27; and the mythological reference in ANET, 105d. For families turning against each other see Josephus, War 5.429–430, and the literary references in ANET, 105d, 459d; and CT 13, 49, cited by A. L. Oppenheim, "Siege Documents from Nippur," *Iraq* 17 (1955): 77–78.

88. Cf. Song 3:9; Mish. Sot. 9:4; S. E. Loewenstamm, s.v. *'apiryon*, EM 1:505. According to Lam. R. 1:47 (to 1:16), the verse refers to a woman for whom tapestry was spread to protect her feet from exposure or scraping on the ground.

89. Lit., "she will be mean to" her husband and children "with regard to her afterbirth and her newborn babies." See Rashbam; Bekhor Shor; Ehrlich, *Mikra*.

90. Cf. Craigie, 350; McCarthy, *Treaty and Covenant*, 179.

91. Daʿat Soferim.

92. Pss. 5:12; 54:8; 61:6; 145:1,2; contrast Mal. 1:6; Isa. 52:5; Ps. 74:10,18.

93. See L. I. Rabinowitz, s.v. "God, Names of," in EncJud 7:683; contrast B. Epstein, *Tosefet Berakhah* (Pinsk, 1937; reprint, Tel Aviv: Moreshet, 1981), ad loc.

94. Josephus, War 5.571; 6.197–198.

95. Abravanel, 269; see Lev. 26:25–26; Jer. 14:18; 21:1–9; 32:1–2,24; 38:2; Ezek. 5:12; 7:15; C. Duffy, *Siege Warfare*, vol. 1 (London: Routledge and Kegan Paul, 1979), 253; H. E. Salisbury, *The 900 Days: The Siege of Leningrad* (New York: Harper and Row, 1969), 376–377, 492, 507.

96. Saadia; Ibn Ezra; Rashbam; Kaspi; R. Meyuḥas.

97. Bekhor Shor; Kaspi.

98. J. J. Finkelstein, "The Genealogy of the Hammurapi Dynasty," JCS 20 (1966): 95, 97.

99. Yohanan Muffs, noting Saadia's translation *qasada* and the similar usage of *sis* in 30:9 and Jer. 32:41 (Jeremiah uses *shaked*, "be watchful," in the parallel passages 31:27–28; 44:27). This volitional sense of *sis*, "delight," corresponds to the same nuance of other terms with the same basic meaning; see Muffs, *Love and Joy*, 121–193; idem, "The Lesson of the Almond Tree," in *Proceedings of the Rabbinical Assembly* 56 (1994; published 1995): 32-34. Cf. Keter Torah here.

100. From *n-s-ḥ*. The cognate verb *nasāḥu* has this sense in Akkadian. See CAD N2, 3d–4b, 14d; M. Held, "The Terms for Deportation in the OB Royal Inscriptions with Special Reference to Yaḥdunlim," JANES 11 (79): 53–67.

101. M. Gruber, "Hebrew *da'abon nepeš* 'Dryness of Throat,'" VT 37 (1987): 365–369. See esp. Ps. 69:4, and cf. Ps. 88:10.

102. Abravanel, 270.

103. Gen. 12:10; 26:1–2; 45:9–11; cf. ANET, 259b, 446a.

104. Meklenburg; NEB; Mayes; cf. NJPS at Isa. 43:14. This interpretation requires revocalizing *bo-'oniyyot* to *ba-'aniyyot*. For the singular see Isa. 29:2; Lam. 2:5; for the abstract form see GKC §124d-f; B. K. Waltke and M. O'Connor, *Biblical Hebrew Syntax* (Winona Lake, Ind.: Eisenbrauns, 1990), §7.4.2.

105. Abravanel, 270.

106. R. Meyuḥas; Ehrlich, *Mikra*; Bekhor Shor; Abravanel.

107. Cf. Lev. 23:37–38; 26:46; Num. 29:39.

108. Abravanel, 7, 271–272; Dillmann; Rofé, *Mavo'*, 178–180; KJV and RSV agree. The reading "And these" at the beginning of v. 69 in SP (von Gall; also reflected in one LXX manuscript and the Ethiopic translation) also implies that the verse introduces what follows, although SP's paragraph divisions connect it with chap. 28. The standard editions of LXX (Rahlfs), Vulg., and Pesh., which number this verse as 29:1, reflect the same interpretation (the Cambridge and Göttingen editions of LXX give both numbering systems).

109. Cf. Exod. 34:28; Deut. 29:8; 2 Kings 23:3; Jer. 11:2,3,6,8; 34:18. See Driver; Hoffmann; Mayes.

110. Moffatt and AT, which number the verse as 29:1, connect it with chap. 28 by translating: "These/Such were the terms. . . ." The issue is summarized well by Smith.

Chapter 29

1. Hebrew texts divide the text of chaps. 29–30 before 29:1,9 (M, SP), 13 and 21 (SP); 30:1,11, and 15 (M and SP), and after 30:20 (M).

2. See particularly 1:30; 2:32–3:6; 4:34; 7:18–19; 8:2–4; 11:2–7.

3. Bekhor Shor at v. 15.

4. "Heart" and "eyes" commonly refer to mental faculties in Hebrew, while "ears" signify "understanding" in Akkadian. Cf. 6:5; Gen. 3:5,7; for "ears" in Akkadian see AHw, s.v. *uznu*. For the same triad see Isa. 6:10; 32:3–4a; Jer. 5:21. On "heart" see Maimonides, Guide 1.39.

5. Ibn Ezra.

6. Av. Zar. 5b; Rashi; Rashbam; Malbim; Bekhor Shor seems to present both possibilities.

7. Mid. Hag.; Ḥazzekuni; R. Meyuḥas.

8. Ibn Ezra.

9. Malbim; Ehrlich, *Mikra*.

10. Abravanel.

11. Hoffmann, based on Shab. 104a and parallels; cf. Malbim.

12. Cf. N. Leibowitz, *Studies in Devarim* (Jerusalem: World Zionist Organization, 1980), 287–293.

13. Exod. 16; 17:1–7; Num. 11:31–32.

14. See 1 Kings 20:13,28; Isa. 52:6; Jer. 16:21; Sarna, *Exodus*, at Exod. 6:3; Rofé, *Mavo'*, 180.

15. *'Ani* appears only in 12:30 and in the non-Deuteronomic verses 32:21,39,49,52.

16. ANET, 532–533, 540–541.

17. Weinfeld, DDS, 103 and s.v. *berit*, TDOT 2:262–264; J. C. Greenfield, "An Ancient Treaty Ritual and its Targumic Echo," in *Salvación en la Palabra . . . Homenaje al Profesor Alejandro Diez Macho* (Madrid: Ediciones Cristiandad, 1986), 391–397.

18. See Comment to 5:2; Rashi; Bekhor Shor; Radak; Driver, 323n. See Abravanel, 278, for other suggestions about the ceremony.

19. Mayes.

20. Driver. Cf. the use of *hityatsev* in Josh. 24:1; 1 Sam. 10:19.

21. The translation "your tribal heads" understands Heb. *ro'sheikhem shivteikhem* as equivalent to, or a scribal error for, *ro'shei shivteikhem* in 5:20 (see LXX; Peshitta; Rashi; Ibn Ezra; Ḥazzekuni; cf. Ehrlich, *Mikra*, and F. Perles, *Analekten zur Textkritik des Alten Testaments* [Munich: Theodor Ackermann, 1895], 53). Literally, the phrase means "your heads, your tribes" or "your heads, your staffs" (*shevet*, "staff," acquired the meaning "tribe" by metonymy because of the use of staffs as tribal insignias). Others take the two words separately, "your heads, that is, your staff-holders" (in other words, "rulers" who hold the staff as an emblem of authority; see Meklenburg; Luzzatto at Gen. 49:16; cf. Sarna, *Genesis* at 49:10 on *meḥokek*). Yet an-

other possibility is that *shivteikhem* is either a variant form of *shofteikhem*, "your judges" or "your chieftains," or a scribal error for it. If that is the sense, the verse would resemble Joshua 24:1: "Joshua assembled all the tribes of Israel. . . . He summoned Israel's elders and *heads, judges/chieftains* and officers; and they presented themselves before God." See also Comment to 33:5, where "*shivtei* Israel" is parallel to "heads of the people." See Z. W. Falk, "Ruler and Judge" (Hebrew), *Leshonenu* 30 (1965–66): 243–247; S. E. Loewenstamm, *Comparative Studies in Biblical and Ancient Oriental Literatures* (Kevelaer: Butzon and Bercker, and Neukirchen-Vluyn: Neukirchener Verlag, 1980), 270–272; C. Begg, "The Reading *Šbty(km)* in Deut. 29:9 and 2 Sam. 7:7," *Ephemerides Theologicae Lovanienses* 58 (1982): 87–105; S. Gevirtz, "On Hebrew *Šebeṭ* = 'Judge,'" in G. Rendsburg et al., eds., *The Bible World: Essays . . . C. H. Gordon* (New York: Ktav, 1980), 61–66.

22. See 2 Kings 23; Neh. 8:1–3; 10:15,29–30; Weinfeld, DDS, 87, 101.

23. Cf. Exod. 19:7,15; 24:3,7–8; Weinfeld, DDS, 291.

24. Cf. Deut. 1:16; 5:14; 14:29; 16:11,14; 24:14,17,19–21; 26:11–13; 27:19; 31:12. See Milgrom, *Numbers*, Excursus 34.

25. See "Inanna and Shukaletudda" (S. N. Kramer, *History Begins at Sumer* [Garden City, N.Y.: Doubleday, 1959], 73); KRT A, iii, 112–113; iv, 214–v, 1 (ANET, 144–145); W. F. Edgerton, "The Strikes in Ramses III's Twenty-Ninth Year," JNES 10 (1951): 142–143.

26. Cf. Gen. 26:28; Num. 5:21–28; Ezek. 16:59; 17:13,18; Neh. 10:30. See Sifra (Weiss 22b, top); Tanḥuma Nitsavim 3; Abravanel, 278; H. C. Brichto, *The Problem of "Curse" in the Hebrew Bible* (Philadelphia: Society of Biblical Literature, 1963), chap. 2; J. Scharbert, s.v. *'alah*, TDOT 1:261–266; Weinfeld, DDS, 62 n. 7; and idem, s.v. *berit*, TDOT 2:256.

27. Tanḥuma Nitsavim 3; Rashi; Ibn Ezra; Bekhor Shor.

28. VTE §§1, 57 (ANET, 534c, 539b); Sefire IA (ANET, 659c).

29. See also, e.g., Num. 25:1–3; Josh. 24:14; Ezek. 20:7.

30. For the disparaging noun see 1 Kings 11:5,7; 2 Kings 23:13. For the verb see Lev. 11:11,13,43. For such disparaging terms see S. Paul, s.v. "Euphemism and Dysphemism," EncJud 6:959–961; M. H. Pope, s.v. "Bible, Euphemism and Dysphemism in," ABD 1:720–725.

31. The noun appears in, e.g., Lev. 26:30; 1 Kings 15:12; Ezek. 6:4.

32. G. A. Cooke, *A Text-book of North Semitic Inscriptions* (Oxford: Clarendon, 1903), 314 l. 11, 321 l. (9) 22, and 334; BDB, 1122a; M. Greenberg, *Ezekiel 1–20* (Garden City, N.Y.: Doubleday, 1983) at 6:4; cf. Aramaic *'even gelal*, "*gelal*-stone," in Ezra. 5:8; 6:4. See H.G.M. Williamson "'*eben gelal* (Ezra 5:8; 6:4) Again," BASOR 280 (1990): 83–88. As a loan-word in Akkadian, *galālu* refers to a type of stone on which inscriptions and pictures are carved (CAD G, 11).

33. Rashi; Ibn Janaḥ, *Sefer Ha-Shorashim*; Radak, *Sefer Ha-Shorashim*; H. D. Preuss, s.v. *gillûlim*, TDOT 3:1–5. See Zeph. 1:17 (cf. Ezek. 4:12,15; Job 20:7).

34. Weinfeld, "The Emergence of the Deuteronomic Movement: The Historical Antecedents," in N. Lohfink, ed., *Das Deuteronomium* (Leuven: Leuven University Press, 1985), 80; idem, DDS, 92.

35. See J. C. Trever, s.v. "Wormwood" and s.v. "Gall," IDB 4:878–879 and 2:350; and M. Zohari, s.v. *ro'sh* and s.v. *la'anah*, EM 7:299–301 and 4:526–527. Cf. Jer. 9:14; 23:15.

36. Heb. *shoresh* usually means "root." The translation "stock" is based on passages in which *shoresh*, or its plural *shorashim*, is the part of a tree from which new branches grow after it has been cut down. See 2 Kings 19:30; Isa. 10:33–11:1; Job 14:7–9; and H. L. Ginsberg, "'Roots Below and Fruit Above' and Related Matters," in D. W. Thomas and W. D. McHardy, eds., *Hebrew and Semitic Studies Presented to G. R. Driver* (Oxford: Clarendon, 1963), 72–76.

37. Thus essentially Rashi; Saadia. This is an example of the "estimative-declarative reflexive"; see GKC §54d; B. K. Waltke and M. O'Connor, *Biblical Hebrew Syntax* (Winona Lake, Ind.: Eisenbrauns, 1990), §28.2f (cf. §§20.21m; 24.2g).

38. Ramban; cf. Bekhor Shor.

39. Judah Halevi, cited by Ibn Ezra; Sforno; Ḥazzekuni; Ehrlich, *Randglossen*, cf. Brichto, *The Problem of "Curse"*, 29 n. 14.

40. See, e.g., Gen. 29:6; Job 5:24; 8:6; 9:4; Ps. 38:4.

41. See Jer. 7:24; 18:12; Ps. 81:13.

42. Based on Arab. *sarirat*, "secret thought." See L. Kopf, "Arabische Etymologien und Parallelen," VT 9 (1959): 283 (see H. Wehr, *A Dictionary of Modern Written Arabic* [Ithaca, N.Y.: Cornell University Press, 1966], 405b). Cf. Targ. Onk.

43. From *shur/sh-r-r*, "see." So Rashi; Radak, *Sefer Ha-Shorashim*, s.v. *sh-r-r*.

44. Based on Aram. *sharir*, "firm." So Ramban; view cited by Radak, *Sefer Ha-Shorashim*, s.v. *sh-r-r*.

45. Driver, comparing Isa. 28:15, "we have made lies our refuge." Cf. 13:3.

46. E.g., Dillmann; NJPS translators. For Moses introducing his own comment into a quotation, see 13:3,7.

47. Jer. 17:6–8. See LXX; cf. Ibn Janaḥ; Ibn Ezra; Judah Halevi cited by Ibn Ezra.

48. Cf. Leeser: "In order that the indulgence of the passions may appease the thirst [for them]."

49. Driver.

50. See 1QS 2:12–16; CD 1:15–16; Rofé, *Mavo'*, 184 n. 29; 197; idem, "Qumranic Paraphrases, the Greek Deuteronomy and the Late History of the Biblcal *nasi*'," *Textus* 14 (1988): 167–169. 4QDeut^c also reads *davkah*.

51. 1 Kings 9:8–9; Jer. 22:8–9 (cf. 5:19; 16:10–13).

52. ANET, 297d, 300a (translation modified); cf. 533c, end of §v. See D. E. Skweres, "Das Motiv der Strafgrunderfragung in Biblischen Texten und Neuassyrischen Texten," BZ 14 (1970): 181–197; P. Vargyas, "Le cylindre de Rassam et la Bible," *Oikumene* 3 (1982): 157–162; B. O. Long, "Two Question and Answer Schemata in the Prophets," JBL 90 (1971): 129–139.

53. Some scholars regard vv. 21–27 as derived from a separate source, or as an interpolation, focusing on the nation as a whole. See Jon D. Levenson, "Who Inserted the Book of the Torah?" HTR 68 (1975): 208; A.D.H. Mayes, "Deuteronomy 4 and the Literary Criticism of Deuteronomy," JBL 100 (1981): 50–51; Rofé, *Mavo'*, 178–197. According to this view, this section is from the exilic period (Rofé argues that it is from after the exile of the northern kingdom; cf. below n. 55). I think that a date after either exile is unlikely unless it can be proved that the land *was* denuded by sulfur and salt and became infertile (Yoma 54a says that it was, for seven years).

54. Pss. 38:14; 78:4,6.

55. Mish. Sanh. 10:3; Tosef. Sanh. 13:12; Sanh. 110b and Rashi on the Mishnah there.

56. Heb. *serefah*, "devastated," is literally "something scorched." Sulfur and salt would not literally scorch the soil but would denude it as a fire would. Or the word may refer to the withering or burning effect salt and sulfur could have on vegetation. See E. P. Deatrick, "Salt, Soil, Savior," BA 25 (1962): 45; M. J. Dietz, *10,000 Garden Questions Answered* (New York: Harper and Row, 1982), 1196: "In very hot weather sulfur should be used [as a fungicide] cautiously, for it is apt to burn the plants."

57. Judg. 9:45. Near Eastern examples are cited by S. Gevirtz, "Jericho and Shechem: A Religio-Literary Aspect of City Destruction," VT 13 (1963): 52–62; Weinfeld, DDS, 109ff. Carthage and later Italian examples are cited by G. F. Moore and C. F. Burney in their commentaries at Judges 9:45. However, the idea that Carthage was salted at the end of the Punic Wars is an invention of modern historians who mistakenly transferred the idea from Judg. 9:45; see R. T. Ridley, "To Be Taken with a Pinch of Salt: The Destruction of Carthage," *Classical Philology* 81 (1986): 140–146 (ref. courtesy of Robert E.A. Palmer).

58. Sefire I, A, 35–36 (ANET, 660a). Cf. Jer. 17:6; Ps. 107:34.

59. Cf. n. 56; Job 18:15.

60. Translation based on J. C. Greenfield, "A Hapax Legomenon: *mimsak ḥarul*," in S. R. Brunswick, ed., *Studies in Judaica, Karaitica, and Islamica Presented to Leon Nemoy* (Ramat Gan: Bar Ilan University Press, 1982), 79–82. Cf. Jer. 49:18.

61. Gen. 10:19; 14:2,8; Hos. 11:8. Cf. Jer. 49:18; 50:40.

62. I. Yeivin, s.v. "Masorah," EM 5:133. Collections of midrashic explanations of majuscules and miniscules are reprinted in J. Eisenstein, *Ozar Midrashim* (reprint, Israel: 1969), 2:432–433.

63. Cited by Hoffmann.

64. Rashi; Bekhor Shor; Ḥazzekuni; Shadal; MdRY Ba-Ḥodesh 5 (Lauterbach 2:230–231); cf. Abravanel, Nitsavim, question 11.

65. Rashi; Ḥazzekuni; Tanḥuma *Nitsavim* 2; MdRY Ba-Ḥodesh 5 (Lauterbach 2:230–231); cf. Sanh. 27b; E. E. Urbach, *The Sages* (Cambridge: Harvard University Press, 1987), 539.

66. Cf. Ibn Ezra; Rashbam at 27:15.

67. Maimonides, cited by Baḥya (cf. Abravanel, Nitsavim, question 10; defended by Meklenburg).

68. Driver; Wright; Moran; Craigie; Mayes.

69. R. Butin, *The Ten Nequdoth of the Torah* (reprint, New York: Ktav, 1969); Lieberman, HJP, 43–46; E. Tov, *Textual Criticism of the Hebrew Bible* (Minneapolis: Fortress Press, 1992), 55–57, 213. According to a talmudic tradition, the dots indicate uncertainty as to whether these words should be retained in Deuteronomy (ARN1 chap. 34; Lekaḥ Tov cited by Butin, *Ten Nequdoth*, 130 no. 8).

70. Sanh. 43b; Rashi; Bekhor Shor; Ḥazzekuni; Hoffmann.

Chapter 30

1. See Mayes; Abravanel, 283; N. Leibowitz, *Studies in Devarim* (Jerusalem: World Zionist Organization, 1980), 310–320.

2. Bekhor Shor; Abravanel; Meyuḥas; Kaspi; Ralbag; Hoffmann; Mayes. Cf. Josh. 23:14–16; 24:20.

3. See Ezek. 16:53 and 55, where the result of *shav shevit* is *tashovna le-kadmatan*, "they shall return to their former state." *Shav shevut/shevit* stands for *heshiv shivah*, "return a return," that is, "restore." See Driver; Shadal; Ehrlich; J. C. Greenfield, "Stylistic Aspects of the Sefire Treaty Inscription," *Acta Orientalia* 29 (1965): 4. It is not clear why, when God is the subject, the verb is usually in the *kal* form *shav*, which is normally intransitive (see, however, Nah. 2:3), nor why the noun is almost always in the form *shevut* or *shevit* (the expected forms *heshiv* [*hiphʿil*] or *shivah* do appear in some passages, such as Jer. 33:7,11,26; Ps. 126:1; equivalents of both appear together in the Aramaic form of the idiom, *hashib shibat*, Sefire 3:24–25 [ANET, 660b]). Perhaps it is because *shav shevut* is more alliterative than *heshiv shivah*. It is possible, moreover, that in biblical times the idiom was pronounced *shav shavut* even when the latter word has a suffix, as here.

4. Meg. 29a; MdRY Pisha 14 (Lauterbach 1:114–115); Bekhor Shor; B. Epstein, *Tosefet Berakhah* (Pinsk, 1937; reprint, Tel Aviv: Moreshet, 1981). E. Z. Melamed argues that this explanation is essentially correct (*Biblical Studies in Texts, Translations and Commentators* [Hebrew] [Jerusalem: Magnes Press, 1984], 131–136), but see the next note.

5. From *sh-b-h*, "capture" (thus Targ. Onk.). That the idiom has nothing to do with the return of captives (which *is* mentioned later) is clear from Job 42:10 and Ezek. 16:53, which use it with reference to Job and Sodom, which were never captured. *Shevut/shevit* is actually from *shuv* (Shadal compares *lazut* from *luz*). The form *shivah* (Aram. *shibat*) is used in Ps.

126:1 and in the Sefire inscription (SP's reading here, *shuvatakh*, is an alternative version of the same form).

6. Heb. *veriḥamkha*, usually rendered "have compassion on you." The translation "take back in love" understands *riḥam* (in *piʿel*) as "love" in the sense of "accept," "acknowledge as one's own." *R-ḥ-m* means "love" in the *kal* conjugation in Ps. 18:2 and in Aramaic. It usually does not have this sense in the *piʿel*. H. L. Ginsberg holds that it does in Hos. 1:6; 2:3,6, and 25, comparing Jer. 12:15; 31:20; 33:26 and the usage of *ʾahav* in Mal. 1:2–3 (Ginsberg, unpublished notes on Hosea, 1965; see NJPS at all those passages, and cf. the use of Aram. *r-ḥ-m* in Aḥikar line 1:11 [AP, 212]; cf. H. J. Stoebe, s.v. *r-ḥ-m*, in E. Jenni and C. Westermann, eds., *Theologisches Handwörterbuch zum Alten Testament*, [Munich: Chr. Kaiser, 1976], 2:763). This translation may be supported by the fact that the verb *follows* "restore your fortunes" rather than *preceding* it as one might have expected if it meant "have compassion." Nevertheless, in view of 13:18 (cf. Isa. 55:7), it cannot be regarded as certain.

7. Bekhor Shor and Ramban, citing Shab. 104a and parallels; Y. Muffs, *Love and Joy*, (New York: Jewish Theological Seminary, 1992), 17; cf. Von Rad.

8. Hos. 2:21; Jer. 24:7; 31:31–34; 32:38–41; Ezek. 11:19–20; 36:25–28. See Ramban; Abravanel, 283–284, argues that God will only remove wrongful appetites from Israel, but not their freedom of choice (cf. 284, end).

9. Job 28:12–28; Eccl. 7:23. See Weinfeld, DDS, 257–260, 264; Thompson.

10. Eccl. 7:23.

11. Contrast "the mind of the god, like the center of the heavens, is remote" ("The Babylonian Theodicy," §XXIV, in ANET, 604a).

12. ANET, 48c, 79d, 438d. See J. Tigay, *The Evolution of the Gilgamesh Epic* (Philadelphia: University of Pennsylvania Press, 1982), 164–165.

13. BM 59b; see E. Berkovits, *Not in Heaven: The Nature and Function of Halakha* (New York: Ktav, 1983).

14. Deut. R. 8:6. Cf. Maimonides, Hilkhot Yesodei Ha-Torah 9:1; Sforno at v. 8 here: future observance of "all His commandments that I enjoin upon you this day" shows that in messianic times the Religion/Law (*dat*) will not be revised.

15. See the texts cited in CAD E, 11cd, such as *Enuma Elish* 7:74, 128; *Gilgamesh Epic* 10:2:22–23; 10:5:27 (ANET, 71b, 72b, 91b, 92d).

16. R. Meyuḥas.

17. Cf. 6:7; 11:19; Isa. 59:21. For "place in the mouth" meaning "teach," probably by heart, see Excursus 28.

18. On the structure of vv. 15–18 see Ibn Ezra; Bekhor Shor. Cf. 11:26–28.

19. Leibowitz, *Studies in Devarim*, 313–315.

20. Ibn Ezra; Sforno. Cf. 26:11 ("bounty").

21. At the beginning of the verse, LXX has the additional clause "If you obey the commandments of the Lord your God," and then continues "*which* I command you." Since LXX takes *ʾasher* in its most common meaning, "which," it requires the additional phrase at the beginning of the verse. If the reading is original, the second part of the verse must be rendered "then you shall thrive and increase, and the LORD . . . will bless you." However, "for" is also a legitimate translation of *ʾasher*. See Gen. 42:21; Josh. 22:31; 1 Sam. 15:15; 1 Kings 15:5; Hos. 14:4; Zech. 1:15; BDB, 83c, §8c; GKC §158b. Another possible rendering would be "In that, inasmuch as I command you" (Smith), as in Josh. 22:31; 2 Kings 17:4.

22. According to Ibn Ezra and Shadal, *huʾ* here means "He," meaning "He [God] is your life." Cf. the Egyptian Hymn to Aten, l. 101: "Thou art lifetime thy own self, For one lives (only) through thee" (ANET, 371b). However, 32:47 and Prov. 4:13 support the NJPS translation.

Chapter 31

1. Hebrew texts have breaks before 31:1 (M), 7 (M, SP), 9 (SP), 14 (M, SP), 16,19,22,25, and 30 (SP), and after v. 30 (M).

2. Note esp. the phrases: "The LORD . . . will cross over before you," "[He] marches with you," "will be with you," "will not fail you or forsake you," "Be strong and resolute," "Be not in fear or dread of them," "Fear not and be not dismayed." Cf. 1:21,29–31; 2:24–25,31; 3:2,21–22; 7:17–24; 9:1–6; 11:22–25; Josh. 10:25; 2 Sam. 10:12; 13:28; 2 Chron. 32:7. See Weinfeld, DDS, 45–51.

3. See, e.g., Gen. 20:8; 44:6; Num. 14:39; Deut. 5:19; 6:6; 12:28; 32:45. Only in instructions to prophets does this phrase sometimes refer to words about to be spoken (Jer. 3:12; 11:6).

4. *V-y-k-l m-sh-h l-d-b-r* (instead of MT's *v-y-l-k m-sh-h v-y-d-b-r*), 1QDeut[b] (1Q5), fragment 13 (DJD 1, p. 59). This reading is reflected in LXX.

5. Ehrlich, *Randglossen*; Smith; Rofé, *Mavoʾ*, 208. For another view cf. Tur-Sinai.

6. If v. 3a is an interpolation, vv. 4–6 may be one, too. See Rofé, *Mavoʾ*, 208.

7. Gen. 21:22; 26:3,28; 28:15,20; 39:2–3; Judg. 6:13; Isa. 8:10.

8. Exod. 3:12; Josh. 1:5,9; Judg. 6:12; Jer. 1:8,19.

9. Some scholars believe that the terms Moses addresses to Joshua are formulas of appointment to office. Technically, this is not so, since the same terms are often used in other circumstances (see v. 6; Josh. 8:1; 10:25; Weinfeld, DDS, 45 n. 5). Nevertheless, addressing them to Joshua publicly in the present situation has the effect of such a formula; see also v. 23 and Josh. 1:5–9,18.

10. Graphically "go" *tavo* and "bring" *tavi* are almost identical, and SP and some medieval manuscripts of the Torah read "bring" in both verses; Targ. Neof., a manuscript of Targ. Onk., Vulg., Pesh., and Samaritan Targ. render likewise (cf. Driver; B. Grossfeld, "Targum Neofiti 1 to Deut. 31:7," JBL 91 [1972]: 533–534; idem, "Neofiti 1 to Deut. 31:7—The Problem Re-analyzed," *Australian Biblical Review* 24 [1976]: 30–34; M. Klein, "Deut. 31:7, *tavo* or *tavi*'?" JBL 92 [1973]: 584–585). However, MT is supported by 1:38 as well as LXX, Targ. Onk., and Targ. Jon., and the reading "bring" is probably due to a common scribal tendency to harmonize inconsistent verses.

11. Mish. Sot. 7:8; Bekhor Shor, Ḥazzekuni; cf. Weinfeld, DDS, 65 n. 1; Rofé, *Mavoʾ*, 210; cf. King Josiah's reading of "the covenant scroll" in 2 Kings 23:2.

12. Josephus, Ant. 4.209. In Neh. 8:1–8 the priest-scribe Ezra reads the Torah to the public, though it is his scribal role that is made explicit there, and he may have been assisted by others who were not priests.

13. In 4QDeut[b] and LXX the verb is plural, but that could be the attempt of a scribe to make the verb fit its subject.

14. According to one version, the king reads 1:1–6:3; 6:4–9, and 11:13–21; 14:22–29 and 26:12–15; 17:14–20; and 28 (Mish. Sot. 7:8).

15. Ḥag. 3a; Rashi. Cf. Aristeas §250.

16. See TJ Ḥag. 1:1, 75d. Cf. Ramban here. See also M. Greenberg, *Studies in the Bible and Jewish Thought* (Philadelphia: Jewish Publication Society, 1995), 434–435.

17. So the *vav* is explained by Ehrlich, *Randglossen*.

18. See Exod. 25:22; 29:42; 30:36; Lev. 16:2; Num. 18:1–7 (all passages assigned by critics to the priestly source in the Torah). Rashi and Ibn Ezra, who accept the identification of the Tent with the Tabernacle, say that the Tent of Exodus 33 was Moses' own, and was used for communication only until the Tabernacle was erected.

19. See also Num. 11:16,23–30; 12:4–5. See von Rad, 189; M. Haran, "The Nature of the ''Ohel Moedh' in Pentateuchal Sources," JSS 5 (1960): 50–65; A. Rofé, "Textual Criticism in the Light of Historical-Literary Criticism: Deuteronomy 31:14–15," EI 16 (1982): 173; Milgrom, *Numbers*, Excursus 28. Several mid-

rashim state that there were two separate tents, a tent of worship (*'ohel ha-'avodot*) and an oracular tent (*'ohel ha-dibberot*). See Sifrei Zuta to Num. 18:4; Yal. 1.737; Tanḥ. Pekudei 5 and parallels.

20. *Be-* means "at" in 1 Sam. 29:1; Ezek. 10:15,20. However, this usage is rare.

21. Exod. 19:19; 34:5; Num. 11:25; 12:5. See Weinfeld, DDS, 202.

22. See Sarna, *Genesis*, at Gen. 15:15; 25:8; 47:30; Milgrom, *Numbers*, at Num. 20:24. "Lying" may refer to the conception of the spirits as lying on beds in Sheol, as in Job 3:13.

23. See, e.g., Exod. 34:15–16; Lev. 17:7; 20:5; Judg. 2:17; 8:27,33; Ezek. 6:9; 20:30; Hos. 1:2; 2:7; 3:1.

24. The phrase can hardly refer to alien gods in the midst of the Israelites while Moses is speaking, as if some of the people are currently worshiping foreign gods. The phrase "will thereupon [*ve-kam*] go astray" implies a future sin. If God knows of alien gods currently in Israel's midst, it would be inexplicable that He does not punish Israel now.

25. The position of *be-kirbo*, lit. "in its midst," is ambiguous. It could also refer to the land, meaning: "the alien gods in the midst of the land that they are about to enter into" (Ibn Ezra; *'erets* is masculine in Gen. 13:6; Isa. 9:18). In either case, the word adds little to the verse and is conceivably nothing but a variant for the preceding word, *shamah*, "that" (lit., "where"). In that case, the text preserves two versions of the phrase identifying the land: *'asher hu' ba' shammah/be-kirbo*, "where/into which they are about to enter" (cf. S. Talmon, "Conflate Readings [OT]," IDBS, 170–172). Yet another suggestion is to emend *be-kirbo* to *be-karov*, "soon" (Ehrlich, *Randglossen*).

26. Cf. Isa. 54:7–8; 59:2; Mic. 3:4; Ps. 27:9. See Saadia; Rashi; Ibn Ezra; Ramban; Sforno; Maimonides, *Guide* 1.23; 3.51; Driver; R. Friedman, "The Biblical Expression *mastir pānim*," HAR 1 (1977): 139–147.

27. Lit. "my God/gods"; the people are speaking collectively.

28. So Shadal; Hirsch; Hoffmann. Cf. Gideon's challenge to the angel who assures him of God's support: "If the LORD is with us, why has all this befallen us? . . . Now the LORD has abandoned us and delivered us into the hands of Midian" (Judg. 6:13).

29. See Exod. 8:18; 17:7; 34:9 (see vv. 5–6); Num. 11:20; 14:14,42; Deut. 6:15; 7:21; 23:15; cf. Josh. 3:10 (see v. 9); Jer. 14:9; Mic. 3:11; Zeph. 3:5,15,17; Ps. 46:6 (see v. 8).

30. See Num. 22:18; Deut. 4:5; 18:16; 26:14. This is almost always the case in biblical prose prior to the Persian period (for which see Ezra 9:6; Neh. 6:14; 7:5; 13:14,22; 13:29). In Gen. 31:30 and Judg. 18:24 *'elohai* without YHVH refers to idols.

31. Abravanel, 294; cf. Jer. 44:18.

32. The main text of 4QDeut^c seems to read *YHVH*, with *'elohai* added above the line.

33. The translation follows Ramban. By suggesting that the verse refers to a *continued* hiding of God's face, it seeks to avoid redundancy with the previous verse.

34. Ps. 40:5; cf. Lev. 19:4, 31 (see Levine, *Leviticus*, ad loc.); 20:6; Isa. 45:22; CAD S, 41–42; Weinfeld, DDS, 83 n. 3; for Aramaic see J. C. Greenfield, "Stylistic Aspects of the Sefire Treaty Inscriptions," *Acta Orientalia* 29 (1965): 7. Cf. "Do not turn your eyes to anyone else" in a Hittite treaty, ANET, 204a.

35. For the singing or oral recitation of written Akkadian poems, see J. Tigay, *The Evolution of the Gilgamesh Epic* (Philadelphia: University of Pennsylvania Press, 1982), 107 n. 72.

36. Cf. Ibn Ezra; Eruv. 54a.

37. In the prologue to LH, col. v, line 20 should be translated "I put law and justice in the mouth of the (people of) the land." See Avigdor Hurowitz, *Inu Anum Ṣirum: Literary Structures in the Non-Juridical Sections of Codex Hammurabi* (Philadelphia: [University Museum:] Samuel Noah Kramer Fund, 1994), 27–29.

38. According to Seforno at v. 29, when the disaster comes, the poem will prevent them from thinking that it was an accident; when they realize that it was caused by their behavior, they will repent. Cf. Radak at Gen. 18:19.

39. Bekhor Shor here and at v. 26; Phillips, 207; so essentially Rofé, *Mavo'*, 214.

40. Isa. 30:8 (cf. 8:16); Hab. 2:2–3.

41. Isa. 48:3–5; see also 43:9–13; 44:6–8.

42. God is the subject. Saadia; Rashi; Ramban (contra Ibn Ezra at v. 15).

43. See, e.g., Deut. 24:1; 2 Sam. 11:14,15; 2 Kings 5:5; Jer. 29:1; 32:11,12; the Lachish letters (KAI nos. 193:5,9–11; 195:6–7), and the Sefire inscriptions (KAI nos. 224:4,14,17,23); J. S. Licht, s.v. *sefer*, EM 5:1080–1081; D. Pardee, "An Overview of Ancient Hebrew Epistolography," JBL 97 (1978): 331.

44. See M. Haran, "Scribal Workmanship in Biblical Times," *Tarbiz* 50 (1980–81): 71–72.

45. N. M. Sarna, s.v. "Bible," EncJud 3:821–822; M. Fishbane, "Varia Deuteronomica," ZAW 84 (1972): 349–352. It is true that "Teaching" (*torah*) can refer to a poetic, prophetic indictment (see Isa. 1:10), and that the poem is in some respects a précis of Deuteronomy's theology, hence a concise version of "the Teaching." This would give the "witness" metaphor in v. 26 the same meaning that it has in vv. 19 and 21.

46. Bertholet and others suggest that in vv. 24 and 26 the text originally *read* "poem" (*sh-y-r-h*) rather than "Teaching" (*t-w-r-h*). Two medieval Hebrew manuscripts of the Bible read thus in v. 24 (see BHS), but the value of such late manuscripts is debatable.

47. For the use of jars see Jer. 32:14; at least some of the Dead Sea scrolls were found in jars. For storage of scrolls in boxes (thus Targ. Jon.; R. Judah according to TJ Shek. 6:1, 49d, end; TJ Sot. 8:3, 22d), see J. Černý, *Paper and Books in Ancient Egypt* (London: H. K. Lewis and Co., 1952), 30; ANET, 495a; R. J. Williams, "Scribal Training in Ancient Egypt," JAOS 92 (1972): 216d; M. Lichtheim, *Ancient Egyptian Literature* (Berkeley: University of California Press, 1973–80), 2:129–131; for book containers in the classical world and talmudic literature, see F. G. Kenyon, *Books and Readers in Ancient Greece and Rome* (Oxford: Clarendon, 1932), 59–30, 129–130; TJ Ber. 3:5, 6d; Meg. 26b; BM 20b. For tablet containers in Mesopotamia see Tigay, *Evolution of Gilgamesh Epic*, 141 ll. 22–25; 263 note on 1, 22; AHw, s.v. *tupšinnu* and *pišannu*.

48. Elsewhere in the Bible, stones are said to be witnesses to agreements made in their presence (Josh. 24:27; Gen. 31:44–52). As a documentary record of the covenant and Israel's acceptance of it, the Teaching is an even more effective witness than mute stones would be.

49. Cf. Exod. 22:12.

50. ANET, 394–396; cf. 2 Sam. 21. See A. Malamat, "Doctrines of Causality in Hittite and Biblical Historiography: A Parallel," VT 5 (1955): 1–12.

51. 2 Kings 22–23; Neh. 8–10.

52. See 1:26,43; 9:6,7,13,23,24.

53. See 1 Sam. 23:3; Ezek. 15:5; Prov. 11:31; cf. Gen. 44:8; Exod. 6:12 (see Rashi at both verses); Gen. R. 92:7.

54. 4QDeut^b.

55. So Driver; Smith; Wright; Rofé, *Mavo'*, 199.

56. Cf. Josh. 8:35; 1 Kings 8:14,22,55; 12:3.

Chapter 32

C. J. Labuschagne, "The Song of Moses: Its Framework and Structure," in I. H. Eybers et al., eds., *De Fructu Oris Sui: Essays in Honour of Adrianus van Selms* (Leiden: Brill, 1971), 85–98; P. W. Skehan, *Studies in Israelite Poetry and Wisdom* (Washington, D.C.: Catholic Biblical Association of America, 1971), 67–77; Rofé, *Mavo'*, chap. 20.

1. Isa. 1:2–3; Jer. 2:4–13; cf. Ps. 50:4 and the address to the mountains and foundations of the earth in Mic. 6:1–8.

2. Sifrei 306 (Finkelstein, 335), end of comment on v. 1; cf. Rashi.

3. Tanḥ. Ha'azinu 1; cf. R. Benaiah in Sifrei 306 (Finkelstein, 333); cf. Rashi, Rashbam.

4. Cf. Jer. 6:18,19; Mic. 6:2. Cf. Jer. 4:28; 51:48, where they are emotionally participating observers.

5. Ehrlich, *Randglossen* at v. 3.

6. See Job 29:21–23; Hos. 14:6; Isa. 55:10; Ps. 72:6–7; Prov. 19:12b; Ecclus. 43:22.

7. Ehrlich, *Randglossen*.

8. Cf. Akkadian *iḫzu* (HALAT).

9. See Sarna, *Genesis*, at 27:28. *Tal* must include rain in the references to irrigation in Isa. 18:4; Hag. 1:10; Zech. 8:12; Prov. 3:20; otherwise rain would be ignored. Note that *ʿ-r-f* is used of rain in Job 36:28.

10. For irrigation by subterranean water, see Gen. 49:25; Deut. 33:13; Ezek. 31:4. The Ugaritic word appears in *Aqhat* C (UT 1 Aqht), i, 44–45 (ANET, 153c), along with cognates of two of the parallel terms for moisture, *tal* and *revivim*: "no moisture [*tl*], no droplets [*rbb*], no welling-up of the subterranean fountains [*shrʿ thmtm*]." See U. Cassuto, *Biblical and Oriental Studies* (Jerusalem: Magnes Press, 1973–75), 2:52, 194 n. 10; E. A. Speiser, "An Analogue to II Sam. 1:21," JBL 69 (1950): 377–378; W. L. Moran, "Some Remarks on the Song of Moses," *Biblica* 43 (1962): 320–322.

11. Shadal.

12. Lit., "give [i.e., ascribe] to him greatness." Cf. 1 Sam. 18:8; Pss. 29:1–2; 68:35; Job 1:22.

13. See 3:24; 9:26; 10:21; 11:2.

14. Num. 14:19; 1 Kings 3:6; Pss. 57:11; 108:5; 145:8; 2 Chron. 1:8; Neh. 9:25.

15. Pss. 22:23–24; 29:1–2; 96:7–8.

16. Rashbam, v. 3; Ibn Ezra, v. 4; Labuschagne, "Song of Moses," 94.

17. Note the parallelism in vv. 15,18,30,37; cf. 1 Sam. 2:2; 2 Sam. 22:32,47; 23:3; Isa. 44:8. LXX renders *tsur* as "god" in the poem. "Rock" (*tsur* [*zur*]) is also an epithet of God in personal names, such as Elizur, Zurishaddai, and Pedahzur in Num. 1:5,6,10.

18. Cf. Isa. 2:10,19,21; Pss. 18:2–3; 27:5; 31:3; 61:3; 62:8; 94:22. Other peoples used the same epithet for their gods. See, e.g., the epithet "great mountain" applied to Sumerian and Akkadian deities (CAD Š, 57bc).

19. 1 Sam. 2:3 and Ps. 18:32 deny that there are other "rocks" or that there are any like the Lord.

20. For this sense of *tamim* (and *tam*), see Gen. 17:1; Pss. 7:9; 102:2,6; Josh. 9:16,19; 2 Sam. 22:24,26; cf. M. Weinfeld, "The Covenant of Grant in the Old Testament and in the Ancient Near East," JAOS 90 (1970): 184–185 nn. 12,15 (following Y. Muffs); J. Tigay, "Psalm 7:5 and Ancient Near Eastern Treaties," JBL 89 (1970): 185 n. 39.

21. Isa. 30:18; Pss. 36:7; 89:15; 119:149.

22. Ps. 7:4; see Tigay, "Psalm 7:5," 185.

23. The related noun *tsedakah* often refers to faithfulness and to acts that deserve a response of loyalty. See Deut. 9:4–6 (note the covenantal context and the contrast with rebelliousness in vv. 6–7); 1 Sam. 12:7; 1 Kings 3:6; Mic. 6:5; Ps. 7:9; Hos. 2:21; Zech. 8:8; Ps. 103:17 (cf. v. 18). In Aramaic, derivatives of *ts-d-k* are used of loyalty and devotion to an ally, and in Arabic they often have the nuance of true and loyal friendship, for fulfilling a covenant with God. See KAI 215:11 (see KAI vol. 2:227). See Weinfeld, "Covenant of Grant," 186 n. 17; Tigay, "Psalm 7:5," 184–185.

24. Heb. *yashar*; Deut. 9:5; 1 Kings 3:6; 9:4; Ps. 7:11; 1 Chron. 29:17; see Tigay, "Psalm 7:5," 185.

25. Mayes.

26. RV (in Smith); cf. RSV; Vulg.

27. OJPS.

28. Ramban.

29. Cf. the Akkadian parallels cited in n. 93.

30. Prov. 9:7; Job 11:15.

31. Cf. *seh tamim* meaning *'ein bo mum* (Ehrlich, *Mikra*).

32. SP's reading *shiḥatu*, plural, is probably correct because the second colon indicates that "children" (or "non-children") is the subject of the first. Since the colon is unusually long, one of the two words *lo lo'* may be a scribal error due to dittography. The context suggests that *mumam* masks a word for loyalty, such as *'emun* in v. 20 (since 20b1 is synonymous with the second half of our verse, 20b2 may well be a clue to the original reading of the first half; cf. *shomer 'emunim*, Isa. 26:2; see Smith; cf. Klostermann cited by Driver).

33. Jer. 3:19; Isa. 63:8; cf. Mal. 3:17. The prophets frequently refer to Israel's being God's children as the basis for His promise to redeem them in the future. See Isa. 43:6; Jer. 31:8,20; Hos. 2:1 (cf. Exod. 4:22).

34. Hos. 11:1–3; Isa. 1:2,4 ("corrupt children" is likely an allusion to our verse [H. L. Ginsberg, s.v. "Isaiah," EncJud 9:50]); 30:1,9; Jer. 3:14,22; 4:22; 31:22.

35. See the collocation of *tamim* (parallel to *ḥasid*) and *'ikkesh* in 2 Sam. 22:26–27. *'Ikkesh* in Proverbs is usually contrasted with blameless and perfect.

36. See Isa. 32:6; Pss. 14:1; 74:18, 22; Job 2:10. Cf. *nevalah*, 22:21.

37. The parallel words, such as "fashioned," show that this is the verb *k-n-h* (*q-n-h*), "create" (also known from Ugaritic), and not its homonym *k-n-h* (*q-n-h*), "acquire." See Gen. 14:19, 22; Ps. 139:13; Prov. 8:22; perhaps Gen. 4:1; Exod. 15:16. See Pope and Habel cited by Sarna, *Exodus*, 248 n. 66.

38. This meaning of *konen* is clear from Ps. 119:73, where it is used alongside "make," and from Ugaritic, which uses *k-n-n* in parallelism with both "father" and *k-n-h* (*q-n-h*), "creator" (UT 51, iv,47–48; 76, iii,6–7). Grammatically, *konen* is causative of *k-n*, which in Phoenician and Arabic is the standard verb for "be."

39. See, e.g., 10:11–13; 1 Sam. 12:7–12; Jer. 2:1–9; Amos 2:9–16; Mic. 6:1–8.

40. Cf. Job 8:8–10; Ps. 78:3; Joel 1:2–3; Judg. 6:13. On oral tradition, see Excursus 28.

41. Job 8:8–10; A. Cavigneaux and B. K. Ismail, "Die Statthalter von Suḫu und Mari im 8. Jh. v. Chr," *Baghdader Mitteilungen* 21 (1990): 400, 403–404. (ref. courtesy Avigdor Hurowitz).

42. Cf. *hafrido* to *nifredu* in Gen. 10:32.

43. For *lemispar* see Josh. 4:4,5; Judg. 21:23; Ezek. 4:5.

44. See, e.g., Targ. Jon., end of verse; Yal. 61 at n. 132 (to Gen. 9:18).

45. See Sarna, *Genesis*, 69; Ginzberg, *Legends*, 5:194–195; D. Sperber et al., s.v. "Nations, the Seventy," EncJud 12:882–886.

46. Rofé, *Mavo'*, 221.

47. Heb. *hanḥel* can take as direct object the thing allotted, the recipient, or—as here—both (Rofé, *Mavo'*, 221).

48. Ehrlich, *Randglossen*; Dillmann.

49. M. Greenberg, "Religion: Stability and Ferment," in WHJP 4/2, 104.

50. See H.W.F. Saggs, *The Greatness That Was Babylon* (New York: New American Library, 1962), 242.

51. Gen. 14:18–22; Num. 24:16; Pss. 18:14; 21:8; 78:17,35,56; 91:1; 92:2; Lam. 3:35,38; cf. Ps. 82:6.

52. Outside the Bible *'El* and *'Elyon* are separate, though associated, deities. The Aramaic Sefire inscriptions mention "El and Elyon" as a pair (ANET, 503–504), and a late, Greek account of Phoenician mythology mentions an "Eliuom, called 'Most High,'" father of heaven and earth and grandfather of El (H. W. Attridge and R. A. Oden, *Philo of Byblos: The Phoenician*

History [Washington, D.C.: Catholic Biblical Association, 1981], 47).

53. Moran; Craigie. In its Greek form *hypsistos*, and perhaps in its Hebrew form as well, Elyon was a popular way for Jews to refer to God in Hellenistic times, perhaps to give them a religious language in common with gentiles (M. Greenberg).

54. See Gen. 18:15, end, 20; 42:16; 49:7; Num. 23:23; Isa. 15:1; Amos 3:7; BDB, 472d; HALAT, 448c; A. Schoors, "The Particle *ki*," OTS 21 (1981): 243–253. LXX reads "And my people Jacob became the LORD's portion," as if the text read *vayehi* rather than *ki*. If that were the original reading one might translate "But His people became the LORD's portion." However, it could be an interpretive translation rather than reflecting a variant reading.

55. SP and LXX make this identification explicit by adding "Israel" at the end of the verse and dividing the colons as follows: "His people Jacob, His own allotment Israel."

56. The text uses the idiom *hevel nahalato*, lit. "His rope-allotment," which is based on the practice of measuring land allotments by rope (*hevel*; see Amos 7:17; Mic. 2:5; Zech. 2:5–6; Ps. 78:55). Eventually *hevel* came to mean "territory" (Josh. 17:14; 19:9; Ps. 105:11). See Driver at 3:4; Musil, cited by H. M. Gevaryahu and S. E. Loewenstamm, s.v. *goral*, EM 2:461.

57. Targ. Onk. and LXX circumvent the problem by translating as if the verb were vocalized *yamtsi'ehu*, "provided for," "maintained," referring to God's provision of food and water in the wilderness. So, too, Sifrei 313; Saadia; Bekhor Shor; cf. Rashi and Rashbam. Cf. Job 34:11, *yamtsi'ennu*, "provides for him" (NJPS) and the use of *m-ts-'* in the *niph'al* to mean "suffice" (Num. 11:22; Josh. 17:16; Zech. 10:10; cf. Akkadian *masu*). SP reads *ye'amtsehu*, meaning that God "strengthened" Israel in the desert.

58. Hos. 9:10 (the reference to Baal-peor proves that the context is the desert period; for earlier Israelite history see Hos. 11:1; 12:4ff; 12:14); Ezek. 16:3–6 (cf. chap. 20 and 33:24; M. Greenberg, *Ezekiel 1–20* [Garden City, N.Y.: Doubleday, 1983], 299–303).

59. Note the mixture of metaphors in Jer. 3:19 (adoption) and 20 (marriage).

60. Ibn Janah.

61. Rashi; Ibn Ezra; Bekhor Shor. T. H. Gaster compares the bedouin idea that shrill winds and other eerie sounds in the desert are the shrieks of demons (*Myth, Legend, and Custom in the Old Testament* [New York: Harper and Row, 1969], 320; cf. Targ. Jon.).

62. See 8:15; cf. Sifrei; Rashi; Ibn Ezra.

63. Cf. Ps. 17:8; Prov. 7:2. Heb. *'ishon* is comparable to Arabic *'insan 'al-'ayin*, "the little man in the eye," referring to one's reflection in the pupil of another (Ibn Janah, *Sefer Ha-Shorashim*; Radak, *Sefer Ha-Shorashim*; HALAT; Gaster, *Myth*, 320).

64. Eagles and other birds catch their young on their backs while initiating them in flying. See Driver, 358; G. R. Driver, "Once Again: Birds in the Bible," PEQ 90 (1958): 56–57; Y. Ahituv and S. Ahituv, s.v. *nesher*, EM 5:978 (see there for the species of eagle indicated here).

65. Cf. Job 8:6.

66. ANET, 19–20.

67. For a systematic study of *bamah*, see P. H. Vaughan, *The Meaning of* Bāmâ *in the Old Testament* (London: Cambridge University Press, 1974).

68. Cf. *tenuvat ha-sadeh*, Ezek. 38:30.

69. See Judg. 14:8ff; 1 Sam. 14:25ff, Ps. 81:17. Rashbam thinks that the text refers to honey from dates that grow in the mountains.

70. Cf. Job 29:6. See Bekhor Shor; Smith; Dalman 4:177; L. Stager, "The Firstfruits of Civilization," in J. N. Tubb, ed., *Palestine in the Bronze and Iron Ages* (London: Institute of Archaeology, 1985), 173.

71. See Dalman 6:307–311; H. Beinart, s.v. *halav u-motsarei halav*, EM 3:137; M. Haran, "Seething a Kid in Its Mother's Milk," JJS 30 (1979): 31 n. 23.

72. So Maimonides, Hilkhot Sefer Torah 8; LXX; Driver; Smith.

73. Gen. 45:18 (parallel to "best"); see also Num. 18:12; Pss. 81:17; 147:14; perhaps Gen. 4:4. See Ibn Ezra; Bekhor Shor; A. Kaplan, *The Living Torah* (New York: Maznaim, 1981), at Lev. 3:9.

74. Radak.

75. See Mic. 7:14; Jer. 50:19; Ezek. 39:18; Ps. 22:13; cf. Amos 4:1.

76. Pss. 81:17; 147:14.

77. Like "heart" of artichoke; cf. Saadia. The view that the grain looks like a kidney is incorrect.

78. Sifrei 317; Rashi; Bekhor Shor (cf. Ta'an. 23a); Abravanel, 304; Sifra, Behukotai, 1 (Weiss 110d).

79. So NEB. If this is correct, the dislocation of "kidneys" may have been an intentional revision to avoid the implication that God fed Israel kidney fat, which is forbidden as food (Lev. 3:17; 7:23–25; cf. Ibn Ezra here). A scribe may have considered the reading impossible for that reason and corrected it by relocating "kidneys" and leaving *helev karim*, which could be understood as "the best of rams." This type of revision has been termed a "nomistic correction," that is, a correction to make a reading consistent with biblical law. See A. Rofé, "The Nomistic Correction in Biblical Manuscripts and Its Occurrence in 4QSam^a," RQ 14 (1989): 247–254.

80. See Gen. 49:11 and Sarna, *Genesis*, ad loc.; cf. Ugar. "blood of trees" (ANET, 133b [the translation "vines" is interpretive]).

81. SP, 4QPhyl^n, and LXX add, before this colon: "Jacob ate and was full" (cf. Neh. 9:25), connecting Israel's rebellion with Moses' frequent warnings that satiety might have this effect (see Comment to 6:11–12). It could be original, but since the phraseology is commonplace in Deuteronomy it may be simply an imitation of Moses' warnings, added to make the connection clear. It would make the verse five colons long, unusual in this poem but not impossible.

82. Deut. 33:5,26; Isa. 44:2.

83. Thus *b-'-t* in rabbinic Hebrew.

84. Rashi and Radak took it as a variant spelling of *kasita* (middle consonant *samekh*), "covered yourself," elliptical for "covered with fat," as in Job 15:27. Ehrlich (*Mikra*) and Ben-Yehudah relate the verb to Arab. *k-s-'*, "eat," "be gorged with food."

85. Heb. *va-yenabbel*; cf. Jer. 14:21; Mic. 7:6.

86. Cf. Rashbam.

87. 2 Sam. 22:47; Ps. 95:1.

88. Cf. Isa. 43:12; Jer. 2:25; 3:13; Pss. 44:21; 81:10.

89. See 7:25; 2 Kings 23:13; Isa. 44:19. Although "abominations" sometimes refers to deeds (e.g., 18:9,12), that is not likely in this context, which is concerned only with idolatry (Ramban).

90. Greenberg, "Religion: Stability and Ferment," 104; Rofé, *Mavo'*, 230.

91. Driver; A. L. Oppenheim, *Ancient Mesopotamia* (Chicago: University of Chicago Press, 1964); cf. LXX *daimones*, as in Ps. 106:37; Isa. 65:11.

92. A somewhat similar deprecation is found in an inscription of the Assyrian king Ashurbanipal, who says that he captured the gods (idols) of the Elamites, treating them like mere ghosts, or turning them into ghosts, that is, powerless beings. See CAD s.v. *zaqiqu* and *manu*.

93. Cf. Jer. 5:7 (cf. 2:11; 16:20); 2 Chron. 13:9. Similar locutions are known in Akkadian for people who are not what they pretend to be or do not act, or are not treated, as their (supposed) status requires. Examples are "non-brother," meaning

"unbrotherly brother" (LFM, no. 115), "non-Babylonians" or "pseudo-Babylonians" (LFM, no. 116; Lambert, BWL, 281).

94. Wisdom boasts of its antiquity in Prov. 8:23–31, and Mic. 5:1 speaks of the ancient origins of the messiah. Anti-Semites in the first century maligned Jews with the charge that they were a new race, not ancient (Josephus, Apion 1.1–2), and Guy Stroumsa informs me that pagans mocked Christianity on the grounds that it was a new religion.

95. Pss. 44:2; 74:12; 77:12, 143:5; Hab. 1:12.

96. The translation "stirred fears" (Radak, Sefer Ha-Shorashim; cf. Sifrei 318 first view and Rashi) overlooks the distinction between s-ʿ-r, "be aghast, appalled" (Jer. 2:12; Ezek. 27:35; 32:10) and yareʾ, "fear," a normal term for worship and reverence.

97. Gk. eideisan; see J. Barth, Etymologische Studien (Berlin: Itzkowski, 1893), 67. Cf. Saadia; Ibn Janāḥ.

98. Isa. 17:7,8; 31:1b; cf. Gen. 4:5; see Sifrei 318, end.

99. Ca. 208 times vs. ca. 22 (BDB, 408bc).

100. See Isa. 51:2; Pss. 29:9; 51:7; Job 39:1; cf. Ps. 90:2. For the association of ḥ-y-l and y-l-d, see M. Held, "Rhetorical Questions in Ugaritic and Biblical Hebrew," EI 9 (1969): 78.

101. ANET, 653d, 654d; cf. ANET, 397b, referring to a Hittite deity.

102. For "spurn" without a direct object see Jer. 14:21. This usage is otherwise unattested, which has prompted various emendations (cf. BHS). NJPS translates as if the text read va-yikhʿas/va-yinʾats be-vanayv u-vi-venotayv. In place of "spurned" (v-y-nʾ-ts), 4Qphylⁿ (reflected in LXX) reads "was incensed" (v-y-k-n-ʾ), a reading that is graphically similar to v-y-n-ʾ-ts and matches the parallelism of "incense" and "vex" in vv. 16 and 21. That reading is also problematic, since k-n-ʾ always takes an object.

103. Shadal; cf. Lam. 2:6, end.

104. Prov. 2:12; 8:13; 10:31; 16:31; 23:33. See J. Greenfield, "The Background and Parallel to a Proverb of Ahiqar," Hommages à A. Dupont-Sommer (Paris: Adrien-Maisonneuve, 1972), 51–52. Cognates of h-p-k are used for betraying and reneging on an oath, treaty, or agreement. See CAD, s.v. abāku; the Syriac of 1 Macc. 6:62; J. Goldstein, "The Syriac Bill of Sale from Dura-Europos," JNES 25 (1966): 2 l. 15; Syriac Ahikar 4:1.

105. E.g., 1 Kings 16:13,26; Jer. 8:19; 14:22; 16:19.

106. J. S. Cooper, The Curse of Agade (Baltimore: Johns Hopkins University Press, 1983), 30–33.

107. Cf. Jer. 15:14; 17:4; Isa. 65:5.

108. Cf. Job 5:19.

109. From ʾ-s-f; cf. Mic. 4:6; thus the Hebrew is read by LXX, Vulg.; Pesh.; Sifrei 321, first two views. Cf. Zech. 14:2.

110. From y-s-f; cf. Ezek. 5:16; Lev. 26:21. So Rashi; Saadia.

111. As if from suf/sof; cf. Amos 4:15. So Sifrei 321 (third view); Rashi (second view); Ibn Ezra; Siftei Ḥakhamim; Ibn Janāḥ; Bekhor Shor; Radak.

112. Ezek. 5:16; Ps. 38:3; Job 6:4; Lam. 3:12–13.

113. Heb. mezei is related to Arab. mazza, "suck out." See Shadal, 562n.; BDB. The translation construes mezei as an active participle, as the context demands.

114. "Ravaging," lit., "consuming" (Heb. leḥumei, an active participle of the paʿul form, again as the context demands).

115. Hab. 3:5; Ps. 91:6. See A. Caquot, "Sur Quelques Démons dans l'Ancien Testament (Reshep, Qeteb, Deber)," Semitica 6 (1956): 53–68; A. Rofé, Israelite Belief in Angels in the Pre-Exilic Period (Hebrew) (Ph.D. diss., Hebrew University, 1969), part 2; Gaster, Myth, 321; W. J. Fulco, The Canaanite God Resep (New Haven: American Oriental Society, 1976); S. E. Loewenstamm, s.v. Reshef, EM 7:437–441; M. Weinfeld, "Divine Intervention in War in Ancient Israel and in the Ancient Near East," in H. Tadmor and M. Weinfeld, eds., History, Historiography and Interpretation (Jerusalem: Magnes Press, 1983), 128–130. Reshef is connected with arrows in some texts, which is comparable to its designation as "arrow" here. Ber. 5a

and Rashi take reshef as a reference to demons (cf. Gaster, Myth, §§242, 269, 275).

116. Heb. meriri, "poisonous." Cf. merorot in v. 32 and Akk. martu; see C. Cohen, s.v. "Poison," EncJud 13:702–704.

117. J. Blau, "Ueber Homonyme und Angeblich Homonyme Wurzeln II," VT 7 (1957): 98.

118. Talmudic-midrashic sources regard ketev, too, as a demon; see Yal. 945; Num. R. 12:3; Rashi; cf. Gaster, Myth, §§ 242, 269, 275.

119. See Judg. 14:5; 1 Kings 13:24; 20:36; 2 Kings 2:24; 17:25; Amos 3:12; 5:19.

120. Cf. Mic. 7:17 and the threat in Jer. 8:17. For ḥemah meaning poison, see Pss. 58:5; 140:4; cf. Akk. imtu; Ugar. ḥmt; see Cohen, "Poison."

121. The blessing of safety from wild animals is promised in Lev. 26:6; Hos. 2:20; cf. Isa. 11:6–8; cf. Job 5:22–23.

122. Cf. Jer. 51:22; Ezek. 7:15; Lam. 1:20; 2 Chron. 36:17.

123. Information courtesy Paul Fink, M.D.

124. Ibn Janāḥ, end of entry; D. H. Müller, "Himjarische Studien," Zeitschrift der Deutschen Morgenländischen Gesellschaft 30 (1876): 701 (ref. courtesy Sol Cohen). Note the reservations of Tur Sinai about derivation from a final heh verb.

125. Cf. Akk. nakāru/nukkuru, "deny, alter, change," Arab. n-k-r, esp. in fourth conjugation, "refuse to acknowledge, deny, renounce."

126. Tur Sinai, who thinks that the error was induced by the frequency of k-ʿ-s in the chapter. If the text read kahash, and a scribe miswrote it as kaʿash, it could easily have been mistaken for kaʿas, which is sometimes spelled with sin (e.g., Job 17:7).

127. So R. Nehemiah in Sifrei, Rashi, and several other medievals; see Smith; Ehrlich, Randglossen; Mayes.

128. Cf. arkatam ḥâtu/lamādu/parāsu/šaʾālu, in CAD A2, 275a, 277d; AHw, 831bc.

129. Abravanel, 307.

130. See Lev. 26:8; Josh. 23:10; Isa. 30:17.

131. Targum; Rashi; Ibn Ezra.

132. E. A. Speiser, "The Stem PLL in Hebrew," JBL 82 (1963): 301–306. The traditional rendering "even our enemies themselves being judges" (e.g., KJV, OJPS, following Targ. Onk., Rashi) is based on the groundless traditional interpretation of pelilim in Exod. 21:22 as judges.

133. Ibn Ezra.

134. AHw, 813b; E. A. Speiser, "PALIL and Congeners: A Sampling of Apotropaic Symbols," Assyriological Studies 16 (1965): 389.

135. There are a few cases in which the order of words in the construct state is reversed, such as tolaʿat shani, "worm of scarlet" (Exod. 25:4) in place of sheni tolaʿat, "scarlet of the worm" (Lev. 14:4); metim ʾevel, "mourning for the dead" (Ezek. 24:17); pishtei ha-ʿets, "stalks of flax" (Josh. 2:6). See Yalon (below, n. 152), pp. 142, 158, 330. However, none of these examples is a possessive genitive fully comparable to ʾoyeveinu pelilim.

136. Jer. 25:15–16; Ezek. 23:31–34; so Isa. 51:17; Ps. 75:9; Lam. 4:21; see Targ. Onk. and Rashi on v. 33; Bekhor Shor; Abravanel, 307 on v. 34; Ehrlich, Mikra; Labuschagne, "Song of Moses," 96–97.

137. See Isa. 16:8; Hab. 3:17; UT 52:10. Saadia interprets as "trellises" or "tendrils," Rashi and Radak (as alternative) as "field." Cf. L. Stager, "The Archaeology of the East Slope of Jerusalem and the Terraces of the Kidron," JNES 41 (1982): 111–121.

138. See n. 116 on poison.

139. LXX; Ehrlich, Mikra.

140. For the grammar, cf. ʾadonim kasheh, Isa. 19:4.

141. "It" refers to the poison wine; see Sifrei 324; Rashi, last comment on v. 43 (giving R. Nehemiah's view); Ibn Ezra; Ramban; Abravanel, 307. For cognates of kamus see Jastrow; CAD, s.v. kamāsu A; C. Cohen, Biblical Hapax Legomena (Missoula, Mont.: Scholars Press, 1978), 39.

142. For wine storerooms, see 1 Chron. 27:27; 2 Chron. 11:11. For the technique of sealing, see the studies of Malamat and Zettler cited in Tigay, "Some Archaeological Notes on Deuteronomy," in D. P. Wright et al., eds., *Pomegranates and Golden Bells: Studies . . . Milgrom* (Winona Lake, Ind.: Eisenbrauns, 1995). The stoppers of indivdual wine jars were also sealed, but that meaning is less likely here in view of the parallel "put away."

143. Romans 12:19.

144. MT's *li* may go back to a manuscript in which *l-y* was written as an abbreviation for *l-y-v-m* (*le-yom*). It is, of course, possible that the reading *le-yom* was created by a scribe who wrongly *thought* that *l-y* was an abbreviation. On abbreviations see chap. 1, n. 89.

145. See, e.g., 2 Kings 9:7. See the treatment by W. T. Pitard, "Amarna *ekēmu* and Hebrew *naqam*," *Maarav* 3 (1982): 5–25.

146. Driver; see Pss. 38:17; 66:9; 94:18; 121:3.

147. The translation "destiny" is probably influenced by the use of ʿatid for the future in rabbinic Hebrew, Aramaic, Syriac, and Arabic, but since this sense is unparalleled in the Bible some have suggested emending the text, based on the parallel "their day of disaster" (*yom ʾeidam*), to *ʿet raʿatamo*, "the hour of their evil [fate]" (cf. Jer. 2:27–28) or *ʿet deḥi*, "the hour of stumbling" (cf. Ps. 56:14). Cf. Jer. 46:21 and see H. L. Ginsberg, "*Siyyum Shirat Haʾazinu*," *Tarbiz* 24 (1954–55): 1–3; idem, "Supplementary Studies in Koheleth," *PAAJR* 21 (1952): 54 n. 64; Tur Sinai.

148. Gen. 30:6; Pss. 43:1; 54:3; Prov. 31:9; cf. Rashi at v. 43, summarizing the Sifrei; Ibn Ezra. That the verse means "judge favorably," and not "give judgment against," is also supported by the fact that it refers to Israel as God's people and servants, and that v. 35 is already implicitly favorable to Israel.

149. Rashi; Milgrom, *Numbers*, chap. 23, n. 54.

150. See Targ. Onk.; Shadal. Cf. NJPS at Gen. 27:42 and Hos. 13:14b.

151. Shadal. Cf. Abravanel, 307.

152. See I. Efros, "Textual Notes on the Hebrew Bible," *JAOS* 45 (1925): 152–153; A. Ahuviah, "ʿAtsur ve-ʿazuv be-yisraʾel," *Leshonenu* 30 (1965–66): 175–178; idem, "ʿAtsur ve-ʿazuv be-yisraʾel," *Leshonenu* 31 (1966–67): 160; H. Yalon, *Pirkei Lashon* (Jerusalem: Bialik Institute, 1971), 322–325; S. Talmon and W. W. Fields, "The Collocation *mashtin bakir veʿatsur veʿazuv* and Its Meaning," *ZAW* 101 (1989): 85–112.

153. Sanh. 97a; Pesh. ("helper or supporter"); cf. Rashi; Sifrei 326, end; Bekhor Shor; cf. Yalon, *Pirkei Lashon*.

154. If so, *ʿatsur* and *ve-ʿazuv* would be active participles. See Comment to 1:13. For ʿ-*ts-r*, "restrain," meaning "govern," see 1 Sam. 9:16–17 (Abravanel, 308); cf. the use of Egyptian *d-ʾ-r*, "control," for ruling a tribe (R. Bullock, *The Story of Sinuhe* [London: Probsthain and Co., ca. 1978], 43). ʿAzuv would not be from the common ʿ-*z-v*, "leave," but from a homonym meaning either "help," "raise up," "restore," or the like, that seems to be attested in a few passages (Exod. 23:5; Neh. 3:8, 34). This interpretation has been supported by Ugar. ʿ-*d-b*, "arrange," and South Arab. ʿ-*d-b*, "repair." The existence of this root in Hebrew and Ugaritic has been challenged; see H.G.M. Williamson, "A Reconsideration of ʿzb II in Biblical Hebrew," *ZAW* 97 (1985): 74–85; Alan Cooper, "The Plain Sense of Exodus 23:5," *HUCA* 59 (1988): 1–22. Note, however, the favorable meaning implied in the El Amarna personal name *Yaḥzib-Adda* (*Yaʿzib-Adda*; *EA* 275:4; 276:4), even if the meaning "May Adda save" (ʿzb) is uncertain.

155. E.g., Judg. 2:16; 3:9.

156. That the speaker introduced in this verse is God is noted by Rashi, Sforno, and Driver, and is supported by the parallel statements in Judg. 10:14 and Jer. 2:28, and by v. 39, where He is still the speaker. 4QDeutᑫ and LXX make this clear by reading "YHVH will say."

157. Rashi.

158. Saadia (see *Neveh Shalom* to Saadia). For this use of "I, I," see Comments to 2:27, "strictly to the highway," and 16:20, "justice, justice."

159. See Isa. 43:10–11,13; 46:4; Hos. 5:14b.

160. This is not necessarily a denial of the existence of other divine beings. Such denials assert that there is no god except for or other than the Lord (see Deut. 4:35,39; 1 Sam. 2:2; 2 Sam. 22:32; Isa. 44:6; 45:5,6,21,22; 46:9).

161. Ps. 30:4b; 1 Sam. 2:6. That God both wounds and heals is also frequently asserted; cf. Isa. 19:22; Hos. 5:14; 6:1–2; Job 5:18.

162. Gen. 14:22; Exod. 6:8; Num. 14:30; Ezek. 20:5; Dan. 12:7.

163. See Num. 14:21; Ezek. 5:11, etc. Grammar favors translating *ḥai ʾadonai/ʾanokhi/ʾani* as a verbal clause, especially here where it is accompanied by the adverb "forever." For a different view, see M. Greenberg, "The Hebrew Oath Particle ḤAY/ḤÊ," *JBL* 76 (1957): 34–39; S. E. Loewenstamm, s.v. *shevuʿah*, *EM* 7:719f. Cf. the comparative material collected by M. R. Lehmann, "Biblical Oaths," *ZAW* 81 (1969): 74–92.

164. As in Exod. 15:3; Isa. 42:13; 59:17; Ezek. 21:11. For flashing weapon cf. Nah. 3:3; Hab. 3:11.

165. MdRY Shirta 4 (Lauterbach 2:33). Some scholars have proposed conjectural emendations of *mishpat* to *kashti*, "my bow," or *benei ʾashpah*, "shafts of the quiver." See Ginsberg, "*Siyyum Shirat Haʾazinu*," 54–55; Ehrlich, *Randglossen* (cf. Lam. 3:13); cf. NAB: *ba-ʾashpah*.

166. Isa. 10:5–26 (cf. v. 10 to v. 13 here); Jer. 25:11–14; Zech. 1:15.

167. 2 Sam. 2:26; 11:25; Isa. 1:20.

168. Many commentators parse the verse differently: "I will make My arrows drunk with blood, and My sword will devour flesh: (My arrows with) blood of the slain and captive and (My sword the flesh of) the enemy chiefs." So Ibn Ezra; Abravanel, 309; Driver; Ehrlich, *Randglossen*.

169. C. Rabin, "The 'Ideology' of Deborah's War," *JJS* 6 (1953): 131. Possibly *peraʿot* has a different meaning here. Various conjectures have been made—such as "the heads of the leaders of the enemy"—based on presumed senses of Arabic cognates (see HALAT). Since *peraʿot* is parallel to ʿam, "people, army" in Judg. 5:1, "leaders" could be correct, or possibly "soldiers." It has even been suggested that *r-ʾ-sh*, "head," is a scribal error for *sh-ʾ-r* (*sheʾer*), "flesh," and that the phrase originally read "flesh of the enemy troops," complementing the second colon of the verse and parallel to the third (Ginsberg, "*Siyyum Shirat Haʾazinu*," 1–3).

170. Driver.

171. Ibid.; cf. Job 29:13 (*piel*).

172. Bekhor Shor; Driver.

173. Cf. 2 Kings 9:7; Ps. 79:10. See Sarna, *Exodus*, at Exod. 21:20; M. Greenberg, s.v. "Avenger of Blood," IDB 1:321.

174. Lit., "His land His people." Ibn Ezra, Ralbag, and others explain the suffix on ʾadmato as comparable to that in phrases like *ḥayeto ʾarets* (Gen. 1:24). 4QDeutᑫ and SP read simply ʾadmat ʿamo; LXX and Vulg. translate thus. Targ. Onk., Rashi, and others interpret the phrase as "His people *and* His land."

175. Cf. Deut. 21:8; Joel 4:19,21. It is less likely that this refers to pollution caused by Israel's idolatry (Ezek. 36:17–18); the poem describes Israel's idolatry at length and never hints at its causing pollution. It does not mention other sins that cause pollution (Deut. 25:4; Lev. 18:24–28; Num. 35:33–34; Jer. 3:1–2,9; Ps. 106:38).

176. Tur Sinai suggests that ʾadmato here means "blood," like Aram. ʾadmaʾ and Akk. adamatu, but this explanation seems to make no difference, since cleansing Israel's blood would presumably mean cleansing the land of it, raising the same problem as the usual interpretation.

177. Following Ginsberg, "*Siyyum Shirat Ha'azinu*," 1–3. For *kipper* meaning "wipe away," Ginsberg cites the usage of *k-p-r* in the Babylonian Talmud, Syriac, and the targum of Prov. 30:20 (rendering Heb. *m-ḥ-h*; cf. the parallelism in Jer. 18:23). Cf. Akk. *kapāru* (used inter alia with "tears") and see B. A. Levine, *In the Presence of the Lord* (Leiden: Brill, 1974), 56–57, 77–78, 123–127.

178. Cf. Exod. 7:10; 10:3; 19:7; 24:3 (also perhaps Gen. 47:1 [cf. 46:29]). The verse would read naturally as an introduction to the poem, a transition between God's instructions to recite it and Moses' compliance. LXX repeats 31:22 before this verse, making clear that it is a recapitulation.

179. As SP, LXX, Vulg. and Pesh. read; so Targs. Onk. and Jon.

180. 2 Kings 17:15; Ps. 81:9; Zech. 3:6; Neh. 9:34. Cf. Weinfeld, Commentary, 261–262.

181. Smith.

182. Rashi; Smith. Cf. Isa. 55:11: God's word will not return *reikam* (without effect?).

183. Bekhor Shor.

184. LH xxvb, §§100–104.

185. TJ Pe'ah 1:1, 15b.

186. Lit., "Ascend this mountain of Abarim, Mount Nebo," meaning either "this mountain in the Abarim range, namely Mount Nebo" or "the peak of the Abarim range, namely Mount Nebo."

187. See B. Oded, s.v. *'Avarim, Har Ha-'Avarim*, EM 6:51.

188. Cf. 11:29; Gen. 25:18; 1 Kings 11:7. See Smith; Driver.

189. Bekhor Shor.

190. The phrase does not refer specifically to death or burial, since it is often distinguished from these, nor to interment in the ancestral tomb, since it is also used of persons who were buried elsewhere. See Gen. 25:8–9; 35:29; 49:33 (burial is later, in 50:1–13); Num. 20:26; 27:13; 31:2.

191. See J. Milgrom, *Numbers*, ad loc. and Excursus 50.

Chapter 33

A. Caquot, "Les bénédictions de Moïse (Deuteronome 33, 6–25)," *Semitica* 32 (1982): 67–81; U. Cassuto, *Biblical and Oriental Studies* (Jerusalem: Magnes Press, 1973), 1:47–70; F. M. Cross and D. N. Freedman, *Studies in Ancient Yahwistic Poetry* (Missoula, Mont.: Scholars Press, 1975), 97–122; D. N. Freedman, "The Poetic Structure of the Framework of Deuteronomy 33," in G. Rendsburg et al., eds., *The Bible World* [New York: Ktav and Institute of Hebrew Culture and Education of NYU], 1980), 25–47; M. Garsiel, *Biblical Names: A Literary Study of Midrashic Derivations and Puns* (Ramat Gan: Bar Ilan University Press, 1981), 104–105, 115, 143, 172, 178; T. H. Gaster, "An Ancient Eulogy on Israel: Deuteronomy 33:3–5, 26–29," *JBL* 66 (1947): 53–62; A.H.J. Gunneweg, "Über den Sitz im Leben der sog. Stammessprüche," *ZAW* 76 (1964): 245–255; J. T. Milik, "Deux documents inédits du désert de Juda," *Biblica* 38 (1957): 245–268; I. L. Seeligmann, "A Psalm from Pre-regal Times," *VT* 14 (1964): 75–92; Z. Weisman, "A Connecting Link in an Old Hymn: Deuteronomy xxxiii 19A, 21B," *VT* 28: 365–367; Y. Zakovitch, *Kefel Midreshei Shem* (M.A. diss., Hebrew University, 1971), 29, 31, 61–64, 127–129, 168–169, 188 n. 4, 216 n. 53; idem, s.v. *shem, midreshei shemot*, EM 8:66.

1. Hebrew texts divide the poem before vv. 1 (M, SP), 7 (M), 8 and 12 (M, SP, 4QDeut^h), 13 (M), 18 (M, SP, 4QDeut^h), 20 (M, SP), 22 (M, SP, 4QDeut^h), 23 (MT var.), 24 (M, SP), 28 (SP), and after 29 (M, SP). There are no breaks between v. 1 and the poem (cf. chap. 1, n. 26), between the exordium and the blessings, or between the blessings and the coda (vv. 25,26).

2. See Gen. 9:27; 49:8,16,19; Isa. 10:31; Amos 5:5; Mic. 1:10–15; Zeph. 2:4.

3. Sensitivity to such potential is clear from passages in which biblical characters' names are explained, such as Gen. 5:29; 27:36; 1 Sam. 25:25. Cf. the talmudic statement *shema' garim*, "the name determines (some of one's future deeds)," Ber. 7b. Not all names were understood or intended thus; see J. Barr "The Symbolism of Names in the Old Testament," BJRL 52 (1969): 11–29.

4. See Josh. 14:6; 1 Sam. 9:6; 1 Kings 13; 17:18; 2 Kings 4:7,9; Ps. 90:1.

5. Josephus, Ant. 4.320; Mid. Hag.; Bekhor Shor citing Joseph Kara; Ibn Ezra; Ramban.

6. Ibn Ezra, comment to v. 3.

7. Judg. 5:4–5; Hab. 3:3–15; Ps. 68:8–9,15–18 (if BHK's emendation in v. 18 is correct); Zech. 9:14; 14:5; see also Pss. 18:8–16; 50:3ff; 77:16–19.

8. See Ibn Ezra; Shadal; S. E. Loewenstamm, "*Re'adat ha-teva' bi-she'at hofa'at ha-shem*," in Y. Kaufmann et al., eds., *'Oz le-Dawid* (Jerusalem: Kiryat Sefer, 1964), 508–520. Traditional exegesis takes v. 2 as a description of the giving of the Torah to Israel at Mount Sinai.

9. Exod. 3:1; 4:27; 18:5; 24:13; Num. 10:33; 1 Kings 19:8.

10. See S. Herrmann, "Der Name JHW? in den Inschriften von Soleb: Prinzipielle Erwägungen," Fourth World Congress of Jewish Studies, *Proceedings*, vol. 1 (Jerusalem: World Union of Jewish Studies, 1967), 213–216; M. Weippert, *The Settlement of the Israelite Tribes in Palestine* (London: SCM, 1971), 105–106 n. 14 (but note idem, "'Heiliger Krieg' in Israel und Assyrien," *Biblica* 55 [1974]: 491 n. 144, where Weippert denies that "Yahwe" is YHVH); B. Mazar, "Yahweh Came Out from Sinai," in *Temples and High Places in Biblical Times* (Jerusalem: HUC-JIR, 1981), 5–7; M. Weinfeld, "The Tribal League at Sinai," in P. D. Miller et al., eds., *Ancient Israelite Religion* (Philadelphia: Fortress Press, 1987), 303–314; S. Ahituv, *Canaanite Toponyms in Ancient Egyptian Documents* (Jerusalem: Magnes Press, 1984), 122 n. 295, 169 n. 491. Cf. F. M. Cross, "Reuben, First-Born of Jacob," ZAW 100 (1988), Supplement, 60 n. 49.

11. See Z. Meshel, *Kuntillet Ajrud* (Jerusalem: Israel Museum, 1978); M. Weinfeld, "Further Remarks on the Ajrud Inscriptions" (Hebrew), *Shnaton* 5–6 (1978–79): 237–239; idem, "Kuntillet 'Ajrud Inscriptions and Their Significance," *Studi Epigrafici e Linguistici* 1 (1984): 121–130.

12. These inscriptions have provoked renewed interest in the old and controversial theory that the Israelites first began to worship YHVH under the influence of the Midianites and/or the Kenites, non-Israelite inhabitants of this region. See Mazar, "Yahweh," and Weinfeld, "Tribal League"; H. H. Rowley, *From Joseph to Joshua* (London: Oxford University Press, 1964), 149–155; contrast R. de Vaux, *The Early History of Israel* (Philadelphia: Westminster Press, 1978), 333–337; Y. Kaufmann, *The Religion of Israel*, trans. M. Greenberg (Chicago: University of Chicago Press, 1960), 242–244.

13. Cf. Isa. 60:1,2; Hab. 3:3; A. L. Oppenheim, "Akkadian *pul(u)ḫ(t)u* and *melammu*," JAOS 63 (1943): 31–34; E. Cassin, *La Splendeur Divine* (Paris: La Haye, Mouton and Co., 1968); Weinfeld, s.v. *kavod*, TWAT 4:27–32. The use of *zaraḥ*, "shone," in connection with Seir may have been prompted by the name of the Edomite (Seirite) clan *zeraḥ*, Gen. 36:13,17,33 (Zakovitch, *Kefel Midreshei Shem*).

14. The Hebrew pronoun *lamo* has no antecedent. Several ancient translations render "upon us," as if the text read *lanu* (LXX; Targ. Onk.; Vulg.; Pesh.). Some modern scholars emend the text to le-'ammo, "to His people" (Ehrlich; BHS; Seeligmann).

15. Rashbam; Radak; Cross and Freedman. See Ezek. 28:7,17; Job 3:4; 10:22; 37:15; cf. Akk. *apú*, "appear," "shine."

16. Pss. 80:2; 94:1; cf. 50:2.

17. See kere; Targ. Onk.; Sifrei 343; Ber. 62a; Vulg.

18. See Shadal.

19. Or *yokedet*, "blazing," or *lapidot*, "torchlike." See BDB,

206d; NAB, notes. For "fire" meaning "lightning," see Exod. 9:23–24.; Pss. 18:13–14; 148:8.

20. Cf. Hab. 3:3–4, "His splendor fills the earth: It is a brilliant light which gives off rays on every side."

21. Cf. ANEP, no. 501.

22. Abu Umar ibn Yaqwi, cited (and rejected) by Ibn Janah, s.v. '-sh-d; Shadal. Four manuscripts of SP read '-sh-d-w-t.

23. Shadal; Smith. *yamin*, "right," is from the same root as *teiman*, "south," in the similar passages cited above.

24. Emending *'eshdat* (spelled '-sh-d-t) to *'isharta* (spelled '-sh-r-t) (Cross and Freedman); cf. Num. 21:15, where SP reads '-sh-r for '-sh-d. The verb '-sh-r is a synonym of *ba'*, "come" (see Prov. 4:14; 9:6). There are other shifts between third and second person in this chapter (see vv. 3,18–19).

25. Thus essentially Targs. Onk., Jon., Neof.; Pesh.; Saadia; Vulg.; Ibn Ezra. Cf. Hab. 3:5 *le fanayv YELEKH dever va-yetse' reshef LERAGLAYV*.

26. Cross and Freedman reach this meaning by emendation.

27. El Amarna letter 147:39–40 (ANET, 484c).

28. Radak; Ramban; Ibn Ezra (at vv. 3 and 4, comparing the use of *nasa'* in Exod. 23:1 [cf. Exod. 20:7 = Deut. 5:11]), all of whom think that v. 4 is part of what the beings/persons mentioned in v. 3 utter.

29. In a footnote, NJPS mentions the possibility that vv. 3–5 apostrophize Moses: "Then were, O lover of the people, / All His worshipers in your care; / they followed your lead, / Accepted your precepts. . . ."

30. *H-b-b* does not otherwise appear in the Bible. It appears in Ecclus. 7:21, MS A (replaced with '-h-b in MS C); 10:25 (MS B). It is known in Aram., Arab., and probably Akk. (see J. Tigay, *The Evolution of the Gilgamesh Epic* [Philadelphia: University of Pennsylvania Press, 1982], 24n.).

31. Also in, e.g., Gen. 35:11; 48:4; Judg. 5:14. See Targs. Onk., Jon., Neof.; Rashi; Ramban; Shadal.

32. Cf. the Egyptian "Ptah who loves his people" (Beyerlin, 27) and the Akk. royal epithet "lover of the people" (*rā'im awīle*, *rā'imu ša niše*), meaning "lover of his subjects" (R. Frankena, *Briefe aus der Leidener Sammlung* [Leiden: Brill, 1968], 21:1; 22:1; R. F. Harper, *Assyrian and Babylonian Letters* [Chicago: University of Chicago Press, 1892–1914], 6: obv. 8). A first-century-C.E. Nabatean king is called "lover of his people" (*r-h-m '-m-h*) (J. Cantineau, *Le Nabatéen* [Paris: Librarie Ernest Leroux, 1930–32], 2:26,29; see G. A. Cooke, *A Text-Book of North Semitic Inscriptions* [Oxford: Clarendon, 1903], 215).

33. See 7:6; 14:2,21; 26:19; 28:9; Num. 16:3. So Ramban, Shadal, Driver.

34. See Ramban; Saadia.

35. See previous note; cf. Rashi. In the light of this view, some suggest that *h-v-v '-m-y-m* be read as *haviv 'ammim*, "best loved of nations," referring to Israel (Gaster, "Ancient Eulogy on Israel"; Milik).

36. For *kadosh* meaning "angel," see Ps. 89:6,8; Job 5:1; 15:15; Zech. 14:5; Dan. 8:13.

37. Some would emend this clause to "they bear your chariot" (*yisse'u merkavtekha*; cf. Isa. 66:15) (Tur Sinai; B. Margulis, "Gen. XLIX, 10/Deut. XXXIII, 2–3," VT 19 (1969): 202–210). Some scholars who believe that the verse refers to God's supernatural entourage argue that the Hebrew terms rendered "indeed" (*'af*), "in your hand" (*be-yadekha*), "in your steps" (*le-raglekha*), and "Your pronouncements" (*mi-dabberoteikha*), really are, or should be emended to, prepositions referring to the position of the angels surrounding God, meaning, respectively, "before Him" (*le-'appayv*), "at His side" (*be-yado*), "at His feet" (*le-raglayv*), and "behind Him" (*mi-dabberotayv*). See Milik, Seeligmann, and A. Rofé, *Israelite Belief in Angels in the Pre-Exilic Period* (Hebrew) (Ph.D. diss., Hebrew University, 1969), 94–97. For *le-'appayv*, cf. Hab. 3:5 (*le-fanayv* // *le-raglayv*) and Ugar. *b'ph* meaning *le-fanayv*. For *mi-*

dabberotayv as "behind," Milik compares Arab. *duburun*, "back" (note Arab. *min dubr*, "behind, in the rear," and cf. Heb. forms like *me-ra'ashotayv*, *ma-rgelotayv*, "at his head/feet"). Some scholars who hold this view revocalize or emend *hovev 'ammim* into a phrase referring to supernatural beings, such as "*hovevei 'ammim*," "those who care for the peoples," namely their angelic patrons (see Excursus 31) (Cross and Freedman) or *seviv 'elim*, "a circle (entourage) of divine beings" (Rofé).

38. Cf. Meklenburg; similarly Cassuto, who assumes that the poem is the libretto of a ceremony in which the people declare renewed allegiance to the Teaching and to God as their king. Saadia neutralizes the seeming change of speaker by rendering: "God, who commanded us the Torah through Moses and gave it as an inheritance to the congregation of Jacob . . . [v. 5] became king. . . ."

39. Gaster, "Ancient Eulogy on Israel"; NEB notes.

40. Suk. 42a (cf. BB 14a and Torah Temimah here); Maimonides, Hilkhot Talmud Torah 1:6; Shulhan 'Arukh, Yoreh De'ah 245:5; cf. Lev. R. 9:3.

41. Sifrei 346; TJ RH 1:3; see also RH 32b; Rashi; Ramban; Driver; Smith; Ehrlich; Mayes; Cassuto; Seeligmann.

42. Cf. Judg. 11:9–10 and the connection between Saul's and David's military victories and their acceptance as king (1 Sam. 8–11; 2 Sam. 5).

43. Exod. R. 2, end; 48:4; 52, beginning; Lev. R. 31:4; 32:2; Num. R. 15:13; Ibn Ezra; Maimonides, commentary to Mish. Shevuot 2:2; S. Talmon, *King, Cult, and Calendar in Ancient Israel* (Jerusalem: Magnes Press, 1986), 48–49; NJPS to v. 3, note c.

44. See also Judg. 8:23; Isa. 33:22; 1 Sam. 8:7; 12:12; Pss. 5:3; 24:7,9; 74:12; 84:4.

45. See Judg. 8:22; 9:6; 1 Sam. 10:17–24; 11:14–15; 2 Sam. 2:4; 3:17–18; 5:3; 1 Kings 1:39; 12:1,20; 2 Chron. 23:1–11. Cf. Ps. 47:6–10.

46. See endnote at 29:9; Weisman, 367–368; cf. Tur Sinai, who reads *shoftei*.

47. Narrated in Gen. 35:22; cf. 1 Chron. 5:1–2. Other reasons for Reuben's loss of status may be its involvement in the insurgency of Num. 16:1 (cf. Deut. 11:6) and its failure to respond to Deborah and Barak's call in Judg. 5:15–16.

48. 1 Chron. 5:3–10.

49. 1 Sam. 13:7; 2 Sam. 24:5; Mesha Inscription, ANET, 320 (see B. Halpern, *The Emergence of Israel in Canaan* [Chico, Calif.: Scholars Press, 1983], 122–123). The Reubenites *are* mentioned in Transjordan in 2 Kings 10:33 (referring to the eighth century, but perhaps simply a traditional designation of the territory) and in 4QSamuel^a, published by F. M. Cross, "The Ammonite Oppression of the Tribes of Gad and Reuben: Missing Verses from 1 Samuel 11 Found in 4QSamuel^a," in H. Tadmor and M. Weinfeld, eds., *History, Historiography, and Interpretation* (Jerusalem: Magnes Press, 1983), 148–158; A. Rofé considers 4QSam^a a late, midrashic composition ("The Acts of Nahash According to 4QSam^a," IEJ 32 [1982]: 129–133).

50. See Sarna, *Genesis*, xvii, 402; Milgrom, *Numbers*, Excursus 70; B. Oded, "The Settlement of the Tribe of Reuben in Transjordania," in *Studies in the History of the Jewish People and the Land of Israel in Memory of Zvi Avneri* (Haifa: University of Haifa, 1970), 11–36 (esp. 20–21); Cross, "Reuben," 46–65; Halpern, *Emergence*, 122–123. That the border between Gad and Reuben fluctuated is implied by the fact that Num. 32:34 assigns the cities of Dibon and Aroer to Gad (cf. 33:45,46 and Mesha 10–11 [ANET, 320]), while Josh. 13:16–17 assigns them to Reuben.

51. Cf. the battlefield prayer and consequent victory in 1 Chron. 5:18–20.

52. *Gilgamesh Epic*, 3:1:12; 3:6:11 (ANET, 81a,d).

53. *Rav*, "strive," masculine singular, cannot be the predicate of "hands," which is feminine plural. Some scholars construe "hands" as adverbial accusative and render "Though he

strives for himself (with) his own hands." Shadal takes *rav* as a noun, as in Isa. 19:20, and renders "his own hands will be the defender of his people." Various emendations have been suggested that do not materially affect the meaning; see Ehrlich, *Randglossen*; D. Christensen, "Dtn 33,11—A Curse in the 'Blessing of Moses'?" ZAW 101:279; Tur Sinai. The NJPS suggestion to read *rab* (with *patah* meaning *rabbeh* as in Judg. 9:29), "Make his hands strong," is unconvincing, since *rabbeh* means "increase," not "strengthen." See A. Berlin "On the Meaning of *rb*," JBL 100 (1981): 90–93.

54. See Exod. 28:30; Num. 27:21; Ezra 2:63. The Urim and Thummim appear under the name *'efod* in 1 Sam. 2:28; 23:9; 30:7, and other passages where they are implied by the use of terms such as "inquire of the LORD" and *lakhad* (Josh. 7:14–18; Judg. 1:1–2; 20:18; 1 Sam. 10:20–22; 14:37–42; 2 Sam. 2:1; 5:23–24). See I. Mendelsohn, s.v. "Urim and Thummim," IDB 4:739–740; A. Toeg, "A Textual Note on 1 Samuel XIV 41," VT 19 (1959): 493–498; Tur-Sinai, s.v. *Urim vetummim*, EM 1:179–183; M. Greenberg, s.v. "Urim and Thummim," EncJud 16:9–9; Sarna, *Exodus*, at 28:30; Milgrom, *Numbers*, Excursus 64; cf. the Egyptian method of presenting questions to an oracle cited by S. Ahituv, s.v. *'atid, haggadat 'atidot*, EM 6:430, top.

55. See Comment to 5:10.

56. Or "Quarrel-Place" (see Comment to 32:51). The meaning of *riv* in the verb *terivehu* (NJPS "challenged") is uncertain. The basic meaning, "quarrel," does not suit the context. "Challenged" attempts to bring the meaning closer to the parallel "test." Pss. 81:8 and 95:8–9 (note chiasm) speak only of testing at Massah and Meribah, and use *b-ḥ-n*, "test," instead of *riv*. They could imply that our verse uses *riv* loosely to express this meaning, perhaps in order to preserve the play on the place name "Meribah" (so S. E. Loewenstamm, *From Babylon to Canaan* [Jerusalem: Magnes Press, 1992], 56). Another possibility is that the verb means "defend" (i.e., "quarrel on behalf of"), implying that when God tested the Levites He also defended them against those who opposed their loyalty to Him. For this meaning see Isa. 1:27; 51:22; Dillmann.

57. See Exod. 32:26–29; Deut. 10:8.

58. Num. 25:1–13.

59. Ezek. 44:15; 48:11.

60. Exod. 17:2–3,7; Num. 20:3,13; Deut. 6:16.

61. Loewenstamm, *From Babylon to Canaan*, 140; Mayes. For other variant traditions in Bible about who tested whom, see Loewenstamm, *From Babylon to Canaan*, 55–65; idem, "The Bearing of Psalm 81 upon the Problem of the Exodus," EI 5 (1958): 80–82. That the Massah-Meribah incident alluded to in Ps. 81:8 involved idolatry is implied by vv. 9–12 there.

62. Moran; Loewenstamm, *From Babylon to Canaan*, 55.

63. The election of the Zadokite priests is described similarly in Ezek. 44:15–16,23–24.

64. See Lev. 10:10–11; Num. 27:21; Deut. 17:8–13; 24:8; 2 Kings 17:28; Ezek. 22:26; 44:23–24; 2 Chron. 19:8–11.

65. See Hag. 2:11–13; Mal. 2:6; cf. Exod. 18:16,19–20; Num. 27:21 (cf. Exod. 28:30); 1 Sam. 14:38–42; Mic. 3:11. Exod. 22:8 presumably involves something like the Urim and Thummim.

66. Num. 17:5; 18:7; 2 Chron. 26:16–18.

67. Exod. 30:1–9,34–38; Lev. 16:12–13.

68. See Num. 17:11–13. See M. Haran, *Temples and Temple Service* (Oxford: Clarendon, 1978), 230–245. Cf. the Canaanite use of incense discussed by O. Keel, "Kanaanäische Sühnenriten auf Ägyptischen Tempelreliefs," VT 25 (1955): 413–469.

69. See J. Milgrom, s.v. *ketoret*, EM 7:113–117; ANEP, nos. 320, 334, 575, 579, 581, 583, 592, 624–628, 640; Keel, "Kanaanäische Sühnenriten"; Haran, *Temples*, 235–241.

70. Heb. *ḥayil*, as in 8:17. Targ. Onk.; Sifrei 352; Ibn Ezra; Shadal: cattle. Sifrei adds: "From this verse it is said 'Most priests are wealthy.'"

71. In the present chapter derivatives of Heb. *r-ts-h*, "accept," are parallel to, and virtually synonyms of, "bless," "bless-

ing," and "bounty" (vv. 16,23,24). See Shadal; cf. Ps. 5:13; Prov. 8:35; 18:22.

72. *B-r-k ma'aseh-yad*; cf. 14:29; 15:10; 16:15; 24:19; 28:12; 30:9. cf. Job 1:10.

73. 1 Sam. 22:17–21.

74. 2 Kings 23:20; cf. 2 Kings 10:18–25; 11:18; 23:5.

75. See, e.g., Ps. 69; cf. O. Eissfeldt, *The Old Testament: An Introduction* (New York: Harper and Row, 1965), 116.

76. Sifrei 352; Rashi; see Num. 16 and Milgrom, *Numbers*, 419–420.

77. 1 Sam. 2:27ff (see Rashi and Radak); 1 Kings 12:31; 13:33. For strife between claimants to the priesthood see F. M. Cross, *Canaanite Myth and Hebrew Epic* (Cambridge: Harvard University Press, 1973), chap. 8.

78. Nah. 2:2,11; Ps. 69:24; Job 40:16; Prov. 31:17. In *motnayim kamayv*, either *motnayim* is adverbial accusative (Ibn Janah, *Sefer Ha-Rikmah*, 360; Rashi; Ibn Ezra; Dillmann; cf. Ps. 3:8; Gen. 3:15) or its final *mem* is an enclitic *mem*, an old emphatic suffix (Cross and Freedman; Ibn Janah's second explanation is close to this; SP omits the *mem*).

79. The rare use of *min* in the sense of "so as not to" enhances the alliteration of *mems* in this verse, as observed by my student, Philip Kaplan. Cross and Freedman vocalize *man yakuman*, "whoever arises" (anticipated by Radak s.v. *min*). 4QTestimonia 20, quoting this verse, reads *bal* (DJD 5:58; cf. Isa. 14:21); 2 Sam. 22:39 uses *ve-lo'* in the same idiom.

80. Student cited by Shadal.

81. See Judg. 3:15; 1 Sam. 7:5–6,16–17; 8:4; 10:17; 11:14–15 (Mizpah in Benjamin; Ramah); cf. Ps. 68:28.

82. Halpern, *Emergence*, 124.

83. Pss. 84:2; 87:2. Traditional commentaries think that the allusion is to the Jerusalem Temple (e.g., Sifrei 352; Rashi; Bekhor Shor); see Josh. 18:16 (cf. 15:8); Judg. 1:21, which put the Temple Mount in Benjaminite territory (but contrast Josh. 15:63). However, it is not clear that the Temple was ever thought to be in Benjaminite territory. Jerusalem was originally assigned to Benjamin, but the Judahites David and Solomon captured the city from the Jebusites and built the Temple; according to Ps. 78:68–69, the Temple was a manifestation of God's love for Judah.

84. Zev. 118b; TJ Meg. 1:14, 72d, top.

85. Bethel (Judg. 20:26–27; on the border between Benjamin and Ephraim [Josh. 16:1], belonged to Benjamin according to Josh. 18:22 but to Ephraim according to Judg. 1:22); Nob (1 Sam. 21–22); Ramah (in Benjamin, according to Josh. 19:25; see discussion by Z. Kallai, s.v. *Ramah, ha-Ramah*, EM 7:373–374).

86. For the idiom, which is always used of humans, see v. 28; 12:10; Lev. 25:18,19.

87. Sifrei 352; Rashi; Bekhor Shor; Smith; Cassuto, 1:78; Caquot, 80 n. 3.

88. GKC §119cc. It means "beside" in the phrase "camping beside," e.g., Num. 2:5,12.

89. This reading may have arisen from alternative readings in the next clause: *'alayv hofef* (as in some medieval Hebrew manuscripts) and *hofef 'alayv* (as in SP and Pesh.); the first *'alayv* was then misconstrued as part of the preceding clause (Driver). 4QDeut[h] replaces it with "God" (*'el*, reflected in LXX) and takes it as the first word of the next clause, which thus reads "God protects him ever." This leaves that clause awkwardly long, as do emendations of the first *'alayv* to *'elyon*, *'-l-y*, or *'-l*, "The Most High" (Driver; BHS; Cross and Freedman; A. Cooper in RSP 3: 455–456).

90. Cf. use of the synonymous *s-b-b* for "surround protectively" in 32:10; cf. Ps. 125:2. *Hofef* might also mean "He spreads, or flaps, (His) wings (over him)" (a protective act; cf. 32:11a), as the verb is used in Aramaic and medieval Hebrew (Ibn Quraish; see E. Kimron, "*hofef alayv kol hayom* [Deut. 33:12]," *Beth Mikra* 24 [1979]: 140–141).

91. Thompson.

92. Cf. Josh. 15:8; 18:16. The translation of Heb. *katef* as "side," "flank," is preferable to "slope" since in its topographical usage it sometimes refers to nonhilly terrain; see Num. 34:11; Isa. 11:14; Ezek. 25:9. In this interpretation, *shakhen* is used in its common sense of the Lord dwelling in His sanctuary as in Exod. 25:8; Isa. 8:18.

93. As in 1 Sam. 17:6, where "between his shoulders" means "on his back, slung from his shoulders." For the same idiom in rabbinic Hebrew and Arabic see Mish. Mak. 3:10; Y. Avishur, "Expressions such as '*bein yadayyim*' and Their Parallels in Semitic Languages," *Beth Mikra* 22 (1977): 204 (nn. 25, 30), 206–208 (Hebrew); M. Ullmann, *Wörterbuch der Klassischen Arabischen Sprache* (Wiesbaden: Harrassowitz, 1970), 1:48. Cf. "between your eyes" meaning "on your forehead" in 6:8.

94. CAD A2, 279b; cf. 276c. Cf. the depictions of the Egyptian god Horus in the form of a falcon perched protectively on the backs of the thrones of pharaohs in ANEP, nos. 377, 379.

95. As in, e.g., Gen. 24:53; Ezra 1:6; so Radak. For "blessing" (*berakhah*) meaning "gift" see, e.g., Gen. 33:11; Josh. 15:19.

96. Song 4:13,16; 7:14.

97. Driver; Ramban.

98. BHK (from Kennicott and de Rossi).

99. Cross and Freedman suggest that the MT may be due to confusion caused by passages like Gen. 27:39; cf. Gen. 27:28.

100. Lit., "bounty from heaven of moisture" (*mi-meged shamayim mi-tal*; for *tal*, "moisture," see Comment to 32:2).

101. If *geresh* comes from *g-r-sh*, "drive out," "toss up," it means that which the earth thrusts forth or tosses up (Driver). Tur Sinai suggests that the text originally read *gadish*, "heap(s) of grain," with *dalet* in place of the similar *resh*. Bekhor Shor explains *geresh* as "that which is sent forth," a metathesized form of *sheger*, "calving" (7:13), used for vegetation; he derives *sheger* from *sh-g-r*, "cast," "throw." If *geresh* does mean *sheger*, the clause could also mean "the bounty of calves, nurtured by the moon." Interestingly, the deity Shaggar (from whose name *sheger* is derived) is identified as a moon god in cuneiform sources (see chap. 7, n. 26; suggestion of Avigdor Hurowitz).

102. Apuleius, *Metamorphoses*, ed. J. A. Hanson (Cambridge: Harvard University Press, 1989), 295 (11:2) (ref. courtesy of Moshe Greenberg). A Sumero-Akkadian hymn also credits the moon god for the fertility of crops (ANET, 386a). The Ruwalah bedouin of Arabia believe that the moon condenses the dew and enables plants to grow (P. K. Hitti, *History of the Arabs*, 8th ed. [London: Macmillan, 1963], 98; ref. courtesy of Joseph F. Angel). The same explanation as Rashi's was expressed earlier by the Karaite Jacob al-Kirkisani (tenth century); see L. Nemoy, *Karaite Anthology* (New Haven: Yale University Press, 1952), 61.

103. Rashi, second interpretation; Bekhor Shor; Ramban (comparing Ezek. 47:12); Shadal. Conceivably the seemingly plural ending -*im* is a misunderstood enclitic *mem* or a dittography of *v-m* at the beginning of v. 15.

104. See N. Waldman, "The Wealth of Mountain and Sea: The Background of a Biblical Image," JQR 71 (1981): 176–180. Note particularly the *Gilgamesh Epic*, 6:17 (ANET, 84a) and the *Baal Myth*, UT 51: v, 77–78 (ANET, 133d); cf. Ps. 72:3.

105. Josh. 17:14–18; the Samaria ostraca refer to the wine and oil of this territory (ANET, 321b). Cf. C. G. Rasmussen, *NIV Atlas of the Bible* (Grand Rapids, Mich.: Zondervan, 1989), 40.

106. See Num. 32:1 (cf. Deut. 32:14); Gen. 37:25; Jer. 8:22; 46:11. Cf. Rasmussen, *NIV Atlas*, 52.

107. Exod. 30:23; Ezek. 27:22; Song 4:14. The related *re'shit* expresses this idea more commonly. See Comment to 18:4.

108. E.g., 34:1; Gen. 8:5; Num. 23:9.

109. Targ Jon.; Ibn Ezra (Yahel Or, ad loc. in *Ḥumash Meḥokekei Yehudah*, ed. Y. L. Krinski [1907–28], adds that mountain fruits are better than valley fruits; cf. Mish. Bik. 1:3,10).

110. Cf. Hab. 3:6; Gen. 49:26 (see Sarna, *Genesis*, ad loc.).

111. T. Jacobsen, "Sumerian Mythology: A Review Article," JNES 5 (1946): 141 (ref. courtesy of Ake W. Sjöberg).

112. Cassuto, 1:61.

113. Ramban; see Isa. 34:1; 42:10; Jer. 8:16; 47:2; Mic. 1:2; Pss. 24:1; 50:12 (implicitly includes animals); 98:7; cf. "city and its fullness" (population, Amos 6:8).

114. Isa. 60:5; cf. v. 16; 66:12; Ps. 72:10.

115. Some manuscripts of SP read "Dweller on Sinai" (*s-n-y*) instead of "Dweller in the Bush" (*s-n-h*).

116. E.g., Joel 4:17,21; Ps. 135:21.

117. Shadal holds that "Dweller in the Bush" must mean "the One who dwells on the mountain [Sinai] that is named after the bush" (*seneh*).

118. Because the epithet is found nowhere else and is not synonymous with the previous phrase, one wonders if the text is correct. Since *'erets u-melo'ah* || *tevel ve-yoshevei vah* in Ps. 24:1, and *yoshevei tevel* || *shokhenei 'arets* in Isa. 18:3, it is conceivable that our clause originally read *shokhenei vah* or the like, meaning "(and the favor) of its inhabitants."

119. Heb. *tavo'tah* seems to be a hybrid of two readings, such as *tavo'* and *te'eteh* (Mayes) or *tavo'* and *tehi* (cf. Gen. 49:26; Cross and Freedman). Cf. *'g'lty* in Isa. 63:3 and *'zkrty* in SP at Exod. 20:21. *Tevu'ot* in v. 14 may have contributed to the confusion.

120. Bekhor Shor. Note that Joshua, Deborah, and Jeroboam I were Ephraimite and Gideon was a Manassite (Num. 13:7,16; Judg. 4:4–5; 6:15). The Northern kingdom is sometimes called "(the House of) Joseph" (Ezek. 37:16; Amos 5:6; Ps. 77:16), as is the entire nation in Pss. 80:2; 81:6. The central sanctuary of Shiloh was in Ephraim (Josh. 18:1; Ps. 78:60,67).

121. Joseph has the same epithet in Gen. 49:26, where Tur Sinai suggests the emendation *negid 'eḥayv*, "ruler, leader of his brothers," based on 2 Chron. 11:22.

122. The Hebrew is literally "*his* firstling bull," referring presumably to Joseph's firstborn. This is contradicted by the end of the verse, which indicates that the bull stands for both Ephraim and Manasseh. The present translation agrees with 1QDeut[b], SP, LXX, Pesh., and Vulg., which lack the pronoun.

123. See *Gilgamesh Epic* 1:1:28 (Tigay, *Evolution of Gilgamesh Epic*, 141, 150, 263) and the passages about Hammurabi and Iahdun-Lim in ANET, 165a, 556b. Cf. the descriptions of heroes and gods fighting like bulls in ANET, 78c and 141c. Cf. Ps. 92:11.

124. Ps. 22:28 and Isa. 52:10 show that the phrase refers to peoples.

125. NJPS explains its translation with a footnote (following Ramban and Driver) stating that "these" are the one horn and "those" the other. However, if the pronouns, which are plural, each referred to a separate horn, it would imply that the ox has at least four horns.

126. In Hebrew parallelism, "thousands" normally precedes "myriads." Here the order is reversed because the larger and pre-eminent tribe is mentioned first (S.E. Loewenstamm, *Comparative Studies* [Kevelaer: Butzon and Bercker, and Neukirchen-Vluyn: Neukirchener Verlag, 1980], 268–269). Elsewhere in the Torah, Ephraim is larger in Num. 1:32–35, but Manasseh is considerably larger in Num. 26:29–37.

127. Gen. 49:13–15; Judg. 5:14–15.

128. B. Mazar, "'They Shall Call Peoples to their Mountain,'" EI 14 (1978): 40. See Josh. 21:34 and 12:22.

129. Ramban; Driver.

130. Suggestion of Moshe Greenberg.

131. In view of references to Zebulun's military activities, the possibility that the reference is to military expeditions cannot be excluded (Targ. Onk.; Ibn Ezra; Shadal; see Judg. 4:6,10; 5:18; 1 Chron. 12:33).

132. Gen. 4:20; 2 Chron. 14:14.

133. Cf. the blessings of dwellings in Num. 24:5 and Job 5:24.

134. In other words, that Zebulun has incorporated the territory of Issachar. This could also be implied by verses that mention only Zebulun where we would expect both tribes (Judg. 4:6 [Issachar's participation is shown by 5:15]; 6:35). This would be a reversal of relations between the tribes if, as some scholars believe, Zebulun began as a group of Issacharite clans that broke away (S. Yeivin, s.v. *Zebulun*, EM 2:898–899; idem, s.v. *Yissachar*, EM 3:950–951). Cf. N. Na'aman, *Borders and Districts in Biblical Historiography* (Jerusalem: Simor, 1986), 192–194. See also Halpern, *Emergence*, 121–122, 124–125.

135. Gen. 9:27 may indicate that dwelling in somebody's tent means being their client or ally. Perhaps Gen. 49:14–15, which describes Issachar as a toiling serf, means that it served Zebulun rather than the Canaanites, as usually thought.

136. Rashi; Targs. Jon. and Yer.

137. Targ. Onk. and Rashi.

138. On Mount Tabor, see Josh. 19:12,22,34; and cf. Y. Aharoni, s.v. *Tavor*, EM 8:406–407; Hos. 5:1 may imply a sanctuary of YHVH on Tabor (Mayes). Mazar, "They Shall Call Peoples," and cited by Aharoni in EM 8:406, favors Mount Carmel, which would suit v. 19b if Zebulun once controlled Mount Carmel.

139. Ps. 4:6 (cf. 50:14); 51:21; thus Ibn Ezra.

140. Ibn Ezra; Craigie.

141. Driver; Smith.

142. Driver; OJPS.

143. Smith; B. A. Levine, *In the Presence of the Lord* (Leiden: Brill, 1974), 135–137.

144. Ehrlich, *Mikra* (citing Isa. 41:2; 49:24 for the sense "victor[y]"); Tur Sinai; Weisman, 365–368. Cf. *tsidkot* in Judg. 5:11 and the evidence cited by Levine, *In the Presence of the Lord*, 135. For *tsedakah* meaning "victory," see also R. Weiss, *Mishut Ba-Mikra'* (Jerusalem: Rubinstein, ca. 1976), 39–40.

145. Meg. 6a with Rashi; Targ. Jon.; Rashi here.

146. See N. Waldman, "Wealth of Mountain and Sea," 176–180.

147. See B. Maisler, "Canaan and the Canaanites," BASOR 102:7ff; M. Eilat, s.v. *tekhelet ve-'argaman*, EM 8:543–546; Milgrom, *Numbers*, 411.

148. E. A. Speiser, *Oriental and Biblical Studies* (Philadelphia: University of Pennsylvania Press, 1967), 324–331; M. Astour, "The Origin of the Terms 'Canaan,' 'Phoenician,' and 'Purple,'" JNES 24 (1965): 346–350.

149. See, e.g., 1 Kings 5:22–23; "The Journey of Wen-Amon," ANET, 28; J. B. Pritchard, "Ships and Sailing in the OT," IDB 4:333–335; J. C. Greenfield, s.v. "Cyprus," IDB 1:753; A. Mazar, *Archaeology of the Land of the Bible* (New York: Doubleday, 1990), 514.

150. The translation presumes that the word is derived from a variant of *ts-f-n* (spelled with *samekh*), "to panel" (assuming that the basic meaning is "cover"; so Rashi) or of *ts-f-n*, "hide" (cf. HALAT). Even if that were the case, things hidden in sand would hardly be suitable objects for the verb "draw" (*y-n-k*, lit. "feed," "suck") in the previous clause.

151. See Smith; Tur Sinai.

152. Smith; Craigie. The older view that this refers to glass is unlikely. The Bible mentions glass only in Job 28:17. There is no evidence that it was manufactured in Israel in biblical times, and there are no glass artifacts to speak of from anywhere in the Near East between the end of the Late Bronze Age and the ninth or eighth century B.C.E.

153. See also Num. 32:16–32; Josh. 1:14; 4:12–13; 22:1–5.

154. Most commentators think that this blessing refers to the size of Gad's territory (Saadia; Rashi; Bekhor Shor; Ramban; Smith). However, the tribe itself is the direct object of "enlarge." Enlarging someone's territory is expressed with the owner as indirect object and the territory as the direct object. See 12:20; 19:8; Gen. 26:22; Exod. 3:8; 34:24; Amos 1:13.

155. Gen. 49:9; Num. 23:24; 24:9. 1 Chron. 12:8 mentions

valiant Gadite warriors who "had the appearance of lions and were as swift as gazelles upon the mountains."

156. "Saw" meaning "chose" (Shadal); see Exod. 18:21 (cf. 25); 1 Sam. 16:1.

157. *Re'shit* has this meaning in 1 Sam. 15:21.

158. Rashi; Bekhor Shor. Alternatively, Gad "chose for himself first"—his was the first tribe to choose land (Ibn Ezra; Radak). Ehrlich, *Mikra*, and Mayes suggest that "the first" is the territory of the firstborn, Reuben, meaning that Gad eventually absorbed parts of Reuben's territory and population (see Comment to v. 6). If so, "the portion of the . . . chieftain" could likewise refer to territory of Reuben who, as firstborn, was originally the chief son.

159. Judg. 5:14 (cf. 9); Isa. 33:22. Cf. Prov. 8:15.

160. Isa. 10:1; 30:8. This usage is presumably based on the practice of engraving laws on stone. This gives the verb the sense "prescribe" and yields the nouns *mehokek*, "commander, ruler," and *hok/hukkah*, "law," "assignment," "prescribed allotment" (e.g., Gen. 47:22; Exod. 5:14; Lev. 6:11; 10:13; Prov. 30:8).

161. Targums; Pesh.; Vulg.; Sifrei 355; Sot. 13b; BB 15a; Yal. 962; Saadia; Rashi; Shadal (final view). That Moses was buried in Reuben's territory (see 34:1,6; cf. Num. 32:38; Josh. 13:20) is not necessarily an objection, since Gad later took over part of Reuben's territory; see Weinfeld, DDS, 153 n. 2.

162. Driver; Smith; Ehrlich.

163. F. Burkitt, "On the Blessing of Moses," JTS 35 (1934): 68; Seeligmann, 84 n. 1. For the syntax cf. *nahalat* YHVH, "a portion provided by God" (Ps. 127:3). Various emendations have been suggested that do not substantially alter the meaning. See NEB; F. Giesebrecht, "Zwei Cruces Interpretum Ps. 45:7 und Deut. 33:21," ZAW 7 [1887]: 291–293; HALAT, 334a.

164. Num. 21:18; perhaps Gen. 49:10.

165. NJPS footnote; cf. Rashi at Meg. 6a.

166. Rashi; Ibn Ezra; Driver; Ehrlich, *Randglossen*. For the plural "heads" cf. 1 Chron. 12:18. "People" (*'am*) could mean "army" here (Craigie).

167. LXX "gathered together with the princes of the people" implies a Hebrew text in which the previous word, *s-p-w-n*, followed *v-y-t-'* and the two formed one word, *v-y-t-'-s-p-w-n* (*va-yit'asefun*). See Giesebrecht, "Zwei Cruces," 291–293.

168. See below, n. 172

169. Rashi; Bekhor Shor; Ibn Ezra; Driver. These commentators interpret "do the LORD's *tsedakah* and *mishpatim*" as "do what is right in His eyes"—namely, fulfilling their promise—or as referring to God's commands to conquer the Canaanites; cf. Smith ("carried out God's judgments on the Canaanites").

170. Judg. 5:11; 1 Sam. 12:7; 2 Sam. 18:19,31; Mic. 6:5; Ps. 36:7. See also Weiss, *Mishut Ba-Mikra'*, 39–40, and Levine, *In the Presence of the Lord*, 135.

171. Mish. Avot 5:18; Sifrei 355; Rashi, second view; Bekhor Shor. "Doing *tsedakah* and *mishpat*" often refers to a king who rules justly (2 Sam. 8:15–18; 1 Kings 10:9; Jer. 22:3,15; 23:5; 33:15; Ezek. 45:9; 1 Chron. 18:14; 2 Chron. 9:8). According to Weinfeld, the idiom means that Moses established social and legal reforms (DDS, 153, and *Justice and Righteousness in Israel and in the Nations* [Hebrew] [Jerusalem: Magnes Press, 1985], 107–108).

172. Cross and Freedman; Freedman, "Poetic Structure"; Tur Sinai; Weinfeld, DDS, 153; idem, *Justice and Righteousness*, 107–108. Weinfeld, for example, thinks that the point is that the Moses instituted a legal reform in the presence of the leaders of the people. Seeligmann and Weisman read (after v. 5) "the leaders of the people came together . . . to recount [*va-yyetannu*] deeds of salvation performed by the LORD, and His acts of deliverance on behalf of Israel."

173. See Josh. 19:40–48; Judg. 1:34–34; 18:1,27–29.

174. Heb. *yezannek*. No other derivatives of *z-n-k* are found in the Bible, and its meanings in postbiblical Hebrew and

cognate languages are not suitable. The translation seems to assume that it is a metathesized cognate of Arab. *nazaka* (*nazaqa*), "be swift, rush forth," used of horses (Ben Yehudah; HALAT; see J. G. Hava, *Arabic-English Dictionary* [Beirut: Catholic Press, 1915], 763). Some suggest emending *yezannek* (*y-z-n-k*) to *y-w-n-k* (*yonek*), "feeding, sucking," meaning that Dan is nourished effortlessly by the cattle and products of the fertile Bashan (Tur Sinai; Ehrlich); *y-n-k* is also used in v. 19 ("draw") and in 32:13 ("fed").

175. Josephus is unrestrained in his praise of the region's fertility and the Talmud describes its fruits as extraordinarily sweet. Josephus, War 3.516–521; Ber. 44a; cf. Targ. Jon.

176. See Targ. Jon.; Tosef. BK 8:18; BK 81a-b.

177. See n. 71 and Ps. 145:16 and cf. 103:5; 104:28.

178. Targ. Onk. Since Heb. *yam*, "west," literally means "sea, lake," the clause could also be translated "Take possession of the lake [Lake Tiberias, as in Isa. 8:23] and (its) south."

179. Thompson. For this road system see Aharoni, LOB, 41–49, esp. 48; Rasmussen, *NIV Atlas*, 27.

180. For the syntax and the meaning *"most blessed"* see Judg. 5:24; 1 Sam. 15:33; cf. Gen. 3:14 and Deut. 7:14. The extraordinary fertility of Asher's territory may have justified this characterization.

181. See Gen. 30:13; Ps. 72:17 (note parallelism and see LXX); Prov. 31:28; cf. Ps. 1:1 to Jer. 17:7.

182. Shadal; Tur Sinai.

183. Sifrei 355; Gen. R. 20:6; S. Krauss, *Talmudische Archaeologie* (Leipzig: Fock, 1910–12), 2:215 and 594 n. 475.

184. Smith.

185. Cf. Pss. 37:31; 40:3.

186. As in Neh. 3:3,6.

187. For bronze and iron gate-bars, see 1 Kings 4:13; Isa. 45:2; Ps. 107:16.

188. LXX; Pesh.; Targ. Onk.; so, too, Saadia.

189. UT 76: ii, 21–22. The word could be a metathesized form of *d-ʾ-b-h* // *ʾoz*, "strength," in Job 41:14. See F. M. Cross, "Ugaritic DBʾAT and Hebrew Cognates," VT 2 (1952): 162–164.

190. Hab. 3:8b; Ps. 68:5; see also 2 Sam. 22:11; Isa. 19:1. Pss. 18:11; 68:34; 104:3. Cassuto, 1:244 notes that these references are always in the context of God punishing evildoers and delivering His servants.

191. See, e.g., ANET, 66c, 84a, 132c, 134a, 138d.

192. Cf. Ps. 146:5; "Happy is he who has the God of Jacob for his help" (*be-ʿezro*).

193. Cross and Freedman, reading *rokhev shamayim be-ʿuzzo rokhev be-gaʾavato shehakim*. The emendation simply divides *b-ʿ-z-r-k* into *b-ʿ-z* and *r-k*, and restores a *beth* lost by haplography, to produce *r-k-b*. Gaster, "Ancient Eulogy on Israel," emends *be-ʿezrekha* to *be-ʿezro*, "in His *ezer*," on the assumption that the latter also has a meaning like "strength," as in Ps. 89:20, where it may mean "warrior." This emendation is simpler and consistent with the parallelism of *ʿezer* and *gaʾavah*, "majesty," in v. 29. But whether *ʿezer* means "strength" is debated (see A. Rainey in RSP 2:74–75, no. 3). Note also the interchanges and word-plays between *ʿ-z-r* and *ʿ-z-z* discussed by G. Brin, "The Roots *ʿzr-ʿzz* in the Bible," *Leshonenu* 24 (1960): 8–14.

194. Hab. 1:12; Ps. 74:12; Isa. 51:9; cf. Prov. 8:23.

195. Radak; Ibn Ezra; Driver.

196. See Cross, *Canaanite Myth and Hebrew Epic*, 15–19, 46–50. Cf. *melekh ʿolam* in Jer. 10:10.

197. Reading *mahaseh* (*m-h-s-h*), "shelter," in place of *mitahat* (*m-t-h-t*), "underneath." These words would have looked fairly similar in the Jewish script of the last two centuries B.C.E. Note *maʿon* // *mahaseh* in Ps. 91:9.

198. *Meʿanneh ʾelohei kedem u-mehattet zeroʿot ʿolam* (Gaster, "Ancient Eulogy on Israel"; NEB). For "shattering the arm" see Ezek. 30:21; Ps. 10:15; Job 38:15.

199. Isa. 27:1; 51:9–11; Pss. 74:10–18; 89:7–11; cf. Hab. 3:8.

200. Although the Bible never calls the ancient powers of the sea "divine beings," they were regarded as such in the pagan myths from which the motif evolved (cf. *Enuma Elish* and the *Baal Myth*). Cf. also the "olden gods" and "gods of olden days" mentioned in Hittite texts; see ANET, 120b, 397b, and F. M. Cross, "The 'Olden Gods' in Ancient Near Eastern Creation Myths," in F. M. Cross et al., eds., *Magnalia Dei* (Garden City, N.Y.: Doubleday, 1976), 329–338.

201. Ehrlich, *Randglossen*, emending *v-y-ʾ-m-r hashmed* to *v-ʾ-m-r-y hishmid*. Cf. Amos 2:9.

202. Heb. *badad*, lit. "alone," meaning either "left alone" or unafraid to dwell alone (Jer. 49:31; Ps. 4:9; cf. Judg. 18:7). See Rashi; Bekhor Shor at 32:12; Driver.

203. Heb. *ʿein* seems to be derived from the same root that underlies *maʿon/meʿonah*, "dwelling" (see Comment to v. 27). The spelling *ʿ-y-n* implies a root *w/yn*; cf. *veʿanah*, "shall abide," in Isa. 13:22 (thus translated by LXX), which implies a root *ʿ-n-h*, perhaps a bi-form.

204. Similar phrases appear in 2 Kings 18:32 and perhaps KAI 14:19 (*ʾ-r-ts-t d-g-n*, taken as "lands of Dagon" [Rosenthal in ANET, 662d] or "lands of grain" [Donner and Röllig in KAI 2:20]).

205. In view of "your protecting [lit., "helping"] shield" below in this verse, note the similar declarations in Ps. 89:16–19, which also refers to God as Israel's shield, and Ps. 146:5, which congratulates the person who has the God of Jacob "as his help"; cf. also the MT of v. 26.

206. See Exod. 15:11; Pss. 35:10; 71:19; 89:9.

207. E.g., Gen. 15:1; Pss. 3:4; 18:3, 31; 28:7 (*ʿuzzi u-magini*); 84:12.

208. In the Hebrew this phrase is preceded by *va-ʾasher*, "and who," which is omitted by the translation because it is awkward and superfluous. It may be a partial dittography of the earlier *ʾashreikha*. Some consider it a misreading of *Shaddai*, "the Almighty," in which case the clause originally meant, "and (by) Shaddai, your sword triumphant." Another possibility is that *ʾasher* here is an epithet of God, and that the passage means: "and (by) the Bestower of Good Fortune, your sword triumphant." *ʾ-sh-r* seems to be the theophoric element in some Hebrew names, synonymous with *gad*, "good fortune," originally "spirit of good fortune" (see Gen. 30:11,13). See N. Avigad, *Hebrew Bullae* (Jerusalem: Israel Exploration Society, 1986), no. 126 (Hebrew; cf. no. 127). In the context of Deut. 33, the Bestower of Good Fortune would be the Lord, as is the spirit of good fortune Gad in names like Gaddiahu (see J. Tigay, *You Shall Have No Other Gods* [Atlanta: Scholars Press, 1986], 65, 69–70). If this is the meaning here, the first half of the verse should probably be parsed as "O happy Israel!/ Who is like you, a people delivered./ The LORD is your protecting shield,/ The Bestower of Good Fortune your sword triumphant." Cf. NEB.

209. Cf. Josh. 10:24; cf. 1 Kings 5:17; Ps. 110:1; Akk. examples cited in CAD K, 7ab; and illustrations in ANEP, no. 249; O. Keel, *The Symbolism of the Biblical World* (New York: Seabury Press, 1978), 253–255; F. J. Yurco, "3,200-Year-Old Picture of Israelites Found in Egypt," BAR 16/5 (September-October, 1990), 30; cf. J. C. Greenfield, "Notes on the Asitawada (Karatepe) Inscription," EI 14 (1978): 74.

Chapter 34

1. Hebrew texts have section breaks before vv. 1 (M, SP), 5, 8, and 10 (SP).

2. Judg. 20:1; 1 Sam. 3:20; 1 Kings 5:5.

3. F. M. Abel, *Géographie de la Palestine* (Paris: Gabalda, 1933–38), 1:381.

4. Smith.

5. See 1:5; 3:29; 4:46; 28:69.

6. Josh. 4:13; 5:10; 2 Kings 25:5.

7. R. Meyuḥas; Ḥazzekuni.

8. Gen. 13:10–12; 2 Kings 7:46.

9. See Josephus, War, 4.452–456 and H. St.J. Thackeray, *Josephus* 4 (Cambridge: Harvard University Press, 1967), 135 n. g. This phrase designates the Jordan Valley from at least as far north as Sukkot (2 Kings 7:46) down to the Cities of the Plain, which were probably around the southern end of the Dead Sea.

10. See Judg. 1:16; 3:13; 2 Chron. 28:15. Josephus, War 4.459–475; M. Avi Yonah, *The Madaba Mosaic Map* (Jerusalem: Israel Exploration Society, 1954).

11. Targ. Jon.; SOR 10; Kid. 38a; Tosef. Sot. 11:7(8). According to Josephus, Ant. 4.327, and Est. Rab. 7:11, end, Moses died on the first of Adar.

12. See 2 Kings 22:12 (high rank is shown by the accompanying officials); Lachish letter 3:19 (ANET, 322b); R. Hestrin and M. Dayagi-Mendels, *Inscribed Seals: First Temple Period* (Jerusalem: Israel Museum, 1979), nos. 3–5; S. Yeivin, s.v. *pekidut*, EM 6:550–551.

13. See Num. 12:6–8; note the parallelism of "servant" and "chosen" in Isa. 42:1 (cf. 41:8) and see Ps. 106:23 (Moses is God's "chosen one"). See also Gen. 24:2 and 34 and H. L. Ginsberg in ANET, 143 n. 6. Sifrei 357 observes: "Scripture speaks [here] in praise of Moses and not in deprecation of him, for we find that the early prophets were called 'servants.'" The term is applied to Abraham, Moses, Caleb, Joshua, David, prophets, all Israel, and the righteous (Gen. 26:24; Exod. 14:31; Num. 14:24; Josh. 1:1–2; Judg. 2:8; 2 Sam. 3:18; 2 Kings 9:7; Amos 3:7; Isa. 41:8; 54:17; Ps. 113:1).

14. Targ. Onk; Targ. Yer.; Ibn Ezra; R. Meyuḥas; Driver; Cf. Num. 3:16; 9:23; Deut. 1:26; 8:3.

15. Ralbag, lesson 15; Ehrlich, *Mikra*.

16. Num. 33:38.

17. BB 17a; MK 28a; Rashi; Targ. Jon.

18. MK 28a; A. Even Shoshan, *Ha-Millon He-Ḥadash* (Jerusalem: Kiryat Sefer, 1975), s.v. *neshikah*.

19. 1 Sam. 28:3–25. See Lekah Tov; Ḥazzekuni; Ralbag; Abravanel, 352; D. Berger, *The Jewish-Christian Debate in the High Middle Ages* (Philadelphia: Jewish Publication Society, 1979), p. 225, §240; Christian writers cited by Ginzberg, *Legends*, 6:164, and S. E. Loewenstamm, *From Babylon to Canaan* (Jerusalem: Magnes Press 1992), 158; M. Greenberg, s.v. "Moses," EncJud 12:387. On the fear in rabbinic literature lest Moses be deified, see further J. Goldin, *Studies in Midrash and Related Literature* (Philadelphia: Jewish Publication Society, 1988), 180–181, 183–185; S. E. Loewenstamm, *From Babylon to Canaan*, 136–166; S. Lieberman, *Texts and Studies* (New York: Ktav, 1974), 206–207 n. 74.

20. In later times there was an Israelite sanctuary of the Lord in the nearby town of Nebo (Mesha inscription, ll. 14–18 [ANET, 320d]; see Rofé, *Mavo'*, 240–241; F. M. Cross, "Reuben, First-Born of Jacob," ZAW 100 [1988], Supplement, 50ff). Rofé considers it "likely that the sanctity of the site was based on the belief that Moses was buried there."

21. See J. Klein, "The 'Bane' of Humanity: A Lifespan of One Hundred Twenty Years," *Acta Sumerologica* 12 (1990). According to Ps. 90:10, a life of seventy to eighty years is normal. In Egyptian literature, the ideal maximal lifespan is 110 years (ANET, 414 n. 33; cf. Gen. 50:26). According to biblical tradition, in earlier generations some people lived much longer, and even in Moses' lifetime, Aaron is said to have lived to 123 (Num. 33:39). These long lifespans should not be rationalized by assuming that "year" means something less than it normally does. This would require interpreting such short years inconsistently. For example, Methuselah's 969 years would have to be divided by ten to become natural, but Abraham's 175 would have to be divided by two or three. Noah's 950 years cannot be divided at all, since the chronology of the flood clearly indicates that his years were twelve-month years (see Gen. 7:11,24; 8:3–5,13–14). There is no evidence that ancient Semitic languages used "years" so inconsistently; had the Bible, which

"speaks in the language of man," done so, how many readers would have understood it? For the literary symbolism of the patriarchal lifespans see N. M. Sarna, *Understanding Genesis* (New York: Jewish Theological Seminary and McGraw-Hill, 1966), 81–85.

22. See Gen. 27:1; 1 Sam. 4:15; 1 Kings 14:4 (contrast 2 Sam. 19:36); ANET, 412b, 561c, 661d.

23. See the supercommentaries on Ibn Ezra by S. Z. Netter (pub. 1859; reprinted in Ḥorev ed. of *Mikra'ot Gedolot* [London and New York, 1948]) and Y. L. Krinski (*Ḥumash Meḥokekei Yehudah*, pub. 1907–28). According to R. Joseph Kimḥi, the verb *nas* is not from *nus* (n-w-s), "flee, depart," but from a cognate of Arabic *nassa* (n-s-s), "dry up" (H. J. Mathews, *Sepher Ha-galuj* [Berlin: M'kize Nirdamim, 1887], 8; for the Arabic verb see G. W. Freytag, *Lexicon arabico-latinum* [Halle: C. A. Schwetschke, 1830–37], 4:270). For detailed discussion, see J. Tigay, "*Lo' nas leho*, 'He had not become wrinkled' (Deut. 34:7)," in Z. Zevit et al., eds., *Solving Riddles and Untying Knots: . . . Studies . . . Greenfield* (Winona Lake, Ind.: Eisenbrauns, 1995), 345–350.

24. See BM 87a; BB 120a; J. C. Greenfield, "A Touch of Eden," in *Orientalia J. Duchesne-Guillemin Emerito Oblata* (Leiden: Brill, 1984), 223–224.

25. Cf. Bezalel's spirit of wisdom from God (technical wisdom in crafts) in Exod. 28:3; 31:3.

26. See Weinfeld, DDS, 181, esp. n. 3. Z. Weisman, "The Personal Spirit as Imparting Authority," ZAW 93 (1981): 225–234, compares this episode with the transfer of Moses' spirit to the elders and the transfer of Elijah's spirit to Elisha.

27. See R. Peter, "L'imposition des mains dans l'Ancien Testament," VT 27 (1977): 48–55; D. P. Wright, "The Gesture of Hand Placement in the Hebrew Bible and in Hittite Literature," JAOS 106 (1986): 433–446. The rite is not the same as laying a single hand on sacrificial animals, as in Lev. 1:4.

28. For detailed discussion, see J. Tigay, "The Significance of the End of Deuteronomy (Deut. 34:10–12)," in M. V. Fox et al., eds., *Temples, Texts, and Traditions: A Tribute to Menahem Haran* (Winona Lake, Ind.: Eisenbrauns, 1995).

29. Ralbag, ad loc. and lesson 15; Sforno; cf. Shab. 104a; Maimonides, "Epistle to Yemen," in A. S. Halkin and Boaz Cohen, eds., *Moses Maimonides' Epistle to Yemen* (New York: American Academy for Jewish Research, 1952), x and 50–51; H. Crescas, *'Or 'Adonai* (Vienna, 1859), 2:4, 3, p. 45a (ref. courtesy Daniel Lasker); cited, with better reading, by Abravanel, 354.

30. Commentary on the Mishnah, Introduction to Sanhedrin, chap. 10.

31. Cf. S. Dean McBride, Jr., in J. L. Mays et al., eds., *Harper's Bible Commentary* (San Francisco: Harper and Row, 1988), 23. McBride suggests that the passage would have the effect of subordinating Ezekiel's "Torah" (Ezek. 40–49) to that of Moses.

32. See 2 Kings 22 and the Introduction to this commentary.

33. This passage would also undermine claims legitimizing the golden calves of Bethel and Dan if such claims were bolstered by a legend that they were manufactured by Aaron with divine approval (see Excursus 12). It would also subordinate aspects of later prophetic teachings that might be inconsistent with those of Moses, such as the classical prophets' critique of sacrifice. Strictly speaking, this passage emphasizes the authority of Moses, not of Deuteronomy, and would not by itself strengthen Deuteronomy's positions on matters where it disagrees with other *Mosaic* traditions in Exodus, Leviticus, and Numbers. However, for Deuteronomy this is a meaningless distinction since the book views itself as the last word on Moses' teachings.

34. ANET, 178–180; Driver and Miles, BL, 97–107 (esp. cols. xxiv, 79–83, and xxvb, 95–102 [Hammurabi's "words" are his laws]). Another important difference between the passages

is that Hammurabi speaks of laws that he himself claims to have written, whereas the Bible always refers to laws ordained by God.

35. Keter Torah. In view of this contrast, Moses' incomparability would subordinate the laws given by Joshua at Shechem (Josh. 24:25–26) to those given by Moses, in case of conflict between them. For other declarations of incomparability in Bible (in deuteronomistic passages) and elsewhere, see 1 Kings 3:12; 2 Kings 18:5; 23:25; Weinfeld, DDS, 358–359; G. N. Knoppers, "'There Was None Like Him.' Incomparability in the Book of Kings," CBQ 54 (1992): 411–431 (ref. courtesy of Avigdor Hurowitz).

36. Gen. 18:19; Exod. 33:12,17; Jer. 1:5; Amos 3:2. See Ram-ban at Gen. 2:9 and Gen. 18:19. Other pertinent nuances of "know" include "care for," "be acquainted with," "be attentive to," and "recognize."

37. Shadal.

38. See Comment to 5:4; Ibn Ezra at 5:4. Abravanel, 354.

39. Cf. Ḥazzekuni ("therefore they believed him"); Crescas cited by Abravanel, 354; Keter Torah.

40. See, e.g., Moses' prophetic signs and the ten plagues (Exod. 4 and 7–12) as well as Exod. 14:21–31; 15:25; 16; 17:5–7,8–13; 19:16–19; 33:29–35; Num. 11:1–2,31–33; 16:30–35.

41. Shadal; Abravanel; cf. Josh. 3:8–4:18; 10:11–14; 1 Sam. 7:5–10; 12:16–18; Isa. 38:8.

42. For the phrases, see Weinfeld, DDS, 329, 330.

Notes to the Appendix

1. The Yiddish term is related to Old French *trop(e)*, "tune," cited by Rashi (commentary to Kid. 71a). It presumably goes back to Latin *tropus* and Greek *tropos*, "mode," "melody."

2. In many codexes and printed editions, such as the Leningrad Codex and BHS, both sets of signs are printed together in the text of the Decalogue, both in Exod. 20 and Deut. 5. Other editions print only the "lower accents" in Exodus and Deuteronomy, and print another copy of the Decalogue, with the "upper accents," at the end of these books or at the end of the Torah.

3. The designations "upper" and "lower" are presumably due to the fact that, in the "upper" set, a slightly larger percentage of the signs is superlinear than in the "lower" set. (In both sets, the majority of the signs are sublinear.)

4. Mak. 24a; Hor 8a.

5. See the detailed study by M. Breuer, "Dividing the Decalogue into Verses and Commandments," in Ben-Zion Segal and G. Levi, ed., *The Ten Commandments in History and Tradition* (Jerusalem: Magnes Press, 1990), 291–330.

6. See Ḥazzekuni at Exod. 20:14; Magen Avraham to Shulhan ʿArukh, ʾOrah Ḥayyim 494:1 (refs. courtesy of Neil Danzig).

7. Ḥazzekuni at Exod. 20:14.

8. See TJ Meg. 74d, top; Eisenstein, *Ozar Dinim u-Minhagim*, 375; L. Jacobs, s.v. "Torah, Reading of," EncJud 15:1253; I. Tishby, *The Wisdom of the Zohar* (Oxford: Oxford University Press, 1989), 3:1037–1039. Cf. Deut. R., *Ki Tavoʾ*, 7:8, end.

EXCURSUSES

The Historical Geography of Deuteronomy

Knowing the location of places named in the Bible is often important for understanding the meaning of a narrative. In this Excursus each place mentioned in the commentary whose site is not obvious is listed alphabetically and, to the extent possible, briefly identified. Identifying biblical places can be difficult because many places were destroyed or abandoned over the centuries or underwent changes of name. Identifying places mentioned in ancient texts is a highly specialized discipline known as historical geography. Sometimes the Bible identifies places or gives their location, particularly when an old name had already been replaced by a newer one that was better known to readers.[1] Because of the Bible's own interest in geography, it contains itineraries and lists of the towns of the Israelite tribes and descriptions of their borders.[2] Frequently, historical geographers begin with less explicit clues in the biblical text, such as the names of nearby places and landmarks and indications of the direction of one place relative to another. Information in the Bible is supplemented from several other sources: references to places in other ancient texts, which are studied by the same methods; archaeological evidence about which sites were occupied in certain periods; identifications of biblical places in ancient translations of the Bible and other postbiblical texts, including Josephus, rabbinic literature, the writings of church fathers, Christian pilgrims, and Arab geographers; and Arabic place names that sometimes preserve the ancient names. All of these sources must be sifted with care, since they are not always reliable and are frequently based on conjecture rather than unbroken tradition.

The results of such research are scattered in an extensive body of scholarly literature. They are periodically summed up in biblical encyclopedias and reference works devoted to historical geography.[3] In preparing the commentary and maps several works have been consulted about each site. The single most useful source is the Hebrew *Entsyklopedia Mikra'it*, published in Israel by the Bialik Institute and the Hebrew University's Museum of Jewish Antiquities, which cites all the major suggestions that had been made about each place, and the evidence on which they are based, as of the time the articles were written. Because the available evidence is incomplete, there is uncertainty and disagreement about the identification of many places. Archaeological exploration regularly opens new options, particularly in Jordan, and several new theories about places in that country have been proposed even since the maps for this commentary were prepared.[4]

Abarim, Heights of (32:49). Probably the mountain range that traverses Transjordan east of the Dead Sea and overlooks the sea.[5]

Ar (2:9). City or region in Moab. The reference to its burning by Sihon favors taking it as a city (see Num. 21:28). Since Ar stands for Moab in 2:9,18 and 29, it must have been an important city, perhaps its capital at the time. It could be identical to Ir-Moab, a city on Moab's northern border mentioned in Num. 22:36,[6] or to Kir-Moab, apparently the capital, mentioned parallel to Ar in Isa. 15:1. Ar and Ir and Kir could be interchangeable terms, all meaning "city."[7]

Argob (3:4). Region in Syria. The name probably had both a narrow and a broader meaning and may have been used for different areas in different periods. In Joshua 13:30 and 1 Kings 4:13 it is a section within Bashan. The targums identify it with Trachonitis, the Leja range east of Bashan. On the other hand, Deuteronomy 3:14 speaks of it as synonymous with all of Bashan and indicates that it abuts Geshur and Maaca, which are on the west.[8]

Aroer (2:36). Doubtless Khirbet Ara'ir, a small tell on the northern slope of the Arnon valley, about a mile from the stream. Remains from the end of the Late Bronze Age indicate that it was a fortress guarding the King's Highway which crossed the wadi nearby (compare Jer. 48:19).[9] "The town in the [Arnon] valley itself" (2:36), near the stream or possibly on an island in it, is always mentioned in conjunction with Aroer; it was likely a suburb of Aroer, perhaps a fort guarding its water supply.[10]

Ashtaroth and Edrei (1:4; 3:1,10). Ashtaroth has been identified as Tell Ashterah, a site along the ancient King's Highway in Syria, about twenty miles east of Lake Tiberias. It is called Ashteroth-Karnaim in Genesis 14:5. It is mentioned as a royal city, ruled by a king with a Semitic name, in the Amarna letters of the Late Bronze Age, and in Ugaritic and Egyptian texts of that age.[11] Edrei has been identified as Deraa, a town south of Ashtaroth near the Jordanian border, about thirty miles east of the Jordan by an eastern tributary of the Yarmuk. Pottery fragments from the Early Bronze Age on have been found at the large tell in the town. It is mentioned in Ugaritic and Egyptian inscriptions of the Late Bronze Age.[12] That Og dwelled or reigned in both Ashtaroth and Edrei is also stated in Joshua 12:4; 13:12,31. A connection between these two cities as twin seats of government seems to be indicated in the Ugaritic text, which speaks of a god dwelling in Ashtaroth and judging (or ruling) in *hdr'y*, apparently a phonetic variant or scribal error for Edrei (*'dr'y*). The god is apparently named Rapi'u, the Ugaritic singular of Rephaim, which is significant in view of Deuteronomy 3:11 which states that Og was the last of the Rephaim.

Bashan (1:4; 3:1–29 passim; 4:43; 29:6; 32:14; 33:22). A mountain range in the territory of modern Syria south of Damascus, extending roughly from the Yarmuk River, or just south of it, to the Hermon range on the north, and from the Golan Heights on the west to the Leja and Hauran (Jebel Druze) mountains on the east. It is not clear whether the mountain ranges on the west and east were considered part of Bashan; in any case, the Israelites did not capture the lands of Maaca and Geshur in the Golan Heights.[13]

Beeroth-bene-jaakan, Moserah, Gudgod, and Jotbath (10:6–7). According to Numbers 33:30–35, where the names are in slightly variant forms, these places were on the way to Ezion-geber, which was two stations beyond Jotbath; whether they are north or south of Ezion-geber is debated. Ezion-geber (q.v.) is near the northern end of the Gulf of Elath, in western Edom. The name Beeroth-bene-jaakan, "the wells of the children of Jaakan," alludes to an Edomite clan mentioned elsewhere in the Bible. Sites containing the Arabic *bir*, "well," have been considered as its location.[14] For Jotbath, sites with Arabic names containing *Taba* have been considered, including places near the al-Taba marsh in the Aravah (near modern Yotvata) and the Wadi Taba, which meets the Gulf of Elath seven miles south of modern Elath.[15] There are no attractive candidates for Moserah or Gudgod.

Beth-peor (4:46; Josh. 13:20; cf. Mount Peor Num. 23:28). A town in the territory taken from Sihon and given to Reuben. Its precise location is unknown. The nearby valley, where the Israelites were encamped when Moses delivered his final addresses, may have been the well-watered Wadi 'Ayun ('Uyun) Musa, "the Valley of Moses' wells."[16]

Bezer (4:43). A town "in the wilderness in the Tableland" of Moab. "The wilderness" suggests that it was in the eastern part of the Tableland. This is probably the Bezer men-

tioned in the inscription of Mesha, King of Moab. The context of the inscription implies that Bezer may have been in the vicinity of Dibon and Aroer, just north of the Arnon.[17]

Dan (34:1). Tell el-Kadi (Tel Dan), at the foot of Mount Hermon. Archaeological excavations have unearthed remains of the city of Dan from the Canaanite and Israelite periods.

Di-zahab (1:1). Perhaps Dahab on the western shore of the Gulf of Elath.

Edom See Seir-Edom.

Edrei See Ashtaroth.

Elath (2:8). Generally identified with either the Jordanian town of Aqabah or Tell el-Kheleifeh, about halfway between Aqabah and the modern Israeli city of Elath. Its name seems to be preserved in Aila, the medieval name of Aqabah. However, since remains of the Iron Age have been found at Tell el-Kheleifeh, but not at Aila, the former is more likely to have been biblical Elath.[18]

Ezion-geber (2:8). A harbor where Solomon maintained a fleet of ships with Phoenician help, possibly located about eight miles south of modern Elath, on the Sinai coast across from Coral Island (Jeziret Fara'un) and on the island itself, where there is a harbor of unknown date which resembles Phoenician harbors. The strait between the coast and the island forms a natural anchorage.[19]

Gilgal (11:30). A place near Mounts Ebal and Gerizim. A likely possibility is a ruin about a mile or so southeast of Tell Balatah (Shechem); its Arabic name, Khirbet Juleijil, may reflect "Gilgal." According to G. A. Smith, it lies on a hill facing the valley between Gerizim and Ebal and contains a circle of large stones.[20] Another suggestion identifies it as El-Unuk, overlooking Wadi Far'ah, four miles east of Mount Ebal and Shechem.[21] It is less likely that the better-known Gilgal, near Jericho, is meant, since that is nearly thirty miles from Mounts Ebal and Gerizim.

Golan in Bashan (4:43). The location of this city is uncertain. Some scholars assume that it was somewhere in the area known today as the Golan Heights, while others identify it with the village of Sahem el-Jawlan a bit further east.[22]

Gudgod See Beeroth-bene-jaakan.

Havvoth-jair (3:14). A group of settlements in northern Transjordan. Literally, 3:14 says "Jair . . . captured the whole Argob district as far as the boundary . . . and named them [that is, Bashan] after himself." "Them" apparently refers to the sixty towns of Bashan (v. 4; see Josh. 13:30).[23] Heb. *Ḥavvot* is usually translated "villages," but if the Havvoth-jair are indeed the sixty towns of Bashan, it cannot literally mean "villages," since the sixty towns were fortified (v. 5). The meaning "villages" is usually supported with reference to Arabic *ḥiwa'*, "circle of tents."[24] However, the Arabic noun is derived from *ḥ-w-y*, "collect," "encompass," "enclose," which theoretically could also yield a noun meaning "enclosed settlement." The entire matter is complicated by other passages referring to Havvoth-jair not in Bashan but in Gilead. Some of them state that Havvoth-jair consists of twenty-three or thirty cities, and one explicitly distinguishes Havvoth-jair from the sixty walled cities in the Argob region of Bashan (1 Kings 4:13; see also Num. 32:39-41; Judg. 10:3-5; 1 Chron. 2:22-23). It seems possible that all these passages reflect changes over time in the number of towns belonging to Havvoth-jair and that this group included towns in Gilead as well as Bashan.[25]

Hazeroth (1:1). The second site at which the Israelites encamped after leaving Mount Sinai, as related in Numbers 11:35 and 33:17. Depending on scholars' theories about the location of Mount Sinai itself, Hazeroth has been identified with either 'Ein Khadra in the southern Sinai or Khadira in northeastern Sinai.[26]

Heshbon (e.g., 1:4; 2:24). Sihon's capital. Its name is preserved in that of Tell Hesban in Jordan, about fifteen miles east of the point where the Jordan meets the Dead Sea. However, excavations at that site have found no remains from the Late Bronze Age, and the excavators conjecture that the Heshbon of the Late Bronze Age was located at Jalul, where remains of the period have been found. Jalul is about seven miles southeast of Tell Hesban and visible from it.[27]

Hor, Mount (32:50). Located on the western border of Seir-Edom, Mount Hor was the first station at which the Israelites stopped after leaving Kadesh, and the place where Aaron died (Num. 20:23–28; 33:37–38). Its exact location is not certain, but it must have been near the present border between Israel and Egypt.

Horeb (e.g., 1:2; 4:10; 5:2). Deuteronomy's usual name for Mount Sinai. It is not clear whether Horeb and Sinai are totally synonymous terms, whether they refer to two different peaks in one mountain range or to two unrelated mountains, or whether one refers to the area and the other to the peak. Some scholars hold that Horeb and Sinai do not necessarily refer to the same place but reflect different traditions about where God's revelation took place. The location of Mount Sinai and/or Mount Horeb remains an unsolved puzzle. Few of the places that the Israelites passed in the wilderness, and none of those close to Mount Sinai, have been identified with certainty. It is not even clear in what part of the Sinai Peninsula the mountain is found. Theories as to its location (see Map 1) have been based on notions about the general route followed by the Israelites in the wilderness.[28] Scholars who believe that they traveled to the southern part of the peninsula after crossing the sea accept the identification of Mount Sinai with one of the high granite mountains in the south, Mount Sirbal, Mount Katherina, or Mount Musa.[29] Mount Musa is the site popularly identified with Mount Sinai today, although there is no evidence that it was so identified any earlier than the fourth century C.E. Other scholars, who believe that the Israelites traveled across the central part of the peninsula, think that Mount Sinai was one of the mountains in that area, perhaps Mount Yaalak or Mount Sinn Bishr; those who think they took a more northerly route identify it as Mount Halal, west of Kadesh-Barnea. Some deny that Mount Sinai is in the Sinai Peninsula and locate it instead in the Negev, or even as far as Midian in northern Arabia.[30] The exact location of the mountain may already have been forgotten in biblical times; apart from Elijah's mysterious journey there (1 Kings 19), the Bible offers no indication that it was ever visited. The name Horeb, apparently derived from *ḥ-r-b*, indicating dryness, is too vague to offer any guidance.

Jahaz (2:32). A city of unknown location in the Moabite part of Sihon's realm, somewhere between Heshbon and the Wilderness of Kedemoth. It is mentioned in the inscription of King Mesha of Moab (ninth century B.C.E.), in a passage implying that it was in the district of Dibon.[31]

Jotbath See Beeroth-bene-jaakan.

Kadesh (1:46). Kadesh-barnea (e.g., 1:2,19) has been identified with the largest oasis in the Sinai Peninsula, just west of the modern Egyptian-Israeli border. It is a site of fertile fields and several springs, including 'Ein Kudeis, which preserves the name Kadesh, 'Ein el-Kudeirat, the richest spring in the Sinai, and 'Ein el-Kuseima. One of these springs or the entire oasis was probably Kadesh-barnea.[32]

Kedemoth (2:26). A city in the formerly Moabite part of Sihon's territory (Josh. 13:18), and a nearby wilderness east of Moab.[33]

Laban (1:1). Since Laban is mentioned next to Hazeroth and near Paran, it is probably the same as Libnah in the Sinai, for the Israelites encamped at both Libnah and the desert of Paran shortly after leaving Hazeroth (Num. 33:17–20; 12:16).[34] Its precise location is

uncertain. Since Laban means "white," it could be one of the places in the Sinai with Arabic names based on the root *b-y-ḍ*, "white." These include some wadis and a mountain in east-central Sinai, in the vicinity of Kuntilla.[35] There was also a city Laban in northeastern Sinai, somewhere between Raphiah and El-Arish.[36]

Moserah See Beeroth-bene-jaakan.

Nebo, Mount (32:49). One of the prominent peaks of the heights of Abarim. Probably Jebel Neba or Ras Siagha, two peaks east of the northeast corner of the Dead Sea. Both command vistas similar to that described in 34:1–3. The first is 3,935 feet above the Dead Sea, the second 3,586 feet. The latter commands the best view of the promised land (see 3:27, 34:1–3).[37]

Oboth (Num. 21:10–11; 33:43–44). In Edom, between Punon and Wadi Zered.[38]

Paran (1:1). "The Desert of Paran" refers to all or part of the Sinai Peninsula and the southern Negev. The context of 1:1 calls for a more specific site, like the others mentioned in the verse. It could be Feiran, the largest oasis in southeastern Sinai and the site of a tell inhabited from the Iron Age on.[39] Compare Mount Paran in 33:2 and Habakkuk 3:3.

Pethor (23:5). Probably Pitru, a city in northern Syria near the confluence of the Euphrates and Sajur rivers, about twelve miles south of Carchemish (Jerablus). It is mentioned in Assyrian inscriptions.[40]

Pisgah (3:17). Refers either to a specific mountain, such as Mount Nebo,[41] or to the heights of Abarim (see above).[42] Since the Hebrew is literally "the *pisgah*" it could also be a common noun, meaning something like "the ridge."

Punon (Num. 33:42–43). The copper mining center Feinan, east of the Arabah in Edom.[43]

Ramoth (4:43). In Gilead. It is generally identified with Tel Ramith (Tell er-Rumeith), southeast of Irbid in northern Jordan.[44]

Salcah (3:10). Generally identified with Tsalkhad (Salkhad), a town on the southwestern edge of Mount Hauran in Syria. If this identification is correct, at least part of Mount Hauran was included in Bashan.

Seir-Edom (1:2; 33:1). As noted in the Comment to 1:2, Seir is practically synonymous with Edom. Edom is best known as the southernmost of the Transjordanian kingdoms, but its territory also extended west of the Aravah into the highlands of the eastern Negev, south of the promised land. Seir usually refers to this part of Edom, which extended northward from just east of Kadesh-barnea to Hormah, near Arad (Num. 20:16; Deut. 1:44). "Mount Halak which ascends to Seir" was on the southern border of the territory conquered by Joshua (Josh. 11:17; 12:7).[45]

Tophel (1:1). Otherwise unknown, but it must be reasonably close to Paran for "between Paran and Tophel" to be a meaningful location.

the westward road (11:30). Must have led west from the Jordan to Mounts Gerizim and Ebal (by Shechem) and perhaps all the way to the Mediterranean. Its eastern segment likely followed the same route as Highway 55 in modern Israel, which runs alongside Nahal Tirza (Wadi Farah) from Damiya on the Jordan (the ford of Adam, Josh. 3:16) and leads to Shechem. It may have followed this wadi all the way to Shechem, or it may have left it and followed another wadi to Shechem.[46] Later, a Roman road followed Nahal Tirza to Shechem, and it is plausible that it was built over an earlier road from biblical times.[47]

Zalmonah (Num. 33:41–42). In Edom, evidently identical to the Roman fort Calamona in the Aravah or east of it.[48]

Zered, wadi (2:13). Generally presumed to be the southern boundary of Moab and identified with Wadi el-Hesa, which is known to have been a border in later periods. It

flows in a west-northwesterly direction into the southern end of the Dead Sea and forms a natural boundary between Edom and Moab.[49]

Zoar (34:3). A city in the south of the promised land, the southernmost of the five cities of the Plain, which included Sodom and Gomorrah (Gen. 10:19; 14:2,8; Deut. 29:22). Its location is uncertain, but most of the evidence suggests that it was south or southeast of the Dead Sea, where a city called Zoar stood in Second Temple and talmudic times.[50]

EXCURSUS 2

Deuteronomy 1–3 and Other Accounts of the Same Events

Chapters 1–3 refer to events recounted elsewhere in the Bible. It is often difficult to reconcile the differences between Deuteronomy and those other accounts. Traditional exegesis generally treats the different accounts as supplementing each other, while modern scholarship assumes that they originate from separate authors or traditions. We shall here survey some of the most important differences and the way they are explained by each approach.

The Northern Border of the Promised Land   (1:7; 11:24)

Deuteronomy 1:7 and 11:24 place the northern boundary of the promised land at the Euphrates river. Other passages in the Torah place it further south at Lebo-hamath, near the northern end of the Bekaa Valley in Lebanon (Numbers 13:21; 34:8). Malbim explained this discrepancy by arguing (on the basis of Exod. 23:30) that Lebo-hamath was a temporary boundary that would be superseded by the Euphrates once the Israelites became numerous enough control a larger territory.[1] Critical theory assigns the passages mentioning Lebo-hamath to the priestly source and those mentioning the Euphrates to the J and E sources or to editors influenced by Deuteronomy.[2]

Both descriptions of the land correspond to ways in which it was perceived in the centuries preceding the Israelites' arrival. With Lebo-hamath as the northern limit, the boundaries correspond to those of Canaan when it was a province in the Egyptian empire. Lebo-hamath was likely part of the northern border set between Egypt and the Hittite Empire ca. 1275 B.C.E. Passages that place the boundary further north, at the Euphrates, reflect a larger conception of the region, a conception held in the fifteenth through thirteenth centuries when the Egyptians sometimes campaigned as far as the Euphrates, attempting to push their empire further north.[3]

The Appointment of the Chiefs   (1:9–15)

The account of the appointment of chiefs to assist Moses differs from that in Exodus 18:13–26 in two main details: (1) here, Moses suggests appointing the chiefs (*sarim*, lit. "officers") and asks the people for nominations, whereas in Exodus Jethro makes the suggestion and tells Moses to choose the chiefs; (2) here, the qualifications for appointment are intellectual, while in Exodus they are primarily ethical and spiritual. In theory, it is possible to reconcile both differences. The Samaritan Pentateuch harmonizes the first

difference by splicing Deuteronomy 1:9–13 into Exodus 18, between verses 24 and 26. In this conflated account, the excerpts from Exodus and Deuteronomy refer to different moments of the episode: first Jethro proposes the appointment, then Moses broaches the idea to the people. This version, however, is not original.[4] The second difference could be harmonized by taking the intellectual qualifications as implying the others. Nevertheless, as M. Weinfeld notes, the intellectual qualifications reflect Deuteronomy's predilection for the values of Wisdom Literature, and Weinfeld argues that Deuteronomy has revised the account in accordance with those values.[5]

Numbers 11, which relates how seventy elders were appointed to assist Moses, complicates our understanding of the role of the chiefs. When that account is read in its own right, it seems that the elders are appointed to help in all areas of leadership. However, when read in connection with Exodus 18 and Deuteronomy 1, the story in Numbers is puzzling. It sounds like another account of the appointment of the chiefs: in Numbers 11:14 Moses complains of his burdens in terms virtually identical to those he uses in Deuteronomy 1:9; and in Numbers 11:17 God says that the elders will share the burden with him, which is exactly what Jethro says the chiefs will do (Exod. 18:22). It is not clear how the elders' functions differ from those of the chiefs who, according to Exodus, were already appointed. Traditional exegesis views both groups as judicial: the chiefs are lower judges and the seventy elders are the high court.[6] However, with 78,600 chiefs already in office, it is hard to see why Moses would have felt that he was bearing the burden of leadership alone, or how the addition of a high court would solve his problem. In short, the institutions of the seventy elders and the chiefs render each other superfluous. In fact, the elders and the chiefs are never mentioned together in the same passage. For these reasons, critical theory regards the narratives about these two groups as variant traditions about the kind of leaders who assisted Moses and about their qualifications. In this view, the phraseology shared by Exodus 18, Numbers 11, and Deuteronomy 1 reflects literary connections between these versions: either they are offshoots of a single original account and the shared phraseology is a residue of the original version, or they developed independently and the shared phraseology was added because they dealt with similar issues.[7]

The institutions of the chiefs and the seventy elders represent two very different types of leadership.[8] Hierarchical systems of appointed officers governing groups of ten and its multiples are characteristic of monarchies; officers with these titles first begin to appear in Israel under Saul.[9] Tribal societies, in contrast, are governed by elders. It is likely, then, that Exodus 18 is projecting back into the period of Moses a system that was established in monarchic times, perhaps originally for the governance of military garrisons. Even the council of elders described in Numbers 11, chosen by Moses and imbued with divine spirit by God, seems to reflect monarchic times. In a tribal society the appointment of elders would not be so described. In such a society, their authority is based on ancient patriarchal tradition and requires no authorization from a national leader or divine inspiration. Hence the narrative in Numbers seems to reflect the royal appointment of a national council of elders at some point in monarchic times. The account in Deuteronomy 1 may reflect a compromise between these two types of authority. Notwithstanding its similarity to Exodus 18, it emphasizes that the officials chosen are already tribal leaders (Deut. 1:13,15), whereas Exodus says, perhaps pointedly, that the appointees were chosen "from among all the people" (Exod. 18:21,25). It is also noteworthy that in Deuteronomy Moses asks the people to nominate the officials, and they express approval of his plan. It seems quite possible that these three narratives reflect different stages in the struggle for power between the ancient tribal leadership and the monarchy in ancient Israel.[10]

The Mission of the Scouts (1:22–25, 36)

This account differs in several respects from its parallel in Numbers 13–14. In Numbers, God commands Moses to send out the scouts to gain intelligence about the population, its defenses, and the resources of the land (Num. 13:2,17–20); in Deuteronomy 1:22 it is the people who suggest sending the scouts, and their assignment is to gather information about the route to follow and the cities to target. Traditional exegesis reconciles the two accounts by assuming that Numbers and Deuteronomy each contains only a partial account and that together they preserve the full course of events. The people suggested that scouts be sent to obtain information of tactical military value, as stated in Deuteronomy. Moses referred their proposal to God, who *consented*—that is the traditional reading of Numbers 13:2. In sending the men out, however, Moses modified their mission. He omitted the request for tactical information, which was superfluous since God would guide the Israelites. Rather, as Deuteronomy states, he charged the men to serve largely as explorers, expecting their report about the land's richness to increase the people's desire for it;[11] that is why the scouts' report in Deuteronomy 1:25 speaks only of the land's goodness. According to this explanation, God consented to the people's proposal either because refusing would have made them suspicious; because the scouts would see how desirable the land was and strengthen the people's resolve to proceed; or because it would expose the people's lack of faith.[12]

In contrast to these explanations, critical theory views the differences between Deuteronomy and Numbers as discrepancies between sources; Deuteronomy either follows variant traditions about the episode, or knew at least some of the traditions on which Numbers is based but modified them for ideological reasons—such as making clear that the scouts' mission, which reflected lack of faith in God and had disastrous consequences, was the people's initiative, not God's.

Deuteronomy raises two further problems. First, it implies that the scouts traveled no further than Hebron. Verse 24 mentions only Wadi Eshcol, near Hebron, and verse 36 says that Caleb would receive the land on which he set foot, and Hebron is what he later received.[13] This conflicts with Numbers 13:21, which states that the scouts traveled north all the way to Rehob at Lebo-hamath. Furthermore, since according to Numbers 14:6 Joshua joined Caleb in pleading with the people, one expects him to be mentioned in Deuteronomy alongside Caleb, as he is in Numbers 14:30 and 32:12. Deuteronomy 1:38 does mention Joshua, but only as Moses' aide and successor; it gives no intimation that he, too, kept faith, or played any role at all, in the incident of the scouts.

Harmonistic exegesis assumes that the scouts split into two groups, one going to the far north and the other, including Caleb, remaining in the south.[14] It explains that Deuteronomy is silent about Joshua's role because he really was less outspoken than Caleb; since he was Moses' attendant, he feared that people would not listen to him.[15] These explanations are unlikely. There is no hint in either book that the scouts split up, and Joshua's reticence is not consistent with Numbers 14:6–7.

Critical theory resolves these problems by positing separate sources for the conflicting data. According to the JE source, the scouts went as far as Hebron, and Caleb attempted to encourage the people. This version of the events, it is presumed, goes back to traditions preserved by Caleb's descendants, who were an important clan in the tribe of Judah and were interested in the role of their ancestor. According to the priestly source, on the other hand, the scouts toured the entire land and Joshua joined Caleb in encouraging the people. Passages from both of these sources were merged in Numbers more or less in their original

forms, which accounts for the inconsistencies within Numbers 13–14. Deuteronomy drew its information only from the JE source, which had not yet been merged with the priestly source.[16]

The Punishment of Moses   (1:37)

Deuteronomy 1:37, to which Moses alludes in 3:26 and 4:21, apparently connects his punishment with the incident of the scouts. However, according to Numbers 20:1–13, Moses (and Aaron) were excluded from the promised land because Moses spoke angrily to the people and extracted water from a rock by hitting it instead of speaking to it as he and Aaron were commanded; in so doing they showed a lack of trust in God and failed to affirm His sanctity in the sight of the people. Most commentators believe that "because of you" in 1:37 refers to that incident, meaning that Moses was punished on account of the people's behavior because it was they who made him so impatient that he hit the rock.[17]

As an explanation of Deuteronomy 1:37, this view raises difficulties. It was Moses, after all, who hit the rock, and even if the people made him irritable, it would be strange for him to refer to the incident three times in Deuteronomy as their fault and ignore his own act entirely. Furthermore, 1:37 is part of Moses' review of the incident of the scouts, which took place in the second year following the Exodus (see 2:14 and Num. 10:11). The incident of the rock took place many years later.[18] That Moses should suddenly mention incidents from so many years later while reviewing the incident of the scouts would be odd. In sum, it is unlikely that 1:37 refers to the incident of the rock.

Abravanel recognizes that Deuteronomy connects Moses' punishment with the incident of the scouts; he holds that Moses was implicated because he modified the scouts' orders and thereby brought about the report that undermined the people's faith. Abravanel argues that Numbers 20:12 mentions Moses' punishment in connection with the rock incident only to protect his honor, since mentioning it in connection with the incident of the scouts might give the impression that he had shared the people's faithlessness at the time of that incident. This argument is forced. Critical theory sees Numbers 20 and our verse as representing two independent traditions explaining Moses' punishment. It assigns the former tradition to the priestly source, which was not followed by Deuteronomy.[19]

The Chronology and Route of the Wanderings from Kadesh to Transjordan   (1:46–2:1,8,14)

According to Deuteronomy, the Israelites left Kadesh in the second year after the Exodus and headed southeastward on the Road to the Sea of Reeds (the Gulf of Elath). They spent the next thirty-eight years skirting the southwestern part of Seir-Edom and then entered the Aravah at its *southern* end (near the gulf), traveled north through the Aravah, and crossed Wadi Zered into Moab. The chronology and route are hard to reconcile with some passages in Numbers. According to the itinerary in Numbers 33, the Israelites camped at Ezion-geber, on the Gulf of Elath, immediately *before* they arrived at Kadesh; to judge from Numbers 20:1 this was in the fortieth year. From Kadesh they proceeded to Mount Hor and from there to Zalmonah, Punon, Oboth, and Iye-abarim on the border of Moab (Num. 33:36–44). Since all the sites following Mount Hor are in the *northern*

Aravah, northern Edom, and Moab, it appears that the Israelites crossed the Aravah into Edom in the *north* without returning to the vicinity of the Gulf of Elath. The *narratives* of Numbers (as distinct from the *itinerary* in Numbers 33) partly agree with this picture and partly differ from it. According to the narratives, the Israelites presumably left Kadesh after the defeat at Hormah (Num. 14:45; cf. v. 25 and 15:32). No further travels are mentioned until Numbers 20:1, when they arrived at Kadesh—apparently for a second time—in the first month of what is presumably the fortieth year. After the king of Edom refused permission for Israel to pass through his territory, the Israelites traveled to Mount Hor (20:14–29) and then took the Road to the Sea of Reeds to skirt Edom (21:1–4). Eventually, they arrived at Oboth, then at Iye-abarim on the eastern border of Moab, and finally at Wadi Zered. This description, too, implies that the Israelites crossed the Aravah into Edom in the *north*, not near the Gulf of Elath.

There are several apparent discrepancies between these descriptions of the Israelites' route.

1. In Numbers 33 the Israelites visit Kadesh in the fortieth year but not the second. Ibn Ezra resolves this problem by identifying one of the earlier stations in Numbers 33, Kibroth Hattaavah, as Kadesh-barnea.[20] This brings the *itinerary* in Numbers 33 into agreement with the *narratives* of Numbers, which also imply two visits to Kadesh. Deuteronomy, however, does not mention a second visit; in 2:14, Israel left Kadesh for good, in the second year. Traditional exegesis resolves this problem by taking the Kadesh visited in the fortieth year as a different place than Kadesh-barnea, which was visited in the second year. The former was in the Wilderness of Zin (Num. 20:1) while the latter was in the Wilderness of Paran (13:26).[21] Deuteronomy, it is implied, simply does not mention the second visit. However, it is clear from Deuteronomy 1:46 that Kadesh-barnea could be called simply Kadesh, and since both Kadesh-barnea and the Wilderness of Zin figure as the southern boundary of the promised land,[22] it seems that Kadesh-barnea and Kadesh in the Wilderness of Zin are the same place, and that the Wilderness of Zin was part of the Wilderness of Paran, which was the collective name for all the wildernesses south and southwest of the promised land.

2. There is no explicit indication in Numbers that the Israelites reached as far south as the Gulf of Elath and entered Edom from the south. Both in the narratives of Numbers and in the itinerary of Numbers 33, the stations mentioned after Mount Hor (Zalmonah, Punon, and Oboth) are east of Mount Hor, which seems to imply that from Mount Hor the Israelites crossed the Aravah in the *north* into northern Edom. Traditional commentators felt no inconsistency here. Since the precise locations of Zalmonah and Punon were not known, Ibn Ezra identified them as places on the perimeter of Edom and assumed that Numbers 21:4 does imply that they circled Edom.[23]

3. According to Deuteronomy 10:6–7, the Israelites traveled from Beeroth-bene-jaakan to Moserah, where Aaron died. According to Numbers, however, they proceeded *from* Moseroth *to* Bene-jaakan and Aaron died at Mount Hor, seven stops later (Num. 33:31,37–39; cf. 20:22–28 and Deut. 32:50). Midrashic exegesis holds that after Aaron died at Mount Hor the Israelites doubled back to Moserah and mourned there so intensely that they later spoke of Moserah as the place where he died.[24] Ibn Ezra argues that Beeroth-bene-jaakan and Moserah are not identical to Bene-jaakan and Moseroth; rather, Beeroth-bene-jaakan is another name for Kadesh and Moserah is the wilderness where Mount Hor was located.

The difficulties with the traditional attempts to harmonize these discrepancies have led critical scholars to posit separate literary sources for the conflicting data. In this view each source had a different conception of the route and chronology of the Israelites' travels. Deuteronomy reflects one conception, assuming a visit to Kadesh in the second year and a circuit of Seir-Edom reaching all the way to the Gulf of Elath. This is based on the JE source. A second, priestly (P) conception, reflected in Numbers 33, has the Israelites visit Kadesh in the fortieth year and proceed from there across the northern Aravah to northern Edom. Each of these conceptions has a counterpart in the *narratives* of Numbers, which blend passages from J and E and some editorial notes from P. The conception that Israel sent scouts from Kadesh in the second year appears in Numbers 13:26b, while that which says that Israel reached Kadesh in the fortieth year appears in 20:1b; but no single source thinks they visited Kadesh twice. Scholars have different ideas as to how each of these versions developed. One view is that the Israelites arrived in Canaan in two separate waves of migration, and that the two routes described in the sources reflect these two waves.[25] Another is that each version reflects one of the routes used in monarchic times by nomads traveling between Egypt and Canaan.[26]

4. A fourth problem relates to the encounter with the descendants of Esau. According to Numbers 20:14–21, Moses sought permission to pass through Edom from Kadesh (west of Edom) and was refused; according to Deuteronomy the Israelites did pass through Edom, but from the south (2:4–8,29). Harmonistic exegesis holds that these were separate incidents. Rashbam and Shadal argue that two different groups of descendants of Esau were involved, those living under a monarch (Num. 20:14), who refused, and "the descendants of Esau," free tribesmen who felt too weak to refuse (Deut. 2:4,8,29). Some modern scholars argue that the Edomites resisted when the Israelites were to their west since Edom's western mountains were steep and defensible, but when Israel came around from the south to the east, where the hills are low, the Edomites lost confidence and agreed. It is, of course, conceivable that there were two separate incidents, but it is strange that each book should mention only one and be silent about the other. W. A. Sumner argues that Deuteronomy 1–3 revised the traditions it had received in accordance with the belief that the Israelites were strong and the Edomites, Moabites, and Ammonites feared them and would not have rebuffed them. Accordingly, Deuteronomy chapter 2 states that the Edomites and Moabites permitted passage (contrary to 23:4–5) and it ignores the Ammonites' refusal (if 23:4–5 implies that).[27]

The Harmonistic and Critical Approaches

In each of the cases reviewed here the commentator is confronted by passages that describe a single phenomenon or event in different ways: there are conflicting statements about the location of the northern border of the promised land, about when Israel visited Kadesh, who first suggested Israel's judicial system, the route from Kadesh into Transjordan, and so forth. Harmonistic exegesis resolves such inconsistencies by three basic arguments: (1) passages that seem to be describing a single subject inconsistently actually refer to different aspects or moments of that subject: there will be different northern borders in different periods; Jethro suggested the judicial system to Moses who then

suggested it to the people; (2) passages that seem to be saying different things about a subject are really saying the same thing in different ways: Kibroth Hattaavah is really Kadesh-barnea; (3) passages that seem unaware of what other passages say are elliptical: the passages that imply a northern route to Edom simply skip the southern loop. The assumption that the entire Torah comes from a single, consistent author makes these methods inevitable, for without them the author would appear to be regularly contradicting himself.

These methods of harmonization were practiced well before the rabbinic period. The first method is reflected in some Torah manuscripts from Qumran and in the Samaritan Torah. In these, verses from Deuteronomy are spliced into episodes of Exodus and Numbers, as in the narrative about the appointment of chieftains (see above), at points which make them appear to refer to different moments within the episodes, not to contradictory versions of them.[28] A technique similar to the second method is reflected in the book of Chronicles, where a seeming contradiction between Exodus and Deuteronomy is resolved. According to Exodus 12:8–9, the Passover offering must be roasted, not boiled (*b-sh-l*) in water, while according to Deuteronomy 16:7 it is to be boiled (*b-sh-l*). This apparent contradiction is resolved in 2 Chronicles 35:13, which says "they *b-sh-l* the Passover offering in fire." This implies that *b-sh-l* really means "cook" and that in Deuteronomy it means the same thing that Exodus expresses by "roast." With these methods, harmonistic exegesis implies that each of the various accounts of an event or a law in the Bible preserves *part* of the event or law, and that by piecing these accounts together and resolving the inconsistencies one gains a fuller picture of the event or the law.

The inconsistencies that require such methods are so common that some of these methods, or similar ones, were formalized in the hermeneutic rules of the rabbis. The first method has a counterpart in the rule that two passages which contradict each other may be harmonized with the help of a third verse: some rabbis used this rule to show that the seemingly inconsistent verses are really referring to different things.[29] The third method is paralleled in the rule that a text may be taken as elliptical.[30]

These are valid principles of interpretation and are often followed by modern historians in dealing with evidence. The first method, for example, is echoed in a manual on historical methodology which advises that "Where statements seem contradictory, it is necessary to determine whether the contradiction is real or only apparent: they may bear on different aspects of a matter."[31] A case in point is the identification of biblical Caphtor (Deut. 2:23): some evidence suggests that it was Crete, while other evidence suggests that it was on the coast of Asia Minor; one historian resolves the discrepancy by assuming that "Caphtor" originally referred to Crete and that later, when Cretans migrated to Asia Minor, they applied the old name to their new home.[32]

Although these methods are in principle valid, in the view of critical scholarship they do not persuasively resolve most of the inconsistencies between Deuteronomy 1–3 and other accounts of the same events. In these cases, the methods require too many unsupported and farfetched presumptions. There is no evidence, for example, that Kibroth Hattaavah was a name for Kadesh or that the scouts split into two groups, and God's instructions to send out the scouts in Numbers 13:2 do not read like the approval of somebody else's proposal. As noted above, the methods in question are compelling if one starts with the assumption that the entire Torah comes from a single author and that it must be consistent; once this is assumed, even the unsupported assumptions seem tolerable. But the essence of the critical approach is to forgo presuppositions about authorship, and without the assumption of single authorship the harmonizing argu-

ments seem like special pleading. Critical scholarship finds it difficult to believe that if the parallel accounts were written by one and the same author they would be worded in such a way as to give two (or more) different ideas of what took place.[33] It considers the idea strange that two different accounts by the same person would both be so incomplete; that each would give so many particulars that the other lacks; and that in the recapitulation the author would fail to indicate that the audience should remember the rest of what happened or could learn about it by consulting the earlier accounts. It finds theories of multiple authorship and revision a more persuasive way to account for the discrepancies.

It is interesting to note that multiple authorship was assumed by the rabbis to explain inconsistencies within the Mishnah. They attributed clauses that are inconsistent and cannot be harmonized to different sages, and they explained contradictory statements of a sage as reflecting different traditionists' accounts of what he said.[34] Since the rabbis did not view the Mishnah the way they viewed the Torah, but knew that it incorporated the views of different authorities, they found multiple authorship a natural explanation for inconsistencies.

It has sometimes been argued that explaining inconsistencies as due to multiple authorship merely transfers the problem from the author to the editor. If we cannot believe that a single, careful author would produce an inconsistent document, why do we assume that an editor would? However, we know that compilers and editors of ancient literary works did not always allow themselves the freedom to rewrite their texts in order to resolve inconsistencies. The comparison of older and younger copies of certain ancient texts shows that in the earlier stages of a work's development, when it was not yet considered classical or sacred, editors felt free to rewrite almost at will, and early revisions of a work show very few inconsistencies even when new matter has been added to them. But once a work acquired sacred or classical status, it became increasingly difficult for editors to revise it even in order to remove inconsistencies. The inconsistencies in the Torah are due, in the critical view, to the fact its source-documents were combined at a time when they already had a quasi-canonical status, and the compilers did not feel free to do much more than juxtapose or interweave the sources and add some transitional phrases. Probably they resolved the inconsistencies exegetically in their own minds, and some of the harmonistic interpretations of the rabbis may well be similar to those of the editors. In any case, editors of sacred or classical texts indeed produced works with inconsistencies, because they preserved the wording of their sources even where they wove them together and rearranged them. As one nineteenth century scholar observed, "It is this way of writing that makes the Bible history so vivid and interesting," for no book written by the modern technique of digesting and rewriting the sources "could have preserved so much of the genuine life of antique times."[35] By not imposing unity and consistency on the sources, the compilers preserved the variety and richness of ancient Israelite belief, tradition, law, and literature.

Underlying the compilers' reluctance to remove inconsistency seems to have been a presumption that "these and those are the words of the living God," in other words, that all the sources they preserved were valid, or at least potentially so. This phrase, in which the Talmud characterizes conflicting opinions of different sages,[36] is certainly applicable as well to what seems to be the biblical editors' evaluation of their sources. No one version of the past, of a law, or of a belief, necessarily preserved the whole truth, and where they felt unable to decide, they preserved what they had received, harmonized inconsistencies as well as they could, and left the rest to posterity.

EXCURSUS 3
The Concept of War in Deuteronomy

As noted in the Comments to 1:6–3:29, the theme of trusting God in battle reflects a concept of war according to which God is the warrior who does the actual fighting for Israel. This concept is expressed from the moment of Israel's escape from the Egyptians: Moses told Israel at the Sea of Reeds that the Lord would fight for them and that the people should hold their peace; the Egyptians, when their chariots got mired, realized that the Lord was fighting for Israel and they sought to flee; and after the Egyptians drowned, the Israelites sang of "The LORD, the Warrior" (Exod. 14:14,25; 15:3).

The concept of God as Israel's warrior was expressed in both belief and practice, especially in the earliest period of Israel's history.[1] God was believed to be present in the Israelite military camp, above the Ark. God Himself was Israel's "myriads of thousands" of troops (Num. 10:36) and the Israelites were "the LORD's ranks" (Exod. 12:41). God defeated the enemy by turning the elements of nature against them or by incapacitating them (see Comment to 2:15). The Israelites either stood by passively or sent the army to assist God by finishing off the enemy, whom God delivered into its hands.[2] These beliefs were expressed in practice by offering prayer and sacrifice before battle, by carrying the Ark and sacred vessels into battle, and by sounding trumpets "to be remembered before the LORD" (Num. 10:9). The camp had to be kept fit for God's presence by avoiding all forms of impurity and defilement. Battles were undertaken at the command of God, issued either on God's initiative, as expressed through a prophet, or in response to an inquiry by Israel through a prophet or oracular means. The army was encouraged before the battle to have no fear, since God would be with them and deliver the enemy into their hands. Refusal to proceed into battle therefore constituted an act of disobedience to God's command and a rejection of His assurances, an act of faithlessness. This explains the gravity of the offense which Moses recounts in chapter 1 and the importance of Israel's obedience in chapters 2 and 3.

This concept was studied at length by Gerhard von Rad in his monograph *Holy War in Ancient Israel*.[3] Unfortunately, the term "holy war" gives the mistaken impression that this type of war was fought for the purpose of spreading one's religion and suppressing others. As the evidence summarized above shows, it was nothing of the sort. In fact, the idea of spreading Israelite religion to foreigners and compelling them to accept it is completely foreign to the Bible. The Bible looks forward to the time when other nations will recognize the Lord's superiority, and ultimately abandon other gods, but it expects this to be a voluntary action on their part in response to witnessing the Lord's greatness.

As indicated, this concept of war was especially prominent in the earliest period of Israel's history. In Deuteronomy, war has been somewhat desacralized. Deuteronomy shares the belief that God fights for Israel, but it never indicates that the Ark accompanies the army in battle and never connects God's presence in the camp with the Ark. It also expects fewer religious practices to accompany war. See the Introduction and the Comments to 1:33, 42; 10:1–2; 20:2; and 23:10–15.

EXCURSUS 4
"The Lord"

In the translation, "the LORD" represents the four Hebrew consonants YHVH (*yod*, *he*, *vav*, *he*), which represent God's name (sometimes called the Tetragrammaton because it consists of four consonants). This translation is not literal and requires an explanation.

YHVH was probably pronounced *Yahweh* (in biblical times the *vav* was pronounced like English 'w'). This conjecture is based on postbiblical transliterations of the name and on the suffixed form *yahu* in personal names such as *Eliyahu* ("Elijah"). Most likely, the name is derived from the root *h-v-h* (a variant of *h-y-h*), "be," and means either "He [who] is/will be . . . [e.g., is/will be present] or exists"[1] or "He [who] causes to exist."[2]

The original pronunciation can only be conjectured because Jews avoided pronouncing it and used substitute words in its place. According to the halakhah, it was not to be pronounced except in special circumstances.[3] Because of this avoidance, the pronunciation was eventually forgotten. There is little evidence that substitutes were used in preexilic times.[4] In those days, God's name was invoked in everyday life and was written even in secular documents such as letters.[5] The practice of rendering it by a title such as Lord or some other substitute developed later. The practice is at least as old as the Dead Sea scrolls, and possibly older.[6]

Avoiding the pronunciation of God's name was an expression of reverence. Philo compares it to the feeling that it is improper to address one's parents by name.[7] There is no evidence for the common view that this avoidance of the name was based on the third commandment.[8] Philo and R. Levi think that it is based on Leviticus 24:15–16, "Anyone who blasphemes his God shall bear his guilt; if he also pronounces the name LORD [YHVH], he shall be put to death . . . if he has thus pronounced the Name, he shall be put to death."[9] However, this view is rejected in the Talmud.[10]

The substitute used most often is *'adonai*, literally, "my Lord." It was a natural choice since it had often been used before God's name, when addressing Him, in the phrase *'adonai YHVH*, "my Lord *YHVH*," as in 3:24; 9:26; and Gen. 15:2. The substitute did not replace the divine name in the written text of the Bible.[11] The consonants YHVH were retained, but instead of pronouncing them, readers said *'adonai*. In the Middle Ages, when the present system of diacritical marks was developed to indicate vowels, the consonants YHVH were given the vowels of *'adonai*, following the method of the *kere*-and-*ketiv* system which signals readers to say the word whose vowels are given in place of the one whose consonants are given.[12]

This explains why English translations have "the LORD" when the Hebrew text has YHVH. What is being translated is not God's name but the substitute, *'adonai*, "my Lord."[13] Actually, the translation is not precise; ever since the Septuagint, translations have customarily replaced "my" with "the."

A different substitute is found in passages like 3:24 and 9:26, where the title *'adonai* already precedes YHVH in the Hebrew text. In such cases, in order to avoid redundancy, the substitute used is *'elohim*. Thus the combination *'-d-n-y YHVH* is vocalized and pronounced as *'adonai 'elohim*, and is translated "Lord GOD." In such cases, "Lord" represents *'-d-n-y* and YHVH is rendered "GOD."

Some Christian students of Hebrew in the Middle Ages and the Renaissance, not realizing that the vowels in printed texts represented a substitute word, took them to be

the vowels of YHVH and mistakenly concluded that the name was pronounced Jehovah (with J pronounced as Y). This became the common representation of the Tetragrammaton in English literature.[14]

The vowels accompanying YHVH in the Leningrad Codex of the Bible, which is the basis of the Hebrew text in this Commentary, are slightly different. Only two vowels are present, and there is no 'o' in the middle of the word. It has been suggested that this manuscript follows a tradition like that of the Samaritans in which the substitute word is not *'adonai* but Aramaic *shema'*, "the name," the equivalent of Hebrew *ha-shem*.[15] (Aramaic *shema'* should not be confused with Hebrew *shema‘*, "hear," as in *shema‘ yisra'el*, "Hear, O Israel.")

EXCURSUS 5
The Promises of Reinstatement   (4:29–31 and 30:1–10)

As noted in the Comments to 4:29–31 and 30:1–10, it is not clear why Moses, in the course of threatening Israel with exile, mentions that God will accept exiled Israel's repentance and restore it to the promised land. It is true, as noted in the Commentary, that God swore to give Israel the land forever. But Moses' purpose in these addresses is not to summarize all the terms of the covenant but to deter Israel from violating it by warning of the consequences. The promise of forgiveness could weaken the effectiveness of the warning.[1] Conceivably, Moses reasons that no generation would dismiss the warning of disaster because of a promise that it could be followed by restoration. However, in 30:1–10, the promises of prosperity after restoration are so glorious that they practically overshadow the threats.

On literary grounds, both of these passages seem to be interpolations in their contexts. Both are followed by paragraphs beginning with the conjunction "for" (*ki*), indicating an explanation or justification of something that has just been said, but in each case nothing in the immediately preceding passage (the promise of reinstatement) is explained or justified. As a result, the NJPS translation had to ignore the conjunction (4:32) or assign it one of its less common meanings ("surely," 30:11). This is because in the present text, 4:29–31 and 30:1–10 have come in between the justifications and the statements that they justify. Since the point of 4:32ff is that the Lord is the only true God, these verses justify verses 25–28, which admonish Israel not to worship false gods lest it be forced to worship such ineffectual deities in exile.[2] They have nothing to do with the promise of restoration in verses 29–31.[3] In chapter 30, verses 11–14 begin: "For [*ki*] this Instruction which I enjoin upon you this day is not too baffling for you, nor is it beyond your reach" (30:11). This does not explain verses 1–10, which tell what will happen if Israel obeys God's commandments later, in the exile. Rather, it justifies God's demand for obedience in the present, and must therefore refer to the end of chapter 29: "it is for us and our children ever to apply all the provisions of this Teaching" (29:28).[4] These considerations suggest that 4:29–31 and 30:1–10 were probably not original parts of the text but were interpolated during the exile to assure the Jews of that time that if they abandoned the sins of which Moses had warned, if they shunned the idolatry of their environment and returned to God, He would accept their repentance and return them to their homeland.[5]

EXCURSUS 6
Moses and Monotheism   (4:32–39)

Deuteronomy 4:32–40 touches upon the part played by Moses in the development of monotheism in Israel. For the sake of clarity it is important that we define the terminology that is used in discussing this issue. The term monotheism refers to the belief that there is only one God. It is sometimes contrasted with monolatry, namely "the worship of but one god when other gods are recognized as existing" (*Random House Dictionary*). These terms figure in the following discussion because scholars debate whether Moses, when he first prohibited the worship of other gods, simultaneously proclaimed that they did not exist; in other words, whether he proclaimed the doctrine of monotheism or only monolatry.

Although Moses tells the Israelites in 4:32–35 and 39 that the events of the Exodus and Mount Sinai show that there are no gods but the Lord, that passage is the first in the Torah to make this point (see also 7:9). None of the narratives about those events in Exodus, nor any passage in Leviticus or Numbers, states that those events taught the lesson of monotheism. Deuteronomy 4:35 could be taken as implying that Israel realized this lesson as soon as the events occurred, but the earlier books do not support such an interpretation. The book of Exodus frequently points out the lessons that were taught immediately by the events of the Exodus and Sinai, such as the fact that the Lord is incomparable and reliable and that Moses is an authentic prophet;[1] nowhere does it say that the Lord is the only God. The laws of Exodus infer from those events only that Israel must not worship other gods;[2] since laws do not normally deal with theological matters, they do not discuss the question of whether other gods exist. From the perspective of the Torah, then, it could be argued that Moses may not have taught the full monotheistic implications of the Exodus and Sinai to the generation that experienced those events, but only to their children forty years later.

Many critical scholars think that the interval between the Exodus and the proclamation of monotheism was much longer. Outside of Deuteronomy the earliest passages to state that there are no gods but the Lord are in poems and prayers attributed to Hannah and David,[3] one and a half to two and a half centuries after the Exodus at the earliest.[4] Such statements do not become common until the seventh century B.C.E., the period to which Deuteronomy is dated by the critical view.[5] Since many critical scholars believe that the laws banning the worship of other gods really do go back to Moses but that the denial of the existence of other gods does not, they conclude that Moses only taught monolatry, not monotheism. And since historical books such as Judges and Kings state that the Israelites continued to worship other gods throughout their history, these scholars conclude that even the requirement of monolatry was not widely accepted in Israel until shortly before the Babylonian exile, or even later. The doctrine of monotheism is thought by these scholars to have originated long after Moses, perhaps as late as the seventh century B.C.E. when it was emphasized by Deuteronomy and the prophets.

The most effective challenges to this view were those of the Israeli biblical scholar Yehezkel Kaufmann and the American archaeologist W. F. Albright.[6] Kaufmann and Albright argued that the explicit statements about monotheism do not tell the whole story. So far as we can tell from the Bible and from archaeological evidence, most Israelites were de facto monotheistic ever since the time of Moses. From its earliest stages biblical religion viewed all gods other than YHVH as ineffective nonentities.[7] Rarely does a biblical

character refer to another deity as doing anything.[8] Most Israelites accused of worshiping other gods seem to have worshiped only images and do not seem to have believed in living powers behind the images as authentic paganism did; they believed, in other words, that the images themselves possessed divine powers and that the gods were the images and nothing more. This seems clear from the fact that when Israelite reformers purged idolatry from the land their efforts were confined to removing images and other objects;[9] they never had to argue against belief in beings that the images represented. Some Israelites also worshiped supernatural beings and phenomena that were part of the Lord's heavenly retinue (see Comment to 3:24), apparently in the belief that God himself required people to honor His subordinates.[10] That the worshipers of these beings believed that God required men to worship them is implied by God's denial that He ever commanded the worship of heavenly bodies (Deut. 17:3). There is no evidence that these worshipers believed these beings to be independent of YHVH or on a par with Him. Furthermore, the number of people who worshiped statues and supernatural beings does not appear to have been large. The book of Judges does not quantify its statements that the Israelites worshiped foreign gods, and the number of specific incidents reported in the book is small.[11] That these incidents were regarded as having such disastrous consequences for Israel is probably not due to their prevalence but to the gravity of the sin and to the biblical doctrine of collective responsibility, which holds the entire nation responsible for the sins of a even a small number of its members.[12] Most of the idolatry reported in Kings was sponsored by the kings themselves, often for political reasons connected with foreign policy; few of these reports indicate that large numbers of common people were involved.[13] Archaeological evidence of polytheism is also scant: few, if any, representations of male deities have ever been found in clearly Israelite contexts, and most of the figurines of females found at Israelite sites represent humans, not goddesses.[14] Israelite inscriptions with religious content rarely mention other gods, and of Israelite personal names that refer to a deity, only six percent refer to deities other than YHVH; the other ninety-four percent mention YHVH.[15] That most Israelites ignored not only the gods of foreign nations, but even the gods of natural phenomena on which all humans depend, can only mean that they did not consider these phenomena to be divine or independently effective.[16] So far as our evidence goes, therefore, ever since the time of Moses most Israelites seem to have regarded only YHVH as an independently effective divine power, and that belief is most simply explained as due to the teachings of Moses himself.[17]

The belief that only YHVH is an independently effective divine power is de facto monotheistic. It reduces all other supernatural beings to the level of angels, spirits, and the like. Since biblical Hebrew generally continued to use words for "gods" (*'elim* and *'elohim*) to refer to those supernatural beings (see Comment to 3:24), whose existence was not denied, we cannot speak of monotheism in the etymological sense of the word but only in the practical, de facto sense just described. As Albright put it, "Mosaic monotheism, like that of the following centuries (at least down to the seventh century [B.C.E.]) was . . . practical and implicit rather than intellectual and explicit. . . . The Israelites felt, thought, and acted like monotheists."[18]

Some biblical passages indicate that the de facto monotheistic belief made it inappropriate to use the same generic terms for both God and lesser beings or idols. Some texts which used these terms for idols pointed out that these objects were not really gods. In 2 Kings 19:17–18, for example, Hezekiah declares that "the kings of Assyria have . . . committed the gods of the nations to flames and have destroyed them" and then adds "for they are not gods, but man's handiwork of wood and stone." Psalm 96:4–5 declares, "All

the gods of the peoples are mere idols." Early Israelite poems contain passages in which the monotheistic creed is explicit, such as "There is no holy being [a term for deity] like the LORD, / Truly, there is none beside You" and "who is a god except the LORD?"[19] Such passages imply, as do Deuteronomy 4:35 and 39, that it is theologically inappropriate to use words meaning "gods" for beings other than the Lord. The weight of linguistic tradition was such that that usage was not abandoned—not even by the Bible itself—during the biblical period. But passages denying that there are any gods but YHVH—denying, in other words, the divinity of lesser supernatural beings—began to multiply in the seventh and sixth centuries B.C.E., especially in the prophecies of Jeremiah and the second part of the book of Isaiah.[20] The need to emphasize the monotheistic idea in this period was probably due to the increased exposure of Israel to the triumphant Assyrian and Babylonian empires, which attributed their victories, including victories over Israel, to their own gods. In any case, what was emphasized in these centuries was the explicit formulation of the monotheistic idea which had been implicit in Israel since the time of Moses.

EXCURSUS 7
The Biblical View of the Origin of Polytheism (4:19–20 and 32:8–9)

As noted in the Commentary, 4:19–20 and 32:7–8 seem to reflect a biblical view that the worship of idols and celestial beings, including the heavenly bodies, began when God divided humanity into separate nations after it built the Tower of Babel. Evidently this view assumes that, as punishment for man's repeated spurning of His authority in primordial times (Gen. 3–11), God deprived mankind at large of true knowledge of Himself and ordained that it should worship idols and subordinate celestial beings, such as heavenly bodies.[1] Then, He selected Abraham and his descendants as the objects of His personal attention to create a model nation and show the others the blessing He bestowed on those who acknowledge His authority.[2]

This view of polytheism reflects the assumption that if the rest of mankind does not worship the true God, that must be God's will. For this reason, it is no sin for other nations to worship idols and the heavenly bodies; it is considered sinful only when done by Israel, to whom God revealed Himself and forbade the worship of these objects.[3]

The implication that worship of the heavenly bodies by other nations was ordained by God struck many traditional commentators as unlikely, since the prophets teach that one day all nations will abandon false religion and recognize the Lord alone.[4] An early attempt to counter this implication is reflected in an addition to 4:19, which refers to the heavenly bodies, reportedly found in the original text of the Septuagint: "which the LORD your God allotted to other peoples *to give light to them*,"[5] in other words to give light, but not to rule. But since the point of verses 19–20 is that God allotted the heavenly bodies to the nations and not to Israel (see also 29:25), this interpretation cannot be correct, since it would imply that the heavenly bodies do not provide light to Israel.[6] Other views suggest that God made the nations worship the heavenly bodies as the first step in elevating them to true knowledge of divinity.[7] However, these explanations are unlikely. The view that the nations will someday abandon idolatry and worship the Lord alone is never expressed in the Torah, and Deuteronomy 4:19 is consistent with this. Only the prophets expect the nations to abandon idolatry in the future. Jeremiah is the first to speak of idolatry as a sin for which the nations will be punished.[8] In the Torah the nations are held guilty for what

they do in the name of their religion, such as child sacrifice, but not for what they worship.[9]

Cross-Generational Retribution (5:9–10 and 7:9–10)

According to 5:9–10, God "visits the guilt of the parents upon the children" and rewards descendants for their ancestors' loyalty and obedience. This idea, also expressed elsewhere in the Bible,[1] is found in Greek and Hittite literature as well.[2] As noted in the Comment to 5:9, the idea corresponds to the concept of family solidarity in ancient societies, especially those with a tribal background. The basic unit of society was the family, not the individual. Individuals were not viewed as separate entities but as inextricably bound up with their kin, including past and future generations. Members of a family expected to share a common fortune, whether good or bad. An adoption contract from Mari states that the adoptive son shall share his adoptive parents' good fortune and their bad fortune.[3] In the light of this concept, it was natural that Saul promised to reward both Goliath's killer and the killer's family, and that grants given to reward loyal servants were to pass on to their descendants in perpetuity.[4] Given the feelings of a person for his family and later descendants, it was recognized that their suffering was indeed painful to him and hence an effective punishment,[5] just as one might reward a person with a benefaction to his family or his descendants.[6] The very threat of harm or promise of benefit to one's family could serve to deter or encourage certain behavior.[7]

Effective as this approach may have been, Deuteronomy 24:16 forbids its application by judicial authorities: "Parents shall not be put to death for children, nor children be put to death for parents: a person shall be put to death only for his own crime." But experience showed that people often do suffer or benefit because of the actions of their ancestors; one modern commentator termed this the "most firmly established of all the lessons of history" (Wellhausen).[8] Accordingly, the cross-generational retribution that was denied to human authorities was recognized as an aspect of divine governance: loyalty to God is rewarded, and rebellion against Him punished, across the generations.[9] Tradition recorded that Noah's entire family was saved along with him, that Abraham's descendants were given the promised land because of his loyalty to God, and that the descendants of Phinehas and David inherited, respectively, the priesthood and the monarchy because of their forebears' loyalty to God.[10] On the other hand, the entire households of Dathan and Abiram perished along with them,[11] while punishments due to David, Jeroboam, and Ahab were carried out on their descendants.[12] Indeed, the generation of the fall of Jerusalem believed that it was being punished for the sins of Manasseh's generation,[13] though not all denied that their own generation, too, had sinned.[14] A popular saying circulated complaining that "fathers have eaten sour grapes and children's teeth are blunted."[15]

Jeremiah and Ezekiel both felt compelled to refer to this attitude when urging their contemporaries to have confidence in a restoration. They apparently found it a hindrance to confidence. Jeremiah asserted that in the future even God would no longer punish descendants for their ancestors' sins; He would punish individuals solely for their own actions, as He requires of human authorities in Deuteronomy 24:16.[16] Ezekiel denied that God operated that way even in the present and was punishing Judah for ancestral guilt:

even now, according to Ezekiel, God rewards and punishes people only for their own deeds.[17] In talmudic times Rabbi Yosi bar Ḥaninah recognized that Ezekiel in effect abrogated the principle of cross-generational punishment expressed in the Decalogue. In his words, "Moses said 'Visiting the guilt of the parents upon the children,' but Ezekiel came and annulled it: 'The person who sins, only he shall die.'"[18]

Jeremiah and Ezekiel were not the only ones to mitigate the doctrine of cross-generational punishment by God. It is partially mitigated in the Torah itself. In the Torah, only Exodus 34:7 and Numbers 14:18 state without qualification that God visits the sins of fathers upon children. In both versions of the Decalogue, the list of generations to be punished and rewarded is qualified by the phrases "of those who hate Me," and "of those who love Me and keep My commandments" (Deut. 5:9-10; Exod. 20:5-6). The phrases most likely refer to the descendants, meaning that cross-generational retribution applies only to descendants who act as their ancestors did; in other words: God "visits the guilt of the fathers on future generations *that reject Him* and rewards the loyalty of ancestors to the thousandth generation of descendants *who are also loyal to Him.*"[19] In other words, God punishes or rewards descendants for ancestral sins and virtues *along with their own* if they—the descendants—"continue the deeds of their ancestors."[20]

This idea of *compound* punishment befalling sinful descendants, attested in Leviticus 26:39 and elsewhere,[21] occupies the middle ground between cross-generational retribution and the principle that individuals should be rewarded and punished only for their own deeds. It recognizes the reality of the former but holds that cross-generational rewards and punishments only come to those who merit similar retribution on their own. This qualification avoids the demoralizing effect that the principle of cross-generational retribution had in its unconditional form ("Why obey if our fate has already been determined by our ancestors' conduct?").

Deuteronomy 7:9–10 goes one step further. According to that passage, God "keeps His covenant faithfully to the thousandth generation of those who love Him and keep His commandments, but instantly requites with destruction those who reject Him—never slow with those who reject Him, but requiting them instantly." Here, only divine rewards are extended down through the generations. God punishes sinners personally and instantly, and not a word is said of His extending the punishment to sinners' descendants. According to this version, God Himself acts in accordance with the principle He established in 24:16.[22]

EXCURSUS 9

"A Land Oozing Milk and Honey"   (6:3 etc.)

The phrase *'erets zavat ḥalav u-devash*, "a land oozing milk and honey," is a favorite one for describing the fertility of the Land of Israel. It appears in Deuteronomy 6:3; 11:9; 26:9,15; 27:3; 31:20, and frequently elsewhere in the Bible.[1] Milk and honey are also mentioned individually in descriptions of plenty in the Bible.[2] They were regarded as necessary and choice foods.[3] They were offered to guests and given as gifts. In the Song of Songs they are used as metaphors for the sweetness of love.[4]

Milk (*ḥalav*) was obtained primarily from goats, and possibly also from cows.[5] It was drunk fresh or perhaps in the form of *leben* (coagulated sour milk) and was processed into dairy products.[6] Honey (*devash*) was eaten as a delicacy and used as the main sweetener,

since sugar was not known. The Bible mentions honey gathered in the wild,[7] but several passages mention it among agricultural products, suggesting that the term sometimes refers to a sweet syrup made from the nectar of fruits, especially of dates, figs, and grapes.[8] This is how the traditional Jewish commentaries generally understand "honey" in the Bible.[9] In rabbinic Hebrew *devash* refers to both bee honey and fruit honey,[10] as does the Akkadian cognate *dishpu*; the Arabic cognate *dibs* is used only for fruit honey. In fact, the word for honey has both meanings in other languages as well, such as Greek. "A land oozing milk and honey" may therefore refer to one or both types of honey.

"A land oozing milk and honey" came to be a proverbial description of the fertility of the land of Israel, representing the products of animals and the earth, of herders and farmers. It is not merely a neutral descriptive phrase, but carries positive overtones.[11] It is not always meant literally. The scouts who toured the promised land brought back grapes, pomegranates, and figs as a confirmation that it was indeed "a land oozing milk and honey" (Num. 14:23,27). Since they did not bring back milk products, they must have meant the phrase as a general reference to fertility rather than specifically to milk and honey.

In Greek literature, milk and honey are mentioned as part of the food of the gods, sometimes produced by magical springs and streams. Apocalyptic and eschatological descriptions of heaven and paradise also speak of such fantastic sources.[12] These descriptions have led some to think that "a land *oozing* milk and honey" hints at the idea of supernatural productivity, as if the ground itself produced these substances. However, the references to milk and honey in the land of Israel are entirely naturalistic. They not only appear in idealized pictures of the land prior to the Israelites' seeing it, but even after they arrived there and knew its actual conditions.[13] Given this purely naturalistic picture, it is not likely that the phrase hints at anything supernatural. Others have thought that the phrase is based on the observation of full udders dripping milk, and beehives leaking honey in hot weather when honeycombs melt, or dates and figs dripping their nectar,[14] but the verb may be simply metaphoric.[15]

The description of the promised land as "oozing milk and honey" may seem puzzling in the light of its condition when Jews returned to redevelop it in the nineteenth and early twentieth centuries. Archaeological evidence, however, indicates that in biblical times the Syro-Palestinian area was far more fertile than it became after the Jews were exiled. Egyptian texts in particular refer to its rich forests, cattle, and fields.[16] The abundance of one region of Syria-Palestine is described as follows:

> It was a good land. . . . Figs were in it, and grapes. It had more wine than water. Plentiful was its honey, abundant its olives. Every [kind of] fruit was on its trees. Barley was there, and emmer. There was no limit to any [kind of] cattle. . . . Bread was made . . . as daily fare, wine as daily provision, cooked meat and roast fowl, beside the wild beasts of the desert . . . and milk was used in all cooking.[17]

In the light of such passages, it seems likely that the land was indeed fertile enough to merit its description as flowing with milk and honey.

EXCURSUS 10

The Shema (6:4)

As noted in the Comment to 6:4, the precise meaning of the Shema is uncertain. The four Hebrew words "YHVH *'eloheinu* YHVH *'eḥad*" literally mean "YHVH our God

YHVH one." Since Hebrew does not have a present-tense verb meaning "is" to link subject and predicate, the link must be supplied by the listener or reader. Where to do so depends on context and is sometimes uncertain. Grammatically, "YHVH our God YHVH one" could be rendered in several ways, such as (1) "YHVH is our God, YHVH alone"; (2) "the LORD our God, the LORD is one" (lit., "YHVH our God, YHVH is one"); (3) "YHVH our God is one YHVH."

The first possibility, which is followed in the NJPS translation, is based on Ibn Ezra and Rashbam.[1] One difficulty with this interpretation is that Hebrew normally expresses "alone" with *levad-*, as in "You alone [*levadekha*] are God of all the kingdoms of the earth" (2 Kings 19:15,19; cf. v. 19 and Ps. 86:10).[2] A few passages have been found in which *'eḥad* seems to have this meaning, but the usage is at best rare (see Comment to 6:4, endnote). There is also a serious syntactic difficulty with this interpretation: it interprets the words "YHVH our God" (*YHVH 'eloheinu*) as a subject and a predicate, meaning "YHVH *is* our God." Although this usage is grammatically possible (see 2 Chron. 13:10), it is rare in the Bible and absolutely anomalous in Deuteronomy, where *YHVH 'eloheinu* occurs nearly two dozen times, consistently as a fixed phrase meaning "YHVH our God."[3] Still, this interpretation seems to be presupposed by Zechariah 14, as noted in the Comment to 6:4. If so, it is the only interpretation that was demonstrably held in biblical times.

The old and familiar translation "the LORD our God, the LORD is one" (2) makes the verse a statement about the nature of God Himself, namely that He is one. This might mean that He is unique (incomparable)[4] or that He is indivisible, that He does not consist of multiple deities (the latter idea is also expressed by translation 3). This translation, however, is problematic because it leaves the second YHVH superfluous; "YHVH our God is one" would have sufficed.

The third possibility, "YHVH our God is one YHVH"—and not many YHVHs—is not as tautologous as it sounds. Pagans referred to some gods by their name and place of worship, such as "Ishtar of Arbela," and in some texts a god's name appears several times, followed each time by a different place. For example, an Egyptian-Hittite treaty invokes both "the Re the lord of the sky" and "the Re of the town of Arinna"; similarly, it invokes "Seth the lord of the sky," "Seth of Hatti," and the Seths of ten other cities.[5] This manner of speaking, based on the many sanctuaries of a deity, was also used by some Israelites. In some Hebrew inscriptions of the ninth–eighth centuries B.C.E. discovered in the Sinai, one refers to "YHVH of Samaria" and two others refer to "YHVH of Teman."[6] Some scholars believe that this manner of speech could imply that there were several deities of each name—several Res, Seths, or YHVHs—and that such a danger was developing in Israel. They believe that the Shema meant "YHVH our God is one YHVH," not many YHVHs, and was intended to counter this kind of disintegration of YHVH into several deities.[7] However, there is no other evidence that such a danger was developing in Israel and we do not even know whether non-Israelites really drew such inferences. Re was the sun, and the Egyptians could hardly have believed that there were two suns. An Egyptian inscription describing offerings to Amon-Re lists his name dozens of times, each time followed by one of his epithets, including local manifestations (e.g., "Amon-Re in Thebes . . . Amon-Re in Heliopolis"), but includes phrases recognizing that all these references are to a single deity (e.g., "Amon-Re in all the places where he wishes to be," "Amon-Re in all his funerary temples," "Amon-Re in all his names").[8] While it is possible that recognition of the unity behind all these names was limited to the intelligentsia and that the common folk thought of these as different deities, there is no evidence to that effect. Furthermore, such a danger

seems foreign to the context of Deuteronomy 6, which is concerned with Israel's relationship to God, not with His nature.

On the basis of present evidence, translation (1) seems the most likely, but it is not certain.[9]

The Shema in Jewish Liturgy

The instruction in 6:7, repeated in 11:18–19, to "speak of . . . these words . . . when you lie down and when you get up" was understood in halakhic exegesis to mean *recite* these words at the times of day when people lie down to sleep and when they arise in the morning. "These words" were identified as 6:4–9 and 11:13–21, the paragraphs in which this instruction is found. The instruction was fulfilled by reciting these two paragraphs, followed by Num. 15:37–41, as part of the morning and evening prayers. They are called the *Keri'at Shema'* ("Recitation of the Shema"), after the first word in verse 4.[10] The practice, known since late Second Temple times, is still followed today.[11]

In the liturgy, the three biblical paragraphs are preceded by blessings praising God for creating light and darkness and bringing on day and night, and for loving Israel and teaching it the Torah. They are followed by blessings praising Him for redeeming and protecting Israel.[12] In rabbinic thought, the first paragraph functions preeminently as a declaration of allegiance to God—as the rabbis called it: "accepting the authority of the kingship of God" (lit., "the yoke of the kingship of Heaven"; Mish. Ber. 2:2).[13] In the context of the liturgy, this is expressed by the addition, after verse 4, of the exclamation "Blessed be the glorious name of His *kingship* forever!" The second paragraph is regarded as "accepting the duty of performing the commandments" (Mish. Ber. 2:2). The blessing that follows the third paragraph begins with the declaration "True, firm, established, obligatory, proper, lasting, satisfactory, favored, agreeable, pleasing, respected, revered, fit, accepted, good and valid is this word" (i.e., this obligation that we have just recited). Many of the adjectives in this declaration are legal terms used in validating legal agreements. They give the recitation of the Shema the force of an oath, meaning: We solemnly affirm that the obligation we have just recited is valid and binding on us in every way.[14] This makes of the Shema a daily affirmation of allegiance to God and to the covenant obligations that allegiance entails.[15]

Although the Shema began as a declaration of allegiance rather than of monotheism, it became the preeminent expression of monotheism (*yihud*) in Judaism.[16] This was undoubtedly fostered by its prominent location in Deuteronomy and its centrality in the liturgy, but it may have been due especially to the word *'ehad*, which normally means "one." This word made the Shema a suitable response to the many theological challenges that Jewish monotheism confronted throughout history: in the face of polytheism it meant that the Divine is one, not many; in the face of Zoroastrian and Gnostic dualism it meant one, not two; in the face of Christian trinitarianism it meant one, not three; and in the face of atheism, one and not none.[17]

The Shema's fundamental significance in Judaism is reflected in the many roles it plays and the special way it is treated. The rules for its recitation are the very first subject dealt with in the Talmud (Tractate Berakhot). Its first verse must be recited with full concentration on its meaning. To prevent distraction one must cover one's eyes when reciting it, and there are restrictions as to whom one may greet while reciting it. A child must be taught the Shema and Deuteronomy 33:4 immediately upon learning to speak.[18] The first para-

graph is recited in bed upon retiring and on one's deathbed.[19] Following the reported precedent of Rabbi Akiba, it has been recited before martyrdom from ancient times through the present.[20] All of this is due to the fact that the Shema serves as the quintessential expression of the most fundamental belief and commitment of Judaism.

The Majuscule Letters in the Shema

In Hebrew texts the letters *ʿayin* in Shemaʿ ("hear") and *dalet* in *ʾeḥad* ("alone") are emphasized, usually by being enlarged.[21] Various explanations have been given for this. The best known is that the two letters spell *ʿed*, "witness," expressing the idea that in reciting the Shema one bears *witness* to God's unity (Abudraham).[22] Another possibility regarding the *dalet* is to prevent confusing it with the similar letter *resh*, which would produce the blasphemous reading *ʾaḥer*, "another," instead of *ʾeḥad*, "one" (Midrash Aggadah).[23]

EXCURSUS 11

Tefillin and Mezuzot   (6:8–9 and 11:18,20)

Tefillin

At least since later Second Temple times (from the second century B.C.E.), and perhaps already in Deuteronomy, Deuteronomy 6:8 and 11:18 along with Exodus 13:9 and 16, have been understood as commanding the wearing of objects by means of which certain of God's words could be fastened to the arm and forehead.[1] For this purpose Jewish law adopted the expedient of writing the requisite words—passages from the Torah—on slips of parchment inserted in small leather capsules called *tefillin*. One is fastened to the forehead, suspended from a leather headband (a *totefet*, as argued in the Comment to 6:8) knotted in the back of the head, with its loose ends hanging down like streamers, as in some of the headbands seen in ancient Near Eastern art. The other is fastened to the upper arm by another leather strap (for "hand" meaning arm, see Judg. 15:14).

Such capsules, in the form of amulets, were a common device for attaching inscriptions to the body. The physical similarity of *tefillin* to amulets was clear to the ancients. Two of the ancient terms for *tefillin*—Hebrew *qemiaʿ* and Greek *phylakterion* ("phylactery")—literally mean "amulet,"[2] and talmudic sources frequently mention *tefillin* and amulets together[3] and speak of the possibility of confusing them with each other.[4] However, *tefillin* resemble amulets only in their external form, not their contents. They contain biblical passages about the Exodus and God's instructions, and thus serve an educational purpose; amulets typically contain magical inscriptions or materials and aim to protect the wearer.[5]

Initially there was some disagreement as to which biblical passages should be placed in the *tefillin*. Since talmudic times they have been limited to the four paragraphs that contain the verses which serve as the basis for the practice: Exodus 13:1–10 and 11–16 and Deuteronomy 6:5–9 and 11:13–21. The *tefillin* found at Qumran included these passages as well as others, most notably the Decalogue. Josephus seems to imply that they contain texts that record God's benefactions, power, and good will.

The wording "bind them" and especially "let them serve as a frontlet" may imply that the parchment (or some other object on which the texts were written) is to be worn directly on the arm and forehead, with the texts visible, instead of being placed in containers affixed to those spots. This would be similar to inscribed armbands known from Egypt and to the inscribed gems and frontlet worn by the Israelite high priest (Exod. 28:9–12,21, 29,36–37).[6] There is evidence that some Jews in talmudic times may have worn the texts this way; some of the church fathers quote reports that certain Jews wrapped the parchment strips around their heads like crowns. In any case, the halakhah did not accept this interpretation but required that the texts be placed in containers.[7]

In talmudic times *tefillin* were worn throughout the day on weekdays. Since the Middle Ages the practice has usually been to wear them only during weekday morning prayers.

The oldest *tefillin* found by archaeologists have come from the caves of Qumran and antedate the destruction of that settlement in 70 C.E. Others were found among the remains of Bar Kochba's forces (132–135 C.E.).

Not all Jews agreed that the biblical texts in question meant to ordain a concrete practice. Although the Pharisees, the Qumran sect, and other Jewish groups did,[8] some of the ancient Greek translations of the Torah take the verses metaphorically to mean that God's teaching should be kept immovably in our attention.[9] The Samaritans also did not accept the precept of *tefillin*.[10] This suggests that prior to the Jewish-Samaritan schism the literal interpretation of the verses was not universally accepted. Similarly, the reference in the Mishnah to "whoever says 'there are no *tefillin*'" (Mish. Sanh. 11:3) must refer to a denial that the biblical verses have *tefillin* in mind. The neglect of the precept reported in some talmudic passages may also reflect a rejection of the literal interpretation.[11]

In the Middle Ages the meaning of these verses was debated by the Rabbanites and the Karaites. The latter stressed a metaphoric interpretation according to which the verses meant that God's commandments and teachings should be remembered well, as if they were bound to our bodies, like a string tied around the finger as a reminder. In favor of this interpretation they cited similar Hebrew metaphors, including "binding" to the body, for remembering teachings (Prov. 1:9; 3:3; 4:9; 6:21; 7:3). Most Rabbanite commentators rejected this argument, on the grounds that analogies from Proverbs, which is explicitly metaphoric in style, have no bearing on the Torah, which is not (Ibn Ezra at Exod. 3:9). Still, no less a Rabbanite authority than Rashbam conceded that the plain sense of the text was metaphoric, meaning "let it be remembered always, as if written on your hand," comparing a similar metaphor in Song of Songs 8:6.[12]

The divergence of interpretations since Second Temple times may go back to different meanings in the biblical texts themselves. It seems that Exodus 13:9 and 16 used "sign," "memorial," and "headband" metaphorically, whereas Deuteronomy 6:8 and 11:18 may have intended them literally. The metaphorical intent of Exodus 13:9 and 16 seems clear when one considers the grammatical subject of "shall be a sign on your hand and a memorial/headband on your forehead" in those verses. The subject cannot be the biblical passages themselves, since they are not mentioned in the texts. The subject must be either (1) the fact "that the LORD brought the Israelites out of Egypt" (vv. 9b,16b); in that case, the verses mean that the Lord's mighty deeds must be remembered well (like a sign on the hand and a memorial or a headband), or (2) the grammatical antecedents of "shall be," namely "this day" or "this practice" or the festival of unleavened bread in Exodus 13:1–10 and the sacrifice/redemption of the first-born in verses 11–16; in that case, the verses mean that these things must be remembered well (like a sign, a memorial, a headband), so that the Lord's

teaching will be remembered well. In neither case does "it shall be a sign" represent an additional observance beyond those mentioned in verses 2–8 and 12–15. ("This institution" in verse 10 explicitly refers to an *annual* practice, namely the eating of unleavened bread in verses 3–8, not to a *daily* rite such as *tefillin*). Hence Exodus 13 seems to be using sign, memorial, and headband metaphorically to indicate that certain historical events and/or certain ceremonies are to be remembered well, much like the metaphoric use of other items of apparel and ornaments that are close or dear to those who wear them (see, in addition to the Proverbs passages, Isa. 62:3; Jer. 2:32; 13:11; 22:24; Hag. 2:23; Job 29:14).[13]

On the other hand, the injunction to "bind" these words in Deuteronomy 6 and 11 seems to be meant literally. Here the reference is to words which, unlike events and ceremonies, can be literally bound to the body, and the following injunction to write these words on the doorposts and gates (Deut. 6:9; 11:20) suggests that something concrete is intended. It is true that even Proverbs speaks of binding teachings and commandments to one's body, and refers to writing them on "the tablet of your heart [i.e., mind]" (Prov. 7:3), but whereas writing words on the heart is a known metaphor,[14] writing them on doorposts and gates is not so known but is a concrete practice (see Deut. 6:9). Hence it is plausible that the accompanying injunction to bind God's words as a sign on the hand and as a headband on the forehead is also meant literally, and that what began as a metaphor in Exodus 13 was interpreted or recast literally as early as the time of Deuteronomy rather than centuries later.[15]

At first glance it might seem surprising for Deuteronomy to give a ceremonial interpretation to something that Exodus meant metaphorically. Deuteronomy normally presents a more abstract approach to religion than do the other books of the Torah. However, the nature of Deuteronomy's "abstractness" may help to explain why it might have been the book to ordain the practice of wearing *tefillin*. Deuteronomy's abstractness is aimed primarily at combating an overly anthropomorphic conception of God and sacrificial worship, and it must have had the effect of reducing the role of sacrifice in daily life, especially in the provinces. In its struggle against idolatry it even outlaws religious artifacts that had once been considered unobjectionable, such as sacred pillars and trees (16:21–22; note also its silence about the cherubs when describing the Ark in 10:1–9). But Deuteronomy does not indiscriminately oppose religious symbols per se. It ordains the precept of *mezuzah* (6:9; see below) and it preserves the injunction to wear fringes on one's garments (22:12; cf. Num. 15:37–41). It opposes only symbols that were too anthropomorphic or that had actual or potential idolatrous associations. The Deuteronomic reformers may well have realized that their reformation would deplete an already small stock of religious symbols in Israelite religion. Concrete, visible symbols are important, and it may be that just as Deuteronomy advocated the precepts of fringes and *mezuzah*, which serve as reminders of God's commandments, it advanced the precept of *tefillin* for the same purpose. Given the current state of evidence, this suggestion is speculative, and whether the precept of *tefillin* goes back to Deuteronomy or only to Second Temple times remains an open question.

Mezuzot

In contrast to the question of *tefillin*, it is certain that Deuteronomy 6:9 means literally to ordain the writing of God's instructions on doorposts and city gates. The verse was understood that way even by the Samaritans, who rejected the precept of *tefillin*,[16] and the practice is attested at Qumran and in literary sources of the late Second Temple period.[17]

It was not unusual to have inscriptions written on the doors, lintels, and doorposts of private houses. Inscriptions of various types have been found at the entrances to ancient Egyptian houses, and to this day invocations, proverbs, and verses from the Qur'an (the Moslem scriptures) are commonly inscribed on or over doors in the Moslem world. No examples of this practice have been found on ancient Israelite houses, but inscriptions on the entrances to tombs, identifying those buried in them, suggest that writing on entrances was known in Israel. The sanctuary at Kuntillet Ajrud in the Sinai Peninsula had inscriptions of religious character in Hebrew and Phoenician script written on its walls and doorposts.[18] In Mesopotamia, Syria, and Hatti royal inscriptions celebrating the accomplishments of the kings, and charters guaranteeing the privileges of certain cities, were sometimes inscribed at city gates.[19]

The closest parallel to what Deuteronomy prescribes—writing God's teachings on the doorposts and gates—is the ancient Egyptian practice of writing instructions at the entrances of temples, enumerating moral and cultic prerequisites for entering the temple.[20] The prescription in Deuteronomy differs in that it is not stating prerequisites for entering the sanctuary but seeking to make people aware of God's instructions at all times and places.

As noted in the Commentary, the text implies that the words are to be written visibly on the doorposts and gates. This is what the Samaritans did, writing on the stone of the building or on stone slabs affixed to it. For an unknown reason, at some point in the late Second Temple period Jewish law modified this practice, ruling that the inscription was to be written on parchment, rolled up, and inserted in a case. The *mezuzah* texts found at Qumran are of this type. The inscription is known as a *mezuzah* (plural *mezuzot*), from the Hebrew word for "doorpost" in 6:9. A *mezuzah* case is affixed, with the top slanting inward, to the upper third of the right-hand doorpost at the entrance of the house and of each residential room in a house.

According to the halakhah, the texts to be written in the *mezuzah* are the two paragraphs that contain the commandment, Deuteronomy 6:4–9 and 11:13–21. As in the case of *tefillin*, there was originally some variation in this practice. The *mezuzah* texts from Qumran (if all of them are really *mezuzot*) include these two paragraphs, but some also include the Decalogue and Deuteronomy 10:12–11:12, and some include parts of Exodus 13, which are also contained in *tefillin*. The Samaritan *mezuzot* contain the Decalogue, and a few add the poem of the Ark from Numbers 10:35–36.

Like many religious objects, *mezuzot* lent themselves to use as amulets (see n. 5). This use was facilitated by their location on doorposts, which suggested that they could serve as amulets to protect the house or city within.[22] No less a figure than Rabbi Judah the Prince sent a *mezuzah* to the Parthian King Ardavan, explaining that it would protect him.[23] To enhance their use for this purpose, other names of God and the names of angels were sometimes added to *mezuzot*. Maimonides forbade this practice, declaring that this not only disqualified the *mezuzah* but turned the instrument of unifying God's name into a mere charm for personal benefit.[24]

The intention of the precepts of *tefillin* and *mezuzah*, along with that of *tsitsit* (fringes), was concisely summed up by Maimonides as follows:

> The ancient sages said, "Whoever has *tefillin* on his head and arm, *tsitsit* on his garment, and a *mezuzah* on his door may be presumed not to sin," for he has many reminders, and these are the "angels" that save him from sinning, as it is said, "The angel of the LORD camps around those who revere Him and rescues them" [Ps. 34:8].[25]

The Golden Calf (9:9–21)

The story of the golden calf, the greatest scandal of the wilderness period, is recalled in 9:9–21, based on the fuller account in Exodus 32. What the calf represented is debated by scholars. Images of bulls and calves were common in Near Eastern religions. In Egypt a bull, Apis, was sacred to the god Ptah and emblematic of him.[1] In Canaanite literature, the chief god El is sometimes called a bull, although this may be no more than an epithet signifying strength, and the storm god Baal sires an ox in one myth.[2] A relief from Asia Minor shows two individuals worshiping at an altar before a bull.[3] Figurines of bulls and calves have been found at several Canaanite sites.[4] At least one was also found at an Israelite site, in the Samaria hills.[5] In some of these the bull or calf represents a deity—usually a storm god—directly. At other times it represents the deity's mount, signifying the deity indirectly.[6]

It is unlikely that Aaron intended the calf to represent another deity, since he proclaimed a festival in honor of YHVH when he finished making it (Exod. 32:5). At first glance the people's declaration, "This is your god, O Israel, who brought you out of the land of Egypt" (Exod. 32:4), seems to imply that they took it as a depiction of YHVH.[7] But in their request to Aaron to make them a god, they explained that they wanted a god to lead them because they did not know what had become of Moses, who led them out of Egypt (Exod. 32:1). This seems to imply that they wanted the calf to replace *Moses*, apparently in his role as mediator of YHVH's presence to the people. In other words, they did not intend the calf to depict YHVH but to function as the conduit of His presence among them, as Moses had functioned previously. Many scholars believe that the calf did so by serving as the pedestal or mount on which YHVH was invisibly present, as did the cherubs in the Holy of Holies (see Comment to 10:1–2).[8] This conception of the calf is illustrated by ancient images of a god standing on the back of a bull or another animal.[9] According to this interpretation, the declaration "This is your god" is not an exact quotation of what the people said at the time, but a paraphrase of their words based on hindsight, reflecting the way they *ultimately* treated the statue. In any case, it is clear from Exodus 32:8 that even if Aaron or the people had legitimate intentions, the people immediately fell to worshiping the calf and violated the Decalogue's prohibition against worshiping idols.

Some scholars believe that the entire golden calf story is a pejorative recasting—also based on hindsight—of a northern cult legend about the origin of the golden calves that Jeroboam erected in Bethel and Dan (1 Kings 12:25–33). In this view, Jeroboam's calves were originally intended as pedestals or mounts for YHVH, like the cherubs, not as idols (see Comment to 4:17–18). With the passage of time people began to venerate them, as shown by Hosea's complaint that people were kissing calves (Hos. 13:2). This development may have been facilitated by the fact that the calves were not kept hidden, as the cherubs were in the Holy of Holies, but stood outdoors in sanctuary courtyards and were visible to the public. This development is analogous to what happened with the copper serpent that Moses made as a charm for healing snakebites: by the time of King Hezekiah, people began to worship it and it had to be destroyed (Num. 21:4–9; see 2 Kings 18:4).

According to this view, the story of Aaron's golden calf originated as a legend about the origin of (one of?) Jeroboam's calves, and originally described its manufacture approv-

ingly, comparable to the account in Exodus about how the people contributed raw materials with which Bezalel and his staff fashioned the Ark and cherubs and the rest of the Tabernacle, following designs provided by God (Exod. 25:9,40; chaps. 35–39). Aaron's statement that he threw the gold into a fire and "out came this calf" (Exod. 32:24) implies that the calf was manufactured with supernatural assistance, which supports the view that the story was originally an approving one.[10] Later, after Jeroboam's calves came to be treated as idols, the manufacture of calves was seen in hindsight to lead inevitably to idolatry, and the story about Aaron's calf was revised to show the phenomenon as sinful from the outset. This, the theory goes, is the version that appears in Exodus and is reflected in Deuteronomy.[11]

EXCURSUS 13
The Arrangement of the Laws in Deuteronomy

The laws of Deuteronomy fall into several groups, some of which share a common theme while others do not. Digressions into relatively unrelated subjects are frequent and it is not always clear where one section ends and the next begins. In the following discussion, we shall refer to the groups and their subdivisions as "sections," "articles," "parts," and "paragraphs." These terms are used for convenience, and do not imply the same degree of connected, topical arrangement which they imply in Western law codes.

The laws may be divided as follows:

Section I. THE SANCTUARY AND OTHER RELIGIOUS MATTERS
(12:2–16:17)

Article A. The Place of Worship (12:2–13:1)

1. Destroying Canaanite sanctuaries (vv. 2–3)

2. Shunning the Canaanite manner of worship by restricting sacrifice to a single place (vv. 4–7)

3. Explication and ramifications of the restriction (vv. 8–28)

4. Shunning Canaanite religious practices (12:29–13:1)

Article B. Punishing instigation to worship other gods (13:2–19)

1. Instigation by a prophet or a dreamer (vv. 2–6)

2. Instigation in secret by a relative or friend (vv. 7–12)

3. Reported subversion of an entire town (vv. 13–19)

Article C. Holiness (14:1–21)

1. Holiness in mourning (vv. 1–2)

2. Holiness in diet (vv. 3–21)

Article D. Periodic Duties at the Chosen Place and Other Periodic Duties
(14:22–16:17)

1. Tithes (14:22–29)

a. Annual tithe (vv. 22–27)

b. Triennial poor tithe (vv. 28–29)

2. Measures to protect the poor (15:1–18)

    a. Remission of debts every seven years (vv. 1–6)

    b. Lending to the poor when the seventh year approaches (vv. 7–11)

    c. Manumission of indentured servants after six years of service (vv. 12–18)

3. The sacrifice of firstborn cattle (15:19–23)

4. The pilgrimage festivals (16:1–17)

Section II. CIVIL AND RELIGIOUS AUTHORITIES (16:18–18:22)

Article A. The judiciary (16:18–17:13)

1. Local judges and officials (16:18–20)

2. Three prohibitions concerning worship (16:21–17:1)

3. Prosecution of apostates (17:2–7)

4. The high court of referral (vv. 8–13)

Article B. The king (17:14–20)

Article C. Endowments of the clergy (18:1–8)

Article D. The prophet (18:9–22)

Section III. JUDICIAL AND MILITARY MATTERS (19–21:9)

Article A. The courts (Chap. 19)

1. Asylum cities (vv. 1–13)

2. The inviolability of boundary markers (v. 14)

3. Witnesses (vv. 15–21)

Article B. Warfare (Chap. 20)

1. Preparing the army (vv. 1–9)

2. Treatment of the population of defeated cities (vv. 10–18)

3. Treatment of trees near besieged cities (vv. 19–20)

Article C. Unsolved murder (21:1–9)

Section IV. MISCELLANEOUS LAWS, MOSTLY ABOUT CIVIL AND DOMESTIC LIFE (21:10–Chap. 25)

Article A. Family laws (21:10–21)

1. Marriage with a woman captured in war (vv. 10–14)

2. The right of the first-born in a polygamous family (vv. 15–17)

3. The punishment of an insubordinate son (vv. 18–21)

Article B. Treatment of the body of an executed criminal (21:22–23)

Article C. Miscellaneous domestic laws (22:1–12)

1. Returning lost animals (vv. 1–3)

2. Assisting with fallen animals (v. 4)

3. Not wearing clothing of the opposite sex (v. 5)

4. Not capturing a mother bird along with her young (vv. 6–7)

5. Building a parapet (v. 8)

6. Forbidden combinations of seed (v. 9)

7. Forbidden combination of animals in plowing (v. 10)

8. Forbidden combination of textiles in garments (v. 11)

9. Tassels on garments (v. 12)

Article D. Marital and sexual misconduct (22:13–29)

1. Accusations of premarital unchastity (vv. 13–21)

2. Adultery with a married woman (v. 22)

3. Adultery with an engaged virgin (vv. 23–27)

4. Rape of an unengaged virgin (vv. 28–29)

Article E. Forbidden relationships (23:1–9)

1. Prohibition of marrying one's father's former wife (v. 1)

2. Restrictions on entry into the Assembly of the Lord (vv. 2–9)

Article F. Miscellaneous laws (23:10–25:19)

1. The sanctity of the military camp (23:10–15)

2. Asylum for escaped slaves (vv. 16–17)

3. Prohibition of prostitution and other abhorrent practices (vv. 18–19)

4. Prohibition of lending at interest (vv. 20–21)

5. Timely fulfillment of vows (vv. 22–24)

6. The right to eat from a neighbor's unharvested crops (vv. 25–26)

7. Forbidden remarriage (24:1–4)

8. Deferral of the new husband from military service (v. 5)

9. Vital implements may not be distrained to compel repayment of a loan (v. 6)

10. Kidnaping (v. 7)

11. Dealing with "leprosy" (vv. 8–9)

12. Taking and holding distrained property (vv. 10–13)

13. Timely payment of wages (vv. 14–15)

14. Transgenerational punishment forbidden (v. 16)

15. Protecting aliens and the fatherless from judicial mistreatment, and widows from distraint of clothing (vv. 17–18)

16. Gleanings for the poor (vv. 19–22)

17. Limits on flogging (25:1–3)

18. Not muzzling an ox while it threshes (v. 4)

19. Levirate marriage (vv. 5–10)

20. Improper intervention in a fight (vv. 11–12)

21. Honest weights and measures (vv. 13–16)

22. Remembering the Amalekite aggression (vv. 17–19)

Section V. LITURGICAL DECLARATIONS (26:1–15)

Article A. The first-fruits ceremony (vv. 1–11)

Article B. The tithe declaration (vv. 12–15)

Several of the laws fall into topical groups, such as those about religious matters in Section I, about civil and religious authorities in Section II, and the laws about family and marital/sexual misconduct in Section III, Articles A and D. Often, however, the organization seems random, especially in Sections III and IV, where laws lacking a common theme are frequently grouped together. In 22:1–12, for example, the laws move from helping in the case of lost and fallen animals to prohibiting transvestism, to collecting birds and their eggs, to constructing parapets, to forbidden combinations, to tassels. The midrash, which often makes ingenious connections between laws, could do no better than say that the latter group is arranged to show that a person who performs one commandment will be rewarded with the opportunity to perform others.[1]

Even within groups of laws about the same topic, the arrangement often does not follow systematic principles of the sort that modern readers expect, such as keeping to a subject and completing it before going on to another, and arranging laws about a subject logically or chronologically, or in some other systematic way.[2] In such an arrangement, for example, in Section I, the laws about bringing all offerings to the chosen sanctuary (Article A) would be followed immediately by the other laws dealing with that obligation, Articles D1, 3, and 4. Instead, however, dietary laws and laws about debt and indentured servants intervene. All the laws about marriage in 21:10–17; 22:13–23; 23:1; 24:1–5; and 25:5–10 would appear together, starting with those that deal with the beginning of marriage (22:13–23 and 24:5) and proceeding through the stages of marriage. They would not be interrupted by laws about execution, distraint, and kidnaping (21:22–23; 24:6–13). There would not be such puzzling transitions as those between the dietary and the tithe laws (14:3–21 and 22–29); between the laws about manumission of slaves and about the consecration of firstlings (15:12–18 and 19–23); and between the laws about the judiciary (16:18–20; 17:2–13) and those about worship sandwiched between them (16:21–17:1).

As early as the first century, Josephus observed that Moses left his laws "in a scattered condition," simply recording them in the order in which he received them from God. In presenting the laws to his readers, Josephus felt obliged to rearrange them, classifying them by subject.[3] A talmudic sage commented that many sections of the Torah "are next to each other but as far from each other [in subject matter] as east from west."[4] Nevertheless, the rabbis agreed that the order of the laws is deliberate, and some held that legal inferences should be drawn from the juxtaposition of laws.[5]

The fact that some of the laws do fall into topically coherent, logically arranged groups such as 22:22–29 shows that Deuteronomy was capable of such an arrangement.[6] In fact, in 14:3–21 Deuteronomy brings together related laws—the dietary laws—that are separated in the earlier sources (see Lev. 11 and Exod. 22:30 and 23:19b). This suggests that where topical arrangement is missing, its absence is intentional and that the arrangement does follow a system of its own. Our difficulty in recognizing this system is due primarily to the fact that our own canons of coherence are almost exclusively topical and linear. In the ancient world, a wider variety of factors was used for organizing subject matter. The arrangement of biblical law has aptly been characterized by S. Kaufman in the following way:

> The individual laws and larger sub-units of each topical unit are arranged according to the ancient Near Eastern method of "concatenation of ideas, key words and phrases, and

similar motifs" so as to form what for the ancient eye and ear were smooth *transitions* between sub-units and frequently, between the various topical units themselves. This procedure has frequently been characterized as "free association," but in reality it is a carefully planned procedure that is anything but free.[7]

Arrangement of literary material by the association of "ideas, key words and phrases, and similar motifs" is well attested in the ancient world. Sometimes the arrangement is even based on factors that are *extrinsic* to the subject matter rather than intrinsic to it. In collections of Sumerian proverbs, for example, some groups are formed by proverbs that begin with identical cuneiform signs.[8] In the Aramaic "Proverbs of Aḥikar," many proverbs are grouped together because of a common theme, while others share a pattern of wording, words from the same root, or from homonymous roots.[9]

The ancient Mesopotamian law corpora show some of the same puzzling features of organization that are found in Deuteronomic law. In the Laws of Hammurabi (LH), for example, the laws about marriage begin by indicating that a marriage with no written contract is invalid (§128), but then turn to adultery, capture of the husband, abandonment, divorce, etc. (§§129ff), and only later do they return to the subject of betrothal (§§159ff). What seems to have prompted this order is the fact that the laws immediately preceding those about marriage are about false claims, including false charges of adultery (§§126–127). This example illustrates what is the predominant principle of organization in the Laws of Hammurabi, namely topical association, or concatenation (meaning a linking together, as in a chain) of topics.[10] "The draftsman effects his transitions from one topic to the next by means of cases in which some of the elements partake of the topic being dropped and of the topic being taken up."[11] These transitional cases are like the points of overlap where the links of a chain are joined. For example, headings in a manuscript of LH indicate that §§26–35 deal with infantrymen and fishermen, while the next sections, §§36ff, deal with real estate.[12] What facilitates the transition is that most of §§26–35 deal with land that the infantrymen and fishermen received as crown fiefs, while §§36ff begin with rules about real estate belonging to infantrymen and fishermen, before going on to other rules about real estate. The family laws of §§128–193 are followed by laws concerning bodily injuries (§§194ff) because the last of the family laws deals with the case of a son who strikes his father and who is punished by having his hand cut off, and many of the injury laws, including the first, punish injuries by talionic mutilation.

Associative principles of organization also figure prominently in rabbinic law. The rabbinic law book *par excellence* is the Mishnah.[13] On the whole it *is* organized in a coherent manner based on the subject matter, in ways that we would not consider puzzling at all. It is divided into six "orders," each of which is further subdivided into tractates that are essentially topical. For example, the order about holy days (*Mo'ed*) has tractates about the Sabbath, Pesaḥ, Sukkot, and Rosh Hashanah. But within these orders, the Mishnah is sometimes tolerant of an arrangement that has nothing to do with the logical connection between subjects. The topical composition of the orders is violated at the outset by the fact that the first order, *Zera'im* ("Seeds"), dealing with religious duties connected with agriculture, begins with the tractate *Berakhot* ("Blessings"), which is about prayer.[14] Within the order about holy days, tractates about holidays that are connected to each other, such as the pilgrimage festivals or Rosh Hashanah and Yom Kippur, are separated from each other because within each order the tractates are arranged by the number of chapters they contain, with the longest tractate first and the shortest last.[15] This is an instructive example of ordering material by factors extrinsic to its content.

More pertinent to the order of the laws within Deuteronomy is the way that laws

within the individual tractates are sometimes arranged by factors extraneous to their topic, or at least their main topic. In some places a law or statement related to the main topic of the tractate is followed by several others unrelated to it, either because they were taught by the same sage or because they share a phrase, a numerical pattern, or a pattern of wording.[16] For example, the tractate *Megillah* deals with Purim and the reading of Megillat Esther. In the fifth paragraph of the tractate, this topic is suddenly interrupted by seven laws dealing in succession with festivals and the Sabbath; vows; bodily emissions and lepers; Bibles, *tefillin*, and *mezuzot*; high priests; high places; and Shiloh and Jerusalem (Mish. Meg. 1:5–11). From the point of view of the subject matter, the grouping seems odd. But there is one thing that all these laws have in common: the wording of each one follows the same pattern, namely: "There is no difference between A and B except . . . ," for example, "there was no difference between Shiloh and Jerusalem except. . . ." The Mishnah's mention of these seven laws was prompted by the fact that the Purim law immediately preceding them was worded in the same way: "There is no difference between the First Month of Adar and the Second Month of Adar except that the reading of the Megillah and giving gifts to the poor must be performed in the second" (Mish. Meg. 1:4). This case, and others like it, are exceptions to the Mishnah's normal, topical arrangement of the laws, and they show how a collection that is perfectly capable of topical arrangement sometimes chooses instead to group laws together because of some incidental detail. It is possible that these laws had already been grouped together prior to the Mishnah, perhaps because the shared features facilitated memorization, and that the Mishnah incorporated them in their entirety because one item in them was pertinent to the matter at hand.[17] The fact that, topically, some of them fit better in other tractates made no difference. Notwithstanding the largely topical arrangement of the Mishnah, its editor felt no need to restrict these laws to the tractates in which they belong topically.

These examples of ancient law collections show that in addition to logical, topic-based arrangement of laws, it was also considered acceptable to arrange laws by the association of topics and of features such as a shared idea or theme, a word, a phrase, or a formula. To moderns, these features seem superficial and extrinsic, but this is not how the ancients viewed them. In the ancient world, verbal similarity was often thought to express an inherent connection between phenomena. According to a Babylonian omen, seeing a raven (*arbu*) in a dream portends income (*irbu*), and according to the Talmud, seeing an elephant (*pil*) portends wonders (*pela'ot*).[18] Names were often thought to portend phenomena that sounded like them or were called by terms that seemed to derive from the same or homonymous roots (see Gen. 49 and Deut. 33). In a world where such omens were taken seriously and people planned their lives around them, verbal similarity was seen as reflecting inherent qualities of phenomena, not as a mere coincidence.

It has long been noted that parts of the Bible, particularly the prophets, are organized around such nontopical factors, among which phraseological connections are prominent. Recently, scholars, particularly Alexander Rofé, have explained the organization of the laws of Deuteronomy by similar principles. In what follows I argue that Deuteronomy is arranged by a mixture of intrinsic, subject-based links and extrinsic, associative ones. The argument follows Rofé's analysis at many points, and in some places where it departs from his specific explanations it follows the same methods.[19] Admittedly, a degree of subjectivity enters into such explanations. This is because in this kind of organization the compiler himself is making subjective links, and sometimes it is difficult to identify what was in his mind.

The Arrangement of the Laws of Deuteronomy

SECTION I. THE SANCTUARY AND OTHER RELIGIOUS MATTERS (12:2–16:17)

The first Section focuses on the sanctuary and the rites and festivals celebrated within it (see particularly 12:2–28 and 16:1–17). Laws about other subjects appear when something in a sanctuary-related law triggers an association with some other subject, after which the text returns to sanctuary-related laws.

Beginning with the sanctuary is particularly fitting in Deuteronomy, in which the single sanctuary chosen by God is a central theme. But starting with the place of sacrifice is not limited to Deuteronomy. The other law collections in the Torah also mention this subject first: the Book of the Covenant, introduced by Exodus 20:19–23; the Priestly Laws, which begin with Exodus 25–31; and the Laws of Holiness (Lev. 17–26), which begin with Leviticus 17:1–9.[20] This probably reflects the fact that all the law collections are religiously oriented, notwithstanding that they include many topics elsewhere considered secular. It may also be that places of worship were sources of laws, or of their teaching.[21] The laws about the place of worship are intimately connected with laws against improper places and means of worship, likewise an association found in all the Torah's law collections.[22]

Article A restricts sacrifice to the single chosen sanctuary. It touches upon uprooting the sanctuaries of Canaanite gods and their abhorrent vestiges; bringing tithes, firstlings, and other sacrifices to the chosen sanctuary; and dietary practices affected by the restriction of sacrifice to this sanctuary. The subsequent articles in Section I expand upon these subjects. Article B supplements the command to uproot Canaanite polytheism, prescribing what is to be done with those who try to reestablish polytheism. The transition to Article B is 13:1, which enjoins Israel not to add to God's laws or subtract any of them. Although this is the conclusion of Article A (prohibiting worshiping the Lord with Canaanite-style rites), it is also an apt introduction to Article B. Clauses about not adding or subtracting often have to do with prophets and scribes faithfully reporting what they have been told.[23] Those who would instigate Israel to worship gods in addition to the Lord would be adding to His commandments or subtracting from them. In fact, the first case in Article B (13:2–6) is apparently one in which the instigator falsely claims that the proposal is a new commandment from God (13:6, "for he lied about the LORD," falsely claiming that He permits the worship of other gods). The placement of this case after 13:1 implies that 13:1 was also understood as a warning against the falsification of God's message by prophets who would claim that He has said more or less than He really has (compare Comment to 4:2). The transitional role of 13:1 is notable for the compiler's methodology: it is like a hinge, serving equally as the conclusion of one article and the introduction to another.

Article C requires holiness in mourning and diet, prohibiting self-mutilation and consumption of "abhorrent" (to'evah) food. These laws are related topically to those of Articles A and B: they clarify the laws about eating meat in chapter 12, indicating which animals may and may not be eaten, and they continue the theme of prohibiting pagan behavior and "abhorrent things" (to'evot, referring to pagan practices in 12:31 and 13:15; eating the flesh of some of these animals is associated with pagan rites in Isaiah 65:3–4 and 66:3,17). Holiness and the uprooting of paganism are also associated in 7:5–6.

Following the dietary laws, Article D, Part 1 deals with tithes of agricultural produce (14:22–29). This topic is thematically related to the dietary laws since it deals with foodstuffs. It also returns the text to the subject of the sanctuary, where the annual tithe is eaten (14:23). Parts 3 and 4 of this article also relate to the sanctuary. Part 2, measures to protect

the poor, does not. It is included here because all the laws of this article are about periodic obligations performed at intervals of a certain number of years or a certain number of times each year, as follows:[24]

Tithe	Every year (14:22–27)
Poor-tithe	Every third year (14:28–29)
Remission of debts	Every seventh year (15:1–11)
Manumission of bondsmen	In seventh year (15:11–18)
Firstlings	Every year (15:19–23)
Pilgrimage festivals	Three times a year (16:1–17)

The transitions within this section are gradual. The annual tithe is followed by the triennial poor-tithe, which is then followed by other measures on behalf of the poor. The first of these, remission of debts (15:1–6), is also related to the poor-tithe phraseologically, since both passages open with the formula "every x years" (15:1 refers to the cycle of seven-year periods to which 14:28 implicitly alludes). The law of remission ends with an exhortation not to deny the poor loans because the debt might be canceled in the seventh year (vv. 7–11), and is followed by another periodic law, this one requiring the release of Hebrew servants in the seventh year after indenture (vv. 12–18). This law is also for the benefit of the poor since it is they who become indentured servants. Like 14:29, each of these parts of chapter 15 promises God's blessing in return for kindnesses to the poor that entail economic loss or risk (see 15:10,18, and cf. v. 6).

The law of firstlings (15:19–23) is another periodic law, since firstlings were sacrificed annually.[25] The phrase "annually" (*shanah be-shanah*, v. 20) joins with "every year" (*shanah shanah*) in 14:22 to form a frame around this group within the periodic laws. This is also a sanctuary-related law, since firstlings were eaten at the sanctuary.

The festival calendar in 16:1–17 is also sanctuary-related, since it prescribes the festivals that require a pilgrimage to the chosen sanctuary; and it is periodic, since these pilgrimages occur three times a year. It is an apt sequel to the firstling law because firstlings were probably sacrificed at the pilgrimage festivals and because the first festival, the Feast of Unleavened Bread, and the sacrifice of firstlings both commemorate the Exodus (see Exod. 13:11–16). The words *pisseaḥ* ("lameness," 15:21) and *pesaḥ* ("passover," 16:1 and elsewhere) create a verbal connection between the calendar and the firstling law.

SECTION II. CIVIL AND RELIGIOUS AUTHORITIES (16:18–chap. 18)

Section II deals with the duties and rights of four main types of authority in Israelite society: judges, the king, priests, and prophets. This topic may follow Section I because some of those about judges and priests refer to the "chosen place," which figured prominently in Section I (12:5–16:17), and the monarchy was also situated in the city where the central sanctuary was located.

Within Article A, Parts 2 and 3 deal with specific cases rather than judicial officials. Part 2 (16:21–17:1) prohibits three unacceptable religious practices. Most likely it appears where it does because of links to Part 3 (17:2–7), which deals with the judicial procedure for apostasy: one of the forbidden practices, sacrificing blemished animals, is called "abhorrent" (17:1), and the blemish is called an "evil thing" (Heb. *davar ra*ʿ), while apostasy is also called "abhorrent" and *davar ra*ʿ (vv. 4–5; the translation renders *davar ra*ʿ in v. 1 as "of a serious kind" and in v. 5 as "wicked thing").[26] Why part 2 precedes Part 3, instead of vice versa, is not clear.

The connection between Parts 2 and 3 (16:21–17:1 and 17:2–7) is even more understandable in the light of Section I, Articles A and B (12:2–13:1 and 13:2–19). Article A requires the destruction of Canaanite cult objects, such as stone pillars and sacred posts, and prohibits the imitation of Canaanite practices in worshiping the Lord (12:3–4, 30–13:1), while Article B prescribes the punishment for those who instigate the worship of other gods. Our passage explicates Article A, indicating that the prohibition of Canaanite practices includes the use of cultic pillars and posts, and it states what Article B presupposes, that individuals who worship other gods are to be prosecuted and executed. Verses 17:2–7 are similar in many details to the cases dealt with in chapter 13, and 16:21–17:7 would fit so well in Part I between Articles A and B that some scholars believe that they were originally located between 13:1 and 2 and formed the transition from Article A to B.[27] If that is the case, their present location is secondary, and is probably the result of a desire to have their rules of judicial procedure (17:4–7) appear in the article that deals with judges and courts and to indicate that enforcement of the first commandment—the primary condition for national welfare—is one of the major responsibilities of the judges.[28]

SECTION III. JUDICIAL AND MILITARY MATTERS (19–21:9)

After introducing the four main types of authorities the text turns to matters under their direct supervision: criminal cases, in which the elders, judges, and priests are involved (Articles A and C), and laws about the conduct of war, in which the priests, officials, and army commanders are involved (Article B). All but one of the criminal cases deal with the avoidance of shedding innocent blood and with purging innocent blood and evil (19:10,13,19; 21:9; 19:14 is discussed below), and the laws of war include the total proscription of the Canaanites in order to avoid the guilt that would come from following their abhorrent influence (20:18).[29]

Parts 1 and 3 of Article A deal with homicide and perjury, matters for the judges. Part 2, about moving a boundary marker (19:14), also deals with a crime, but it has no inherent connection to the other parts. Some similarity probably made this seem a convenient location for it. One possibility is because Parts 1 and 2 both deal with the division of territory (see 19:3).[30] Another is because the word *gevul* appears in both parts (it means "boundary marker" in v. 14 and "territory" in vv. 3 and 8).[31] A third possibility is that since the offense is a form of theft, it was placed between laws about homicide and perjury because murder, theft, and perjury appear in that order in the Decalogue (5:17).[32]

Parts 1 and 3 both seek to prevent wrongful punishment, the first of accidental killers and the second of innocent defendants. Both contain the injunctions to purge/sweep away (Heb. *b-ʿ-r*) bloodguilt or evil, and to take no pity on the guilty (vv. 13 and 21). The connection between Parts 1 and 3 is further clarified by Numbers 35, where asylum cities and the requirement of two witnesses are part of the same law. In that context, the point is that the guilt of the killer, who seeks refuge in an asylum city, must be proven by the testimony of witnesses before he may be surrendered to the blood avenger (see v. 30 there). This was important to state because blood vengeance was originally not supervised by the state, and relatives of the victim, in their anger, were often unconcerned about objective proof that the killing was intentional.

Article A, about judicial matters, is followed by Article B, about warfare. One reason for this may be the association of judging and military leadership as the primary roles of government.[33] Another possibility is that capital punishment and war are instances in which the taking of human life is permitted.[34] The most explicit, though superficial, link

454

between the two articles is their shared references to cutting down trees with an axe (19:5; 20:19–20).

Article C (21:1–9), like Article A, seeks to protect the nation from the bloodguilt that would be caused by an unpunished homicide. Since the killer is unknown and punishment impossible, this article provides instead for ritual removal of the bloodguilt. It is puzzling that the order of Articles B and C is not reversed. Article C would make a natural sequel to Article A, and if that were the original order, then Article B and Section III Article A— both about war—would also be contiguous.[35] As it is, Article C stands as a sort of appendix to those dealing with public officials.

SECTION IV. MISCELLANEOUS LAWS, MOSTLY ABOUT CIVIL AND DOMESTIC LIFE (21:10–chap. 25)

Whereas Sections II and III dealt with public officials and matters concerning the nation as a whole, Section IV deals primarily with private matters concerning individuals, their families, and their neighbors.

Article A (21:10–21), deals with family matters. Part 1 (vv. 10–14), about marriage to a woman captured in war, is probably placed first because of its connection to war, dealt with near the end of the previous Section. It appears in this section because it focuses on marital relations, not the war in which the woman is captured.[36] Part 2 (vv. 15–17) protects the rights of a man's firstborn son whose mother he dislikes. It echoes the end of Part 1, which deals with the possibility of the captive wife's husband disliking her (note the contrasting phrases "desire . . . no longer want" in Part 1 and "loved . . . unloved" in Part 2).[37] Part 3 (vv. 18–21) also deals with a son, in this case one who is intolerably insubordinate and is executed.

The execution of the insubordinate son leads to Article B (vv. 22–23), which is also about execution. Another possible connection between these two laws is that a father might use the charge of misbehavior as grounds for disinheriting the son of an unloved wife.[38] There is also a phraseological connection between this article and the last two parts of the preceding one:

> "If a man has" (*ki tiheyena le'ish*, v. 10)
> "If a man has" (*ki yiheyeh le'ish*, v. 15)
> "If a man is guilty of" (*ki yiheyeh be'ish* [lit., has against him], v. 22)

Article C (22:1–12) consists of nine laws, dealing mostly with property. They cover two groups of subjects, with additional laws attached because of incidental similarities to the main groups. Three of the four laws in the first group deal with kindness concerning animals: returning lost animals (as well as clothing and other property), helping lift a pack animal if it falls on the road (vv. 1–3 and 4; these laws are formulated similarly), and sparing the mother bird in a nest that is likewise found fallen on the road (vv. 6–8). Interwoven among these, probably because verse 3 refers to lost clothing, is a prohibition on wearing clothing of the opposite sex (v. 5). The second group deals mostly with domestic matters. Its first law requires building parapets on the roofs of houses to prevent people from falling off (v. 8); the theme of falling may be the link that connects it with the first group.[39] This is followed by three laws prohibiting the mixing of species in planting a vineyard, plowing, and in garments (vv. 9–11); appended to the latter is a requirement that garments have tassels (v. 12; here, again, we have two unrelated laws connected because both mention garments).[40] The connection of building houses and the forbidden mixtures

is due to a combination of intrinsic and extrinsic factors: the group of laws about forbidden combinations begins with planting a vineyard. Following this group (and its appendage about tassels) comes a group about marriage and sexual relationships (22:13–29). These three activities—building a house, planting a vineyard, and marrying—were the standard triad of domestic activities in biblical times. They are mentioned in the same order in 20:5–8.[41] These subjects are therefore combined because of their intrinsic connection in life. Within the group about forbidden combinations, however, other topics are introduced because of an extrinsic connection to the law about vineyards: the law about a forbidden combination of plow animals is related to that about vineyards both intrinsically (plowing is also an agricultural activity) and extrinsically (it deals with forbidden combinations); the following law, about clothing, is connected to the preceding ones by an exclusively extrinsic factor (forbidden combinations), and the law about tassels is connected to the latter by an extrinsic factor (clothing).

Article D (22:13–29), as noted, begins with marital relations. It opens, in a chronologically appropriate fashion, with a law about the inception of marriage (22:13–21). Like the immediately preceding law, it too refers to a garment, this time as evidence of virginity. The remainder of this article deals with sexual misconduct, arranged in decreasing order of legal gravity: clear-cut consensual adultery, cases in which the woman's consent is not certain, and nonadulterous rape.

Article E (23:1–9) deals with various types of forbidden relationships. Part 1 (23:1), prohibiting a man from marrying his father's former wife, continues the theme of marital misconduct from Article D. Its opening clause, "No man shall marry . . . wife," echoes the beginning of that Article, "If a man marries a wife . . ." (22:13),[42] and its reference to his father's garment (*kanaf*, lit. the "corner" of the garment) echoes the references to garments and garment corners (*kanfot*) in 22:12 and 17.[43] Part 2 (vv. 2–9) deals with eligibility for admission to "the Assembly of the Lord." It appears here because such eligibility included permission to marry Israelites. Its first two laws are particularly close to the subject of marriage, since the first refers to persons of impaired fertility and the second refers to the "misbegotten" (*mamzer*) who, according to rabbinic law, is the product of a forbidden marriage.[44] The regulations in Part 2 appear in ascending and then descending order of the periods of time they mention: the first states a prohibition that has no effect on future generations, the second states one that extends even to the tenth generation, the third mentions one of the same length, but adds that this means forever, and the fourth terminates the prohibition with the third generation. The people covered by these regulations appear in decreasing order of the degree of personal responsibility for their exclusion or acceptance: members of the first group are banned because of—apparently—their own actions, the second because of an act by their parents, and the rest are excluded or accepted because of a historical act by their ancestors.[45]

Article F (23:10–25:19) is a lengthy series of laws about various subjects. No central theme unites them, and many follow each other without obvious topical connection. This may have to do with the fact that this is the final section of the laws (apart from 26:1–15), and it is common for miscellaneous subjects to be placed together at the end of a work.[46] Nevertheless, certain subjects do appear more than once, such as further laws about marriage (24:1–4,5; 25:5–10), laws requiring farmers to give strangers some of their crops (23:25–26; 24:19–21; cf. 25:4; 26:12), and laws protecting or benefiting debtors, laborers, and the poor and disadvantaged (23:20–21; 24:6,10–15,17–18).[47] These and other laws seem in many cases to follow each other because of some incidental phrase or theme that they share. Since the preceding articles deal with marriage, it may be convenient for us to view

Article F as essentially a continuation of that subject (24:1–5; 25:5–10), with various digressions to topics related by incidental details. This is not necessarily the design intended by the text, but it will help maintain a sense of coherence as the text proceeds from topic to topic.

Parts 1–6 have several links to 23:2–9.[48] The reference to the Assembly of the Lord may have prompted Part 1, about the military camp, since the Assembly of the Lord sometimes is comprised of the adult, arms-bearing males assembled for war (as in Judg. 20:1–2; 21:5,8). Since refugees permitted to reside in Israel would become resident aliens, Part 2 may have been placed here because it is resident aliens whose eligibility for membership in the Assembly is discussed in vv. 2–9. Parts 3 and 4, about certain rights and duties of citizens that do not apply to aliens, may have been placed here because membership in the Assembly is tantamount to citizenship. Several of the laws in Article F 1–6 contain language or refer to actions that relate to types of entry and admissibility, linking them to the subject of entering/not entering (*yavo'/lo' yavo'*) the Assembly of the Lord in 23:2–9. Part 1 one temporarily denies a soldier entry (*lo yavo'*) to a military camp and permits him to return when the sun sets (lit., "enters," *be-vo' ha-shemesh*, vv. 11–12).[49] Part 2 grants escaped slaves entry into Israel (vv. 10–17).[50] In Part 3, one of the laws about abhorrent practices refers to the inadmissibility (*lo' tavi'*) of two types of donations to the Temple, including "the price of a dog" (v. 19). Part 4 (vv. 20–21) digresses to interest on loans, possibly because the terms for interest seem to be derived from the verb "bite" and are thus called to mind by "dog" (also, v. 21 ends with *ba' shamah*, "entering into"). The digression continues in Part 5 with further laws about vows (vv. 22–24), prompted by that theme in the laws about abhorrent practices. The chapter then returns to laws about entry, dealing with entering a neighbor's vineyard and field (*ki tavo'*, vv. 25–26).

Following these digressions, the text returns to the subject of marriage.[51] Parts 7–8 deal with unrelated aspects of marriage, but they begin with identical clauses: "When a man takes a wife" (vv. 1,5). Part 7 prohibits a man from remarrying his former wife if she was married after their divorce. Part 8 defers a newly married man from military service for a year in order to give happiness to his wife. It is similar to the rules about draft deferral in 20:6–8, but because its concern is with the married couple rather than the soldier alone, it appears here and not in chapter 20.

Parts 9–16 are mostly laws of a humanitarian character, intended to protect or benefit the disadvantaged. They seem to be linked by incidental verbal and thematic connections. Part 9 (v. 6), prohibiting the distraint of vital implements, such as a handmill, to compel repayment of a loan, has a thematic connection with Parts 7 and 8 because grinding, the function of a mill, is a metaphor for sexual relations (Job 31:10). The subjects of marriage and handmills are also juxtaposed in Jeremiah 25:10, perhaps because of the same metaphor: "the sound of mirth and gladness [cf. Deut. 24:5], the voice of bridegroom and bride, the sound of the handmill . . ."[52]

The location of Part 10, about kidnaping (v. 7), invites speculation. There is a verbal connection between its opening clause (lit., "stolen a person [*nefesh*] from among his brethren . . .") and the end of the previous law ("distraining someone's life [*nefesh*]").[53] However, the connection is more than verbal, since distraint and theft, though described by different verbs, both involve depriving a person of his property or freedom against his will, and some prophetic and wisdom passages regard them as similar acts. Most telling is Job 24:9, which describes the wicked who "steal the fatherless from the breast, and distrain the infant of the poor."[54] The juxtaposition of verses 6 and 7 is therefore natural and convenient because of the similarity of the actions. It seems at least possible that these laws

were also juxtaposed in order to make a point about the distraint of humans. Although the Torah does not explicitly deal with this practice elsewhere, and may not have considered it legal, we know that in practice children were sometimes distrained for the debts of their parents, in Israel and elsewhere (see, e.g., 2 Kings 4:1). In Mesopotamia, the children, wives, and slaves of debtors were subject to distraint.[55] The point of the juxtaposition here may be to indicate that distraining humans, and then selling or enslaving them in satisfaction of the debt, is legally tantamount to kidnaping. This might explain Deuteronomy's restriction of the law to Israelite victims (unlike Exod. 21:16), since two other laws in Deuteronomy which are explicitly for the benefit of Israelites alone also deal with the protection of debtors: Israelites may not be charged interest and their debts must be canceled in the seventh year (15:3; 23:21).[56] The location of the present law would thus imply that, in addition to other protections for Israelite debtors, they could not be distrained and then sold for debts, though foreigners could be.[57]

Part 11 (vv. 8–9) digresses to the subject of leprosy. One possible explanation for this is that the requirement in the next law, that a creditor remain outside the house of a debtor whose property he wants to distrain (v. 5), is reminiscent of the requirement that a leper reside outside the camp during his observation period and outside his tent during his purification.[58]

Following the digression, Part 12 (vv. 10–13) returns to the subject of distraint following default on a loan. It includes the provision that a distrained night garment must be returned to the debtor by sunset every day so that he may sleep in it, and a promise that the grateful debtor will bless the creditor to God. Part 13 (vv. 14–15) requires timely payment of wages. It shares a deadline of sunset with the preceding law and, in contrast to the concluding promise of that law, warns that an aggrieved laborer will cry out to God against an employer who delays wages.[59]

Part 14 (v. 16) prohibits the execution of parents and children for each other's crimes. It interrupts the laws dealing with maltreatment of the poor (vv. 10–15 and 17). It was placed here perhaps because, like verse 15, it refers to guilt (*het'*, translated as "crime" in this verse).[60]

Part 15 (vv. 17–18), protecting the rights of aliens, the fatherless, and widows, returns to the theme of prohibiting maltreatment of the poor and disadvantaged. Part 16 (vv. 19–22) contains further measures for the benefit of aliens, widows, and orphans, requiring farmers to leave gleanings for them in their fields. Both parts end with the same motive clause, "Remember that you were a slave in Egypt (v. 18 adds: "and that the LORD your God redeemed you from there"); therefore do I enjoin you to observe this commandment."[61]

Part 17 (25:1–3) sets limits on the flogging of criminals and Part 18 (v. 4) prohibits muzzling an ox when it threshes.[62] What unites these two laws and Part 16 is the fact that all involve types of beating: the olive harvesters' beating of the olive tree (*ḥ-b-t*, 24:20), the flogging of the criminal (*n-k-h*), and the striking of threshing animals with staffs and switches to prod them.[63]

Parts 19–22 (25:5–19) form a unit of four laws that is framed by the idiom "blot out the name" (vv. 6,19). Part 19, about levirate marriage, introduces the theme of reproduction, which is echoed in Part 20's reference to genitals (v. 11), and in terms of imagery, perhaps, in Part 21's reference to weightstones in a pouch (v. 13; compare 24:1–6, where two laws about marriage are followed by a law about millstones, recalling the metaphor of grinding for sexual relations).[64] Part 22, requiring Israel to "blot out the name of Amalek," echoes the reason given for levirate marriage, that the dead man's "name not be blotted out"

(vv. 6,19). Verbal and thematic connections link these four laws with each other and with the two that precede them in the chapter. These include the word *'aḥ*, "brother," "fellow" (vv. 3,5,6,7,9,11), verbs meaning "approach" (*niggash*, vv. 1,9, and *karav*, v. 11), acts of humiliation (vv. 3,9–10,11), and the theme of two men quarreling (vv. 1,11). Parts 19 and 20 begin with similar clauses, "*If brothers dwell together*" and "*If two men fight together*, a man and his *brother*."

SECTION V. TWO LITURGICAL DECLARATIONS (26:1–15)

This Section prescribes liturgical declarations that the farmer is to recite when he brings the first fruits to the Temple and after he gives the poor-tithe to the strangers, orphans, and widows every third year. Several factors may explain why these two ceremonies are mentioned here. Both are to be performed after the Israelites settle in the land, like the immediately preceding law, 25:17–19. In fact, the condition for carrying out the latter, "when the LORD your God grants you safety from all your enemies around you" (25:19), is the condition for bringing offerings to the chosen sanctuary (26:2; see 12:10). The declaration "I have not neglected [lit., "forgotten"] any of Your commandments" in 26:12 echoes the command in 25:19, "Do not forget!" There is also a structural reason for this location, for it gives the laws of Deuteronomy a framework like that which frames the Book of the Covenant: just as both of these law collections begin with a law about the place of worship (Exod. 20:19–23; Deut. 12), both have a law about bringing the first fruits to the Temple as their penultimate law (see Exod. 23:19).[65]

EXCURSUS 14

The Restriction of Sacrifice to a Single Sanctuary (Deuteronomy 12)

The twelfth chapter of Deuteronomy ordains a religious reformation that includes the provision that sacrifices may be offered to the Lord only in a single sanctuary, one chosen by Him for that purpose.[1] The historical narrative in 2 Kings 23 and its parallel in 2 Chronicles 34 describe how King Josiah (639–609 B.C.E.) enforced this law in 622 B.C.E. by destroying all other sanctuaries and restricting sacrifice to the Temple in Jerusalem.[2] Approximately a century earlier a similar reform was carried out by King Hezekiah (late eighth–early seventh century B.C.E.), though there is no indication that he, likewise, was motivated by Deuteronomy.[3]

This law is the most singular, and one of the most pervasive, of all the laws in Deuteronomy. It is also one of the most puzzling laws in the Bible. It transferred virtually all important activities that were previously performed at sanctuaries throughout the country—sacrifice, festivals, rites of purification, and certain judicial activities—to the central sanctuary in the religious capital. Given the universality of God's power, the idea that He would accept sacrifice in only one place is puzzling. Furthermore, the law must have been extraordinarily disruptive to popular religion since most of the public lived far from the Temple and could not often travel there, and would have to decrease, delay, or forgo vital services that it provided for them.[4] Eventually the synagogue came to take its place for most purposes. But why was this reformation called for?

To compound the puzzle, Deuteronomy, which explains its laws so frequently, gives no explicit reason for this law, although it implies that there is something pagan about

sacrificing at many sanctuaries without explaining what that is. Commentators have speculated about the motives for the reform, but no theory has been able to marshal enough supporting evidence to win widespread assent.

The major approaches to the question are the following.

Instrumental Reasons: Religious and Moral

1. *To curtail sacrifice*. Maimonides held that the purpose of the law is to minimize the role of sacrifice in worship. This is part of his overall view that prayer, not sacrifice, is the ideal form of worship. In his view, God permitted sacrifice to continue since it was so ingrained that prohibiting it would have caused great confusion; but He sought to limit it as much as possible, while permitting prayer at all times and places.[5] Since enforcement of the law did drastically diminish the role of sacrifice in the religious life of most people, the likelihood must be taken seriously that this was indeed its intention, or one of its intentions, and not merely its by-product. G. von Rad and M. Weinfeld hold, similarly, that "the very purpose of the book of Deuteronomy was to curtail and circumscribe the cultus."[6]

2. *To preserve the Temple's ability to inspire people by keeping it unique*. The medieval *Sefer Ha-Ḥinnukh* holds that the sanctuary can inspire people only if it is unique—not if there are temples everywhere.[7]

Instrumental Reasons: Political and Economic

1. *Unity*. Several scholars see the restriction as originating in Hezekiah's political goals. T. H. Robinson attributes it to Hezekiah's aim to concentrate national enthusiasm on the preservation of the capital from the invading Assyrians.[8] Similarly, Weinfeld has argued that Hezekiah sought to secure the loyalty of the Judahite countryside to Jerusalem in the face of Assyrian aggression; by making the provincial population more dependent religiously on Jerusalem, he hoped to deter it from going over to the Assyrians.[9] E. Nicholson holds that Hezekiah's aim was to reunify the nation around Judah and Jerusalem by removing competing sanctuaries and the foreign cults that were sapping nationalistic fervor; he presumes that the local sanctuaries were where these cults were gaining ground.[10]

That attachment to a place of worship might indeed foster political loyalty is indicated by the actions of Jeroboam when he led the secession of the northern tribes from Judah, with its capital in Jerusalem. Jeroboam established sanctuaries in Dan and Bethel because he feared that if the northern tribes continued to offer sacrifices in Jerusalem, their attachment to the city might eventually lead them to reunite with Judah and overthrow him (1 Kings 12:26–33). However, it is not clear whether Hezekiah could have realistically expected centralization to foster loyalty to Jerusalem. Jeroboam did not close down local sanctuaries near people's homes as Hezekiah (and Josiah did). This drastic move, which deprived the other cities of the ability to sacrifice at all, might well have engendered resentment and caused the move to backfire. In fact, the Assyrian Rabshakeh may have been voicing popular resentment, or seeking to foment it, when he publicly called on Jerusalem to

surrender and cited Hezekiah's closing of the local sanctuaries as a reason Hezekiah could not expect God to prevent an Assyrian victory (2 Kings 18:22).

2. *Economic*. W. E. Claburn sees the restriction of sacrifice to Jerusalem as an attempt by Josiah to wrest control of "the largest possible proportion of the peasantry's agricultural surplus" from the rural Levites so as to use it for royal purposes such as defense.[11] Against this approach two considerations seem telling: (1) While Deuteronomy brings all sacrifices to the capital, it gives a considerable proportion of them not to the king or the Jerusalem clergy under his control, but to the nation at large, requiring pilgrims to consume their own offerings during festivals in the capital (Deut. 12,14,16); the direct beneficiaries of this policy are the pilgrims and the local economy of Jerusalem, not the king. (2) Deuteronomy is hardly designed to advance royal interests: it portrays the monarchy as a grudging concession to human initiative, pejoratively describing it as a desire to be like other nations (17:14). It assigns no significant role to the king (such as appointing judges or commanding the army), but severely restricts the king's freedom to accumulate capital and describes him as a figurehead whose main role is studying God's Teaching so that he will not become arrogant (Deut. 17:13–20).

Theological Approaches

Most theological approaches hold that this restriction was intended to advance the cause of *monotheism*, *monolatry*, or *monoyahwism*. Three such views often blend with each other:[12]

1. *Monotheism*. The oldest known view, expressed as early as Josephus (first century C.E.), connects the requirement for a single sanctuary to the belief that there is only one God. In the Middle Ages, Abravanel argued that having many sanctuaries would suggest that there are many gods, while having but a single sanctuary indicates that God is one.[13] But Deuteronomy, which emphasizes monotheism frequently, does not mention it at all in connection with this demand, and Abravanel's logic is hardly compelling. The existence of many synagogues, churches, and mosques has never suggested a multiplicity of gods. The universality of the one God argues all the more readily for multiple places of worship: If His power reaches everywhere, it should be possible to worship Him everywhere. Note Malachi 1:11: "For from where the sun rises to where it sets, My name is honored among the nations, and everywhere incense and pure oblation are offered to My name; for My name is honored among the nations."[14]

2. *Monolatry*. A second view sees the law as more concerned with religious behavior than theology. Abravanel, like Ramban, saw Deuteronomy's law as a continuation of that in Leviticus 17:1–10.[15] Leviticus forbids the Israelites in the wilderness to slaughter animals unless they first render them as sacrifices at the Tabernacle;[16] sacrifices may not be offered elsewhere. This is to force the people to bring to the Lord the sacrifices that they have been making out in the field, so that "they may offer their sacrifices no more to the goat-demons after whom they stray" (v. 7). In other words, all slaughter of these animals—even for food—must take place at the Tabernacle in order to prevent sacrifice to goat-demons (satyrs). However, despite a certain similarity, the laws of Leviticus and Deuteronomy are apparently quite distinct. Had Deuteronomy 12 likewise sought to prevent sacrifice to goat-demons,

or to other gods, it could have accomplished this by restricting slaughter to *any* legitimate sanctuary *of the Lord*. Instead, it does away with the key provision of Leviticus 17 by permitting slaughter for food to take place *anywhere*. It might even be argued that Deuteronomy's law would increase the likelihood of sacrifice to demons or other gods. For unlike Leviticus 17, which assumes that all Israelites live together in one camp, near the Tabernacle, Deuteronomy legislates for the period after settlement when most Israelites will live far from the sanctuary. By making it impossible for most Israelites to sacrifice regularly to the Lord, yet permitting slaughter everywhere, Deuteronomy might well have increased the temptation and opportunities to sacrifice to other gods.

A broader version of this approach holds that restricting sacrifice to the Lord to one place is an aspect of Deuteronomy's effort to prevent the worship of other gods (not only demons). In this view, the various local sanctuaries of the Lord around the country were centers of syncretism, and by centralizing all worship in one place, the priests could exercise greater control and prevent such corruption.[17] This view is problematic for several reasons. There is little evidence that the local sanctuaries were corrupted by syncretism; as Y. Kaufmann noted, "the waves of foreign influence that occasionally swept over Judah and Israel radiated from the royal centers—Samaria and Jerusalem."[18] But even if the local sanctuaries were paganized, could Deuteronomy have reasonably expected that restricting the number of sanctuaries where *the Lord* could be worshiped would deter those who wished to worship other gods? In this case, too, it might be argued that the law would actually encourage the worship of other gods, since it prevented most Israelites from sacrificing regularly to the Lord. In addition, a single, central sanctuary was no less subject to corruption than were those in outlying places. Just before the law of Deuteronomy was put into effect by Josiah, the Temple in Jerusalem had been co-opted for the worship of pagan gods alongside the Lord, and the syncretism reported at it is far more extensive than anything ever said about the outlying sanctuaries.[19] Restriction of sacrifice to the capital was thus no guarantee against its corruption. Furthermore, the Temple in Jerusalem was rehabilitated by purging it of paganism; why did this solution not suffice for the other corrupted sanctuaries? Why did they have to be abolished instead? Finally, and most telling: the provision in Deuteronomy 12 seems to have nothing to do with the worship of other beings. Its stated point is not to prevent the worship of other gods but to prohibit certain ways of worshiping the Lord Himself (12:4, 31).

3. *Monoyahwism.* A modern variant of the first two views is that many sanctuaries of YHVH might sooner or later suggest that there are several deities named YHVH, just as several humans bear the same personal name.[20] This theory is based on a phenomenon described in Excursus 10. Pagans often referred to each of their gods by its name and place of worship, and in many texts a god's name appears several times, followed each time by a different place. Some scholars believe that this manner of speech, based on the many local sanctuaries of each deity, could imply that each name actually referred to several deities. Some scholars believe that the Hebrew inscriptions from Kuntillet Ajrud (Sinai Peninsula, ninth–eighth centuries B.C.E.) referring to "YHVH of Samaria" and "YHVH of Teman" show that a belief in many YHVHs was developing in Israel. However, there is no other evidence that such a belief was developing in Israel (no prophet warns against it), and we do

not know whether ancient pagans actually drew such inferences either; as noted in Excursus 9, there is reason to believe that they did not. As an analogy we may note that the Christian practice of referring to Mary by the names of places where sanctuaries have been built in her honor, such as "Our Lady of Lourdes," "Our Lady of Fatima," and "Our Lady of Guadalupe," never led Christians to imagine that these names refer to different Marys.

4. *Multiple worship sites inherently pagan*. The view that enjoys the clearest textual support is that of M. Greenberg, according to whom Deuteronomy perceives sacrificing at multiple places as an inherently pagan practice. In chapter 12, after the requirement to destroy "all the sites" where the Canaanites worshiped their gods, including their altars, pillars, sacred posts, and images, the text continues, literally, "Do not act thus toward the LORD your God, but look only to the site that the LORD your God will choose. . . . There you are to bring your burnt offerings and other sacrifices" (12:4–6). The command "Do not act thus" means "do not act as the Canaanites did," by sacrificing in many places. This is clear from the use of the phrase later in the chapter. After a detailed explication of the rule, including the admonition not to sacrifice "in any place you like" (v. 13), the chapter concludes with the injunction that Israel should not inquire how the Canaanites worshiped their gods and act "thus"—that is, as the Canaanites did—but rather must "not act thus toward the LORD your God," since the Canaanites "performed for their gods every abhorrent act that the LORD detests," including child sacrifice (vv. 30–31). In other words, in this chapter "acting thus" refers to imitating the Canaanites. In verses 4–6 it implies that sacrificing at multiple sites is forbidden because that is what Canaanites do.[21]

This meaning is also clear from the indictment of northern Israel in 2 Kings 17:9–11: "The Israelites . . . built for themselves shrines in all their settlements . . . they set up pillars and sacred posts for themselves on every lofty hill and under every luxuriant tree; and they offered sacrifices there, at all the shrines, like the nations whom the LORD had driven into exile before them." The Qumran *Temple Scroll* makes this understanding of Deuteronomy 12:4 explicit, stating "Do not do in your land as the nations do; everywhere they sacrifice and plant sacred trees for themselves and erect stone pillars and place figured stones to worship upon" (11QTemple 51:19–21, combining Deut. 12:2–4 and 16:21–22). This implies that multiplicity of worship sites is so typically pagan that it is considered *ipso facto* pagan.

This idea is not entirely unlike the theory that the prohibition of sacrificing at multiple sites is related to monotheism. But in this view the point is not that prohibiting the practice serves the practical end of protecting monotheism. It is rather that the practice has negative associations: it smacks of paganism. Admittedly, this view does not explain why this particular imitation of paganism was considered so objectionable, and required such vehement opposition, when other means of worship used by pagans, such as sacrifices and altars, were accepted. But this is not an insuperable obstacle to the theory. The fact is that various practices were considered indelibly pagan and rejected, while other practices performed by pagans were considered compatible with monotheism and adopted. For example, while images of calves were forbidden, images of cherubs were acceptable. Often, we cannot say why such decisions were made. It is likely that in some cases the forbidden phenomena had ineradicable pagan associations of which we are no

longer aware. In other cases, the decision may have been intuitive.[22] Whatever the reason, the view that sacrificing at multiple sites was considered inherently pagan is the only one that can claim explicit textual support from the very passage that forbids the practice.

It is possible that Hezekiah, Josiah, and Deuteronomy all had different reasons for imposing this restriction. It is interesting to recall that ancient lawgivers, in order to prevent challenges to their enactments, sometimes did not immediately reveal the reasons for their rulings, and sometimes announced reasons for public consumption that were not their essential reasons.[23] Conceivably, the reason implied by the text masks a deeper reason that seemed inadvisable to reveal.

EXCURSUS 15
Child Sacrifice and Passing Children through Fire (12:31 and 18:10)

Deuteronomy 12:31 refers to the Canaanite practice of child sacrifice. Written evidence for this practice comes from classical writers, some quoting an older Canaanite source, describing the religion of Phoenicia and its Mediterranean colonies, especially Carthage (Phoenicia was part of Canaan, as explained in Comment to 1:7). According to them, people would sacrifice one of their children (by fire, as some of the writers specify), or would vow to do so, when they wanted some great boon from the gods, especially to avert a calamity such as plague or imminent defeat in war. Archaeological evidence for this practice comes from special precincts in Phoenician colonies, such as Carthage, where hundreds of urns have been found containing charred bones of young children and, in some cases, of animals. These precincts are not normal cemeteries for people who died a natural death, as shown by the facts that some of the burials are of animals and that the human burials are limited to children. Moreover, many of the urns, from the eighth to second centuries B.C.E. are buried beneath steles inscribed with dedications to the gods, thanking them for answering the offerers' prayers. Reliefs from ca. 500 B.C.E., found at Pozo Moro, Spain, show a two-headed monster receiving offerings of small people in bowls. Since some of the cultural influences identified at the site are Phoenician, these reliefs may also reflect Canaanite practice.[1]

Earlier evidence of Canaanite child sacrifice is found in Egyptian reliefs of the thirteenth century B.C.E. that show besieged Canaanite cities. As the Egyptians attack, the people of the city are engaged in a religious ceremony, praying toward heaven and dropping the bodies of dead children, who had apparently been sacrificed, over the walls. In these reliefs, the victims are not burned; but under identical circumstances King Mesha, of Moab, in the ninth century B.C.E., stood atop the walls of his embattled city and offered his son as a burnt offering in the hope of preventing defeat.[2]

Underlying child sacrifice was the belief that for the most earnestly desired benefactions from the gods, the most precious gifts had to be offered. The biblical reverence for human life made the Bible view this as the most outrageous of the Canaanites' abominations. But, as the case of Jephthah and others cited in the Prophets indicate, there were times when some Israelites accepted the gruesome logic of child sacrifice and actually practiced it.[3]

Deuteronomy 18:10 forbids the practice of "consign[ing] one's son or daughter to the fire." It not clear whether this also refers to sacrificing them, like 12:31, or to a nonlethal ceremony. It is likewise unclear whether it is related to the practice of "giving" children to Molech, which is forbidden in Leviticus 18:21 and 20:2–5.

The uncertainties are partly due to the ambiguity of the phrase translated "consign to fire," *ma'avir ba-'esh*. Literally, the phrase means "make pass through fire." In Deuteronomy 18:10 it is not clear whether the phrase is meant literally or is short for "make pass to a deity by means of fire." The latter meaning is inferred from Exodus 13:11–15, which states that Israel must pass (NJPS translates "set apart") all firstborn males to the Lord. The firstborn of cattle must then be sacrificed, while those of humans must be redeemed. Since "making pass" can *result* in sacrifice, Deuteronomy 18:10 can be understood as referring to child sacrifice, like 12:31. This is how the verb, and the full phrase, are used by the prophets to describe the human sacrifices that were performed in the valley of Ben-Hinnom.[4] In light of this usage, 18:10 is generally thought to prohibit sacrificing children to any deity, even the Lord, as Jephthah apparently did (Judg. 11:30–40).[5] If this is the meaning, the case of King Mesha of Moab, mentioned above, may explain why the verse lists this practice among magical and divinatory practices. Mesha was surrounded by three armies, and he sacrificed his eldest son in an act of desperation. This led to "a great wrath" upon the attackers, causing them to abandon the siege (2 Kings 3:27). The text does not say that the "wrath" came from Mesha's deity (though that may be how Mesha understood it). This is consistent with the fact that the Bible does not assume that pagan gods are capable of action. It appears that the book of Kings understands Mesha's sacrifice as essentially a magical act designed to produce some kind of supernatural outburst against the enemy. Seen in this light, "making children pass through fire" may have been considered a magical act—albeit a desperate one—like some of the others in Deuteronomy 18:10.[6]

However, sacrifice is not the only possible implication of "passing through fire." Exodus 22:28–29 shows that "making a child pass" to a deity is synonymous with "giving a child" to a deity. In 1 Samuel 1:11 "giving a child" to a deity means consecrating him to serve God in a sanctuary. Even the full phrase "make pass through fire" need not imply sacrifice. It is not normally used for burning. In Numbers 31:23 it refers to nondestructive purging of utensils; though they are brought into contact with fire, they are not consumed. In light of this usage, some commentators understand passing children through fire as a nonlethal ceremony in which children are passed between rows of fire or leap over it, either as a means of consecrating them to a deity as servants or worshipers, or for a magical purpose such as purification or divination. Practices of this type are known from the classical world and elsewhere.[7] In the state of Orissa in India, worshipers of the goddess Kali annually walk or hop over a path of burning coals as a test of their faith in the power of the goddess to protect them. Often, the worshipers "have asked the goddess to cure their own illnesses or those of close relatives, and in return . . . they have pledged to perform some act involving the risk of physical harm. Parents of a sick child often pledge that the child will travel over the hot coals, walking alone if he is old enough or being carried by one of the participating adults if he is not."[8]

Modern scholarship has not been able to resolve the question of whether Deuteronomy 18:10 refers to a lethal or a nonlethal practice. Because of this, we cannot say whether or how passing children through fire is related to the dedication of the first-born, to Canaanite child sacrifice, or to the worship of Molech.[9]

The Laws of Deuteronomy 15

The Relationship between Deuteronomy 15, Exodus 21–23, and Leviticus 25

The subjects dealt with in 15:1–18, the seventh year and manumission of indentured servants, are also found in Exodus 21–23 and Leviticus 25. The laws of Exodus and Deuteronomy are very close in detail and terminology. In both books, for example, the slave is called a Hebrew, he is set "free" (*ḥofshi*), and the activity of the seventh year is called "dropping" or "releasing" (*shamat/shemittah*). Both books set the term of servitude at six years and prescribe a ceremony for the servant who chooses to remain for life (the "awl" is mentioned in the Bible only in these two passages). Furthermore, as we have seen in the Comments to 15:1–18, even where the two books differ from one another, their provisions are not incompatible: Exodus's provisions for the fallowing of the land in the seventh year and for the release of daughters sold for marriage can be reconciled with Deuteronomy, and Deuteronomy may intend both of these laws to continue.

It is less clear that Exodus expects debts to be remitted in the seventh year. Exodus does have rules about loans to the poor (Exod. 22:24–26), and in that context it might have been expected to allude to the possibility that the debts would be forgiven after six years. This is not a compelling argument, but it raises the possibility that debt-remission is an innovation in Deuteronomy. This would be perfectly understandable in light of the critical view that the laws of Exodus 21–23 address a pre-monarchic society while Deuteronomy is a product of the eighth–seventh centuries B.C.E.[1] Although poverty existed in every age, it was exacerbated in Israel by a century of wars with the Aramaean kingdoms in the ninth and eighth centuries. Deuteronomy's remission of debts may therefore be the result of the need for more radical steps to counter this increased poverty.

These considerations imply that Deuteronomy 15 is based on laws like those that appear in Exodus 21–23[2] and that it adds supplementary provisions in accordance with more recent needs and its own humanitarian emphasis (such as giving provisions to the newly freed servant).

The provisions of Leviticus 25 are more difficult to reconcile with those of Exodus and Deuteronomy. The most notable inconsistency between the texts is the fact that Deuteronomy and Exodus require the manumission of servants after six years of service, whereas Leviticus mentions manumission only as part of the fiftieth, or jubilee, year.[3] Harmonistic exegesis seeks to reconcile the difference by taking the jubilee year as complementary to the six-year term: the servant serves for six years unless the jubilee comes first, in which case he goes free at the jubilee; if he chooses to remain a servant beyond six years, he must go free at the jubilee.[4] However, this is far-fetched. Jubilees come infrequently, and most servants would go free after six years. Leviticus would, by this theory, ignore the date when most servants go free and emphasize a date when only a small number would. This view is also inconsistent with Leviticus's system of calculating the price for early redemption of a servant on the basis of the years remaining until the jubilee, a system which assumes that

serving until the jubilee is the norm.[5] And, finally, if the harmonistic explanation were correct, it would be strange that the texts are all written so as to give two different ideas of when servants are freed, with no cross-reference to one another. It is hard to escape the conclusion that Leviticus does not recognize a six-year limit on indentured servitude.[6]

It is also very unlikely that the remission of debts is operative in Leviticus. Leviticus 25:25–45 deals with several stages of indebtedness, calls upon the creditor to treat the debtor as a kinsman, and provides for his indenture and his eventual manumission. If Leviticus were aware that a debtor might eventually gain relief through the remission of his debt, its failure to mention this would be a glaring, inexplicable omission.

It therefore seems likely that Leviticus 25 represents a system for the relief of poverty that is independent of the one in Exodus and Deuteronomy. This conclusion is consistent with the fact that Leviticus 25 seems textually unrelated to Exodus 21–23. It lacks the terminological similarities, noted above, that connect Deuteronomy to Exodus, and it uses different terms to say the same things. It describes the activity of the seventh year, for example, as the land "having a sabbath" rather than the farmer "dropping" or "releasing" it.

The orientation of Leviticus's system is indicated by the fact that it allows an indentured servant to serve for as long as fifty years before he and his family go free. Since the average number of years served would be twenty-five, it is clear that many indentured servants would regain their freedom only in old age, and some would not live long enough to go free at all. This implies that the system in Leviticus is designed to benefit families more than individuals. Even though an individual might not regain his freedom, his family eventually would. This system seems to approach the problem from the perspective of tribal society, which thought of itself as an aggregate of clans and families rather than individuals. Leviticus's provisions for the return of land reflect the same perspective: land that is sold because of poverty or to satisfy debts is to be returned to its original owners in the fiftieth year (that is, the jubilee year).[7] In this case, too, it would often be the descendants of the owner who benefit, not the owner himself. That the interests of the tribe or clan are paramount in Leviticus is also clear from the law calling upon the owner's kinsmen to redeem the land from the purchaser earlier than the jubilee; for the purchaser, not the owner, would then hold the land until the jubilee.[8] The aim of the law is to prevent the clan or tribe from losing part of its land, just as daughters who inherited their father's land were required to marry within their tribe for this very reason.[9] Leviticus's law of manumission, likewise, aims to prevent any of the family units of the tribe from being reduced to permanent servitude. Exodus and Deuteronomy, in contrast, seek to protect individuals.

In sum, the laws of Leviticus 25 are not based on those of Exodus 21–23, and in important respects are incompatible with them. They represent an independent system for dealing with similar problems. From a literary viewpoint, this system is part of the Holiness Code (Leviticus 17–26), which is associated with the priestly source of the Torah. It is not clear if this system is derived from a geographical or chronological background different from that of Exodus 21–23 and Deuteronomy, or if it simply reflects the approach of another school of thought.[10]

Fallowing of Fields

It is difficult to tell whether Deuteronomy expects fallowing of fields to be part of the seventh year, as prescribed in Exodus 23:10–11. In early Second Temple times, the people pledged to "forgo [the produce of] the seventh year, and every outstanding debt" (Neh.

10:32), indicating that both practices were combined then. Talmudic exegesis presumes that the seventh year included both types of release.[11] Some scholars argue that Deuteronomy's silence on fallowing indicates that it intends to abandon the practice.[12] Others, however, note a logical connection between the two practices: debts commonly came due at harvest time, when farmers realized their income; it therefore made sense to remit debts in a year when there would be no harvest.[13]

The Seventh Year According to Jeremiah

Deuteronomy refers to two different seventh years. According to Deuteronomy 15:12, indentured servants were to be released in the seventh year, after six years of service; this "seventh year" varied in each case, depending on when the servant began to serve. In verse 1 of the same chapter the seventh year refers to the year of remission, publicly proclaimed and identical for everybody (see v. 9 and cf. 31:10). The two laws appear near each other because they both refer to a seventh year, even though that means something different in each case.

The book of Jeremiah seems to imply that toward the end of the First Temple period, the two seventh years were taken to be identical and that all servants were to be freed simultaneously, in the year of remission. According to Jeremiah 34, when Jerusalem was besieged by the Babylonian army in 588 B.C.E., the people agreed to release their indentured servants, a practice that had apparently been neglected for a long time. No sooner was the siege lifted than they impressed them into service again. Jeremiah rebuked the people for disregarding the law of Deuteronomy 15, which he paraphrased as follows: "In the seventh year (literally, "After a period of seven years"), each of you must let go any fellow Hebrew who may be sold to you; when he has served you six years, you must set him free" (Jer. 34:14). Jeremiah's opening phrase comes from Deuteronomy 15:1, where "the seventh year" refers to the national year of remission; the rest of his citation is a paraphrase of verse 12. This combination of verses suggests that he took the seventh year, in which servants are released, to be the same as the seventh year of remission.[14] This interpretation—an ancient halakhic midrash—may have been inspired by the juxtaposition of the two laws in Deuteronomy.[15]

Observance and Modification of the Laws in Later Times

There is evidence for the remission of debts in the Second Temple period. Nehemiah, who governed Judah on behalf of Persia in the fifth century B.C.E., canceled all debts owed him by fellow Jews and persuaded the nobles and prefects to do likewise, and to return property and children they had seized as collateral. It is not known whether this took place in a sabbatical year, but under Nehemiah's leadership the people later ratified the pledge, mentioned above, to "forgo [the produce of] the seventh year, and every outstanding debt," which suggests that, at least in the future, the cancellation of debts would take place in the seventh year.[16] Of interest in this connection is an Aramaic inscription of the fourth century B.C.E. written on an ostracon found at Arad. The first line reads "whoever has a claim for money against. . . ." This could be a copy of a decree proclaiming remission of debts (there is no indication whether this took place in the seventh year).[17]

In late Second Temple times the law of remission did indeed become a deterrent to lending, as Deuteronomy 15:9 anticipated. In order to protect those who needed loans, and

to prevent violation of verses 9–10, the sage Hillel (end of first century B.C.E. and beginning of first century C.E.) devised a legal means for circumventing the remission. The means was the *prosbul*, a document or declaration in which the lender declares to the court that a particular loan will not be subject to remission.[18] By this means Hillel ensured that the law would not undermine its own purpose.

EXCURSUS 17

The Name of the Feast of Booths (16:13 and 16)

According to Leviticus 23:42–43, the Feast of Booths is named for the practice of dwelling in booths, or bowers, during the seven-day festival. Booths (Heb. *sukkot*, singular *sukkah*) are temporary structures made of branches and foliage that are used for shelter in various circumstances: by soldiers in the field, by herdsmen to protect their cattle, by watchmen guarding fruit trees, and particularly by grape harvesters who live in the vineyards during the grape harvest season.[1] According to Leviticus, the practice is intended to remind future generations that God "made the Israelites live in booths" when He brought them out of Egypt.

The meaning of the explanation in Leviticus has been the subject of considerable speculation because in the wilderness the Israelites lived in tents, not booths.[2] According to Rabbi Akiba, while in the desert, in summertime, the Israelites built booths for shade in addition to their tents.[3] This is unlikely, since branches and foliage were not available in the wilderness except, in small quantities, at oases. Rashbam holds that the verse is using "booths" loosely for "tents," and that dwelling in booths on the festival of ingathering serves to remind the Israelites of the time when they had no land or harvest, so that they will remember that God gave them all that they have and will not think that their prosperity is due to their own efforts.[4]

However, the commemorative symbols prescribed by the Torah normally commemorate miracles, and there is nothing miraculous about living in booths or tents.[5] Since *sukkah* literally means a protective cover or shelter, some commentators, both midrashic and modern, believe that Leviticus does not mean that the Israelites literally dwelt in booths, but that God's protective cloud shielded them in the wilderness as a booth protects one from the elements. In Psalm 105:39 the cloud is called a *massakh*, "screen, cover," from the same root as *sukkah* (s-k-k), and in Isaiah 4:5–6 the prophet promises that God will cover Mount Zion with clouds, smoke, and fire that will "serve as a booth [*sukkah*] for shade from heat by day and as a shelter for protection against drenching rain."[6] In this view, then, the booths of the festival merely symbolize the protective cloud.

This view does not account for the reason the Feast of Booths should be the time for commemorating the protective cloud, which shielded Israel year-round.[7] Modern scholars have noted that booths are in use particularly in the summer months leading up to the Feast of Booths, when grapes and other fruit are ripening and being harvested. Therefore, it has been suggested that dwelling in them was originally chosen as a rite for celebrating the ingathering, because doing so symbolized the harvest season that has just been concluded.[8] In this view, the explanation given in Leviticus 23:43 represents an adaptation of the practice so that the festival can serve as a reminder of God's beneficence toward Israel in historical events as well as nature.[9] It makes the Feast of Booths an apt counterpart to the Feast of Pesaḥ and Unleavened Bread.

This is a trend that is quite well established in the Bible and in postbiblical Judaism.[10] Another example is the historical significance assigned to the Feast of Weeks as a commemoration of the giving of the Torah in addition to its role as a harvest festival (see introductory Comment to 16:9–12). Yet another is the Torah's preference for numerical names of the months. According to Exodus 12:2, the month in which the Exodus occurred is the first month. Since the month numbers allude to the Exodus, they serve as constant reminders of that pivotal event.[11] The other system of month names current in Israel in preexilic times, which the Bible uses rarely, consisted of names based on the state of nature during each month, such as "Abib" in 16:1.[12] The Torah's preference for the numerical system and the historical symbolism of the festivals are both in keeping with the Bible's emphasis on historical and social events, such as Israel's liberation from bondage, even more than nature as the sphere of life in which God's will is most manifest. This is in contrast to pagan religions in which the harmonious integration of man and nature was the main focus of attention.[13]

EXCURSUS 18
The Proscription of the Canaanites   (7:1–2, 7:16 and 20:15–18)

According to Deuteronomy 7:1–2, 7:16 and 20:15–18, when the Israelites enter the promised land they are to wipe out the Canaanites living there. The terms referring to this requirement are the verb *haharem*, "proscribe," and the noun *herem*, "proscription," "a thing proscribed." Deuteronomy states this as an unconditional mandate and leaves no room for sparing any Canaanites in the promised land. Modern critical scholars and traditional Jewish exegesis hold, each for different reasons, that at the time when Israel entered the promised land there was actually no such policy of unconditional proscription of the Canaanites. Traditional exegesis holds that Deuteronomy in fact does not require *unconditional* proscription. Modern scholars hold that it does, but that this policy is purely theoretical and did not exist when Israel entered the land.

In 7:1–2, 7:16, the command to doom the Canaanites is clearly unconditional and offering them terms of submission is prohibited. That 20:15–18 is also meant unconditionally is indicated by its opening clause, "Thus you shall deal with all towns that lie very far from you," that is, *with foreign, non-Canaanite* cities. "Thus" refers back to verse 10, which requires Israel to offer to spare cities that surrender. Verses 15–17 indicate that this offer is made only to cities *outside* the promised land and that the Canaanites *in the land* are to be denied this option. This interpretation of the law is consistent with Joshua 6–11 (except for 11:19–20, mentioned below), according to which surrender was not offered to the cities of Canaan when Joshua conquered them.

According to 20:18, the aim of this unconditional requirement is to rid the land of Canaanites, who might influence Israelites to adopt their abhorrent rites, such as child sacrifice and various occult practices (12:31; 18:9–12). Note that it is particularly abhorrent rites, and not beliefs, that prompt this policy. By itself, worship of astral bodies and other gods by Canaanites and other pagans is not counted against them as a sin, since Deuteronomy holds that God assigned such worship to them (see 4:19; 32:8; and Excursuses 7 and 31). Exodus, too, requires ridding the land of the Canaanites to prevent them from influencing Israel, though it prescribes expulsion rather than annihilation.[1] The aim of these policies is defensive, and no action is prescribed against idolatry or idolaters outside

Israelite territory. These policies are not based on ethnicity; Deuteronomy prescribes the same treatment for Israelite cities that lapse into idolatry (13:13–19).

Modern scholars hold that this law is purely theoretical and was never in effect. In their view, the populations of only a few Canaanite cities were annihilated, but most were not. There is much evidence in favor of this view. Archaeology has found only a few Canaanite cities that seem to have been destroyed by the Israelites when they arrived in the land at the beginning of the Iron Age (ca. 1200 B.C.E.).[2] As noted above, pre-Deuteronomic laws, in Exodus, speak of the Canaanites being expelled rather than annihilated, and the narratives of Judges, Kings, and Joshua 15–17 indicate that many were neither expelled nor annihilated but were spared and subjected to forced labor.[3] Some scholars suggest that even Deuteronomy did not originally require annihilating the Canaanites. In their view, Deuteronomy's original law consisted only of 20:10–14, according to which *all* cities are to be offered terms of submission. They note that Joshua 11:19, Joshua 15–17, and Judges all reflect this form of the law. In this view the following paragraph in Deuteronomy, verses 15–18, is a later supplement that modifies the original law by restricting the requirement to offer the option of surrender to foreign, non-Canaanite cities.[4] This supplement is reflected in Deuteronomy 7:1–5, 16–26, and the narratives of Joshua 6–11 (except for Joshua 11:19–20), but it is based on a theoretical reconstruction, conceived at a later time when the Canaanites had ceased to exist as a discernible element of the population in Israel, to account for their disappearance.

If this is the case, where did the idea of proscribing the Canaanites come from? The historical books, as noted, indicate that the invading Israelites did proscribe some Canaanite cities. Proscription was a well-known practice in the ancient world. One type of proscription was the religious practice of devoting property, cattle, or persons (perhaps the victims of sacrificial vows, such as Jephthah's daughter) irrevocably to a deity, that is, to a sanctuary and the priests, sometimes by destruction or killing.[5] Another type was punitive proscription, which consisted of executing those who committed severe offenses against the gods. This type is prescribed by Exodus 22:17 for individual idolaters, and by Deuteronomy 13:13–18 for idolatrous cities.[6] Proscription of enemy armies and populations to the gods is known from various places in the ancient world. King Mesha of Moab proscribed the Israelite inhabitants of some towns in Transjordan to his god when he recaptured former Moabite territory there.[7] Other parallels are known from Mesopotamia and ancient Europe.[8] In the context of ancient warfare, in which the gods were believed to be the main fighters and human antagonists their enemies, proscription of the enemy's population seemed to be a natural way for an army to express devotion to a deity. A case in point is God's command to Saul to proscribe the Amalekites to avenge their ancient ambush of the Israelites.[9] Proscription was not considered necessary or obligatory in most cases, but was something that an army might vow to do to induce divine aid in critical circumstances, such as before a crucial battle or a counterattack following a defeat. Examples of this are Israel's proscription of Arad and Ai after initial defeats by them, and the proscription of Jericho at the start of Israel's campaign for the promised land.[10]

Deuteronomy appears to have inferred from cases like these that the disappearance of the Canaanites was due to a systematic policy of proscription.[11] Aware that there were no discernible Canaanites left in Israel, aware from Exodus and Numbers that the land was to be rid of them, aware of Exodus 22:17, which requires proscription of Israelite idolaters, and mindful of its own law requiring proscription of idolatrous Israelite cities, Deuteronomy must have assumed that God, in His zeal to protect Israel from exposure to pagan abominations, had required eliminating the Canaanites by the same means. It is interest-

ing, however, that Deuteronomy never speaks of proscribing the victims *to God*.[12] It uses proscription in a purely secular way, meaning simply "destruction." It is not a sacrifice to God but a practical measure to prevent the debasement of Israelite conduct.

Traditional Jewish commentators, as mentioned, do not believe that Deuteronomy means to proscribe the Canaanites unconditionally. The Sifrei and other halakhic sources reason that since the express purpose of the law is to prevent the Canaanites from influencing the Israelites with their abhorrent religious practices (v. 18), if they abandoned their paganism and accepted the moral standards of the Noachide laws they were to be spared.[13] Maimonides holds that verse 10 requires that Israel offer terms of surrender to *all* cities, Canaanite included. In his view, when verse 15 says "*thus* you shall deal" with non-Canaanite cities, it is not referring to, and limiting, verse 10, but verse 14, which calls for sparing the women and children of a city taken in battle. In his view this means that *all* cities must be given the option of surrender; the difference between Canaanite and foreign cities is only that if foreign cities reject the offer, only their men are to be killed, but if Canaanite cities reject the offer, their entire population is to be killed.[14] This view is compatible with Joshua 11:19, which implies that Canaanite cities could have saved themselves by surrendering: "Not a single city made terms [*hishlimah*] with the Israelites; all were taken in battle."[15]

These arguments notwithstanding, it is clear from 7:1–2 and 16 that Deuteronomy's demand for proscription of the Canaanites is indeed unconditional.[16] The rabbis' rejection of this view is a reflection of their own sensibilities. As M. Greenberg has observed, they must have regarded this understanding of the law as implausible because it is so harsh and inconsistent with other values, such as the prophetic concept of repentance and the prediction that idolaters will someday abandon false gods, and the halakhic principle that wrongdoers may not be punished unless they have been warned that their action is illegal and informed of the penalty.[17] In effect, they used interpretation to modify and soften the law in deference to other, overriding principles.

EXCURSUS 19

The Ceremony of the Broken-Necked Heifer (21:1–9)

The ceremony described in Deuteronomy 21:1–9 seeks to protect the nation from the bloodguilt that would befall it in the case of a homicide by an unknown killer. Since it is impossible to punish the killer and eliminate the bloodguilt that way, the law provides instead for its ritual removal. As noted in the Commentary, the ceremony consists of several elements, most of which are puzzling. The elders of the nearest town break the neck of a heifer in a wadi, the priests approach, and the elders wash their hands over the heifer, declare their innocence, and pray for absolution.

The expiatory character of the ceremony is clear from the statement in verse 8b that it will absolve the people of bloodguilt. A rite with a similar purpose was performed among the Hittites, whose laws also include a parallel to the practice of measuring to determine which city is closest to where a corpse is found (v. 2). According to a letter from the Hittite king to the king of Babylonia, when the killer *is* known, he is seized and handed over to the family of the victim, which then has two choices: it can accept monetary compensation from the killer or it can execute him. If it accepts compensation and does not execute the killer, the town where the killing took place has to be purified.[1] This

implies (as does Num. 35:33) that executing the killer serves the same purpose as purification. Inferably, in a case where the killer cannot be executed, purification is the only option. This is the purpose that the biblical rite serves.

While the overall expiatory goal of the ceremony is clear, only the prayer in verse 8a is unambiguous. The meaning of all the other elements is ambiguous. They resemble other rites known from the Bible or elsewhere, but the resemblance is incomplete. Slaughtering the heifer resembles certain types of sacrifice and magic, but it is neither of these. The elders' washing hands over the heifer is comparable but not identical to the act of laying hands on sacrificial animals, including the goat used in the ritual of the Day of Atonement (Lev. 16:21–22). The elders' declaration of innocence strongly resembles oaths uttered by potential suspects in a crime, and yet it is not worded as an oath. The priests are present for only part of the ceremony, but have no specific role.

Because of its puzzling elements, rabbinic texts list this ceremony, along with the goat sent to Azazel on the Day of Atonement and the red heifer (Lev. 16; Num. 19), among the commandments for which there is no apparent reason and which other nations and the impulse for evil challenge.[2] Rabbinic sources report that the ceremony was abolished in the first century C.E. because murder had become common and was committed openly; even if the authorities did not know who the killer was, it was highly unlikely that nobody knew, as verse 1 requires.[3]

Since Deuteronomy explains a good half of its laws,[4] the fact that it leaves such puzzling elements unexplained looks intentional. It probably implies that Deuteronomy does not believe that these rites themselves expiate bloodguilt. To Deuteronomy, the prayer of verse 8, which asks God to remove the bloodguilt, is the key to absolution. The other elements appear to be remnants of traditional practices that Deuteronomy has preserved, in modified form, perhaps only because popular feeling considered them indispensable for purging bloodguilt.

What might these elements have meant originally? Let us examine each of them.

The slaughter of the heifer. The main theories about killing the heifer have been summarized as follows: it is either "a sacrifice, a symbolic or vicarious execution of the murderer, the representation of the penalty the elders will suffer if their confession of innocence is not true, the means of preventing the animal laden with guilt from returning to the community, or a reenactment of the murder which removes blood pollution from the inhabited to an uninhabited area."[5]

The theory easiest to eliminate is that killing the heifer is a sacrifice. Everything speaks against it: the priests are not present for its slaughter, it is not slaughtered at an altar, the method of slaughter is nonsacrificial, its blood is not sprinkled, and it is neither eaten nor burnt.[6] The view that the slaughter is intended to prevent the guilt-laden animal from carrying the guilt back to the community is also problematic. It relies partly on the assumption that in washing their hands over the calf the elders transfer guilt to it. The timing of the hand-washing speaks against this assumption, for in comparable cases, as when the priest places his hands on the goat for Azazel and confesses the Israelites' sins, the act takes place before the animal is slaughtered or sent away.[7] In the present case, since the elders slaughter the animal *before* washing their hands, it would carry no guilt at the time of slaughter.

There is something to be said for each of the other views. In essence they amount to saying that the heifer represents either the murderer, the elders, or the victim.

The view that slaughtering the heifer is a symbolic or vicarious execution of the murderer[8] finds some support in the fact that the elders wash their hands immediately afterward, for there is a Hittite practice requiring the citizens of a town to bathe after an

execution.[9] Some comments in midrashic texts show how easily the ceremony lent itself to interpretation as an act of punitive magic. According to Targum Jonathan, a swarm of worms from the heifer finds the killer and seizes him so that the authorities can bring him to justice; according to Midrash Aggadah, the worms themselves kill him.[10]

The view that slaughtering the heifer represents the penalty the elders will suffer if their declaration is false may be supported by the use of such a symbol in the treaty between Ashurnirari V of Assyria and Mati'ilu of Arpad (eighth century B.C.E.). At the time the treaty was made, a lamb was beheaded and declared to represent the vassal, who was to suffer the same fate if he should violate the treaty. Similarly, in the *Iliad* an exculpatory oath is accompanied by the slaughter of a boar, which is then thrown into the sea, representing the fate of the oath taker if he is lying.[11] Another argument in favor of this view is considered below, in the discussion of the elders' declaration of innocence.

The view that the slaughter of the heifer at the wadi is a reenactment of the murder in a place where the bloodguilt will be harmless is supported by the timing of the hand-washing ceremony. As noted above, since this is done after the heifer is executed, it cannot be a means of transferring guilt to the heifer. In some of the Psalms "washing the hands" is an idiom expressing innocence.[12] In this rite, literally doing so over the calf and saying "our hands did not spill this blood" could mean that the calf represents the victim and that the elders are dramatizing their (and their townspeople's) innocence.

Of these three views, taking the act as a reenactment of the murder seems the most likely, since it alone suggests a reasonable explanation of why it must take place at a barren wadi: that is, so that the imitation bloodguilt is kept far from civilization. Nevertheless, this view is far from certain.

The hand-washing. As noted above, the timing of the hand-washing speaks against the assumption that it is a means of transferring guilt to the heifer. The act could be comparable to the Hittite procedure of washing hands after an execution, if the killing of the heifer symbolizes the execution of the killer, or it could be a dramatic expression of the town's innocence of the murder. Another possibility is that the rite is purgative, literally removing the bloodguilt that has adhered to the townspeople's hands due to their inability to atone for it with the killer's blood (Num. 35:33).

The elders' declaration of innocence. As noted in the Comment to verse 7, the elders' declaration, "Our hands did not shed this blood, nor did our eyes see it," means "We really do not know who the killer is (and are not protecting him)" or "We did not see it happening and stand idly by." It has been suggested that their declaration is an exculpatory oath, comparable to the oaths taken by the likely suspect in cases of lost or damaged property (Exod. 22:6–7,9–10).[13] In Deuteronomy it is not worded as an oath: that would require the conditional particle *'im*, so that it would mean "We *swear* that we did not shed this man's blood and do not know who the killer is." But in a case similar to the present one, the king of Carchemish instructs his vassal, the king of Ugarit, to have the townspeople take an oath that is very similar to the elders' declaration: "We swear that we did not kill so-and-so. . . ; none of us knows who killed him."[14] In this case, if they take the oath the matter is closed and the townspeople do not have to indemnify the victim's widow. Although Deuteronomy does not word the declaration as an oath, the parallel from Ugarit, reflecting earlier practice in the region, suggests that the elders' declaration may have been an oath in an earlier form of the Israelite procedure for dealing with unsolved murder, but that Deuteronomy has modified it. And if the declaration once was an oath, the slaughter of the heifer might well represent a dramatization of the fate of the elders in case they were lying (see above). We can only speculate why Deuteronomy

would have modified an oath into a declaration. It could be because exculpatory oaths exempted those who took them of all responsibility. In the present case, that would have left the bloodguilt unabsolved. Perhaps by changing the oath into a declaration of innocence Deuteronomy left room for the prayer for absolution in verse 8.

The presence of the priests. The text states that the priests are present because of their normal duties (v. 5; see Comments to 10:8; 17:9; 18:5), but it does not indicate what they do in this rite. Since their normal duties include performing rites of expiation, including the ritual of the Day of Atonement, they may be present because of the similarity of the present ceremony to those rites. The text also mentions their role in judging lawsuits and cases of assault. Although they issue no ruling here, they are traditionally involved in insoluble cases (see Comment to 17:9). If the elders' declaration in verse 7 represents an oath, one might surmise that the priests are present to administer it, since exculpatory oaths were normally taken in the presence of priests at a sanctuary.[15]

It is noteworthy that the priests step forward only after the heifer is slaughtered. This may be Deuteronomy's way of depriving the slaughter of the sanctity that their participation would lend to it, and it may indicate that their role is to ensure that the ceremony does not end with the slaughter, which the unlearned might regard as magically efficacious and sufficient, but that it continues with the declaration and prayer of verses 6–8, thereby making it clear that absolution can come only from God.

All the views we have considered are far from being proven. It is not clear that Deuteronomy attributes any meaning at all to the elements preceding the final prayer. Since to Deuteronomy the prayer is what counts, it appears that the other elements of the procedure are vestigial and may have been modified by Deuteronomy to deprive them of their original meaning. What we are trying to understand, therefore, is their pre-Deuteronomic meaning, and if Deuteronomy has modified them significantly, it may be impossible to recognize the proper ancient parallels and use them to identify the meaning.

It seems likely, in any case, that the ceremony has combined several complementary, and perhaps partly redundant, means of expiating bloodguilt: the prayer on the one hand, and the slaughter of the heifer, the hand-washing and the elders' declaration, which may originally have been separate rites or parts of a single rite. In its abundance of elements with similar aims the ceremony is comparable to the complex of rites that characterized the Ten Days of Penitence in later Judaism. Traditionally these days involved six elements:

1. Prayers for forgiveness (*seliḥot*), recited from the month before Rosh Hashanah through Yom Kippur.

2. Confession of guilt (*viddui*), also recited from the month before Rosh Hashanah through Yom Kippur.

3. *Tashlikh*, going to a body of water and reciting Micah 7:19 ("You will hurl all their sins into the depth of the sea") and other prayers and shaking out one's pockets, on the afternoon of Rosh Hashanah.[16]

4. *Kapparot*, swinging a hen or rooster around over one's head a day or two before Yom Kippur and reciting the formula "A life for a life . . . this is my substitute, this is my replacement, this is my atonement; this hen/rooster shall go to death but I shall go on to a long and pleasant life and peace," after which the rooster is slaughtered, its intestines are thrown to the birds and whatever remains is donated to the poor. This popular practice was opposed by many authorities but survived and was widely accepted. In some places plants were used instead of fowl. Others, particularly in modern times, replaced the practice with gifts to charity.[17]

5. *Malkot*, ritual flagellation, practiced by some Jews on the day before Yom Kippur.[18]

6. Fasting on Yom Kippur (the Day of Atonement) and at other times between Rosh Hashanah and Yom Kippur.

Like the ceremony of the broken-necked heifer, these prayers and ritual actions are complementary means of expiating guilt. In both cases, it is because expiation of guilt is so vital that numerous means were employed and redundance was not only disregarded but was considered a virtue. If we are right in supposing that Deuteronomy preserved aspects of the ceremony of the broken-necked heifer only because popular feeling considered them indispensable for purging guilt, the survival of *kapparot* despite rabbinic opposition makes it a particularly apt parallel.

EXCURSUS 20

Accusations of Premarital Unchastity (22:13–22)

There are several puzzling features in the law about accusations of premarital unchastity. The first paragraph (22:13–19) enables the bride's parents to rebut the husband's charge by producing a cloth or garment that was spotted with blood when the marriage was consummated. But such a cloth could easily be faked by the bride or her parents, as recognized in medieval commentaries and talmudic sources.[1] On the other hand, the second paragraph (vv. 20–21) implies that the absence of a blood-stained cloth is sufficient to convict the bride. This seems to disregard the normal requirement of two witnesses to a crime for conviction and execution (17:2; 19:15). It also overlooks the fact that not all virgins have intact hymens or bleed the first time they have sexual relations, a fact also recognized in talmudic sources.[2] Furthermore, the law treats the girl's premarital sex as a capital crime, although verses 23–24 and Exodus 22:15–16 indicate that such misconduct calls for execution only if she is engaged.

Halakhic exegesis resolves these difficulties by reading the law in the light of the other biblical laws just cited and subordinating it to them, as follows: This is a case where the husband claims that, finding no evidence of virginity, he investigated and learned from others that his fiancée had engaged in sexual relations after becoming engaged to him. He must produce two witnesses who testify that they saw her about to sin and warned her that she was committing a capital crime. The parents can disprove the charge only by producing evidence to discredit this testimony; although some authorities of the talmudic period interpret the cloth literally, the halakhah adopted the view that the "cloth" stands for evidence provided by defense witnesses who counter the prosecution witnesses, thus laying out the facts "like a cloth."[3]

As an interpretation of the biblical law the halakhic view is forced, but it is a testimony to the impracticability of the law as stated in Deuteronomy. Even the avowedly literalistic Karaite exegesis agrees that the matter cannot hinge on the cloth alone and that witnesses (attendants who examined the cloth or the bride at the time of the marriage) are required.[4] A fragmentary paraphrase of this law from Qumran states that the matter is to be determined on the basis of a physical examination of the bride by trustworthy women shortly after consummation of the marriage.[5]

An interesting defense of the literal interpretation of the cloth is offered by Shadal, who suggests that the Torah intentionally relies on the cloth, despite its inconclusiveness, in order to protect nonvirgin brides from excessive punishment. In his view, although the

Torah does not require judicial punishment of girls who lose their virginity before engagement (Exod. 22:15–16; Deut. 22:28–29), popular sentiment would have demanded their execution if they did and then married under false pretenses.[6] Hence, he holds, the law is designed to protect these girls from popular sentiment; to do so, it discouraged husbands from bringing charges by making the charges easy to rebut and thereby exposing the husbands to punishment for making them.[7] Because making the girl's offense a capital crime and permitting conviction without two witnesses is inconsistent with other laws in Deuteronomy, Rofé argues that verses 20–21 are a late interpolation in the book, by a writer who advocates sterner treatment of prebetrothal intercourse than do those verses that treat it as a noncapital offense. He holds that this writer is also responsible for the law condemning the rebellious son to death (21:18–21), and that both laws aim to strengthen family authority. In Rofé's view, rabbinic exegesis effectively abrogated this interpolation because of its severity and its inconsistency with the rest of the Torah.[8]

Another possibility, albeit speculative, is prompted by a scholarly theory about Mesopotamian law. Some scholars believe that certain harsh penalties in Mesopotamian contracts and law corpora are meant merely "in terrorem," as a deterrent, with no intention that they would actually be carried out.[9] This theory is comparable to the rabbinic view that the law about the rebellious son was not enforced but was merely for educational purposes.[10] One might, then, theorize that verses 20–21 of the present law are not intended for enforcement but are simply a rhetorical means of condemning premarital intercourse and of deterring girls from engaging in it.[11] By implying that nonvirgin brides can be executed, it would provide ammunition for parents to use in warning their daughters against unchastity, much as they could have used 21:18–21 in warning sons against insubordination. This could explain why the first paragraph does not have the husband executed for his false accusation; if his bride really faced execution if convicted, 19:16–19 would have required executing him if his accusation proved false (cf. the Arab practice cited in the Comment to 22:14). It is true that the deterrent effect is reduced by the fact that the bride might escape conviction by fabricating false evidence. Nevertheless, the law would still have a chilling effect, and no girl could be certain that she or her parents would not be caught if they falsified the evidence. If this hypothesis is correct, *in practice* matters may have been handled more or less as the halakhah prescribes, in agreement with the other pertinent laws about sexual offenses and judicial procedure: only fornication during engagement would have led to execution, and then only on the testimony of two witnesses.

EXCURSUS 21

The Background and Development of the Regulations about Admission to the Assembly of the Lord   (23:2–9)

Historical Background

The attitudes reflected in 23:2–9 toward certain neighboring peoples and types of individuals have prompted scholarly attempts to date these regulations by identifying one or more periods when Israel's relations with its neighbors would have led to a determination

to exclude them and their descendants. The text explains these laws with reasons related to experiences of the Mosaic period, but this is problematic. It is hard to understand why, just a few decades after the Exodus, the Egyptian oppressors would have been viewed more benignly than Ammon and Moab, and why the latter two peoples' relatively minor offenses of inhospitality and attempted cursing should have justified harsher treatment than generations of enslavement by Egypt. It seems more likely that these reasons are later explanations that aim to explain the laws in terms of the text's assumed Mosaic date.

A date for these regulations in the period of the Chieftains (the "Judges") or right after it could be defended on the ground that Ammon and Moab were hostile to Israel in that period while Egypt and Edom were not.[1] Their descendants might have been feared as potential fifth-columnists who had to be excluded from the governing Assembly where they might influence public policy.

J. Milgrom sees these regulations as a northern Israelite polemic, from the time of the divided monarchy, against the Davidic dynasty. He argues that the Moabites and Ammonites were enemies of the northern kingdom, that the ban on *mamzerim* (23:3) is implicitly directed against those nations because of the tradition that they are the offspring of incest (Gen. 19:30–38), and that the targets of the laws are the most important ancestors of the Davidic dynasty: David himself, a descendant of Ruth the Moabite, and his grandson Rehoboam, whose mother was Naamah the Ammonite. Thus the kings of the south are shown to be descended from women who were doubly prohibited. That the Davidic dynasty was compromised by such ancestry is reflected, in Milgrom's view, in an aggadic statement that the halakhic interpretation permitting Ammonite and Moabite women "loosed the bonds" of David.[2]

The presumption underlying these and other attempts to date the regulations in verses 2–9 is that the regulations reflect attitudes current when Deuteronomy was composed, or when these particular laws were composed, which may have been earlier than Deuteronomy as a whole. This presumption is reasonable, but the results have been highly speculative since relations between Israel and its neighbors fluctuated during the six centuries preceding the Babylonian exile. There are many occasions when the attitudes reflected in these regulations could have been natural, probably including occasions of which historians are unaware.

Later Development

Deuteronomy 23:2–9 was the focus of considerable literary and exegetical attention in exilic and postexilic times.

Lamentations 1:10 bemoans the fact that when the Temple was destroyed, it was entered by "nations of whom You [God] said that they may not enter Your Assembly." This clearly invokes the language of Deuteronomy 23. Conceivably the allusion is simply ironic, meaning "You said that they may not enter Your Assembly, and here they have gone further and entered your very Temple!" It is also possible, however, that this allusion is based on a legal interpretation according to which those excluded from the Assembly were also excluded from the Temple. In either case, since the Temple was destroyed by the Babylonians, who are not mentioned in Deuteronomy 23:4–9, Lamentations evidently assumes that the four nations that *are* mentioned in Deuteronomy 23:4–9 stand for *all* foreigners. This is clearly the intention of a text from Qumran that uses phrases from Deuteronomy 23:2–9 in rules prohibiting foreigners, resident aliens, the emasculated, and *mamzerim* from entering the

future Temple.[3] Rules banning foreigners from the Temple are known from Ezekiel 44:5–9,[4] to which the Qumran text also alludes, and rules banning certain types of people from temples are also known outside the Bible.[5] However, this cannot be the original meaning of Deuteronomy 23. In banning people from the Temple, Deuteronomy would undoubtedly have called it "the place which the LORD your God has chosen"; "assembly," or "congregation," does not refer to a sanctuary in Deuteronomy or anywhere else in the Bible.[6]

The law is cited again in 1 Kings 11:1–2 in describing King Solomon's sin of intermarriage: "King Solomon loved many foreign women in addition to Pharaoh's daughter—Moabite, Ammonite, Edomite, Phoenician, and Hittite women, from the nations of which the LORD had said to the Israelites, 'None of you shall join them and none of them shall join you, lest they turn your heart away to follow their gods.'" This passage draws its phraseology from the prohibitions of intermarriage with the Canaanites in Deuteronomy 7:1–4 and Joshua 23:12 and the list of foreign nations excluded from the Assembly in Deuteronomy 23:4–9, but it adds the Phoenicians (lit., "Sidonians"), who are not mentioned in either. Here, too, then, the list in Deuteronomy 23 (and the lists of Canaanites) has been construed as standing for all foreigners.

The same broad construction of the law was evident during the period of the Return to Zion in the fifth century B.C.E. At that time, many Jewish men were found to have married foreign women, including Ammonites and Moabites but also others such as Ashdodites (from Philistia). Based on their interpretation of Deuteronomy 23:4–9 in combination with 7:1–4 and other verses in the Torah, Ezra, Nehemiah, and the leaders of the community insisted on the dissolution of all intermarriages.[7]

What seems to have been new in the interpretation of Deuteronomy 23 in the books of Lamentations, Kings, and Ezra-Nehemiah is primarily the breadth of their interpretation, whereby the law is construed as referring to all foreigners. Some scholars believe that interpreting it as dealing with marriage was also new, and that "not being admitted into the *kahal* of the LORD" did not have that meaning in Deuteronomy.[8] Certainly, the phrase does not literally refer to marriage. In the Commentary, however, we argue that exclusion from the *kahal* is tantamount to exclusion from citizenship and, in the light of citizenship rights in Athens, that at least some noncitizens were denied the right to marry Israelites. In other words, while "may not be admitted into the *kahal* of the LORD" does not *mean* "may not marry an Israelite," it implies it.

Conversion and Marriage

One of the reasons why Ezra, Nehemiah, and their associates demanded the dissolution of intermarriages is that they saw no other way to comply with the law as they understood it. So far as is known, there was as yet no formal procedure for converting foreigners to Judaism. In preexilic times, foreigners became Israelites only by the informal, generations-long process of ethnic assimilation that resulted from living in the land of Israel or marrying Israelites, which no source other than Deuteronomy prohibited (except with regard to Canaanites).[9] Ezra, Nehemiah, and their associates knew of no way by which they could have speeded up the process if they had wished to. There is evidence that some of their contemporaries felt that foreigners could be accepted. In Babylonia, there were foreigners who "attached themselves to the LORD" and served Him, and the prophet of the exile assured them of acceptance.[10] Eventually, this attitude prevailed and procedures for religious conversion were created.[11]

The later halakhic interpretation of the regulations in verses 2–9 is predicated on three presumptions: (1) that these verses do deal with marriage; (2) that any foreigner may convert to Judaism; and (3) that "the congregation of the LORD" refers to native-born Jews who are the products of legal unions. The salient points of the halakhic interpretation are as follows.

The law about emasculated men (v. 2) applies to any man whose testes, penis, or genital ducts are removed or destroyed, unless the condition was congenital or resulted from illness. The men covered by the restriction may not marry native-born Jewish women, but they may marry women who have converted to Judaism.[12] The *mamzer* (v. 3) may not marry a native-born Jew, but he or she may marry another *mamzer* or someone who has converted to Judaism. In other respects the *mamzer* was not shunned. For example, in religious ceremonies where status determines who receives an honor or goes first, a learned *mamzer* is given precedence over an ignorant high priest.[13]

Once a formal process of conversion had been developed and converts from all nations were accepted, this law was taken to mean that Jewish women could not marry *male* converts from Ammon and Moab (since the law uses the masculine forms of Ammonite and Moabite), but Jewish men could marry females (such as Ruth).[14] The third generation in verse 9 was taken as referring to generations after the conversion of one's ancestors; thus, the grandchildren of Edomite and Egyptian converts could marry Jews.[15] The talmudic sages recognized, however, that the law of verses 4–9 had in any case become a dead letter, since Ammonites and Moabites had by now blended with other nations and no gentile was an identifiable descendant of the original Ammonites and Moabites.[16]

EXCURSUS 22

The Alleged Practice of Cultic Prostitution in the Ancient Near East (23:18–19)

Scholars who believe that cultic prostitution was practiced in the ancient Near East and that it is the target of Deuteronomy 23:18 have used the concept in a confused and confusing way to refer to several different phenomena. The term "prostitution" is inappropriate for most of them, and some probably never existed in the ancient Near East. Since these phenomena are mentioned frequently in commentaries and reference works, it is worth clearing up the confusion.[1]

Some scholars connect the *kedeshah* of 23:18 with the sacred marriage ceremony ("hierogamy," or *hieros gamos*) performed in ancient Mesopotamia. This ceremony, symbolizing the sexual union of the goddess Inanna with Dumuzi, a god or deified king, was expected to secure the land's fertility and welfare. In it, the role of Dumuzi was played by the king, and scholars believe that it included ritual intercourse between him and a woman—the queen or a priestess—representing the goddess, in order to produce the desired results by sympathetic magic.[2] No text actually states that the goddess was represented by a woman; possibly she was represented by a statue or was thought to be present invisibly, as in hierogamies described in classical sources.[3] If a real woman did take part, she could hardly be called a "prostitute," though she could be called a *kedeshah* in the literal sense of the term, "holy woman" or "priestess." In any case, the rite is not known to have

been practiced after the nineteenth century B.C.E., and there is no evidence that it was ever practiced in Canaan or Israel.[4]

Some scholars refer also to a type of prostitution mentioned in Greek and Latin sources of the fifth century B.C.E. and later, beginning with Herodotus. These sources describe two types of prostitution that scholars call cultic or sacred, though "temple prostitution" would describe the matter more clearly: (1) brothels, occupied by temple prostitutes (hierodules), were maintained by the temples of certain goddesses as income-producing enterprises; a famous example is the temple of Aphrodite in Corinth; (2) in some places individual women, usually prior to marriage, were required to serve as prostitutes temporarily for various purposes, such as honoring a goddess or in place of some other religious obligation. Herodotus (fifth century B.C.E.) describes one such practice on Cyprus and at Babylon, and Lucian (second century C.E.) describes another at Byblos. Both of these types were cultic primarily in the sense that the income they generated went to the sanctuary. Although the goddess of sex was honored by the sexual act, the prostitutes' customers were men from the street whose motive was essentially sexual, not religious.[5] There is no unambiguous evidence that this kind of institutionalized temple prostitution was practiced earlier in the ancient Near East, though a few passages may imply it.[6] The only thing remotely resembling this in the Bible is the practice forbidden in Deuteronomy 23:19, which indicates that street prostitutes might, on their own initiative, make donations to temples. But these women were not temple employees or prostituting as a religious obligation.[7]

Scholars have assumed that worshipers of fertility gods "through the use of imitative magic, engaged in ritual intercourse with devotees of the shrine, in the belief that this would encourage the gods and goddesses to do likewise" and thereby fructify crops, herds, and families.[8] This practice would constitute a sort of democratization of sacred marriage: not (or not only) the king or priest, but every man would seek in this way to enhance the fertility of the land, or of himself and his crops or herds. Some scholars assume that male cult prostitutes were also employed for this purpose. If such a rite existed, it could hardly be termed "prostitution." In any case, it is a fantasy: there is no evidence that it existed anywhere in the ancient world. The assumption that it did is based largely on an unwarranted combination of sacred marriage and temple prostitution with Hosea 4:14, where the prophet blames widespread adultery on the fact that men "turn aside [or "dismember sacrificial animals"] with whores [*zonot*] / and sacrifice with prostitutes [*kedeshot*]."[9] In the absence of any other evidence that commoners would consort with prostitutes as an act of worship, it is more likely that Hosea is simply describing debauchery at festivals, with men picking up prostitutes and bringing them to the banquets accompanying the sacrifices; their act is no more cultic than is the fornication at threshing floors mentioned in Hosea 9:1.[10]

There is probably no subject in the field of ancient Near Eastern religion on which more has been written, with so much confidence, on the basis of so little explicit evidence, than "cultic prostitution." It is a case of conjectures that have been repeated so often, without examination of the evidence, that they have turned into "facts." There is, in fact, no evidence available to show that ritual intercourse was ever performed by laymen anywhere in the ancient Near East, nor that sacred marriage, even if it involved a real female participant, was practiced in or near Israel during the biblical period. There is a bit of uncertain evidence that may imply the practice of income-producing temple prostitution in Mesopotamia, and postbiblical evidence for the practice in Byblos, but no evidence that this is what the biblical *kedeshah* did. There is little reason to believe that the women mentioned in Deuteronomy 23:18–19 are anything but common prostitutes.

EXCURSUS 23
Levirate Marriage   (25:5–10)

According to Josephus, whose view is echoed by some modern scholars, the purpose of levirate marriage is to prevent men's households from dying out and their property passing to relatives, and to provide for their widows.[1] The practice undoubtedly had these effects, but the Bible's own explanation, as noted in the Commentary to 25:5–10, is that levirate marriage aims to provide a dead man with a son in order to prevent his name from being blotted out. This reflects the belief that death does not put an absolute end to an individual's existence. In biblical times it was believed that dead people's spirits continue a kind of shadowy existence in Sheol (the netherworld, beneath the earth), and that the living could assist them in various ways. Many of these methods involved keeping a deceased man's name present on earth, thus perpetuating his spirit's contact with the living.[2] Perhaps the reasoning was that just as the mention of a person's name can conjure up a very real mental picture of him, wherever a person's name was present his spirit was present. In this respect, a name functioned more or less as an image was thought to function. Hence in some places it was the custom to place a person's image, or an inscription bearing his name, in a sanctuary, thus keeping him before the deity at all times; conversely, one's enemies could be harmed by writing their names on bowls and then smashing the bowls, just as effigies are used in voodoo.[3]

Having descendants was one way in which a man's name was kept present among the living, at least for a generation or two. A person who had no descendants had no "name or remnant."[4] This idea may be based on the fact that sons bore their father's name as a patronym (they were called "so-and-so son of X"): each time a son was mentioned by his full name, his father's name would be pronounced. The inheritance of a man's land by his sons also facilitated the mention of his name, since the son's property would be referred to as "property of so-and-so son of X."[5] When a man left no son, other means were employed. Numbers 27:1–11 provides that when a man leaves only daughters, they may inherit his property and thus preserve his name. This may have been accomplished by the daughters' husbands or sons receiving the property and taking the deceased man's name as a patronym (such a case is mentioned in the books of Ezra and Nehemiah: a priest married the daughter of a man and was then called by the latter's name, doubtless as a patronym).[6] Another means of perpetuating a man's name was by erecting a memorial pillar. The childless Absalom erected one and named it "Absalom's Pillar" since he had no son "to mention [his] name" (2 Sam. 18:18); the inscription on the pillar kept his name present on earth.[7] The reference to a son who could have mentioned Absalom's name probably reflects another means by which a son would aid his father posthumously, that is, the performance of vital services for his spirit. This is indicated by Mesopotamian texts in which "mentioning the name" of the deceased refers to invoking their names in connection with offerings of food and water to their spirits (for a similar practice in Israel, see Comment to 26:14).[8]

These practices were the duty of children toward their deceased parents, which is one reason why dying childless was considered a terrible curse.[9] People who were childless often adopted children to perform these rites for them. Some texts refer to the performance of such rites on behalf of women as well,[10] and this may have been done in Israel, too. It is possible, however, that the spirits of women were thought to depend on the rites performed for the men with whom they had been associated in life.

Levirate marriage is part of the same complex of practices. It provides a man with a son posthumously, to assist his father's spirit in the ways just described. Given the importance of perpetuating the name of the deceased, it seems likely that the son would not only be legally attributed to the deceased man, but would also take his name as a patronym (see Comment to 25:6).

Marriage of a widow to a member of her husband's family is also mentioned in Genesis 38 and in the book of Ruth. In Genesis, Judah, the father of the dead husband, is still living, and it is his responsibility to ensure that another of his sons marries the widow.[11] The second son, Onan, is unwilling to provide a son for his brother, but he goes through the motions of performing the levirate with the widow, Tamar. The fact that Onan does not simply refuse to marry Tamar may mean that the law at that time denied him the option of refusing, but he may have been simply yielding to pressure from Judah or seeking to obtain his dead brother's share of Judah's estate. After Onan's death, Tamar tricked Judah into impregnating her. This may imply that in that period the deceased man's father was one of those who might perform this duty, as in the Middle Assyrian Laws and the Hittite Laws.[12] Possibly, however, this was not the norm and Tamar was improvising out of desperation, since Judah had failed to give her to his surviving son. In Ruth 4, a more distant relative of the dead man who left no sons or brothers must marry his widow, at least if he wishes to redeem the dead man's property. Since Deuteronomy 25:5 imposes the obligation only on the deceased's brother, the practice in Ruth could be a variant custom, perhaps one Deuteronomy intends to abolish. It may be, however, that Deuteronomy merely describes the standard situation and would not object to the practice described there.[13]

The narratives in Genesis and Ruth reflect the role of levirate marriage in different stages of Israelite history. In Genesis, where the Israelite patriarchs are living as semi-nomadic herdsmen, the aim is to "provide offspring for the deceased" (Gen. 38:8). In Ruth, with the Israelites settled in towns and owning farmland, the aim is "to perpetuate the name of the deceased upon his estate, so that [his] name not disappear from among his kinsmen and from the gate of his town" (Ruth 4:5,10). It is not clear where the law of Deuteronomy stands in this picture. Since it does not explicitly mention the dead man's estate, it may have been worded so as to cover seminomadic as well as landed Israelites. This is uncertain because the condition that the two brothers must be "living together" (25:1) may be related to the future son's inheriting the dead man's land.

The practice of marrying the widow of a childless man to a member of his family is known in various forms around the world, but its function varies in different societies.[14] In the Hittite Laws it is mentioned as an exception to the laws of incest: a widow may, or must, be married to her husband's brother, father, or husband's brother's son. In the Middle Assyrian Laws, the father of a man who dies may, under certain circumstances, give the widow or fiancée to another of his sons or to a son of the deceased by another wife; he may also, apparently, marry her himself. In the Hittite Laws and most of the Assyrian Laws it is immaterial whether the deceased man left children. The aim of the practice is not to provide him with a son, but to maintain the investment of his father, who had paid a bride-price for the widow, and to provide support for her. Similar motives prevail among Arabs, where levirate marriage is a voluntary rather than obligatory practice. The biblical concern with providing a son for the deceased man is partially paralleled in the Hindu Laws of Manu, according to which the dead man's relative must unite with the widow, but the union is only temporary, until she bears a son.

EXCURSUS 24

Improper Intervention in a Fight   (25:11–12)

What is puzzling about the law concerning a woman who seizes a man's genitals while trying to save her husband is the fact that the punishment seems out of all proportion to what she has done. Her act is motivated by what seems—at least from a modern point of view—to be a legitimate concern, and her method is one of the only means by which an unarmed woman can disable a man. That her act seems immodest, or humiliating to her victim, would seem to be mitigated by these considerations.

These problems led talmudic and medieval commentators to explain the crime and/or the punishment in ways that seem far-fetched but, if correct, would make the law more understandable:

1. The woman was wrong to use a method that humiliated her victim, but her punishment is not really mutilation; "cut off her hand" refers to *fining* her the monetary value of her hand, just as the complete talionic formula refers, according to rabbinic exegesis, to monetary compensation (see Comment to 19:21).[1]

2. Seizing a man's genitals endangers his life, and cutting off the woman's hand is not meant as a punishment for the court to impose later, but a means available to bystanders to save her victim in case she won't release him. The real intent of the law is to illustrate the moral duty of bystanders to save the life of a person being pursued, if possible without killing the pursuer, but otherwise by killing him. In this reading, oddly, the wife represents the pursuer and her husband's opponent the victim. The meaning is: If a person is attacking another in a potentially lethal way (such as seizing his genitals, which is considered a lethal spot), you may even wound the attacker if that is necessary to save the victim ("you may *even* cut off her hand"); if that doesn't suffice, you may kill the attacker ("show no pity").[2]

3. The law only refers to fights where there is no danger to the woman's husband and her brazen, dangerous means of helping him are uncalled for; if her husband *is* in danger, she may save him by any means necessary. This view is based on the wording of the protasis, in which "If two men get into a fight with each other" is followed by the seemingly superfluous "a man and his fellow [lit., brother]"; the latter phrase is taken to mean that the men are not mortal enemies.[3]

These explanations all imply a presumption that the woman's seizing her victim's genitals in order to save her husband was not, in and of itself, a crime worthy of mutilation, and the law would not have treated it so if that were all that was involved. These explanations hardly express the original intent of the law. They illustrate, however, that puzzlement about the law is not solely the result of a modern outlook.

The issues involved in explaining this law were well summarized by the Karaite Jacob al-Kirkisani (tenth century):

> The reason for the obligation of this amputation [of the woman's hand] is doubtful. The Rabbanites thought that the reason is that the woman desired to cause mayhem, since if someone's sexual organs are seized, this causes him intense pain, depending on how roughly they are seized. Others thought that the reason was that the woman had extended her hand to the [male] genitals, which she is forbidden to touch. The Rabbanite view seems more reasonable, since the Torah informs us that she sought to save her husband, and this could be accomplished only by hard pressure on the assailant's sexual organs. This is a

matter of [common] experience: If two men are fighting, and the weaker one cannot prevail against the stronger, he will grab at the stronger one's sexual organs, whereupon the stronger must release his hold, thus enabling the weaker to gain victory over him. If one thinks that both aforementioned reasons together are behind this rule, he may well be right.

One may by analogy make this rule to apply to men also; that is to say, if a man extends his hand to seize another man's sexual organs in order to accomplish the same purpose as was intended by the woman, he must likewise have his hand cut off, since the reason [for this act] was [to inflict] pain and discomfort. It is possible that [this rule] mentions only women because at this time it was women—Egyptian or other—who practiced this mode of attack against Egyptian or other men, so that when quarrels broke out among the men, the women would grab the attacker's sexual organs in order to save their husbands. And that is why the rule mentions only women. . . .

As for those who hold that the reason for this rule is [concern about] indecency, they say that the rule applies by analogy to any indecent gesture toward either men or women, as well as to anyone, male or female, who performs such a gesture—once he touches another person's sexual parts, his hand must be cut off. One might retort that the uncertainty of understanding this rule is increased by its application only to women, which seems to imply that touching the sexual organs is not meant to cause pain or damage, for had it been so, the rule would not apply to women only, since rules applicable to men are applicable to women also, so that in this case what has been said [in this work] about analogy does not apply—the rule here applies only to a woman who grabs a man's genitals, and not to anyone [and anything] else.[4]

A provision similar to Deuteronomy 25:11–12 appears in the Middle Assyrian Laws. MAL §8 and the preceding paragraph read as follows:

> If a woman has laid hand on a man [and] a charge has been brought against her, she shall pay thirty minas of lead and shall be beaten twenty times with staves.

> If a woman has crushed a man's testicle in an affray, one of her fingers shall be cut off. And if, even though a physician has bound it up, the other testicle has become affected along with it and becomes inflamed, or if she has crushed the other testicle in the affray, they shall tear out both of her [the last word is missing].[5]

In the Assyrian law, it is clear that the woman has injured the man's testicles. She has probably kicked or squeezed hard enough to cause a hematoma or, perhaps, orchitis, which is even more painful and could last for a few weeks.[6] The explicit reference to injury is consistent with the view that the biblical law has injury of the genitals in mind, a conclusion also supported by the fact that the preceding law in Deuteronomy deals with a man who dies childless. This would explain the severity of the punishment in Deuteronomy. The fact that the biblical law does not explicitly mention the damage may mean that the woman is guilty even if she only seizes the man's genitals. By squeezing hard enough, she could cause him extreme pain and even cause him to pass out, which would be sufficient for her purposes. Apparently she is guilty because her action risked injuring the man's genitals, and hence his ability to produce children.[7]

The Assyrian and biblical laws are not similar in every respect. The preceding paragraph in the Assyrian collection singles out women who hit men, not men who hit women. This may imply that in the Assyrian ethos, for a woman to hit a man is itself a crime, presumably because it violates his superior status and humiliates him. This may imply that the following law singles out women who injure men's genitals because it, too, was a crime only when committed by women. The biblical law does not address this issue. Lacking a provision that penalizes women who strike men, it leaves open the possibility, mentioned by Kirkisani, that the law about seizing genitals would also apply to males, and

that it mentions the female only because women were more likely to resort to this tactic; men, because of their greater strength, would rely on fisticuffs or wrestling.[8]

The Assyrian law deals with a case in which the woman is a principal in the fight, not a bystander trying to assist one of the principals. In essence, it means that women may not use one of the few means they have for defending themselves against stronger men. The Bible imposes no such restriction, but penalizes women only for using this tactic when they are not attacked but are intervening in a fight between others.

<h2>EXCURSUS 25</h2>

Deuteronomy 27

Chapter 27 raises several difficult questions of coherence, it interrupts the connection of chapters 26 and 28, and its three main sections are introduced by different combinations of speakers. These sections seem inconsistent and redundant both internally and in relation to each other. Here we shall note some of the major difficulties and some attempts to resolve them, although in the end many questions will remain.

When are the Steles to be Erected?

Verses 2–3 seem to require that the steles be erected, plastered, and inscribed immediately upon entering the land, on the day that Israel crosses the Jordan. This is implied by the temporal clauses "on the day when you cross" in verse 2 and "when you cross over" (be-'ovrekha) in verse 3. This means that the ceremony is to be performed at a site near the Jordan. The timing and location are what give the ceremony its significance: Israel's very first act in the promised land is to dramatize how its life there must be based on Moses' Teaching.

This understanding is complicated by verse 4, which repeats that the steles are to be erected "upon crossing" (be-'ovrekhem), but adds that they are to be erected on Mount Ebal, which is too far from the Jordan to reach on the same day as the crossing. Read in the context of verse 4, the temporal clauses in verses 2–3 must be understood loosely, meaning "once you have crossed," not necessarily on the same day.[1] However, this is not the natural way to construe verse 2. The phrase "on the *day* when" (ba-yom 'asher), with the definite article and the relative particle, commonly refers to a specific day, and in the context of a law it is not likely to refer to an undefined future time.[2] The immediacy of the command is so clear that a manuscript of Joshua from Qumran places the story of how Joshua carried it out right after the crossing of the Jordan in Joshua 3–4, instead of later in the book as in the Masoretic Text (Josh. 8:30–35).[3] Likewise, most of the rabbinic commentators felt obliged to adopt farfetched explanations of how the Israelites reached Ebal and Gerizim in a single day. According to one view, a miracle made it possible; according to another, these were not the well-known Mounts Ebal and Gerizim by Shechem, but a smaller pair of mountains with the same names, located near Gilgal, where the Israelites entered the promised land![4]

It appears, then, that Deuteronomy 27:4 goes against the natural sense of verses 2–3. Furthermore, apart from adding that the steles are to be erected "on Mount Ebal," the verse is completely redundant after verses 2–3. This suggests that it is an interpolation that

aims to override the plain sense of verses 2–3. By repeating the clause "upon crossing the Jordan" and then adding "on Mount Ebal," verse 4 implies that the time when Israel reaches Mount Ebal also counts as "the day when you cross the Jordan."

What was the aim of this revision? Why was the location of the ceremony, with its dramatic immediacy, changed to Mount Ebal? Verses 2–3 must have intended the ceremony to take place at Gilgal, near Jericho. This was the Israelites' first camp in the promised land. According to Joshua 4, when the Israelites crossed the Jordan they took twelve stones from the river and set them up at Gilgal as a memorial of the event. While Israel was encamped there, several momentous firsts occurred: Joshua circumcised all the males who had been born in the wilderness, the people celebrated the first Pesah in the land, the manna ceased, the people ate the produce of the land, an angel appeared to Joshua, and the Israelites launched their military campaign for the land from there.[5] Later, Gilgal was the site of an important sanctuary in the days of Samuel and Saul. In the eighth century it was one of the most frequented sanctuaries in the northern kingdom of Israel.[6]

It seems likely, given the clear meaning of verses 2–3 and all the firsts that occurred at Gilgal, that verses 2–3 stem from a tradition that the Israelites were commanded to erect inscribed steles at Gilgal.[7] But for some unknown reason, the north Israelite circles in which Deuteronomy developed (see the Introduction) believed that Mount Ebal, by Shechem, was the more suitable location for the ceremonies prescribed in chapter 27. Shechem, too, had played a venerable role in Israel's early history, not the least because it was the first place in the promised land where Abraham built an altar to God (see Comment to 27:4). Perhaps, because of its central location, the Deuteronomic movement originally intended Mount Ebal to become "the place that the LORD will chose to establish His name." For this or some other reason, 27:2–3 were "overwritten" with verse 4 so as to replace Gilgal with Mount Ebal.

Which Stones are to be Inscribed?

Verse 27:8 seems to imply that the Teaching was to be written on the stones of the altar,[8] since they are the stones mentioned last before this verse (vv. 5–6). If that is the case, the stones of the altar would be identical to the inscribed stones of verses 2–4. But this is unlikely for several reasons: the altar stones must be left uncut, which would make them rough and unsuitable for writing on; furthermore, had the stones of the altar been those of verses 2–4, the requirement that they be uncut would have been introduced in verse 2, where the other characteristics of the inscribed stones are given, and verse 5 would have begun "And you shall take *those* stones and build an altar."[9] It seems clear, then, that the inscribed steles and the altar stones are different stones, just as the stones and the altar in the covenant ceremony in Exodus 24 are separate.

These two views have been debated since ancient times. A minority rabbinic view holds that the Teaching is to be written on separate stones. The Mishnah and other ancient sources hold that it is to be written on the altar.[10] The book of Joshua, which describes the fulfillment of this instruction, may be the earliest source to adopt the latter view. Joshua 8:30–32 states: "At that time Joshua built an altar to the LORD . . . on Mount Ebal . . . as Moses . . . had commanded . . . an altar of unhewn stone upon which no iron had been wielded. They offered [sacrifices] on it. And there, on the stones, he inscribed a copy of the Teaching that Moses had written for the Israelites." In Joshua's abbreviated account, no other stones are mentioned, which suggests that the stones are those of the altar.[11]

If, as we claim, verses 2–4 do not mean that the writing is on the altar, how are we to explain why verse 8 gives the impression that it is? There are several possibilities:

1. Verse 8 is simply recapitulating the point of verse 2 to emphasize that the terms of the Teaching, not the altar and the sacrifice, are the most important part of the ceremony; the impression is the unintentional result of the recapitulation.

2. Some scholars suggest that verses 5–7 are an interpolation and that verse 4 was originally followed by verse 8.[12] If so, the impression is the unintentional result of the interpolation.

3. M. Fishbane holds that the impression is likely intentional and correctly divined by Joshua 8. He agrees that the law of the altar in verses 5–7 is an interpolation and that verse 8 resumes the interrupted command of verses 2–4, but he holds that the verse also means to reinterpret the stones of those verses as altar-stones in order to suppress their original character as *matsevot*, sacred pillars, like those used in the covenant ceremony of Exodus 24:4. Deuteronomy reinterprets the stones because it considers such pillars illegitimate (Deut. 16:22).[13] If this is the case, then the ceremony is an old, pre-Deuteronomic one that Deuteronomy is revising, and verses 1–8 in their present form do indeed mean to imply that the inscribed stones of verses 2–4 are those of the altar, not separate, free-standing steles.

Chapter 27 in its Context

As noted above, chapter 27 interrupts the connection of chapters 26 and 28, which clearly belong together. In those chapters, Moses is the speaker; here, three headings refer to him in the third person, and other speakers accompany him. Only verses 9–10 deal with the covenant being made in Moab at this point in the book, as shown by "today" / "this day" in those verses. In them, Moses and the priests seem to restate what Moses himself says in 26:16–19. The rest of the chapter is about covenant ceremonies that the Israelites are to perform *later*, when they arrive in the promised land.

What unites the three sections of the chapter with each other, and with the surrounding chapters, is that they are all about covenant ceremonies. There seem to have been numerous independent traditions about precisely when Israel formally became God's people and concluded the covenant with Him.[14] These traditions included Exodus 19–24 and Deuteronomy 4–5, according to which God established His covenant with Israel at Mount Sinai-Horeb; Deuteronomy 28:69 and 29:9–28, according to which He did so in Moab; and Deuteronomy 27 and Joshua 24, which state in different ways that the covenant was established at or near Shechem, after the conquest of the promised land. Deuteronomy reconciles these traditions by showing that they are all aspects of the same covenant. Chapters 5:19–6:3 show that the covenant made in Moab is a reaffirmation, with further details, of the one made at Sinai-Horeb. Chapter 27, by weaving the instructions about the covenant ceremonies at Mount Ebal into Moses' speech about the Moab covenant, shows that the ceremonies at Ebal are a reaffirmation of the Moab covenant, and hence of the Sinai-Horeb covenant.

The multiplicity of ceremonies that Deuteronomy 27 prescribes for Mounts Ebal and Gerizim may be due to the momentous nature of the event these ceremonies mark: Israel's long-awaited arrival in the promised land. In its importance, this event is comparable to the Exodus, which is also accompanied and commemorated by ceremonies that are

described with seemingly redundant and overlapping details (Exod. 12–13). It seems that momentous events were felt to require various ceremonies to express their significance, that there were different traditions about what was required, that these variations required editorial skill to harmonize them, and that continuing reflection in the light of later experience attracted revisions of earlier writings about them.

EXCURSUS 26

The Structure and Style of Deuteronomy 28

Chapter 28 contains two main sections, (A) blessings and promises (vv. 1–14) and (B) curses and threats (vv. 15–68). (For brevity we will sometimes refer to these as simply "blessings and curses," although technically these terms refer only to the explicit blessings and curses that contain the words "blessed" and "cursed," vv. 3–6 and 16–19). Section B has three parts, all introduced by similar introductory verses: (B1) 15–44, (B2) 45–57, and (B3) 58–68.

Several aspects of the chapter raise interesting questions about its composition and history. The unequal number of blessings as compared with curses makes section B seem too long. In addition, whereas sections B2 and B3 describe a natural sequence of disasters in which each leads to the next, there is no obvious order to the threats in section B1, verses 20–44. For example, the nation and king are exiled in verses 36–37, but in verses 38–44 the people are still in the land. Verse 35, threatening a skin disease, seems out of place, in the midst of a series of social disasters, and redundant, since verses 22 and 27 already mention skin inflammation and other diseases. Verse 41 says that children will be carried off in captivity, but verse 32 had already said as much. Because of these features, several verses in this section have been perceived as dislocated or intrusive.

In addition to these difficulties within section B1, section B2 also speaks of the people still living in the land, despite the exile of verse 36, and B3 again mentions diseases (vv. 59–61) and exile (vv. 63–68).

Scholars once assumed that these problems were the result of interpolations by later writers who sought to make the chapter more vivid or to incorporate allusions (some borrowed from Jeremiah and Lamentations) to the Babylonian defeat and exile of Judah. These writers were thought to have been careless about the way they disturbed the logical organization of the text. By removing the disturbing elements, scholars sought to reconstruct the "original" text of the chapter, which would be much better organized. Since sections B2 and B3 refer to the siege and exile, they were partly or entirely eliminated as interpolations that updated the chapter after the defeat by Babylonia. Some verses in B1 were eliminated because of redundancy and disturbance of the order. With these omissions, section B would correspond more closely in length and content with its counterpart, section A.[1]

Today, much more is understood about the literary style of the Bible, particularly about the types of literary structure it follows, and more is known about the genre of blessings and curses and its ancient Near Eastern background. Numerous examples of the genre have been found in Hittite, Mesopotamian, and Aramaic treaties, legal texts, and other genres, and they display some of the features that have puzzled scholars in Deuteronomy 28. In this genre it is typical for threats to outnumber promises, because the main point is to deter violation of the instructions to which they are appended.[2] Repetition serves the same purpose, because the genre does not aim to present a systematic analysis of what would happen but to make a palpable, unforgettable impression on those addressed.[3] Hence, there is no need to arrange

punishments in a natural sequence. Sometimes the curses seem to be presented in simply random order. Often, ancient Near Eastern documents organize curses in a theological order based on relationships between the gods who inflict each one.[4] As a result of this lack of concern for natural order, some texts mention disasters befalling people in their homeland *after* mentioning deportation, as in Deuteronomy 28.[5] As we shall see, parts of the chapter follow another nonnatural system based on chiastic structure.

Similar blessings and curses elsewhere in the Bible and in other ancient Near Eastern texts make it clear that Deuteronomy 28 also draws on the content and wording of traditional threats, both individual ones and groups of threats. The use of older material in the chapter is clear from the parallels surveyed in Excursus 27. This information helps us to formulate realistic hypotheses that account for the seeming disorder of the threats. It seems likely, for example, that whole groups of threats, each sharing a common theme or pattern such as those in verses 30–33 and 38–41, were taken intact from older collections. Various collections probably had some identical threats, such as enslavement of children. For the purposes of the chapter there was no need to eliminate duplication, to group the similar threats together, or to arrange the threats in a chronologically consistent sequence. This method of compilation would explain why similar curses are dispersed throughout the chapter and why some threats seem to disregard what others have already said. In sum, it is reasonable and realistic to presume that the chapter was originally composed of materials drawn from various sources, rather than being carelessly revised after it was initially completed.

Structure

Sections A and B1 are essentially catalogues. The blessings and curses are arranged in a literary order rather than a natural, cause-and-effect sequence. Each of these sections begins with a brief series of six explicit blessings or curses and continues with a longer series of promises and threats elaborating on them. The curses in B1 (vv. 15–19) are the converse, virtually verbatim, of the blessings in A (vv. 3–6). The promises and threats that follow are arranged in chiastic structures in which the elements form a thematic symmetry. This style goes a long way toward explaining the order, since chiasm requires repetition of themes and their separation into symmetric locations in the structure.

The promises of verses 7–13a identify five different phenomena that are mentioned or implied in the blessings of verses 3–6 and refer back to them chiastically. Each promise relates to a successively earlier blessing as follows:[6]

    A. economic success (v. 3a)
        B. fertility of soil (v. 3b)
            C. fertility of humans and animals (v. 4)
                D. abundant food (v. 5)
                    E. military success (v. 6)
                    E'. military success (v. 7)
                D'. abundant food (v. 8)
            C'. fertility of humans and animals (v. 11)
        B'. fertility of soil (v. 12a)
    A'. economic success (v. 12b–13)

This arrangement highlights selected aspects of certain blessings that are not their only meanings, or not necessarily the ones intended in verses 3–6. For example, verses 12b–13a

relate to the city of verse 3a as the locus of financial activity, though the verse probably has in mind a wider range of activities. Verse 7 relates to the "comings and goings" of verse 6 as military activity, though that is not necessarily what verse 6 itself intends.[7]

In section B1, the threats are likewise arranged in an order that seems mostly chiastic, though they do not relate to the curses in a chiastic order. The section begins with a summary introduction (v. 20) and then introduces a standard triad of plagues: disease, famine (represented by its causes, drought and hardened soil), and defeat (vv. 22–26).[8] The latter two plagues form the first elements of the chiasm, which then continues as follows:

> A. agricultural disaster (drought and hardened soil) (vv. 23–24)
> B. defeat leading to becoming byword (vv. 25–26)
> C. inflammation (v. 27)
> D. madness, blindness (vv. 28–29a)
> E. constantly abused and robbed (v. 29b)
> F. oppression (vv. 30–33a)
> E'. continually abused and downtrodden (v. 33b)
> D'. madness from what one sees (v. 34)
> C'. inflammation (v. 35)
> B'. exile leading to becoming a byword (vv. 36–37)
> A'. agricultural disaster (crop-destroying pests) (vv. 38–42)

Following the chiasm, section B1 ends with loss of economic superiority (vv. 43–44), reversing the corresponding promises at the end of section A (vv. 12b–13a).[9]

Unlike sections A and B1, sections B2 and B3 are arranged in a natural, cause-and-effect sequence, each developing a single sequence of events over several verses.

Section B2 opens with an introduction (vv. 45–46) like that in verse 15 and then states its main theme in verses 47–48: servitude, starvation, and poverty under a conqueror. It describes a natural sequence of events: invasion, pillage of crops, siege, starvation, and cannibalism. It alludes to several of the explicit curses, such as those concerning "the produce of your soil," "the calving of your herds and the calving of your flocks," and "the issue of your womb" (translated as "your own issue") (v. 17; see vv. 51,53); and the military defeat and the siege of the cities illustrate the curses of "coming and going" and of the city (vv. 16,19).

Section B3 also follows a natural sequence of events, starting with another consequence of siege, disease (the theme stated in v. 59). It describes the resultant decimation of the population, deportation, dispersion, and desperate conditions in exile. Decimation and deportation illustrate the curses of "issue of the womb" and "coming and going" in war.

Sections B2 and B3 have sometimes been thought to be, or to contain, later additions to the chapter because they seem to allude to the events surrounding the Babylonian conquest. Nothing in the text requires this inference. Siege, cannibalism, and exile were common experiences in the ancient world. They are mentioned in ancient Near Eastern treaties (see Excursus 27) and could easily have been included in Deuteronomy 28 long before the fall of Judah.[10] The fact that the only place of exile mentioned explicitly is Egypt (v. 68) argues against revision after the defeat of Judah, since most of those who left were deported to Babylonia, which is not mentioned at all.[11] Nor do verses that resemble passages in Jeremiah argue for revision. Deuteronomy's influence on the book of Jeremiah is well known and it is more likely that this, and not the reverse, is the explanation for the similarities.

Although sections B2 and B3 are not demonstrably later than the Babylonian conquest, their different type of organization does raise questions about their relation to the rest of the chapter. So does their opening verse (v. 45), which would read well as a conclusion to

the threats in section B1 (vv. 15–44). Unlike the introductions to sections B1 and B3, verse 45 is not a conditional sentence but an unconditional one, and since it echoes verse 15, the two verses together can be seen as a frame around the section, with verse 45 matching, in reverse, the conclusion of the promises (v. 13b; note how vv. 45 and 13b are both immediately preceded by very similar verses describing economic superiority and subjugation).

If verse 45 (and perhaps its sequel, v. 46) was in fact composed as a conclusion to section B1, does it imply that, to its author, the curses were concluded and that sections B2 and B3 were not an original part of the chapter? It is certainly possible that they were original. The composition of speeches and literature is a subjective matter, and authors often bring their remarks to a seeming conclusion and then continue (frequently, to the grief of their audience). In the Assyrian treaty of Esarhaddon, a whole series of curses is summed up by reiterating the conditions that will bring them on, and then a new set of curses begins, some duplicating earlier ones.[12] The new series could have been drawn from a different source, but the fact remains that it is part of Esarhaddon's treaty, not a later addition. Perhaps something similar is true of our sections B2 and B3. The author/compiler of Deuteronomy 28 may have chosen to conclude the chiastic, catalogue-like presentation at this point and then give a chronologically organized description of exactly how the disasters would come about. He used verse 45 as a hinge, to conclude the preceding description as well as introduce the new one. The different method of organization in sections B2 and B3 could indicate that he drew the description from a different source than section B1, though this is not necessarily the case since one writer can employ different styles. Whatever the source of sections B2 and B3, it is possible that the entire chapter was created as a single unit from the outset, and is not the result of accretions or repeated redactions. However, we cannot be certain, and the possibility that section B2, and possibly B3, is a later addition—though not necessarily later than the exile—cannot be ruled out.

Style

The blessings and curses are formulated in a variety of ways.

The explicit blessings and curses read "blessed/cursed shall you be in . . ." or "blessed/cursed shall your . . . be" (vv. 3–6,16–19).

The promises and threats fall into two main groups. The first specifies God as their cause, and the second simply describes the condition or experience:

a. God as cause:
  i. The Lord will ordain/let loose a particular phenomenon referred to by a noun (blessing, curse, etc.) (vv. 8,20).
  ii. The Lord will do the following for/to you, referred to by a verb (put to rout, establish, give, strike, etc.) (e.g., vv. 8–9,11,22,27,49,59).

b. condition or experience:
  i. You/your children/your cattle, etc., shall be slaughtered, carried off, etc. (e.g., vv. 26,30–34,53), and you will have no (deliverer/power, etc.)/be unable to (be cured, succeed, etc.) (vv. 26,27,29,31,32,35).
  ii. You shall (do something), but somebody else shall enjoy the results of your efforts (v. 30), or: You shall (do something), but (shall not succeed) because your normal pursuits will be frustrated (vv. 38–41).[13]

These two types of promise and threat are interwoven. In some cases, conditions whose cause is not stated are clearly the result of a previously mentioned divine activity (e.g., vv. 7,9–10,25–26). Even where that is not obvious, the overall context of the chapter makes it clear that all that is promised and threatened is the result of God's actions (e.g., vv. 22–23).

Several recurrent motifs and refrains appear throughout the chapter or in parts of it. Three verses describe reactions to Israel's plight by other nations (vv. 10,25,37). Each part of section B has a cluster of verses that use the verbs "destroy/be destroyed" (*sh-m-d*) and "perish/wipe out" ('-*v-d*), which are "repeated with knell-like effect" (vv. 20,24; 45,48,51; 61,63).[14] Two sections refer to psychological reactions caused "because of what your eyes shall see" (vv. 34,67) and section B2 has the refrain "because of the desperate straits to which your enemy shall reduce you" (vv. 53,55,57).

The number seven is mentioned in verses 7 and 25 and figures as the number of calamities in lists (vv. 22,27–28) and as the number of times that the root *sh-m-d*, "destroy/ be destroyed," appears (vv. 20,24,45,48,51,61,63).[15]

The effect of the chapter on its audience is heightened by the aural impact of assonance. The explicit blessings and curses are replete with alliteration and repetition of the key words *barukh* and '*arur*. There are strings of words containing the same sound: *sh* in verses 23 and 37, *ts* in verses 53, 55, 57, *alephs* in verse 30, and *b* in verses 30, 47, 52–53. Several lists are shaped by considerations of assonance and number: verse 20 lists three alliterative disasters (*ha-me'erah*, *ha-mehumah*, *ha-mig'eret*), verse 28 three rhyming disasters (*shig-ga'on*, '*ivvaron*, *timhon levav*), and verse 22 seven diseases falling into three rhyming or alliterative groups (*shahefet*, *kaddahat*, and *dalleket*; *harhur* and *herev*; *shiddafon* and *yerakon*). Various other disasters are referred to by rhyming pairs of words: '*avak ve-'afar* (v. 24), '*ashuk ve-gazul* (v. 29), '*ashuk ve-ratsuts* (v. 33), *be-ra'av u-ve-tsama'* (v. 48), *be-matsor u-ve-matsok* (vv. 53,55,57).

Another effective device is contrast. Several threats contrast Israel's undertakings with their unwanted results: "If you pay the bride-price for a wife, another man shall enjoy her," etc. (v. 30); "Though you take much seed out to the field, you shall gather in little," etc. (vv. 38–41). Others contrast Israel's former blessedness with its punishment: "Because you would not serve the LORD . . . in joy and gladness over the abundance of everything, you shall have to serve your enemy in hunger and thirst and nakedness and lack of everything" (vv. 47–48); "You shall be left a scant few, after having been as numerous as the stars in the skies" (v. 62); "As the LORD once delighted in making you prosperous and many, so will the LORD now delight in causing you to perish and in wiping you out" (v. 63). Some blessings and curses contrast Israel's fate with that of its enemies: "They will march out against you by a single road, but flee from you by seven roads" (v. 7); "You shall march out against them by a single road, but flee from them by seven roads" (v. 25). Finally, others emphasize a blessing or a curse by saying the same thing in positive and negative ways: "You will be creditor to many nations, but debtor to none" (v. 12, reversed in v. 44); "the head, not the tail . . . at the top and never at the bottom" (v. 13, reversed in vv. 43–44).

Many of these devices are poetic in nature. Deuteronomy employs them here, at the conclusion of the laws, to make a strong, emotional impact on its audience, to teach as effectively and unforgettably as possible that obeying or disobeying the laws has far-reaching and serious consequences.

The Literary Background of Deuteronomy 28

Deuteronomy 28 is the longest example in the Bible of the literary genre of blessings and curses, which invokes divine rewards and punishments to sanction compliance with legal and other types of obligations. This genre was well known in the ancient world. Its aim was to encourage adherence to obligations by adding divine sanctions to those provided by human authorities, which were (and are) often insufficient. It is rooted in oaths, by which one or both parties signify their commitment to a promise by calling divinely inflicted punishments down upon any of them who would violate it. From this simple beginning the genre grew into lengthy lists of punishments for disobedience and, often, shorter lists of rewards for obedience. Attested as early as the third millennium B.C.E. in Sumer, the genre is commonly attached to international treaties and is also used with laws, border agreements, domestic boundary markers, loyalty oaths, and with warnings against disturbing tombs, tampering with inscriptions and monuments, and, in more recent times, violating copyrights.[1] The contents of the promises and threats are not limited to this genre. They also appear in omens, indicating that ultimately they express the common hopes and fears of people, especially those living in close contact with the agricultural and cattle-raising base of their subsistence and with the danger of war.

Other examples of the genre in the Bible are the brief lists of promises in Exodus 23:20–33 and Deuteronomy 7:12–16; the threats in Deuteronomy 4:25–28; and the long list of both in Leviticus 26. Passages of similar style and content also appear in the prophets, particularly in the book of Jeremiah, which was heavily influenced by Deuteronomy. Foreign parallels come from as far away as Greece, but most are from Near Eastern texts such as the Babylonian *Laws of Hammurabi* (1792–1750) and the Vassal Treaties of Esarhaddon, king of Assyria (680–669).[2] (All dates are B.C.E.) There are numerous similarities in content, and sometimes in wording, between Deuteronomy 28, parallel texts in the Bible, and those from elsewhere in the ancient world. Some of these similarities indicate that Deuteronomy drew on earlier sources and traditions in composing chapter 28.

Here is a sampling of some of the more notable parallels.

In Exodus 23:25–27, God promises, "You shall serve the LORD your God, and He will bless your bread and your water. And I will remove sickness from your midst. No woman in your land shall miscarry or be barren. I will let you enjoy the full count of your days. . . . I will throw into a panic all the people among whom you come, and I will make all your enemies turn tail before you."

In Leviticus 26, God promises, "Your threshing shall overtake the vintage, and your vintage shall overtake the sowing; you shall eat your fill of bread and dwell securely in your land" (v. 5); and He warns, "I will wreak misery upon you—consumption and fever, which dry out the eyes and dry the throat; you shall sow your seed to no purpose, for your enemies shall eat it. . . . I will send pestilence among you, and you shall be delivered into enemy hands. . . . You shall be routed by your enemies. . . . You shall flee though none pursues. . . . You shall eat the flesh of your sons and the flesh of your daughters" (vv. 16,17,25,29).

Jeremiah's predictions include, "Lo, I am bringing against you, O house of Israel, a nation from afar. . . . A nation whose language you do not know—you will not understand what they say. . . . They will devour your harvest and food . . . your sons and

daughters . . . your flocks and herds . . . your vines and fig trees. They will batter down with the sword the fortified towns on which you rely"; "Their houses shall pass to others, fields and wives as well"; "The carcasses of this people shall be food for the birds of the sky and the beasts of the earth";[3] "I will make them a horror to all the kingdoms of the earth"; "I will make them . . . a disgrace and a proverb, a byword and a curse in all the places to which I banish them"; "I will make you a slave to your enemies in a land you have never known"; and "I will cause them to eat the flesh of their sons and the flesh of their daughters, and they shall devour one another's flesh—as a result of the desperate straits to which they will be reduced by their enemies, who seek their life."[4]

Turning to foreign parallels, the epilogue to Hammurabi's laws[5] includes such curses as, "May Enlil . . . incite turmoil against him [that is, against the king who changes or abolishes Hammurabi's laws or effaces the stele on which they are written] that cannot be suppressed";[6] "May Enlil . . . order . . . the destruction of his city, the dispersion of his people"; "May Enlil order . . . the scattering of his people"; "May Ea . . . deprive him of knowledge and understanding and constantly lead him in the dark";[7] "May [the gods] . . . shatter his weapons on the field of battle . . . strike down his warriors"; "May [his enemies] carry him away in bonds to a land hostile to him";[8] "May Ninkarrak . . . inflict upon him in his body a grievous malady, an evil disease, a serious injury which never heals, whose nature no physician knows, which he cannot allay with bandages";[9] "May . . . these curses . . . overtake him quickly."[10]

Mesopotamian omens include such promises as, "That cattlefold will become increased" and "The king will attack and overthrow the land of his enemy"[11] and warnings such as, "An enemy will enjoy the harvest of the land," "besiege the city," "take the elders of the land," and "enjoy the treasures of your land," and "the members of the family will be taken as booty, and their mother will mourn over them."[12] Babylonian boundary stones contain such curses as, "May his corpse be cast aside and may there be no one to bury him,"[13] "May Sin . . . clothe his whole body with 'leprosy' that never departs," [14] and "May somebody else take over the house he may build."[15]

A fourteenth-century-B.C.E. Hittite treaty states, "If you obey these words, may these gods . . . graciously protect you, your wife, your sons, grandsons, your lands, your cities, your threshing places, your vineyards, your pastures, your cows, your sheep, and all of your possessions, and may you see good prosperity . . . and live to old age. . . . If you . . . violate these words . . . may these oaths destroy you, your wife, your sons, your lands, your cities, your vineyards, your threshing places, your pastures, your cows, your sheep, and all of your possessions, and may they destroy your progeny from the earth."[16] Another adds, "The curses shall pursue you relentlessly."[17]

The Vassal Treaties of Esarhaddon contain the following warnings:[18] "Keep this treaty . . . lest . . . you deliver your land to destruction, your people to be deported"; "May Anu . . . rain upon all your houses disease, exhaustion, *di'u*-disease, sleeplessness, worries, ill health"; "May Sin . . . clothe you in 'leprosy'";[19] "May Shamash [the sun god], the light of heaven and earth, not give you an accurate, reliable oracle; may he take away your vision and may you walk about in darkness!"[20] "May Ninurta . . . fell you with his fierce arrow, and fill the plain with your corpses, give your flesh to eagles and vultures to feed upon"; "May Venus . . . let your wives lie in the embrace of your enemy before your very eyes, may your sons not take over your house, may a foreign enemy divide your possessions";[21] "May locusts, which diminish the [produce of] the land, [devour] your crops"; "Mother shall [bar the door to] her daughter, may you eat in your hunger the flesh of your children, may one man eat the other's flesh through want and famine";[22] "May Ishtar, lady

of battle, break your bow in a heavy battle, tie your arms, and have you crouch at the feet of your enemy"; "May Nergal [god of fever and pestilence] . . . extinguish your life with his merciless dagger, may he plant carnage and pestilence among you"; "so may you never rest nor sleep."

An Aramean monument, dated to some time within the eleventh to ninth century, contains the curse, "May he sow but let him not reap, may he sow a thousand [measures] but get one . . . [measure] in return."[23] The Aramaic treaty from Sefire, Syria, ca. 750, threatens "Seven years shall the locust eat. Seven years shall the worm eat. Seven years shall *t-w-y*-pests come upon the face of the land, and no grass shall sprout, so that nothing green can be seen and its rushes do not [grow]. . . . The gods shall let loose caterpillar, vermin [of the field], crop consuming devourer against Arpad and its people."[24]

Turning to the Greek world, a fifth-century oath declares, "If I observe what is written in the oath, my city will be free of disease: if not, it shall be sick; [if I observe . . .], my city shall remain undestroyed: if not, it shall be destroyed; [if I observe . . .], my [land] shall bear [fruits]: if not, it shall be barren; [if I observe . . .], the women shall bear children like their parents: if not they shall bear monsters; [if I observe . . .], the cattle shall bear like the cattle: if not [they shall bear] monsters."[25] A sixth-century Greek oath warns, "If any one should violate this [oath] . . . let them be under the curse . . . that their flocks yield not their natural increase; that defeat await them in camp and court and their gathering place."[26]

The foregoing parallels make it abundantly clear that promises and predictions of blessing and curse were a common feature of ancient practice and literature. They were used to sanction obligations of various types and to predict the future. Most of the passages we have reviewed are not verbatim parallels and do not by themselves imply a close literary relationship among the various texts. They deal with types of fortune and misfortune—hopes and fears—that would naturally occur to different writers living in the same or similar societies. Some of the biblical blessings and curses have unmistakably Israelite touches, such as the blessing of making Israel a holy people (Deut. 28:9) and the use of idolatry and return to Egypt as curses (vv. 36,64,68). However, a few passages show signs of close international literary connections. The imagery of verse 23, and Leviticus 26:19, is so similar to an Assyrian curse that a literary relationship among the three passages is hardly questionable. Verse 23 warns, "The skies above your head shall be copper and the earth under you iron," while Leviticus 26:19 says, "I will make your skies like iron and your earth like copper" (cf. Deut. 11:17). In the treaties of Esarhaddon we find: "May all the gods . . . turn your soil into iron, so that no one may cut a furrow [?] in it. Just as rain does not fall from a copper sky, so may there come neither rain nor dew upon your fields and meadows, but let it rain burning coals in your land instead of dew."[27] There is also a very close parallel to Leviticus 26:26, "Ten women shall bake your bread in a single oven, they shall dole out your bread by weight, and though you eat, you shall not be satisfied": a curse on an Aramean statue reads "One hundred women will bake bread in a single oven and not fill it."[28] These parallels point to a literary tradition of curses, in treaties and various other genres, shared by Israelites, Arameans, and Assyrians, and it is quite possible that many other biblical curses are also part of this tradition.[29]

Another type of similarity applies to the curses in Deuteronomy 28:26–33, which are paralleled in almost identical order in the treaty of Esarhaddon. The respective orders are as follows:

Deut. 28	Curse	Esarhad. par.	Responsible god
v. 26	carcasses carrion for animals	41	Ninurta
v. 27	skin inflammations	39	Sin
vv. 28–29	madness, "blindness,"[30] and dismay	40	Shamash
v. 30	fiancée raped, loss of house, vineyard	42A	Venus
vv. 31–33	possessions and children plundered	42B	Venus

There is one difference in the order of these curses: had Deuteronomy followed Esarhaddon's order, verse 26 would have *followed* verses 27–28. This exception could be intentional, since it enables Deuteronomy to place verse 26 in a chiastically suitable location (see Excursus 26). The similar outlines could be mere coincidence; they involve only four of twenty-one paragraphs in the Esarhaddon treaty, and other parallels between Deuteronomy 28 and Esarhaddon's treaty appear in different places in the two texts with no similarity in the order. What suggests a relationship between the two texts at this point is the fact that while there is no inherent reason for this order in Deuteronomy, the order seems to correspond to traditional groupings of the gods in Mesopotamian texts. Thus, plagues imposed by Sin (the moon god) and Shamash (the sun god) appear next to each other because those two deities, and the punishments they impose, are commonly paired in Mesopotamian texts.[31] However, only the *order* of the curses is shared; their wording is too different to suggest that Deuteronomy copied them from Esarhaddon's treaty. It is not even as similar as the parallel to verse 23, mentioned above, which is found elsewhere in Esarhaddon's treaty. The details of verse 30 are clearly inspired by Deuteronomy 20:5–7, not by the Assyrian text.

What may have happened is this: Assyrian scribes used longer and shorter lists of curses for various occasions. They had an outline of topics, the order of which was based on traditional groupings of the gods who inflicted each curse; following the outline was more important than the exact wording of the curses. One segment of this outline, similar or identical to that followed in §§39–42 of the Esarhaddon treaty, became known to Israelite scribes, perhaps from a treaty between Assyria and Israel or some nearby state, but possibly from some other literary genre such as a monument. Deuteronomy drew on this outline but worded the curses in its own way and possibly modified the order to suit the chiastic structure of its section B1.

The parallels within the Bible itself show that blessings and curses of this sort, even if some were ultimately inspired by foreign models, were part of Israelite tradition from early times, and the immediate source of most or all the blessings and curses within Deuteronomy (and Leviticus) was undoubtedly this local Israelite tradition. Even if some curses were drawn more directly from foreign models, they were freely modified in keeping with Israelite ideas. Most uniquely Israelite is the use of blessings and curses to sanction biblical religion and law, based on the view that God is Israel's true king. Although the metaphor of kingship was also used by other ancient religions, in Israel it was used in unique ways: God was considered to be the author of Israel's laws (a role attributed only to human kings elsewhere) and Israel saw itself as bound to Him by a covenant. The ancient practice of sanctioning obedience to obligations with blessings and curses, and their use in treaties for sanctioning loyalty to the suzerain, made it natural for the Bible to use them to express the consequences of fidelity or infidelity to the divine King and His laws.

The Writing and Reading of the Teaching (31:9–13)

The writing of the Teaching by Moses, and his instructions for reading it to the people every seven years (31:9–13), culminate his exhortations to the people to learn the Teaching, to discuss it constantly, and to teach it to their children as a guide for their lives (see 4:9–10; 5:1; 6:6–9,20–25; 11:18–20). These exhortations embody Deuteronomy's profound concern to impress the Teaching on the mind of all Israelites in order to shape their character as individuals and as a nation. This concern is one of the most characteristic and far-reaching ideas of the Bible, particularly of Deuteronomy. It reflects several premises and aims of Biblical religion:

a. The Teaching is divinely inspired and authoritative, hence sacred and canonical.

b. The entire people, and not only a spiritual, intellectual, or clerical elite, are God's children and consecrated to Him. Hence, biblical religion is for the people as a whole (cf. 33:4). All must live a holy way of life, like priests among the nations. Therefore, the entire people must be taught about God and His laws. This aspect of biblical religion was expressed artistically at Dura-Europos in Syria, as perceived by E. J. Bickermann:

> The sacred books of all other religions . . . were ritual texts to be used or recited by priests. In the Mithra temple at Dura it is a Magian in his sacred dress who keeps the sacred scroll closed in his hand. [But] in the synagogue of Dura a layman, without any sign of office, is represented reading the *open* scroll.[1]

c. The entire citizenry must be trained in the nature of justice, including civil and criminal law, so as to live in accordance with it.

d. The entire citizenry must know its own rights and duties as well as those of its leaders. This, as observed by M. Greenberg, enables all to judge the leaders' actions and prevents all from excusing failures to perform their duties by claiming ignorance of them. See the introductory Comment to 16:18ff.[2]

The first steps taken toward achieving these goals are recorded in Exodus and Numbers. The Israelites are told to teach their children about God's benefactions in freeing them from slavery, explaining that various rites are reminders of those benefactions (Exod. 12:26–27; 13:8,14–15; cf. Num. 15:37–41; Josh. 4:5–7,20–24). The Decalogue is addressed to the entire people, and Moses reads the Book of the Covenant to them (Exod. 20:1; 24:7). In Leviticus and Numbers, even some instructions about priestly procedures are addressed to the public at large (Lev. 1:1–5; 21:24; Num. 28–29), implying that the people as a whole must know the procedures that the priests perform on their behalf and even the rules that apply to the priests alone.[3]

Deuteronomy systematizes these beginnings and develops them much further, providing for regular teaching of God's instructions to the entire nation both privately and publicly.

Private Teaching

The family is the most natural educational institution, especially in an ancient society in which formal schooling was probably mostly for professional purposes rather than general

education. Hence, Moses' exhortations are frequently addressed to parents, urging them to impart the Teaching to their children on their own initiative and in response to children's questions about rites and commandments (4:9–10; 5:1; 6:6–9,20–25; 11:18–20).[4]

The Public Reading of the Teaching

Imparting the Teaching is not left solely in private hands. As 31:9–13 ordains, the entire public, including women, children, and strangers, must assemble to hear it read every seventh year at an impressive, festive occasion. This will make it clear that the Teaching is a public and not merely private concern, and will give it the full prestige of a national interest.

Deuteronomy does not mention whether the Teaching is to be read publicly on other occasions, but its homiletic style (see the Introduction) seems designed for public presentation. Deuteronomy 14:23 may presume public readings, since it expects other visits to the Temple to have the same inspirational effect that the septennial reading is designed to achieve in 31:12–13. If the local religious gatherings that 16:8 seems to imply are indeed forerunners of the synagogue service, the Teaching may well have been taught on such occasions, just as the reading of the Torah became a central feature in the synagogue service in postbiblical times.

Outside of Deuteronomy, the Bible mentions public reading of the Teaching on a number of occasions. The Book of Joshua reports that Joshua, after performing the ceremonies prescribed in Deuteronomy 27, read the entire Teaching "to the entire assembly of Israel, including the women and children and strangers," seemingly in fulfillment of the present instruction (Josh. 8:34–35). 2 Kings 23:2 describes a public reading of Deuteronomy by King Josiah shortly after the book's discovery in 622 B.C.E. The reading took place some time before Pesaḥ (not on the Feast of Booths). After the Babylonian Exile, in the fifth century B.C.E., Ezra read the Teaching to the assembled people on the first day of the month of Tishri and then for all seven days of the Feast of Booths (Neh. 8), applying the law of Deuteronomy 31:10–13 as he understood it. (By his time the Teaching included not only Deuteronomy, but also the older, separate documents that now constitute Genesis through Numbers; in other words, "the Teaching" consisted of essentially the entire Pentateuch, the Torah as the term is used today.)

The ceremonies that accompanied the reading, on the second day of the Feast of Booths in late Second Temple times, are summarized by Maimonides as follows:

> Trumpets are blown throughout all Jerusalem to assemble the people. A high pulpit made of wood is brought and set up in the midst of the Court of Women. The king goes up and sits on it so that people may hear his reading, and all Israel who go up to observe the feast gather around him. The minister of the [Temple Mount] synagogue takes a Torah scroll and gives it to the chief of the synagogue, the chief of the synagogue gives it to the prefect, the prefect to the High Priest and the High Priest to the king, to honor him by the service of many men. The king receives it standing, but if he wishes he may sit. He opens it, looks in it and recites a benediction in the way that all who read the Torah in the synagogue do. He reads the [assigned] chapters until he finishes. Then he rolls up the scroll and recites a benediction after it in the way in which it is recited in synagogues.[5]

The Writing of the Teaching

According to Deuteronomy 31:9, Moses wrote down the Teaching just before his death. A number of texts had been written earlier: records of some Israelite victories

(Exod. 17:14; Num. 21:14) and the Decalogue and the Book of the Covenant (Exod. 24:7; 31:18; 32:15–16; 34:27–29). Particularly noteworthy is the people's unanimous public pledge to obey the terms of the Book of the Covenant, thereby ratifying and canonizing it (Exod. 24:1–11). These written texts were the first stage in the creation of *Scripture*, a collection of sacred, canonical *books* which ultimately came to embrace the entire Bible ("Bible" is derived from Greek *ta biblia*, "the books [*par excellence*]"). In time, Scripture became the primary medium by which people learned God's teachings. The devotion of Jews, and Christians after them, to the written Scripture led the Arabs, in the Middle Ages, to call them *'ahl al-kitab*, "people(s) of the Book."

However, written texts were not originally studied by the people. Only after a gradual development did they become the primary medium for imparting the Teaching. The main form of publication in the ancient world was oral presentation.[6] This is Moses' method as well. He stores the tablets of the Decalogue in the Ark (Exod. 25:16,21–22; Deut. 10:1–2) and reads the Book of the Covenant to the people (Exod. 24:7), but makes no arrangements for people to study them or the records of Israelite victories (Exod. 17:14; Num. 21:14). Although he ordains that the Teaching be written on the doorposts of homes, on city gates, on steles on Mount Ebal, and apparently in *tefillin* (6:8–9; 11:18, 20; 27:3,8), he does not have copies made on parchment or papyrus, a form convenient for study. The written copy made in chapter 31 is to be stored and taken out periodically and read to the people. All of this points to the fact that even in Deuteronomy the dissemination of the Teaching remains primarily oral, with teachers either reciting it from memory or reading aloud from the written text (see also 4:9–10; 6:7,20–25; 11:19; 30:14; cf. 32:7).[7] Only the king is required to study the written text (17:18–19; it seems likely that other officials responsible for the enforcement of the Teaching also read it). Doubtless, in the First Temple period the written text of Scripture was used primarily for preservation, copying and verification, memorization, and for reading to others, as in Mesopotamia, early Greece, and Arabia.[8] Even in talmudic times, when the written text became the primary means of Bible study, the Torah continued to be read aloud in the synagogue, with most of the congregation following it aurally (hence one of the names for the Bible, *mikra'*, "that which is read"). Only centuries later, when printing made large numbers of copies affordable, could the entire congregation follow in written texts.

Parallels

The public reading of the Teaching on the Feast of Booths has some partial counterparts in the ancient world. Since the Teaching embodies the covenant between God and Israel, the requirement that it be read publicly is parallel to a requirement found in some Hittite treaties that the treaty be read to the vassal periodically (such as three times a year) to ensure that the vassal is aware of his obligations.[9] Reading the Teaching publicly at a festival is paralleled by the public recitation of the Homeric epics every fourth year at the Great Panathenea festival in ancient Athens. According to the Greek orator Lycurgus, the purpose of the recitation was to inspire the people to emulate the nobility of the Homeric heroes.[10]

There are few, if any, counterparts elsewhere in the ancient world to the idea of educating the entire people in religious and civil law. King Hammurabi of Babylon (eighteenth century B.C.E.) claimed that when the god Marduk instructed him "to bring justice to the people of the land and teach them proper conduct, [he] placed law and justice in the mouth" of the land, meaning that he taught it to the people, probably by

heart.[11] Whether he actually did so is questionable, since his laws are never cited in records of Babylonian legal proceedings. Later, Sargon II of Assyria (721–705) appointed officials to teach the exiles whom he settled in his capital the proper ways of serving the gods and the king.[12] It is not clear whether this really refers to educating the public in religious law. What Sargon had taught may have been nothing more than the duty of paying taxes to temples and the king,[13] and in any case there is no information indicating that he had his own citizens taught the same thing. In any case, nowhere else do we find a systematic program for putting this ideal into practice, nor evidence that it was actually put into practice, such as we find in the Torah and in postbiblical Judaism.

Later Developments

Several ideas in Deuteronomy 31 were developed further in later times, and some had a far-reaching effect on the entire character of Judaism.

By talmudic times (70–500 C.E.) the public reading of the Teaching was expanded into a year-round system—still followed today—of reading the Torah aloud in the synagogue. Babylonian Jewish communities completed the entire Torah in one year. Until some time in the Middle Ages Jews in Israel completed it in the course of three to three-and-a-half years, reading shorter sections each week and leaving time for commentary and sermons. Consecutive sections of the Torah are read every Sabbath morning and afternoon and on Monday and Thursday mornings. Pertinent excerpts are also read on holidays, the first day of each month, and public fast days. On Sabbath mornings, holidays, and fast days selections from the prophets and other parts of the Bible are read as well.[14] Some of the procedures for the reading are derived by halakhic interpretation from 31:9–13. For example, when the Torah is read, descendants of the priests (*kohanim*) are called up first, then Levites, and finally other Jews because of the order in which they are mentioned in verse 9 ("priests, sons of Levi . . . elders of Israel"). The Torah must not be read in translation but in Hebrew, because verse 11 says to read "this" teaching, that is, in this very form.[15]

The ultimate expression of the primacy of the written text of the Torah appears in the last of the traditional 613 commandments that halakhic tradition considers biblical in origin: every Jewish male must make a personal copy of the entire Torah or have one written for him (this commandment can be fulfilled by purchasing Bibles, since this encourages their production). This is based on a reading of Deuteronomy 31:19 as addressed to every Jewish male (hence the plural verb). This interpretation presumes the halakhic rule that sections of the Torah may not be written as separate excerpts and reasons that the passage must mean "write a copy of the entire Torah *including* the following poem."[16]

The idea that the entire people must be instructed in God's law eventually led to the intellectualization of Judaism. No other religion is so dependent on all of its adherents being learned. Judaism has been aptly characterized as "a religion which expects each adherent to develop judicial qualities,"[17] to know the law and how to apply it. The study of Torah (*talmud Torah*) is considered equal, if not superior, to all other commandments because, as the prerequisite to their performance, it alone leads to all the others.[18] In the same spirit Hillel said, "The ignorant cannot fear sin, nor can the unlearned be pious,"[19] meaning that they do not have a complete idea of what is sinful or how to express their piety; for that reason, when Hillel epitomized the entire Torah as "what is hateful to you do not unto others," he added: "The rest is its commentary—go and learn it."[20]

The religious education of the entire public also led to the democratization of leadership in Judaism. The fact that even laws about the priests were addressed to the public as a whole put the public in a position to supervise the priests, as the rabbis perceived.[21] As a result, expertise in religion did not remain confined to the hereditary priesthood, and it became possible for any Jew who had the intellectual qualifications, irrespective of family background, to master it. This is the significance of the fact that rabbis rather than priests are the religious leaders in Judaism.[22]

The Composition of Deuteronomy 31

One of the most important endeavors of biblical scholarship in the past two centuries has been the source criticism of the Torah. Starting from the simple question of how to reconcile inconsistencies in the text, and refusing to accept forced explanations to harmonize them, scholars eventually arrived at the theory that the Torah was composed of selections woven together from several, at times inconsistent, sources dealing with the same and related subjects. The reasoning followed in this kind of analysis is somewhat similar to that of the talmudic sages and later rabbis who held that inconsistent clauses and terminology in a single paragraph of the Mishnah must have originated with different sages,[1] and who recognized that Moses could not have written passages of the Torah that contain information unavailable to him, such as the last chapter of Deuteronomy, which describes his death and its aftermath; such passages, they held, had doubtlessly been written by different authors, such as Joshua or later prophets.[2]

Today it is clear that many ancient texts were indeed composed in the manner reconstructed by source critics. Earlier and later versions of certain works are known, and by comparing them we can see that the later versions have incorporated two or more accounts of the same event or theme, sometimes placing the accounts side-by-side and sometimes interweaving them with each other. While we do not have such empirical evidence in the case of the Torah, knowing that it exists for other works makes the kind of analysis employed in the source criticism of the Torah seem very plausible.[3]

Chapter 31 of Deuteronomy provides an opportunity to see how this aspect of biblical scholarship works. More than any other chapter in Deuteronomy, it is characterized by doublets, inconsistencies, interruptions, and variations in vocabulary and concepts that scholars take as evidence of different literary sources.

Doublets are superfluous repetitions of what are essentially the same events or ideas. In Chapter 31, Moses publicly appoints Joshua as his successor, as God had instructed him earlier (vv. 1–8; see 3:28); then, unexpectedly, God Himself appoints Joshua, without referring to Moses' action or explaining why He repeats it (vv. 14–15,23). Moses hands over the Teaching twice, once to the priests and elders (v. 9) and later to the priests alone (vv. 25–26). There are two introductions to the poem of chapter 32, one by God to Moses (vv. 16–21) and one by Moses to the people (vv. 28–30). God tells Moses that the *poem* will be a witness (v. 19). Moses does not mention this in his introduction to the poem, but in giving the Teaching to the Levites he tells them that the *Teaching* will be a witness (v. 26). God states that He knows the people are sure to sin in the future (vv. 16–21); then we discover that it is Moses who knows of their coming sin, and he does not say that God told

him of it (vv. 27,29). Finally, verse 30 reports that Moses recited the poem to the people, which seems to duplicate his teaching it to them in verse 22.

In addition to these inconsistencies and redundancies, the order of the events is puzzling. It would have been natural for Moses to instruct the Levites to keep the Teaching by the Ark at the same time that he tells them to read it every seven years (vv. 9–13), but his instructions about the Teaching are interrupted by God (vv. 14–23). God also interrupts His own actions. After He summons Moses and Joshua to the tent for Joshua's appointment (vv. 14–15), He digresses to tell Moses about Israel's future sin and punishment and to instruct him about the poem (vv. 16–21). Only after the poem is written down and taught to the people (v. 22), all of which would take a good deal of time, does God finally appoint Joshua, who has been waiting in the Tent all this time (v. 23). And only after this does Moses tell the Levites where to keep the Teaching (vv. 24–27).

The Sources of the Chapter

The inconsistencies and redundancies suggest that the chapter incorporates materials from different literary sources. This is indicated by the fact that in each of the doublets, one version displays language and themes typical of Deuteronomy and related literature, while the other displays language and themes characteristic of the passages in Genesis–Numbers attributed by critical scholars to the source that they call "JE" (JE is itself a combination of two earlier sources, "J" and "E", standing for the "Yahwistic" source and the "Elohistic" one; these designations are based on the name of God that each prefers).[4]

For example: The account of Joshua's appointment in verses 1–8 is consistent with earlier parts of Deuteronomy. In 3:28 God says "Appoint Joshua and say to him, 'Be strong and resolute,' for he shall go across at the head of this people, and he shall apportion to them the land" and here Moses says to Joshua, "Be strong and resolute, for it is you who shall go with this people into the land . . . and it is you who shall apportion it to them" (v. 7; cf. 1:38; 3:21). On the other hand, according to verses 14–15 and 23, the appointment of Joshua by God takes place in the Tent of Meeting, to which God descends in a pillar of cloud. Neither the tent nor the pillar of cloud is mentioned elsewhere in Deuteronomy, but they appear frequently in Exodus–Numbers.[5] The pillar of cloud is mentioned only in the JE source, and the vocabulary of these verses also includes phrases, such as "children of Israel"[6] (instead of "all Israel" or "this people"),[7] that are common in the JE source but appear rarely or never in Deuteronomy.

The brief introduction to the poem in verses 28–30 is shown to be rooted in Deuteronomy by such characteristically Deuteronomic phrases as "gather to Me,"[8] "call heaven and earth to witness against them,"[9] the verb *hishḥit* ("act wickedly"),[10] and "having done evil in the sight of the LORD and vexed Him."[11] The longer introduction in verses 16–22 has, instead, phraseology that is characteristic of the other sources of the Torah, such as "go astray"[12] instead of "follow" after other gods,[13] "alien gods"[14] instead of "other gods,"[15] "break My covenant"[16] instead of "transgress" or "forsake" God's covenant,[17] "then" (lit., "on that day")[18] instead of "at that time,"[19] and, again, "children of Israel."

This analysis suggests that chapter 31 has incorporated two separate accounts of Moses' preparations for his departure. One, from the JE source, was an account of how God appointed Joshua in the Tent of Meeting, informed Moses that Israel would betray Him and meet disaster, and had Moses write the poem and teach it to the people (vv. 14–23). The other, from the Deuteronomic school, recounted how Moses, following God's in-

structions, appointed Joshua, told the people that Moses knew they would sin and incur punishment, and summoned them to hear the poem (vv. 1–8,28–30).

The Deuteronomic source of this chapter included both of the paragraphs in which Moses gives the Teaching to the priests (vv. 9–13,24–27). This is indicated by the thoroughly Deuteronomic phraseology in both and by the fact that their subject, the Teaching, appears in the Torah only in Deuteronomy.[20] However, it seems unlikely that these two paragraphs are originally from the same author since they give different impressions of what Moses did once he finished writing the Teaching: one says that he gave it to the priests and elders with instructions to read it every seven years; the other, that he gave it to the Levites for storage. While these are not incompatible actions, had both accounts been written by the same author, they would probably have been recounted in a single paragraph in which Moses finishes writing the Teaching, gives it to the priests, tells them to store it in the Ark, and then tells them and the elders to take it out and read it once every seven years.[21] Furthermore, these paragraphs also assign different functions to the Teaching, based on inconsistent premises. The first sees the Teaching as a device to encourage loyalty to God and expects it to be effective; the second (like the material from JE) is certain that the people will sin—in other words, that the Teaching will fail to bring about loyalty to God. The impression that these paragraphs stem from separate sources is heightened by the fact that each refers to the priests differently: the first calls them "the priests, sons of Levi" while the second calls them "the Levites." Hence, although these two paragraphs are both clearly from the Deuteronomic school, it seems that Deuteronomic literature was not a single, monolithic source. Rather, it was a collection of materials that shared certain concepts and stylistic features but also contained variations and, over time, was revised and supplemented.[22]

The final unit preceding the poem, verses 28–30, is also curious. Certainly verse 30 introduces the poem, but verses 28–29 make no explicit reference to it and their relationship to it is uncertain. Some of the terms in verses 28–29 do have counterparts in verse 30 and in the poem: cf. *hak-hilu*, "gather," from the same root as *kahal*, "congregation" in verse 30; "speak . . . to" (lit., "speak . . . in the hearing of") (cf. 30); "heaven and earth" (cf. 32:1), "act wickedly" (*hashhet tashhitun*; cf. *shihet*, "baseness" [?], 32:5), and "vexed" (*k-ʿ-s*; cf. 32:16,19,21).[23] But, as noted above, these terms are all found elsewhere in Deuteronomy without reference to the poem.[24] In fact, Moses has twice before "call[ed] heaven and earth to witness" the consequences of disobeying the Teaching (4:26; 30:19), and he uses the phrase "these words" so often with reference to the Decalogue and the Teaching[25] that, for all its nonspecificity, the phrase is practically a Deuteronomic synonym for them and not the poem. Two other features of verses 28–29 are also inconsistent with its referring to the poem: they refer to something that Moses intends to address to Israel's leaders, whereas the poem is addressed to the entire people (v. 30; 32:44); and verse 29, referring to Moses' expectations, seems suited to introduce something he says on his own initiative, not the poem, which is composed by God and taught on His initiative (vv. 16–21).[26] These considerations have given rise to a suggestion that verses 28–29 were originally part of an introduction to the Teaching or to an exhortation to observe the Teaching, and that their counterpart in 32:45–47 originally served as the conclusion to the same. In this view, these two passages have been co-opted to serve here as Deuteronomy's introduction and conclusion to the poem.

If that is the case, the question arises as to where verses 28–29 and 32:45–47 originally stood—or what originally stood between them—since they now frame the poem instead of the Teaching. This question has been answered with reconstructions of the supposed

original text that could be correct but are too speculative to be proven.[27] For present purposes it is sufficient to note that Deuteronomy is not only a creative editorial arrangement of originally disparate materials, but also displays features that imply that these materials may once have appeared in a different order.

The Structure of the Chapter

Ibn Ezra notes that the events recounted in this chapter could not have taken place in the order in which they are related. Invoking the rabbinic principle that "there is no earlier and later in the Torah"—that is, the Torah does not always intend us to assume that events took place in the order in which it presents them—he states that all of Moses' actions involving the Teaching (vv. 9–13 and 24ff.) must have taken place at the same time, and that God had finished appointing Joshua (vv. 14–15 and 23) before He made His statement to Moses (vv. 16–22). This would certainly be a more natural sequence of events,[28] and one wonders why the chapter relates them in so puzzling an order. This is no less a question if parts of the chapter are drawn from separate literary sources, for a compiler, too, could have arranged the material in a more natural sequence.

A. Rofé holds that the narrative originally did follow a more natural sequence, but that the text was accidentally rearranged in the course of its transmission. In his view, God's summons to Moses and Joshua in verses 14–15 was immediately followed by Joshua's appointment and Moses' instructions in verses 23–27; these were in turn followed by verses 16–22 and then verses 28–30. The present confusing order was caused by the accidental transfer of verses 23–27 to their present location between verses 22 and 28. Rofé explains that this could have happened if verses 23–27 constituted a single, full column in a manuscript (this is quite plausible given the size of columns in some Qumran manuscripts). Under that circumstance, one of two things could have happened: (a) a copyist accidentally skipped this column and, after realizing his mistake, inserted it two columns later; (b) this column was the only one on a small sheet of parchment and the sheet became separated from the rest of the scroll (as happens when the threads deteriorate) and was sewn back in the wrong place.[29]

This is a plausible theory, though it does not account for another disturbance, namely the interruption of Moses' instructions about the Teaching by God's appointment of Joshua (even in the proposed original order, verses 14–15 and 23 interrupt verses 9–13 and 24–27). More importantly, it does not account for the chiastic order of subjects in verses 9–27:

    A. The Teaching (vv. 9–13)
      B. Appointment of Joshua (vv. 14–15)
        C. The poem (vv. 16–22)
      B'. Appointment of Joshua (v. 23)
    A'. The Teaching (vv. 24–27)

This pattern suggests that the chapter was more likely formed by design than by accident. The compiler may have structured the chapter chiastically for purely esthetic purposes, but the design has other effects that may also have been intentional. The problematic element in the structure is the unit from the JE source, verses 14–23, which is both disrupted and disruptive. It is disrupted because God's introduction to the poem appears in the middle of His appointment of Joshua. The effect of this order is to imply that Joshua was present

when God told Moses of Israel's future apostasy, and hence bears a special responsibility to resist the people's defiance and rebelliousness as Moses had (and as Joshua subsequently did; see Joshua 24).[30] The unit is disruptive because it interrupts the two paragraphs dealing with the Teaching. The effect of this is twofold: (a) it makes these paragraphs serve as a frame around Joshua's appointment, implying that Joshua must lead the people in accordance with the Teaching, as does Joshua 1:7–8; (b) it relates the message of the poem to the Teaching, reinforcing the point that violation of the covenant (verses 16,20) violates the Teaching since the Teaching is the embodiment of the covenant (see Comment to 31:26).

The Poem and the Teaching as Witnesses

Verse 31:19 characterizes the poem of chapter 32 as a witness to Israel's guilt and God's justice in punishing it. As noted in the Comment to that verse, the idea of a text serving as a witness that a disaster was foretold is known from the prophets Isaiah and Habakkuk.[31] The witness metaphor is a natural one for the first part of the poem in 32:1–25. However, this characterization disregards the second part of the poem, which predicts that God will eventually deliver Israel and punish its enemies (vv. 26–43). Those verses imply that the poem was not composed to serve solely as a prediction and explanation of disaster, as it does in 31:16–21.[32] It was probably composed after a disaster to explain it and offer the hope of deliverance (see Excursus 30). Since 31:16–21 does see it solely as a prediction and explanation of disaster, it was probably adopted for use in Deuteronomy because it explains the predicted disaster in theologically meaningful terms.

Since the characterization of the poem as a witness appears in a passage drawn from the JE source, which is older than Deuteronomy, the use of the witness metaphor to characterize *the Teaching* (v. 26) must have been borrowed by Deuteronomy from the JE passage.[33] However, as noted in the commentary, Deuteronomy does not use the metaphor in the same way. Rather, it uses it as an appropriate way to characterize itself as a witness to, or as evidence of, the covenant.

The Compiler of the Chapter

That the compiler of chapter 31 incorporated conflicting versions of the same events in his narrative suggests that he did not regard them as inconsistent, but rather as descriptions of different moments in an unfolding sequence of events. He seems to have believed that by arranging the variants in the order in which he presented them, he was restoring the original complexity of the events that his sources had reported incompletely.[34] It seems likely that he had explanations in mind to reconcile some of the inconsistencies, but did not feel free either to add these explanations to the text or to omit inconsistent details in order to create a smoother narrative. This implies that in his mind his sources were already fixed and virtually inviolable.[35]

This suggests that the compiler who put these parallel sources together was probably not the author, or authors, of Deuteronomy 1–30.[36] Although those chapters also rely on earlier literary sources, they do not incorporate them verbatim but recast them in Deuteronomic style, add comments, and edit out details that are unacceptable.[37] This difference in

approach could have one of two explanations: the author(s) of Deuteronomy 1–30 lived closer to the time of composition of the earlier sources, when their wording had not yet become fixed; or the author(s) of Deuteronomy 1–30 and the compiler of chapter 31 simply had different attitudes to "classical" texts.

Textual Revisions in the Chapter

Apart from the question of the origin of the different sections of the chapter, it seems that some smaller details were modified during the course of the transmission of the text. Two of the more convincing examples are the following.

Syntactically, the two halves of verse 3 fit together awkwardly[38] and give alternate answers to the question of who will succeed Moses: "The LORD your God is the one Who will cross over before you; and He Himself will wipe out those nations from your path and you shall dispossess them [v. 3a]. Joshua is the one who shall cross before you, as the LORD has spoken [v. 3b]." The answer in verse 3b is the natural one: Joshua will be Moses' successor. The statement in verse 3a is not really an answer to the same question: God is not Moses' successor—He has been behind the events all the time and that will not change. That verse 3b is the intended sequel to verse 2 is confirmed by 3:23–28 where God's refusal to permit Moses to "cross yonder Jordan" is followed by the statement that Joshua will "go across before this people." It is not that verse 3a is irrelevant—certainly the people needed assurance that God would continue to lead them—but had that point been part of the original text, it would probably have been made after verse 3b and in a syntactically smoother manner, such as: "Joshua is the one who shall cross over before you, and I shall be with him just as I was with you." Hence it is likely that verse 3a is an interpolation in the text (in the spirit of 1:30–33) by a writer who sensed the people's need for such assurance. Since verses 4–6 expand on this theme, they may have been interpolated along with verse 3a. If so, the original text probably resumed with the appointment of Joshua in verse 6. If these verses are interpolations, they must have been added to the text relatively early, since they are present in the Septuagint and all other ancient witnesses to the text.[39]

As noted in the Commentary, the two halves of verse 15 may reflect different conceptions of where God appears when he descends to the Tent of Meeting. Verse 15a may locate Him inside the Tent, consistent with the passages that equate the Tent with the sanctuary, and have Him speak in a cloud within the Holy of Holies—that is, the passages from the priestly source. According to verse 15b, God remained at the entrance, as He does in passages describing the Tent as a separate oracular tent—that is, passages from the JE source. As noted in the Comment, the first part of the verse could be translated "The LORD appeared *at* the Tent," although the use of *be-* for "at" is rare. The inconsistency is absent in the Septuagint, where the first half of the verse reads: "The LORD came down in a cloud and stopped at the entrance of the Tent of Meeting." If this reading is the original one, and the text represented God only as remaining in the cloud outside the Tent, the MT reading "in the Tent" is secondary, and may be due to an attempt to harmonize the verse with the priestly conception of the Tent, as noted by A. Rofé.[40] However, it is also possible that the Masoretic reading is original—reflecting a conflation of priestly and JE conceptions—and that the Septuagint reading is a secondary attempt to harmonize the text in accordance with Exodus 33:9 and Numbers 12:5.

EXCURSUS 30
The Poem Ha'azinu   (32:1–43)

The poem *Ha'azinu* (*Shirat Ha'azinu*) is written in the style characteristic of biblical poetry. Most of its lines contain at least two colons consisting of an equal or nearly equal number of stress units, usually three, such as the following:

> *ya'aróf ka-matár likḥí*   *tizzál ka-tál 'imratí*   (v. 2)
>
> *zekhór yemót 'olám*   *bínu shenót dor-va-dór*   (v. 7)

The most notable feature of biblical poetry is parallelism, whereby the colons in each line are related to each other in one of several ways. In most instances they express the same or similar ideas, with the second colon sometimes intensifying the first; in some cases the second colon contains a contrast with the first; in others, it complements the first. These three types are usually termed, respectively, "synonymous," "antithetic," and "synthetic" parallelism.[1] For example:

Synonymous
Give ear O heavens, let me speak
Let the earth hear the words I utter. (v. 1)

Antithetic
Our own hand has prevailed
None of this was wrought by the LORD. (v. 27b)

Synthetic
He fixed the boundaries of peoples
In relation to Israel's numbers. (v. 8)

The first two types of parallelism create a sort of "thought rhyme," in place of the sound rhyme that is customary in Western poetry and relatively infrequent in biblical poetry.

Biblical poetry shares these features with other ancient Near Eastern poetry, especially Canaanite. Just as modern poets have rhyming dictionaries to assist them in composing, ancient poets drew on a repertoire (not necessarily a written one) of traditional parallel terms. Many of these occur in parallel and often in the same order elsewhere in biblical poetry as well as Canaanite. Examples in *Ha'azinu* include the Hebrew words translated as "Give ear" and "hear" (v. 1),[2] "rain," "dew," "showers," and "droplets" (v. 2),[3] "create" and "make endure" (rather, "bring into existence," v. 6),[4] "of old" and "ages past" (v. 7),[5] "curd" and "milk" (v. 14),[6] "foe(s)," "enemy," and "those who reject" (vv. 27,41),[7] "thousand" and "ten thousand" (v. 30),[8] "vine" and "vineyards" (v. 32);[9] and "asp" and "viper" (v. 33).[10]

Other poetic features in *Ha'azinu* are assonance and similarly formulated phrases and themes. Examples of assonance are the words *kanekha* and *yekhonenekha* and other words ending with the suffix *-ekha* in verse 6, *havleihem–naval* and *kine'uni–'akni'em* in verse 21, *kadḥa–va-ttikad* in verse 22, and *shadmot–Sedom* in v. 32. The negative particles *lo'* and *'ein* abound in the poem,[11] supplemented by the privative terms "void," "gone," and "not left"

(vv. 28,36). Several phrases are coined consisting of the negative *lo'* attached to nouns and adjectives: "not-His-sons," "witless," "no-gods," "no-folk" (vv. 5,6,17,21). Individual words and derivatives of the same root recur, such as the divine appellation *tsur*, "Rock" (vv. 4,15,18,30,31,37) and the root *n-b-l* (vv. 6,15). Many of these features would have been particularly effective when the poem was recited orally. That it was composed for oral delivery is indicated by its frequent direct addresses to Israel (vv. 6,7,18,38,39).

Like many poems, *Ha'azinu* contains a goodly number of rare words and forms.[12] In some cases this may be due to the fact that the poem is relatively ancient and uses vocabulary that later fell out of use. Rabbinic Hebrew and cognate languages help us approximate the meaning of some of them.

As noted in the Commentary, *Ha'azinu* is usually laid out in explicitly poetic form. In some copies from Qumran, colons are separated from each other.[13] According to the halakhah,[14] in a Torah scroll the poem must be written with two colons per line, separated by a blank space; this does not apply to the text printed in books. In the present Hebrew edition this colon system is followed in principle, with an exception: there is an odd number of colons in verse 14, and from that point on the halakhic layout detaches the parallel colons from each other, placing them on separate lines through verse 39, where there is again an odd number of colons. In this edition the odd colons are printed on separate lines so that the other pairs can be kept together.

Genre

Ha'azinu is a psalm and, like many biblical psalms, it displays features of several different genres. The introductory summons is paralleled in didactic psalms, prophecies, and proverbs;[15] similar summonses to heaven and earth and other elements of nature appear in prophetic indictment speeches.[16] Its didactic retrospective on Israel's history has counterparts in hymnic historical psalms and in prophecies.[17] The challenge to let Israel's false gods save it (vv. 37–39) and the ringing declaration of the Lord's exclusive divinity are paralleled in prophetic speeches.[18] The poem's descriptions of the slaughter of the enemy are paralleled in prophecies of calamity, particularly against Israel's enemies.[19] Its concluding invitation to praise the Lord for delivering His people has parallels in hymns.[20] Various features of wisdom literature appear throughout the poem, such as its characterization as a "teaching" (v. 2), its attribution of sin to foolishness (vv. 6,28–29), its appeal to elders (v. 7), and terminology characteristic of wisdom literature, such as *tahappukhot*, "treachery, turnabout" (v. 20).[21]

In recent years, under the impact of studies of Near Eastern treaties and biblical covenants, scholars have proposed that the poem belongs to a genre that they call the "covenant lawsuit."[22] This genre is supposedly based on the literary form that a suzerain would use in appealing to the gods to condemn a vassal for violating the terms of a treaty that they had witnessed; the suzerain would do so prior to declaring war on the vassal to punish that violation. In this view, key elements in the genre are the enumeration of the suzerain's past benefactions, the statement of the vassal's ingratitude and betrayal, and the appeal to the gods and other entities that had witnessed the treaty and would punish violators. Hence it is proposed that heaven and earth are invoked here to testify that Israel did indeed accept covenant obligations to God, which it violated, or to judge and punish Israel. One or both of these roles do seem to be reflected in 4:26 (see Comment there), 30:19, and 31:28. However, *Ha'azinu* never mentions the covenant. It speaks of the relation-

ship and moral responsibilities created by God's treatment of Israel in terms of the relationship between father and child, not suzerain and vassal,[23] and it portrays Israel as a perfidious child rather than a rebellious vassal.[24] Heaven and earth offer no testimony in the poem about the existence of the covenant or its violation (according to 31:19–21 these are attested by the poem itself). Nor are they appealed to as judges and punishers. That is God's role, and His agents are human enemies and natural disasters, not heaven and earth. For whatever reason, heaven and earth are summoned only to hear. Hence the argument that the poem is modeled on a "lawsuit" for breach of covenant is unconvincing.[25]

Literary Affinities

Ha'azinu has affinities with other parts of Deuteronomy, particularly with chapters 4 and 29–31.[26] There are a few linguistic and phraseological affinities, such as the terms and phrases "abominations" (for idols), "gods they had never known," "act corruptly," and the verb "incense/vex."[27] There are thematic and conceptual affinities with other parts of the book, such as the theme that satiety leads to apostasy (31:20; 6:10–13; 8:12–20; 11:16), a theme also known outside of Deuteronomy. The overall message of the first part of the poem—that God's past benefactions to Israel morally oblige Israel to serve Him loyally—is the central theme of Deuteronomy's view of history.

These shared elements do not necessarily indicate that the poem is of one piece with the rest of the book, for there are significant differences in the way that some of the common themes and concepts are used.[28] Although the appeal to heaven and earth in 32:1 is anticipated in 4:26 and elsewhere, here they are not summoned to testify or punish. The idea of God's parceling out nations (vv. 8–9) has counterparts in 4:19 and 29:25, but these differ significantly from verses 8–9 where, according to what is probably the original reading, God allots the other nations to different divine beings. Elsewhere the allocation is in the opposite direction: according to 29:25 He allotted other "gods" (defined as mere statues in 29:16) to the nations, and in 4:19 He allotted the heavenly bodies to other nations. The latter formulations seem to be ways of revising the concepts of Deuteronomy 32 to eliminate any suggestion that the gods of the nations are supernatural beings who own or govern the other peoples, as *Ha'azinu* implies, and to show them as nothing but man-made statues and natural objects created by the Lord.

There are other significant differences between the poem and the rest of Deuteronomy. As noted above, the theme of covenant, so central to Deuteronomy, is not mentioned at all in the poem, even though 31:20 says that the poem will testify to Israel's guilt in violating the covenant. The frequent Deuteronomic references to the Exodus and the patriarchs and the fact that God promised the land have no echo here. The conception of the punishment is also different; in *Ha'azinu* it is limited to war and natural disasters in the land, whereas elsewhere in Deuteronomy these are followed by exile.

Ha'azinu must be an independent composition, older than the rest of Deuteronomy, since it is mentioned in 31:19, a passage drawn from the older JE source (see Excursus 29). Since the poem not only attests to Israel's guilt, as 31:19 says it will, but also predicts that God will rescue Israel and punish its enemies (vv. 26–43), it could not have been composed to serve solely as a prediction and explanation of disaster, as 31:16–21 says. Its concluding description of Israel's deliverance implies that it was probably composed after a particular disaster to offer an explanation and hope of deliverance. Quite likely, it was adopted by Deuteronomy because it explained the disaster in theologically meaningful terms.

That the poem is older than Deuteronomy is also suggested by its affinities with several other books of the Bible. Among several parallels in the Book of Hosea,[29] note particularly Hosea 13:4–10:

> Only I the LORD have been your God
> Ever since the land of Egypt;
> You have never known a [true] God but Me,
> You have never had a helper other than Me. [Cf. Deut. 32:12]
> I looked after you in the desert,
> In a thirsty land. [Cf. Deut. 32:10]
> When they grazed, they were sated;
> When they got sated, they grew haughty;
> And so they forgot Me. [Cf. Deut. 32:13–15]
> . . . .
> You are undone [or: Your corruption], O Israel! [Cf. Deut. 32:5]
> You had no help but Me. [Cf. Deut. 32:12]
> Where now is your king?
> Let him save you! [Cf. Deut. 32:37–39]

Compare also Deuteronomy 32:39 with Hosea 5:14: "I, I will attack and stride away, carrying the prey that no one can rescue" [cf. Isaiah 43:13, "Ever since day was, I am He; None can deliver from My hand"]; Deuteronomy 32:18 with Hosea 8:14: "Israel has ignored [forgotten] his Maker"; and Deuteronomy 32:10 with Hosea 9:10: "I found Israel [as pleasing] as grapes in the wilderness."

There are also affinities with other books. Isaiah 1:2–4, for example, has been taken as a summary of Deuteronomy 32:1–18:

> Hear, O heavens, and give ear, O earth, [Cf. Deut. 32:1]
> For the LORD has spoken:
> I reared children and brought them up—
> And they have rebelled against Me! [Cf. Deut. 32:5–18]
> . . . .
> Ah, sinful nation!
> People laden with iniquity!
> Brood of evildoers! [*zeraʿ mereʿim*]
> Depraved [corrupt] children! [*banim mashḥitim*] [Cf. Deut. 32:5]
> They have forsaken the LORD,
> Spurned the Holy one of Israel,
> Turned their backs [on Him].

Other parallels in the prophets include Jeremiah 2:28, "And where are those gods you made for yourself? Let them rise up and save you, if they can" (cf. Deut. 32:38), and Isaiah 58:14, "I will set you atop the highlands, and let you enjoy the heritage of your father Jacob" (cf. Deut. 32:13). Note also the parallels in Psalm 78:58, "They vexed Him with their high places, they incensed Him with their idols. God heard it and was enraged; He utterly rejected Israel" (cf. Deut. 32:16,19) and Psalm 106:37, "They sacrificed their own sons and daughters to demons" (cf. Deut. 32:17).

These parallels probably indicate that *Haʾazinu* was written earlier than the prophets and Psalms 78 and 106, for it seems more likely that several prophets and psalmists were influenced by one classic poem (widely known by heart, according to 31:19,21) than that the poem borrowed from several prophets who lived centuries apart and whose prophecies may not have been well known beyond their own disciples.[30] The fact that *Haʾazinu* shows no trace of the distinctive prophetic ideas, such as repentance (see Comment to

4:30) and the idea that the entire nation is punished for socio-moral sins as well as idolatry,[31] also argues against its having borrowed from the prophets.

Date

A relatively early date for the poem is suggested by its contents and language as well. Commentators have long sought to date the poem by identifying the enemy and the events it describes. For traditional commentators who ascribe the poem to the time of Moses, dating the events was an exegetical exercise and a religious one as well, since the deliverance promised in verses 34ff. might refer to the commentator's own time.[32] For critical commentators, the date of the events might provide a clue to the date and historical context in which the poem was composed.

From a critical point of view the poem seems post-Mosaic since it refers to the settlement in the promised land and Israel's apostasy as past events and is addressed to the guilty generation. But the apostasy occurred recently enough that there are still fathers and elders to consult for religious truth (v. 7). Although the description of Israel's punishment is in the future tense, it is so circumstantial as to suggest that it, too, was written after the disaster had begun, as does the fact that punishment of the enemy is said to be imminent (v. 35). Unfortunately, the poem offers few firm clues for dating the events precisely. The enemy has been identified variously as the Canaanites (twelfth or eleventh century B.C.E.) the Philistines (eleventh century), the Arameans (tenth and ninth centuries), the Assyrians (eighth century), the Babylonians (seventh and sixth centuries), the Samaritans (fifth century), or even later enemies. Most of these identifications seem unlikely. The poem makes no reference to the deportation of the northern tribes by Assyria or of Judah by the Babylonians, and it is unlikely that those highly organized empires, or even the Arameans, would be described as a "no-folk," a term more suited to a nomadic people.

Some details suggest that the poem may describe an event in the period of the Chieftains (the "Judges"). Verse 17 attributes the calamity to the worship of "new" gods, as does Judges 5:8, "When they chose new gods, then was war in the gates" (the second clause is admittedly difficult to translate). God's mocking challenge to Israel to let its false gods save it (vv. 37–39) is paralleled by His challenge in Judges 10:14. The difficult phrase *ʿatsur ve-ʿazuv* (v. 36), although used elsewhere in connection with the monarchic period, seems to be equivalent to *shofet* and *moshiaʿ*, the terms used of the leaders of the period of the Chieftains. Canaanites and Philistines were a threat in that period, but the description of the enemy as a "no-folk" might better suit such nomadic raiders of that period as the Midianites, Amalekites, and Kedemites (Judg. 6:2–6). This would suggest that the poem may have been written in the period of the Chieftains (twelfth–eleventh centuries B.C.E.), during a time of attacks by one or more such enemies.

The language of the poem is also compatible with an early date, although not necessarily as early as the period of the Chieftains.[33] Several features characteristic of early biblical poetry (ca. thirteenth–tenth centuries B.C.E.) cluster together in the poem: the use of the imperfect (prefix) tense without *vav*-consecutive to narrate past events (e.g., *yimtsaʾehu*, "He found him," v. 10), the third-person masculine plural suffix *-mo* (as in *ʿaleimo*, v. 23, and *tsareimo*, v. 27), the preservation of the original root-consonant *yod* before the suffix on a verb (*ḥasayu*, from *ḥ-s-y*, v. 37), the old third-person feminine verb ending *-at* (*ʾazlat*, v. 36), and the third-person masculine singular pronominal suffix *-enhu* (*yesovevenhu, yitsrenhu*, v. 10).

Evaluating this evidence is complicated by the fact that the poem also contains the later counterparts of these features, those that appear in the poetry of the eighth and following centuries: *vav*-consecutive verbs and perfect (suffix) tense verbs to narrate past events (e.g., *va-yishman* and *shamanta* in v. 15), the third-person masculine plural suffix *-am* (as in *tsuram*, v. 30; it appears more frequently than *-mo*), elision of the original root-consonant *yod* before the suffix on a verb (as in *yishtu*, v. 38), and the feminine verbal ending *-ah* (as in *kadhah*, v. 22).

It is not known whether these alternative features also existed in the earlier period—in which case they are compatible with an early date for the poem—or whether they first developed later and, if so, when. If they are later developments, they may indicate that the poem was written or revised during a period of transition from the older forms to the later ones (perhaps between the tenth and eighth centuries), or that the poem was written later and consciously, but inconsistently, imitated the older style. Whatever may be the case, it is probably significant that *Ha'azinu* is one of the handful of biblical poems that exhibits the greatest concentration of such ancient features. That it is older than Deuteronomy 1–31 and 34, perhaps considerably older, is likely.

The Use of the Poem in Second-Temple Times

According to Josephus, copies of *Ha'azinu* and other biblical poems were kept in the Temple.[34] Rabbinic sources report that the Levites read parts of the poem in the Temple while the Additional Offering (*musaf*) was being made on Sabbaths. They completed it over a six-week cycle and then began again.[35] Conceivably, the copy mentioned by Josephus was used for this purpose.[36] It is interesting to note in this connection that one of the Qumran manuscripts (4QDeut^q) apparently contained only the poem and was not part of a longer Torah scroll.[37] Perhaps it was used for reading the poem on some similar occasion, or for teaching the poem by heart, as chapter 31 commands.

Nowadays, *Ha'azinu* or the preceding Torah portion, *Va-yelekh*, is read on the Sabbath between Rosh Hashanah and Yom Kippur. In the Sephardic liturgy, it is read on the Ninth of Av (the anniversary of the destruction of both Temples) during the morning service, in place of the Song at the Sea (Exodus 15).[38]

EXCURSUS 31

Text and Theology in Deuteronomy 32:8 and 43

The most significant variant readings found in the Qumran scrolls and Septuagint of Deuteronomy are in verses 8 and 43 of *Ha'azinu*.[1] To facilitate comparison of readings in the following discussion of these variants, we shall translate the key terms in question more literally than they are meant, as follows:

'elohim: "divinities"

benei 'elohim, *benei 'elim* ("divine beings" in the translation), and Greek *huioi theoi*: "sons of the divine"

Greek *angeloi theoi*: "angels of the divine"

benei yisra'el ("Israel[ites]" in the translation): "sons of Israel"

Deuteronomy 32:8

As noted in the Commentary, the variant reading of verse 8, "equal to the number of sons of the divine" (*le-mispar benei 'elohim*),[2] obviates several problems that are raised by the Masoretic reading "equal to the number of the sons of Israel" (*le-mispar benei yisra'el*). For this reason, the variant is most likely the original reading.

According to Job 1–2, the "sons of the divine" are a group that periodically present themselves before God to report on their assignments. One of them, called "the Adversary" (the *satan*), is a sort of roving investigator and prosecutor who reports to God what he has seen on earth. In Hebrew these beings are called *benei 'elohim*, "sons of *'elohim*," meaning "members of the *'elohim* class." The equivalent term in other Canaanite languages is *benei 'el(im)*, and according to Ugaritic mythology there are seventy such beings.[3] Although *'elohim* and *'el(im)* literally mean "god/gods," they also refer to various types of supernatural beings and heavenly bodies that form God's retinue, as noted in the Comment to 3:24. These include spirits, angels (*mal'akhim*, lit., "emissaries"), the sun, moon, stars, and "the host of heaven."[4]

In some passages one encounters traces of a belief that these beings and bodies govern the earth for God. Genesis 1:16 and 18 say that God created the sun and moon "to rule" (*le-memshelet, li-mshol*) over the day and night. The existence of such beliefs is also reflected in passages that criticize or combat them. For example, in Psalm 82 God rebukes the "divinities" (*'elohim*) for judging unjustly and the psalmist calls upon God to judge *all* nations personally and take them *all* as His allotment.

The idea stated in the variant reading, that the number of nations equals the number of "sons of the divine," suggests that each of these beings is paired with a nation. Jewish sources of the Hellenistic and talmudic periods elaborate on this picture, indicating that God appointed divine beings to govern the nations on His behalf. Ben Sira paraphrases our passage as follows:

> In dividing up the peoples of all the world,
> Over every people He appointed a ruler,
> But the LORD's portion is Israel.[5]

The "rulers" are Ben Sira's equivalent of Deuteronomy's "sons of the divine." The book of Daniel, from the same period as Ben Sira, refers to them as "governors" or "princes" (Heb. *sarim*) and describes them as angelic patrons and champions of various nations.[6] It mentions those of Persia and Greece and—here it disagrees with Deuteronomy and Ben Sira—one for Israel, too. The same picture is also known in a variety of forms in Jewish Hellenistic and rabbinic literature, where the number of these beings is seventy.[7]

The sources indicate that the "sons of the divine" were angel-like beings under God's authority, a belief compatible with the monotheistic viewpoint expressed in Deuteronomy 32:17,21, and 39. The designation *benei 'elohim*, "sons of the divine," may even have been chosen to emphasize their inferiority. Nevertheless, the concept seemed problematic. At the very least, it indicates that God shared the world with supernatural beings associated with individual nations and seems to imply that He intended the other nations to worship those beings (see Excursus 7). The scribes responsible for transmitting the text of the Bible were probably concerned that readers not envisage them as having the power and authority that would encourage Jews to worship them along with God, an act completely incompatible with Deuteronomy's opposition to angelology (see Comments to 4:19,37 and

13:6). They may also have considered the concept too reminiscent of polytheistic pantheons, such as the Canaanite "assembly of *benei 'el*"[8] (it may, in fact, have evolved from such a concept). For one or both of these reasons, they eliminated the reading *benei 'elohim*, "sons of *'elohim*," and replaced it with *benei yisra'el*, "sons of Israel." This reading preserved the numerical aspect of the verse, for according to Deuteronomy 10:22 there were seventy Israelites at a key point in Israel's history, equal to the number of divine beings and nations. Hence the text still meant that God divided the human race into seventy nations.

The original reading of verse 8 survived in the Septuagint, which was made for Greek-speaking Jews and preserved by Greek-speaking Christians (it is still used today in the Greek Orthodox Church). Traces of it survived among Jews as well. Targum Pseudo-Jonathan actually reflects both readings, as indicated by italics here:

> When the Most High allotted the world to the peoples that came forth from the sons of Noah, when he gave separate scripts and languages to humanity in the Generation of the Division, at that time He cast lots with *the seventy angels, princes of the nations*, with whom He revealed himself [when going down] to see the city [where the Tower of Babel was being built], and at the same time He established the boundaries of the nations equal to the number of *seventy Israelite persons* who went down to Egypt.

What is more, the version of this story related in the eighth-century-C.E. work Pirkei de-Rabbi Eliezer tells of God casting lots with the seventy angels and appointing them over the seventy nations, and says nothing about the number seventy matching the number of Israelites, even though it alludes to our verse. Apparently this is an old tradition that goes back to a text of Deuteronomy that stated that the number of nations was based on the number of "sons of the divine."[9] As late as the tenth century C.E. Saadia Gaon felt compelled to rebut the view that the text implies that God shared the world with other supernatural beings.[10]

The issues raised in verse 8 are also involved in 4:19 which implies that God took Israel for Himself and allotted the heavenly bodies to other peoples to worship. Allotting the heavenly bodies to other peoples is the converse of the idea in 32:8 that God allotted the nations to the "sons of the divine."[11] As noted in the Comment to 4:19 and in Excursus 30, the statement that God allotted the sun, moon, and stars to other nations, instead of allotting the nations to the divine beings, seems to be a way of revising 32:8 (or the tradition underlying it) so as to eliminate any suggestion that the gods of the nations are supernatural beings who own or govern the other peoples. However, as noted in Excursus 7, even the formulation of 4:19, implying that worship of the heavenly bodies by other nations was ordained by God, struck many as unlikely, and according to a tradition in rabbinic literature, the original Septuagint revised the text of that verse to read that the Lord allotted the heavenly bodies to other peoples "*to give light* to them," in other words to give light, but not to rule.

The idea that God distributed the nations among the angels is unique to the Bible. Elsewhere we hear of the major gods dividing the regions of the universe among themselves by lot,[12] or of a chief deity distributing cities, lands, and regions to other gods.[13] These myths are concerned with the allotment of residences and cult centers to the gods, not with relationship of the gods to the people of these places. In the Bible the motif serves to express God's relationship to humanity and his election of Israel.

Deuteronomy 32:43

It is likely that divine beings were also eliminated from the text of verse 43. As noted in the Commentary, three different versions of this verse are known—the Masoretic text, the Qumran text, and the Septuagint—and it is possible that none of them reflects the original version exactly. The Masoretic text is almost certainly incomplete since the first and fourth colons, unlike any others in the poem, lack parallel colons. These are supplied in the Qumran manuscript and the Septuagint, which have, respectively, three and four pairs of colons, or bicolons. Here are the three texts, with the bicolons designated by letters and their component colons by numbers:

	Masoretic Text	*4QDeut^q*	*Septuagint*
a1.	O nations, rejoice His people	O heavens, rejoice with Him	O heavens, rejoice with Him
a2.		Bow to Him, all divinities	Bow to Him, all sons of the divine.
a3.			O nations, rejoice with His people
a4.			And let all angels of the divine strengthen themselves in Him.
b1.	For He'll avenge the blood of His servants,	For He'll avenge the blood of His sons,	For He'll avenge the blood of His sons,
b2.			Be vengeful
	And wreak vengeance	And wreak vengeance	And wreak vengeance and recompense justice
	on His foes,	on His foes,	on His foes,
c1.		Requite those who reject Him,	Requite those who reject Him,
c2.	And will	And will	And the Lord will
	cleanse His people's land.	cleanse His people's land.	cleanse His people's land.

In the Qumran and Septuagint texts, every colon has a parallel: a1 is parallel to a2 (and, in the Septuagint, a3 // a4), and the colons in b and c are chiastically parallel (b1 // c2 and b2 // c1). Since the rest of the poem consists almost entirely of parallelistic bicolons, the original text of the verse probably had a structure like this.

The most notable colon in these texts is a2, "Bow to Him, all divinities" (*'elohim*; the Septuagint reflects a virtually synonymous reading "sons of the divine [*benei 'elohim*]"). It is identical to Psalm 97:7b and similar to Psalm 29:1, "Ascribe to the LORD, O sons of the divine [*benei 'elim*] . . . glory and strength . . . bow down to the LORD." This colon was probably part of the original text, like the reading "sons of the divine" in verse 8, and, like it, eliminated from the Masoretic text to prevent an angelological or polytheistic interpretation.[14]

Most of the other differences between the three texts are probably due to the fact that they derived from alternative versions of the original, in which the same ideas were expressed in slightly different ways. It was common for slightly different versions of a text to develop as it was transmitted; there are, for example, similar differences between 2 Samuel 22 and Psalm 18, which are alternative versions of the same poem. In the present case, in colon a1 the alternatives were "heavens" and "nations,"[15] and in b1 "sons" or "servants.[16] The Septuagint's colons a3–a4 are to be explained the same way; they are simply a variant of a1–a2.[17] They are probably based on a Hebrew text that originally read "O nations, rejoice with Him, / Let all sons of the divine [*benei 'elohim*] exult," but had

become corrupted to "O nations, rejoice with His people, / Let all sons of the divine strengthen themselves in Him." "With Him" became "with His people" by dittography: *ʿ-m-v*, "with Him," was miswritten as *ʿ-m ʿ-m-v*, "with His people."[18] "Exult" probably became the awkward "strengthen themselves in Him" by a transposition of letters: the original reading was probably *v-y-ʿ-l-v-z-v*, "let them exult," which was miscopied, or misread, as *v-y-ʿ-z-v l-v*, "let them be strong to Him."[19] "Angels of the divine" in a4 is a variant *translation* of a2's *benei ʾelohim*, "sons of the divine"; the Septuagint commonly uses either "angels of the divine" or "sons of the divine" for the Hebrew phrase (see note 2). This translation indicates that a3–a4 were translated into Greek by someone other than the person who translated a1–a2; it is unlikely that a single translator would have rendered the same phrase differently in the same context. All this implies that a scribe/editor of the Septuagint found an extra copy of *Haʾazinu* in Greek that contained a variant version of a1–a2, based—without his realizing it—on a corrupt Hebrew text, and added it to the text as a3–a4.[20]

The absence of colon c1 can be explained by haplography—the scribe's eye skipping from the *vav* at the beginning of c1 to that at the beginning of c2.

Textual changes of the type found in verses 8 and 43 were part of a process that is reflected elsewhere in the Bible. Psalm 29:1, "Ascribe to the Lord, O sons of the divine" (*benei ʾelim*)," is revised in Psalm 96:7 (and in 1 Chron. 16:28) to read "Ascribe to the Lord, O families of peoples."[21] The revision of 4:19 in the Septuagint, according to rabbinic tradition, was also motivated by concern over polytheistic misinterpretation of the text. Personal names in the Bible were sometimes revised for the same reason. According to the Book of Chronicles, several individuals, including members of the family and associates of David and Solomon, had names containing the element Baal, such as Eshbaal and Beeliada (Baaliada).[22] In the Masoretic text of the Book of Samuel, however, all these names were revised, becoming Ish-bosheth, Eliada, and the like.[23] Apparently the word *baʿal*, literally "lord," was once considerered a legitimate epithet of God, like its synonym *ʾadon*, and was used as such in personal names.[24] Later, however, when the cult of the Canaanite storm god, who was also called *baʿal*, became a serious threat in Israel, the epithet was shunned, and manuscripts mentioning such names were revised to avoid giving the impression that Saul and David had honored the Canaanite god. The Masoretic text of the Book of Samuel derives from manuscripts that underwent such revision, whereas that of Chronicles does not.

Such revisions were not made systematically throughout the Bible. There were varying attitudes toward such passages. References to the *ʾelohim* (divinities) in God's retinue were not inherently problematic since *ʾelohim*, in addition to its use for "God" and for pagan gods, sometimes meant angel, as noted above. Since the term had this innocuous meaning, it was allowed to remain in many biblical passages, such as Psalm 97:7, cited above, and 4QDeutq.[25] The same is true of the synonymous *ʾel*, *benei ʾelim*, and *benei ʾelohim*, as in Psalm 29:1; Job 1–2; and 4QDeutj, cited above, as well as Deuteronomy 3:24, "You whose powerful deeds no divinity [*ʾel*] in heaven or on earth can equal"; Exodus 15:11, "Who is like You, O Lord, among the divinities" (*ʾelim*); and the strange story about the *benei ʾelohim* in Genesis 6:1–4.[26] It is not always clear why a particular reference was preserved or revised. The case of Deuteronomy 32:8 is understandable, since the original reading seems to imply that God shares His authority with other divine beings. But it is not clear why the account of marriage between *benei ʾelohim* and humans in Genesis 6:1–4 was allowed to remain. Nor is it clear why Deuteronomy 32:43 was revised when an identical phrase was preserved in Psalm 97:7. The inconsistent treatment of these references, and of names with the element *baʿal*, seems to imply that as individual books of the Bible were copied and

recopied, the decision in each case depended on the judgment of individual scribes, or scribal schools, as to whether or not the reference might give rise to theological misunderstanding, and that such judgments varied depending on conditions in different times and places and the scribes' personal, perhaps subjective evaluation of those conditions.

By rabbinic times, the text of the Bible was fixed and no longer subject to revision. Remaining passages that might be misunderstood were handled by interpretation instead of revision. For example, the *benei 'elohim* of Genesis 6:2 were interpreted as sons of officials or judges, and the *benei 'elim* in Exodus 15:11 were explained as "the mighty," "those who minister to God in heaven," and in other ways.[27] The rabbis were probably unaware that the textual revisions discussed here had taken place. But they did believe that something similar had happened in other passages. There is a rabbinic tradition that several readings in the Masoretic text are the result of small corrections by the scribes (*tikkunei soferim*) to alter expressions that might seem disrespectful toward God. For example, they stated that "Abraham remained standing before the LORD" (Gen. 18:22) is a revision of "the LORD remained standing before Abraham," which seemed to put God in a subservient position, and that "[Eli's] sons scorned themselves" (*la-hem*, 1 Sam. 3:13) is a euphemistic correction of "scorned God" (*'elohim*, a reading reflected in the Septuagint).[28] The assumption underlying this tradition—that the sanctity of the biblical text was not so inviolable as to risk disrespect for God—is very similar to the belief that must have motivated earlier scribes who made the revisions discussed here: the sanctity of the text is not so inviolable as to risk misleading people in ways that might compromise monotheism.

EXCURSUS 32

The Sources of 32:48–52

Deuteronomy 32:48–52 is thoroughly inconsistent with the rest of Deuteronomy. As noted in the Commentary, it follows Numbers 27:12–14, which is from the priestly source of the Torah, almost verbatim. Accordingly, in both language and content it agrees with the priestly source. It gives Mount Hor as the place of Aaron's death, in agreement with Numbers 20:20–28 and 33:38, but not Deuteronomy 10:6, and it attributes the punishment of Moses and Aaron to the incident at Meribah, as does Numbers 20:12–13, whereas Deuteronomy connects Moses' punishment to the incident of the scouts (1:37) and Aaron's to that of the golden calf (9:20; 10:6).

Linguistic and idiomatic affinities[1] with the priestly source include "on that very day" (v. 48) instead of "at that time";[2] *'ani* rather than *'anokhi* for "I";[3] "children of Israel" (vv. 49,51,52) instead of "all Israel" or "this people";[4] *'ahuzzah* (v. 49) rather than *nahalah* or *yerushah* for the promised land as a "possession";[5] "be gathered to one's kin" (v. 50);[6] *ma'al*, "break faith," instead of *himrah*, "rebel";[7] and *be-tokh* (v. 51) rather than *bekerev* for "among."[8] Based on this evidence, critical scholarship presumes that most, if not all, of this paragraph was composed, on the model of Numbers 27, by a post-Deuteronomic editor in order to reestablish the link between Numbers 27 and the death of Moses that was broken by Numbers 28–36 and Deuteronomy 1:1–32:47.[9]

EXCURSUS 33

The Blessing of Moses (Deuteronomy 33)

Poetic Style

Although Deuteronomy 33 is not explicitly called a poem, nor laid out in Torah scrolls in a poetic format like chapter 32, it too is written in the style characteristic of biblical poetry. Most lines contain at least two parallel colons consisting of an equal or nearly equal number of stress-units, usually three, and many of the parallel terms are drawn from a repertoire of traditional pairs.[1] It features rhyme in verses 8 and 10b (the sounds *-kha* and *-ah*) and alliteration (*mems* in v. 6 and *alephs* in v. 9). Wordplay is prominent in several of the blessings, and the coda is framed by similar and similar-sounding language in its opening and closing verses, as noted in the Commentary. Animal imagery is used metaphorically to characterize Joseph, Gad, and Dan.

Like *Ha'azinu*, the blessing contains several unique and rare words.[2] Here, too, their presence may be due to the fact that the poem is relatively ancient and uses vocabulary that later fell out of use. It is also possible that the poem uses words or forms from regional variations of Hebrew spoken by the individual tribes. Some unique words are probably due to textual error, such as *tavo'tah* (v. 14) and perhaps *sefunei* (v. 19).[3]

Genre and Literary Affinities

Verse 1 characterizes the poem as a "blessing" of the Israelites. Like Jacob's final words to his sons in Genesis 49:1–27, which are also called "blessings" (Gen. 49:28), it combines features of several genres: blessings of various types,[4] the father's final blessing or testament,[5] the leader's farewell address,[6] the tribal aphorism,[7] and the hymn.[8] The blessings vary in length and are formulated in a variety of styles: petitions or exhortations addressed to God (vv. 6–7,8a,11,16b,24b) or to the tribe (vv. 18,23b,25), a blessing of God for His benefactions to the tribe (v. 20a), and descriptions of the tribes or their territories (vv. 8a,10,12,13–16a,17,19,20b,22,23a,26–29).

The closest analogue to these blessings is the last words of Jacob in Genesis 49. A few verses, particularly verses 13b, 16b, and perhaps 15, are almost verbatim parallels to Genesis 49:25–26 in the blessing of Joseph (see also Isaac's blessings in Gen. 27:28,39). Verse 22 describes Dan as "a lion's whelp," the same simile that Genesis 49:9 uses of Judah. On the whole, however, Deuteronomy 33 has a character of its own. Its exordium and coda, unparalleled in Genesis, refer to all of Israel and unite the individual blessings into a whole. Each blessing except the first is introduced by a heading that identifies the tribe to which it refers. Its blessings are uniformly positive (with the possible partial exception of v. 6b), whereas some of those in Genesis 49 are actually curses or censorious. Most of its blessings refer to the tribe's religious activities or God's role in the blessing, whereas only one blessing in Genesis 49 mentions the latter.

The blessings bear a more general similarity to the Song of Deborah, which likewise

contains a description of God's approach from the southland to assist Israel and which lists ten of the tribes and characterizes them (Judg. 5:4–5,14–18). There, however, the content of the sayings is limited to the tribes' conduct during the rebellion of Deborah and Barak against the Canaanites. Six of the tribes are praised for taking part in the battle and four are criticized for their absence.[9] None of the comments is similar to the blessings in Deuteronomy 33.

Some of the imagery and language of the blessings is paralleled in Balaam's blessings of Israel: Here Joseph has "horns like the horns of a wild ox" (v. 17), there "God . . . is like the horns of the wild ox" for Israel (Num. 23:22; 24:8); here Gad is "poised like a lion, to tear off [*taraf*] arm and scalp" (v. 20), there Israel is "a people that rises like a lion . . . [it] rests not until is has feasted on prey" (*teref*, lit. what is torn) (23:24; cf. v. 9); here Moses calls Issachar to "Rejoice . . . in your tents" (v. 18), and there Balaam exclaims "How fair are your tents, O Jacob, your dwellings, O Israel!" (Num. 24:5).

The exordium and the coda have many affinities with psalms and other biblical poems. Close parallels to verse 2 are cited in the Commentary. Parallels to the coda are especially numerous. Israel's dwelling "untroubled, in a land of grain and wine, under heavens dripping with dew" (v. 28) is close to Balaam's declaration that Israel is "a nation that dwells untroubled" and Isaac's blessing of Jacob, "May God give you of the dew of heaven and the fat of the earth, abundance of grain and wine" (Num. 23:9; Gen. 27:28). Also common are declarations of God's incomparability, descriptions of His riding through the skies, epithets and descriptions of Him as ancient, a refuge, and a shield, and declarations exclaiming Israel's good fortune (*'ashrei*), all noted in the Comments to the coda and to 3:24.

Since most of these parallels are not verbatim, they do not imply literary interdependence of Deuteronomy 33 and the other texts. They reflect, rather, a common fund of phrases and motifs that were traditionally used in blessings, psalms, and similar literary genres. The few parallels that are nearly verbatim must have been particularly popular in blessings and hence known virtually by heart.

The affinity to the psalms suggests that the poem originally had a liturgical function. Because of its contents it is reasonable to suppose that it was recited at a pilgrimage festival at which all the tribes, or their representatives, gathered. The prominence of Joseph in the blessings has convinced some scholars that the festival was held at a sanctuary in the territory of Ephraim or Manasseh, such as Shiloh or Shechem. But other clues in the poem may point to Jerusalem or a sanctuary in Benjaminite territory, to Mount Tabor in the north, or to Mount Nebo in Transjordan.[10] The general theme of such a festival, and whether it was one of those mentioned in biblical liturgical calendars, is a matter of speculation.[11]

The Poem and Deuteronomy

Moses' blessing has little in common with other parts of Deuteronomy. It lacks characteristic Deuteronomic phraseology and it makes no explicit reference to the historical themes on which the book is based: God's promises to the patriarchs; the Exodus; the events at Mount Sinai-Horeb; Israel's election and the covenant; nor to the book's theological concerns, monotheism and the dangers of idolatry. Nor does the poem explain that the good fortune which it describes depends on obeying God's commandments, which is the main point of Deuteronomy.

The poem, along with verse 1, not only lacks these Deuteronomic features, but in several respects is inconsistent with other parts of Deuteronomy. The terms "children of Israel" (v. 1) and "Sinai" (v. 2), instead of "all Israel" and "Horeb," are typical of the JE and P sources, not Deuteronomy,[12] and the reference to Moses as "the man of God" (v. 1) is unprecedented in Deuteronomy or anywhere else in the Torah. The absence of a blessing for Simeon is inconsistent with that tribe's presence among those pronouncing blessing in 27:12. That God "drove out" the Canaanites (v. 27b1) agrees with the non-Deuteronomic sources which command that they be expelled, but is inconsistent with Deuteronomy's command that they be destroyed (7:2,16; 20:15–18).[13] Verse 8 seems to reflect a different tradition than 10:8 concerning when the Levites were awarded the priesthood, and verse 11's assumption of Levitical wealth does not square with Deuteronomy's picture of them as needy. In addition, the priestly duties that verses 8–10 mention differ partly from those listed in 10:8 and 21:5; those passages include carrying the Ark and blessing in God's name and omit the Urim and Thummim, probably because Deuteronomy sees God's will as communicated exclusively through prophecy.[14] Verse 8 also disagrees with 6:16, and the rest of the Torah, about what happened at Massah and Meribah.[15]

These differences between chapter 33 and the rest of Deuteronomy indicate that the chapter was originally independent of Deuteronomy and was not edited to harmonize it with the book when it was incorporated into it. It must have been put into the book because it was attributed to Moses and, by looking back on a successful conquest of the promised land, effectively foretells the conquest. Since it does not serve the admonitory aims of the book, it was in all likelihood not inserted by the author of Deuteronomy but by the editor who integrated Deuteronomy with the JE and P materials of chapters 31–34.[16]

The Tribes

The poem contains ten separate blessings covering twelve tribes. Curiously, there is none for the tribe of Simeon. Various conjectures have been proffered to find allusions to Simeon. Some manuscripts of the Septuagint add a blessing for Simeon to that of Reuben by reading verse 6b as "And let *Simeon* be many in number."[17] Rabbinic sources see an allusion to Simeon in verse 7, in the opening phrase of Judah's blessing, *shema' YHVH*, "Hear, LORD," since those were Leah's first words in explaining Simeon's name, *shim'on*, which is derived from *sh-m-'*, "hear": she said, *ki shama' YHVH*, "Because the LORD heard" (Gen. 29:33).[18] Some modern scholars, attracted by the appropriateness of *shema' YHVH* to *shim'on*, assume that verse 7 originally included a blessing for Simeon as well as Judah (like vv. 18–19, which combine two tribes), but that it fell out of the text by accident.[19] It would indeed have been logical for Simeon and Judah to share a blessing since Simeon's territory was within Judah's (see Josh. 19:1–9 and Judg. 1:3). However, it is possible that Simeon was intentionally omitted precisely because its territory was within Judah's and it was an insignificant tribe.[20] The same situation may be reflected in the fact that Simeon is cursed with dispersal in Genesis 49:7.

The tribes are listed in a geographic order, as befits the fact that many of the blessings refer to the territories in which they are soon to settle.[21] The order is based on contiguity. Beginning with Reuben, in whose territory the Israelites stood as Moses blessed them, the blessings move west across the Jordan to Judah and then, after Levi, follow a northward course through Benjamin, Ephraim and Manasseh (the Joseph tribes), and Zebulun, including the latter's neighbor to the east, Issachar,[22] then farther east, back across the

Jordan to Gad, then north to Dan, south to Naphtali, and west to Asher. Levi, which had no territory, is mentioned between Judah and Benjamin, apparently because the Levites served as priests in Jerusalem, which straddled the border between those two tribes, or elsewhere in the region (see below).[23]

Although arranging the tribes geographically precludes following the standard order, based on the order in which the tribes' eponymous ancestors were born according to Genesis 29–30 and 35:16–18, the subgroups of the standard order (which are also roughly geographic) are preserved. The list begins with the tribes descended from the first group that Leah bore, Reuben, Judah, and Levi (Simeon, as noted, is omitted); it then mentions the two descended from Rachel's sons, Benjamin and Joseph, though in reverse order; it continues with the two descended from Leah's later sons, Zebulun and Issachar; and it concludes with the tribes descended from the sons of the concubines: Gad, Dan, Naphtali, and Asher. All the deviations from the birth sequence are explicable by the geographic order.

The Unity of the Poem

Some scholars have questioned whether the entire poem was composed at the same time.

The affinities between the exordium and the coda, and the difference between their style and that of the blessings, have led some to suggest that the exordium and coda originally constituted an independent hymn, and that the blessings were likewise an independent composition without a poetic framework, like Genesis 49. According to this view, the blessings were later inserted into the hymn at the point where "the tribes of Israel" are mentioned.[24] This is possible, but because biblical poetry often mixes genres the stylistic argument is not decisive. The coda and at least part of the exordium do form a coherent hymn celebrating the Lord's coming to Israel's aid, becoming its king, and enabling it to conquer the promised land.[25] But, as noted in the Commentary, the coda has its own literary frame. This could suggest that it was composed in the first place to serve as a distinct section of a larger work, such as the present poem, and was not originally the immediate sequel to the exordium. As noted in the Commentary, it aptly sums up the main themes of the blessings and, along with the exordium, puts the blessings in the larger context of Israel's history. The exordium and the coda may well have been composed for that purpose.[26]

The difficulty in finding a coherent line of thought in verses 2–5 has led some scholars to question whether all of these verses originally belonged together. Verse 2, and perhaps verse 3, belong to a well-attested motif that does not elsewhere include the themes of verses 4–5. Some hold that all of verse 4 is an interpolation, added to connect the description of God's approach *from* Sinai to aid Israel (vv. 1–3) with the theophany *at* Mount Sinai.[27] If "the Teaching" (*torah*) in this verse is the Deuteronomic teaching, it may well be an interpolation, since the rest of the poem is unrelated to Deuteronomy. It could, however, refer to God's teachings in general rather than to Deuteronomy in particular. Yet another view is that verses 4–5 were the original introduction to the blessings, a poetic equivalent of verse 1, identifying Moses as the speaker.[28] In that case, "Moses charged us with the *torah*" might mean "Moses charged us with [the following] testament" (as in "last will and testament"; note the parallel "heritage," that is, "inheritance").[29]

Although the exordium (at least in part) and the coda may have been composed to serve as the framework for the blessings, the blessings themselves may have been com-

posed earlier. It has even been suggested that the differences between them in length and style indicate that individual blessings were composed separately and at different times, perhaps by each tribe for itself.[30] This might explain why it is so difficult to find a single historical period that is compatible with all the blessings. That tribes composed sayings and blessings about themselves is certainly possible. However, there are enough similarities in meter, style, wording, and imagery between several of the blessings in the chapter, and between them and some of the sayings in Genesis 49 and Judges 5, to make it implausible that all the tribes composed these blessings independently.

Finally, some scholars have argued, on linguistic and stylistic grounds, that all or part of verses 8–10, which refer to the Levites' priestly duties, is later than the rest of the poem. Verses 8–10 contain particles that are relatively uncommon in poetry and are virtually absent from the rest of this poem, namely the relative pronoun *'asher* (v. 8), which appears again only in verse 29, where it is problematic, and the accusative particle *'et* (v. 9, twice), which does not appear again. Stylistically verses 8–10 use the standard 3:3 meter much less than the other blessings do. In this view only verse 11, which is similar to the other blessings and, like Genesis 49:5–7 refers to Levi as a secular rather than priestly tribe, is the original blessing of Levi.[31]

The Date of the Poem

The reference to Moses—if the reading is correct—in the third person in verse 4 suggests that the poem is not Mosaic. Possible references to Moses and his grave site in verse 21 would also imply a post-Mosaic date. That the poem was composed after the conquest of Canaan is implied by the fact that it looks back upon the conquest as a past event (v. 27), and by its reference to Dan in the far north, where the tribe migrated in the period of the Chieftains (the "Judges") (see Comment to v. 22). On the other hand, its description of the tribes as presently living in their territories rules out a date after the exile of the northern tribes ca. 720 B.C.E.

Evidence that would permit a more precise dating is equivocal. Several factors suggest a relatively early date. The absence of any hint of the secession of the northern tribes and the attendant rivalry between them and the south[32] points to a date prior to the death of Solomon (ca. 922). The reference to Thummim and Urim (v. 8) points in the same direction, since these fell out of use after David's reign.[33] But the modest blessing of Judah suggests an even earlier date; it is hardly compatible with a date in the reign of Solomon or David (ca. 1000–922), when Judah dominated all the tribes. In fact, since the poem mentions only God, or possibly Moses, as king (v. 4) it seems to be even earlier than the first king, Saul (ca. 1020–1000).

However, a number of other considerations point to relatively later dates.

1. If the belovedness of Benjamin refers to its being the tribe of the first king, it would imply a date in the reign of Saul. This implication would be obviated if the verse refers to the status of Benjamin in the days of Ehud or Samuel or to an early sanctuary in Benjamin's territory (see Comment to v. 12).

2. The date of the blessing of Levi is entangled with the complex history of the Levites, about which there is much uncertainty. If the tribe's location in the poem presumes that it is based at the Temple in Jerusalem, then the poem cannot be earlier than the period of Solomon, who built the Temple. Conceivably, however,

the location reflects the service of Levites in older sanctuaries in Judah, Benjamin, and Ephraim in the period of the Judges.[34]

Even if the blessing of Levi is from the monarchic period, it does not necessarily mean that the rest of the poem is also from that period. If parts of the blessing point to a Solomonic or later date, they may not have been part of the original poem and do not necessarily imply that the other parts are late.

3. The preeminence of Joseph, as reflected in the length of its blessing and its designation as "the elect of his brothers" and "a firstling [that is, first-born] bull," could be allusions to the northern kingdom, "the House of Joseph," centered in Ephraimite territory and whose first king was the Ephraimite Jeroboam son of Nebat (ca. 922–901).[35] However, the blessing does not necessarily presuppose the northern kingdom. It focuses on fertility and military prowess rather than royal power. In Genesis 49, too, Joseph has the longest blessing and is designated "the elect of his brothers," yet it is Judah who is promised royal authority and tribute, and in much more explicit terms (v. 10).[36] In comparison, the blessing of Joseph here seems to refer to something less than monarchic rule over all the tribes. It may allude to Joseph's earlier preeminence as the leader of a coalition of northern tribes in the period of the Chieftains, as in the days of Gideon the Manassite.[37]

4. The language of the poem does not show the same concentration of archaic features as found in *Ha'azinu*.[38] The few archaic features present are balanced by features typical of the standard poetic Hebrew that predominates in the poetry of the eighth and following centuries. As noted in Excursus 30, some of these features that preponderate in later poetry conceivably existed earlier, in which case they are compatible with an early date for the poem. Otherwise, they indicate that the poem was either written or revised during a period of transition from the older forms to the later ones (perhaps between the tenth and eighth centuries) or when the later ones predominated (from the eighth century on).

> The poem's archaic features are three imperfect (prefix) tense verbs without *vav*-consecutive for narrating a past event (*yissa'*, "[they were] accepting," verse 2; *terivehu*, "you challenged," verse 8b2; *yintsoru*, "they kept," verse 9);[39] three cases of the third-person masculine plural suffix *-mo* (*lamo*, "to them," v. 2, twice; suffix *-eimo*, "their," v. 29) and none of the standard biblical Hebrew form *-am*;[40] a participle ending in *-i* (*shokhni*, v. 16);[41] and possibly at least one enclitic *mem* (if *motnayim* in v. 11 is read as *motnei-ma*).[42] The standard poetic Hebrew features in the poem are the following: for narrating a past event, imperfect verbs *with* *vav*-consecutive outnumber those without it;[43] the form *-ennu* for the third-person masculine singular pronominal suffix on imperfect verbs appears (v. 7), but not its earlier counterpart *-enhu*;[44] and the original root consonant *yod* is elided before the suffix on *yoru* (original root *w-r-y*) in verse 10.

All of these considerations indicate that the poem was composed prior to the exile of the northern tribes ca. 720 B.C.E., possibly during the time of Solomon or (perhaps excepting part of the blessing of the Levites) earlier in the United Monarchy, or conceivably in the pre-monarchic period. Some time after it was composed, it may have undergone a linguistic-stylistic revision and the blessing of Levi may have been expanded. The poem is certainly older than Deuteronomy 1–31 and 34, perhaps considerably older.

Simḥat Torah

The poem and the following chapter are the last two chapters in the Torah. They are read in the synagogue on *Simḥat Torah*, the "Celebration of the Torah," the festival at which the annual cycle of reading the Torah is completed with great rejoicing and is immediately begun again. A unique feature of the festival is the practice of marching and dancing with all the Torah scrolls in the synagogue and then reading the subsections of verses 1–26 several times so that every adult member of the congregation may be called to the Torah and, following them, all the minors as a group. After this, a distinguished adult is called as the *ḥatan Torah*, the "Torah's Bridegroom," for the reading of the final verses of the Torah, Deuteronomy 33:27–34:12, and then another distinguished adult, the *ḥatan Bere'shit*, the "Bridegroom of Genesis," is called for the reading of the beginning of Genesis. The festival is one of the most popular and memorable of the Jewish liturgical year.

NOTES TO THE EXCURSUSES

Excursus 1

1. See, e.g., Gen. 2:11–14; 14:2,3,7,17; 23:2; Deut. 4:48; 11:30; Josh. 15:9,15,49,60; Judg. 21:19.

2. See, e.g., Num. 33; 34; Josh. 13–21; N. Na'aman, *Borders and Districts in Biblical Historiography* (Jerusalem: Simor, 1986).

3. See particularly F. M. Abel, *Géographie de la Palestine* (Paris: Gabalda, 1933–38); G. A. Smith, *The Historical Geography of the Holy Land* (reprint; New York: Harper and Row, 1966); G. A. Smith and J. G. Bartholomew, *Atlas of the Historical Geography of the Holy Land* (London: Hodder and Stoughton, 1915); J. J. Simons, *The Geographical and Topographical Texts of the Old Testament* (Leiden: Brill, 1959); Y. Aharoni and A. F. Rainey, LOB; Y. Aharoni and M. Avi-Yonah, *The Macmillan Bible Atlas*, rev. ed. (New York: Macmillan, 1977) (a third edition, completely revised by A. F. Rainey and Z. Safrai, appeared in 1993, too late to be utilized); Z. Kallai, *Historical Geography of the Bible* (Jerusalem: Magnes Press, 1986); C. G. Rasmussen, *Zondervan NIV Atlas of the Bible* (Grand Rapids, Mich.: Zondervan, 1989).

4. See J. M. Miller, "The Israelite Journey Through Moab," JBL 108 (1989): 590–595; J. A. Dearman, "The Levitical Cities of Reuben and Moabite Toponymy," BASOR 276 (1989): 55–57.

5. B. Oded, s.v. *'Avarim, Har Ha-'avarim*, EM 6:51.

6. The proposed translation in 2:17 "crossing the border" may imply that Ar was situated near that border on the Wadi Arnon. That would support identifying Ar as Ir-Moab.

7. "City" is one meaning of Kir and the normal meaning of Ir (*'-y-r*), and Ar (*'-r*) could be a variant form of Ir. In fact, the Samaritan Pentateuch reads Ar for Ir in Num. 21:15, and a scroll of Isaiah from Qumran reads Ir for Ar in Isa. 15:1. For the location see B. Oded, s.v. *'Ar, 'Ar-Mo'ab*, EM 6:343–344; Miller, "Israelite Journey," 590–595.

8. See S. E. Loewenstamm, s.v. *'Argov* 1, EM 1:528–529.

9. EAEHL 1:98–100; Driver, 45. The phrase "on the edge of the Arnon valley" (2:36) distinguishes this Aroer from "Aroer which is close to Rabbah" (Josh. 13:25). Since the Arnon was the border between Moab and Sihon's territory, some scholars believe that Aroer is the border town Ir-Moab (Num. 22:36; see comment to v. 9, above). But that town was accessible to the king of Moab (ibid.) and was presumably in territory under his control and therefore south of the stream, in territory Israel was not to conquer. See B. Oded, s.v. *'ir, ha-'ir 'asher ba-nahal*, EM 6:215; Y. Tsafrir, s.v. *'Aro'er* 2, EM 6:398–399.

10. "The town" (*ha-'ir*) could be a common noun or the name of the town. For possible sites see Miller, "Israelite Journey," 595 n. 42.

11. See ANET, 242, 329, 486c; S. Ahituv, s.v. *'Ashtarot*, EM 6:404–406; idem, *Canaanite Toponyms in Ancient Egyptian Documents* (Jerusalem: Magnes Press, and Leiden: Brill, 1984), 72–73; M. Avi-Yonah, s.v. "Ashtaroth, Ashteroth-Karnaim, Karnaim," EncJud 3:737; the Ugaritic reference is in B. Margulis, "A Ugaritic Psalm," JBL 89 (1970): 292–294; M. Pope, "Notes on the Ugaritic Rephaim Texts," in M. deJ. Ellis, ed., *Ancient Near Eastern Studies in Memory of Jacob Joel Finkelstein* (Hamden, Conn.: Archon Books, 1977), 169–170.

12. See ANET, 477c and note on 676; M. Avi-Yonah, s.v. "Edrei," EncJud 6:381; B. Mazar, s.v. *'Edre'i*, EM 1:119–120; Ahituv, *Canaanite Toponyms*, 90–91. For the Ugaritic text, see the previous note.

13. See S. E. Loewenstamm, s.v. *Bashan*, EM 2:366–368.

14. See Gen. 36:27 (note LXX); 1 Chron. 1:42; Abel, *Géographie*, 2:262; M. Avi-Yonah, s.v. *Be'erot benei ya'akan*, EM 2:9.

15. See M. Avi-Yonah, s.v. "Jotbath, Jothbatah," EncJud 10:300–301; M. Broshi, s.v. *Yatevatah*, EM 3:673; Weinfeld, Commentary, 420.

16. Smith, *Historical Geography*, 381; H. Gevariahu, s.v. *Beit Pe'or*, EM 2:98–99; Rofé, *Mavo'*, 238; F. M. Cross, "Reuben, First-Born of Jacob," ZAW 100 (1988), Supplement, 51–52.

17. ANET, 320–321; men from Dibon were employed to rebuild Bezer. See S. E. Loewenstamm, s.v. *Betser*, EM 2:308–309; Dearman, "Levitical Cities"; Weinfeld, Commentary, 231.

18. N. Glueck, s.v. *'Eilat, 'Eilot*, EM 1:268–272; EAEHL 713–717; Abel, *Géographie*, 2:311–312; J. Braslavi, *'El Eilat ve-'el Yam-Suf: Ha-yada'ta 'et ha-arets*, vol. 4 (Ain Charod, Israel: 1952), 4:460; K. Baedeker, *Palestine and Syria* (Leipzig: Baedeker, 1906), 209–210; A. Flinder, "Is This Solomon's Seaport," BAR 15/4 (July-August, 1989): 31–43.

19. See esp. 1 Kings 9:26; 2 Chron. 8:17; S. Ahituv, s.v. *'Etsyon gever*, EM 6:332–333; Flinder, "Solomon's Seaport," 31–43.

20. Smith, *Historical Geography*, 153–154. See Smith and Bartholomew, *Atlas*, pl. 25, section A-2; T. K. Cheyne, ed., *Encyclopedia Biblica* 2:1732; Driver, "Addenda and Corrigenda," xxi; H. Gevariahu, s.v. *Gilgal*, EM 2:489; M. Haran, "Shechem Studies," *Zion* 38 (1973): 14–15; Rofé, *Mavo'*, 24.

21. A. Zertal, "Israel Enters Canaan—Following the Pottery Trail," BAR 17/5 (September-October, 1991): 38–45.

22. See Loewenstamm, s.v. *Golan*, EM 2:458.

23. For a plural pronoun referring back to an *implied* plural antecedent see Jonah 1:3 ("with them," the sailors on "the boat"); cf. GKC §440p.

24. BDB, 295; HALAT, 284; Wehr, 219.

25. For discussion see B. Mazar, s.v. *havvot Ya'ir*, EM 3:66–67; Weinfeld, Commentary, 176–177, 185.

26. See S. E. Loewenstamm, s.v. *hatserot*, EM 3:277.

27. M. Haran, "The Historical Framework of the Exodus: Data and Suggestions," in Y. Avishur and J. Blau, eds., *Studies in the Bible and the Ancient Near East* (Jerusalem: Rubinstein, 1978), 164–165 n. 23.

28. See B. Oded, s.v. "Exodus," EncJud 6:1048–1050 (on the map in cols. 1043–1044 the locations of Jebel [Mount] Sinn Bishr and Jebel Ya'allaq are mistakenly switched); M. Avi-Yonah, s.v. "Sinai," EncJud 14:1593–1596; O. Lifschitz, s.v. "Sinai, Mount," EncJud 14:1597–1600; M. Har-el, s.v. *Sinai, har Sinai*, EM 5:1020–1022. For further literature see N. M. Sarna, *Exploring Exodus* (New York: Schocken, 1986), 233 n. 16.

29. In 1838, Edward Robinson, the great explorer of the Holy Land, traveled by camel from Mount Musa via Aqaba to the vicinity of Kadesh-barnea in eleven days (see Edward Robinson, *Biblical Researches in Palestine*, 3rd ed. [London: John Murray, 1867], 2:565–567 [the fifth and sixth stations on April 10 were near Kadesh]). This has been taken as consistent with the eleven-day distance from Horeb to the promised land mentioned in Deut. 1:2. However, it is not certain that 1:2 refers to a route via Aqaba. More importantly, the Israelites' rate of travel would have been determined by the speed of those traveling by foot, which is less than half the speed of camels.

30. See, recently, Cross, "Reuben," 58–59.

31. ANET, 320d. See Dearman, "Levitical Cities," 276; Miller, "Israelite Journey," 589–590.

32. See Y. Aharoni, s.v. *Kadesh 5, Kadesh barnea'*, EM 7:39–42. Note the doubts of Cross, "Reuben," 58–59.

33. See Dearman, "Levitical Cities," 276; contrast Miller, "Israelite Journey," 590.

34. For the alternative forms Laban/Libnah, cf. Geba/Gibeah (1 Sam. 13:15–16; Judg. 20:4, 10); Bezer/Bozrah (Deut. 4:43; Jer. 48:24).

35. See Abel, *Géographie*, 2:214.

36. ANET, 286d; see Ahituv, *Canaanite Toponyms*, 129; Weinfeld, Commentary, 127.

37. See B. Oded, s.v. *Nevo, Har Nevo*, EM 5:687–690; Smith, *Historical Geography*, 563ff.

38. See S. E. Loewenstamm, s.v. *'ovot*, EM 1:69–70.

39. See Y. Aharoni, s.v. *Pa'ran, Midbar Pa'ran*, EM 6:433–434.

40. See I. Eph'al, s.v. *Petor*, EM 6:638–639; T. Jacobsen, s.v. "Pethor," IDB 3:772.

41. Driver and Smith take it as E and D's synonym of Mount Nebo; Cross considers Pisgah-Nebo a poetic double name ("Reuben," 50n).

42. See B. Oded, s.v. *Pisgah, ha-pisgah*, EM 6:513–514.

43. See Aharoni and Rainey, LOB, 202; S. Abramsky, s.v. *Punon, Pinon*, EM 6:445–446.

44. B. Oded, s.v. *Ramot Gil'ad*, EM 7:378–380.

45. Smith, *Historical Geography*, 359–360; Abel, *Géographie*, 1:389–391; H. Liver, *Se'ir* 1, EM 8:324–325; Keil-Delitzsch, 250–251, 281; J. R. Bartlett, "The Land of Seir and the Brotherhood of Edom," *Journal of Theological Studies*, N.S. 20 (1969): 4–7; Ahituv, *Canaanite Toponyms*, 169. For the Negev highlands see E. Orni, s.v. "Negev," EncJud 12:925–926.

46. Kaufmann, *Sefer Yehoshua'*, 2nd ed. (Jerusalem: Kiryat Sefer, 1963), 132; Aharoni and Rainey, LOB, 34, 60 (describing the road from west to east); M. Haran, "Shechem Studies," *Zion* 38 (1973): 14–15; Rofé, *Mavo'*, 24.

47. Smith and Bartholomew, *Atlas*, pl. 25, section A-2.

48. See s.v. *Tsalmonah*, EM 6:736.

49. Y. Tsafrir, s.v. *Nahal Zered*, EM 5:811–812. Since Num. 21:11–13 indicates that the Israelites reached Wadi Zered after leaving "the wilderness bordering on Moab to the east," some scholars believe that Wadi Zered must be east of Moab and identify it with one of the north-south tributaries of Wadi Arnon. If, however, the wilderness referred to in Numbers 21 is *southeast* of Moab, there is no difficulty in assuming that Wadi Zered was the southern boundary.

50. For the location see Sarna, *Genesis*, Excursus 13; Driver; S. Ahituv, s.v. *Tso'ar*, EM 6:695–696. For a possible reference in the Amarna letters see W. L. Moran, *Les lettres d'el Amarna* (Paris: Editions du Cerf, 1987), 552, 604; for later times, see Smith, *Historical Geography*, 325–326; N. Lewis et al., *The Documents from the Bar Kochba Period in the Cave of Letters* (Jerusalem: Israel Exploration Society, Hebrew University, and the Shrine of the Book, 1989), 21 (citing G. W. Bowersock and M. Avi Yonah). The question is complicated by Gen. 13:10, which seems to imply that Zoar was near the Jordan River or the northern end of the Dead Sea, since it was visible from Bethel.

Excursus 2

1. Malbim at Num. 34:2–12.

2. See S. R. Driver, *Introduction to the Literature of the Old Testament* (reprint; New York: Meridian, 1957), 15, 31, 62, 69; M. Noth, *The Deuteronomistic History* (Sheffield: University of Sheffield, 1981), 110 n. 17.

3. On the boundaries of Canaan see B. Mazar, *Cities and Districts* (Hebrew) (Jerusalem: Mosad Bialik, 1975), 167–181; idem, s.v. *'erets yisra'el*, EM 1:607–616.

4. J. Tigay, ed., *Empirical Models for Biblical Criticism* (Philadelphia: University of Pennsylvania Press, 1985), 61–68.

5. See Weinfeld, DDS, 244–319.

6. See Mish. Sanh. 1:6; Maimonides at 1:5; Mid. Hag. at Deut. 1:15; Maimonides, Hilkhot Sanhedrin 2:7.

7. For the second possibility cf. Y. Zakovitch, "Assimilation in Biblical Narratives," in Tigay, ed., *Empirical Models*, 175–196.

8. For the following see H. Reviv, "The Traditions Concerning the Inception of the Legal System in Israel: Significance and Dating," ZAW 94 (1982): 566–575; S. E. Loewenstamm, s.v. *mishpat*, EM 5:629–630.

9. See chap. 1, n. 55.

10. Verse 16:18, in which the judges are to be appointed by the people and not by the head of the nation, seems to reflect a different social and historical background than 1:9–13.

11. SP implies this sequence of events by inserting Deut. 1:22–23a before Num. 13:1.

12. See Tanḥ. Shelaḥ Lekha, 7 (cf. Rashi at Deut. 1:23); Rashi and Ramban at Num. 13:2; Abravanel here.

13. Josh. 14:13–14; 15:13–14.

14. Shalag at Num. 13:22 and Deut. 1:24.

15. Shadal at Num. 13:30.

16. See G. B. Gray, *Numbers* (reprint; Edinburgh: T. and T. Clark, 1956), 128–134; Driver, *Introduction*, 62–63; J. Liver, s.v. *kalev*, EM 4:106–110. For another case in which Deuteronomy drew upon one of the Pentateuchal sources before it was merged with another, see Comment to 11:6.

17. The earliest text to connect 1:37 with Numbers 20 is Ps. 106:32–33, "They provoked wrath at the waters of Meribah and Moses suffered *on their account* [this phrase alludes to Deut. 1:37], because they rebelled against Him, and he [Moses] spoke rashly." For midrashic and other ancient discussions of the reason for Moses' death, see Chap. 1 n. 112.

18. The incident of the rock occurred perhaps as late as the fortieth year (SOR 8–9; Rashi and Ibn Ezra at Num. 20:1; Gray, *Numbers*, 256–257).

19. Deut. 32:51, which does mention the rock incident, is also assigned to P. See Excursus 32.

20. The assumption that a place may have several names is often invoked by the medieval commentators to resolve discrepancies; see Ibn Ezra at Deut. 1:2; Abravanel at Deut. 1:2 (p. 12) and at Numbers 33 (p. 160, end).

21. See Ibn Ezra at Num. 20:14; Ramban and Abravanel at 20:1.

22. See Num. 13:21; 34:3–4; Josh. 15:1,3.

23. Ibn Ezra at Num. 21:4,10; 33:43. Conceivably 21:4 does mean that the Israelites reached the Gulf of Elath, as explicitly assumed by Keil and Delitzsch (*Numbers*, 138, 142). This is a tolerable argument in the case of the narratives in Numbers, which might have skipped the entire southern loop of the journey if it was uneventful. It is less plausible in the case of Num. 33, which mentions countless places at which nothing is known to have happened. Still, that chapter does skip other stages of the journey (stations must be missing between Eziongeber and Kadesh [Num. 33:36], since these are about seventy miles apart), and if one is willing to assume a major omission in the route in both Numbers 21 and 33, they need not be taken as clashing with Deuteronomy.

24. See Rashi following MdRY Vayassa 1 (Lauterbach 2:85–86); TJ Yoma 1:1, 38b. For modern attempts at harmonization see Hoffmann. SP removes the problem by replacing vv. 6–7 with a paraphrase of Num. 33:31–38. See Weinfeld, Commentary, 404, 419.

25. Y. Aharoni, LOB, 201–206.

26. M. Haran, *Ages and Institutions in the Bible* (Hebrew) (Tel Aviv: Am Oved, 1972), 41.

27. W. A. Sumner, "Israel's Encounters with Edom, Moab, Ammon, Sihon, and Og According to the Deuteronomist," VT 18 (1968): 216–228.

28. See Tigay, ed., *Empirical Models*, 53–95; E. Tov, "The

Nature and Background of Harmonizations in Biblical Manuscripts," JSOT 31 (1985): 3–29.

29. D. Weiss Halivni, *Sources and Traditions: Tractate Shabbath* (Hebrew) (Jerusalem: Jewish Theological Seminary, 1982), 110–113.

30. See H. Strack, *Introduction to Talmud and Midrash* (New York: Meridian and Philadelphia: Jewish Publication Society, 1959), 96, no. 9.

31. H. C. Hockett, *The Critical Method in Historical Research and Writing* (New York: Macmillan, 1955), 69.

32. See R. de Vaux, *The Early History of Israel* (Philadelphia: Westminster Press, 1978), 506.

33. Driver, xxxv.

34. See Samuel in BK 14a and 36b; R. Yohanan in BM 41a (see Steinsaltz ad loc.) and Sanh 62b; Ber. 3a; cf. Tigay, ed., *Empirical Models*, 14 n. 48.

35. W. Robertson Smith, *The Old Testament in the Jewish Church*, 3rd ed. (New York: Appleton, 1892), 328–329. For the evidence see Tigay, ed., *Empirical Models*, chap. 1.

36. Eruv. 13b; Git. 6b.

Excursus 3

1. See Exod. 14:24; Num. 10:9, 35–36; 31:6; Deut. 1:30; 20:1–4; 23:10–15; Josh. 6:2–20; 10:10,14,42; 23:3,10; Judg. 1:1–2; 4:6–7,14–16; 5:20,23; 7:2–8,22–23; 1 Sam. 4:1–7; 7:9–11; 13:9–12; 14:6–20,36–37; 17:47; 21:6; 28:5–6; 30:7–8; 2 Sam. 5:19,22–25; 1 Kings 20:13–14,28; 22:2–25; 2 Kings 3:11–19; Ps. 18:15; 20:8; 44; 60:12–14. For brief summaries of the evidence see R. de Vaux, *Ancient Israel* (New York: McGraw-Hill, 1961), 258–267; M. Greenberg, "Religion: Stability and Ferment," in WHJP 4/2, 97–98. For analogous concepts elsewhere in the ancient world see Weinfeld, "Divine Intervention in War," in H. Tadmor and M. Weinfeld, eds., *History, Historiography, and Interpretation* (Jerusalem: Hebrew University, Institute of Advanced Studies and Magnes Press, 1983), 121–147. Assyrian reliefs show King Ashurnasirpal II (883–859) advancing in battle with his bow drawn while above him a winged figure of the god Ashur advances pointing his bow in the same direction (see G. E. Mendenhall, *The Tenth Generation* [Baltimore: Johns Hopkins University Press, 1973], 45–46). Aramaic inscriptions describe the deity Hadad as "walking before" the king to grant him victory and the booty of his enemies (I. Eph'al and J. Naveh, "Hazael's Booty Inscriptions," IEJ 39 [1989]: 194; A. Biran and J. Naveh, "An Aramaic Stele Fragment from Tel Dan," IEJ 43 [1993]: 81–98; cf. 1:30; 20:2,4,14).

2. A. Rofé distinguishes between battles in which Israel is totally passive and those in which it participates. See "Ephraimite versus Deuteronomistic History," in D. Garrone and F. Israel, eds., *Storia e Tradizioni di Israele. Scritti in Onore di J. Alberto Soggin* (Brescia: Paideia Editrice Brescia, 1991), 229–231.

3. G. von Rad, *Holy War in Ancient Israel* (German ed., 1958; English ed., Grand Rapids, Mich.: Eerdmans, 1991). Reuven Firestone studied the similarities and differences of this concept and the Islamic *jihad* in a lecture, "Conceptions of Sanctified War in the Scriptures of Judaism and Islam," delivered to the 1991 meeting of the Association for Jewish Studies.

Excursus 4

1. Rashbam and Bekhor Shor at Exod. 3:14–15. Maimonides conjectures that YHVH may "indicate the notion of a necessary existence," though he denies that the name is based on any known verbal root (see Maimonides, Guide 1.61). Derivation from *hvh/hyh* is suggested by Exod. 3:14–15; see Rashi and Exod. R. 3:6 on v. 14; Seforno on v. 15; and Ber. 9b.

2. Abravanel on Exodus, 186, and most moderns. See J. F.

McCurdy, "Names of God: Biblical Data," JE 9:160–161; Ben Yehuda 4:1984–1988 n. 1; Cassuto, s.v. *'elohim, shemot 'elohim ba-mikra'*, EM 1:307–311; W. F. Albright, *Yahweh and the Gods of Canaan* (Garden City, N.Y.: Doubleday, 1968), 168–172; F. M. Cross, *Canaanite Myth and Hebrew Epic* (Cambridge: Harvard University Press, 1973), 60–71. Both interpretations of the name are compatible with the form *Yahweh*, which could represent either the *kal* (simple) or the *hiph'il* (causative) conjugation and either the present (continuous) or future tense.

3. Kid. 71a; Pes. 50a; Av. Zar. 17b–18a; Exod. R. 3:6, end; Mish. Ber. 9:5; Mish. Sot. 7:6; Mish. Sanh. 10:1. See Albeck, *Nashim*, 387; J. D. Eisenstein, s.v. "Names of God: In Rabbinical Literature," JE 9:162–163; A. Marmorstein, *The Old Rabbinic Doctrine of God, Vol. I: The Names and Attributes of God* (reprint; New York: Ktav, 1968), 17–40.

4. Amos 6:10 refers to a special circumstance.

5. See, e.g., Ruth 2:4; ANET, 322, 569.

6. The practice is found in Christian copies of the LXX, which render YHVH by *kyrios*, "Lord." The LXX of the Torah was composed in the third century B.C.E., but it is not certain that this practice was followed in the original LXX; it could be a later, Christian modification. See P. W. Skehan, "The Divine Name at Qumran, in the Masada Scroll, and in the Septuagint," *Bulletin of the International Organization for Septuagint and Cognate Studies* 13 (1980): 14–44.

7. 2 Mos., 207. It was considered respectful to refer to one's father as *'abba' mari*, "my father, my lord," rather than by name (Kid. 31b; Maimonides, Hilkhot Mamrim 6:3; Shulḥan 'Arukh, Yoreh De'ah 240:2). According to Sanh. 100a, Gehazi was punished for speaking of his master Elisha by name.

8. See Ehrlich, *Randglossen*, at Exod. 20:7.

9. 2 Mos., 203–208; PdRK 148a. Thus LXX and Targ. Onk.

10. Sanh. 56a.

11. This did happen in some passages, such as Exod. 15:17 and Ps. 38:16, where *'adonai* is spelled *'-d-n-y*. It is difficult to tell when such readings were part of the original text and when they are due to scribal alteration.

12. Since the first consonant in *'adonai* is a guttural letter (*alef*), Hebrew grammar requires that its first vowel, which would otherwise be a *sheva*, become a *hataf-patah* (a clipped *a*, something like the *a* in "alone"). When accompanying YHVH that vowel follows a *yod* and therefore reverts to *sheva* (rendered as "e" in "Jehovah," to be discussed below).

13. The grammatically plural form *'adonai* instead of the singular *'adoni* is simply a plural of rank or majesty, a form used for terms referring to authorities, such as *be'alim*, *'adonim*, "master," and *'elohim*, "a god," "God" (e.g., Exod. 21:29,36; Isa. 19:4; Mal. 1:6; 1 Kings 11:33; Gen. 1:1; thus Ibn Janah, *Sefer Ha-Shorashim*, s.v. *'-d-n*; idem, *Sefer Ha-Rikmah*, ed. Wilensky, 295–296, sec. 26; Maimonides, Guide 1.61 (see Crescas ad loc.); GKC §§ 124g–i.

14. See E. G. Hirsch, s.v. "Jehovah," JE 7:88; s.v. "Jehovah," *Oxford English Dictionary*; G. F. Moore, *Judaism* (Cambridge: Harvard University Press, 1958–59), 3:61.

15. See Z. Ben-Hayyim, "On the Pronunciation of the Tetragrammaton by the Samaritans," EI 3 (1954): 147–154; *The Literary and Oral Tradition of Hebrew and Aramaic Amongst the Samaritans*, Vol. 3, Part 2 (Jerusalem: The Academy of the Hebrew Language, 1967), 170, 237.

Excursus 5

1. H. L. Ginsberg, *The Israelian Heritage in Judaism* (New York: Jewish Theological Seminary, 1982), 80.

2. Ramban; cf. Bekhor Shor at v. 31; Ḥazzekuni; see also Driver, lxxvi; Smith.

3. Some commentators hold that *ki* does refer back to v. 31, explaining that vv. 32ff. prove God's compassion and faithful-

ness, supporting the message of v. 31 that He will not abandon Israel (Sforno; R. Meyuḥas; R. Nissim Gerondi [cited by Abravanel, 36, question 16]; Keil-Delitzsch; Driver at 4:32 [but see his comment on lxxvi]; Craigie). This misses the point of vv. 32ff., which explicitly state that the experiences they cite prove the sole divinity of YHVH; although v. 37 states that God acted out of love for the patriarchs, the text does not present this as the lesson of the events.

4. Driver at 30:11 and lxxvi.

5. Smith; Driver, lxxvi; H. W. Wolff, "Das Kerygma des deuteronomistischen Geschichtswerks," *ZAW* 73 (1961): 180–183. For similar passages, related to those in Deuteronomy 4 and 30, see 1 Kings 8:46–50; Jer. 29:13–14. For the preexilic background of the "theology of repentance," see Weinfeld, Commentary, 217–221 (this does not affect the literary arguments favoring the conclusion that the verses in Deuteronomy are exilic interpolations; cf. Weinfeld, 209). Given the likelihood that these verses are interpolations, their exilic date cannot by itself be used to date all of chapters 4 and 30 to that period. For another example of a prophecy of exile (of temple vessels) being revised to include reference to restoration, see Jer. 27:22 and E. Tov in J. Tigay, ed., *Empirical Models for Biblical Criticism* (Philadelphia: University of Pennsylvania Press, 1985), 221–222.

Excursus 6

1. See esp. Exod. 8:6; 9:14; 14:31; 15:11; 18:11; 19:9.

2. Exod. 20:2–3; 22:19; 23:13,24; 34:14.

3. 1 Sam. 2:2; 2 Sam. 7:22; 22:32. The antiquity of the clauses denying the existence of other gods in these verses is debated. "Truly there is none beside you" in 1 Sam. 2:2 interrupts the parallelism of the first and third clauses of the verse; it renders superfluous the rest of the verse, which says that God is incomparable; and it differs grammatically from the rest of the poem, which speaks of God in the third person. The fact that the location of this clause in the verse differs in the MT and the LXX may also indicate that it is an interpolation. The clause is found, however, in 4QSamuel[a] as well as the LXX. 2 Sam. 7:22 is considered to be Deuteronomistic in style (see Weinfeld, DDS, 331 no. 5) and if so may have been added to the text in the course of editing the book in the seventh century B.C.E. or later. 2 Sam. 22:32 (and its duplicate text, Ps. 18:32) is part of a unit (vv. 31–32) that some consider intrusive between vv. 30 and 33 and therefore an interpolation. (On all of these verses, see S. R. Driver, *Notes on the Hebrew Text and the Topography of the Books of Samuel* [Oxford: Clarendon Press, 1913; reprint, 1960]; P. K. McCarter, *I Samuel* and *II Samuel* [Garden City, N.Y.: Doubleday, 1980, 1984]; M. H. Segal, *Sifrei Shemu'el* [Jerusalem: Kiryat-Sefer, 1956].) Conceivably all of these clauses were added to the text in the seventh century B.C.E. or later when explicit assertions of monotheism became common (see below), but there is no manuscript evidence against any of them. Because there is a degree of subjectivity in the arguments cited above, it is not certain that any of the passages are interpolations.

4. Assuming that the Exodus took place toward the end of the thirteenth century B.C.E., that Hannah lived around the mid-eleventh century, and that David reigned from about 1000–961 B.C.E.

5. See, e.g., Jer. 2:11; 5:7; 16:20; Isa. 44:6,8; 45:5,21. Similar statements appear in such passages as 2 Sam. 7:22, 1 Kings 8:60, and 2 Kings 19:15, which many scholars consider to be Deuteronomistic and from the seventh century B.C.E. or later (see Weinfeld, DDS, 331).

6. See Y. Kaufmann, *The Religion of Israel*, trans. M. Greenberg (Chicago: University of Chicago Press, 1960), esp. 122–149; W. F. Albright, *Archaeology and the Religion of Israel*, 4th ed. (Baltimore: Johns Hopkins University Press, 1956), 116, 155, 177–178; idem, *The Archaeology of Palestine and the Bible* (rep-

rint; Cambridge, Mass.: American Schools of Oriental Research, 1974), 163–167; idem, *History, Archaeology, and Christian Humanism* (New York: McGraw-Hill, 1964), 266–267.

7. Genesis describes the patriarchs as worshiping only YHVH. Although the patriarchs use a variety of names for Him, such passages as Gen. 14:22; 21:33; and Exod. 6:2–3 understand all of them as names of YHVH, and Jacob insists that the members of his household dispose of the images of alien gods they were carrying (Gen. 35:2–4). We are not told what the patriarchs believed about other gods. Genesis is concerned instead with the patriarchs' devotion to YHVH as expressed in their trust and obedience.

8. Jephthah's statement to the king of the Ammonites that the latter's god had given the Ammonites their land (Judg. 11:24) is probably an appeal to the Ammonite's belief, not a reflection of Jephthah's.

9. See, e.g., 1 Sam. 7:3–4; 2 Kings 23:4–15.

10. This reasoning of the polytheist is spelled out by Maimonides, Hilkhot ʿAvodah Zarah 1:1. Cf. M. Smith, *Palestinian Parties and Politics* (New York: Columbia University Press, 1971), 218 n. 111. As Kaufmann observed: "Monotheism need not inevitably [prohibit the worship of lower divine beings]. . . . The One is not necessarily 'jealous' in a cultic sense. There is room in monotheism for the worship of lower divine beings—with the understanding that they belong to the suite of the One. Thus Christianity knows the worship of saints and intercessors, as does Islam. Nor did later Judaism shrink from conceiving the scapegoat as a propitiatory offering to Sammael. . . . [But] the bearers of biblical religion sensed that for the folk the cult is decisive: whatever is worshiped is divine. A plurality of worshiped objects is calculated to foster the erroneous notion of a plurality of divine realms; hence the monotheistic idea needed to be complemented by a monolatrous cult. Even if the cult of idols, satyrs, the dead, etc., did not intend to encroach on the domain of the One, such an outcome was virtually inevitable. The monotheistic idea could never be firmly established with the folk at large unless it were complemented by cultic exclusiveness" (Kaufmann, *Religion*, 137, 147).

11. See Judg. 6:25–32, referring to Gideon's town of Ophrah, and 9:4 and 46, referring to Shechem; it is not certain that the Shechemites of this period were Israelites. The references to polytheism in the introduction to Judges and in the transitional passages between the episodes of the book do not indicate the numbers of people involved, nor does a similar statement in Judg. 5:8.

12. The biblical concept of collective responsibility meant that entire groups shared responsibility for the deeds of their individual members. As a result, when the Bible says "Israel sinned," as in Judges, it is often referring to the actions of small numbers of people. When one man, Achan, violated the ban on booty at Jericho, God told Joshua, "Israel has sinned! They have broken the covenant . . . they have taken of the proscribed . . ." (Josh. 7:11; cf. v. 1); thirty-six Israelites died for the sin. Similarly the sins involving the golden calf and Baal Peor were attributed to "the people," though Moses' commands to execute the guilty make it clear that only some of the people were involved (Exod. 32; Num. 25). A. J. Heschel paraphrased this concept as "Few are guilty, all are responsible" (Heschel, *The Prophets* [New York: Harper and Row, 1962], 14). This is the original meaning of the saying *kol yisrael ʿarevin zeh la-zeh*, "all Israelites are responsible [i.e., surety] for each other" (Sanh. 27b and parallel texts; see E. E. Urbach, *The Sages: Their Beliefs and Opinions* [Cambridge: Harvard University Press, 1987], 538–541). For further discussion of the subject see Heschel, *Prophets*, 14–16; Kaufmann, *Religion*, 135, 229–230, 270; W. Eichrodt, *Theology of the Old Testament* (Philadelphia: Westminster Press, 1961–67), 2:231–240, 435–437.

13. The involvement of the public is mentioned in such verses as 1 Kings 18:22,30; 19:10,14,18; 2 Kings 17:7–17. The

prime examples of polytheism cited in the book, however, are the chapels that Solomon built for his foreign wives and his eventual worship of their gods, Jeroboam's golden calves, Ahab's tolerance of Jezebel's zeal for Baal, and the paganizing activities of Manasseh.

14. These figurines usually represent women as pregnant, holding babies, or with breasts full of milk, and it is a reasonable conjecture that they were used as charms which were intended to aid women in conceiving, giving birth, and producing sufficient milk. See J. Tigay, *You Shall Have No Other Gods* (Atlanta: Scholars Press, 1986), Appendix F, Section 2.

15. See ibid.

16. In other words, monolatry presupposes monotheism; note that Naaman decides to become monolatrous (2 Kings 5:17) after he becomes a monotheist (v. 15).

17. Albright, *Archaeology and the Religion of Israel*, 177.

18. See also Deut. 4:28; 28:64; Jer. 2:11.

19. 1 Sam. 2:2; 2 Sam. 22:32; Ps. 18:32. See n. 3.

20. See n. 5.

Excursus 7

1. The punitive character of being forced to worship lesser heavenly beings is suggested by passages in which being dealt with by angels is compared unfavorably to being dealt with by God Himself (Exod. 32:34; 33:1–5,12–16). A pertinent example in talmudic folklore is the belief that God gives rain to foreign lands through an emissary, while to the land of Israel He gives rain personally (Ta'an. 10a; Sifrei 42 [cf. Ta'an. 25b and Yoma 21a for Ridya, the bull-like angel of rain, and see A. Kohut, *Aruch Completum* (Vienna, 1928), 7:257]; for this and other passages expressing the theme "not by means of an angel but by God Himself" see J. Goldin, *Studies in Midrash and Related Literature* [Philadelphia: Jewish Publication Society, 1988], 163–173).

2. See Y. Kaufmann, *The Religion of Israel*, trans. M. Greenberg (Chicago: University of Chicago Press, 1960), 221, 294–295, 358; M. Greenberg, "Biblical Attitudes Toward Power," in E. B. Firmage et al., eds., *Religion and Law: Biblical-Judaic and Islamic Perspectives* (Winona Lake, Ind.: Eisenbrauns, 1990), 103. That idolatry began when humanity was divided into different language groups also seems to be implied by Zeph. 3:9, according to which the nations will be (re)united in the worship of the Lord when He makes them all "pure of speech" (lit., "clear of speech"), presumably meaning that they will once again speak a mutually intelligible language.

3. See Kaufmann, *Religion*, 128, 164.

4. See, e.g., Isa. 2; Jer. 16:19–20; Zech. 14:9.

5. See the list of Septuagint readings in Meg. 9a–9b and parallels discussed by E. Tov, "The Rabbinic Tradition Concerning the 'Alterations' Inserted into the Greek Pentateuch and Their Relation to the Original Text of the LXX," JSJ 15 (1984): 65–89; A. Geiger, *Ha-Mikra' Ve-Targumav* (reprint; Jerusalem: Bialik Foundation, 1972), 285–286 (cf. Vulg.); the same interpretation is given in Mid. Hag., Saadia, and Rashi on the verse.

6. Abravanel.

7. See Hoffmann and the patristic view cited by Driver, 71.

8. Jer. 50:35–39; cf. 12:14–17. See Kaufmann, *Religion*, 424.

9. See Deut. 12:29–31; 18:9–12; 20:18 (cf. 7:4).

Excursus 8

1. Exod. 20:5–6; 34:6–7; Num. 14:18; Jer. 32:18.

2. ANET, 207–208, 395d; the Greek texts are cited in Weinfeld, Commentary, 298.

3. ARM 8, 1:4–5; this translation is preferable to that in ANET, 545, no. 13.

4. 1 Sam. 17:25; M. Weinfeld, "The Covenant of Grant in

the Old Testament and the Ancient Near East," JAOS 90 (1970): 189–190.

5. Gen. 9:25; Num. 16:32; Deut. 11:6; 1 Sam. 2:30–36; 2 Kings 5:27; 9:7–10.

6. 2 Sam. 9:1; 10:2; 19:32–40.

7. Judg. 14:15; 18:25; cf. Shadal at Exod. 20:5; cf. ANET, 207d. Job protests that if this is true, it is no real punishment or deterrent (Job 21:19–21,31).

8. J. Wellhausen, *Prolegomena to the History of Ancient Israel* (New York: Meridian, 1957), 307; cf. Shadal at Exod. 20:5.

9. Exod. 22:20–23; 34:7; Num. 14:18; Deut. 7:9; 2 Sam. 24:17; Jer. 18:21; 32:18; Ps. 103:17–18; 109:9–15. See M. Greenberg, "Some Postulates of Biblical Criminal Law," in M. Haran, ed., *Yehezkel Kaufmann Jubilee Volume* (Jerusalem: Magnes Press, 1960), 20–27.

10. Gen. 6:28; 7:1; 26:4–5; Num. 25:7–13; 1 Kings 3:6.

11. Num. 16:32; Deut. 11:6 (contrast Num. 26:11).

12. 1 Sam. 12:10; 1 Kings 14:7–18; 15:29–30; 21:21–29; 2 Kings 9:7–9.

13. 2 Kings 23:26–27; 24:3; Jer. 15:4; Lam. 5:7; cf. ANET, 395cd.

14. Lam. 5:16.

15. Jer. 31:29–30; Ezek. 18:2.

16. Jer. 31:29–30.

17. Ezek. 18:1–20.

18. Mak. 24a.

19. For a summary of views on these clauses see M. Weiss, *Mi-Ba'ayot "Torat ha-Gemul" ha-Mikra'it, Tarbiz* 32 (1963): 6–11.

20. See Targums Onk. and Jon.; Ber. 7a; Sanh. 27b; Rashi, Rashbam, Ramban, Abravanel, Sforno, Keil-Delitzsch, and Mayes.

21. See Isa. 65:7; Jer. 16:11–13; Ps. 109:2–20; Lam. 5:7 and 16; Neh. 9:2; Dan. 9:16.

22. For further discussion see Milgrom, *Numbers*, Excursus 32.

Excursus 9

1. Exod. 3:8,17; 13:5; 33:3; Lev. 20:24; Num. 13:27; 14:8; 16:13–14; Josh. 5:6; Jer. 11:5; 32:22; Ezek. 20:6,15.

2. Joel 4:18 and Job 20:17. In Greek and Canaanite mythology, the skies rain oil and the wadies and plains flow with honey at the presence of the god of fertility (T. H. Gaster, *Thespis*, rev. ed. [Garden City, N.Y.: Doubleday, 1961], 222, 459; ANET, 140d).

3. Gen. 18:8; 43:11; Judg. 4:19; 14:8–9; 2 Sam. 17:29; 1 Kings 14:3; Jer. 41:8; Ecclus. 39:26.

4. Song 4:11; 5:1.

5. Prov. 27:27; Deut. 32:14; Isa. 7:21–22.

6. M. Haran, "Seething a Kid in Its Mother's Milk," JJS 30 (1979): 30–31.

7. Judg. 14:8–9; 1 Sam. 14:27–29; cf. Ps. 81:17 and possibly Deut. 32:13. Although beekeeping was known elsewhere in the ancient Near East, and by talmudic times in Israel, there is no evidence for it in Israel in biblical times.

8. Gen. 43:11 (see Sarna, *Genesis*); Lev. 2:11–12 (see Levine, *Leviticus*); Num. 13:27 (n.b. v. 23; see Milgrom, *Numbers*); Deut. 8:8; it is frequently mentioned next to olive oil, as in Ezek. 16:19; 2 Chron. 31:5.

9. See, e.g., Targ. Jon. Deut. 8:8; 27:3; Sifrei 297; MdRSbY (ed. J. N. Epstein and E. Z. Melamed, p. 38) and Mid. Hag. (ed. S. Fisch, p. 228), where the issue is debated; TJ Bik. 1:3, 63d; Rashi, Rashbam, and Ibn Ezra at Lev. 2:11 (see Meḥokekei Yehudah there); Rashi at Deut. 26:2.

10. Mish. Ned. 6:9; Mish. Ter. 11:3; Bek. 7b; Ket. 111b with reference to our phrase.

11. Cf. Exod. 3:8; Num. 14:7–8; Ezek. 20:6.

12. See also the Qur'an, 47:16, which promises believers rivers of water, milk, wine, and honey in the Garden of Paradise (ref. courtesy Sarah Stroumsa).

13. Gen. 43:11; Deut. 26:9; 32:13–14; 2 Kings 18:32; Jer. 11:5; Ezek. 27:17; cf. ANET, 19–20. The date honey of the Jordan Valley near Jericho was well known in Second Temple times; see Josephus, War 4.468–469; Pliny, *Natural History* 13:44–45, in H. Rackham, *Pliny: The Natural History* 4 (Cambridge: Harvard University Press, 1945), 125.

14. Cf. Ket. 111b; Tosef. Toh. 2:5; Pliny, *Natural History*, 13:45.

15. See further S. E. Loewenstamm, s.v. *devorah*, EM 2:584–587; 4:547, 553.

16. ANET, 237–238, 477a. See S. D. Waterhouse, "A Land Flowing with Milk and Honey," *Andrews University Seminary Studies* 1 (1963): 152–166.

17. ANET, 19–20. For the final clause, see H. Fischer, *Varia* (New York: Metropolitan Museum of Art, 1976), 97–98. This area (called Yaa or Araru) was perhaps in the Bekaa Valley or northern Transjordan; cf. Ahituv, *Canaanite Toponyms in Ancient Egyptian Documents* (Jerusalem: Magnes Press, and Leiden: Brill, 1984), 66–67.

Excursus 10

1. Followed by Shadal and Ehrlich.

2. Ehrlich, *Randglossen*, claims that *levad* is not used in nominal sentences, such as the Shema, but see 2 Kings 19:19 and Ps. 86:10.

3. As in 1:6,19–20; 2:33,36; 4:7; 5:2; 6:24–25; 29:14,17,28. The same is true of "the Lord *your* God," which occurs far more often (see chap. 5, n. 28); 29:5 is a possible exception. That the copula belongs only in the last clause of the verse is recognized in the Nash Papyrus, Targum Neof., the fragment targum (MS V), and Pesh., which add *hu'* at the end of the verse, and in LXX and Vulg. which add "is" there.

4. For *'eḥad* meaning "unique" see 2 Sam. 7:23. Cf. Akkadian "unique one" (ANET, 386b). Some Egyptian texts seem to describe gods as "one" on this sense; see ANET, 365b, 366c; J. Bergman, s.v. *'eḥad*, in TDOT 1:194f (cf. C. Gordon, "His Name is 'One,'" JNES 29 [1970]: 198–199).

5. ANET, 201a; cf. the Hittite treaties in ANET, 205ab (several Ishtars) and 205d–206a (several Telepinuses and Hebats), the Assyrian treaty in ANET, 533cd (two or three Adads, two Ishtars), and the South Arabian inscription in ANET, 667b (three "'Attars"). Cf. W. Eichrodt, *Theology of the Old Testament* (Philadelphia: Westminster Press, 1961–67), 1:200. (Place names of the form *ba'al* plus place name [e.g., Exod. 14:2; Josh. 11:17] have also been taken to indicate a multiplicity of gods named Baal, but since *ba'al* is originally a common noun for "lord," these names may simply refer to unnamed local spirits.) Eissfeldt rejects the view that the various Canaanite Baals were viewed as different beings (cited by G. von Rad, *Old Testament Theology* [New York: Harper and Row, 1962–65], 1:209 n. 44); cf. also E. Bevan, *Holy Images* (London: George Allen and Unwin, 1940), 20.

6. Z. Meshel, *Kuntillet Ajrud* (Jerusalem: Israel Museum, 1978).

7. W. F. Bade, "Der Monojahwismus des Deuteronomiums," ZAW 30 (1910): 81–90; G. F. Moore in *Encyclopaedia Biblica* 1 (1891): 1091–1092; Driver, 89–90; Eichrodt, *Theology*, 1:105 n. 5, 226 n. 2; von Rad, *Old Testament Theology* 1:227; G. Fohrer, *History of Israelite Religion* (Nashville: Abingdon, 1972), 297 n. 1; see the recent discussion by P. Kyle McCarter in P. D. Miller et al., eds., *Ancient Israelite Religion* (Philadelphia: Fortress Press, 1987), 139–142. If such a danger existed, it might have been acute in the seventh century, as Deuteronomy was developing, when refugees from Samaria were migrating into Judah.

Two other phenomena that might theoretically have posed a similar danger—although there is no evidence that they actually did—are the multiplicity of names used for YHVH in Genesis (see, e.g., Gen. 14:18–19; 16:13; 17:1; 21:33; 31:13; cf. also the epithet *YHVH zeh Sinai*, "YHVH of Sinai," Judg. 5:5; Ps. 68:9) and a type of theological speculation known from Babylonia in which several deities were identified as aspects or parts of a single deity (see T. Jacobsen, *Treasures of Darkness* [New Haven: Yale University Press, 1976], 234–236).

8. Nili Fox, "One God? A Study of DNs and Their GNs" (unpublished University of Pennsylvania seminar paper, 1991), 4. The text is partially translated into English by H. Nelson, "The Egyptian Temple," in G. E. Wright and D. N. Freedman, ed., *Biblical Archaeologist Reader* (Garden City, N.Y.: Doubleday, 1961), 153.

9. For a recent discussion of the issue and a new suggestion, see J. G. Janzen, "On the Most Important Word in the *Shema* (Deuteronomy VI 4–5)," VT 37 (1987): 280–300.

10. See Tractate Berakhot; Maimonides, Sefer Ha-Mitsvot, positive no. 10; Sefer Ha-Ḥinnukh, no. 419.

11. Aristeas 158–160; Josephus, Ant. 4.212–213; the practice is also reflected at Qumran (M. Weinfeld, "Traces of 'Qedushat Yozer'" [Hebrew] *Tarbiz* 45 [1975–76]: 15–26; S. Talmon, *The World of Qumran from Within* [Jerusalem: Magnes Press, 1989], 226, 229). Whether the Nash papyrus, which includes the Shema, was a liturgical text or part of *tefillin* or a *mezuzah* is not certain. Recitation of the third paragraph (Num. 15:37–41) in the morning prayer is reflected in Josephus, Ant. 4.212–213. Whether it was to be recited at night was long debated; see Mish. Ber. 1:5; R. Kimelman, "The *Shema* and Its Rhetoric: The Case for the *Shema* Being More than Creation, Revelation, and Redemption," *Journal of Jewish Thought and Philosophy* 1 (1992): n. 15; I. Elbogen, *Ha-Tefillah be-Yisrael* (Tel Aviv: Devir, 1972), 18.

12. See Kimelman, "*Shema* and Its Rhetoric."

13. Ber. 13a (J. Goldstein, *I Maccabees* [Garden City, N.Y.: Doubleday, 1976], 133 n. 171, compares the Shema's role to that of an oath of loyalty such as the Roman soldier's oath).

14. Judah Halevi, *Kuzari*, 3:17; Elbogen, *Ha-Tefillah be-Yisrael*, 17; M. Weinfeld, "The Loyalty Oath in the Ancient Near East," UF 8 (1976): 410–412.

15. H. L. Horowitz, "The Sh'ma Reconsidered," *Judaism* 24 (1975): 476–481.

16. Maimonides, Hilkhot Keri'at Shema' 1:2; Sefer Ha-Ḥinnukh, no. 419. For a comprehensive collection of Jewish sources on the Shema, see M. M. Kasher, *Sefer Shema' Yisrael* (Jerusalem: Beth Torah Shelemah, 1980). See also S. D. McBride, "The Yoke of the Kingdom," *Interpretation* 27 (1973): 273–306.

17. Milton Steinberg, *Basic Judaism* (New York: Harcourt, Brace and World, 1947), 42ff.; Hertz, 920–921. Daniel J. Satlow observes that Deut. 6:4–9 is a more suitable expression of Israelite belief than the Bible's explicit declarations of monotheism because it expresses the one God's connection to Israel as well as a fuller range of religious thought (D. Satlow, "Why the *Shema*?" [unpublished University of Pennsylvania seminar paper, 1985]).

18. Suk. 42a; Maimonides, Hilkhot Talmud Torah 1:6; Shulḥan 'Arukh, Yoreh De'ah 245:5.

19. See S. Singer, *The Standard Prayerbook* (New York: Bloch, 1951), 438, 458.

20. See Ber. 61a; Hertz, 922–923.

21. Masorah; Minḥat Shai; Midrash Aggadah, ed. S. Buber; Ḥazzekuni. For confusion of enlargement, suspension, and strange forms of writing letters, see M. M. Kasher, *Torah Shelemah* 29:98–99.

22. *Sefer Abudraham Hashalem*, ed. S. Wertheimer (Jerusalem, 1963), 80. Cf. Josephus, who calls the recitation "bearing witness" (Greek *martyrein*) to God's bounties (Ant. 4.212–213).

23. Midrash Aggadah, ed. S. Buber; cf. Lev. R. 19:2 (ed. Margulies, 418, 422); Tanḥ. Genesis sec. 1. Note that in Exod. 34:14 the enlarged *resh* in *ʾaḥer* can be explained similarly, so as to prevent the blasphemous reading "You shall not bow down to *the one* God" instead of "to another god." For other explanations see Baal Ha-Turim; *Midrash ʾOtiot Ketanot U-Gedolot*, in J. D. Eisenstein, *ʾOtzar Midrashim*, 2:432–433; Kasher, *Sefer Shemaʿ Yisraʾel*, 22:15; 26:43; appendix, 245ff.

Excursus 11

1. The earliest explicit reference to this interpretation is Aristeas 158–159; see also Josephus, Ant. 4.212–213; Matt. 23:5; the targums, MdRY, and Sifrei Deut. on the biblical verses; and Men. 34b–37b. N. G. Cohen argues that Philo also refers to *tefillin* in Spec. 4, xxvi, §§137–139; see "Philo's Tefillin," *Proceedings of the Ninth WCJS*, Division A, The Period of the Bible (Jerusalem: World Union of Jewish Studies, 1986), 199–206.

2. See Tractate Tefillin 9 and 12; Matt. 23:5.

3. E.g., Mish. Shab. 6:2.

4. Eruv. 96b–97a.

5. When amulets do contain biblical verses, they are of apotropaic content, such as Ps. 91 or the priestly blessing (Num. 6:24–26; see G. Barkai, *Ketef Hinom* [Jerusalem: Israel Museum, 1986], Eng. 29–31, Heb. 34–37). That the purpose of *tefillin* as a commandment is educational and spiritual is clear from the content of the passages that the halakhah requires them to contain. This does not rule out the possibility that earlier such capsules were filled with magical inscriptions and used as amulets. Indeed, even *tefillin* containing nothing but the required passages attracted a superstitious veneration for presumed protective powers, being sometimes worn in the privy for protection from demons or placed on a child who could not sleep (Ber. 23a–b; TJ Shab. 6:2, 8b; Targum to Song 8:3). But this kind of veneration is commonly accorded to sacred objects and practices and is no more indicative of the meaning of *tefillin* as a commandment than is similar treatment of the Torah, the *mezuzah*, the Second Tithe or the coins into which it has been converted, and the scriptures of other religions. See J. Tigay, "On the Term Phylacteries (Matt. 23:5)," *Harvard Theological Review* 72 (1979): 51–52.

6. Cf. the (uninscribed) pendants attached to frontlets shown by O. Keel, "Zeichen der Verbundenheit: Zur Vorgeschichte und Bedeutung der Vorderungen von Deuteronomium 6,8f. und Par.," in P. Casetti et al., eds., *Mélanges Dominique Barthélemy* (Göttingen: Vandenhoeck und Ruprecht, 1981), 193–215.

7. See A. M. Habermann, *ʿAl ha-Tefillin Bi-ymei Qedem*, EI 3 (1954): 176–177; G. Vermes, "Pre-Mishnaic Jewish Worship and the Phylacteries from the Dead Sea," VT 9 (1959): 70.

8. Mish. Meg. 4:8; Shab. 108b.

9. Aquila, Theodotion, and some manuscripts of LXX.

10. Men. 42b; Git. 45b.

11. Shab. 130a; TJ Ber. 2:3, 4b.

12. In keeping with his view that Jewish law is independent of the literal meaning of Scripture, Rashbam held that such an interpretation would not cancel the halakhah; see his introduction to his commentary on Exod. 21.

13. See J. Tigay, "On the Meaning of *Ṭ(W)ṬPT*," JBL 101 (1982): 321–331.

14. Jer. 31:32; ANET, 476b.

15. For fuller discussion see J. Tigay, s.v. *tefillin*, EM 8:883–895.

16. For Samaritan *mezuzot* see Keel, "Zeichen der Verbundenheit," 175–178.

17. For Qumran texts identified by scholars as *mezuzot*, see DJD 3 (1962): 158–161; DJD 6 (1977): 80–85; Keel, "Zeichen der Verbundenheit," 166–168 (he thinks that the Nash Papyrus is

also a *mezuzah*). See also Aristeas 158; Philo, Spec. 4.142; Josephus, Ant. 4.213.

18. See Keel, "Zeichen der Verbundenheit," 183–192; IR, nos. 14, 139, 140; Z. Meshel, *Kuntillet Ajrud* (Jerusalem: Israel Museum, 1978), 12–13. Lachish letter no. 4 mentions writing on the *delet*, meaning either on the door or in a column of a scroll. See ANET, 322c; DOTT, 216.

19. M. Cogan, s.v. *shaʿar*, EM 8:234 (see EM 4:387–390; ANET, 653–654); H. G. Güterbock, "Hittite Historiography: A Survey," in H. Tadmor and M. Weinfeld, eds., *History, Historiography, and Interpretation* (Jerusalem: Magnes Press, 1983), 22–23.

20. Keel, "Zeichen der Verbundenheit," 183–192; Weinfeld, Commentary, 256; idem, "Instructions for Temple Visitors," in S. Israelit-Groll, ed., *Egyptological Studies* (Jerusalem: Magnes Press, 1982), 224–250.

21. The Sifrei considers and rejects writing the *mezuzah* on stone.

22. See J. Trachtenberg, *Jewish Magic and Superstition* (Cleveland and New York: World Publishing Society; Philadelphia: Jewish Publication Society, 1961), 146–152; cf. Targum to Song 8:3; J. Hastings, ed., *Encyclopedia of Religion and Ethics* (reprint; New York: Scribner's, 1951), s.v. "Charms and Amulets," 440.

23. TJ Peʾah 1:1, 15d; cf. the story about Onkelos in Av. Zar. 11a.

24. Maimonides, Hilkhot Tefillin u-Mezuzah 5:4.

25. Ibid., 6:13.

Excursus 12

H. C. Brichto, "The Worship of the Golden Calf: A Literary Analysis of a Fable on Idolatry," HUCA 54 (1983): 1–44; N. M. Sarna, *Exploring Exodus* (New York: Schocken, 1986), 215–219; J. R. Spencer, s.v. "Golden Calf," ABD 2:1065–1069; H. Motzki, "Ein Beitrag zum Problem des Stierkultes in der Religionsgeschichte Israels," VT 25 (1955): 470–485.

1. L. H. Lesko, "Egyptian Religion: An Overview," in M. Eliade, ed., *The Encyclopedia of Religion* (New York: Macmillan, 1987), 5:49; ANEP, fig. 570.

2. ANET, 129d, 142c.

3. ANEP, fig. 616. Cf. the scene on the Anatolian cylinder seal reproduced in L. Stager, "When Canaanites and Philistines Ruled Ashkelon," BAR 17/2 (March-April, 1991): 28.

4. See ANEP, figs. 832, 835 (a statue of a deity standing on a bull, from Hazor), 828 (Ugarit); Stager, "Canaanites and Philistines," 25–29 (Ashkelon); R. Hestrin, "The Cult Stand from Taʿanach and its Religious Background," in E. Lipinski, ed., *Studia Phoenicia* 5 (1987): 61–77, and more briefly in "Understanding Asherah: Exploring Semitic Iconography," BAR 17/5 (September-October, 1991), 55–56 (Taanach, tenth century; it is not certain whether Taanach was Israelite or Canaanite at the time).

5. A. Mazar, "The 'Bull Site'—An Iron Age I Open Cult Place," BASOR 247 (1982): 27–42.

6. See ANEP, figs. 500, 501, 519–521, 531, 537, 570, 616, 828, 832, 835.

7. See M. Haran, *Temples and Temple Service* (Oxford: Clarendon, 1978), 29 n. 28; H.-J. Kraus, *Worship in Ancient Israel* (Richmond: John Knox Press, 1966), 150.

8. See Comment to 4:17–18; Radak at 1 Kings 12:28; W. F. Albright, *From the Stone Age to Christianity*, 2nd ed. (Garden City, N.Y.: Doubleday, 1957), 299–300; Y. Kaufmann, *The Religion of Israel*, trans. M. Greenberg (Chicago: University of Chicago Press, 1960), 271; W. Eichrodt, *Theology of the Old Testament* (Philadelphia: Westminster Press, 1961–67), 1:107–108; Weinfeld, Commentary, 424–426.

9. See ANEP, figs. 470–474, 479, 486, 500–501, 519–521, 530–531, 534, 537, 835; Mazar, "'Bull Site.'"

10. See S. E. Loewenstamm, "The Making and Destruction of the Golden Calf," *Biblica* 48 (1967): 481–490.

11. H. L. Ginsberg, "Hosea's Ephraim: More Fool than Knave," *JBL* 80 (1961): 345–346; Weinfeld, *Commentary*, 424–426. For a possible Assyrian reference to Jeroboam's calves, see J. Tigay, *You Shall Have No Other Gods* (Atlanta: Scholars Press, 1986), 35, and cf. Hos. 10:5–6.

Excursus 13

H. M. Wiener, "The Arrangement of Deuteronomy 12–26," JPOS 6 (1926): 185–195, reprinted in H. Loewe, ed., *Posthumous Essays* (London: Oxford University Press, 1932), 26–36; Steven Kaufman, "The Structure of the Deuteronomic Law," *Maarav* 1 (1978–79): 105–158; idem, "The Second Table of the Decalogue and the Implicit Categories of Ancient Near Eastern Law," in J. H. Marks and R. M. Good, ed., *Love and Death in the Ancient Near East: Essays in Honor of Marvin H. Pope* (Guilford, Conn.: Four Quarters Publishing Co., 1987), 111–116; Rofé, *Mavo'*, chap. 17, "The Arrangement of the Laws in Deuteronomy" (Hebrew; Eng. trans. in *Ephemeridum Theologicarum Lovaniensium* 64 [1988]: 265–287); G. Braulik, "Die Abfolge der Gesetze in Deuteronomium 12–26 und der Dekalog" in N. Lohfink, ed., *Das Deuteronomium* (Leuven: Leuven University Press, 1985), 252–272; idem, "Zur Abfolge der Gesetze in Deuteronomium 16,18–21,23: Weitere Beobachtungen," *Biblica* 69 (1988): 63–92; B. Levinson, "The Hermeneutics of Innovation: The Impact of Centralization upon the Structure, Sequence, and Reformulation of Legal Material in Deuteronomy" (Ph.D. diss., Brandeis University, 1991).

1. Tanḥuma Ki Tetse' 1; Abravanel, 201.

2. For the kind of order modern readers expect, note the following advice from a well-known guide for writing college papers:

> Consider the organization of the material—in what arrangement and what order you will present it . . . and . . . [keep in mind] the controlling idea of the paper . . . while the outline is taking shape. *Arrangement* calls for separation of the material into categories. . . . Using some logical basis of separation—chronological, spatial, logical, general-to-particular . . . cause-to-effect (to name but a few), determine how the . . . material is to be grouped. . . . *Chronological order* means that the ideas are presented in the order of their happening . . . *logical order* is one in which the presentation of each idea depends for its comprehension upon the reader's grasp of the idea preceding it.

K. L. Turabian, *Student's Guide for Writing College Papers*, 2nd ed. (Chicago: University of Chicago Press, 1972), 47–48.

3. Josephus, Ant., 4.197. Josephus may have followed an order he found in proto-rabbinic sources; see D. M. Goldenberg, "The Halakha in Josephus and in Tannaitic Literature," JQR 67 (1976): 30–43. Modern scholars have likewise remarked on the scattered nature of the arrangement; see those quoted by Levinson, "Hermeneutics of Innovation," 2–3.

4. Sifrei Num. sec. 131.

5. According to Rabbi Akiba (early second century), "every section that is juxtaposed to another draws meaning from it" (Sifrei Num. 131). Not all the rabbis agreed that this method should be applied throughout the Torah, but it is notable that those who did not nevertheless agreed that in the case of Deuteronomy it should (*be-mishneh torah darshinan semukhin*; Ber. 21b; Yev. 4a; see further W. Bacher, *'Erkhei Midrash* [reprint; Jerusalem: Carmiel, 1970], 1:91; 2:247). An example of a legal inference from juxtaposition is Rabbi Judah the Prince's interpretation of Deut. 23:1, "No man shall marry his father's [former] wife [lit. woman]." According to R. Judah, this includes not only one's father's former wife, but also women he had raped or seduced, since the immediately preceding laws deal with seduction and rape (Deut. 22:23–28; see Ber. 21b). A similar inference from the juxtaposition of these passages is found in 11QTemple 66:9ff., which apparently takes the location of 23:1 as indicating that it qualifies 22:29: the rapist is to marry his victim only if she is legally permitted to him by the laws about incest. This implies that the sectarians who do not draw inferences from juxtaposition, addressed in Berakhot, are not the Qumran sect.

6. On the coherence and order of 22:13–29, see G. J. Wenham and J. G. McConville, "Drafting Techniques in Some Deuteronomic Laws," VT 30 (1980): 248–252. Elsewhere in the Torah, Exodus 21:12–22:16 and Leviticus 1–7 are good examples of coherently, topically ordered collections of rules dealing with a single group of closely related subjects. On the former, see S. M. Paul, *Studies in the Book of the Covenant in the Light of Cuneiform and Biblical Law* (Leiden: Brill, 1970), 106ff.

7. See Kaufman, "Structure," 115; the first quotation is from Paul, *Studies*, 106, referring to the laws of Exod. 21:12–22:16.

8. Steven J. Lieberman. Associative links are also discernible in the arrangement of Mesopotamian omen literature. See S. M. Moren, *The Omen Series Shumma Alu, A Preliminary Investigation* (Ph.D. diss., University of Pennsylvanaia, 1978).

9. See J. M. Lindenberger, *The Aramaic Proverbs of Ahiqar* (Baltimore: Johns Hopkins University Press, 1983), 21 (N.B.: proverbs 11–12 are more likely connected by the homonymous roots spelled *ḥmr* than by *rḥm*; perhaps the latter is a misprint).

10. See H. Petschow, "Zur Systematik und Gesetzestechnik im Codex Hammurabi," ZA 23 (1965): 146–172; cf. idem, "Zur 'Systematik' in den Gesetzen von Eschnunna," in *Symbolae Iuridicae et Historicae Martino David Dedicatae*, 2 (Leiden: Brill, 1968): 131–143. Petschow suggests that in a few cases the connections are based on "key words" (*Stichwörter*; see 151 and 169 n. 137), but in most if not all of the cases he cites the verbal link reflects a topical one. For example, LH §113 and the nearby §120 are indeed linked by the word "granary," but that is because both deal with losses that occur at granaries.

11. J. J. Finkelstein, "A Late Old Babylonian Copy of the Laws of Hammurapi," JCS 21 (1967): 43.

12. Ibid. These ancient headings show that the original classification and paragraphing of the laws by their first modern editor, V. Scheil, were sometimes off the mark. Since dividing the laws into classes is a prerequisite for explaining their arrangement, this discovery is a sobering reminder of how easy it is for moderns to miss what the ancients considered the intrinsic subject of a law.

13. Such principles are also prominent in nonlegal rabbinic literature. Max Kadushin characterized the coherence of sections of midrashic literature as follows:

> Even in those instances in which haggadic statements are connected, they are connected only through an association of ideas. Such an instance in the Mekilta, consisting of a number of statements, begins with one telling that God spoke to Moses in Egypt not in the city but outside of it because the city "was full of abominations and idols," and closes with the declaration that the patriarchs and prophets offered their lives in behalf of Israel [Lauterbach, 1:3–11, ll. 35–113]. The statements in this passage are connected, to be sure, but the connection is from statement to statement only, so that the last has no connection whatever with the first, nor indeed with any but the one immediately preceding it. Essentially, each statement in the passage is an independent entity.

M. Kadushin, *A Conceptual Approach to the Mekilta* (New York:

Jonathan David for the Jewish Theological Seminary, 1969), 19–20.

14. Maimonides suggests that this is because the agricultural laws are essentially about food, and one may not eat before reciting a blessing over the food. See his Introduction to the Commentary on the Mishnah (ed. Y. Kafih, Hebrew edition, 14); Albeck, *Zera'im*, 1–2.

15. H. Danby, *The Mishnah* (London: Oxford University Press, 1933), xxiv (see n. 2 there for seeming exceptions); J. N. Epstein, *Mavo' le-nusah ha-mishnah*, 983–989. In the Qur'an, too, following the introductory chapter, the remaining chapters are arranged in order of length, from the longest to the shortest. The same is true of the first five books of the minor prophets in the Septuagint. For a similar principle in the order of the Prophets and Hagiographa, see L. Blau, s.v. "Bible Canon," in JE 3:143–144; H. L. Ginsberg, s.v. "Job, The Book of," EncJud 10:111–112.

16. Danby, *Mishnah*, xxv. Certain passages found in the Babylonian Talmud hold that the sequence of the tractates in the Mishnah is also because of shared patterns of formulation. See Shevuot 2a; Sotah 2a.

17. Danby, *Mishnah*, xxv.

18. A. L. Oppenheim, *The Interpretation of Dreams in the Ancient Near East* (Philadelphia: Transactions of the American Philosophical Society, N.S. 46/3, 1956), 241; Ber. 56b, end, 57b; cf. J. Tigay, "An Early Technique of Aggadic Exegesis," in H. Tadmor and M. Weinfeld, eds., *History, Historiography, and Interpretation* (Jerusalem: Magnes Press, 1983), 177–179.

19. See Rofé, *Mavo'*, chap. 17, "The Arrangement of the Laws in Deuteronomy." I have also found convincing explanations of specific links in Kaufman, "Structure," 105–158, but I am not persuaded that the provisions of Deuteronomy as a whole follow the order of the Decalogue (cf. Levinson, 19 n. 28; for earlier explanations of the Book of the Covenant as based on the order of the Decalogue, see Paul, *Studies*, 107 n. 1).

20. Driver, 136; Paul, *Studies*, 34–35.

21. J. Blenkinsopp, in R. E. Brown et al., eds., *The Jerome Biblical Commentary* (Englewood Cliffs, N.J.: Prentice Hall, 1968), 1:110.

22. Paul, *Studies*, 34–35. Cf. Exod. 23:24; 34:12; Num. 33:51–52; Deut. 7:5.

23. See Chap. 13 n. 5.

24. The unity of this section is reflected in its selection as the Torah reading on the last days of Passover and the Feast of Weeks (if they fall on a Sabbath) and on Shemini 'Atseret.

25. Exod. 34:18–23 also juxtaposes firstlings and Pesah.

26. Note also "the LORD detests," 16:22. Others suggest that the prohibition on asherahs and pillars at the altar is located here because some aspects of judging took place at sanctuaries or the like; cf. Hoffmann, 296; Kaufman, "Structure," 155 n. 88.

27. See Driver; O. Eissfeldt, *The Old Testament: An Introduction* (New York: Harper and Row, 1965), 131, 174; Weinfeld, DDS, 92; Rofé, *Mavo'*, 57–59, 61 n. 5, 164, 170, 206 n. 31. (If this is the case, the use of pillars, posts, and blemished sacrificial animals would be the original referent of 13:1.) Others, in contrast, think that 13:2–19 were originally located with the material in chap. 17 (see scholars cited by P. E. Dion, "Deuteronomy 13: The Suppression of Alien Religious Propaganda in Israel during the Late Monarchical Era," in B. Halpern and D. W. Hobson, ed., *Law and Ideology in Monarchic Israel* [JSOT Supplement 124; Sheffield: Sheffield Academic Press, 1991], 147–216). Placing the two passages together is not without problems. Verses 17:2–7 lack many of the consistent characteristics of 13:2–19, such as the phrase "whom you have not experienced" after "other gods," which appears in all three cases in chap. 13 (see also Levinson, "Hermeneutics of Innovation," chap. 4). Dion holds that the two passages were not originally connected, but that 17 is a late derivative of 13 (see esp. 159 n. 2). In 11Q Temple 54–57, the paraphrase of 17:2–7 (as well as the

following verses) immediately *follows* that of chap. 13; this does not imply anything about the original location of the passage, since 11Q Temple regularly gathers together laws about related subjects; see Y. Yadin, *Megillat Ha-Mikdash* (Jerusalem: Israel Exploration Society and others, 1977), 1:62. Since 17:2–7 do fit with the subject matter of their present context, their present location, even if secondary, is not necessarily the result of a textual accident. However, if their location is intentional, why were 16:21–17:1 also included here and not left in 13, which they would fit better? Possibly this is because passages excerpted from their original context often draw in more material than is needed in their new context; see S. Lieberman, HJP, 7, 33; cf. J. Tigay, "On Evaluating Claims of Literary Borrowing," in M. Cohen, et al., eds., *The Tablet and the Scroll: . . . Studies . . . Hallo* (Bethesda, Md.: CDL Press, 1993), 255 n. 29.

28. Cf. Abravanel, 116b (at 17:2ff.); Hoffmann, 298.

29. See Abravanel at 19:1; 20:1 and 10; 21:1 and 10; Sforno at 19:2; Rofé, *Mavo'*, 75, 130, 165, 176.

30. M. Greenberg.

31. Rofé, *Mavo'*, 165. The basic meaning of *gevul* is "boundary." "Boundary marker" and "territory within boundaries" are derived meanings.

32. Mayes. For "theft" of fields, see Mic. 2:2. In the MT of the Decalogue, adultery intervenes between murder and theft, but in some other versions the order is murder-theft-perjury, as here, *preceded* by adultery (Nash Papyrus, LXX of Deuteronomy, Philo).

33. In 1 Sam. 8:20 these are the main roles of the king. Although Deuteronomy assigns neither to him, assuming that the laws were given their present order during the monarchy, the association could have been implicit in the mind of the compiler (Rofé, *Mavo'*, 164, notes that judges are followed by kings in 17:13–20). However, these two roles were also sometimes combined in the same individual in the premonarchic period, as in the case of Deborah in Judg. 4:5ff.

34. Kaufman, "Structure," 135. But seeing all of 19:1–22:8 as parts of a unit on taking life, corresponding to the sixth commandment, is forced.

35. See Rofé, *Mavo'*, 165 and 176. In the present order, Articles B and C are "connected by the parallel imagery of the *felled tree* of the *field* [20:19] and the body *fallen* in the *field* (21:1)" (C. Carr, cited by Kaufman, "Structure," 156 n. 96), and by the assonant phrases *ha-'adam 'ets ha-sadeh* and *ba-'adamah . . . nofel ba-sadeh* (Rofé, *Mavo'*, 176). Rofé's suggestion that A-C-B-IIIA was actually the original order is tempting. However, it is difficult to believe that, if that were the case, an editor created the present order because he considered these tenuous connections preferable. It would be more likely that the present order is due to haplography: after copying chap. 19, a scribe's eye jumped from the next word, *ki*, in 21:1, to that in 20:1, and the scribe then restored the skipped 21:1–9 after completing chap. 20 (the confusion could have been abetted by the fact that the words following *ki* in both verses have identical endings).

36. Mayes, 283.

37. Another reason that Part 2 follows Part 1 perhaps hinges on the possibility that the captive wife might become the loved one, because the marriage was based on lust, or she might become the unloved one should her husband later reject her, as v. 14 contemplates.

38. A. H. Freimann, s.v. *ben sorer u-moreh*, EM 2:161–162, citing LH §§168–169.

39. Kaufman, "Structure," 136. Rofé suggests that the link is between birds and roofs, where birds often nest (Rofé, *Mavo'*, 165–166).

40. There may be another reason as well; as J. Milgrom has noted, according to early rabbinic sources the tassels are an exception to the ban on mixing wool and linen: they were originally *supposed* to be made of *sha'atnez*, and this may be

another reason that they are mentioned right after v. 11 (Milgrom, *Numbers*, 413).

41. See also 28:30; Jer. 29:5–6. For the first two domestic activities, cf. Prov. 24:27 (order: prepare field, build house). For these plus the law about plowing, note also the order in which property is listed in Deut. 5:18 (house, field . . . ox and ass). The fact that this triad of domestic activities is preceded by a group of laws mentioning oxen and asses (22:1,4), and includes one about plowing with these animals (v. 10), may be due to the fact that oxen were essential for the farmer's work. In Deut. 28:30–31, the same triad is followed by a reference to farm animals, and Hesiod, *Works and Days*, ll. 405–406, recommends: "First build a house and get an ox for the plow, and a woman, not a wife but a slave woman, to follow the plow." Cf. Luke 14:18-20.

42. Because of this connection Vulg. and some English translations count this as the last verse of chapter 22. SP and 11QTemple do likewise; the latter, as noted above, indicates that the prohibition appears here to qualify 22:29: the rapist is to marry his victim only if she is legally permitted to him by the laws concerning incest. (Since 23:1 is connected to the laws that precede and follow it, it forms a "hinge" between them, as does 13:1 in its context.)

43. Cf. Rofé, *Mavo*', 166.

44. Kaufman holds that v. 2 is prompted by v. 1's reference to the father's genitals. The sequence of these laws is an interesting parallel to the first two "blessings" by Jacob in Genesis 49; there he denounces Reuben for sleeping with his father's concubine and then dissociates himself from the violent Simeon and Levi, asking never to "enter their council nor . . . be counted in their congregation [assembly]" (Gen. 49:4,6). Note also Lev. 22:13–24, in which laws about whom the high priest may marry are followed by laws about bodily defects which disqualify priests from service (including crushed testes, v. 20).

45. See Z. W. Falk, *Ha-'asurim lavo' bakahal*, BM 62 (1975): 342–351.

46. 2 Sam. 21–24.

47. Other topics include justice (24:16; 25:1–3), calls for remembering past events (23:25; 24:9; 25:17–19) or the bondage in Egypt (23:8; 24:18,22), and recurrent phrases such as *'ervat davar* (23:15; 24:1), *hyh b . . . het*'.

48. Several observations about the progression of topics in 23:10–26 are based on Rofé, *Mavo*', 166–167 (among other things, Rofé notes that a law is sometimes not connected to the one immediately preceding it, but to the one before that); see also Kaufman, "Structure," 138–139 (note also his argument that 23:10ff. continue the concern of vv. 1 and 2ff. with sexual purity).

49. Moran: 10–15 come after 2–9 because the exclusion is only temporary.

50. Rofé, *Mavo*', 130–131, 166. (Rofé says that *be-shivtekha huts* in v. 14 prompted *'imekha yeshev be-kirbekha* in v. 16). There is also a phraseological connection between Parts 1 and 2: God accompanies the camp to "save" Israel (*le-hatsil*) and the slave escapes "to save himself" (*le-hinnatsel*) (C. Carmichael, *The Laws of Deuteronomy* [Ithaca: Cornell University Press, 1974], 187).

51. Like chap. 23, chap. 24 begins with laws about marriage (vv. 1–5) and ends with laws providing for the sharing of crops with those in need (vv. 19–22).

52. Kaufman, "Structure," 139–140, 156 n. 108; Rofé, *Mavo*', 167; cf. Ibn Ezra. Other possible connections: grinding is usually women's work (J. C. Greenfield); *rehayim* ("millstone") is reminiscent of *rehem*, "womb" (D. M. Goldenberg).

53. Abravanel.

54. For the text of Job 24:9 see the commentary of Driver and Gray, part 2, 167; Seeligmann, *Studies in Biblical Literature*, ed. A. Hurvitz et al. (Jerusalem: Magnes Press, 1992), 281, n. 37. For the association of distraint and stealing see also Ezek.

18:7,12, and esp. 16 (see M. Greenberg, *Ezekiel 1–20* [Garden City, N.Y.: Doubleday, 1983]).

55. Driver and Miles, BL, 1:208–221; Goetze, *The Laws of Eshnunna* (New Haven: American Schools of Oriental Research, 1956), 68–73; CAD N s.v. *nepú* and *nipútu*.

56. Cf. also 15:7,12; Lev. 25:35–46, all of which have their background in insolvency.

57. Another possibility, though I think less likely, is that the juxtaposition implies that the law deals with unlawful distraint, that is, distraint where there is no debt or obligation, as in LH §§114 and LE §§22–24. The point would then be that unlawful distraint and selling is tantamount to kidnaping.

58. Rofé, *Mavo*', 167–168 (Rofé holds that this law is in any case an interpolation). See Lev. 13:46; 14:8.

59. Rofé, *Mavo*', 168.

60. Mayes; Rofé, *Mavo*', 168. Mayes notes that Exod. 22:21ff., following a law that is parallel to vv. 14–15 here, says that God will punish the oppressors' children; this law would be the antithesis of that if we read *yamutu*, with several versions, instead of *yumetu*. But such a theological statement would be out of place in a context of laws about what human authorities are supposed to do, and Mayes believes that *het'* in vv. 15 and 16 is enough to explain the location. In Ezek. 18:18–20, *'oshek* and *gezel* are followed by transgenerational punishment (divinely imposed) (my student, Mina Glick), but that is probably a coincidence.

61. The repetition of v. 18 in v. 22 may be a *Wiederaufnahme* (my student, Sonya Starr), implying that vv. 19–21 are a digression. If so, the main, or original, thread of the text was judicial laws, 24:16–18 followed by 25:1–3. Another possibility is that vv. 19–22 are an interpolation, placed here because of the shared motive clause.

62. M and SP, which lack a parashah division between vv. 3 and 4, may imply recognition of a strong thematic connection between the verses. Abravanel saw the two laws as sharing the theme of compassion—toward the criminal and toward the threshing ox. Somewhat similarly, S. Kaufman sees the two laws as part of a series prescribing fairness to one's fellow. He understands the juxtaposition of criminals and animals as part of an intentional arrangement of the series to descend from the highest to the lowest types of fellow as judged by socioeconomic criteria (Kaufman, "Structure," 141).

63. See the threshing scenes in Egyptian art, in ANEP, figs. 89, 122 row 6. This suggestion is close to that of Rofé, who holds that the striking implied in v. 4 is that of the oxen's hooves on the grain (Rofé, *Mavo*').

64. Cf. Job 31:10. See Rofé, *Mavo*', 168–169; Kaufman, "Structure," 157 n. 113; Seforno, Hoffmann, and Smith on vv. 1–12.

65. Hoffmann, 2:483; Rofé, *Mavo*', 169. In some respects, the law preceding Section V echoes the beginning of Section I: "when the Lord your God grants you safety from all your enemies around you" (25:19) echoes 12:10 (cf. Rofé, *Mavo*', 169) and "blot out the memory of Amalek" (25:19) echoes 12:3, "obliterating their [the Canaanite gods'] name" (my student, Mina Glick).

Excursus 14

1. Some scholars have argued that Deuteronomy does not mean to limit sacrifice to a single place, claiming on the basis of 23:17 that the phrase *ba-makom 'asher yivhar YHVH* means "in any place the LORD chooses," the point of the law being that one may not sacrifice in places chosen by humans, only in those chosen by God. This view was refuted, contextually and grammatically, long ago, and recent attempts to revive it are unconvincing. See J. A. Bewer, "The Case for the Early Date of Deuteronomy," JBL 47 (1928): 309–313; L. B. Paton, "The Case

for the Post-Exilic Origin of Deuteronomy," *JBL* 47 (1928): 347; E. König, "Stimmen Ex 20:24 und Dtn 12:13f. zusammen?" *ZAW* 42 (1924): 337–346; idem, "Der generelle Artikel im Hebräischen," *ZAW* 44 (1926): 172–175; K. Budde, "Das Deuteronomium und die Reform König Josias," *ZAW* 44 (1926): 184–189. Laws such as 17:8–13 and 31:11 clearly presuppose a single place.

2. Questions about the historicity of this account are discussed in the Introduction.

3. Archaeologists have discussed whether traces of the destruction of local sanctuaries by Hezekiah and Josiah are identifiable at certain sites in Judah. See the sources cited by J. Bright, *A History of Israel*, 3rd ed. (Philadelphia: Westminster Press, 1981), 282 n. 38; 319 n. 26; N. Lohfink, "Recent Discussion on 2 Kings 22–23: The State of the Question," in D. L. Christiansen, ed., *A Song of Power and the Power of Song: Essays on the Book of Deuteronomy* (Winona Lake, Ind.: Eisenbrauns, 1993), 40.

4. For comments on the negative impact of centralization, see M. Buber, *The Prophetic Faith* (New York: Harper, 1960), 168–169; cf. Rowley, *Worship in Ancient Israel* (Philadelphia: Fortress Press, 1967), 240. In the Comments to 12:2–28 (introductory Comment) and 16:8 I have suggested that Deuteronomy expected the place of sacrifice to be taken by prayer and study in locations throughout the country. Conceivably, incense and meal offerings were also permitted to continue outside of the chosen sanctuary; see chap. 12, n. 6.

5. Maimonides, Guide 3.32; cf. Leviticus R. 22:8 (see the comment of Margulies, 317).

6. Cf. M. Weinfeld, Commentary, 37; DDS, 190, 210–224; von Rad, cited by Weinfeld, 190n. See also Weinfeld, "The Emergence of the Deuteronomic Movement," in N. Lohfink, ed., *Das Deuteronomium* (Leuven: Leuven University Press, 1985), 85–86, citing Hosea 8:11–14 as underlying Deuteronomy's attitude. In this he follows H. L. Ginsberg, *The Israelian Heritage of Judaism* (New York: Jewish Theological Seminary, 1982), 21–22, but, in my view, explains Hosea's reasoning more convincingly than Ginsberg does.

7. Sefer Ha-Ḥinnukh (ed. C. Chavel), nos. 187, 438.

8. T. H. Robinson and W.O.E. Oesterley, *A History of Israel* (Oxford: Clarendon, 1932), 1:392–393; cf. Hertz, at Deut. 12:5.

9. M. Weinfeld, "Cult Centralization in Israel in the Light of a Neo-Babylonian Analogy," *JNES* 23 (1964): 202–212. For a critique of the Babylonian analogy on which Weinfeld based his argument, see M. Cogan, *Imperialism and Religion* (Missoula, Mont.: Society of Biblical Literature and Scholars Press, 1974), 33 n. 67; cf. W. E. Claburn, "The Fiscal Basis of Josiah's Reforms," *JBL* 92 (1973): 11 n. 1.

10. E. Nicholson, "The Centralisation of the Cult in Deuteronomy," *VT* 13 (1963): 380–389. Cf. 1 Kings 12:26–27.

11. Claburn, "Fiscal Basis," attempts to meet the first objection by claiming that the populace was not granted the entire offering, but was merely allowed to deduct travel expenses from the amount of the tax due; he implies that the remainder would then be handed over to the king (16–17). There is not a hint of this in the text. Admittedly, this would be a neat solution to the problem discussed in the Comment to 14:26.

12. On these three views in general, cf. Driver, 138, and H. Preuss, *Deuteronomium* (Darmstadt: Wissenschaftliche Buchgesellschaft, 1982), 12–19, 132.

13. Josephus, Against Apion, 2.193. Cf. Abravanel at Lev. 17, p. 102b, top, and at Deut. 12:5, p. 120b, top; cf. Ralbag at Deut. 12 and at Josh. 22:10. Cf. Preuss, *Deuteronomium*, 132, and see J. Wellhausen, *Prolegomena to the History of Ancient Israel* (New York: Meridian, 1957).

14. If Deuteronomy's position is rooted in Hosea's objection to multiple *altars*, could this be based on a fear of the hypostatization of altars? A few altars in the Bible are actually given names which could suggest something of the sort: Jacob's altar *'el 'elohei Yisra'el*, "God/El, God of Israel" (Gen. 33:20), Moses' *YHVH-nissi*, "YHVH is my standard" (Exod. 17:15), and Gideon's altar *YHVH shalom*, "YHVH, All-is-well" (Judg. 6:24). In rabbinic times "The Altar" was an oath handle, used as a surrogate for God's name (Mish. Ned. 1:3; Matthew 23:18). Note also the personification of the altar in Mish. Suk. 4:5; Tosef. Suk. 3:1 (for the concerns raised by such personification, see Tigay, "A Second Temple Parallel to the Blessings from Kuntillet Ajrud," *IEJ* 40 [1990]: 218).

15. Abravanel at Lev. 17, p. 102a, end; Ramban at Lev. 17:2.

16. This applies to domestic animals that are acceptable for sacrifices, not to game animals like deer and gazelles.

17. E.g., Driver, 138; Bright, *History*, 282; Preuss, *Deuteronomium*, 15–16; Nicholson, "Centralisation of the Cult," 381 n. 1; 384. Some add that the local shrines were also centers of debauchery which the restriction of sacrifice likewise aimed to eliminate; see J. Milgrom, "Profane Slaughter and a Formulaic Key to the Composition of Deuteronomy," *HUCA* 47 (1976): 16; Kennett cited by Nicholson, "Centralisation of the Cult," 381n.

18. Y. Kaufmann, *The Religion of Israel*, trans. M. Greenberg (Chicago: University of Chicago Press, 1960), 288–289.

19. 2 Kings 21:5,7; 23:4,6,11,12.

20. See Wellhausen, *Prolegomena*, 26–27, and sources cited in Excursus 10, n. 7; A. Rofé, "Jerusalem: The City Chosen by the Lord," in D. Amit and R. Gonen, eds., *Jerusalem in the First Temple Period* (Hebrew) (Jerusalem: Ben Tzvi Institute, 1990), 52–62. See the discussion of this issue by P. Kyle McCarter in P. D. Miller et al., eds., *Ancient Israelite Religion* (Philadelphia: Fortress Press, 1987), 139–142.

21. M. Greenberg, "Religion: Stability and Ferment," in *WHJP* 4/2, 119. According to Greenberg, the principle "Do not act thus toward the Lord your God" is based on Exod. 23:24, "Do not act thus," referring to the worship of foreign gods. He argues that Deuteronomy has expanded the principle to cover anything that resembles pagan manners of worship, not only idols and the like, but even multiple places of worship.

22. Kaufmann, *Religion of Israel*, 136–137. Kaufmann later argues that Deuteronomy bans multiple worship sites in order to desacralize nature. In his view, considering all places as acceptable for worship reflects the pagan tendency to deify all of nature (since the gods are personifications of the forces of nature) and to regard sanctity as a natural, potentially ubiquitous phenomenon. This is contrary to the biblical view that God is outside of nature. Nature itself is devoid of divinity, and sanctity is determined solely by God's sovereign choice. The most unambiguous way to express this is by limiting sanctity to a single place, as does Deuteronomy. (Theoretically God might choose to sanctify several places, as Exod. 20:21 implies, but this would leave the point that holiness is solely a matter of divine choice less obvious.) See Kaufmann, *Religion of Israel*, 288–290; cf. 161–162; Moran, 267; R. J. Clifford, *Deuteronomy* (Wilmington, Del.: Michael Glazier, 1982), 76. However, it is not necessarily true that paganism considers every place legitimate for sanctuaries. At least in Mesopotamia specific divine authorization was sometimes required for building sanctuaries.

23. See S. Lieberman, HJP, 139–143; cf. Boaz Cohen, *Jewish and Roman Law* (New York: Jewish Theological Seminary, 1966), 1:53.

Excursus 15

1. See Philo, Abr. 178–191; R. de Vaux, *Studies in Old Testament Sacrifice* (Cardiff: University of Wales Press, 1964), 52–90; L. E. Stager, "The Rite of Child Sacrifice at Carthage," in J. G. Pedley, ed., *New Light on Ancient Carthage* (Ann Arbor: University of Michigan Press, 1980), 1–11; L. E. Stager

and S. R. Wolff, "Child Sacrifice at Carthage," *BAR* 10/1 (January-February, 1984): 30–51; M. Almagro-Gorbea, "Les Reliefs Orientalisants de Pozo Moro," in J. Duchemin, ed., *Mythe et Personification: Travaux et Mémoires. Actes du colloque du Grande Palais (Paris) 7–8 Mai 1977* (Paris: Société d'Édition "Les Belles Lettres," 1980), 123–136; C. A. Kennedy, "The Mythological Reliefs at Pozo Moro, Spain," *Society of Biblical Literature Seminar Papers* 20 (1981): 209–216; idem, "Tartessos, Tarshish, and Tartarus: The Tower of Pozo Moro and the Bible" (forthcoming).

2. P. Derchain, "Les plus anciens témoignages de sacrifices d'enfants chez les sémites occidentaux," *VT* 20 (1970): 351–355; A. Spalinger, "A Canaanite Ritual found in Egyptian Reliefs," *Journal of the Society for the Study of Egyptian Antiquities* 8 (1978): 47–60 (cf. *ANEP*, no. 334).

3. For Jephthah and Mesha see Judg. 11:30–40; 2 Kings 3:26–27; further instances are cited in the next note. In the story of the Akedah (Gen. 22), Abraham implicitly recognizes that God, the author of life, has the right to demand such a sacrifice. What biblical law denies is that He exercises that right or approves such offerings.

4. See esp. Jer. 32:35 and Ezek. 20:26,31 (that these texts refer to actual human sacrifice is clear from Jer. 7:31; 19:5; Ezek. 16:20–21; 23:37,39); cf. 2 Kings 23:10. If the passages in Jeremiah are by Jeremiah himself, they are the testimony of an eyewitness. Weinfeld regards them as inauthentic Deuteronomic additions to the book and dismisses their testimony, together with that of Ezekiel, Ps. 106, and Isa. 57, as exaggerations of late "moralizing literature whose tendentiousness and poetical fantasy tend to blur the . . . reality to which it refers" (Weinfeld, "The Worship of Molech and the Queen of Heaven and its Background," *UF* 4 (1972): 141; idem, "Burning Babies in Ancient Israel," *UF* 10 (1978): 413 n. 4). But even if these are Deuteronomic additions in Jeremiah, their evidence is not necessarily impugned, for Weinfeld concedes elsewhere that most of the sins listed in these additions, including the cult in the Valley of Ben-Hinnom, did take place in an earlier period (Weinfeld, DDS, 29–30).

5. For the view that the verse refers to Molech worship and that the latter consists of human sacrifice, see Targ. Jon. at Lev. 20:2; the Sages cited in Mid. Hag.; Tanh. B. Deut. 8a and Yal. Jer. 277; Ramban at Lev. 18:21; cf. 2 Chron. 28:3 (cited in n. 6); Josephus, Ant. 9.243; Wisdom 12.3–6. For a recent defense of this view, see M. Smith, "On Burning Babies," *JAOS* 95 (1975): 477–479. For other explicit references to human sacrifice in the Bible, see 2 Kings 17:31 (by the foreign Sepharvites); Isa. 57:5; Ps. 106: 37–38; and the passages cited in the preceding notes.

6. The practice is cited again with divination in 2 Kings 17:17 and 21:6 (the reading "burned" [*va-yav'er*] in 2 Chron. 28:3 is either interpretive or a scribal error for *va-ya'aver*, "made pass"). Note also the collocation of Molech worship and divination with necromancy in Lev. 20:1–6. According to Ramban at Lev. 18:21, the ceremony was both lethal and used for divination.

7. See Sanh. 64b; Mid. Hag.; Sifrei Deut. 171; LXX; Vulg.; Rashi; Bekhor Shor; and Rashi and Ibn Ezra at Lev. 18:21. See esp. Weinfeld, "Worship of Molech," 142–143, as well as Driver (cf. Ibn Ezra at Lev. 18:21); T. H. Gaster, *Myth, Legend and Custom in the Old Testament* (New York: Harper and Row, 1969), 586–588; D. Plataroti, "Zum Gebrauch des Wortes MLK im alten Testament," *VT* 28 (1978): 286–300. "Burning children to a god" is mentioned in Assyrian texts of the ninth through seventh centuries B.C.E., but it appears only as a punishment for violation of contracts, and whether it refers to nonlethal dedication or to sacrifice is debated. See Weinfeld, "Worship of Molech" and "Burning Babies," and Smith, "On Burning Babies."

8. James M. Freedman, "Trial by Fire," *Natural History* 83/1 (New York: American Museum of Natural History, 1974): 57.

9. See also M. Buber, *Kingship of God* (New York: Harper

and Row, 1967), 98, 177–184; Weinfeld, "Worship of Molech" and "Burning Babies," and Smith, "On Burning Babies"; M. Cogan, *Imperialism and Religion* (Missoula, Montana: Society of Biblical Literature and Scholars Press, 1974), 78–83; G. C. Heider, *The Cult of Molek: A Reassessment* (Sheffield: JSOT Press, 1985); P. G. Mosca, "Child Sacrifice in Canaanite and Israelite Religion: A Study in *Mulk* and Molech" (Ph.D. diss., Harvard University, 1975).

Excursus 16

1. See S. M. Paul, *Studies in the Book of the Covenant* (Leiden: Brill, 1970), 44; S. E. Loewenstamm, in WHJP 3:238–240.

2. As noted in the Introduction, Deuteronomy draws on laws from a collection that must have resembled Exod. 21–23, though it was not identical to it.

3. Lev. 25:10,13,28, and 39–55.

4. MdRY Nezikin 2 (Lauterbach 3:17); Mish. Kid. 1:2; TJ Kid. 1:2, 59b.

5. Lev. 25:47–54.

6. B. L. Eichler explains the difference between the laws on other grounds. In his view, Exodus and Deuteronomy deal with debt slaves, while Leviticus deals with individuals who sell themselves voluntarily because of poverty (s.v. "Slavery," in P. J. Achtemeier et al., eds., *Harper's Bible Dictionary* [San Francisco: Harper and Row, 1985], 959); cf. chap. 15, n. 24.

7. Lev. 25:10,13,28.

8. Lev. 25:25–28. See J. Pedersen, *Israel: Its Life and Culture* I–II (London: Oxford University Press, 1940), 84–85; S. Japhet, "The Laws of Manumission of Slaves," in Y. Avishur and J. Blau, eds., *Studies in the Bible and the Ancient Near East* (Jerusalem: Rubinstein, 1978), 242.

9. Num. 36. Note, too, that the land is apportioned to clans, not individual families (Num. 26:52; 33:54; see Milgrom, *Numbers*, 512).

10. Note Weinfeld's suggestion that the priestly literature reflects a provincial background (Commentary, 36).

11. Git. 36a, end, and see also Levine, *Leviticus*, Excursus 9.

12. H. L. Ginsberg, *The Israelian Heritage*, 64; cf. S. Kaufman, "A Reconstruction of the Social Welfare Systems of Ancient Israel," in W. B. Barrick and J. R. Spencer, eds., *In the Shelter of Elyon* (Sheffield: JSOT Press, 1984), 282.

13. Hoffmann, 234. For the due date at harvest time, see K. R. Veenhof, "An Ancient Anatolian Money-Lender: His Loans, Securities, and Debt-Slaves," in B. Hruška and G. Komoróczy, eds., *Festschrift Lubor Matouš* (Budapest: Eotvos Lorand University, 1978), 285.

14. In that case, he must have understood "he shall serve you six years" to mean "he shall serve you for a maximum of six years."

15. For the rabbinic principle that legal inferences may be derived from the juxtaposition of laws in the Torah, see Excursus 13 n. 5. N. M. Sarna holds that legal issues underlie Jeremiah's interpretation. He argues that the released slaves had entered slavery for debt, that the episode in Jer. 34 took place during a sabbatical year in which debts were remitted, and hence that the slaves were released because their debts were now canceled ("Zedekiah's Emancipation of Slaves and the Sabbatical Year," 143–149 in H. A. Hoffner, Jr., ed., *Orient and Occident* [Kevelaer: Butzon and Bercker, and Neukirchen-Vluyn: Neukirchener Verlag, 1973]). Jeremiah's interpretation was considered, but rejected, in talmudic times and in the Middle Ages; see MdRY Nezikin 1 (Lauterbach 3:7); TJ Kid. 1:2, 59a; Sarna, "Zedekiah's Emancipation," 148. It is advocated today by Mayes, 250; Levine, *Leviticus*, 271.

16. See Neh. 5:1–13; 10:32. See E. M. Yamauchi, "Two Reformers Compared: Solon of Athens and Nehemiah of Jeru-

salem," in G. Rendsburg et al., eds., *The Bible World: Essays . . . Gordon* (New York: Ktav and Institute of Hebrew Culture and Education of NYU, 1980), 269–292.

17. J. Naveh in Y. Aharoni, *Ketovot Arad* (Jerusalem: Bialik Institute and Israel Exploration Society, 1975), 192 no. 41; M. Weinfeld, *Justice and Righteousness* (Jerusalem: Magnes Press, 1985), 99–100.

18. See Mish. Shev. 10:2–4 (with *Mele'khet Shelomo*); Albeck, *Zera'im*, 383; Sifrei 113; Git. 36a–37b; Torah Temimah to Deut. 15:3; s.v. "Prosbul" in JE and EncJud.

Excursus 17

1. See 2 Sam. 11:11; 1 Kings 20:12,16; Gen. 33:17; Isa. 1:8; Job 27:18; cf. Jonah 4:5; Pss. 31:21; 27:5; 18:12; Suk. 8b.

2. See Exod. 18:7; Lev. 14:8; Num. 11:10; 16:26–27; Deut. 1:27; Josh. 3:14.

3. Suk. 11b and Rashi ad loc.

4. Rashbam at Exod. 23:16 and Lev. 23:43.

5. Levush, cited by Y. Weingarten, *Ha-Mahazor Ha-Meforash le-Hag Ha-Sukkot* (Jerusalem: Gefen, 1989), 13–14. Examples are all the symbols of the Exodus (Exod. 12–13), the jar of manna (Exod. 16:33–34), the altar plating commemorating the supernatural destruction of Korah and his cohorts (Num. 17:1–5), and the rods symbolizing the supernatural election of Aaron for the priesthood (Num. 17:25). An exception is fringes that serve as reminders of God's commandments (Num. 15:37–41).

6. See Suk. 11b; Rashi; Ramban; D. Z. Hoffmann, *Sefer Va-Yikra* (Jerusalem: Mosad Harav Kook, 1953–54), at Lev. 23:42–43 (2:207); N. H. Tur Sinai, *Ha-Lashon ve-Ha-Sefer* (Jerusalem: Bialik Institute, 1948–55), 3:78ff.; Weingarten, *Ha-Mahazor Ha-Meforash*, 13ff. Note the metaphoric *"sukkah* of peace" in the *Hashkivenu* prayer.

7. This is also the problem with the suggestion that the booths are used on the festival because they are the temporary lodgings for the pilgrims (J. Licht, s.v. *sukkot*, EM 5:1042). Pilgrims would need lodging at all the festivals, even shorter ones, and booths would not necessarily typify this one alone (Rofé, *Mavo'*, 44 n. 30). Note also that even the residents of Jerusalem, who needed no special lodgings, erected booths and dwelled in them during Sukkot in the days of Nehemiah (Neh. 8:13–19).

8. See, e.g., J. Licht, s.v. *sukkot*, EM 5:1041; R. de Vaux, *Ancient Israel* (New York: McGraw-Hill, 1961), 501; J. B. Segal, *The Hebrew Passover* (London: Oxford University Press, 1963), 179. That the practice symbolizes the harvest season just concluded obviates Tur-Sinai's objection that the festival falls after the grape harvest when booths are no longer in use (*Ha-Lashon ve-Ha-Sefer*, 3:81). There are Greek parallels to the practice of dwelling in huts on certain agricultural festivals. See Segal, *Hebrew Passover*, 120 n. 1; M. P. Nilsson, s.v. "Cernea," OCD 206.

9. Dalman 1/1, 160–161.

10. See T. H. Gaster, *Festivals of the Jewish Year* (New York: William Sloane, 1964).

11. See Bekhor Shor's paraphrase of God's command in Exod. 12:2: "This month shall be the first of your freedom, and you shall make it first in counting months so that you may count from the hour of freedom and thus remember the hour of freedom and My kindness to you, and you will thereby take care to revere Me, love Me, and serve Me."

12. See also Exod. 13:4; 23:15; 34:18. Three other names from this system appear in the book of Kings: the month of Ziv ("brightness," falling in April-May), the month of Ethanim, ("steadily flowing wadis" [?], in October-November), and the month of Bul (probably "flooding," in November-December; see 1 Kings 6:1,37,38; 8:2). At least two of these names are also

known in Phoenician, and they were probably adopted from the Canaanites. See HALAT on the four month names and de Vaux, *Ancient Israel*, 183.

13. See H. Frankfort et al., *Before Philosophy* (Harmondsworth and Baltimore: Penguin, 1949). On the religious significance of the month names, see also Sarna, *Exodus*, at 12:2. For further discussion see J. Tigay, "The Calendar and Theology," in memorial volume for Albert Elazar, ed. Daniel J. Elazar (in press).

Excursus 18

S. E. Loewenstamm, s.v. *herem*, EM 3:290–292; M. Greenberg, s.v. *herem*, EncJud 8:345–350; N. Lohfink, s.v. *haram*, TDOT 5; M. Weinfeld, "The Ban on the Canaanites and Its Development in Israelite Law," *Zion* 53 (1988): 135–147; Milgrom, *Numbers*, Excursus 44; Philip D. Stern, "A Window on Ancient Israel's Religious Experience: The Herem Re-investigated and Re-interpreted" (Ph.D. diss., New York University, 1989).

1. Exod. 23:27–31; cf. 33:2; 34:11–16 (see also Lev. 18:24–25; 20:23; Deut. 33:27; Josh. 24:12,18; Judg. 2:3; 6:9). Strictly speaking, Exodus states that *God* will expel the Canaanites, but the fact that it prohibits Israel from making a pact that would allow the Canaanites to remain implies that the Israelites were to be God's agents in doing so. Num. 33:50–56 also requires ridding the land of the Canaanites, but whether by expulsion or annihilation is unclear (see Weinfeld, "Ban on the Canaanites," 139). On Numbers' motive see Milgrom, *Numbers*, Excursus 44, and Weinfeld, "Ban on the Canaanites," 139. According to Genesis and Leviticus, the Canaanites are to be expelled because of sexual immorality, occult practices, and child sacrifice (see Gen. 9:22–27; 15:16; 19:4–5; Lev. 18; 20).

2. W. G. Dever, *Recent Archaeological Discoveries and Biblical Research* (Seattle: University of Washington Press, 1990), 56–61.

3. Judg. 1:19,27–36; 1 Kings 9:20–21; Josh. 15:63; 16:10; 17:12–13; cf. Ps. 106:34–35. Cf. Gen. 9:25–27, which probably reflects the enslavement of the Canaanites by the Israelites and the Philistines.

4. A. Biram, *"mas 'oved," Tarbiz* 23 (1952): 138; A. Toeg, "Exodus 22:4: The Text and the Law in the Light of the Ancient Sources," *Tarbiz* 39 (1969–70): 229; I. L. Seeligmann, *Studies in Biblical Literature*, ed. A. Hurvitz et al. (Jerusalem: Magnes Press, 1992), 121–122; Weinfeld, "Ban on the Canaanites," 140–141 n. 22; Rofé, *Mavo'*, 131–132; M. Fishbane, *Biblical Interpretation in Ancient Israel* (Oxford: Clarendon, 1988), 199–209. Toeg, for example, reasons that if vv. 10–14 originally referred only to foreign cities, they would hardly have been placed *before* the law about the Canaanites—with whom war was imminent—and worded as a universal policy.

5. Lev. 27:28–29; Num. 18:14; Ezek. 44:29.

6. See also Judg. 21:5–11.

7. Mesha ll. 10–21 (ANET, 320).

8. See Loewenstamm, s.v. *herem*; Greenberg, s.v. *herem*, 8:348; Lohfink, s.v. *haram*, 5; Stern, "Ancient Israel's Religious Experience," 19–129 (see esp. 45 and 116–117). The European examples are attested among the Celts, Gauls, Teutons, and Romans. These are usually ad hoc decisions; it is possible, though not certain, that some of these peoples regularly proscribed enemies.

9. 1 Sam. 15:3,18,33; 1 Kings 20:42; Mic. 4:13.

10. Num. 21:1–3; Josh. 6–8.

11. The view that God destroyed the Canaanites appears already in Amos 2:9, a product of the eighth century B.C.E., and it is therefore possible that Deuteronomy owes this idea to an earlier source. 1 Chron. 4:39–43 mentions the practice in Hezekiah's time.

12. Rofé, *Mavo'*, 129 and n. 14. Deut. 13:17 speaks of burning the idolatrous Israelite city "*kalil* to the LORD." Even if this means "as a holocaust," it is the city and its spoil that are so described. The inhabitants are "proscribed," but not "to the LORD" (v. 16).

13. Sifrei 202; Tosef. Sot. 8:7; Sot. 35b; Maimonides, Hilkhot Melakhim 6:1.

14. Maimonides, Hilkhot Melakhim 6:1; followed by Ramban here. This view makes explicit the view of talmudic-midrashic sources which state that Joshua announced even before entering the promised land that those who wanted to emigrate or surrender would be permitted to do so (Deut. R. 5:13–14; TJ Shev. 6.1, 36c; Lev. R. 17:6). According to Maimonides, the Canaanites could save themselves by agreeing to perform forced labor and to accept the seven Noachide commandments, including the prohibition of polytheism (on these commandments see Sarna, *Genesis*, Excursus 3). Even after the siege began, he ruled, the city was to be surrounded only on three sides so that those who wished to save themselves by fleeing could escape via the fourth side (Hilkhot Melakhim 6:7; other authorities limit this rule to foreign wars).

15. Thus Maimonides and Ramban (see previous note); Lohfink, s.v. *ḥaram*, 197.

16. See also Rashi at Sot. 35b, s.v. *ve-khatevu mi-le-mattah*; Meklenburg at Deut. 20:16.

17. M. Greenberg, *Ha-Segullah ve-Ha-Koaḥ* (Tel Aviv: Ha-Kibbutz Ha-Me'uḥad and Sifriyat Po'alim, 1986), 20. See also Meklenburg at Deut. 20:16.

Excursus 19

R. Patai, "The 'Egla 'Arufa or the Expiation of the Polluted Land," JQR NS 30 (1939–40): 59–69; A. Roifer (Rofé), "'eglah 'arufah," *Tarbiz* 31 (1962): 119–143; S. E. Loewenstamm, s.v. *'eglah 'arufah*, EM 6:77–79; J. Milgrom, s.v. "'Eglah 'Arufah," EncJud 6:475–477; D. P. Wright, "Deuteronomy 21:1–9 as a Rite of Elimination," CBQ 49 (1987): 387–403; Z. Zevit, "The 'egla Ritual of Deuteronomy 21:1–9," JBL 95 (1976): 377–390.

1. The Hittite letter is translated in LFM, but for the pertinent passage see *CAD* D, 26a; *CAD* E, 82b ("they purify the [city] in which the person was killed"). Cf. J. J. Finkelstein, "The Goring Ox," *Temple Law Quarterly* 46/2 (Winter 1973), 281 n. 345. The letter does not describe the rite of purification. Several Hittite texts are described as "ritual for purification of a city," "ritual concerning a crime," and "ritual for the expiation of a murder(?)" by E. Laroche, *Catalogue des textes hittites* (Paris: Klincksieck, 1971), nos. 400, 401, 405, 441, 454. Unfortunately they have not yet been edited.

2. Tanḥ. Mishpatim 7, end; Yoma 67b variant; S. Lieberman, *Texts and Studies* (New York: Ktav, 1974), 254; cf. Ramban at 21:4, end; Maimonides, Hilkhot Me'ilah 8:8. Rational explanations are offered by Maimonides, Guide 3.40; Abravanel, 195–196. Other commandments so characterized include Deut. 14:8,21b; 22:11; and 25:9.

3. Mish. Sot. 9:9 with commentary of Bertinoro; Tosef. Sot. 14:1 with commentaries of Ḥasdei David and S. Lieberman, TK, 8:750–751; Mid. Hag.; cf. also Sifrei 205.

4. See R. Sonsino, *Motive Clauses in Biblical Law* (Chico, Calif.: Scholars Press, 1980), 98, 102, 221.

5. See Wright.

6. Von Rad. The requirement that the heifer be one that has never been worked does not make it a sacrifice: the same requirement also applies to the red cow, which is not a sacrifice (Num. 19:2), and to the cows that the Philistines sent to pull the wagon in which they returned the Ark to Israel (the Philistines did not intend these for sacrifice, though the Israelites later did sacrifice them; 1 Sam. 6:7,14).

7. Lev. 16:21–22.

8. Sot. 47b; Eccl. R. 7:16; Midrash Tanna'im, 126; see Hoffmann to v. 9. Several moderns agree: e.g., Driver; Loewenstamm, s.v. *'eglah 'arufah*, 6:77; Mayes.

9. ANET, 211a; cf. Patai, "'Egla 'Arufa," 68.

10. See Targ. Jon. to v. 8, Midrash Aggadah to vv. 3 and 8, and Baḥya to v. 1; cf. Keter Torah to vv. 8–9. Cf. H. J. Elhorst and C. Steuernagel, cited by Roifer, "'eglah 'arufah," 127. On punitive magic against an unknown assailant see E. A. Hoebel, *The Law of Primitive Man* (Cambridge: Harvard University Press, 1964), 270. The ceremony could be a sort of ceremonial expression of an *'alah* pronounced against an unknown offender (as in Judg. 17). This could fit either the symbolic or the magical interpretation.

11. ANET, 532d; cf. Sefire 1:40 (ANET, 660b); cutting the neck of a sheep in an oath ceremony accompanying a gift of cities to a vassal (D. J. McCarthy, *Treaty and Covenant*, 2nd ed. [Rome: Biblical Institute Press, 1981], 86–96, 307); *Iliad* 19:252–268 (cf. 3:268–301). Cf. also the Babylonian "oath sworn by slaughtering a sheep and touching the wound" (Shurpu 3.35). Cf. the ceremonies accompanying oaths in Jer. 34:17–21; Neh. 5:12–13; ANET, 354a-b (cf. H. A. Hoffner, Jr., "Symbols for Masculinity and Femininity," *JBL* 85 [1966]: 332); J. G. Frazer, *Folklore in the Old Testament* (London: Macmillan, 1918), 1:395–396; A. Kohut, *Arukh Completum*, 2nd ed. (Vienna: Menorah, 1926), 3:229, s.v. *h-s-t*.

12. Ps. 26:6: "I do not consort with scoundrels. . . . I wash my hands in innocence"; Ps. 73:13: "I kept my heart pure and washed my hands in innocence." Hands full of blood are a well-known symbol of guilt (Isa. 1:15).

13. R. de Vaux, *Ancient Israel* (New York: McGraw-Hill, 1961), 157.

14. *Šumma . . . ina ālim nidūkū; iānu-ma ša idūkušu nīdēmi*; J. Nougayrol et al., *Ugaritica* 5 (Paris: Imprimerie Nationale and Librarie Orientaliste Paul Geuthner, 1968), 95 ll. 45–50. Oaths are sworn in similar cases in documents from Ugarit and among the later Arabs; see H. Reviv, "On Urban Representative Institutions and Self-Government in Syria-Palestine," JESHO 12 (1969): 292; Smith, cited by Driver, 241.

15. Exod. 22:7,10; 1 Kings 8:31; LH §§23, 106–107, 120, 266, 240, 281; ANET, 544d–545b; see BL 1:467–468.

16. See H. Schauss, *Guide to Jewish Holy Days* (New York: Schocken, 1964), 148–149, 160–164; s.v. "Tashlikh," EncJud 15:829–830.

17. See J. D. Eisenstein, s.v. *kapparot*, in *Ozar Dinim U-Minhagim* (New York: Hebrew Publishing Co., 1938), 183–184; Schauss, *Guide to Jewish Holy Days*, 149–151, 164–167; S. Y. Agnon, *Days of Awe* (New York: Schocken, 1965), 147–150; s.v. "Kapparot," EncJud 10:756–757; Y. Weingarten, *Ha-Maḥazor Ha-meforash*, Yom Kippur (Jerusalem: Gefen, 5747), 9–15. I thank my mother, Ethel Yollick, and my aunt, Helen Miller, for sharing with me their recollections of the practice from their childhood.

18. See Schauss, *Guide to Jewish Holy Days*, 152, 167.

Excursus 20

1. Abravanel; Shadal. Talmudic sources report that in some places the bride was searched to make certain that she did not bring an already stained cloth into the nuptial chamber (the groom was likewise searched to ensure that he did not bring a clean cloth to switch with the legitimately stained one in order to destroy the evidence of virginity in case he should later decide to bring false charges). The possibility that the bride used blood from a bird is also mentioned. See Tosef. Ket. 1:4ff.; TJ Ket. 1:1, 25a; 4:4, 28c; and Ket. 12a.

2. Mish. Ket. 1:7 (*mukkat 'ets*, "accidentally deflowered," lit. "injured by a piece of wood"); J. Preuss, *Biblical and Talmu-*

dic Medicine, trans. F. Rosner (New York: Sanhedrin Press [Hebrew Publishing Company], 1978), 477, 479.

3. Sifrei 237; Ket. 11b, 46a; Maimonides, Hilkhot Na'arah Betulah 3; Torah Temimah; Rofé, *Mavo'*, 147–148. The Boethusians, too, held that "cloth" is meant literally (*Megillat Ta'anit*, ed. H. Lichtenstein, "Die Fastenrolle," HUCA 8–9 [1931–32]: 331). According to Rofé, 149 n. 27, the rendering of v. 20 in LXX, Vulg., and Pesh. ("But if the charge proves true *and* [evidence of] virginity was not found in her") is in the spirit of the halakhic view that conviction does not depend on the cloth alone. Josephus, Ant. 4.246, speaks vaguely of "what evidence [the husband] may have."

4. Keter Torah.

5. See J. Tigay, "Examination of the Accused Bride in 4Q159: Forensic Medicine at Qumran," in E. L. Greenstein and D. Marcus, eds., *Comparative Studies in Honor of Yohanan Muffs* JANES 22 (1993): 129–134.

6. According to E. Westermarck, *Marriage Ceremonies in Morocco* (London: Macmillan, 1914), 236, among the Tsul in Morocco, absence of blood would lead to the bride's execution by her family (other places in Morocco did not do this [240]).

7. Cf. H. C. Brichto's explanation of the *sota* ritual in Num. 5: "The Case of the *Sota* and a Reconsideration of Biblical 'Law,'" HUCA 46 (1975): 55–70.

8. Rofé, *Mavo'*, 147–150.

9. See, G. R. Driver and J. C. Miles, *The Babylonian Laws* (Oxford: Clarendon, 1960) 1:204 n. 3, 400.

10. See chap. 21 n. 52.

11. This possibility is considered by Rofé, *Mavo'*, 148–149 n. 26, but he thinks it unlikely.

Excursus 21

Y. Kaufmann, *The Religion of Israel*, trans. M. Greenberg (Chicago: University of Chicago Press, 1960), 206, 300–301, 449, 451; idem, *History of the Religion of Israel*, vol. 4, trans. C. W. Efroymson (New York: Ktav, 1977), 136–139, 331–349, 384–385; Z. Falk, "Ha-'Asurim Lavo' Ba-Kahal," BM 62 (1975): 342–351; K. Galling, "Das Gemeindegesetz in Deuteronomium 23," in W. Baumgartner et al., eds., *Festschrift A. Bertholet* (Tübingen: J.C.B. Mohr, 1950), 176–191; M. Fishbane, *Biblical Interpretation in Ancient Israel* (Oxford: Clarendon, 1988), 114–143.

1. See Judg. 3:12–30; 10:7–12:7. Apart from Egyptians, the law deals only with the three Transjordanian neighbors with whom the Israelites felt the closest kinship (see Deut. 2:2–19,37). Nothing is said about the Midianites, Arameans, or the Philistines.

2. J. Milgrom, "Religious Conversion and the Revolt Model for the Formation of Israel," JBL 101 (1982): 173–174.

3. 4QFlorilegium (DJD 5:174), ll. 3–4. See Fishbane, *Biblical Interpretation*, 129, 142.

4. S.J.D. Cohen, "From the Bible to the Talmud: The Prohibition of Intermarriage," HAR 7 (1983): 32, thinks that Isa. 56:3ff., Neh. 13:1–9, and some rabbinic passages may also reflect an interpretation of Deut. 23:4–9 as excluding foreigners from the Temple. According to Neh. 13:1–9, Nehemiah expelled Tobiah the Ammonite from the Temple in connection with the separation of all aliens from Israel, based on an interpretation of Deut. 23:4. In later Second Temple times gentiles were barred from the inner courts of the Temple in Jerusalem (Mish. Kel. 1:8; Josephus, War 5.193–194; cf. Josephus, Ant. 12.145–146; J. Fitzmeyer, *A Wandering Aramean* [Missoula, Mont.: Scholars Press, 1979], 35). No such prohibition is known in preexilic times (cf. Milgrom, *Numbers*, 402).

5. See Falk, 347. In Athens, a citizen disfranchised for some offense was not allowed to enter a temple (D. M. MacDowell, *The Law in Classical Athens* [Ithaca: Cornell University Press, 1978], 72). A law from Eresus (on Lesbos) barred eunuchs from

a sanctuary (see F. R. Walton, s.v. "Eunuchs, Religious," OCD, 416). Such an interpretation of Deut. 23:2 would be in the spirit of Lev. 21:20, which lists certain bodily defects as disqualifying priests from officiating (cf. Lev. 22:24).

6. This is the primary objection to Galling's thesis that these laws have to do with allowing foreigners to participate in worship at Israelite border sanctuaries.

7. Ezra 9–10; Neh. 13:1–3,23–29. See Kaufmann, *History*, and Fishbane, *Biblical Interpretation*.

8. See Fishbane, *Biblical Interpretation*, 117.

9. See Kaufmann, *Religion*, 206, 300–301; Milgrom, "Religious Conversion," 169–176. Circumcision qualifies a resident alien to take part in the *pesah* offering, but he remains a resident alien, not an Israelite (Exod. 12:48–49; v. 49 means that he becomes like the Israelite in respect of the sacrifice, not in every respect; see Milgrom, *Numbers*, 399).

10. Isa. 56:3–9.

11. See S.J.D. Cohen, "Conversion to Judaism in Historical Perspective: From Biblical Israel to Postbiblical Judaism," *Conservative Judaism* 36 (1982–83): 31–45.

12. Mish. Yev. 8:2; Maimonides, Hilkhot 'Issurei Bi'ah 16. According to Sefer Ha-Mitsvot, negative no. 360 and Sefer Ha-Hinnukh, no. 575, it applies only to those whose condition makes them infertile.

13. Mish. Yev. 8:2; Maimonides, Hilkhot 'Issurei Bi'ah 15:7,33; Sefer Ha-Hinnukh, no. 576; Mish. Hor. 3:8. Eisenstein, *Ozar Dinim U-Minhagim* (New York: Hebrew Publishing Co., 1938), 236.

14. Sifrei 249; Mish. Yev. 8:3.

15. Maimonides, Hilkhot 'Issurei Bi'ah 12:17–19.

16. Mish. Yad. 4:4; Ber. 28a; Maimonides, Hilkhot 'Issurei Bi'ah 12:25.

Excursus 22

D. Nussbaum, *The Priestly Explanation of Exile and its Bearing Upon the Portrayal of the Canaanites in the Bible* (M.A. thesis, University of Pennsylvania, 1974), 52–89; I. M. Haase, *Cult Prostitution in the Hebrew Bible?* (Ph.D. diss., University of Ottawa, 1990); T. H. Gaster, in J. G. Frazer, *The New Golden Bough*, ed. Gaster (Garden City, N.Y.: Doubleday, 1961), 223; E. J. Fisher, "Cultic Prostitution in the Ancient Near East," *Biblical Theology Bulletin* 6 (1976): 225–236; M. Gruber, "Hebrew *qedeshah* and her Canaanite and Akkadian Cognates," UF 18 (1986): 133–148; idem, "The *Qedesah*: What Was Her Function?" *Beer-Sheva* 3 (1988): 45–51; R. Oden, *The Bible Without Theology* (New York: Harper and Row, 1987), chap. 5; Jo Ann Hackett, "Can a Sexist Model Liberate Us? Ancient Near Eastern 'Fertility' Goddesses," *Journal of Feminist Studies in Religion* 5 (1989): 65–76; J. G. Westenholz, "Tamar, *Qedesha*, *Qadishtu*, and Sacred Prostitution in Mesopotamia," HTR 82 (1989): 245–265; E. A. Goodfriend, s.v. "Prostitution," ABD 5:507–509; K. van der Toorn, s.v. "Cultic Prostitution," ABD 5:510–513.

1. For examples of the confused usage, see von Rad; O. J. Baab, "Prostitution," IDB 3:932–933; J. L. Mays, *Hosea* (London: SCM, 1969), 71, 75; cf. James A. Michener, *The Source* (New York: Random House, 1965), chap. 3, "Level XIV: Of Death and Life."

2. See J. Renger and J. Cooper, "Heilige Hochzeit," RLA 4:251–269; S. N. Kramer, *The Sacred Marriage Rite* (Bloomington: Indiana University Press, 1969); T. Jacobsen, *The Treasures of Darkness* (New Haven: Yale University Press, 1976), 32–47; Frazer, New *Golden Bough*, 50–57.

3. H. Frankfort, *Kingship and the Gods* (Chicago: University of Chicago Press, 1948), 296; Kramer, *Sacred Marriage*, 79; Jacobsen, *Treasures of Darkness*, 39; Renger and Cooper, "Heilige Hochzeit," 4:250 §15; J. Bottéro, "La Hiérogamie après l'époque 'sumérienne,'" in S. N. Kramer, *Le Mariage Sacré á*

Sumer et à Babylone (Paris: Berg International, 1983), 175–214; cf. Milgrom, *Numbers*, Excursus 61. In none of the examples of sacred marriage in the ancient world cited by Frazer, *New Golden Bough*, §§127–130, do two human partners have intercourse; see also OCD, 651.

4. The sacred marriage in the first millennium apparently did not involve human participants at all; see Frankfort, *Kingship*, 330–331.

5. Herodotus 1:199; Lucian, *The Syrian Goddess (De Dea Syria)*, ed. H. W. Attridge and R. Oden (Missoula, Mont.: Scholars Press, 1976), §6; OCD, 890; Frazer, *New Golden Bough*, 171–172, 223; H. Licht, *Sexual Life in Ancient Greece* (London: Routledge and Kegan Paul, 1932), 388–395; E. M. Yamauchi, "Cultic Prostitution: A Case Study in Cultural Diffusion," in H. A. Hoffner, Jr., ed., *Orient and Occident* (Kevelaer: Butzon and Bercker; Neukirchen-Vluyn: Neukirchener Verlag, 1973), 219.

6. One contract specifies that the violator of the contract will have to give his daughters to Ishtar as prostitutes (cited by M. Weinfeld, "The Worship of Molech and the Queen of Heaven and its Background," UF 4 [1972]: 145; the meaning of the terms translated "sacred prostitute" on p. 144 is debated); for prostitutes connected with goddesses and a temple official see Rivka Harris, *Ancient Sippar* (Leiden: Nederlands Historisch-Archaeologisch Instituut te Istanbul, 1975), 173, 182–183, 332; M. L. Gallery, "Service Obligations of the *kezertu*-Women," *Orientalia* 49 (1980): 338; J. Renger, "Untersuchungen zum Priestertum in der altbabylonischen Zeit," ZA 58 (1968): 184 (but on the use of evidence from lexical lists see Gruber, "Hebrew *qedeshah*," 149). Various types of women associated with Mesopotamian temples have been considered cultic prostitutes; in most cases there is no decisive evidence that they were prostitutes or that prostitution was inherent in their office or connected with the cult. See Renger, "Untersuchungen zum Priestertum," 58–59; Harris, *Ancient Sippar*, 302–332. As Gruber notes, the assumption that some of these women were sacred prostitutes owed much to "scholars being unable to imagine any cultic role for women in antiquity that did not involve sexual intercourse" ("Hebrew *qedeshah*," 138). According to M. A. Dandamaev, *Slavery in Babylonia*, rev. ed. (DeKalb: Northern Illinois University Press, 1984), 135, the Ishtar temple at Uruk hired out some of its lower female personnel as concubines to private citizens in the latters' homes.

7. K. van der Toorn interprets Prov. 7:5–23 and Deut. 23:19 as indicating that women who had made vows which their husbands wouldn't give them money to fulfill might turn to prostitution to earn what they needed ("Female Prostitution in Payment of Vows in Ancient Israel," JBL 108 [1989]: 193–205). This is conceivable but it was hardly common, at least no more so than women turning to prostitution to earn money for anything else they wanted. In any case, it is not a cultic act.

8. Baab, "Prostitution," 933. Baab implies that the action of Eli's sons, who "lay with the women who performed tasks at the entrance of the Tent of Meeting" at Shilo (1 Sam. 2:22), is an example of the sacred marriage rite. However, if the practice were part of the cult at Shilo, why would Eli, the high priest of that sanctuary, protest against it? It is far more likely that Eli's sons were simply taking advantage of women over whom they had influence.

9. See, e.g., Mays, *Hosea*, 75.

10. See Gruber, "Hebrew *qedeshah*," 134 n. 5; idem, "The *Qedešah*: What Was Her Function?," 45–51; H. L. Ginsberg, "Lexicographical Notes," SVT 16 (1967): 75 n. 2; idem, s.v. "Hosea, Book of," EncJud 8:1019; van der Toorn, "Female Prostitution," 202–203; idem, s.v. "Cultic Prostitution," 510–511.

Excursus 23

E. Neufeld, *Ancient Hebrew Marriage Laws* (London:

Longmans, Green, 1944), 23–55; S. E. Loewenstamm, s.v. *yibbum, yavam vi-yvamah*, EM 3:444–447; L. I. Rabinowitz, s.v. "Levirate Marriage and ḥalisah," EncJud 11:122–131; R. de Vaux, *Ancient Israel* (New York: McGraw-Hill, 1961), 37–38; H. H. Rowley, "The Marriage of Ruth," in *The Servant of the Lord and Other Essays on the Old Testament* (Oxford: Blackwell, 1952), 171–194; T. and D. Thompson, "Some Legal Problems in the Book of Ruth," VT 18 (1968): 79–99; H. C. Brichto, "Kin, Land, Cult, and Afterlife—A Biblical Complex," HUCA 44 (1973): 1–54.

1. Josephus, Ant. 4.254; cf. Driver; Mayes, 328; Z. Falk, *Hebrew Law in Biblical Times* (Jerusalem: Wahrmann, 1964), 159; Neufeld, *Ancient Hebrew Marriage Laws*, 29–30.

2. 2 Sam. 18:18; Syriac Ahikar 4:15; ANET, 431d–432a; CAD Z, 18bc; J. J. Finkelstein, "The Genealogy of the Hammurapi Dynasty," JCS 20 (1966): 114–115; M. H. Farbridge, *Studies in Biblical and Semitic Symbolism* (1923; reprint, New York: Ktav, 1970), 239–244. On the afterlife, see A. Heidel, *The Gilgamesh Epic and Old Testament Parallels* (Chicago: University of Chicago Press, 1946), 191–207; M. Bayliss, "The Cult of Dead Kin in Assyria and Babylonia," *Iraq* 35 (1973): 115–125; T. J. Lewis, *Cults of the Dead in Ancient Israel and Ugarit* (Atlanta: Scholars Press, 1989); Brichto, "Kin, Land, Cult, and Afterlife," 22ff.; Pope, "The Cult of the Dead at Ugarit," in G. D. Young, ed., *Ugarit in Retrospect* (Winona Lake, Ind.: Eisenbrauns, 1981); E. Bloch-Smith, "The Cult of the Dead in Judah: Interpreting the Material Remains," JBL 111 (1992): 213–224.

3. See Aqhat A, i, 27–28 and parallels (ANET, 150; see Lewis, *Cults of the Dead*, 54–60) and the Egyptian execration texts in ANET, 328–329, and ANEP, fig. 593; cf. S. Lieberman, *Texts and Studies* (New York: Ktav, 1974), 263 n. 72.

4. 1 Sam. 24:21; 2 Sam. 14:7; Isa. 14:22; 66:22; Job 18:16–19; cf. Akkadian *šumu*, "name," which sometimes means "son," (cf. ANET, 117 n. 40; the idiom *šumu u zēru*, "son and seed," means "progeny"; see LH, xxviii, 44–49); Aramaic *šm*, "name," in KAI 228A:14.

5. Cf. Num. 27:4; Ruth 4:10; cf. Ps. 37:18 and Brichto, "Kin, Land, Cult, and Afterlife," 26–27.

6. Ezra 2:61; Neh. 7:63 (see NJPS); cf. Milgrom, *Numbers*, Comment to 27:4.

7. Note also *yad vashem*, "monument and name," referring to an inscribed monument to perpetuate people's names "even better than sons and daughters" would (Isa. 56:5; see S. Talmon, "Yad washem: An Idiomatic Phrase in Biblical Literature and its Variations," *Hebrew Studies* 25 [1984]: 8–17). See also Lewis, *Cults of the Dead*, 118–120; for the importance of preserving inscribed names, note the curses against those who would erase a person's name: ANET, 179a, 654bc, 655a, and CAD N1, 259c.

8. See CAD Z, 18bc; KAI 214:16–17, 21–22; Finkelstein, "Genealogy of the Hammurapi Dynasty," 114–115; J. C. Greenfield, "*adi baltu*—Care for the Elderly and its Rewards," in AfO Beiheft 19 (1982): 310d, 311bc; Lewis, *Cults of the Dead*, 53ff., 72ff., 96, 119. See also Comment to 26:14.

9. Gen. 15:2–3; 30:1; Lev. 20:20–21; Jer. 22:30.

10. Greenfield, "*adi baltu*," 311bc and n. 20; M. Bayliss, "The Cult of Dead Kin in Assyria and Babylonia," *Iraq* 35 (1973): 119.

11. As in MAL; see below.

12. See MAL §§30, 33, 43 (see discussion in G. Cardascia, *Les Lois Assyriennes* [Paris: Les Éditions du Cerf, 1969]); HL §193; C. H. Gordon, "The Status of Women Reflected in the Nuzi Tablets," ZA 43 (1936): 163, citing E. A. Speiser and E. Chiera, "Selected 'Kirkuk' Documents," JAOS 47 (1927): 43 no. 6 (an apparently optional provision in a marriage contract).

13. See T. and D. Thompson, "Some Legal Problems," 79–99. Note that Ruth 1:11–13 implies that a brother would have been preferable.

14. In addition to MAL and HL, see M. Tsevat, "Marriage and Monarchical Legitimacy in Ugarit and Israel," JSS 3 (1958):

237–243 (Ugarit, in royal family); W. Robertson Smith, *Kinship and Marriage in Early Arabia* (Boston: Beacon, 1903), 104–106; H. Granqvist, *Marriage Conditions in a Palestinian Village* (Helsinki: Akademische Buchhandlung, 1931), 1:86, 146; 2:291, 299–310; G. Bühler, *The Laws of Manu* (Oxford: Clarendon, 1886), 337ff.; Driver; J. G. Frazer, *Folklore in the Old Testament* (London: Macmillan, 1919), 2:263–341; T. H. Gaster, *Myth, Legend, and Custom in the Old Testament* (New York: Harper and Row, 1969), 593 (American Indians).

Excursus 24

1. Sifrei 292; BK 27a; Rashi; R. Meyuḥas.

2. Sifrei 293; Maimonides, Hilkhot Rotseaḥ 1:7-8; R. Meyuḥas.

3. Abravanel; Ehrlich. Cf. BK 28a: she is guilty only if there was another way to save her husband.

4. Yaʿqub al-Qirqisani, *Kitab al-Anwar wal-Maraqib*, ed. Leon Nemoy (New York: Alexander Kohut Memorial Foundation, 1941), Part 6, chap. 70, pp. 710-711, kindly translated by Leon Nemoy and Daniel Lasker. I have paraphrased slightly.

5. MAL §8. The translation is based on that of S. M. Paul, "Biblical Analogues to Middle Assyrian Law," in E. B. Firmage et al., eds., *Religion and Law* (Winona Lake, Ind.: Eisenbrauns, 1990), 336–337; see also ANET, 181a; G. R. Driver and J. C. Miles, *The Assyrian Laws* (Oxford: Clarendon, 1935), ad loc.; CAD I/J, 251b; CAD N1, 273b. The final clause is conjecturally restored with "eyes," "hands," or "nipples." See also Weinfeld, DDS, 292 n. 4; C. H. Gordon, "A New Akkadian Parallel to Deuteronomy 25:11–12," JPOS 15 (1935): 29–34.

6. Information courtesy Dr. Philip Marrone, Sports Medicine Center, Jefferson Hospital, Philadelphia.

7. Possibly, the law regards the risk as even more serious: According to Sifrei 292, injury to the genitals can be lethal and in the present law "genitals" stands for any *lethal* spot on the body.

8. Alternatively, we might reason that the law deals only with women injuring men's genitals because other injuries, whether caused by men or women, can be punished by talion, as prescribed by laws such as Lev. 24:19–20. Even the present injury, if caused by a man, could be punished by talion. Only in the case of injury to men's genitals by women is it impossible to inflict talion on the offender. Hence, a special law is required, to show what is to be done in place of literal talion (cf. Shadal; Craigie).

Excursus 25

1. Josephus and R. Ishmael go so far as to hold that they are to be performed several years later, after the conquest of the land is complete. Josephus, Antiq. 4.305–308; 5.68–70 (but cf. 5.20); TJ Sot. 7:3, 21c.

2. See Driver; Num. 15:23; Deut. 4:10,32; Judg. 4:14; 1 Sam. 24:5; 2 Sam. 19:20,25; Jer. 20:14 (twice); 38:28; Hag. 2:18; Est. 9:1.

3. In G. J. Brooke, ed., *New Qumran Texts and Studies* (Leiden: Brill, 1994), see A. Rofé, "The Editing of the Book of Joshua in the Light of 4QJoshᵃ," 73–80, and E. Ulrich, "4QJoshᵃ and Joshua's First Altar in the Promised Land," 89–104.

4. Ginzberg, *Legends* 4:6–7; 7:172; Y. M. Grintz, s.v. "Gerizim, Mount," EncJud 7:436; Mish. Sot. 7:5; Tosef. Sot. 8:1; R. Shela in Sanh. 44a; SOR 11; R. Mana in TJ Sot. 7:3, 21c; Lieberman, TK 8:702, ll. 80–82.

5. Josh. 5.

6. Hos. 4:15; 9:15; 12:11; Amos 4:4; 5:5.

7. The command in Deut. 27:2–3 to erect stones immediately after crossing the Jordan is tantalizingly similar to the tradition reported in Joshua 4 and suggests that the two are

somehow related. Perhaps they are two variant traditions. See Moran; Weinfeld, DDS, 164–165; M. Haran, "Schechem Studies," *Zion* 38 (1973): 13–14. Contrast Hoffmann, 496. Mish. Sot. 7:5 etc. think that the same stones were used at Ebal and then returned to Gilgal.

8. Plato mentions sacrifices offered over a pillar inscribed with laws and with an oath invoking curses upon the disobedient (*Critias*, 119).

9. Shadal; Malbim; Hoffmann; Driver. Cf. the wording of Num. 17:2–3.

10. Mish. Sot. 7:5; Josephus, Ant. 4.308; TJ Sot. 7:5, 21d (see Lieberman, TK 8:699–701).

11. Josh. 8:24 implies that Joshua read the Teaching aloud from the altar stones. His reading the Teaching seems to be based on combining Deut. 27 with 31:10–13.

12. Driver; D. J. McCarthy, *Treaty and Covenant*, rev. ed. (Rome: Biblical Institute Press, 1981), 195 n. 17.

13. M. Fishbane, *Biblical Interpretation in Ancient Israel* (Oxford: Clarendon, 1988), 161–162; cf. A. Rofé, "The Nomistic Correction in Biblical Manuscripts," RQ 14 (1989): 249 n. 11.

14. See J. Licht, "The Biblical Claim of Establishment," *Shnaton* 4 (1980): 98–128.

Excursus 26

M. Noth, *The Laws in the Pentateuch and Other Essays* (Philadelphia: Fortress Press, 1966), 118–131; D. R. Hillers, *Treaty Curses and the Old Testament Prophets* (Rome: Pontifical Biblical Institute, 1964), 12–42; D. J. McCarthy, *Treaty and Covenant* (Rome: Biblical Institute Press, 1981), 172–182; J. G. Plöger, *Literarkritische, formgeschichtliche und stilkritische Untersuchungen zum Deuteronomium* (Bonn: Hanstein, 1967) Part 3, 130–217; G. Seitz, *Redaktionsgeschichtliche Studien zum Deuteronomium* (Stuttgart: Kohlhammer, 1971), Part 4, 254–302.

1. See, e.g., Smith; Wright; Moran; Noth, *Laws in the Pentateuch*, 120–121; M. H. Segal, *The Pentateuch* (Jerusalem: Magnes Press, 1967), 96; Hillers, *Treaty Curses*, 30–32.

2. K. A. Kitchen, *Ancient Orient and Old Testament* (Chicago: Inter-Varsity Press, 1966), 97 n. 41; McCarthy, *Treaty and Covenant*, 173, 176.

3. Wright; Thompson, 271.

4. See Excursus 27.

5. See LH, xxvi, 73–75; xxvii, 7–13, and the treaty of Esarhaddon with Baal of Tyre (ANET, 534b).

6. Rofé, *Mavo'*, 23.

7. Internally vv. 7–13a also display a chiastic pattern independent of their relation to vv. 3–6. See Thompson.

8. See introductory Comment to 28:21–26.

9. These threats spell out virtually all of the curses of vv. 16–19, though in less structured ways. They also reverse most of the promises of section A, often verbatim though in a different order. Thus, section B1 can be viewed as an elaboration, in reverse, of practically the same basic promises found in section A.

10. Israel knew what sieges were like from several previous experiences (Thompson, 271). See 1 Kings 14:25; 2 Kings 6:24; 16:5; 17:5; 18:9; 24:10.

11. A small group did migrate to Egypt; see Jer. 42:7–43:7.

12. In VTE, §57 sums up the conditions of the treaty and the curses, and §58 is clearly a new beginning, partly duplicating what was said in earlier sections (McCarthy, *Treaty and Covenant*, 176, following Hillers, *Treaty Curses*, 32ff.).

13. Hillers, *Treaty Curses*, 28ff., 36; cf. Rofé, *Mavo'*, 136. Laboring only to have the wrong person reap the benefit of one's efforts is also found in Job 27:16–17; 31:8 (cf. Isa. 62:8–9; 65:21–22). The inability to enjoy the fruits of one's labors is found in Amos 5:11; Mic. 6:15; Zeph. 1:13.

14. Driver.

15. Weinfeld, DDS, 125, notes the use of the typological number seven in Lev. 26 and Sefire I, A: 21–24 (ANET, 659d).

Excursus 27

D. R. Hillers, *Treaty Curses and the Old Testament Prophets* (Rome: Pontifical Biblical Institute, 1964); R. Frankena, "The Vassal-Treaties of Esarhaddon and the Dating of Deuteronomy," OTS 14 (1965): 122–154; Weinfeld, DDS, 116–129; idem, "Traces of Assyrian Treaty Formulae in Deuteronomy," *Biblica* 46 (1965): 417–427; D. J. McCarthy, *Treaty and Covenant*, 2nd ed. (Rome: Biblical Institute Press, 1981), 172–182.

1. See S. N. Kramer, *The Sumerians* (Chicago: University of Chicago Press, 1963), 310–313, 315; L. W. King, *Babylonian Boundary-Stones* (London: British Museum, 1912); ANET, 161, 178–180, 201, 205, 206, 327, 353–354, 532–534, 538–541, 654–656, 659–662; *Sefer Abudraham* (Warsaw, 1878; reprint, Israel, 1973), 3; cf. Weinfeld, DDS, 61–62.

2. Translations of the epilogue to LH and VTE are found in ANET, 177–180, 534–541 (the treaty is usually referred to as "treaties" because copies have been found for several vassals of Esarhaddon; see ANET, 534d n. 1). The main surveys of parallels are those of Hillers, McCarthy, Frankena, and Weinfeld.

3. Cf. Goliath's boast, "I will give your flesh to the birds of the sky and the beasts of the field" and David's retort "I will give the carcasses of the Philistine camp to the birds of the sky and the beasts of the earth" (1 Sam. 17:44,46).

4. Jer. 5:15–17; 6:12; 7:33; 15:4; 24:9; 17:4; 19:9. For cannibalism, see also Ezek. 5:10.

5. LH rev. xxvi, 59, 73–74; xxvii, 5–6, 86; xxviii, 2–9, 22–23, 50–62, 84–91.

6. LH rev. xxvi, 59. In this passage, as often in Akkadian, turmoil is associated with rebellion and anarchy. See citations in CAD and AHw, s.v. *ešātu, ešītu, dilḫu, dalāḫu, ippiru, saḫmaštu, tēšū/tēšītu* (befalls kings, army, enemy: CAD M1, 248b; CAD N1, 88d). Cf. also CAD A1, 204c.

7. LH rev. xxvii, 5–6; see M. Held, "A Faithful Lover in an Old Babylonian Dialogue," JCS 15 (1961): 15; CAD M2, 126b.

8. LH rev. xxviii, 22–23. See also ANET, 612d, 614d 615ab (ref. courtesy Sol Cohen).

9. LH rev. xxviii, 50–62. For more on incurable wounds see Hillers, *Treaty Curses*, 64ff.

10. LH rev. xxviii, 84–91; see Weinfeld, DDS, 108.

11. E. V. Leichty, *The Omen Series Šumma Izbu* (Locust Valley, N.Y.: J. J. Augustin, 1970); 172:89; 180:2; cf. 206:48.

12. Ibid., 41:94; 43:117; 82:95; 162:39; 174:5; CAD L, 73d–74a. For other Mesopotamian omens similar to the blessings and curses, see ibid., 3–4; 39:78; 46:5; 78:52; 104:33; 131:1,4,9; 202:6.

13. CAD Q, 202c; more in Hillers, *Treaty Curses*, 68–69.

14. Cited by Hillers, *Treaty Curses*, 15.

15. BBSt. no. 6, ii, 53, cited in CAD B, 201a.

16. J. Friedrich, *Staatsvertraege des Hatti-Reiches*, Part 2 (Leipzig: Hinrichs'sche Buchhandlung, 1930), 81–83. These blessings and curses are the only known extrabiblical case of perfectly parallel curse and blessing formulae. Some scholars compare them to the almost perfectly parallel blessings and curses in Deut. 28:3–6, 16–19.

17. Weinfeld, DDS, 108.

18. See VTE §§25, 38A–42, 47–49, 97; cf. §§59, 85 (ANET, 537–549). Cf. the Treaty of Ashurnirari V with Mati'ilu of Arpad, i, 16–20 (ANET, 532d), and the Treaty of Esarhaddon with Baal (ANET, 534b).

19. VTE §39. As in the Bible, the term translated "leprosy" refers to dermatological conditions, but not to the disease known as "leprosy" today (see Comment to 24:8).

20. VTE §40. For the text see Weinfeld, *Biblica*, 46:419 n. 1; for the translation "accurate, reliable oracle" (rather than "fair and equitable judgment"), see CAD D, 152 b–d; CAD K, 470b,d. Blindness and darkness symbolize ignorance due to unreliable oracles, rather than the absence of law and justice.

21. VTE §42. Cf. the Egyptian prophecy of social upheaval, "Men take a man's property away from him, and it is given to him who is from the outside. I show thee the possessor in need and the outsider satisfied" (ANET, 445c), and contrast the blessings "you shall enjoy the fruit of your labors" (Ps. 128:2) and "He who plows his harvest will eat it" (Egyptian Hymn of Merneptah, ANET, 378a).

22. See introductory Comment to 28:53–57; VTE §47; see also §§69, 75, and ANET, 533b and 300a; omens and prophecies cited in CAD A1, 204b (an Egyptian parallel is cited by A. L. Oppenheim, "Siege Documents from Nippur," *Iraq* 17 [1955]: 78 n. 34).

23. J. C. Greenfield and A. Shaffer, "Notes on the Akkadian-Aramaic Bilingual Statue from Tell Fekherye," *Iraq* 45 (1983): 112–113 ll. 31–32.

24. Sefire Treaty IA, 27–30 (ANET, 659d–660a; see Weinfeld, DDS, 123–124; Tawil BASOR 225: 59–61).

25. P. Siewert, *Der Eid von Plataiai* (Munich: C. H. Beck'sche Verlagsbuchhandlung, 1972), 5–7 (translation from Weinfeld, "The Emergence of the Deuteronomic Movement: The Historical Antecedents," in N. Lohfink, ed., *Das Deuteronomium* [Leuven: Leuven University Press, 1985], 80, slightly modified).

26. Quoted by Weinfeld, "Emergence," 80.

27. VTE §§63–64 (ANET, 539c).

28. Greenfield and Shaffer, "Akkadian-Aramaic Bilingual Statue," 112–113 l. 36.

29. For discussion of the role of treaties in transmitting knowledge of the curses, cf. D. R. Hillers, *Treaty Curses*, 86–87; idem, *Covenant: The History of a Biblical Idea* (Baltimore: Johns Hopkins University Press, 1969), 138–140; J. Tigay, review of D. R. Hillers, *Lamentations*, JNES 35 (1976): 140; J. C. Greenfield, "Aramaic Studies and the Bible," *Congress Volume, Vienna, 1980* (Leiden: Brill, 1981), 113. For ancient Near Eastern curse traditions in Canaanite, see A. Demsky, "Mesopotamian and Canaanite Literary Traditions in the Ahiram Curse Formula," EI 14 (1978): 7–11.

30. Several ancient curses call for actual blindness. In the commentary it is argued that Deuteronomy more likely uses blindness metaphorically for incomprehension, stupefaction, or disorientation, though panic-induced psychosomatic blindness is also possible. For curses of actual blindness, see ANET, 155a (Aqhat C, iv, 167), 354a, 533c, 660a; T. H. Gaster, *Thespis* (Garden City, N.Y.: Doubleday, 1961), 367. For madness, cf. Zech. 12:4; Euripides' "Those whom God wishes to destroy he first makes mad" (E. M. Beck, *Bartlett's Familiar Quotations*, 14th ed. [Boston: Little, Brown, 1968], 86a and n. 6), and the Erinyes, "the Greek spirits of punishment [that] regularly work by disturbing the mind" (H. J. Rose, s.v. "Erinyes," OCD, 407a; cf. Leichty, *Šumma Izbu*, 32 note to line 6).

31. Cf. Weinfeld, DDS, 119 (cf. Hillers, *Treaty Curses*, 13; Frankena, "Vassal-Treaties," 129). Although in a general way the gods are listed in VTE in order of rank, with the chief Assyrian god Ashur first, it may be too much to say that the order is strictly hierarchical. If there was an exact hierarchy of the gods in the Assyrian pantheon, it is not known. The gods are listed three times in VTE; the order varies each time, as well as in variant manuscripts of the treaty (see Frankena, 147) and in other Assyrian treaties (see ANET, 533d). On the order of the curses in the epilogue to Hammurabi's laws, see Avigdor Hurowitz, *Inu Anum Šīrum: Literary Structures in the Non-Juridical Sections of Codex Hammurabi* (Philadelphia: Samuel Noah Kramer Fund, 1994), 40–43, 74–76.

Excursus 28

M. Greenberg, "Three Conceptions of the Torah in Hebrew Scriptures," in E. Blum at al., eds., *Die Hebräische Bibel und ihre zweifache Nachgeschichte* (Neukirchen-Vluyn: Neukirchener Verlag, 1990), pp. 365-375.

1. E. J. Bickermann, *Studies in Jewish and Christian History*, Part 1 (Leiden: Brill, 1976), 199 [emphasis added], and note further comments there.

2. The public as a whole was instructed in the details of the judicial reform undertaken by King Jehoshaphat, 2 Chron. 17:7ff.

3. In contrast, Babylonian priestly instructions state that they may not be shown to nonpriests (see ANET, 331b, 336a); cf. Bickermann, *Studies*, 199 n. 84.

4. Cf. Gen. 18:19; Exod. 12:26-27; 13:8, 14-15; Josh. 4:5-7, 20-24; Judg. 6:13; Ps. 44:2; 78:1-6. On education in ancient Israel see A. Demsky, s.v. "Education, in the Biblical Period," EncJud 6:382-398; A. Lemaire, *Les écoles et la formation de la Bible dans l'Ancien Israël* (Fribourg: Éditions Universitaires, and Göttingen: Vandenhoeck and Ruprecht, 1981); s.v. "Education, Ancient Israel," ABD 2:305-312.

5. Maimonides, Hilkhot Ḥagigah 3:1, based on Mish. Sotah 7:8; Tosef. Sotah 7:15 (ed. Zuckermandel).

6. M. Hadas, *Ancilla to Classical Reading* (New York: Columbia University Press, 1954), 50-60.

7. Cf. the oral transmission of tradition in Exod. 12:26-27; 13:8, 14-15; Josh. 4:5-7, 20-24; Judg. 6:13; Pss. 44:2; 78:1-6. Cf. S. Gandz, "Oral Tradition in the Bible," in S. W. Baron and A. Marx, eds., *Jewish Studies in Memory of George A. Kohut* (New York: Alexander Kohut Memorial Foundation, 1935), 253-261. For the simultaneous writing and oral transmission of the same material see Exod. 17:14. For study of the written text see Neh. 8:14; Dan. 9:2.

8. Cf. F. G. Kenyon and C. H. Roberts, "Books, Greek and Latin," OCD, 173bc; J. Tigay, ed., *Empirical Models for Biblical Criticism* (Philadelphia: University of Pennsylvania Press, 1985), 7 n. 22; idem, *The Evolution of the Gilgamesh Epic* (Philadelphia: University of Pennsylvania Press, 1982), 102 n. 72.

9. See ANET, 205d; D. J. McCarthy, *Treaty and Covenant*, 2nd ed. (Rome: Biblical Institute Press, 1981), 2 no. 4; Weinfeld, DDS, 64-66.

10. See G. Murray, *The Rise of the Greek Epic* (New York: Oxford University Press, 1960), 188ff., 299ff., 307ff.; J. O. Burtt, *Minor Attic Orators* (Cambridge: Harvard University Press, 1980), 2:91, 93. Some Babylonian myths were also recited before an audience, but we have no idea of who the audience was or what the occcasion was.

11. ANET, 165d; Avigdor Hurowitz, *Inu Anum Ṣirum: Literary Structures in the Non-Juridical Sections of Codex Hammurabi* (Philadelphia: Samuel Noah Kramer Fund, 1994), 27-29. Hammurabi also had his laws displayed in the temple so that a citizen who thought he had been wronged might consult them (ANET, 178b). Later, the Roman Twelve Tables of law were published (on tablets) in the Forum so that they could be known beyond patrician circles; they were learned by heart by "schoolboys" for centuries, even in Cicero's time (A. Berger and B. Nicholas, s.v., "Twelve Tables," OCD, 1100), although these may have been students in professional schools.

12. S. Paul, "Sargon's Administrative Diction in II Kings 17:27," JBL 88 (1969): 73-74. Paul compares 2 Kings 17:24ff.

13. M. Cogan, *Imperialism and Religion* (Missoula, Mont.: Society of Biblical Literature and Scholars Press, 1974), 51.

14. L. Jacobs, s.v. "Torah, Reading of," EncJud 15:1246-1255; Josephus, Apion 2.175; IR, no. 182.

15. Git. 59a-b; Maimonides, Hilkhot Ḥagigah 3:5.

16. Sanh. 21b; Maimonides, Sefer Ha-Mitsvot, positive no. 18; Sefer Ha-Ḥinnukh (ed. C. Chavel), no. 613; Torah Temi-

mah, note 26 to 31:19; A. Kaplan, *The Living Torah* (New York: Maznaim, 1981); Ralbag.

17. L. Finkelstein, introduction to S. Schechter, *Aspects of Rabbinic Theology* (New York: Schocken, 1961), xiv; cf. Hoffmann at Deut. 4:6; Maimonides, Hilkhot Talmud Torah 1:11.

18. Mish. Pe'ah 1:1; Kid. 40b.

19. Avot 2:5.

20. Shab. 31a.

21. Sifra to Lev. 21:24 (Emor, 3:12; Weiss 96a); so, too, Rashi at Lev. 21:24.

22. A. Rofé, "The Nomistic Correction in Biblical Manuscripts and its Occurrence in 4QSamᵃ," RQ 14 (1989): 247.

Excursus 29

Driver, lxxiii-lxxvii; M. Noth, *The Deuteronomistic History* (Sheffield, England: Sheffield University, 1981), 34-35, 115; N. Lohfink, "Der Bundesschluss im Land Moab: Redaktionsgeschichtliches zu Dt. 28:69-32:47," BZ 6 (1962): 32-56; Rofé, *Mavo'*, 198-215; J. Levenson, "Who Inserted the Book of the Torah?" HTR 68 (1975): 209-212.

1. Sifrei 357; BB 15a; Mish. Eduyot 1:3 (see J. Tigay, ed., *Empirical Models for Biblical Criticism* [Philadelphia: University of Pennsylvania Press, 1985], 168).

2. See Samuel in BK 14a and 36b; R. Yohanan in BM 41a (see note of Steinsaltz ad loc.) and Sanh. 62b. Cf. Tigay, ed., *Empirical Models*, 15 n. 48, and see the Introduction to this Commentary.

3. See Tigay, ed., *Empirical Models*.

4. Critics believe that Deuteronomy has a particularly strong, and some would say exclusive, affinity to E. That affinity is not especially pronounced in Deut. 31.

5. Tent of Meeting: Exod. 33:7-10; Num. 11:16; 12:5 (JE; the phrase also appears in "P," the priestly source); pillar of cloud: Exod. 13:21-22; 33:9-10; Num. 12:5; 14:14; and elsewhere (JE).

6. Cf. Exod. 2:23; 12:37; 19:1.

7. Cf. vv. 1,7 in this chapter; 1:1; 3:28; 29:1. See Driver, 337-338. Another account of Joshua's appointment, from P, appears in Num. 27:15-23.

8. Cf. 4:10.

9. Cf. 4:26; 30:19.

10. Cf. 4:16,25.

11. Deut. 4:25; 9:18. For these and further examples see Klostermann, *Der Pentateuch* (Leipzig: Deichert, 1893), 240-241.

12. Cf. Exod. 34:15-16.

13. Cf., e.g., Deut. 6:14; 8:19; 11:28.

14. Cf. Gen. 35:2,4.

15. Cf., e.g, Deut. 6:14; 8:19; 11:28.

16. Cf. Gen. 17:14; Lev. 26:15,44. In the Torah this idiom is found only in P, but was probably not limited to it; see Driver, 340-341.

17. Cf. Deut. 17:2; 29:24 (see Weinfeld, DDS, 340, 341 citing, e.g., 1 Kings 17:2; 9:2-9).

18. Cf. Gen. 15:18.

19. Cf. Deut. 1:9; 10:1.

20. The Deuteronomic themes and phraseology in the two paragraphs include "the Ark of the LORD's Covenant," "the priests, sons of Levi," "every seventh year," "remission," "the place which LORD your God will choose," "the stranger within your gates," the verbs "hear" and "learn," and "the land which you are about to cross the Jordan to possess." See the tables of Deuteronomic phraseology in Weinfeld, DDS, Appendix A.

21. If Moses' actions *had* to be separated for some literary purpose, one would have at least expected the second paragraph to refer back to his instructions to the priests and elders, or to his giving them the Teaching; one would not expect it to refer

all the way back to his writing of the Teaching as if he had done nothing after that.

22. See Rofé, *Mavo'*, 209–214.

23. Ibid., 199–200.

24. See 4:10,16,25,26; 5:1; see also the next note.

25. Deut. 5:19; 6:6; 11:18; 12:28; 30:1; 31:1. "These words" in 32:45 must mean this, too, since it refers to words that include commandments (see v. 46).

26. Cf. Abravanel, 296. In the poem itself, the speaker is sometimes God and sometimes Moses.

27. See the views of Dillmann and others, cited (and opposed) by Driver, lxxiii–lxxv, 343, and 382.

28. For an imaginative attempt at reconstructing the original order or the text, see M. Naor, "Deut. 31–34: A Reconstruction of the Text," in I. Ben-Shem et al., eds., *Sefer Yosef Braslavi* (Jerusalem: Kiryat-Sefer, 1970), 216–229.

29. Rofé, *Mavo'*, 202.

30. Hoffmann, 568.

31. Isa. 30:8; Hab. 2:2–3.

32. Mayes; Phillips.

33. Weinfeld, DDS, 10 n. 2; Rofé, *Mavo'*, 213 par 2.

34. See Tigay, ed., *Empirical Models*, 53–89 and the comments of M. Greenberg cited there, 54.

35. Cf. ibid., 44–45, and the comments of Greenberg cited there.

38. Or, if one accepts Noth's attribution of 1–3 or 1–4 (and more) to a later writer than D, he was not the Deuteronomistic historian; see Levenson, "Who Inserted the Book of the Torah?"

37. Ibid., 211.

38. SP, LXX, and Vulg. smooth the transition by adding a conjunction before "Joshua"; this is obviously secondary.

39. Rofé, *Mavo'*, 208 n 36.

40. See A. Rofé, "Textual Criticism in the Light of Historical-Literary Criticism: Deuteronomy 31: 14–15," EI 16 (1982): 171–186.

Excursus 30

Poetry: G. B. Gray, *The Forms of Hebrew Poetry* (1915; reprint, New York: Ktav, 1972); J. Muilenburg, s.v. "Biblical Poetry," EncJud 13:671–681; B. Hrushovsky, s.v. "Prosody, Hebrew," EncJud 13:1195–1203; J. Kugel, *The Idea of Biblical Poetry* (New Haven: Yale University Press, 1981); R. Alter, *The Art of Biblical Poetry* (New York: Basic Books, 1985); L. Alonso Schökel, *A Manual of Hebrew Poetics* (Rome: Pontifical Biblical Institute, 1988); J. C. Greenfield, "The Hebrew Bible and Canaanite Literature," in R. Alter and F. Kermode, eds., *The Literary Guide to the Bible* (Cambridge: Harvard University Press, 1987), 545–560; idem, "The 'Cluster' in Biblical Poetry," *Maarav* 5–6 (1990): 169–168.

Deuteronomy 32: W. F. Albright, *Yahweh and the Gods of Canaan* (Garden City, N.Y.: Doubleday, 1968), 17–19; idem, "Some Remarks on the Song of Moses in Deuteronomy," VT 9 (1959): 339–346; O. Eissfeldt, *The Old Testament: An Introduction* (New York: Harper and Row, 1965), 226–227; U. Cassuto, s.v. *Devarim (Sefer)*, EM 2:615–617; idem, *Biblical and Oriental Studies* (Jerusalem: Magnes Press, 1973–75), 41–46, 95–100; Y. Kaufmann, *Toledot ha-'Emunah ha-Yisre'elit* (Jerusalem: Bialik Institute and Dvir, 1955), 2:287–290; R. Meyer, "Die Bedeutung von Deuteronomium 32 8f, 43 (4Q) für die Auslegung des Moses Liedes," in A. Kuschke, ed., *Verbannung und Heimkehr* (Tübingen: J.C.B. Mohr, 1961), 197–209; H. L. Ginsberg, *The Israelian Heritage of Judaism* (New York: Jewish Theological Seminary, 1982), 93–94, 101 n. 131, 104 n. 135, 108 n. 136; M. Frank, "Shirat 'Ha'azinu,'" *Tarbiz* 18 (1947): 129–136. See also bibliography to chapter 32.

1. This classification is overly simple, but it will suffice for present purposes.

2. See Num. 23:18; Isa. 1:2; UT 6:22–23.

3. 2 Sam. 1:21; Mic. 5:6; Ps. 72:6; UT 1 Aqhat (AQHT C) i, 41, 44–45.

4. Job 31:15; UT 76, iii, 6–7.

5. Exod. 3:15; UT 68:10.

6. Judg. 5:25; UT 52:14.

7. Ps. 13:5; UT 68:9; 51, vii, 35–36.

8. 1 Sam. 18:7,8; Ps. 91:7; UT 51, i, 28–29.

9. Hab. 3:17; UT 52:10–11.

10. Ps. 91:13; UT *'nt* iii, 37–38.

11. For *lo'* see vv. 6,17,20,27,30,31,34; for *'ein* see vv. 4,12,28,39. See also *lulei* (27), *lu* (29).

12. Several are *hapax legomena*. Some, such as *petaltol* (v. 5), *'emun* (v. 20), *meriri* (v. 24), *nasikh* (v. 38), *sitrah* (v. 38), *yenakkeru* (v. 27), and *pelilim* (v. 31), are from roots that are known in different forms. Others have no related words in the Bible at all: *se'irim* (v. 2), *kasita* (v. 15), *mezei* (v. 24), *'af 'eihem* (v. 26), and *kamus* (v. 34).

13. Some Qumran copies have one or four colons per line: 4QDeut^q (see Excursus 31); 1QDeut^b, frags. 16–19 (1Q5, in DJD 1:60 and pl. X). According to DJD 1:60, 1QDeut^b frags. 16–19 is written in stichs. 4QDeut^j (v. 8) is not written stichometrically.

14. Soferim 12:8–9; Maimonides, Hilkhot Sefer Torah 8 (see *Mishneh Torah*, ed. Y. Kafih [Kiryat Ono, Israel: Mekhon Mishnat Ha-Rambam, 1985], 2:406–407). SP also writes two colons per line, but its extra colon in v. 15 changes all the points of division afterwards.

15. Pss. 49:2; 78:1; Isa. 28:23; Prov. 4:1.

16. Isa. 1:2; Mic. 6:1–2; cf. Jer. 6:19.

17. Pss. 78, 105, 106; Ezek. 20, 16, 23.

18. Judg. 10:14; Jer. 2:28.

19. Isa. 34:5–6; 49:26; 63:1–6; Jer. 12:12; 25:30–33; 46:10; 50:25–32.

20. Exod. 15:21; Pss. 96:1; 98:1.

21. Driver, 348; J. R. Boston, "The Wisdom Influence upon the Song of Moses," JBL 87 (1968): 198–202.

22. H. B. Huffmon, "The Covenant Lawsuit in the Prophets," JBL 78 (1959): 285–295; G. E. Wright, "The Lawsuit of God: A Form-Critical Study of Deuteronomy 32," in B. W. Anderson and W. Harrelson, eds., *Israel's Prophetic Heritage* (New York: Harper and Brothers, 1962), 26–67; J. Harvey, "Le '*rib*-pattern,' réquisitoire prophétique sur la rupture de l'alliance," *Biblica* 43 (1962): 172–196; Moran, 275c; idem, "Some Remarks on the Song of Moses," *Biblica* 43 (1962): 317–320; M. Delcor, "Les attachés littéraires, l'origine et la signification de l'expression biblique 'prendre à témoin le ciel et la terre,'" VT 16 (1956): 8–25.

23. A few terms describing the relationship—*shihet*, *tamim*, and *ts-d-k*—are also found in covenant contexts but this is because the terms describing treaties and family relationships have much in common; see J. Tigay, "Psalm 7:5 and Ancient Near Eastern Treaties," JBL 89 [1970]: 183 n. 36). Nor is the father-child relationship a metaphor here for the covenant; father-child and covenant partners are separate metaphors for the relationship between God and Israel.

24. The same is true of Isa. 1:2ff., which may be based on Deut. 32 (see H. L. Ginsberg, s.v. "Isaiah," EncJud 9:50).

25. C. J. Labuschagne, "The Song of Moses: Its Framework and Structure," in I. H. Eybers et al., *De Fructu Oris Sui: Essays in Honour of Adrianus van Selms* (Leiden: Brill, 1971), 93; Boston, "Wisdom Influence," 198–202.

26. See A. Rofé, *Israelite Belief in Angels in the Pre-Exilic Period* (Hebrew) (Ph.D. diss., Hebrew University, 1969), 98–99; Weinfeld, DDS, 10 n. 2, and 364; J. Levenson, "Who Inserted the Book of the Torah?" HTR 68 (1975): 215ff. I am not referring to details in which chapter 31 intentionally anticipates 32: "alien gods" (31:16) as in 32:12 instead of Deuteronomy's usual "other

gods"; "hide My countenance from them" (31:17–18) as in 32:20. See also 31:28–29.

27. Vv. 5,16,17,21 (cf., e.g., 4:16,25; 7:25–26; 9:18; 11:28; 13:3,15; 31:29).

28. There is a subtle difference in the use of terminology. Elsewhere in Deuteronomy, "abomination" refers to idolatrous acts; here it refers to the idol itself (as in 2 Kings 23:13; Jer. 16:18; Isa. 44:19).

29. See Cassuto, *Biblical and Oriental Studies*, 1:95–100.

30. See Y. Kaufmann, *The Religion of Israel*, trans. M. Greenberg (Chicago: University of Chicago Press, 1960), 157–158, 397n.

31. See ibid., 158–160, 345–347, 365–367.

32. See Abravanel, 305–306, 307–310; Sifrei 317, 318, 320, 328.

33. David A. Robertson, *Linguistic Evidence in Dating Early Hebrew Poetry* (Missoula, Mont.: Society of Biblical Literature, 1972).

34. Josephus, Ant. 4.303; cf. 3.38; 5.61.

35. RH 31a; TJ Meg. 3:7, 74b, end; see Maimonides, Hilkhot Temidin u-Musafin 6:9.

36. Cf. H. St. J. Thackeray, *Josephus: The Man and the Historian* (New York: Jewish Institute of Religion Press, 1929), 90.

37. See P. Skehan, "A Fragment of the 'Song of Moses' (Deut. 32) from Qumran," BASOR 136 (1954): 12–15.

38. M. Ydit, s.v. "Av, the Ninth of," EncJud 3:938.

Excursus 31

Julie Duncan, "A Critical Edition of Deuteronomy Manuscripts from Qumran, Cave IV. 4QDt^b, 4QDt^e, 4QDt^h, 4QDt^j, 4QDt^k, 4QDt^l" (Ph.D. diss., Harvard University, 1989), 110 and Plate 6; P. W. Skehan, "A Fragment of the 'Song of Moses' (Deut. 32) from Qumran," BASOR 136 (1954): 12–15; idem, "Qumran and the Present State of Old Testament Text Studies: The Masoretic Text," JBL 78 (1959): 21; DJD 14 (1995) as cited below.

1. For v. 8, see 4QDeut^j in Duncan, "Critical Edition" and in DJD 14:90 and plate XXIII. For v. 43, see 4QDeut^q, published by Skehan in BASOR 136:12–15 and in DJD 14:137–142 and plate XXXI. For discussion see Skehan, *Studies in Israelite Poetry and Wisdom* (Washington, D.C.: Catholic Biblical Association of America, 1971), 67–77; F. M. Cross, *The Ancient Library of Qumran and Modern Biblical Studies*, 2nd ed. (Garden City, N.Y.: Doubleday, 1961), 182–184; Rofé, *Mavo'*, 222–228; J. M. Grintz, *Motsa'ei Dorot* (Israel: Ha-kibbutz Ha-meuchad, 1969), 242–257; P.-M. Bogaert, "Les trois rédactions conservées et la forme originale de l'envoi du Cantique de Moïse," in N. Lohfink, ed., *Das Deuteronomium: Entstehung, Gestalt, und Botschaft* (Leuven: Leuven University Press, 1985), 329–340; Mayes. I am grateful to Emanuel Tov for his advice on matters discussed in this Excursus.

2. So 4QDeut^j (the text is sometimes quoted as if it read *b-n-y '-l* because that is all that was known when it was first quoted by Skehan in BASOR 136:12; the additional fragment, containing the final three letters *h-y-m* was quoted by him later in JBL 78:21, but it escaped the notice of many scholars). Some LXX manuscripts read "sons of God" (Göttingen ed.) and others "angels of God" (Rahlfs and Cambridge eds.). Both translations reflect the same Hebrew text, since LXX uses the latter phrase for *benei 'elohim* in Gen. 6:2 (Codex A); Job 1:6; 2:1; 38:7; cf. Dan. 3:25.

3. T. H. Gaster, s.v. "Sons of God," IDB 4:426. See UT 51: vi, 46 and iv, 50–51 (ANET, 134c, 133b); KAI 26A: iii, 19 (ANET, 654c); 27:11 (if authentic).

4. On the *benei 'elohim*, see summary of views by A. Cooper in RSP 3:434–435. For *'elohim* meaning "angels," see Judg. 13:22. When Manoah is convinced that he and his wife have seen an angel, he declares "We shall surely die, for we have seen an

'elohim" (Judg. 13:22). Cf. Gen. 32:29,31. For Canaanite *benei 'el* as stars, note the parallelism with *phr kkbm* in UT 76 (CTCA 10), i, 3–4 (cf. Ibn Ezra at Ps. 29:2).

5. Ecclus. 17:17(14). The first line is not present in all manuscripts, but the dependence of the rest on Deut. 32:8 is in any case unmistakable.

6. Dan. 10:13,20,21; 12:1. See also Ps. 82:7 (cf. Weinfeld, Commentary, 206).

7. Jub. 15:31–32; PRE 24; see Ginzberg, *Legends* 1:181; 5:204–205 n. 91.

8. UT 51: iii, 14; 137: 14, 15 etc. (ANET, 132c, 130a); KAI 26A: iii, 19 (ANET, 654c) and 27:11–12 (if authentic).

9. PRE 24; Yalkut Gen. 62, text preceding n. 45; cf. the Hebrew Testament of Naphtali in M. M. Kasher, *Torah Shelemah* 7 (New York: American Biblical Encyclopedia Society, 1950), 1889.

10. I. Davidson, *Saadia's Polemic Against Hiwi al-Balkhi* (New York: Jewish Theological Seminary, 1915), 58–59; cf. 87, 96–97.

11. That the stars are divine beings is implied by the parallelism in Job 38:7 and UT 76 (CTCA 10), i, 3–4; cf. Weinfeld, Commentary, 206–207.

12. Atrahasis I, 11–18 (in W. G. Lambert and A. R. Millard, *Atra-hasis: The Babylonian Story of the Flood* [Oxford: Clarendon, 1969], 43); *Iliad* 15:184–193.

13. See the Sumerian Deluge story, ll. 92–98 (ANET, 43d); Sanchunyaton's account of Phoenician mythology, in H.W. Attridge and R. A. Oden, *Philo of Byblos: The Phoenician History* (Missoula, Mont.: Scholars Press, 1976), 56–59.

14. See Rofé, *Mavo'*, 221–222, n. 20, 224 n. 29; idem, *Israelite Belief in Angels in the Pre-exilic Period* (Hebrew) (Ph.D. diss., Hebrew University, 1969), 92ff. Dillmann and Grintz argue that the MT of vv. 8 and 43 is original and that the variants were introduced late to give textual grounding to the role of the angelic patrons of nations (Dillmann ad loci; Grintz, *Motsa'ei Dorot*). This is hardly likely. The tendency of scribes was to eliminate such troublesome readings, not to add them. If the variants were added later, they ought to have read *sarei 'elohim*, the term used in Daniel, and not the problematic *benei 'elohim*, the type of reading that was in the process of being eliminated from the biblical text in the Second Temple period.

15. "Heavens" is probably more original than "nations," since it is a more apt parallel to "sons of the divine" or "divinities" (cf. Ps. 89:6–7) and the reading is comparable to such verses as Isa. 44:23; 49:13; Pss. 69:35–36; 96:11; 148:1,11ff.

16. As noted in the Commentary, "His sons" is consistent with the metaphor of Israel as God's children that prevails in the first part of the poem, whereas "servants" corresponds to the metaphor used in v. 36. The use of "avenge" instead of "redeem" *may* support "servants" (see Commentary). The extra "Be vengeful" at the beginning of b2 in the Septuagint can be explained easily as reflecting a reading *v-y-k-w-m*, a dittography of the end of b1.

17. Rofé, *Mavo'*, 225.

18. MT's "His people" (*'ammo*) is probably also an error. The parallelism in a1–a2 and a3–a4 shows that the consonants *'-m-v* should be vocalized *'immo*, "with Him," as implied by LXX, not *'ammo*. This is confirmed by the rest of the verse, which talks about God's deeds, not Israel's. However, once a2 was removed from the text, it was easy to read *'-m-v* as *'ammo*, since *harnin* takes a direct object in such verses as Ps. 32:11 and 81:2.

19. Rofé, *Mavo'*, 223–228. This makes a3–a4 more synonymous with each other than a1–a2 are.

20. The practice of presenting two or more translations of the same clause or verse is attested in LXX and in the targums. See S. R. Driver, *Notes on the Hebrew Text and Topography of the Books of Samuel* (Oxford: Clarendon, 1913), lv–lvii; Z. Talshir, "Double Translations in the Septuagint," in C. E. Cox, ed., *VI*

Congress of the International Organization for Septuagint and Cognate Studies (Atlanta: Scholars Press, 1987), 21–63; Y. Komlosh, *The Bible in the Light of the Aramaic Translations* (Tel Aviv: Dvir, 1973), 154–155, 365–366; R. Weiss, *The Aramaic Targum of Job* (Tel Aviv: Chaim Rosenberg School for Jewish Studies, Tel Aviv University, 1979), 288–293. Whereas modern editions place alternative translations in footnotes, ancient ones commonly placed them in the text itself, or sometimes in the margin. For another example in Deuteronomy, see LXX to 23:18.

21. "Assembly of nations" in Ps. 7:8 is likewise probably a revision of "assembly of divinities." See R. Tournay, "Les psaumes complexes," VT 56 (1949): 47–55; I. L. Seeligmann, "A Psalm from Pre-regal Times," VT 14 (1964): 81 n. 1; Rofé, *Israelite Belief in Angels*, 90–94 (following Budde). Cf. H. L. Ginsberg, "A Strand in the Cord of Hebraic Hymnody," *EI* 9 (1969):46.

22. 1 Chron. 8:33; 9:39; 14:7. For a fuller list see E. Tov, *Textual Criticism of the Hebrew Bible* (Minneapolis: Fortress Press, 1992), 267–269.

23. E.g., 2 Sam. 2:12,15; 5:16. For discussion and other examples see J. Tigay, *You Shall Have No Other Gods* (Atlanta: Scholars Press, 1986), 7–8, 14, 68.

24. Cf. Hos. 2:18.

25. Other examples are Pss. 95:3; 96:4; 97:9; 135:5; Job 38:7.

26. See also Ps. 89:7.

27. Targ. Onk. Gen. 6:2; Gen. R. 26:5; Rashi ad loc.; MdRY Shirta 8:8 (Lauterbach 2:60–61). The rabbis made it clear that they solved other problems exegetically that SP solved by textual revision; see TJ Sot. 7:3, 21c, and E. S. Rosenthal, "*Leshonot Soferim*," in B. Kurzweil, ed., *Yuval Shay* (Ramat Gan: Bar Ilan University, 1958), 319–320 n. 186.

28. See S. Lieberman, HJP, 28–37; Tov, *Textual Criticism*, 64–67.

Excursus 32

1. For details see Smith and Driver.

2. See Gen. 7:13 vs. Deut. 1:9.

3. See Lev. 26:16 (ʼ*ani*, common in P, is used in Deuteronomy only in 12:30 and 29:5) vs. Deut. 4:1, etc.

4. See Exod. 12:37 vs. Deut. 1:1; 3:29.

5. E.g., Lev. 14:34 vs. Deut. 4:21; 2:9,12.

6. E.g., Lev. 25:8; 35:29; Num. 20:2.

7. See Lev. 26:40 vs. Deut. 1:26.

8. See Exod. 29:45 vs. Deut. 11:6.

9. Details added by the editor consist mainly of more particular instructions concerning Moses' ascent of Mount Nebo. See discussion by Driver; Weinfeld, DDS, 181.

Excursus 33

W. J. Pythian-Adams, "On the Date of the 'Blessing of Moses' (Deut. XXXIII)," *JPOS* 3 (1923): 158–166; U. Cassuto, s.v. *Devarim (Sefer)*, EM 2:617–618; O. Eissfeldt, *The Old Testament: An Introduction* (New York: Harper and Row, 1965), 227–231; A. Rofé, *Mavoʼ*, 234–249; Y. Zakovitch, *Kefel Midreshei Shem* (M.A. thesis, Hebrew University, 1971), 61ff. See also bibliography to chapter 33.

1. Examples include the terms translated as (1) "came" and "approached" (v. 2; cf. Prov. 1:27; Job 3:25; Mic. 4:8); (2) "observed" and "kept" (v. 9; cf. Pss. 12:8; 140:5; Prov. 2:8); (3) "law" and "instruction" (v. 10; cf. Isa. 51:4; Pss. 19:10; 119 passim); (4) "Jacob" and "Israel" (v. 10; cf. Gen. 49:7; Num. 23:7); (5) "bless/blessing/bounty" and "favor" (vv. 11,16,23,24; cf. Ps. 5:13; Prov. 8:35; 18:22); (6) "heaven" and "deep" (v. 13; cf. Gen. 7:11); (7) "sun" and "moon(s)" (v. 14; cf. Ps. 104:19; RSP 1, no. 577); (8) "head" and "crown" (meaning the top of the head) (v. 16; cf. Num. 24:17 [see SP]; Ps. 68:22; RSP 1, no. 511);

9. "myriads" and "thousands" (v. 17; see Excursus 30; RSP 1, no. 44); (10) "judgments" and "decisions" (v. 21; cf. Pss. 72:1,3; 106:3); (11) "heavens" and "the skies" (v. 26; cf. Isa. 45:8; Ps. 36:6); and (12) "in safety" and "untroubled" (v. 28; cf. Jer. 49:31; Ps. 4:9). Some of these pairs are also found in Canaanite and Akkadian poetry. See the RSP citations; M. Held, "Studies in Biblical Homonyms in the Light of Akkadian," JANES 3 (1970–71): 47–55; J. C. Greenfield, "Some Phoenician Words," *Semitica* 38 (1990): 156.

2. Some are variants or derivatives of words known from elsewhere in the Bible, such as *dabberot* (v. 3), *hitʼasef* (v. 5), *ketorah* (v. 10), *hofef* (v. 12), *shefaʻ* (v. 19), *minʻal* (v. 25), and possibly ʼ*eshdat* (v. 2) and *geresh* (v. 14). Others, such as *hovev* (v. 3), *tukku* (v. 3) *zannek* (v. 22), and *doveʼ* (v. 25), have no related words in the Bible at all.

3. Cf. G. Rendsburg, *Linguistic Evidence for the Northern Origin of Selected Psalms* (Atlanta: Scholars Press, 1990).

4. Cf. Gen. 9:26–27 (cf. v. 20a); Num. 6:24–26 (priestly blessing, addressed to recipient, like vv. 18,23b,25); and the blessings of Balaam in Num. 22–24.

5. Gen. 27:7; 28:1–4,39–40; and the blessings in Genesis 49.

6. Josh. 23–24; 1 Kings 2:1–9.

7. Gen. 49; Judg. 5.

8. See the parallels to the exordium and the coda, cited in the Commentary.

9. B. Halpern, *The Emergence of Israel in Canaan* (Chico, Calif.: Scholars Press, 1983), 117–118, challenges the view that they are criticized.

10. See the views summarized by Rofé, *Mavoʼ*, 237.

11. Several scholars believe that the poem, or at least the framework, was part of a festival, held once or repeatedly, to celebrate the Lord's kingship. See S. Mowinckel, *The Psalms in Israel's Worship* (New York: Abingdon, 1962), 114–115, 154–155; U. Cassuto, *Biblical and Oriental Studies* (Jerusalem: Magnes Press, 1973–75), 1:48–49; I. L. Seeligmann, *Studies in Biblical Literature*, ed. A. Hurvitz et al. (Jerusalem: Magnes Press, 1992), 83; Rofé, *Mavoʼ*, 236–243. On the whole I think that the kingship theme is not emphasized enough to believe that it reflects the original occasion of the poem.

12. "Children of Israel," JE and P; "Horeb," E (Driver, 6).

13. See introductory Comment to 20:15–18 and Excursus 18. On the other hand, the verb *hashmed* in v. 27b2 is consistent with Deut. 2:12, 21ff.; 7:23–24; and 9:3, unless we assume that it has here the looser meaning of "ruin" that it seems to have in chapter 28; see Comment to 28:20.

14. The poem's list of priestly duties is closer to those of 1 Sam. 2:28 and 1 Chron. 23:13.

15. On this the poem agrees with Ps. 81:8. See S. E. Loewenstamm, *From Babylon to Canaan* (Jerusalem: Magnes Press, 1992), 55.

16. Driver, 389; Eissfeldt, *Old Testament*, 231; Moran.

17. LXX A and manuscripts.

18. Sifrei 348 (see R. Hammer, *Sifre: A Tannaitic Commentary on the Book of Deuteronomy* [New Haven: Yale University Press, 1986], 508 n. 6); Yal. 954; Lekah Tov; Pesikta de-Rav Kahana (ed. B. Mandelbaum), 442; Rashi; Abravanel, 325, 326; cf. Mishnat R. Eliezer §20.

19. M. Heilprin, cited by Smith, 365; Tur Sinai; Zakovitch, *Kefel Midreshei Shem*, 61ff.; cf. Ehrlich, *Randglossen* (v. 11 is Simeon's blessing); Cassuto, *Biblical and Oriental Studies* (v. 7 is Simeon's, v. 11 Judah's). Philo, *On the Change of Names*, 200, says that Simeon is included in Levi's blessing.

20. Yal. 954; R. Joshua of Sikhnin in Mid. Psalms 90:3, cited and rejected by Abravanel, 325. Most of Simeon's cities in Josh. 19:1–8 are listed in 15:26–32,42 as Judah's. In Num. 26, Simeon's population is less than half of what it was in Num. 1, the largest loss suffered by any tribe (Milgrom, *Numbers*, 220). On the history of the tribe, see S. Ahituv, s.v. *Shimʻon* 2, EM 8:132–136.

21. Abravanel, 323–324; Mayes; H. Weippert, "Das Geographische System der Stämme Israels," VT 23 (1973): 76–89.

22. Zebulun also precedes Issachar in Num. 34:25–26, where the order is again geographic, but also in Gen. 49:13–15 and Josh. 19:10–23, where it is not. In those cases, the order might reflect a time when Zebulun was superior, while cases in which Issachar precedes reflect a time when Issachar was.

23. Ibn Ezra and Ramban at v. 6; Abravanel, 323–324.

24. Gaster, "An Ancient Eulogy on Israel," JBL 66 (1947): 53–62; Eissfeldt, *Old Testament*, 227–228; Mowinckel, *Psalms*, 154–155; Seeligmann, *Studies in Biblical Literature*; Z. Weisman, "A Connecting Link in an Old Hymn: Deuteronomy xxxiii 19A, 21B," VT 28 (1978): 365–367; Mayes, 396.

25. F. M. Cross, *Canaanite Myth and Hebrew Epic* (Cambridge: Harvard University Press, 1973), 99–111; Halpern, *Emergence of Israel in Canaan*, 126ff.; idem, *The Constitution of the Monarchy in Israel* (Chico, Calif.: Scholars Press, 1981), 69ff.

26. Smith.

27. Seeligmann, who sees this as the earliest reflex of the tradition that interprets vv. 2–3 as a description of the theophany and lawgiving at Sinai; cf. M. Fishbane, *Biblical Interpretation in Ancient Israel* (Oxford: Clarendon, 1985), 75–77.

28. Moran; P. D. Miller, *The Divine Warrior in Israel* (Cambridge: Harvard University Press, 1973), 82.

29. Note the use of *tsivvah*, "charge," "command," in the context of giving final instructions concerning one's household before dying, 2 Sam. 17:23; 2 Kings 20:1.

30. Mayes, 397.

31. F. M. Cross and D. N. Freedman, *Studies in Ancient Yahwistic Poetry* (Missoula, Mont.: Scholars Press, 1975); Moran; Mayes; A. Cody, *A History of Old Testament Priesthood* (Rome: Pontifical Biblical Institute, 1969), 114–115; L. Ruppert, "Das Motif der Versuchung durch Gott in Vordeuteronomischer Tradition," VT 22 (1972): 56–59. The fact that vv. 8–10 lack the linguistic and textual problems present in the rest of the chapter would be explained if those verses were not yet part of the chapter when it was subject to the conditions that caused these difficulties.

32. V. 7 hardly reflects the isolation of Judah after the secession of the northern tribes (so Smith, 361, 266 and others); it was, after all, the north that seceded.

33. Sot. 48a-b; Cody, *History of Old Testament Priesthood*, 115–116. There are no references to the Urim and Thummim being used after David's reign.

34. It is likely that Levitical priests served in those territories in that period, since Levites lived there (Judg. 17:7,9; 19:1; 1 Sam. 6:15) and were preferred as priests even though others were considered eligible to serve (see Judg. 17–18). Whether the priestly family of Eli, that served at Shiloh and later elsewhere in Benjamin, were Levites is debated (Cross, *Canaanite Myth*, 196ff.; Cody, *History of Old Testament Priesthood*, 70–71).

35. See Amos 5:6,15; 1 Kings 11:26.

36. Cf. 1 Chron. 5:1–2: Joseph acquired the birthright but Judah acquired leadership.

37. Judg. 6–8. The coalition led by Deborah was centered in Ephraimite territory (Judg. 4:5). See also Rofé, *Mavo'*, 242–243.

38. See David A. Robertson, *Linguistic Evidence in Dating Early Hebrew Poetry* (Missoula, Mont.: Society of Biblical Literature, 1972), 49–50, 138, 148, 150.

39. See ibid., 28.

40. Ibid., 66–68; there is also one instance of the chronologically neutral *-hem* (v. 17).

41. See ibid., 69–75.

42. Ibid., 79ff., esp. 81–82, 108–109; he cites uncertain cases in vv. 2 and 3 (twice) on 94, 98, 102. Perhaps the plural suffix on *yerahim*, v. 14, is another case.

43. With *vav*-consecutive in vv. 5,21 (twice), 27 (twice), 28. They are all in initial position, while the imperfects *without vav*-consecutive are medial and follow perfects. According to Robertson, ibid., 28, this situation is reminiscent of standard biblical Hebrew, suggesting later archaizing rather than earliness.

44. The form *-ehu*, in v. 8, is irrelevant because it is not connected to the verb with *-n-*.